Hong Kong
Macau & Guangzhou

Damian Harper
Robert Storey

Hong Kong, Macau & Guangzhou

9th edition

Published by
Lonely Planet Publications
Head Office: PO Box 617, Hawthorn, Vic 3122, Australia
Branches: 150 Linden Street, Oakland, CA 94607, USA
10a Spring Place, London NW5 3BH, UK
1 rue Dahomey, 75011 Paris, France

Printed by
SNP Printing Pte Ltd, Singapore

Photographs by

Jon Davison	William Cheung	Tristy Fairfield
Patrick Horton	Hong Kong Tourist Association	Glenn Beanland
Mark Kirby	Siren Entertainment	
Tony Wheeler	Richard I'Anson	

Front cover: Candles at the Kun Iam Temple, Macau (Richard I'Anson, Lonely Planet Images)

First Published
1978

This Edition
January 1999

Although the authors and publisher have tried to make the information as accurate as possible, they accept no responsibility for any loss, injury or inconvenience sustained by any person using this book.

National Library of Australia Cataloguing in Publication Data

Harper, Damian
Hong Kong, Macau & Guangzhou

9th ed.
Includes index.
ISBN 0 86442 584 8.

1. Hong Kong (China) – Guidebooks. 2. Macao – Guidebooks
3. Canton (China) – Guidebooks. I.Title

915.125046

Damian Harper

After six years in the book trade (London, Paris and Dublin), Damian threw it in to study Chinese at London's School of Oriental and African Studies. He spent a year in Beijing as part of his course and there he met his Qingdao-born wife, Dai Min. After graduating, Damian fled England for Hong Kong and found temporary work at Sotheby's in the ceramics department. After working for a period as an editor and translator, Damian and his wife packed their bags and hit the road to help update the 6th edition of *China* and the 2nd edition of the *Hong Kong city guide*. He is a regular returnee to Hong Kong.

Robert Storey

After graduating from the University of Nevada with a worthless liberal arts degree, Robert pursued a distinguished career as a slot machine repairman in a Las Vegas casino. He later worked for the government bureaucracy, though he is not quite sure what his job was. Seeking the meaning of life, Robert became a backpacker and drifted around Asia before he finally reached nirvana in Taiwan. He is the author or co-author of numerous Lonely Planet guides, including *Taiwan*, *China* and *Korea*. Robert Storey is also the author of the novel *Life in the Fast Lane*.

From Damian

Thanks to all the people who helped in the preparation of this book. I am naturally indebted to my wife Dai Min for all her help and patience. Cheers to John Silver for his hospitality. Thanks also to Peggy Yu and Dai Lu – sorry that it was all *magwai faan*! Laura and Tony helped out with a much needed camera – ta. Thanks also to the BBC, Sotheby's, the HKTA, the MGTO, *HK Magazine* and apologies if I have overlooked anyone else.

This Book

The 1st edition of this book was researched and written by Carol Clewlow, and since then it has gone through several incarnations under the influence of a number of people. The 2nd edition was updated by Jim Hart, with a Guangzhou section added by an Australian student who had lived and studied in China for some time. The 3rd and 4th editions were updated by Alan Samalgalski, and the 5th, 6th, 7th and 8th editions were rewritten and updated by Robert Storey. This 9th edition was updated by Damian Harper.

From the Publishers

The 9th edition of *Hong Kong, Macau & Guangzhou* was pulled together in Lonely Planet's Melbourne office with the expertise of a cast of thousands. Lara Morcombe coordinated the editing, with assistance from Isabelle Young, Tony Davidson, Paul Harding and Emily Coles. The rough edges were swept away in proofing by Mic Looby and Russell Kerr. Chris Thomas coordinated the mapping, design and layout, with expert assistance from Leanne Peake and Glenn Beanland.

Quentin Frayne breezed through the language section, with Charles Qin assisting on Chinese script and Sally Steward casting a trained eye over the Portuguese accents. To create the glamorous illustrations, Mick Weldon scratched and Jenny Bowman scribbled. Leonie Mugavin sacrificed quiet nights and prime time TV to check prices and embassy phone numbers. Kristin Odijk, Sharon Kaur, Rachel Scott and Chris Love waltzed through the layout checks, Valerie Tellini scanned the images, and Dan Levin tweaked the fonts. Tim Uden held the team's sanity together during layout and Margie Jung created the lovely front cover.

A very special thank you to Ryan Law for writing the superb Hong Kong Film section, on short notice, and for assisting Lonely Planet in Hong Kong by acquiring images. Thanks also to Paul Wiegard and Siren Entertainment for the Hong Kong film images, and Mark Morrison for his contribution to the Hong Kong Film section.

Thanks also to Jody Fenn for the design advice and Margot Morcombe for the history tips, and Victoria Hung, Stanley Yip and the Hong Kong Tourist Association for their help and the use of their images. And finally, many thanks to Grandmaster William Cheung for graciously allowing us to reprint his personal martial arts photos.

Warning & Request

Things change – prices go up, schedules change, good places go bad and bad places go bankrupt – nothing stays the same. So, if you find things better or worse, recently opened or long since closed, please tell us and help make the next edition of this guide even more accurate and useful.

We value all of the feedback we receive from travellers to Hong Kong. Julie Young coordinates a small team who read and acknowledge every letter, postcard and email, and ensure that every morsel of information finds its way to the appropriate authors, editors and publishers.

Everyone who writes to us will find their name in the next edition of the appropriate guide and will also receive a free subscription to our quarterly newsletter, *Planet Talk*. The very best contributions will be rewarded with a free Lonely Planet guide.

Excerpts from your correspondence may appear in new editions of this guide; in our newsletter, *Planet Talk*; or in updates on our Web site – so please let us know if you don't want your letter published.

Thanks

All those involved in producing this book greatly appreciated the contributions of travellers who put so much effort into writing and telling us of their experiences. With thanks to everyone and apologies to anyone who's been left out, we'd like to mention the following people:

Sharon Adams, Scott Anderson, John Anderson, Jackie Ashe, Bob Barratt, Roger Beard, John MC Beath, Marshall Berdan, Rikki Bewley, Ulrike Bohm, David Boyall, Roger Boyes, Mark Brennan, Mathieu Bringer, Michael Brodrip, R Brooks, Sarah Butcher, NS Cadet, Annfielde Chan, Mike Charles, MeiLing Chua, Kwok Chung On, Nicole Clark, Laura Cloniger Smith, Gerry Connolly, Dan Coultas, Mark Cowell, Ake Dahllof, Jay Davidson, Andrew Davies, Kara Davis, K de Bruijn, Dr Ernest Deubelli, Kelsey Dorogi, Gaby Eidenberg, John Fender, Effie Fletcher, Ruby Foon, Markus Fussel, Michael Fysh, Melanie Gafield, Barbara & Bill Gallager, Geielula Geipel, Kristina Gidlof, Barbara Gilbert, Charlotte Glasser, NM Golchha, Rich Gordon, Richard E Graves, Rick Graves, Martin Gray, Harald Hagg, A Hagquist, Ken Haley, Paul Harding, John Harkness, Korey Hartwich, John E Hazel, Jennifer Henderson, Nick Hickton, Sasha Hilowitz, Janet Hilowitz-Schweda, Sally Hopkins, Douglas & Mary Ann Irvin, Helga & Ross Ivers, Mr Arved Jacast, Jean-Luc, Peter Jenkins, Ian Johnson, Barry Jones Hon, Soraya Jourdan, Scott Kerwin, Anu Kirjasuo, Carsten Koeppen, GF Kortschak, Gerhard Kotschenreuther, Kris Kwymenga, Paule Lamarque, Emma Langstaff, Alan Leahy, Dr Bernard Leeman, J Lewis, Torng Lih, Sam Lin, Will Linsdell, Klaus Ludwig, Maureen Lyons, Brent MacNeil, Amy & Dan Marcus, Gabriela Maya, James McDonald, Greg McElwain, Annette McGloin, Ciara McPartland, Alison McShanag, Jonathan Meltz, David Miller, RF Monch, Kim Morofke, Jon Morris, Dr David C New, Tracey Nicholls, Gregory O'Neil, Gillian Otlet, Andy Parkinson, Richard Peace, Mattijs Perdeck, E Philipson, Kevin Phillipp, B Pieters, Mr Christophe Pointreau, Jimmy Poole, Amanda Roll-Pickering, Keren Roman, Frank Ross, Inaki Salaberria, Stefan Samuelsson, Livraria Sao Paul, Viv Saunders, Mark Schaeffer, Karl Scharbert, Marianne Schuppe, Hartmut Schweda, Craig Scott, JA Searle, M Segal, Gideon Sheps, Jason Shumate, Lyle Sinrod Walter, Elaine Slade, David Sloan, Dr Sharon Smith, James Smith, David Steinke, Vanessa Sterling, Donal & Eva Stuart-Tsang, Andreas Suhrbier, Ken Sui, John Sweet, Jon Taffs, Phil Thomas, Eric Tilleson, Dr Joseph YS Ting, Mark Tinker, Catherine Twek, Hideaka Ueda, Kevin Utting, Derek van Pelt, Mr Tse Wai Man, Owen Walker, J Walker, Geoffrey Waters, Margaret & Nev Williams, Robert Williams, Jane Williams, Joanne Williams, Kathleen Williams, John Wilson, Yan Wong, Robert Woo, Alison & Rodney Woodcock

Contents

MACAU

FACTS ABOUT MACAU **340**

FACTS FOR THE VISITOR **351**

GETTING THERE & AWAY **371**

GETTING AROUND **375**

Map Legend

BOUNDARIES

▬▬·▬·▬·▬	.... International Boundary
─·─·─·─·	.... Provincial Boundary
─ ─ ─ ─	.... Disputed Boundary

ROUTES

════A25═	..... Freeway, with Route Number
═══════	.... Major Road
═══════	.... Minor Road
═══════	.... Minor Road - Unsealed
───────	.... City Road
───────	.... City Street
───────	.... City Lane
┼┼┼┼┼─●─┼	.... Train Route, with Station
─────Ⓜ──	.... Metro Route, with Station
╫─╫─╫─╫─╫	.... Cable Car or Chairlift
───────	.... Ferry Route
──────····	.... Walking Track/Tour

AREA FEATURES

	.... Building
++++++	.... Christian Cemetery
××××××	.... Non-Christian Cemetery
	.... Hotel
	.... Market
✿	.... Park, Gardens
	.... Pedestrian Mall
	.... Urban Area

HYDROGRAPHIC FEATURES

	.... Canal
	.... Coastline
	.... Creek, River
	.... Lake, Intermittent Lake
»» ╫╫ ∈	.... Rapids, Waterfalls
	.... Salt Lake
⊥ ⊥ ⊥ ⊥ ⊥ ⊥	.... Swamp

SYMBOLS

✪	CAPITAL	.... National Capital	✈	.... Airport	�🏛	.... Museum
◉	CAPITAL	...... Provincial Capital	∿	... Ancient or City Wall	♣	.... National Park
●	CITY	.... City	❻	.... Bank	←	.... One Way Street
●	Town	.... Town	⚓	.... Beach	🅿	.... Parking
●	Village	.... Village	🛡	.... Castle or Fort	)(	.... Pass
			⌒	.... Cave	⛽	.... Petrol Station
■		.... Place to Stay	⛪	..... Cathedral, Church	★	.... Police Station
▲		...... Camping Ground	∼∼∼	.... Cliff or Escarpment	✉	.... Post Office
⚏		.... Caravan Park	◥	.... Dive Site	❖	.... Shopping Centre
⌂		.... Hut or Chalet	◐	.... Embassy	▣	.... Shrine
			⊕	.... Hospital	▭	.... Swimming Pool
▼		.... Place to Eat	☀	.... Lighthouse	☎	.... Telephone
⛾		.... Pub or Bar	※	.... Lookout	▦	.... Temple
			Ⓜ	... Metro Entrance/Exit	⊙	.... Toilet
			⚱	.... Monument	❶	.... Tourist Information
			☪	.... Mosque	⊖	.... Transport
			▲	.... Mountain	🐾	.... Zoo

Note: not all symbols displayed above appear in this book

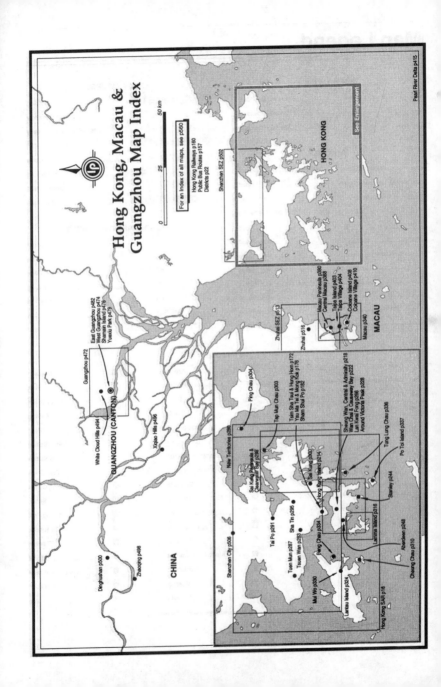

Hong Kong, Macau & Guangzhou Map Index

For an Index of all maps, see p560

Hong Kong Railways p160
Public Bus Routes p157
Districts p22

0   25   50 km

Pearl River Delta p15

See Enlargement

HONG KONG

MACAU

Macau Peninsula p380
Central Macau p388
Taipa Island p403
Taipa Village p404
Coloane Island p408
Coloane Village p410

Macau p340

Shenzhen SEZ p502

Zhuhai SEZ p13

Zhuhai p516

CHINA

Dinghushan p500

Zhaoqing p498

Guangzhou p472
East Guangzhou p482
West Guangzhou p474
Shamian Island p476
Yuexiu Park p479

GUANGZHOU (CANTON)

White Cloud Hills p494

Xiqiao Hills p496

Shenzhen City p506

Tai Po p291

Tsuen Wan p283

Sha Tin p295

Tuen Mun p287

Mui Wo p330

Lantau Island p324

Cheung Chau p310

Aberdeen p248

Peng Chau p304

Lamma Island p316

Stanley p244

Ping Chau p298

Tap Mun Chau p304

New Territories p268

Sai Kung Peninsula &
Clearwater Bay p298

Tsim Sha Tsui & Hung Hom p172
Yau Ma Tei & Mong Kok p176
Sham Shui Po p182

Sheung Wan, Central & Admiralty p218
Wan Chai & Causeway Bay p222
Lan Kwai Fong p265
Around Victoria Peak p228

Tung Lung Chau p336

Po Toi Island p337

Hong Kong Island p216

Hong Kong SAR p18

Introduction

The handover of power from Britain to the People's Republic of China, marked the final chapter in Hong Kong's 150 year colonial saga. Prophets of gloom had much in store for Hong Kong on midnight 30 June 1997, but despite the pessimists, Hong Kong (under a new name Hong Kong SAR, or Special Administrative Region) was quickly back to business, albeit under new management.

The city is an exciting fusion of east and west. The vast majority of people are Chinese, and their customs, folklore and language are Cantonese. The world of the Chinese – the noise, chaos, food and language – is everywhere. Intruding into this Chinese universe are familiar western symbols – Christian churches share the religious landscape with Taoist and Buddhist temples, while cosmopolitan restaurants punctuate the avenues of Cantonese food stalls. The meeting of these two worlds blends into a ripe and invigorating cocktail of colour, aroma and sensation.

Hong Kong has something for everyone. Shoppers will trip over themselves to reach the huge malls in Central, Admiralty, Causeway Bay and Kowloon. Romantic travellers will enjoy the nocturnal view over the waters of Victoria Harbour, and museums abound for those who wish to dig a bit deeper into local history and culture. Admirers of modern architecture can view Hong Kong's arresting Central district and for those who need more space, a bus ride can take you away to sandy beaches and secluded walks.

Hong Kong has surprising natural retreats for lovers of the big outdoors. A short ferry ride away is Lamma Island, an overgrown idyll that nature enthusiasts will find hard to resist. The New Territories cuts a huge swathe to the north, offering bracing walks among dramatic and spectacular countryside.

Hong Kong at night offers yet more. Lovers of good food will be spoilt for choice

in the city's eclectic eateries. A recent revolution in the restaurant scene has turned the map of Hong Kong even more into an atlas of the world's food. Hong Kong's bars colour the spectrum from the alternative and the chic to the refined. And to see the early hours in, Hong Kong's nightclubs offer an energetic fusion of rhythms and moods.

An hour away across the water is charming Macau, a sleepy Portuguese territory hanging onto southern Guangdong Province. Not officially a Portuguese colony, Macau has all the trappings of one: gaily painted Catholic churches, traditional buildings, narrow streets and splendid Portuguese food. The door is set to close on Portugal's foot on 20 December 1999, when this small enclave returns to China, Hong Kong style, to become a SAR. If you can visit beforehand, do so – Macau is brimming with atmosphere and is so much more than a charming diversion from Hong Kong.

Last, but by no means least, is mainland China. Shenzhen and Zhuhai are the most accessible cities, but for the most part are business destinations. Most travellers head to Guangzhou (formerly known as Canton), capital of Guangdong Province and an energetic city on the cutting edge of China's opening up to the outside world. Not far from Guangzhou is Zhaoqing, an attractive town with scenic limestone towers, and Dinghushan, a wooded area of restful walks and streams.

Facts about Hong Kong

HISTORY

'Albert is so amused at my having got the island of Hong Kong', wrote Queen Victoria to King Leopold of Belgium in 1841. While her husband could see the funny side of this apparently useless little island off the south coast of China, the British foreign secretary, Lord Palmerston, was less amused. He considered the acquisition of Hong Kong a massive bungle. 'A barren island with hardly a house upon it!' he raged in a letter to the man responsible for the deal, Captain Charles Elliot.

Western Traders

The British were not the first westerners to open trade with China. Regular Chinese contact with modern European nations began in 1557, when the Portuguese were given permission to set up a base in nearby Macau. Jesuit priests arrived in 1582 and established themselves at Zhaoqing, a town west of Guangzhou. Their scientific and technical knowledge aroused the interest of the imperial court, and a few priests were permitted to live in Beijing.

Guangzhou began trading with the Europeans in 1685. British ships began to arrive regularly from the East India Company bases on the Indian coast, and traders were allowed to establish 'factories' (offices and residences) near Guangzhou to export tea and silk. From the end of the 17th century the British and French were trading regularly at Guangzhou, followed by the Dutch, Danes, Swedes and Americans.

The opening of Guangzhou is an indication of how unimportant the Imperial court considered trade with the west. Guangzhou was far from Nanjing and Beijing, which were the centres of power under the isolationist Ming (1368-1644) and Qing (1644-1911) dynasties. It was considered to exist on the edge of a wilderness, and its inhabitants were regarded somewhat suspiciously and referred to as the 'southern barbarians'. It was

therefore fitting that Guangzhou traded with the 'western barbarians' – as far as the Chinese were concerned, only the Chinese empire was civilised and the people beyond its frontiers were barbarians.

In 1757 the fuse to the Opium Wars was lit when, by imperial edict, the Co Hong (a Guangzhou merchants' guild) gained exclusive rights to China's foreign trade. Numerous restrictions were placed on the western traders: it became illegal for foreigners to learn Chinese or to deal with anyone except the Co Hong; they could only reside in Guangzhou from September to March; they were restricted to Shamian Island on Guangzhou's Pearl River; and they had to leave their wives and families downriver in Macau. The traders complained about the tight restrictions, but nevertheless, trade flourished.

Trade in favour of China was not what the western merchants had in mind and, in 1773, the British unloaded a thousand chests at Guangzhou, each containing almost 70kg of Bengal opium. The intention was to change the balance of trade, as British purchases of tea, silk and porcelain far outweighed Chinese purchases of wool and spices. This manoeuvre was successful and opium sales skyrocketed.

Emperor Dao Guang, alarmed at the drain of silver from the country (the Chinese paid for purchases of tea, silk and opium with silver) and the increasing number of opium addicts, issued an edict in 1796 totally banning the drug trade. This was ignored by the foreigners, who continued to trade with the help of the Co Hong and corrupt Chinese officials.

In 1839 the emperor dispatched Lin Zexiu, an official of great personal integrity, to Guangzhou with orders to stamp out the opium trade. It took Lin a week to surround the British in Guangzhou, cut off their food supplies and demand the surrender of all opium in their possession. The

British held out for six weeks until they were ordered by Captain Charles Elliot to surrender 20,000 chests of opium – Elliot was under instructions from Lord Palmerston to solve the trade problem. Lin then had the 'foreign mud' publicly destroyed in the small city of Humen.

This, along with other minor incidents, was the pretext that hawkish elements in the British government needed to win support for military action against China. An expeditionary force under Rear Admiral George Elliot (a cousin of Charles Elliot) was sent to extract reparations and secure favourable trade arrangements.

The force arrived in June 1840 and besieged Guangzhou before sailing north and occupying or blockading a number of ports and cities along the coast and Yangzi River. To the alarm of the emperor, the force threatened Beijing, and Qi Shan was sent to negotiate with the Elliots. The British were persuaded to withdraw from northern China, and in return Qi agreed to the Convention of Chuan Bi which unofficially ceded Hong Kong Island to the British.

Neither side recognised the convention, but despite this the British commodore Gordon Bremmer led a contingent of naval men ashore and claimed Hong Kong Island for Britain on 26 January 1841.

In late February, Captain Charles Elliot successfully attacked the Bogue forts at Humen, took control of the Pearl River and laid siege to Guangzhou. He withdraw in May after extracting Y6 million and various other concessions from the merchants of Guangzhou city.

In August 1841, a powerful British force sailed north and seized Xiamen, Ningbo, Shanghai and other ports. With the strategic city of Nanjing under immediate threat, the Chinese were forced to accept the Treaty of Nanjing which, among other things, officially ceded the island of Hong Kong to the British 'in perpetuity'.

In 1856 war broke out again after Chinese soldiers boarded the British merchant ship *Arrow* to search for pirates. French troops joined the British in this war, while Russia and the USA lent naval support. The war was brought to an end by the Treaty of Tianjin, which permitted the British to establish diplomatic representation in China.

Despite Chinese warnings, in 1859 a flotilla carrying the first 'British envoy and minister plenipotentiary' to Beijing attempted to force its way up the Pei Ho River. It was fired upon by the Chinese and sustained heavy losses. Using this as an excuse, a combined British and French force invaded China and marched on Beijing. Another treaty, the Convention of Beijing, was forced on the Chinese, ceding the Kowloon Peninsula and Stonecutters Island to the British.

Britain made a final land grab 40 years later under the pretext that it needed more land to protect the colony, as China was on the verge of being parcelled up into 'spheres of influence' by the western powers and Japan. In June 1898 the Second Convention of Beijing presented Britain with a 99 year lease for the New Territories, beginning 1 July 1898 and ending 1 July 1997.

War & Revolution

Just before WWII Hong Kong began a shift away from trade to manufacturing. This move was hastened by the civil war in China during the 1920s and 30s, and by the Japanese invasion of the country – when Chinese capitalists fled with their money to the safety of British colony. The crunch finally came during the Korean War in the early 1950s, when a USA embargo on Chinese goods threatened to strangle the colony economically. To survive, the colony had to develop industries such as banking and insurance, as well as some manufacturing outlets.

When the communists came to power in China in 1949, many people were sure that Hong Kong would be overrun. Militarily, Beijing could have overrun Hong Kong in less time than it takes to make fried rice. But while the communists denounced the 'unequal treaties' which created a British colony on their soil, they recognised Hong Kong's economic importance to China.

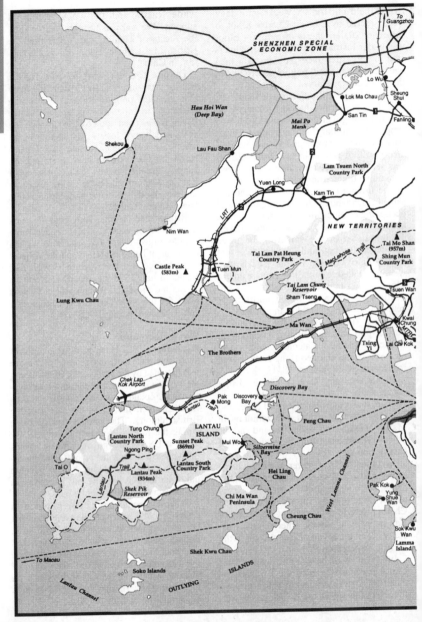

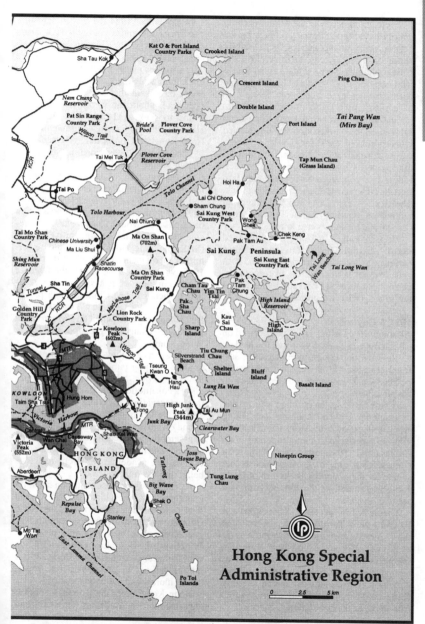

Hong Kong Special
Administrative Region

0   2.5   5 km

Even without force, the Chinese could simply have ripped down the fence on the border and sent the masses to peacefully settle on Hong Kong territory. In 1962 China actually staged what looked like a trial run for this, sending 70,000 people across the border in a couple of weeks.

In 1967, at the height of the Great Proletarian Cultural Revolution, Hong Kong again seemed doomed when riots by disgruntled workers rocked the colony. Several bombs were detonated. In the same year, a militia of 300 armed Chinese crossed the border, killing five policemen and penetrating 3km into the New Territories before pulling back. The then governor, David Trench, kept an aircraft on stand-by at Kai Tak airport in case he and his family had to flee.

Property values in Hong Kong plunged sharply, as did China's foreign exchange earnings as trade and tourism ground to a halt. Perhaps it was the loss of foreign exchange that sobered China for, by the end of the 1960s, order had been restored.

1997 & Beyond
Although Hong Kong and China depend on each other economically, during the lead up to 1997 the population of Hong Kong suffered considerable anxiety at the possible political and economic consequences of the handover.

For the Chinese, the problem was not one of economics, but of keeping face. Hong Kong will go down in history as the last survivor of a period of foreign imperialism on Chinese soil. That period is seen by most Chinese as a time of great weakness and shame for their country; the return of Hong Kong was to deliver the country from that sense of disgrace.

Theoretically at least, the expiry of Britain's New Territories lease meant that the Chinese border would move south as far as Boundary St on the Kowloon Peninsula, taking in the whole territory, except for Hong Kong Island, Stonecutters Island and Kowloon. It was hard to see how Hong Kong could remain viable when severed from most of the population.

In September 1984 the British agreed to hand back the entire colony – lock, stock and skyscrapers – to China in 1997. An alternative was to divide it – leaving each side with a useless piece, and Britain hanging on to a colony which, arguably, it did not want. Some have said that Britain should have kept quiet about the whole issue, forcing China to seek a Macau-style solution – allowing the British to continue running Hong Kong with no formal agreement.

The agreement, enshrined in a document known as the Sino-British Joint Declaration, theoretically allows Hong Kong to retain its pre-handover social, economic and legal systems for at least 50 years after 1997. Hong Kong as a colonial possession of England would disappear and re-emerge as a Special Administrative Region (SAR) of China. Hong Kong would be permitted to retain its capitalist system after 1997, while across the border the Chinese would continue with a system that it labelled socialist. The Chinese catch phrase for this was 'one country, two systems'. Deng Xiaoping also called this 'gangren zhi gang', or 'Hong Kong people governing Hong Kong'.

In 1988, as a follow-up to the Joint Declaration, Beijing published *The Basic Law for Hong Kong*, a hefty document resembling a constitution. The Basic Law permits the preservation of Hong Kong's legal system, and guarantees the right of property and ownership. It also includes the rights of assembly, free speech, association, travel and movement, correspondence, choice of occupation, academic research, religious belief and the right to strike.

As China's internal constitution has lofty guarantees of individual freedoms and respect for human rights, few Hong Kong Chinese had faith in the agreement. The guarantees were seen as empty promises. Effectively the Basic Law provided Beijing with the means to interfere in Hong Kong's internal affairs to preserve public order, public morals and national security.

Hong Kong under the British was never anything more than a benign autocracy, and

Beijing made it abundantly clear that it also would not allow Hong Kong to establish its own democratically elected government. The chief executive was to be chosen by a Beijing appointed panel of delegates, while some lower officials would be elected by the people.

Beijing demanded that Britain remove its Ghurkha battalion, to be replaced by the People's Liberation Army (PLA). This generated both fear and scepticism. The Chinese government said it was a matter of 'national sovereignty', but sceptics claimed it was an attempt to suppress democracy and dissent. Besides, the British military and Ghurkha battalion were sitting on extremely valuable real estate, such as the HMS Tamar Naval Centre in Central. Attempts to transfer these bases to civilian use before the handover were adamantly rejected – the PLA were set to gain property worth billions of US dollars.

Hong Kong's fledgling pro-democracy movement denounced the Joint Declaration as the new 'unequal treaty' and the Basic Law as a 'basic flaw'. Hong Kong residents never had any opportunity to vote for or against these agreements – the negotiations were held entirely behind closed doors. Some accused Britain of selling out the best interests of the people of Hong Kong in order to maintain good economic relations with China.

Forebodings of other grim possibilities emerged with the massacre of pro-democracy demonstrators at Tiananmen Square in Beijing on 4 June 1989. In Hong Kong, more than one million people attended protest rallies – a figure that represents one in six people (the anniversary continues to be remembered every year at a candlelight vigil held in Victoria Park). Chinese officials, based in Hong Kong, who had spoken out against the Tiananmen killings, were removed from their posts, or sought asylum in the USA and Europe. The residents who had money and skills emigrated to any country that would take them and newspapers began to warn of a 'brain drain' that would cripple the economy.

The Gate of Heavenly Peace

In the week leading up to the 4 June 1998 anniversary of the Tiananmen (Gate of Heavenly Peace) massacre, Hong Kong residents weren't pulling punches. The demonstrations were significantly different from previous years in that they were the first ever held on Chinese soil. The fact that the demonstrations were allowed to proceed at all has huge implications for the future of the ex-colony and for China. The situation facing Beijing is starkly simple: there is one part of China where people can dissent and express their discontent, and another (the rest of the mainland) where they cannot. This is the sort of tension that tends to quickly unravel a society's fabric. Many are hoping that the controversial new law on sedition and subversion, that is due to be passed by the Provisional Legislature, will not infringe upon the right to protest. Beijing will somehow have to neuter the pro-democracy camp if it wants to avoid such ideals being exported across the border to a land ravenous for political freedoms.

Jiang Zemin may have found it hard to stomach the sight of the radical April 5th Action Group parading a coffin daubed with the words 'the political power that kills, stinks for ten thousand years', but this is the legacy that is handed to him. Hong Kong offers the Chinese Communist Party (CCP) wealth and power on a plate, but with this comes the unappetising side salad of responsibilities. It takes political maturity to seize this kind of nettle, a kind of maturity and confidence that the CCP is yet to demonstrate. Jiang Zemin has no doubt taken a keen interest in recent developments in Indonesia.

Luckily for the powerbrokers in Beijing, urban councillors in Hong Kong voted 19 to 18 to stop a sculpture called the 'Pillar of Shame' being erected in public. The 8m effigy of contorted human bodies and faces, sculpted by the Danish sculptor Jens Galschiot, commemorates those who died in the Tiananmen massacre. The vote was a close call and the pro-democracy camp has responded symbolically by burying the statue until full democracy comes to Hong Kong, when it will be dug up again.

After the massacre confidence plummeted – the Hong Kong stock market fell 22% in one day, and a great deal of capital headed overseas. In the aftermath the Hong Kong government took steps to rebuild confidence by launching an Airport and Port Project estimated at HK\$160 billion and designed to lure foreign investors.

Sino-British relations worsened with the arrival in 1992 of Chris Patten, Hong Kong's last British governor. Patten set out to give Hong Kong a democratic foundation at the eleventh hour. He pushed through a series of legislative reforms that eventually led to direct elections for both lawmakers and municipal officials. Hong Kong residents were largely sceptical, with many wondering why Britain had chosen to wait until this late date to start experiments in democracy. China reacted badly, first levelling daily verbal attacks on Patten, then threatening the post-1997 careers of any pro-democracy politicians or officials. When these tactics didn't work, it targeted Hong Kong's economy. Negotiations on numerous business contracts straddling 1997 suddenly dragged to a halt, and Beijing successfully scared off foreign investors by boycotting all talks on the new airport program.

Sensing that it had alienated even its supporters in the colony, China backed down, and in 1994 gave its blessing to the new Chek Lap Kok airport. Its hostility toward direct elections remained, and China vowed to throw out all democratically elected legislators post-1997 and replace them with a 'provisional legislature', which would serve until further elections were held under the new government.

On 31 August 1994, China adopted a resolution to terminate the terms of office of Hong Kong's three tiers of elected bodies (district boards, municipal councils and the legislature). A Provisional Legislative Council (Linshi Lifahui) was elected by Beijing to prepare itself to replace the existing Legislative Council – it operated from nearby Shenzhen, as it had no authority until the transferral of power. The Democratic Party in Hong Kong, which had 19 seats in the Legislative Council, was the strongest opponent of the Provisional Legislative Council.

As for the executive branch of power, Beijing-led elections were held in 1996 for the position of Chief Executive – this position would replace that of governor. The former shipping tycoon Tung Chee Hwa was chosen. For Hong Kong residents he was the acceptable face of China – being largely affable, a speaker of English and Cantonese (although born in Shanghai) and an expert businessman.

Despite the outrage from the Democrats, who claimed that the Provisional Legislature was illegal, the panic as the 1997 handover drew near gave way to pragmatism. The feeling was that Hong Kong would have to make the most of the situation – that pessimism would get it nowhere and that optimism would generate stability and hope.

The picture before the handover was rosy, the financial outlook for Hong Kong was good and the economy strong. This paved the way for a smooth transfer of power and a gracious exit for the departing colonial power.

China agreed to a low-key entry into Hong Kong and kept the PLA troops off the streets. On the night of 30 June 1997, Chris Patten sailed emotionally away from a city holding its breath as the new rulers perused their domain. The handover celebrations were watched by millions around the world. Prince Charles was stoic, Patten wept and Chinese Premier Jiang Zemin tried to restrain his happiness.

Initially, the new Hong Kong SAR started out on a good footing, and the hordes of photojournalists that had been propping up the bars of Central for weeks decided to screw on the lens cap and head home. There were no stories. Nothing untoward was happening and the world started to look elsewhere for news. The expected political storm did not appear – China had adopted a sensible hands-off policy and it appeared to be working well.

Taiwan and Hong Kong

The hands-off approach that China has successfully adopted in its management of Hong Kong (so far) isn't just to keep Hong Kong residents from marching on the streets. The Chinese government wants to prove that it can manage one incredibly rich piece of real estate (Hong Kong), so that it can manage another (Taiwan). So, Hong Kong has been left to run itself according to the timeless principles of market forces; this is exactly what the powerbrokers in Beijing think the Taiwanese want to see. China wants Taiwan to return to the flock of provinces that make up the People's Republic of China under an extension of the 'one country, two systems' approach that is currently in vogue.

Unfortunately, Hong Kong's Chief Executive, Tung Chee Hwa, couldn't quite restrain himself from ordering the pulling down of Taiwanese flags on the Taiwanese double tenth celebration on 10 October 1997. Tung Chee Hwa quickly rushed to massage everyone's feelings with the cryptic words: 'We are a free society and of course shall have freedom of speech'.

GEOGRAPHY

Hong Kong's 1070 sq km is divided into four main areas – Kowloon, Hong Kong Island, the New Territories and the outlying islands.

Kowloon is a peninsula on the north side of the harbour. The southern tip of this peninsula (Tsim Sha Tsui) is the biggest tourist area and is where most of the hotels are situated. Kowloon proper only includes the land south of Boundary Rd – a mere 12 sq km. North of Boundary St is New Kowloon, which is part of the New Territories.

Hong Kong Island covers 78 sq km, or roughly 7% of Hong Kong's land area. The island is on the south side of the harbour and is the main business area, with numerous tourist hotels and sightseeing spots. Towering above the skyscrapers is the Peak, Hong Kong's premier scenic viewpoint.

The New Territories occupies 980 sq km, or 91% of Hong Kong's land area, and are sandwiched between Kowloon and the Chinese border. It is home to about one third of Hong Kong's population. Foreign visitors rarely make the effort to visit the New Territories, even though there is much to offer.

The outlying islands refers to any island apart from Hong Kong Island. Officially, they are part of the New Territories and make up about 20% of Hong Kong's total land area. There are actually 234 islands

and while many are tiny rocks, the largest (Lantau) is nearly twice the size of Hong Kong Island. The islands offer a taste of tranquil village life and in some ways are the best part of Hong Kong. Some of the larger islands, including Lantau, Cheung Chau and Lamma, are well served by commuter ferries and offer both residents and visitors an escape from Hong Kong's blistering urban pace. They are also home to some excellent country parks.

Within these four main areas are numerous neighbourhoods. Hong Kong Island is divided into Central, Wan Chai, Causeway Bay, Quarry Bay and so on, while Kowloon districts include Tsim Sha Tsui, Yau Ma Tei, Mong Kok, Hung Hom etc.

CLIMATE

Hong Kong is perched on the south-east coast of China just a little to the south of the Tropic of Cancer. It's on the same latitude as Hawaii and Calcutta, but the climate is not as tropical. A powerful Arctic wind blows across the huge land mass of Asia during winter, and in summer monsoons blow from the south, bringing humid tropical air.

Winter is chilly, windy and frequently cloudy. It rains infrequently, but when it does, it's usually a chilly, depressing drizzle that lasts for days on end. It never snows or freezes, but it's cold enough to wear a warm

HONG KONG

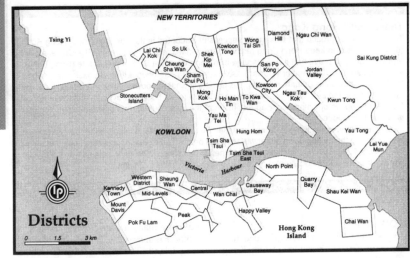

Districts

0   1.5   3 km

NEW TERRITORIES

Tsing Yi

Lai Chi Kok
So Uk
Shek Kip Mei
Cheung Sha Wan
Sham Shui Po
Kowloon Tong
Wong Tai Sin
Diamond Hill
Ngau Chi Wan
Sai Kung District
San Po Kong
Jordan Valley
Stonecutters Island
Mong Kok
Ho Man Tin
To Kwa Wan
Kowloon City
Ngau Tau Kok
Kwun Tong
Yau Ma Tei
KOWLOON
Hung Hom
Yau Tong
Tsim Sha Tsui
Tsim Sha Tsui East
Lei Yue Mun
Victoria Harbour
North Point
Western District
Sheung Wan
Central
Wan Chai
Causeway Bay
Quarry Bay
Shau Kei Wan
Kennedy Town
Mid-Levels
Happy Valley
Chai Wan
Mount Davis
Peak
Pok Fu Lam
Hong Kong Island

sweater or coat. Many travellers arrive at the airport totally unprepared in shorts and a T-shirt. A low cloud ceiling leaves the mountains often shrouded in mist, and making it pointless to visit the Peak and other scenic outlooks. Winter usually continues into March, often ending when the Arctic wind stops.

Spring is a short season and is a good time to visit. It's generally warm by the end of March and stays pleasant until the end of May. In March or April, an occasional wind will swoop out of the north and send temperatures plummeting for a few days. Big thunder showers become more frequent as

June approaches. June tends to be the wettest month and the beginning of the summer monsoon. The Chinese call this the 'plum rain'. Summer (July and August) is sunny, hot and humid, with an occasional thunder shower.

September brings just a hint of cooler weather, but is also the month during which Hong Kong is most likely to be hit by typhoons. These vary in size from tropical storms to severe super-typhoons. If the typhoon passes by Hong Kong at a distance, it will bring a little rain and wind that might only last for half a day. If it scores a direct hit (ie within 100km of the city), the winds can be deadly and it may rain for days on end. You can't go outside during a bad typhoon and most businesses shut down. When the spectre of a typhoon becomes a possibility, warnings are broadcast continuously on the TV and radio. You can also contact the Royal Observatory typhoon hotline (☎ 2835-1473) for information.

Autumn is from October until early December and is the best time to visit. The weather is generally sunny and dry.

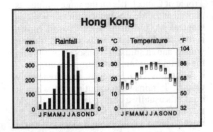

Hong Kong

mm Rainfall in   °C Temperature °F

Typhoons

Almost every year a typhoon heads for Hong Kong. Despite the awesome capacity typhoons possess for major flooding and destruction, many residents in Hong Kong welcome the odd tempest blowing into town, as it can virtually guarantee time off work. But what exactly is a typhoon?

A typhoon is a violent tropical cyclone, a massive whirlpool of air currents often tens of kilometres high and hundreds of kilometres wide. Feeding off rising moisture, tropical cyclones can only survive over warm oceans and once they hit land, typhoons quickly die out.

The 'eye' of the cyclone is generally tens of kilometres wide and basically a column of descending air, which is much calmer than the surrounding vortex.

Cyclones can last for as long as a few weeks, but not all will mature into typhoons. Only about half of the cyclones in the South China Sea ever reach typhoon ferocity. The gradation of ferocity of tropical cyclones ascends as follows: tropical depression (up to 62km/h); tropical storm (63 to 87km/h); severe tropical storm (88 to 117km/h); and typhoon (118km/h or more).

Hong Kong is a small target, so the chances of a direct hit (when typhoon intensity winds pass within 100km of the city) by a typhoon is actually small. Only a dozen or so have struck in the past 50 years, despite the 15 or so that are in the vicinity each year. The No 10 signal goes up when this happens, as hurricane force winds are expected, along with widespread damage.

Some famous typhoons have included: Typhoon Wanda (1962), which delivered hourly mean wind speeds of 133km/h and peak gusts of 259km/h; Typhoon Ellen (1983), which killed 22 people and injured over 300 (insurance claims totalled over HK$300 million); Typhoon Wayne (1986), which blew in and out of town like a boomerang that wouldn't go away; and Typhoon Brenda (1989), which came heavily laden with rain and caused widespread flooding.

ECOLOGY & ENVIRONMENT

Hong Kong is an urbanised, consumer-oriented, throw-away society with a *laissez-faire* stance towards business and economic growth that has ensured that few or no measures exist to control water, waste or air pollution. After nearly 150 years of ignoring the issue, in 1989 the Hong Kong government suddenly realised that Hong Kong was in danger of becoming a vast, densely populated cesspool.

The Environmental Protection Department was established as a regulatory body to deal with the 15,700 tonnes of municipal waste and 32,000 tonnes of construction waste generated daily in Hong Kong. An aggressive public service campaign was implemented to remind locals not to treat the roads, waterways and parks as rubbish bins, though judging by the rubbish on the streets, not everyone is getting the message; the waste figures have leapt by 83% since 1986.

Most construction waste comes not from the erection of new buildings, but from the demolition of old ones. Landfills are being opened to absorb the enormous amount of trash and solid waste.

Water pollution has become one of Hong Kong's most serious ecological problems. Victoria Harbour is in a pitiful state, suffering from years of degradation from pollution and sewage. Factories, farms and restaurants in the New Territories are now being criticised for dumping untreated waste into freshwater streams or the sea. Unfortunately, a great deal of damage has already been done and the government admits that some New Territories' streams are 'no better than open sewers'.

In early 1998, Hong Kong's newspapers announced a 'red tide' of toxic algae that was culling half of the territory's fish stocks. The 'red tide' referred to the colour imparted into the water by the build-up of toxic microscopic plankton. The government set up a monitoring system for swimming beaches based on the amount of disease-causing bacteria in the water; as a result, five popular beaches were closed. The cause was traced to increasing pollution levels in the Pearl River Delta, especially from the illegal dumping of sewage and industrial waste into rivers in Guangdong, north of Hong Kong. For details on the risk that this could pose to your health, particularly if you're considering swimming at one of Hong Kong's many beaches, refer to the Health chapter.

Pollution is also a concern for a number of Hong Kong's animal species. The population of Chinese White Dolphins is under threat from chemical pollution, increased boat traffic and the destruction of the natural shoreline to make way for land reclamation schemes. The huge nature reserve and bird haven of Mai Po Marsh is seriously threatened by both the untreated pig sewage that has flooded into Deep Bay for years and the increase in waste from Shenzhen. The bird sanctuaries in the wetland areas of Tin Shui Wai, Kam Tin and Kwu Yung around Mai Po, are being threatened by government plans to build huge residential housing estates in the New Territories to satisfy the increasing demand for apartments.

Another of Hong Kong's most serious problems is air pollution. Smoke-belching factories, ceaseless construction and a high proportion of diesel vehicles have made for dangerous levels of particulate matter and nitrogen dioxide. Case numbers of asthma and bronchial infection have soared in recent years, and doctors blame the poor air quality. Travellers with respiratory conditions should take this into consideration if planning to stay for a prolonged period. See the Health chapter for more details.

It remains to be seen whether China will continue to support the fight against pollution in Hong Kong. There is little cause for optimism, considering China's appalling track record on environmental protection and its apparent desire to turn itself into an industrial wasteland.

Not all of Hong Kong is ravaged by pollution. Around 40% of the territory's total land area is in protected country parks. These areas are off-limits to development and private motor vehicles, and contain all

of Hong Kong's 17 freshwater reservoirs. Hikers, campers, birdwatchers and other nature-lovers all benefit from this protection. Most of the country parks are in the New Territories and the outlying islands, but even the higher mountainous slopes of Hong Kong Island are protected.

FLORA & FAUNA

Hong Kong is home to a wide variety of animal and plant life. While the constant expansion of new towns has decreased the number of larger animals, there are smaller mammals, amphibians, reptiles, birds and insects in large numbers.

One of the largest natural habitats for wildlife conservation is the Mai Po Marshes, which together with the Inner Deep Bay area are listed as a 'Wetland of International Importance' under the Ramsar Convention of 1995. Mai Po is a network of ponds and mudflats that attract almost 70,000 waterbirds every winter. The mudflats of Deep Bay and Mai Po combined form an essential stopping-off place for migratory birds. Roughly 300 species of bird have been spotted in the area, among the shrimp ponds and dwarf mangroves.

Kowloon and the New Territories provide homes to quite a number of Long-tailed Macaques and Rhesus monkeys – one of these monkeys made it to Kennedy Town on Hong Kong Island in early 1998 and was regularly spotted hanging from lampposts and traffic lights. Wild boars, sometimes weighing over 100kg, are found in some rural spots and are regarded as pests because they dig up crops. Much more aesthetic, and rarely seen, are the barking deer (also called muntjaks) and black-and-white quilled Chinese porcupines. The latter can even be found on the high slopes of Hong Kong Island. Small mammal species include Chinese leopard cats, civet cats, masked palm civets, ferret badgers, otters, porcupines, shrews and bats. Leopards and tigers, some of which were seen in Hong Kong's initial years, were all but wiped out at the beginning of the 20th century. The last tiger seen in the New Territories was said to have been shot in 1915, though there were claims of sightings in later years.

An interesting creature is the Chinese pangolin, a scaly mammal that resembles an armadillo. When attacked, it rolls itself up into an impenetrable ball. Unfortunately, its existence is threatened because the Chinese use its flesh as a medicinal tonic and aphrodisiac. Frogs, lizards and snakes appear in large numbers in the New Territories and the outlying islands – a massive Burmese Python was caught on Lantau Island in 1997.

A walk in the New Territories or a trip to one of the outlying islands will provide the eager entomologist or botanist with a splendid selection of insects and plant life. Hong Kong is home to more than 200 species of butterfly, many of which are unusually elegant. Dragonflies, spiders and large moths also inhabit the territory, including giant silkworm moths (one type of which has a wingspan of over 20cm!).

Hong Kong waters are rich in sealife, including sharks – the popular beaches are equipped with shark nets. Hong Kong is also visited by four species of whale and 11 species of dolphin, including Chinese White Dolphins (Sousa chinensis), which are actually pink in colour. The dolphins are also known as the Indo-Pacific Humpbacked dolphin. About 100 to 150 of these lovely mammals inhabit the coastal waters around Hong Kong, finding the brackish, though increasingly polluted, waters in the vicinity a perfect habitat. See the boxed text 'Hong Kong's Vanishing Pink Dolphins' in the Outlying Islands chapter for more details. Endangered green turtles still pay a call to Sham Wan beach on Lamma Island to lay eggs, but the eggs are considered a delicacy by the locals, so this hatching ground is under threat. See the boxed text 'Green Turtles' in the Outlying Islands chapter for more details.

A walk along the more secluded beaches (eg on Lamma Island) can turn up cowries, limpets, cone shells, helmet shells, turban shells and bearded ark shells. Cone shells should be approached with caution as these can be very poisonous if alive – some species can kill. The venomous textile cone shell finds a habitat on the shores of Hong Kong. Such beaches are also the home to a wide variety of plant life, including creeping beach vitex (vitex trifolia), rattlebox (croatalaria retusa), beach naupaka (scaevola sericea) and screw pine (pandanus tectorius).

Lamma Island, Cheung Chau, Lantau Island and the New Territories are thick with vegetation. Lamma has an amazing variety of plant life that even the most casual observer can appreciate. To see such richness of foliage and grass so close to Hong Kong Island is a wonder. A nocturnal walk on Lamma Island is accompanied by a host of noises from the undergrowth, and the croaking of frogs and toads. The dry racket of cicadas can be heard on the islands and the New Territories during summer.

GOVERNMENT & POLITICS

The Hong Kong SAR is a unique phenomenon within China, or for that matter, anywhere else in the world.

Hong Kong is not politically democratic, nor has it ever been. Democratic elements exist within its political structure, but this is by no means across the board, and it is highly unlikely that democracy will develop any further. Business rather than politics has always governed Hong Kong, and political power is said to be drifting more towards the business sector. Hong Kong's society is extremely unpoliticised – the last British governor of Hong Kong tried to change this, though with limited success.

The executive branch of power is led by the Chief Executive, who is currently Shanghai business tycoon Tung Chee Hwa. The position of Chief Executive is supported by an Executive Council that advises on policy matters. Other positions answerable to the Chief Executive are the Chief Secretary for the administration (who is responsible for the formulation of government policies and their implementation), a Financial Secretary (who is responsible for the fiscal and economic policies of the government) and the Secretary for Justice (who is responsible for drafting all legislation).

The legislature controls public expenditure, legislates and supposedly moderates the power of the administration. The pre-handover legislature (Legislative Council) was shadowed by a Beijing appointed Provisional Legislature, which was installed on 1 July 1997. This provisional body served until May 1998, when a new Legislative Council was elected partially by the people of Hong Kong, partially by the business constituencies and partially by powerbrokers in Beijing.

The judiciary interprets the law as enacted by the legislature. It is an independent branch of government. The Court of Final Appeal has the power of final adjudication.

The Urban Council is in charge of the day-to-day running of services in Hong Kong Island and Kowloon, including street cleaning, garbage collection, food hygiene, hawkers' licences and public recreation. In the New Territories, the Regional Council provides services similar to those provided by the Urban Council.

In 1982, 18 District Boards were established to give Hong Kong residents a degree of control in their local area. These boards consist of government officials and elected representatives, but have little power.

The Hong Kong Civil Service employs approximately 173,000 people. Up until recently, several thousand of these employees were expats, many of whom held top policy-making positions. The number of expats in positions of power has dwindled dramatically. British professionals are no longer recruited for top administrative posts in the territory's police force. The Joint Declaration decrees that expats cannot head major government departments, nor hold deputy positions in some departments.

Politically, things have gone surprisingly smoothly, but there are subtle changes afoot. Many say that power is drifting into the hands of Tung Chee Hwa. The leader of the Democratic Party, Martin Lee, has called this process 'the beginning of the Singapore-isation of Hong Kong'. An important amount of new legislation is being pushed through the Provisional Legislature, a body which people are worried is becoming a rubber-stamping office.

Legislation was quickly passed on the changes to the system for the legislative elections held in May 1998. This system dramatically reduced the franchise and seriously cut back the number of seats that the Democratic Party hoped to win. The changes mean that more influence now lies in the hands of business constituencies and powerbrokers in Beijing, with only twenty of the sixty seats voted for by the common voter (10 of the seats were voted for by an 800 strong electoral council and 30 seats voted for by business constituencies).

Even so, the May elections returned Martin Lee to the Legislature (which he was ignominiously ejected from when the Provisional Legislature was established) on a wave of public enthusiasm; the Democrats won a total of 13 seats. He promptly called for full democracy for Hong Kong by the year 2000. The 53% voter turnout was a success for the democratic foundations of Hong Kong.

Leung Kwok Hung

Sometimes seen at the 64 Club in Lan Kwai Fong, Leung Kwok Hung is a very familiar face to Hong Kong residents, especially the police. Banned from entering China and also banned from the Provisional Legislative Council in 1997, Leung is an unflagging member of the April 5th Action Group. Having a reputation for extreme unruliness and revolt, Leung is in fact a Trotskyist-Marxist who attends virtually all public demonstrations in his bid to bring about a socialist democratic system. He's normally on the front page of the *South China Morning Post* or the *Hong Kong Standard* being carried horizontally away from some demonstration by the police. Befriended by neither the west nor China, the danger is that he will find little support if he contravenes Hong Kong protocol too seriously.

Many say that the shift towards the executive means that it will be able to make decisions that will be immune from the law. Furthermore the civil service and the bureaucracy is becoming less open and accountable, with a corresponding fear of the return of the corruption that dogged it in the past. However the Independent Commission Against Corruption (ICAC) maintains that it will continue to exercise its right to probe all levels in its pursuit of fairness and the application of the law. The ICAC was given far-reaching powers to prosecute – needing only to show that a civil servant has wealth disproportionate to their income. Already, ICAC has seen a sharp increase in the number of cases it prosecutes.

The new political hegemony is working, but Beijing has yet to be tested – the big question is, will Beijing be content to sit back and leave things alone if there is large scale political dissent?

ECONOMY

Hong Kong is a competitive and money-oriented society. Its *laissez faire* economic policies are a capitalist's dream – free enterprise and free trade, low taxes, a hard working labour force, a modern and efficient port, excellent worldwide communications and a government famous for a hands-off approach.

When it comes to regulating business, 'positive non-intervention' has always been the policy of the government. Hong Kong is one of Asia's 'four little tigers' (also called 'four little dragons'). The other economic powerhouses in this weight division are Korea, Singapore and Taiwan. While China's per-capita Gross National Product is around US$500, in Hong Kong it's about US$23,000.

Hong Kong has moved towards capital-intensive rather than labour-intensive industries. Industries like telecommunications, banking, insurance, tourism and retail sales have pushed manufacturing to the background, and most of the manual labour is now performed across the border in southern China. The shift from manufacturing to

services has been accompanied by a dramatic increase in wages.

The living standards and wages of most people in Hong Kong are much higher than those in China and most other Asian countries – only Japan ranks higher. Maximum personal income tax is no more than 15%, company profit's tax is 16.5%, and there are no capital gains or transfer taxes. These excellent tax conditions attract dynamic businesses and professionals to the economy.

With a low unemployment rate (but one that is currently rising), Hong Kong has traditionally suffered from a labour shortage, which is something of a rarity in the Asian region. Most of the menial work (domestic, construction etc) is performed by imported labour, chiefly from the Philippines. However, with the current influx of Chinese labour, many of these foreigners may be kicked out of their jobs (and out of Hong Kong).

Only about 350,000 people of the 2.5 million-strong workforce are unionised, which appears to suit Hong Kong capitalists as much as the Chinese government. It's argued that the PRC believes a strong independent union movement could become the focus of mass political discontent, and therefore upset Hong Kong's 'stability and prosperity'.

The growth in the services sector is underpinned by trade, which has expanded 37 fold over the past two decades. As entrepôt for the flood of goods into and out of China, Hong Kong has become the world's eighth largest trading entity. The total annual value of visible trade (which excludes trade in services) had risen to more than US$300 billion by 1995. Domestic exports (products made and sent out from Hong Kong) only account for around 20% of total exports. The bulk of goods sent out from Hong Kong are re-exports – semi-finished and finished goods imported into the territory for additional processing or transhipment.

Tourism has traditionally been Hong Kong's second largest earner of foreign exchange (after textiles), but is currently in decline. In July 1997 there was a 35%

plunge in visitors compared to the same month in 1996. There was a 68% drop in Japanese tourists after the news that a number of hotels had been charging the Japanese up to three times the usual rate. As tourism earned UK£8.3 billion in 1996 and employs 12% of the workforce, the potential for disaster is huge. The Chief Executive, Tung Chee Hwa, has given the Hong Kong Tourist Association (HKTA) HK$100 million to sort out this problem.

Hong Kong has a very small agricultural base. Only 9% of the total land area is suitable for crop farming and less than 2% of the population is engaged in agriculture or fishing. Most of the food is imported from the mainland – even McDonald's gets its potatoes and vegetables from China.

Hong Kong depends on imports for virtually all its requirements. This includes water, and more than 50% is pumped from China. To pay for these imports Hong Kong has to generate foreign exchange through exports, tourism and overseas investments. So far, there has been no problem paying bills, and one of the government's 'problems' has been what to do with the surplus revenue!

China has become the No 1 investor in town, having pumped billions of US dollars into the local economy during the 1990s. By the end of 1995, China had made a direct investment in Hong Kong of HK$108 billion (US$14 billion). Chinese firms have become major players in the property and financial markets, and long-time Hong Kong blue-chip firms, such as Hongkong Telecom and Swire Pacific, now count companies from the mainland among the key shareholders. These Chinese companies have also invested heavily in key infrastructure projects related to the Chek Lap Kok airport program. Hong Kong has reciprocated this investment by pouring HK$774 billion (US$100 billion) into mainland China – particularly into Guangdong Province.

This capital does not necessarily cheer Hong Kong's business community. On the Chinese mainland, the government's policy has frequently been to invite foreign companies to invest, learn their technology secrets and then strangle them with red tape. Some foreign companies that have survived in China have been forced into highly unfavourable joint-venture operations.

POPULATION & PEOPLE

Hong Kong's official population is about 6.4 million, with an annual growth rate of 2.1%. It is also expected that each year around 50,000 Chinese immigrants will move to the territory.

The average population density is approximately 5800 people per sq km, but this figure is rather deceiving as the density varies from area to area. Some urban areas have tens of thousands of people stacked into multi-block, high-rise housing estates, while other areas are genuinely rural or uninhabited.

In 1851, at the time of colonisation, the territory's population was a mere 33,000. By 1931 this had grown to 880,000 people. This growth was largely due to China's tumultuous history in the first half of this century. The collapse of the Qing dynasty in 1911, Chinese warlords and the civil war motivated thousands of Chinese to flee to the safer shores of Hong Kong.

A further 700,000 people fled to Hong Kong when the war between China and Japan erupted in 1937. The Japanese attacked the colony on 8 December 1941, the same time as the attack on Pearl Harbour, and occupied Hong Kong for the next three and a half years. To relieve the colony's food shortage the Japanese deported thousands of Chinese civilians, reducing the population to 600,000 by 1945. These people returned after the war along with 750,000 people escaping from the communists, bringing the total population to about 2.5 million.

From the 1950s to the 1970s there was a flow of immigrants across the border from China. In two years alone at the end of the 1970s, the population rose by a quarter of a million as a result of Chinese immigration– some legal, but most of it not.

About 98% of Hong Kong's population is ethnic Chinese, most of whom can trace their origins to China's Guangdong Province – about 60% were born in the colony. The distribution of the population varies, with around 35% living in Kowloon, 21% on Hong Kong Island, 42% in the New Territories and 2% in the outlying islands.

If any group can truly claim to belong to Hong Kong, it is the Tankas, the nomadic boat people who have fished the local waters for many centuries, and the Hakka (literally, Guest), who farm the New Territories. The Hakka emigrated from north to south China centuries ago to flee persecution. Hakka women can be recognised in the New Territories by their distinctive spliced-bamboo hats with wide brims and black cloth fringes.

Hong Kong has a large expat community which numbered 146,400 in July 1997. Of this number, the three largest groups were as follows: 146,400 Filipinos, 40,900 Americans and 34,300 Indonesians. Some of the remainder are half or quarter Chinese. Beijing has indicated that citizenship can only be endowed on Hong Kong residents of 'pure Chinese descent'. In other words, race is the deciding factor, not place of birth. This also poses a problem for other nationalities, such as Hong Kong's longstanding Indian residents, who are now stateless. The 15,000 Indians who live in the territory are looked down upon by many Hong Kong Chinese. The Indians fear that Beijing may harbour a similar attitude and expel them. Even if they're allowed to stay, many doubt China will allow them to travel freely. The Filipinos and Nigerians are likely to be expelled on mass – they have no legitimate citizenship claim and China would rather replace them with cheap Chinese labour.

EDUCATION

Hong Kong's education system is based on the British model. Primary education is free and compulsory. At secondary level students begin to specialise – some go into a university or college preparatory programs, while others select vocational education combined with apprenticeships.

At the tertiary level, education is fiercely competitive. Only about 5% of students who sit university entrance exams actually gain admission. This is less of a problem for wealthy families, who simply send their children abroad to study.

A number of secondary schools were recently in revolt at the policy adopted by Tung Chee Hwa to impose educational instruction in Cantonese, rather than in English. Many schools use English as the medium of instruction, as they consider English a useful language for success in life. The Chief Executive insisted that government assisted schools make the change; however a compromise was reached whereby a number of schools retained the right to continue education in English.

Campuses

Hong Kong has five universities. Hong Kong University, established in 1911, is the oldest. Its campus is on the west side of Hong Kong Island in the Mid-Levels area. The Chinese University of Hong Kong is at Ma Liu Shui in the New Territories – it was officially established in 1963 on a beautiful campus. The Hong Kong University of Science & Technology admitted its first students in 1991, and is situated in Tai Po Tsai in the south-east of the New Territories.

The newest institute is the City University of Hong Kong. The campus is on Tat Chee Ave, very close to Kowloon Tong MTR station. This school was formerly known as City Polytechnic of Hong Kong. This is not to be confused with the Hong Kong Polytechnic University, in the Hung Hom area, which was established in 1972.

ARTS
Lion Dance

The lion is an animal that is much respected in Chinese culture, although it is not indigenous to China. Lions are considered to bring good fortune and ward off evil, and that is why they often guard (in pairs) the entrance to houses and large buildings. The origin of the Lion dance is uncertain,

HONG KONG

though some say it was brought to China from India, in the Tang dynasty (618-907), by entertainers and circus troupes.

Whatever the origins, the Lion dance is an essential ceremony for the opening of new businesses, or even at weddings. As an extreme degree of athleticism is needed to perform a Lion dance, the dance troupe always belongs to a kungfu school. The lion is animated by two performers and the whole spectacle is accompanied by music, which matches the tempo of the lion's movements. The lion's mouth and eyes open and close and a beard hangs down from the lion's lower jaw – the longer the beard, the more venerable the school that performs the dance. At the opening of new businesses and restaurants, the lion is sometimes rewarded with a lettuce hanging on a string, which it must reach up and grab between its jaws.

Lions vary over China, with northern lions performing all sorts of difficult and skilful acrobatics such as balancing with all four feet on a large ball, while the southern lion is very colourful, lovely and ferocious.

Lion dances are common in late January or February, during the Chinese New Year. Lion dance troupes are also hired for the opening ceremony of new businesses and restaurants, as the lion is believed to scare away evil spirits.

Music

Hong Kong's popular music is generically known as 'Canto-pop', a saccharine arrangement of romantic melodies and lyrics. Rarely radical, the songs invariably deal with teen issues such as unrequited puppy love, loneliness and high emotion. The music is polished and compulsively singable (hence the explosion of karaoke parlours).

Big names in the music industry are the thespian/crooner Andy Lau, the excellent Mr nice guy Jackie Cheung, ex-Beijing waif Wang Fei and the immortal Sally Yip. Bands that have made it big include Beyond and Grasshopper. Records from the mainland, Taiwan and Japan also fill up space at His Master's Voice (HMV) music stores.

Art in Hong Kong

Hong Kong's artists are hardly typical of the larger Hong Kong society. They have always fought against a deep-seated apathy to art in a community that makes business success the ultimate ambition. Many artists complain that the colonial structure encouraged people to make money rather than art. It goes without saying that Hong Kong is famous for its wealth rather than for its art production.

Those in Hong Kong who turn to producing art find themselves exploring the hybrid landscape left to them by a schizophrenic culture. And it is art that has recently found itself a mouthpiece for the unsettling reunion of the ex-colony with China.

Under the new regime, artists now have a new set of concerns, including limits on artistic expression, and the competition posed by mainland artists. There is also a danger that artists will either start to devote more time to opposition and rebellion (both valid functions of art) at the expense of other areas or that they may develop a culture of fawning and toadying to the powers that be, which will result in a celebration of banality.

One example of the latter has already caused much controversy in Hong Kong. Liu Yuyi was chosen as painter by appointment to memorialise the return of Hong Kong to the PRC. His resulting creation was seen by some as a shrill, candy-coated piece of propaganda featuring a sea of dignitaries (including Deng Xiaoping, Jiang Zemin and Tung Chee Hwa) toasting Hong Kong's future. Notable for their absence from the vapid mass of smiling faces were democratic politicians.

But there are artistic undercurrents moving against such prevailing tides. The excellent Fringe in Central promotes the arts by providing up and coming artists with a foothold and a space to display their works. This is an excellent place to witness explorative Hong Kong art; from the intensely personal to concerns about the future of the city. The Dragon's Back Gallery at the Fringe has a host of challenging exhibitions from the local scene – recent shows have included Sonia Pang-Washfords' collages which communicate her experiences as a Eurasian returning to Hong Kong after 21 years.

Canto-pop won't mean much to you unless you make deliberate inroads into Cantonese culture, eg by learning the language. If you manage to learn a few Canto-classics and reel them off at your local karaoke lounge, you will be friends with the boss ('*bohsee*' in Cantonese) for life.

Chinese Opera

Few Chinese festivals are complete without an opera performance. There are probably more than 500 opera performers in Hong Kong, and opera troupes from China make regular appearances. Chinese opera is a world away from the western variety. It is a mixture of singing, speaking, mime, acrobatics and dancing that can go on for five or six hours.

Four types of Chinese opera are performed in Hong Kong. Top of the line for Chinese culture enthusiasts is the Beijing opera. This opera has a highly refined style that uses a variety of traditional props and almost no scenery. The Cantonese variety of opera is more like 'music hall' theatre. It usually has a 'boy meets girl' theme, and incorporates modern and foreign references. The most traditional, but least performed opera, is Chaozhou. This opera is staged almost as it was in the Ming dynasty, with morality tales from Chaozhou legends and folklore.

Since the handover you can now see Chinese revolutionary opera classics like *The White-Haired Girl* and *Taking Tiger Mountain by Strategy*.

Costumes, props and body language reveal much of the meaning in Chinese opera, so a little homework beforehand may make things easier to understand and enjoy. The HKTA offers a handout entitled *Hong Kong's Musical Heritage* – Chinese Opera that gives a good summary of the origins, symbols and workings of performances. An excellent introduction to the mysterious world of Chinese opera is offered by Chen Kaige's wonderful film, *Farewell my Concubine*, starring Gong Li and Zhang Guoying.

The best times to see Chinese opera are during one of the many festivals. The annual Hong Kong Arts Festival is held in summer (February/March), the biannual Festival of Asian Arts is in October/November, and the Urban Council staged the first ever Chinese Opera Festival from October to November in 1997. The HKTA has leaflets giving full details of the festivals, and *bc* and *HK Magazine* also publish complete listings.

Puppets

Puppets are the oldest of the Chinese theatre arts. Styles include rod, glove, string and shadow puppets. The rod puppets, visible only from waist up, are fixed to a long pole with short sticks for hand movements. The puppets are made from camphor wood and the main characters have larger heads than the rest of the cast. The shadow variety are made from leather and cast shadows onto a silk screen. Shadow and glove puppet performances are musically accompanied by the erhu or pipa instruments. Most performances relate tales of past dynasties. The most likely place to see performances is on TV – live shows are somewhat rare these days.

SOCIETY & CONDUCT
Traditional Culture

Face Much of the southern Chinese obsession with materialism is often attributed to gaining face. Owning nice clothes, a big car, a piano, imported cigarettes and liquor, will all help gain face. Therefore, when taking a gift to a Chinese friend, try to give something like a bottle of imported liquor, perfume, cigarettes or chocolate.

Face is no different from what others call 'the presentation of self'. And the presentation of this face varies according to class. One buys what is socially respectable as well as what one can afford. There are always people who buy gifts with snob appeal, but these people are not the norm in Hong Kong.

Charlotte Kwok Glasser

Chinese Zodiac Astrology has a long history in China and is integrated with religious beliefs. As in the western system of astrology, there are 12 zodiac signs. These signs are based on the year of your birth, rather than the time of year you were born, though the exact day and time of birth is also carefully considered in charting an astrological path.

If you want to know your sign in the Chinese zodiac, look up your year of birth in the chart. However, it's a little more complicated than this because Chinese astrology goes by the lunar calendar. The Chinese Lunar New Year falls in late January or early February, so the first month will be included in the year before.

It is said that the animal year chart originated from when Buddha commanded all the beasts of the earth to assemble before him. Only 12 animals came and they were rewarded by having their names given to a specific year. Buddha also decided to name each year in the order in which the animals arrived – the first was the rat, then the ox, tiger, rabbit and so on.

Many festivals are held throughout the year in accordance with the lunar calendar. Some festivals only occur at the end of the 12 year cycle, and some occur only once in 60 years. This is because each of the 12 animals is influenced at different times by five elements: metal, wood, earth, water and fire. The full cycle thus takes 60 years and at the end of this time there is a 'super festival'.

Being born or married in a particular year is believed to determine one's fortune. In this era of modern birth-control techniques and abortion, Chinese parents will often carefully manipulate the birth times of their children. The year of the dragon sees the biggest jump in the birth rate, closely followed by the year of the tiger. A girl born in the year of the pig could have trouble getting married!

Five Elements Also important in determining your character is the five element theory *(nghang)*, according to which you are born in a year that belongs to one of the five elements (wood, water, fire, earth, metal).

The elements belong to a cycle of creation and destruction whereby wood creates fire, fire creates earth (ash), earth creates metal (ore), metal creates water (through condensation on metal) and water creates wood (through growth). Conversely, earth destroys water (by damming it), water destroys fire, fire destroys metal (melting), metal destroys wood (axe), and wood destroys earth (by breaking it up with roots).

If you are born in a metal year, it might be bad news to marry someone who is born in a wood year. However, each element is sub-divided into 12 more degrees, so you can be of a very weak metal and marry someone of a strong wood nature, and get on fine! Many Chinese couples determine which is the best year to have a child so that it will harmonise with their elemental signs.

continued on page 38

Chinese Zodiac								
Rat	1924	1936	1948	1960	1972	1984	1996	2008
Ox/Cow	1925	1937	1949	1961	1973	1985	1997	2009
Tiger	1926	1938	1950	1962	1974	1986	1998	2010
Rabbit	1927	1939	1951	1963	1975	1987	1999	2011
Dragon	1928	1940	1952	1964	1976	1988	2000	2012
Snake	1929	1941	1953	1965	1977	1989	2001	2013
Horse	1930	1942	1954	1966	1978	1990	2002	2014
Goat	1931	1943	1955	1967	1979	1991	2003	2015
Monkey	1932	1944	1956	1968	1980	1992	2004	2016
Rooster	1933	1945	1957	1969	1981	1993	2005	2017
Dog	1934	1946	1958	1970	1982	1994	2006	2018
Pig	1935	1947	1959	1971	1983	1995	2007	2019

Chinese Martial Arts

WILLIAM CHEUNG ACADEMY

HONG KONG TOURIST ASSOCIATION

WILLIAM CHEUNG ACADEMY

WILLIAM CHEUNG ACADEMY

WILLIAM CHEUNG ACADEMY

A	
B	C
D	

A: *Taiji quan* is the gentle cousin of *kungfu*. It's mainly used for exercise.
B: Training with the *wing chun* wooden dummy.
C: *Wing chun* punches are delivered with great rapidity and in a straight line.
D: Armed combat with twin *wing chun* butterfly knives.

Chinese Martial Arts

Many westerners have been bewitched by the spell of *kungfu*, plunging into its world of legends, myth and mystery. For the novice, however, it promises a way that becomes more labyrinthine with every step, and the skills it promises seem daily more distant. But for those who take to the art, it becomes a rewarding part of their lives, a long journey with a unique destination.

Often misinterpreted, kungfu teaches an approach to life that stresses patience, endurance, magnanimity and humility; when two people get together and discover they share an interest in martial arts, it's the cue for an endless exchange of techniques and anecdotes. It's a club mentality for members only.

The first well known missionary of this ancient art was Bruce Lee. Despite having genuine skill, his films projected little more than a violent cinematic form of kungfu, a distortion of the original. Kungfu, or *gongfu,* means skill and can be applied to any artistic achievement that has been reached through hard work. It's the difficult journey towards mastery that gives kungfu its mystery and grace.

The stories and legends that circulate around the martial arts community keep adherents on the gruelling path to achievement – like the one about the Malaysian Five Ancestors master who broke the leg of a Thai boxer, with his finger!

One of the best books on the spirit of the martial arts is John F Gilbey's *The Way of a Warrior.* The following is a thumbnail sketch of a few of the arts that you may see while travelling in Hong Kong, Macau or mainland China.

Bruce Lee, an on-screen legend, an off-screen enigma. Mystery still surrounds his life and untimely death.

Taijiquan – Supreme Ultimate Fist

The most popular martial art in the world, *taijiquan* is generally practised in China by the elderly, who find it invaluable for flexibility, good circulation, leg strength and good balance. A major part of studying taijiquan is the development of *qi*, or energy, that can be used for healing, or in fighting.

The most popular form of taijiquan is the Yang style, which is not too difficult to learn in its simplified form (though the full form has 108 postures and takes 20 minutes to perform) and is not strenuous. Other styles, such as the Chen style, call for a wider array of skills as the postures are painfully low and the kicks high, so endurance and flexibility are important. Chen style is popular with younger exponents and clearly has its roots in Shaolin, mixing slow movements with fast, snappy punches.

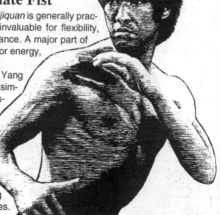

Other styles include the Sun and Wu styles.

After learning the empty hand form (a smooth, continuous set of movements), the practitioner goes on to learn weapons forms, generally including the *taiji* sword and maybe the *taiji* pole, depending on the skills of the teacher. Practitioners can also be trained in the use of other weapons.

A student of taijiquan will be introduced to pushing hands, a two person exercise that opens the door to the fighting side of taijiquan. Pushing hands teaches students how to interpret the force of their opponents and to react accordingly. The correct interpretation of, and reaction to, force is the main weapon in the taiji armoury. Resistance to force is educated out of the student and instead a yielding to pressure is trained. Through yielding, force can be controlled and redirected away from the target; this aspect is very hard to train as it goes against natural inclinations to resist force with force. The highest point of taijiquan, being able to evade all attacks, is reserved for a precious few who have devoted themselves to the art. If fighting or self-defence is what you are after, learn *karate*, kickboxing or *wing chun*, which emphasise the martial aspect.

Nonetheless, for those who learn taijiquan, the art promises a lifelong interest that constantly surprises with its lessons in re-educating the body. Strength, speed, suppleness and health are all physical benefits enjoyed by students of taijiquan, and the slow movements promote relaxation as an antidote to stress.

Wing Chun

Invented by a woman (a Buddhist nun from the Shaolin Temple called Ng Mui, who taught her skills to a young girl called Wing Chun), wing chun is a ferocious and dynamic system that promises reasonably quick results for those learning. This was the style that taught Bruce Lee how to move and, although he ultimately moved away from it to develop his own style, wing chun had an enormous influence on him.

Grandmaster William Cheung demonstrates wing chun kungfu.

THE WILLIAM CHEUNG ACADEMY

Wing chun emphasises speed rather than strength. Evasion, subterfuge and rapid strikes are the hallmarks of the wing chun system. The forms are simple and direct, doing away with the pretty flourishes that characterise other styles. While some say that this makes the art unattractive, it is typical of the nature of this boxing style that it accentuates effectiveness rather than glamour.

The theory of wing chun is enshrined in its 'centre-line theory' that draws an imaginary line down the human body and centres all attacks and blocks on that line. The line runs through the sensitive regions: eyes, nose, lips, mouth, throat, heart, solar plexus and groin. Any blow that lands on any of these points is debilitating and dangerous; the three empty hand forms train arm and leg movements that both attack and defend this line. None of the blocks stray beyond the width of the shoulders, as this limits the range of possible attacks, and punches follow the same theory. This gives the forms of wing chun its distinctive simplicity. The sweeps of western boxers are removed and instead the punch takes its strength mainly from the shoulders, elbows and wrist. Punches are delivered with great rapidity in a straight line, along the shortest distances between the puncher and the punched. A two person training routine called *chi sau*, or sticking hands, teaches the student how to be soft in response to attacks; softness promotes relaxation in the practitioner and fosters speed in counterattacking.

Weapons in the wing chun arsenal include the twin wing chun butterfly knives, which are sharp and heavy, and an extremely long pole, which requires considerable strength to handle with skill.

Despite being an excellent system for self-defence, wing chun practitioners are often over-confident and cocky, which is contrary to the spirit of the system. Wing chun forms are not especially strenuous and often do not build up the stamina necessary for students who want to fight professionally. For your average punter, however, the study of wing chun can provide a whole range of useful skills.

Bagua Zhang – Eight Trigram Boxing

This intriguing art is probably one of the strangest to witness, and is certainly one of the most esoteric. The practitioner wheels around in a circle, changing speed and direction, occasionally kicking or thrusting out a palm strike. This is the art of *bagua zhang*, or eight trigram boxing, one of the soft or internal styles of Chinese boxing.

Trigrams are used by the bagua walker to practice the rotary motions and rhythms required to master this martial art.

Eight trigram boxing draws its inspiration from the trigrams (an arrangement of three broken and unbroken black lines) of the classic *Book of Changes* or *I Ching*, the oracle used in China for divination. The trigrams are often arranged in circular form, and it is this pattern that is traced out by the bagua walker.

The practitioner of bagua zhang must display all the skills of subterfuge, evasion, speed and unpredictability that are the motifs of this style. Force is generally not met with force, but deflected by circular movements that are built into students through their meditations upon the circle. Circular forms are the mainstay of all movements, radiating from torque at the waist. Arcing, twisting, twining and spinning describe the rotary motions of the Bagua Zhang student, reflecting a circular pattern that is as natural as the orbits and shape of the planets. The usual Taoist interpretation of bagua zhang reveals an obviously Shamanistic origin, which gives the art its dance-like structure, mesmerising appeal and depth.

A further hallmark of the style is the exclusive use of the palm instead of the fist as the main striking weapon. This may appear strange and even ineffectual, but in fact the palm can transmit a surprising amount of power – consider a thrusting palm strike to the chin, for example. The palm is also far better protected than the fist, as it is cushioned by muscle. The fist has to transmit the power of a punch through a myriad of bones which have to be correctly aligned to avoid damage. If you had to punch a brick wall as hard as you could, would you use your fist or your palm? In fact, bagua fighters were feared among Chinese boxers for their ferocity and unorthodox moves.

The art of Bagua Zhang is deeply esoteric and almost off-limits to non-Chinese. There are practitioners who teach foreigners, but they are not nearly as prolific as teachers of bagua's sister art, taijiquan. Anyone who finds a teacher of worth must be prepared for an intense schooling in a difficult art. Those who do become proficient in bagua zhang will inherit a disappearing legacy of old China.

Xingyi Quan – Body-Mind Boxing

Xingyi quan is another soft, or internal martial art that is often mentioned in the same breath as taijiquan, despite being different in many ways. Like taijiquan the training emphasises the development of qi, or energy; however, the movements of xingyi quan are dynamic and powerful, and the fighting philosophy is not passive, like that of taijiquan.

Jackie Chan, a well known and respected practitioner of Chinese martial arts.

SIREN ENTERTAINMENT

Possibly the oldest martial art still in existence in China, xingyi quan was developed in imitation of the fighting techniques and spirit of twelve animals. There are different schools of xingyi quan which consist of different animal styles, but the standard form consists of the dragon, tiger, horse, monkey, chicken, harrier, Chinese ostrich, swallow, eagle, bear, water lizard and snake. Each animal must be understood in terms of its shape and intention or idea, which gives the name to this style of boxing.

Before studying the animal forms, the student must start with the five punches that are the building blocks of xingyi quan. The five punches are *pi*, *beng*, *zuan*, *pao* and *heng*; each one must be studied in turn until perfected. In general, each punch is practised while stepping up and down in a straight line and then put together into a linking set.

Each punch represents one of the five elements of Chinese philosophy – pi (metal), beng (wood), zuan (water), pao (fire) and heng (earth). The punches reflect the cycle of conquest and creation implicit in the life of the five elements: fire conquers metal, metal conquers wood, wood conquers earth, earth conquers water and water conquers fire. Alternatively, fire produces earth, earth produces metal, metal produces water, water produces wood and wood produces fire. This is the relationship between the five elements or phases that is also reflected in the art of xingyi quan. For example, pi conquers beng, yet is itself conquered by pao.

Xingyi quan is performed in a relaxed state, emphasising a calm but observant mind. The movements are quick, intelligent and direct, assisted to their target by a body that must unite all its movements into a threaded whole. Training in the art is punishing and consists of many postures that must be held for a long time, in order to develop qi. Attacks are generally met with force rather than with evasive manoeuvring. Like bagua zhang, teachers of xingyi quan are hard to find, and are often reticent about the art.

Other Martial Arts

Dozens of other styles exist in China, each reflecting their own fighting philosophy and spirit. You can take your pick according to your persuasion: drunken boxing, white crane boxing, white eyebrow boxing, monkey boxing, tiger boxing, five ancestors boxing and many, many more. Each style is a distillation of fighting experience and contains a deep and rewarding link with the past.

THE WILLIAM CHEUNG ACADEMY

Grandmaster William Cheung demonstrates an armed variation of wing chun.

HONG KONG

continued from page 32
Your Age Are you sure you know how old you are? You might be less than certain after seeing how the Chinese work it out. Since the Chinese calculate age from the moment of conception, a baby is already going on one year when it leaves the womb. The seventh day on the Chinese lunar calendar is also 'everyone's birthday'.

Fungshui The Cantonese word *fungshui* (*fengshui* in Mandarin) literally means 'wind-water'. Westerners call it geomancy, the art (or science if you prefer) of manipulating or judging the environment to produce good fortune. If you want to build a house or find a suitable site for a grave, you call in a geomancer. The Chinese warn that violating the principles of good fungshui can have serious consequences. Therefore, fungshui masters are consulted before an apartment block is built, a highway laid down, telephone poles erected or trees lopped.

Trees may have a spirit living inside, and for this reason some villages and temples in the New Territories still have fungshui groves to provide a place for the good spirits to live.

Attempts to cut down fungshui groves to construct new buildings have sometimes led to massive protests and even violent confrontations – the solution may be a large cash payment to the village to 'placate the spirits'.

Businesses that are failing may call in a fungshui expert. Sometimes the solution is to move a door or window. If this doesn't do the trick, it might be necessary to move an ancestor's grave. The location of an ancestor's grave is an especially serious matter. If the grave is in the wrong spot, or facing the wrong way, then there is no telling what trouble the spirits might cause. If a fungshui master is not consulted, and the family of the deceased suddenly runs into an episode of bad luck, then it's time to see a Taoist priest who knows how to deal with the troublesome ghosts.

Hong Kong produces some architectural wonders, but no matter how attractive or in-novative, any office tower built without the blessings of a fungshui expert could be a financial disaster – no one but foreigners would rent the offices.

One prominent building had to be completely renovated and worked over by Taoist priests after it was 'discovered' that the faces of wolves could be seen in the marble decor. Evidently, the spirits of the wolves had been trapped in the marble and the tenants quickly moved out of this haunted building. Fortunately, the priests were able to save the building and prevent the landlord from going bankrupt.

Construction of Hong Kong's underground Mass Transit Railway (MTR) began with an invocation by a group of Taoist priests who paid respects to the spirits of the earth whose domain was about to be violated.

Dos & Don'ts
Clothing Hong Kong is a very fashion conscious city. Still, Hong Kong is cosmopolitan – they've seen it all, so you can get away with wearing almost anything. Revealing clothing is OK – shorts, miniskirts and bikinis (at the beach only) are common; nude bathing is a definite no-no.

There is one exception to this tolerance – thongs (flip flops). Thongs are OK to wear in hotel rooms, but most definitely not in its lobby or outdoors (except around a swimming pool or beach).

Some restaurants and hotels will not let you in the door wearing thongs. Many westerners ignore this unwritten rule and, although the police won't arrest you for wearing thongs in public, you will be looked upon with contempt.

Oddly, sandals are perfectly acceptable. The difference between sandals and thongs is the strap across the back of the ankle. As long as the strap is there, it's OK. No strap, and you're dressed indecently.

Handy Hints Always hand a piece of paper to somebody using both hands. This shows respect. This especially rings true if the receiver is somebody important, like a public official, your landlord or a business associate. You will notice that Hong Kong Chinese always hand business cards with two hands (coupled with a slight lowering of the head). If you use one hand, you will be considered rude.

Colour Codes Every colour is symbolic to the Chinese. Red is normally a happy colour, though red ink is an exception. Messages written in red convey anger, hostility or un-friendliness. If you want to give someone your address or telephone number, write in any colour but red.

White is the colour of death and it is appropriate to give white flowers only at funerals. Colour symbols can be a little obscure, eg a man should never wear a green hat because this indicates that his wife is having an affair!

Killer Chopsticks Leaving chopsticks sticking vertically into the bowl is a bad omen. This resembles incense sticks in a bowl of ashes, a sure death sign.

Gift Giving It's good manners when visiting people to bring some sort of gift, such as flowers or chocolates, especially if you've been invited for a meal. Money is generally not appropriate (and indeed would be an insult), but there are times when you are supposed to give money – weddings, funerals and (for children) the Chinese Lunar New Year. The money should be given in a red envelope (sold in stationery shops all over Hong Kong). The equivalent of the *hongbao,* or red package containing money given at the time of the Chinese spring festival, is called *laisee* in Hong Kong.

To complicate matters further, a Chinese person with good manners is supposed to refuse (at least once, maybe twice) any gift you offer. You are supposed to insist. They will then 'reluctantly' accept. To accept a gift too readily is considered greedy and will cause the recipient to lose face. This makes it really hard to know if the person is trying to refuse the gift because they don't want it,

or if they want it but must make a token refusal to save face. If you receive a present that is gift-wrapped, it is customary not to open it in front of the giver. If you open it immediately, it makes you look greedy.

RELIGION

In Chinese religion, Taoism, Confucianism and Buddhism have become inextricably entwined. Ancestor worship and ancient animist beliefs have also been incorporated into the religious milieu.

In Hong Kong there are approximately 600 temples, monasteries and shrines. Most are tiny but some are enormous, such as the Po Lin Monastery on Lantau Island, the Ten Thousand Buddhas Monastery at Sha Tin and the Sik Sik Yuen (Wong Tai Sin Temple) in Kowloon.

Buddhism

Buddhism was founded in India in the 6th century BC by Siddhartha Gautama of the Sakya clan. Siddhartha was a prince who became discontented with the physical world when he was confronted with the sights of old age, sickness and death. He despaired of finding fulfilment on the physical level, since the body was inescapably subject to these weaknesses.

Around the age of 30 Siddhartha broke from the material world and sought 'enlightenment' by following various yogic disciplines. After several failed attempts he devoted the final phase of his search to intensive contemplation. One evening as he sat beneath a banyan tree, he slipped into a deep meditation and emerged after achieving enlightenment. His title 'Buddha' means 'the awakened' or 'the enlightened one'.

Buddha founded an order of monks and preached his ideas for the next four decades until his death around 480 BC. To his followers he was known as Sakyamuni, the 'silent sage of the Sakya clan'. It is said that Gautama Buddha was not the only Buddha – the fourth, in fact – and is not expected to be the last.

The cornerstone of Buddhist philosophy is the view that all life is suffering. Everyone is

Chinese Gods

Chinese religion is polytheistic, ie having many divinities. Every Chinese house has its kitchen or house god, and trades have gods too. Students worship Wan Chung, the deified scholar. Shopkeepers pray to Tsai Shin, God of Riches. Every profession has its own god, and numerous temples in Hong Kong and Macau are dedicated to certain gods. The following are some of the important local divinities.

Tin Hau Queen of heaven and protector of seafarers, she is one of the most popular gods in Hong Kong. She was born on an island in Fujian Province between 900-1000. After her death the cult of Tin Hau spread along the coast of China. In Macau she is known as Ah Ma, or Mother, and in Taiwan she is known as Matsu. In Singapore she is Ma Chu Po, or Respected Great Aunt.

In Hong Kong about 250,000 fishing people are followers of Tin Hau and there are about two dozen temples dedicated to her. The most famous temple is Tai Miu (literally Great Temple) at Joss House Bay in the New Territories east of Hong Kong Island. Others are on Cheung Chau Island, at Sok Kwu Wan on Lamma Island, on Market St in Kowloon's Yau Ma Tei district, on Tin Hau Temple Rd in Causeway Bay, and at Stanley on Hong Kong Island. Tin Hau was a real person.

Kwun Yum The Buddhist equivalent of Tin Hau is Kuanyin (Kwun Yum in Hong Kong), the God of Mercy, who stands for tenderness and compassion for the unhappy lot of mortals. Kwun Yum temples are at Repulse Bay and Stanley on Hong Kong Island, and at Cheung Chau in the outlying islands. There are some temples in Macau also, where the god is called Kuan Iam.

Kuanti Soldiers pray to Kuanti, the red-faced God of War. Kuanti was a great warrior who lived at the end of the Han dynasty (206 BC to 220 AD) and is worshipped not only for his might in battle but because he is the

HONG KONG TOURIST ASSOCIATION
Numerous Buddhist temples in Hong Kong are dedicated to Kwun Yum, the popular God of Mercy.

subject to the traumas of birth, sickness, old age, fear and death. The cause of suffering is desire – the desires of the body and the desire for personal fulfilment. Happiness can only be achieved if these desires are overcome.

Buddhism developed in China during the 3rd to 6th centuries AD. In the middle of the 1st century AD the religion gained the interest of the Han emperor Ming, who sent a mission to the west. The mission returned in 67 AD with Buddhist scriptures, two Indian monks and images of Buddha. Centuries later other Chinese monks, like Xuan Zang,

journeyed across to India and returned with Buddhist scriptures.

Buddha wrote nothing – the writings that have come down to us date from around 150 years after his death. By the time these texts emerged, divisions had already appeared within Buddhism. There was a split into two major schools – Theravada and Mahayana.

The Theravada, or 'doctrine of elders', holds that the path to nirvana is an individual pursuit. It centres on monks and nuns who make the search for nirvana a full-time profession. This school maintains embodiment of right action, integrity and loyalty. The life of Kuanti is told in an old Chinese legend called *The Story of the Three Kingdoms*.

Kuanti is not a cruel tyrant delighting in battle and the slaying of enemies. Rather, he can avert war and protect people from its horrors. He is also the patron god of restaurants, pawn shops and literature, as well as the Hong Kong police force and secret societies such as the Triad organisations.

Kuanti temples are at Tai O on Lantau Island and the Man Mo (literally, civil and military) Temple on Hollywood Rd, Hong Kong Island.

Pak Tai Like all gods for special localities, Pak Tai keeps an eye out for his area, Cheung Chau Island. Like Kuanti, Pak Tai is a military protector of the state and there are various stories about his origins. Chinese ancestors are the spiritual guardians of their descendants, and Pak Tai is the guardian of peace and order.

On Cheung Chau, Pak Tai is revered as a life-giver, having intervened to end a plague which hit the island at the end of the last century; consequently a large temple, the Temple of Jade Vacuity, is dedicated to him.

Tam Kung This god is worshipped only on a small stretch of the southern Chinese coast which includes Macau and Hong Kong. One theory is that he was actually the last emperor of the Southern Song dynasty (1127-1279), which was overrun by Kublai Khan's Mongol armies. The emperor was a boy of eight or nine years and is now worshipped under the pseudonym of Tam Kung. A temple for Tam Kung can be seen in Shau Kei Wan on Hong Kong Island and Coloane village in Macau.

Wong Tai Sin This god watches over the housing settlement of the same name in Kowloon. Wong Tai Sin's popularity had a meteoric rise in Hong Kong after a man and his son brought a painting of him from Guangdong Province in 1915. They installed the painting and an altar in a small temple in Wan Chai. A temple was built in Kowloon in 1921 and his popularity grew further.

For all that, Wong Tai Sin had a humble beginning as a shepherd boy in Zhejiang Province. At 15 he was taught by an immortal how to make a herb that could cure all illnesses – thus, he is worshipped by the ill. Wong Tai Sin also spent 40 years in seclusion doing various miraculous things like turning white boulders into sheep (which perhaps explains why he is worshipped by business people, who want to turn white elephants into profitable companies).

that people are alone in the world and must tread the path to nirvana on their own – Buddha can only show the way. The Theravada school is the Buddhism of Sri Lanka, Myanmar (Burma), Thailand, Laos and Cambodia.

The Mahayana, or 'Greater Vehicle', school holds the belief that since all existence is one, the fate of the individual is linked to the fate of others. Buddha did not just point the way and float off into his own nirvana, but continues to offer spiritual help to others seeking nirvana. Mahayana is the Buddhism of Vietnam, Japan, Tibet, Korea, Mongolia and China.

Taoism
Originally a philosophy, Taoism (or Daoism) evolved into a religion. Unlike Buddhism, which was imported from India, Taoism is Chinese. While Buddhism is found throughout East Asia, Taoism is seldom practised by non-Chinese.

The philosophy of Taoism originated with Laozi (Laotse), who lived in the 6th century BC. Very little is known about

HONG KONG TOURIST ASSOCIATION
Buddhist Monks follow either the Theravada or Mahayana school of buddhist philosophy in their seach for nirvana.

Laozi and some have questioned whether or not he existed. His name simply means the old one. Laozi is believed to have been the custodian of the imperial archives for the Chinese government, and Confucius is supposed to have consulted him. It is doubtful that Laozi ever intended his philosophy to become a religion. Chang Ling is more or less credited with formally establishing the Taoist religion in 143 BC.

Laozi left behind a record of his beliefs in a slim volume entitled the *The Way and its Power (Dao De Jing)*. The book is brimming with profound insight.

Understanding Taoism is not simple. The word *tao* (pronounced 'dao'), means 'the way'. It is considered indescribable, but might be interpreted as the guiding path, the truth or the principle of the universe. Many say that appreciation of the

tao can be felt by reading Laozi's book, as it emanates through the language, leaving an impression of its timelessness.

One of the main principles of Taoism is the concept of *wuwei*, or 'doing nothing'. A quote, attributed to Laozi, 'Do nothing, and nothing will not be done', emphasises this principle. The idea is to remain humble, passive, non-assertive and non-interventionist. Sima Qian, a Chinese historian who lived from 145 to 90 BC, put it another way: 'Do not take the lead in planning affairs or you may be held responsible'.

Non-intervention or 'live and let live' ideals are the keystones of Taoism. Harmony and patience are needed, and action is obtained through inaction. Taoists like to note that water, the softest substance, will wear away stone, the hardest substance. The soft martial arts of China (the most famous of which is Taijiquan, or T'ai Chi) take their inspiration from Taoism and apply its principles in their quest for power and a long life. It is said by many practitioners that the practise of Taijiquan creates a physical sensation of and a physical adjustment to 'the way'.

Just as there have been different interpretations of Tao, there have also been different readings of *De*. De is commonly taken to mean the expression of the Tao in a persons daily life, although the Chinese character for de literally means morality. De can be understood as meaning magic or power, qualities that evolve in those who follow 'the way'.

In the book *Tao: the Watercourse Way*, author Alan Watts pursues the meaning of Taoism and its metaphors.

Unlike philosophical Taoism, which has many western followers, Chinese Taoism is a religion. It has been associated with alchemy and the search for immortality. *The Secret of the Golden Flower* written by Richard Wilhelm (Arkana) is a classic of Taoist alchemy.

As time passed, Taoism increasingly became wrapped up in the supernatural, self-mutilation, hot-coal dances, witchcraft, fortune telling and magic. All this is evident if you visit a Taoist temple during the ghost month or certain other festivals.

Confucianism

Confucius is regarded as China's greatest philosopher and teacher. The philosophy of Confucius has been borrowed by Japan, Korea, Vietnam and other neighbours of China. Confucius never claimed to be a religious leader, prophet or god, but his influence has been so great in China that Confucianism is regarded by many as a religion.

Confucius (551-479 BC) lived through a time of great chaos known as the Warring States Period. He emphasised devotion to parents and family, loyalty to friends, justice, peace, education and humanitarianism. A great reformer, Confucius preached the virtues of good government. His philosophy led to China's renowned bureaucracy, and the system of civil service and university entrance examinations, where a person gained position through ability and merit rather than through noble birth and connections.

Confucius preached against such evils as corruption, war, torture and excessive taxation. He was the first teacher to open his school to all students on the basis of their eagerness to learn.

The philosophy of Confucius is most easily found in the *Lunyu* or *The Analects*. Many quotes have been taken from this work, the most famous perhaps being the Golden Rule. The western version of this is 'Do unto others as you would have them do unto you'. The eastern Confucian version is written in the negative, 'Do not do unto others what you would not have them do unto you'.

The glorification of Confucius began after his death and eventually his ideas permeated every level of Chinese society. During the Han dynasty (206-220 AD), Confucianism effectively became the state religion. In 130 BC it was made the basic discipline for training government officials, and remained so almost until the end of the Qing dynasty in 1911.

In 59 AD sacrifices were ordered to Confucius in all urban schools. In the 7th and 8th centuries, during the Tang dynasty, temples and shrines were built to him and his original disciples. During the Song dynasty *The Analects* became the basis of all education.

Although Confucius died almost 2500 years ago, his influence remains strong in China. The Chinese remain solidly loyal to their friends, family and teachers. The bureaucracy and examination system still thrives, and a son is generally favoured over a daughter. It can be said that much of Confucian thought has become what is generally considered Chinese culture.

Chinese Religion Today

On a daily level, the Chinese are much less concerned with the high-minded philosophies and asceticism of Buddha, Confucius or Laozi than they are with the pursuit of worldly success, the appeasement of the dead and the spirits, and the seeking of hidden knowledge about the future.

The most important word in the Chinese religious vocabulary is *joss*, meaning luck. The Chinese are too astute to leave something as important as luck to chance. Gods have to be appeased, bad spirits blown away and sleeping dragons soothed to keep joss on your side. No house, wall or shrine is built until an auspicious date for the start of construction is chosen and the most favourable location is selected. Incense must be burnt, gifts presented and prayers said to appease the spirits inhabiting the construction site.

Integral parts of Chinese religion are death, the after-life and ancestor worship. Chinese funerals are usually lavish and drawn-out events. The body can only be buried on a special day and this day is signalled by the clash of cymbals and the moan of oboes. A clover-shaped coffin is carried by grief-stricken mourners (sometimes they have been paid to weep) and many wear ghost-like outfits with white hoods. A fine spread of roast pig and other foods to be offered to the gods accompanies the funeral.

A grave site is chosen on the side of a hill with a good view for the deceased. At the grave the mourners burn paper models of material treasures like cars and boats, as well as bundles of paper money, to ensure that the dead person is taking the good things from their life. Just as during the Shang dynasty, when the dead were said to look after the welfare of the living, the living continue to take care of the dead.

Other Religions

Hong Kong has a cosmopolitan population, and many religious denominations are represented. There are around 500,000 Christians (55% Catholic, 45% Protestant), 50,000 Muslims, more than 1000 Jews, and Indian Sikhs.

If you want to pursue non-Buddhist and non-Taoist religions, you can contact one of the following places of worship:

Anglican
(☎ 2523-4157) St John's Cathedral, 4-8 Garden Rd, Central

Baha'i
(☎ 2367-6407) flat C-6, 11th floor, Hankow Centre, Middle Rd, Tsim Sha Tsui

Christian Scientist
(☎ 2524-2701) 31 MacDonnell Rd, Central

Hindu
(☎ 2572-5284) Happy Valley

Jewish
(☎ 2801-5440) Ohel Leah Synagogue, 70 Robinson Rd, Mid-Levels

Methodist
(☎ 2570-8709) North Point Methodist Church, 11 Cheung Hong St, North Point

Mormon
(☎ 2559-3325) Church of the Latter Day Saints, 7 Castle Rd, Mid-Levels, Central

Muslim
(☎ 2575-2218) Islamic Union, 40 Oi Kwan Rd, Wan Chai

Quaker
(☎ 2697-7283) Society of Friends, 3rd floor, Conference Room, Mariners Club, Middle Rd, Tsim Sha Tsui

Roman Catholic
(☎ 2552-3992) St Joseph's, 37 Garden Rd, Central

Facts for the Visitor

HIGHLIGHTS
The Best
The trip on the Peak Tram to Victoria Peak has been practically mandatory for visitors since it opened in 1888. It's fascinating to take a 30 minute ride on a sampan through one of Hong Kong's fishing harbours (Cheung Chau's is best). Equally interesting is a ride on Hong Kong Island's trams. Exploring the outlying islands by ferry is one of Hong Kong's best kept secrets – the walks are truly excellent. Hong Kong has some amazingly good beaches – and the best way to reach them is by boat or as part of a hiking trip. Similarly, no hiker could resist the MacLehose, Lantau or Hong Kong trails – all offer some of the world's most breathtaking views. Amusement park enthusiasts will find Ocean Park hard to beat. Party animals can eat, drink and dance the night away at Lan Kwai Fong and Wan Chai. Lunch at a good dim sum restaurant is one of the great pleasures of this region and, of course, Hong Kong is famous for shopping.

Lastly, there are many who insist that the highlight of their visit to Hong Kong was Macau. See the Macau chapters of this book for details.

The Worst
The lifts at the Chungking Mansions – if you ever get stuck in one of these, say your prayers and chew on that cyanide capsule. The stairwells at Chungking Mansions. Low-hanging street signs, especially the sharp ones. The 'no change given' policy on Hong Kong buses. Hong Kong air conditioners that constantly drip on your head as you walk down the street. The coffee on Hong Kong ferries. The words 'copy-Rolex' shouted into your ear on Nathan Rd. Cockroaches that fly in summer. Hong Kong's public telephones – when you eventually find one it's likely to be next to a deafening bus lane.

PLANNING
When to Go
In terms of weather, April to May and October to November are probably the best times to visit Hong Kong. Temperatures are moderate, and there's a good chance of clear skies and sunny weather. December to March tends to see a lot of rain, and from June to September the sweltering heat and humidity can make sightseeing sweaty. For more details, see the climate section in the Facts about Hong Kong chapter.

Under normal conditions, Hong Kong hotels have a high season from March to June and September to January. During this time the rates go up, rooms are often hard to find and the airfares to Hong Kong are usually higher. This was the golden rule until the handover, but the subsequent slumping of the tourist market has seen fierce competition in the airline and hotel industries. In winter 1997 there were cuts of up to 50% to hotel room prices and vast slashes in airfares (see the Hong Kong Getting There & Away chapter and the Places to Stay sections for more details).

Travel in and out of Hong Kong can be difficult during Chinese New Year, which falls in late January to early February. Flights are usually full, and the border with China becomes a living hell as millions of locals flood to the mainland to visit relatives. On the other hand, the crowds are absent and a growing number of shops and restaurants only close for one day during the holiday (instead of the traditional three to seven day break).

If you're planning to leave Hong Kong for the UK or the USA in August, book your flight early. You will be competing for seats with tens of thousands of Hong Kong students going back to universities abroad.

What Kind of Trip
You can tackle Hong Kong solo; with friends and family; with a tour; do a mad

dash; or stay in one spot and pursue special interests. Hong Kong's diversity lends itself to just about any type of journey.

Maps

Good maps are easy to get in Hong Kong. The Hong Kong Tourist Association (HKTA) hands out free copies of its *Official Hong Kong Map* booklet at its offices at the Chek Lap Kok airport, the Star Ferry terminal in Tsim Sha Tsui and Jardine House in Central. Maps are divided by district, list hotels and shopping centres, have both English and Chinese script, and are easy to read. Similar maps can be found on the back pages of HKTA's *The Official Hong Kong Guide* and *Hong Kong Now!*, and are usually available in hotels as well as the HKTA offices.

A series of free maps is produced by The Map Company Ltd (☎ 2537-7605). In addition to an overall *Map of Hong Kong* there are separate maps of the main centres, but these are not very detailed. These maps can usually be found at hotels, some bars and Oliver's Super Sandwich stores.

If you're looking for greater detail, topographical accuracy and excellent colour reproduction, it's worth investing in the *Hong Kong Guidebook*, published by Universal Publications and regularly updated. Although it's HK$60, it's worth it for the quality and legibility. Compiled in both English and Chinese, it also includes useful information such as bus routes, timetables and hotel lists. The 1998 version comes with a free Public Transport Boarding Guide. It is available from most bookshops.

The *Hong Kong Official Guide Map* (produced by the government) has both overall and district maps, and is available from most bookshops. Other maps worth looking for are the *Hong Kong Touring Map* published by Universal Publications (HK$18), the *Detailed City Map of Hong Kong Island* also published by Universal Publications (HK$22) and the *Hong Kong* map published by Berndston & Berndston (HK$55), an all-weather map wrapped in plastic.

The government also sells a series of countryside maps that are extremely useful if you plan to go hiking in the hills. These are available at the Government Publications Office (☎ 2537-1910) in the Government Office building, Queensway Government Offices, 88 Queensway, Admiralty. You'll find the office open from 9 am to 4 pm on weekdays (Monday to Friday), and 9 am to 1 pm on Saturday.

Those of you who are seriously into maps can try the Map Publications Centre (☎ 2848-2480) at either the 14th floor, Murray building, Garden Rd, Central (near the Peak Tram terminus), or at 382 Nathan Rd, Yau Ma Tei. Universal Publications produces a series of waterproof maps of the New Territories and outlying islands that are reasonably priced (HK$22) and wonderfully detailed.

Unfortunately there are no good bus maps. The Citibus Information Centres have maps – there is one just outside the Star Ferry terminal in Central. Citibus also publishes a book, but it is large and unwieldy and doesn't list the routes of the opposition bus companies. Your best option may be Universal Publications' *Hong Kong Guidebook*.

Hong Kong is full of free maps, but Cheque-Point moneychangers do charge for theirs (HK$30) without saying so! Among your given paperwork will be hidden a receipt for the map, but most travellers don't realise they've been charged until too late (sorry, no refunds).

Rudy Samson

What to Bring

As little as possible. Many travellers try to bring everything and the kitchen sink. Keep in mind that you can and will buy things in Hong Kong and elsewhere, so don't burden yourself with a lot of unnecessary junk. If you arrive in summer (or even late spring) you'll wish you only had a lunchbox and your toothbrush – the slightest effort will bring you out in a flood of sweat.

That advice having been given, there are some things that you will want to bring from home. The first consideration is the bag you will use to carry all your goods. Backpacks are the easiest type of bag to carry and a frameless or internal-frame pack is the easiest to manage on buses and trains. Packs that close with a zipper can usually be secured with a padlock. Of course, any pack can be slit open with a razor blade, but a padlock will usually prevent pilfering.

A daypack can be handy when you leave your main luggage at the hotel or in lockers. A beltpack is OK for maps, extra film and other miscellanea, but don't use it for valuables such as your travellers cheques and passport, as it's an easy target for those dreaded pickpockets.

If you don't want to use a backpack, a shoulder bag is much easier to carry than a suitcase. Well designed shoulder bags can double as backpacks by rearranging a few straps. If you must have a suitcase, get one with wheels. Cases with wheels and a pull-out handle are even better.

'Lightweight' and 'compact' are two words that should be etched in your mind when you're deciding what to bring. Saw the handle off your toothbrush if you have to – anything to keep the weight down! You only need two sets of clothes – one to wear and one to wash. You will, no doubt, be buying clothes along the way and you can find some real bargains in Hong Kong, Macau and China.

Nylon running or sports shoes are best as they are comfortable, washable and lightweight. If you're going to be in cold weather, buy them oversized and wear with heavy wool socks rather than carrying a pair of boots. A pair of thongs (flip flops) is useful footwear for indoors and shower rooms.

A Swiss army knife (even if it's not made in Switzerland) comes in handy, but you don't need one with 27 separate functions. Basically, you need a small sharp blade, a can opener and a bottle opener – a built-in magnifying glass or backscratcher isn't necessary.

The secret of successful packing is plastic bags or nylon stuff bags – these not only keep things separate, but also keep them clean and dry.

Airlines do lose bags from time to time, but there's a much better chance of it not being yours if it is tagged with your name and address inside as well as outside the bag. Other tags can always fall off or be removed.

TOURIST OFFICES
Local Tourist Offices
The enterprising Hong Kong Tourist Association (HKTA) is definitely worth a visit. Staff are efficient and helpful and have reams of information, most of it free. At the time of writing each of the HKTA offices offered a free phone service. The HKTA also sells (at reasonable cost) a few useful publications, postcards, T-shirts and other souvenirs.

You can call the HKTA hotline (☎ 2807-6177) from 8 am to 6 pm Monday to Friday, and from 9 am to 5 pm on weekends and holidays. You'll find HKTA offices at the following addresses:

Central
  Shop 8, basement, Jardine House, 1 Connaught Place. Open from 9 am to 6 pm weekdays, and 9 am to 1 pm on Saturday. Closed on Sunday and holidays.
Star Ferry terminal
  Tsim Sha Tsui, Kowloon. Open from 8 am to 6 pm Monday to Friday, and from 9 am to 5 pm on weekends and holidays.
Head Office
  (☎ 2807-6543) 11th floor, Citicorp Centre, 18 Whitfield Rd, North Point. This is a business office and is not for normal tourist inquiries.

There are three HKTA offices at Chek Lap Kok airport. These are open daily from 6 am to midnight and are located in the transit area and Buffer Halls A & B on the arrival level. The HKTA has a hotel booking service, which doesn't deal with the really cheap accommodation, but can usually find you a room starting from the two star to five star level. As an added benefit, booking through the HKTA (or most other travel agencies for that matter) nets you a discount of 20% to 30% off the walk-in rate.

HONG KONG

If you have access to a fax, you can take advantage of the HKTA's Infofax service. The data available includes HKTA member hotels, restaurants, places to shop and so on. If dialling from within Hong Kong, the fax number is 11 digits (fax (9006) 2077-1128), but from abroad it's only 10 digits including the country code (fax (852) 177-1128). To use this service, either pick up the handset on the fax machine and dial or set it to polling mode before dialling. After you connect you'll receive a list of topics and the appropriate fax numbers to call to receive the data. You can call this service from abroad and there is no charge beyond what you pay for an international phone connection. If calling from within Hong Kong, the local phone company charges HK$2 per minute from 8 am to 9 pm, and HK$1 per minute from 9 pm to 8 am.

Tourist Offices Abroad
HKTA offices abroad willingly supply brochures and information about Hong Kong. You'll find HKTA offices at the following locations:

Australia
  (☎ (02) 9283 3083) level 4, 80 Druitt St, Sydney, NSW 2000
Canada
  (☎ (416) 366-2389) 3rd floor, Hong Kong Trade Centre, 9 Temperance St, Toronto, Ontario M5H 1Y6
China
  (☎ (8610) 6465-1603) C211A Office building, Beijing Lufthansa Centre, No 50 Liangmaqiao Rd, Chaoyang District, Beijing 100016
France
  (☎ 01 47 20 39 54) Escalier C, 8th floor, 53 Rue François 1er, 75008 Paris
Germany
  (☎ (069) 959-1290) Humboldt Strasse 94, D-60318 Frankfurt am Main
Italy
  (☎ (06) 6880-1336) c/o Sergat Italia Srl, Casella Postale 620, 00100 Roma Centro
Japan
  (☎ (03) 5219-8288) 2/F, Kokusai building, 3-1-1 Marunouchi, Chiyoda-ku, Tokyo 100; (☎ (06) 229-9240) 8th floor, Osaka Saitama building, 3-5-13 Awaji-machi, Chuo-ku, Osaka 541

Korea (South)
  (☎ (822) 778-4403) c/o Glocom Korea, suite 1105, Paiknam building, 188-3 Eulchiro 1-Ka, Chung-Gu, Seoul
New Zealand
  (☎ (09) 575-2707) PO Box 2120, Auckland
Singapore
  (☎ (65) 336-5800) 9 Temasek Blvd, 34-03 Suntec Tower Two, 038989
South Africa
  (☎ (011) 339-4865) c/o Development Promotions, PO Box 30615, Braamfontein 2017
Spain
  (☎ (03) 414-1794) c/o Sergat España SL, Pau Casals 4, 08021 Barcelona
Taiwan
  (☎ (02) 581-2967) 9th floor, 18 Chang'an E Rd, Section 1, Taipei; (☎ 02-581 6061) Hong Kong Information Service
UK
  (☎ (0171) 930-4775) 5th floor, 125 Pall Mall, London, SW1Y 5EA
USA
  (☎ (630) 575-2828) suite 200, 610 Enterprise Drive, Oak Brook, IL 60521; (☎ (212) 869-5008) 5th floor, 590 Fifth Ave, New York, NY 10036-4706; (☎ (310) 208-4582) suite 1220, 10940 Wilshire Blvd, Los Angeles, CA 90024-3915

VISAS & DOCUMENTS
Passport
A passport is essential for visiting Hong Kong, and if yours is within a few months of expiration get a new one immediately. Losing your passport is very bad news – getting a new one means a trip to your embassy or consulate and usually a long wait while faxes or telexes are sent (at your expense) to confirm that you exist. If you'll be staying a long time in Hong Kong, it's wise to register your passport with your consulate or embassy – this makes the replacement process much simpler if you lose it or it is stolen.

Visas
Most of the rules remain the same as before the handover. Future changes are difficult to predict and undoubtedly will reflect the political situation in Beijing. For the foreseeable future, however, it is likely that things will remain much the same.

The only real changes affect British travellers. Currently, British citizens who hold UK passports can stay for up to six months without a visa and this can be extended. Citizens of Commonwealth countries (including British Dependent Territories citizens, British Overseas citizens, British subjects and British protected persons) do not require a visa for a stay of up to three months. If you have any queries, you can contact the British Citizens Unit on the 6th floor of Immigration Tower, 7 Gloucester Rd, Wan Chai. Citizens of most western European countries are also permitted to stay for three months without a visa. Americans, Japanese, South Africans and Germans (and the majority of Latin American countries) do not require visas for a visit of one month or less.

Officially, visitors have to show that they have adequate funds for their stay and that they have an onward ticket or a return ticket to their own country. In practice, this rule is seldom enforced, except in the case when a visa is required. Visitors from the following countries must have a visa: Afghanistan, Albania, Bulgaria, Cambodia, CIS (former USSR), Costa Rican provisional passports, Cuba, Czech Republic, Hungary, Iran, Iraq, Laos, Lebanon, Libya, Mongolia, Myanmar (Burma), North Korea, Panamanian special passports, People's Republic of China (PRC), Romania, Slovak Republic, Somalia, Sudan, Syria, Taiwan, Tonga, Vatican service passports, Vietnam, Yemen, Yugoslavia and all stateless persons. If you do need a visa, apply to the nearest Chinese consulate.

Visitors are not permitted to take up employment, establish any business or enrol as students. If you want to engage in employment, education or residence you must have a work visa beforehand. It is very hard to change visa status after you have arrived in Hong Kong. Anyone wishing to stay longer than the visa free period must apply for a visa before travelling to Hong Kong. Also be aware that this information is just a guide and (although it is very unlikely) that immigration authorities have the right to refuse permission to enter Hong Kong.

Work Visas You need a company on your side to get a work visa for Hong Kong. The Hong Kong Immigration Department requires proof that you have been offered employment, usually in the form of a contract. The prospective employer is also obligated to show that the work you plan to do cannot be performed by a local. Usually, visitors must leave Hong Kong in order to obtain a work permit, returning only when it is ready. Exceptions are made, however, especially if the company explains that it urgently needs to fill a position. Work visas are generally granted for between one and three years. Extensions should be applied for a month before the visa expires.

From overseas, applications for work visas can be made at any Chinese consulate. For more information in Hong Kong, contact the Hong Kong Immigration Department (hotline ☎ 2824-6111, fax 2877-7711, email, enquiry@immd.gcn.gov.hk, www.info.gov.hk/immd/), 2nd floor, Immigration Tower, 7 Gloucester Rd, Wan Chai.

Visa Extensions In Hong Kong, inquire at the Hong Kong Immigration Department (☎ 2824-6111), 2nd floor, Immigration Tower, 7 Gloucester Rd, Wan Chai.

In general, visa extensions are not readily granted unless there are special circumstances – cancelled flights, illness, registration in a legitimate course of study, legal employment, marriage to a local etc.

Travel Insurance

There are various types of travel insurance policies. Some will cover losses due to theft, accident, illness and death. The best policies might reimburse you for an air ticket if you're forced to fly home in an emergency. Many healthcare programs do not cover travel abroad for more than a certain period, so check to find out if you are properly covered.

Travel insurance is something you should arrange before you venture abroad. You can, of course, purchase an insurance policy after arrival in Hong Kong. Rates vary, so shop around. Some of the banks are in the business of selling medical and travellers' insurance – HongkongBank is one such place. Banks produce brochures in English describing the available policies. If you are being sent or relocated to Hong Kong by your company, you should be aware that many companies will include your medical coverage as part of the deal. See the Health chapter in this book for information about health insurance policies.

Driving Licence & Permits

Driving Licence Any foreigner over the age of 18 with a valid International Driving Permit can drive in Hong Kong for up to 12 months. If you're staying longer, you'll need a Hong Kong licence. Apply to the Transport Department Licensing Division (24 hour hotline ☎ 2804-2600), 41st floor, Immigration Tower, 7 Gloucester Rd, Wan Chai. There are four licensing offices spread throughout the territory. There is another licence issuing office on the 3rd floor of the United Centre, 95 Queensway, Wan Chai. A 10 year licence costs HK$900. If you have a licence from your home country bring it along, as it may save you having to get a learner's permit, taking a driving course or doing the driving test. The learner's-permit-driving course routine is a drag – it takes lots of time and costs lots of money.

International Driving Permit If you plan to drive abroad, get an International Driving Permit from your local car association or motor vehicle department before you leave home. Although a scant few countries will issue an International Driving Permit if you just show a licence from your home country, Hong Kong is definitely not one of those places.

In many countries International Driving Permits are valid for one year only, so there's no sense getting one far in advance of departure. However, some countries issue permits valid for three years.

Hostel Card

An International Youth Hostel Federation (IYHF) card is of limited use in Hong Kong

and nearby Macau. You can still spend the night at affiliated youth hostels without a IYHF card, but you will pay more for your bed. For information on Hong Kong's hostels, see the Accommodation section in this chapter.

Student & Youth Cards

If you're a student or you're under 27, you can get an STA Youth Card. If you're aged 13 to 26, you qualify for an International Student Identity Card (ISIC), which entitles you to a number of discounts on airfares, trains, museums etc. To get this card, inquire at your campus – cards can also be issued by the Hong Kong Student Travel Bureau. A small discount (10%) is offered at the STB Hostel to holders of an ISIC card.

International Health Certificate

Useful (though not essential) is an International Health Certificate to record your vaccinations. This can also be issued in Hong Kong.

Other Documents

Visitors and residents are advised to carry identification at all times as the immigration authorities do frequent spot checks to catch illegal workers and those who overstay their visas. If you have no ID, you could find yourself being 'rounded up'. It needn't be a passport – anything with a photo is acceptable. Anyone staying in Hong Kong for more than three months is required to have a Hong Kong Identity Card. If you wish to register for an identity card, phone the 24 hour telephone appointment service on ☎ 2598-0888 or go to the Identity Card issuing office on the 24th floor of Immigration Tower, 7 Gloucester Rd, Wan Chai. Be sure to take your passport.

Business cards make a good impression and can be made cheaply in Hong Kong. It costs about HK$300 for 200 cards. Business card printing shops can be found in many places, and Sheung Wan is a good place to start. Alternatively, make use of the 'Express Card' machines, which can whip out customised cards in less than 10 minutes. The machines are found mostly in MTR and KCR train stations – Central MTR station has several. For HK$25 you get 40 cards.

Photocopies

It's wise to keep photocopies of vital documents in a separate place. You should include a copy of your passport's data pages, birth certificate, credit cards, airline tickets and a list of your travellers cheque serial numbers. To this you might as well add an emergency stash of US$50 or more. Also leave a copy of all these things with someone at home.

If you're travelling with your spouse, a photocopy of your marriage licence might come in handy should you become involved with the law, hospitals or other bureaucratic authorities.

If you're planning on working or studying in Hong Kong, it could be helpful to have copies of transcripts, diplomas, letters of reference and other professional qualifications. However, be warned, customs officials can be tough on job-seekers arriving without work visas. For more information see the Work section in this chapter.

CONSULATES
Consulates in Hong Kong

There's a complete list of consulates in the *Yellow Pages* under the heading Consulates. Some of the smaller countries are represented by honorary consuls who are normally businesspeople employed in commercial firms – so it's advisable to phone beforehand to find out if the consul is available. Beijing – keen to keep consulate powers limited to the 'SAR' of Hong Kong – is slowly phasing out diplomats who hold dual accreditation in mainland China. The following are some of the diplomatic missions in Hong Kong.

Australia
(☎ 2827-8881) 23rd and 24th floor, Harbour Centre, 25 Harbour Rd, Wan Chai
Canada
(☎ 2847-7420) 11th to 14th floor, Tower I, Exchange Square, 8 Connaught Place, Central

China
(☎ 2827-1881) 5th floor, lower block, Visa Office of the Ministry of Foreign Affairs, 26 Harbour Rd, Wan Chai
France
(☎ 2529-4316) 26th floor, Tower II, Admiralty Centre, 18 Harcourt Rd, Admiralty
Germany
(☎ 2529-8855) 21st floor, United Centre, 95 Queensway, Admiralty
Indonesia
(☎ 2890-4421) 127-129 Leighton Rd, Causeway Bay
Japan
(☎ 2522-1184) 46th floor, Tower I, Exchange Square, 8 Connaught Place, Central
Korea (South)
(☎ 2529-4141) 5th floor, Far East Finance Centre, 16 Harcourt Rd, Admiralty
Macau
(☎ 2523-0176) British Trade Commission, Bank of America Tower, Lambeth Walk, Admiralty
Malaysia
(☎ 2527-0921) 24th floor, Malaysia building, 50 Gloucester Rd, Wan Chai
Myanmar (Burma)
(☎ 2827-7929) room 2421, Sung Hung Kai Centre, 30 Harbour Rd, Wan Chai
New Zealand
(☎ 2877-4488) room 2705, 27th floor, Jardine House, Connaught Place, Central
Philippines
(☎ 2823-8500) room 602, United Centre, 95 Queensway, Admiralty
Russian Federation
(☎ 2877-7188) room 2932, 29th floor, Sun Hung Kai Centre, 30 Harbour Rd, Wan Chai
Singapore
(☎ 2527-2212) room 901, 9th floor, Tower I, Admiralty Centre, 18 Harcourt Rd, Admiralty
South Africa
(☎ 2577-3279) Great Eagle Centre, 23 Harbour Rd, Wan Chai
Taiwan
(☎ 2525-8315) Chung Hwa Travel Service, 40th floor, Tower I, 89 Queensway, Admiralty
Thailand
(☎ 2521-6481) 8th floor, Fairmont House, 8 Cotton Tree Drive, Central
UK
(☎ 2901-3000) 1 Supreme Court Rd, Admiralty
USA
(☎ 2523-9011) 26 Garden Rd, Central
Vietnam
(☎ 2591-4510) Visa office, 15th floor, Great Smart Tower, 230 Wan Chai Rd, Wan Chai

CUSTOMS

Even though Hong Kong is a duty-free port, there are items on which duty is still charged. In particular, there are high import taxes on cigarettes and alcohol. The duty-free allowance for visitors is 200 cigarettes (or 50 cigars or 250g tobacco) and 1L of alcohol. Apart from these limits there are few other import taxes, so you can bring in reasonable quantities of almost anything. An exception is ivory, which requires a bureaucratic tangle of permits.

Of course, you can't bring anything deemed illegal into Hong Kong. This includes fireworks. Hong Kong residents returning from Macau and China are often vigorously searched for this reason. Not surprisingly, firearms are strictly controlled and special permits are needed to import them. Non-lethal weapons like chemical mace and stun guns are also prohibited.

Customs officers are on the alert for drug smugglers. If you're arriving from Thailand or Vietnam, expect a rigorous examination of your luggage.

Have some sympathy for the enormous job that customs officials perform. Aside from air passengers, more than 700 ships a day pass through Hong Kong's harbour. Obviously, not all ships can be inspected. One customs official mentioned that the biggest problems are with ships from South-East Asia (carrying heroin) and from the USA (smuggling guns and ammunition). This is in addition to small speedboats from China, which bring in guns, drugs and illegal immigrants.

BAGGAGE STORAGE

If you're going to visit Macau, Guangzhou or points beyond but will be returning to Hong Kong, consider the virtues of leaving your heavy junk behind. Most hotels and even some budget hostels have left-luggage rooms. There is usually a charge for this service, which can be anything from cheap to totally outrageous – be sure to inquire first to avoid any unpleasant surprises when you come back to pick up the bag.

The last option is lockers, but you'll have to search hard. There are a few in the major KCR train stations and at the Macau and China ferry piers. Hong Kong's lockers are high-tech – rather than using keys, when you close the locker door, a machine will spit out a numbered ticket. You have to punch in this number if you ever want to see your bag again, so keep the ticket where you won't lose it or write the number down elsewhere. Watch out for thieves in the area who snatch a quick glance at the ticket, or try and help as the *gwailo* attempts to work out how it all operates. If the thief knows your number, they'll get your bag. Some lockers have a maximum storage time of three days, so read the instructions carefully.

MONEY
Currency

The local currency is the Hong Kong dollar, which is divided into 100 cents. Bills are issued in denominations of HK$20 (grey), HK$50 (blue), HK$100 (red), HK$500 (brown) and HK$1000 (yellow). Coins are issued in denominations of 10 cents, 20 cents, 50 cents, HK$1, HK$2, HK$5 and HK$10. There is also a HK$10 note (green) but it is now being phased out in favour of the HK$10 coin.

Hong Kong currency is issued by three local banks, rather than by the government. The Hongkong and Shanghai Bank (often shortened to HongkongBank) and the Standard Chartered Bank have long been Hong Kong's two designated note issuers. Though the bills issued by each share the same colours, the designs are different. In May 1994 the Bank of China became the third note-issuing bank. The two British banks have stopped issuing notes carrying references to the British monarchy, instead switching to designs that are more palatable to the Chinese government.

By the end of 1997, approximately one quarter of the 4.5 billion coins issued in Hong Kong had already left for the mainland. Of the remaining 3.3 billion in local circulation, 800 million were minted in the colonial era! Coins bearing the image of the Queen's head were still plentiful at the time of writing. Watch out for fake HK$500 and HK$1000 notes — in 1997 the market was swamped with forgeries, prompting many retailers to refuse any large denomination bills.

Exchange Rates

Since 1983, the Hong Kong dollar has been pegged to the US dollar at a rate of US$1 to HK$7.80, though it is allowed to fluctuate within a narrow range of this level. This move deterred the rampant speculation in the currency that had been threatening the local economy. The 'peg', as it's called, frequently comes under attack by analysts, as it limits Hong Kong's fiscal policy options. At the moment the Hong Kong dollar generally moves against other currencies in line with the direction of the US dollar. If the peg goes, then wild fluctuations will occur as the Hong Kong dollar devalues. Many argue that it is likely to disappear by the year 2000, as China will almost certainly have to devalue its own currency, the Renminbi, which has appreciated to levels that are destroying China's export market.

The following exchange rates were current at the time of publication:

Australia	A$1	=	HK$4.60
Canada	C$1	=	HK$5.11
China	Y1	=	HK$0.93
France	Ffr1	=	HK$1.29
Germany	DM1	=	HK$4.31
Japan	¥100	=	HK$5.30
New Zealand	NZ$1	=	HK$3.91
Singapore	S$1	=	HK$4.41
Switzerland	Sfr1	=	HK$5.14
Taiwan	NT$1	=	HK$0.22
Thailand	B1	=	HK$0.18
UK	£1	=	HK$12.54
USA	US$1	=	HK$7.75

Exchanging Money

Hong Kong has no exchange controls – locals and foreigners can send large quantities of money in or out as they please. Hong Kong is the financial centre of Asia simply because it is unregulated.

Cash Banks generally offer the best rates, while the moneychanging counters at the airport offer the worst. Some banks charge non-account holders a commission. The HongkongBank, Hang Seng Bank and Standard Chartered Bank all levy fees of HK$50 for each transaction. If you're changing several hundred US dollars or more you'll be given a better rate, which makes up for the fee. Hong Kong is saturated with branches of these banks, so you should have little trouble finding one.

Your best bet is probably Dao Heng Bank, which not only gives a slightly better rate than most other banks, but also does not charge a commission. One of Dao Heng's most convenient locations for visitors is its foreign exchange counter on the main floor of Towers I and II, Exchange Square, 8 Connaught Rd, Central. Bank hours are from 9 am to 4 pm Monday to Friday, and until noon or 1 pm on Saturday.

Travellers Cheques Most banks will cash travellers cheques, and all charge a fee, often irrespective of whether you are an account holder or not. The best deal is probably the Dao Heng Bank, which charges a flat rate of HK$20. The HongkongBank charges 0.375% of the total amount, Standard Chartered tacks on a HK$50 commission and Hang Seng charges HK$60 an encashment. Licensed moneychangers don't levy a commission, but sometimes give a slightly lower rate for travellers cheques – this may improve if you are changing a significant sum.

Hong Kong is a good place to buy travellers cheques. Generally the fee is 1% of the total value of cheques purchased.

If your travellers cheques are lost or stolen, try the following places for replacements: American Express (☎ 2885-9331); Citicorp (☎ 2821-7215); Thomas Cook (☎ 2854-0575, 2854-1388); and Visa (☎ 2523-8152).

ATMs Using an ATM or debit card is one of the cheapest ways to get money from overseas, as the only fees levied are those by your home bank for ATM withdrawals.

There are two major ATM networks in Hong Kong. HongkongBank and Hang Seng Bank operate one network which accepts a fairly large number of international ATM systems, such as GlobalAccess, Plus and Cirrus, as well as Visa credit and debit cards. The Jetco network is used by Standard Chartered and a host of smaller Hong Kong banks, and accepts Cirrus ATM cards and MasterCard credit and debit cards.

The ATM systems accepted are displayed above ATM's. Payment is in Hong Kong dollars only. Midland Bank customers can use cashpoint cards with HongkongBank machines to draw from their account in the UK, as Midland is part of HongkongBank.

If you decide to stay in Hong Kong long-term, obtaining a HongkongBank ETC ATM card will give you access to the HongkongBank ATM system (over 800 machines) as well as the Hang Seng Bank. HongkongBank also issues a card called Mondex which you can use when shopping.

Credit Cards The most widely accepted credit cards are American Express (Amex), Visa, Diners Club, JCB and MasterCard.

Some shops may try to add a surcharge to offset the commission charged by credit companies. In theory this is prohibited by the credit companies, but to get around this many shops will offer a 5% discount if you pay cash.

The following companies are the major issuers of plastic money:

American Express International Inc
  (Amex, 24 hour hotline ☎ 2885-9366) 1st floor, Henley building, 5 Queens Rd, Central
Citibank
  (24 hour hotline ☎ 2860-0333) 11th floor, Dorset House, Tai Koo Place, 979 King's Rd, Quarry Bay
Diners Club
  (24 hour hotline ☎ 2860-1888) 11th floor, Dorset House, Tai Koo Place, 979 King's Rd, Quarry Bay
JCB
  (☎ 2366-7211) 28 Hankow Rd, Tsim Sha Tsui; room 507-509, Hong Kong Pacific Centre, Connaught Rd, Central

MasterCard International
  (☎ 2598-8038) suite 1401-4, Dah Sing Financial Centre, 108 Gloucester Rd, Wan Chai
Visa
  (24 hour hotline ☎ 2810-8033) Lippo Tower, Tamar St, Admiralty

International Transfers International telegraphic transfers are fast and efficient. All of the major banks in Hong Kong provide this service – the two most popular being HongkongBank and Hang Seng Bank. The fees usually range from HK$100 to HK$150. HongkongBank's international transfer desk (customer service centre ☎ 2748-3322) is on the 3rd floor of the main branch, 1 Queen's Rd, Central.

A specialist in telegraphic transfers is Western Union (☎ 2528-5631), shop 2038, 2nd floor, United Centre, 95 Queensway, Admiralty.

If you're having money wired, it's useful if the sender includes your passport number along with your name. You can also have the money wired directly into a bank account. Anyone can open a bank account in Hong Kong – there is no need to have a residency visa. Accounts can be opened in Hong Kong dollars or almost any other major currency, including gold.

Black Market No foreign currency black market exists in Hong Kong. If anyone on the street does approach you to change money, assume it's a scam.

Moneychangers Licensed moneychangers, such as Thomas Cook and Chequepoint, are abundant in tourist areas like Tsim Sha Tsui. The moneychangers are open on Sunday, holidays and late into the evenings. There is no commission, but the exchange rates offered are equivalent to a 5% commission. These rates are clearly posted, though if you're changing several hundred US dollars or more you should be able to bargain for a better rate. Before the actual exchange is made, the moneychanger is required by law to give you a form to sign clearly showing the amount, exchange rate and any service charges.

The moneychangers operating at Chungking Mansions on Nathan Rd in Tsim Sha Tsui usually offer the best rates. Streetside moneychangers in tourist areas (Cheque-Point is the best known) give relatively poor rates, though you can often bargain over a large transaction (you'd still do better at a bank).

Try to avoid changing money at hotels as the rates are only marginally better than those offered by the airport moneychangers.

Security

Hong Kong has its share of pickpockets. Rather than lose your precious cash, travellers cheques and passport, keep them far from sticky fingers. Devices which can thwart pickpockets include pockets sewn onto the inside of your trousers, Velcro tabs to seal pocket openings and money belts or pouches under your shirt.

Costs

Many argue that one reason for Hong Kong's abrupt decline in tourism is that it has priced itself out of the market. A four course dinner for two with a few beers at a mid-range international restaurant in Soho could set you back HK$700. Hong Kong has lost its edge when it comes to picking up bargains – it takes a lot of searching to find a shop with good prices.

For those of more humble means, it's possible to survive in Hong Kong for under HK$200, but it will require a good deal of self-discipline. Accommodation is the biggest expense, but you can get it down to HK$60 a night by staying in grotty dormitories. The true Spartan could, theoretically, spend the night on a dorm bed, have three fast-food meals, travel on the tram and ferry, and only spend about HK$130 a day. Food is actually quite reasonable if you choose your restaurants carefully – you can keep the eating bill down to HK$60 a day if you patronise budget eateries or buy your own from supermarkets. Transport is cheap only because distances are short – on a per kilometre basis, Hong Kong's prices are world class.

One of the easiest ways to empty your wallet is to visit Hong Kong's bars. Prices for beer and cocktails are on a par with those in Tokyo. A beer usually costs HK$30 to HK$50, and cocktails are slightly more. One way around these prices is to target happy hours, usually held between 4 and 8 pm (although times vary), when the prices are either halved, or you get two drinks for the price of one. If you like to drink but don't fancy the prices, you will find the beers and spirits in the two supermarket chains, Wellcome and Park N'Shop, good value. Cigarettes are reasonably cheap if you avoid buying them in bars.

The main way to cut costs is to control yourself – shopping in Hong Kong can be addictive. Many people find all those cameras and electronic goodies irresistible and suddenly decide they need to buy all sorts of things they don't need at all! Nightlife is also a temptation – discos, pubs and expensive restaurants have been the downfall of many budget travellers.

The good news for consumers is that property prices fell dramatically in early 1998 and this should have an effect on the prices of goods and services in general.

Tipping & Bargaining

Although tipping was never customary for the Chinese, westerners have introduced this vulgar practise to Hong Kong. Feel no obligation to tip taxi drivers, but it's almost mandatory to tip hotel porters at least HK$10. If you make use of the porters at the airport, HK$2 a suitcase is normally expected.

Fancy hotels and restaurants have a 10% service charge. Many staff members expect more, especially from free-spending tourists. Check for hidden extras before you tip – some mid-range hotels charge HK$5 for each local call (when it should be free) and some restaurants consistently get the bill wrong.

Many bars have a policy of forcing you to sit down and then sending a waitress to serve you, expecting a tip. If you don't want this, just order the drink yourself and sit at a table.

Let your conscience be your guide. If you think the service was great, you might want to leave something. Otherwise don't bother – there's no need to reward unsatisfactory service.

Bargaining is expected in Hong Kong's tourist districts, but not as much elsewhere. Sadly, some people turn it into a ruthless contest of 'in your face' east-west rivalry. Some tourists operate on the theory that you can get the goods for half the price originally quoted. Our philosophy is that if you can bargain something down to half price, then you shouldn't buy from that shop anyway. If the business is that crooked (and many are, particularly in the Tsim Sha Tsui tourist ghetto), it will probably find other ways to cheat you – like selling electronics with missing components, or second-hand cameras instead of new ones. In an honest shop, you shouldn't be able to bargain more than a 10% discount.

Bargaining is definitely out in the department stores and clothing chain stores, such as Giordano and U2. You can certainly try at the jewellery stores – you could well get 10% off, which makes quite a difference when the price tag is HK$18,000.

Price tags should be displayed on all goods. If you can't find a price tag you've undoubtedly entered one of those business establishments with 'flexible' (read rip-off) prices. For more details, see the Shopping section in this chapter, and the Shopping sections in the Kowloon and Hong Kong Island chapters.

Taxes & Refunds

There is no sales tax in Hong Kong. The only tax visitors are likely to run into is a 5% government tax on hotel rates. Hotels add this to the 10% service charge, making for a total surcharge of 15%.

Many shops will exchange defective goods, or in the case of clothing, if the garment doesn't fit. Be sure to keep receipts and go back to the store as soon as possible.

Refunds are almost never given in Hong Kong, but most shops will give you credit towards another purchase.

POST & COMMUNICATIONS

Hong Kong's postal system is generally excellent – letters are sometimes delivered the same day they are sent! Postage rates are on a par with most developed countries. Mail boxes and post offices are clearly marked in English, and the postal staff generally speak very good English.

Postal Rates

Airmail The Hong Kong postal service divides the world into two distinct zones. Zone 1 is China, Indonesia, India, Japan, South-East Asia, South Korea and Taiwan and Zone 2 is the rest of the world. The rates for letters and postcards are HK$2.10 (Zone 1) and HK$2.60 (Zone 2) for the first 10g; and HK$1.10 and HK$1.20 respectively for each additional 10g. Aerogrammes are HK$2.10 for both zones.

International Surface Mail The rates vary widely depending on the destination country. Parcels shipped by surface take six to 10 weeks to reach the USA or UK, and are around half the cost of airmail. Post offices also sell different sized cardboard boxes, allowing you to pack and send on the spot.

Sending Mail

On Hong Kong Island, the General Post Office (GPO) is on your right as you disembark from the Star Ferry. In Kowloon the most convenient post offices are at 10 Middle Rd, east of the Ambassador Hotel and Nathan Rd, Tsim Sha Tsui (this office has a stamp vending machine outside which is useful after hours). Another good post office is in the basement of the Albion Plaza, 2-6 Granville Rd, just off Nathan Rd, Tsim Sha Tsui. All the major post offices are open Monday to Friday from 8 am to 6 pm, Saturday until 2 pm, and are closed on Sunday and public holidays.

Allow five days for delivery of letters, postcards and aerogrammes to the UK and the USA. Speedpost reduces delivery time by about half. Sea mail is slow, so allow from six to 10 weeks for delivery to the UK and USA.

Speedpost Hong Kong's Speedpost (☎ 2921-2277, fax 2541-4868) is often called Express Mail Service (EMS) elsewhere. Letters and small parcels sent by Speedpost should reach almost any destination in the world within four days. Furthermore, anything sent by Speedpost is automatically registered. An advantage of using Speedpost is that the customs declaration is simple (though the pick-up service is limited to account holders).

The rates for Speedpost vary enormously according to destination. Every post office has a schedule of fees and a timetable is available on request. Rates are listed in HK$.

Weight Not Over	Letters & Postcards	Printed Matter	Small Packet
20g	2.30	2.10	4.60
50g	4.00	3.60	4.60
100g	5.30	4.60	4.60
250g	10.50	9.40	9.40
500g	20.00	17.50	17.50
1kg	35.00	31.00	31.00
2kg	56.00	45.00	45.00

Courier Service Private companies offering rapid document and small parcel service (32kg limit) include DHL (☎ 2765-8111), Federal Express (☎ 2730-3333) and TNT Express (☎ 2331-2663). All three companies have numerous pickup points and many MTR stations have DHL suboffices, including Central, Admiralty and Causeway Bay. DHL also offers a 24 hour collection service.

Receiving Mail

There are poste restante services at the GPO and other large post offices. Mail is held for two months. If you address an envelope c/o Poste Restante, GPO Hong Kong, it will go to the GPO on Hong Kong Island. If you want letters to go to Kowloon, address them to Poste Restante, 10 Middle Rd, Tsim Sha Tsui, Kowloon.

If you decide to take up residence or do business, there is a very long waiting list for post office boxes.

Telephone

Hongkong Telecom has until quite recently enjoyed a monopoly on phone services. In 1994 three other companies were permitted into the market: Hutchison (☎ 2807-9011), New T&T (☎ 2112-1121) and New World (☎ 2138-2200). The lucrative long-distance monopoly will continue until the year 2006. Monopolies usually charge high rates for poor service, but Hongkong Telecom is something of an exception – the service is good and the long-distance rates are the lowest in Asia.

All calls made within Hong Kong are local calls and therefore free, except for public pay phones which cost HK$1 a call. The pay phones accept HK$1, HK$2 and HK$5 coins.

Hong Kong has very few public phones. Your best bet is to try indoors – check the hotel lobbies, convenience stores, ferry terminals, MTR stations and post offices. There are free courtesy phones in the airport and many shops have phones placed outside on the street.

If you want to phone overseas, it's cheapest to use an International Direct Dialling (IDD) telephone. You can place an IDD call from most phone boxes, but you'll probably need a 'phonecard'. Phonecards can be bought at Hongkong Telecom Service Centres, branches of 7-Eleven and OK convenience stores, and come in denominations of HK$50, HK$100 or HK$250.

ElephantTalk and Hongkong Telecom Hello phonecards are also widely available. The difference between these phonecards and the ones mentioned previously is that you can call from any phone by punching in a PIN code. Cards come in HK$100, HK$200 and HK$300 denominations. Hello phonecards can be picked up at Hongkong Telecom Service Centres. ElephantTalk cards can be bought at a reduced rate (eg HK$80 for a HK$100 card) from a number of shops and some of the cheap guesthouses in Chungking Mansions.

To make an IDD call from Hong Kong, first dial 001, then the country code, area code and number. If the area code begins with a zero, you must omit the zero. To call Melbourne (area code 03) in Australia (country code 61) you would dial 001-61-3-5555 5555. If you're using someone else's phone and you want to know the cost of the call, dial 003 instead of 001 and the operator will call back to report the cost.

If you go to Hongkong Telecom, there are various options for overseas phone calls. These are: operator-connected calls (paid in advance with a minimum of three minutes); IDD (which you dial yourself after paying a deposit, and the unused portion of your deposit is refunded); reverse charges (which requires a small deposit that is refundable if the charge is accepted or if the call doesn't get through); or simply buying a phonecard. You can place international calls at the following Hongkong Telecom Service Centres (listed more-or-less in order of convenience for travellers):

Hong Kong Island
Shop 116, Prince's building, Chater Rd, Central; 290-292 Hennessy Rd, Wan Chai – open from 10 am to 8 pm Monday to Saturday, closed public holidays; 2nd floor, Jusco Department Store, Kornhill Plaza North, 1 Kornhill Rd, Quarry Bay – open from 10 am to 7 pm daily, including public holidays
Kowloon
Hermes House, 10 Middle Rd, Tsim Sha Tsui – open 24 hours daily, including public holidays; shop 43f, ground floor, Ma Tau Wai Rd, Hunghom – open from 9 am to 7 pm Monday to Saturday and public holidays
New Territories
Shop 303-313, ground floor, Castle Peak Rd, Tsuen Wan – open from 9 am to 7 pm Monday to Saturday, closed public holidays; shop 31b-e, level 3, Sha Tin Centre, Sha Tin – open from 9 am to 7 pm Monday to Saturday, 12 am to 6 pm Sunday and public holidays

For those who make frequent calls, it makes sense to join a call-back service to take advantage of the cheaper phone rates of other countries (although look out for the hidden costs and long delays in connection). Companies that can provide this service include Primecall (☎ (800) 698-1232, email primecal@compumedia.com),

Global Access (☎ 2651-8466) and Mastercall International (☎ 2722-6118).

Another option is to make use of the home-direct service, which connects you directly to a local operator in the country dialled. You can then make a reverse-charge or credit card call with a telephone credit card valid in that country. See the boxed text 'International Dialling Codes' for the home-direct dialling codes for some countries. A few places, including Chek Lap Kok airport, some hotels and shopping centres, have home direct phones where you simply press a button labelled USA, UK, Canada etc to be put through to your home operator. For details dial ☎ 013. You may want to check whether your home telephone company supports home-direct services before leaving for Hong Kong.

For long-termers in Hong Kong, residential line rental is HK$67 per month, plus HK$13 for a basic push-button telephone.

International Dialling Codes

Country	Direct Dial	Home Direct
Australia	001-61	800-0061
Canada	001-1	800-1100
France	001-33	800-0033
Germany	001-49	800-0049
Indonesia	001-62	800-0062
Italy	001-39	800-0039
Japan	001-81	800-0181
Korea	001-82	800-0082
Malaysia	001-60	800-0060
Netherlands	001-31	800-0031
New Zealand	001-64	800-0064
Singapore	001-65	800-0065
Spain	001-34	800-0034
Sweden	001-46	800-0046
Taiwan	001-886	800-0886
Thailand	001-66	800-0066
UK	001-44	800-0044
USA	001-1	800-1111*

*Through AT&T you can also dial 800-1121 (MCI) or 800-1877 (Sprint), and for Hawaii you can dial 800-1188.

The installation fee is HK$530. For more information, call ☎ 2888-2888.

To phone Hong Kong from overseas, use your country's international dialling code plus Hong Kong's country code (852), followed by the local eight digit number.

Some useful telephone numbers and prefixes include the following:

Ambulance, Fire, Police, Emergency
  ☎ 999
Free Ambulance Service (St John)
  ☎ 2576-6555 (Hong Kong Island)
  ☎ 2713-5555 (Kowloon)
  ☎ 2639-2555 (New Territories)
Calls to China
  ☎ 012
Credit Card Billing
  ☎ 011
Crime Report, Police Business
  ☎ 2527-7177
Directory Assistance
  ☎ 1081
Fire Hazard Complaints
  ☎ 2723-8787
Hong Kong's Country Code
  ☎ 852
IDD Prefix
  ☎ 001
Information hotlines
  ☎ 1000 (general)
International Directory Assistance
  ☎ 013
International Operator
  ☎ 010
Taxi Complaints
  ☎ 2527-7177
Time & Weather
  ☎ 18501
Tropical Cyclone Warning Inquiries
  ☎ 2835-1473

Telephone Directories There are more phone directories than you would expect! Currently, the line-up includes the *Yellow Pages for Consumers* (three volumes, in English and Chinese), the *Yellow Pages for Businesses* (one volume, English only), the *Business White Pages Telephone Directory* (one volume, English or Chinese), the *Residential Directories* (three volumes, in English and Chinese) and the *Hong Kong Fax Directory* (one volume, in English and Chinese). These guides are available from Telecom CSL shops (see the Telecom CSL Shops entry in this section for details). The *Hong Kong Yellow Pages* is now available on the Internet at www.hkt.com/directory.

Mobile Phones & Pagers Hong Kong boasts the world's highest per-capita usage of mobile telephones and pagers. Even if you don't take up permanent residence, it might be worth knowing that you can rent this equipment. Hongkong Telecom can rent or sell you a mobile phone. It offers three reasonably priced rental packages (minimum period one week) which can be rented on the spot from one of the Hongkong Telecom CSL shops. For more information, call ☎ 2911-1783. Another place where you can rent mobile phones is Rentel (☎ 2881-2688).

Pagers can be rented from a wide variety of sources. Hongkong Telecom charges a fairly low monthly fee, but tacks on usage fees and a large deposit. Phone ☎ 2883-0333 for details. Other companies rent and sell pagers at slightly lower prices. Look in the *Yellow Pages* under Pagers to find an extensive list. You could start with ABC Communications (☎ 2710-0333), Star Paging (☎ 2771-1111), Hong Kong Star Internet (☎ 2781-6552) and Hutchison Paging (☎ 2332-1123, 2770-8233). Mobile phones and pagers do work inside the MTR.

Telecom CSL Shops This is where you apply for service, pay bills, rent pagers, and purchase equipment and phone directories. The full list of shops is extensive and some of the major ones include: shop 116 Prince's building, Chater Rd, Central; ground floor, 68 Percival St, Causeway Bay; ground floor, Hermes House, 10 Middle Rd, Tsim Sha Tsui; shop 2, ground floor, Omega Plaza, 32a-34a Dundas St, Yau Ma Tei.

Fax
Hongkong Telecom offers fax services and the fully digital fibre-optic lines ensure good quality transmission within Hong Kong. Per-page rates range from HK$15 (Hong

HONG KONG

Kong) to HK$45 (Europe), depending on the destination country. You can receive faxes for HK$10 a page. Most hotels and even many youth hostels allow guests to send and receive faxes. The surcharge for sending is usually 10% above the cost, and receiving is normally HK$10 a page. If dialling your own fax for an overseas transmission, use the international prefix 002 (for a data line) rather than 001 (for a voice line).

Email & Internet Access

Hong Kong is a good place to log on. There are more than 80 Internet Service Providers (ISP) including, CompuServe (☎ 3002-8332) and America Online (☎ 2519-9040) – two of the world's largest online services. If you want to dial direct to overseas online services, you can try Datapak – Hongkong Telecom's packet switching network. Hongkong Telecom's Internet access service is Netvigator (☎ 2888-1278).

Other ISPs are ABC Net (☎ 2710-0363), Asia Online (☎ 2837-8888) and Hong Kong Star Internet (☎ 2781-6552). Star Internet also has an office next to World Wide House on Des Voeux Rd, Central, where you can use the Internet for free – though the terminals are usually occupied by anxious stockmarket watchers. Other places you can use the Internet for free include the Trade Development Council Business Library (☎ 2584-4333) and the British Council Library (☎ 2913-5125).

If you're staying in Hong Kong for an extended period, you may want to look into Hong Kong Internet and Gateway Services (☎ 2527-4888, email aaron@hk.net), which charge an initial fee of HK$100, and a monthly subscription rate of HK$100. The online fee is HK$18 per hour and you get issued with a roaming number so you can access your email at local rates from abroad.

The Last Governor

Relinquishing his post as governor of Hong Kong, and charting a course on the night of 30 June 1997 to relative political obscurity, Chris Patten left behind a five year career hallmarked by discord with the People's Republic of China. Locking horns with Beijing was his métier and it wasn't just for the sake of a good scrap – his job was to represent the people of Hong Kong. Kowtowing to the totalitarian clique in northern China was something for which he didn't have the stomach.

It is convincingly argued that the first spasms of democracy should have come to Hong Kong earlier than it did, but at the end of the day, most agreed that proto-democracy was better than no democracy. The skeletal apparatus of democracy in Hong Kong may, with time, gather about itself the flesh and blood of a full franchise – this was the gamble.

Leaving the Hong Kong political arena winded but self-assured, Chris Patten retreated to the comfort of his farm in the south of France to put quill to paper and naturally reflect upon his experiences. The summary of these reflections was to be a book that would be titled *East and West*.

HarperCollins paid Patten an advance of UK£125,000 for the book and it all seemed hunky-dory. Chris Patten never for a moment imagined that he would face censorship in his native land the UK, but he hadn't reckoned on the intricate pro-China manoeuvring of HarperCollin's owner, Rupert Murdoch.

It seems that it was Mr Murdoch's business sense that was affronted by various anti-China swipes in Patten's book, rather than any deep-seated love of the Middle Kingdom. China was the focus of the Murdoch group's hydra-headed ambition to make a mint out of cable TV and satellite opportunities in the country as it surged towards its post-socialist future. As *guanxi*, or 'connections', with the nation's establishment was the best way to realise his aims in China, any critical rhetoric that might scupper his networking plans was anathema.

HarperCollin's pro-China bias had already raised eyebrows with its 1995 publication of the honey-tongued biography of Deng Xiaoping, written by his daughter. It was also argued that other

If your hotel doesn't have email facilities, don't despair. Kublai's Cyberdiner (☎ 2529-9117) on the 3rd floor, One Capital Place, 18 Luard Rd, Wan Chai (the entrance is on Jaffe Rd), is a great Mongolian barbecue eatery, offering email access. You can sit down with a coffee, get an email address and chat online. The service is free, and the Cyberdiner is open from noon to 11 pm daily.

Xyberia cybercafe (☎ 2984-1008, fax 2984-7618, email sahr@xyberia.com) is on hand for those who want to surf the Net, espresso in hand. You'll have to take the ferry to find it, however, as it's at shop C, Sea View building, 1 Ngan Wan Rd, Mui Wo, Lantau (the first Internet cafe in the outlying islands).

Telegraph
Hongkong Telecom (☎ 2888-2888, 24 hour hotline ☎ 1000) is the place to go for sending international or local telegrams.

INTERNET RESOURCES
There are heaps of online services dealing with Hong Kong issues, and a simple Net search on the words 'Hong Kong' will turn up all sorts of intriguing possibilities. Lonely Planet contributes to this medium – check out the Web site at www.lonelyplanet.com.

You'll find *bc Magazine* has the scoop on Hong Kong's vast entertainment and nightlife scene. The website is (email bconline@netvigator.com, www.netvigator.com/bconline).

Information changes on the Internet so quickly that it's impossible to say what the hottest sites will be at the time you read this. At the moment, some good possibilities include:

Asian Sources Online
　the centre of Asian trade on the World Wide Web, www.asiansources.com
Hong Kong government information
　www.info.gov.hk

ships of the Murdoch fleet, including the flagship *Times* newspaper, revealed true colours by dishing up scant reports on China issues. But the picture was far from clear. HarperCollins was the publisher of Jung Chang's *Wild Swans*, the bible of fledgling China watchers. She was also apparently signed up with HarperCollins to paint Mao in, no doubt, less than flattering colours in a forthcoming biography. Even so, Patten's book was targeted and HarperCollins pulled the plug.

Designed as a defensive manoeuvre behind which the bulging truth could shelter, the Murdoch press declared Patten's book 'boring'. The manoeuvre was a goner from the start. The book's editor, Stuart Proffitt, had recently publicly declared the book 'lucid' and one of the best reads of its genre; any hope of a collected front was wrenched apart. Damage limitation was the only option left to HarperCollins PR department. The *Times* newspaper's attempt at damage limitation – not reporting the incident at all – backfired horribly; rival newspapers swept down like vultures onto twitching prey.

Proffitt quit in disgust and managed to find a job still editing the book on a freelance basis with the book's new publisher, Macmillan. Friends and foes came rapidly out of the woodwork, applying balms and sharpening knives respectively. Andrew Neil, former editor of the *Sunday Times* and one of Murdoch's former colleagues, got stuck in. Writing an article in the *Guardian*, he conducted an incisive analysis of Murdoch's techniques of business, describing the man as a 'serial kowtower'. A leading literary agent indicated a reconsideration of a relationship with HarperCollins and a number of HarperCollin's authors rallied in support of Patten. Labour Party MPs also voiced concerns at what was seen as a major threat to free speech.

It was never a question of whether the book would be published or not, just a question of by whom. The publicity has possibly guaranteed good sales figures. Chris Patten stands to do well out of his new arrangement with Macmillan and he's also possibly in the running for the position of Mayor of London. But, to many, the case was a sad admission that business interests had taken precedence over intellectual freedom.

Hong Kong information page
   www.geog.hkbu.edu.hk/hkwww.html
Hong Kong Tourists Association
   www.hkta.org

BOOKS
Lonely Planet
Other guides relevant to Hong Kong published by Lonely Planet are the *Beijing city guide*, *China*, *Hong Kong city guide*, *South-West China*, the *Cantonese phrasebook* and the *Mandarin phrasebook*.

Lonely Planet guides to countries in the region include *Australia*, *Indonesia*, *Japan*, *Korea*, *Laos*, *Mongolia*, *Myanmar*, *The Philippines*, *Taiwan*, *Thailand* and *Vietnam*. Regional guides include *Malaysia, Singapore & Brunei*, *North-East Asia* and *South-East Asia*. City guides include *Bangkok*, *Ho Chi Minh city*, *Kyoto*, *Singapore* and *Tokyo*.

Guidebooks
The following special interest guidebooks offer handy advice if you stay in Hong Kong for a while.

The Leisure Guide to Hong Kong is a recent guide that has proven popular. *The Guide to Shopping in Hong Kong* (FDC Services Ltd Publishing, 1996) by Fiona Campbell is an essential guide for the tireless shopper, and hopefully will come out in a new edition.

Hong Kong's Best Restaurants (Illustrated Magazine Publishing) is published annually by Hong Kong Tatler Magazine.

Living in Hong Kong (American Chamber of Commerce) has quite an American slant, but it's regularly updated and has loads of useful information for anyone planning to move to Hong Kong.

Establishing an office in Hong Kong (American Chamber of Commerce) is a regularly updated reference work that, despite being primarily for Americans, is full of up-to-date, useful information. *Associations & Societies in Hong Kong*, which is published by the HKTA, has a self-explanatory title.

Culture Shock! Hong Kong. A Guide to Customs and Etiquette (Kuperard) by Betty Wei & Elizabeth Li is an excellent introduction to Hong Kong culture.

The Hong Kong Guide, 1893 is available as a reprint and makes fascinating reading. The travel information is somewhat out of date.

Travel
The Taipan Traders by Anthony Lawrence (one of the Formasia series of books) is a large sketchbook containing portraits by Asia's finest painters. *Great Cities of the World – Old Hong Kong* is another interesting Formasia book.

Times Editions' *Hong Kong* by Ian Lloyd & Russell Spurr is a good pictorial book.

History & Politics
Hong Kong's brief but colourful history makes for good reading. One of the best is Jan Morris' *Hong Kong – Epilogue to an Empire*. The excellent book moves seemlessly between past and present Hong Kong in an effort to explain what made the colony so unique among the possessions of the British empire.

A History of Hong Kong by GB Endacott, published in 1958, is a classic covering everything you'd ever want to know about Hong Kong's past. It's not to be confused with *A History of Hong Kong* by Frank Welsh.

The Last Governor by Jonathan Dimbleby is an acclaimed account of Chris Patten's historic mission to Hong Kong. Patten's own book *East and West*, will be essential reading for those interested in recent Hong Kong history. Originally to be published by HarperCollins, Rupert Murdoch apparently couldn't decide between gutsy political commentary or his own interests in China, so the manuscript went to Macmillan.

The government's annual report is entitled *Hong Kong 1995*, *Hong Kong 1996* etc. In addition to the excellent photographs, the text is a gold mine of information about the government, politics, economy, history, arts and just about any other topic relevant to Hong Kong.

Maurice Collis' *Foreign Mud* tells the sordid story of the Opium Wars. Another version of the same story is *The Opium War* by the Foreign Language Press in Beijing.

Hong Kong Illustrated, Views & News 1840-1890, compiled by John Warner, is a large sketchbook and shows the colony's history.

The Taipans – Hong Kong's Merchant Princes tells the story of the western managers *(taipans)* who profiteered during the Opium Wars. *The Other Hong Kong Report* is a fascinating and somewhat cynical rebuttal to the government's optimistic annual report.

Nature Guides

The Government Publications Centre sells nature guides to Hong Kong's flora, fauna, geography and geology. Try starting with *Hong Kong Animals* by Dennis Hill & Karen Phillipps.

There are also quite a few other 'Hong Kong Fill-in-the-blank' guides, including *Hong Kong Insects*, *Hong Kong Trees*, *Hong Kong Shrubs* and *Hong Kong Poisonous Plants*.

The Urban Council produces the *Illustrated Guide to the Venomous Snakes of Hong Kong*. Audubon Society types should take a look at the *New Colour Guide to Hong Kong Birds* by Viney & Phillipps. *Hong Kong Country Parks* by Stella Thrower is an excellent introduction to walking in the countryside, as is *The Hong Kong Countryside* by CAC Herklots. *Magic Walks* by Kaarlo Schepel is a good guide to walking in the New Territories and the outlying islands and can be picked up from commercial bookshops.

Also worth looking out for is *Hong Kong Pathfinder* (Asia 2000) by Martin Williams.

Humour

Larry Feign doesn't pull any punches in his hilarious political cartoons – these graced the pages of the *South China Morning Post* before Feign was given the boot in the pre-handover political environment (an era of shrill, knee-jerk press self-censorship).

His best works have been released in a series of books which include *The World of Lily Wong* and *The Adventures of Super Lily*. Feign's latest book *Let's All Shut Up and Make Money* includes cartoons covering Hong Kong's final 100 days under British sovereignty.

You can find many of these books in shops all over Hong Kong, including (ironically) the South China Morning Post Family Bookshop. Feign's work can also be accessed at his Web site: www.feign.demon.co.uk. Nuri Vittachi, a writer for the *Far Eastern Economic Review* has published many humorous tracts, including *The Hong Kong Joke Book*, *Only in Hong Kong* and *Travellers' Tales*.

Author George Adams writes books with a humorous bent, including *True Hong Kong Confessions*, *Games Hong Kong People Play*, *Wicked Hong Kong Stories*, *The Great Hong Kong Sex Novel* and *Hong Kong Watching*.

General

Certainly the most famous novel set in Hong Kong is *The World of Suzie Wong* by

©1993,1998 Larry Feign. Reproduction forbidden. For full-color Lily graphics, books and more, go to: http://www.asiaonline.net/lilywong

Richard Mason. It was written in 1957 and the movie was produced in Hong Kong in 1960.

Spy-thriller author John Le Carré wrote *The Honourable Schoolboy*, which is a story of espionage set in the early 1970s.

Kowloon Tong by Paul Theroux is a recent novel that explores expat insecurities on the eve of the handover.

Tai-Pan by James Clavell is almost as thick as the yellow pages and is an easy way to pass idle hours. It's an unrealistic version of ships and traders in Hong Kong's early days. The sequel to *Tai-Pan* is another epic-length book, *Noble House*.

Triad by Derek Lambert is a violent fictional account of the Chinese underworld.

Hong Kong Babylon: An Insiders guide to the Hollywood of the East by Frederic Dannen & Barry Long is a rollicking ride through the Byzantine world of Hong Kong movies. It includes plot summaries and excellent reviews for such classics like *Hard Boiled*, *City on Fire* and *Chungking Express*. This book should be read with a good dose of popcorn.

The Occult World of Hong Kong by Frena Bloomfield delves into the unsettling world of ghosts, superstition and occult belief in the territory. It will either fascinate you or give you nightmares.

The private lives of Hong Kong families are captured in *Chinese Walls* by Sussy Chako and *The Monkey King* by Timothy Mo. *An Insular Possession*, also by Timothy Mo, is a novel set in pre-colonial Hong Kong.

Getting to Lamma by Jane Alexander (Asia 2000) is a fictional adventure that ends up on the wonderful Lamma Island.

Bookshops

Hong Kong has a reasonable if unimaginative selection of bookshops. These shops are too often stocked to the hilt with stale hardbacks (usually business or law books), so it may be advisable to take your own paperbacks.

If you want to order a book, you'll experience a long wait and it'll inevitably be expensive.

Bookshops in Hong Kong are also arranged with little imagination or forethought, and the general approach to bookselling is dated – it's infuriating to go into shop after shop and find all the books (and magazines) sealed in plastic. Stationery can generally be found in bookshops such as Bookazine, Jumbo Grade and Times.

Libraries

Hong Kong has a fairly extensive public library system. The most useful for travellers is the main library (☎ 2921-2555) at City Hall, High Block, Central, just east of the Star Ferry terminal. With a passport and a HK$130 deposit, foreign visitors can get a temporary library card allowing them to take out books. The library is open Monday to Thursday from 10 am to 7 pm, Friday until 9 pm, Saturday until 5 pm and Sunday until 1 pm. It is closed on public holidays. For the location of other libraries, call the City Hall main library.

The Trade Development Council Business Library (☎ 2584-4333) on the 38th floor, Office Tower, Convention Plaza, 1 Harbour Rd, Wan Chai, is well stocked with relevant books and CD ROMS. It's open from Monday to Friday 9 am to 6 pm and Saturday until 1 pm.

If you are doing research and need academic information, you may find the library of the University of Science and Technology (HKUST) useful. HKUST is situated at Clear Water Bay, Sai Kung and can be reached on bus No 298 from Lam Tin MTR station. There are also a few terminals with Internet access. The library is open to the public but (you can't) borrow materials unless you're a student, staff member or affiliated with the library. There are however, card operated copy machines and (you) can buy stored value cards from the counter.

SY Yung

Various cultural centres, including the Alliance Française, British Council and Goethe Institut, also maintain libraries. See the Cultural Centres section in this chapter for telephone and address information.

continued on page 80

Hong Kong Food

RICHARD I'ANSON

RICHARD I'ANSON

PATRICK HORTON

RICHARD I'ANSON

RICHARD I'ANSON

A	B
C	
D	E

A: Temple Street Night Market
B: Reclamation Street Market
C: Chinese grocery shop
D: Preserved eggs
E: Typical market produce

Hong Kong Food

The Chinese don't ask 'Have you eaten yet?'. Instead they say 'Have you eaten rice yet?'. Rice is an inseparable part of Chinese culture – the key to survival in a long history. Among older, more conservative Chinese, wasting rice is practically a sin. If they see you've left half your rice uneaten, they may regard you with disdain.

Despite this apparent parsimony, there are few places on earth with a more cosmopolitan cuisine than Hong Kong, and the locals like to boast that their city has the best food in the world. Hong Kong has been witness to an increasingly inventive restaurant world, offering a wider and more exotic range of foods each year. The last few years has seen a clutch of new eateries flinging open doors and cooking up flavours from all over the world.

Unfortunately, eating well in Hong Kong is not cheap. Budget eating will leave a lot of change in your pocket if you're willing to eat from pushcarts and Styrofoam boxes while standing or sitting on wobbly, plastic stools. Plush, spacious surroundings are expensive, mainly because a high proportion of the price of a restaurant meal goes into paying for the space occupied by the customer's bottom.

It's easy enough to eat on a budget in Hong Kong. Almost every residential and commercial neighbourhood has cheap noodle shops. During lunchtime keep your eyes peeled for sidewalk signs advertising set lunches. These usually belong to Hong Kong-style western restaurants where you can get soup, main course, dessert and tea or coffee for as low as HK$30, though HK$35 is closer to the average.

Travellers often find themselves eating a lot more fast food than they originally intended. Cost is one reason, as fast food is significantly cheaper than a meal at many Chinese restaurants. Another reason is

---

Yum Cha-rged

Chinese restaurants often try to overcharge customers. Once you enter, staff feel it's a licence to charge you any price. I'm referring to the more expensive restaurants and not to the cheap ones. Besides a 10% service bill, you may be charged for tea you didn't order or drink. One place charged me for tea because the beer I ordered was served in a tea glass. Of course, I was charged for the beer too. Another place tried to force me to accept a whole pitcher of beer just for myself, when I had only ordered a glass. When Chinese restaurants make a mistake, the general practice is to try to force the customer to take and pay for the item.

If a bar or a restaurant brings an appetiser such as peanuts, you will be charged for it even though you didn't ask for it or eat any. It's a good idea to check the bill before paying because the mistakes are in favour of the restaurant. Unless I was getting together with friends, I would only eat at the low-priced Chinese joints.

John Harkness

that after a few months in Asia many travellers find that they can't stand the sight of another noodle. Fast food is also easy and ordering is simpler than in many hole-in-the-wall Chinese restaurants.

Bad levels of English fluency in Hong Kong's cheap restaurants also often push travellers to the sanctuary of fast-food outlets. Many Chinese restaurants only list western food in the English menu and Chinese food in Chinese characters. Unable to decipher the Chinese menu, frustrated travellers turn to the English menu and end up eating hot dogs and spaghetti, while the Chinese at adjacent tables feast on Peking duck, egg rolls and steamed dumplings. If you follow the restaurant recommendations in the following chapters, you will be able to sample a tasty range of food in generally user-friendly surroundings.

The best hunting grounds for budget diners are the little back streets uphill from Central (such as Stanley and Wellington Sts), Sheung Wan, Wan Chai, Causeway Bay and Tsim Sha Tsui. Most of these areas have the steady flow of commuters or residents needed to support a large number of noodle shops, fast-food joints and so on. All these areas have plenty of mid-range restaurants, and this is where Hong Kong truly comes into its own. You can get almost any Asian or western cuisine, from Scandinavian to Vietnamese. Unfortunately, like the hotels, Hong Kong's mid-priced restaurants charge more than you would expect. Lunch at a nice Chinese or western restaurant can easily cost HK$600 for three people.

Finding top-notch Chinese restaurants is easy, but finding one that's cheap can take perseverance. It's especially hard to find a cheap but good restaurant with an English menu. One possible solution is to explore the street stalls, known as *dai pai dong* in Cantonese. There are no menus to struggle with, so just point to what you want. You can do this as well if eating dim sum in a Chinese restaurant – the food is usually wheeled around on trolleys, so it's a case of using a chopstick to point at what catches your eye. See the Dim Sum entry in this section.

Dedicated diners may want to pick up the annual *HK Magazine Restaurant Guide*. Covering more than 500 restaurants (including Macau), this is one of the most lively guides to Hong Kong dining. At HK$50 a copy, it's well worth the money if you plan to go restaurant hunting. To get a copy, call *HK Magazine's* editorial office (☎ 2850-5065, fax 2543-4964, email aisacity@hk.super.net). *Hong Kong's Best Restaurants* is an annual edition put out by *Hong Kong Tatler*. The HKTA also produces the *Official Dining and Entertainment Guide* which includes many of its member restaurants.

Food Etiquette

The Chinese are by and large casual about etiquette at the table, and they don't expect foreigners to understand all of their dining customs. But there are a few rules that are good to know.

Chinese meals are social events. Typically, a group of people sit at a round table and order dishes (at least one per person) from which everyone partakes. Ordering a dish just for yourself appears selfish, unless you're with close friends. Most Chinese pick food from these communal dishes with their own chopsticks. But if you notice someone

HONG KONG TOURIST ASSOCIATION

At a Chinese banquet, many small dishes are served in seemingly endless succession. The trick is to pace yourself!

carefully placing a pair next to each plate of food, then use these 'public chopsticks' to serve yourself. Some dishes will come with a serving spoon, in which case use this.

Toasts in Hong Kong are not usually the variety with tedious speeches that occasionally befalls western diners, but are considerably more succinct. Sometimes a toast is limited to the words *'yam seng'* (this roughly translates as down the hatch). Raising your tea or water glass is not very respectful so unless you have deep-rooted convictions against alcohol, its best to drink your booze with the rest of the crowd. If you are the guest of honour at dinner don't be surprised if you're called on to down a few glasses.

When the food is served, it's best to wait for some signal from the host before digging in. You will likely be invited to take the first piece if you are the invited guest. Often your host will serve it to you, placing a piece of meat, fish or chicken in your bowl. When eating fish, don't be surprised if the head gets placed on your plate: the head is considered to have the tastiest meat. It's all right if you decline, as someone else will gladly devour the delicacy.

Apart from the communal dishes, everyone gets an individual bowl of rice or a small soup bowl. It's considered polite to hold the bowl near your lips and shovel the contents into your mouth with chopsticks (or spoon for soup). Soup is usually eaten at the end of the meal, rather than as an appetiser.

Eating is generally a hearty affair and often there is a big mess after the end of a meal. Restaurants are prepared for this – tablecloths are changed after each customer leaves. In Hong Kong it is also acceptable for Chinese diners – depending on the situation of course – to spit bones from their food out on to the tablecloth.

Power Eating

The Chinese love banquets and look for any excuse to have one. Not all banquets are free, however; especially at weddings, you're expected to bring a cash gift placed in a red envelope. Find out in advance if you are supposed to do this and how much you should give.

When the banquet begins, you may at first be disappointed. It will seem as if there isn't enough food on the table. Nevertheless, eat slowly to avoid feeling satisfied because one course will follow another. You will often be urged to eat more and more, no matter how full you are. About 10 to 12 courses is considered normal at a banquet.

At banquets, eat little or no rice. Rice is considered a filler, and if you're eating a 12 course meal you'll soon become full with seven courses yet to go.

There is plenty of toasting between courses. The host raises a glass and says *gam bei* (literally, dry glass), which basically means 'bottoms up'! You do not have to empty your glass; just take small sips, especially since Chinese liquor is powerful. Some people who can't handle strong alcohol fill their glass with tea instead. However, you definitely must go along with the toast.

When tea is served you can thank the waiter by tapping your middle finger lightly on the table. Use one finger if you are single, and two fingers (index and middle) if you are dining with your partner. This is only used for tea and not for food. If you want to indicate to the waiter that you want more tea, take the lid slightly off the teapot.

Another good rule to remember is not to stick your chopsticks upright into your rice – this is how rice is offered to the dead, and the connotations at meal time are not pleasant for Chinese people. Chinese habitually make use of toothpicks after, and even between, courses. The polite way is to cover one's mouth with one hand while using the toothpick with the other.

Finally, if you absolutely can't manage chopsticks, don't be afraid to ask for a fork. Nearly all Chinese restaurants have these – better a little humility and a full belly than intact pride and an empty stomach.

Main Dishes

Being a large country, China can be divided into many geographical areas, and each area has a distinct style of cooking. The ingredients used in the food tend to reflect the agricultural produce available in a region. For example, northern China is suitable for raising wheat, so noodles, dumplings and other wheat-based dishes are common. In the south, where the climate is warm and wet, rice is the basic staple. Coastal areas have great seafood dishes. The Sichuan area, where spices grow well, is famous for fiery hot dishes. Other provinces that serve foods with chilli are Hunan and Hubei.

It is not only geography that determines the ingredients used – tradition and culture play a part. The Cantonese, the least squeamish among the Chinese, are known for their ability to eat virtually anything. Consequently, animals with physical and possible sexual prowess are widely sought. Snake meat, for example, is considered good for your health. The more venomous the snake, the greater its reputation as a revitaliser. Five step snake is a delicacy, so named because if it bites

Chinese banquets are often a social affair – everyone shares the meal. Ordering your own meal is considered rude and selfish.

HONG KONG TOURIST ASSOCIATION

you, you don't have a lot of time to make it to the anti-venom cabinet. Little old ladies drink snake blood because they believe it cures arthritis. Some men are convinced the blood is an aphrodisiac, so it's often mixed with Chinese wine. Everyone knows that tigers are strong, so tiger meat is much in demand. Being a protected animal, the meat is very expensive – especially the sexual organs.

Of course, not all Hong Kong residents are interested in eating the testicles of endangered species. Generally you will be eating dishes that include pork, duck, beef and fish. Dishes are served together, though you will often have to remind the waiter to bring the rice. The soup, meat and vegetables will all appear in the middle of the table, which will soon fill up, depending on how many there are in your group. Tables are often equipped with a glass turntable on which the food is placed. It's not unusual for a meal to be served with small dishes filled with various sauces – hot mustard sauce is the most popular with Cantonese food. Chilli sauce (laatjiu jeung) is usually served, as well as soya sauce (seeyau).

HONG KONG TOURIST ASSOCIATION

Yum Cha is often presented in small bamboo containers.

It's rare to see salt shakers in a Chinese restaurant, though pepper is sometimes available. Often you will find several small bottles on the table containing soy sauce, vinegar and sesame oil. The Chinese often mix all three together. The vinegar is usually a dark colour and is easily confused with soy sauce, so taste some first before dumping it on your food. The Chinese don't dump sauces on food – instead the food is dipped into a separate dish.

If a Chinese restaurant has recently opened, it will probably be offering a special promotion such as free beer or half a chicken for only HK$1. As the competition is stiff in Hong Kong, such techniques are commonly used to attract diners. Kennedy Town, west of Hong Kong Island, often suffers from outbreaks of a restaurant price war.

China's regional variations are well represented in Hong Kong. There are five major styles of Chinese cuisine; Beijing-Shandong, Sichuan-Hunan, Shanghainese, Cantonese and Chaozhou, so you can target the type of Chinese food that best suits your palate.

Beijing & Shandong

Beijing and Shandong cuisine is from the wheatbelt in the cold north of China. Steamed bread, dumplings and noodles figure more prominently than rice.

The better Beijing restaurants put on quite a show of noodle making for the tourists. This is done by hand – the chef adroitly twirls the dough, stretches it, divides it into two strands, stretches, divides into four and so on until the noodles are as thin as threads.

The most famous speciality is Peking duck, served with pancakes and plum sauce. Another northern speciality is Mongolian hotpot, which is composed of an assortment of meats and vegetables cooked in a burner on the dining table – it's so good in Hong Kong that it's hard to believe it can be so bad in Mongolia. Hotpot is usually eaten during winter.

Another popular dish, beggar's chicken, was supposedly created by a pauper who stole a chicken, but had no cooking pot, so he baked it smothered in clay. The chicken is stuffed with mushrooms, pickled Chinese cabbage, herbs and onions, then wrapped in lotus leaves, sealed in clay and baked all day in hot ashes.

Bird's-nest soup is a speciality of Shandong cooking. Other dishes include:

bàkgìng fùngcháu làimīn – noodles fried with shredded pork and
    bean sprouts
bàkgìng tinngap – Peking duck
bàkgùpa jùnbākchoi – Tianjin cabbage and black mushrooms
chòngyau béng – pan-fried spring onion cakes
foogwai gài – beggar's chicken
gònchàu ngauyōksì – fried shredded beef with chilli sauce
gòngbau dàihà – sautéed prawns in chilli sauce
sànsìn tòng – clear soup with chicken, prawn and abalone
sìnyōk síulong bàu – steamed minced pork dumplings

Cantonese Originating in neighbouring Guangdong Province, Cantonese food is the most popular in Hong Kong. The flavours are more subtle than other Chinese cooking styles, the sauces are rarely strong and some dishes almost have a sweet taste.

The Cantonese are almost religious about the importance of fresh ingredients. It is common to see fish tanks in seafood restaurants. Those familiar with the sights of Chinatowns around the world will recognise the practice of stir-frying using a wok over a searing hot flame. This is known in Cantonese as *wok hei*.

Expensive dishes that have a 'look-what-I'm-eating' value include abalone and shark's fin. Pigeon is a Cantonese speciality served in various ways, including plain roast (a gourmet's delight), with lemon or oyster sauce. Below is an introduction to the world of Cantonese cuisine:

chà sìu – barbecued pork
cháu dāumiu – stir-fried pea sprouts
chìngcháu gailán – stir-fried kale (cabbage)
chìngjìng sēkbànyue – steamed garoupa (fish) with soy sauce
    dressing
dàibāk juiyùng hà – 'drunken' prawns (steamed in rice wine)
jìuyim ngaupai – deep-fried salt-and-pepper spareribs
sìjiu ngauhó – fried rice noodles with beef and green peppers
sàilanfà daijí – stir-fried broccoli with scallops
sàng sìu gap – roast pigeon
sìnning jìnyūengài – pan-fried lemon chicken

Chaozhou In some cases Chaozhou dishes are lighter than Cantonese dishes, and make heavy use of seafood. Sauces can border on sweet, using orange, tangerine or sweet beans for flavour. Among the most famous specialities are shark's fin and bird's nest. Duck and goose, cooked in an aromatic sauce which is used again and again (known as *lo sui*, or old water), are also popular. Chaozhou chefs are known for their skills in carving raw vegetables into fancy floral designs. Try the following dishes:

bàkgù sàilanfà – stewed broccoli with black mushrooms
bìngfà gòngyin – cold sweet bird's nest soup (dessert)
chuenjìu gōklunghà – baked lobster in light pepper sauce

chìngjìu ngauyōksì – fried shredded beef with green pepper
dāi yuechi tòng – shark's fin soup
fòngyue gailán – fried kale with dried fish
gàiyung sīuchoi – stewed Tianjin cabbage with minced chicken
jang hèungngap – deep-fried spiced duck
jìng hai – steamed crab
seisèk pingpán – cold appetiser platter of four meats

Dim Sum Dim sum is a uniquely Cantonese dish that is served for breakfast or lunch. The term dim sum means 'a snack'. If the characters are translated literally, dim sum means 'to touch the heart'. The act of eating dim sum is usually referred to as *yum cha*, which literally means 'to drink tea' (it is always served with dim sum meals).

Eating dim sum is a social occasion and something you should do in a group. If you're by yourself, try to round up three or four other travellers for a dim sum lunch. Of course, you can eat dim sum alone, but it consists of many separate dishes which are meant to be shared. You can't simply order a plate with a variety of dim sum. Having several people to share with you means you can try many different dishes.

Dim sum delicacies are normally steamed in a small bamboo basket. Typically, each basket contains four identical pieces, so four people would be an ideal number for a dim sum meal. You pay by the number of baskets you order. The baskets are stacked up on pushcarts and rolled around the dining room.

You don't need a menu, just stop the waiter or waitress and choose something from the cart, and it will be marked down on your bill. Don't try to order everything at once. Each pushcart has a different selection, so take your time and order a selection of dishes. It's estimated that there are about 1000 dim sum dishes. Usually dim sum is not expensive – HK$30 per person is average for breakfast, or perhaps HK$45 for a decent lunch.

Dim sum restaurants are normally brightly lit and very large – it's rather like eating in an aircraft hangar. Nevertheless, it can get very crowded, especially at lunch time. Dim sum dishes include:

Delicious sweet barbecued pork buns.

chà sìu bàu – barbecued pork buns
chéung fán – steamed rice flour rolls with shrimp, beef or pork
chìng cháu sichoi – fried green vegetable of the day
chùn gúen – fried spring rolls
fán gwó – steamed dumplings with pork, shrimp and bamboo
    shoots
fūng jáu – fried chicken's feet
gàisì cháumīn – fried crispy noodles with shredded chicken
gòn sìu yìmīn – dry-fried noodles
hà gáu – shrimp dumplings
ham súi gok – fried rice flour triangles (usually with pork inside)
ho yīp fān – rice wrapped in lotus leaf
pai gwàt – steamed spare ribs
sàn jùk ngau yōk – steamed minced beef balls
sìu mai – pork and shrimp dumplings
wōo gok – deep-fried taro puffs

Shanghainese Shanghainese cooking (including Hangzhou and Suzhou) contains more oil and is generally richer and sweeter than

HONG KONG TOURIST ASSOCIATION

A typical feast of many small and tasty dishes.

other Chinese cuisine. Seafood, preserved vegetables, pickles and salted meats are widely used, and there are lots of dumplings on the menu. Another speciality is the cold-meat-and-sauce dishes. There are a large number of Shanghai and Hangzhou restaurants in Hong Kong, so you won't have a problem finding one. Here are a few dishes to get you started:

> *chìngcháu dāumiu* – sautéed pea sprouts
> *fēichui yukdai* – sautéed scallops with vegetables
> *fótúi síuchoi* – Shanghai cabbage with ham
> *hongsìu sìjítau* – braised minced pork balls with vegetables
> *ja jígài* – deep-fried chicken
> *jui gài* – 'drunken chicken' in cold rice wine marinade
> *nghèung ngauyōk* – cold spiced beef
> *sēunghói chòcháu* – fried Shanghai noodles with pork
> *sùenlāt tòng* – hot-and-sour soup
> *sungsúe wongyue* – sweet-and-sour yellow croaker fish

Sichuan & Hunan This area is known for having the most fiery food in China. Chillies are widely used along with aniseed, coriander, fennel seed, garlic and peppercorns. Dishes are simmered and soaked to give the chilli peppers time to work into the food. However, not all dishes from Sichuan are hot (eg Camphor smoked duck).

Hunanese cooking, on the other hand, can be excruciatingly hot. In Hunan they *chila bu chima* (literally, eat hot, but not numb), which means that Hunanese cooking is very fiery, but lacks the herbs used in Sichuan cooking that anaesthetise and numb the mouth. These provinces are miles from the sea, so pork, chicken and beef are staple meats, while seafood is uncommon. Hong Kong has some decent restaurants that specialise in Hunanese food, but Sichuan restaurants consistently fail to capture the genuine flavour. Hubei is also noted for its spicy food.

> *chìngjìu ngauyōksì* – sautéed shredded beef and green pepper
> *chuipei wongyuepin* – fried fish in sweet-and-sour sauce
> *dan daṇ mīn* – noodles in spicy peanut soup
> *gònbìn seigwai dāu* – pan-fried spicy string beans
> *gòngbau gàidìng* – sautéed diced chicken and peanuts in chilli sauce
> *gòngbau mínghà* – sautéed shrimp in chilli sauce
> *jèungcha háu ngap* – duck smoked in camphor wood
> *mapo dāufōo* – 'grandma's beancurd' in spicy sauce
> *sùenlāt tòng* – peppery hot-and-sour soup with shredded meat
> *yuehèung kéijí* – sautéed eggplant in spicy fish sauce

Vegetarian The Chinese are masters at adding variety to vegetarian cooking. Strict Buddhists (a distinct minority in Hong Kong) are traditionally vegetarian. Large monasteries often have vegetarian restaurants, though you can also find a few restaurants in Kowloon and on Hong Kong Island.

Vegetarian food is based on soybean curd *(tofu)* to which the Chinese do some miraculous things. Not only is it made to taste like any food you could think of, it's also made to look like it as well. A dish that is sculptured to look like a fish or a chicken can either be made from layered pieces of dried bean curd or fashioned from mashed taro root. Vegetarian dishes include:

bòlo cháufān – fried rice with diced pineapple
chìngdūn bàkgù tòng – black mushroom soup
chùn gúen – spring rolls
fōopei gúen – spicy bean-curd rolls
gàmgù súnjìm – braised bamboo shoots and black mushrooms
jàilōumēi – mock chicken, barbecued pork or roast duck
lohon choi – stewed mixed vegetables
lohonjài yìmīn – fried noodles with vegetables
yehchoi gúen – cabbage rolls

An option you shouldn't overlook is Hong Kong's Indian restaurants. Indian vegetarian cuisine is considerably spicier than its Chinese counterpart. Some Indian restaurants are exclusively vegetarian, but most offer a combined menu. Even if you're not vegetarian, it's worth trying tasty meatless dishes such as *biryani*.

There are also a number of healthy-eating type restaurants run by the Hare Krishna community. See the Places to Eat section in the Hong Kong Island and Kowloon chapters for details.

Other Asian Food Indian food used to be one of the great budget options in town, but Hong Kong's ridiculously high rents and stiff competition from fast-food joints have taken a toll. Now a good lunch or dinner will cost between HK$60 and HK$90 at the cheaper spots. Don't turn your nose up at the Indian restaurants in Chungking Mansions. Among the grime and barbarism at the Chungking Mansions some fantastic Indian restaurants have won a well-deserved reputation for great food and huge portions.

Japanese food is never cheap unless you go for the sushi served on a conveyer belt. A Japanese meal will cost at least double what you'd spend for a similar level of service in a Chinese restaurant. Bring a credit card or a suitcase full of cash.

A glut of Thai eateries fields the diner with a lot of choice. Vietnamese, Filipino and Korean cuisine will also spice up your stay. The latter can be found almost everywhere, with Korean barbecues being particularly good fun and very popular. Many restaurants have a set-price, all-you-can-eat barbecue. Pile up a griddle or two with slabs of meat and seafood and clog up your arteries.

HONG KONG TOURIST ASSOCIATION

Seafood is a highlight of the Chinese cuisine, especially around the coastal regions.

Desserts

The Cantonese have always been the best Chinese bakers. There are certain specialities which seem to be distinctly home-grown. Desserts to look for include custard tarts (best when served hot), steamed buns with sweet bean-paste inside, coconut snowballs (sweet rice-flour balls dressed with coconut slices), and various other sweets dressed with coconut and sesame seeds.

Incidentally, you do not find fortune cookies in Cantonese or any other real Chinese cuisine. These are a foreign invention.

Fast Food

The landscape is not as bleak as this name might suggest. In Hong Kong people do everything quickly, so there's a good market for places that can turn out quality food in a hurry.

Of course, the usual international chain food-food outlets are available: McDonald's, KFC, Hardee's etc. In fact, Hong Kong has earned a special place on the McDonald's corporate map – at the last count four of the world's 10 busiest McDonald's restaurants were in Hong Kong. McDonald's is exceptionally good value in Hong Kong, with set meals (Big Mac, fries and soft drink) at HK$17 (more affordable than in many other countries), which makes it the cheapest meal provider in the city.

Hong Kong has several home-grown fast-food chains, serving both western and Chinese food. Breakfast usually features *congee* (watery rice porridge), fried noodles or western-style ham and eggs. For lunch and dinner there is a range of different dishes, from pepper steak to home-style bean curd. Most chains also have afternoon tea menus – a chicken leg, hot dog or fried radish cake with tea or coffee. Breakfasts average around HK$20, lunch and dinner HK$35 to HK$50, and afternoon tea HK$15.

The four major fast-food chains are Cafe de Coral, Fairwood, Dai Ga Lok and Maxim's. All are very similar in price and quality. Some, like Maxim's, have special value meals after 5.30 pm, where you can get a bowl of vermicelli noodles with pork strips in a tasty soup for only HK$15.

One of the brightest fast-food choices is the Oliver's Super Sandwiches chain. Originally started as a gourmet food store in Central, these have evolved into a network of clean, reasonably priced sandwich shops. The sandwich ingredients are fresh and tasty. Waffles, soup, baked potatoes, salad and toasted sandwiches are also served. In Central, Oliver's has branches in Exchange Square, Prince's Building and Citibank Plaza. In Causeway Bay there's an Oliver's in Windsor House.

Delifrance offers decent coffee, sandwiches, croissants, cheese puffs, soup and other titbits. The restaurants are spacious and clean, and there are newspapers on wooden rods for customers to read. Branches are throughout Hong Kong, including Central, Sheung Wan and Wan Chai.

An excellent place to eat sandwiches, daily set meals (cottage pie, quiche lorraine and pasta) and coffee is Pier One (☎ 2526-3061), in the basement arcade under Jardine House. There's a secret to eating at Pier One, and that is arrive early for lunch (about noon) before all the suits from above descend en masse, or alternatively, come just after lunch (2 pm).

Wan Chai is also home to thriving, hole-in-the-wall sandwich parlours. These businesses are all pretty good and offer great fillings and decent coffee. Little Italy has made a name for itself at 88 Lockhart Rd, and is open till 6 am on Friday and Saturday (there's another branch at 13 Lan Kwai Fong). Fidi (the name means 'make it swift' in Cantonese) does the same sort of fare at 87-91 Lockhart Rd, Wan Chai. The Chop Chop Cafe (☎ 2526-1122), 17 Wing Wah Lane, Lan Kwai Fong, is a small but cheap eatery where you can fill up on baked potatoes and other speedy cuisine.

Clinching the trophy for most exotic fast-food chain is Genroku Sushi. Sushi is very cheap and served on a conveyor belt. Though obviously not in the same league as the delicacies served in a good Japanese restaurant, the sushi is still OK. The only drawback is that there can be long queues for seats, especially during the 1 to 2 pm lunch hour. For locations of some Genroku Sushi branches, check the Central, Causeway Bay and Tsim Sha Tsui maps.

Fruit

Besides peaches, pears and apples, Hong Kong imports a wide variety of fruit from Australia and South-East Asia. Many of these are excellent, though some tropical varieties spoil rapidly after being picked. You'll also find that prices are several times higher than in the Philippines, Thailand or Vietnam. Treats to look for include:

carambola – This is also known as star fruit, because that's what it looks like from an angle.

durian – This large fruit has tough spiky skin which looks impenetrable. After breaking it open with a big knife and peeling off the skin (not difficult), you'll encounter the next obstacle, a powerful odour that many can't stand. The creamy fruit is actually delicious and even used to make ice cream in South-East Asia. The durian season is approximately from April to June. Durians spoil fairly easily and cost a bundle.

jackfruit – This large segmented fruit is fine stuff when ripe, but positively awful if it's not.

longan – The name means 'dragon eyes' in Chinese. The skin is brown, but otherwise the taste is similar to lychees. It's season is from around June through early August.

lychee – This red pulpy fruit with white flesh and a single large (inedible) seed is one of the main agricultural exports of China. It grows well in Guangdong Province, just across the border from Hong Kong. There is even a lychee carbonated soft drink, which is fine stuff. China's lychee season is from April through June. The name comes from the Cantonese lai jee.

mango – These are sweet, pulpy and very messy to eat. Although the mango season is late spring and summer, you can easily buy dried mango at any time of year. The Chinese also eat green (unripe) mangos out of season, but pickled and sweetened – the taste is sour but not bad.

mangosteen – Cut these in two and scoop out the delicious pulp with a spoon.

papaya – This delicious fruit is available year-round in Hong Kong. The abundant black seeds from the centre of the fruit can be dried and used as herbal medicine. The seeds have been successfully used to treat amoebic dysentery, but the taste is awful. By contrast, the fruit is delicious stuff and is even used to make milk shakes.

pomelo – The pomelo is similar to a large grapefruit but tougher.

rambutan – This fruit is very similar to the lychee except for the 'hairy' skin.

Self-Catering

Wellcome and Park N' Shop, the two major supermarket chains, have branches all over Hong Kong. In stock are staples like bread, milk, eggs, tinned and frozen foods, as well as wines and spirits. The selection is generally large. 7-Eleven convenience stores are ubiquitous and open 24 hours, but the prices are high.

More upmarket do-it-yourselfers may want to check out the basement floors of the Japanese department stores in Causeway Bay. The supermarkets there have all manner of exotic items and high-quality foods, as reflected by the prices. The basement level of the Seibu department store, in the Pacific Place Mall in Admiralty, has one of the best markets in town, with dozens of imported cheeses, meats, snacks and luxury foods.

Delicatessens are blossoming in Hong Kong. Gastronomes can head to a number of quality outlets, pungent with the aroma of herbs, spices, cheeses, dried sausages, patés and fine wines. Oliver's Food Stores, associated with the sandwich fast-food chain, is stuffed with European delicacies – the prices are steep. There are Oliver's stores in the Prince's Building in Central, Harbour City in Tsim Sha Tsui and the Repulse Bay Shopping Arcade.

For fresh bread and wholemeal ingredients, The Source of Health (☎ 2869-7383) obliges with a pastoral selection of breads and cakes, including banana and raisin muffins, organic whole wheat loafs and French baguettes. Follow the crispy aroma to 18, Yip Fung Building, D'Aguilar Street, Central.

Snacks There are loads of bakeries around that sell western snacks and titbits, such as croissants, hot dogs, cheese turnovers, pizzas and freshly baked bread. There are also a growing number of cafes that serve excellent coffee and pastries.

The more traditional Chinese snacks are various seafood, often

Amazing amounts of effort and skill go into the preparation of food and garnish.

HONG KONG TOURIST ASSOCIATION

served on a bamboo skewer. Squid on a stick is one such example. Fish ball soup served in a styrofoam cup is a modern variation of a traditional snack. You mostly buy these Cantonese munchies from pushcarts. These tend to gather late at night in strategic locations, like in front of the off-track betting parlours or the ferry piers.

Thousand-year-old eggs (also known as hundred-year-old eggs) are a Cantonese speciality – these are duck eggs soaked in a chemical solution for several days. This turns the white of the egg green and the yolk a greenish-black. In the past, the eggs were soaked in horse urine. Most westerners say these eggs smell and taste like ammonia. Salty duck eggs are really tasty and cheap. The egg is soaked in a saline solution for a long period which crystallises the yolk and imparts a lovely flavour to the interior. Generally eaten for breakfast, they are very filling.

Drinks

Nonalcoholic Drinks

Tea In Chinese restaurants tea is often served free of charge, or at most you'll pay HK$1 for a big pot which can be refilled indefinitely. On the other hand, coffee is seldom available except in western restaurants or coffee shops, and it is never free.

When your teapot is empty and you would like a refill, signal this by taking the lid off the pot. To thank the waiter or waitress for pouring your tea, tap your fingers on the table. You needn't say thank you. The finger-tapping is only done for tea, and not for food.

There are three main types of tea: green or unfermented; *bolai*, which is fermented and also known as black tea; and *oolong*, which is semi-fermented. There are many varieties of tea, including jasmine *(heung ping)*, which is a blend of tea and flowers served without milk or sugar.

There are also some good English teas available, though you usually have to go to a upmarket hotel if you want it served properly. The Chinese places are cheaper and also serve western-style tea, but with a Hong Kong twist. Milk tea *(nai cha)* uses an extremely strong brew so the flavour can punch through the heavy dose of condensed milk. Lemon tea *(ningmeng cha)* is also strong, and is often served with several whole slices of fresh lemon.

Most of the tea is imported from China, but some comes from India and Sri Lanka. Hong Kong has only one tea plantation (at Ngong Ping on Lantau Island) and it's basically a tourist attraction.

HONG KONG TOURIST ASSOCIATION

Your dining experience can be less damaging to the hip pocket if you take your own wine.

Coffee The last few years have seen a miniature explosion of cafes in Hong Kong, and the range of coffee now available is quite rich. Cafes are expensive in Hong Kong, but offer blessed retreat from pavement pounding. Hong Kong Chinese also enjoy chilled coffee *(dong gafei)*, which can also be bought everywhere in cans, usually manufactured by Nescafé. The cans come in gradations of strength and consistency.

Fleecy No, *fleecy* is not just what shopowners on Nathan Rd do to tourists – it's also the name of a sweet cold drink. The distinguishing feature of a fleecy is that it contains some sort of lumpy mixture, usually red or green mung beans, and sometimes pineapple or other fruits, and black grass jelly. Milk or ice cream is usually part of the mixture, but not always. You can sample these drinks almost anywhere, even in Chinese fast-food restaurants.

Soft Drinks In any convenience store or supermarket you'll find a whole range of juice, soft drink and milk products. Most restaurants have cola and juice at the very least.

Roadside stalls sell a whole range of made-on-the-spot fruit juices that cost about HK$7. You can custom make your own brew according to the fruits stocked. Sugarcane juice is delicious but a real tooth-rotter – the cane is stripped with a knife and pulverised in a grinder for its juice.

Alcoholic Drinks

Beer is by far the most popular alcoholic beverage, and there's a wide range of choice in bars, convenience stores and supermarkets. Hong Kong has two major breweries – Carlsberg (Denmark) and San Miguel (Philippines). These are the most widely available brands, along with those the breweries produce under licence, including Lowenbrau and Kirin.

Microbrewery beers are sold at a number of bars in Hong Kong. Hong Kong's original microbrewery, the South China Brewing Co Ltd, produces a selection of local concoctions that you may see about town. These include Red Dawn, Tai Koo Brew, Aldrich Bay Pale Ale,

---

Bottoms Up

Hong Kong boasts the world's most dense concentrations of restaurants per square metre of paving slab. This all sounds fine to the migrant gastronome out in search of fine dining – unless they want to wash all that fine food down with a decent wine. With alcohol licence application enmeshed in a thicket of red tape, many a restaurateur watches pitifully as diners bring their own wine. Without an alcohol licence, many restaurants lose out on a huge slice of profits. You'll have to twist the restaurateur's arm pretty hard if you want a clandestine tipple – the maximum penalty for serving alcohol without a licence is two years in the slammer plus a fine of HK$1 million. Cheers.

But this is all good news for the diners who select their restaurants with care. You can save a bundle on taking along your own wine, normally sold at nearby corner shops or whipped out of the drinks cabinet before leaving home. Considering the mammoth mark up on wines bought in Hong Kong restaurants, you'll be more than chuffed to try out your Swiss army knife corkscrew. A wander around the restaurants in Soho should present you with a crop of restaurants, horns locked tight with the licensing authorities. Pop into one of the enterprising wine merchants in the locality and stock up.

Stonecutter's Lager and Dragon's Back India Pale Ale.

Imported beers are popular, and most bars have a selection, mostly in bottles but in some cases on tap. There are good English bitters and ales on tap, though the taste suffers a bit from having spent several weeks in a cargo ship. Irish and German beers are also available, and Tsingtao, China's main export beer, is sold everywhere.

Drinking beer in the bars is ridiculously expensive, unless you target happy hour. Buying beers at the supermarket, however, is cheap with cans of beer ranging from HK$2 upwards!

Among Hong Kong's more wealthy drinkers, cognac is the liquor of choice. Hong Kong accounts for nearly 11% of the worldwide market for cognac brandy, and has the world's highest per capita consumption. Hong Kong residents generally drink it neat, but rarely sip – sometimes you'll even see a group of enthusiastic diners downing it shot style! Supermarkets, departments stores, restaurants and bars usually have a decent selection of other spirits and wines. Certain spirits can also be bought cheaply at supermarkets – no-name brands are excellent value. Wine is popular and is becoming increasingly prized.

Chinese alcohol is available in restaurants and a few bars. The easiest on the palate is probably *siu hing jau*, more commonly known by its name in Mandarin, *shao xing jiu*. Other options may not go down so smoothly. Though the Chinese tend to refer to all home-grown alcohol as 'wine' in English, the majority are hard alcohol distilled from grains like rice, sorghum or millet. Most are potent, colourless and extremely volatile. The best known, and most expensive, is *mao tai*, distilled from millet. Another delicacy is *goh leung* (*gao liang* in Mandarin), which is made from sorghum. Have fun with these drinks, but if your dining companions start repeating the phrase *gon bui* (literally, drain your glass), you may want to start looking for an escape route.

Happy Hour During certain hours of the day, several bars, discos and nightclubs give substantial discounts on drinks. Some places give you drinks for half-price during happy hour, while others let you buy one drink and give you the second one free. Usually, happy hour is in the late afternoon or early evening, but the times vary too much for there to be any hard rule. If you enter a bar during happy hour, take note of the time it ends, otherwise, you may linger too long and wind up paying more than you expected.

continued from page 64
CD ROMS

Hong Kong produces a number of interactive CD ROMS for the local market. These are mostly in Cantonese, though English subtitles are not uncommon. A quick browse of the CD racks at a computer arcade in Kowloon produced this list of locally made titles: *Karaoke Canto-Pop*, *God of Gambling*, *Triad Women*, *Daughter of Darkness*, *Blood Lust*, *I Ching – Book of Erotic Changes*, *Woman with Four Husbands*, *Sex School* and *Kung Fu Devil*.

NEWSPAPERS & MAGAZINES

Hong Kong has long been a bastion of media freedom in Asia. This will almost certainly change, as China has little patience with media criticism. Some Hong Kong newspaper publishers and TV stations have already started exercising self-censorship to avoid ruffling feathers in Beijing.

Most journalism in Hong Kong focuses on business and finance, and hence usually only skirts the sensitive issues. This is not always the case, at least not in Beijing's eyes. In 1994 a Hong Kong reporter working in Beijing was jailed for 12 years after he wrote a story on interest rates and central bank gold sales, which China (after the fact) deemed state secrets.

In January 1996, China announced new controls on foreign wire services disseminating economic and financial news in China, Hong Kong, Macau and (arrogantly) Taiwan.

For the time being, the media in Hong Kong continues to struggle with new realities. The local English-language newspapers are the *South China Morning Post* and the *Hong Kong Standard*. The *South China Morning Post* (HK$7), also known as the 'Pro China Morning Post', has the largest distribution, and is read by more Hong Kong Chinese than expats. Its classified advertisement sales make it the world's most profitable newspaper. The *Hong Kong Standard* (HK$6) is generally more rigorous in its reporting. Both papers are available on the Net: *Hong Kong Standard's* Web site is at www.hkstandard.com; and *South China Morning Post's* Web site is at www.scmp.com.

Three international newspapers produce Asian editions that are printed in Hong Kong. These are the *Asian Wall Street Journal*, *USA Today* and the *International Herald Tribune*. *Asia Times* is a relative newcomer to the market. Overseas newspapers are flown in on a regular basis, but are expensive. You can find these in bookshops that sell magazines and papers.

Hong Kong also has its share of news magazines, including *Asiaweek*, *Far Eastern Economic Review* and a slew of Asian-

Mad Dogs & Chinamen

Released on the streets with a snarl in March 1996, *Mad Dog Daily* is a vehemently anti-communist Cantonese newspaper. Published by Huang Yumin, an ex-professor in the department of current affairs at Zhuhai University, *Mad Dog Daily* is deliberately confrontational – the name and the logo is a vociferous bulldog pointing to its role as a watchdog for Hong Kong society.

Mad Dog represents an attempt to turn the tide against the growing tendency towards self-censorship that typifies both the English and Chinese-language press. Newspapers increasingly reflect the Chinese mainland attitude of *baoxi, bubaoyou* (report the good news, not the bad). *Mad Dog Daily* aims to challenge Beijing, and it's not afraid of being silenced – Huang Yumin has said, 'I am only too happy to provide a test case'. The only way the paper can be closed down is if draconian laws are put into effect. Beijing must be more than keen to slip a sedative overdose into this particular dog's dinner, but, with the rest of the world watching, China's hands are tied.

Other newspapers and periodicals on Beijing's blacklist include *Cheng Ming*, *Ming Pao*, *Apple Daily*, *Next*, *Hong Kong Economic Journal*, *Front-Line Magazine* and *Open Magazine*.

focused business magazines. *Time, Newsweek* and the *Economist* are all available in the current edition. On the leisure side, *Hong Kong Tatler* and *Home Journal* are for those interested in local lifestyle issues.

All this is a drop in the bucket compared with the local Chinese-language print media. There are nearly 50 Chinese-language newspapers in Hong Kong, giving the city the world's highest per capita ratio of newspapers. Most of these cover general news, although there are five or six devoted solely to finance, and more than a dozen that report nothing but horse-racing! Some of these papers have colourful names, such as *Mad Dog*.

If you want to see what's happening in Hong Kong's entertainment and nightlife, pick up a copy of the excellent *HK Magazine*. It's on the ball with local gossip and behind-the-scenes stories, all dished up in fine writing. It's published weekly and is available free in bars, some restaurants, Oliver's Super Sandwich stores and hotels. In addition to music, cinema and performing arts listings, *HK Magazine* carries lively articles on current trends in the city, reviews of restaurants and bars, and a classified ad section that makes for interesting reading.

Also worth checking out is *bc Magazine*, a monthly guide to Hong Kong's entertainment and partying scene. One of the most useful features in this highly visual and glossy publication is the complete listing of bars and clubs. It is also free and can usually be found alongside *HK Magazine* racks. If you're staying on the outlying islands, look for *The Islands' Orbital*, a free rag covering the bohemian island culture.

The HKTA has several free information publications, including the monthly *Official Hong Kong Guide* and the weekly *Hong Kong Now!* These are available at HKTA information centres, hotels and shopping malls.

RADIO & TV

Radio Television Hong Kong (RTHK) is funded by the government, but is an editorially independent broadcasting system. In 1996 the Chinese government upset everyone by demanding access to RTHK to broadcast Beijing's viewpoint. The British authorities refused to cooperate, but how much longer RTHK can maintain its independent editorial content is a big question.

In 1998 Xu Simin, a leftist and friend of Tung Chee Hwa, assailed the radio station with the accusation that it was a 'remnant of British rule'. A stinging backlash from the general public followed, leaving few in doubt about the popularity of RTHK.

The most popular English-language radio stations are RTHK Radio 3 (567 kHz AM, 1584 kHz AM, 97.9 mHz FM, 106.8 mHz FM); RTHK Radio 4 (classical music, 97.6 to 98.9 mHz FM); RTHK Radio 6 (BBC World Service, 24 hours, 675 kHz AM); Commercial Radio (864 kHz AM); Metro News (1044 kHz AM); Hit Radio (99.7 mHz FM); FM Select (104 mHz FM); and Quote AM (alternative and dance music, 864 kHz AM). The English-language newspapers publish a daily guide to radio programs.

Hong Kong's terrestrial TV stations are run by two companies, Television Broadcasts (TVB) and Asia Television (ATV). Each company operates one English-language and one Cantonese-language channel. The two English stations are TVB Pearl (channel 3) and ATV World (channel 4). The two Cantonese stations are TVB Jade (channel 1) and ATV Home (channel 2). The program schedule is listed daily in the English-language newspapers.

As people in Macau also read Hong Kong newspapers, programs from the Macau TV station (TdM) are listed, but the signal is too weak to be received in Hong Kong. TdM has wanted to broadcast to Hong Kong for years, but the Hong Kong government has strenuously objected, claiming that this would cause interference. Many suspect the real reason is that the existing stations would prefer not to have any competition.

Hong Kong's own satellite TV station, STAR TV (☎ 2621-8888), is available at most hotels and is free for anyone who owns a satellite dish (about 500,000 people). STAR TV broadcasts across Asia and its sports, music and Chinese drama channels can be seen throughout China. Other regional broadcasters based in Hong Kong include NBC, TBS and the sports channel, ESPN.

As if this city-state of six million people needed more television, Wharf Cable (☎ 2112-6868) entered the scene in 1993. Started by the local conglomerate Wharf Holdings, the station currently offers 20 channels and has plans to expand.

VIDEO SYSTEMS

Due to the influence of Britain, Hong Kong subscribes to the PAL broadcasting standard. The three most common standards are PAL (used in Australia, Hong Kong, New Zealand, UK and most of Europe), SECAM (France, Germany and Luxembourg) and NTSC (Canada, Japan, Korea, Latin America and USA). For more details see the Video entry in the Shopping section later in this chapter.

PHOTOGRAPHY & VIDEO
Film & Equipment

Almost everything you could possibly need in the way of photographic accessories is available in Hong Kong. Stanley St on Hong Kong Island is the place to look for reputable camera stores.

If you don't want to be weighed down by 10kg of heavy metal, the best option may be to invest in a pocket-sized electronic point-and-shoot camera. Connoisseurs of photography will no doubt moan and groan at this advice, but it should be pointed out that some of the more expensive models come with an amazing variety of features. A high-end point-and-shoot camera should have a zoom lens (preferably 28mm to 120mm), fill flash, self-timer, remote control, and special modes for night photos and exposure compensation. The latter feature allows you to manually brighten or darken the exposure. This is particularly important if you use slide film – slides tend to come out too dark when used in automatic cameras.

Technical Tips

Hong Kong has visually striking scenery, but getting good pictures can often be challenging. The first problem is the fickle weather – it can be cloudy for months on end. In mountainous areas such as Victoria Peak, you may encounter fog as thick as pea soup. Indoor photography can be complicated by poor lighting and cramped spaces. This can be remedied with a wide-angle lens and a flash or fast film.

Real enthusiasts may want to buy two or three cameras – one for colour slide film, one for colour prints and one for black and white. While it is possible to get prints made from slides (or even slides made from prints) and black and white made from colour, the best results are achieved when you use the proper film.

If you're heading up to the Peak to catch the stunning views, the late afternoon, when the sun is shining down on the city, is the best time to go.

Hong Kong's bright lights can often be very photogenic at night, assuming you understand the intricacies of night-time photography. If you have a tripod, a nocturnal shot of Central across from Tsim Sha Tsui makes classic material.

Making a good travel video is a complex subject that would require a book in itself (indeed, such books are available in Hong Kong and elsewhere). For the budding amateur, general considerations include equipment, light, sound and avoiding the dreaded camera shudder.

For a more detailed discussion of video equipment see the Video entry in the Shopping section of this chapter.

Restrictions

For visitors, there are few restrictions when taking photos. Politically sensitive photo opportunities are few and far between, due to the clandestine PLA presence and the general business-as-usual feel of post-97 Hong Kong. The PLA used to travel at hours like 3 am so as to remain unseen, but have started to appear with more frequency during daylight hours.

You can't photograph customs and immigration procedures at the airport, ferry terminals and overland border crossings. There are signs advising you of this fact. Nor can you photograph security measures, such as x-ray machines, metal detectors, machine gun-toting airport police etc.

Those with a keen sense of photography will find a treasure chest of photographic opportunities in Hong Kong. However, when walking about, think before you take photos. Places like pawn shops and mahjong parlours want to keep a low profile and aiming your camera could invite an angry response.

Photographing People

There are three basic approaches to photo-graphing people. One is the polite 'ask for permission and pose it' shot, which is some-times rejected. Another is the 'no-holds barred and upset everyone' approach. The third is the surreptitious photo – standing half a kilometre away with a metre-long tele-photo lens.

Not being a particularly friendly place, asking permission to photograph people in Hong Kong seldom produces any coopera-tion. Fortunately, the locals are used to camera-clicking foreign tourists, and won't normally throw a fit if you take a photo. Young students seem to enjoy having their photo taken and may even ham it up for the camera. Many older Chinese people strong-ly object to having their picture taken, so please be considerate.

When it comes to being photographed by family and friends, Hong Kong Chinese are generally big on people shots. Most have a collection of several thousand photos of themselves, standing in front of something (a temple, boat, karaoke lounge etc). Hong Kong Chinese tend to be unimpressed by photos which lack people, no matter how beautiful the scenery. Some foreigners have been taken aback when showing prize (but people-less) pictures to Hong Kong friends, who take a quick look and pronounce the photos 'boring'.

Airport Security

The dreaded x-ray machines are officially marked 'film-safe', and most travellers will not need to worry about film being fogged by x-rays. Professional photographers using ultra-sensitive film (such as ASA 1000) do need to worry about this, especially if the film is repeatedly exposed to even mild x-rays. One way to combat the problem is to use lead-lined bags, though it's probably safer and easier to get the film physically inspected.

TIME

Hong Kong Standard Time is eight hours ahead of GMT/UTC. Hong Kong does not have daylight-saving time. When it's noon in Hong Kong it's 11 pm the previous day in New York; 8 pm the previous day in Los Angeles; 4 am in London; noon in Singa-pore, Manila and Perth; and 2 pm in Melbourne and Sydney.

ELECTRICITY
Voltages & Cycles

The standard is 220V, 50 Hz (cycles per second) AC. Electrical shops in Hong Kong and elsewhere sell handy pocket-sized transformers that step down the electricity to 110V, but most mini-transformers are only rated for 50W. This is sufficient for an electric razor or laptop computer but not for those electric heater coils that some travellers carry to make tea and coffee. If in doubt, most appliances have a wattage rating printed somewhere on the bottom. Overloading a transformer can cause it to melt. Luxury tourist hotels often have razor outlets with multi-fittings to suit different plugs and voltages.

Apart from needing the right voltage, a few electric motors need the right frequency of current to work properly. For example, your 60 Hz clock will run slow on 50 Hz current, although it shouldn't harm the motor.

Plugs & Sockets

Hong Kong's plug and socket system is a nightmare. Some electric outlets are de-signed to accommodate three round prongs, others are wired for three square pins of the British design and others for two prong plugs! Not surprisingly, inexpensive plug adaptors are widely available in Hong Kong supermarkets, though this is not much comfort when you find you can't plug in your hairdryer in the morning. Remember that adaptors are not transformers. If you ignore this warning and plug a 110V appliance into a 220V outlet, there'll be sparks and fireworks.

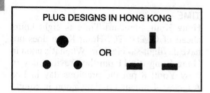

PLUG DESIGNS IN HONG KONG

OR

WEIGHTS & MEASURES

Although the international metric system is in official use in Hong Kong, in practice traditional Chinese weights and measures are still common.

If you want to shop in the local markets, become familiar with Chinese units of weight. Things are sold by the *leung*, which is equivalent to 37.8g, and the *gan* (catty), where one gan is about 600g. There are 16 leung to the gan.

Gold is sold by the *tael*, which is exactly the same as a leung. Many banks sell gold in Hong Kong as the Chinese have a long history of putting wealth into gold – the Chinese generally have little faith in paper money.

Hong Kong currently uses both the British and Chinese system of counting floors in a building. In the British system the street level is the ground floor and the next one up is the 1st floor. In the Chinese system the street level is the 1st floor. The use of both can be confusing.

LAUNDRY

Laundry services are easy to find in all areas of Hong Kong except the business district, Central. Most hotels, and even the cheap youth hostels, have a laundry service. Prices at the private laundrettes are normally HK$28 for the first 3kg, and then HK$7 for each ad-

ditional kilo. If your load is less than 3kg, you still pay the same, so you might want to combine your washing load with a friend's.

Drycleaners are easy to spot and some laundrettes offer the service. Drycleaning a shirt costs around HK$15, a skirt HK$30 and trousers HK$35 to HK$40.

TOILETS

You need a strong bladder to visit Hong Kong – the city suffers from a scarcity of public toilets. You'll find some of the toilets indicated on the area maps for the city.

It is irritating that all the major shopping malls have toilets, but keep the doors locked so only employees with keys can use them. Ocean Centre, arguably the busiest tourist mall, is a notorious example and even goes so far as to put a sign on the rest room doors saying 'staff only'. The only recourse is to seek out the toilets in fast-food outlets (though not all have them) and in some of the large department stores.

There are public toilets in: the Central Market on Hong Kong Island; a basement off Lan Kwai Fong; past the turnstiles of the Star Ferry; and in some of the parks. The ferries to the outlying islands are all equipped with toilets.

If you find a public toilet you probably won't find toilet paper, so bring your own.

WOMEN TRAVELLERS
Safety Precautions

Principles of decorum and respect for women are deeply ingrained in Chinese culture, despite the Confucianist sense of superiority accorded men, Chinese women often call the shots and wield a tremendous amount of influence (especially within marriage). There is a strong sense of balance between men and women in Hong Kong.

The experience of most women travellers is that Hong Kong is a safe city. Few women complain of bad treatment, intimidation or aggression, and for the most part your Hong Kong experience should be hassle-free. That having been said, it is still important to keep your wits about you, especially if you're wandering about alone at night. You may also want to be wary of agencies advertising for western women to work as models, escorts and extras in films; these agencies can be fronts for prostitution.

Women's Organisations

Hong Kong has heaps of organisations catering to the interests of women. The following list presents just a few:

Family Planning Association of Hong Kong
(☎ 2575-4477)
Harmony House
(24 hour hotline ☎ 2522-0434) – a shelter for women and their children.
Hong Kong Council of Women
(☎ 2386-6255) 4 Jordan Rd, Yau Ma Tei, Kowloon – open from Monday to Friday from 9.30 to 11.30 am, 2 to 4 pm and 7 to 9 pm, and can offer general advice to women.
Hong Kong Federation of Women
(☎ 2833-6131, fax 2833-6909) flat B, 10th floor, Jonsim Place, 228 Queen's Rd East, Wan Chai
Hong Kong Federation of Women's Centres
(☎ 2386-6256, fax 2728-0617) S8-9, 2nd floor, Lai Kwai House, Kai Kwok Estate, Kowloon
Hong Kong Women's Welfare Club – Eastern District
(☎ 2561-3409, fax 2811-5982) 4th floor, 210 Java Rd, North Point
Hong Kong Women's Welfare Club – Western District
(☎ 2548-1536, fax 2540-5003) 60 Bridges St, Sheung Wan
International Women's Forum
(☎ 2507-9300, fax 2827-2929) c/o 3rd floor, Sun Hung Kai Centre, 30 Harbour Rd, Wan Chai
International Women's League
(☎ 2782-2207, fax 2782-2839) 1st floor, 28 Ferry St, Jordon, Kowloon
Mother's Choice
(☎ 2868-2022) – provides information on childcare.
Rape Hotline
(☎ 2572-2222)

GAY & LESBIAN TRAVELLERS

The PRC's official attitude to gays and lesbians in mainland China is ambiguous, with responses ranging from draconian penalties to tacit acceptance. The official attitude in Hong Kong is far more positive. In July 1991 the enactment of the Crimes (Amendment) Ordinance removed criminal penalties for homosexual acts between male adults. Since the amendment, gay groups have been lobbying for anti-discrimination legislation to address the issue of discrimination on the grounds of sexual orientation. Despite this apparent liberalisation, Hong Kong Chinese are fairly conservative and it can still be risky for gays and lesbians to 'come out' to family or employers.

Visitor information specific to gay travellers can be gained through *Contacts Magazine* (☎ 2817-9447). One group providing a phone-line counselling service is Horizon's (☎ 2815-9268), which is a switchboard service run by volunteers offering advice to local and visiting gays, lesbians and bisexuals.

There are no specific laws preventing people with HIV/AIDS from travelling to Hong Kong. Numerous government and volunteer groups provide services for HIV positive people and these include: the Hong Kong Department of Health AIDS Unit (24 hour hotline ☎ 2780-2211); Hong Kong AIDS Foundation (helpline ☎ 2513-0513, inquiries 2560-8528, emailhkaf@asiaonline.net), 5th floor, Shau Kei Wan Jockey Club Clinics, 8 Chai Wan Rd, Shaukewan, Hong Kong; and the HIV Information and Drop-In Centre (☎ 2523-0531) at St John's Cathedral, Battery Path.

The gay 'scene' in Hong Kong has seen a small revolution take place over the last few years. A cluster of bars and clubs has opened around Glenealy and Wyndham Sts. See the Entertainment section in the Hong Kong Island chapter for more details.

DISABLED TRAVELLERS

Disabled persons have to cope with substantial obstacles, such as the stairs at the MTR stations, narrow crowded footpaths and steep hills. People whose sight, hearing or walking ability is impaired must be extremely cautious of Hong Kong's crazy drivers, who almost never yield to pedestrians. Crossing Hong Kong's busy thoroughfares on a pedestrian overpass will also be a problem for some disabled travellers.

On the other hand, taxis are not hard to find and most buildings have lifts. Wheelchairs can negotiate most of the ferries (lower deck only), but don't attempt to move around on hoverferries.

In some (but not all) upmarket hotels there are specially designed rooms for disabled people. Those that provide such rooms are indicated in the Places to Stay section in the Kowloon and Hong Kong Island chapters.

Chek Lap Kok airport has been designed with facilities for passengers with disabilities. A free porter service is available, ramps make moving between levels simple and lifts are equipped with audible indicators. Electric carts are also available in the terminal (ask your airline for details); check-in counters and immigration and custom areas are also equipped with facilities for those with special needs. Built-in features include disabled toilets, telephones and drinking fountains. For those who are blind or partially blind, a tactile guide path has been incorporated into the departures kerb, and from the airport express platform to information counters and help phones.

If you have any further queries, contact the Joint Council for the Physically and Mentally Disabled (☎ 2864-2931, fax 2864-2962).

SENIOR TRAVELLERS

Hong Kong is just about as user-friendly to senior travellers as any western city. With decent medical care, pharmacies, air conditioning and good public transport, Hong Kong offers most of the usual modern conveniences that make travel safe and comfortable. However, some senior travellers may have difficulty negotiating the steep hills or the steps on pedestrian overpasses and in the MTR stations.

There are half-price discounts for seniors (age 65 and over) on buses and ferries, and on MTR and KCR trains. There are also discounts for seniors (age 60 and over) in museums and on organised tours. Some upmarket hotels have discounts for seniors, though these are somewhat bogus because

anyone can get good discounts at a hotel by booking through a travel agent.

If you would like further information, contact the Hong Kong Society for the Aged (☎ 2511-2235), room 1601, Tung Sun Commercial Centre, 194 Lockhart Rd, Wan Chai. Helping Hand (☎ 2522-4494) is another organisation that deals with issues relating to the elderly.

TRAVEL WITH CHILDREN

Except for the dangers posed by traffic, Hong Kong is a pretty good travel destination if you want to bring the kids along. Food and sanitation is of a high enough standard that you needn't fear for their health, and there is plenty to keep them amused (Ocean Park, the Peak Tower, video games and STAR TV being some examples).

A number of upmarket hotels give special concessions for families with children (reduced rates or free extra bed etc). Most public transport offers half-price fares for children under the age of 12.

If your children are teenagers, useful summer camp programs are offered through the Outward Bound School (☎ 2792-4333, 2792-0055).

Lonely Planet publishes a guide entitled *Travel with Children* which has useful tips.

USEFUL ORGANISATIONS

The Hong Kong Information Services Department (☎ 2842-8777) can answer specific questions or direct you to other government agencies that can handle your inquiry. It's best to try the HKTA before resorting to the Information Services Department.

If you feel that you were defrauded, there are a few agencies that might be able to help you. The first place to try is the HKTA (☎ 2807-6177): if the shop is a member, HKTA can apply pressure, but don't expect miracles. If not, the HKTA can at least advise you on who to contact for more help.

Another place to try is the Hong Kong Consumer Council's (HKCC) complaints and advice hotline (☎ 9229-2222). HKCC advice centres are located in Central (☎ 9221-

6228), ground floor, Harbour building, 38 Pier Rd, and Kowloon (☎ 9226-4011), ground floor, Morning Joy building, 141-143 Kau Pui Lung Rd, Tokawan.

If you get robbed, you can obtain a loss report for insurance purposes at the Central Police Station, 10 Hollywood Rd (at the top end of Pottinger St) in Central. There is also a crime hotline (☎ 2527-7177), but this is not for emergencies.

The Community Advice Bureau (☎ 2815-5444, fax 2815-5977) is where volunteer expats answer questions for new Hong Kong foreign residents. Since it's a volunteer organisation, don't bother the staff with trivia. If you've been living in Hong Kong for a while, perhaps you'd like to volunteer some time too.

The Royal Asiatic Society (RAS, ☎ 2849-6113, fax 2849-6113), GPO Box 3864, is dedicated to helping its members or visitors learn more about the history and culture of Hong Kong. The RAS organises lectures and field trips, operates a lending library and puts out publications of its own. The RAS was founded in London in 1823 and has branches in several Asian countries.

If you've been ripped off by your employer, take your complaint to the Labour Department (24 hour ☎ 2717-1771), or drop by its office in the Harbour building, 38 Pier Rd, Central. Of course, that's assuming you're working legally to begin with.

A lot of westerners go to work in Hong Kong and it's pretty easy to get a job in the pubs and nightclubs. However, quite a few of these places are not adverse to treating staff pretty badly because they'll be moving on and are usually desperate for the money. Some pubs are notorious for making deductions from wages for any reason. However, Hong Kong does have quite strong employment protection legislation. The Labour Department has a 24 hour hotline for answering questions. One pub tried to deduct HK$600 from my wages, but a quick phone call told me my rights and I eventually got my money.

Clive Searle

If you're in the publishing, music or software business and your goods are being pirated, you can try complaining to the Intellectual Property Department (☎ 2961-6800), 24th and 25th floors, Wu Chung House, 213 Queen's Rd East, Wan Chai. This is also the place for registering copyrights, trademarks and patents.

If you're interested in doing business in Hong Kong, the largest and most visible presence is the Hong Kong Trade Development Council (TDC), which for 30 years has been promoting Hong Kong as a trading and manufacturing partner for foreign businesses. Facilities in its top-notch office include its TDC Business Library (☎ 2584-4333), and more than 70 CD ROM databases where you can access essential world trade information (you can also get online for free). The TDC (☎ 2584-4188) phone/fax service provides a list of over 100,000 Hong Kong manufacturers – the information will be sent to you by fax (although there is a charge per record so have your credit card handy).

The TDC also co-sponsors or takes part in numerous trade fairs each year (the Convention and Exhibition Centre was hugely expanded in 1997), and publishes a wealth of literature on Hong Kong markets and products. *HK Enterprise Internet* is TDC's electronically published magazine, posted on the TDC home page (www.tdc.org.hk). The TDC head office (☎ 2584-4333) is on the 38th floor, Office Tower, Convention Plaza, 1 Harbour Rd, Wan Chai. The council also has more than 50 representative offices in numerous countries.

Another source for trade information, statistics, government regulations and product certification is the Hong Kong Trade Department (☎ 2392-2922), Trade Department Tower, 700 Nathan Rd, Mong Kok. The Hong Kong Industry Department offers information and assistance to overseas investors at its One Stop Unit (☎ 2737-2434), 14th floor, Ocean Centre, 5 Canton Rd, Tsim Sha Tsui. Other organisations that could be of interest to those in Hong Kong on business are the Employers' Federation of Hong Kong (☎ 2528-0536), 1001 East Town building, 41 Lockhart Rd, Wan Chai, and the Hong Kong Industrial Technology

HONG KONG

Centre Corporation (☎ 2788-5400), 78 Tat Chee Ave, Kowloon.

Hong Kong is well served by both local and overseas chambers. The largest chamber is the Hong Kong General Chamber of Commerce (☎ 2529-9229), 22nd floor, United Centre, 95 Queensway, Admiralty. It has more than 4000 members and boasts 10 offices throughout the territory. In addition to its various member services, the chamber offers a host of services for foreign executives and firms such as translation, serviced offices, secretarial help and printing.

The Chinese General Chamber of Commerce (☎ 2525-6385, email cgcc@cgcc.org.hk, www.cgcc.org.hk) is authorised to issue Certificates of Hong Kong origin for trade purposes. Its address is 7th floor, Chinese General Chamber of Commerce building, 24-25 Connaught Rd, Central. The Chinese Manufacturers' Association of Hong Kong (☎ 2545-6166), operates testing laboratories for product certification, and can also issue Certificates of Hong Kong origin. It is on the 3rd floor, CMA building, 64-66 Connaught Rd, Central.

The American Chamber of Commerce (☎ 2526-0165, fax 2537-1682, email amcham@amcham.org.hk) is on the 19th floor of the Bank of America Tower, 12 Harcourt Rd, Central. For a complete listing of both local and overseas chambers check the *Yellow Pages Commercial/Industrial Guide*.

If you know of any corrupt government officials you can call the Report Centre of the Independent Commission Against Corruption (ICAC, ☎ 2526-6366).

In the event of a medical emergency dial ☎ 999: operators speak English. St John's offers free ambulance service in Hong Kong (☎ 2576-6555), Kowloon (☎ 2713-5555) and the New Territories (☎ 2639-2555).

Some people find life in Hong Kong difficult to adapt to, especially long-term residents. There are a few places who can help out: try phoning St John's Counselling Service (☎ 2525-7207) or the Community Advice Bureau (☎ 2815-5444).

Other useful helplines and organisations include AIDS Concern Helpline (☎ 2898-4422); HIV Information and Drop-In Centre (☎ 2523-0531); AIDS Unit (☎ 2780-2211); Alcoholics Anonymous (☎ 2522-5665); Rape Hotline (☎ 2572-2222); Drug Abuse Hotline (☎ 2366-8822); Narcotics Anonymous (☎ 2813-7343); and the Samaritans (☎ 2896-0000).

DANGERS & ANNOYANCES
Rudeness
The biggest complaint made by travellers is that Hong Kong people are often rude, pushy and impatient. This impression partly results from the fact that most foreigners deal mainly with people in the tourist trade rather than the typical Hong Kong resident. However, this is a thin excuse. Sales clerks in Taiwan, Korea, Japan or the Philippines are generally cheerful and friendly, but this is seldom the case in Hong Kong.

You may encounter sales clerks who pretend you don't even exist – go into a supermarket and ask a clerk 'where can I find coffee' and they pretend to have a hearing problem. At other times, you get half way through your question when the clerk cuts you off abruptly with the reply 'out of stock'. The excuse that they don't speak English is also a thin one – even in countries where English is nonexistent, clerks who don't understand what you're saying just smile, laugh or shrug their shoulders. In Hong Kong, the reaction is more likely to be irritation and hostility. When you do get a smile, it usually means that the person is Thai or Filipino.

The HKTA is aware of the problem, and has attempted to educate people to smile, say 'hello' and 'thank you'. Unfortunately, the HKTA's efforts have been less than stunningly successful.

It's not just tourists who complain. Many native Hong Kong residents also feel that their home town is far less friendly than it should be. Furthermore, Chinese from other parts of China feel that not only Hong Kong residents, but also the Cantonese in general are the least hospitable people in the entire country.

This doesn't mean that you will never encounter an amiable person in Hong Kong. Within this sea of frowning faces, there are smiles. You might even meet someone who will be polite, helpful, friendly and generous, and not expect anything in return. Sadly, such experiences are all too rare, especially if you're a short-term visitor.

Crime

Despite Hong Kong's obvious prosperity and low unemployment rate, there are plenty of people who live on the margin of society and will resort to crime to earn a living. This includes western travellers, some of whom arrive in Hong Kong totally broke with no prospects for employment. There have been disturbing reports of foreigners having had their backpacks burgled by their room mates in youth hostels. One fellow had his wallet, passport and travellers cheques lifted during the two minutes he spent taking a shower at a hostel – the only other people in the place were travellers. So if something of yours is stolen, don't automatically assume that the guilty party is a local.

If you set a bag down and don't keep an eye on it, the whole thing may disappear in seconds. A number of people had their luggage stolen in the old Kai Tak airport when they wandered off for a minute to use the toilets or change money. You probably wouldn't leave your bags unattended in a developing country, so don't assume that it's OK in wealthy Hong Kong. The same principle applies in restaurants and pubs – if your bag doesn't accompany you to the toilet, don't expect to find it when you return.

Hong Kong now has a serious drug problem. There are estimated to be more than 40,000 drug addicts in Hong Kong, 90% of whom are male. Some female addicts finance their habit by working in the sex industry, and some of the men resort to crimes such as pickpocketing, burglary and robbery. The effect on travellers is that you have to be careful with your valuables.

It is generally safe to walk around at night, though it's best to stick to well-lit areas.

Tourist districts like Tsim Sha Tsui are heavily patrolled by the police.

Scams

Increasingly, we're getting letters from gullible travellers who have become the victims of scams. Typically, a traveller is approached by a 'trustworthy' man or woman who offers 'friendship'. Under a pretext, the tourist is lured to the new friend's place and introduced to some more friends. Next, the traveller is offered a part in a 'get-rich-quick scheme'. At first it's claimed that the tourist need not provide any money. Later, more money is needed for the operation than was originally thought and they ask the tourist to hand over a hefty amount. Alone against a band of complete strangers, the tourist is likely to give money in a despairing attempt to stay alive.

Smuggling

Professional smugglers often target westerners to carry goods into countries like Vietnam and India where the goods are prohibited or the import taxes are high. The theory is that customs is less likely to stamp the goods on a western passport. These small-time smuggling expeditions are commonly known as 'milk runs'. The westerner either gets a fee and heads back to Hong Kong to do it again, or else gains a free air ticket to another destination.

Smuggling is far more risky than travellers are led to believe by their prospective 'employer'. A traveller living in Chungking Mansions was solicited to smuggle 7kg of gold into Nepal and was offered US$2000 for his trouble. He got caught and was given four years in prison. Another traveller got caught at Seoul airport wearing three mink coats under his jacket – he was fined and given two months in jail before being booted out of the country. There are also cases of travellers being used as 'mules' to carry drugs hidden inside electronic goods.

LEGAL MATTERS

Most foreigners who get into legal trouble in Hong Kong are usually involved with drugs, either as a consumer or dealer. All forms of dope are highly illegal in Hong Kong. It makes no difference whether it's heroin, opium or marijuana – the law makes no distinction. If police or customs officials find dope or the smoking equipment in your possession, you can expect to be arrested immediately. Police sometimes spot check the bars in the Lan Kwai Fong drinking area and the passengers debarking the ferry at Lamma Island. Don't forget that, although Hong Kong possesses a more benign legal system than that over the electrified fence to the north, Hong Kong is now under Chinese rule, and in China drug runners are routinely shot.

Drink driving has long been overlooked in Hong Kong, but the police are starting to crack down. Patrol cars are being equipped with breathalysers and stiffer penalties.

If you run into legal trouble and don't have the funds to hire a lawyer, the Legal Aid Department (☎ 2537-7677) provides both residents and non-residents with representation, subject to a means and merits test.

BUSINESS HOURS

Office hours are Monday to Friday from 9 am to either 5 or 6 pm, and on Saturday from 9 am to noon. The lunch hour is from 1 to 2 pm and many offices simply shut down and lock the door at this time. Banks are open Monday to Friday from 9 am to 4.30 pm and on Saturday from 9 am to 12.30 pm.

Many Hong Kong companies still run on a 5½ day working week, but this concept is beginning to fall out of favour. Some companies use the promise of a five day week in their 'help wanted' ads to lure employees.

Stores and restaurants that cater to the tourist trade keep longer hours, but almost nothing opens before 9 am. Even tourist-related businesses shut down by 9 or 10 pm, and many will close for major holidays, especially Chinese New Year.

Restaurants generally open from 11.30 am to 2.30 pm for lunch and 6 to 11 pm for dinner. Of course, there are many exceptions to this rule. Some pubs keep the kitchen open until 1 am and Chinese noodle shops often run from early in the morning until the wee hours. Bars generally open at noon or 6 pm and close anywhere between 2 to 6 am. Happy hours at bars are generally from 4 to 8 pm, but you will find some that are more flexible.

PUBLIC HOLIDAYS & SPECIAL EVENTS

Western and Chinese culture combine to create an interesting mix of holidays. Trying to determine the exact date of each is a bit tricky as there are two calendars in use in Hong Kong – the Gregorian solar and the Chinese lunar. These calendars do not correspond exactly because a lunar month is only 28 days. To keep the two calendars in relative harmony, an extra month is added to the lunar calendar once every 30 months. The result is that the Chinese New Year, the most important Chinese holiday, can fall anywhere between 21 January and 28 February on the Gregorian calendar.

The return of Hong Kong to China has seen a shake up of the public holiday system. Gone is the revelry usually seen on the Queen's birthday, instead Hong Kong grinds to a halt on 1 October, National Day. The day after National Day also merits a vacation. SAR Establishment Day (1 July) is held on the anniversary of the handover of Hong Kong to China. The eviction of Japanese forces from Hong Kong at the end of WWII by allied forces (after Nagasaki and Hiroshima were blitzed) is now revised to the Sino-Japanese War Victory Day. The rewriting of history has begun in earnest. The Taiwanese double tenth anniversary on 10 October will not evolve into a joyous celebration – the event in 1997 saw Taiwanese flags being pulled down by the police.

Many of the Chinese festivals go back hundreds, perhaps thousands, of years – the true origins are often lost in the mists of time. The reasons for each festival vary and you will generally find that there are a couple of explanations. The HKTA's free leaflet *Chinese Festivals & Special Events* has the exact dates that festivals are celebrated in the current year.

New Year The first week day in January is a public holiday.

Chinese New Year The first day of the first moon is the Chinese New Year, also known as the Spring Festival. The first, second and third day of the first moon are public holidays. It's worth bearing in mind that many shops take a three day holiday at this time.

This is a festival for the family, with little for the visitor to see except a fireworks display on New Year's Eve. You may also see a lion dance either in the street or in a top tourist hotel.

Starting the New Year well is said to ensure good fortune for the entire year. Therefore, houses are cleaned, debts paid off and feuds, no matter how bitter, are ended – even if it's only for the day. Pictures of gods are pasted around the front doors of houses to scare off bad spirits, along with messages of welcome on red paper to encourage the good ones.

By tradition, everyone asks for double wages. The garbage collector, the milkman, the postman and so on get *lai see* (lucky money) in red envelopes as tips. The traditional Chinese New Year greeting *kung hey fat choi* literally means 'good wishes, good fortune'.

Hotels crank the prices up at New Year and you may find all the hotels full. It's certainly not the time to go to China, as hordes of Hong Kong people cram the trains and every other form of transport to get there. Macau is similarly besieged, but the atmosphere is much more fun than in Hong Kong.

It is worth seeing the huge flower fairs where, on Chinese New Year's Eve, the Chinese buy lucky peach blossoms, kumquat trees and narcissi from the hundreds of flower sellers. Victoria Park in Causeway Bay is the place to go for this, although it's jam-packed.

The first day of the first moon usually falls at the end of January or the beginning of February. For the next two years, it will fall on 16 February 1999 and 5 February 2000.

Lantern Festival The Lantern Festival (Yuen Siu) is not a public holiday but is more interesting than the Chinese New Year. At the end of the Chinese New Year celebrations, customarily the 15th day of the first moon (middle or end of February), lanterns in traditional designs are lit in homes, restaurants and temples. In residential areas, you'll see people carrying lanterns through the streets.

Easter In Hong Kong, Easter is a public holiday held over three days starting from Good Friday and running through to Easter Sunday. Although many westerners don't realise it, the date of Easter is fixed by the lunar calendar, falling somewhere in March or April. The Easter holiday is often close to Ching Ming festival, and is locally known as the 'foreigner's Ching Ming'.

Ching Ming Ching Ming is a family affair. It is when the Chinese visit and clean the graves of ancestors. Food and wine is left for the spirits, and incense and paper money is burned. Some people follow the custom of pasting long strips of red and white paper to the graves to indicate that the rituals have been performed. The festival is thought to have its origins during the Han dynasty, about 2000 years ago, when ancestors' tombs were swept, washed and repaired.

Ching Ming is a public holiday and is not a particularly good time to visit Hong Kong, though not nearly so bad as the Chinese New Year. Many people take a three or four day holiday. Banks and many other businesses close, public transport is extremely crowded and the border crossing into China is a near riot.

Ching Ming was traditionally celebrated at the beginning of the third moon, but the calendar has been slightly adjusted so that it always falls during the first week of April.

Tin Hau Festival Although it's not a public holiday, this is one of Hong Kong's most colourful occasions. Tin Hau is the patron of fishing people and is one of the territory's most popular gods.

Junks are decorated with flags and sail in long rows to Tin Hau temples to pray for clear skies and good catches. Often Tin Hau's image is taken from temples and paraded through the streets. Shrines from the junks are carried to the shore to be blessed by Taoist priests.

The best place to see the festival (and the fortune telling, lion dances and Chinese opera that follow) is at the site of Tin Hau's best known temple, the Tai Miu Temple in Joss House Bay. It's not accessible by road and is not on the normal ferry route, but at festival time the ferry company puts on excursion trips that get very crowded.

The Tin Hau temple at Stanley on the south coast of Hong Kong Island was built in 1767 and is said to be the oldest building in Hong Kong. Another main Tin Hau temple is at Sok Kwu Wan on Lamma Island.

The Tin Hau Festival is traditionally held on the 23rd day of the third moon, and will fall on 8 May 1999 and 27 April 2000 for the next two years.

Cheung Chau Bun Festival The Bun Festival of Tai Chiu is held in May on Cheung Chau Island, traditionally on the sixth day of the fourth moon. Precise dates are decided by village elders on the island about three weeks before it starts. This is a Taoist festival and there are three or four days of religious observances.

While not a public holiday, it's a good reason to visit Cheung Chau. Festival information is in the Outlying Islands chapter.

Birthday of Lord Buddha This is also referred to as the Bathing of Lord Buddha and is not a public holiday. Like most Buddhist festivals, it's more sedate than the Taoist celebrations. Buddha's statue is taken from monasteries and temples and ceremoniously bathed in water scented with sandalwood, ambergris (a waxy substance secreted from the intestine of a sperm whale and often found floating in the sea), garu wood, turmeric and aloes (a drug used for clearing the bowels, made from the fleshy, spiny-toothed leaves of the aloe plant). The

mixture is drunk by the faithful, who believe it has great curative powers.

While Lantau Island is the best place to observe this event, most people visit only Po Lin, the largest and best known temple. Extra ferries operate for the crowds.

The New Territories has several Buddhist temples worth visiting at this time, such as the Ten Thousand Buddhas Monastery in Sha Tin, or the Miu Fat Monastery at Lam Tei.

The festival is celebrated on the eighth day of the fourth moon. For the remainder of this century it will fall on the 22 May 1999 and 11 May 2000.

Dragon Boat Festival Double Fifth (Tuen Ng, fifth day, fifth moon) or the Dragon Boat Festival is a public holiday and is normally held in June. It's a lot of fun despite the fact that it commemorates the sad tale of Qu Yuan, a poet-statesman of the 3rd century BC who hurled himself into the Mi Lo River in Hunan Province to protest against a corrupt government. The people who lived on the banks of the river raced to the scene in their boats in an attempt to save him but were too late. Not unmindful of his sacrifice, the people later threw dumplings into the water to keep the hungry fish away from his body.

Traditional rice dumplings are still eaten in memory of the event and dragon-boat races are held in Hong Kong, Kowloon and the outlying islands. See the races at Shau Kei Wan, Aberdeen, Yau Ma Tei, Tai Po and Stanley, and on Lantau and Cheung Chau Islands. The boats are rowed by teams from Hong Kong's sports and social clubs. International dragon-boat races are held at Yau Ma Tei.

This lunar holiday will fall on the 18 June 1999 and 6 June 2000 for the next two years.

SAR Establishment Day This public holiday (1 July) celebrates the resumption of China's sovereignty over Hong Kong.

Birthday of Lu Pan, Master Builder Legends say that Lu Pan was a real person, born around 507 BC and later deified. A master architect, magician, engineer, inventor and designer, Lu Pan is worshipped by anyone connected with the building trade. Ceremonies sponsored by the builders' guilds are held at Lu Pan Temple in Kennedy Town, Hong Kong Island. The celebration occurs around middle to late July. It's a minor holiday.

Maidens' Festival This is a minor holiday and you might not even notice anything special taking place. Also known as the Seven Sisters Festival, this is a celebration for girls and young lovers and is held on the seventh day of the seventh moon (about mid-August).

It has its origins in an ancient Chinese story about two celestial lovers, Chien Niu, the cowherd and Chih Nu, the spinner and weaver. One version says that they became so engrossed in each other that they forgot their work. As a punishment the Queen of Heaven decided that they should be separated by being placed on either side of a river which she cut through the heavens

with her hairpin. The King of Heaven took pity on the lovers and said they could meet once a year – but provided no bridge across the river. So magpies (regarded as birds of good omen) flocked together, spread their wings and formed a bridge so the lovers could be reunited.

At midnight on the day of this festival prayers are offered by unmarried men and women to Chien Niu and Chih Nu. Prayers are also directed to Chih Nu's six sisters, who appear in another version of the story. The main offerings made to the seven sisters are cosmetics and flowers.

Sino-Japanese War Victory Day This is held on a Monday in middle to late August and replaces Liberation Day.

Ghost Month On the first day of the seventh moon (late August or early September), the gates of hell are opened and 'hungry ghosts' are freed for two weeks to walk the earth. Hungry ghosts are the spirits of those who were either unloved,

HONG KONG TOURIST ASSOCIATION
Dragon Boat racing is normally held in June; the local events are held in waters around the outlying and Hong Kong islands, while international races are held at Yau Ma Tei.

abandoned and forgotten by the family or suffered a violent death. On the 14th day (called the Yue Lan Festival) paper cars, houses and money are burnt for the ghosts, and food is offered.

People whose relatives suffered a violent death are particularly concerned to placate the spirits. Many people will not swim, travel, get married, move house or indulge in other risky activities during this time.

The ghost month is an excellent time to visit Taoist temples in Hong Kong, as they are usually packed with worshippers burning incense and making offerings. There are also Cantonese opera performances – presumably to give the ghosts one good night out before they go down below for another year. This is not a public holiday.

Mid-Autumn Moon Festival This festival is held in September, on the 15th night of the eighth moon. This festival begins at night and the day after is a public holiday.

Although the observance of the moon is thought to date back to much earlier times, today the festival recalls an uprising against the Mongols in the 14th century when plans for a revolution were passed around in cakes.

Moon cakes are still eaten and there are many delicious varieties. The various fillings include coconut, dates, nuts, lotus, sesame seeds and sometimes an egg.

Everyone heads for the hilltops, where they light special candle lanterns and watch the moon rise. The Peak Tram and the transport to the New Territories is always crowded. For young couples, it's a romantic holiday – a time to be together and watch the moon.

The Mid-Autumn Moon Festival will be celebrated on 24 September 1999 and 12 September 2000 for the next two years.

National Day This festival, held on 1 October, celebrates the establishment of the People's Republic of China. The following day is also a holiday.

Birthday of Confucius Confucius' birthday is in early October and religious observances are held by the Confucian Society in the Confucius Temple at Causeway Bay. It's a minor holiday that usually passes unnoticed by most Hong Kong residents.

Cheung Yeung Festival This festival is based on a story from the Eastern Han dynasty (in the first two centuries AD). An old soothsayer advised a man to take his family away to a high place for 24 hours to avoid disaster. When the man returned to his village he found every living thing had been destroyed and only he and his family had survived. Many people head for the high spots again to remember the old man's advice. The Cheung Yeung Festival is held in middle to late October.

While not an especially interesting occasion, the Cheung Yeung Festival is a public holiday.

Christmas & Boxing Day Christmas (25 December) and the day after (Boxing Day) are public holidays. The frantic shopping spree and general jubilation that accompanies the event should guarantee the holiday a long future under the new management, even though the sending of Christmas cards was banned on the mainland a few years ago.

Other Events
There are literally hundreds of cultural and special-interest events throughout the year. The HKTA publishes a complete schedule every month. Exact dates vary from year to year, so if you want to time your visit to coincide with a particular event, it would be wise to contact the HKTA beforehand. A brief rundown of important annual events includes:

Hong Kong Fringe Festival
    The Fringe Club sponsors three weeks of performances by an eclectic mix of up-and-coming artists and performers from Hong Kong and overseas; held in late January/early February.
Hong Kong Golf Open
    This is held at the Royal Hong Kong Golf Club, usually in February.

Hong Kong Arts Festival
  A month of music, performing arts and exhibitions by hundreds of local and international artists; held in February/March.
Hong Kong International Marathon
  Organised by the Hong Kong Amateur Athletic Association, this major event is held in Sha Tin, usually in March.
Hong Kong Food Festival
  Sponsored by the HKTA and usually held in March.
Hong Kong International Film Festival
  This festival brings in hundreds of films from around the world and is used to showcase new, local and regional productions; held in March or April.
Hong Kong International Handball Invitation Tournament
  Organised by the Hong Kong Amateur Handball Association, this event is held in March or April.
Rugby Sevens
  Famous three day rugby event that attracts teams from all over the world; held in March or early April.
Sotheby's and Christie's Auctions
  These usually occur in Spring (March to May) and Autumn (September to November).
Hong Kong Computer Expo
  This takes place in May.
International Dragon Boat Festival
  This international festival is usually held in June, the week after the Chinese dragon-boat races.
Davis Cup
  This tennis tournament is held in July.
International Arts Carnival
  This unusual summer festival promotes performances by children's groups. The carnival usually falls in July or August.
Asian Regatta
  Organised by the Hong Kong Yachting Association, this event is usually held in October.
Festival of Asian Arts
  One of Asia's major cultural events, bringing in musicians, dancers, opera singers and other performance groups from all over the region; held every other year in October or November.
Hong Kong Folk Festival
  The Hong Kong Folk Society brings together well known international acts and local musicians; held in November.

ACTIVITIES

Hong Kong may be a sea of concrete and asphalt, but there are a surprising number of ways to keep fit and have fun. One excellent, all-round option is the South China Athletic Association (SCAA; ☎ 2577-6932, fax 2890-9304), 88 Caroline Hill Rd, Causeway Bay. The SCAA has facilities for billiards, bowling, tennis, squash, table tennis, gymnastics, fencing, yoga, judo, karate, golf and dancing. Membership is cheap and there is a discounted short term membership available for visitors (HK$50 per month). Another excellent contact is the Hong Kong Amateur Athletic Association (☎ 2504-8215, fax 2577-5322), room 1017, Sports House, 1 Stadium Path, So Kon Po, Causeway Bay. It's a venue that houses all sorts of sports clubs.

Billiards, Snooker & Pool

The Chinese are crazy about these games, but most facilities are rather makeshift. Many billiard and snooker clubs seem to open and close on a regular basis, so your best bet is to phone the Hong Kong Billiards and Snooker Control Council (☎ 2576-1272, fax 2834-5198). The Kowloon Cricket Club (☎ 2367-4141) has snooker tables, although the cost of joining the club may be prohibitive, unless you plan to stay in Hong Kong for a while. Two bars in the same building in Wan Chai, the Flying Pig (☎ 2865-3730) and Ridgways (☎ 2865-6608), have pool tables.

Bowling

Some of the best facilities are at the SCAA (☎ 2577-6932), 88 Caroline Hill Rd, Causeway Bay.

In Kowloon, bowling alleys tend to be located in the backwaters. One of the most accessible is the AMF Bowling Centre (☎ 2732-2255) in the New East Ocean Centre, Tsim Sha Tsui East. Further away is the AMF Mei Foo Bowling Centre (☎ 2742-5911), 1st floor, 95C Broadway St, Lai Chi Kok.

Canoeing

To find enthusiasts of this sport, contact the Canoe Union (☎ 2572-7008, fax 2838-9037), room 1010, Queen Elizabeth Stadium, 18 Oi Kwan Rd, Wan Chai. Canoeing facilities are available through the

Tai Mei Tuk Water Sports Centre (☎ 2665-3591), Regional Council, Tai Mei Tuk, Tai Po, New Territories. You can also inquire at the Wong Shek Water Sports Centre (☎ 2328-2370), Wong Shek pier, Sai Kung, New Territories. Alternatively, there is the Chong Hing Water Sports Centre (☎ 2792-6810), West Sea Coffer Dam, High Island Reservoir, Sai Kung, New Territories.

Computer Clubs & BBSs

Hong Kong's economic prosperity and low-priced computer equipment make this an ideal place for computer hobbyists. You can seek the company of fellow computer freaks by joining a computer club, or plug in a modem and dial up an electronic Bulletin Board System (BBS).

Like BBSs, computer clubs come and go, but the HKTA publication *Associations & Societies in Hong Kong* lists a few. One of the biggest is the Computer Club Hong Kong Ltd (☎ 2374-1328, fax 2374-0859), room 9A, 9th floor, Go Up Commercial building, 998 Canton Rd, Mong Kok, Kowloon. Another is the Hong Kong Computer Society (☎ 2834-2228, fax 2834-3003, email hkcs@hkcs.org.hk, www.hkcs.org.hk), unit D, 1st floor, Luckifast building, 1 Stone Nullah Lane, Wan Chai.

The *South China Morning Post* has a small computer section every Tuesday that publishes information on activities for computer buffs.

Cricket

Cricket is increasingly popular with the locals. The club waiting lists are long and you may have to be recommended. In addition the joining fees are expensive, which makes it only worth considering if your stay is long term.

Information can be obtained from the Hong Kong Cricket Association (☎ 2504-8102, fax 2577-8486, email hkca@hkabc.net), room 1019, Sports House, 1 Stadium Path, So Kon Po, Causeway Bay.

On Hong Kong Island, north of Deep Water Bay, is the Hong Kong Cricket Club (☎ 2574-6266). On the other side of Victoria

Harbour is the Kowloon Cricket Club (☎ 2367-4141) – a wonderful, though expensive, patch of greenery. There is also a cricket club (☎ 2723-8721) on Lamma Island.

Cycling

There are bicycle paths in the New Territories, mostly around Tolo Harbour. The paths run from Sha Tin to Tai Po and continue up to Tai Mei Tuk. You can rent cycles in these three places, but the paths get very crowded on the weekends. During the week you may have the paths to yourself. Bicycle rentals are also available at Shek O on Hong Kong Island and Mui Wo on Lantau Island.

Although the Hong Kong Cycling Association (☎ 2573-3861), room 1013, Queen Elizabeth Stadium, 18 Oi Kwan Rd, Wan Chai, mainly organises cycling races, you can call it for information. To find out about areas for mountain biking or for equipment, ask the staff at Flying Ball Bicycle Co (☎ 2381-3661), 201 Tung Choi St, Mong Kok. Another decent area for purchasing cycling gear and accessories is Garden St in Mong Kok and Wan Chai Rd in Wan Chai.

Fishing

Sport fishing from small yachts is a popular activity. To organise a trip, contact the Hong Kong Amateur Fishing Society (☎ 2730-0442), Yau Ma Tei. While there are virtually no restrictions on sea fishing, it's a different story with fishing at freshwater reservoirs. The fishing season is from September to March and there are limits on the quantity and size of fish taken. A licence from the Water Supplies Department (☎ 2824-5000), Wan Chai, is required. It costs HK$24 and is valid for six months from 1 September to 31 March.

Fitness Centres

Getting fit is big business in Hong Kong, with the largest slices of the pie shared out between a few big names. T.L.C. Fitness Chain has branches in Admiralty (☎ 2866-9968), Causeway Bay (☎ 2576-7668) and Jordan (☎ 2730-5038), and the monthly subscription starts at HK$415. Ray Wilson California Fitness Centre has two branches:

(☎ 2522-5229) 1 Wellington St, Central; and (☎ 2877-7070) 88 Gloucester Rd, Wan Chai. New York Fitness (☎ 2543-2280) in Hollywood Rd offers aerobics, personal training, physiotherapy, massage and beauty therapy.

Golf

There are five golf courses in Hong Kong. Green fees vary for visitors, and range anywhere from HK$450 (Deep Water Bay Golf Club) to HK$1400 (Fanling) for an 18 hole course. If you are signed in by a member, it can be considerably cheaper. On weekends, the courses are crowded and you pay more. The Hong Kong Golf Club has two courses. The less expensive one is the nine hole course at Deep Water Bay (☎ 2812-7070) on the south side of Hong Kong Island. Considerably nicer is the course at Fanling (☎ 2670-1211) in the New Territories. The Discovery Bay Golf Club (☎ 2987-7271) on Lantau Island is perched high on a hill, offering impressive views. So does the Shek O Country Club (☎ 2809-4458), which is situated on the south-eastern tip of Hong Kong Island. The Clearwater Bay Golf and Country Club (☎ 2719-1595) is on the Sai Kung peninsula in the New Territories. If you want to purchase golf equipment, try Nevada Bob's Golf Stores in Central (☎ 2868-4234) and Kowloon (☎2368-6805).

Handball

You can play at the Indoor Handball Court in Kowloon Park in Tsim Sha Tsui, or at Victoria Park in Causeway Bay. Otherwise, contact the Hong Kong Amateur Handball Association (☎ 2504-8119, fax 2577-5570), room 1013, Sports House, 1 Stadium Path, So Kon Po, Causeway Bay.

Hiking

Although trekking in Hong Kong is less challenging than the Nepalese Himalayas, some basic equipment is necessary. Most important is a full water bottle. Other useful items include food, a rainsuit, sun hat, toilet paper, maps and compass. Boots are not necessary – indeed, some people suffer lower back pain after hiking in heavy boots. The best footwear is generally a good pair of running shoes. If you're prone to getting blisters, take some plaster. Of course, just how much equipment you decide to drag along depends on how far you plan to walk.

Good maps will save you a lot of time and trouble. The Government Publications Office (see the Maps section at the beginning of this chapter) has a series of excellent topographical maps. The Universal Publications maps of the New Territories and outlying islands are detailed, easy to read and waterproof. The Country Parks Authority (☎ 2733-2132) in Kowloon and the HKTA also have useful leaflets detailing good hikes. If you really want to scour the trails, consider picking up a copy of Kaarlo Schepel's *Magic Walks in Hong Kong*, which has three different volumes. Another helpful volume is *Hong Kong Pathfinder* by Martin Williams, available in most Hong Kong bookshops.

Track conditions vary widely – not all are concrete paths. *Countryside* maps may describe a track as 'unmaintained/impassable'. This term may mean as little as the path is not concrete, to as much as the path is genuinely difficult or impossible to locate.

Serious walkers should remember that the high humidity during spring and summer is tiring. November to March are the best months for strenuous treks. At high elevations, like at the youth hostel at Ngong Ping on Lantau, it can get very cold so it's essential to bring warm clothes and even a down sleeping bag if you're staying the night.

The sun can be merciless, so a hat and UV lotion are essential. Even if there is cloud cover and no visible sun, you can still get bad sunburn at this latitude. There is little shade as there are few trees on the slopes of Hong Kong's mountains. One consequence of this is that landslides still occur during heavy rainstorms.

Very few hiking areas in Hong Kong are dangerous, but there have been several injuries and some deaths. The victims are mostly inexperienced walkers taking foolish risks. It is wise to stick to the established trails and heed the signs saying 'Steep and Seasonally Overgrown' or 'Firing Range'.

Snakes are rarely encountered, and can be avoided by sticking to the trails and not walking through dense undergrowth. If you see a snake, the best thing to do is to walk away. Most snakes are shy of large creatures, including humans, but will attack only when cornered. Hikers tend to get bitten when accidentally stepping on a snake or attempting to beat it with a stick.

Mosquitoes are a nuisance, so a good mosquito repellent is essential. Autan and Off! are popular brands available from Hong Kong drugstores. Mosquito coils (incense) are also effective when you're resting, but should not be used inside a tent or any other enclosed area – these are both a fire hazard and the smoke contains a poison that isn't particularly good for your lungs.

Hiking in Hong Kong has become so popular that many trails are crowded on weekends, so try to schedule your walks during weekdays. The four longest trails are (in descending order): the MacLehose Trail (New Territories), Wilson Trail (Hong Kong Island and New Territories), Lantau Trail (Lantau Island) and the Hong Kong Trail (Hong Kong Island). See the relevant chapters in this book for details.

To contact hiking clubs, call the Federation of Hong Kong Hiking and Outdoor Activities Groups (☎ 2720-4042) in Sam Shui Po. More serious climbers should try the Hong Kong Mountaineering Union (☎ 2747-7003, fax 2770-7115) which has training courses for leisure climbing, rock-climbing, sport climbing and mountain craft. Also contact the YMCA (☎ 2369-2211) and the YWCA (☎ 2522-3101), which regularly arrange a series of adventurous walks around such areas as Silvermine to Pui O, Shek O to Chai Wan and other popular routes. The Green Lantau Association (☎ 2985-5099) organises walks on Lantau Island.

Serious walkers can join in the annual Trailwalker event, a gruelling race across the MacLehose Trail in the New Territories. This 100km walk is a real challenge, but it cuts through some of the most exciting countryside in Hong Kong. For more information, call the Trailwalker Charitable Trust (☎ 2520-2525), c/o Oxfam.

Horseback Riding

Opportunities for horseback riding are limited. The Hong Kong Riding Union (☎ 2488-6886), Kowloon Tong, organises rides in the New Territories. On Hong Kong Island, riding lessons are available at the Pok Fu Lam Riding School (☎ 2550-1359). Classes are HK$340 per hour and there is a long waiting list. Other possibilities include the Lo Wu Saddle Club (☎ 2673-0066) and the Hong Kong Rider Club (☎ 2522-2142) – the latter organises outings for two days and a night for HK$880.

Karting

The big event of the year for karting enthusiasts is the Hong Kong Kart Grand Prix, held in late November or early December. For more details contact the Hong Kong Kart Club (☎ 2504-8293, fax 2577-8885), room 1015, Sports House, 1 Stadium Path, So Kon Po, Causeway Bay.

Lawn Bowling

Victoria Park in Causeway Bay has facilities for lawn bowling. These are open in the afternoon on week days and all day on weekends. There is a Lawn Bowls Association (☎ 2504-8249, fax 2577-5621)

HONG KONG TOURIST ASSOCIATION
The mountainous terrain on Lantau Island makes for some spectacular views.

in room 1022, Sports House, 1 Stadium Path, So Kon Po, Causeway Bay.

Martial Arts

Chinese *gongfu,* or kungfu as it's often called in the west, has formed the basis for many Asian martial arts. There are several organisations offering training in various schools of Chinese martial arts *(wushu),* as well as other Asian disciplines. Popular Chinese martial arts include taijiquan *(t'ai chi)* and wing chun, while karate, judo and aikido are Japanese, and taekwondo is Korean. Wing chun was Bruce Lee's original style, and is indigenous to the Hong Kong area. See the Martial Arts special section in the Facts about Hong Kong chapter.

It is a good idea to check the classified pages of the English newspapers and magazines for contact numbers. You could also go to the parks in the early morning in search of someone who will teach you. Among those listed below, the Hong Kong T'ai chi Association charges HK$500 a month for weekly classes (but the staff do not speak good English) and the Hong Kong Wushu Union only has classes for children. Relevant addresses include:

Chinese Martial Arts Association
(☎ 2504-8164)
Hong Kong Amateur Karatedo Association
(☎ 2891-9705) room 1006, Queen Elizabeth Stadium, 18 Oi Kwan Rd, Wan Chai
Hong Kong Chinese Martial Arts Association
(☎ 2394-4803) 9th floor, 687A Nathan Rd, Kowloon
Hong Kong Taekwondo Association
(☎ 2504-8116) room 1014, Sports House, No 1, Stadium Path, Causeway Bay
Hong Kong T'ai chi Association
(☎ 2395-4884) 11th floor, 60 Argyle St, Kowloon
Hong Kong Wushu Union
(☎ 2504-8226) 3rd floor, 62 Castle Peak Rd, Kowloon
South China Athletic Association
(☎ 2577-6932) 88 Caroline Hill Rd, Causeway Bay
Wing Chun Kung Fu Club
(☎ 2385-5908) 1st floor, No 12, Man Yuen House, Jordan Ferry Point, Kowloon

Wing Tsun Martial Arts Association
(☎ 2385-7115) 8th floor, A block, 440-442 Nathan Rd, Kowloon
YMCA
(☎ 2369-2211) 41 Salisbury Rd, Tsim Sha Tsui

If you want to stock up on butterfly knives, a wing chun pole, a wooden dummy, *Escrima* sticks, punchbags, a nine section staff, kungfu slippers, swords or just want to thumb through a decent collection of books on the martial arts, try Kung Fu Supplies Co (☎ 2891-1912), flat A, 6th floor, 188 Johnston Rd, Wan Chai.

Outward Bound

The Outward Bound School (☎ 2792-4333, 2792-0055) organises orienteering courses, camping, barbecues and teaches wilderness survival. It's geared towards helping young adults build character and self-esteem, though it is not limited to teenagers. The address is Tai Mong Tsai, New Territories.

Parachuting

It's not the cheapest of sports, but you can't beat it for thrills. If you enjoy diving out of aircraft, contact the Hong Kong Parachute Association (☎ 2791-4550). Jumps take place when the weather is good.

Running

Nothing beats the path around Victoria Peak on Harlech and Lugard Rds for a morning jog with spectacular views. Part of this is a 'fitness trail' with various exercise machines (parallel bars and the like). The jog along Bowen Rd, which is closed to traffic and runs in an east-west direction in the hills above Wan Chai, is almost as spectacular.

As long as there are no horse races, the racecourse at Happy Valley is an excellent place to run. There is also a running track in Victoria Park in Causeway Bay.

In Kowloon, a popular place to run is the Promenade which runs along the waterfront in Tsim Sha Tsui East. It's not a very long run, but the views are good and it's close to many of the hotels.

The Hong Kong International Marathon is held on the second day of the Chinese New Year. This has become a cross-border event and part of the course passes through China. The Coast of China Marathon is held in March. Contact the HKTA for more information on marathons.

For easy runs followed by beer and good company, consider joining Hash House Harriers (☎ 2857-7008, fax 2857-7226), GPO Box 1057. You do not need to be in particularly good shape to participate. The Hash is an international organisation geared towards the young and the young at heart.

Contact the Distance Runners Club (☎ 2579-8674, fax 2503-0003), GPO Box 10368, which can organise other people for you to run with. There is also a Ladies Road Runners Club (☎ 2537-4593, fax 2849-7854), PO Box 20613, Hennessy Rd Post Office, Wan Chai.

Every Thursday morning from 7 to 8.30 am, there is a running clinic. For information, call the Adventist Hospital (☎ 2574-6211 ext 777). If you take running seriously, contact the Triathlon Association (☎ 2504-8282, fax 2576-8253), room 1020, Sports House, 1 Stadium Path, So Kon Po, Causeway Bay.

Sauna & Massage

This is a great way to relax following any activity, whether it's been a strenuous hike through the hills or a frantic day of dodging fellow shoppers in Causeway Bay. Sauna baths are popular in Hong Kong and many offer a legitimate massage service. Most are for men only, but the hotels and a few of the saunas have facilities for women.

On Hong Kong Island one of the biggest places is the New Paradise Health Club (☎ 2574-8807), 414 Lockhart Rd, Wan Chai. Services include a sauna, steambath, Jacuzzi, and massage for both men and women. Sauna and massage, plus one drink, costs HK$238. Nearby the elaborate Sunny Paradise Sauna (☎ 2831-0123), 339-347 Lockhart Rd, is for men only and saunas start at HK$340. One of the oldest places in town is the funky Hong Kong Sauna (☎ 2572-8325) at 388 Jaffe Rd,

Wan Chai. This place is tiny and looks really seedy, but it's improving. Again, it only takes men and a one hour sauna and massage will cost you HK$218.

In Kowloon, another reputable establishment is Crystal Spa (☎ 2722-6600), basement 2, Harbour Crystal Centre, 100 Granville Rd, Tsim Sha Tsui. Go with a friend for HK$480. In Tsim Sha Tsui East is VIP Sauna (☎ 2311-2288), 13th floor, Autoplaza, 65 Mody Rd.

Scuba Diving

Diving in Hong Kong is not very rewarding as pollution has destroyed most of the interesting sea life and muddied the water. There are organisations that put together dives to reefs and islands further out from Hong Kong. Bunn's Diving Equipment (☎ 2893-7899) in Wan Chai organises dives every Sunday from 9 am to 4.30 pm for HK$280 – most of the dives are in Sai Kung. Bunn's also has branches in Mong Kok (☎ 2380-5344) and Kowloon (☎ 2382-0828). Other contacts to try are Scubamania (☎ 2792-0805) at 269 Hennessy Rd. Mandarin Divers (☎ 2554-7110) offers advanced, rescue, divemaster and instructor courses, as well as a whole range of other diving activities. Another company that can provide an array of courses from beginner to advanced is Pro Dive Education Centre (☎ 2890-4889, www.divehk.com), 2nd floor, 27 Paterson St, Causeway Bay. Equipment can be bought at Ming's Sports Co (☎ 2376-0031) in Kowloon.

Skating

One of the best ice skating rinks in Hong Kong is on the 1st floor of Cityplaza Two (☎ 2885-4697), Cityplaza Shopping Centre, 18 Tai Koo Shing Rd, Quarry Bay. The easiest way to get there is to take the MTR to Tai Koo station.

In Kowloon, the best rink is Whampoa Super Ice (☎ 2774-4899) in basement 2 of the Whampoa Gardens Shopping Complex in Hung Hom. Further afield is Riviera Ice Chalet (☎ 2407-1100), 3rd floor, Riviera Plaza, 28 Wing Shun St, Tsuen Wan, New Territories.

For ice dancing or ice hockey, contact the Hong Kong Ice Activities Association (☎ 2893-8443, fax 2827-5050), room 906, 18 Oi Kwan Rd, Wan Chai. This is also the location of the Ice Hockey Association.

If you prefer wheels to blades, visit the Rollerworld at Cityplaza Shopping Centre in Quarry Bay. There's also a roller rink in Telford Gardens shopping mall, next to Kowloon Bay MTR station. The Hong Kong Amateur Roller Skating Association (☎ 2504-8203, fax 2577-5671) should be able to provide information on other venues if you're feeling enthusiastic.

Soccer

Soccer has caught the imagination of the Chinese. The competition for playing fields on the weekends or holidays is keen, though you won't have much trouble getting a pitch during working hours. There are over 130 soccer pitches in Hong Kong, and you can call the Urban Services Department to locate those nearest to you. The Urban Services Department is itself segmented into neighbourhood divisions, so look in the Business Telephone Directory to find the relevant branch. Some notable soccer pitches include:

Blake Garden
   Po Hing Fong, Sai Ying Pun, Hong Kong Island
King George V Park
   Hospital Rd, Sai Ying Pun, Hong Kong Island
Kowloon Park
   Tsim Sha Tsui
Kowloon Tsai Park
   La Salle Rd, Shek Kip Mei
MacPherson Playground
   Sai Yee St, Mong Kok
Morse Park
   Fung Mo St, Wong Tai Sin
Southern Playground
   Hennessy Rd, Wan Chai,
Victoria Park
   Causeway Bay

To get serious about competing in matches contact the Football Association (☎ 2712-9122, fax 2760-4303), 55 Fat Kwong St, Ho Man Tin, Kowloon. The association has a women's division.

Squash

There are about 600 public squash courts in Hong Kong. These are full in the evening or on holidays. The most modern facilities are at the Hong Kong Squash Centre (☎ 2521-5072), next to Hong Kong Park in Central. It costs HK$27 per half hour, and you should book in advance. This is also the home of the Hong Kong Squash Rackets Association, which has done much to promote the sport. There are squash courts in the Queen Elizabeth Stadium (☎ 2591-1331) in Wan Chai.

In Sha Tin in the New Territories, you can play squash at the Jubilee Sports Centre (☎ 2605-1212).

Other venues include Kowloon Tsai Park (☎ 2336-7878) and Lai Chi Kok Indoor Sports Games Hall (☎ 2745-2796) in Kowloon. Also in Kowloon, the Kowloon Cricket Club (☎ 2367-4141) has squash facilities. The squash event of the year is the Hong Kong Squash Open, held in September.

Surfing

Not strictly allowed in Hong Kong, you do however find surfers holding their own at Big Wave Bay, Shek O.

Swimming

The most accessible beaches are on the south side of Hong Kong Island, but some of these are becoming increasingly polluted. The best beaches can be found on the outlying islands and in the New Territories. The longest beach in Hong Kong is Cheung Sha on Lantau Island. Some beaches verge on the idyllic – Hung Shing Ye beach on Lamma Island is fantastically serene in the early morning, despite the hulking power generating station opposite. The other thing to be wary of are shark attacks. The major beaches have shark nets (some in a state of disrepair), and you should think twice about swimming wherever you feel like (eg off the side of a pleasure boat).

There is an official swimming season from 1 April to 31 October. During this time, the 42 designated public beaches in Hong Kong are staffed with lifeguards and the shark nets are inspected daily. From the first day of the official swimming season until the last, expect the beaches to be chock-a-block on weekends and holidays. When the swimming season is officially declared finished, the beaches become deserted no matter how hot the weather.

At most of the beaches you will find toilets, showers, changing rooms, refreshment stalls and sometimes restaurants.

Hong Kong's Urban Council also operates 13 public swimming pools. There are excellent pools in Kowloon Park (Tsim Sha Tsui) and Victoria Park (Causeway Bay). Many pools shut for the winter, but heated pools exist, such as the South China Athletic Association (☎ 2890-7736), 88 Caroline Hill Rd, Causeway Bay, and Morrison Hill Swimming Pool (☎ 2575-3028), 7 Oi Kwan Rd, Wan Chai. For more information contact the Amateur Swimming Association (☎ 2572-8594) in Wan Chai or the Winter Swimming Association (☎ 9017-6685).

Table Tennis & Badminton
It's widely acknowledged that the Chinese are the best table tennis players in the world. Phone the Hong Kong Table Tennis Association (☎ 2575-5330) for information. It's not so widely known that the Chinese are also badminton enthusiasts. Contact the Badminton Association (☎ 2504-8318), room 2005, Sports House, 1 Stadium Path, So Kon Po, Causeway Bay, for details. There are similar facilities at the South China Athletic Association (☎ 2577-6932), 88 Caroline Hill Rd, Causeway Bay. You can also find facilities at the Aberdeen Indoor Games Hall (☎ 2553-6663), 168 Wong Chuk Hang Rd, Aberdeen.

Tennis
The Hong Kong Tennis Centre (☎ 2574-9122) is at Wong Nai Chung Gap, a spectacular pass in the hills between Happy Valley and Deep Water Bay on Hong Kong Island. It's open from 7 am until 11 pm, but it's only easy to get a court during working hours. It costs HK$42 per hour during the day and HK$57 per hour during the evening.

There are 14 courts, open from 7 am to 10 pm, in Victoria Park (☎ 2570-6186) that can be booked. There are four courts open from 7 am until 5 pm at Bowen Road Sports Ground (☎ 2528-2983) in the Mid-Levels – the cost is HK$42 per hour. The South China Athletic Association (☎ 2577-6932) also operates tennis courts at King's Park, Yau Ma Tei.

Other facilities in Kowloon are at Tin Kwong Rd Playground in Kowloon City and at Kowloon Tsai Park in Shek Kip Mei. In the New Territories, you can play tennis at the Jubilee Sports Centre (☎ 2605-1212) in Sha Tin.

The Hong Kong Tennis Association (☎ 2504-8266) is in Victoria Park. This is the place to ask questions about available facilities and upcoming events. In October, the Hong Kong Tennis Classic is held in Victoria Park.

Toastmasters Club
The purpose of this organisation is to give you practice in public speaking, to practice English (if it's not your native language) and to meet people. For some, it's a sort of dating service.

Actually, Toastmasters is not one organisation – there are many informal clubs that use the same name or some variation. The sponsors of the clubs are often companies who want to teach speaking skills to employees and thus build self-confidence. One is Victoria Toastmasters Club (☎ 9485-3236, fax 2847-7441), GPO Box 6038. Another is Hong Kong Toastmasters Club (☎ 2826-3489, fax 2352-2355), GPO Box 9384.

Waterskiing
The main venues for waterskiing are on the south side of Hong Kong Island at Deep Water Bay, Repulse Bay, Stanley and Tai Tam. The south side of Lamma Island also attracts waterskiers. The Deep Water Bay Speedboat Company (☎ 2812-0391) charges HK$580 per hour for boat and ski hire. Contact the Hong Kong Waterski Association (☎ 2504-8168) for more information.

Windsurfing

Windsurfing is extremely popular in Hong Kong; giving the city its first gold medal at the Atlanta Olympics in 1996. The best months for windsurfing are September to December when a steady north-east monsoon blows. Windsurfing during a typhoon is not recommended!

Around December, Stanley Beach becomes the venue of the Hong Kong Open Windsurfing Championship. At Stanley Main Beach on Hong Kong Island try the Pro Shop (☎ 2723-6816), which has a windsurfing course for HK$800 (four to five hours), or you can rent a board hourly for much less. Rental fees are typically from HK$60 to HK$80 per hour. The Stanley Windsurfing Centre (☎ 2813-2882) is an alternative. Shek O is another good place on Hong Kong Island for windsurfing.

Equipment rentals are available in the New Territories at the Windsurfing Centre (☎ 2792-5605), Sha Ha (just past Sai Kung). On Cheung Chau Island try the Cheung Chau Windsurfing Centre (☎ 2981-8316), Tungwan Beach – it's cheap but communication can be a problem. Also phone the Windsurfing Association of Hong Kong (☎ 2504-8255) which has courses from HK$800 (for children).

Yachting & Sailing

With water on all sides, it makes sense that sailing is an extremely popular activity in Hong Kong. The most prominent club is the august Royal Hong Kong Yacht Club, which has facilities throughout the territory. Even if you're not a member, you can check with any of the following clubs to see if races are being held and whether an afternoon's sail aboard one of the entrant vessels is possible: Aberdeen Boat Club (☎ 2552-8182); Aberdeen Marina Club (☎ 2555-8321); Hebe Haven Yacht Club (☎ 2719-9682); Royal Hong Kong Yacht Club (☎ 2832-2817); and the Hong Kong Yachting Association (☎ 2504-8158). Some clubs hire vessels, others just let you use club facilities where you can moor your boat.

If smaller sailboats or hobie cats (a type of small boat) are more your style, you may be able to rent one down at St Stephen's Beach, near Stanley. Hobies rent for around HK$150 to HK$200 per hour, depending on the size.

If there is a group of you, consider hiring a junk for the day or evening. This is a great way to see the outlying islands and New Territories, or sail out to Lamma or Lantau islands for seafood lunches or dinners. Included in the price is usually eight hours of vessel hire, plus a captain and deckhand. Charterboats (☎ 2555-8377) in Aberdeen hire out junks for HK$2500 (weekdays) and HK$3500 (weekends), which gives you a vessel that can seat 35 people. It is also possible to hire cruisers that can take up to 60 people. More expensive is the Aberdeen Marina Club (☎ 2555-8321), which hires junks for HK$5200 (weekdays) and HK$6200 (weekends). Other outfits that rent junks include The Boatique (☎ 2555-9355), Aberdeen, and Rent-A-Junk (☎ 2780-0387), Mong Kok.

One of the major events is the Hong Kong-Manila yacht race, which takes place every two years. Phone the Royal Hong Kong Yacht Club (☎ 2832-2817) for more details.

Other Activities

The following is a list of associations and clubs which offer activities that could be of interest:

Amnesty International	☎ 2300-1250
Archery Association	☎ 2504-8148
Astronomical Society	☎ 2547-4543
Backgammon Club	☎ 2782-2721
Balloon & Airship Club	☎ 2812-7847
Basketball Association	☎ 2504-8181
Birdwatching Society email hkbws@hkstar.com	
Bobsleigh Association	☎ 2827-5050
Bodybuilding Association	☎ 2504-8246
Boxing Association	☎ 2504-8130
Buddhist Association	☎ 2574-9371
Fringe Festival	☎ 2521-7251, fax 2868-4415
Golf Association	☎ 2522-8804
Human Rights Commission	☎ 2713-9165
International Kite Association	☎ 2443-2768
Mensa	☎ 2534-2999

Orienteering Club	☎ 7684-2842
Photographic Society	☎ 2527-5186
Raja Yoga Centre	☎ 2806-3008,
	fax 2887-0104
Rugby Football Union	☎ 2504-8311
Scout Association	☎ 2377-3300
Sport Climbing Association	☎ 2645-0341

COURSES

Hong Kong is a good place to brush up on your Chinese culture, whether it is learning how to make a decent pot of hot-and-sour soup, painting a classic landscape or speaking Cantonese. The following section includes some options for study. If you can't find what you're looking for, contact the Community Advice Bureau (☎ 2524-5444).

The YMCA (☎ 2369-2211) and YWCA (☎ 2522-3101) both offer a broad range of cultural classes and three month courses. Courses include just about anything – Basic Cantonese, Continuing Cantonese, cooking, Mahjong, watercolour painting, cardplaying, computer courses, qigong, taijiquan, wine tasting, tennis and loads more.

For the visual arts, check with the Hong Kong Museum of Art (☎ 2734-2167, 2734-2141), the Hong Kong Visual Arts Centre (☎ 2521-3008) and the Hong Kong Arts Centre (☎ 2582-0219).

Calligraphy

Most calligraphy courses in Hong Kong are given in Chinese, but the Hong Kong Arts Centre has some in English as well. You can also check with the School of Professional and Continuing Education at Hong Kong University (☎ 2547-2225).

Chinese Painting

Classes are dependant on demand, and you can check with the Hong Kong Arts Centre, the YWCA, and the School of Professional and Continuing Education at Hong Kong University (☎ 2547-2225).

Cuisine

Continuous classes in a vast range of Chinese, Thai and western cuisine are offered by the Towngas Cooking Centre (☎ 2576-1535) in Causeway Bay (Towngas also has classes in flower arranging).

The Home Management Centre (☎ 2510-2828) in North Point has classes on Wednesday morning, where you can learn three Chinese dishes in two hours for HK$85. The Oriental Culinary Institute (☎ 2882-3000) in Pok Fu Lam offers basic and advanced courses in Chinese and other Asian dishes, including dim sum, stirfry, abalone and bird's nest soup. Classes are HK$200, and are taught in Cantonese and English. In Mong Kok, Chinese cooking lessons are given at the Chopsticks Cooking Centre (☎ 2336-8433). To learn how to cook the perfect cake, try Baker's Dozen (☎ 2826-9283) at room 403, Yu Yuet Lai building, 43-55 Wyndham St, Central.

Dance

The Jean M Wong School of Ballet (☎ 2886-3992) has seven schools throughout the territory that offer courses in Chinese ethnic minority dance as well as Balinese dance, ballet, jazz dance and other western styles. Prices are reasonable at HK$150 per hour.

Salsa, Latin, ballroom, rock and roll, and disco classes are offered at Teresa Woods Dance Studios (☎ 2987-0592, the Web www.terrsawood.com), 18-20 Lyndhurst Terrace, Central. Check the classified pages of *HK Magazine* for other schools and dance routines.

Language

Not too many people take the time and considerable effort needed to learn Cantonese. With China's economy booming, demand for Mandarin classes has soared. However, Hong Kong is a not a brilliant place to learn Mandarin as you risk picking up an atrocious accent. Often the Chinese practise their Mandarin on foreigners rather than speaking Cantonese.

The Chinese University in Hong Kong offers regular courses in Cantonese and Mandarin. Classes can be arranged through the New Asia Yale centre in the China Language Institute. There are three terms a year – one 10 week summer term and two regular 15 week terms. Classes are also held by the School of Professional and Continuing Education at Hong Kong University (☎ 2547-2225). The British Council (☎ 2913-5500), the YMCA (☎ 2369-2211), the YWCA (☎ 2522-3101) and Venture (☎ 2507-4985) are good places to study Cantonese and Mandarin.

There are a number of private language schools that cater to individuals or companies. These informal schools offer more flexibility and even dispatch teachers to companies to teach the whole staff. Considering all the native Chinese speakers in town, tuition is not cheap, often running at around HK$300 plus for one-on-one instruction. Language schools to consider include the Chinese Language Institute of Hong Kong (☎ 2524-8678) in Central and the Chinese Language Society of Hong Kong (☎ 2529-1638) in Wan Chai.

Another approach is to look for schools and individual teachers in the classified sections of the *South China Morning Post*, *Hong Kong Standard* and English-language magazines. Alternatively, advertise yourself, looking for a teacher.

Pottery

The Pottery Workshop (☎ 2525-7949) at the Fringe, 2 Lower Albert Rd, Central, has classes as well as exhibitions.

WORK

Stretching the cash? It used to be the case that British citizens, British passport holders and registered British subjects did not need work visas. This has changed and everyone who wants to work in Hong Kong now has to obtain a work visa first.

Ironically, it has been even harder for mainland Chinese to come to Hong Kong to work (legally) since 1 July 1997 than it was before the handover (the last thing China wants is hundreds of thousands of Chinese relocating to Hong Kong in search of the much higher salaries and standards of living). Even so, about 50,000 mainland Chinese are legally moving to Hong Kong every year.

It is possible to obtain under-the-table employment, but there are stiff penalties for employers who are caught hiring foreigners illegally (the penalties are routinely advertised on TV and threaten a large fine and a stint in the slammer). These rules are vigorously enforced against employers who hire labourers from China. Despite the rules, westerners can still find temporary illegal work in Hong Kong, but there are considerable risks.

If you arrive as a visitor and get a job, you will probably have to leave at some point, apply for a visa and return when it is obtained – the easy-fix, quick run to Macau and back is no longer foolproof. Westerners are normally granted a work visa for six months and extensions should be applied for a month before the visa expires.

Success in finding work depends largely on your skills. Professional people such as engineers, computer programmers and accountants will have no problem landing a job, especially now that Hong Kong's well-educated class is emigrating in droves to Canada, Australia and elsewhere. However, those who do not possess these high technology skills are at a distinct disadvantage.

The job market in Hong Kong is adapting to the new realities of the post-handover period. The situation is far from stable, and it is impossible to predict future trends, but one consequence of all the uncertainty before the handover was that many skilled and talented Chinese people fled Hong Kong. While large numbers of these people returned or are returning, there are still professional positions available for foreigners in certain companies. This, however, does not apply to all companies, and some big names are only taking on people of Chinese descent.

In general, the Hong Kong job market is still energetic, dynamic and diverse. It's worth bearing in mind that job loyalty is a dirty concept in Hong Kong – some residents change jobs four times a year. The quest is always for a higher salary and employees are regularly enticed away from positions. This creates a swiftly changing job market, with bundles of choice – just look at the jobs section of the *South China Morning Post* on any Saturday for an idea of the range and volume of available jobs.

Many of the professional Hong Kong Chinese who made the permanent move away from the territory took with them their excellent English-language skills. This, coupled with an increasing emphasis on the use of Mandarin (in business and in the classroom), has led to a swift decline in the level of spoken English. This is creating job opportunities for foreigners trained as racecourse commentators, English language teachers, financial editors, magazine editors, TV and radio presenters and tour guides. Those with English-language teaching training (eg TEFL) will find a bountiful market for their skills (see the following Teaching section).

For professional jobs, registering with Hong Kong personnel agencies or headhunters is important. Drake (☎ 2848-9288) is a popular employment agency that often advertises – it's worth getting on the company's list. One can always check classified ads in the local newspapers. The Saturday edition of the *South China Morning Post* or the Friday edition of the *Hong Kong Standard* are particularly helpful. *Recruit*, a free job hunters' magazine is available after 5 pm on Friday and Monday in MTR stations. *HK Magazine* also has a useful jobs section.

The tax system has a highest marginal tax rate of 15%, and you don't pay any tax for your first year – though it's retrieved in your second year. Your first HK$100,000 is tax free. Many employers offer medical schemes and other incentives.

Living expenses in Hong Kong are quite high, especially rent, so be sure to reach an agreement on salary before you begin any job. In general, unskilled foreign labourers can negotiate salaries from HK$50 to HK$80 per hour. Your nationality makes a difference – unfair as it might seem, Filipinos and Thais earn considerably less than westerners for doing the same work.

Teaching

It's fairly easy to pick up work teaching con-

versational English, though you may find yourself doing a lot of commuting between part-time jobs. Teaching English is not always as easy as it sounds. If your students are good, it can be a pleasure, but if their English is poor, teaching can be both boring and frustrating.

At the time of writing, the Hong Kong Department of Education was advertising for native teachers of English (with school experience) to move to Hong Kong, enticed by the prospect of a HK$15,000 a month housing allowance and a basic salary in excess of HK$25,000 per month (the average salary in Hong Kong is about HK$12,000 a month). This led to an outcry from local teachers who do not receive a housing allowance.

If you don't have teaching qualifications, you can still contact schools about conversational classes. Alternatively you could advertise yourself as a one-on-one teacher of conversational English – you can expect to earn at least HK$200 an hour (many Hong Kong Chinese have their company pay for extra-curricular English lessons). A good idea is to advertise yourself locally (eg on Wellcome and Park N'Shop supermarket noticeboards). This way you can have all your students in the same area.

Qualified teachers with British passports, or a British spouse, could also apply to the British Council (☎ 2879-5138), ground floor, Easey Commercial building, 255 Hennessy Rd, Wan Chai, for full or part-time teaching posts.

Translating

If you're fluent in one or more foreign languages, you might get work as a translator. You can find dozens of companies listed in the *Yellow Pages for Consumers* under Translators and Interpreters. Some of these include KERN (☎ 2850-4455), Multilingual Translation Services (☎ 2581-9099), Polyglot Translations (☎ 2851-7232) and Language Line (☎ 2511-2677).

Bars & Restaurants

Good places to start looking for work in the

catering industry are bars and western restaurants in Lan Kwai Fong, Wan Chai, Tsim Sha Tsui and Yung Shue Wan on Lamma Island. Besides finding catering work, you may meet people in gwailo bars and restaurants with tips on English-teaching opportunities, modelling jobs, secretarial work and so on. Be warned that bars are coming under increasing pressure to recruit English-speaking Chinese bar staff and the number of vacancies is consequently drying up.

Movies & Modelling
Occasionally westerners can find work standing around as extras in Hong Kong movies (long hours and little pay). If you are a repository of terrific martial arts techniques, have a great sense of humour, possess appalling acting skills and a love of adventure, look out for parts as the baddie gwailo in Hong Kong's frenetic cinema industry.

Modelling is another possibility for both men and women. Modelling agencies are listed in the *Yellow Pages for Businesses*, but contacts are vital and the agencies are of limited help. Stunning looks and an impressive portfolio help.

MOVING TO HONG KONG
Moving Companies
If you're moving a household, consider the services of a moving company. The following companies handle both international and local moves:

Asian Express	☎ 2893-1000
Columbia International	☎ 2547-6228
International Worldwide Removal	☎ 2690-2829
Jardine International	☎ 2563-6653
Prudential Moving	☎ 2648-9282
Santa Fe Transport	☎ 2574-6204

Storage
A number of moving companies offer both short-term and long-term storage of household and commercial items. For a fee, these companies are happy to move the items in question and place them in a warehouse. Many of the warehouses (or *godowns* as they are known in Hong Kong) are in the To

Kwa Wan district of Kowloon, near Kai Tak airport. Some companies in this market include:

Fortune International	☎ 2770-2077, ☎ 2676-5981
Lap Sing Transportation	☎ 2571-8177, fax 2887-8147
Superior Removal	☎ 2545-7883, fax 2854-2746
Yan Yan Transportation	☎ 2891-4388, fax 2783-0715

ACCOMMODATION
In Hong Kong there are three basic accommodation categories: cramped guesthouses; adequate but uninspiring mid-range hotels; and luxury hotels, some of which are considered the world's finest. Within each category there is a good deal of choice, and you should be able to find a comfortable place to stay.

The prices, even for budget accommodation, are higher than most other Asian cities, and you don't get a whole lot for your money (except in some of the top-end hotels). It's worth bearing in mind that there was a turnaround in prices post handover, due to a decline in tourists. Many mid-range and luxury hotels were offering 'winter packages' to attract customers. Hotels were slashing up to 50% off the rate for single and double rooms. The general consensus is that if the tourist slump continues, prices will drop permanently.

The HKTA publishes a *Hotel Guide* that lists more than 80 Hong Kong hotels, complete with prices and photos. To get a hold of this before you leave home, contact the nearest HKTA overseas office (see the Tourist Offices section earlier in this chapter).

Reservations
Making a reservation for your hotel room is not essential, though you can save a lot of money if you do it the right way. If you fly into Hong Kong needing a place to stay, the Hong Kong Hotels Association (☎ 2383-8380, email hkha@att.net.hk) has reservation centres at the airport. Its staff can get you into

HONG KONG

a mid-range or luxury room sometimes 50% cheaper than if you were to walk in yourself. The HKTA deals with a total of 75 hotels and has a selection of brochures for each hotel so you can compare facilities. The centre does not handle any budget accommodation.

Booking hotels through a travel agent can also garner substantial discounts, sometimes as much as 40% off the walk-in price. If you're in Hong Kong and want to book either a mid-range or luxury hotel, call Phoenix Services (☎ 2722-7378, fax 2369-8884), room A, 7th floor, Milton Mansion, 96 Nathan Rd, Tsim Sha Tsui, which can often get you 20% to 30% off what you would expect to pay at the hotel. Another company that handles hotel bookings is Traveller Services (☎ 2375-2222, fax 2375-2233, www.traveller.com.hk), room 1012, Silvercord Tower 1, 30 Canton Rd, Tsim Sha Tsui. Also remember that, at the time of writing, many airlines and hotels were slashing prices to attract business. Airlines such as British Airways and Cathay Pacific were offering super-cheap return flights (for one or two) to Hong Kong with a set number of nights in a hotel.

Like anywhere else in the world, Hong Kong hotels require deposits for advance reservations.

Camping
Camping is permitted next to most International Youth Hostels Association (IYHA) youth hostels (it's prohibited at the Ma Wui Hall and Bradbury Lodge hostels). You have to pay a camping fee of HK$25 which permits you to use the hostels' toilet and washroom facilities.

Camping is generally prohibited on the 42 public beaches patrolled by lifeguards, but is OK on remote beaches.

Also, several government and independent campsites exist on Lantau Island and in the New Territories (see the New Territories chapter for details). Some campsites are listed in a HKTA camping leaflet.

The availability of fuel is limited, so the most useful kind of camping stove is the type that uses throw-away gas canisters – though

be sure to carry out your litter. A few high-tech camp stoves can use diesel fuel, which is readily available. Kerosene is very difficult to find and ditto for 'white gas'. Hong Kong locals use bags of charcoal for cooking in picnic and camping areas.

Hostels
The Hong Kong Youth Hostels Association (HKYHA, ☎ 2788-1638, fax 2788-3105), room 225, block 19, Shek Kip Mei Estate, Kowloon, sells IYHF cards for HK$110 to Hong Kong residents (HK$180 for non-residents). It can also give you a members' handbook which shows the locations of the hostels, and is the place to purchase various hostel paraphernalia (guide books, patches etc). The office is inconveniently located in a hideous housing estate near Shek Kip Mei MTR station. It is possible to buy membership cards at the hostels – be sure to bring a visa-sized photo along and some ID.

As at youth hostels in other countries, you are required to own a special IYHF sleeping sheet (you can buy or rent these at the hostels) and you must do a few simple cleaning chores.

Prices for a dormitory bed range from HK$35 to HK$65 a night, and a few hostels have family rooms for two/four persons at HK$220/260 a room. If you're not a member of the IYHF, you can still stay at the hostels, but you'll be charged considerably more – it pays to get a membership card if you're staying more than a few days.

Except for Ma Wui Hall (which is open all day), hostels close from 10 am to 4 pm on weekdays (some may stay open all day on weekends). All hostels are shut between 11 pm and 7 am – forget about late-night partying. Normally, travellers are not permitted to stay more than three days, but this can be extended if the hostel has sufficient empty beds.

Some of the more remote hostels shut down during mid-week, especially in winter. On the other hand, many are full to overflowing during the school holidays. For these reasons, you'd best ring up in advance to make sure a bed is available. If making a booking more than three days in advance, ring the HKYHA head office and secure a booking reference number. You can take this number to the hostel head office or any branch of the HongkongBank and pay into account No 002-645414-004 – be sure to keep the receipts to give to the hostel manager. International computerised bookings are also possible. To reserve a bed less than three days before your anticipated stay, call directly to the hostel and make the booking with the manager. The phone numbers of the individual hostels are listed in the Places to Stay sections of the relevant chapters in this book.

Warning Theft is a constant worry in any dormitory-style accommodation. The problem is your fellow travellers, not the management of the hostels. Most hostels have lockers available – be sure to use them. Remember, it only takes a minute for your camera or Walkman to walk away.

Guesthouses

Dominating the lower end of the market are the so-called guesthouses, usually a block of tiny rooms squeezed into a converted apartment or two. Often there are several guesthouses operating out of the same building. Even the cheapest option, a bed at one of the youth hostels, is no bargain at HK$50. The picture brightens if there are two of you. Find a room in a clean guesthouse for around HK$200 and your accommodation cost falls to a more bearable level. Even though the room may be a glorified closet, at least it's yours. Generally there is a public phone (although your room may have its own), which is free to use. Some guesthouses offer a fax service and email facilities.

Try and haggle for the best offer, as a lot of places may be eager to fill rooms. Some guesthouses are swish, with doubles for HK$500 or more. Prices are much cheaper in Macau – if it's budget accommodation you're after, it could well be cheaper (and more fun) to pop over to Macau on the ferry, spend a few days there and head back (just

don't gamble away your savings in the process!).

Hotels

Except in the outlying islands, there are no hotels that could be called 'budget accommodation'. Low-end places in the city are all guesthouses. Furthermore, there seem to be fewer and fewer hotels in the mid-range category – as time goes by, everything is moving upmarket and luxury hotels are abundant in Hong Kong. Don't forget the advice mentioned earlier in this section about booking your room through the Hong Kong Hotels Association or a travel agent where you can make a large saving.

Hong Kong's mid-range hotels are as expensive as the top-end places in other cities. High demand and soaring property values keep the accommodation costs high. Prices range anywhere from HK$600 (relatively scarce) to over HK$2000 for a double room. Singles are sometimes priced a bit lower. The average price you're likely to encounter is HK$1000, though there is little to distinguish one room from another.

At the very least rooms will have a built-in bathroom with shower, bath and toilet, air conditioning, telephone and TV. Some hotels also supply in-house cable TV systems, mini refrigerators, toiletries and other small amenities. Many have business centres, email facilities and other funky, modern gadgets. The Kowloon Hotel has small rooms, but bristles with technology. You get free email access (your own email address comes with your key), the TV doubles as a computer screen and the in-room fax can be used as a printer.

There are a few mid-range hotels that might be considered good deals. On Hong Kong Island, the Newton Hotel Hong Kong in North Point is quite nicely furnished and, once you're inside, feels a bit like a luxury hotel. It also has a rooftop pool with a great view. Over in Kowloon, the Eaton Hotel Hong Kong has comfortable rooms and good service, despite its relatively low rates. Staying at the Kowloon Hotel (which is run by the Peninsula group) allows you to use the pool, health club and other gorgeous facilities at the nearby Peninsula. The New Kings Hotel has recently had a facelift and has singles for HK$550 and doubles for HK$650 to HK$750. The International Hotel has similarly priced rooms. If you can manage to book a room at the Salisbury YMCA you'll be rewarded with courteous, professional service, a comfortable room and excellent exercise facilities.

Be warned that some mid-range hotels charge for local calls. You may get charged HK$5 a call, which is ridiculous considering the hotel does not get charged. Often this is not clearly stated, so check this out beforehand.

For those who can afford HK$2000 or more for a room, a stay in one of Hong Kong's luxury hotels is an experience worth savouring. Of course, you should be selective – there are plenty of average hotels that charge top-end rates. A few, such as the Peninsula, Island Shangri-La and Mandarin Oriental, offer comfort, amenities and service that can compete with the world's finest five star hotels. All of these hotels have an elegant range of suites, for those who want both space and comfort.

All of the top-end hotels are in the best locations and are set to a backdrop of stunning views. Typically facing Victoria Harbour, your room will look onto a wonderful nocturnal view of Hong Kong. As well as offering the finest in terms of comfort, many of these excellent hotels are home to some of the most famous restaurants and bars in Hong Kong. The Peninsula is crowned by Felix, creation of the French designer Philip Stark. An experiment in theatrical design and ingenuity, the restaurant has won plaudits not just for its form, but also for its fabulous international cuisine. The Peninsula also boasts Gaddi's – still holding onto its reputation as *the* French restaurant in Hong Kong. On the 25th floor of the Mandarin Oriental is Vong, a famous newcomer that offers Vietnamese, French and Thai food in sumptuous surroundings.

If shopping is on your itinerary, Hong Kong's best hotels have all the big names in fashion and style under one roof in elegant shopping malls. Speciality stores at these hotels are the place to go for that rare bottle of wine or long-sought after cigar.

If you stay in hotels you will find a 10% service charge and a 5% government tax added to your bill, but you won't be troubled with either in the guesthouses.

Homestays
Currently, the only homestay is the Tung O Bay Homestay (☎ 2982-8461, fax 2982-8424) on Lamma Island; an excellent retreat miles from pollution and noise and perched on the edge of a sandy beach.

See the Lamma section in the Outlying Islands chapter for more details.

Rental Accommodation
For definition purposes, a long stay means a month or more. Many hotels and guesthouses offer big discounts for monthly rentals.

See the Places to Stay section of the Outlying Islands chapter for details on the cheap retreats away from the overpriced stranglehold of Hong Kong Island and Kowloon.

Apartments It is worth looking at the 'flats' advertised almost daily in the property pages of the English press, starting at around HK$4000 a month (usually in the Kowloon area). These are whole floors in apartment blocks that have been converted by landlords into makeshift rooms that have a bathroom (no kitchen), TV, air-con and a phone. These apartments are not very attractive or clean and are not worth the money but are central.

It is worth remembering that Hong Kong Chinese prefer to live in the tall, modern, lift-equipped high-rises and shun the old, smaller tonglau, or 'Tang buildings', which are usually five to seven storeys tall and often don't have lifts. The tonglau are much cheaper than the high-rises and sometimes have more character (being older) though, are generally not as clean. There are no management fees, usually just a monthly cleaning fee which is only about HK$100. Tonglau buildings give you the opportunity to find an apartment at the top of a building which could give you a terrace on the roof. The Hong Kong Chinese are not wild about living in apartments with rooftop terraces, so these are not difficult to find and are only marginally more expensive than an apartment without a terrace. This gives you double the space (essential in Hong Kong) plus the chance to have endless barbecues.

In upmarketsville, the trendy gwailo housing estates all boast excellent surroundings, fine sea views, security guards and prices to match. Rents start at around HK$9000 a month for a studio flat and move up to around HK$20,000, or even HK$30,000 for three bedrooms. Management fees are a monthly extra. Many westerners who can afford such accommodation don't pay for it – their company does. On Hong Kong Island, you can find these estates on the Peak, the Mid-Levels, Pok Fu Lam (especially Baguio Villa), Happy Valley (Stubbs Rd), South Horizons, Deep Water Bay, Repulse Bay, Stanley and Shek O. In the New Territories, check out Tai Po (Hon Lok Yuen), Yuen Long (Fairview Park), Clearwater Bay and Sai Kung. In the outlying islands, only Discovery Bay on Lantau Island falls into this category.

A one bedroom apartment in the Mid-Levels will cost anywhere from HK$15,000 to HK$55,000 a month. That same apartment will go for somewhat less in Tsim Sha Tsui or Wan Chai. The districts on eastern Hong Kong Island, western Hong Kong Island (eg Kennedy Town is a popular expat refuge) and north-eastern or north-western Kowloon, are more affordable – you may find a 600 sq foot one bedroom apartment for HK$8000 a month. The most expensive place is the Peak, where rents can easily top HK$100,000 a month (nearly US$13,000). Also be aware that apartments are measured in square feet and the measurement in Hong Kong is taken from the outside wall surface *in*, so if the apartment looks smaller than you thought it would, this is the reason (especially if the block has thick walls).

The cheapest apartments are in the ugly public housing estates that tend to be concentrated in Kowloon. Half of all Hong Kong residents live in these places. Pets, particularly dogs, are prohibited, though people raise them surreptitiously.

A much better option is to find an apartment on Lamma Island. Most Chinese want to move from Lamma and live in a high-rise, leaving very cheap apartments behind. Lamma is a beautiful island that's very popular with gwailos. It's well serviced by restaurants and pubs. See the Places to Stay section in the Outlying Islands chapter for more details.

Apartments are generally rented with little or no furniture, but used furnishings can sometimes be bought from departing foreigners. Check the noticeboards at expat pubs or around expat housing areas (Lamma Island, for example, has a noticeboard by the ferry pier). Also check the classified advertisements of the weekend English-language papers.

One little trick that many gwailos have discovered is that practically all Chinese have a strong fear of anything associated with death. The result is that apartments with views overlooking cemeteries are always cheaper and almost always rented by foreigners. If you understand the principles of fungshui, then finding an apartment with bad fungshui gives you bargaining power over the landlord when deciding your rent.

If you are stuck for accommodation, 'leave' apartments are worth investigating. Employees on contract are rewarded every couple of years with long holidays and usually rent their apartments while away. The usual duration is three months, during which time you are responsible for the rent and the wages of the *amah* (servant). Some people even offer the apartment rent-free with only the amah's wages to pay. Leave apartments are listed under a separate heading (leave flats) in the classified advertisements section of the *South China Morning Post*.

Then, of course, there are the real estate agents. The agent's fee is generally equivalent to one month's rent. Other upfront expenses will include a deposit, usually equal to two months rent, and the first month's rental payment. This can add up to a lot of money. For contact details look in the *Yellow Pages* under Estate Agents.

Short-termers may be interested in 'serviced apartments', which are high-priced flats rented out for a short term (maybe one to three months). Thumb through the *Yellow Pages* under Serviced Apartments. Occasionally the property sections of the English-language newspapers also carry advertisements.

Residential burglaries are a problem in Hong Kong, so keep security in mind. Change the locks when you move in. A steel door helps and many places have bars on the windows. Even the apartments in the high-rises staffed by security guards have steel cage doors and grills on the windows – burglars have been seen climbing, spiderman-like, up the outer walls of such buildings, crowbar between teeth.

Offices If you're doing business in Hong Kong, a number of companies can rent you an instant office. You can rent an office with phone and fax, or you can rent secretaries and translators as well. Prices depend on how many staff you want, size, location, the length of the lease etc. Most places require a three month minimum. The HKTA can supply you with a list of companies that rent business offices.

As for buying property, Hong Kong's property prices are among the highest in the world. Another problem is the uncertainty about whether China will continue to respect the property rights of foreigners. Currently, an apartment in a public housing estate goes for about HK$1 million – if you can find one. Apartments elsewhere usually sell for a mere HK$5 million.

ENTERTAINMENT

The Saturday and Sunday English-language newspapers have weekend entertainment inserts listing current plays, films, cultural events and nightspots. Alternatively you can use either *HK Magazine* or *bc Magazine*. The HKTA publishes the *Dining and Nightlife* pamphlet, which lists the telephone numbers, addresses and operating

hours of businesses, but unfortunately only gives a vague idea of the service.

For cinemas, concerts and various cultural performances, you can book tickets over the phone from Cityline (☎ 2317-6666) – you book using a credit card and then collect the ticket at the theatre from a vending machine.

Canto-Pop, Rock & Jazz

Canto-pop is the name for the local pop music. Concerts by Hong Kong stars such as Andy Lau, Faye Wong, Aron Kwok, Jackie Cheung, Beyond and Li Ming are frequent. If you give Canto-pop a chance, you will find some excellent tunes.

A few bars, most notably the Jazz Club, bring in well known artists from time to time. Most of these are jazz and blues musicians.

There are usually a few decent rock bands playing around town, and there are numerous bars with house bands that play dance tunes.

Hong Kong is not a friendly environment for musicians. The few bars that dare to book original bands are usually small or lack a decent sound system. With the high rents in the bar districts, you can be sure that a lot of musicians are on stage for little, if any, pay. However, things do seem to be picking up as more and more bars feature live music. The local audience is increasingly receptive to bands that play something other than pop tunes or classic rock. At the time of writing, one of the most popular local bands, with a cult following, is The Bastards.

A number of pubs and clubs have Filipino bands who can play 'Hotel California' in their sleep, and yours. Other places have more experimental evenings. Some pubs have jam nights, so take your guitar along and practise your chords. See the Entertainment sections in the Hong Kong Island and Kowloon chapters for more information.

Cultural Events

In Hong Kong there are cultural performances every week, often featuring foreign ensembles. Chinese classical or folk music concerts are less frequent.

It's cheaper to go to performances by local ensembles like the Hong Kong Philharmonic or the Hong Kong Chinese Orchestra. The Hong Kong government subsidises the cost of bringing in foreign acts, so the prices are sometimes reasonable. Tickets range from as low as HK$50 for a seat at the back of a local performance to HK$300 for something like the English Chamber Orchestra.

In addition to the Hong Kong Cultural Centre, classical music concerts are often held at City Hall (☎ 2921-2840) in Central and the Hong Kong Academy for Performing Arts (☎ 2584-8514) in Wan Chai.

Hong Kong has a diverse number of gallery exhibitions. Take time to visit a few and avail yourself of the opportunity to find out more about not only contemporary Chinese art, but also Vietnamese, Japanese, Korean, Russian and western art. The Fringe Gallery (☎ 2521-7251) at the Fringe Club has regular exhibitions. Consult *HK magazine* and *bc Magazine* for a comprehensive list of galleries and exhibitions.

The *South China Morning Post* and *Hong Kong Standard* have cultural sections that will give you the latest scoop on art exhibitions, film festivals, opera, meetings, concerts, beauty pageants, lion dances and so on.

The HKTA, the Urban Council and the Arts Centre have cultural programs that include events such as performances by Cantonese opera troupes, piano recitals, Fujianese puppet shows, Chinese folk singers and exhibits of Chinese watercolours. Information can be obtained from the Arts Centre or HKTA offices. For information on arts festivals see the Public Holidays & Special Events section in this chapter.

HK Magazine, *bc Magazine*, the HKTA's *Hong Kong Diary* and the entertainment sections of the English-language newspapers all have details on venues, performance times, ticket prices and bookings.

Many performances are held at the Hong Kong Cultural Centre (☎ 2734-2010) in Tsim Sha Tsui, so it may be worth stopping there to pick up a monthly schedule.

Bookings for most cultural events can be made by telephoning URBTIX (☎ 2734-9009) from 10 am to 8 pm. Tickets can either be reserved with an ID card or passport numbers (and picked up within three days of ordering), or paid for in advance by credit card. You can collect tickets at one of the many URBTIX outlets throughout the city. Bring your passport or ID for proof of identity. There are URBTIX windows at the City Hall in Central, the Hong Kong Arts Centre in Wan Chai and the Hong Kong Cultural Centre in Tsim Sha Tsui. Some Tom Lee Music stores also have URBTIX facilities. *HK Magazine* lists all URBTIX outlets.

Cultural Centres

You can ring up Hong Kong's cultural centres to ask about upcoming performances. However, it would seem that this doesn't always work too well:

I rang up the Coliseum to find out who would be playing at the evening concert and was told 'a bunch of gwailos'. I said 'well yes, but what's the name of the band?'. They said 'just some gwailos from England, with long hair and guitars'.

Jenny Chan

There are two main cultural centres in Kowloon. The Hong Kong Cultural Centre (☎ 2734-2010), 10 Salisbury Rd, Tsim Sha Tsui, is home to the Philharmonic Orchestra and Chinese Orchestra. The Ko Shan Theatre (☎ 2334-2331), Ko Shan Rd, Hung Hom (near the KCR station) holds small performances.

Cultural centres on Hong Kong Island include the following: the Academy for the Performing Arts (☎ 2584-8514), 1 Gloucester Rd, Wan Chai; the Hong Kong Arts Centre (☎ 2877-1000), 2 Harbour Rd, Wan Chai; City Hall Theatre (☎ 2921-2840), Edinburgh Place, next to the Star Ferry terminal in Central; the Institute for Promotion of Chinese Culture (☎ 2559-4904), room 1001-5, 5 Shun Tak Centre, 200 Connaught Rd, Sheung Wan; the Sheung Wan Civic Centre (☎ 2853-2678), 5th floor, 345 Queen's Rd, Sheung Wan; and the Sai Wan Ho Civic Centre (☎ 2568-3721), 111 Shau Kei Wan Rd, adjacent to Sai Wan Ho MTR station.

The New Territories has three cultural centres: Sha Tin Town Hall (☎ 2694-2536), 1 Yuen Ho Rd, Sha Tin; Tuen Mun Town Hall (☎ 2452-7300), 3 Tuen Hi Rd, Tuen Mun; and Tsuen Wan Town Hall (☎ 2414-0144), Yuen Tun Circuit, Tsuen Wan.

Several countries have set up centres in Hong Kong to promote an understanding of culture and society. All of them offer language courses, and most show films or host seminars. A few also have libraries.

The largest of these centres is the British Council (☎ 2913-5125), recently relocated in new offices at 3 Supreme Court Rd, Admiralty. Its main role is to provide English- language classes and community access to British expertise in science and technology, but it also sponsors cultural programs and has a library that can be used for free (though you have to be a member of the library to take out books, CDs and videos). The library also offers free Internet access. This is a good place to leaf through recent papers and magazines from the UK.

The Alliance Française (☎ 2527-7825), 2nd floor, 123 Hennessy Rd, Wan Chai, also has a library and offers a wide range of cultural activities. Dante Alighieri (☎ 2573-0343), 704 Trinity House, 165-171 Wan Chai Rd, Wan Chai, is the Italian cultural society and offers courses in language and other subjects.

For German books, films or just the chance to meet a fellow German speaker, contact the Goethe Institut (☎ 2802-0088) on the 14th floor, Hong Kong Arts Centre, 2 Harbour Rd, Wan Chai.

La Sociedad Hispanica de Hong Kong (☎ 2407-8800) offers classes in Spanish language and culture and organises Spanish meals, video evenings and so on. Its address is GPO Box 11751, Hong Kong.

Concerts

The live music scene is improving as new concert halls and venues open. In previous years there were no decent band venues. The territory had stadiums, but none were large enough to pack in the numbers needed by profit-conscious band managers. There were problems with noise pollution and neighbours complaining.

Misunderstandings between artists and ticket organisers were common. In 1997 Michael Jackson's lawyer had to write to a Hong Kong concert organiser, threatening to sue if the organisers continued to claim that the megastar was going to perform in Hong Kong. However, an increasing number of bands and solo acts do perform in Hong Kong without drama, including Sting, Primal Scream, Oasis and Prodigy.

Concerts are usually held either at the HITEC Rotunda (☎ 2620-2222) in Kowloon Bay or in the new extension to the Convention and Exhibition Centre in Wan Chai. These are not huge venues, so the ticket prices are exorbitant – HK$480.

Another venue is the Hong Kong Coliseum (☎ 2355-7233), 9 Cheong Wan Rd, Hung Hom. This is a 12,500 seat indoor facility next to Kowloon KCR station. The sound is abysmal, but this is where some of the big international acts play.

Smaller acts are sometimes booked into the Ko Shan Theatre (☎ 2334-2331) on Ko Shan Rd, Hung Hom. In this venue the sound isn't great, but the back portion of the seating area is open-air, and the theatre is fairly small so most seats give you a good view.

Known mainly as the site of the wildly popular Hong Kong Rugby Sevens event, the Hong Kong Stadium (☎ 2895-7895) at Eastern Hospital Rd, Causeway Bay, is Hong Kong's largest venue for sporting and cultural events. It was expanded recently to seat 40,000 rugby fans, but the government figured that it would also be a good way to attract big-name music acts from abroad.

Unfortunately the planners didn't take into account the local residents, who after the first few concerts raised a tremendous stink about the noise and crowds. Bureaucrats scrambled to find a solution, and at one point someone suggested turning off the stage speakers and issuing concert-goers with earphones!

The only other big place to see a band is Queen Elizabeth Stadium (☎ 2591-1347), 18 Oi Kwan Rd, Wan Chai. This stadium is OK for sporting events, but it's a lousy place to see a concert – you'd get better acoustics in an empty aircraft hanger.

Clubs & Discos

Hong Kong has developed an active club scene, and many bars have started offering dance and thematic club nights. This evolution has been aided by the arrival of good, professional DJs whose sole mission is to dream up ever more seamless, innovative mixes to keep people on their feet. Most of the club nights take place on Friday and Saturday, but there are some mid-week venues. Cover charges range from HK$50 to HK$150, but look out for theme nights where you might be allowed in free if you're among the first 50 through the door in 70s gear (or whatever). As with most bars and clubs in Hong Kong, beer and drinks range from HK$30 to HK$70 at the really expensive places.

Both *HK Magazine* and *bc Magazine* have club night listings, and the latter also boasts a regular column, 'Club Scene'. It's a good idea to check as things are fluid – club nights come and go, and venues fall in and out of fashion.

Serious clubbers should look at the possible schedules in *HK Magazine* and *bc Magazine* for upcoming events in Shenzhen, Guangzhou and even Taiwan. Every now and then raids over the border are made by organisers (with DJs in tow) to widen the frontiers of clubland. The border with Shenzhen closes at 10.45 pm and reopens at 7 am, which fits in just fine with club hours. See the Shenzhen section in the Guangzhou chapter for more details.

For the non-raver, there are plenty of straightforward discos where you can dance till you drop, or the sun rises, whichever comes first. See the Entertainment sections in the Hong Kong Island and Kowloon chapters for a list of addresses.

Hostess Clubs

How does it feel to be legally mugged in Hong Kong? To find out, just visit one of the many sleazy-looking topless bars along Peking Rd (and adjacent streets) in Tsim Sha Tsui.

Be wary of places where an aggressive tout, sometimes female, stands at the front door, and tries to persuade you to go inside. In the past touts would grab travellers by the arm and try to pull them inside, but the government finally banned this practice after numerous complaints. However, the rules are suspended during the Chinese New Year, when you practically have to beat them off with a stick. By the way, touts often solicit couples, not just males.

It's very likely that there will be signs on the front door promising 'Drinks Only HK$40' and naughty pictures to stimulate interest. Inside, a cocktail waitress, usually topless and often wearing nothing but her knickers, will serve you a drink. She will probably be friendly and chat for a few minutes. It will be one of the most expensive conversations of your life – after a pleasant five minute chat you will be presented with a bill for about HK$500.

When you protest, staff will undoubtedly point to the tiny sign posted on the wall behind a vase which informs you of the HK$400 service charge for talking to the waitress. If you balk at paying this fee, don't be surprised if two muscular thugs suddenly happen to be standing by your elbows. Congratulations, you've now met Hong Kong's notorious Triads. The bill can be paid with travellers cheques and if you really don't have enough money, try bargaining – it works anywhere else in Hong Kong.

Hostess clubs come in two varieties – the sleaze-pits mostly found in Tsim Sha Tsui, and the 'respectable establishments' in Tsim Sha Tsui East. The difference is that the sleaze-pits blatantly try to cheat customers, while the respectable pits don't need to cheat – these businesses are very upfront about the high prices. The line-up of Mercedes and Rolls-Royces outside the door should suggest just what sort of clientele frequents these places. The respectable hostess clubs offer live music, featuring Filipino bands and topless dance shows (that is, the dancers are topless, not the Filipino bands). An evening out in any of these places could easily cost a cool HK$1000 or

The Triads

At one time the Triads, or secret societies, may have been a positive influence in China. It is said the Triads opposed the corrupt and brutal Qing (Manchu) dynasty and aided the revolution that brought down the Qing in 1911. The fact that Kuanti, the God of War, has been adopted by the Triads has probably lent some respectability to these organisations.

Unfortunately, the Triads that exist now are the Chinese equivalent of the Mafia. Sporting such catchy names as Bamboo Union and 14K, the Triads have been increasingly successful at recruiting disaffected teenagers in Hong Kong's high-rise housing estates. Initially offering young people a bit of companionship and adventure, the 'fun' soon turns to illegal gambling, extortion, protection rackets, the smuggling of drugs and weapons, prostitution, loan sharking, and sometimes robberies of banks and jewellery shops. Like most such organisations, once you join a Triad you cannot quit. *Gwailos* are not welcome – even the Triad-controlled prostitution business centred in Mong Kok and Sham Shui Po shuns foreign clientele.

Membership in a Triad is illegal in Hong Kong – it's even illegal to claim to be a member. Yet the Triads seem to be growing and have been trying to use wealth to muscle into legitimate businesses: a recent target has been Hong Kong's movie industry. Many fear that the growing influence of the Triads will drive out legitimate businesses and hurt Hong Kong's economy in the long term.

It was the Communists who smashed the Triad-controlled opium selling business in Shanghai after the 1949 revolution. The Triads have not forgotten this and in 1997 many Hong Kong-based criminals moved operations to ethnic Chinese communities in countries like Australia, Canada and the USA. Even the poverty-stricken Philippines has received some of this 'overseas investment' – Triad-arranged kidnappings of wealthy Chinese families living in the Philippines has become a growth industry. Ironically, some Triads are expanding into mainland China, establishing links with corrupt government officials and high-ranking soldiers in the People's Liberation Army (PLA).

Foreigners visiting Hong Kong seldom encounter Triad members directly except possibly in two places – the 'copy-watch' spruikers along Nathan Rd and the bouncers in sleazy hostess clubs. Fortunately, it's easy enough to avoid doing business with these unpleasant characters – buy a Swatch instead, and do your drinking in Lan Kwai Fong or Wan Chai.

---

more. This is beyond the means of most middle-class Hong Kong residents.

Karaoke

The word *karaoke* (empty orchestra) is borrowed from the Japanese. Basically, it's sing-along video tapes. Most of the songs are in Chinese. English versions are also available. If you are learning Chinese, this could be your chance to learn to sing in Cantonese:

Somehow amazed that I could speak Cantonese, these two guys at the Fountainhead Bar in Yung Shue Wan invited me to sing a few numbers at the karaoke parlour nearby. Struggling through four numbers by Andy Lau and Jackie Cheung in Mandarin and Cantonese had an immediate effect; I returned to my table to find it stacked with free drinks, courtesy of the management. The manager also invited me for lunch at his brother's restaurant down the road the next day.

Mahjong

If you walk down the side streets of Hong Kong, sooner or later you are bound to hear the rattle of mahjong pieces. Mahjong is so popular in Hong Kong that there are licensed mahjong centres where you can meet other players and gamble all day. Hong Kong is a good place to play mahjong, but there is a lot of local talent and you'll be up against the professionals. If you want to visit a mahjong centre, it may be a good idea to take a Chinese person along.

Theatre

Local theatre groups mostly perform at the Hong Kong Arts Centre, the Academy for Performing Arts or the Hong Kong Cultural Centre (see the Cultural Events section in this chapter for details). Performances are mostly in Cantonese, though summaries in English are usually available. Tickets range between HK$60 and HK$200, depending on the seats and the venue.

Smaller theatre companies occasionally present plays at the Fringe Club (☎ 2521-7251), 2 Lower Albert Rd, Central. Often the themes are local and feature amateur actors.

Pubs

Since there is substantial British influence in Hong Kong, it's not surprising that British-style pubs are plentiful – especially in the tourist areas. Often the owners are British or Australian, and you can expect authentic decor, meat pies, darts and sometimes Aussie bush bands.

Depending on where you go, beers typically cost HK$35 a pint (unhappy hour), which is likely to be more expensive than the shirt you'll be wearing if you've bought any clothes in Hong Kong. Overall, Lan Kwai Fong on Hong Kong Island is the best area for pubs, but there are also plenty in Kowloon.

SPECTATOR SPORTS

Sporting events are well covered in the sports section of Hong Kong's English-language newspapers. These sporting events don't fall on the same day every year, so contact the HKTA for further information.

Cricket

The Hong Kong International Cricket Series is held in late September to early October every year. This two day event at the Hong Kong Stadium sees teams from Australia, England, India, New Zealand, Pakistan and the West Indies battling it out in a speedy version of the usually long and drawn out game.

Horse Racing

Gambling is deeply ingrained in Chinese culture, though, to be fair, it was the British who introduced horse racing to Hong Kong. Without a doubt, horse races are now Hong Kong's biggest spectator sport.

Apart from mahjong games and the twice weekly Mark Six Lottery, which generates money for the government, racing is the only form of legal gambling in Hong Kong. The first horse races were held in 1846 at Happy Valley racecourse on Hong Kong Island, and became an annual event. Now there are about 65 meetings a year at Hong Kong's two racecourses, and around 450 races in total. The newer and larger track is at Sha Tin in the New Territories, and has seats in an air conditioned enclosure which can accommodate 70,000 people (see the New Territories chapter for more details).

While you don't need your passport to attend a race, you do need one if you want to get a tourist ticket. These tickets are worthwhile, especially when the race track is crowded – there have been times when up to 50,000 race fans have been turned away! If you qualify for a tourist ticket, you'll be admitted despite the crowds – you can also walk around next to the finish area. In order to qualify, your passport must show that you've been in Hong Kong for less than 21 days.

The HKTA has Come Horse Racing tours to Happy Valley and Sha Tin. See the Organised Tours section in the Hong Kong Getting Around chapter for details.

The racing season is from late September to June. Normally, races at Sha Tin are held on Saturday from 1 to 6 pm. At Happy Valley, races are normally on Wednesday evening from about 7 to 11 pm; however this schedule isn't followed religiously. Sometimes extra races are held on Sunday or holidays. Check with the HKTA in late September or early October to get the schedule for the coming season.

Betting is organised by the Hong Kong Jockey Club (HKJC). Many types of betting combinations are available, including: the quinella (picking the first and second); or double quinella (picking the first and second from two races); the treble (picking the winner from three specific races); and the six-up (picking the first or second from all six of the day's races). Off-track betting is also permitted. The HKJC maintains off-track betting centres at 39-41 Hankow Rd in Tsim Sha Tsui, at 64 Connaught Rd, Central.

If you want to attend the races, a seat in the public stands at Happy Valley costs HK$10. A visitor's badge to sit in the members' box costs HK$50. These badges can be purchased at the gate on the day of the race, or up to two days in advance at any branch of the HKJC.

You are not allowed to bring mobile phones into the track, but special small lockers are available for storage!

Rugby

The Seven-A-Side Rugby Tournament, popularly known as the Rugby Sevens, sees teams from all over the world come together in Hong Kong every March (or early April) for three days of lightning fast (15 minute) matches. Even non-rugby fans scramble to get tickets, for in addition to the sport, there's a lot of action in the stands. For many, the Rugby Sevens is a giant, international, three day party.

Getting tickets is the hard part, as many are reserved for the members of overseas rugby clubs. Hong Kong companies, public relations firms and society's upper-crust also get sizeable allocations, leaving little for ordinary fans. Information on ticket sales is carried in the local newspapers, usually sometime in mid-February.

For details on the tournament and buying tickets, contact the Hong Kong Rugby Football Union (☎ 2504-8311), room 2001, Sports House, 1 Stadium Path, So Kon Po, Causeway Bay. The HKTA's overseas offices may also be able to provide you with information.

Soccer

Hong Kong has a fairly lively amateur soccer league. Games are played on the pitches inside the Happy Valley Horse Racing Track and at Mong Kok Stadium. The sports section of the English-language papers carries information on when and where matches are held. Alternatively you can contact the Hong Kong Football Association (☎ 2712-9122), 55 Fat Kwong St, Ho Man Tin, Kowloon.

Tennis

Several international tennis tournaments are held annually in Hong Kong. The largest is the Salem Open (held in April) and the Marlboro Championship (usually in October). The tournaments are held in Victoria Park in Causeway Bay. Check the local English-language newspapers for information on times and ticket availability.

SHOPPING

'Shop till you drop' is the motto of many visitors to Hong Kong. While it's true that the city resembles one gigantic shopping mall, a quick look at the price tags should convince you that shopping in Hong Kong is not a bargain. Imported goods like Japanese cameras and electronic gadgets can be bought for roughly the same price in many western countries. What makes Hong Kong shine is the variety – if you can't find it in Hong Kong, it probably doesn't exist.

There are some good deals on clothing, footwear, luggage and other items that are made in China and require little technology to produce. Though even these prices are on the rise as China's rampant inflation continues to drive up workers' wages and other production costs.

There could well be a shake up in the future, as retailers have been hit hard by the dismal tourist figures after the handover. The collapsing prices of shares, the rapidly depreciating property market and the overall negativity compounded the damage. To make things worse, newspapers revealed that the Japanese were being seriously ripped off by hotels and shops. The Japanese responded by taking holidays elsewhere. Realistically speaking, falling property prices should drag down retail rents and prices.

The HKTA can give you information to get you started, but don't accept it as gospel. The HKTA produces both a handy little booklet called *Shopping* which recommends shops that are HKTA members – though we have found some of these members to be less than charitable – and the *Official Shopping Guide*. Another reference, Fiona Campbell's *The Guide to Shopping in Hong Kong*, is a thorough introduction on where to shop.

Duty Free

Hong Kong is a duty-free port, and the only imported goods on which there is duty are alcohol, tobacco, perfumes, cosmetics, cars and some petroleum products. In general, almost anything – cameras, electronics, jewellery and so on – will be cheaper when you buy it outside duty-free shops.

If you want to buy duty-free cigarettes and liquor, you might do better buying these on the aircraft. The other option is to buy from the duty-free shops in Macau (at the ferry pier) or at the border crossing at Shenzhen. Alternatively, just wait until you get to another country – most other airports in Asia offer better deals on duty-free items than what you'll find in Hong Kong's airport.

Guarantees

There are too many cases of visitors being sold defective equipment and retailers refusing to honour warranties. Every guarantee should carry a complete description of the item (including model and serial numbers), as well as the date of purchase, the name and address of the shop it was purchased from, and the shop's official stamp.

Many imported items come with a warranty registration with the words 'Guarantee only valid in Hong Kong'. If it's a well known brand, you can often return this card to the importer in Hong Kong to get a warranty card for your home country. It's best to do this while you're still in Hong Kong, as doing it by post from abroad is risky.

A common practice is to sell grey-market equipment (ie imported by somebody other than the official local agent). Such equipment may have no guarantee at all, or the guarantee might only be valid in the country of manufacture (which will probably be either China or Japan).

If you buy goods such as cameras and computers at discount prices, make sure – if you really need the latest model – that the model hasn't been superseded. Contacting an agent is one way of obtaining a detailed explanation of what each model actually does, though many agents won't be interested in talking to you. The HKTA *Official Shopping Guide* has a list of sole agents and phone numbers in the back of the pamphlet.

Always check prices in a few shops, take your time and return to a shop several times if necessary. Don't buy anything expensive in a hurry and always get a manufacturer's guarantee that is valid worldwide. When comparing camera prices, for example, make sure you're comparing not only the same camera body but also the same lenses and any other accessories.

Refunds & Exchanges

Many shops will exchange defective goods, or in the case of clothing, if the garment simply doesn't fit. Be sure to keep receipts and go back to the shop as soon as possible.

Forget about refunds. These are almost never given in Hong Kong. This applies to deposits as well as the final payment. There is really no reason to put a deposit on anything unless it is being custom-made, like a fitted suit or a pair of glasses. Some shops might ask for a deposit if you're ordering an unusual item that's not normally stocked, but this isn't a common practice.

If you put a deposit on something, don't ever expect to see the money again.

Receipts Receipts can often just be a scrap of paper with an illegible Chinese scrawl, but it is in your interest for it to be printed and legible. This will pay off if you need to change the purchased item later, or if customs question you on the price of goods purchased abroad (ask your consulate in Hong Kong for exact rules and regulations concerning customs and duties) or for insurance purposes upon your return home. Insist on getting an itemised receipt and avoid handing over the cash until you have both the goods and a receipt.

Rip-Offs

Caveat emptor, or 'buyer beware', are two words which should be embedded in your mind while shopping in Hong Kong, especially during that crucial moment when you hand over the cash.

Rip-offs do happen. While most shops are honest, there are plenty which are not. The longer you shop in Hong Kong, the more likely it is that you'll run into a shopkeeper who is crooked. It would be wise to learn how to recognise the techniques of rip-off artists.

The HKTA recommends that you only shop in shops which display the HKTA membership sign. This sounds like great advice except that many of the best shops are not HKTA members.

The most common way to cheat tourists is to simply overcharge. In the tourist shopping district of Tsim Sha Tsui, you'll rarely find price tags on anything. Checking prices in several shops therefore becomes essential. However, shopkeepers know that tourists compare prices in several locations before buying, so staff will often quote a reasonable or ridiculously low price on a big-ticket item, only to get the money back by overcharging on small items or accessories.

You may be quoted a reasonable price on a camera, only to be gouged on the lens cap, neck strap, case, batteries and flash. If you realise that you are being ripped off and casually ask why you're being charged 10 times the going rate for a set of batteries, you'll probably be told in no uncertain terms to 'get the hell out'.

Overcharging is easy to spot, but so many dishonest shopowners are even more sneaky. These shopowners sometimes remove vital components that should have been included free (like the connecting cords for the speakers on a stereo system) and demand more money when you return to the shop to get them.

You should be especially wary if staff want to take the goods into the back room to 'box it up'. This provides ample opportunity to remove essential items. The camera case, included free with most cameras, will often be sold as an accessory. Another tactic is to replace some of the good components with cheap or defective ones. Only later will you discover that the 'Nikon' lens turns out to be a cheap copy. When it's time to put your equipment in the box, it's best if you do it yourself.

Another sneaky ploy is to knowingly sell defective merchandise. Your only safeguard is to inspect the equipment carefully before handing over the cash.

Also be alert for signs of wear and tear – the equipment could be second-hand. Here are two experiences of dissatisfied customers:

They took a deposit and demanded an extra $800 for the camera when I came for delivery ... used abusive language and started fights.

I signed a receipt for a US$200 disc player. The staff member had another receipt underneath the first one and produced a $30 record player when he went to put the disc player in a box. So I ended up with a $30 record player which cost $200 and a receipt for a record player (switched!).

Getting Help There isn't much you can do if a shop overcharges, but if you discover that the goods are defective or something is missing, return to the shop immediately with the goods and receipt. Sometimes it really is an honest mistake and it'll be cleared up at once. Honest shopkeepers will exchange defective goods or replace missing components. On the other hand, if the shop intentionally cheated you, expect a bitter argument.

If you feel you were defrauded, don't expect any help from the police. There is an unfortunate lack of consumer protection in Hong Kong. There are a few agencies that might be able to help you. The first place to try is the HKTA (☎ 2807-6177). If the shop is a member, the HKTA can apply pressure, but don't expect miracles. If you file a written complaint, the only penalty the HKTA can impose is to revoke the shop's membership (which incidentally, costs HK$15,000 in annual dues).

Another place to try is the Hong Kong Consumer Council's (HKCC) complaints and advice hotline (☎ 9229-2222). HKCC has advice centres, including: ground floor, Harbour building, 38 Pier Rd, Central (☎ 9221-6228); and ground floor, Morning Joy building, 141-143 Kau Pui Lung Rd, Tokawan, Kowloon (☎ 9226-4011). The Small Claims Tribunal (☎ 2825-4667) is the place to contact for claims less than HK$15,000. The Community Advice Bureau (☎ 2815-5444) can help you find a lawyer.

As a last desperate measure, you can take matters into your own hands. By this we don't mean you should punch the shopkeeper, which might be satisfying but isn't legal. It is entirely legal to stand outside the shop and tell others about your experience. Some pickets have successfully had their money returned after driving away other customers. This can be an exhausting way to spend your time in Hong Kong and results are by no means guaranteed.

Fake Goods Watch out for counterfeit-brand goods. Fake labels on clothes are the most obvious example, but there are fake Rolex watches, fake Gucci leather bags, fake jade, fake jewellery, fake herbal medicines and even fake electronics. Some fakes are better than others – we saw a tracksuit top emblazoned with its interpretation of Adidas – 'Adiads'. Obviously there's more risk buying electronic goods than buying clothes, shoes or luggage. The pirated music tapes and CDs are often poor quality and have a tendency to rapidly deteriorate. One of the big retail scams at the time of writing was the sale of dodgy Guangdong-made speakers for HK$10,000 a pair, advertised as a top of the range model from the USA. The speakers were worth HK$250 at the most. This sort of thing happens on a regular basis. If you haven't heard the brand name and the goods are expensive, don't buy.

Hong Kong's customs agents have been cracking down on the fake electronics and cameras, and the problem has been pretty

much solved. However, counterfeit brand name watches seem to be very common. If you discover that you've been sold a fake brand name watch when you thought you were buying the genuine article, it would be worthwhile contacting the police or customs because this is definitely illegal.

Shipping Goods

Goods can be sent home by post, and some shops will package and post the goods for you, especially if it's a large item. Also, find out whether you will have to clear the goods at the country of destination. If the goods are fragile, it is sensible to buy 'all risks' insurance. Make sure you keep all the receipts.

Sometimes doing it yourself can save money, though it may not be worth the hassle. Smaller items can be shipped from the post office. United Parcel Service (UPS, ☎ 2735-3535) also offers services from Hong Kong to 40 other countries. It ships by air and accepts parcels weighing up to 30kg. UPS has an office in the World Finance Centre, Canton Rd, Tsim Sha Tsui.

Among the better known companies are DHL (☎ 2765-8111). Check the *Yellow Pages Commercial/Industrial Guide* for further listings.

Shopping Hours

There are no hard and fast shopping hours in Hong Kong, but shops in the four main shopping areas are generally open as follows: Central and Western districts from 10 am to 6 pm; Causeway Bay and Wan Chai from 10 am to 10 pm; Tsim Sha Tsui, Yau Ma Tei and Mong Kok from 10 am to 9 pm; and Tsim Sha Tsui East from 10 am to 7.30 pm. Causeway Bay is the best part of town for late-night shopping.

Most shops are open seven days a week, but on Sunday or holidays many only open from 1 to 5 pm. Street markets are open every day and well into the night (with the exception of the Jade Market in Kowloon, which is open from 10 am to 3.30 pm). Almost everything closes for two or three days during the Chinese New Year holiday period. Just before the Chinese New Year is the best time to make expensive purchases – everything goes on sale during this time so shops can clear out old stock.

Where to Shop

The three major shopping districts are Causeway Bay, Tsim Sha Tsui and Mong Kok. Each has something different to offer, though all have one thing in common – constant, dense crowds.

Causeway Bay has perhaps the largest weekend crowds and the broadest spectrum in terms of price. The high-end is well represented by numerous designer clothing shops and a cluster of Japanese department shops (Sogo, Mitsukoshi, Daimaru and Matzusakaya). Times Square is a vast shopping experience. There are plenty of shops selling medium-priced clothing, electronics, sporting goods and household items. In this area you can also stumble upon lively street markets. Tower records and HMV can both be found in Causeway Bay. Jardine's Bazaar and the area behind it are home to stalls and shops peddling cheap clothing, luggage and footwear.

Tsim Sha Tsui is a curious mixture of tackiness and sophistication. Nathan Rd itself is a huge avenue of camera, watch and electronics shops, and leather and silk emporiums. Despite being the worst part of town for bargain hunters it is also strong in luxury and quality goods, and a large number of designer and signature shops congregate in the area. Some of these lie along Nathan Rd, but the bulk are found in Harbour City – an enormous labyrinth of a shopping complex that stretches nearly 1km from the Star Ferry terminal north along Canton Rd. For middle and low-priced clothing you can try the back streets east of Nathan Rd.

Mong Kok caters mostly to local shoppers, and it offers good prices on clothing, sporting goods, camping gear, footwear and daily necessities. There's nothing very exotic, but for everyday items it's a popular spot.

Hong Kong's finest luxury offerings are mostly found in the glittering shopping malls in Central and Admiralty. The Landmark, Galleria and Pacific Place, among others, have branches of most international luxury retailers as well as some homegrown varieties. Some of Hong Kong's top jewellery and accessories shops are also in these districts. Tsim Sha Tsui East has a string of mostly upscale shopping malls, the biggest being the Tsim Sha Tsui Centre at 66 Mody Rd.

For antiques, head to Hollywood Rd in Sheung Wan, where there is a long string of shops selling Chinese and Asian items. Some of the really good spots have genuine finds, but be careful what you buy.

Wan Chai is another good spot for medium and low-priced clothing, sporting goods and footwear, but like Mong Kok, the area caters mainly for locals. Wan Chai has no glamour, but it's well worth sifting through for bargains. Being further from the main business districts, these malls charge retailers lower rents, which can translate into lower prices for consumers. One of the biggest of these is Cityplaza, an enormous shopping complex in Quarry Bay at Tai Koo MTR station. Up in the New Territories the Sha Tin New Town Plaza is another mammoth mall, and can be easily reached by taking the train to Sha Tin KCR station.

For budget shopping, there's no better place to start than at one of Hong Kong's street markets. Hong Kong's biggest street market is the night market held on Temple St, which basically runs parallel to Nathan Rd in Yau Ma Tei. If it's cheap (and in many cases shoddy) it'll be available: clothes, cassettes, fake designer goods, watches, leather goods, pens, alarm clocks, radios, knives, cheap jewellery, pirate CDs and tapes, illegal porn, potions, lotions and hundreds of other downmarket items. Alongside the market are numerous noodle and seafood restaurants and stalls where you can grab a bite in between purchases. The market runs roughly from 6 pm to midnight.

The Tung Choi St market, two blocks east of Mong Kok MTR station, mainly sells cheap clothes. People start setting up their stalls as early as noon, but it's better to arrive between 6 and 10 pm, when there's a lot more on offer. Another bustling market is on Apliu St (open from noon to 9 pm) in Sham Shui Po, one block west of Sham Shui Po MTR station.

If you're looking strictly for clothing, try Jardine's Bazaar in Causeway Bay. A bit more upscale and fun is the Stanley market, located in the village of Stanley on southern Hong Kong Island.

At any of these markets, it's good to check out the shops on the sides of the street, which are hidden behind all the street stalls. This is often where you'll find the real bargains, if there are any, and the staff are generally less pushy.

Another possible bargain option is going to one of Hong Kong's factory outlets. Most of these deal in ready-to-wear garments, but there are a few that also sell carpets, shoes, leather goods, jewellery and imitation antique pieces. Often prices aren't that much less than in retail shops. It's important to always check purchases carefully, as refunds are rarely given and many articles are factory seconds and imperfect.

If you decide to shop in the factory-outlets, it's highly advisable to invest HK$69 in a copy of *The Complete Guide to Hong Kong Factory Bargains* by Dana Goetz & Caroline Radin, sold in most bookshops. This gives a thorough rundown on what to expect and could save you a lot of time. The HKTA also has a useful handout on factory outlets.

Shopping Malls
Malls provide convenient shopping, and the scale of Hong Kong's malls means that you can find most of what you want all in one place. Most malls are open seven days a week. The following list contains the largest of Hong Kong's shopping malls.

Citiplaza
  111 King's Rd, Tai Koo, Quarry Bay. The largest shopping centre in eastern Hong Kong and directly linked up to the MTR.
Harbour City
  5 Canton Rd, Tsim Sha Tsui. A vast conglomeration of malls fused into one.

New World Centre
  20 Salisbury Rd, Tsim Sha Tsui. This is one of Kowloon's major malls.
Prince's building
  Chater Rd, Central. A quieter and more civilised shopping experience.
The Galleria
  9 Queens Rd, Central. A classy enclave of top-end shopping.
The Landmark
  16 Des Voeux Rd, Central. Lots of classy designer labels all under one roof.
The Mall
  Pacific Place, 8 Queensway, Admiralty. Easily reached by MTR, this mall has everything, including a handy UA cinema complex. It's crowded on weekends.

What to Buy
Antiques & Curios Hong Kong has a rich and colourful array of Asian antiques and curios – treasures await both the serious and not-so-serious collector. Serious collectors of art and antiques, including ceramics, will probably restrict themselves to the reputable antique shops and auction houses.

Caution is the by-word for this game, for Hong Kong is the receptacle of a whole array of forgeries and expert reproductions. Among this ersatz crowd shine some gems from China and South-East Asia, including, genuine examples of Ming and Qing furniture, Tibetan carvings, beautiful ceramics and works of art, Korean and Japanese treasures, traditional Chinese landscape paintings, calligraphic scrolls and snuff bottles. Just remember that most of the really good pieces are in private collections and are often sold either through Christie's or Sotheby's.

Most of Hong Kong's antique shops are bunched along Hollywood Rd in Sheung Wan. The shops make for a fascinating stroll – religious statues and carvings lean against each other among a jumble of antique furniture, screens and wall-hangings. The shops at the western end of Hollywood Rd tend to be cheaper in price and carry more dubious antiques, however, these shops also stock a wide range of old books and magazines, propaganda posters, badges from the

Cultural Revolution, and all sorts of bric-a-brac from China and Hong Kong.

The more reputable places should have price tags that state the antique's name, age and whether any restoration work has been done. If you're interested in a piece, ask if the vendor can supply a certificate of authenticity. Try to haggle the price down and ask for trade terms if you are in the business yourself.

Serious antique buyers should check out the auction houses. Sotheby's Hong Kong (☎ 2524-8121), 18th floor, Tower Two, Lipo Chun Chambers, 189 Des Voeux Rd and Christie's (☎ 2521-5396), 28th floor, Alexandra House, 16-20 Chater Rd hold two sales yearly, in April and November – check the Shopping section of the Hong Kong Island chapter for more details.

For Chinese arts and crafts the main places to go are the large China-run department shops scattered throughout the territory. You can get all sorts of hand-carved wood pieces, ceramics, paintings, enamel and *cloisonné*, calligraphy, jade, silk garments and even bolts of silk. Many pieces are garish, modern souvenir items, and are much cheaper to buy in China.

One of the biggest chains is Chinese Arts & Crafts – which occasionally stocks valuable pieces. A bit more pedestrian is the Yue Hwa Chinese Products Emporium, but it is a great place to pick up little gifts for friends. Similar in quality and selection are CRC department shops.

There are also a few antique shops in the Harbour City complex in Tsim Sha Tsui, but getting a good price there is said to be considerably difficult. These antique shops are mainly concentrated in a corridor of shops called The Silk Road. Along this road you will find cloisonné, bronzes, jade, lacquer, ceramics, rosewood furniture and screens.

Serious antique shoppers should pick up a copy of *Hong Kong Antique, Fine Art and Carpet Galleries* by Barbara Anderson. It's available at most bookshops and, although it's dated, it's still a comprehensive pocket guide.

Hong Kong is also an excellent place to buy fine art. The city's galleries display a rich and varied selection of Chinese modern and traditional art, regional and South-East Asian art, and Russian and western art. Galleries also provide a perfect opportunity to relax after the hustle and bustle of Hong Kong streets. For information on specific shops that deal in antiques, consult the Shopping sections in the Kowloon and Hong Kong Island chapters.

Appliances & Electronics Sham Shui Po is a good neighbourhood to search for electronic items. You can even buy (and sell) second-hand goods. If you take any of the west exits from the MTR at Sham Shui Po station, you'll find yourself on Apliu St. This is one of the best areas in Hong Kong to search for the numerous permutations of plug adapters you'll need if you plan to use your purchase in Hong Kong, Macau or mainland China.

Mong Kok is another very good neighbourhood to look for electronic gadgetry. Starting at Argyle St and heading south, explore all the side streets running parallel to Nathan Rd, such as Canton Rd, Tung Choi, Sai Yeung Choi, Portland, Shanghai and Reclamation Sts.

There are also quite a few electronics shops in Causeway Bay, with windows stuffed full of camcorders, CD players and other goodies. Locals generally avoid these places – apparently many of these shops are under the same ownership, ensuring that the prices are high throughout the area. Also, it's probably best to avoid the shops in Tsim Sha Tsui, many of which are skilled at fleecing foreign shoppers.

Though the selection isn't as good, the Fortress group of shops is quite reliable, and will always give you a warranty with your purchase. There are branches all over Hong Kong, including Central, Causeway Bay, Sheung Wan, Tsim Sha Tsui and Wan Chai.

Remember that most electrical appliances in Hong Kong are designed to work with 220V. Some manufacturers now equip computers, stereos and video machines with an international power facility that automatically senses the voltage and adapts to it. Others include a little switch for 110/220V operation. Also make sure you have the correct plug for wherever you plan to use your equipment.

Cameras When shopping for a camera, keep in mind that you should never buy one that doesn't have a price tag. This will basically preclude 99% of the shops in Tsim Sha Tsui. The best place to look for cameras is Stanley St in Central (see the Shopping section in the Hong Kong Island chapter). Tsim Sha Tsui has a couple of shops on Kimberley Rd dealing in used cameras. See the Photography & Video section in this chapter for photography tips and the Rip-offs entry in this chapter for shopping tips.

Carpets Carpets are not really that cheap in Hong Kong, but there is a good selection of silk and wool (new and antique) carpets. Imported carpets from Afghanistan, China, India, Iran, Pakistan, Tibet and Turkey are widely available. The best carpets have a larger number of knots per square inch (over 550) and are richer in detail and colour than cheaper carpets. Silk carpets are generally hung on the wall rather than used on the floor. Older carpets are dyed with natural vegetable dye. The bulk of Hong Kong's carpet and rug shops are clustered on Wyndham St in Central. There are also a few places in Ocean Terminal, Tsim Sha Tsui.

Clothes & Shoes The emphasis in Hong Kong is on slick and neat fashion, the chic rather than the radical, and the result is a very well-dressed and stylish city.

For bargain clothes, one of the best known places is Granville Rd in Tsim Sha Tsui. The eastern end is not much more than a row of down-market shops with bins and racks of discount clothing, including a fair amount of factory rejects. Clothes are definitely cheap, but the selection isn't great, and you need to check carefully for any flaws.

In general the shops with permanent signs carry better stock, and this is where

you'll have a better chance of getting something that is really good value for money. Also take the effort to check the upstairs shops: some of these places have good deals on silk garments. There are cheap places on Nathan Rd that veteran Hong Kong shoppers avoid. Most of the brand name items are fake, and fall apart after several washes.

On Hong Kong Island, Jardine's Bazaar in Causeway Bay has low-cost garments, though it may take some hunting to find anything decent. There are several sample shops and places to pick up cheap jeans in Lee Garden Rd and Li Yuen St in Central.

The street markets at Temple St (Yau Ma Tei), Tung Choi St (Mong Kok) and Apliu St (Sham Shui Po) have the cheapest clothes, both in terms of price and quality. These are OK places to pick up T-shirts and you may find something else you like, especially in the shops that are hidden behind the stalls. Tung Choi St and adjacent Sai Yeung Choi St South are also good places to hunt for sports shoes and hiking boots.

For mid-priced items, Causeway Bay and Tsim Sha Tsui, particularly east of Nathan Rd, are good hunting grounds. Take the time to pop into one of the dozens of Bossini, Baleno, Giordano, U2 or Esprit clothing chain stores. These specialise in well made and affordable mainstream fashion items. Marks & Spencer also has a number of branches in Hong Kong.

The section of Lockhart Rd near the Sogo department store in Causeway Bay is a good place to look for footwear. Check around though, as some places have considerably better prices than others on the same product. It's also worth taking a stroll down Johnston Rd in Wan Chai, which has lots of mid-priced and budget clothing outlets.

For top-end choice, head to the shopping malls in Central and Tsim Sha Tsui and the Japanese department stores in Causeway Bay. Nearly all the world's top international designers are represented in Hong Kong, and there are some interesting local fashions as well.

In Central, the best places for top-end garments, accessories and footwear are the

Landmark, the Galleria, the Prince's building and the Pedder building. In Admiralty, the Pacific Place shopping mall has an impressive array of mid-range and top-end shops. In Tsim Sha Tsui, the Harbour City complex has many clothing and shoe shops. Locals say that the shops in Central, while expensive, generally give better value for money than those in Harbour City.

Although people still flock to Hong Kong's tailors, getting a suit or dress made is no longer a great bargain. For a quality piece of work you'll probably pay close to what you would in New York or London. An exception might be some of the Indian tailors on the streets of Tsim Sha Tsui; however, remember that you usually get what you pay for; the material is often decent, but it may be a shoddy construction job. Some of these places offer same-day suits. Bear in mind that most tailors will require a 50% non-refundable deposit. The more fittings you have, the more comfortable you will feel.

Computers Hong Kong is a popular place to buy personal computers. While prices are competitive, it is also important to pay careful attention to where and what you buy. Computers are prone to breakdowns, so finding a shop with a good reputation for honesty is vital. Before leaving Hong Kong it's important to run the computer continuously for several days to make sure it's free of defects.

You may have your own ideas about what kind of computer you want to buy, but if you're leaving Hong Kong you would be wise to choose a brand name portable computer with an international warranty, such as Hewlett-Packard, Compac or Acer.

Many shops will be happy to sell you a generic desktop computer custom-designed to whatever configuration you desire. Buying a generic machine might make sense if you will be living in Hong Kong for at least a year (the typical warranty period). Assuming that the shop stays in business for a year, the warranty will probably be honoured. However, if the dealer proves to be inept or dishonest, you may have to go else-where for repairs and pay for the service. In general, buying a brand name is safer.

You may be hit with a steep import tax when you return to your home country. Save your receipt because the older the machine, the less you're likely to pay in import duty. The rules in many countries say that the machine is tax-exempt if over one year old, and some shops in Hong Kong will even write you a back-dated receipt on request for this purpose!

Some Hong Kong computer shops still sell pirated computer software, although the authorities have cracked down on this. Bear in mind that besides being illegal, pirated programs often contain computer viruses – there is even one called 'AIDS' and wearing a condom offers no protection whatsoever.

Ivory Ivory jewellery, chopsticks and ornaments used to be big sellers in Hong Kong, fuelling the demand for tusks and contributing to the slaughter of Africa's already depleted elephant population. In 1989 the Hong Kong government signed the Convention on International Trade in Endangered Species (CITES) treaty which effectively bans the import of raw ivory.

In the meantime, the only carved ivory products being sold in Hong Kong are those which were supposedly manufactured before the ban went into effect. Ivory retailers need to have all sorts of documentation proving where and when the goods were made. Many countries now ban the importation of ivory altogether, no matter how or when it was manufactured.

If you want to purchase ivory pieces while in Hong Kong (no matter how small), you have to obtain an import license from your home country and an export license from Hong Kong. If you are in Hong Kong and want to purchase ivory, check with your consulate for advice and with the Hong Kong Agriculture and Fisheries Department (☎ 2733-2282).

Jade The Chinese attribute various magical qualities to jade, including the power to prevent ageing and keep evil spirits away.

It's a pity then that jade doesn't have the magical ability to prevent lying. Fake jade exists – the deep green colour associated with some jade pieces can be achieved with a dye pot, as can the white, green, red, lavender and brown of other pieces. Green soapstone and plastic can be passed off as jade too.

Most so-called Chinese jade sold in Hong Kong comes from Australia, New Zealand, South Africa and the USA. One trick of jade merchants is to sell a supposedly solid piece of jade jewellery which is actually a thin slice of jade backed by green glue and quartz.

It is said that the test for jade is to try scratching it with a steel blade – real jade will not scratch. Another story is that water dropped on real jade will form droplets if the stone is genuine.

There are two different minerals which can be called jade: jadeite from Myanmar (Burma) and nephrite (commonly from Canada, China, New Zealand and Taiwan). Unfortunately, you would have to know your Burmese jade pretty well to avoid being fooled. While the colour green is usually associated with jade, a milk-white shade is also highly prized. Shades of pink, red, yellow, brown, mauve and turquoise come in between.

The circular disc with a central hole worn around many necks in Hong Kong represents heaven in Chinese mythology. In the old days, amulets and talismans of jade were worn by Chinese court officials to denote rank, power and wealth. One emperor was reputed to have worn jade sandals, and another gave his favourite concubine a bed of jade.

If you're interested in looking at and possibly purchasing jade, head to the jade market in Yau Ma Tei, about 10 minutes walk from Yau Ma Tei MTR station. Unless you're fairly knowledgeable about jade, it's probably wise to limit yourself to modest purchases. The jade market is open daily from 10 am to 3.30 pm.

Serious buyers will probably stick with jewellery dealers of repute and, of course, with the Sotheby's and Christie's auctions, which sparkle with some of the finest jade specimens in the far east. The modern jade and jadeite jewellery sales have spectacular

pieces. The advantage of buying through auction is that you can easily research the history of the piece (through previous auction catalogues and certificates of authenticity) and the auctions attract international dealers of standing, which means the word generally gets around if there is a fake or a piece of doubtful authenticity on view.

Jewellery If you have ever tried to sell a second-hand diamond ring to a jewellery shop, you no doubt already know that the price of used jewellery is a fraction of what it costs new. Yet shops that buy second-hand jewellery turn around and sell it for close to what it costs new.

The moral of the story is that buying jewellery as an investment is a non-starter. Don't buy jewellery in Hong Kong (or anywhere else) with the idea that you can sell it for more in your home country. The only way to make money from jewellery is to be well connected with a supplier and to have your own retail outlet.

One of the great myths of the jewellery business is that the high prices in the shops reflect the rarity of the materials. While it's true that uncut diamonds sold in bulk cost far more than zircons, the high prices charged reflect the fact that people are willing to pay a lot for shiny rocks and metals. A ring with US$5 worth of raw materials can sell for US$100 in the shops. If the materials are worth US$100, the retail price can be US$1000, and so on.

Part of what you pay for is the labour involved in making the rocks look good. The jewellery export business is big in Hong Kong. This is because gemstones are imported, cut, polished, set and re-exported using cheap Chinese labour. In theory, this should make Hong Kong a cheap place to purchase jewellery. In practice, retail prices are only marginally lower than elsewhere.

Your only real weapon in getting a decent price is the intense competition in Hong Kong. Jewellery has a large mark-up and there is considerable latitude for bargaining. However, the jewellers have a weapon, namely the inability of the common tourist to judge good quality jewellery from bad. Can you distinguish a pure diamond from a zircon? A flawed diamond from a perfect one? Most people cannot. To become an expert on jewellery requires considerable training. The law requires jewellers to stamp the content on gold and platinum products, but that isn't much help when it comes to judging gems.

If you don't think you can spot a real from a fake, at least be sure about where you buy. If the items you want to buy do not have price tags attached, that's a serious danger sign and you should go elsewhere. Shops in the trendy shopping arcades of the Tsim Sha Tsui tourist combat zone are going to be the most expensive.

Opals are said to be the best value in Hong Kong because this is where opals are cut. Diamonds are generally not a good deal, because the world trade is mostly controlled by a cartel. Hong Kong does not have a diamond-cutting industry and must import from Belgium, India, Israel and the USA.

A couple of reputable jewellers will issue a certificate that not only states exactly what you are buying, but guarantees that the shop will buy it back at a fair market price. It's worthwhile buying from one of these places – if you later become dissatisfied with your purchase, you can at least get most of your money back on a trade-in. Two chain stores which give this guarantee are King Fook and Tse Sui Luen.

Finally, after you've bought something and want to find out its value, you can have it appraised. This is a service you get charged for, and some stones (such as diamonds) may have to be unset for testing. You can contact the Gemmological Association of Hong Kong (☎ 2366-6006) for the current list of approved appraisers. One company that does appraisals is Valuation Services (☎ 2869-4350), 11 MacDonnell Rd, Central.

Leathers & Luggage As with clothing, the manufacture of luggage and leather goods is low-tech and labour intensive, which means that China is the perfect place to open a factory. Lots of what gets produced in main-

land China is pure junk – zippers and straps that break instantly, and 'leather' that often proves to be vinyl.

Fortunately, most of what gets sent to the Hong Kong market is export quality, but check carefully because there is still a lot of rubbish on sale. All the big brand names like Gucci and Louis Vuitton are on display in Hong Kong department stores, and you'll find some local vendors in the leather business with odd names like Mandarina Duck and Companion Reptile. To be sure, you'll find a wide selection and a big spread in price.

The best advice for buying this kind of stuff is to take your time to carefully inspect zippers, straps and stitching. Look on the inside of the luggage, as the outside may be tough leather or nylon but the inside could be cheap vinyl. Decide early on if you need an expensive label or just durability at the lowest possible price.

Music Hong Kong is pretty much on the ball when it comes to tunes. HMV (inquiries ☎ 2377-9797) is constantly flinging open the doors to larger and larger music supermarkets. The Central building branch is massive, and is open seven days a week from 10 am to 10 pm. You can listen to a whole range of CDs before purchasing – this means it's easy to spend the whole day wearing headphones and staring at the carpet. CDs are cheap – with chart discs selling for around HK$110. HMV also does a large range of video CDs, Digital Video Discs (DVDs) and music/film mags. Don't expect to find tapes anywhere though – it's CDs only. HMV can be found in: the Central building, Pedder Street, Central; Swire House, Central; Windsor House, Causeway Bay; Sands building, Peking Rd, Tsim Sha Tsui; and New Town Plaza, Sha Tin. Tower Records (☎ 2506-0811) is also in town, in Times Square, 1 Matheson Street, Causeway Bay.

It's worth looking out for are the KPS video rental stores, some of which also have a pretty good range of CDs for sale. The best branch is in the Silvercord Shopping Centre on Canton Rd in Tsim Sha Tsui.

continued on page 137

林青霞　張敏　Hong Kong Film

天龍八部

God of Gamblers

Days of Tomorrow

City Hunter

A Taste of Killing and Romance

When you hear the term 'Hong Kong film', what is your first thought? Jackie Chan? Bruce Lee? Kungfu splatter spectaculars?

Hong Kong films have become more and more popular in the west in the past few years. Hong Kong films have recently won several international awards. For example, Maggie Cheung Man Yuk was selected as the Best Actress for the Berlin Film Festival, while Wong Kar Wai's *Happy Together* was selected as the Palme d'Or at the Cannes Film Festival in 1997.

The new wave of Hong Kong films in the 1990s has attracted fans worldwide, particularly since John Woo's blood-soaked heroic epics *Hardboiled* and *The Killer*. Spurred on by this success, some of the performers and directors are developing their talents in Hollywood. In 1998 Jackie Chan made his first American film *Rush Hour*, while John Woo has become one of the most popular directors in Hollywood with the success of *Face/Off*. Hong Kong superstars Chow Yun Fat and Jet Li made their US debuts in 1998, in *The Replacement Killers* and *Lethal Weapon 4* respectively.

Hong Kong has long been regarded as an 'Eastern Hollywood'. There are around 100 films produced in Hong Kong each year – reputedly the third highest amount after Hollywood and India. This seems remarkable, as Hong Kong is only a small place with limited resources for a film industry.

Many people think that Hong Kong only produces films about martial arts. This is not completely true, but Hong Kong is famous for a series of kungfu films produced in the 1970s and early 1980s, as well as the bullet-riddled action films of the 1980s and 1990s.

Some people have preconceptions about Hong Kong films (or just foreign films in general for that matter), and believe that they are boring, cheap and dumb. Well, cheap they may sometimes be, and dumb – definitely! But boring? Never!

A Brief History of Hong Kong Film

Before we discuss the history, we need to define Hong Kong films. A Hong Kong film is one made by a company established in Hong Kong. Though Hong Kong produced its first fiction film *Stealing the Roasted Duck* in 1909, it is not regarded as a Hong Kong film as its production company was based in Shanghai.

The first Hong Kong film was *Chuang Tze Tests His Wife* in 1913, produced by Li Bei Hai and directed by his brother Li Beihai. The director overcame problems with limited resources by playing the part of the wife himself!

The development of the Hong Kong film industry can be divided into several stages and each has its special characteristics. The first stage is before WWII. During this time, films were still new to people in Hong Kong so the production of films was limited. Between 1935-1941 many film companies produced anti-war propaganda films in reaction to the Japanese invasion of Hong Kong.

The second stage is from WWII to the late 1960s. The films of this period were principally concerned with social relationships and family values, influenced by a wave of emigration from mainland China to Hong Kong. The island became overcrowded and living standards dropped, which led to general social problems, family quarrels etc. The producers and directors mirrored these problems in social realist films. Some examples include *Parents' Love/The Great Devotion* (1960) and *Father and Son* (1954).

Xi Hu films were also common in the post-war years. Xi Hu is often referred to as Chinese Opera, and was the most famous entertainment of the day, but difficult for an ordinary family to afford, as the ticket price could cost up to half the monthly salary of a worker. Producers took this as an opportunity

East is Red –
Brigitte Lin & Joey Wong

to film Xi Hu performances so that audiences could still enjoy the show at an affordable cost. Even some of the most famous opera performers made lots of Xi Hu films. For example, Ren Jian Hui appeared in more than 300 films in only 20 years!

The production periods for films in the 1950s and 1960s were very short. This trend continues. Nowadays it takes a Hollywood film around one to two years to complete, but in Hong Kong it takes only two to six months. The average production cycle for Hong Kong films in the 1960s was only two weeks! Some of the films were finished within seven days! Hence, some people nicknamed the films of this era as 'Seven Day Fresh'.

The third stage of the Hong Kong film industry was between the late 1960s and the early 1970s. This was a dark age for Cantonese Hong Kong films. The production of Xi Hu films decreased with the death of Tang Di Sheng, a leading script writer, in 1959 and the early retirement of Ren Jian Hui and Bai Xue Xian in 1968. In Xi Hu films, the scripts were more important than directions – usually script writers were onsite to edit the scripts. Social films became less popular in the late 1960s, and films in Mandarin from the mainland and Taiwan became the norm.

Hong Kong films returned to prominence with the popularity of Bruce Lee, who appeared in *The Big Boss* in 1971. Though Bruce Lee only made four films and suddenly passed away during the production of *The Game of Death*, his contribution to Hong Kong films was enormous as he drew the attention of the North American market.

Three directors should be acknowledged for the films of the 1970s and 1980s. The first is Jackie Chan. He made many kung-fu films in the late 1970s, such as *Snake in the Eagle's Shadow* (1978) and *Drunken Master* (1978). His 1980s films were mostly police-related stories, such as *The Protector* (1985) and the highly popular *Police Story* series.

The second director is King Hu, who directed several stylish Mandarin kungfu films in the early 1970s. The films of today still take King Hu's films as a reference point for action design, as he choreographed the action scenes. His successful approach enabled him to cast the actress Cheng Pui Pui as the lead role in a number of his films, and indeed other action directors of this period sometimes preferred a female in the lead role.

The third director, Michael Hui, with his brother Sam Hui, produced many popular social comedies, including *Private Eyes* (1976) and *The Pilferers' Progress* (1977) – the latter was directed by John Woo.

In the early 1980s, Hong Kong filmmakers tried to put the issues arising from the imminent handover of power to China into their films. For example, the vampire films of the time expressed a fear of the future. But overall Hong Kong films declined as the market share for local films decreased.The silence of the Hong Kong film industry in the mid-1980s ended with John Woo's *A Better Tomorrow* series as well as the historical action films by Tsui Hark – a typical example being the *Once Upon a Time in China* (Wong Fei Hung) series.

In the early 1990s, the popularity of comedy actor Stephen Chow soared. He starred in several famous TV series and the film *Fight Back to School* (1991). Chow is the master of *mo lai to* comedy, in which the previous scene or plot need bear no relation to the next, as long as it's funny. Hong Kong audiences certainly enjoy the humour, and Chow's success has redefined the comedy genre in the 1990s.

Excellence in Hong Kong films is recognised each April with the presentation of the Hong Kong Film Awards (HKFA), which was established in 1981. The selection criteria was revised in the early 1990s and the HKFA Co Ltd was set up in 1995 to make the awards independent. HKFA represents the opinions of professionals in the industry. The winners of the best film category in recent years are *Summer Snow* (1995), *Comrades, Almost a Love Story* (1996) and *Made in Hong Kong* (1997).

Sad State of the Industry Today

In 1998 the Hong Kong film industry is in a new and dangerous slump, with a decrease in the number of local productions as well as poor returns at the box office. There were 94 films made in Hong Kong in 1997, as compared to 164 completed in 1994. Hong Kong films are faced with many internal and external problems.

The local box office has been badly affected by pirated Video Compact Discs (VCDs). You cannot imagine how fast these can be produced – when the film's grand opening is on Thursday, you can find a pirated version on VCD on Friday afternoon! As the price for a pirated VCD in Hong Kong is only half the normal ticket price, many prospective cinema-goers buy these VCDs instead, regardless of the poor quality.

Another internal problem is that there are no replacements for the crew in the industry, due to a lack of any long-term training plan. In the past it was very hard to enter the film industry without a good relationship with someone already working in film. The result is that most of the crew listed in the credits are more or less the same as those in the films of the 1980s.

The price of tickets is another factor affecting the box office. Ticket prices for films in Hong Kong have increased by more than 70% from 1992 to 1998. When compared with other forms of entertainment, audiences consider films too expensive and so visit cinemas less.

Hong Kong people have also lost their confidence in Hong Kong films. In 1993 and 1994 some large budget but poor quality films flopped at the box office (despite the presence of big stars such as Andy Lau and Anita Yuen). Nowadays many in Hong Kong prefer Hollywood films, as they assume that Hong Kong films are inferior, even though it may not be the case.

Externally, Hong Kong films are losing markets in Taiwan and South-East Asia. This is partially due to the economic crisis of 1997 and 1998, but also because those audiences, like the local ones in Hong Kong, have come to prefer Hollywood fare. The Taiwanese market has also declined as Taiwanese companies made heavy losses after investing in Hong Kong films in 1993 and 1994.

The Adventurers – Andy Lau

Forecast for Hong Kong Films

It is difficult to forecast the future of Hong Kong films, but we know that the industry has reacted to the situation. Formal training courses for film crews have begun. The industry is producing fewer films but of a higher quality, to win back the confidence of the audience. At the same time, the industry has asked the Hong Kong government to take action against the pirate industry.

The Motion Picture Industry Association (MPIA) has organised Filmmark to attract overseas distribution companies to buy the rights for Hong Kong films. At the same time, producers are trying to break into new markets like Russia and South America.

Hopefully these and other efforts will lead to a resurgence of Hong Kong filmmaking, as has been the case several times in its 90 year history.

Some Good Hong Kong Films

Before arriving in Hong Kong, check out some Hong Kong films. It won't be easy to choose, as over 8000 Hong Kong films have been produced already. Here is a selection of 10 titles from the 1980s and 1990s that give a broad selection of filmmaking, Hong Kong style:

Mr Vampire (1985)

Director: Ricky Lau Koon Wai

Cast: Lam Ching Ying, Chin Siu Ho, Moon Lee Choi Fung, Ricky Hui Koon Ying

One of the classic vampire stories, blending horror, humour and action. Eastern vampires do not behave like Hollywood ones, so should you meet one in the dark, this film will prepare you. This role stereotyped the late Lam Ching Ying into a career of ghost-busting, but when you see his cool Taoist moves, you'll agree that you'd rather have no-one else doing the job.

Mr Vampire

Once Upon a Time in China 2 (1991)

Director: Tsui Hark

Cast: Jet Li, Lian Jie, Max Mok Siu Chung, Rosamund Kwan Chi Lam, Donnie Yen Ji Dan

Wong Fei Hung is an enduring Chinese hero, and films about his life are one of the most popular topics in Hong Kong films. This is the second of the series produced by Tsui Hark and it elevated Jet Li to the status of action superstar. It has great action design as well as a stirring score.

Sex & Zen (1991)

Director: Michael Mak Tong Kit

Cast: Lawrence Ng Kai Wah, Amy Yip Chi Mei, Kent Cheng Juk Si, Shadow Ip

This is an erotic film, but most of the scenes are played for laughs. Sex & Zen simply takes the usual excesses and vigour of Hong Kong film-making and applies them to a bedroom setting. The result may not be quality viewing, but it is unique.

Sex & Zen

C'est la Vie, Mon Cherie (1993)

Director: Derek Yee Tung Sing

Cast: Anita Yuen Wing Yee, Lau Ching Wan, Carrie Ng Ka Lai, Carina Lau Ka Ling

This is a tragedy about the love between a poor saxophone player and a performer in Temple St. A similar story has been filmed several times in the past, but this one has an outstanding script. Anita Yuen and Lau Ching Wan were newcomers when they were cast in the film but their performances were beyond expectation. An extremely impressive film.

Crime Story (1993)

Director: Che Kirk Wong Chi Keung

Cast: Jackie Chan, Kent Cheng Juk Si, Au Yeung Pui Shan, Ken Lo Wai Kwong,

Jackie Chan is the best known of all Hong Kong stars, except perhaps Bruce Lee. His blend of kungfu and comedy is loved the world over, with the added excitement that he performs all of his own stunts. There are many Jackie Chan films in video stores, but this one is not only an action story but also offers an in-depth exploration of the characters.

Chung King Express (1994)
Director: Wong Kar Wai
Cast: Brigitte Lin Ching Hsia, Tony Leung Chiu Wai, Faye Wong Ching Man, Takeshi Kaneshiro
Wong Kar Wai is a famous Hong Kong art-film director. His films are heavy on dialogue, and some people enjoy them while others totally hate them. Prepare yourself before watching as Wong's films are different from the mainstream. *Chung King Express* presents an insight into the crowded nature of modern Hong Kong life.

Comrades, Almost a Love Story (1996)
Director: Peter Chan Ho San
Cast: Maggie Cheung Man Yuk, Leon Lai Ming, Kristy Yeung Kung Yu, Eric Tsang Chi Wai
Another successful Hong Kong love story. The script is well written and powerful, and you will keenly experience the feelings of the leading characters.

Naked Killer – Chingmy Yau

Young and Dangerous (1996)
Director: Andrew Lau Wai Keung
Cast: Dior Cheng Yee Kin, Jordan Chan Siu Chun, Gigi Lai Chi, Francis Ng Chun Yu
This film is adapted from a popular local comic series about the Triad society. *Young and Dangerous'* fresh new angle captured the hearts of film-goers, and its tremendous success at the box office has spawned more than 10 films of a similar nature. The film has been criticised for setting a bad example to youth by glamorising a criminal lifestyle.

Places to See Films in Hong Kong

Like all films, Hong Kong films are made for the big screen. What could be finer than checking out a Hong Kong film in a Hong Kong cinema?

There are altogether over 90 cinemas in Hong Kong. There are three Cinema Circuits: Golden Harvest, Newport and Empire. As some of these cinemas are multiplex cinemas, the total number of screens is over 200. Around 40% of these cinemas show Hong Kong films. Due to the rapid increase in rents, most of the traditional cinemas (with dress circles) have been re-developed. Most of the cinemas in Hong Kong are multiplex cinemas with less than 500 seats for each screen.

Cinemas in Hong Kong are quite small and the seat between each row is only 35 inches (about 90cm). For most of the cinemas, seats are allocated at the same level without any slopes. Hence, if you are over 6ft, please be considerate and try to sit low. Another thing to note about Hong Kong audiences is that they are quite likely get up

The First Shot - Maggie Cheung

and leave if the film fails to grab them in the first 10 minutes; thus, Hong Kong films often start with a bang. Similarly, when the credits roll, most of the audience will leap to their feet. Jackie Chan and Stephen Chow films often feature hilarious out-takes during the credits as an incentive for the audience to stay and watch.

You have to choose seats when you book tickets. If you are late booking tickets for a popular film, you may find yourself sitting in the first row. Most of the cinemas offer advanced bookings, varying from two to seven days.

Ticket prices are around HK$40 to HK$60, depending on the location and the policy of the cinema. In February 1997, the MPIA introduced 'Tuesday Movie Day'. Ticket prices for all cinemas in Hong Kong are HK$30 on Tuesday. Some cinemas also provide a special morning show at 10.30 am from Monday to Friday, showing films from the past few years, at the special price of HK$12 to HK$20.

On Monday to Friday, cinemas usually screen five sessions: 12.30, 2.30, 5.30, 7.30 and 9.30 pm. Some of the cinemas may have a midnight show at 11.30 pm. On weekends and public holidays, most of the local cinemas will have an additional special screening at 4 pm. The actual showing time will depend on the running time of the film.

Almost all Hong Kong films showing in Hong Kong have Chinese and English subtitles. You can confirm that the film has English subtitles by checking its Censorship License in the cinema.

The *South China Morning Post* and the *Hong Kong Standard* have listings for film screenings in Hong Kong, as does *Hong Kong Magazine*. However, these publications lack detailed information about the cinemas showing Hong Kong films. The best way to check is via the Internet, at Movieworld Hong Kong (www.movieworld.com.hk/) or Netvigator (www.netvigator.com/).

Ryan Law

All photographs reprinted with the permission of Siren Entertainment

Fist of Legend – Jet Li

continued from page 128
The branch on Jaffe Rd in Wan Chai isn't bad either, and there is another branch on the 3rd floor of Prince's building in Central. You can also buy CDs at the street markets on Temple St, Yau Ma Tei, and Tung Choi St, Mong Kok, but these are usually pirated and the sound quality is poor.

Unless you really must, don't bother buying any musical instruments in Hong Kong. There's not a great selection, and the prices are truly outrageous. If you absolutely need something, your best bet is Tom Lee music stores, with branches in Causeway Bay, Tsim Sha Tsui and Wan Chai.

If you're looking to buy Chinese instruments, again Hong Kong is not a great place. There are a few shops along Wan Chai Rd between Johnston and Morrison Hill Rds in Wan Chai, but what is on offer is generally not good value for money. It might even be cheaper to buy a train ticket to Guangzhou in neighbouring Guangdong Province.

Watches Shops selling watches are ubiquitous in Hong Kong and you can find everything from a Rolex to Russian army timepieces and scuba-diving watches. As always, you should avoid the shops which do not have price tags on the merchandise. The big department stores are quite all right, but compare prices.

It's worth knowing that watch cases do not have to be expensive to ensure a quality watch: the internal workings (simply known as the 'movement') are 90% of the battle. There is a thriving industry in Hong Kong which puts top-quality Swiss movements into cheap made-in-China cases. While you do want to find a case that isn't going to rust, you can easily solve the green-wrist syndrome if you buy a leather rather than metal watchband. A waterproof watch is another ball game – if it's made in China, let the seller dunk it into a glass of water to prove that it is indeed waterproof.

About every third person you'll encounter on Nathan Rd in Tsim Sha Tsui will be yelling 'copy watch!' in your ear. This is not some sort of traditional Chinese greeting but an attempt to sell you a fake Rolex or Seiko. Just why this is tolerated by the Hong Kong authorities is mystifying – after all, it is illegal and the government claims to be 'cracking down' on counterfeiters. The police have even found fake watches in shops displaying the HKTA logo.

Perhaps you don't mind buying counterfeit merchandise, but consider this: these fake Rolexes have a nasty habit of losing 10 to 15 minutes of time per day, and then stop working after a month. If by some miracle it lasts longer, then the 'gold' watchband starts to turn your wrist green.

Video This catch-all term 'video' refers to a number of commercial products: a TV set, video tape player (also known as video cassette recorder or VCR), the video tapes and a video camera (camcorder).

In and around the Tsim Sha Tsui rip-off zone, practically every video store has a demonstration TV set up in the rear of the store. You can expect a demonstration in which only the most expensive 'digital' video camera produces a crisp image. What you won't be told is that the TV is rigged so that it will only work properly with the overpriced digital model. You also won't be told that the 'digital' model is not digital at all, but an ordinary camera for which you get to pay double.

This problem can best be avoided by not shopping in Tsim Sha Tsui. However, life isn't so simple – it is also important to understand a few basics of TV broadcasting if you want to purchase a VCR, video tapes or a camcorder.

Hong Kong's standard for video and TV broadcasting is PAL. Unfortunately, there are additional complications to consider – a PAL-standard TV bought in Hong Kong may not work for you, even if your home country uses PAL, because the stations might be adjusted to different frequencies. A few manufacturers have started offering multi-standard TVs that can be adjusted to PAL, NTSC or SECAM with the flick of a switch, but these models cost more. Some multi-standard systems show colour in one mode only, so read the manuals carefully before purchasing.

If multi-standard TVs and multi-standard VCRs exist, is there also such a thing as a multi-standard camcorder? The answer is no. If you want to buy a camcorder, you must decide which standard you want, PAL, NTSC or SECAM. A wrong choice would be a costly mistake, so pay careful attention to the labels.

Again, you've got the same problem when purchasing video tapes. If you buy a pre-recorded video tape off the shelf in Hong Kong, it will almost certainly be PAL standard. If your home country uses NTSC or SECAM, you won't be able to view this tape unless you have one of those new multi-standard VCRs.

Video tapes come in two main sizes (with a third currently entering the market): VHS and 8mm. Virtually all pre-recorded tapes and all VCRs are VHS size. The 8mm tapes are very small and are ideal for use in small hand-held camcorders. If you produce a movie on 8mm tape, many companies offer a service to transfer it to a VHS tape for home viewing. A more important complication is the new improved 'super-video' (S-video) variation. This is a high-resolution variation of the VHS and 8mm standard, called Super-VHS (S-VHS) and Hi-Band 8mm (Hi-8), respectively. You cannot play an S-video tape on a standard VCR; however, an S-VCR can play standard video tapes. A recently introduced and compact version of VHS, known as VHS-Compact (VHS-C), is smaller than standard VHS but larger than 8mm.

If you've managed to digest all this, you still have one more hurdle to clear – audio standards. Video tapes come with the ability to reproduce sound, and the latest rage is stereo quality sound.

In the VHS format there is VHS Hi-Fi and in the 8mm format there is the new PCM audio format. If you want to enjoy this improved sound quality, you have to buy equipment that can record and play back.

Laser disk (more accurately called a video disk) offers a few advantages over tapes: longevity, the ability to jump from one point in a movie to another, and freeze frames that don't flutter. The drawback is that you can't make your own recordings on laser disks unless you invest in expensive equipment (slowly getting cheaper). The real reason to buy laser disks and a laser disk player is to watch quality pre-recorded movies. Hong Kong has a well-developed market for video disks and video disk players, but if you want to buy a video disk player then first make sure that you can buy films on disk back home. You may end up having to get your films from Hong Kong.

Confused? You ought to be.

Getting There & Away

AIR
Airports & Airlines

Hong Kong is the main gateway to China and much of East Asia. Consequently, the international air service is excellent and competition keeps the fares relatively low compared to neighbouring countries.

The days of daredevil landings at Hong Kong's Kai Tak airport finished on 6 July 1998 when the technicians, air traffic controllers and airport staff had had enough and left to migrate over to Hong Kong's brand new and gremlin-infested airport at Chek Lap Kok on Lantau Island. The move was done in six hours, during which no flights entered Hong Kong. The new airport was supposed to be an adventurous reassertion of Hong Kong's cutting edge lead as a regional transport centre, but sadly it quickly lurched from one blunder to another, further besmirching Hong Kong's already tarnished post-handover reputation. Computers crashed, offices were unfinished, and huge delays confronted passengers, while Hong Kong was left contemplating the dire choice of either using Shenzhen airport or re-opening Kai Tak so that air cargo could get into the territory.

Businesses lost vast amounts of money waiting for supplies that had no point of entry into Hong Kong. Critics of the airport scheme questioned the logic of a new airport to deal with a shrinking number of tourists and a diminishing amount of air cargo supplying a less than robust economy. Strong regional airport competition would also test the foresight of building such a huge and expensive alternative to Kai Tak. And to top it all off, the glass perimeter wall of the new terminal building unexpectedly started to bubble, requiring replacement.

But despite the mixed feelings surrounding the demise of Kai Tak airport, the breathtaking descents over Kowloon were never worth the overall inefficiency that was its hallmark. Tai Tak's single runway was one of the world's busiest, with aircraft movements separated by only a few minutes during peak times of the day. There were long lines at immigration and customs. The only benefit of Kai Tak was its central location.

The new airport at Chek Lap Kok is the result of a HK$156.4 billion airport core program that sees air traffic landing on a huge patch of reclaimed land on the north of Lantau Island. The passenger terminal consists of eight levels, 120 shops (including moneychanging desks and banks), 288 check-in counters. The terminal is the design work of Sir Norman Foster, architect of the seminal Hongkong and Shanghai Bank building in Hong Kong's Central district.

HONG KONG TOURIST ASSOCIATION
Tsing Ma Bridge is one of the world's largest road and rail suspension bridges. It connects Chek Lap Kok with Kowloon.

The airport is connected to the mainland by one of the world's largest suspension bridges (the 2.2km long Tsing Ma Bridge, linking the islands of Tsing Yi and Ma Wan), capable of supporting road and rail. Massive new highways have been constructed, including the 12.5km North Lantau Expressway. A monumental harbour reclamation project made way for the 2km Western Harbour Crossing can accommodate six lanes of traffic, connecting Sai Ying Pun (Sheung Wan) and West Kowloon. Also constructed is the Airport Railway Tunnel which has been laid on the seabed of Victoria Harbour. The airport railway is 34km long and will connect the airport with Hong Kong Island via Kowloon and Tsing Yi. It takes 23 minutes to get to Hong Kong Island by rail, and the hours of operation for the airport railway are from 6 am to 1 am. Another rail link will connect Tung Chung (a new town to the south of the airport and on Lantau Island) with Hong Kong Island, taking trains to Tung Chung via Kowloon, Olympic, Lai King and Tsing Yi.

Tung Chung was originally a village with a few points of interest (see the Outlying Islands chapter), but it used to be isolated transport-wise. As part of the territory's plans to solve the housing crisis, Tung Chung has now become a huge, residential estate, taking advantage of the increased transport opportunities provided by the adjacent airport. It is essentially part of the airport project, even though it has no practical function that connects it to the operation of the airport (apart from providing housing for those who work at the airport). The airport was originally due to open to coincide with the handover of Hong Kong to China, but a series of delays set back the schedule.

The airport's expanded facilities have cut down the time departing passengers spend checking in and waiting, and the time arriving passengers spend in immigration and baggage claim. The airport is able to handle 40 aircraft movements in an hour at maximum capacity, and the terminal is a state-of-the-art world of moving walkways, conveying you through a tempting backdrop of facilities and shops.

After landing, look out for the Hong Kong Tourist Association's (HKTA) information centre, where you can supply yourself with maps and heaps of information on transportation, dining, sights and a host of other subjects concerning Hong Kong. These are all free and worth taking.

Also a must is a visit to the Hong Kong Hotels Association (HKHA). If you're looking for mid-range or top-end hotel accommodation and you're not booked in anywhere, the HKHA can often get you a room at half to two-thirds the price you would pay if you went directly to the reception desk in a hotel. The HKHA represent a huge number of hotels and stock all the hotels' brochures. The office does not handle hostels, guesthouses or other budget accommodation.

If you need money, try to change as little as possible with the airport moneychangers: the rates are the worst in town. If you have an ATM card you might want to try the ATMs in the arrival hall, which support global networks, including Plus System and Cirrus, and dispense Hong Kong dollars.

To keep your return seat, make sure to reconfirm your onward or return ticket at least 72 hours before your flight. If you don't there's a good chance you'll get bumped from your flight. The heavy volume of traffic through Hong Kong means there's almost always someone else who wants your seat.

If you are flying either Cathay Pacific Airways or United Airlines you can take advantage of city check-in services offered by these companies, which allow you to check your bags and receive your boarding pass in advance. This is also a good way to get a window or aisle seat. For United Airlines, you must go to its office (see the following Airline Offices list) in Central with your passport and you'll be issued with a boarding pass. Cathay Pacific Airways lets you check in either the day before or the same day if it's at least three hours before departure. On Hong Kong Island, the city check-in counter is at the Pacific Place Mall in Queensway, Admiralty, and at China Hong Kong City in Tsim Sha Tsui.

Northwest Airlines allows you to collect your boarding pass from its office in Central. Dragonair offers a phone check-in facility for club members, and Malaysian Airline offers the same service to 1st and business-class passengers.

Chek Lap Kok airport levies a departure tax of HK$50 (provisionally) per person, so be sure to have at least this much Hong Kong currency on hand when you check in – don't blow all your money and end up with HK$5 only as you sprint for the plane. Charges for overweight checked baggage are high, so check with your carrier about weight limits before you go on a serious shopping spree.

Over 2000 display panels and monitors (in both English and Chinese) are situated in the Arrival and Departure levels, giving constantly updated information on flight arrivals and departures.

Flight information is also available from the numerous passenger information kiosks situated throughout the terminal. See the Hong Kong Getting Around chapter for information on getting from the airport into town.

The following is a list of the major airline offices in Hong Kong. Where applicable, reservation and reconfirmation telephone numbers (res) are followed by flight information numbers (info).

Aeroflot
(☎ res 2845-4232, info 2769-8126) room 22, New Henry House, 10 Ice House St, Central
Air Canada
(☎ 2522-1001) room 1002, Wheelock House, 20 Pedder St, Central
Air France
(☎ res 2524-8145, info 2769-6662) room 2104, Alexandra House, 7 Des Voeux Rd, Central
Air India
(☎ res 2522-1176, info 2769-6558) 42nd floor, Gloucester Tower, 11 Pedder St, Central
Air New Zealand
(☎ res 2524-9041, info 2769-8571) 1601 Fairmont House, 8 Cotton Tree Drive, Central
Alitalia
(☎ res 2543-6998, info 2769-6448) 806 Vicwood Plaza, 199 Des Voeux Rd, Central

All Nippon Airways
(☎ res 2810-7100, info 2769-8609) room 2512, Pacific Place Two, 88 Queensway, Admiralty
American Airlines
(☎ 2826-9269) room 1738, Swire House, 9 Connaught Rd, Central
Ansett Australia
(☎ 2527-7883) unit A, 26th floor, United Centre, 95 Queensway, Admiralty
Asiana Airlines
(☎ res 2523-8585, info 2769-7782) 34th floor, Gloucester Tower, 11 Pedder St
British Airways
(☎ res 2868-0303, info 2868-0768) 30th floor, Alexandra House, 7 Des Voeux Rd, Central
Civil Aviation Administration of China (CAAC)
(☎ 2840-1199) ground floor, 17 Queen's Rd, Central; (☎ 2739-0022) ground floor, Mirador Mansion, 54-64B Nathan Rd, Tsim Sha Tsui; (☎ 2398-2683) room 906, 9th floor, Argyle Centre, 688 Leighton Rd, Mong Kok
Canadian Airlines International
(☎ res 2868-3123, info 2769-7113) room 1702, Swire House, 9 Connaught Rd, Central
Cathay Pacific Airways
(☎ res 2747-1888, info 2747-1234) ground floor, Swire House, 9 Connaught Rd, Central; shop 53, New World Shopping Centre, Tsim Sha Tsui
China Airlines (Taiwan)
(☎ res 2868-2299, info 2769-8361) 3rd floor, St George's building, Ice House St; Connaught Rd, Central
Continental Micronesia
(☎ res 2524-8638, info 2383-6094) room M1, New Henry House, 10 Ice House St, Central
Dragonair
(☎ res 2590-1188, info 2769-7728) World Wide House, 19 Des Voeux Rd, Central; 22nd floor, Devon House, Tai Koo Place, Quarry Bay
Emirates
(☎ 2526-7171) Gloucester Tower, 11 Pedder St, Central
EVA Airways
(☎ 2810-9251) Gloucester Tower, 11 Pedder St, Central
Garuda Indonesia
(☎ res 2840-0000, info 2769-6689) 7th floor, Henley building, 5 Queen's Rd Central
Gulf Air
(☎ 2881-8993) room 2508, Caroline Centre, 28 Yun Ping Rd, Causeway Bay
Japan Airlines
(☎ res 2523-0081, info 2769-6524) 20th floor, Gloucester Tower, 11 Pedder St, Central

KLM-Royal Dutch Airlines
(☎ 2808-2118) room 2201, World Trade Centre, 280 Gloucester Rd, Causeway Bay
Korean Air
(☎ res 2368-6221, info 2769-7511) 11th floor, South Seas Centre, Tower II, 75 Mody Rd, Tsim Sha Tsui East
Lufthansa Airlines
(☎ 2868-2313, info 2769-6560) room 1109-1110, Wing Shan Tower, 173 Des Voeux Rd, Central
Malaysia Airlines
(☎ res 2521-8181, info 2769-6038) 23rd floor, Central Tower, 28 Queen's Rd, Central
Northwest Airlines
(☎ res and info 2810-4288) 29th floor, Alexandra House, 7 Des Voeux Rd, Central

Philippine Airlines
(☎ res 2369-4521, info 2769-6253) room 6, ground floor, East Ocean Centre, 98 Granville Rd, Tsim Sha Tsui East
Qantas Airways
(☎ res 2842-1438, info 2842-1400) room 1433, Swire House, 9-25 Chater Rd, Central
Scandinavian Airlines
(☎ res 2865-1370, info 2769-7017) room 1401, Harcourt House, 39 Gloucester Rd, Wan Chai
Singapore Airlines
(☎ res 2520-2233, info 2769-6387) 17th floor, United Centre, 95 Queensway, Admiralty
Swissair
(☎ res 2529-3670) 8th floor, Tower II, Admiralty Centre, 18 Harcourt Rd, Central

Air Travel Glossary

Baggage Allowance This will be written on your ticket and usually includes one 20kg item to go in the hold, plus one item of hand luggage.

Bucket Shops These are unbonded travel agencies specialising in discounted airline tickets.

Bumped Just because you have a confirmed seat doesn't mean you're going to get on the plane (see Overbooking).

Cancellation Penalties If you have to cancel or change a discounted ticket, there are often heavy penalties involved; insurance can sometimes be taken out against these penalties. Some airlines impose penalties on regular tickets as well, particularly against 'no-show' passengers.

Check-In Airlines ask you to check in a certain time ahead of flight departure (usually one to two hours on international flights). If you fail to check in on time and the flight is overbooked, the airline can cancel your booking and give your seat to somebody else.

Confirmation Having a ticket written out with the flight and date you want doesn't mean you have a seat until the agent has checked with the airline that your status is 'OK' or confirmed. Meanwhile you could just be 'on request'.

ITX An ITX, or 'independent inclusive tour excursion', is often available on tickets to popular holiday destinations. Officially it's a package deal combined with hotel accommodation, but many agents will sell you one of these for the flight only and give you phoney hotel vouchers in the unlikely event that you're challenged at the airport.

Lost Tickets If you lose your airline ticket an airline will usually treat it like a travellers cheque and, after inquiries, issue you with another one. Legally, however, an airline is entitled to treat it like cash and if you lose it then it's gone forever. Take good care of your tickets.

MCO An MCO, or 'miscellaneous charge order', is a voucher that looks like an airline ticket but carries no destination or date. It can be exchanged through any International Association of Travel Agents (IATA) airline for a ticket on a specific flight. It's a useful alternative to an onward ticket in those countries that demand one, and is more flexible than an ordinary ticket if you're unsure of your route.

No-Shows No-shows are passengers who fail to show up for their flight. Full-fare passengers who fail to turn up are sometimes entitled to travel on a later flight. The rest are penalised (see Cancellation Penalties).

Thai Airways International
(☎ res 2529-5601, info 2769-6038) 24th floor, United Centre, 95 Queensway, Admiralty; shop 124, 1st floor, World Wide Plaza, Des Voeux Rd and Pedder St, Central

Trans World Airlines (TWA)
(☎ 2851-1411) mezzanine floor, Sun House, 90 Connaught Rd, Central

United Airlines
(☎ res 2810-4888, info 2769-7279) 29th floor, Gloucester Tower, 11 Pedder St, Central

Vietnam Airlines
(☎ 2810-6880) Peregrine Tower, Lippo Centre, 89 Queensway, Admiralty

Virgin Atlantic
(☎ 2532-6060) 27th floor, Kinwick Centre, 32 Hollywood Rd, Central

Buying Tickets

Judging prices for flights to Hong Kong has always been predictable. At the time of writing, however, everything was in the air, so to speak. Major airlines teamed up with hotels to offer amazing bargains to lure tourists back to Hong Kong. If the tourism slump continues to decline, the prices will only get lower. The prices listed in this chapter should be taken with a pinch of salt, and you should check the market thoroughly.

You will have to choose between buying a ticket to Hong Kong, then making other travel arrangements when you arrive, and

---

On Request This is an unconfirmed booking for a flight.

Onward Tickets An entry requirement for many countries is that you have a ticket out of the country. If you're unsure of your next move, the easiest solution is to buy the cheapest onward ticket to a neighbouring country or a ticket from a reliable airline which can later be refunded if you do not use it.

Open Jaw Tickets These are return tickets where you fly out to one place but return from another. If available, this can save you backtracking to your arrival point.

Overbooking Airlines hate to fly empty seats and since every flight has some passengers who fail to show up, airlines often book more passengers than they have seats. Usually excess passengers make up for the no-shows, but occasionally somebody gets bumped. Guess who it is most likely to be? The passengers who check in late.

Point-to-Point Tickets These are discount tickets that can be bought on some routes in return for passengers waiving their rights to a stopover.

Reconfirmation At least 72 hours prior to departure time of an onward or return flight, you must contact the airline and 'reconfirm' that you intend to be on the flight. If you don't do this the airline can delete your name from the passenger list and you could lose your seat.

Restrictions Discounted tickets often have various restrictions on them – such as needing to be paid for in advance and incurring a penalty to be altered. Others are restrictions on the minimum and maximum period you must be away, such as a minimum of 14 days or a maximum of one year.

Stand-by This is a discounted ticket where you only fly if there is a seat free at the last moment. Stand-by fares are usually available only on domestic routes.

Transferred Tickets Airline tickets cannot be transferred from one person to another. Travellers sometimes try to sell the return half of their ticket, but officials can ask you to prove that you are the person named on the ticket. This is less likely to happen on domestic flights, but on an international flight tickets are compared with passports.

Travel Periods Ticket prices vary with the time of year. There is a low (off-peak) season and a high (peak) season, and often a low-shoulder season and a high-shoulder season as well. Usually the fare depends on your outward flight – if you depart in the high season and return in the low season, you pay the high-season fare.

buying a ticket allowing various stopovers in Asia – such a ticket could fly you from Sydney to London, with stopovers in Denpasar, Jakarta, Hong Kong, Bangkok, Calcutta, Delhi and Istanbul.

Whatever you do, buy air tickets from a travel agent as the airlines don't deal directly in discount tickets. There are a host of deals that travel agents offer and fares will vary according to your point of departure, the time of year, how direct the flight is and flexibility. Not every travel agent offers discount tickets and those that do can vary widely. It's a good idea to call the airline first for the cost of the cheapest tickets – use that as your starting point when talking to travel agents. With the cheapest tickets, you often have to pay the travel agent first and

then collect the ticket at the airport. Nevertheless, these tickets may be worth the extra trouble. If you want the cheapest flight, tell the agent, and then make sure you understand the restrictions on the ticket. As a result of intense competition, most tickets sold these days are discounted, and considering the current economic climate in Hong Kong, you should be able to net a really good deal.

It's important to realise that when you buy a discounted air ticket from a travel agent, you must also go back to that agent if you want to obtain a refund – the airlines will not refund your money directly unless you paid full fare. This can be quite a hassle if you decide, half way through your travels, to change your route. In this case, you'd

Chek Lap Kok Airport

The opening of Chek Lap Kok airport has seen the curtain close on one of the largest civil engineering projects in the world. The area of reclamation that the airport sits upon is about the same size as the Kowloon peninsula; the whole airport core program has cost HK$156.4 billion, and work was not limited to the airport alone. Also thrown in was the building of the world's largest suspension bridge capable of supporting road and rail (the 2.2km long Tsing Ma Bridge, linking the islands of Tsing Yi and Ma Wan), the construction of massive new highways (including the 12.5km long North Lantau Expressway) and another harbour reclamation project to make way for the 2km Western Harbour Crossing, connecting Sai Ying Pun (Sheung Wan) and West Kowloon – this can accommodate six lanes of traffic. A railway tunnel has been laid on the seabed of Victoria Harbour, and the 34km railway connects the airport with Kowloon, Tsing Yi and Hong Kong Island.

The whole show was put together with more than 20,000 workers (almost 3000 of whom lived in specially constructed workers' villages) from a host of countries. It is predicted that the airport will be able to handle an annual volume of 87 million passengers per year by 2040. On hand to cope with such a huge volume of planes is a HK$975 million air traffic control system. It hasn't all been plain sailing however – Chek Lap Kok was originally supposed to open in time for the handover.

All of this effort and cost was made to circumvent the limitations of Kai Tak. In 1997, Kai Tak was the world's busiest airport in terms of cargo and the third busiest for international passengers. Kai Tak was too small and couldn't operate 24 hours a day because of its close proximity to residential areas. It was estimated that Kai Tak in 1995 lost a potential 2.5 million passengers (and a corresponding loss of tourist revenue) as a result of these restrictions. It is hoped that Chek Lap Kok will reverse these figures; but by how much is questionable considering the slowdown in economic performance in early 1998 and the collapse of the tourist industry that followed the handover.

When you step into the terminal at Chek Lap Kok, take a good look around – it's designed by Sir Norman Foster, architect of the Hongkong and Shanghai Bank Building in the Central district of Hong Kong.

have to return to the place of purchase to recoup your money. Of course, you could mail the ticket to a reliable friend, who could try to get it refunded, but don't count on this working. Some travel agents (and airlines) are extremely slow to issue refunds – delays of up to a year are not uncommon!

Most airlines divide the year into 'high' or 'peak' (expensive), 'shoulder' (less expensive) and 'low' or 'off' (cheapest) seasons. In the northern hemisphere, the high season is June to September and the low season is November to February. The holidays (Christmas and Chinese Lunar New Year) are treated as high season even though these come during the low season. In the southern hemisphere, the seasons are reversed.

Despite the name, 'normal economy-class tickets' are not the most economical fares. Essentially, these are full-fare tickets. On the other hand, these give you maximum flexibility and are valid for 12 months. Also, these are fully refundable, as are unused sectors of a multiple ticket.

'Group tickets' are well worth considering. You usually do not need to travel with a group. However, once the departure date is booked it may be impossible to change – you can only depart when the group departs, even if you never meet another group member. There could be other restrictions – you might have to complete the trip in 60 days, or perhaps only fly during the low season or on weekdays. It's important to ask the travel agent what conditions and restrictions apply to any tickets you intend to buy. The good news is that the return date can usually be left open.

Advance Purchase Excursion (APEX) tickets are sold at a discount but will lock you into a rigid schedule. Such tickets must be purchased two or three weeks ahead of departure, do not permit stopovers, and may have minimum and maximum stays as well as fixed departure and return dates. Unless you must return at a certain time, it's best to purchase APEX tickets on a one way basis only. There are stiff cancellation fees if you decide not to use your APEX ticket.

Round-the-World (RTW) fares are put together by two or more airlines and allow you to make a circuit of the world using a combination of routes. A typical RTW ticket is valid for one year, allows unlimited stopovers along the way and costs about UK£1200, A$1800 or US$2000. An example, including Hong Kong, would be a British Airways and United Airlines combination flying from London to New York, to Los Angeles, to Sydney, to Hong Kong and returning to London. There are many options involving different combinations of airlines and routes. Generally, routes which stay north of the equator are usually a little cheaper than routes that include destinations like Australia or South America. Most packages require you to keep moving in the same direction.

Enterprising travel agents put together RTW fares at much lower prices than the joint airline deals but, of course, these will involve unpopular airlines and less popular routes.

One thing to avoid is a 'back-to-front' ticket. These are best explained by example – if you want to fly from Japan (where tickets are relatively expensive) to Hong Kong (where tickets are much cheaper), you can pay by check or credit card and have a friend or travel agent in Hong Kong mail you the ticket. In theory this sounds great, but in reality the airline's computer records will show that the ticket was issued in Hong Kong rather than Japan, and the airline will refuse to honour the ticket. Consumer groups have filed lawsuits over this practice with mixed results, but in most countries the law protects the airlines, not consumers. In short, the ticket is only valid starting from the country of issue. The only exception to this rule is if you purchase a full-fare (non-discounted) ticket, but this robs you of the advantage you gain by purchasing a back-to-front ticket.

If the ticket is issued in a third location (such as the USA), the same rule applies. You cannot fly from Japan to Hong Kong with a ticket mailed to you from the USA – if you buy a ticket in the USA, you can fly from there to Japan and then to Hong Kong and thus enjoy the discounted price, but you can't start the journey from Japan. Again, an exception is made if you pay the full fare.

'Frequent-flier' plans have proliferated in recent years and are now offered by most airlines. Basically, these allow you a free ticket if you chalk up so many kilometres with the same airline. The plans aren't always good – some airlines require you to use all your frequent-flier credits within one year or you lose the lot. Sometimes you find yourself flying on a particular airline just to get frequent flier credits, and the ticket may well be considerably more expensive than what you might have got elsewhere. Many airlines have 'blackout' periods – peak times when you cannot use the free tickets you obtained under a frequent-flier program. When you purchase the ticket be sure to give the ticket agent your frequent-flier membership number, and again when you check in for your flight. A common complaint seems to be that airlines forget to record your frequent-flier credits – save all your boarding passes and ticket receipts, and be prepared to push if no bonus is forthcoming.

Some airlines offer student card holders discounts of up to 25% on tickets. In some countries, an official-looking letter from the school is also needed. You also must be aged 26 or less. These discounts are generally only available on ordinary economy-class fares. You wouldn't get one, for instance, on an APEX or a RTW ticket as these are already discounted.

Courier flights can be a bargain if you're fortunate enough to find one. The way it works is that an air freight company takes over your entire checked baggage allowance. You are only permitted to bring along a carry-on bag. In return, you get a steeply discounted ticket. These arrangements usually have to be made a month or more in advance and are only available on certain routes. Such flights are occasionally advertised in the newspapers, or contact air freight companies listed in the phone book.

Buying Tickets in Hong Kong One of the best places to buy tickets in Hong Kong is Phoenix Services (☎ 2722-7378, fax 2369-8884), room A, 7th floor, Milton Mansion, 96 Nathan Rd, Tsim Sha Tsui. The staff are friendly, patient and work hard to get you the best possible price. Bookings can be made for anywhere in the world, but Phoenix Services specialises in Vietnam. Another honest agent with good reviews is Traveller Services (☎ 2375-2222), room 1012, Silvercord Tower 1, 30 Canton Rd, Tsim Sha Tsui. In the same neighbourhood is Shoestring Travel (☎ 2723-2306), flat A, 4th floor, Alpha House, 27-33 Nathan Rd, Tsim Sha Tsui.

Many travellers use the Hong Kong Student Travel Bureau (☎ 2730-3269), room 835, 8th floor, Star House, Tsim Sha Tsui. This business doesn't offer the bargain fares of earlier years, but is still worth a try. If you hold an ISIC card you can get a discount. Offices in Hong Kong include: Argyle Centre (☎ 2390-0421), room 1812, 688 Nathan Rd, Mong Kok; (☎ 2833-9909), room 608, Hang Lung Centre, Patterson St, Causeway Bay.

If you need a ticket quickly, Hong Kong Four Seas Tours Ltd (☎ 2722-6112) has branches all over the place. The prices usually aren't as low as the discount operations listed previously, but you'll almost always get the seat you want and you can have the ticket delivered.

On the Hong Kong Island, Natori Travel (☎ 2881-8145, fax 2576-0311), room 2102A, Goldmark, 502 Hennessy Rd, Causeway Bay, gets good recommendations.

Warning Be careful about Hong Kong travel agencies – rip-offs do occur. It happens less now than it used to, but Hong Kong has long been plagued with bogus travel agents and fly-by-night operations that appear shortly before peak holiday seasons and dupe customers into buying non-existent airline seats and holiday packages. One way to tell is to check if the fly-by-night operator is listed in the telephone book – these businesses usually don't stay around long enough to get listed.

The most common trick is a request for a non-refundable deposit on an air ticket. You pay a deposit for the booking, but when you go to pick up the tickets the staff claim that the flight is no longer available. You will then be offered a seat on another flight at a higher price – sometimes 50% more! This sales tactic is commonly referred to as 'bait and switch' – it's illegal in many countries, but apparently perfectly legal in Hong Kong.

It is best not to pay a deposit, but rather to pay for the ticket in full and get a receipt clearly showing that there is no balance due, and that the full amount is refundable if no ticket is issued. Tickets are normally issued the next day after booking, but you must pick up the really cheap tickets (ie group tickets) yourself at the airport from the 'tour leader' (who you will never see again once you've got the ticket). One caution: when you get the ticket from the tour leader, check it carefully because occasional errors occur. For example, you may be issued a ticket with the return portion valid for only 60 days when you paid for a ticket valid for one year etc.

If you think you have been ripped off, and the agent is a member of the HKTA the organisation can apply some pressure (and apparently has a fund to handle cases of out-right fraud). Unfortunately, even agents who are members of the HKTA, do not have to comply with any set of guidelines.

Travellers with Special Needs

Most international airlines can cater to special needs – travellers with disabilities, people with young children and even children travelling alone. Check with the airline to be sure.

Special dietary needs (vegetarian, kosher etc) can also be catered to with advance notice. However, the 'special meals' usually aren't very special – these often consist of salad, fruit, bread and dessert.

Airlines usually carry babies up to two years of age at 10% of the relevant adult fare; a few may carry babies free of charge. Reputable international airlines usually provide nappies (diapers), tissues, talcum and all the other paraphernalia needed to keep babies clean, dry and half happy. For children between the ages of four and 12, the fare on international flights is usually 50% of the regular fare or 67% of a discounted fare.

Departure Tax

Airport departure tax at Chek Lap Kok is HK$50. It's free if you can persuade the airport personnel that you're under the age of 12.

Australia

Depending on where you depart from, flights to Hong Kong from Australia take between eight and 12 hours. Although this is still a fairly long flight, there is only a two hour time change between Sydney and Hong Kong, so jet lag is not a worry.

Ticket prices are generally expensive, and the cheapest tickets to purchase are APEX tickets, which have set return dates. The published return fares on Qantas Airways and Cathay Pacific Airways usually cost A$1359 but are often discounted to around A$1200. Fares on Ansett start around A$950 to A$1100. You can also usually get free stopovers in either Singapore, Bangkok or Kuala Lumpur if you fly with Singapore Airlines, Thai Airways International or Malaysia Airlines.

It's possible to get reductions on the cost of APEX and other fares by going to the student travel offices and/or some of the travel agents in Australia that specialise in discounting. The weekend travel sections of newspapers like the *Age* (Melbourne) or the *Sydney Morning Herald* are good sources of travel information.

In Melbourne, the Flight Centre is well worth trying, with offices throughout the inner city (☎ (03) 131 600). The main office is at 353 Little Collins St, Melbourne. There are Flight Centre branches in central Sydney (☎ (02) 9235 3522), Brisbane (☎ (07) 3221 9211) and Darwin (☎ (08) 8941 8002).

Canada

With so many ex-Hong Kong residents living in Vancouver, you would expect to find year-round super-cheap airfares on this route. However, fares are not terribly low, and there is a considerable variation by season. Fares from Vancouver can often match those of San Francisco in the USA, though eastern destinations such as Toronto or Montreal tend to cost more than flying to New York.

Getting discount tickets in Canada is much the same as in the USA – go to the travel agents and shop around until you find a good deal. There are a number of good agents in Vancouver for discounted tickets. Travel Cuts offers cheap return and one-way fares to Hong Kong, and has offices in a number of Canadian cities, including Vancouver, Edmonton, Toronto and Ottawa. Fares are slightly cheaper if you fly Northwest Airlines, though you are obliged to make a transit stop in Seattle, USA.

If you're thinking of heading to Canada from Hong Kong, a return ticket to Toronto will cost about HK$7950 and to Vancouver will cost about HK$5600. Prices may be lower during October to November and May to June.

China

There are no bargain fares into China. The Chinese government sets the prices, and all the domestic airlines toe the line, as does Dragonair, a joint-venture airline between Cathay Pacific Airways and the PRC's CAAC. Flights can be difficult to book due to the enormous volume of business travellers and Asian tourists, so plan ahead if possible. Some one year return fares are: Beijing HK$4660; Chengdu HK$4550; Guangzhou HK$1020; Kunming HK$3130; and Shanghai HK$3290. One-way fares are exactly half the return price.

Europe

The Netherlands, Switzerland and Belgium are good places for buying discount air tickets. In Antwerp, WATS has been recommended. In Zurich, try SOF Travel and Sindbad. In Geneva, try Stohl Travel. In the Netherlands, NBBS is a reputable agency. Frankfurt is Germany's gateway to Hong Kong, with direct flights on Lufthansa.

In Germany there are some quarterly magazines available which specialise in price information for flights all over the world (*Reise & Preise*, *Reisefieber* etc).

From most cities in Western Europe, general return fares to Hong Kong are about US$800.

Guam

Guam has emerged as a popular honeymoon spot, and a favoured location for Chinese and Japanese film crews making karaoke movies. Although Guam is a four hour flight from Hong Kong, air fares cost as much as a flight to the US west coast (a 13 hour flight)!

Continental Micronesia has a monopoly on direct Hong Kong to Guam flights, but other airlines can sometimes offer lower fares if you make a stopover. A return flight on Continental Micronesia is HK$5200, and a return flight on Asiana Airlines is HK$5160 with a stopover in Seoul.

Indonesia

Garuda Indonesia has direct flights from Jakarta to Hong Kong, and from Denpasar to Hong Kong via Jakarta. Cheap discount air tickets out of Indonesia can be bought from travel agents in Kuta Beach in Bali and in Jakarta. There are numerous airline ticket discounters around Kuta Beach – several are on the main strip, Jalan Legian. You can also buy discount tickets in Kuta for departure from Jakarta. In Jakarta, there are a few discounters on Jalan Jaksa. Budget return prices from Hong Kong to Jakarta are currently HK$7630.

Japan

Japan is not a good place to buy cheap air tickets. The cheapest way to get out of Japan is by ferry to either Taiwan or Korea. However, if you need an air ticket, some well-established English-speaking Tokyo travel agents include STA Travel (☎ 5269-0751) and Ikebukuro (☎ 5391-2922).

The cheapest fares start at around ¥550,000 for a round-trip on United Airlines or Northwest Airlines. Japan Airlines and All

Nippon Airways usually charge ¥560,000 to ¥575,000. Prices out of Hong Kong to Japan are usually around HK$6560. The flight from Tokyo to Hong Kong takes around five hours.

Korea (South)
Some of the best deals are available from Joy Travel Service (☎ (02) 776-9871, fax 756-5342), 10th floor, 24-2 Mukyo-dong, Chung-gu (directly behind City Hall). The Korean International Student Exchange Society (KISES, ☎ (02) 733-9494), room 505, YMCA building, Chongno 2-ga, Seoul, is also very good. Otherwise you could try Top Air Travel Co (☎ 2736-5111, fax (82) 2725-3687), suite 301, Sunil building, 231 Insa-dong, Chongro-ku.

Korea's Asiana Airlines usually has the cheapest flights between Hong Kong and Seoul at around HK$2800 for a 14 day return. Cathay Pacific Airways is considerably more expensive at HK$3600 for a 14 day return ticket, but at the time of writing it had a promotion for two people for HK$3100. Ticket prices out of Seoul are usually higher than from Hong Kong. At the time of writing return tickets to Seoul could be picked up for HK$2100. It's approximately five hours flying time between Hong Kong and Seoul.

New Zealand
Air New Zealand and Cathay Pacific Airways fly directly from Auckland to Hong Kong. APEX fares are the cheapest way to go, but you have to pay for your ticket at least 21 days in advance and spend a minimum of six days overseas. The lowest-priced return tickets available from Auckland to Hong Kong are NZ$1780. Ninety day return fares from Hong Kong to Auckland are HK$6620 on Singapore Airlines. One-way tickets are priced at around 75% of the return airfare.

Singapore
The three hour flight from Hong Kong to Singapore can cost anywhere from HK$2020 for a 30 day return on Cathay Pacific Airways to HK$3000 for a 30 day return on United Airlines (daily flights). At the time of writing, Qantas Airways was offering flights from Hong Kong for HK$2550. Prices out of Singapore are about the same. In Singapore try Airmaster Travel, 46 Bencoolen St, and check in the *Straits Times* for agents. Other agents also advertise in the *Straits Times* classified columns.

Taiwan
There are something like 15 flights a day between Taiwan and Hong Kong, with many of the seats taken by Taiwanese businessmen shuttling to and from China. This frequency will definitely drop off if direct flights between China and Taiwan begin – this has been in the planning stage for some time. The cheapest return fares on the Hong Kong to Taipei or Hong Kong to Kaohsiung routes are HK$2780. Flying time is about 1½ hours.

With an International Student Identification Card (ISIC) or STA Travel youth card, discounts are available from Youth Travel International (☎ (02) 2721-1978), suite 502, 142 Chunghsiao E Rd, Section 4, Taipei. This place can also issue these cards to qualified individuals.

Otherwise, look for discount travel agencies that advertise in the local English-language newspapers, the *China Post* or *China News*. An agent we've dealt ,with and found to be very reliable is Jenny Su Travel (☎ (02) 2594-7733, fax (02) 2592-0068), 10th floor, 27 Chungshan N Rd, Section 3, Taipei.

Thailand
The Hong Kong to Bangkok route offers some of the best deals in Asia. Cheap tickets abound, with return flights to Bangkok costing HK$1800 on Gulf Air and HK$1900 on Qantas Airways. At the time of writing you could purchase a return flight to Bangkok for HK$1500 on Cathay Pacific Airways. The flight takes three hours.

Prices from Bangkok to Hong Kong are about the same; try the travel agents on Khao San Rd for the cheapest fares. Student Travel in the Thai Hotel is helpful and efficient.

Discounted one-way/return fares start at 3485/5454B.

The UK

Flight times range anywhere from 13 hours for direct flights from London to 20 hours or more for cut-rate excursions on cash-hungry East European or Middle Eastern carriers.

It's impossible to accurately judge future trends for air tickets, but at the time of writing, prices were almost freefalling – the best advice is to scout around as many places as possible, and plan early. You used to be able to fly economy return for around UK£500 on tickets valid for 14 days to six months. Virgin Atlantic, British Airways and Cathay Pacific Airways would occasionally thrash out a brief price war and then things would return to normal. At the time of writing, it was possible to fly return to Hong Kong and stay for three nights at a decent mid-range hotel for around UK£420. Radical deals like this were in response to what was a massive corrosion of profits for the airline and hotel industries in the wake of a decline in tourism.

In general, airfare discounting in the UK is a long-running business – agents advertise fares openly. There are a number of magazines in Britain that have good information about flights and agents. These include *Time Out*, the Sunday papers, *Evening Standard*, *TNT Magazine* and *Southern Cross*.

It's an excellent idea to ask around for the best deals in London's Chinatown (in the Charing Cross Rd area). Significant bargains are usually offered as the Chinese community are regular fliers to Hong Kong. Some of these outlets only deal with Chinese customers, but Reliance (☎ (0171) 435-0503) at 12 Little Newport Street is a good bet, as is Samtung Travel (☎ (0171) 437-888), 12 Newport Place. Even before the price-slashing started, you could pick up return tickets in Chinatown for around UK£450.

Trailfinders is well organised and reliable, and is located at 215 Kensington High St, London W8 (☎ (0171) 937-5400), and at 42 Earl's Court Rd, London W8 (☎ (0171) 938-3366). Another good agent is The Travel Bug (☎ (0171) 835-1111), 125 Gloucester Rd, London SW7. STA Travel (☎ (0171) 361-6262, fax (0171) 938-4478) has several offices dotted around.

Good deals from London or Manchester can be found with British Airways, Air France, Alitalia, Gulf Air, Malaysia Airlines, KLM-Royal Dutch Airlines, Singapore Airlines and Thai Airways International. These airlines often do not charge extra if passengers want to stopover en route, and some encourage this by offering stopover packages. Just remember that in general, the cheaper the airfare the more inconvenient (or interesting) the route. Gulf Air and Singapore Airlines offer the best value for money in terms of comfort and attention to passenger's needs (even though flights go via Dubai and Singapore, respectively).

At the time of writing, Singapore Airlines was offering return tickets to London for HK$3450 (via Singapore), though this usually costs more like HK$6000. Virgin Atlantic and British Airways were offering return tickets for HK$4480 for a six month return – prices are generally much higher. One-way flights are generally about half the price of return tickets.

The USA

Direct flights to Hong Kong from the US west coast take around 13 hours nonstop. Flying from the east coast will require at least one stopover, which usually stretches the flight to a mind-numbing 20 hours. Jet lag hits hard after these flights, what with a time difference of between 12 and 15 hours and a date change after crossing the international date line.

There are some good open tickets that remain valid for six months or one year, allow multiple stopovers and don't lock you into any fixed departure dates. For example, there are cheap tickets between the US west coast and Hong Kong with stopovers in Japan and Korea for a little extra money – the departure dates can be changed and you have one year to complete the journey.

Usually, and not surprisingly, the cheapest fares are offered by bucket shops. San

Francisco is the bucket shop capital of the USA, though some good deals can be found in Los Angeles, New York and other cities. Discounters can be found in the *Yellow Pages* or the major daily newspapers. A more direct way is to wander around San Francisco's Chinatown – especially in the Clay St and Waverly Place area. Many of the bucket shops are staffed by recent arrivals from Hong Kong and Taiwan who speak little English. Inquiries are best made in person. One place popular with budget travellers is Wahlock Travel in the Bank of America building on Stockton St.

It's not advisable to send money (even cheques) through the post unless the agent is well established – some travellers have reported being ripped off by fly-by-night mail-order ticket agents. Nor is it wise to hand over the full amount to 'Shady Deal Travel Services' unless the business can give you the ticket straight away – most US travel agencies have computers that can produce the ticket on the spot.

Council Travel, with an office on Bush St, is the largest student travel organisation. You don't have to be a student to use Council Travel, but the staff can do specially discounted student tickets.

One of the cheapest and most reliable travel agents on the west coast is Overseas Tours (☎ (800) 222-5292), room 206, 475 El Camino Real, Millbrae, CA 94030. It is quite trustworthy for mail-order tickets.

If you're heading to Hong Kong during the low season, carriers like Asiana Airlines, Korean Air or China Airlines can get you there from San Francisco or Los Angeles for US$680, excluding tax. Canadian Airlines International also offers a flight via Vancouver for CAN$1500. Most of these flights make a stop in the carrier's home country: Asiana Airlines and Korean Air take you through Seoul, China Airlines through Taipei. This is not always such a bad thing, as it's usually easy to arrange a stopover for little or no extra charge.

Fares from other parts of the USA depend on whether you are flying from a major domestic airport. Flying from large cities like Atlanta, Chicago or Denver shouldn't cost too much more than from New York. If you're coming from somewhere off the major air routes, be prepared to pay more.

Other Asian Countries

For one-way/return tickets purchased in Hong Kong, some sample fares include: Kuala Lumpur HK$1400/2850; Kathmandu HK$2000/3600; Manila HK$950/1600; Pnomh Penh HK$1300/2750; and Yangon (Rangoon) HK$800/2750. A sample return fare to Vietnam is HK$549 to Hanoi or Ho Chi Minh City (Saigon).

Other Regions

There are also numerous flights between Hong Kong and Russia (Moscow, HK$4950 return), the Middle East (Dubai, HK$6700 return), Africa (Johannesburg, HK$8400 return) and South America (Rio de Janeiro, HK$13,500 return).

LAND
China

Bus The only way in and out of Hong Kong by land is through mainland China. Several transport companies in Hong Kong offer bus services to Guangzhou, Shenzhen and several other destinations in Guangdong Province. The best of these is Citybus, which also operates a domestic bus network in Hong Kong.

There are five buses daily to Guangzhou, leaving from Citybus stations at China Hong Kong City in Tsim Sha Tsui and Shatin City One in the New Territories. Tickets are HK$180 one way. Buses from Guangzhou to Hong Kong depart from major hotels, popular ones being the Garden Hotel and the Victory Hotel. Citybus also runs eight buses daily to Shenzhen, including two departures from the Shangri-La Hotel in Admiralty. Tickets are HK$65 on weekdays (Monday to Friday), HK$85 on weekends. Information and credit-card ticket bookings are handled by Citybus (☎ 2736-3888), China Travel Service (CTS, ☎ 2853-3888) and MTR Travel Services Centre (☎ 2922-4800). The latter also has offices in MTR subway stations at Admiralty, Causeway

Bay, Mong Kok, Tsim Sha Tsui, Taiku and Tsuen Wan.

CTS (the PRC's government-owned travel agency) also runs frequent buses to Guangzhou and Shenzhen, leaving approximately hourly from Wan Chai, Hung Hom, Mong Kok and Tsuen Wan. The adult one-way fare to Guangzhou is HK$185 and child fares are HK$135 (discounts available if there are three or more of you). For more information call ☎ 2764-9803. There are numerous other small bus companies that run regular coaches to Guangzhou. A one-way ticket with Chenda Yongan Travel Company (☎ 2336-1111) is HK$150.

If you take the bus, don't forget to get your visa first! For details, see under the China Visas entry in this chapter.

Train By far the most convenient mode of land transport is the Kowloon-Guangzhou express train (some trains go via Changping), which covers the 182km route in approximately two hours.

There is a direct rail link between Kowloon, Shanghai and Beijing. Trains to Beijing (via Guangzhou, Changsha, Wuchang and Zhengzhou) leave on alternate days, take 30 hours, and cost HK$706 (hard sleeper), HK$934 (soft sleeper) and HK$1191 (deluxe soft sleeper). The trains to Shanghai (via Guangzhou and Hangzhou) also leave on alternate days, take 29 hours, and cost HK$627 (hard sleeper), HK$825 (soft sleeper) and HK$1039 (deluxe soft sleeper). There is also one departure daily to Zhaoqing via Foshan.

From Hong Kong you catch trains at the Kowloon-Canton Railway (KCR) station in Hung Hom, Kowloon. Immigration formalities are completed before boarding; passengers are requested to arrive at Hung Hom station 45 minutes before boarding the train. To get to the station from Tsim Sha Tsui by public transport, take the 5C bus from the Star Ferry terminal, the 8A bus from nearby on Salisbury Rd or the No 8 green minibus from Middle Rd.

Timetables change, but current departure times for the high-speed train from Hong Kong are 8.35, 9.25, and 11.35 am and 12.55 pm. In the other direction, trains leave from Guangzhou for Hong Kong at 8.40 and 10 am, and 3.15 and 5.45 pm. Trains for Hong Kong depart from the Guangzhou East Train Station. The train to Zhaoqing leaves at 3.35 pm.

In Hong Kong, tickets can be booked up to seven days in advance at CTS or the KCR station in Hung Hom. Phone ☎ 2947-7888 to purchase your ticket over the phone; if bought over the phone, passengers must collect the tickets at least one hour before the train departs from the Hung Hom KCR station. Tickets can also be bought at Mong Kok, Kowloon Tong and Sha Tin station ticket offices. Return tickets will not be issued within five days of departure. The gate closes 20 minutes before the train departs, so get there in good time.

The one-way 1st class tickets for the high-speed express trains cost HK$250 and the 2nd class tickets cost HK$220 (child HK$110). Prices can increase across the board by HK$40 during the high season (usually during public holidays or whenever Guangzhou hosts a major trade fair). CTS does not accept credit cards, so bring cash or go through a travel agent. There is also a luggage consignment charge from Hung Hom to Guangzhou of HK$4.90 per 5kg.

A cheaper but less convenient option is to take the KCR commuter train to the station at Lo Wu, cross through immigration into the Chinese border city of Shenzhen and catch a local train to Guangzhou. There are around 20 trains to and from Guangzhou daily, and the ride takes between 2½ to three hours. Hard seats (the Chinese equivalent of 2nd class) cost anywhere from HK$92 to HK$112 depending on the type of train. Soft seats (1st class) cost between HK$103 and HK$118. There is also a high-speed double-decker express train that connects Lo Wu (at the border with Shenzhen) with Hung Hom in Kowloon. See the Hong Kong Getting Around chapter for details

If you're thinking of heading into China from Hong Kong, CTS can help book onward train connections from Guangzhou.

This is worth looking into, as buying a ticket in Guangzhou (for say, Beijing or Chengdu) can be a nightmare of long lines, pickpockets and frustration. CTS can also buy tickets for you between larger destinations in China, outside of Guangzhou (for example, from Shanghai to Beijing), but not for less travelled routes.

CTS offices in Hong Kong are open from 9 am to 5 pm on weekdays and until 1 pm Saturday. Only the Tsim Sha Tsui and Mong Kok offices are open from 9 am to 1 pm Sunday. Locations include:

Head Office
    (☎ 2853-3888) 2nd floor, 78-83 Connaught Rd, Central
Central
    (☎ 2521-7163) mezzanine, China Travel building, 77 Queen's Rd
Mong Kok
    (☎ 2789-5970) 2nd floor, 62-72 Sai Yee St
North Point
    (☎ 2565-8610) ground floor, 196-202 Java Rd
Tsim Sha Tsui
    (☎ 2315-7188) 1st floor, Alpha House, 27-33 Nathan Rd
Wan Chai
    (☎ 2832-3866) ground floor, Southorn Centre, 138 Hennessy Rd

China Visas

These can be arranged by CTS and most travel agents; many guesthouses and hotels can also arrange visas, for a small fee. If you want to save a little money and don't mind spending the time to do it yourself, go the Visa Office of the PRC (☎ 2827-9569), 5th floor, Lower Block, 26 Harbour Rd, Wan Chai. At the time of writing, visas processed in two days cost HK$180, and in a single day (express) HK$430. US passport holders are charged HK$340 and HK$590 respectively for the service. You must supply two photos, which can be taken at the visa office for HK$35.

South-East Asia

The Vietnam-China border has finally opened up to train travellers, and overland travel by bus between Cambodia and Vietnam (at Moc Bai) is now reasonably safe. Things are still dicey on the Thai-Cambodian border, but if that gets sorted out then rail and road journeys from Singapore and Bangkok to Hong Kong would be entirely feasible.

Europe

From Europe, you can reach Hong Kong by rail, though most travellers following this route also tour China. Don't take this rail journey just to save money – a direct flight from Europe to Hong Kong works out to be about the same price or less. The idea of an overland trip is to get a good, long look at Russia, Mongolia and China.

It's a long haul. The most commonly taken routes are from western Europe to Moscow, then on to Beijing via the Trans-Manchurian or Trans-Mongolian Railway. From Beijing there are trains to Kowloon every other day (see the China section in this chapter). The minimum time needed for the whole journey (one way) is roughly 10 days, though most travellers spend some time in China.

In Hong Kong, tickets for the Beijing to Moscow journey can be booked at Moonsky Star (☎ 2723-1376, fax 2723-6653, email 100267.2570@compuserve.com), 4th floor, flat 6E, E block, Chungking Mansions, 36 Nathan Rd, Tsim Sha Tsui. The staff are helpful and can organise visas and tailor your ticket to include stops en route. Although Moonsky has an office in Beijing, arranging trips through China and Russia can be very difficult, so make allowances if the staff have trouble getting you exactly what you want. You can also try Time Travel (☎ 2366-6222, fax 2739-5413) in the same building, on the 16th floor, A block, Chungking Mansions, 36 Nathan Rd, Tsim Sha Tsui.

If you're travelling from Europe, Travel Service Asia (☎ (069) 07371-4963, fax 07371-4769), Kirchberg 15, 7948 Dürmentingen, Germany, is highly recommended for low prices and good service. In the UK, one of the experts in budget train travel is Regent Holidays (☎ (0117) 921-

1711, fax 925-4866), 15 John St, Bristol BS1 2HR. Another agency geared towards budget travellers is Progressive Tours (☎ (0171) 262-1676), 12 Porchester Place, Connaught Square, London W2 2BS. Several travellers have recommended Scandinavian Student Travel Service (SSTS), 117 Hauchsvej, 1825 Copenhagen V, Denmark. One agent in Germany catering to the Trans-Siberian market, with tours of Mongolia included, is Mongolia Tourist Information Service (☎ (030) 784-8057), Postfach 62 05 29, D-1000 Berlin 62.

A popular book about the journey is the *Trans-Siberian Handbook* by Bryn Thomas (Trailblazer Publications). More details are provided in the following guides produced by Lonely Planet – *China, South-West China, Mongolia* and *North-East Asia on a Shoestring.*

It can be hard to book this trip during the summer high season. Low season shouldn't be a problem, but plan as far ahead as possible.

SEA
Like buses and trains, most boats leaving Hong Kong are bound for China. The only exceptions are the luxury cruise ships which sometimes pass through Hong Kong on world-wide journeys.

From the China ferry terminal, you can board daily jet catamarans and hovercraft to destinations in neighbouring Guangdong Province, including Shenzhen, Nanhai, Zhuhai, Huizhou, and Guangzhou. Tickets for the hovercraft to Guangzhou (over two hours) are HK$190 and for the jet catamaran (three hours) HK$183. Boats to Guangzhou aren't much faster or convenient than trains or buses, but the river scenery is nice. Turbo Cat has two trips daily to East River Guangzhou (the Guangzhou Economic Zone), departing at 7.15 am and 1.30 pm; tickets cost HK$250 from Kowloon and HK$225 from Guangzhou – the journey takes two hours. Phone Turbo Cat on ☎ 2851-1700 for more details.

The China ferry terminal also has daily morning jet boats to Wuzhou in Guangxi Province (10 hours, HK$410), from where you can link up with buses to Guilin, Yangshuo and Nanning. If you have time, you can even take a ship up the eastern China coast to Xiamen or Shanghai. There are usually only four to five departures monthly for each destination. There are also three to four ships a month to Haikou, Hainan Island.

The Hong Kong & Yaumati Ferry Co (☎ 2525-1108) has two morning and two evening boats to Shekou in Shenzhen. The tickets are HK$110 from Hong Kong and HK$90 from Shekou. Departures are from the China ferry terminal in Tsim Sha Tsui.

For information on getting to Macau by sea, see the Macau Getting There & Away chapter.

Sailing times and ticket prices are subject to frequent change. For the latest information, as well as bookings, you can either go to the ticket windows at the China ferry terminal in Tsim Sha Tsui or contact CTS.

Departure Tax
If leaving by sea, there is a departure tax of HK$26, but it's an 'invisible' tax as it's included in the price of the ticket.

ORGANISED TOURS
It's so easy to organise a tour yourself after you've arrived in Hong Kong that it hardly pays to do so beforehand. See the Hong Kong Getting Around chapter for details.

WARNING
Remember that all prices published in this book are subject to change. Inflation is the scourge of travel writers – today's quoted prices start to look very quaint six months after publication. Furthermore, travel agents recommended in this book can go bad or bankrupt, or get swallowed up in corporate raids.

In addition, the travel industry is highly competitive and there are many lurks and perks. In other words, you may have to do a bit of research yourself to find out who's offering the best deals on tickets this year.

Getting Around

Hong Kong is small and crowded, and therefore public transport is the only practical way to move people. Consequently public transport is cheap, fast, widely used and generally efficient. It is mostly privately owned and operates at a profit.

TO/FROM THE AIRPORT
The new airport at Chek Lap Kok opened in early July 1998, replacing Kai Tak airport. Chek Lap Kok airport sits on a huge chunk of reclaimed land off Lantau. It's much further away from the town centre than Kai Tak and getting into town has become an expensive affair. The Airport Railway is probably the most popular transport choice for most people, although taxis (which are not cheap) and buses also connect with Kowloon and Hong Kong Island.

Airport Railway
Regular departures take passengers to Central on Hong Kong Island at speeds of up to 135km/h in approximately 23 minutes. The Airport Railway consists of two lines, but the one of most use to travellers is the Airport Express, with departures every 4½ minutes when fully operational.

The Airport Express stops at Tsing Yi, West Kowloon and Central. The train is a comfortable ride, with individual TV sets (nine channels in four languages) relaying flight information, world news and entertainment programs. There is an in-town check-in service whereby you can check in your baggage on Hong Kong Island and Kowloon, leaving you free to go shopping. Flight information screens have been installed at the Airport Express stations so you can check on the status of your flight. One-way adult fares to/from the airport are HK$100 for Hong Kong Island and HK$90 for Kowloon. Children's tickets are approximately half price. A number of hotels offer a free shuttle bus service to hotels from the stations in Central and Kowloon.

The other line is the Tung Chung line, which runs from Tung Chung New Town to Tsing Yi, to Lai King, to Olympic, to Kowloon, to Central. Trains on this line are not as hi-tech as the Airport Express, and are generally for local passengers rather than international arrivals.

Airbus
Hong Kong Island and Kowloon are connected to the airport by airbus, the routes of which are in the following list. The most useful for travellers are the A11, A12 and the A21, which take you to most of the major hotel and guesthouse areas. The buses are air conditioned and have plenty of room for luggage. English and Chinese announcements notify passengers of hotels serviced at each stop. No change is given on the buses, although change is available at the airport bus service centre.

A11 – Sheung Wan, Central, Admiralty, Wan Chai, Causeway Bay (HK$40); buses leave every 12 minutes

A12 – Sheung Wan, Central, Admiralty, Wan Chai, Causeway Bay, Tin Hau, Fortress Hill, North Point, Quarry Bay, Tai Koo, Sai Wan Ho (HK$45); buses leave every 15 minutes

A21 – Mong Kok, Yau Ma Tei, Jordan, Tsim Sha Tsui, Kowloon-Canton Railway (KCR) station (HK$33); buses leave every 10 minutes

A22 – Jordan, Hung Hom, To Kwa Wan, Kowloon Bay, Ngau Tau Kok, Kwun Tong, Lam Tin (HK$39); buses leave every 15 minutes

A31 – Tsing Yi, Kwai Chung, Tsuen Wan (HK$17); buses leave every 15 minutes

A41 – Tsing Yi, Sha Tin (HK$20); buses leave every 20 minutes

There are also a number of routes that run from the airport throughout the night, these include:

N11 – Sheung Wan, Central, Admiralty, Wan Chai, Causeway Bay (HK$35); buses leave every 20 minutes

HONG KONG

N21 – Tsing Yi Rd West, Mei Foo, Lai Chi Kok, Cheung Sha Wan, Sham Shui Po, Prince Edward, Mong Kok KCR Station (HK$23); buses leave every 20 minutes

N22 – Tung Chung, Mong Kok, Yau Ma Tei, Jordan, Tsim Sha Tsui Ferry pier (HK$28); buses leave every 20 minutes

N31 – Tung Chung, Tsing Yi, Tsuen Wan (HK$20); buses leave every 20 minutes

Taxi

Taking a taxi is the only other public transport option. The taxi stand is just outside the transportation centre, at the main terminal building (it is clearly signposted). Only take a taxi if you have to, as it is an expensive affair with Chek Lap Kok being so far away from hotel clusters in the centre of town. It is far cheaper (and quicker) to take the Airport Express: only consider a taxi if you are part of a large group. To Tsim Sha Tsui and Kwun Tong in Kowloon it costs HK$285 and HK$340 respectively. To Central, Wan Chai, Causeway Bay and Aberdeen in Hong Kong Island it costs HK$350/370/380/430 respectively. To Tsuen Wan and Sha Tin in the New Territories is costs HK$235 and HK$325 respectively (please note that all taxi prices are estimates). It is useful to remember that red taxis serve Hong Kong Island, green taxis the New Territories and blue taxis Lantau Island.

Boat

There is a ferry link between the airport and Tuen Mun in the New Territories. Ferry services operate from 6 am to 10 pm daily and services leave at approximately 30 minute intervals. The one-way fare is HK$15 for adults and HK$10 for children. The trip takes about 15 minutes. There are plans to expand the ferry service to take in other destinations around Hong Kong in the future.

BUS

The extensive bus system offers a bewildering number of routes that take you just about anywhere in Hong Kong. Most visitors use the buses to explore the south side of Hong Kong Island and the New Territories. The north side of Hong Kong Island

and most of Kowloon are well-served by the Mass Transit Railway (MTR).

In Central, the most important bus station is on the ground floor under Exchange Square. From this station you can catch buses to Aberdeen, Repulse Bay, Stanley and other destinations on the south side of Hong Kong Island. In Kowloon, the Star Ferry Bus Station is the most crucial, with buses to the KCR station and points in eastern and western Kowloon.

Finding the bus station is the easy part; figuring out which bus you want may take more effort. One useful fact to memorise is that any bus number ending with the letter K (78K, 69K etc) means the route connects to the Kowloon-Canton Railway. Similarly, bus numbers ending with M (51M, 68M etc) go to other MTR stations. Those ending with R are recreational buses and normally run on Sunday, public holidays or for special events like the races at Happy Valley. Buses with an X are express. Air conditioning is used without mercy even in winter – bring gloves so you don't get frostbite. Whether you want it or not, air conditioning costs extra. Children under the age of four can ride for free if accompanied by an adult; children aged five to 11 pay half fare.

Buses are run by two private operators. The majority of Citybuses are plush air-con coaches, and the drivers tend to be a bit more sedate than some those from other companies. Unfortunately most bus drivers drive maniacally and crashes are not infrequent. In 1998 there was a bus crash in the Aberdeen tunnel and a serious Citybus crash that left three dead (the driver was taking a bend too fast).

Kowloon and the New Territories are served by Kowloon Motor Bus (KMB). Citybuses are yellow and KMB buses are red and cream.

Most buses run from about 6 am until midnight, but Nos 121 and 122 are night buses that operate through the Cross-Harbour Tunnel every 15 minutes from 12.45 to 5 am. Bus No 121 runs from Macau Ferry pier on Hong Kong Island, then through the tunnel to Chatham Rd in Tsim

Public Bus Routes

0   2.5   5 Km

Sha Tsui East before continuing to Choi Hung on the east side of the airport. Bus No 122 runs from North Point on Hong Kong Island, through the Cross-Harbour Tunnel, Chatham Rd South in Tsim Sha Tsui East, the northern part of Nathan Rd and on to Lai Chi Kok in the north-west part of Kowloon. You can catch these near the tunnel entrances on either side of the harbour.

Fares range from HK$2.50 to HK$30. Payment is made into a fare box upon entry, so have plenty of change handy as no change is given. A typical trip will cost around HK$5. Otherwise, invest in an Octopus card, which you can use on the majority of KMB and Citybus cross-harbour routes (see the Mass Transit Railway section in this chapter for more information on Octopus cards). There are no ticket collectors. To alight, push the bell strip or button just before your stop.

If you can't find the bus you need, the Hong Kong Tourist Association (HKTA) has leaflets and an information hotline (☎ 2807-6177). You can also contact Citybus (☎ 2873-0818) or KMB (☎ 2745-4466). For buses to specific sights around Hong Kong, see the Things to See & Do section in the relevant chapter.

Minibus

Minibuses are cream-coloured with a red roof or stripe down the side, and seat 16 people. Minibuses can be handy to go short distances, such as from Central to Wan Chai or Causeway Bay, and you can always get a seat – standing passengers are not allowed by law. The destination is displayed on the front in largish Chinese characters, and although there is sometimes a smaller English translation below, it can be hard to read. The price to the final destination is displayed on a card propped up in the window, but this is also often only in Chinese.

You can hail a minibus just as you do an ordinary taxi. It will stop almost anywhere, but not at the stops for the large KMB buses or in the restricted zones where it's unsafe to stop. The fares are not much higher than on the large buses.

The real trick lies in getting off. There are no buttons or bells, so you must call out before your stop. This is no easy task if you're not really sure where you want to get off. Moreover, minibus drivers rarely speak English. If you call out, 'stop here please', there is a pretty good chance the driver will do so, but otherwise try the Cantonese version, which sounds like 'yow lok'.

Fares range from HK$2 to HK$10, but tend to increase on rainy days and at night. You pay the driver when you get off.

If you're in Central on Hong Kong Island, the best place to catch minibuses to Wan Chai and other points east is on the ground level of Exchange Square. If heading west towards Kennedy Town, walk up to Stanley St, near Lan Kwai Fong. There are a few buses that cross the harbour late at night, running between Wan Chai and Mong Kok. On Hong Kong Island, minibuses can be found on Hennessy and Fleming Rds. In Kowloon you may have to trudge up Nathan Rd as far as Mong Kok before you'll find one. Minibuses to the New Territories can be picked up at the

Jordan Rd ferry pier in Kowloon or at Choi Hong MTR station.

One last point, if you're in a hurry, do not jump on an empty or near-empty minibus. Drivers will sit for as long as 20 minutes waiting for passengers, and if the minibus doesn't fill up, the driver will cruise the streets, stopping constantly to try and pull in riders. When this happens, you're better off taking the bus, MTR or simply walking.

Maxicab

Maxicabs (or Green minibuses) have a green stripe, operate on fixed routes and stop at designated places. Fares vary, according to distance, between HK$1.50 and HK$18. You pay when you get on and no change is given. In Tsim Sha Tsui the No 1 maxicab runs from the Star Ferry terminal to Tsim Sha Tsui East every five minutes or so between 7.20 am and 10.20 pm. The fare is HK$2.50. On Hong Kong Island, a useful route is from Edinburgh Place (near City Hall and the Star Ferry terminal) to the Peak. Hours of operation are from 7 am to midnight.

TRAM

Hong Kong's trams are tall and narrow double-decker streetcars that trundle along the northern side of Hong Kong Island. The tram line was built in 1904 on what was then the shoreline of Hong Kong Island, which helps you appreciate just how much land Hong Kong has reclaimed from the sea.

The trams are not fast but are cheap and fun. For a flat fare of HK$2 (dropped in a box beside the driver when you leave) you can go as far as you like, whether it's one block or to the end of the line. Trams operate between 6 am and 1 am, and on each route trams run at a frequency of one every two to seven minutes, but often arrive bunched together. If the wait is much longer then there's probably been a backup somewhere down the line, so be prepared to elbow your way through the crowd to squeeze aboard when it arrives. You may have to do the same when it comes time to alight.

Try to get a seat at the front window upstairs to enjoy a first-class view while rattling through the crowded streets. Tall passengers will find it uncomfortable standing up as the ceiling is low, but there is more space at the rear of the tram. Watch out for trams when crossing the road; although most make a grinding sound which alerts you to the tram's lumbering approach, some are stealth versions and the driver may not be looking ahead carefully (some drivers eat their lunch and dinner while driving).

The routes often overlap. Some start at Kennedy Town and run to Shau Kei Wan, but others run only part of the way and one turns south to Happy Valley. The longest run, from Shau Kei Wan to Kennedy Town, takes about 1½ hours. The eight routes are as follows:

From (west)	To (east)
Kennedy Town	Causeway Bay
Kennedy Town	Happy Valley
Kennedy Town	North Point
Kennedy Town	Shau Kei Wan
Shau Kei Wan	Happy Valley
Western Market	Causeway Bay
Western Market	Shau Kei Wan
Whitty Street	North Point

TRAIN
Mass Transit Railway (MTR)

The MTR is clean, fast and safe, and one of the world's most modern subway systems. Though it costs a bit more than other forms of public transport, it is the quickest way to get to most urban destinations. Trains run every two to four minutes from 6 am to 1 am daily on three lines. Fares range from HK$4 to HK$13.

For short hauls, the MTR is not great value. If you want to cross the harbour from Tsim Sha Tsui to Central, the MTR is about five times the price of the Star Ferry with none of the views, and is only marginally faster. If your destination is further away (say North Point or Tsuen Wan), the MTR is considerably faster than a ferry or a bus, air conditioned and about the same price. The MTR also connects with the Kowloon-

Canton railway (KCR) at Kowloon Tong station. If possible, it's best to skirt rush hours: 7.30 to 9.30 am and 5 to 7 pm. Some 2.4 million people use the MTR every day, most of them at these times. Joining the crowd is no fun.

Riding the MTR is easy; just follow the signs. Everything is automated, from the ticket vending machines to the turnstiles. Ticket prices range from between HK$4 and HK$13. Ticket machines take HK$5, HK$2, HK$1 and 50 cent pieces, and give change; a handful of machines take HK$20 notes. The machines have a touch-sensitive screen with highlighted destinations. There are also change machines that accept coins only – notes must be changed at the ticket offices or the Hang Seng minibanks located in the stations. Once you pass through the turnstiles, you have 90 minutes to complete the journey before the ticket becomes void.

The MTR uses 'smart tickets' with a magnetic coding strip on the back. When you pass through the turnstile, the card is encoded with the station identification and time. At the other end, the exit turnstile sucks in the ticket, reads where you came from, the time and how much you paid, and lets you through if everything is in order. If you underpaid by punching the wrong button on the ticket machine, you can pay the difference at the other end.

You can't buy a return ticket, but you can purchase an 'Octopus' card if you're going to do quite a bit of travelling during your stay in Hong Kong. This clever device allows you to travel on the MTR, the KCR East Rail, LRT (including the LRT shuttle bus), most of the KMB and Citybus cross-harbour routes and all outlying islands and New Town routes of the Hong Kong & Yaumati Ferry Co (HKF) ferries. This one card gives you access to six different modes of transport in Hong Kong. All you do is touch fare-deducting processors installed at stations with the Octopus card and the fare is deducted (it will show you how many credits you have left). Octopus cards can be purchased from ticket offices or customer service centres in MTR, KCR East Rail and

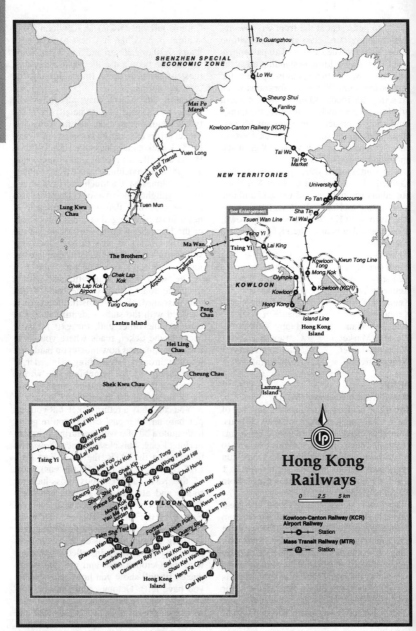

To Guangzhou

SHENZHEN SPECIAL
ECONOMIC ZONE

Lo Wu

Sheung Shui
Fanling

Mai Po
Marsh

Kowloon-Canton Railway (KCR)

Tai Wo
Tai Po
Market

Yuen Long

Light Rail Transit (LRT)

NEW TERRITORIES

University

Fo Tan Racecourse

Lung Kwu
Chau

Tuen Mun

Sha Tin

Tsuen Wan Line   Tai Wai

Tsing Yi

Ma Wan

Tsing Yi Lai King

The Brothers

Kowloon
Tong Kwun Tong Line

Chek Lap
Kok

Airport Railway

Olympic Mong Kok

KOWLOON

Chek Lap Kok
Airport

Kowloon Kowloon (KCR)

Tung Chung

Hong Kong

Peng
Chau

Island Line

Lantau Island

Hong Kong
Island

Hei Ling
Chau

Cheung Chau

Shek Kwu Chau

Lamma
Island

Tsuen Wan
Tai Wo Hau

Kwai Hing
Kwai Fong
Lai King

Tsing Yi

Mei Foo Lai Chi Kok Kowloon Tong Wong Tai Sin
Cheung Sha Wan Shek Kip Mei Diamond Hill
Sham Shui Po Lok Fu Choi Hung
Prince Edward Kowloon Bay
Mong Kok Ngau Tau Kok
Yau Ma Tei Kwun Tong
Jordan Lam Tin

KOWLOON

Tsim Sha Tsui

Sheung Wan Fortress
Central Hill North Point Quarry Bay
Admiralty Tai Koo
Wan Chai Sai Wan Ho
Causeway Bay Tin Hau Shau Kei Wan
Heng Fa Chuen
Chai Wan

Hong Kong
Island

**Hong Kong
Railways**

0   2.5   5 km

Kowloon-Canton Railway (KCR)
Airport Railway
├──◉── Station

Mass Transit Railway (MTR)
── Ⓜ ── Station

LRT stations, and certain piers of the HKF. Cards come in the following denominations: Adult, HK$150; children and senior citizens, HK$70 (a refundable deposit of HK$50 is included in the price). Octopus cards are reloadable; just go to one of the add value machines or ticket offices located at every station (you can add value to the amount of HK$1000). The card has a maximum negative value of HK$35 which is recovered the next time you reload (hence the deposit). There may well be a tourist Octopus in the future. If you have any queries, call the Octopus hotline on ☎ 2993-8880.

Avoid the MTR 'tourist ticket' which costs HK$25 but is only good for HK$20 worth of travel. For your extra HK$5 you get to keep the ticket as a second-rate souvenir.

Children aged two or under can travel free and there are special child/student tickets (for children aged three to 11) which are much cheaper than adult prices. Passengers aged 12 or over can only use the child/student tickets if they are carrying a Hong Kong Student Identity Card – an International Student Identity Card (ISIC card) is not acceptable.

Smoking, eating and drinking are not permitted in MTR stations or on the trains, and violators are subject to heavy fines if caught. You are not supposed to carry large objects (like bicycles) aboard trains either, though backpacks and suitcases are OK.

Unfortunately there are no toilets in either the trains or the stations. If you leave something on the train, you might be able to reclaim your goods at the lost property office at Admiralty station between 11 am and 6.45 pm, Monday to Saturday. For other queries, call the passenger information hotline (☎ 2750-0170).

Kowloon-Canton Railway (KCR)

KCR is a single-line commuter railway running from Kowloon to the border with mainland China at Lo Wu. The tracks are the same as used by the Kowloon-Guangzhou express, but the trains are different, bearing more of a resemblance to subway train carriages. The KCR is a quick way to get up to the New Territories, and the ride offers some nice views.

The KCR is cheap, with a half hour ride to Sheung Shui costing just HK$9 (HK$18 for 1st class), although the trip to the border at Lo Wu costs HK$33 (HK$66 for 1st class). Trains run every five to 10 minutes, except during rush hour, when there is a train every three minutes. The trip to Lo Wu takes about 45 minutes. Children under three years travel free, with a reduced fare for three to 12 year olds.

A new double-decker high-speed train has been introduced that speeds from Hung Hom on a nonstop journey to Lo Wu. This cuts the journey time by 15 minutes; tickets are HK$66.

You can change from the MTR to the KCR at Kowloon Tong station. The southernmost station on the line at Hung Hom is easily reached from Tsim Sha Tsui by taking green minibus No 8 from Middle Rd. You can use your Octopus card (see Mass Transit Railway in this chapter for information on Octopus) on the KCR and you can ride to Lo Wu station if you plan to cross the border into China (see the Getting There & Away chapter on Hong Kong for more details). The KCR customer services hotline number is ☎ 2602-7799.

Light Rail Transit (LRT)

The latest addition to the alphabet soup of Hong Kong trains is the LRT. This is rather like a modern air-con version of the tram. The LRT runs on the road and stops at designated stations. However, it's much faster than the tram, at times reaching speeds of up to 70km/h.

Most visitors never set foot on the LRT, as it only runs in the western New Territories, connecting the city of Tuen Mun with Yuen Long. There are plans to connect it with the MTR and KCR networks.

There are five LRT lines connecting various small suburbs. The system operates from 5.30 to 12.30 am Monday to Saturday, and from 6 am to midnight on Sunday and public holidays. The LRT station in Tuen Mun is at the hoverferry pier, from where you can catch a ferry to Central. Fares on the LRT are HK$4 to HK$5.80 for adults and tickets are purchased from vending machines (change is available from change booths). Octopus cards can be used on the LRT (see Mass Rail Transit in this chapter for more information on Octopus). The system of fare collection is unique for Hong Kong – there are no gates or turnstiles and customers are 'trusted' to pay. However, that 'trust' is enforced by occasional police spot checks. Fines for those who haven't purchased a ticket are HK$290 plus possible prosecution.

TAXI

Hong Kong taxis are not too expensive when compared with other major developed cities. With more than 18,000 cruising the roads, taxis are usually easy to flag down.

When a taxi is available, there should be a red 'For Hire' sign displayed in the windscreen and the 'Taxi' sign on the roof will be lit up at night. It's important to realise that taxis cannot stop at bus stops or in restricted stopping zones where a yellow line is painted next to the kerb.

In Kowloon and Hong Kong Island, taxis are red with silver tops. In the New Territories taxis are green with white tops. New Territories taxis are not permitted to pick up or put down passengers in Kowloon or Hong Kong Island. On Lantau Island, taxis are blue. Hong Kong Island taxis and Kowloon taxis tend to avoid each others' territory as the drivers' street geography on the other side of the water gets very shaky.

The flag fall for taxis in Hong Kong and Kowloon, is HK$15 for the first 2km and HK$1.40 for every additional 200m. In the New Territories, flag fall is HK$12 for the first 2km, and HK$1.20 for every 0.2km thereafter. There is a luggage fee of HK$5 per bag, but not all drivers insist on this payment. Most drivers carry very little change, so keep a supply of coins and HK$10 bills.

If you go through either the cross-harbour or eastern harbour tunnels, you'll be charged an extra HK$20. The toll is only HK$10, but you have to pay for the driver's return toll as

well. You will be charged a mammoth HK$45 for using the new Western Harbour Tunnel. There is no double charge for other tunnels; the tolls are as follows: Aberdeen costs HK$5; Lion Rock costs HK$6; Shing Mun costs HK$5; Tate's Cairn costs HK$4; and Tseung Kwan O costs HK$3.

It's often hard to get taxis during rush hour, when it rains or during driver shift changes (around 4 pm). Taxis are also in higher demand after midnight. Officially, there are no extra late-night charges and no extra passenger charges. Unofficially, during heavy rains and after midnight some drivers try to charge double, which is illegal; just pretend you 'don't understand' and pay the meter fare.

Many taxis have a card that lists the top 50 destinations in Cantonese, English and Japanese – this is useful as many taxi drivers don't speak English. Even if the card doesn't list your specific destination, it will certainly have some nearby place. However, it's never a bad idea to have your destination written down in Chinese.

If you feel a taxi driver has ripped you off, get the taxi number and call the police hotline (☎ 2527-7177) to lodge a complaint with the relevant details about when, where and how much. Drivers have some reason to fear the police as getting a taxi licence is extremely difficult and can be revoked if the driver breaks the rules.

Also contact the police if you leave something of value in a taxi – the majority of drivers will turn in lost property.

CAR & MOTORCYCLE
Road Rules

Driving is on the left side of the road, the same as in Australia and Britain but the opposite to China. Seat belts must be worn by the driver and all front-seat passengers. Police are strict and give out traffic tickets at the drop of a hat.

Driving in crowded Hong Kong brings little joy. The traffic often slows to a crawl and finding parking is a nightmare. On top of this, the government has deliberately made driving expensive as a discouragement. For a local resident to get a driving licence, he or she must take an expensive driving course and then wait about 18 months. The motor vehicle import tax is 100% and the petrol tax is more than 100%. Vehicle registration (based on engine size) averages about HK$8000 annually and liability insurance is compulsory.

For details about driving licences, see the Visas & Documents (Driving Licence & Permits) in the Facts for the Visitor chapter on Hong Kong.

Car Rental

There's not much need to rent a car in Hong Kong, unless you are planning an excursion to the New Territories. Even then, unless the place is quite out of the way, you may do better with public transportation. It still can be fun though.

Car rental firms require either an International Driver's Permit or one from your home country, and a credit card deposit of HK$5000 and up (the slip is torn up upon the return of an undamaged vehicle). Drivers must be at least 25 years of age. Daily rates run from HK$650 for a small car like a Honda Civic to HK$2500 for an upmarket Mercedes or BMW model. Reputable car rental outfits in Hong Kong include Ace (☎ 2560-8689), 16 Min Fat St, Happy Valley, and Avis (☎ 2890-6988), 85 Leighton Rd, Causeway Bay.

You normally get unlimited kilometres at no extra cost and discounts if you rent for a week or more. Many car-rental outlets and the big hotels offer chauffeur-driven cars, but using this service for one day could easily cost more than your hotel room. Motor cycles seem impossible to rent, but can be bought if you're staying long enough.

Motorcycle

It's impossible to rent motorcycles in Hong Kong, but if you're staying for a while you can buy one. In truth, Hong Kong is not a great place to ride: traffic is fierce, exhaust fumes are heavy and other drivers don't give a damn about motorcyclists. Registration is expensive and somewhat of a hassle.

The best place to look for a motorcycle, new or used, is on Caroline Hill Rd in Causeway Bay. There is a string of shops, most of which have at least one person who can speak English. Unless you have a good job, you may only be able to window-shop; Hong Kong's soaring import duties make motorcycles ridiculously expensive.

BICYCLE

Cycling in Kowloon or Central would be suicidal, but in the quiet areas of the islands or the New Territories a bike can be quite a nice way of getting around. The bike-rental shops tend to run out of bikes early on weekends.

Some places where you can rent bikes and ride in safety include: Shek O on Hong Kong Island; Sai Kung, Sha Tin and Tai Mei Tuk (near Tai Po) in the New Territories; Mui Wo (Silvermine Bay) on Lantau Island; and on the island of Cheung Chau.

WALKING

Much of Hong Kong is best seen on foot, however walking around isn't necessarily easy or relaxing, especially in the business districts. Poorly designed crosswalks, crushing masses of people and hurtling buses can make your stroll anything but casual. The complexity of pedestrian flyovers around Central, Admiralty and Wan Chai can drive visitors insane, but there's often no other way to cross the road. If you find you can't cross the road normally, look up and you will probably see a flyover nearby. Finding the stairs up, however, can be bewilderingly difficult – stairs are often hidden away in neighbouring buildings.

Sometimes it seems that the other side of the road is completely inaccessible. You also have to be constantly on your guard against the dangers of traffic – the heat, humidity and general chaos of the streets of Hong Kong can create a stubborn lethargy in the pedestrian shopper that can be as lethal as some of the driving. If you persevere you will be rewarded with the sights, sounds and smells that define Hong Kong.

HONG KONG

Where have all the Rickshaws gone?

Rickshaws must have appeared in Hong Kong soon after being invented as the Japanese *jinriksha*. There were already 700 registered and licensed in the colony of Hong Kong by 1895 and there were probably more than 5000 by WWI. In the mid-1920s, despite competition from buses, trams and other mechanised transport, rickshaws still numbered more than 3000 and were a vital part of the colony's transport network. Over the next 15 years rickshaws dwindled away until there were only a few hundred left at the start of WWII, but the numbers must have swollen dramatically during the war and in the tough years that followed

HONG KONG TOURIST ASSOCIATION
A rickshaw puller, central Hong Kong.

because there were about 8000 registered in the late 1940s. It was the peak before a rapid decline as taxis, and increased traffic congestion, swept rickshaws off the roads in the 1950s and 1960s. By the early 1970s rickshaws had ceased to be a means of transport and became a tourist attraction.

It's said the last rickshaw licence was issued in 1975, when there were still nearly 100 left in the colony. But the rickshaw pullers still seem to have current licences. Although there is no campaign to get rid of the rickshaws, the remaining rickshaw 'boys' are now old men, and are ready to entertain offers from any rickshaw collector who might care to buy their steeds.

Wealthy families and businesses often had a rickshaw, much as a car is kept today. Towards the end of WWI there were even 60 rickshaws registered in the name of brothels. These were used to deliver courtesans to their customers. There was a busy trade to the bars and brothels of Wan Chai for a time during the Vietnam R&R years of the 1960s and into the 1970s. By the early 1980s the numbers had dropped to less than 50 and the rickshaws eventually contracted to the small group that hangout at the Star Ferry pier on the Hong Kong Island side, waiting to take visitors on a short jog around the car park or to pose for photographs. By the early 1990s rickshaw numbers had fallen to less than 20 and by late 1997 these were truly an endangered species, just eight rickshaws remained and a 'for sale' sign hung over the whole collection.

Tony Wheeler

Rural Hong Kong offers some outstanding walks and hikes. Try the 100km MacLehose trail in the New Territories for starters. Even Hong Kong Island has a 50km 'Hong Kong Trail' that spans the length of the island and takes you up and out of the city and into the trees and hills. If this daunts you, just stick to the 3.5km circuit around the Peak or head out to the islands to experience tranquillity and beauty.

TRAVELATOR

Hong Kong's latest transport scheme is attracting widespread attention. Officially dubbed the 'Hillside Escalator Link', but commonly known as the 'travelator', this looks like something out of a science fiction movie. Basically, the system consists of elevated escalators and moving walkways. It's 800m long at present, making it the longest escalator in the world.

One of Hong Kong's long-standing problems is that many well-to-do residents live in the Mid-Levels, the lower portion of the Peak, but work in the skyscraper forest below. The roads are narrow and the distance is more vertical than horizontal, making the walk home a strenuous climb. The result is a rush-hour nightmare of bumper-to-bumper taxis, minibuses and private cars. The travelator is aimed at solving this problem by getting people out of vehicles entirely. To judge from the rush-hour crowds, the project has been a smashing success.

Although construction ran 500% over budget, no one is complaining and there's talk of expanding the system.

BOAT

Hong Kong's ferries are almost always faster and cheaper than the buses and there are discounts for children under 12. As long as you are not prone to seasickness, the boats are fun and the harbour views are stunning when the weather cooperates. These rides also furnish you with great photo opportunities.

Though you'll find that many people break the rules, smoking is prohibited on all ferries and the fine is HK$5000. If you travel on the Aberdeen to Sok Kwu Wan ferry you will notice that the captain is smoking, as are the ship's mate and the ticket collector and half of the passengers.

Sad to say, all of the cross-harbour ferries now prohibit bicycles. This means that the only way to get a bicycle across the harbour is in the boot (trunk) of a taxi. Bicycles are permitted on the outlying islands ferries, but not on the hoverferries.

The ferries to the outlying islands and the longer haul boats have small galleys where you can buy appalling food and coffee – beer and soft drinks are also for sale.

Bear in mind that temperatures on the open sea are often much lower than on land. If you are in Hong Kong in winter and are planning to journey by ferry, take a few extra layers as the thermometer can drop rapidly.

Cross-Harbour Ferries

Practically every visitor takes a ride on the Star Ferry, which is also an essential mode of transport for commuters. The ferries have names like Morning Star, Evening Star, Celestial Star, Shining Star, Twinkling Star etc. You should definitely take the trip on a clear night if possible.

There are three Star Ferry routes, but by far the most popular is the one running between Tsim Sha Tsui and Central. The trip takes seven minutes, and there are frequent departures – leaving every five to 10 minutes

at peak time. Fares for the lower and upper deck are HK$1.70 and HK$2.20 respectively. Those 65 years of age and over ride for free. The coin-operated turnstiles do not give change but you can get this from the ticket window. A special tourist ticket is available for HK$20, which allows unlimited rides on the Star Ferry and Hong Kong's trams. Given how cheap the normal fare is, you'd have to do at least 14 trips in four days to make this worthwhile. The Star Ferry also links Tsim Sha Tsui with Wan Chai, and Central with Hung Hom. Frequencies and operating hours are as follows:

Central (Edinburgh Place)-Hung Hom: every 12 to 20 minutes (every 20 minutes on Sunday and public holidays) from 7 am to 7.20 pm
Central (Edinburgh Place)-Tsim Sha Tsui: every five to 10 minutes from 6.30 am to 11.30 pm
Wan Chai-Tsim Sha Tsui: every 10 to 20 minutes from 7.30 am to 11 pm

Hong Kong Island-Kowloon-New Territories Ferries

The Hong Kong Ferry (HKF) Company operates a number of useful ferries and hoverferries.

Hoverferries are twice as fast as conventional boats and are far more modern, with aircraft-type seats, no-one standing, and air conditioning. These are exciting to ride but not particularly smooth. When the water is rough, hoverferries bounce along like a stone skipping across a pond. If you're prone to seasickness, don't get on a hoverferry after eating a big plate of greasy pork chops or lasagne – you won't have the option of getting rid of any unpleasant mess over the side as the windows don't open. The following schedules are for ferries and hoverferries connecting Hong Kong Island to Kowloon and the New Territories.

Ferry
Central-Yau Ma Tei (Jordan Rd): every 15 to 20 minutes from 6.10 am to midnight
North Point-Hung Hom: every 20 minutes from 6.55 am to 9 pm
North Point-Kowloon City: every 20 minutes from 6.50 am to 8.50 pm

North Point-Kwun Ton: every 20 minutes from 7 am to 8 pm

Wan Chai-Hung Hom: every 15 to 20 minutes from 7 am to 8 pm, Monday to Friday; and every 20 to 30 minutes from 7.10 am to 8.15 pm on Saturday

Hovercraft (Hoverferry)

Central (Queen's pier)-Tsim Sha Tsui East: every 20 minutes from 8 am to 8 pm

Central (outlying islands ferry piers)-Tsuen Wan: every 20 minutes from 7 am to 6.40 pm

Central (outlying islands ferry piers)-Tuen Mun: every 15 to 20 minutes from 6.45 am to 8.30 pm

Central-Tuen Mun by jet catamaran: four services from the outlying islands ferry piers, every morning between 7.20 and 8.35 am

At sporadic intervals, there are also early morning ferry departures from Wan Chai via Central to Tuen Mun and return. Another service operates from Tsuen Wan to Central and Wan Chai via Tsing Yi.

Outlying Islands Ferries

HKF runs a series of ferry services to Hong Kong's more populous islands including Lantau, Cheung Chau, Peng Chau and Lamma Island. Departures are from the outlying islands ferry piers, which sit on a plot of newly reclaimed land in front of Exchange Square in Central. These piers are all clearly signposted.

On weekends there are a few ferries to Lantau and Cheung Chau from the Star Ferry terminal in Tsim Sha Tsui.

The larger boats are separated into ordinary and deluxe classes. The deluxe class includes an air conditioned top deck that can induce frostbite, and a small open-air deck on the fantail. This last spot is one of the nicest places to be in Hong Kong on a warm sunny day, and is the main reason why you'd want to shell out extra for the deluxe ticket.

Fares are generally reasonable, except on weekends when the prices nearly double. From Monday to Saturday morning, adult fares to Mui Wo (Lantau) are HK$9.70 (HK$17 deluxe); on Saturday afternoon and Sunday fares rise to HK$17 (HK$32 deluxe). Ferries to Lamma cost HK$9.20 (H$17

deluxe) from Monday to Saturday morning, and HK$12.50 (HK$32 deluxe) on Saturday afternoon and Sunday. Prices for children and senior citizens are about half.

Beverages and snacks are available on board. If you decide to venture out to one of the islands, try and do so during the week, as it's cheaper and the boats are packed to the gunwales on weekends. For more information on the outlying islands, see the Outlying Islands chapter.

Lantau is also served by ferries linking Central with Discovery Bay, a dormitory community sitting on the eastern side of Lantau Island. Ferries run every 20 minutes during the day and every hour or so throughout the night. The one-way fare is HK$20, and boats depart from the eastern side of the Star Ferry terminal in Central.

Amusingly (or not), ferries from Central occasionally have a problem navigating the short distances involved. A ferry en route to Lamma Island recently strayed into Chinese waters in foggy weather (its engine also caught on fire) and was escorted back to Hong Kong waters by a Chinese vessel. Another ferry from Lamma Island to Aberdeen decided to go the long way around via Stanley on the south-east of Hong Kong Island.

Times are subject to change. For the latest information, pick up a seasonal schedule at the HKF information office next to the outlying islands ferry piers in Central or phone the inquiries hotline ☎ 2542-3081. HKTA information centres also have up-to-date ferry schedules. Basic schedules for some of the major outlying islands ferries are in the following list:

Central-Cheung Chau: approximately hourly from 5.35 am to 12.30 pm, with more frequent trips during rush hours

Central-Cheung Chau: there are five hoverferry services in either direction between 8.50 am and 4.50 pm Monday to Friday

Tsim Sha Tsui-Cheung Chau: ferry leaves for Cheung Chau at 4 pm Saturday, and at 8 and 10 am Sunday; ferry leaves for Tsim Sha Tsui at 12.45 pm Sunday

Central-Lantau (Mui Wo): approximately hourly from 6.10am to 12.20 am

Central-Lantau (Mui Wo) via Peng Chau: there are four hoverferry services a day each way from 9.40 am and 5.10 pm

Central-Lantau (Tai O): on Saturday there are two services a day at 9.15 am and 2.15 pm; and one service a day at 8.15 am on Sunday and public holidays

Tsim Sha Tsui-Lantau (Mui Wo): every one to two hours from 1 to 7 pm Saturday and from 9 am to 7 pm Sunday

Central-Peng Chau: approximately hourly from 6.30 am to 12.20 am

Central-Peng Chau: there are four hoverferry services each way between 9.40 am and 5.20 pm Monday to Friday

Central-Lamma Island (Yung Shue Wan): approximately every 1½ hours from 6.20 am to 12.30 am

Central-Lamma Island (Sok Kwu Wan): every two to three hours from 6.50 am to 11 pm

Yung Shue Wan on Lamma Island is also connected to Central by Pollyferries and a HKF hoverferry service that runs between Central and Yung Shue Wan in the morning and afternoon, from Monday to Friday; there is also a Yung Shue Wan, to Pak Kok Tsuen, to Kennedy Town boat that leaves approximately every two hours, and occasional boats from Pak Kok Tsuen to Central.

Other Boats

A *kaido* is a small to medium-sized ferry that can make short runs on the open sea. Few kaido routes operate on regular schedules, preferring to adjust supply to demand. There is a sort of schedule on popular runs like the trip between Aberdeen and Lamma Island. Kaidos run most frequently on weekends and holidays when everyone tries to 'get away from it all'.

A *sampan* is a motorised launch that can only accommodate a few people. A sampan is too small to be considered seaworthy, but can safely zip you around typhoon shelters like Aberdeen Harbour. Bigger than a sampan, but smaller than a kaido, is a *walla walla*. These operate as water taxis on Victoria Harbour. Most of the customers are sailors living on ships anchored in the harbour.

Even if you're not a sailor, walla wallas are useful to late-night carousers who need to get across the harbour after the MTR and regular ferries stop running. Your other late-night options are taxis or bus Nos 121 and 122 (see Bus in this chapter for details). On Hong Kong Island you can catch walla wallas from Queen's pier (east side of the Star Ferry pier). On the Kowloon side, walla wallas can be found at the Kowloon Public pier (just east of Star Ferry pier).

HELICOPTER

This is not exactly for the typical commuter or tourist; however, if you want a spectacular flight over the city with tremendous views to accompany it, contact Heliservices (☎ 2802-0200). You have to charter the chopper for at least half an hour, and a 45 minute flight over to Lantau and back is a mere HK$11,205.

ORGANISED TOURS

Tourism is one of Hong Kong's main money earners, so it's no surprise that there is a mind-boggling number of tours available to just about anywhere in Hong Kong. These are run by specialised tour outfits, hotels, bus companies, ferry operators, and even the MTR.

Some of the best tours are offered by the HKTA. Tours take in some genuinely worthwhile sights, and are well run. If you only have a short time in Hong Kong, or are not in the mood to deal with public transport, these may be just what you're looking for. Some tours are standard excursions covering major sights on Hong Kong Island such as Victoria Peak, while other tours take you on harbour cruises, out to the islands, or through the New Territories.

The HKTA also has a series of thematic tours covering subjects such as horse-racing, Chinese folk customs and lifestyles, sports and recreation, and life in Hong Kong's public housing estates, where you are given the opportunity to visit a Chinese family. Prices range from about HK$275 to HK$500 per person, and there are discounts for children and seniors. The HKTA also arrange tours of Macau and Guangdong Province. For further details pick up a copy of the *HKTA Tours* pamphlet at a HKTA information centre or call the tour operations department (☎ 2807-6390, www.hkta.org) Monday to Saturday from 9 am to 5 pm, and on Sunday (☎ 2807-6177) from 9 am to 5 pm. Another company operating tours in Hong Kong and to Macau, Shenzhen and Guangzhou is Gray Line (☎ 2368-7111).

Watertours (☎ 2724-2856), owned by the venerable Hong Kong trading conglomerate Jardine Matheson, is another well established outfit. As the name implies, the company specialises in water-borne sightseeing, and offers nearly 20 different harbour tours, island excursions and dinner and cocktail cruises. Prices range from HK$200 for the Afternoon Eastern Harbour Cruise to HK$630 for the Highlight of the Night Cruise. If you want to take in the enormity of the Tsing Ma Bridge, Watertours can take you there. Prices are considerably lower for children. You can book through Watertours, a travel agent or, in many cases, your hotel.

Hong Kong Tramways and Star Ferry offer daily tours on trams and boats. There are seven ferry tours a day, costing HK$180 for adults and HK$140 for children 12 and under. Open-top tram tours, which use special luxury trams, leave five times daily (there is one evening departure) and cost HK$180 for adults and HK$140 for kids. For information and bookings, call Hong Kong Tramways on ☎ 2118-6235. If you want something different, then why not hire out a tram for a party. Trams cost HK$530 per hour unless you opt for the antique model, which costs HK$830 per hour. You often see these trundling down the road at night with balloons, music and laughter spilling from the upper deck. You can even hire a 'Star' Ferry by the hour for HK$1300. Further details can be found by phoning Star Ferry (☎ 2118-6241, 2118-6242).

Kowloon

The name Kowloon is thought to have originated when the last emperor of the Song dynasty passed through the area during his flight from the Mongols. He is said to have counted eight peaks on the peninsula and commented that there must therefore be eight dragons there – but was reminded that since he himself was present there must be nine. Kowloon is thus derived from the Cantonese words *gau,* meaning nine, and *long,* for dragon.

It covers a mere 12 sq km of high-rise buildings extending from the Tsim Sha Tsui waterfront to Boundary St. Apart from a few notable exceptions, Kowloon is architecturally unexciting. Height restrictions for buildings (because aircraft bound for Kai Tak airport had to skim Kowloon rooftops) give the district a much lower skyline than in Central. Central is also Hong Kong's financial heart, shown off as its most prized asset, while Kowloon is more a crowded province of mercantile mayhem. There is none of the slickness of Central (except the pockets of glamour in top-end hotel shopping arcades), and for the most part Kowloon is a riot of tourist commerce set to a gritty backdrop of crumbling tenement blocks.

There are impressive buildings, none the less, supported by intriguing sights. Love or hate its design, the Hong Kong Cultural Centre is a bold stab at turning Hong Kong into something more than a city obsessed with wealth. The Peninsula is one of Hong Kong's great colonial buildings and, at night, the Promenade along Victoria Harbour is a stunning technicolour vista of Central and Wan Chai – the subject of countless postcards. Kowloon Park is a blessed haven for the tired denizens of Nathan Rd and the Hong Kong History Museum is a must-see for those who want a colourful and imaginative guide through the Hong Kong of yesterday.

Kowloon's districts are best seen on foot. Unlike on Hong Kong Island, there's no tram to ferry you around; but areas of interest are not spaced too far apart, and these are the areas with the highest concentration of hotels, restaurants and amenities.

TSIM SHA TSUI (MAP 1)

The tourist ghetto of Tsim Sha Tsui (pronounced 'jim sa joy') lies at the very tip of the Kowloon Peninsula. About 1 sq km of shops, restaurants, pubs, topless bars, fast-food places and camera and electronics shops are clustered on either side of Nathan Rd.

Clock Tower

Between the Star Ferry pier and the new Cultural Centre, the 45m clock tower is all that remains of a train station that once existed at the tip of the Kowloon Peninsula. The station – the southern terminus of the Kowloon-Canton Railway (KCR) – was built in 1916 and torn down in 1978. The clock tower was built in 1922. The original building, which had columns and was in colonial style, was too small to handle the large volume of passenger traffic. The new Kowloon KCR station, where many travellers begin their journey to China, is a huge, modern building in Hung Hom to the north-east of Tsim Sha Tsui.

Hong Kong Cultural Centre

Adjacent to the Star Ferry terminal is one of Hong Kong's distinctive landmarks, the Cultural Centre (☎ 2734-2009). It is in many ways a world class venue, including a 2100 seat concert hall, a theatre that seats 1800, a smaller 300 seat theatre, rehearsal studios, an arts library and an impressive main lobby. The concert hall even has a pipe organ (with 8000 pipes), the largest in South-East Asia. The presence of the Cultural Centre has enabled Hong Kong to regularly book high-profile international artists. On the south side of the building is a viewing area where you can admire Victoria Harbour, also known as Hong Kong Harbour. The Cultural Centre is open from

9 am to 11 pm on Monday to Saturday, and from 1 to 11 pm on Sunday and public holidays. There are daily tours from 12.30 to 1 pm; tickets for adults are HK$10, and for children, disabled and senior citizens, HK$5.

Hong Kong Museum of Art
The Cultural Centre complex incorporates the Museum of Art (☎ 2734-2167). There are six galleries exhibiting Chinese antiquities; Chinese fine arts; historical pictures, paintings and lithographs of old Hong Kong; and the Xubaizhi collection of painting and calligraphy. The sixth gallery houses temporary international exhibitions on a rotational basis. The exhibits are quite tastefully displayed, giving one the feeling that funding isn't a major problem for this particular museum. When your feet are sore, take a seat in the hallway and enjoy the harbour vista. There is a shop on the ground level that has a commendable collection of art books and prints, including an extensive section on Chinese art. The museum is closed on Monday; operating hours are Tuesday to Saturday from 10 am to 6 pm, and Sunday and public holidays from 1 to 6 pm. Admission is HK$10 for adults, HK$5 for kids and seniors, but why not go on a Wednesday, when it's free?

Hong Kong Space Museum
This is the peculiar building, shaped like half a golf ball, at 10 Salisbury Rd, adjoining the Cultural Centre. It's divided into three parts: the Space Theatre (planetarium), the Hall of Space Science and the Hall of Astronomy.

Exhibits include a lump of moon rock, models of rocket ships, telescopes, time lines and videos of moon walks – all very educational and worth a look. The Mercury space capsule piloted by astronaut Scott Carpenter in 1962 is also displayed.

Opening times for the exhibition halls are weekdays (closed on Monday) from 1 to 9 pm, and from 10 am to 9 pm on weekends and public holidays. Admission is HK$10 for adults and kids, HK$5 for students and seniors.

The Space Theatre has several 'sky shows' daily (except Monday), some in English and some in Cantonese. Headphone translations are available for all shows. The museum also shows Omnimax (giant screen) films. These films are projected onto the rounded dome of the theatre, and the effect is more laughable than dramatic. Space Theatre shows generally start at 11.30 am, with the last show usually at 8.30 pm. Both sky shows and Omnimax films cost HK$30 for adults and HK$15 for children. To find out what's playing and when, stop by the ticket window or call the museum. Advance bookings can be made up to one hour before show time by calling ☎ 2734-9009.

The Peninsula
Directly opposite the Space Museum on Salisbury Rd stands one of Hong Kong's landmarks, the Peninsula Hotel. Looking like a huge throne, the hotel is a stunning addition to the architecture of Tsim Sha Tsui. Before WWII it was one of several prestigious hotels across Asia where everybody who was anybody stayed. The list of premier hotels included the Raffles in Singapore, the Taj in Bombay, the Cathay (now called the Peace) in Shanghai and the Strand in Yangon (Rangoon).

Land reclamation has robbed the hotel of its prestigious waterfront location, but the breathtaking interior is worth a visit. Afternoon tea at the Peninsula is still one the best experiences in town. If you can ever afford to stay, do so; there is a commitment to excellence that makes for a rare experience that you won't forget. The exclusive shops and main lobby are usually packed with tourists rather than guests. For more details on the Peninsula, see Places to Stay in this chapter.

Ocean Terminal
Next door to Star House shopping arcade on Canton Rd, the long building jutting into the harbour is the Ocean Terminal. There always seems to be an ocean liner moored there full of elderly millionaires. To meet their needs, the terminal and adjoining Ocean Centre are crammed with ritzy shops in endless arcades. It's not the place for

cheap souvenir hunting but it's interesting for a stroll. Incurable shoppers will be in seventh heaven, and non-shoppers in the third circle of hell. On the waterfront is a small park, built on a pier, which has benches and good views of the harbour.

Nathan Rd

The main drag of Kowloon was named after the governor, Sir Matthew Nathan, around the turn of the century. It was promptly dubbed 'Nathan's Folly' since Kowloon at the time was sparsely populated and such a wide road was thought unnecessary. The trees that once lined the street are gone and some would say the folly has remained.

Now the lower end of the road is known as the **Golden Mile**, after both its real estate prices and its ability to suck money out of tourists' pockets. While unable to boast any sights per se, lower end Nathan Rd is an experience in itself. Seedy guesthouse ghettoes awkwardly rub shoulders with top-end hotels, Indian tailors ply their trade on street corners and every other person seems intent on divesting you of wads of cash. Those living in Chungking Mansions will have Nathan Rd on their doorstep. This should furnish them with some pretty lurid memories that the Hong Kong Tourist Association is reluctant to advertise.

Kowloon Park

Once the site of the Whitfield Barracks for British and Indian troops, this area has been reborn as a park that is an oasis of green and a refreshing escape from the clutter and bustle of Nathan Rd. In a curious mixture of nature and artifice, pathways and walls crisscross the grass, birds hop around in cages, and towers and viewpoints dot the landscape. **Sculpture Walk** is an interesting addition, featuring works by local sculptors. The **Hong Kong Museum of History** is also there, as well as the excellent Kowloon Park Swimming Complex complete with waterfalls. If you want to swim (between April and October when the pools are open), go in the morning or afternoon on a weekday: on weekends there are so many bathers it's

tough to make out the water. The park is open from 6 am to midnight.

Hong Kong Museum of History

A visit to the Hong Kong Museum of History (☎ 2367-1124) is almost essential for anyone who hopes to gain a deeper understanding of Hong Kong. This excellent museum is in the grounds of Kowloon Park, not far from the Haiphong Rd entrance. The museum takes the visitor on a fascinating walk through Hong Kong's past, from prehistoric times (about 6000 years ago, give or take a few years) to the present. In addition to a large collection of 19th and early 20th century photographs, there are replicas of village dwellings, traditional Chinese costumes and a re-creation of an entire street block from 1881, including an old Chinese medicine shop. It's an attractive exhibit and does a fine job of telling the fascinating story of Hong Kong. The museum is open from Tuesday to Saturday from 10 am to 6 pm, and on Sunday and public holidays from 1 to 6 pm. It is closed on Monday. Admission costs HK$10, HK$5 for students and seniors, and is free on Wednesday.

Kowloon Mosque & Islamic Centre

Near the intersection of Nathan and Cameron Rds, the Kowloon Mosque and Islamic Centre is the largest mosque in Hong Kong. The present building was completed in 1984 and occupies the site of the an earlier mosque, which was built in 1896 for Muslim Indian troops garrisoned in the now demolished barracks at Kowloon Park.

The mosque is interesting to admire from the outside, but you can't simply wander in and take photos like you can in Buddhist or Taoist temples. If you are a Muslim, you can participate in the religious activities. Otherwise, you must obtain permission to visit the mosque. Permission isn't always granted, but you can inquire (☎ 2724-0095).

TSIM SHA TSUI EAST (MAP 1)

This big piece of land to the east of Chatham Rd didn't even exist until 1980.

continued on page 179

Public Square Street

1
2

Yau Ma Tei

Kansu Street

Pak Hoi Street

Saigon Street

Temple Street

Ning Po Street

Nanking Street

Bowring Street

Tak Shing Street

Austin Road

Hillwood Road

Observatory Road

Kimberley Road

Kimberley Street

Granville Road

Cameron Road

Cameron Lane

Humphreys Ave

Haiphong Road

Kowloon Park Drive

Peking Road

Middle Road

Salisbury Gardens

Clock Tower

Harbour Sightseeing Cruises Pier

To Central / Star Ferry Terminal

To Wan Chai

Victoria   Harbour

To Central

Canton Road

Gascoigne Road

To Yau Ma Tei & Mong Kok

Wylie Road

King's Park Sports Ground

Princess Margaret Road

Gascoigne Road

Mau Lam Street

Chi Wo Street

Jordan Road

Cox's Road

Jordan Path

Kowloon Cricket Club Ground

Cheong Wan Road

Austin Avenue

Chatham Court

Chatham Road South

Knutsford Terrace

Observatory Road

Granville Square

Science Museum Road

Granville Road

TSIM SHA TSUI EAST

Mody Road

Mody Square

Tsim Sha Tsui East

Tsim Sha Tsui East Ferry Pier

Salisbury Road

Prat Ave

Hart Avenue

Hanoi Road

Cornwall Avenue

Mody Road

Minden Ave

Minden Road

Signal Hill Garden

Nathan Road

Tak Hing Street

Tak Shing Street

Pilkem Street

Parkes Street

Woosung Street

Temple Street

Kwun Chung Street

Battery Street

Shanghai Street

Shanghai Street

Reclamation Street

Wai Ching Street

Ferry Street

Kowloon Park Swimming Complex & Indoor Games Hall

Kowloon Park

TSIM SHA TSUI

Tsim Sha Tsui

Carnarvon Road

Lock Road

Hankow Road

Canton Road

China Ferry Terminal

MTR Tsuen Wan Line

Victoria Harbour

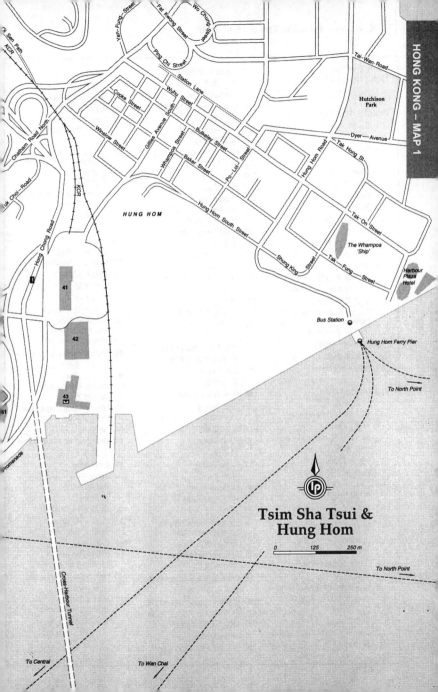

Tai-Wan-Road

Hutchison
Park

Yen-Fung-Street

Fat-Kwong-Street

Wo-Chung-Street

Ping-Chi-Street

Station-Lane

Dyer—Avenue

Cooke-Street

Wuhu-Street

KCR

Sen Path

Chatham—Road-North

Winslow-Street

Gillies-Avenue-South

Whampoa-Street

Bulkeley-Street

Pau-Lok-Street

Baker-Street

Hung-Hom-Road

Tak-Hong-St.

Tak-On-Street

HUNG HOM

Hung Hom South Street

Tak—Fung—Street

The Whampoa
'Ship'

Tuk-Choi-Road

KCR

Hong-Chong-Road

Shung-King-Street

Harbour
Plaza
Hotel

1

41

42

43

Bus Station

Hung Hom Ferry Pier

To North Point

Promenade

**Tsim Sha Tsui &
Hung Hom**

0   125   250 m

To North Point

Cross-Harbour-Tunnel

To Central

To Wan Chai

Tsim Sha Tsui & Hung Hom (MAP 1)
尖沙咀與紅磡

PLACES TO STAY

4 Eaton Hotel
香港逸東酒店

6 Nathan Hotel
彌敦酒店

8 Majestic Hotel
大華酒店

11 New Lucky Mansions
華豐大廈

12 Shamrock Hotel
新樂酒店

13 Prudential Hotel
恆豐酒店

15 Bangkok Royal Hotel
曼谷貴賓酒店

17 BP International House
龍堡國際賓館

19 Royal Pacific Hotel & Towers
皇家太平洋酒店

29 Miramar Hotel
美麗華酒店

32 Kimberley Hotel
君怡酒店

33 Windsor Hotel
溫莎酒店

37 Stanford Hillview Hotel
仕德福山景酒店

39 Ramada Hotel Kowloon
九龍華美達酒店

49 Hilton Towers
希爾頓大廈

51 Nikko Hotel
日航酒店

52 Grand Stanford Harbour View Hotel
海景嘉福酒店

53 Regal Kowloon Hotel
富豪九龍酒店

54 Royal Garden Hotel
帝苑酒店

58 Kowloon Shangri-La Hotel
九龍香格里拉大酒店

61 Park Hotel
百樂酒店

62 International Hotel
國際酒店

72 Marco Polo Hotel
香港馬哥孛羅酒店

78 Victoria Hostel

80 Hyatt Regency Hotel
香港凱悦酒店

84 New Astor Hotel
新雅圖酒店

97 Holiday Inn Golden Mile
金域假日酒店

102 Lucky Hotel
幸運酒店

107 Hong Kong Renaissance Hotel
華美達新酒店

110 Hong Kong Hotel
香港酒店

115 Imperial Hotel
帝國酒店

117 Chungking Mansions
重慶大廈

123 Sheraton Hotel
香港喜來登酒店

126 Kowloon Hotel
九龍酒店

127 YMCA Salisbury Hotel
香港基督教青年會

134 The Regent
麗晶酒店

136 New World Hotel
新世界酒店

PLACES TO EAT

5 Food Stalls
食品攤

16 Snow Garden
雪園飯店

20 La Rose Noire

21 Hard Rock Cafe
硬石

22 Happy Garden Noodle & Congee Kitchen
臺灣雞家莊

23 Taiwan Beef Noodle
臺灣牛肉麵

24 Oliver's Super Sandwiches
利華超級三文治店

28 Oliver's Super Sandwiches
利華超級三文治店

30 MC2 Media Café

35 Tutto Bene

36 El Cid/Tapas Bar

38 Fook Lam Moon
福臨門

47 Taiwan Beef Noodle
臺灣牛肉麵

60 North Sea Fishing Village Restaurant
北海漁村

63 Kung Tak Lam Vegetarian Restaurant
功德林上海素食有限公司

64 Oliver's Super Sandwiches
利華超級三文治店

74 Jimmy's Kitchen
占美餐廳

75 Gaylord
爵樂印度菜館

77 Sawadee Thai Restaurant

79 Java Rijstaffel
爪哇餐廳

85 Valentino
華倫天奴意大利餐廳

89 Delicious Food Co Chiu Chow Restaurant
好味道潮州餐廳

90 Shanghai Restaurant
上海喬家柵飯店

91 Tai Fung Lau Peking Restaurant
泰豐樓酒家

93 Higher Taste Vegetarian Dining Club

94 Genroku Sushi

96 Shanghai No1 Restaurant
上海第一菜館

98 Delifrance

104 Three-Five Korean Restaurant
三五亭

105 Osaka Restaurant

111 Planet Hollywood
繽麗好萊塢

118 Koh-I-Noor Indian Restaurant
寶軒印度餐廳

120 Spring Deer Restaurant
鹿鳴春飯店

121 Siu Lam Kung Seafood Restaurant
小杬公海鮮菜館

OTHER

1 Jade Market
玉器市場

2 Kowloon Central
Post Office
九龍郵局

3 Queen Elizabeth Hospital
伊利莎伯醫院

7 Temple Street Night
Market (South Section)
廟街夜市（南部）

9 Jordan Ferry Bus
Terminus

10 Yue Hwa Chinese
Products Emporium
粵華

14 Gun Club Hill Barracks
槍會山軍營

18 China Hong Kong City
(Passenger Ship Terminal)
中港城（客運站）

25 Hong Kong
Museum of History
香港博物館

26 Hongkong Bank
匯豐銀行

27 Kowloon Mosque;
Islamic Centre
清真寺

31 Miramar Cinema
美麗華戲院

34 Bahama Mama's
Coconut Bar

40 Hong Kong
Science Museum
香港科學館

41 Kowloon-Canton
Railway Terminus
(Kowloon KCR Station)
九龍火車總站

42 Hong Kong Coliseum
香港體育館

43 Hong Kong Mail Centre
國際郵遞中心

44 Club Boss
大富豪夜總會

45 Chinachem Plaza Cinema
華懋廣場戲院

46 Lost City
迷城夜總會

48 New Mandarin Plaza
新文華商業中心

50 Peninsula Centre
半島中心

55 Hongkong Bank
匯豐銀行

56 KPS Video
金獅

57 Tsim Sha Tsui Centre
尖沙咀中心

59 Auto Plaza
安達中心

65 Kirin Plaza

66 Wellcome Supermarket
惠康超級市場

67 Citibank
萬國寶通銀行

68 Curio Alley
古董街

69 Kangaroo Pub

70 Fuk Tak Temple
福德廟

71 Silvercord Cinema
新港戲院

73 Silvercord Shopping
Centre; KPS Video; China
Arts & Crafts
新港中心、金獅、
中藝有限公司

76 Amoeba Bar

81 Mirador Arcade
美麗都

82 Watering Hole Pub

83 China National Aviation
Corp Ticket Office

86 Biergarten

87 Delaney's

88 Schnurrbart

92 Jouster II

95 Rick's Café

99 Swindon Books
辰沖圖書有限公司

100 First Cup Coffee

101 Bottoms Up
露臀夜總會

103 HMV Record Store

106 Ned Kelly's Last Stand
力嘉利絲餐廳

108 Ocean Centre
海洋中心

109 Ocean Terminal
海運大廈

112 Watson's
屈臣氏

113 Park N' Shop Supermarket
百佳超級市場

114 China Travel Service
中國旅行社

116 Mad Dog's Pub

119 Lyton Building
麗東大廈

122 Post Office; Hongkong
Telecom Service Centre
郵局、香港電
訊服務中心

124 The Peninsula
半島酒店

125 Hongkong Bank
匯豐銀行

128 Star House
星光行

129 Kowloon Star Ferry Bus
Terminal
天星碼頭巴士總站

130 HKTA Information Centre
香港旅遊協會

131 Hong Kong
Cultural Centre
香港文化中心

132 Hong Kong
Space Museum
香港太空館

133 Hong Kong
Museum of Art
香港藝術館

135 New World Centre
新世界中心

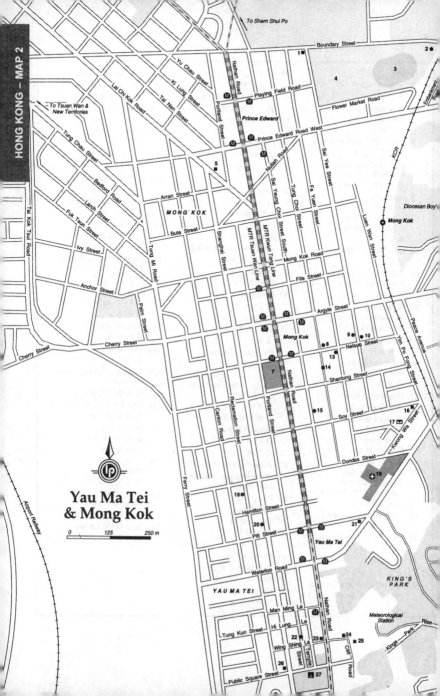

To Sham Shui Po

Boundary Street

1

2

3

4

Playing Field Road

Yu Chau Street

Ki Lung Street

Tai Nan Street

Portland Street

Nathan Road

Lai Chi Kok Road

Flower Market Road

To Tsuen Wan & New Territories

Prince Edward

Prince Edward Road West

Tung Chau Street

Bedford Road

Larch Street

Fuk Tsun Street

Ivy Street

Anchor Street

Arran Street

MONG KOK

Bute Street

Tong Mi Road

Shanghai Street

Sai Yeung Choi Street South

MTR Tsuen Wan Line

MTR Kwun Tong Line

Nullah Road

Sai Yee Street

Tung Choi Street

Fa Yuen Street

Luen Wan Street

KCR

Diocesan Boy's

Mong Kok

5

Tai Kok Tsui Road

Palm Street

Cherry Street

Cherry Street

Mong Kok Road

Fife Street

Argyle Street

Mong Kok

9 10

8

13

14

7

Reclamation Street

Canton Road

Ferry Street

Nathan Road

Portland Street

Nelson Street

Shantung Street

15

Soy Street

16

17

Kwong Wa Street

Yim Po Fong Street

Peace Avenue

Dundas Street

19

Yau Ma Tei
& Mong Kok

0   125   250 m

Airport Railway

18

Hamilton Street

20

Pitt Street

21

Yau Ma Tei

Waterloo Road

YAU MA TEI

Man Ming La

Hi Lung La

Tung Kun Street

22

Wing Shing Street

26

23

Temple Street

Public Square Street

27

24

25

Cliff Road

Nathan Road

KING'S PARK

Meteorological Station

Kings Park Rise

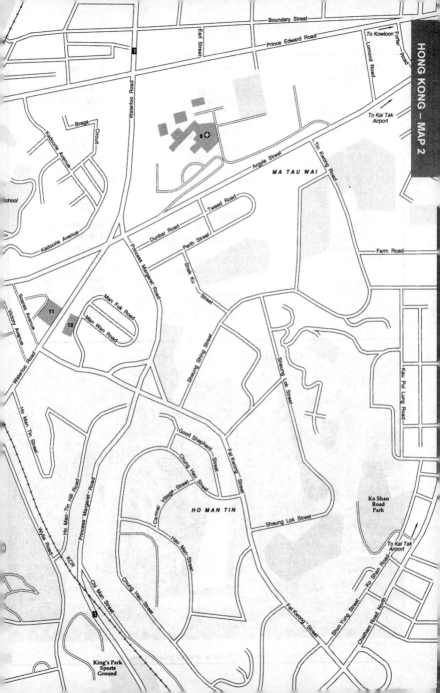

HONG KONG – MAP 2

**Yau Ma Tei &
Mong Kok (MAP 2)**
油麻地及旺角

PLACES TO STAY
1 Newton Hotel Kowloon
　　九龍麗東酒店
5 Concourse Hotel
　　京港酒店
7 Grand Tower Hotel
　　雅蘭酒店
11 Metropole Hotel
　　京華國際酒店
12 Anne Black Guest
　　House (YWCA)
　　柏顏露斯賓館
　　（女青年會）
16 Stanford Hotel
　　仕德福酒店
18 STB Hostel
　　學聯旅舍
21 YMCA International House
　　香港中華基督教
　　青年會國際賓館

23 New King's Hotel
　　高雅酒店
24 Booth Lodge
　　(Salvation Army)
　　卜維廉賓館
25 Caritas Bianchi Lodge
　　明愛白英奇賓館
26 Pearl Seaview Hotel
　　明珠海景酒店

OTHER
2 Bird Garden
　　雀鳥花園
3 Mong Kok Stadium
　　旺角大球場
4 Boundary Street Sports
　　Ground
　　界限街運動場
6 Kowloon Hospital
　　九龍醫院
8 Well Mount Sporting
　　Goods Shop
　　華輝運動用品中心

9 Wise Mount Sporting
　　Goods Shop
　　惠峰運動用品公司
10 China Travel Service
　　中國旅行社
13 Mong Kok Computer
　　Centre
　　旺角電腦城
14 Tung Choi Street Market
　　女人街（通菜街）
15 Broadway Cinema
　　百老匯戲院
17 Post Office
　　郵局
19 Kwong Wah Hospital
　　廣華醫院
20 Chamonix Alpine
　　Equipment
22 Temple Street Night
　　Market (North Section)
　　廟街夜市（北部）
27 Tin Hau Temple
　　天后廟

HONG KONG TOURIST ASSOCIATION

Every weekend Victoria Harbour is awash with colourful spinnakers.

continued from page 171
Built entirely on reclaimed land, Tsim Sha Tsui East is a cluster of shopping malls, hotels, theatres, restaurants and nightclubs. Everything is new – there are none of the old, crumbling buildings of nearby Tsim Sha Tsui.

Tsim Sha Tsui East caters to Hong Kong's middle class and *nouveaux riches*. The area has a few office towers, but mainly caters to an affluent selection of shoppers, diners and night-owls. If you get curious and decide to venture into a night club, be prepared to burn a hole in your pocket.

The Promenade
Along with the Peak, this amazing waterfront walkway offers some of the best views in Hong Kong. It's a lovely place to stroll during the day, and at night the view of Central lit up in neon is mesmerizing. You'll find yourself accompanied by lovers, joggers, musicians, photographers with tripods and, believe it or not, people fishing right off the Promenade. The Promenade becomes a sea of people during the Chinese New Year fireworks display and again during the Dragon Boat Festival.

The Promenade officially starts at the New World Centre, though you can walk along the water starting from the Star Ferry terminal. It goes all the way to the Hong Kong Coliseum and Kowloon KCR station. Midway along the Promenade is a ferry pier where you can catch a hoverferry across the harbour to Hong Kong Island.

Hong Kong Science Museum
The Science Museum (☎ 2732-3232) is at 2 Science Museum Rd (near the corner of Chatham Rd South and Granville Rd). It's a multi-level complex with more than 500 displays on computers, energy, physics, robotics, telecommunications, transportation and more. About 60% of the exhibits are 'hands-on', which helps to keep younger visitors interested. All in all it's a great place for the kids.

Admission is HK$25 for adults, and HK$12.50 for kids, students and seniors.

Opening hours are 1 to 9 pm Tuesday to Friday, and 10 am to 9 pm on weekends and public holidays. The museum is closed on Monday.

HUNG HOM (MAP 1)
The many features of Hung Hom include the Whampoa, the Hong Kong Polytechnic (☎ 2766-5111) and the 12,500 seat Hong Kong Coliseum, which hosts concerts and sporting events.

The Whampoa
In the middle of a high-rise housing estate in Hung Hom is the Whampoa, a full-sized concrete model of a luxury cruiser. While not very seaworthy, the 'ship' is impressive – 100m long and four decks tall. The whole thing is actually a fancy shopping mall with shops, restaurants, a cinema and playground (top deck). The basement houses more shops and a car park. It was built by one of Hong Kong's largest companies, Hutchison Whampoa.

The good ship Whampoa is a little off the beaten tourist track, but not difficult to reach. It's at the corner of Shung King and Tak Fung Sts. You can get there from Tsim Sha Tsui by taking green minibus No 6 from Hankow Rd (south of Peking Rd). There is also a Star Ferry from Central to Hung Hom that lands at the waterfront a couple of blocks away from the Whampoa; ferries also ply the route to Hung Hom (an adjacent pier) from Wan Chai and North Point on Hong Kong Island.

YAU MA TEI (MAPS 1 & 2)
Immediately to the north of Tsim Sha Tsui – and indistinguishable from it – is the Yau Ma Tei district (pronounced 'yow ma day'). In Cantonese, Yau Ma Tei means 'place of sesame plants'. The name obviously dates from years gone by; now the only plants you'll find in this urban district are in the window boxes of grimy, crumbling tenements. The area's attractions are the Jade Market, the Temple St night market and the Chinese emporiums along Nathan Rd.

There are many interesting walks to take

along the streets between Jordan Rd and Kansu St. These include Canton Rd (ivory and mahjong shops), Saigon St (a street market) and Ning Po St (paper items such as kites and paper houses, and luxury items for the dead).

The best way to see this area is to set off by foot and take whichever turn beckons. It's just a short walk from Yau Ma Tei Mass Transit Railway (MTR) station.

If you want a detailed guided tour, pick up a copy of the Hong Kong Tourist Association's (HKTA) *Yau Ma Tei Walking Tour*, available at HKTA information centres for HK$35.

Jade Market

Jade Market is on Kansu St, near the Gascoigne Rd overpass, just west of Nathan Rd. It's open daily from 10 am to 3.30 pm, but go early as you may find the jade sellers packing up at about 1 pm. It's more for Chinese than for foreign tourists, but you can get some good deals.

A few sellers are reasonably honest and will quote a decent price; with others you may have to engage in a marathon bargaining session just to get items down to shopping mall prices (so why bother?). Furthermore, all the vendors use a 'members only' sign language to communicate prices between each other; outsiders are quite likely to be fleeced.

To get there take bus No 9 from the Kowloon Star Ferry bus station and get off at Kowloon Central Post Office. You can also take the MTR and get off at either Jordan or Yau Ma Tei stations.

Tin Hau Temple

Between Market and Public Square Sts, a block or two north of the Jade Market, is a good sized temple dedicated to Tin Hau, the God of Seafarers. To the right, as you face the main temple, is a long row of fortune-tellers.

The temple complex also houses an altar dedicated to Shing Wong (God of the City) and To Tei (God of the Earth). The temple is open daily from 8 am to 6 pm.

Temple St

Temple St (named after the Tin Hau Temple) is the liveliest night market in Hong Kong, and the place to go for cheap clothes, food, watches, pirate CDs, fake labels, footwear, cookware and everyday items; everything seems to end up there. It used to be known as 'Men's St' because the market only sold men's clothing. Though there are still a lot of men's items on sale, vendors don't discriminate – anyone's money will do.

Temple street extends all the way from Man Ming Lane in the north to Ning Po St in the south, and is divided in two by the Tin Hau Temple. For street food, head to the section of Temple St north of the Tin Hau temple. You can get anything from a simple bowl of noodles to a full meal, served at your very own table on the street. There are also a few seafood and hotpot restaurants. Also on Temple St are all sorts of food stalls selling huge fried sausages *(heungcheung)* and fried kebabs with chicken *(gai)* and aubergine *(ayegwa)*.

Temple St hawkers set up at 6 pm and leave by midnight. The market is at its best in the evening from about 8 to 11 pm when it's clogged with stalls and people.

MONG KOK (MAP 2)

Aside from housing a ridiculous number of people in shabby apartment blocks, Mong Kok is also one of Hong Kong's busiest shopping districts: the name in Cantonese aptly means 'prosperous corner'.

This is not a place for designer fashion, ritzy jewellery and hovering salespeople. This is where locals come to buy everyday items like jeans, tennis shoes, kitchen supplies, computer accessories and so on. Take a look at Fife St, which has an amazing collection of stalls selling old records, books, ceramics, machinery and music scores. Mong Kok is also a good place to buy backpacks, hiking boots and other travel gear. Even if none of these items are on your shopping list, it's worth taking a look around.

Most of the action is east of Nathan Rd. Two blocks walk from Mong Kok MTR station is the Tung Choi St night market, open every night of the week. Similar to Temple St market in Yau Ma Tei, but not as much fun, Tung Choi St used to also be known as 'Women's St', selling only goods for females. Like Temple St, it now caters to both sexes.

The streets west of Nathan Rd reveal Hong Kong's seamier side, for this is where you'll find some of the city's seediest brothels. Mostly run by Triads, these places are often veritable prisons for young women and teenage girls, usually brought to Hong Kong on false pretences and then forced into prostitution. The Hong Kong Police routinely raid these places, but a look at the rows of brightly coloured signs shows that business goes on as usual. This is not a great part of town to hang around after midnight, though there's little risk of violent crime.

Yuen Po St Bird Garden

The bird market has flown from its original location in Hong Lok St and is now in Yuen Po St Bird Garden. The Chinese have long favoured birds as pets; you can often see local men walking around airing their birds. They especially like birds that can sing and the singing prowess of a bird often determines its price. Some birds are also considered harbingers of good fortune, which is why you'll see some men carrying birds to the horse races.

Aside from the hundreds of birds on display, elaborate cages carved from teak and bamboo, and ceramic water and food dishes are also on sale. The birds seem to live pretty well: the Chinese use chopsticks to feed live grasshoppers to their feathered friends, and give them honey nectar to gild their vocal cords.

To get to the Bird Garden, take the MTR to Prince Edward Station, come out of the Prince Edward Rd West exit and walk east for about 10 minutes.

NEW KOWLOON

Surrounding Kowloon proper is an area of about 30 sq km known as New Kowloon. It includes places such as Sham Shui Po and Lai Chi Kok (pronounced 'lie zhee gok') in

the west, and Kwun Tong in the east. Strictly speaking, these places are part of the New Territories, but tend to be included in Kowloon in everyday usage of the name. Boundary St marks the division between Kowloon and the New Territories, and this would have become the new border had Britain and China failed to reach an agreement on Hong Kong's future.

Wong Tai Sin Temple (Sik Sik Yuen)

This large and active Taoist temple was built in 1973 and is adjacent to the Wong Tai Sin housing estate, in the west of New Kowloon. It is dedicated to the god of the same name. The image of the god in the main temple was brought to Hong Kong from China in 1915 and installed in a temple in Wan Chai, where it remained until being moved to the present site in 1921. For information on Wong Tai Sin see Religion in the Facts about Hong Kong chapter.

Like most Chinese temples, this one is an explosion of colour, with red pillars, bright yellow roofs and blue lattice work. Bright flowers and shrubs add to the effect. If you come in the late afternoon or early evening, you can watch hordes of businessmen and secretaries praying and divining the future with *chim* (sticks that must be shaken out of a box on to the ground and then read). Friday evening is the busiest time for such worshippers. Behind the main temple are the **Good Wish Gardens**, replete with colourful (though concrete) pavilions, curved pathways and an artificial waterway. Adjacent to the temple is an arcade filled with dozens of booths operated by fortune tellers. Some of the fortune tellers speak good English, so if you really want to know what fate has in store for you, this is your chance to find out. Just off to one side of the arcade is a small open area where you can look up and get a magnificent view of **Lion Rock**, one of Hong Kong's prominent natural landmarks.

The temple recently catapulted into the news when one of the monks, collecting donations at the main gate, kicked a beggar in the head for some indiscretion. He must have had Shaolin training (the Shaolins are a Buddhist monastic order famous for their martial arts).

The temple is open daily from 7 am to 5.30 pm. The busiest times are around the Chinese New Year, Wong Tai Sin's birthday and weekends. There is no admission fee for visiting this or any other temple in Hong Kong, but the temple has become used to tourists dropping a few coins (HK$1 will do) into the donation box by the entrance. Getting there is easy. Take the MTR to Wong Tai Sin station, use exit B to leave the station, and then follow the signs.

Lei Cheng Uk Museum (Han Tomb)
The Lei Cheng Uk Museum (☎ 2386-2863) at 41 Tonkin St, Lei Cheng Uk Estate, is a branch of the Museum of History. The site is a late Han dynasty (25-220 AD) burial vault.

The Han Tomb is one of Hong Kong's earliest surviving historical monuments; it was discovered in 1955 when workers were levelling the hillside for a housing estate. The tomb consists of four barrel vaulted brick chambers in the form of a cross, set around a domed central chamber. It is estimated to be more than 1600 years old and is encased in a concrete shell for protection.

While somewhat interesting, it's kind of a long way to come for an anticlimactic peek through perspex.

It is open daily (except Monday) from 10 am to 1 pm and from 2 to 6 pm. On Sunday and most public holidays it's open from 1 to 6 pm. Admission is free. To get there, take bus No 2 from the Kowloon Star Ferry bus station Tsim Sha Tsui and get off at Tonkin St. The nearest MTR station is Cheung Sha Wan, a five minute walk from the tomb.

Sham Shui Po
Follow the signs at Sham Shui Po (pronounced 'sam soy po') MTR station to Apliu St and you can't miss the enormous street market, which features everything from clothing to CDs at rock bottom prices.

Descend back into the MTR and come up on the north-east side of the tracks to find the Golden Shopping Centre, 146-152 Fuk Wa St, the place to see the latest in computers and other high-tech wizardry. Two blocks further north-east at 85-95 Un Chau St (between Kweilin and Yen Chow Sts) is the New Capital Computer Plaza.

There is a chic, multi storey shopping mall called the Dragon Centre above the bus depot on the west corner of Yen Chow St and Cheung Sha Wan Rd; it's sign-posted in

Sham Shui Po 深水

1   New Capital Computer Plaza
    新高登電腦廣城
2   Post Office
    郵局
3   Golden Shopping Centre
    高登
4   McDonald's
    麥當勞
5   Dragon Centre; Bus Depot
    西九龍中心及巴士站
6   Apliu Street Market
    鴨寮街市
7   Sam Tai Tsz Temple
8   Market
    市場

the MTR. It doesn't look like a shopping centre at first glance, but an external escalator will take you from street level beside the bus depot up to the first shopping level.

The Dragon Centre towers above the surrounding apartment blocks and from the top level you can see the tall buildings in Central! The conveyers are all glass-sided (you can see the return steps going underneath the escalators) and each floor has a choice of escalator. You can go up one floor or skip the next and go up two: this is useful if you're aiming for the excellent food hall on the top floor where food is cheap and plentiful (HK$20 to HK$30 buys a huge meal of soup, egg, pork and rice). It's packed with family groups on weekends and it can be hard to find a seat during lunchtime. There's also a skating rink on the floor below the food centre, and a roller coaster suspended above the shopping floors (though it's not always operating).

Lei Yue Mun

To the east of Kai Tak airport is a residential neighbourhood called Kwun Tong, and a bit further south-east is a rapidly modernising fishing village called Lei Yue Mun. *Lei yue* means 'carp' and *mun* is 'gate', and 'carp gate' refers to the channel separating eastern Kowloon from neighbouring Hong Kong Island.

While you aren't likely to find the 'village' reminiscent of ancient China, it's one of Hong Kong's prime seafood venues. Although the seafood isn't necessarily better than anywhere else, it makes for a nice eating excursion. The neighbourhood is colourful and lively at night when the diners arrive en masse. You can get there on bus No 14C from Kwun Tong MTR station – take it all the way to the end of the line which is Lei Yue Mun MTR station.

PLACES TO STAY

Kowloon is home to an incredible cross section of society, taking in all extremes of the wealthy and poor. Students and backpackers will be impressed by the sheer volume of guesthouses stacked vertically in the crumbling mansion blocks of Nathan Rd. Chungking Mansions and Mirador Mansions may affront the senses with its flawless downward mobility, but these are cheap and part and parcel of the true Hong Kong experience. Many an expat will confess that they spent their first nights in Hong Kong at Chungking. Some never checked out.

All sorts of gradations exist between the grimy bottom rung of guesthouses and the shameless opulence at the top of the hotel ladder. The Peninsula is in the same neighbourhood as the lowest of the low and may not be on the average backpacker's agenda, but it's probably the last word in elegance and sophistication. A world of choice, catering to all budgets, can be found between these two poles.

What's more, with the number of tourists visiting Hong Kong decreasing, the high prices that usually milk foreigners dry are also falling, (and this trend will probably continue). Now is probably the best time to check in.

Also remember that if you are arriving in Hong Kong by air, the Hong Kong Hotels Association (☎ 2383-8380, email hkha@att. net.hk, www.hkta.org.hkha) has a counter at Chek Lap Kok airport where you can leaf through a huge number of hotel brochures and make large savings (up to 50% off) on mid-range and top-end hotel rooms. See Accommodation in the Facts for Visitors chapter for more details.

PLACES TO STAY – BUDGET

For definition purposes, budget in Hong Kong is any place where you can get a double room for under HK$500. The cheapest doubles usually start at about HK$150; there is nowhere as spectacularly cheap as some of the antiquated doss houses of Macau, but with patience and determination, you should be able to haggle the price down.

Chungking Mansions

There is probably no other place in the world like *Chungking Mansions*, the budget accommodation ghetto of Hong Kong. This huge high-rise dump at 36-44 Nathan Rd, in the heart of Tsim Sha Tsui, is almost a city in itself. Virtually all needs in life can be catered for there – everything from finding a room to eating, shopping and getting your hair cut.

Chungking Mansions is like a medieval town that has been under permanent siege since the 1600s, surrounded by a netherworld of sleaze and horrifying odours. Don't seek sanctuary in the lifts unless you have to; these are like steel coffins on cables.

If your curiosity is piqued, then we suggest that before you check in you first watch Wong Kar Wai's 1994 film *Chungking Express*. This absolutely fantastic film captures all the sleaze of the Mansions and its labyrinthine environs in a haunting yet captivating series of stories. You'll be whistling the soundtrack as you queue up for the B Block lift.

For years there has been talk about tearing down Chungking Mansions because it's an eyesore and a fire trap, but the cost would be huge and the Hong Kong government tends to take a 'hands off' approach to private enterprise.

A crackdown on fire safety violations finally came at the end of 1993, and many tinderbox guesthouses were shut down. Others survived by upgrading standards – the new building codes require smoke alarms, sprinklers and walls made of fireproof material. However, the recent political upheaval has allowed fire safety codes to slacken once again.

There has been an increase in hostels featuring walls made of plywood and sprinkler systems consisting of a bucket of water. If you stay in a guesthouse with smoke lights and slightly more than just a fireaxe propped against the wall, it'll be included in the price. If you're going to stay, at least tap on the wall of your room to be sure it isn't made of cardboard.

The character of Chungking has changed in other ways in recent years. The place now serves as a long-term boarding house for workers from developing countries. This has actually driven prices and standards down, and matchbox rooms are often occupied by two, three or even four persons. Backpackers have started migrating to guesthouses in other buildings, but Chungking is still the cheapest place to stay in Hong Kong. Some residents have been in the building for years, trapped by low wages and an inability to return to the real world. We heard of one poor soul who spent six years in dormitory accommodation in Chungking Mansions.

Adding some spice to your stay are the occasional midnight raids by the police. Mostly the police are looking for illegal immigrants – if your passport is at some embassy awaiting visa stamps, this could create a problem. At least try to have a receipt for your passport from the travel agency, a photocopy of your passport and some other picture ID card. Another purpose of the police raids is supposedly to round up foreign prostitutes, though the police do little more than hassle them if they haven't overstayed their visas. One thing travellers really have to watch out for is drugs; a few grams of hashish in your

Unmansionables

For a real-life vision of hell, take a look down the light wells of Chungking Mansions' D block. It's dark, dirty, festooned with pipes and wires, and covered in what looks like the debris of half a century. Why bother to put rubbish in the bin when it's so much easier to throw it out the window? Discarded plastic bags fall only halfway before lodging on a ledge or drainpipe. Soon these are joined by old newspapers, used toilet paper, underwear, half-eaten food and an expired rat.

In 1993, the building's electric transformer blew up, blacking out the Mansions for a whole week.

The lifts are a little slice of hell. A buzzer sounds when one too many people have clambered aboard, and a sign inside one helpfully announces: 'The Irresponsible for Accident due to Overloading'.

backpack could leave you with a lot of explaining to do.

The entrance to Chungking Mansions is via Chungking Arcade facing Nathan Rd. Wander around and you will find lifts labelled A to E. There are only two, tiny, overworked lifts for each 17 storey block. Long lines form in front of the lifts in A and B blocks. You can join the queue and wedge yourself into a coffin-sized metal lift that shudders from floor to floor in 98% humidity, or you can take the stairs, usually piled high with rotting refuse. The choice is yours.

Despite the dilapidated appearance of the building, most of the little hotels are OK – generally clean and often quite comfortable, though rooms are the size of closets. Standards do, however, vary. Your best bet is to opt for the hotels that have a high density of foreign travellers.

Chungking is a good place to eat cheaply too: there are several low priced restaurants, mostly run by Indians and Pakistanis (see Places to Eat in this chapter). The ground floor is filled with shops selling everything imaginable, though the mezzanine floor has better deals. You can pick up all sorts of electrical goodies like alarm clocks and radios, made in mainland China and dirt cheap.

Bargaining for a bed is possible when business is slack. You can often negotiate a cheaper price if you stay a long time, but never do that on the first night. Stay one night and find out how you like it before handing over two weeks rent. Once you pay, there are no refunds. Be certain to get a receipt. Paying for a room in advance so that you can have it on a certain day is not advised. If that cheap room suddenly becomes 'not available', threaten to call the police.

If you're too tired to go from door to door looking for a room, just wait in the lobby with your luggage. There are plenty of touts who will approach you with offers of cheap rooms.

I arrived at the Mansions in the late afternoon, dripping with sweat from the swelter that swamps Hong Kong every summer. I avoided the first two salesmen who came at me hawking cheap suites, but couldn't shake the third one. Sighing, I went upstairs with him to see his 'luxury room dorms',

which turned out to be about the size of a large hotel's toilet stall. Needing to be centrally located to catch an early morning flight, I gave in to the extortion and went in to lie down. Sitting on a bunk all the way across the room from me (about half a metre), was my new roommate, Bill.

Mark W Pickins

Prices listed in this book are only a guide and vary with the season, peaking in summer and during certain holidays such as Easter. As a general guide, a single room in Chungking Mansions starts in the HK$150 to HK$180 range, reaching about HK$250 or higher for larger rooms with attached bath. A double (two people in one bed) costs about HK$20 more, but it can be HK$50 more if you require twin beds.

Rooms will typically come with air-con and TV, although the phones are usually communal and located in the lobby. Calls are free in Hong Kong, so be suspicious if staff charge you. Many guesthouses can get you a Chinese visa quickly, although it's cheaper to do it yourself. Some, like the *Fortunate Guesthouse* on the 11th floor of A block, have a laundry service. Also, be prepared for varying levels of English fluency among guesthouse concierges. It's best to choose a guesthouse where you can communicate, so you can complain effectively (if need be) without any misunderstandings.

Dormitories There's a dwindling number of dormitories in Chungking Mansions, though there are dormitories elsewhere in Tsim Sha Tsui (see Other Budget Accommodation in this section). One popular favourite is the *Travellers' Hostel* (☎ 2368-7710), 16th floor, A block, which is a landmark in this building. Dorm beds cost HK$70. Cooking facilities are available. There are also double rooms with/without attached bath for HK$150/170; singles (without shower) are HK$120.

The *Fortunate Guesthouse* (☎ 2366-5900), 11th floor, A block, is a friendly place with a range of rooms and dorm beds for HK$60. On the 12th floor of A block is the friendly *Super Guesthouse*. The only other dormitories are in the *Splendid Asia Guesthouse* (☎ 2724-1313) in 4th floor, B block.

Guesthouses – A Block

This block has the densest concentration of guesthouses. The main drawback is the frequent long queues to get into the lifts. You may find yourself using the stairs more than you expected, which wouldn't be so terrible except that the stairwells are like snapshots of hell and the cockroaches show no fear. Still, A block is popular. Below is a selection of what's on offer; bear in mind that the shifting sands of the Chungking guesthouse world constantly turn up new names.

16th floor
Travellers' Hostel (☎ 2368-7710) is a popular guesthouse with double rooms, with/without attached bath, for HK$150/170; singles (without shower) are HK$120.
15th floor
Kyoto Guesthouse (☎ 2721-3574) has doubles (without shower) from HK$130; doubles with a shower start at HK$160.
The *Park Guesthouse* (☎ 2368-1689) is clean, airconditioned and friendly; rooms with shared bath are HK$120, and with private bath HK$160.
14th floor
Hawaii Guesthouse (☎ 2366-6127) has cheap doubles at HK$120 and rock bottom singles at HK$100.
Tokyo Guesthouse (☎ 2367-5407) has singles for HK$150 without shower.
Himalaya Guesthouse (☎ 2368-7276) has expensive doubles (with shower) for HK$230 and cheap singles at HK$150.
13th floor
Rhine Guesthouse has doubles with attached bath for HK$150.
12th floor
Peking Guesthouse (☎ 2723-8320) has friendly management and is very clean. All rooms have air conditioning and start at HK$180 (with bath).
11th floor
Fortunate Guesthouse (☎ 2366-5900) is very clean, the rooms are big and the owner friendly. The cheapest singles (with shower) are HK$120; doubles start at HK$200.
8th floor
New Mandarin Guesthouse (☎ 2366-1070) is clean and has singles for HK$140 with a shared bath and HK$180 with an attached private bath.

Tom's Guesthouse (☎ 2722-4956) has small rooms with attached bath starting at HK$170.
7th floor
The *Double Seven Guesthouse* (☎ 2367-1406) has singles from HK$150.
The *Welcome Guesthouse* (☎ 2721-7793) has singles (no shower) at HK$130, and doubles at HK$220; it has a laundry service.
First Guesthouse has singles for HK$120 (no shower).
6th floor
London Guesthouse (☎ 2724-5000) is not bad. Singles (with shower) are HK$150.
4th and 5th floors
Chungking House (☎ 2366-5362, fax 2721-3570) is pretty swish by Chungking standards with singles from HK$299 and doubles at HK$400.

Guesthouses – B Block

This block has almost as many guesthouses as A block, so you may still have to queue for the lifts. The stairwells support a rather large amount of wildlife, including a rare species of aggressive cockroach indigenous to this region of Chungking Mansions. Be grateful for the stray cats as they keep the rats in check. If you see a dead cat, take the lift.

17th floor
Amar Guesthouse (☎ 2368-4869) has singles for HK$150.
16th floor
Tom's Guesthouse has doubles at HK$200.
15th floor
Carlton Guesthouse (☎ 2721-0720) is quite clean and friendly, with singles at HK$200.
14th floor
Da Shing Guesthouse has singles at HK$120 and more expensive doubles.
13th floor
New Washington Guesthouse (☎ 2366-5798) is friendly, clean and popular; singles with shower start at HK$130, and doubles from HK$200.
12th floor
Hong Kong Guesthouse (☎ 2723-7842) has singles for HK$150 and doubles for HK$220.
10th floor
Kowloon Guesthouse (☎ 2369-9802) offers singles at HK$130 and doubles at HK$250; it is one of the larger places in this block and seems to be popular with Nigerians.
9th floor
Happy Guesthouse (☎ 2368-0318) has HK$120 singles and HK$200 doubles.

8th floor
  Hollywood Guesthouse (☎ 2732-2155) offers singles from HK$170.
7th floor
  New York Guesthouse (☎ 2724-3696) offers HK$130 singles (no shower) and doubles with shared bath for HK$160.
6th floor
  Kamal Guesthouse (☎ 2739-3301) calls itself 'A Name In Chungking', and has cheap singles at HK$100 (without shower).
4th floor
  Splendid Asia Guesthouse (☎ 2724-1313) has dorm beds for HK$40 and singles/doubles for HK$120/150.
3rd floor
  Dragon Inn (☎ 2368-2007) is a clean option, with singles at HK$150, doubles from HK$220 and triples from HK$300.

Guesthouses – C Block The one great advantage of staying in C block is that the queues for the lifts are shorter. Also, the stairwells and hallways are much cleaner than elsewhere in Chungking Mansions. Just why is uncertain; perhaps C block has its own indigenous culture.

16th floor
  Tom's Guesthouse (☎ 2367-9258) is clean, friendly and popular, with good singles for HK$200.
  Garden Guesthouse (☎ 2368-0981) is clean, with singles at HK$200 (with shower).
15th floor
  Carlton Guesthouse (☎ 2366-9951) is a bit shifty, with doubles at HK$180.
13th floor
  Osaka Guesthouse and *New Grand Guesthouse* (☎ 2311-1702) have the same owner; all rooms have private bath and TV, and the price ranges from HK$150 to HK$250.
10th floor
  Kowloon Guesthouse has rooms with shared/private bath for HK$160/180.
7th floor
  New Chungking Guesthouse (☎ 2368-0981) is very clean and pleasant with doubles for between HK$200 and HK$300.

Card Tricks

An extremely innocent looking Filipino struck up a casual conversation with me as I was awaiting a ferry at the Tsim Sha Tsui terminal. He asked where I was from, and when I said Vancouver, Canada, he remarked on what a coincidence it was that his sister was going to study there. As she had never gone so far away before and just happened to be with him in Hong Kong, he asked if it might be possible for me to come back to his hotel and speak with her. Being a good sport, I agreed.

When we arrived at his guesthouse in the lovely Chungking Mansions, his 'sister' wasn't there but his 'brother', who just happened to be a croupier in Macau, was. Since we had some time to kill before the sister returned, the croupier was quite eager to show me some card tricks. We started with a basic tutorial on blackjack and then got onto the topic of how easy it was to cheat, with him using card-shark techniques and me playing along. He emphasised how these techniques were secret and how he might 'lose his job' if it were revealed that he had shown these methods to me.

The conversation, naturally, turned to the scam. Essentially he proposed that he could loan me some money and we would perpetrate the scheme at the casino in Macau then split the profits 50:50 afterwards. First, of course, we had to practise. He was quite eager for me to stick around until 7 pm, when an informal card game with his friends would be taking place. Unfortunately for him, it just so happened that I had to return to the hostel that night to meet a friend for dinner. I was, 'of course', still interested in the idea so I promised to meet him at the ferry terminal at 9 am the next day. This never did quite materialise as I 'slept in', missed the appointment and caught my evening flight out of Hong Kong.

Robert Meyer

6th floor
> New Brother's Guesthouse (☎ 2368-9943) is good but all rooms have shared bath only; prices start at HK$180.

4th floor
> Maharaja Guesthouse (2722-6917). Ranjeet Guesthouse (2368-9943) has singles at HK$150.

Guesthouses – D Block

This part of Chungking is almost as tattered and dirty as A and B blocks. It rates fourth in terms of the number of guesthouses, but there seems to be a lot of traffic and you sometimes have to queue for the lifts.

17th floor
> Dragon Garden Guesthouse (☎ 2366-2121) has HK$180 singles (with shower) and HK$250 doubles.

16th floor
> New Shanghai Guesthouse (☎ 2311-2515) is a clean and friendly guesthouse; singles (with shower) are HK$188.

8th floor
> Fortuna Guesthouse (☎ 2366-4524) is quite clean, with singles/doubles at HK$160/200.

6th floor
> Regent Inn Guesthouse

5th floor
> Royal Inn and Royal Plaza Inn (☎ 2367-1424) have a sign that says 'deluxe rooms'; these aren't, but the English spoken by the staff is good. Singles with shared bath are HK$150, and with attached bath HK$250.

4th floor
> Head Sun Guesthouse has a bizarre name and is pretty grungy.
> Lai Wei Guesthouse, is a well-kept place.
> Mt Everest Guesthouse is slap-bang next to a sweat shop.

3rd floor
> Princess Guesthouse (☎ 2367-3101) has cheap singles for HK$80 and HK$120, and doubles at HK$150 (this place has been going since 1964, if that's good news).

Guesthouses – E Block

Like C block, this area is a backwater which is relatively clean and quiet. The guesthouses are thinning out, especially after the fire safety crackdown. There are light to moderate queues for the lifts, a breeze from the southeast if your room has windows and a chance of showers if the plumbing is working.

13th floor
> Mandarin Guesthouse (☎ 2366-0073) is a so-so place with singles for HK$150 (with shower).
> Maharaja Ranjeet Guesthouse (☎ 2368-4631) has singles for HK$120 (without air-con) and HK$220 (with air-con).

6th floor
> Regent Inn Guesthouse (☎ 2722-0833) is a smart sort of place but pricey for Chungking Mansions, with singles for HK$200 and doubles for HK$250.

Mirador Arcade

Mirador Arcade at 58 Nathan Rd is like a scaled down version of Chungking Mansions, but considerably cleaner and roomier. It's on Nathan Rd between Mody and Carnarvon Rds, one block north of Chungking Mansions. The place caught on fire in 1988, but that actually did it some good – the building has since had a pretty thorough renovation. Much of the backpacker clientele has moved there in recent years, with the result that there can be heavy queues for the lifts during peak hours (daytime). Ask about discounts if you want to rent long-term.

Dormitories Hostels in Mirador typically charge HK$50 to HK$60 for a dorm bed. A decent place is the Cosmic Guesthouse (☎ 2739-4952), flat A2, 12th floor, which is clean and has dorm beds for HK$60. Others with dorm beds include:

Ajit Guesthouse (☎ 2369-1201), flat F3, 12th floor; HK$50
Blue Lagoon Guesthouse (☎ 2721-0346), flat F2, 3rd floor; HK$60/70/80
Lily Garden Guesthouse (☎ 2366-2575), flat A9, 3rd floor; HK$60
Mini Hotel (☎ 2367-2551), flat F2, 7th floor, has dorm beds for HK$50 and doubles for HK$140.
New Garden (☎ 2311-2523), flat F4, 13th floor, has expensive dorms at HK$70.
Oriental Pearl Hostel (☎ 2723-3439), flat A3, 6th floor; HK$65
Star Guesthouse (☎ 2311-9095), flat F2B, 4th floor, has four bed dorms at HK$55 per bed.

Guesthouses Starting from the top floor, there's the clean, bright and friendly First-Class Guesthouse (☎ 2724-0595, fax 2724-0843), flat D1, 16th floor. Rooms all have an attached bath with singles/doubles at HK$150/180.

Man Hing Lung (☎ 2722-0678, fax 2311-8807) on the 14th floor in flat F2 is a decent place. The rooms are clean and the atmosphere is good. Singles cost HK$120 to HK$180, or you can arrange to live there from HK$3000 a month. If you arrive by yourself and want a room mate, the very friendly management can put you in with another traveller.

On the 13th floor are the *Kowloon Hotel* and the *New Garden Hostel* (☎ 2311-2523), a joint venture with over 65 rooms, including HK$100 singles (shared bath), HK$150 singles/doubles (with bathroom), HK$200 twin bedroom (with a phone and fridge and a great view over to Central) and excellent HK$400 doubles on the 10th floor.

Ajit Guesthouse (☎ 2369-1201), flat F3, 12th floor, is deservedly popular with travellers. Clean rooms with shared bath cost HK$150; with private bath it's HK$250.

Also on the 12th floor is *Cosmic Guesthouse* (☎ 2739-4952, fax 2311-5260), flat A2. This is a very clean, recently refurbished, quiet guesthouse with a polite owner. Singles (with shower) are HK$160, doubles HK$200, big doubles HK$220.

The *Tristar Guesthouse* (☎ 2301-3018), flat E3, 9th floor, has cheap singles for HK$120/150 and more expensive doubles from HK$220.

A new, clean and friendly place is the *Hung Kiu Guesthouse* (☎ 2312-1505), flat C3, 8th floor. Singles (with shower) are HK$180, doubles HK$280.

Also new, clean and tidy is the *Lucky Guesthouse* (☎ 2367-3522), flat A11, 7th floor, with singles for HK$200 and triples at HK$150 per bed.

On the 6th floor, flat A3, is the *Oriental Pearl Hostel* (☎ 2723-3439, fax 2723-1344). Nothing special, the place has HK$250 doubles and dorm beds at HK$65. Also on the 6th floor is the *Man Lee Tak Guesthouse* (☎ 2739-2717), flat A1, which has HK$200 singles and HK$280 doubles. Flat F2 on the 6th floor is *Charles Inn* (☎ 2301-3078), a clean and tidy place

boasting HK$200 singles and HK$250 doubles.

Cheap HK$130/180 singles/doubles (with shower) can be found at the *Lai Wei Guesthouse* (☎ 2368-0663, fax 2191-9438, email joanyikh@netvigator.com), flat F1, 5th floor. *Loi Loi Guesthouse* (☎ 2367-2909, fax 2723-6168), also on the 5th floor, flat A2, is clean and very nice. Singles (no shower) are HK$150, doubles are HK$220/280 and triples are HK$300/400. The *Mei Lam Guesthouse* (☎ 2721-5278), flat D1, 5th floor, has singles from HK$180 and doubles at HK$250.

Star Guesthouse (☎ 2311-9095, fax 2312-0085), flat F2B, 4th floor, is a friendly place dishing up cheap singles/doubles for HK$130 without shower. Dorm beds are available at HK$55.

Garden Hostel (☎ 2311-1183), flat F4, 3rd floor, is decent (the staff speak good English) with dorm beds at HK$60 (split male and female dorms), and a patio. Doubles are HK$170 (with shower).

Lily Garden Guesthouse (☎ 2366-2575), flat A9, 3rd floor, has small but clean rooms, although it's not a very friendly place. Singles (with shower) come in at HK$180, triples are HK$300. This is part of a group of guesthouses under the same management that also include the *New Osaka Guesthouse*, flat F2, 5th floor, *Nagoya Guesthouse*, flat A11, 8th floor, *City Guesthouse*, flat F2, 9th floor, and *Mickey Garden Guesthouse*, flat E1, 15th floor.

The *Blue Lagoon Guesthouse* (☎ 2721-0346, fax 2721-0216), flat F2, 3rd floor, has dorm beds for HK$60/70/80 (depending on the size of the dorm), and singles for HK$120. There is a free email facility that's for incoming messages and costs from HK$15 to HK$20 if you want to send.

Other Budget Accommodation

At 33 Hankow Rd is the *Victoria Hostel* (☎ 2376-0621, fax 2376-2609), which has dorm beds starting at HK$90. Reasonable singles start at HK$350 and doubles at HK$450. The hostel offers free daily email access and you get a 15% discount if you book your room through the hostel's Web site.

Salisbury YMCA (☎ 2369-2211), 41 Salisbury Rd, Tsim Sha Tsui, is certainly *not* a budget hotel. However, it's intriguing to backpackers because on the 5th floor there are dorm beds for HK$190 each (four beds per room) plus 10% tax. That's more than three times what you'd pay in the Mirador Arcade, but 'the Y' is plush. There are restrictions however: check in is at 2 pm and check out at 11 am, no one can stay more than seven consecutive nights and walk-in guests aren't accepted when their passports show that they have been staying in Hong Kong for more than 10 days. The YMCA also has more expensive doubles for HK$730.

The *STB Hostel* (☎ 2710-9199, fax 2385-0153, email stbhoste@netvigator. com), operated by the Hong Kong Student Travel Bureau, has 12 single dorm beds at HK$160 each per night (eight male, four female). It also has doubles/triples with bathroom for HK$460/$540. Suites are HK$600. It's clean and relatively quiet and the staff speak decent English, although some travellers have encountered less than friendly management in the past. If you have an International Student Identity Card (ISIC) you can get a 10% discount. Lockers are available (for a fee) and there is a photocopier, fax and email facilities for guest use. The hostel is on floors 1-3, Great Eastern Mansion, 255-261 Reclamation St, Mong Kok, just to the west of Yau Ma Tei MTR station.

Golden Crown Court, 66-70 Nathan Rd (opposite the south-east corner of Kowloon Park), Tsim Sha Tsui, has a few guesthouses that were once popular and cheap. It has undergone a transformation and offers a host of clean and smart guesthouses that are more expensive than Chungking Mansions or Mirador Mansions, but it may suit you better. Some, like the Fuji Hotel, are very dapper indeed.

On the top floor is the *Fuk Lam Travel Guesthouse* (☎ 2739-0021), flat A, 10th floor; expensive for what you get, singles/doubles are HK$250/300.

The clean *Golden Crown Guesthouse* (☎ 2369-1782), 5th floor, has a friendly owner who speaks good English. On offer are a few dorm beds (HK$80), HK$250 singles (without shower) and HK$350 singles (with shower).

Also on the 5th floor of Golden Crown Court (but hidden at the back) is the spotlessly clean and highly recommended *Wah Tat Guesthouse* (☎ 2366-6121, fax 2311-7195). The very friendly owner has singles/doubles that both cost HK$250 (or HK$300 if you stay less than three nights) and triples for HK$450.

On the 4th floor is the very smart and new *Fuji Hotel* (☎ 2367-2883). Once you've sidled past the oil paintings and inspected the wood panelling with a white-gloved finger, you'll find that the doubles cost HK$520 (but you get a 10% discount if you stay for more than two days). Very plush indeed.

Star Guesthouse (☎ 2723-8951), 6th floor at 21 Cameron Rd, Tsim Sha Tsui, is immaculately clean. *Lee Garden Guesthouse* (☎ 2367-2284) is on the 8th floor, D block, 36 Cameron Rd, close to Chatham Rd South. Both guesthouses are run by the same owner, the charismatic Charlie Chan. Both are well kept and managed; small singles are HK$300, doubles (with bath) HK$350 and triples are HK$500.

There are more guesthouses to be found in Tsim Sha Tsui along Cameron Rd, near the intersection with Chatham Rd. The *Lyton building*, 32-40 Mody Rd, also has several average guesthouses, all with private bath, air-con and TV. Examples include the *Frank Mody House* (☎ 2724-4113) on the 7th floor (take lift No 4 at the back), which has doubles/triples with shower for HK$400/500; and the *Lyton House Inn* (☎ 2367-3791) on the 6th floor, with doubles from HK$300 to HK$350.

In Hankow Rd you will find the *Lucky Hotel* (☎ 2926-3220), whose friendly owner has doubles without a shower for HK$300. If you are wandering the streets of Tsim Sha Tsui looking for hay for the night, occasionally glance up at the thicket of neon above you and you will no doubt see other new guesthouse arrivals.

The *New Lucky House*, 300 Nathan Rd (entrance on Jordan Rd), near Jordan MTR station in Yau Ma Tei, is in a slightly better neighbourhood than most of the other guesthouses. There are eight places to choose from in various price ranges. From the top to the bottom floor, the rundown is as follows:

Great Wall Hotel (☎ 2388-7675, fax 2388-0084), also known as *Sky Guesthouse*, 14th floor; singles/doubles HK$300/350

Ocean Guesthouse (☎ 2385-0125, fax 2782-6441), 11th floor; singles/doubles at HK$270/320

Nathan House (☎ 2780-1302), 10th floor; doubles cost HK$400; usually full

Overseas Guesthouse, 9th floor; singles/doubles with shared bath for HK$180/200; clean and friendly

Tung Wo Guesthouse, 9th floor; singles HK$180; cheap but not so nice

Hilton Inn (☎ 2770-4880), 3rd floor; singles/doubles at HK$200/250; a bit dreary

Also in Yau Ma Tei (but right above Jordan MTR station) is *Cumberland House* at 227 Nathan Rd. On the 5th floor you'll find *International House* (☎ 2730-9276), with rooms in the HK$400 to HK$500 range. On the 6th floor is the friendly *City Guesthouse* (☎ 2730-0212), where singles/doubles are HK$300/350, although, at the time of writing, rooms were cheaper as the guesthouse was undergoing repairs.

Possibly also worth looking out for are the 'flats' advertised almost daily in the property pages of the English-language press, starting at around HK$4000 per month and usually in Tsim Sha Tsui. These are actually rooms with bathroom (no kitchen), TV, aircon and phone that are generally let out on a long-term basis. These are not very good value, but put you in the middle of town.

PLACES TO STAY – MID-RANGE

A double room at a mid-range hotel costs between HK$650 and HK$1200 per night, and from HK$1300 to HK$2500 or more at one of the more expensive mid-range places. Some medium-priced hotels are as expensive

as top-end choices, but lack the overall quality of the more elegant hotels. If you stay in a mid-range hotel, the average price you're likely to encounter is HK$1000.

In Kowloon and Hong Kong Island, mid-range hotels are all pretty much the same. Some, however, can be recommended for offering something different such as inhouse cable TV systems and mini refrigerators. Many have business centres. Some mid-range hotels have email facilities and other funky, modern amenities. The *Kowloon Hotel* has minute rooms, but because it is owned by the Peninsula group you can use the splendid facilities at the Peninsula nearby. The rooms include attractive features such as free email access and personal email addresses; the TV doubles as a computer screen and the in-room fax doubles as a printer.

At the cheaper end of the market, the *New Kings Hotel* offers value for money, as does the *Salisbury YMCA*, which offers a high standard of service for an inexpensive price (see the list in this entry for prices). The *International Hotel* has similarly priced rooms. The *Dadol Hotel* is very cheap and only just classifies as a mid-range hotel. Also fairly cheap is the hostel style accommodation offered by several non-profit organisations, such as the Salvation Army's *Booth Lodge* in Yau Ma Tei. There is also the *Caritas Bianchi Lodge* in Yau Ma Tei and the *Caritas Lodge* in Mong Kok. The *YMCA International House* in Yau Ma Tei and the *Anne Black Guest House (YWCA)* in Mong Kok are two other options.

Be warned that some mid-range hotels (eg the *Concourse Hotel*) charge for local calls; guesthouses and top-end hotels don't. If you are going to make local calls, you may get charged HK$5 a call, which is ridiculous considering the hotel does not get charged. Often this is not clearly stated, so ask beforehand.

Worth bearing in mind before you decide to stay in a better class mid-range hotel are the packages that were being offered by the majority of top-end hotels at the time of writing. Two examples were the *Holiday Inn Golden Mile,* which was offering the standard singles for HK$1399 instead of the usual HK$2200, and the *New World Hotel* which down-priced its 'superior' singles from HK$2200 to HK$1250. Also worth bearing in mind are the deals that combine air tickets with hotel rooms.

The following hotels range enormously in price, and have doubles in the HK$580 to HK$2700 range:

Anne Black Guesthouse (YWCA, ☎ 2713-9211, fax 2761-1269) is badly located near Pui Ching and Waterloo Rds in Mong Kok. The official address is 5 Man Fuk Rd, uphill from and behind a Caltex petrol station. There are 169 rooms, reserved for women only. Single rooms range from HK$363 to HK$600 and doubles start at HK$550. It is near the Yau Ma Tei MTR station.

Bangkok Royal Hotel (☎ 2735-9181, fax 2730-2209), 2-12 Pilkem St, Yau Ma Tei, has singles from HK$500 to HK$660, and doubles from HK$580 to HK$740. Near Jordan MTR station.

Booth Lodge (☎ 2771-9266, 2385-1140), 11 Wing Sing Lane, Yau Ma Tei, is run by the Salvation Army and is spartan, but comfortable. Doubles and twins range from HK$620 to HK$1200. It is near the Yau Ma Tei MTR station.

BP International House (☎ 2376-1111, fax 2376-1333), 8 Austin Rd, Tsim Sha Tsui, has doubles from HK$1300 to HK$1900 and family rooms from HK$1050 to HK$1230. It is near the Jordan MTR station.

Caritas Bianchi Lodge (☎ 2388-1111, fax 2770-6669), 4 Cliff Rd, Yau Ma Tei. Singles are offered for HK$720, doubles HK$820 and triples HK$1020. It is near the Yau Ma Tei MTR station.

Caritas Lodge (☎ 2339-3777, fax 2338-2864), 134 Boundary St, Mong Kok, is not as fancy as the Bianchi, but it is less expensive, with singles at HK$540 and doubles/twins at HK$620. It is near the Prince Edward MTR station.

Concourse Hotel (☎ 2397-6683, fax 2381-3768, email concours@hkstar.com, www.hkstar.com/concourse), 20 Lai Chi Kok Rd, Mong Kok; doubles are HK$1280 to HK$1580 and suites are HK$2800. It is near the Prince Edward MTR station.

Dadol Hotel (☎ 2369-8882), 1st floor, Champagne Court, 16-20 Kimberley Rd, Kowloon, has doubles from HK$600. It is near the Tsim Sha Tsui MTR station.

Eaton Hotel (☎ 2782-1818, fax 2782-5563), 380 Nathan Rd, Yau Ma Tei, has doubles from HK$1350 to HK$2700. It is near the Jordan MTR station.

Evergreen Hotel (☎ 2780-4222, fax 2385-8584), 42-52 Woosung St, Yau Ma Tei, has doubles from HK$800 to HK$850 and triples at HK$980. Near Jordan MTR station.

Grand Tower Hotel (☎ 2789-0011, fax 2789-0945), 627-641 Nathan Rd, Mong Kok, has doubles from HK$1500 to HK$2300. It is near the Mong Kok MTR station.

Guangdong Hotel (☎ 2739-3311, fax 2721-1137), 18 Prat Ave, Tsim Sha Tsui, offers doubles from HK$1587 to HK$1780, and suites from HK$1900. It is near the Tsim Sha Tsui MTR station.

Imperial Hotel (☎ 2366-2201, fax 2311-2360, email imperial@imperialhotel.com.hk, www.imperialhotel. com.hk), 30-34 Nathan Rd, Tsim Sha Tsui, has singles from HK$950 to HK$1700 and doubles from HK$1100 to HK$2000. It is near the Tsim Sha Tsui MTR station.

International Hotel (☎ 2366-3381, fax 2369-5381), 33 Cameron Rd, Tsim Sha Tsui, offers singles/doubles from HK$580/780 to HK$880/1080. It is near the Tsim Sha Tsui MTR station.

Kimberley Hotel (☎ 2723-3888, fax 2723-1318, email kh-resv@kimberley.com.hk, www.kimberley.com.hk), 28 Kimberley Rd, Tsim Sha Tsui, has singles/doubles from HK$1550/1650 to HK$2050/2150 and suites at HK$2450. It is near the Tsim Sha Tsui MTR station.

Kowloon Hotel (☎ 2369-8698, fax 2739-9811, email khh@peninsula.com), 19-21 Nathan Rd, Tsim Sha Tsui, has singles/doubles from HK$1500/1600 to HK$2550/2650 and suites from HK$3600. It is near the Tsim Sha Tsui MTR station.

Majestic Hotel (☎ 2781-1333, fax 2781-1773), 348 Nathan Rd, Yau Ma Tei, has doubles from HK$1450 to HK$1900. It is near the Jordan MTR station.

Metropole Hotel (☎ 2761-1711, fax 2761-0769, email hotel@metropole.com.hk, www.metropole.com.hk), 75 Waterloo Rd, Yau Ma Tei, has doubles from HK$1330 to HK$1650. It is near the Yau Ma Tei MTR station.

Miramar Hotel (☎ 2368-1111, fax 2369-1788, www.great-china.net/hotelmiramar), 130 Nathan Rd, Tsim Sha Tsui, has doubles from HK$1800 to HK$2200 and suites from HK$3200. It is near the Tsim Sha Tsui MTR station.

Nathan Hotel (☎ 2388-5141, fax 2770-4262), 378 Nathan Rd, Yau Ma Tei, has singles for HK$780, doubles for HK$880 and triples for HK$1200. It is near the Jordan MTR station.

New Astor Hotel (☎ 2366-7261, fax 2722-7122), 11 Carnarvon Rd, Tsim Sha Tsui, has doubles from HK$880 to HK$1800 and suites from HK$3600. It is near the Tsim Sha Tsui MTR station.

New Kings Hotel (☎ 2780-1281, fax 2782-1833), 473 Nathan Rd, Yau Ma Tei, has singles/doubles from HK$550/650 to HK$600/750. It is near the Yau Ma Tei MTR station.

Newton Hotel (☎ 2787-2338, fax 2789-0688, email kwlnewton@asiansources.com), 58-66 Boundary St, Mong Kok, has doubles from HK$1060 to HK$1640. It is near the Prince Edward MTR station. (There's also a Newtown Hotel of a similar standard in North Point on Hong Kong Island.)

Park Hotel (☎ 2366-1371, fax 2739-7259), 61-65 Chatham Rd South, Tsim Sha Tsui, has singles/doubles from HK$1200/1300 to HK$2100/2200. It is near the Tsim Sha Tsui MTR station.

Pearl Seaview Hotel (☎ 2782-0882, fax 2388-1803), 262-276 Shanghai St, Yau Ma Tei, has singles/doubles from HK$880/1280 to HK$1280/1580 and suites from HK$2400. It is near the Yau Ma Tei MTR station.

Prudential Hotel (☎ 2311-8222, fax 2311-4760), 222 Nathan Rd, Yau Ma Tei, has doubles from HK$1480 to HK$2980. It is near the Jordan MTR station.

Ramada Hotel Kowloon (☎ 2311-1100, fax 2311-6000, email hotel@ramada-kowloon.com.hk), 73-75 Chatham Rd South, Tsim Sha Tsui, has doubles from HK$1300 to HK$2050 and suites from HK$2800. It is near the Tsim Sha Tsui MTR station.

Royal Pacific Hotel (☎ 2736-1188, fax 2736-1212, email htl@royalpacific.com.hk, www.royalpacific.com.hk), China Hong Kong City complex, 33 Canton Rd, Tsim Sha Tsui, has singles/doubles from HK$1300/1500 to HK$2450/2650 and suites from HK$2500. It is near the Tsim Sha Tsui MTR station.

Salisbury YMCA (☎ 2369-2211, fax 2739-9315), 41 Salisbury Rd, Tsim Sha Tsui, has singles from HK$880, doubles from HK$1030 to HK$1270 and suites from HK$1720. It is near the Tsim Sha Tsui MTR station.

Shamrock Hotel (☎ 2735-2271, fax 2736-7354, email shamrock@iohk.com), 223 Nathan Rd, Yau Ma Tei, has doubles from HK$630 to HK$1070. It is near the Jordan MTR station.

Stanford Hillview Hotel (☎ 2722-7822, fax 2723-3718, email sfhvhkg@netvigator.com), 13-17 Observatory Rd, Tsim Sha Tsui, has doubles from HK$910 to HK$1310. It is near the Tsim Sha Tsui MTR station.

Stanford Hotel (☎ 2781-1881, fax 2388-3733, email sfhkg@netvigator.com), 118 Soy St, Mong Kok, has singles/doubles from HK$1200/1200 to HK$1800/1800. It is near the Mong Kok MTR station.

Windsor Hotel (☎ 2739-5665, fax 2311-5101, email windsor@windsorhotel.com.hk, www. windsorhotel.com.hk), 39-43A Kimberley Rd, Tsim Sha Tsui, has doubles from HK$1400 to HK$1800 and suites from HK$2900. It is near the Tsim Sha Tsui MTR station.

YMCA International House (☎ 2771-9111, fax 2771-5238), 23 Waterloo Rd, Yau Ma Tei, has doubles from HK$800 to HK$1000 and suites from HK$1130 to HK$1500. It is near the Yau Ma Tei MTR station.

PLACES TO STAY – TOP END

Mention Hong Kong and many people think of the *Peninsula*, which opened in 1928 and has become the patriarch of the territory's luxury hotels. Near the Peninsula, is *The Regent*, flagship hotel of the Regal International Hotels chain. It is much more modern in feel, though like the Peninsula, it bows to a few colonial traditions, such as its fleet of Rolls-Royces and Daimlers. This hotel is a favourite with business travellers, and its outdoor swimming pool has outstanding views.

Other Kowloon notables include the *New World Hotel,* which has an outdoor pool set in a huge garden with a spectacular view, and the *Nikko Hong Kong,* where you'll find all the amenities and attention typical of fine Japanese hotels.

You can get as much as a 30% discount at many hotels by booking your room through a local travel agency or by booking through the Hong Kong Hotels Association (see Accommodation in the Facts for the Visitor chapter for more details). Top-end hotels are as follows:

Grand Stanford Harbour View (☎ 2721-5161, fax 2732-2233, email gshv@netvigator.com), 70

Mody Rd, Tsim Sha Tsui East, has singles/doubles from HK$2350/2500 to HK$3250/3400 and suites from HK$4800. It is near the Tsim Sha Tsui MTR station.

Harbour Plaza (☎ 2621-3188, fax 2621-3311), 20 Tak Fung St, Hung Hom, has doubles from HK$2200 to HK$2850 and suites from HK$4200.

Holiday Inn Golden Mile (☎ 2369-3111, fax 2369-8016, email goldenmile@asianvoyage.com, www.goldenmile.com), 46-52 Nathan Rd, Tsim Sha Tsui, has singles/doubles from HK$1900/2300 to HK$2450/2550 and suites from H$5500. It is near the Tsim Sha Tsui MTR station.

The Hong Kong Hotel (☎ 2113-0088, fax 2113-0011, email mphkh97@asiaonline.net, www.marcopolohotels.com), Harbour City, Canton Rd, Tsim Sha Tsui, has singles/doubles from HK$2300/2400 to HK$3530/3630 and suites from HK$3960 to HK$15,000. It is near the Tsim Sha Tsui MTR station.

Hong Kong Renaissance Hotel (☎ 2375-1133, fax 2375-6611, email renhotel@hk.linkage.net), 8 Peking Rd, Tsim Sha Tsui, has doubles from HK$2600 to HK$3600. It is near the Tsim Sha Tsui MTR station.

Hotel Nikko (☎ 2739-1111, fax 2311-3122, email nikko@hotelnikko.com.hk), 72 Mody Rd, Tsim Sha Tsui East, has doubles from HK$2200 to HK$3100 and suites from HK$5500. It is near the Tsim Sha Tsui MTR station.

Hyatt Regency (☎ 2311-1234, fax 2739-8701, email general@hyattregency.com.hk), 67 Nathan Rd, Tsim Sha Tsui, has doubles from HK$2800 to HK$3600 and suites from HK$4400. It is near the Tsim Sha Tsui MTR station.

Kowloon Shangri-La (☎ 2721-2111, fax 2723-8686, www.Shangri-La.com), 64 Mody Rd, Tsim Sha Tsui East, has singles/doubles from HK$2300/2550 to HK$3600/3850 and suites from HK$4400 to HK$17,000. It is near the Tsim Sha Tsui MTR station.

The Marco Polo (☎ 2113-0888, fax 2113-0022, email mphkgbc@wlink.net), Harbour City, Canton Rd, Tsim Sha Tsui, has singles/doubles from HK$1950/2050 to HK$2200/2300 and suites from HK$3450. It is near the Tsim Sha Tsui MTR station.

New World Hotel (☎ 2369-4111, fax 2369-9387, email nwhtlbc@netvigator.com), 22 Salisbury Rd, Tsim Sha Tsui, has singles/doubles from HK$2200/2350 to HK$2850/2850 and suites

from HK$3300 to HK$7500. It is near the Tsim Sha Tsui MTR station.

Peninsula (☎ 2366-6251, fax 2722-4170, email pen@peninsula.com), Salisbury Rd, Tsim Sha Tsui, has doubles from HK$2900 to HK$4600 and suites from HK$5200 to HK$39,000. It is near the Tsim Sha Tsui MTR station.

Prince (☎ 2113-1888, fax 2113-0066), Harbour City, Canton Rd, Tsim Sha Tsui, has doubles from HK$2050 to HK$2400 and suites from HK$3200. It is near the Tsim Sha Tsui MTR station.

Regal Kowloon Hotel (☎ 2722-1818, fax 2369-6950, email rkh@regalhotels.com, www.regalhotels.com), 71 Mody Rd, Tsim Sha Tsui East, has singles/doubles from HK$2100/2200 to HK$2900/3050 and suites from HK$5000 to HK$12,000. It is near the Tsim Sha Tsui MTR station.

The Regent (☎ 2721-1211, fax 2739-4546), 18 Salisbury Rd, Tsim Sha Tsui, has doubles from HK$2600 to HK$4150 and suites from HK$4650. It is near the Tsim Sha Tsui MTR station.

The Royal Garden (☎ 2721-5215, fax 2369-9976, email htlinfo@theroyalgardenhotel.com.hk, www.theroyalgardenhotel.com.hk), 69 Mody Rd, Tsim Sha Tsui East, has singles/doubles from HK$2300/2450 to HK$2900/3050 and suites from HK$4000 to HK$15,600. It is near the Tsim Sha Tsui MTR station.

Sheraton Hotel (☎ 2369-1111, fax 2739-8707, email res_hongkong@ittsheraton.com, www.sheraton.com/quickview/h0482.html), 20 Nathan Rd, Tsim Sha Tsui, has doubles from HK$2800 to HK$3400 and suites from HK$3600. It is near the Tsim Sha Tsui MTR station.

PLACES TO EAT

You will find that Kowloon doesn't have the same range of restaurants as Hong Kong Island. That said, you can still find an imaginative range of food in Tsim Sha Tsui and its environs, and the prices are slightly lower than south of Victoria Harbour.

Main Dishes

Chinese Working from the bottom up, *Happy Garden Noodle & Congee Kitchen* at 76 Canton Rd, Tsim Sha Tsui, is a budget option, where you can fill up on great soup noodles and congee (HK$28 to HK$30). And next door is the *Taiwan Beef Noodle*,

78-80 Canton Rd, a decent restaurant chain with good Taiwanese style beef noodles (HK$26). Another cheap option is *Hau Fook St*, a few blocks east of Nathan Rd, which isn't included on many tourist maps. Walking north from the intersection of Carnarvon and Cameron Rds, it's the first lane on your right. Unfortunately, most of the places don't have English menus.

A traditional place for cheap eats is the *Temple St* night market in Yau Ma Tei. The street market starts at about 8 pm and begins to close down at 11 pm. Market cuisine, served from a pushcart, includes fish balls or squid on skewers and other less identifiable delicacies (maybe you're better off not asking). There are also plenty of mainstream indoor restaurants. Although many locals are drawn by the seafood restaurants, any Hong Kong resident will tell you that fresher marine cuisine is served up in the outlying islands and New Territories (see the Outlying Islands and New Territories chapters for more information).

Going more upmarket, *Siu Lam Kung Seafood Restaurant* (☎ 2721-6168) at 17-21 Minden Ave has long been a local favourite and is known for its shellfish specialities. This place is a bit more expensive than most, but that doesn't deter the crowds, so you may want to book ahead. Also frequented by local seafood lovers is the *North Sea Fishing Village Restaurant* (☎ 2723-6843), located in the 1st basement of the Auto Plaza, 65 Mody Square, Tsim Sha Tsui East. If you can ignore the cheesy nautical decor, this place has good dim sum.

The *Jade Garden Restaurant* (☎ 2730-6888), 4th floor, Star House (right across from the Tsim Sha Tsui Star Ferry terminal), is also a good deal. The restaurant offers a consistently fine choice of Cantonese dishes, including pan-fried stuffed bean curd.

The traditional rosewood furniture and ambience of *Dynasty* (☎ 2369-4111) at the New World Hotel provide an authentic Cantonese dining experience. It's not cheap and specialities include steamed sliced pork with preserved shrimp paste and fresh salmon with rice noodle strips.

On the 2nd floor of the Tsim Sha Tsui Centre, Mody Rd, is the Kowloon branch (☎ 2368-7266) of Maxim's *Chiu Chow Garden,* where you can taste a lighter, more subtle variation of Cantonese cooking for a modest sum. Just east of the Guangdong Hotel, on Prat Ave, the *Delicious Food Co Chiu Chow Restaurant* also seems worth trying, though the decor is a bit basic.

Next door is the *Shanghai Restaurant* (☎ 2739-7083), which presents food the authentic Shanghai way; heavy with lots of oil. If you don't mind the oil, and a somewhat high bill, it's probably worth trying. One door over is the *Great Shanghai Restaurant* (☎ 2366-8158), which while it is a bit more touristy and less authentic, it is also cheaper and easier to negotiate for non-Chinese speakers. The stir-fried fresh water shrimps are a speciality. The *Snow Garden* (☎ 2736-4341) at 229 Nathan Rd is another popular venue for Shanghai food – go there for drunken pigeon, braised sea cucumber and sauteed fresh water shrimps, or just try the 'siu long bao', traditional Shanghai meat-filled buns cooked in a steamer.

Tsim Sha Tsui is home to what is probably Hong Kong's most famous Peking restaurant, the *Spring Deer* (☎ 2366-4012). Tucked away in a nondescript building at 42 Mody Rd, this place serves some of the crispiest Peking duck in town. At HK$280 for a whole bird, it's not exactly budget dining, but won't break the bank either. This place is extremely popular, so you may have to book several days in advance. If you can't get in, try the *Tai Fung Lau Peking Restaurant* (☎ 2366-2494), 29-31 Chatham Rd, Tsim Sha Tsui, which serves some fine northern specialities; HK$240 for a whole Peking duck. If it's full, try the lamb hot-pot restaurant next door for more north Chinese cooking, or the inexpensive *Peking Restaurant* (☎ 2730-1315) at 227 Nathan Rd.

If you are hunting for spicy Sichuan cuisine, Tsim Sha Tsui is not the best neighbourhood to be looking in, but you can try the *Fung Lum Restaurant* (☎ 2367-8686), 1st floor, Polly Commercial building, 21-23 Prat Ave, Tsim Sha Tsui.

If you really want to experience the finest of Chinese food in Hong Kong, Tsim Sha Tsui has a number of restaurants happy to serve up as much abalone and shark's fin as you can handle. One of Hong Kong's top Cantonese restaurants, the *Fook Lam Moon* (☎ 2366-0286), 55 Kimberley Rd, makes sure you're taken care of from the minute you walk out of the elevator, with hostesses wearing *cheong sam* (a formal tight-fitting Chinese dress) to escort you to and from your table. Sample the pan-fried lobster balls, a house speciality.

The *Spring Moon* (☎ 2366-6251) in the Peninsula is a grand and impressive restaurant. Complementing the high standards of the hotel, the food is excellently prepared and the ambience is stunning.

It may not win any awards for its name, but *The Chinese Restaurant* (☎ 2311-1234) has acquired a good reputation for its Cantonese food. Seafood is, like elsewhere, a speciality, but the high ceilings and traditional booth seating – based on Chinese teahouses of the 1920s – make for an unusual dining experience. It's on the 2nd floor, Hyatt Regency Hong Kong, 67 Nathan Rd, Tsim Sha Tsui.

On the harbour side of the Regent Hotel, the *Lai Ching Heen* (☎ 2721-1211) has repeatedly won awards for its refined Cantonese cuisine (though the elegant interior and stunning view may have influenced the judges somewhat). The menu changes with each lunar month, and if the selections get confusing there's always a waiter hovering nearby to act as a guide.

Dim Sum Restaurants normally serve dim sum from around 11 am to 3 pm, but a few places are also open for breakfast. The following places offer reasonably priced meals:

Canton Court (☎ 2366-6469), Guangdong Hotel, 18 Prat Ave, Tsim Sha Tsui; dim sum served from 7 am to 3 pm
Eastern Palace (☎ 2730-6011), 3rd floor, Omni Hongkong Hotel, Shopping Arcade, Harbour City, Canton Rd, Tsim Sha Tsui; dim sum served from 11.30 am to 3 pm

Harbour View Seafood (☎ 2722-5888), 3rd floor, West Wing, Tsim Sha Tsui Centre, 66 Mody Rd, Tsim Sha Tsui East, has stunning harbour views. It closes at midnight; dim sum served from 11 am to 5 pm
New Home (☎ 2366-9243), 19-20 Hanoi Rd, Tsim Sha Tsui, specialises in Hakka cuisine; dim sum served from 7 am to 4.30 pm
North China Peking Seafood (☎ 2311-6689), 2nd floor, Polly Commercial building, 21-23 Prat Ave, Tsim Sha Tsui; dim sum served from 11 am to 3 pm
Orchard Court (☎ 2317-5111), 1st and 2nd floors, Ma's Mansion, 37 Hankow Rd, Tsim Sha Tsui; dim sum served from 11 am to 5 pm
Oriental Harbour Restaurant (☎ 2723-3885), 2nd floor, Tsim Sha Tsui Centre, 66 Mody Rd, Tsim Sha Tsui East; good harbour views (try to get a table by the window); dim sum served from 11 am to 3 pm
Wu Kong Shanghai (☎ 2366-7244), basement, Alpha House, 27 Nathan Rd, Tsim Sha Tsui. The crispy fried eels are excellent; dim sum served from 11.30 am to midnight (most unusual)

American At *Dan Ryan's Chicago Grill* (☎ 2735-6111), shop 200, Ocean Terminal, Harbour City, Canton Rd, Tsim Sha Tsui, the theme is 'Chicago', including a model elevated rail system (the MTR is faster though). Dan Ryan's has made a serious name for itself as *the* place for burgers in Hong Kong.

The *San Francisco Steak House* (☎ 2735-7576), 7 Ashley Rd, Tsim Sha Tsui, specialises in surf-and-turf, setting you up for the night with steaks, barbecue ribs, lobsters, kebabs, burgers, clams et al. Only for the serious carnivore (bring a tungsten tipped toothpick).

US pop culture elbowed its way into the restaurant scene with the arrival of *Planet Hollywood* and the *Hard Rock Cafe*. Planet Hollywood (☎ 2377-7888), 100 Canton Rd in Tsim Sha Tsui, attracts long queues eager to sample the standard American fare. The Hard Rock Cafe is, as you all know, a stamping ground for homesick Americans desperate to escape noodlesville and hit home turf, burger and beer in hand and baseball cap screwed on tight. There is another Hard Rock Cafe branch in Central. Of the two, the Central restaurant is better

HONG KONG

– the Kowloon branch doubles as a dance club and the service suffers.

The Bostonian (☎ 2375-1133) inside the Hong Kong Renaissance Hotel, 8 Peking Rd, Tsim Sha Tsui, is ostensibly a seafood restaurant. However, it has the most knock-out lunchtime buffet in Kowloon (Monday to Saturday HK$178, Sunday HK$220).

Continental *Jimmy's Kitchen* (☎ 2376-0327), 1st floor, Kowloon Centre, 29 Ashley Rd, has a generous menu that has given it an established and loyal fan-base. On top of that it's also steeped in an old colonial nostalgia that may be particularly appealing now that the Union Jack is yesterday's scene.

Undeniably the territory's most fantastic restaurant setting, both inside and out, is at *Felix* (☎ 2366-6251) on the 28th floor of the Peninsula. The experience begins before you even set foot in the restaurant, with a ride in the restaurant lift steeped in special mood lighting. High ceilings, vast windows and hulking copper-clad columns surround the Art Deco table setting. At either end of the dining room are what look to be giant metal washtubs enclosing a bar, a mini disco and a wine-tasting room. Then there are the bathrooms, which are the talk of Hong Kong (you can find out for yourself). The food, if you even notice it, is east meets west. It is, of course, very tasty, but portions are not generous. At least your eyes won't go away hungry. Felix is open from 6 pm to 2 am daily.

Filipino The *Mabuhay* (☎ 2367-3762), 11 Minden Ave, serves good Filipino and Spanish food. Many Filipino expatriates eat in Mabuhay.

French *Gaddi's* (☎ 2366-6251), still holds onto its reputation as *the* French restaurant in Hong Kong. Located in the Peninsula, this place has boasted virtually the same menu (and some of the same staff) for its entire three decades. Obviously the system doesn't need fixing. The atmosphere is a bit stiff, making it hard to relax, but the food will probably keep you excited.

Another option for those seeking elegant French cuisine is *Au Trou Normand* (☎ 2366-8754), 6 Carnarvon Rd, Tsim Sha Tsui.

German & Austrian German grub is available at the *Biergarten* (☎ 2721-2302), 8 Hanoi Rd, and the Kowloon branch of *Schnurrbart* (☎ 2366-2986) at 9 Prat Ave, Tsim Sha Tsui. If you're near the Star Ferry terminal, a *pfannengebratener fleischkase* (pan fried meat 'cheese') awaits at *Weinstube* (☎ 2376-1800) on the 1st floor of the Honeytex building, 22 Ashley Rd, Tsim Sha Tsui.

Indian There are some excellent Indian restaurants in Kowloon which are often very good value. The greatest concentration of cheap Indian and Pakistani restaurants is in Chungking Mansions at 36-44 Nathan Rd. Despite the grotty appearance of the entrance to the Mansions, many of the restaurants are surprisingly plush inside. The food cooked in these establishments varies in quality, but if you follow the recommendations below, you should be in for a cheap and very filling meal. A good lunch or dinner will cost from about HK$50. Chungking Mansions has an avid fan base, so why not give it a bash.

The Taj Mahal Club (☎ 2722-5454), 3rd floor, B block, is a popular destination for those who like to choke on blindingly hot curries and pay little for the experience. The chicken masala is HK$38 and excellent value. On the 3rd floor of C block is *The Delhi Club* (☎ 2368-1682), which does very good value Indian Nepali food. Try the chicken tandoori at HK$20. Also in C block on the 4th floor is the *Islamabad Club* (☎ 2721-5362), a spartan sort of place that will fill you up without emptying your pockets. Another well known spicy eatery is the *Swagat Restaurant* (☎ 2722-5350). The food at Swagat is really very good, the portions huge and the decor is a cut above the rest of the Chungking crowd.

Others to look out for within the bowels of Chungking Mansions include the *Islamabad Club* (☎ 2721-5362), 4th floor, C block, which cooks up Indian and Pakistani halal food; the *Khyber Pass Club Mess* (☎ 2721-2786), 7th floor, E block, which has good food served in more-or-less acceptable surroundings; and the *Nanak Mess* (☎ 2368-8063), flat A4, 11th floor, A block, which is decent but isn't one of the top spots.

If you can't handle the stigma of dining at the Chungking Mansions, *Woodlands* (☎ 2369-3718), 5-6 Mirror Tower, 61 Mody Rd, provides cheap Indian meat-free meals. The setting is unpretentious, simple and fun, and the food is good.

The *Koh-I-Noor* (☎ 2368-3065) on the 1st floor of 3-4 Peninsula Mansion, 16C Mody Rd, Tsim Sha Tsui, is one of a chain of restaurants. It is cheaper and less stylish than its counterpart in Central, but the food is great and the staff friendly. The speciality is North Indian food, although there are often buffets laid on of food from other regions (value for money).

The popular *Branto Indian Pure Vegetarian Club* (☎ 2366-8171) at 9 Lock Rd is cheap and excellent. This is the place to go if you want to try an alternative to chicken and lamb and still savour some fine food. Great value.

Surya Restaurant (☎ 2366-5961) is buried among the shops inside the Lyton building at 34-48 Mody Rd. It's as good a place as any to get your mutton biryani, lamb keema sali and chicken tikka. The restaurant is open from noon until midnight.

The venerable *Gaylord* (☎ 2376-1001) in Ashley Rd, Tsim Sha Tsui, has been going strong since 1972. Dim lighting, booth seating and live Indian music usher you into an aromatic and cosy world of spicy dining.

Indonesian The *Java Rijsttafel* (☎ 2367-1230), Han Hing Mansion, 38 Hankow Rd, Tsim Sha Tsui, serves *rijsttafel* (literally, rice table). This place packs out with Dutch expats, most of whom complain that the same food is a lot cheaper in Amsterdam. The menu is extensive, but if you get overwhelmed just order a serving of the rijsttafel, which gives you 16 tasty dishes for under HK$150.

Irish *Delaney's* (☎ 2301-3980) is in 3-7 Prat Ave, Tsim Sha Tsui, if you fancy Irish pub grub and a mellow pint of Guinness.

Italian *Valentino* (☎ 2721-6449) at 16 Hanoi Rd, Tsim Sha Tsui, is a great Italian restaurant. *La Taverna* (☎ 2376-1945), Astoria building, 36-38 Ashley Rd, Tsim Sha Tsui, is highly rated. *Pizza World* (☎ 2367-1983) ground floor, New World Centre, 22 Salisbury Rd, is also very popular.

In another price bracket altogether is *Sabatini* (☎ 2721-5215), 3rd floor, The Royal Garden, 69 Mody Rd, Tsim Sha Tsui East. A direct copy of its namesake in Rome, on offer are classic Italian heavyweights like fettuccine carbonara (a creamy pasta with bacon) and exquisite desserts.

Japanese If you want cheap Japanese food, make it yourself. Japanese restaurants charge Japanese prices. You can economise by looking for informal ones without the fish ponds and young Filipinos in geisha costumes playing ukuleles. There are also a couple of top-end options for those in pursuit of fine Japanese cuisine.

Gomitori (☎ 2367-8519), 92 Granville Rd, Tsim Sha Tsui East, is a restaurant frequented by Japanese expats, which is always a good sign, despite the fact that this restaurant is tiny. Meals seem to be good value.

Kyo-Zasa (☎ 2376-1888), 20 Ashley Rd, is a colourful and cosy Japanese restaurant that oozes real authenticity. The food is equally spot-on and the price is reasonable. If you want a quiet evening with intimacy on the menu, the *Nishimura* (☎ 2775-6899), 6th floor, Hong Kong Hotel, 2 Canton Rd, Harbour City, is probably the perfect place. Despite being expensive, the surroundings are a real treat.

Finally, in the basement of the Kowloon Shangri-La Hotel is the *Nadaman* (☎ 2721-2111); its authentic, traditional setting has won a deserved reputation. It is very expensive, although the set meals at lunch time are excellent value (there is another branch in the Island Shangri-La Hotel (☎ 2820-8570), Pacific Place, Admiralty).

Korean There are several excellent and easily accessible Korean restaurants. Many of these are barbecue restaurants, where you sit around a table with a griddle in the middle, upon which you fling strips of pork, lamb, beef, chicken, squid and fish (plus the odd vegetable) and watch as the whole lot catches fire, spitting oil in all directions. It's actually great fun, especially with loads of beer, and makes for an excellent party.

Many restaurants have special 'all-you-can-eat' menus which are a good deal.

Arirang (☎ 2956-3288), 210 The Gateway, 25 Canton Rd, Tsim Sha Tsui, is a large barbecue outfit, perfect for group bookings. The restaurant wins a lot of praise for its barbecues and traditional food. Also in Tsim Sha Tsui is the small but sizzlingly popular *Three-Five Korean Restaurant* (☎ 2376-1545), 6 Ashley Rd.

Other popular Korean restaurants include *Seoul House* (☎ 2314-3174), 35 Hillwood Rd, Yau Ma Tei, and *Korea House* (☎ 2367-5674), Empire Centre, 68 Mody Rd, Tsim Sha Tsui East.

Malaysian *Banana Leaf Curry House* (☎ 2721-4821), 3rd floor, Golden Crown Court, 68 Nathan Rd, dishes up Malaysian food served on a banana leaf. The spicy Singapore noodles go down well with the delicious range of fruit juices.

Pan-Asian One of the great bargains in town is the lunch/dinner buffet at *Salisbury's Dining Room* (☎ 2369-2211) on the 4th floor of the Salisbury YMCA in Tsim Sha Tsui. The food is not exquisite, but it's value for money, the atmosphere is cheery and it has a prime location.

Portuguese *Hideaway* (☎ 2926-3098), 86-98 Canton Rd, has authentic Portuguese food. There is another branch in Wan Chai (☎ 2923-5038).

Spanish A long-time favourite with the expats, *El Cid* (☎ 2312-1989), 14 Knutsford Terrace, Tsim Sha Tsui, does justice to Spanish classics such as paella and fritas,

and has an excellent assortment of tapas (appetisers). The restaurant has a healthy selection of Spanish wine. Actually there are two restaurants: one that just serves tapas and another which has both tapas and appetisers.

Thai Thai food can be devastatingly hot but delicious. An excellent Thai restaurant is *Royal Pattaya* (☎ 2366-9919), 9 Minden Ave, Tsim Sha Tsui. This place has a vegetarian menu. Authentic, flavoursome Thai food can be found at the *Red Chilli Thai Food Restaurant* (☎ 2363-5723) at 27 Man Tai St, and another good option is *Wong Chun Chun* (☎ 2721-0099), 21-23 Prat Ave, Tsim Sha Tsui.

The neighbourhood, Kowloon City, near the old passenger terminal at Kai Tak airport, has an unusually high concentration of Thai residents and Thai restaurants. There are also a few Indian restaurants in the neighbourhood. The selection of places to eat is so good and the prices are so reasonable (by Hong Kong standards) that it's almost worth a trip out there for a meal. Some of the more popular Thai eateries include the *Cambo Thai* (☎ 2716-7318), 15 Nga Tsin Long Rd; *Golden Orchid Thai* (☎ 2716-1269), Nos 6 and 12, Lung Kong Rd; *Golden Wheat Thai* (☎ 2718-1801), 34 Nam Kok Rd; and the *Wong Chun Chun Cantonese-Thai* (☎ 2383-4680) – which has a branch at 70-72 Nga Tsin Wai Rd and at 29-33 Lung Kong Rd.

Vegetarian Massage that meat-free conscience with a trip to *The Higher Taste Vegetarian Dining Club* (☎ 2723-0260), on the 6th floor, 27 Chatham Rd, where you are invited to take off your shoes and mumble 'Hare Krishna' through mouthfuls of cheap vegetable offerings. You can pass on the street dance if you want, but the food is excellent, great value and the restaurant attracts a colourful assortment of types.

Cheap Indian meat-free meals are cooked up at *Woodlands* (☎ 2369-3718), 5-6 Mirror Tower, 61 Mody Rd. The setting is unpretentious, simple and fun, and the food is good.

Many of the other Indian restaurants mentioned earlier in this chapter have a wide selection of meat-free dishes.

Like its sister branch in Causeway Bay, the *Kung Tak Lam* (☎ 2367-7881), 1st floor, 45-47 Carnarvon Rd, attracts a loyal clientele who wouldn't eat anywhere else. This is Shanghai vegetarian cuisine and we can guarantee you'll love it.

Worth a detour if you're in the area is the rather good *Pak Bo Vegetarian Kitchen* (☎ 2380-2681) at 787 Nathan Rd, Mong Kok.

Vietnamese *W's Paris 13th* (☎ 2723-6369), Toyo Mall, 94 Granville Rd, Tsim Sha Tsui East, wins no points for decor, but the food is delicious and the prices should make you happy as well. *Huong Viet* (☎ 2384-9790) at 5 Man Wai St is also worth hunting down, although the menu is only in Chinese and Vietnamese. Another branch (☎ 2730-4866) exists in shop 101, Ocean Centre, Tsim Sha Tsui. *Café de La Paix Vietnamese Cuisine* (☎ 2721-2747), Hermes Commercial Centre, corner of Hillwood and Nathan Rds, is also worth noting.

Breakfast
If you are looking for a pick-me-up coffee, great muffins, pastries and baguettes, then *Espresso Americano* (☎ 2377-0876), with its rich range of coffees, is an excellent place for breakfast. It can be found on the ground floor of Star House on Salisbury Rd and opens at 7.30 am.

La Rose Noire Patisserie (☎ 2956-1222), on the ground floor of the Gateway at 254 Canton Rd, serves up excellent coffee and breakfasts. Tucked away at shop 5 in Cameron Lane, *Kona Coffee Specialists* (☎ 2724-3709) sell some fantastic coffees. On offer are 14 different concoctions including a Blue Mountain brew which will set you back HK$32 and an espresso for HK$15.

The *Deli Corner* (☎ 2311-8288) provides an enclave of calm away from the grind of Nathan Rd, in the basement of the Holiday Inn Golden Mile. This is an excellent (but pricey) spot to pause for a pastry and coffee while thumbing through the morning papers. Deli Corner opens at 7.30 am.

The window of the *Wing Wah Restaurant* (☎ 2721-2947) is always filled with great looking cakes and pastries. It's at 21A Lock Rd, Tsim Sha Tsui, near Swindon bookshop and the Hyatt Regency. Either take it away or sit down with some coffee. Inexpensive Chinese food is also served and – a rare treat for a Hong Kong budget Chinese cafe – there is an English menu.

Deep in the bowels of every MTR station you can find *Maxim's Cake Shops*. The cakes and pastries look irresistible, but don't sink your teeth into the creamy delights until you're back on the street as it is prohibited to eat or drink anything in the MTR stations or on the trains – there is a HK$1000 fine.

Delifrance is a coffee shop notable for its pastries, muffins, submarine sandwiches, quiche and bouillabaisse, not to mention coffee. You'll find one branch in the Hyatt Arcade at 67 Nathan Rd and another in Carnarvon Plaza, 20 Carnarvon Rd, Tsim Sha Tsui.

Fast Food
Oliver Super Sandwich Stores has a branch on the ground floor of the Ocean Centre on Canton Rd, Tsim Sha Tsui. It's a great place for breakfast – inexpensive bacon, eggs and toast. The sandwiches are equally excellent; the bread is so good you'll probably take home a loaf from the adjacent delicatessen. The restaurant packs out during lunch hour, but is blissfully uncrowded at other times.

McDonald's occupies key strategic locations in Tsim Sha Tsui. Late night restaurants are amazingly scarce in Hong Kong, so it's useful to know that two McDonald's in Tsim Sha Tsui operate 24 hours a day (at 21A-B Granville Rd and 12 Peking Rd). There is also a McDonald's at 2 Cameron Rd, and another in Star House opposite the Star Ferry terminal.

Domino's Pizza (☎ 2765-0683), Yue Sun Mansion, Hung Hom, does not have a restaurant where you can sit down to eat. Rather, pizzas are delivered to your door within 30 minutes of phoning in your order.

If the pizza arrives even a few minutes late, you get a HK$10 discount. If it's 45 minutes late, the pizza is free.

Pizza Hut has a number of branches: lower basement, Silvercord Shopping Centre, corner Haiphong and Canton Rds, Tsim Sha Tsui; shop 008, Ocean Terminal, Harbour City, Canton Rd, Tsim Sha Tsui; and 1st floor, Hanford House, 221C-D Nathan Rd, Yau Ma Tei.

Other fast food outlets in Kowloon include *KFC*, Cameron Rd, Tsim Sha Tsui; *Café de Coral*, mezzanine floor, Albion Plaza, 2-6 Granville Rd, Tsim Sha Tsui; and *Fairwood Fast Food*, 6 Ashley Rd, Tsim Sha Tsui. *Hardee's* have a branch in the Ocean Terminal; and *Jack in the Box* is on the ground floor of the Tsim Sha Tsui Centre, 66 Mody Rd, Tsim Sha Tsui East.

Self-Catering

If you're looking for the best in cheese, bread and other imported delicacies, check out the delicatessen at *Oliver's* (☎ 2730-9233) on the ground floor of Ocean Centre on Canton Rd. You'll find exotica such as blue cheese, Melba toast, imported Belgian chocolate cookies and German black bread. For a larger concentration of delicatessens, refer to Places to Eat in the Hong Kong Island chapter.

For true backpackers' cuisine like muesli, yoghurt and peanut butter, you've got to go to the supermarkets – and Hong Kong's are exceedingly well stocked. The biggest surprise is that prices are very reasonable. Kowloon and Yau Ma Tei are well-supplied with branches of the two popular supermarket chains, *Park N' shop* and *Wellcome*.

Branches of Park N'Shop can be found on the south-west corner of Peking Rd and Kowloon Park Drive; and in the 2nd basement, Silvercord Shopping Centre, 30 Canton Rd. Branches of Wellcome are inside the Dairy Farm Creamery, 74-78 Nathan Rd (open until 10 pm); on the north-west corner of Granville and Carnarvon Rds; and in the basement of Star House (next to the Star Ferry terminal).

ENTERTAINMENT

Kowloon's entertaiment scene plays second fiddle to the entertainment hot spots of Hong Kong Island. That's not to say you won't find anything to do in Kowloon – the district is littered with bars and pubs – but it's all just a bit tackier, less imaginative and more rundown.

Cinemas

Probably the most accessible cinema for westerners in Kowloon is the *Silvercord* cinema (☎ 2317-1083), 30 Canton Rd, Tsim Sha Tsui. It is not far from the Star Ferry terminal and has two theatres that screen the latest western films. *Chinachem Golden Plaza Cinema* (☎ 2311-3000), 77 Mody Rd, Tsim Sha Tsui East, also has showings of mainstream western flicks. The *Broadway Cinematique* (☎ 2332-9000), Prosperous Garden, 3 Public Square St, Yau Ma Tei, hosts more high-brow films for those in need of cerebral entertainment. The *Astor Classics* (☎ 2781-1833), Eaton Hotel, Astor Plaza, 380 Nathan Rd, Jordan, tries to provide more original presentations. The *Hong Kong Space Museum* (☎ 2734-2722) also sporadically hosts film forums and festivals that showcase arthouse material. Other cinemas in Kowloon worth considering include the *Empire* (☎ 2332-1939), 60 Soy St, Yau Ma Tei; *London* (☎ 2736-8282), 219 Nathan Rd, Yau Ma Tei; *Majestic* (☎ 2782-0272), 348 Nathan Rd, Yau Ma Tei; *Miramar* (☎ 2736-0108), Park Lane Square, 1 Kimberley Rd, Tsim Sha Tsui; *Ocean* (☎ 2377-2100), 3 Canton Rd, Tsim Sha Tsui; and *UA Whampoa* (☎ 2303-1040), Whampoa Garden, Hung Hom.

Don't forget that you can book tickets for screenings at any of the above cinemas through *Cityline* (☎ 2317-6666). Use your credit card and collect tickets at the theatre before the film commences.

Night Markets

The biggest and most popular night market among tourists is the Temple St market in Tsim Sha Tsui (near Jordan MTR station). The market opens at 8 pm and closes around midnight. See Yau Ma Tei in this chapter for more details.

Another big market is at Tung Choi St in Mong Kok. It is geared more towards selling clothing and is open mainly during the daytime.

Discos & Clubs

Tsim Sha Tsui does not have a great deal to offer when it comes to dancing. One of the better known venues is *Rick's Cafe* (☎ 2367-2939), 4 Hart Ave, Tsim Sha Tsui. The decor is cheesy Casablanca, complete with palm trees and Bogie and Bergman photos decorating the walls; check out the frightful ad on local TV. The dance floor is usually a writhing knot of western men and Filipino girls. Entry is free from Monday to Thursday and costs HK$120 on Friday and Saturday nights. Women get free shots every Wednesday night.

Bahama Mama's Caribbean Bar (☎ 2368-2121), 4-5 Knutsford Terrace, Tsim Sha Tsui, is also popular. The theme is (can you guess) tropical isle, complete with palm trees and surf boards. It really is a friendly spot and stands apart from most of the other late-night watering holes. On Friday and Saturday nights there is a DJ spinning songs to get folks onto the bonsai-sized dance floor. From 5 to 9 pm the music slouches back into a reggae beat. There's a HK$100 minimum cover charge after 11 pm on Friday and Saturday nights. Jazz bands grace the stage after 9 pm on Sunday.

Catwalk (☎ 2369-4111), on the 18th floor of the New World Hotel, 22 Salisbury Rd, Tsim Sha Tsui, is the hot spot for Hong Kong's monied young things. There's live music (usually quite good) in one section, disco in another (and we mean disco), and yes, karaoke in several other areas. Mobile phones, designer watches and Cognac are the order of the day. Catwalk also features one of Hong Kong's highest cover charges: HK$200 on Friday and Saturday, though this does include two drinks. The fee falls to HK$120 during the rest of the week for men, and entry is free for women.

Nearby, in the Regent hotel, the posh *Club Shanghai* (☎ 2721-1211) usually has an American house band cranking out dance tunes five to six nights a week. The place is decked out à la 1930s Shanghai, down to the opium pipes (not filled) on each table. Cover is HK$120 from Sunday to Thursday, and HK$150 on Friday and Saturday (but includes one drink).

Though a miserable venue for big name gigs, the *Hard Rock Cafe* (☎ 2377-8118), 100 Canton Rd, Tsim Sha Tsui, is not a bad spot to hit the dance floor. The decor of guitars and rock memorabilia spice up the place, and there is usually a live band playing. If not, the cafe hosts a DJ to entertain the crowd, playing from about 10.30 pm onwards. Cover is HK$80 for men, and women get in free.

Rock & Jazz

Ashley Rd has its own little time warp in the form of *Ned Kelly's Last Stand* (☎ 2376-0562), 11A Ashley Rd, Tsim Sha Tsui. A great tradition continues with Colin Aithison and the Kelly Gang playing Dixieland jazz Tuesday to Sunday from 9.15 pm to 1.45 am the next morning. Ken Bennett and the Kowloon Hongkers play on Monday.

Chasers (☎ 2367-9487), 2-3 Knutsford Terrace, Tsim Sha Tsui, has live music every night. Most nights the guitars and drumsticks are in the hands of resident band Square Eyes, who have a repertoire of rock-based covers and mainstream hits.

For mellow 40s and 50s jazz, take your smoking jacket along and sip cognac at *The Bar* (☎ 2315-3135) at the Peninsula, Salisbury Rd, Tsim Sha Tsui. The music starts at 9.30 pm.

Pubs & Bars

Bars are spread out in Tsim Sha Tsui, but there are three basic clusters: along Ashley Rd; within the triangle formed by Hanoi, Prat and Chatham Rds; and up by Knutsford Terrace. In addition to the bars listed in this section, don't forget to check out other Entertainment sections for Kowloon bars such as the *Hard Rock Cafe*, *Chasers*, *The Bar*,

Rick's Cafe, *Bahama Mama's Caribbean Bar* and the *Catwalk*. There are also other nondescript watering holes scattered about. Should you decide to go exploring, bear in mind that a few of the smaller places are more for Hong Kong Chinese than foreigners. If you're treated to a chilly welcome, just continue on to another bar; there are plenty of options.

Jouster II (☎ 2723-0022), shops A and B, Hart Ave Court, 19-23 Hart Ave, Tsim Sha Tsui, is a fun multi-storey place with mediaeval decor; check out the knight in shining armour and miniature drawbridge. The crowd is mostly Chinese and the noise can be deafening when several tables start playing drinking games.

Up on Prat Ave is the Kowloon branch of *Delaney's* (☎ 2301-3980). This offshoot seems even more authentically Irish than the original Delaney's in Wan Chai: lots of dark wood, green felt and a long bar that you can really settle into for the long haul. Just up the street a bit is *Schnurrbart* (☎ 2366-2986), 9-11 Prat Ave, Tsim Sha Tsui, a smaller and somewhat more restrained version of its counterpart in Lan Kwai Fong. The beer is just as good, though. Armies of Germans descend on *Biergarten* (☎ 2721-2302), 8 Hanoi Rd, Tsim Sha Tsui, for porknuckle, sauerkraut and the selection of excellent beers on tap. Any of these places would make for a fine afternoon breather after a day of shopping or sightseeing.

Amoeba Bar (☎ 2376-0389), 22 Ashley Rd, Tsim Sha Tsui, has local live music in the basement from around 9 pm, and the place doesn't close until about 6 am. It draws a mainly Cantonese crowd.

The *Kangaroo Pub* (☎ 2376-0083), 1st and 2nd floors, 35 Haiphong Rd, Tsim Sha Tsui, is an Aussie pub in true tradition. This place does a good Sunday brunch.

MC2 Media Cafe (☎ 2369-9997) in the Mirimar shopping centre, 1-23 Kimberley Rd, Tsim Sha Tsui, has a decent selection of microbrewery beers, and at the time of writing was staging a beer buffet (where you can drink as much as you want for HK$55). The *Watering Hole* (☎ 2312-2288) in the basement of 1A Mody Rd, Tsim Sha Tsui, is a kind of grotty, salt-of-the-earth place where local expats sometimes congregate for a swilling session.

Mad Dogs Pub (☎ 2301-2222), basement, 32 Nathan Rd, Tsim Sha Tsui, is a popular Aussie style pub. From Monday to Thursday it's open from 7 am until 2 am the next morning. Over the weekend (from Friday to Sunday) it doesn't close at all.

Bottoms Up (☎ 2367-5696), basement, 14 Hankow Rd, Tsim Sha Tsui, has a particular appeal for James Bond fans. Duty brought 007 there on one of his Asian sojourns, and the club is still milking it for all it's worth. Just because Mr Bond made it there, it doesn't mean you have to; this place is a true sleazepit. Park your Aston-Martin elsewhere.

Finally, if you can no longer stand the low-life sleaze, noise and general barbarity of Tsim Sha Tsui, and you're willing to pay anything for peace and quiet, then the *Bar* (☎ 2315-3135) on the 1st floor of the Peninsula can oblige. Disturbed only by the sounds of the soft and gentle clinking of wine glasses, the tinkle of the top notes of the bar's piano or the muffled cough from the waiter at your side to signal that the bar is about to shut for the night, it all seems somehow worth the massive financial outlay. It is open from noon until 1 am.

Hostess Clubs

Tailor-made for those on expense accounts, these are best avoided unless you want to pick up a chit a yard-long and riddled with hidden extras. You can emerge from one of these clubs a month's salary worse off if you aren't careful. The clubs in Tsim Sha Tsui are particularly bad, but business seems to be more above board in Tsim Sha Tsui East. See Entertainment in the Facts for the Visitor chapter for details of hostess bar scams.

All of the following establishments are considered respectable, but expensive. A popular place with Chinese tycoons is *China City Night Club* (☎ 2723-0388), 4th floor, Peninsula Centre, 67 Mody Rd, Tsim

Sha Tsui East. It's open daily from noon to 4 am.

Club Bboss (☎ 2369-2883), New Mandarin Plaza, 14 Science Museum Rd, Tsim Sha Tsui East, bills itself as a 'Japanese style nightclub'. Certainly the prices are Japanese style. With more than a thousand hostesses of 'various nationalities', it's a good place to practise your Tagalog or Thai (if you don't mind paying HK\$1000 an hour for lessons).

Club Deluxe (☎ 2721-0277), L-301, New World Centre, Salisbury Rd, Tsim Sha Tsui, is a good place to burn money, especially in the VIP karaoke suites. Opening hours are from 8 pm to 3 am. The club has an indoor waterfall, among other exotic features.

SHOPPING

In Tsim Sha Tsui, you don't have to look for a place to shop, the shopping comes to you – people are constantly trying to stuff advertisements into your hands. Finding a place to buy a loaf of bread is almost impossible along the streets crammed with shops peddling clothes, watches, cameras, jewellery, eyeglasses and electronics. It's capitalism run amok, and more than a few travellers who are only in Hong Kong to pick up a China visa, suddenly catch the buying fever. Try to exercise some restraint, or attend a local meeting of Shopperholics Anonymous.

If you've decided that you need to do some serious shopping, then Hong Kong is as good a place as any to go on a buying binge. However, if you're looking to make some expensive purchases like cameras, video and stereo equipment, please memorise the following mantra: Tsim Sha Tsui is a rip-off. While it's quite all right to purchase clothing, you should look elsewhere when buying pricey hi-tech items.

That said, shopping in Kowloon is a bizarre mix of the down at heel and the glamorous, and an afternoon's stroll through its shopping quarters should yield a few surprises. Die-hard shoppers can spend the whole day in Harbour City (made up of five shopping arcades) without ever seeing the light of day. From the boutique shopping arcade of the Peninsula to the stalls of the Temple St night market, you can find just about anything, if you are prepared to look hard enough.

Antiques

Most of the rich pickings lie south of Victoria Harbour (most notably along Hollywood Rd and Wyndham St), but there are a few places of note in Kowloon. There are a few antique shops in the Ocean Terminal/Harbour City complex in Tsim Sha Tsui, but getting a good price is said to be considerably more difficult there than on Hong Kong Island. Antique shops are mainly concentrated along a corridor called the Silk Road; there you can find cloisonné, bronzes, jade, lacquer, ceramics, rosewood furniture and screens. Art Orient at room 342 has a fine selection of Buddhist and Tibetan artefacts. The whole arcade makes for an intriguing stroll.

Well known among dealers in Hong Kong is Charlotte Horstmann & Gerald Godfrey Ltd (☎ 2735-7167), shop 104, Ocean Terminal. This shop has a great clutter of textiles, ceramics, jade, furniture and sculpture on display; more than can be looked at in a single afternoon's viewing. Eileen Kershaw (☎ 2366-4083) in the Peninsula has a splendid collection of porcelains and carpets.

Appliances & Electronics

Whatever you do, don't ever buy anything electrical on Nathan Rd; you could be seriously burnt.

Sham Shui Po is a good neighbourhood to search for electrical and electronic goodies. You can even buy and sell secondhand appliances. If you take any of the west exits from the MTR at Sham Shui Po station, you'll find yourself on Apliu St where there are numerous good shops. Apliu St is one of the best areas in Hong Kong to go searching for the numerous permutations of plug adaptors you'll need if you're heading to China.

Mong Kok is another good neighbourhood for electronic gadgetry. Starting from Argyle St and heading south, explore all the side streets running parallel to Nathan Rd, such as Tung Choi, Sai Yeung Choi,

Portland, Shanghai and Reclamation Sts. In this area you can buy just about anything imaginable.

Backpacks

Hong Kong is a good place to pick up gear for hiking, camping and travelling. Outdoor International (☎ 2314-4454), shop B1B in the basement of Star House, is one shop in Tsim Sha Tsui with a decent range of camping and hiking gear, stocking brands such as Berghaus and Gore-tex.

Mong Kok is a good neighbourhood for camping gear, though there are also a couple of places in nearby Yau Ma Tei. Some places worth exploring include Chamonix Alpine Equipment (☎ 2388-3626), On Yip building, Shanghai St; Mountaineer Supermarket (☎ 2397-0585), 395 Portland St; Tang Fai Kee Military (☎ 2385-5169), 248 Reclamation St; and the Three Military Equipment Company (☎ 2395-5234), 83 Sai Yee St.

Bookshops

One of the biggest and best bookshops is Swindon Books (☎ 2366-8001), 13 Lock Rd, Tsim Sha Tsui. There are also smaller branches at shop 346, 3rd floor, Ocean Terminal, Tsim Sha Tsui; and at the Star Ferry terminal, Tsim Sha Tsui.

Times Books (☎ 2367-4340) is hidden in the basement of Golden Crown Court at 66-70 Nathan Rd, Tsim Sha Tsui. The South China Morning Post Family Bookshop has branches on the 3rd floor, Ocean Terminal, Tsim Sha Tsui; and on the ground floor of the Tung Ying building, Granville Rd (at Nathan Rd).

Books related to the arts can be found at the Performing Arts Shop (☎ 2734-2091) in the Hong Kong Cultural Centre in Tsim Sha Tsui. Tai Yip Company (☎ 2732-2088) have an excellent and extensive range of art books and cards in the shop on the 1st floor of the Hong Kong Museum of Art in Tsim Sha Tsui.

Cameras

Tsim Sha Tsui is perhaps the most expensive place in Asia, if not the world, to buy photo-

Lais, Damned Lais

China has a tendency to politicise everything – a point made perfectly clear to a Hong Kong entrepreneur, Jimmy Lai. He founded Giordano (named after a New York pizza parlour), which has become one of the most successful clothing retailers in the world. The chain has spread quickly across Asia and beyond. It also seems to have inspired a close competitor, Bossini.

Giordano clothing is made in China, and in recent years Giordano outlets have opened in most major Chinese cities. One would think the Chinese authorities would be pleased with Giordano's success. After all, the jobs created in the clothing factories go to Chinese workers and the foreign exchange earned by exporting the clothes goes into China's coffers.

But unfortunately for Giordano shareholders, founder Jimmy Lai also decided to start a Chinese-language newspaper in Hong Kong. Unlike most Hong Kong newspapers, which kowtow to Beijing, Lai's paper made some very unflattering remarks about the former Chinese Premier, Li Peng. The Chinese authorities swooped on Giordano outlets in China, shutting down stores and harassing the employees. For the good of the company, Lai stepped down. However, the Chinese police have continued their campaign against the company. Giordano shareholders have tried unsuccessfully to convince the authorities that Lai no longer has a financial interest in the company.

Lai has many supporters in Hong Kong – both expat gwailos and Hong Kong locals flock to Giordano stores, partially as an act of defiance against China. But it's hard to be optimistic about Lai's future, unless he emigrates. His newspaper is certainly a target for government retaliation, as are Giordano stores in Hong Kong. And if rumours are true, Lai needs continuous protection against Hong Kong's Triads, who have put a contract out on him.

graphic equipment. This particularly applies to Nathan Rd. Shops don't put price tags on the equipment and charging double or more is standard.

In this neighbourhood, camera equipment is only 'reasonably priced' when it's broken, second-hand or components are missing. Stanley St in Central is probably the best neighbourhood for camera equipment (see Hong Kong Island chapter), or go up to Mong Kok or the shopping malls in Sha Tin (see the New Territories chapter).

From our experience, the two best camera shops in Tsim Sha Tsui are in Champagne Court at 16 Kimberley Rd. One is Kimberley Camera Company (☎ 2721-2308) and the other is David Chan (☎ 2723-3886). There are price tags on the equipment, a rare find in Tsim Sha Tsui. These places also sell used equipment and there is some latitude for bargaining.

Carpets
In this game, it's worth knowing what you're buying; if you're in doubt then do not buy. There are a few places in Ocean Terminal that stock a decent range. The Chinese Carpet Centre (☎ 2735-1030), shop 178, Deck 1, Ocean Terminal, has a huge selection of new carpets and rugs. You can custom order from Hong Kong's Tai Ping Carpets Ltd, which has a showroom (☎ 2522-7138) on the ground floor of Wing On Plaza, 62 Mody Rd, Tsim Sha Tsui. The Royal Rug Company (☎ 2721-4978), room 704-5, Grand Centre, 8 Humphreys Ave, is a trusted carpet retailer and also has a massive selection.

Children's Clothing & Toys
Mothercare (☎ 2735-5738) can be found at shop 137, Ocean Terminal, Harbour City, Canton Rd, Tsim Sha Tsui. Chicco (☎ 2377-3369) at shop 023a, Marina Deck, Ocean Terminal, Tsim Sha Tsui, sells exclusive kiddies clothing. On the toys front, Toys R Us (☎ 2730-9462) have a branch at shop 032, Ocean Terminal, Harbour City, 5 Canton Rd.

Chinese Emporiums
Most of the emporiums sell an eclectic range of ceramics, furniture, souvenirs and clothes. One branch of Yue Hwa Chinese Products (☎ 2311-1987) is at Park Lane Boulevard on Nathan Rd, Tsim Sha Tsui, just north of the Kowloon Mosque. Look for the two storey block that looks like the world's longest garage.

The PRC owns Chinese Arts & Crafts. There are branches at Star House (☎ 2735-4061), 3 Salisbury Rd, Tsim Sha Tsui, and 239 Nathan Rd, Yau Ma Tei (near Jordan MTR station). Everything has price tags and no bargaining is necessary.

Chung Kiu Chinese Products is also worth investigating. Branches are at 17 Hankow Rd, Tsim Sha Tsui; 528-532 Nathan Rd, Yau Ma Tei; and 47-51 Shantung St, Mong Kok.

Cigars
You can probably get your cigarettes cheaper elsewhere, but Davidoff (☎ 2724-8984) at shop EL3 in the Peninsula has an excellent range for those who find smoking cigars an indispensable joy.

Clothing
You'll find the best buys at the street markets on Tong Choi St in Mong Kok and in Apliu St in Sham Shui Po. If you want to search around Tsim Sha Tsui, the best deals are generally found at the eastern end of Granville Rd. Giordano's has an outlet at Golden Crown Court, 66-70 Nathan Rd. Bossini has one of its many shops at Granville House, 53 Granville Rd, Tsim Sha Tsui. Another name in the mass market fashion industry is U2, with branches in the Tsim Sha Tsui Centre and at 202 Nathan Rd, Tsim Sha Tsui. Another good place is on the mezzanine floor of Chungking Mansions (not the ground floor). There are many factory outlets in Hung Hom, especially in Kaiser Estates. If you want to track them down, consult Dana Goetz's book, *Hong Kong Factory Bargains*.

On Nathan Rd there are packs of Indian tailors waiting to charge after you with offers of on-the-spot tailoring. Some manage to put the whole suit together (plus tailor-made shirts) in the space of an afternoon. If you want a suit made up, be sure to communicate exactly how you want it made and skip the 'just add water', instant suit approach. Some of these tailors can actually put together decent suits, but allow for a few days. Needless to say, these suits are very cheap.

Britain's well known Marks & Spencer chain (☎ 2377-1051) has a branch in Tsim Sha Tsui at shops 102 and 254, Ocean Terminal, Harbour City, Canton Rd.

There are many amazingly fancy and expensive boutiques in Tsim Sha Tsui and the prices don't seem to faze the hordes of free-spending Hong Kong residents. The shopping arcade at the Peninsula is a maze of luxury names and price tags, and the other top-end hotels have similar arcades.

Among the top names are: Salvatore Ferragamo (☎ 2831-8457), shop 111, Regent Shopping Arcade, 18 Salisbury Rd, Tsim Sha Tsui; and Nina Ricci Boutique (☎ 2721-4869), with shops in room 149, lobby floor, Regent Shopping Arcade and shop BE 13-15 in the basement of the Peninsula, Salisbury Rd, Tsim Sha Tsui (☎ 2311-5922). Hermes Boutique (☎ 2315-3262) has a shop at BE 7-9, also in the basement of the Peninsula.

Computers

Star Computer City, on the 2nd floor of Star House at 3 Salisbury Rd, Tsim Sha Tsui, is the largest complex of computer shops in Tsim Sha Tsui. While it's not the cheapest place in Hong Kong to find computers, it's also not the most expensive (that honour goes to nearby Nathan Rd). Bargaining is advised; honesty is in short supply in this neighbourhood. The highest mark-ups (blatant overcharging) are on small items like floppy disks and printer cartridges; you can often get a 50% discount just by asking for it.

From the outside of the building it's not immediately obvious how to get inside this complex; as you face Star House from the harbour side, there are two main entrances with escalators leading up to the mezzanine

level. The computer shops are all cleverly concealed in there.

Mong Kok Computer Centre has three floors of computer shops. It's geared more towards the resident Cantonese-speaking market than foreigners, but you can generally get better deals than in Tsim Sha Tsui. The computer centre is at the intersection of Nelson and Fa Yuen Sts in Mong Kok.

The Golden Shopping Centre, basement and 1st floor, 146-152 Fuk Wah St, Sham Shui Po, has a good selection of computers, accessories and components. The nearby New Capital Computer Plaza, 85-95 Un Chau St, is also excellent. Both places are signposted in the Sham Shui Po MTR station.

Department Stores

A favourite department store in Hong Kong is the main branch of Yue Hwa Chinese Products at 301 Nathan Rd, Yau Ma Tei (corner of Nathan and Jordan Rds). Unlike the touristy branch in Tsim Sha Tsui, this store has a wide assortment of practical, everyday, locally produced and imported items (not just from China). There are also some Chinese exotica like herbal medicines. However, it's not a high fashion store – if it's famous labels you crave, look elsewhere.

Wing On is an upmarket department store where you can find Gucci handbags, Calvin Klein underwear, Chanel No 19 perfume and Rolex watches (real ones). There are three branches in Kowloon: 361 Nathan Rd, Yau Ma Tei; 620 Nathan Rd, Mong Kok; and Wing On Plaza, Mody Rd, Tsim Sha Tsui East. Another Hong Kong department store is Sincere, 83 Argyle St, Mong Kok. Lane Crawford has a store in Manson House, 74 Nathan Rd, Tsim Sha Tsui. Dragon Seed operates a three storey department store at Albion Plaza, 2-6 Granville Rd, Tsim Sha Tsui.

Eyeglasses

Nathan Rd in Tsim Sha Tsui is lined with opticians charging high prices for low quality eyewear, but the rude service is free. On the 3rd floor of Yue Hwa Chinese Products, 301 Nathan Rd, Yau Ma Tei.

Herbal Medicine

Western visitors often become so engrossed buying cameras and electronic goods that they forget Hong Kong is famous for something else – herbal medicine.

Nearby Guangzhou is a less expensive place for buying Chinese medicines, but in Hong Kong there are more chemists who can speak English and prices really aren't much higher. Also, in Hong Kong it's easier to find everything you want in one place and there's less problem with counterfeit medicines. Chinese herbalists have all sorts of treatments for stomach aches, headaches, colds, flu and sore throat. Herbalists also have herbs to treat long-term problems like asthma. Many of these herbs seem to work. Whether or not Chinese medicine can cure more serious illnesses like cancer and heart disease is debatable.

In general, Chinese medicine works best for the relief of unpleasant symptoms (pain, sore throat etc) and for some serious long-term conditions which resist western medicines, such as migraine headaches, asthma and chronic backache. A well known Chinese cure-all, the ganoderma mushroom, seems to work well on certain chronic intestinal diseases. And in the case of migraine headaches, herbs may well prove more effective than western painkillers. But for acute life-threatening conditions, such as heart problems or appendicitis, it's still wise to see a doctor trained in western medicine.

When reading about the theory behind Chinese medicine, the word 'holistic' appears often. Basically, this means that Chinese medicine seeks to treat the whole body rather than focusing on a particular organ or disease.

Another point to be wary of when taking herbal medicine is the tendency of some manufacturers to falsely claim that a product contains potent and expensive ingredients. For example, some herbal formulas may list the horn of the endangered rhinoceros. Widely acclaimed as a cure for fever, sweating and hot flushes, rhino horn is so rare it's practically impossible to buy. Any formula listing rhinoceros horn may, at best, contain water buffalo horn. In any case, it's best to avoid contributing to the slaughter of an endangered species.

One benefit of Chinese medicine is that there are generally few side-effects. Compared to a drug like penicillin which can produce allergic reactions and other serious side-effects, herbal medicines are fairly safe. Nevertheless, herbs are still medicines, and not candy. There is no need to gobble herbs if you're feeling fine.

In Chinese medicine, a broad-spectrum remedy such as snake gall bladder may be good for treating colds, but there are many different types of colds. The best way to treat a cold with herbal medicine is to see a Chinese doctor and get a specific prescription. The pills on sale in herbal medicine shops are generally broad-spectrum, while a prescription remedy will usually require that you

Gems

Opal Mine (☎ 2721-9933), Burlington House Arcade, 92 Nathan Rd, Tsim Sha Tsui, has a truly vast selection of Australian opals that makes for fascinating viewing, even for the mildly curious. It's more like an opal factory than a jewellery shop, where you can see stones still embedded in the original rock alongside polished specimens.

If you are worried about mistakenly forking out a fortune for fake diamonds, Blunco of Hong Kong (☎ 2375-1489), 13th floor, Hanley House, 68-80 Canton Rd, Tsim Sha Tsui, has a wide selection of simulation rocks at simulation prices. At least you know what you're getting.

If you're shopping for pearls, Om International (☎ 2366-3421), 1st floor, Friend's House, 6 Carnarvon Rd, has a fine selection of saltwater and freshwater specimens.

Jewellery

There's more to Hong Kong than copy Rolex watches. In fact, if you are planning take home a bunch of specific herbs and cook them into a thick broth.

If you visit a Chinese doctor, you might be surprised by what he or she discovers about your body. For example, the doctor will almost certainly take your pulse and may tell you that you have a 'slippery' or 'thready' pulse. Chinese doctors have identified more than 30 different kinds of pulses. A pulse can be 'empty', 'leisurely', 'bowstring', or even 'regularly irregular'. The doctor may then examine your tongue and pronounce that you have 'wet heat', as evidenced by a slippery pulse and a red, greasy tongue.

HONG KONG TOURIST ASSOCIATION

Chinese Herbalists practise a holistic approach to ailment remedy, where the whole body is treated. They prefer not to focus on just one organ or disease.

Many Chinese medicines are powders that come in vials. Typically, you take one or two vials a day. Some of these powders taste OK, but others are very bitter and difficult to swallow. If you can't tolerate the taste, you may want to buy some empty gelatin capsules and fill them with the powder.

A good place to purchase herbal medicines is Yue Hwa Chinese Products Emporium at the north-west corner of Nathan and Jordan Rds, just above Jordan MTR station. Before buying anything, explain your condition to a Chinese chemist and ask for a recommendation.

There are plenty of books available to learn more about Chinese medicine. One of the easiest to understand is *The Web That Has No Weaver: Understanding Chinese Medicine*, by Ted Kaptchuk.

If you want a more advanced text, *The Theoretical Foundations of Chinese Medicine*, by Manfred Porkert, is good.

to buy a (genuine) Rolex, it's possible to get at least 10% off the price tag from a number of jewellers, so there's no harm in haggling.

Bear in mind that Chinese gold is almost pure, and this is what gives many pieces that dark orangey colour. Jewellers' display windows are usually piled high with gold ornaments, with good luck trophies, Chinese zodiac animals and the odd gold bar. The lack of finesse in window arrangement is made up for by its overbearing garishness.

King Sing Jewellers (☎ 2735-7021), shop 14, ground floor, Star House, 3 Salisbury Rd, Tsim Sha Tsui, is a reputable dealer with a wide selection of diamonds, pearls and gold items. Ming's Jewellery (☎ 2721-3907), room 31, The Regent Shopping Arcade, 18 Salisbury Rd, Tsim Sha Tsui, also has a stunning selection of imaginatively crafted pieces. The Danish jeweller Georg Jensen (☎ 2724-1510) has a shop full of expertly crafted silver in the basement of the Peninsula, Salisbury Rd, Tsim Sha Tsui.

King Fook and Tse Sui Luen are two chain stores which guarantee to buy back any jewellery at its wholesale price. Of course, be sure you get the certificate and realise that you need to be in Hong Kong to take advantage of the buy-back plan. There isn't supposed to be any difference in price from one branch to another, but you might do better to avoid Tsim Sha Tsui. Branches of King Fook are in Tsim Sha Tsui (☎ 2313-2768) in the Hotel Miramar Princess Shopping Plaza, 118-130 Nathan Rd; in Mong Kok (☎ 2789-2008) on the ground floor, 644 Nathan Rd; and in Yau Ma Tei (☎ 2735-1017), shop A-C, ground floor, 26 Jordan Rd.

Tse Sui Luen branches can be found in Yau Ma Tei (☎ 2332-4618) on the ground floor, 315 Nathan Rd; and in shop A and B, ground floor, 190 Nathan Rd (☎ 2926-3210). There is a branch in Mong Kok (☎ 2770-2322) in shop G1 and G2 on the ground floor of the Nathan Centre, 580 Nathan Rd; and in Hung Hom (☎ 2333-4221) on the ground floor, Summit building, 30 Man Yue Street.

Music & Software

HMV is a chain store with a large branch in Tsim Sha Tsui at the north-west corner of Hankow and Peking Rds. There is an excellent and wide-ranging selection of CDs, Video CDs and DVDs, racks of magazines, informative staff and a vast index of all CDs in existence. This shop offers a respite from the endless trudge around Tsim Sha Tsui; just pop in and sample a CD of your choice at one of the listening posts provided. It's worth asking the staff for news of upcoming concerts in town. The shop is open from 10 am until midnight. Also worth exploring is the branch in Central building, Central, which is open from 10 am to 10 pm, seven days a week.

The chain store KPS is another good place to buy CDs and Video CDs. Computer software (legal copies, that is) are also sold at substantial discounts. There are several branches, but the easiest one to find is in the basement of Silvercord Shopping Centre (☎ 2730-3055) at 30 Canton Rd, and is open from 10 am to 10 pm. There are other branches in Tsim Sha Tsui East (☎ 2724-3737) on the 1st floor of Tsim Sha Tsui Centre, 66 Mody Rd; in Mong Kok (☎ 2388-1380) on the 3rd floor, Chong Hing Square, 601 Nathan Rd; and in Hung Hom (☎ 2330-7702), shop 6, site 4, Whampoa Gardens.

You can also pick up cheap CDs at the Temple St night market and from shops in Mong Kok, but the selection is limited.

Pharmaceuticals

Hong Kong is a good place to stock up on everyday practical items, especially if you're headed into the backwaters of China, where shaving cream and deodorant are luxuries. Watson's is Hong Kong's biggest chain store in the pharmaceutical arena; there seems to be one on every street corner. However, we have found prices to be somewhat better at Mannings, a much smaller chain. There is one in Tsim Sha Tsui on the lower ground floor, shop 37-47, Silvercord Shopping Centre, 30 Canton Rd.

Worth bearing in mind (but be cautious) is that many of the smaller independent chemists seem happy to dish out prescription drugs whether you have a receipt or not. This could be useful if you need a new prescription but don't want to spend HK$100 for a consultation.

Sporting Goods

Ocean Terminal in Tsim Sha Tsui has a number of outlets where you can pick up sports equipment and clothing. These include Gigasports (☎ 2992-0389), shop 33, and the Sporting Edge (☎ 2735-4255), shop 104a.

Diving equipment can be obtained from Ming's Sports Co (☎ 2376-0031), ground floor, 53 Hankow Rd, Tsim Sha Tsui; and at Bunn's Diving Equipment (☎ 2380-5344), ground floor, 217 Sai Yee St, Mong Kok.

The Golf Gallery Ltd, shop 17-19, ground floor, 28 Hankow Rd, Tsim Sha Tsui, specialises in, you've guessed it, golf equipment; and if you want to try your luck fishing, have a word with the staff at Po Kee Fishing Tackle Co Ltd (☎ 2730-4562), 150 Ocean Terminal, Tsim Sha Tsui.

Serious cyclists can take in the selection of the Flying Ball Bicycle Co (☎ 2381-3661), 201 Tung Choi St, Mong Kok (near Prince Edward MTR station).

Shops which sell windsurfing equipment include Pro-Shop (☎ 2723-6816), 1st floor, front unit, Ocean View Court, 31 Mody Rd, Tsim Sha Tsui; Windsurf Boutique (☎ 2366-9911, fax 2369-8403), shop 19-23, Rise Commercial building, 5-11 Granville Circuit, Tsim Sha Tsui; and Wind 'N' Surf (☎ 2366-9293), Flat 3, Block A, 1st floor, Carnarvon Mansion, 10 Carnarvon Rd, Tsim Sha Tsui.

Tourist Shopping Malls
Exploring the malls in tourist land is not a total waste of time. True, you can probably find what you need for less money in other areas of Kowloon, but sometimes it is worth paying more in Tsim Sha Tsui to avoid having to track down the same goods elsewhere. The malls are also interesting tourist attractions in themselves.

In the tourist zone of Tsim Sha Tsui, there are three big complexes in a row on Canton Rd: Ocean Terminal (nearest the Star Ferry), Ocean Centre and Harbour City. Across the street at 30 Canton Rd is Silvercord. The New World Centre is on Salisbury Rd, adjacent to the New World Hotel.

In Tsim Sha Tsui East, the biggest mall is the Tsim Sha Tsui Centre at 66 Mody Rd (between Salisbury and Mody Rds). There are other malls that you could probably spend days exploring.

Hong Kong Island

The commercial heart of Hong Kong pumps away on the northern side of Hong Kong Island, where banks and businesses, high-rise apartment blocks and hotels cover a good part of its 78 sq km. Since the hand-over, the sights and scenes on Hong Kong Island have remained for the most part unaltered. Visible changes have remained discreet but are nevertheless symbolic, like the occasional red and gold flag of the People's Republic of China (PRC), fluttering in the breeze. Snatches of Mandarin can be heard on the wind, before being swallowed up by the chorus of Cantonese. But for the traveller, Hong Kong Island remains as it was before – a city where pockets of preserved history are hemmed in by an upwardly mobile skyline of dazzling modernity and prosperity.

Though the island makes up only 7% of Hong Kong's total land area, its importance

as the historical, political and economic centre of Hong Kong far outweighs its size. It was there, after all, that the original settlement, Victoria, was founded. Most of the major businesses, government offices, expensive hotels and restaurants and exclusive residential neighbourhoods are there. The island is home to the ex-governor's mansion, the stock exchange, the legislature, the territory's premier shopping district, the original horse-racing track and a host of other places that define Hong Kong's character. Not surprisingly, a good deal of Hong Kong's sights are also on the island.

Looking across from Tsim Sha Tsui shows how unbelievably crowded the northern side of the island is. About the only natural places left to build on are the steep hills rising up behind the skyscrapers. As well as moving up, Hong Kong keeps on moving out. Reclamation along the harbour edge continues to add the odd quarter kilometre every so often, and buildings once on the waterfront are now several hundred metres back. The latest round of reclamation is altering the shorelines of the Sheung Wan, Central, Admiralty and Wan Chai districts, prompting some wags to predict that the harbour will soon be completely filled.

One of greatest ways to see the north side is to jump on one of the wobbly double-decker trams that trundle between Kennedy Town and Shau Kei Wan. Try to go during mid-morning or mid-afternoon, when there's a better chance of grabbing a front seat on the upper deck. The trams are slow, and while this may not be ideal for rushed commuters, if you want to sit back and get a feel for Hong Kong city life, this is the way to do it. For HK$2, it's also one of the best bargains.

The south side of Hong Kong Island is of a very different character to the north. For one thing, there are some fine beaches and the water is actually clean enough to swim in. The best beaches are at Big Wave Bay,

HONG KONG TOURIST ASSOCIATION
Double decker trams are a unique way to see Hong Kong Island.

Deep Water Bay, Shek O, Stanley and Repulse Bay. Expensive villas are perched on the hillsides, and the impression is more of the French Riviera than over-crowded Hong Kong. It's easy to circumnavigate the island by public transport, starting from Central and taking a bus over the hills to Stanley, then heading clockwise along the coast back to the Star Ferry terminal.

CENTRAL

Nearly every visitor to Hong Kong passes through Central whether for sightseeing, taking care of errands such as changing money, or en route to the bars and restaurants of Lan Kwai Fong. Many business travellers spend all their time in this district, where most of Hong Kong's larger international companies have offices. Not surprisingly, Central has some impressive architectural treasures that can appear quite magnificent, especially in the right light conditions. An eclectic assortment of historical remnants, churches, parks and gardens contribute to a surprising harmony of ancient and modern themes.

A good place from which to start exploring Central is the Star Ferry terminal. Once leaving the terminal, on the right-hand side, is **Jardine House**, a 40 storey silver monolith covered with circular porthole-style windows. This building, otherwise known as the 'House of a Thousand Orifices' in honour of its appearance, is the headquarters of Hong Kong's venerable trading house, Jardine Matheson. In the basement is the Hong Kong Travel Association (HKTA), where you can pick up scores of leaflets on sights, accommodation, public transport and just about anything else relating to visiting Hong Kong. To the east of the building, in a small plaza, is the sculpture 'Double Oval', by Henry Moore.

West of Jardine House is **Exchange Square**, home to the Stock Exchange of Hong Kong and one of Central's more elegantly designed structures. The entire complex of three office towers is elevated. Access is via a network of pedestrian walkways that stretches west to Sheung Wan and has links to many of the buildings on the other side of Connaught Rd. The ground level is given over to the Exchange Square bus station and minibus stop. The stock exchange is located at the main entrance to Towers I and II. Tours of the stock exchange (☎ 2840-3859) are possible but are generally intended for business groups. Outside Exchange Square Towers I and II is a seating area surrounding a fountain, which is an excellent place to relax, especially in the early evening.

The statue in front of the Forum shopping mall is of a *taijiquan* (t'ai chi) posture known as 'Snake creeps down', although the sculpture is simply called 'Taiji'. It's by the Taiwanese sculptor, Zhu Ming.

Take the pedestrian walkway over Connaught Rd and you will find yourself in the heart of Central. Most of the buildings are office towers, but those with an eye towards shopping can check out Prince's building and the Landmark, both of which cater to more well-heeled consumers.

Tsui Museum of Art

The Tsui Museum of Art (☎ 2868-2688) is on the 4th floor of the Henley building, 5 Queen's Rd, Central. The collection is the pet project of a Hong Kong tycoon and is interesting though modest in size. It has a good display of *sancai* (or three colour) pottery from the Tang dynasty (618-907), bronzes from as far back as the late Shang dynasty (1700-1100 BC) and a few paintings and calligraphy scrolls. Admission is HK$30 for adults, HK$15 for children; operating hours are from 10 am to 6 pm on weekdays and from 10 am to 2 pm on Saturday.

Cenotaph

To reach the main part of Central you have to cross Connaught Rd. Straight ahead as you leave the Star Ferry is the pedestrian underpass which surfaces at the side of the Cenotaph in Statue Square. This forlorn looking monument is a memorial to Hong Kong residents who died in WWI and WWII.

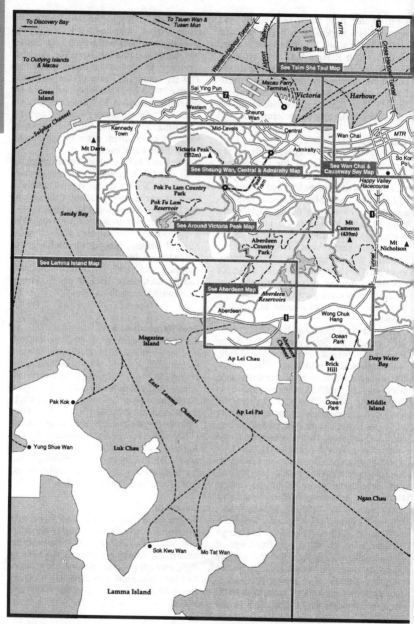

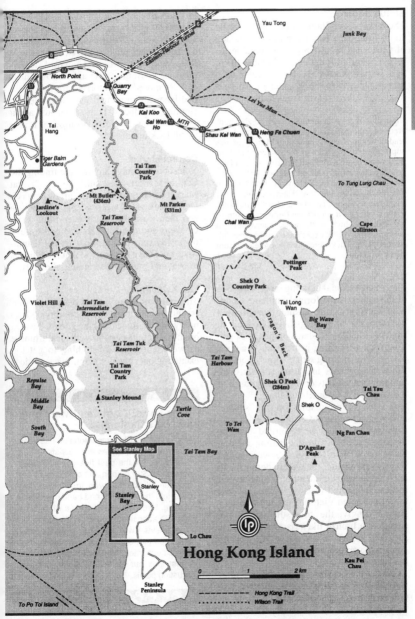

Hong Kong Island

0   1   2 km

–––––––– Hong Kong Trail
········· Wilson Trail

HONG KONG

Statue Square

The main part of Statue Square is across the street from the Cenotaph on the south side of Chater Rd. Statue Square is notable for its collection of fountains and places to sit, and is best known in Hong Kong as a meeting place for thousands of Filipino migrant workers on the weekend.

On my last day I was moved. Every Sunday hundreds of Filipino maids gather in Central. I had read of this in *Hong Kong* by Jan Morris but was unprepared for the scale of the gathering and for the emotional impact. I had planned to spend my last day sunning myself on a beach but instead was infected by the joy these women had in each others' company and stayed amongst them for some hours. They chatted ceaselessly, the noise of the chatter giving a strange fascinating, almost musical, loud hum to the area. There were so many of them yet the experience was so peaceful, so energising. They were like birds released from cages for a time.

Liz Storrar

The ornate colonial building on the east side of the square is the former Supreme Court, now serving as the **Legislative Council building**, seat of the Legislative Council. In front is a blindfolded statue of the Greek god Themes, representing justice: this is a good place to watch Hong Kong's grassroots political movements in action (protests are routinely staged outside the east entrance of the Legislative Council building).

No longer on display in the square, however, are numerous effigies of England's royalty. The statues were spirited away by the Japanese during the occupation of Hong Kong in WWII. Though all were found intact in Japan after the war, in deference to anti-colonialist sentiment, only Queen Victoria was restored to Hong Kong, and not to Central but to Victoria Park in Causeway Bay. Fittingly, the sole survivor in the square is a bronze likeness of Sir Thomas Jackson, a particularly successful former chief manager of the Hongkong and Shanghai Bank.

East of the Legislative Council is **Chater Garden**, where Chinese residents practise taijiquan exercises in the early morning.

Li Yuen St

Actually this is two streets: Li Yuen St East and Li Yuen St West, which run parallel to each other between Des Voeux and Queen's Rds, opposite the Lane Crawford department store. Both streets are narrow alleys and are closed to motorised traffic. These two lanes are crammed with shops selling clothing, handbags, fabrics and just about everything else. Nearby Pottinger St is also worth looking into.

Central Market

You shouldn't have any trouble finding the Central Market – just sniff the air. Central Market is a large four storey affair between Des Voeux and Queen's Rds. It's more a zoo than a market, with everything from chickens and quail to eels and crabs, alive or freshly slaughtered. Fish are cut lengthwise, but above the heart so that it continues to beat and pump blood around the body.

Lan Kwai Fong

This is Hong Kong's chief disco, pub, bar, restaurant and party neighbourhood. Formerly an expatriate drinking ghetto, the area has now become popular with local Chinese as well. The bars are nothing to get too excited about, but it's a fun place to do a

Elvis Lives! .... in Lan Kwai Fong, and he's Cantonese

Melvis (42), an Elvis impersonator, has been serenading the yuppies and tourists of Lan Kwai Fong for the past five years. Usually earning HK$20 a song, his best targets are drunken Elvis fans, who instinctively dig deep into their pockets and hand over wads of cash. Usually dressed up in a white jump suit with adhesive side-burns clinging to his face, Melvis Kwok Lam has a whole array of getups that span the King's career. The best time to track him down is on weekends – just look out for the bouffant quiff and thrusting pelvis.

little pub-crawling. See Entertainment in this chapter for details. Lan Kwai Fong also has a number of good places to eat. On weekday lunchtimes the area becomes a swirling, dizzying mass of office workers trying to squeeze a decent meal into short lunchbreaks.

St John's Cathedral

Built in 1847, this is one of the few colonial structures left in Hong Kong. Criticised for marring the oriental landscape of the colony when it was built, this Anglican church is now lost in the forest of skyscrapers that make up Central. Services have been held continuously since the church opened, except between 1942 and 1944 when the Japanese Imperial Army used it as a social club. The building was ravaged during the occupation. The wooden front doors were rebuilt after the war, using timber salvaged from HMS *Tamar*, a British warship that used to guard the entrance to Victoria Harbour.

The church is still quite active, and in addition to weekly services runs a number of community and social services, as well as a small bookshop.

Behind the cathedral is the **French Mission building**, a charming structure dating from 1917 and now home to Hong Kong's new Court of Final Appeal. Both the cathedral and the French Mission building are on Battery Path, a tree-lined walk that takes you back into the heart of Central.

A flight of steps opposite the southern face of the Hongkong and Shanghai Bank building takes you up to the cathedral and the French Mission building.

Government House

This is the former residence of the governor of Hong Kong, located on Upper Albert Rd opposite the Zoological & Botanical Gardens. The original sections of the building date back to 1858. Other features were added by the Japanese during the occupation of Hong Kong in WWII, including the rectangular eaved tower.

The current Chief Executive, Tung Chee Hwa, turned down the offer to make it his abode, saying the fung shui wasn't satisfactory. Government House is closed to the public except for one day in March (always a Sunday), when the azaleas are in bloom. It really should be opened up as a museum. It is still worth a visit to see, at least from the outside, the last seat of colonial administrative power.

Zoological & Botanical Gardens

First established in 1864, these excellent gardens are a pleasant collection of fountains, sculptures, greenhouses, aviaries, a zoo and a playground. There are hundreds of species of birds, exotic trees, plants and shrubs on display. The zoo is surprisingly comprehensive and is also one of the world's leading centres for captive breeding of endangered species.

The gardens are divided by Albany Rd, with the plants and aviaries in one area, off Garden Rd, and most of the animals in the other. It really is worth going there; some of the animals are hypnotisingly watchable. If you go to the gardens before 8 am the place will be packed with people toning up with a bit of taijiquan before heading off to work. Opening hours are from 6 am to 10 pm daily (6 am to 7 pm for the zoo). Admission is free.

The gardens are at the top end of Garden Rd (heading away from the harbour). It is an easy walk from Central, but you can also take bus No 3 or 12 from the stop in front of Jardine House on Connaught Rd. The bus takes you along Upper Albert and Caine Rds on the northern boundary of the gardens. Get off in front of the Caritas Centre (at the junction of Upper Albert and Caine Rds) and follow the path uphill to the gardens.

Hong Kong Park

This is one of the most unusual parks in the world – it was deliberately designed to look anything but natural, emphasising synthetic creations such as its fountain plaza, conservatory (greenhouse), aviary, artificial waterfall, indoor games hall, visual arts centre, playground, viewing tower, museum and taiji garden.

Continued on page 226

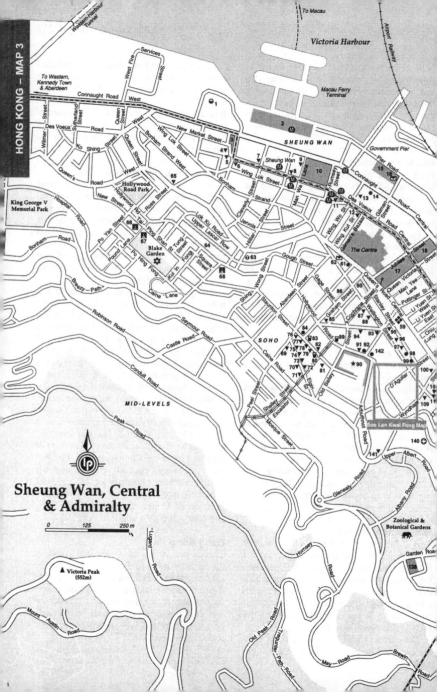

Victoria Harbour

To Macau

Airport Railway

Western Harbour Tunnel

West Fire Services Street

Macau Ferry Terminal

To Western, Kennedy Town & Aberdeen

Connaught Road West

Queen Street

Des Voeux Road West

Sutherland Street

Wing Lok Street

New Market Street

SHEUNG WAN

Government Pier

Wilmer Street

Ko Shing Street

Bonham Strand West

Wing Lok Street

Sheung Wan

Pier Road

Queen's Road West

Bonham Strand

Wing Lok Street

Man Wa Lane

Rumsey Street

Connaught

Hollywood Road Park

Bonham Strand

Jervois Street

Strand

Man Wa Lane

Des Voeux

Wing Wo St

Wing Kut St

Gilman's Bazaar

Road Central

King George V Memorial Park

Hospital Road

New Street

Hollywood Rd

Po Yan Street

Ladder St

Upper Lascar Row

Lok Ku Road

Hillier

Jervois Street

Gilman's Bazaar

The Centre

Jubilee Street

Bonham Road

Tai Ping Shan St

Pound Lane

Po Hing Fong

Square Street

Ladder St

Gough Street

Queen Victoria St

Queen's Road Central

Man Yee Lane

Pottinger Street

Breezy Path

Blake Garden

Kui In Fong

Caine Lane

Shing Wong Street

Aberdeen Street

Hollywood Road

Graham Street

Cochrane Street

Wellington Street

Stanley Street

D'Aguilar Street

Li Yuen St East

U Lam Terrace

Robinson Road

Seymour Road

Castle Road

SOHO

Staunton Street

Gage Street

Peel Street

Elgin Street

Shelley Street

Caine Road

Old Bailey Street

Chiu Lung

Conduit Road

Peak Road

MID-LEVELS

Mosque Street

Escalator

Old Bailey Street

Arbuthnot Road

Wyndham

See Lan Kwai Fong Map

Upper Albert Road

Glenealy Road

Ice House St

Zoological & Botanical Gardens

Sheung Wan, Central & Admiralty

0   125   250 m

▲ Victoria Peak (552m)

Mount Austin Road

Hornsey Road

Garden Road

Tramway Path

Old Peak Road

May Road

Glenealy

Albany Road

Brewin Road

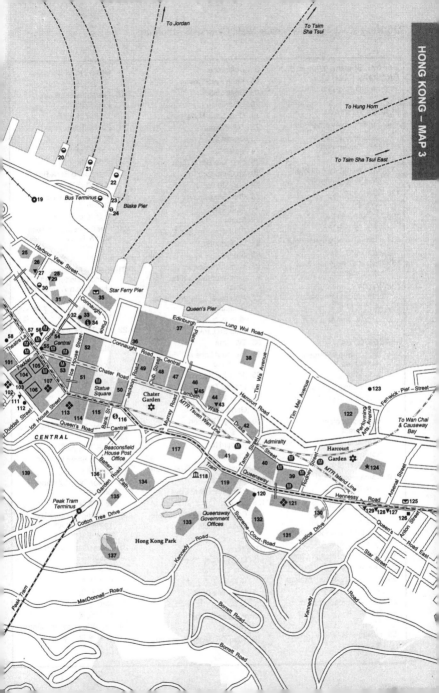

To Jordan

To Tsim
Sha Tsui

To Hung Hom

To Tsim Sha Tsui East

20

21

22

23
24

19

Bus Terminus

Blake Pier

25

26
27
28
29

30

31

32
33
34

35

Star Ferry Pier

Queen's Pier

Connaught

Edinburgh

37

Lung Wui Road

58

57 56
55
54

Theatre Lane

Peddar

101

104
105
103 106
102
111
112

107

36

Connaught Road Central

52

Chater Road

Ice House Street

51

50

Statue
Square

49
48

47

Club Street

Chater
Garden

Duddell Street

113

114

115

116

Queen's Road Central

Bank St

38

46
45
44
43

Lambeth
Walk

42

Harcourt Road

Tim Wa Avenue

Tim Mei Avenue

123

122

Fenwick Pier Street

To Wan Chai
& Causeway
Bay

Performing
Arts Avenue

CENTRAL

139

136

Beaconsfield
House Post
Office

134

135

Peak Tram
Terminus

Cotton Tree Drive

Garden Road

Battery Path

137

133

117

118

119

Queensway

Queensway
Government
Offices

Supreme Court Road

41

40

39

Admiralty

Drake Street

Tamar Street

Rodney Street

Harcourt
Garden

124

MTRI Island Line

120

121

130

132

131

Justice Drive

Hennessy Road

125

129 128 127
126

Arsenal Street

Queen's
Road East

Star Street

Anton Street

Hong Kong Park

Kennedy Road

Peak Tram

MacDonnell Road

Borrett Road

Borrett Road

Kennedy Road

MTRI Tsuen Wan Line

Murray Road

Jackson Road

Tram

Central, Sheung Wan and Admiralty (MAP 3)

中環、上環、金鐘

PLACES TO STAY

47 Furama Kempinski Hotel
富麗華酒店
48 Ritz-Carlton Hotel
麗嘉酒店
52 Mandarin Oriental Hotel
香港文華東方酒店
126 Wesley Hotel
衛蘭軒
130 JW Marriot Hotel
香港萬豪酒店
131 Conrad International Hotel
港麗酒店
132 Island Shangri-La Hotel
港島香格里拉大酒店
138 YWCA Garden View International House
花園國際賓館
（香港基督教女青年會）

PLACES TO EAT

4 Golden Snow Garden Restaurant
金雪園飯店
5 Hsin Kuang Restaurant
上環新光酒樓
6 Delifrance
7 Ho Choi Seafood Restaurant
好彩海鮮酒家
8 Korea Garden
梨花苑韓國料理
9 Korea House Restaurant
高麗莊
11 Oliver's Super Sandwiches
利華超級三文治店
12 Law Fu Kee Noodle Shop
羅富記粥麵專家
13 The Original Health Café
27 Le Fauchon
29 Oliver's Super Sandwiches
利華超級三文治店
43 Secret Garden Korean Restaurant
秘苑
56 Haagen-Dazs
喜見達

57 Delifrance
65 Kaffa Kaldi Coffee
69 Casa Lisboa
70 2 Sardines
71 Club Casa Nova
72 The Bayou
73 Desert Sky
74 Caramba!
75 Red Star Bar & Café
76 La Comida
77 Café au Lac
78 Club Scandinavia
北歐餐廳
79 Nepal
80 Stauntons Bar and Café
81 Le Fauchon
82 Sherpa
85 Miyoshiya Ramen Shop
87 Jim Chai Kee Noodle Shop
88 Fat Heung Lam Vegetaria Restaurant
佛香林素菜館
91 Club Sri Lanka
93 TW Café
94 Petticoat Lane & Vegitable
95 Jim Chai Kee Noodle Shop
96 Luk Yu Teahouse
陸羽茶室
97 Genroku Sushi
100 Jimmy's Kitchen
占美餐廳
108 Aujourd'hui
109 City Café
110 Tandoor Indian Restaurant
111 Delifrance
127 Yoshinoya Beef Bowl
128 Baccus
129 Cosmic Noodle Bar & Café
141 Mozart Stub'n

OTHER

1 Macau Ferry Terminal Bus Terminus
港澳碼頭巴士總站
2 Shun Tak Centre
信德中心
3 Western Market
西港城
10 Wing On Department Store
永安中心

14 China Travel Service
中國旅行社
15 Government Offices & Post Office
海港政府大廈
16 Post Office
郵局
17 Central Market
中環街市
18 Hang Seng Bank Building
恆生銀行總行
19 Airport Railway Central Station
機場鐵路香港站
20 Pier 5 – Ferries to Tuen Mun & Tai O
五號碼頭——
往屯門及大澳之船
21 Pier 6 – Ferries to Lamma Island Hoverferries to Tuen Mun, Tsuen Wan & Tsing Yi
六號碼頭——往荃灣、屯門、青衣及南丫島之船
22 Pier 7 – Ferries to Lantau, Peng Chau & Cheung Chau Islands
號碼頭——往梅窩、坪洲、長洲之船
23 Ferries to Jordan
往佐敦道碼頭
24 Public Toilets
公用廁所
25 Tower Three, Exchange Square
交易廣場三座
26 Forum Shopping Mall
富臨閣
28 Tower Two, Exchange Square
交易廣場二座
30 Exchange Square Bus Terminus (Ground Level)
交易廣場巴士站
31 Tower One, Exchange Square
交易廣場一座
32 Pier One
海舫餐廳
33 Jardine House
怡和大廈
34 HKTA Information Centre
香港旅遊協會

35 General Post Office
郵政總局

36 City Hall (Upper Block);
Public Library
大會堂高座、圖書館

37 City Hall (Lower Block)
大會堂低座

38 Prince of Wales Building
威爾斯親王大廈

39 United Centre
統一中心

40 Queensway Plaza
金鐘廊

41 Lippo Centre
力寶大廈

42 Far East Finance Centre
遠東金融中心

44 Bank of America Tower
美國銀行中心

45 Bull & Bear Pub
牛和熊酒吧

46 Hutchison House
和記大廈

49 Hong Kong Club Building
香港會

50 Legislative Council Building
立法會大樓

51 Prince's Building
太子大廈

53 Alexandra House
歷山大廈

54 Swire House
太古大廈

55 HMV

58 Queen's Theatre
皇后戲院

59 Lane Crawford Department
Store
連卡佛

60 Night Market
(Dai Pai Dong)
夜市(大排檔)

61 Eu-Yan Sang Pharmacy
余仁生有限公司

62 Post Office
郵局

63 Public Toilets
公用廁所

64 Cat Street Shops
古玩街

66 Pak Sing Temple

67 Kuan Yin Temple

68 Man Mo Temple
文武廟

83 Club 1911

84 Hop Hing Vintners
合興

86 Fresh Food Market

89 Globe Cafe & Bar

90 Central District Police
Station & Victoria Prison
中區警署,
域多利監獄

92 Propaganda

98 Color Six

99 Photo Scientific

101 Pedder Building
畢打大廈

102 Marks & Spencer
馬莎

103 HMV

104 Central Building
中建大廈

105 Gloucester Tower
告羅士打大廈

106 Edinburgh Tower
公爵大廈

107 Landmark Shopping Centre
置地廣場

112 American Express
Traveller Services
美國運通卡旅遊服務

113 Galleria Shopping Centre
愛美高廣場

114 Standard Chartered Bank
Building
渣打銀行

115 Hongkong & Shanghai
Bank Building
香港上海匯豐
銀行總行大廈

116 Bank of China
中國銀行

117 Bank of China Tower
中銀大廈

118 Flagstaff House Museum
茶具文物館

119 Supreme Court
高等法院

120 Government Publications
Office
政府刊物銷售處

121 Pacific Place Shopping
Mall; UA Queensway
Cinema
太古廣場、UA金鐘戲院

122 Citic Tower

123 Helicopter Landing Ground

124 Police Headquarters

125 Post Office
郵局

133 British Council
英國文化協會

134 Citibank Plaza
萬國寶通大廈

135 Murray Building
美利大廈

136 St John's Cathedral
聖約翰座堂

137 Aviary
觀鳥園

139 Ex-Government House
舊督憲府

140 Hong Kong Central Hospital
港中醫院

142 The Mughal Room
莫臥兒餐廳

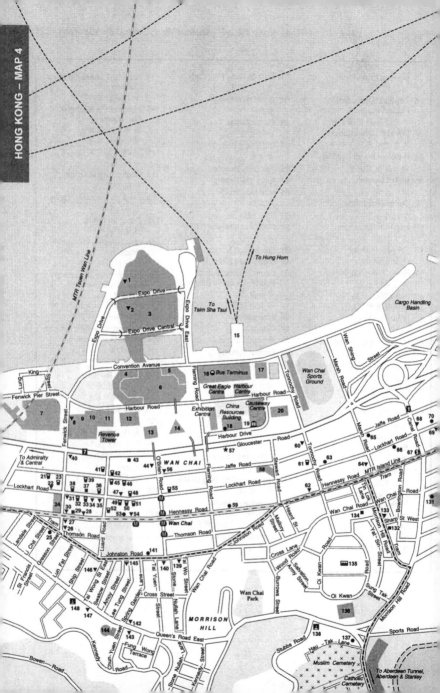

MTR Tsuen Wan Line

▼ 1

Expo Drive

▼ 2   3

Expo Drive Central

Expo Drive East

To Hung Hom

To Tsim Sha Tsui

15

Cargo Handling Basin

Convention Avenue

King Street

Lung King Street

Fenwick Pier Street

4   5   Fleming Road   16 ⊖ Bus Terminus   17

Great Eagle Centre   Harbour Centre

6

Wan Chai Sports Ground

Wan Shing Street

Marsh Road

Harbour Road

7   ▼ 9 10   11   12   Exhibition Centre   China Resources Building   Causeway Centre   20

Fenwick Street

▼ 8   Revenue Tower   13   14   Harbour Drive   18   19 ▥

Tonnochy Road

Harbour Road

Jaffe Road   Lockhart Road   68   70

Gloucester   Road   60 ▼   65   66   69

★ 57   Canal Road

▼ 40   WAN CHAI   56   Jaffe Road   63   67

▼ 7   O'Brien Road   58   Stewart Street   61 ▼   64 ▼

41 ▼   ▼ 42   44 ▼   55   Lockhart Road   62 ▼   Hennessy Road

21 ▼ 23   38   ▼ 39   37   ▼ 45   ▼ 46   Fleming Road   Jaffe Road   MTR Island Line   Tram

22 ▥   33 34 35   36   47 ▼   ▼ 48   Wan Chai Road   133   131

Lockhart Road   ▼ 31 ▼ 9   ▼ 49 ▥   50   59   Lin Lok Street

24   ▼ 30   32   49 ▥   51   Mallory Street   134 ▥   ▥ 132

▼ 29 ▼ 28   52   53 ▼ 54   Hennessy Road   Morrison Hill Road   Sharp St West

▼ 27   Ⓜ Wan Chai   Heard St   Bowrington Road

25   Thomson Road   Johnston Road   Yat Sin Street

26   Thomson Road   Cross Lane   Sung Tak Street   Tram

Ⓜ   141   Johnston Road   Wood Road   135

Landale Street   Lee Tung Street   146 ▼   145   140   139   Salvation Army Street   Oi Kwan Road

St Francis Street   Gresson Street   Lun Fat Street   Ship Street   Swatow Street   Amoy Street   Spring Garden Lane   Tai Wo Street   Stone Nullah Lane   Burrows Street

148   147   142   Cross Street   Wan Chai Park   136   Morrison Hill Road

144   143   Queen's Road East   MORRISON HILL   138   137   Sports Road

Chun-Yuen Street   Fung Wong Terrace   Kennedy Road   Stubbs Road   Hau Tak Lane

Bowen   Road   Stone Nullah Lane   Kennedy Street   Muslim Cemetery   Catholic Cemetery   To Aberdeen Tunnel, Aberdeen & Stanley

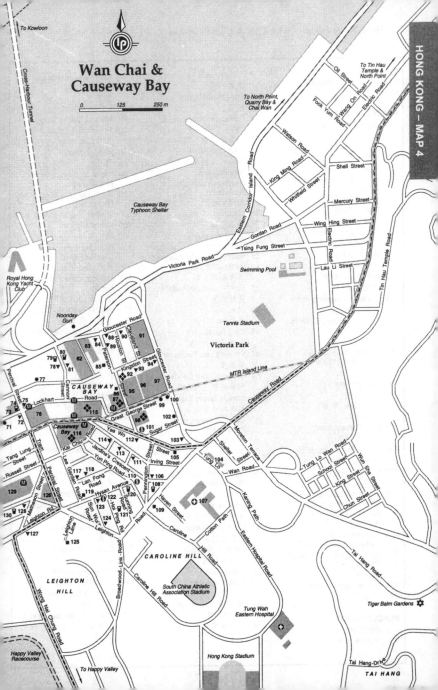

Wan Chai & Causeway Bay (MAP 4)
灣仔和銅鑼灣

PLACES TO STAY

4 Grand Hyatt Hotel
君悅酒店

5 New World Harbour View Hotel
新世界海景酒店

10 Harbour View International House
灣景國際賓館

24 Empire Hotel
皇悅酒店

29 New Harbour Hotel
星港酒店

37 Wharney Hotel
華美酒店

43 Luk Kwok Hotel
六國酒店

58 Century Hongkong Hotel
世紀香港酒店

83 Excelsior Hotel; Dicken's Bar
怡東酒店

85 Payless Inn & Jetvan Travellers' House
創之傑賓館

86 Noble Hostel
高富旅館

97 Park Lane Hotel
柏寧酒店

104 New Cathay Hotel
新國泰酒店

105 Regal Hongkong Hotel
富豪香港酒店

109 Leishun Court
禮信大廈

119 Phoenix Apartments; Wan Lai Villa; Garden Guest House; Dragon Inn
鳳鳴大廈

125 Causeway Bay Guesthouse; The Bar Pub

132 South Pacific Hotel; South Pacific Cinema
南洋酒店

134 Charterhouse Hotel
利景酒店

PLACES TO EAT

1 Port Café
維港咖啡閣

2 Trader's Grill
商悅扒房

8 The Open Kitchen
雅廚

22 Portucale Restaurant & Pub
葡萄牙餐廳酒吧

26 Fook Lam Moon
福臨門魚翅海鮮酒家

27 Thai Delicacy

28 Healthy Vegetarian Restaurant
康健素食

30 Cinta
金蒂餐廳

31 Beirut Lebanese Restaurant

34 Saigon Beach Vietnamese Restaurant
濱海越南小館

35 Brett's Seafood Restaurant
寶鮮漁家

40 Cinta J
金蒂J餐廳

44 3.6.9 Restaurant
上海三六九 漫

47 Yin King Lau Restaurant
燕京樓

54 Oliver's Super Sandwiches
利華超級三文治店

56 Oliver's Super Sandwiches
利華超級三文治店

60 Carriana Chiu Chow Restaurant
佳寧娜潮州菜

62 Oliver's Super Sandwiches
利華超級三文治店

64 Late-Night Food Stalls; Noodle Shops
大排檔、麵店

68 Sui Sha Ya
水車屋日料理有限公司

69 Sze Chuan Lau Restaurant
四川樓川菜館

72 Tai Woo Seafood
太湖海鮮城

75 Snake King Two

78 Yuet Hing Yuen
越興園越南食品

81 Yin Ping Vietnamese Restaurant
燕萍餐廳

84 King Heung Peking Restaurant
京香樓

88 Brewery Tap

89 Martino Coffee Shop

90 Vegi Food Kitchen
香齋廚素菜館

93 Haagen Dazs
喜見達

94 Paper Moon American Restaurant

103 Kung Tak Lam Vegetarian Restaurant
功德林上海素食有限公司

106 Kublai's
鐵木真

111 Night Market (Dai Pai Dong)
夜市（大排擋）

112 McDonald's; KFC; King Kebab
麥當勞及肯德雞

113 Watson's & KPS CD Store
屈臣氏及金獅

114 Fat Mun Lam Vegetarian Restaurant
佛滿林素菜館

117 Red Pepper
南北樓

118 Ichiban
一級棒

123 Queen's Café

124 Forever Green Taiwanese Restaurant
欣葉台灣料理

127 Indonesian Restaurant
印尼餐廳

128 Genroku Sushi
元氣壽司

133 Ichibantei Ramen Shop

139 Lung Moon Restaurant
龍門大酒樓

140 Vegetarian Garden
素真圍

142 3.6.9 Restaurant
上海三六九飯店

143 Harry Ramsden's

145 Jo Jo Mess Club

146 Steam & Stew Inn
蒸燉炆棧

147 Oliver's Super Sandwiches
利華超級三文治店

OTHER

3 Hong Kong Convention &
  Exhibition Centre Extension
  香港會議展覽中心
6 HK Convention & Exhibition
  Centre
  香港會議展覽中心
7 Hong Kong Academy for
  the Performing Arts
  香港演藝學院
9 Hong Kong Arts Centre
  香港藝術中心
11 Shui On Centre; La Bella
   Donna
   瑞安中心
12 Wan Chai Tower
   灣仔政府大樓
13 Immigration Tower
   移民局大廈
14 Central Plaza
   中環廣場
15 Wan Chai Ferry Pier
   灣仔渡海碼頭
16 Bus Terminus
   巴士總站
17 Harbour Road Indoor
   Games Hall
   港灣道室內運動館
18 Visa Office of People's
   Republic of China
   中華人民共和國
   大使館簽証處
19 Museum of Chinese
   Historical Relics
   中國文物展覽館
20 Sun Hung Kai Centre;
   Viceroy; Cine-Art House
   新鴻基中心
21 The Wanch
23 New Pussycat
25 Cosmos Books
   天地圖書
32 Neptune Disco
   海皇星酒廊
33 Royal Arms
36 Flying Pig & Ridgeways
38 Carnegie's
39 Rick's Cafe
41 Joe Bananas
42 Big Apple
   大蘋果的士高酒廊
45 Delaney's & Kublai's
   鐵木真

46 Neptune II
   海皇星酒廊II
48 Horse & Carriage
49 New Makati
50 Old China Hand
51 bb's; The Blue Lizard
   Lounge
52 Country Club 88
53 Alliance Française
   香港法國文化協會
55 Horse & Groom
57 Wan Chai Police Station
   灣仔警署
59 Lockhart Road Market
   駱克道街市
61 New Tonnochy
   新杜老志夜總會
63 Sunny Paradise Sauna
   新瀛閣桑拿
65 Hong Kong Sauna
   香港桑拿
66 New Paradise Health Club
   新瀛閣桑拿
67 Dao Heng Bank
   道亨銀行
70 New York Cinema
   紐約戲院
71 Hideaway II Portuguese
   Barbecue Pub
   賊竇葡國餐廳燒烤酒家
73 Causeway Bay Plaza Two
   銅鑼灣廣場II
74 The Jump
76 Causeway Bay Plaza
   銅鑼灣廣場
77 Wellcome Supermarket
   惠康超級市場
79 Royal's Pub
80 Shakespeare Pub
82 World Trade Centre; Times
   Bookshop
   世貿中心
87 Daimaru Department Store
   大丸
91 Daimaru Household
   Square; Asahiya;
   Supermarket
   大丸
92 Marks & Spencer
   馬莎
95 Pearl & Jade Cinemas;
   Spaghetti House
   明珠翡翠戲院

96 Wellcome Supermarket
   惠康超級市場
98 Matsuzakaya Department
   Store
   松板屋
99 HMV CD Store
100 Windsor House; Windsor
    Cinema
    皇室大廈、皇室戲院
101 HongkongBank
    匯豐銀行
102 7-Eleven
107 St Paul's Hospital
    聖保祿醫院
108 Brecht's Circle
110 Citibank
    萬國寶通銀行
115 Sogo Department Store
    崇光
116 Mitsukoshi Department
    Store
    三越商場
120 Piccadilly Tavern
121 King's Arms
122 Dao Heng Bank
    道亨銀行
126 Lee Theatre Plaza
    利舞台廣場
129 Times Square; Delifrance
    時代廣場
130 Times Bar
131 UA Times Square Cinema
    UA時代廣場戲院
135 Morrison Hill Swimming
    Pool
    摩理臣山游泳池
136 Queen Elizabeth Stadium
    伊利沙伯體育館
137 Xinhua News Agency
    新華社
138 Sikh Temple
    錫克教廟
141 Southorn Playground
    修頓球場
144 Hopewell Centre &
    Hongkong Bank
    合和中心及匯豐銀行
148 Tai Wong Temple
    洪聖廟

HONG KONG

continued from page 217

For all its artifice, the park is beautiful in its own weird way and, with a wall of skyscrapers on one side and mountains on the other, makes for some dramatic photography.

Perhaps the best feature of the park is the **aviary**. Home to more than 600 birds (and 30 different species), the aviary is huge. To enter is to have the impression of wandering into a world of birds. Visitors walk along a wooden bridge suspended about 10m above the ground and on eye-level with the tree branches, where most of the birds are to be found.

Within the park is the **Flagstaff House Museum** (☎ 2869-0690), the oldest western-style building still standing in Hong Kong, dating from 1846. The museum houses a Chinese tea-ware collection, including pieces dating from the Warring States period (473-221 BC) to the present, and a gallery exhibiting some rare Chinese ceramics and seals. It is open daily, except Monday (and some public holidays), from 10 am to 5 pm. Admission is free.

Hong Kong Park is an easy walk from either Central or Admiralty. Bus Nos 3, 12, 23, 23B, 40 and 103 will also get you there. Alight at the first stop on Cotton Tree Drive.

SHEUNG WAN

West of Central (to the right as you go off the Star Ferry) is Sheung Wan (the Western District), which once had something of the feel of old Shanghai about it. The comparison is a bit forced now since much of old Sheung Wan has disappeared under the jackhammers of development, and old stairway streets once cluttered with stalls and street sellers have been cleared away to make room for more buildings or the Mass Transit Railway (MTR). Nevertheless, the area is worth exploring.

From Queen's Rd, Central, head south to **Hollywood Rd**. This street has wreath and coffin makers and several funeral shops, selling everything for the best-dressed corpses. It is also full of furniture shops with antiques of all kinds, from the genuine article to modern reproductions made before your very eyes. This is the street to find if you are on the prowl for ceramics and works of art.

Travelling west along Hollywood Rd, Cat St (Lascar Row) used to be famous in Hong Kong for its arts and crafts, but many dealers are now at the **Cat Street Galleries**, Casey building in nearby Lok Ku Rd. The galleries contain five floors of arts and crafts, antiques and souvenirs, plus an exhibition hall and auction room.

Man Wa Lane, near Sheung Wan MTR station, is a good location if you want to get a name chop carved. A name chop is a stone that has a name carved in Chinese on the base. Chops are sometimes made of jade or wood. When dipped in ink, the chop can be used as a stamp.

Near the intersection of Bonham Strand and Queen's Rd West is **Possession St**. The name recalls that somewhere around there the flag was planted for England after Captain Elliot sealed his unofficial deal with Qi Shan and formally annexed Hong Kong. The area just to the west of Possession St is known as Possession Point, once Hong Kong's shoreline.

Man Mo Temple

This temple, on the corner of Hollywood Rd and Ladder St, is one of the oldest and most famous in Hong Kong. The Man Mo – (literally civil and military) is dedicated to two deities. The civil deity is a Chinese statesman of the 3rd century BC and the military deity is Kuanti, a soldier born in the 2nd century AD and now worshipped as the God of War (see Religion in the Facts about Hong Kong chapter). Kuanti is also known as Kwan Tai or Kwan Kung.

Outside the entrance are four gilt plaques on poles which are carried at procession time. Two plaques describe the gods being worshipped; the others request quietness and respect and warn menstruating women to keep away. Inside the temple are two antique chairs shaped like houses, used to carry the two gods at festival time. The coils suspended from the roof are incense cones burnt by worshippers. A large bell on the right is dated 1846 and the smaller ones on the left were made in 1897.

The exact date of the temple's construction has never been agreed on, but it's certain it was already standing when the British arrived to claim the island. The present Man Mo Temple was renovated in the middle of the last century.

The area around the Man Mo Temple was used extensively for location shots in the film *The World of Suzie Wong*, based on a novel of the same name by Richard Mason. The building to the right of the temple appears as Suzie's hotel, although the real hotel Luk Kwok (called Nam Kok in the film) is in Wan Chai, several kilometres to the east.

HONG KONG UNIVERSITY

West of Sheung Wan takes you through Sai Ying Pun and Shek Tong Tsui districts to Kennedy Town, a residential district at the end of the tram line. The chief attraction of this area is Hong Kong University's Fung Ping Shan Museum. To get to Hong Kong University, see the directions for getting to Fung Ping Shan Museum, explained in the following section.

Fung Ping Shan Museum

This museum (☎ 2859-2114) houses collections of ceramics and bronzes, plus a lesser number of paintings and carvings. The bronzes are in three groups: Shang and Zhou dynasty ritual vessels; decorative mirrors from the Warring States period to the Tang, Song, Ming and Qing dynasties; and Nestorian crosses from the Yuan dynasty (the Nestorians were a Christian sect that arose in Syria, and at some stage arrived in China, probably during the Tang dynasty). Its collection of Yuan dynasty bronzes is the largest in the world.

A collection of ceramics includes Han dynasty tomb pottery and recent works from the Chinese pottery centres of Jingdezhen and Shiwan in the PRC.

The museum is in the Hong Kong University, 94 Bonham Rd. Take bus No 3 from Edinburgh Place (adjacent to city hall), or bus No 23 or 103 coming from Causeway Bay, and get off at Bonham Rd, opposite St Paul's College. The museum is open Monday to Saturday, 9.30 am to 6 pm, and is closed on Sunday and several public holidays. Admission is free.

VICTORIA PEAK

If you haven't been to the Peak, then you haven't been to Hong Kong. Every visitor tries to make the pilgrimage, and for good reason: the view is one of the most spectacular in the world. It's also a good way to get Hong Kong into perspective. It's worth repeating the Peak trip at night as the illuminated view is superb. Bring a tripod for your camera if you want to get some sensational night photos. Legend has it that the illuminated foot-hills of Central were the inspiration behind the film *Blade Runner*. Whether this story is true or apocryphal, you decide. Anyway, due to the recent construction of some hallmark buildings, the view is far more stunning now than it was in 1982, when the film appeared.

The Peak has been *the* place to live ever since the British moved in. The *taipans* (company bosses) built summer houses there to escape the heat and humidity (it's usually about 5°C cooler than down below). The Peak is still the most fashionable place to live in Hong Kong, as reflected by the astronomical real estate prices (ditto for the prices charged in some of the cafes).

HONG KONG TOURIST ASSOCIATION
The Peak Tower is an impressive structure when emerging from the Peak's morning mists.

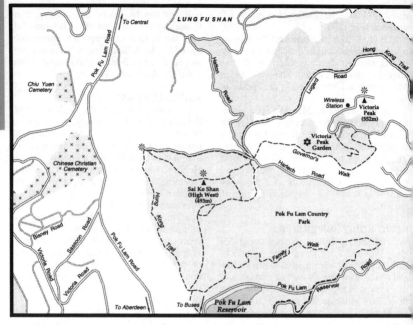

Unfortunately, the area has been robbed of some of its charm by insensitive development. Developers couldn't resist throwing up the **Peak Galleria**, an overblown, overpriced four level shopping plaza, the **Peak Tower**, looking like a huge titanium anvil, is a further questionable addition to the Peak skyline.

The top of the tram line is at 400m elevation. The tram offloads passengers at a station situated inside the Peak Tower. This could be a place to bring the kids; there are a couple of adventure simulators to keep the children amused – the 'Peak Explorer' (a futuristic ride in space and time), the 'Rise of the Dragon' (a car-ride through Hong Kong history) and 'Ripley's Believe it or Not!' odditorium. Apart from that, there are loads of shops and restaurants, a viewing terrace and even a post office.

The Peak Galleria is right next to the station. The place is designed to withstand

winds of over 270km/h, theoretically more than the maximum velocity of a typhoon. The viewing deck is reached by taking escalators up to the 3rd level. Inside the mall you'll find a number of expensive restaurants and retail shops, from art galleries to duty free. If you're looking for a bite to eat, see if there's a free table at the Peak Cafe, which offers a much better dining experience than many of the other restaurants on the Peak. See the Places to Eat section in this chapter for more details.

When people refer to the Peak, this generally means the Peak Galleria and surrounding residential area. Victoria Peak is actually the summit – about half a kilometre to the west and 140m higher. You can walk around Victoria Peak easily without exhausting yourself. Harlech and Lugard Rds encircle it: Harlech Rd is on the south side while Lugard Rd is on the north slope and together these roads form a loop. For

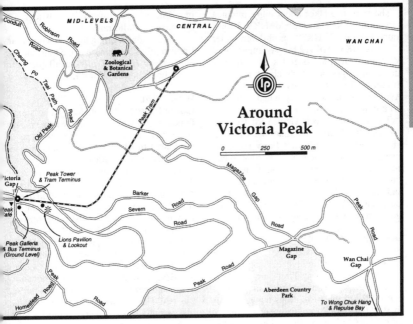

those who would rather run, not walk, this makes a spectacular jogging route.

You can walk from the Peak Cafe to the remains of the **old governor's mountain lodge** near the summit (550m elevation). The lodge was burnt to the ground by the Japanese during WWII, but the gardens remain and are open to the public. The views are particularly good and there is a topo-scope identifying Hong Kong's various geographical features.

If you feel like a longer walk, you can continue for a further 2km along Peak Rd to Pok Fu Lam Reservoir Rd, which leaves Peak Rd near the car park exit. This goes past the reservoir to the main Pok Fu Lam Rd, where you can get the No 7 bus to Aberdeen or back to Central.

Another good walk is down to Hong Kong University. First walk to the west side of Victoria Peak by taking either Lugard or Harlech Rd. After reaching Hatton Rd,

follow it down. The descent is very steep but the path is obvious.

If you're going to the Peak, you should go by the **Peak Tram** – at least one way. It's an incredibly steep ride, and the floor is angled to help passengers getting off at the midway stations. In the summer, packed with people, the inside of the trams can get pretty hot.

Running for more than a century, the tram has never had an accident – a comforting thought if you start to have doubts about the strength of the cable. In 1885 everyone thought the Honourable Phineas Kyrie and William Kerfoot Hughes were quite crazy when they announced their intention to build a tramway to the top, but it opened three years later, wiping out the scoffers and the sedan-chair trade in one go. Since then, the only occurrences which have stopped the tram have been WWII and the violent rain-storms of 1966, which washed half the track down the hillside.

HONG KONG

The tram trip takes about eight minutes and costs HK$18 one way, or HK$28 for a round trip (HK$5/HK$8 for children under 12 years; HK$6/HK$12 for passengers over 65 years). The tram operates daily from 7 am to midnight, and runs about every 10 minutes with three stops along the way. Avoid going on a Sunday when there are usually long queues.

The tram station is in Garden Rd, Central, south of the Murray building and Citibank Plaza, 650m from the Star Ferry terminal. Every 20 minutes there is a free shuttle bus between the Star Ferry and the Peak Tram station from 9 am to 7 pm (8 pm on Sunday and public holidays); however, it is often late. Between 8.05 and 11.35 pm, the No 15C shuttle bus ferries passengers to the station.

HONG KONG TRAIL

For those who like a challenge, it is possible to walk the entire length of Hong Kong Island. The Hong Kong Trail starts from the Peak Tram station on Victoria Peak, follows Lugard Rd to the west, drops down the hill to Pok Fu Lam Reservoir, near Aberdeen, before turning east and zigzagging across the ridges. The trail traverses the four country parks of Hong Kong Island: **Pok Fu Lam Country Park** on the south side of Victoria Peak; **Aberdeen Country Park** on the east side of the Peak; **Tai Tam Country Park** on the east side of the island; and **Shek O Country Park** in the south-east near Shek O. It's not likely that you'll want to hike the entire length of the trail in one day, since it's a rugged 50km. There are no designated camping sites along the trail.

Tai Tam is the largest of the country parks on Hong Kong Island, and arguably the most beautiful. The Hong Kong Trail skirts along the northern side of **Tai Tam Reservoir**, the largest lake on the island.

If you intend to do this hike, it would be wise to purchase the *Hong Kong Trail* map published by the Country Parks Authority (CPA), or the *Countryside series* map for Hong Kong Island. Both maps are available from the Government Publications Office in the Government Offices build-

ing, Queensway Government Offices, 66 Queensway, Admiralty.

There is also a bilingual map without an English title (the Chinese name translates as *Hong Kong Hiking Trails*), available from many bookshops in Hong Kong.

WAN CHAI

East of Central is one of Hong Kong's most famous districts, Wan Chai (the name means 'little bay' in Cantonese). In the hype of the tourist brochures, Wan Chai is still inseparably linked with the name of Suzie Wong – not bad considering that the book dates back to 1957 and the movie to 1960. Although Wan Chai had a reputation during the Vietnam War as a seedy red-light district, today it is mainly a business centre and shopping district.

It is still, however, a pretty interesting place to explore. The rows of narrow streets, sandwiched between Johnston Rd and Queen's Rd East, harbour all sorts of interesting shops and mini-factories where you can see the 'real' Hong Kong at work: watchmakers, blacksmiths, shoemakers, printers, signmakers and so on.

Nestled in an alley on the south side of Queen's Rd East is **Tai Wong Temple**, also known as Hung Sing Temple, where fortune-tellers used to do a brisk trade. It is still active, if somewhat subdued. Just east of the temple, also on Queen's Rd East, the **Hopewell Centre** is another one of Hong Kong's rather unique office towers. Basically a 40 storey cylinder, it is the flagship building of the Hong Kong property and construction magnate Gordon Wu. The centre has a tacky revolving restaurant at the top, which is accessed by two bubble-shaped external elevators. Though it's a short trip, the elevator ride is a great way to get an aerial view of Wan Chai.

Hong Kong Arts Centre

Also in the Wan Chai district is the Arts Centre (☎ 2582-0200) on Harbour Rd. The Pao Sui Loong Galleries (☎ 2582-0256) are on the 4th and 5th floors of the centre and international and local exhibitions, with an emphasis on contemporary art, are held year round. Opening hours are 10 to 8 pm daily. Admission is free. To get there take the MTR to Wan Chai station and follow the signs.

Police Museum

This museum (☎ 2849-7019) at 27 Coombe Rd relates the history of the Royal Hong Kong Police Force, which was formed in 1844. Intriguingly, the museum also houses a Triad Societies Gallery. Operating hours are from 9 am to 5 pm, Wednesday to Sunday, and from 2 to 5 pm on Tuesday; it is closed on Monday. Admission is free.

You can get there on bus No 15 from Central. Get off at the intersection of Peak and Stubbs Rds.

Museum of Chinese Historical Relics

This museum (☎ 2827-4692) houses cultural treasures unearthed during the course of archaeological digs in China. Two special exhibitions each year focus on artefacts from specific provinces.

The museum is on the 1st floor of the

Jardine Matheson

For a long time Jardine Matheson was Hong Kong's largest and most powerful *hong* (big company). It set up shop in Causeway Bay in 1844, after moving its headquarters from Macau. Now Jardine Matheson resides in the World Trade Centre, next to the Hotel Excelsior.

The area is still full of company names and memorials. Percival St, which crosses Hennessy Rd, is named after Alexander Percival, a relative of Sir James Matheson who joined the firm in 1852 and ended up a partner. Matheson St leads off Percival. Hennessy Rd becomes Yee Wo St; Yee Wo being the name under which Jardine traded in Shanghai. Jardine's Corner is just south of Victoria Peak and Jardine's Lookout is to the south-east, in the hills overlooking the harbour.

Jardine Matheson bought heavily in the first land sale in the colony in 1841. It bought a large tract of land on what was then the waterfront at Causeway Bay and hewed a whole township out of the rock. It built *godowns* (warehouses), offices, workshops, a slipway, homes and messes for employees. All that remains of the East Point establishment is an old gateway with a couple of plaques. You'll find it on a side street from Yee Wo St. It's still owned by Jardine Matheson but is now full of modern warehouses.

Two streets to the right behind Yee Wo St you'll find Jardine's Bazaar and Jardine's Crescent, names which recall the old firm. A Chinese bazaar was once on the former street. A hint of the past is still visible – the area has Chinese provision shops, herb shops and cooked-food stalls. Jardine's Crescent is still one big street market, which nowadays mostly sells clothes. Between Jardine's Bazaar and the crescent is the short Fuk Hing Lane, an interesting shopping alley with leather handbags, silk scarves, Chinese padded jackets and designer jeans.

The handover of Hong Kong to China has heralded Jardine's decline as top business dog in Hong Kong. The company fell into disfavour with the Chinese government shortly after the 1984 Sino-British Joint Declaration was signed. Sensing that a Communist government was bad business, Jardine's moved its headquarters to Bermuda. In the 1990s it further angered China by backing efforts to introduce democracy in Hong Kong. China retaliated by refusing to approve construction of Container Terminal Nine because it was to be built by a consortium headed by Jardine's.

While other hongs, such as Swire and Hutchison Whampoa, have entered into potentially lucrative joint-venture deals with the Chinese government, Jardine's has found itself on the outer. Nevertheless, the firm's management is unrepentant, and has indicated that the other hongs may yet rue the day a decision was made to let China's state-run firms into the business. But at least for some harried British executives, Bermuda is looking better all the time.

Causeway Centre, 28 Harbour Rd, Wan Chai. Enter from the China Resources building. Operating hours are 10 to 6 pm weekdays and Saturday, and 1 to 6 pm on Sunday and public holidays. From Central, take bus No 10A, 20, 21 or 104. Admission is free.

CAUSEWAY BAY

Catch the tram that goes through Wan Chai and let it take you to Causeway Bay. This area was the site of a British settlement in the 1840s and was once a *godown* (warehouse) area for merchants and a harbour for fishermen. The geography of the old Causeway Bay – Tung Lo Wan (meaning Copper Gong Bay in Chinese) – has almost disappeared as a result of reclamation.

The new Causeway Bay, one of Hong Kong's top shopping and nightlife areas, was built up from swampland and the bottom of the harbour. Jardine Matheson, one of Hong Kong's largest companies, set up shop there, which explains some of the street names: Jardine's Bazaar, Jardine's Crescent and Yee Wo St (Yee Wo is Jardine Matheson's Chinese name).

In addition to buying things, people go to Causeway Bay to dine out and, to a lesser extent, go drinking. The rush of consumers, diners and drinkers gives this district a vibrant feel at almost any time of the night or day. Several shopping centres can be found south of Hennessy Rd. Chief among these is **Times Square**, an enormous retail/office/restaurant complex that jars sharply with the decrepit 1950s low-rise tenements around it. Defying critics who said the location would doom the project, Times Square and its shops, restaurants, cinema and office towers have turned Causeway Bay into one of the city's centres.

Typhoon Shelter

The waterfront used to be a mass of junks and sampans huddling in the Causeway Bay Typhoon Shelter, but these days it's nearly all *gwailo* (foreign devil) yachts. This should be no surprise, as the Royal Hong Kong Yacht Club has its headquarters there.

The land jutting out is **Kellett Island**, which has been a misnomer ever since a causeway connected it to the mainland in 1956, and further land reclamation turned it into a peninsula. The cross-harbour tunnel surfaces there.

Noonday Gun

Satirist Noël Coward made the noonday gun famous with his 1924 song *Mad Dogs and Englishmen* about colonists who brave the heat of the noonday sun while the natives stay indoors:

In Hong Kong they strike a gong, and fire off a noonday gun, to reprimand each inmate, who's in late.

HONG KONG TOURIST ASSOCIATION
The traditional firing of the Noon Day Gun in Causeway Bay.

Built in 1901, this recoil-mounted three-pounder is the best known landmark in Causeway Bay. It stands in a small garden in front of the Excelsior Hotel on Gloucester Rd and is fired daily at noon.

Exactly how this tradition started is unknown. Some suggest that Jardine Matheson fired the gun without permission to either farewell a departing managing director or welcome an incoming ship. The authorities were so enraged by the company's insolence that, as a punishment, Jardine's was ordered to fire the gun every day.

continued on page 241

Hong Kong Architecture

Hong Kong's famous skyline is in a constant state of flux. The sheer imagination channelled into its architectural achievements makes Hong Kong an exciting and vibrant city to visit. History is not completely plundered – preserved chunks of traditional architecture remain in an assortment of temples, old government buildings and walled villages. However, the predominant aspiration of Hong Kong business is to ascend and this statement is enshrined in the city's vertical form.

The verticality of Hong Kong's Central district is both a statement of power and function – real estate in this area of largely reclaimed land is at a premium – the only way is up. This is the logic behind the most recent architecture in Hong Kong – creating space in one of the densest cities in the world. Some buildings seize height at all costs (Central Plaza); others are smaller but revel in elaborate detail and sophistication (Hongkong and Shanghai Bank building); while others (in case you feel lost in this forest of sheer glass walls and perpendicular monuments to finance) are horizontal (Hong Kong Convention and Exhibition Centre New Wing). Whatever your feelings, Hong Kong is an inspiring and dramatic city.

The Bank of China Building

Still the architectural symbol of Hong Kong, this 70 storey building was completed in 1990. Impressive and daring as it is, the building is very much a brash and hard-edged synopsis of the 1980s. In purely physical terms, the building dominates not just its immediate environment, but also the whole Hong Kong skyline. The Bank of China building had to be bigger than the nearby Hong Kong and Shanghai Bank building, as it represented the new power in town (the People's Republic of China) and did its best to dwarf the symbol of the exiting power (Great Britain). From 1986, the old Bank of China building had been looked down upon by Norman Foster's Hongkong and Shanghai Bank building, and it was time to turn the tables.

The asymmetry of the building is puzzling at first sight, but is in reality a simple geometric exercise. Rising from the ground like a cube, it is successively reduced, quarter by quarter, until the south-facing quarter is left to rise upwards. The staggered cutting off of each triangular column creates a crystalline beauty and a prismatic allure.

The interior of the building is ingeniously freed from the mass of structural supports. Weight-bearing columns are positioned in each of the four corners of the building, with a fifth running down the centre of the tower, but only to the 25th floor, from where it feeds into the four columns at each corner. This liberates space on each floor to benefit the work environment. The fabric and design of the support structures (steel and concrete) had to be built to withstand wind pressures exerted at typhoon intensity.

Despite being designed by a Chinese-born architect Ieoh Ming Pei, the building is clearly western in inspiration. Chinese elements are incorporated but muted. The segments of the building rising upwards are claimed to be analogous to bamboo sections, but this metaphor is lost in the overall steel and glass composition; likewise, the angularity of the construction conflicts with the round form of natural bamboo. Flanking the tower are two landscaped gardens that successfully pay allegiance to traditional Chinese aesthetics and add a natural dimension to the geometric display. A notable absence, for a building of this size, is the lack of Chinese lions by the main door (the old Bank of China building has two sets, one traditional, the other, Art Deco). Even the Hongkong and Shanghai Bank building has two huge bronze lions, reclining on the north side of the building.

HONG KONG TOURIST ASSOCIATION
Bank of China Building.

The granite lobby is impressive and the banking hall on the 3rd floor, with its vast marble floor, is illuminated by a 15 storey, light-filled atrium. But position-wise, the Bank of China building is impeded by its location as it is stranded in a web of flyovers and can't be accessed easily by pedestrians.

Many local Hong Kong Chinese see the building as a huge violation of the principles of fungshui. For example, the bank's four triangular prisms are negative symbols in the fungshui guidebook; being the opposite to circles, these contradict what circles suggest – money, perfection and prosperity. Furthermore, the huge crosses on the sides of the building suggest negativity and its shape has been likened to a praying mantis (a threatening symbol), as the radio masts look like insect's antennae.

Even more sinister are the triangular angles on the surface of the building – these are associated with daggers or blades and it is claimed that these cut into neighbouring buildings. One angle cuts across the former governor's residence (which previously had enjoyed fungshui protection) and this was used by some people to explain the run of bad luck that afflicted Chris Patten and his two predecessors.

Take the express lift to the 43rd floor (it doesn't stop at any other floor) for a panoramic view of Hong Kong.

Hongkong & Shanghai Banking Corporation Headquarters

Hong Kong & Shanghai Banking Corporation Headquarters.

Visiting this building (178.8m) is an unforgettable experience. It is a masterpiece of construction precision, sophistication and innovation. It was also extremely expensive; it cost nearly US$1 billion to construct, making it the world's most expensive building when it was completed in 1985. It cost much more to construct than the nearby, and much taller, Bank of China building.

This glass and aluminium structure is the fourth HongkongBank building at 1 Queen's Rd, Central, since the bank's founding in 1865. Indeed the need to fit a huge office tower on the original site is what pushed renowned British architect Norman Foster to adopt the unique design.

Locals call this place the 'Robot building', and it's easy to see why – it resembles one of those clear plastic models built so you can see how everything inside works. The gears, chains, motors and other moving parts of the escalators and lifts are all visible. The stairwells are only walled in with glass, affording dizzying views to workers inside the building. Structurally, the building is equally radical, built on a 'coat-hanger' frame.

The framework of the building is a staggering achievement. Observable, from outside the building, are five huge trusses from which the floor levels hang. Supporting the trusses are eight groups of four-column steel clusters, wrapped in aluminium. Using this technique, Foster eliminated the need for a central core. The resulting atrium gives the building a sense of space and light. If you stand in the atrium and look up, you can see how the whole structure hangs, rather than ascends. The building is flexible – the flooring, for example, is constructed from movable panelling. Most of the building's major components were assembled overseas and brought together on site.

The building reveals Foster's desire to create areas of public and private space and to break the mould of previous bank architecture. The ground floor is public space, that people can traverse without entering the building. From there, escalators rise to the main banking hall. The building gives the impression that it is inviting to enter and not guarded and off-limits. This sensation is encouraged by the imaginative use of natural light. Hung on the south side of the building are 480 computer controlled mirrors that reflect natural light into the atrium (it's called a sunscoop in architectural vernacular).

On a more traditional note, the building also makes concessions to fungshui orthodoxy. A Chinese geomancer was called in to approve the overall design and ensure that conventions were appeased. For example, the escalators on the ground floor were carefully positioned so as to maximise the flow of *qi* or *hei* (energy) into the building. A pair of 1930s bronze lions (that used to guard the doors of the previous Hongkong and Shanghai Bank) were deliberately placed in a position that harmonised with the fungshui of the locality.

It's definitely worth riding up the escalator to the 1st floor to gaze at the cathedral-like atrium and the natural light filtering through. The bank does not conduct tours of its masterpiece, but staff are accustomed to tourists wandering in; there is a reception desk on the 1st floor where you can pick up an information booklet on the building. The bank is open from 9.00 am to 4.30 pm Monday to Friday, and from 9.00 am to 12.30 pm on Saturday.

Hong Kong International Airport Passenger Terminal

Probably the first or the last building you'll pass through during your stay in Hong Kong, this magnificent new terminal at Chek Lap Kok airport replaces the legendary relic at Kai Tak in Kowloon.

Designed by the Mott Consortium (comprising Mott Connell, Foster and Partners and BAA plc), the new terminal is the largest single airport building in the world with an overall length of 1.27km and a floor area of 500,000 sq metres; this also represents the world's largest enclosed public space (equivalent to ten times the size of Wembley Stadium in the UK). The baggage hall of the terminal is the size of Yankee Stadium in New York, USA, so don't lose sight of your bag. Construction required 370,000 cubic metres of concrete (constituted with granite from nearby former hills).

SIR NORMAN FOSTER

Aerial photograph of Chek Lap Kok airport under construction.

Sir Norman Foster has brought his experience and distinctive architectural philosophy to the scheme. The planning is open and wide, with a welcoming interior for those in transit. Elements of human scale were not overlooked. Norman Foster says of the terminal: 'It will be large – the largest in the world, but it will also be friendly and accessible to all who use it. It will be grand and majestic – but never overwhelming. Above all, it will be flexible to grow and change, so that it can always meet the future needs of Hong Kong'.

From the air the terminal has the appearance of a massive bird or aeroplane. Once through passport control and security, passengers will enter the East Hall, which has the largest retail space (housing shops, cafes and restaurants) in an international airport. You may never need to check out. The airport's 38 boarding gates are on a 'Y' shaped concourse leading from the central base.

The vaulted roof is a light-weight steel membrane (a repeating grid of steel shells) covering an area of 18 hectares, spanning the entire building in a complex geometry of linked vaults. Roof supports had to be designed to withstand vast structural forces – up to 300 tonnes in some places. Two of the world's largest cranes were employed to install the square roof bays. At the side, the roof hangs over the terminal's glass perimeter (a circumference of

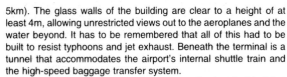

SIR NORMAN FOSTER
Chep Lap Kok airport.

5km). The glass walls of the building are clear to a height of at least 4m, allowing unrestricted views out to the aeroplanes and the water beyond. It has to be remembered that all of this had to be built to resist typhoons and jet exhaust. Beneath the terminal is a tunnel that accommodates the airport's internal shuttle train and the high-speed baggage transfer system.

If you like figures, here are some more: the terminal building features over US$140 million worth of communications and computer-based electronic systems. Passengers have access to 2000 monitors for flight information and 12,000 smoke detectors conspire to make sure you stub out your cigarettes. The 1.7km tunnel that houses the Automated People Mover (APM, in hi-tech parlance) is as wide as a motorway (but you can't drive your car in) and as deep as a two storey building. Its roof is strong enough to carry the weight of a fully laden jumbo jet. The terminal plans to service 80 million passengers annually within a few decades, which will make the airport the busiest in the world.

Lippo Centre

Costing HK$468 million and designed by American architect Paul Marvin Rudolph (a former student of Walter Gropius of Bauhaus fame), the Lippo Centre solidifies the rather brash naivety of the 1980s (rapidly becoming nostalgia territory) in steel and reflective glass. One glance at the structure's lumpy protrusions and robotic outline and you know you're in 'shoulder pad land'.

RICHARD I'ANSON
Lippo Centre.

Diagonally opposite Pacific Place, the building's two towers are different heights: one is 36 floors and the other 40 floors. The protrusions hanging from the sides of the building are clumped in three groups and consist of 'sky-rooms'. The overall design is challenging and commands attention, but sadly the building, once brimful with 1980s vigour and enthusiasm, is looking a bit tarnished and weather-beaten.

Pacific Place

Designed and constructed by Wong & Ouyang Ltd, Pacific Place is an impressive feat of organised form. Pacific Place is, in many ways, typical of Hong Kong's blueprints for large-scale commercial development. However, the harmonies of shape and the originality of style reveal the concern of the Pacific Place architects in producing novel solutions to the problem of space in this crowded territory.

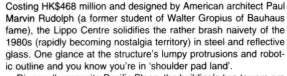

HONG KONG TOURIST ASSOCIATION
Pacific Place.

Constructed in two phases, Phase I consisted of a huge podium for shops and cinemas (currently the UA Queensway cinema), topped by an office tower and the JW Marriot Hotel. The poetry comes from the harmonious outlines of the Phase II buildings (the Island Shangri-La Hotel and the Conrad Hotel), which soften the hard angles of Phase I. The curved lines of the two hotels add beauty to the complex, delivering a balanced aesthetic. Against the predominantly squarish outline of Hong Kong architecture, the ellipses of the two Phase II buildings add grace and a certain measure of mystery. Naturally, the interiors of each of the two Phase II hotels are splendid.

Central Plaza

Once the tallest tower in Asia, Central Plaza (374m) was designed in 1989 and completed in 1992. If you are looking across Victoria Harbour to Hong Kong Island at night, this is the vast tower way off to the left of the Bank of China building. The glass skin of the tower has three different colours – gold, silver and ceramic-coated sheets. The result is rather garish.

RICHARD I'ANSON
Central Plaza.

The tower is triangular in design with indented corners. Sitting atop the building is a 64m mast standing on a tripod. The base of the building is notable for the landscaped garden and public plaza. Though isolated by major roadways, the building is successfully connected to other buildings by numerous overhead public walkways (including the Hong Kong Convention and Exhibition Centre and Wan Chai MTR station).

The colonnade at the base of the tower is made from vast granite columns. It's a warning of what's in the lobby – an overdone marbled attack on the senses. Altogether the construction is very Hong Kong: upwardly mobile, crisp and forthright.

If you want some fantastic views, jump into one of the elevators and journey to the Sky Lobby (on the 46th floor) for a breathtaking panoramic sweep over Victoria Harbour to Kowloon.

Hong Kong Convention & Exhibition Centre New Wing

The bird-like extension to the Hong Kong Convention and Exhibition Centre (costing HK$4.8 billion) was the site of the 1997 handover ceremony. This wonderful piece of architecture is not to everyone's taste. Low and horizontal, the structure has an uplifting design that gives the impression that the building is preparing for flight (no doubt the intended metaphor for Hong Kong's post-colonial future). The building's curves add potential movement to an otherwise static shoreline.

HONG KONG TOURIST ASSOCIATION
Hong Kong Convention & Exhibition Centre New Wing.

Inside the new wing is a cavernous interior given over to five exhibition halls, two convention halls, two foyers, two theatres, seven restaurants, two car parks and 52 meeting rooms. Maybe the best aspect is outside – the promenade surrounding the wing offers wonderful views over to both Central and Tsim Sha Tsui. Hong Kong Island has long lacked an equivalent to the promenade that runs along Victoria Harbour in Tsim Sha Tsui and this extension successfully liberates space from the waters of the harbour. The promenade also features a huge, golden sculpture of Hong Kong's new symbol, the Bauhinia flower.

The Peak Tower

This challenging building, designed by Terry Farrell & Co (designer of the excellent new British Council building), is a sign of vitality in the world of Hong Kong architecture.

Whatever your interpretation of the design, this is a building you cannot ignore. It is situated at the terminus of the Peak Tram and is a regular podium (containing shops and theme rides) covered by a striking roof. The best time to see the structure is as it emerges from the mist – a common climatic phenomenon on the Peak.

HONG KONG TOURIST ASSOCIATION
The Peak Tower.

Exchange Square

Exchange Square is the seat of the stock exchange (hence the name), and is elevated above the fray of Central. The buildings are finished in reflective glass and polished granite, lending a certain solidity and nobility to the structures. The buildings, designed by P&T Architects & Engineers Ltd, incorporate curved and straight elements. Most notable is the magnificent plaza in between the Forum and Exchange Square I and II that is decked out with seating, sculptures and fountains. The complex is accessible from Swire House and Jardine House, via overhead pedestrian walkways, and the Exchange Square bus terminal, which is beneath the square.

HONG KONG TOURIST ASSOCIATION
Exchange Square.

Hong Kong Cultural Centre

The Hong Kong Cultural Centre is a dynamic focus for the arts in Hong Kong and a challenge to the notion that the territory is devoid of culture.

Occupying a prime piece of the Tsim Sha Tsui waterfront, the Cultural Centre is asymmetrically weighted and wave-like. The pronounced shape lifts upwards at the sides in a celebratory gesture, facing the reserved traditionalism of the old KCR clock tower opposite. Leading away from the Cultural Centre is the excellent promenade that looks out over Victoria Harbour to the magnificent architectural spectacle of Hong Kong's Central District.

RICHARD I'ANSON
Hong Kong Cultural Centre.

An evening view of Hong Kong.

HONG KONG TOURIST ASSOCIATION

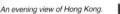

continued from page 232
Victoria Park

Victoria Park is one of the biggest patches of green grass on the northern side of Hong Kong Island. It is one of the territory's most popular parks. Hong Kong teams play football in the park on weekends and the Urban Services League puts on music and acrobatic shows. Also in the park is the statue of Queen Victoria that used to sit in Statue Square.

Victoria Park is the site of the annual Tiananmen Square massacre vigil held on the evening of June 4th. It is a very moving occasion, accompanied by songs and speeches, while everyone sits on the ground with candles of remembrance.

The best time to stroll around the park is on a weekday. Early in the morning its a good place to see the slow-motion choreography of taiji practitioners. In the evening the park is given over to Hong Kong's young lovers. Between April and October you can take a dip in the Victoria Park swimming pool for HK$17.

A few days before the Chinese New Year, Victoria Park becomes a flower market. The park is also worth a visit during the evening of the mid-Autumn (Moon) Festival when people turn out en masse carrying lanterns. Other events in the park include the Hong Kong Tennis Classic and the Hong Kong International Kart Grand Prix.

Causeway Bay Sports Ground

This is the most popular sports ground in Hong Kong and the home of the Chinese Recreation Club. The sports ground is on the south side of Causeway Rd, just to the south of Victoria Park. The ground has football, volleyball, badminton and tennis facilities open to the public.

Tin Hau Temple

One more site worth a look in Causeway Bay is a tiny temple built in honour of the god of fishing people, Tin Hau, on Tin Hau Temple Rd (at the junction with Dragon Rd), on the east side of Victoria Park (near Tin Hau MTR station). Before reclamation, the Tin Hau Temple stood on the waterfront. The bell inside dates back to the 15th century, but the temple itself is about 200 years old.

Tiger Balm Gardens

Not actually in Causeway Bay but in the adjacent Tai Hang district are the famous (or perhaps more appropriately, infamous) Tiger Balm Gardens, officially known as the Aw Boon Haw Gardens. A pale relative of the better-known park of the same name in Singapore, Hong Kong's Tiger Balm Gardens are three hectares of grotesque statuary in appallingly bad taste. These concrete gardens were built at a cost of HK$16 million (and that was in 1935!) by Aw Boon Haw, who made his fortune from the Tiger Balm cure-everything medication. Aw is widely described as having been a philanthropist, though perhaps his millions could have been put to a more philanthropic use.

The gardens are just off Tai Hang Rd near **Jardine's Lookout**. It's a rather long trudge from Happy Valley. It's best to take bus No 11 which you can catch at Exchange Square, Admiralty MTR station or Yee Wo St, Causeway Bay. The gardens are open daily from 9.30 am to 4 pm and admission is free.

HAPPY VALLEY

There are two neighbourhoods on the north side of Hong Kong Island that have been colonised by gwailos with expense accounts. One is the Mid-Levels and the other is Happy Valley, south of Wan Chai.

However, gwailo-watching is not the main reason for going there. There are two horse-racing tracks in Hong Kong – one at Shatin in the New Territories and the other at Happy Valley. The racing season is from late September to May. For details, see Activities in the Hong Kong Facts for the Visitor chapter.

Of some historical interest are several **cemeteries** that stand across the street from the spectator stands. These are divided into Catholic, Protestant and Muslim sections and date back to the founding of Hong Kong as a colony. The placement is somewhat ironic, as is Happy Valley's name, for the area was a malaria-infested bog that led to a fair number of fatalities before the swamps were drained. Many of the victims of the huge fire at Happy Valley racecourse 80 years ago are also buried there.

Racing buffs can wallow in history at the **Hong Kong Racing Museum** (☎ 2966-8065) on the 2nd floor of the Happy Valley Stand at the racecourse. It's open from 10 am to 5 pm, Tuesday to Saturday, and on Sunday from 1 to 5 pm. It's closed on Monday. Admission is free. Getting to Happy Valley is easy. A tram marked Happy Valley runs from Central.

QUARRY BAY

Sights really start to thin out east of Causeway Bay, with the landscape dominated by apartment towers and industrial blocks. The main attraction of Quarry Bay is one of Hong Kong's finest shopping malls, the Cityplaza Shopping Centre. Although not normally considered a tourist attraction, it has much to be recommended. Shopping is much more pleasant once you get out of the tourist zones. Shops have price tags on merchandise and there is no bargaining; yet prices are generally lower than you could bargain for in Tsim Sha Tsui, Kowloon.

To get to Cityplaza, take the MTR to Tai Koo station, from where you can exit directly into the shopping mall.

CHAI WAN

Out at the east end of Hong Kong Island's MTR is Chai Wan, a region of nondescript office buildings, warehouses and workers' flats. Gwailos in this neighbourhood are rare, and if you have a western face you may even be a local tourist attraction yourself. However, other than seeing what's at the end of the MTR line, there is one small museum out there that might be worth tracking down.

Law Uk Folk Museum

This is Hong Kong's newest museum, though the building, itself, is over 200 years old. The Law Uk Folk Museum (☎ 2896-7006), 14 Kut Shing St, is a restored Hakka village house. The Hakka (literally, guest people) migrated from the north in the 13th century. The museum has been dressed up with a few wax figures in traditional Hakka dress. Furniture and farming tools are also on display. It's open from 10 am to 1 pm and from 2 to 6 pm, Tuesday to Saturday. On Sunday and public holidays it opens from 1 to 6 pm. It's closed on Monday and some public holidays. Admission is free. Take the MTR to Chai Wan station.

SHEK O

Shek O, on the south-east coast, has one of the best beaches on Hong Kong Island. And because it takes around two hours to get there, it's usually less crowded than the other south island spots. On weekdays the town is sometimes almost deserted, and it's easy to spend the afternoon lazing on the beach, snacking at the open-air restaurants or gawking at the mansions dotting the Shek O headlands.

Shek O is a small village, so it's easy to get your bearings. From the bus stop it takes five minutes to walk to the beach. En route you'll pass a few good restaurants (see Places to Eat in this chapter). If you take the road leading off to the left you'll enter a maze of small homes, which gradually grow in size and luxury as you head out along the peninsula to the east of the beach. This is the **Shek O headlands**, home to some of Hong Kong's wealthiest families. If you traipse down to the tip of the peninsula, you'll find a viewpoint where you can look out over the South China Sea: next stop, the Philippines.

Walking is possible around Shek O beach, though the terrain is steep and the underbrush quite thick in spots. Better yet, take advantage of the bicycle rental shops and pedal down to **Big Wave Bay**, another fine beach located 2km to the north of Shek O. To get there just follow the road out of town, past the Shek O Country Club and Golf Course, turn right at the traffic circle and keep going until the road ends.

Getting There & Away

To get to Shek O, take the MTR or tram to Shau Kei Wan, and from Shau Kei Wan take bus No 9 to the last stop. It's a long ride but quite scenic and (depending on your driver) potentially exciting.

STANLEY

Stanley (the name in Cantonese means red pillar) is the trendy, suburban gwailo place to live. It's on the south-east side of the island, just 15km as the crow flies from Central. Once the village was indeed a village. About 2000 people lived there when the British took over in 1841, making it one of the largest settlements on the island at the time. The British built a prison near the village in 1937 – just in time to be used by the Japanese to intern the expatriates. Now it's used as a maximum security prison.

Hong Kong's contingent of British troops was housed in Stanley Fort at the southern end of the peninsula, which is off-limits to the public at the time of writing.

There is an OK beach (not as crowded as the one at Repulse Bay) at Stanley Village. It's also possible to rent windsurfers there. **Stanley Market** dominates the town. On weekends it's bursting with both tourists and locals, so it's better to go on a weekday. The market is open daily from 10 am to 7 pm.

On a short walk westwards, out of town along Stanley Main St, is yet another **Tin Hau Temple**. Although the original building dates back to 1767, it has undergone complete renovation and is now a bit of a concrete hulk – however, the interior is traditional. Behind the temple a huge residential estate is being built, but if you follow the path that passes the Tin Hau Temple and continue up the hill, you reach the **Kwun Yum Temple**. Above the temple is a pavilion housing a massive statue of Kwun Yam (the 48 armed God of Mercy who is also known as Kuanyin and Guanyam) looking out to sea. The pavilion was built in 1977, following a claim by a woman and her daughter that they saw the statue move and a bright light shine from its forehead; maybe Stanley isn't such a dull place after all.

From town you can walk south along Wong Ma Kok Rd to **St Stephen's Beach**,

which has a cafe, first aid unit, showers and toilets, umbrella, boat and windsurfer hire (in the summer months); lording over it all is a lifeguard. This lovely, shady walk takes about 25 minutes. Turn right when you finally get to a small road leading down to a jetty. At the end, turn left and walk past the boathouse to the beach. You can also hop on bus No 73A which takes you close to the intersection with the small road. Opposite the bus stop is a **military cemetery** for military personnel and their families; the oldest graves date from 1843, but the cemetery was reopened in 1942 for the burial of those who died in WWII during internment by the Japanese.

Getting There & Away

To get to Stanley from Central take bus No 6, 6A, 6X or express bus No 260 from the Exchange Square bus station. Bus No 6 climbs over the hills separating the north and south sides of the island. It's a scenic, winding ride. Bus No 260, which goes via the Aberdeen tunnel, is quicker and perhaps better for those prone to motion sickness. From Hoi Ping Rd in Causeway Bay you can take the No 40 green minibus. If you're coming from Shau Kei Wan (eastern station of the tram), an exciting ride on bus No 14 takes you to Stanley via the Tai Tam Tuk reservoir. Bus No 73 connects Stanley with Repulse Bay and Aberdeen.

One note of warning. If you visit Stanley during the weekend, you may have a tough time catching a bus back to Central between 5 and 8 pm, when everybody else is also trying to get home. If queues for the Nos 6 and 260 buses are too long to endure, consider the No 73 to Aberdeen, or check the queue for the No 40 green minibus to Causeway Bay.

WILSON TRAIL

This trail traverses the island and is a bit odd because the southern section (28.7km) is on Hong Kong Island and the northern section (49.3km) is in the New Territories. The trail was named after former Hong Kong governor, Sir Wilson.

HONG KONG

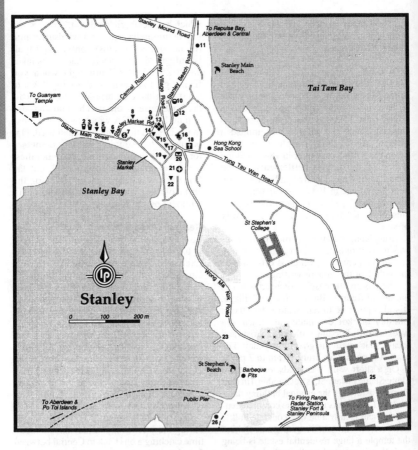

Stanley

0   100   200 m

Stanley Mound Road

To Repulse Bay, Aberdeen & Central

●11

Stanley Main Beach

Tai Tam Bay

To Guanyam Temple

■1

Carmel Road

Stanley Village Road

Stanley Beach Road

●10

●12

Stanley Market Rd

8
9
13
2 3 4 5 6
14
7
●16
18
▼15
17
19 ▼
20
21
22

Hong Kong Sea School

Stanley Main Street

Stanley Market

Stanley Bay

Tung Tau Wan Road

St Stephen's College

H

Wong Ma Kok Road

23

24

St Stephen's Beach

Barbeque Pits

25

To Aberdeen & Po Toi Islands

Public Pier

26

To Firing Range, Radar Station, Stanley Fort & Stanley Peninsula

The trail begins about 1km to the north of Stanley; if you jump on either bus No 6, 6A, 6X or 260, to or from Central, you will pass the beginning of the trail which leads north from Stanley Gap Rd. Coming from Central, you want to alight from the bus about 2km from Repulse Bay. The first, steeply rising section of the trail is all concrete steps. You soon reach the summit of Stanley Mound (385m), topped by a pavilion. The summit is also known as the Twins, or Ma Kong Shan in Chinese. On a clear day you'll have an excellent view of

Stanley, Repulse Bay and over to Lamma Island. The trail continues north over Violet Hill, intersects the Hong Kong Trail, passes Mt Butler, drops down into the urban chaos and terminates at Quarry Bay MTR station. Actually, the 'trail' becomes a road and goes straight through the Eastern-Harbour Tunnel to Lam Tim MTR station in the New Territories. Forget about walking through the tunnel; just take the MTR. For details on the northern section of this trail, see the New Territories chapter.

Stanley
赤柱

1 Tin Hau Temple
  天后廟
2 Beaches
3 Lord Stanley's Bar &
  Bistro
4 Stanley's Oriental
  Restaurant
  赤柱東方餐廳
5 Smuggler's Inn
6 Stanley's French
  Restaurant
  赤柱法國式餐廳
7 HongkongBank
  匯豐銀行
8 Cooked Food Stalls
  (Dai Pai Dong)
  大排檔

9 Public Toilets
  共用廁所
10 Minibuses to
   Causeway Bay
   往銅鑼灣之巴士
11 Changing Rooms;
   Showers; Shop
12 Stanley Bus
   Terminal
   赤柱巴士總站
13 Welcome
   Supermarket
   惠康超級市場
14 Delifrance
15 Lucy's
16 Stanley Police
   Station
   赤柱警察局
17 Tables 88
18 St Anne's Church

19 At Village
   Restaurant
20 Stanley Post
   Office
   郵局
21 Medical Clinic
   診所
22 Domino's Pizza
23 Pier
   碼頭
24 Stanley Military
   Cemetery
   赤柱軍人墳場
25 Stanley Prison
   赤柱監獄
26 Sailboat Rental
   租小船處

REPULSE BAY

Repulse Bay's long, somewhat white, beach is the most popular on Hong Kong Island. Packed on weekends, it's a good place if you like people watching, but not ideal if you're hoping for solitude. During summer, the beach is crowded even on weekdays. Middle Bay and South Bay, respectively about a 10 and 30 minute walk along the shore to the east, have beaches that are usually less crowded. The water is pretty murky and the slimy feel of the seafloor underfoot is enough to turn you into a 'land-lubber'.

Toward the eastern end of Repulse Bay beach is an unusual **Kwun Yum Temple** popularly known as the Life Saver's Club. The temple area is full of statues and mosaics of Kwun Yum (in Mandarin she is known as Kuanyin), the God of Mercy, and inside is a cafe and the headquarters of the Royal Life-saving Society. The sprawling temple houses an amazing assembly of figures, deities and figures, including a four-faced Buddha and statues draped in pearl necklaces and ornaments. Garish but fascinating. In front of the temple is Longevity Bridge – crossing it is supposed to add three days to your life.

Repulse Bay is also home to some of Hong Kong's most rich and famous, and hills behind the beach are saturated with luxury apartment towers. One dwelling worth noting is a pink, purple and yellow monstrosity with a giant square cut out of the middle. Apparently this unique design feature was added at the behest of a fung shui expert, though in Hong Kong such a stunt might also have been devised to push up the property's value. The **Repulse Bay Shopping Arcade** at 109 Repulse Bay Rd is a popular forum of shops and restaurants.

Getting There & Away

Bus Nos 6, 6A, 61, 260 and 262 from Central's Exchange Square bus station all pass by Repulse Bay. Shuttle buses to Repulse Bay leave every 15 minutes (peak time) from a stop just to the left as you exit from the Central Star Ferry terminal. To get to Repulse Bay from Aberdeen take bus No 73.

OCEAN PARK & WATER WORLD

A stimulating cultural experience this is not, but these two fun parks are set in a nice location just to the east of Aberdeen and are quite entertaining. These are also good places to see modern Hong Kong at play.

Hong Kong residents are quite proud of Ocean Park (information and inquiries ☎ 2552-0291), a fully fledged amusement park, complete with Dragon roller coaster, space wheel, octopus, swinging ship and other stomach-turning rides. It is also something of a marine park, with a wave cove that houses seals, sea lions and penguins, daily dolphin and killer-whale shows and an aquarium that features a walk-through shark tank and atoll reef. The **Atoll Reef** is particularly impressive, with around 4000 fish on display including the mammoth Napoleon fish (it looks about six foot in length!), tawny nurseshark, whitetip reef shark and cowtail ray – you can get right up close. The **Shark Aquarium** has hundreds of different sharks on view and scores of rays. The park also caters for birdwatchers, with aviaries and a flamingo pond.

The complex is built on two sides of a steep hill and is linked by a very scenic seven minute cable car ride. The park entrance is on the 'lowland' side, which also has children's attractions like a dinosaur discovery trail, kid's world and miniature rides. The main section of the park sits on the 'headlands' and affords a beautiful view of the South China Sea and southern Hong Kong Island. This is where you'll find the rides and marine attractions.

At the rear entrance is **Middle Kingdom**, a sort of Chinese cultural village with temples, pagodas, traditional street scenes and staff dressed in period garments. There are also arts and crafts demonstrations, live theatre and Cantonese opera. This is a highly whitewashed version of ancient China, but it's harmless enough.

Entrance fees are HK$140 for adults, or HK$70 for kids aged three to 11 years. Opening hours are from 10 am to 6 pm daily. It's best to go on a weekday as the weekends are amazingly crowded. A map comes with the ticket, so it's not difficult to find your way around.

Water World is right next to the front entrance of Ocean Park. With a full complement of swimming pools, water slides and diving platforms, it's a great place to go and splash around in during the searing heat of summer. Water World is open from June to October. During July and August, operating hours are from 9 am to 9 pm. During June, September and October it is open from 10 am to 6 pm. Admission for adults/children costs HK$65/33 during the daytime, but in the evening falls to HK$44/22.

Getting There & Away

Probably the most convenient way to get to Ocean Park and Water World is via a special Citybus that leaves from the bus station next to Admiralty MTR station. Buses leave every 15 to 20 minutes from 9.10 am and cost HK$11 (HK$5.50 for children). Citybus sells a package ticket that includes transportation and admission to Ocean Park for HK$150 for adults (HK$75 for children); however, it doesn't actually save you very much. There is also a special Ocean Park Citybus that leaves from the Star Ferry terminal and costs the same as the Admiralty Citybus. It leaves every 15 to 20 minutes from 10 am to 3.30 pm; the last bus back to the Star Ferry terminal departs at 4.30 pm, except on Sunday, when it leaves at 6.30 pm.

A cheaper way to get there is to catch bus No 70 from the Exchange Square bus station in Central and get off at the first stop after the tunnel. From there it's a 10 minute walk. The No 6 green minibus (HK$7.50) from Central's Star Ferry terminal takes you directly to Ocean Park and Water World, but does not run on Sunday and public holidays. Bus No 73 connects Ocean Park with Aberdeen to the west and Repulse Bay and Stanley to the east.

DEEP WATER BAY

This is a quiet little beach with a generous dose of shade trees located a few kilometres east of Aberdeen. There are a few nice places to eat and have a drink and there is a barbecue pit at the east end of the beach. If you want a dip in the water, this spot is usually less crowded than Repulse Bay.

To get there from Central, take bus No 6A, 260 or 262 from the Exchange Square bus station. Bus No 73 connects Deep Water Bay with Aberdeen to the west and Repulse Bay and Stanley to the east.

ABERDEEN

For many years Aberdeen Harbour was one of Hong Kong's top tourist attractions because of the large number of people (estimated at over 6000) who lived and worked on the junks moored there. Over the years the number of boats has dwindled as more and more of the 'boat people' have moved into high-rises or abandoned fishing as a career. The harbour is still worth a look, but these days the best fishing harbour is on Cheung Chau Island (see the Outlying Islands chapter for details).

Also moored in Aberdeen Harbour are three luxury palace-like floating restaurants. Sampan tours can be arranged at the Aberdeen Promenade. You can have your choice of private operators, which generally mill around the eastern end of the promenade, or licensed operators sponsored by the HKTA, like the Aberdeen Sampan Co (☎ 2873-0310). The private sampans usually charge HK$50 to HK$60 per person for a 30 minute ride, though you should easily be able to bargain this down if there are several of you. If you are by yourself, just hang out by the harbour; the old women who operate the boats will leap on you and try to get you to join a tour. Once on a tour, you can get a close up of the *zhuga teng* (houseboats) upon which families make a living. Watertours does a 25 minute trip around the harbour for about HK$50 per person, but it's usually more fun to charter your own sampan. If you don't mind missing out on close-up shots of boat life, you can get a free 10 minute tour by hopping on one of the boats out to the floating restaurants and then riding back. These leave every four or five minutes.

On one side of the harbour is the island of **Ap Lei Chau** (Duck's Tongue Island). The island used to be a junk-building centre, but now it's covered with housing estates. There's not much to see there, but a walk across the bridge to Ap Lei Chau affords good views of the harbour and some nocturnal shots of the fiery lights of the Jumbo restaurant. Alternatively, you can get a boat across for HK$1.50.

If you've got time to spare, a short walk through Aberdeen will bring you to a **Tin Hau Temple**, at the junction of Aberdeen Main and Aberdeen Reservoir Rds. Built in 1851, it's a sleepy spot, but still an active place of worship. It's also one of Hong Kong's more important altars to the patron deity of Hong Kong's boat people; appropriate, given Aberdeen's harbour community. Close to the harbour, near Aberdeen Main Rd, is the Hung Hsing Shrine, a collection of ramshackle altars and incense pots.

If you're feeling vigorous, the entrance to Aberdeen Country Park and Pok Fu Lam Country Park is about a 15 minute walk along Aberdeen Reservoir Rd. From there you can walk up to Victoria Peak and catch the Peak Tram or the bus down to Central.

Getting There & Away

A tunnel linking Aberdeen with the northern side of Hong Kong Island provides rapid access to the town. From the Exchange Square bus station, take bus No 7 or 70 to Aberdeen. Bus No 7 goes via Hong Kong University, and No 70 goes via the tunnel. Bus No 73 from Aberdeen will take you along the southern coast to Ocean Park, Repulse Bay and Stanley.

PLACES TO STAY – BUDGET

At the budget end, things aren't wildly exciting on Hong Kong Island. Most of the well known cheap guesthouses are located in Kowloon. There are a few good-value options available on Hong Kong Island, however, don't take the prices listed as gospel. A general down-turn in the number of tourists has created a fluctuating price structure; and don't be afraid to haggle. Guesthouses are often struggling to fill up beds and many will offer discounts for long stays.

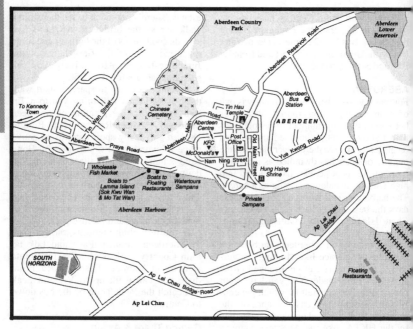

Youth Hostels

On top of Mount Davis, not far from Kennedy Town, is *Ma Wui Hall* (☎ 2817-5715, fax 2817-5715), the only dormitory accommodation on Hong Kong Island. The advantage of this place is that it's very clean and quiet and has great views of the harbour; beds only cost HK$65 for members (or HK$95 for non-members) per night. There are cooking facilities and secure lockers and a new block under construction will include a TV and recreation room. The hostel has 112 beds and is open from 7 am to 11 pm. Call ahead to make sure there's a bed before you make the trek out there.

The hostel now offers a shuttle bus from the Macau ferry terminal in Sheung Wan, but there are only four departures a day, so phone first and get the time of the next service.

If you arrive from the airport, take the A2 bus to Central, then change to bus No 5B or 47 bus. Bus No 5B runs from Paterson St in Causeway Bay to Felix Villas (though it only runs from 5.55 to 10.15 am and from 4.40 to 8.20 pm). Bus No 47 starts at the Exchange Square bus station. You're least likely to take bus No 77, which runs westwards through to Aberdeen. All these buses will drop you off at Felix Villas (the 5B terminus) on Victoria Rd. From the bus stop, walk back 100m. Look for the YHA sign and follow Mt Davis Path (not to be confused with Mt Davis Rd) – there is a shortcut to the hostel which is signposted halfway up the hill. The walk takes 20 to 30 minutes.

Guesthouses

Just about all of the guesthouses on Hong Kong Island are located in Causeway Bay. The excellent *Wang Fat Hostel* (☎ 2895-1015) is on the 3rd floor, flat A2, 47 Paterson St, just above the Daimaru Department Store in Causeway Bay. Rooms with shared/private bath are HK$280/350.

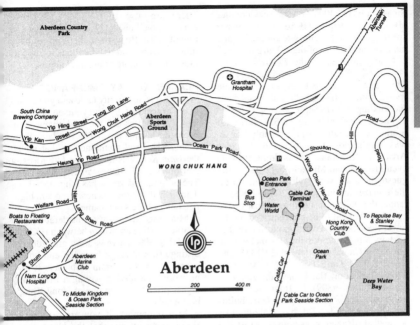

Aberdeen

Each room has a private phone. The hostel is quiet and clean and the friendly owner speaks good English.

In terms of value, *Noble Hostel* (☎ 2576-6148, fax 2577-0847) is certainly one of the best guesthouses in Hong Kong. Every room is squeaky clean and is equipped with a private phone and air conditioning. The hostel continues to expand and has now spread into five different buildings; the main office is flat A3, 17th floor, 27 Paterson St (above the Daimaru Department Store). Singles/doubles with shared bath are HK$240/300. With private bath it's HK$300/400.

Also at 27 Paterson St is *Wonderful Well* (☎ 2577-1278, 9480-6481, fax 2577-6639) on the 4th floor in flat A5. This pleasant accommodation owes much of its appeal to the charming Angela Hui, who runs the place. Superb double rooms cost HK$400. The singles cost HK$250 and are often full.

Yet another hostel at 27 Paterson St is *Kai Woo Hung Wan Co* (☎ 2890-5813, fax 2890-5725). It's on the 11th floor in flat A1, and it has good singles/doubles for HK$350/380, though not much English is spoken.

Close by is Fairview Mansion at 51 Paterson St. On the 5th floor in flat A you'll find *Payless Inn* (☎ 2808-1030, fax 2890-7798), which has singles/doubles without bath for HK$280/350, or doubles with attached bath for HK$500. Down on the 4th floor of the same building is *Jetvan Travellers' House* (☎ 2890-8133), which has singles/doubles without a bath for HK$300/400.

Located on the south side of Causeway Bay and next door to a church is the *Causeway Bay Guest House* (☎ 2895-2013), flat B, 1st floor, Lai Yee building, 44A-D, Leighton Rd. With only seven rooms, it's easily booked up, but if you can get one you'll probably be happy with it. All are quite clean and have attached bathrooms.

Singles are HK$400 (with shower), doubles HK$500 and triples HK$600. The owner speaks good English; the guesthouse is quite near the No 10 stop of the A3 airport bus.

Nearly adjacent is the *Emerald House* (☎ 2577-2368), 1st floor, 44 Leighton Rd. This guesthouse features clean double rooms with a private bath and round beds (no kidding) for HK$450.

The *Central* building at 531 Jaffe Rd (corner with Cannon St) is probably Causeway Bay's closest contender to Mirador Arcade in Kowloon. The building itself is even grottier than Mirador, but most of the guesthouses are very stylish. Rooms in all these places are in the HK$200 to HK$500 range, depending on facilities. Most of the guesthouses tend to be concentrated on the lower floors, but it's worth exploring further upstairs too. Some possibilities include the *Lung Tin Guesthouse* (☎ 2832-9133), 2nd floor, flat F; *Lung Poon Villa* (☎ 2838-9868), 2nd floor, flat L; and the *Empress House* (☎ 2831-9809), 1st floor, flat A.

Nearby, the *Phoenix Apartments* building, 70 Lee Garden Rd, has a plethora of somewhat sleazier guesthouses. Most are 'love hotels' where rooms are rented by the hour; ambiguous messages like 'special for after midnight' decorate the business cards of these hotels. Nevertheless, love hotels are also available for overnighters and offer rooms with intriguing features such as pink wallpaper, mirrored ceilings and circular beds. The staff are not always friendly and often speak diabolical English. Prices are more expensive on the weekends (when the 'love-weekenders' are in residence) and the hotels also charge more for daytime use. Make sure to confirm the checkout time before paying, as it can be early. One of the cheapest places is the *Wah Lai Villa* on the 4th floor, where HK$220 will get you a round bed with mirrored headboard for the night. The *Garden Guest House* (☎ 2577-7391) is a quiet, clean establishment with doubles at HK$450. *Dragon Inn* (☎ 2576-3849) in flat G on the 2nd floor is equipped with English speaking staff and doubles cost HK$380 from Monday to Friday.

There are also more guesthouses/love motels in the Leishun Court building at 116 Leighton Rd. Be warned, these places have little character and few facilities to support those staying more than a few nights.

PLACES TO STAY – MID-RANGE

Wan Chai is now pretty tame and you're unlikely to accidentally find yourself checking into a brothel as did the lead character in Richard Mason's novel *The World of Suzie Wong*. The hotel mentioned in that novel, the *Nam Kok*, was in fact the *Luk Kwok*, a real hotel at 67 Gloucester Rd, Wan Chai. The original *Luk Kwok* has long since been demolished, but there is now a modern highrise hotel of the same name.

Mid-range prices vary considerably, with doubles costing anywhere between HK$600 and HK$1800. There is not a great deal to distinguish mid-range from top-end hotels, except perhaps a certain ambience. It may be worth considering paying a marginally higher price to stay in one of Hong Kong's best hotels.

Also remember, if you are arriving in Hong Kong by air, that the Hong Kong Hotels Association (☎ 2383-8380, email hkha@att.net.hk, www.hkta.org.hkha) has a counter at Chek Lap Kok airport where you can leaf through a huge number of hotel brochures and seek a large discount (up to 50% off) on hotel rooms. See Accommodation in the Facts for Visitors chapter for more details.

Bishop Lei International House (☎ 2868-0828, fax 2868-1551), 4 Robinson Rd, Mid-Levels; singles/doubles from HK$1080/HK$1280, suites from HK$2080.

Charterhouse (☎ 2833-5566, fax 2833-5888, email info@charterhouse.com, www.charterhouse.com), 209-219 Wan Chai Rd, Wan Chai; singles/doubles from HK$1400/1750 to HK$1750/1850, suites from HK$2500. It is near the Causeway Bay and Wan Chai MTR stations.

City Garden (☎ 2887-2888, fax 2887-1111), 9 City Garden Rd, North Point; doubles from HK$1700 to HK$3500. It is near the Fortress Hill MTR station.

Empire (☎ 2866-9111, fax 2861-3121, email booking@empire-hotel.com, www.empire-hotel.com), 33 Hennessy Rd, Wan Cha; doubles are from HK$1400 to HK$2200, suites from HK$2800. It is near the Wan Chai MTR station.

Grand Plaza (☎ 2886-0011, fax 2886-1738), 2 Kornhill Rd, Quarry Bay; doubles are from HK$1500. It is near the Tai Koo MTR station.

Harbour View International House (☎ 2802-0111, fax 2802-9063), 4 Harbour Rd, Wan Chai; doubles are from HK$1050 to HK$1550. It is near the Wan Chai MTR station.

Luk Kwok (☎ 2866-2166, fax 2866-2622, email lukkwok@lukkwokhotel.com), 72 Gloucester Rd, Wan Chai; singles/doubles are from HK$1700/1880 to HK$1980/2180, suites from HK$4000. It is near the Wan Chai MTR station.

New Cathay (☎ 2577-8211, fax 2576-9365), 17 Tung Lo Wan Rd, Causeway Bay; singles HK$700 and doubles HK$800 to HK$1130, suites from HK$1870. It is near the Causeway Bay MTR station.

New Harbour (☎ 2861-1166, fax 2865-6111), 41-49 Hennessy Rd, Wan Chai; doubles HK$1080 to HK$1680, suites from HK$1980. It is near the Wan Chai MTR station.

Newton (☎ 2807-2333, fax 2807-1221), 218 Electric Rd, North Point; doubles from HK$1400 to HK$1950. It is near the Fortress Hill MTR station.

South China (☎ 2503-1168, fax 2512-8698), 67-75 Java Rd, North Point; doubles from HK$1610 to HK$1800. It is near the North Point MTR station.

South Pacific (☎ 2572-3838, fax 2893-7773, email hinfo@southpacifichotel.com.hk, www.southpacifichotel.com.hk), 23 Morrison Hill Rd, Wan Chai; singles/doubles from HK$1550/1700 to HK$2200/2200, suites from HK$3900. It is near the Causeway Bay MTR station.

Wesley (☎ 2866-6688, fax 2866-6633), 22 Hennessy Rd, Wan Chai; doubles from HK$1250 to HK$2900. It is near the Admiralty MTR station.

Wharney (☎ 2861-1000, fax 2865-6023), 57-33 Lockhart Rd, Wan Chai; singles/doubles from HK$1400/1500 to HK$4500/4500. It is near the Wan Chai MTR station.

YWCA Garden View International House (☎ 2877-3737, fax 2845-6263), 1 MacDonnell Rd, Central; doubles from HK$880 to HK$990, suites from HK$1512 to HK$1815. The closest MTR station is Central, but from there it's a steep walk uphill. The hotel is uphill from the Zoological & Botanical Gardens.

PLACES TO STAY – TOP END

Prices for Hong Kong's luxury hotels are as high as anywhere on earth. But in some cases, the money you spend brings a level of comfort and service not often matched. Hong Kong's top flight hoteliers are constantly trying to match or better hotels in Bangkok, London, New York, Paris and Tokyo. So far Hong Kong's hotels are doing a fine job. This assessment does not extend to all hotels in the top-end category. Some merely have top-end prices; the amenities, location and service are good, but not outstanding. If you're going to spend this amount of money, anyway, try and book one of the six or seven hotels that take service to that next rarefied level.

The Peninsula's counterpart on Hong Kong Island is the *Mandarin Oriental,* owned by none other than Jardine Matheson, Hong Kong's most famous trading house. While not architecturally as impressive as the Peninsula, The Mandarin has a healthy dose of old-world charm. Styling is subdued, and in some rooms a bit outdated, but the service, food and facilities are still excellent, and you get all the atmosphere that comes with staying at one of Hong Kong's landmarks. Needless to say, the views are fantastic. The Mandarin harbours some of the best restaurants in Hong Kong.

The crisp and somewhat sterile exterior of the *Island Shangri-La* conceals an elegant sophistication. Placing a strong emphasis on personal service, this is the kind of hotel where you will find everything and staff seem genuinely interested in making your stay pleasant. This tasteful hotel has some nice touches, like a library where you can take afternoon tea, an outdoor Jacuzzi and a 24 hour business centre. For shopping purposes, the Pacific Place adjacent has a huge collection of fashionable shops.

The Island Shangri-La Hotel has a wonderful atrium on the 41st floor and bubble elevators from the 41st to the 56th floor. Gliding up in the elevator, it is possible to see one of the biggest paintings in the world (around 60m high!) – a wonderful picture of a very mountainous Chinese landscape.

Gunter Quaisser

The nearby *Conrad International Hong Kong*, is a member of the Hilton Hotels group. While not quite as elegant as the Island Shangri-La, the hotel has received enthusiastic reviews for its attention to business travellers' needs.

Winning the prize for the most overblown lobby is the *Grand Hyatt Hong Kong*. A swirl of black marble, oriental rugs and palm trees, this vast foyer inspires either admiration or amusement. But the hotel itself can be taken seriously. The rooms are tastefully and comprehensively furnished, the service attentive and the recreational facilities among the most complete of any Hong Kong hotel.

While hotels in this category have price tags that start from HK$1800 and rise to mortgageable heights, room prices reflect the astronomical cost of Hong Kong real estate, especially in areas with a premium on Hong Kong's best views. Obviously, all of these places have excellent facilities. Hotels in this category include:

Century Hong Kong (☎ 2598-8888, fax 2598-8866), 238 Jaffe Rd, Wan Chai; singles/doubles from HK$1850/2050 to HK$2050/2150. It is near the Wan Chai MTR station.

Conrad International (☎ 2521-3838, fax 2521-3888, email info@conrad.com.hk, www.conrad.com.hk), Pacific Place, 88 Queensway, Admiralty; singles/doubles from HK$2850/3050 to HK$3900/4150, suites from HK$5200 to HK$25,000. It is near the Admiralty MTR station.

Excelsior (☎ 2894-8888, fax 2895-6459), 281 Gloucester Rd, Causeway Bay; doubles from HK$2400 to HK$3400, suites from HK$4200 to HK$8500. It is near the Causeway Bay MTR station.

Furama Kempinsk (☎ 2525-5111, fax 2845-9339, email furamahk.china.com), 1 Connaught Rd, Central; doubles from HK$2500 to HK$3500, suites from HK$3700 to HK$10,000. It is near the Central MTR station.

Grand Hyatt (☎ 2588-1234, fax 2802-0677, www.hyatt.com), 1 Harbour Rd, Wan Chai; singles/doubles from HK$2900/3150 to HK$25,000. It is near the Wan Chai MTR station.

Island Shangri-La (☎ 2877-3838, fax 2521-8742, www.shangri-la.com), Pacific Place, Supreme Court Rd, Admiralty; doubles from HK$2700 to HK$3850, suites from HK$5300 to HK$26,000. It is near the Admiralty MTR station.

JW Marriot (☎ 2810-3000, fax 2845-0737), Pacific Place, 88 Queensway, Admiralty; doubles from HK$2800 to HK$3950, suites from HK$6000. It is near the Admiralty MTR station.

Mandarin Oriental (☎ 2522-0111, fax 2810-6190), 5 Connaught Rd, Central; doubles from HK$3300 to HK$5300, suites from HK$7000 to HK$25,000. It is near the Central MTR station.

New World Harbour View (☎ 2802-8888, fax 2802-8833), 1 Harbour Rd, Wan Chai; singles from HK$2700, doubles for HK$3000, HK$18,800 for the presidential suite. It is near the Wan Chai MTR station.

Park Lane (☎ 2890-3355, fax 2576-7853, email info@parklane.com.hk), 310 Gloucester Rd, Causeway Bay; singles/doubles from HK$2480/2780 to HK$3680/3980, suites from HK$4880. It is near the Causeway Bay MTR station.

Regal Hongkong (☎ 2890-6633, fax 2881-0777, email rhk@regal-hotel.com, www.regalhotels.com), 88 Yee Wo St, Causeway Bay; doubles from HK$2800 to HK$3800, suites from HK$6000 to HK$22,000. It is near the Causeway Bay MTR station.

Ritz-Carlton (☎ 2877-6666, fax 2877-6778, email ritzrchk@hk.super.net, www.ritz-carlton-hong kong.com), 3 Connaught Rd, Central; singles/doubles from HK$2850 to HK$4200 (same rate for both), suites from HK$4500. It is near the Central MTR station.

PLACES TO EAT

Besides what is listed here, please refer to Nightlife in this chapter to find pub grub and other assorted late-night munchies.

Central, Admiralty & Soho

Chinese Dim sum is relatively cheap, but it's usually served for breakfast and lunch only. In the evening restaurants drag out pricey Cantonese fare like pigeon, snake and shark-fin soup. You can easily find expensive Cantonese restaurants in big hotels. The following places are in the low to medium price range:

Luk Yu Tea House (☎ 2523-5464), 26 Stanley St, Central; dim sum served from 7 am to 6 pm. This restaurant has lots of traditional character.

Tai Woo (☎ 2524-5618), 15-19 Wellington St, Central; dim sum served from 11 am to 4.30 pm

Yung Kee Restaurant (☎ 2522-1624), 32-40 Wellington St, Central; dim sum served from 2 to 5pm

The Lan Kwai Fong area has some wonderful examples of Zhejiang and Shanghai cuisine. The *Ning Po Residents Association* (☎ 2523-0648), 4th floor, Yip Fung building, 10 D'Aguilar St, offers some tasty dishes and is extremely popular with both expats and locals.

The *Red Star Bar & Cafe* (☎ 2804-6939), 26-30 Elgin St, Soho, is more difficult to categorise. Definitely a product of the strange culture of handover 1997, this place features postmodern Chinese food served against a trendy backdrop of TV sets, geometric tables and poseurs. This is Chinese food with a western kick.

Hunan Garden (☎ 2868-2880) is a more upmarket restaurant perched between the towers of Exchange Square on the 3rd floor of the Forum shopping mall. This elegant, expensive establishment specialises in spicy Hunan cuisine. The fried chicken with chilli is excellent and the seafood dishes (unusual in Hunan cuisine) are recommended. The setting, looking out on views of the harbour and into the heart of Central, adds to the atmosphere.

The *Island* restaurant (☎ 2848-7305) on the 4th floor of the Furama Kempinski Hotel on Connaught Rd serves classy (but pricey) Cantonese food. If you want to let your hair down and spend with abandon, try the deep-fried squid stuffed with mashed shrimp or the sliced pigeon with bamboo shoots; delicious.

American *American Pie* (☎ 2877-9779) is hidden away on the 4th floor of the California Entertainment building in Lan Kwai Fong. Featuring home-style dishes like turkey with gravy, fresh salads and even meatloaf, this place has become so popular you almost always need to book a table in advance. Try the Sunday brunch, a real bargain. If you're craving a fat slab of ribs, hit *Tony Roma's* (☎ 2521-0292), next door, on the 1st floor of the California Tower.

Dan Ryan's Chicago Grill (☎ 2845-4600), unit 114, Pacific Place, 88 Queensway, is an international chain with outstanding food. This place features a big-screen video showing sports shows, and packs out during the American World Series baseball games. Operating hours are from 8.30 am until midnight and it's not terribly cheap.

British Pubs are everywhere, though many have 'gone native'. One place that stays true to its roots is the *Bull and Bear* (☎ 2525-7436) on the ground floor of Hutchison House on Lambert Walk, Central. All the standards are on the menu, at prices even the English should be able to stomach. More expensive is *Bentley's Seafood Restaurant and Oyster Bar* (☎ 2868-0881), firmly established in the basement of the Prince's building, 10 Chater Rd, Central. Among the medley of seafood served up is lobster bisque, oyster and mushroom pie, fresh Scottish salmon and smoked eel.

Cajun & New Orleans A popular new name in the Soho neighbourhood is the *Bayou* (☎ 2526-2118) at 9-13 Shelley St. This new establishment has gone down well with expats and picked up good reviews (although it's not cheap). Try the cajun barbecue ribs or the voodoo pasta.

European High on nostalgia and one of the oldest names in the game is *Jimmy's Kitchen* (☎ 2526-5293), at 1 Wyndham St, Central, which at 60 years of age has become a Hong Kong institution. The chargrilled king prawns, the baked onion soup, black pepper steak and a whole medley of desserts all compete for the diner's approval. Bear in mind that this is not cheap eats territory. There's also a Tsim Sha Tsui branch (☎ 2376-0327) on the 1st floor of the Kowloon Centre, 29 Ashley Rd.

Post 97 (☎ 2810-9333), 1st floor, 9 Lan Kwai Fong, has good music, plush, comfy couches and muted decor. It's a good place to unwind, sip wine and read a book, although, during lunch and dinner and on weekend nights, it gets pretty lively.

French Unpretentious yet refined French dining can be had in Central at *Aujourd'hui* (☎ 2869-1132), 4-6 On Lan St, an attractive side street off Wyndham St. This relative newcomer is a touch on the expensive side, but has proved popular.

La Rose Noire Patisserie (☎ 2877-0118, www.la-rose-noire.com) is on the 3rd floor of the Pacific Place in Admiralty. Lunch and dinner menus feature a delicious range of cheap salads, quiches, puffs and pizzas, plus an extravaganza of cakes and French pastries. Food can even be ordered online and picked up later.

The smart *2 Sardines* (☎ 2973-6618) at 43 Elgin St, Soho, serves authentic French cuisine. An escargot's throw away is *Café Gypsy* (☎ 2521-0000) at 29 Shelley St. Prices are not cheap but where else can you order goat's cheese marinated in olive oil and herbs. *Le Fauchon* (☎ 2526-2136) at 6 Staunton St near Central is also almost certain to satisfy (although the bill may shock). *Pierrot* (☎ 2522-0111), on the 25th floor of the Mandarin Oriental, 5 Connaught Rd, Central, has excellent food and views.

German & Austrian If you're yearning for a good bockwurst and maybe even some German conversation, don't give up hope. In Lan Kwai Fong both *Schnurrbart* (☎ 2523-4700) and *Bit Point* (☎ 2523-7436) serve up hearty bierstube fare. These are bars however, where German beer drinking is taken seriously, and the cigarette smoke can get pretty thick at times. Another alternative is the *Mozart Stub'n* (☎ 2522-1763) at 8 Glenealy, Central: a cosy little Austrian spot with good food and wines and a delightful atmosphere.

Indian The *Spice Island Club*, 63-69 Wellington St, has good Indian and Nepali food; prices are quite reasonable for lunch, but not so great for dinner.

Nestled on the 3rd floor of 10 Wing Wah Lane, next door to Club 64 in Lan Kwai Fong, the *Curry Club* (☎ 2523-2203) is another cheap, longstanding expat hangout,

and with good reason. The food is good value and the staff always obliging. Also in Lan Kwai Fong is the Central branch of the *Koh-I-Noor* restaurant chain (☎ 2568-8757) on the 1st floor of the California Entertainment building.

Costing a bit more but worth the extra expense is *Club Sri Lanka* (☎ 2526-6559), basement, 17 Hollywood Rd, Sheung Wan. This place features an excellent Sri Lankan buffet for around HK$85. There's also a vegetarian buffet that costs a bit less. Note that alcohol is not served on the premises, but you can take your own. The ever popular *Ashoka* (☎ 2524-9623), 57 Wyndham St, still has a well-deserved reputation.

The Mughal Room (☎ 2524-0107), 75-77 Wyndham St, serves idyllic samosas and all the food is an exercise in harmonic flavouring. Recommended dishes include the dahi papri chat and the paneer dilbahar.

Tandoor (☎ 2845-2299), 3rd floor, On Hing building, 1-9 On Hing Terrace in Central, is another local favourite, and has an open kitchen so you can see how it's all done. Prices are a bit high, but are not unreasonable. *India Today* (☎ 2801-5959) at 26-30 Elgin St is a new arrival to the area south of eastern Hollywood Rd – a district which is fast becoming a new restaurant centre for Hong Kong Island.

International No one seems to have a bad thing to say about *M at the Fringe* (☎ 2877-4000), which is hidden in the basement of the Fringe Club at 2 Lower Albert Rd, Lan Kwai Fong. The menu is constantly changing. The soups are excellent, and it's worth saving room for dessert. Reservations are a must.

One of the best restaurants in Hong Kong, and one of the most expensive, is *Petrus* (☎ 2877-3838) on the 56th floor of the Island Shangri-La Hotel in Central (close to the clouds). Many diners opt for the seven course set dinner (HK$720), probably because this lets them focus on the view and the extensive wine list. Petrus is open daily for lunch and dinner, except Sunday when only dinner is served.

The *Rickshaw Club* (☎ 2525-3977), 22 Robinson Rd (at the intersection with Mosque St), is spread out over three floors. This unconventional restaurant offers such dishes as Greek salad on pita bread; the 'Rickshaw Pizza' is truly superb.

Italian Along with American restaurants, a bevy of new Italian places have flooded onto the scene in recent years. Most aren't bad, but there are only a few that really justify the money you have to shell out for a taste of old Italy.

In the Lan Kwai Fong area, *Tutto Meglio* (☎ 2869-7833) is beautifully decorated and the food excellent, hailing principally from Florence. Also in Lan Kwai Fong is *Va Bene* (☎ 2845-5577), at the top end of Lan Kwai Fong. Elegantly appointed, with pastel walls and wooden venetian blinds, the (decent) food has a hefty price tag. If you're not yet spoilt for choice, *Tutta Luna* (☎ 2869-0099), 12 Lan Kwai Fong, has a rich range of ingredients and flavours and all for a very reasonable price.

In the Landmark in Central is the attractive *La Trattoria* (☎ 2524-0111), an exorbitantly expensive although admittedly excellent Italian restaurant. Duck lasagne, spaghetti with clams in white wine sauce and other exotic Italian dishes make this a rare treat. *Club Casa Nova* (☎ 2869-1218), 46B Elgin St, is a popular place, but the servings are minuscule for what you pay (and we were overcharged).

Grappa's (☎ 2868-0086) is a further top-notch venue for perfect antipasti, fettucini and a cornucopia of Italian flavours. You can find it at 132 Pacific Place, Queensway.

Japanese Eating Japanese cuisine can quickly lead to bankruptcy, so if you don't have deep pockets, eat elsewhere.

Two great places for lunch in Central are *Hanagushi* and *Fukuki*, both in the Lan Kwai Fong area. Hanagushi (☎ 2521-0868), 19 Lan Kwai Fong, is a bit cramped and really fills up from 1 to 2 pm on weekdays, but the skewered yakitori, soba noodles and sushi are all crowd-pleasers. Fukuki

(☎ 2877-6668) in Wellington St is more refined, with tatami mats and private dining enclaves; it also costs more. Close by, *Tokio Joe* (☎ 2525-1889), 16 Lan Kwai Fong, strives to make the Japanese dining experience accessible to new initiates and is not dauntingly expensive. Also in the area is *Yorohachi* (☎ 2524-1251), 5-6 Lan Kwai Fong, which offers an excellent teppanyaki grill and great-value lunch boxes.

Kosher The *Shalom Grill* (☎ 2851-6300), 2nd floor, Fortune House, 61 Connaught Rd, serves up kosher and Moroccan cuisine. If you're in the mood for a Jerusalem felafel or a Casablanca couscous, this is the place.

Malaysian Malaysian food fans will be happy to discover that, at the time of writing, a Malaysian restaurant, *Melaka,* was about to open its doors for business at 32C Staunton St.

Mexican Several places in town claim to serve Mexican food. With the following exceptions, these should all be given a wide berth. In Lan Kwai Fong *Zona Rosa* (☎ 2801-5885) has been known to impress serious Mexican food fans. The food is fresh, the sauces and chillies quite hot, but the high prices may cool you down a bit. *Caramba!* (☎ 2530-9963), 26-30 Elgin St, with a somewhat blinding selection of tequila, provides a cosy and intimate Mexican dining experience in the heart of Soho.

Middle Eastern *Desert Sky* (☎ 2810-7318), 36 Elgin St, is an atmospheric oasis of Arabic spices and shades. It serves a bargain buffet lunch for HK$78 and has a performance of belly dancing on Tuesday nights. *Beirut* (☎ 2804-6611) at 27-39 D'Aguilar St, Lan Kwai Fong, continues to provide excellent and extremely filling Lebanese food. Another branch can be found at 48-50 Lockhart Rd, Wan Chai (☎ 2865-7271).

Nepalese The *Nepal* restaurant (☎ 2869-6212), 14 Staunton St, Soho, is worth seeking out. Savour a feast of Nepalese

HONG KONG

flavours, including such novelties as chicken lali gurash, mutton gorkhali, steamed vegetable dumplings and yak cheese. The set dinner costs a healthy HK$178. Waiters rush across the road with loaded plates to the sister restaurant *Sherpa* (☎ 2973-6886), which shares the same menu. Nepalese souvenirs are available for sale.

Portuguese If you don't have the time to make it to Macau, you might consider the *Casa Lisboa* (☎ 2869-9631) at 21 Elgin St in Soho. Where better to chomp your way through roast suckling pig, African chicken, ribs and baked seafood rice? It costs a lot more than a Portuguese meal in Macau, but then you don't have to buy a ferry ticket either or have the hassle of changing your patacas.

Scandinavian Yes, there is a Scandinavian restaurant in Hong Kong (of all places). It's called *Club Scandinavia* (☎ 2525-2621) and, as you can imagine, strongly features seafood. You can find it at 15 Staunton St, Soho.

Spanish A Lan Kwai Fong landmark for years, *La Bodega* (☎ 2877-5472) in Wyndham St serves up quirky Spanish food in large helpings. The menu is a blackboard brought to your table where you can work your way through pasta with vegetables and garlic prawns, seafood paella and barramundi with green tomatoes.

Just about every national cuisine under the sun is represented in the Central/Sheung Wan borderland of Soho, including Spain. *La Comida* (☎ 2530-3118) is a cosy little affair at 22 Staunton St; and *Rico's* (☎ 2840-0937), 44 Robinson Rd, offers a refreshing dining experience in a pleasant Mediterranean atmosphere.

Thai With a glut of Thai eateries in this area, the diner is presented with a lot of choice.

For an excellent weekend night, sink a few beers at Club 64 and then fight your way over to the *Good Luck Thai* restaurant (☎ 2877-2971) at 13 Wing Wah Lane,

spilling out into the street opposite. It's cheap, chaotic and fun and only a brief stagger away from further beers at Club 64 and the rest of Lan Kwai Fong.

Also in Lan Kwai Fong, but at the opposite end of the spectrum, is *Supatra's* (☎ 2522-5073), 50 D'Aguilar St. This place is super trendy, but all of the food is done perfectly. It gets a bit loud when the after-work crowd starts flowing in, but the mood is cheerful enough. *Lemongrass* (☎ 2905-1688) in the basement of the California Tower at 30-32 D'Aguilar St is a quiet, smart and discreet place that serves up such treats as pomelo salad, spicy green Papaya salad and mussels in red curry.

Phukets has branches in the Mid-Levels (☎ 2868-9672), 30-32 Robinson Rd, and in Wan Chai (☎ 2527-2568).

The *Mid-Levels restaurant* is a cosy spot with a mural of a Thai beach to enhance the atmosphere. The food is good (mainly seafood) and the menu seems regularly to expand.

The *Golden Elephant* (☎ 2522-8696), shop 234, Pacific Place, Queensway, allows you to savour fantastic food in elegant Thai surroundings. Go as a group so you can order a table-load of dishes from the extensive menu. Other branches are in Times Square (☎ 2506-1333) Causeway Bay and Harbour City (☎ 2735-0733), Kowloon.

Vegetarian *Vegi-Table* (☎ 2877-0901) has cheap, no-nonsense food, great choice and no MSG. It's at 1 Tun Wo Lane, Central. To get there, walk under the Mid-Levels escalator as it cuts between Lyndhurst Terrace and Hollywood Rd. Tun Wo Lane is to the left as you walk uphill.

The *Fringe Club* (☎ 2521-7251) at 2 Lower Albert Rd, Lan Kwai Fong, does a vegetarian lunch buffet where you can crunch your way through ultra-healthy salads.

Also in the Central/Sheung Wan district is the *Original Health Café* (☎ 2815-0398) at 2702-3, 27th floor, Wing Shan Tower, 173 Des Voeux Rd. This place specialises in cheap, high-fibre new-age food. Meals

RICHARD I'ANSON

RICHARD I'ANSON

Top: A walk along the esplanade provides one of the best views of Victoria Harbour and Hong Kong Island.
Bottom: A Star Ferry worker taking a break. Star Ferries ply the waters between Hong Kong Island and Kowloon.

HONG KONG TOURIST ASSOCIATION

HONG KONG TOURIST ASSOCIATION

HONG KONG TOURIST ASSOCIATION

HONG KONG TOURIST ASSOCIATION

HONG KONG TOURIST ASSOCIATION

HONG KONG TOURIST ASSOCIATION

TRISTY FAIRFIELD

RICHARD I'ANSON

HONG KONG TOURIST ASSOCIATION

A	B	C
D	E	F
G	H	I

A: Junk sailing on Victoria Harbour.
B: Night time, Victoria Peak.
C: Chinese calligraphy.
D: Dragon boat races on Victoria Harbour.
E: Chinese opera makeup.

F: Collecting peach blossoms.
G: Fishing buoy.
H: Mong Kok bird market.
I: Junk at sunset.

are created in an organic frenzy of wholesome Puritanism.

Vietnamese *Bon Appetit* (☎ 2525-3553), 14B Wing Wah Lane, is a Vietnamese restaurant that serves up cheap but scrumptious meals for those on a rock-bottom budget.

Indochine 1929 (☎ 2869-7399) on the 2nd floor of the California Tower in Lan Kwai Fong is not cheap, but the mood of colonial Vietnam may well bewitch you. The old photographs, lighting and memorabilia serve as an appetiser for the remarkable, well presented food that follows. Try the spring rolls and the beef and papaya salad.

The coterie of Soho eateries wouldn't be complete without the exotic Vietnamese elegance of *Café Au Lac* (☎ 2526-8889), 20 Staunton St. This is authentic Vietnamese food for the well heeled; female waiters wearing traditional clothing add to the rarefied atmosphere.

Mixed Asian *Vong* (☎ 2825-4028) on the 25th floor of the Mandarin Oriental is a newcomer with Vietnamese, French and Thai food on the menu. The food is expensive (and it is easy to get carried away), but the view alone makes it worthwhile.

Amid all the glitter and lights of Central's Pacific Place is *Tiger's* (☎ 2537-4682). The decor is a bit off-beat, but the food is right on target. Indonesian, Thai, Indian and other South-East Asian dishes are all included on the menu; the South-East Asian buffet is reasonable value at HK$138 for lunch and HK$198 for dinner.

Breakfast An excellent place for breakfast is *Pier One* (☎ 2526-3061) in the basement arcade under Jardine House. This is also an excellent place to pick up lunch – filling sandwiches, daily set meals (cottage pie, quiche lorraine, pasta and other reliables) and excellent coffee are all on the menu.

Oliver's Super Sandwiches does excellent breakfasts until 11 am. There's a branch on the ground floor of Tower I, Exchange Square. Along with cooked western breakfasts, Oliver's Super Sandwiches provide

newspapers for patrons to browse through. Other branches can be found in the Prince's building, 10 Chater Rd, Central, next to Oliver's Delicatessen, and in Citibank Plaza, 3 Garden Rd.

A good venue for coffee is *Fauchon*, in shops 4 and 5, The Forum, Exchange Square Tower III. A small coffee will set you back HK$15, but the tasty pastries are not to be missed.

The central branch of *Delifrance* is in Pacific House, Zetland St. There is another small Delifrance outlet in the arcade at Queensway Plaza, Queensway (next to Admiralty MTR station).

La Rose Noire Patisserie (☎ 2877-0118) on the 3rd floor of the Pacific Place in Admiralty serves excellent French pastries and coffee.

Fast Food You can find *Hardee's* in the Grand building, Connaught Rd, Central, opposite Exchange Square. *KFC* lurks at 6 D'Aguilar St; *Maxim's* has a branch in the Prince's building, 10 Chater Rd, Central.

McDonald's can be found all over the place: in the basement of 37 Queen's Rd Central; at 38 D'Aguilar St (up in Lan Kwai Fong); in the Sanwa building, 30-32 Connaught Rd; and at shop 124, level 1, Pacific Place, 88 Queensway.

Pizza Hut has a branch at B38, basement 1, Edinburgh Tower, the Landmark, 17 Queen's Rd; and *Spaghetti House* is on the lower ground floor, 10 Stanley St. *Domino's Pizza* (☎ 2521-1300), 9 Glenealy, has no restaurant facilities but delivers to any address within a 2km radius. Delivery is supposedly guaranteed within 30 minutes, even in Hong Kong's horrendous traffic.

As the name implies, late-night hours are kept at *Midnight Express* (☎ 2525-5010), 3 Lan Kwai Fong. This place has a combination menu of Greek, Indian and Italian food, with deliveries available every day of the week, except Sunday. The kebabs are outstanding and cost around HK$35 to HK$45. Opening hours are from 11.30 am to 3 am, except on Sunday, when it opens at 6 pm. *Little Italy*, at 13 Lan Kwai Fong, is a popular sandwich parlour that is also open until the very wee hours.

Ice Cream *Haagen-Dazs,* the American ice-cream outlet with the Scandinavian name, is in World Wide House on Pedder St (between Des Voeux and Connaught Rds). There is another branch at 1 Lan Kwai Fong (see the Lan Kwai Fong map).

Self-Catering If you want fresh bread and wholemeal ingredients, *The Source of Health* (☎ 2869-7383), Yip Fung building, 18 D'Aguilar St, Central, makes a selection of breads and cakes including blueberry muffins, banana and raisin muffins, organic whole-wheat loafs and French baguettes.

The *Central Market* on Queen's Rd, between Jubilee and Queen Victoria Sts, has three floors of meat, vegetables, fish and poultry. The daily prices are posted on a large noticeboard. If you really want to rub elbows with the proletariat, this is the place to do it.

Delicatessens are blossoming in Hong Kong. Gastronomes can head to a number of quality outlets, pungent with the wonderful aroma of herbs, spices, cheeses, dried sausages, patés and fine wines. *Oliver's Delicatessen,* associated with the sandwich fast food chain, is stuffed with European delicacies, though prices are steep. There are Oliver's Delicatessens in the Prince's building in Central, in Harbour City in Tsim Sha Tsui and in the Repulse Bay Shopping Arcade.

Other delis to look out for are *Vino and Olio* (☎ 2523-4483) at 54 D'Aguilar St, Lan Kwai Fong, and (also in Lan Kwai Fong) the *Wyndham Street Deli* (☎ 2522-3499) at 36 Wyndham St, Central – a smart and relaxing restaurant/deli *Euro-mart* (☎ 2810-8021), 27-29 Elgin St, is a European-style convenience store full of choice ingredients. *L'Épicerie* (☎ 2522-1577), 31-37 Mosque St, is a convenient source of delicatessen food if you're near the Mid-Levels.

Seibu Department Store, level LG1, Pacific Place, 88 Queensway (near Admiralty MTR station), has the largest stock of imported foods in Hong Kong, supplying a range of imported cheeses, breads and chocolates. Tucked away in a corner of the department store is the Pacific Wine Cellar. This is a good place to get wine, and there are frequent sales of wine by the case. It's open from 11 am until 8 pm.

Of special interest to chocolate addicts is *See's Candies,* with two stores in Central: B66 Gloucester Tower, the Landmark, 11 Pedder St; and shop 245, Pacific Place, Queensway (near Admiralty MTR station).

Sheung Wan

Chinese A popular destination for dim sum and Cantonese seafood is the *Ho Choi Seafood Restaurant* (☎ 2850-6722) at 287-291 Des Voeux Rd, Central. The menu is a maze of Chinese characters, so just join the fray and point. For the full aircraft-hanger Cantonese restaurant experience, try the *Hsin Kuang Restaurant* (☎ 2541-3233), a multi-storey affair next to the Western Market. The food isn't all that memorable, but the atmosphere is pure Hong Kong. Next door is the *Golden Snow Garden Restaurant* (☎ 2815-8128), steeped in the flavours of Shanghai, the Sichuan Province and Beijing. Dim sum is from 11 am to 3 pm.

Korean Sheung Wan is where the local Korean expats eat. The *Korea House Restaurant* (☎ 2544-0007) in the Korean Centre building, 119-21 Connaught Rd, is acknowledged as having some of the most authentic Korean barbecue, kimchi (grated vegetables mixed with other ingredients) and appetiser dishes in Hong Kong. Prices are very reasonable, too. Enter from Man Wa Lane. In the same building, the *Korea Garden* also seems to draw a steady crowd of Korean diners.

The Peak

International The food at the *Peak Cafe* (☎ 2849-7868) is always delicious. The menu includes Chinese, Indian, Thai and some western dishes (the Indian food is usually the best pick). But what really makes this place is the amazing setting: the vaulted ceiling, elegant decor and one of Hong Kong's best-looking bars. It's also perfect for outdoor dining and was voted by readers of *HK Magazine* in 1997 as Hong Kong's most romantic dining experience.

Across the road, housed in the hulking Peak Galleria, is the *Cafe Deco Bar and Grill* (☎ 2849-5111). This place also does the east meets west thing, though with neither the class nor the warmth of the Peak Cafe. Still the food is good, if overpriced, and you can't argue with the jaw-dropping view of Hong Kong and Kowloon, especially at night.

Wan Chai

Chinese Queue up behind Mr Spock at the *Cosmic Noodle Bar and Café* (☎ 2527-1686) at 8-12 Hennessy Rd, Wan Chai (see the Sheung Wan, Central and Admiralty map). In fact, noodles are just a few of the dishes cooked at this trendy establishment. Also on the list is a galaxy of burgers, salads, pancakes, sandwiches, cakes, muffins and desserts. Out of this world.

Johnston Rd in Wan Chai has a couple of well-frequented, very traditional restaurants. The dining experience at the *Lung Moon Restaurant* (☎ 2572-9888) has not changed a great deal since the 1950s, and the prices, while not at 1950s levels, are still reasonable. Not a lot of English is spoken there.

Nearby, the *Steam and Stew Inn* (☎ 2529-3913) at 21-23 Tai Wong St East serves up 'homestyle' Cantonese food, most of which is steamed, stewed or boiled. Pinned to the windows are the inevitable yellowing photos of the last governor, Chris Patten, chomping away on location. The food is good and MSG free; try the steamed mushroom stuffed with minced pork and crab meat sauce. The place is popular, so it may be a good idea to call ahead.

Excellent Beijing food can be had at *American* (☎ 2527-1000), 20 Lockhart Rd. Don't be put off by the name or by its grimy appearance; the restaurant has been around for over 50 years and most of the customers are regulars.

3.6.9. Restaurants are definitely worth a visit for reasonably-priced, traditional

Shanghai food and polite and resourceful (although a bit doddery) service. The tangy sweet and sour soup is thick with chunks of chicken, mushroom, tofu strips and peas – almost a meal in itself. The aubergine fried with garlic is excellent. There are two branches in Wan Chai: one on O'Brien Rd and the other on Queen's Rd East, across from the Hopewell Centre.

If you don't mind a steeper bill, *One Harbour Road* (☎ 2588-1234) is a beautifully designed Cantonese restaurant in the Grand Hyatt Hotel. In addition to a harbour view, you can choose from six pages of gourmet dishes and dine in spacious surroundings. Not a bad combination. You'll need little tempting to sample the pan-fried tofu stuffed with shrimp mousse, but go easy on the abalone unless you've endless credit. *Dynasty* (☎ 2802-8888) in the New World Harbour View Hotel is another gem; it has outstanding dim sum.

Yin King Lau Restaurant (☎ 2520-0106), 113 Lockhart Rd, is OK but will leave the real Sichuan food enthusiasts unmoved and yearning for more authentic cuisine. The best Sichuan food we found was actually in Macau, which is a bit of a way to go for the experience (see the Macau chapter for more details).

Australian & British While the cuisine of Australia and the UK have not taken the world by storm, Hong Kong has a dedicated following of expat fish and chip lovers. *Brett's Seafood* (☎ 2866-6608), 72-86B Lockhart Rd and 71-85B Hennessy Rd, is an Australian fast-food hangout that gets fine reviews.

For Hong Kong's best fish and chips, there's really no other contender to *Harry Ramsden's* (☎ 2832-9626) at 213 Queen's Rd East. The place is cheery, cheap and the food consistently good; the service is a bit slow and sloppy, but the fish is excellent. HK$98 gets you a fine haddock and chips and a soft drink. Brits trip over each other to get in. Highly recommended.

Filipino *Cinta* (☎ 2529-9752), 41 Hennessy

Rd, does excellent Filipino and Indonesian food. There is also a newer branch, *Cinta-J* (☎ 2529-4183) in the Malaysia building, 50 Gloucester Rd. Both are fairly expensive; calculate spending HK$300 per person. Both Cintas also offer late-night cocktail-lounge entertainment. Opening hours are from 11 am to 2 am.

Greek *Bacchus* (☎ 2529-9032), basement, 8 Hennessy Rd, is a place to go and have a good time; the food is deliciously different and the service friendly and upbeat. On some nights there is live entertainment and every Tuesday you can smash a plate in honour of Greek Party Night. The experience will cost you, but it's almost always worth it.

Indian *Jo Jo Mess Club* (☎ 2527-3776), 86 Johnston Rd, has great Indian food, including vegetarian dishes. There are also numerous vegetarian places nearby.

Ashoka (☎ 2891-8981) is on the ground floor, shop 1, Connaught Commercial building, 185 Wan Chai Rd. Prices are reasonable for big luncheon and dinner buffets.

Indonesian *Shinta* (☎ 2527-8780) on the 1st floor of the Kar Yau building, 36-44 Queen's Rd East, near the intersection with Hennessy Rd, is a dimly lit and laid-back restaurant that serves up a pretty good nasi goreng.

International For stunning views over Victoria Harbour and Central, fabulous decor and smooth design, try the new *Port Café* (☎ 2582-7731) in the Hong Kong Convention and Exhibition Centre. While not cheap, this is a stylish, sophisticated addition to the Hong Kong dining scene; a relaxed, quiet place to linger and eat scrumptious Euro-Italian dishes. It will also provide you with a good excuse to have a look around the Exhibition Centre.

On a similar note, *Trader's Grill* (☎ 2582-8888) is also in the Exhibition Centre. Trader's is a sleek, stylish and good-value restaurant kitted out with modern lines and efficient service. The emphasis is on

seafood and quiet dining, with only an occasional rattle of pans from the open kitchen.

The Open Kitchen (☎ 2827-2923) on the 6th floor of the Arts Centre, 2 Harbour Rd, is a new addition to this somewhat eclectic category of restaurants. It is a well-lit, smart restaurant serving Indian, Malaysian, Japanese and Italian food. If you're taking in a show or a play at the Arts Centre, this is an excellent spot to meet friends and have dinner.

Camargue (☎ 2525-7997), 128 Lockhart Rd, serves outstanding meals. *HK Magazine* routinely gives this place its highest 'not to be missed' rating, so perhaps you should take this advice. Near the Camargue restaurant, *bb's* (☎ 2529-7702), 114-120 Lockhart Rd, has a popular seafood menu.

Irish *Delaney's Ale* is about as close to real Irish pub grub and silky smooth Guinness draught as you're going to get outside of Dublin. There are two branches: in Wan Chai (☎ 2804-2880), 2nd floor, One Capital Place, 18 Luard Rd; and in Tsim Sha Tsui (☎ 2301-3980), 3-7 Prat Ave. The Tsim Sha Tsui pub, with an impressively long bar that stretches the length of the restaurant, has the better atmosphere. But food in both places is always reliable. Also on tap is Delaney's Irish Ale, which is specially brewed for the bar by the South China Brewing Co.

Italian You can try the pleasantly relaxed *Rigoletto's* (☎ 2527-7144) at 14 Fenwick St. *La Bella Donna* (☎ 2802-9907) on the 1st floor of the Shui On Centre, 6-8 Harbour Rd, is a less expensive option. The food is not spectacular, but you should walk away full and happy.

Mongolian *Kublai's* is a fast growing chain of places that does a refined version of Mongolian barbecue. Head to the food counter, pick out whatever meat, vegies, spices and sauces you want (there's a lot to choose from), hand it through a hole in the wall to the cook and return to your table to await your creation. It's all you can eat for HK$98 (lunch) and HK$138 (dinner), and for the taste and the experience, this is a fine price. It's best if you can go with a group, as it's a very social atmosphere. Diners are allotted time blocks (two hours after 9.30 pm) due to the high demand, so call ahead to book your spot. An Internet access area exists for those eager to fraternise with distant nomads on line. There are three branches: in Wan Chai (☎ 2529-9117) on the 3rd floor of One Capital Place, 18 Luard Rd; in Causeway Bay (☎ 2882-3282) at 1 Keswick St; and in Tsim Sha Tsui (☎ 2722-0733) at 55 Kimberley Rd.

Thai The *Chili Club* (☎ 2527-2872) is another old haunt of Thai aficionados. Some say it's slipped a few notches, but it's still a popular destination on the Hong Kong spice route. It's located on the 1st floor, 88 Lockhart Rd.

Nearby at 44 Hennessy Rd, *Thai Delicacy* (☎ 2527-2598) has some of Hong Kong's most authentic tasting Thai food, and at prices that few other places can match. The decor is strictly utilitarian, but you'll probably be too busy feasting to notice.

Vegetarian The *Vegetarian Garden* (☎ 2833-9128) at 128 Johnston Rd, one of the plentiful Buddhist restaurants in town, has a take away on the ground floor and a restaurant downstairs. It serves a great range of veggie dishes (with an English menu). Two dishes will cost about HK$100; the menu includes vegetarian squid, veggie sweet and sour pork and seaweed rolls.

Also in Wan Chai is the *Healthy Vegetarian Restaurant* (☎ 2527-3918), 51-53 Hennessy Rd, another Buddhist veggie establishment (sporting the Buddhist swastika on its business card) that is more popular with Chinese vegetarians.

Vietnamese *Saigon Beach* (☎ 2529-7823) at 66 Lockhart Rd is one of the best and most well known of the Vietnamese restaurants in this area. You'll walk in and say 'what a dump!' and you'll be right. If it's crowded and there are only one or two of

you, chances are you'll be sharing your table with strangers. Don't worry, it's all worth it. Prices are higher than you might expect for a place of this size and appearance, but if you don't want to eat there, there are plenty of others who will grab their seat.

Mixed Asian The *Viceroy* (☎ 2827-7777) on the 2nd floor of the Sun Hung Kai Centre, 30 Harbour Rd, Wan Chai, almost goes overboard on its mixed-Asian lunchtime buffet; a swish pot-pourri of Indian, Vietnamese, Thai and Indonesian dishes.

Fast Food Wan Chai has a good range of fast food. Choices include *Fairwood Fast Food*, 165 Wan Chai Rd, and *Domino's Pizza* (☎ 2833-6803), Canal Rd East. Domino's has no sit-down restaurant but delivers to any address within 2km (which in this case means Causeway Bay as well). *Hardee's* is at 101 Wan Chai Rd and *McDonald's* is in the CC Wu building, 302-308 Hennessy Rd. *Spaghetti House* has branches on the 1st floor, 68 Hennessy Rd, and on the 1st floor of 290 Hennessy Rd.

Oliver's Super Sandwiches are in force in the area, with numerous, easy-to-find branches. Wan Chai is also home to many thriving, hole-in-the-wall swift-sandwich parlours, popular with local gwailo workers during lunch break.

The shops are all pretty good and serve up great fillings and decent coffee. *Little Italy* has made a name for itself at 88 Lockhart Rd and is open till 6 am on Friday and Saturday; perfect for post-club munchies. There is another branch at 13 Lan Kwai Fong. *Fidi* (the name means 'make it swift' in Cantonese) does the same sort of fare at 87-91 Lockhart Rd.

Causeway Bay
Chinese *Sze Chuen Lau* (☎ 2891-9027), 466 Lockhart Rd, is a so-so Sichuan restaurant. Specialities include orange beef, smoked duck and chilli prawns. This place is open from noon until midnight and is extremely popular with the expat community. It's often full.

Much better, but more expensive, is the long-established *Red Pepper* (☎ 2577-3811) restaurant, 7 Lan Fong Rd. If you want to set your palate and set your tonsils aflame, try the sliced pork in chilli sauce, accompanied by Sichuan noodles. Spicy food lovers may also want to try the *Yunnan Kitchen* (☎ 2506-3309) in a vertical food court (you'll understand when you see it) on the 12th floor of the Times Square shopping complex. This place does a pretty good job of capturing the taste of Yunnan cuisine; specialities include Yunnan ham, fried Dali-style vermicelli and fresh prawns stuffed in bamboo. Like all the restaurants in Times Square, this one's a bit pricey, but the midday buffet is good value at HK$78.

Decent Hangzhou cuisine can be found at the *Shanghai Village* (☎ 2894-9705) at 9 Lan Fong Rd. Though often crowded, the restaurant has a quiet back room where you can sometimes escape the masses.

The one place in town to go for Taiwanese food is *Forever Green* (☎ 2890-3448). This place does a good job with traditional Taiwanese specialities like oyster omelette, fried bean curd and three-cup chicken *(sanbeiji)*. Prices are fairly high. There is another branch in Yau Ma Tei (☎ 2332-7183), 18 Cheung Lok St.

Burmese Hong Kong has only one place to sample Burmese food, *Rangoon Restaurant* (☎ 2893-0778), ground floor, 265 Gloucester Rd. Don't expect the place to echo old Burma; the trim plays second fiddle to the wide selection of Burmese food. Vegetarians will find more than enough on the menu to make the trip worthwhile.

Indonesian If you can ignore the decor of Formica and fake wood panelling, *Indonesian Restaurant* (☎ 2577-9981), 28 Leighton Rd, Causeway Bay, serves very authentic meals. The service won't have you jumping for joy, but the fried chicken and super-spicy roasted fish with chilli might.

The *Indonesia Padang Restaurant* (☎ 2576-1828), 85 Percival St, is another popular option.

International *W's Entrecote* (☎ 2506-0133), shop 1303, the Food Forum, Times Square, 1 Matheson St, does nothing other than serve steak. In the price is included bread, a salad with vinaigrette and as many french fries as you can squeeze onto your plate.

Japanese Causeway Bay caters to a large number of Japanese tourists and is perhaps the best area in Hong Kong to look for Japanese food. It is never cheap, but you can save a bit by looking in the basements of Japanese department stores. *Daimaru Household Square* on Kingston St and Gloucester Rd has takeaway Japanese food but nowhere to sit and eat.

Isshin (☎ 2506-2220) in Times Square is not cheap but does rate among the best of Hong Kong's Japanese restaurants. For a more down-to-earth atmosphere, try *Ichiban* (☎ 2890-7720), 21 Lan Fong Rd. It has the atmosphere of an *izakaya* (a Japanese-style pub), and seems to tolerate enthusiastic bouts of sake drinking. Though the service can be a bit negligent, the food does not disappoint.

Tomokazu (☎ 2833-6339) is in shop B, Lockhart House, 441 Lockhart Rd. For Japanese food, consider it a bargain. The set lunches for two people cost HK$200 and the amount of food is more than most people can finish.

Upon entering *Sui Sha Ya* (☎ 2838-1808) you will be greeted by a character in full Samurai armour. Once recovered from the shock, you can indulge in a wonderland of (expensive) Japanese delights. The restaurant is on the 1st floor, Lockhart House, 440 Jaffe Rd.

Korean *Korea Restaurant* (☎ 2577-9893), 58 Leighton Rd, is a good place for an authentic Korean barbecue. *Sorabol Korean Restaurant* (☎ 2881-6823), 99 Percival St, Causeway Bay, is the Korean's Korean restaurant, with helpful staff to boot. The barbecue is excellent. Also in Causeway Bay, in the Food Forum at Times Square, is *Arirang* (☎ 2506-3298), a large, brightly lit restaurant that may not be the place for a romantic ménage à deux, but great for a party.

It's a barbecue outfit, and why not; these are a lot of fun. Get a plate-load of *segyubsahl gooi* (pork belly slices) or the *boolgogi* (marinated beef slices) and sizzle up. Arirang has another branch at 210 The Gateway, 25 Canton Rd, Tsim Sha Tsui (☎ 2956-3288).

Vegetarian *Vegi Food Kitchen* (☎ 2890-6660), ground floor, Highland Mansions, 8 Cleveland St, has a sign warning you not to bring meat or alcohol onto the premises. If you're carrying a meat loaf in your backpack, check it in at the door.

The excellent and usually packed out *Kung Tak Lam* (☎ 2890-3127) at 31 Yee Wo St appears to hold hostage most of Hong Kong's vegetarian population. with a huge range of inexpensive, well-prepared Shanghai vegetarian food. The dishes are prepared to resemble meat in appearance and texture, but without a shred of the real thing. The mock goose, mock duck and sweet and sour fish are recommended. All the vegetables are grown organically, it's MSG free and the only drawback is it's a bit noisy. There is also a branch in Tsim Sha Tsui (☎ 2367-7881) at 45-47 Carnarvon Rd. The *Fat Mun Lam Vegetarian Kitchen* (☎ 2577-5518) at 43 Jardine's Bazaar is said to have good dishes, but all the places look about the same.

Vietnamese *Yuet Hing Yuen* (☎ 2832-2863), 17 Cannon St, makes few concessions to decor, but the food is a triumph. It's all a bit chaotic and noisy, but the price is reasonable and you could well find yourself going back for seconds. The deep-fried butter and garlic chicken wings is a simple and sure choice. If it's packed out, just across the way is the *Yin Ping Vietnamese Restaurant* (☎ 2832-9038) at 24 Cannon St.

Mixed Asian The 'Food Forum' occupies the top three floors of the Times Square shopping mall and is dedicated entirely to restaurants (expensive ones!). From the 9th floor of the shopping mall you can catch the escalator up. There are two or three restaurants on each floor.

The 10th floor contains the *Chrysanthemum Seafood Restaurant* (☎ 2506-3033) and *Elegant Banyan Restaurant* (☎ 2506-2866).

The 11th floor Times Square restaurants specialise in mixed Asian dishes. You can contact the *Golden Elephant Thai Restaurant* (☎ 2506- 1333), *Arirang* Korean restaurant (☎ 2506-3298) and *Roy's at the New China Max* (☎ 2506-2282).

The top floor of Times Square is home to the *Nam Garden Chinese Restaurant* and *Yunnan Kitchen*.

Breakfast *Delifrance* is located in The Marketplace, in the basement of Times Square shopping mall (near the MTR station entrance). While lunch and dinner are served there, the emphasis is on croissants, pastry, soup, sandwiches and coffee.

Fast Food The following fast-food outlets can be found in Causeway Bay: *Jack in the Box*, 53 Paterson St; *KFC*, 40 Yee Wo St; and *McDonald's* in the McDonald's building (no kidding) at 46 Yee Wo St and at basement 2, Mitsukoshi Department Store, 500 Hennessy Rd.

Ice Cream *Haagen-Dazs* has small shops in the Marketplace, a shopping arcade in the basement of Times Square, and in Kirin Plaza, Kingston St.

Happy Valley
One of the biggest bargains in Hong Kong is the vegetarian cafeteria on the 6th floor of the *Adventist Hospital* at 40 Stubbs Rd. Opening hours are short: breakfast 6 to 7.30 am, lunch noon to 1.30 pm and dinner 5 to 6.30 pm.

Quarry Bay
The Continental (☎ 2563-2209) in Quarry Bay is a proud example of Australian restaurateurship in this far-flung outpost of the Australian food empire. *HK Magazine* heaped praise upon praise on its carrot soup and rigatoni pasta. An imaginative, no-holds barred menu keeps all and sundry drifting back. The restaurant is on the ground floor, 2 Hoi Wan St. To get there, take the MTR

to Quarry Bay, take the exit to Tong Chong St and Devon House. Hoi Wan St is near the end of Tong Chong St on the left.

Q (☎ 2960-0994) at 33 Tong Chong St, is a reasonably recent arrival that has attracted some attention for its good value, ever-changing continental menu (with strong Italian tendencies).

Shek O

Black Sheep (☎ 2809-2021), 452 Shek O Village, is an extremely popular restaurant with an international menu.

Stanley

If you can't resist Indian food, *The Curry Pot* (☎ 2899-0811), 6th floor, 90B Stanley Main St, can oblige. *Pepperoni's* (☎ 2813-8605), 64 Stanley Main St, is right in the bustling market area. While not as famous as its cousin in Sai Kung, nevertheless, the pizzas are very good. *Domino's Pizza* (☎ 2813-9239) has established an outlet at 30A Stanley Main St.

Stanley's Oriental (☎ 2813-9988), 90B, Stanley Main St, serves up Chinese as well as a whole host of other Asian dishes. A whole concoction of flavours makes the waterfront location even more unique and memorable.

Lucy's (☎ 2813-9055), 64 Stanley Main St, wins consistent praise for its low prices and light weight menu of European delights.

In terms of high-priced, high-class establishments, *Stanley's French Restaurant* (☎ 2813-8873), 86 Stanley Main St, with its seaside setting, attentive staff and, above all, fine food will more than justify the trip out to Stanley. Dishes include spinach and lobster bisque, braised veal shank in creamy potato puree and a vegetarian set lunch.

Another place with a memorable waterfront setting and fairly good food is *Stanley's Oriental Restaurant* (☎ 2813-9988), 90B Stanley Main St. It's a good place to relax with a drink, though it may take some time before it's brought to you. Bear in mind that you're paying as much for the view as for the food.

Tables 88 (☎ 2813-6262), 88 Stanley Village Rd, is housed in what used to be the local police station. Though the building dates back to 1854, you wouldn't guess so from the love-it or hate-it decor. The menu is continental and the food is worth the price. The restaurant is diagonally opposite the Stanley bus station.

Repulse Bay

If you're in the mood for dim sum or a fancy Cantonese meal you can try the *Hei Fung Terrace Chinese Restaurant* (☎ 2812-2622), 1st floor, Repulse Bay Shopping Arcade.

The Verandah (☎ 2812-2722), 109 Repulse Bay Rd, serves continental food, although you may have to book well in advance as it's popular (and rightly so).

Travellers will be pleased to find one of Hong Kong's best delicatessens, *Oliver's Delicatessen* (☎ 2812-7739), at 109 Repulse Bay Rd.

Aberdeen

Floating Restaurants There are three floating restaurants moored in Aberdeen Harbour, all specialising in seafood. The food gets bad press and these outfits are not really recommended except as a spectacle. Dinner will cost about HK$200 and upwards.

The best of the floating restaurants is the *Jumbo Floating Restaurant* (☎ 2553-9111), which also serves relatively cheap dim sum from 7.30 am to 5 pm. The adjacent *Floating Palace Restaurant* (☎ 2554-0513) also does dim sum but is more expensive. Nearby is the *Tai Pak Floating Restaurant* (☎ 2552-5953) which has no dim sum but plenty of seafood. Another alternative is to catch a ferry over to Sok Kwu Wam on Lamma Island and sample both its seafood and atmosphere (see the Outlying Islands chapter for details).

ENTERTAINMENT

Central, Admiralty & Soho

Cinemas There are only a couple of cinemas in Central geared towards English-language films. A good one is *Queen's* (☎ 2522-7036), Luk Hoi Tung building (rear entrance), 31 Queen's Rd.

UA Queensway (☎ 2869-0322) at Pacific Place in Admiralty is the plushest cinema in Hong Kong and has the best sound system. This cinema has a large number of screens and gets the best presentations. It's also very easy to get to; just take the MTR to Admiralty. Don't forget that you can buy tickets on your credit card through Cityline (☎ 2317-6666) and collect them at the theatre before the performance.

Lan Kwai Fong Running off D'Aguilar St is a narrow L-shaped alley closed to cars. This is Lan Kwai Fong, and along with neighbouring streets and alleys it is Hong Kong's No 1 eating and drinking venue, despite the challenge from Soho. The street has changed over the years. Refugees from Chungking Mansions can no longer afford the pricey food, and many of the bars and discos have moved to Wan Chai. The clientele tends to be upwardly mobile, sporting cellular phones, trendy suits and slick cars. Nevertheless, the people you see walking the street are mixed: businessmen in suits hand-in-hand with Filipino bar girls, fashionably dressed western women in slit gowns and high heels, backpackers in sandals and T-shirts; African traders, Russian sailors and Chinese yuppies (invariably called 'chuppies').

There is no place quite like it in the world. Disco music thumps in the background everywhere, the alleys are packed with people and everybody is there to see and be seen. Just how Lan Kwai Fong ever got started is a mystery. Equally uncertain is how it will end. High rents, the tourist downturn and a slow drift of restaurants and clientele west to the nearby Soho axis could be the beginning of the end for Lan Kwai Fong.

Some night spots in this stratified part of town have a dress code, which basically means no shorts, sandals or T-shirts. Many travellers have run afoul of this rule, particularly during the scorching summer months. If you demand to be comfortable, you'll just have to forego the most chic clubs. Otherwise, carry a fancy set of clothes and change in the nearest rest room or phone booth.

Lan Kwai Fong became world famous (or rather, infamous) on New Years' Eve, 31 December 1992. The street was so thoroughly mobbed with drunken revellers that 21 people were trampled to death and many others were injured. Since then, the authorities have instituted 'crowd control'. The number of customers permitted inside a business establishment is supposedly limited, sidewalk cafes have theoretically been banned (some continue to resist), the authorities are getting very tough with liquor licences and so on. Some places were judged unsafe and closed, and business has definitely experienced a downturn. Oddly, the bars have retorted by moving even further upmarket and squeezing more dollars out of a smaller crowd. Halloween is another festival that is taken seriously in Hong Kong, with Lan Kwai Fong as the focal point for party-goers.

Discos & Clubs *JP Encounter* (☎ 2521-0309) on the ground floor of the Bank of America Tower, Harcourt Rd, Central, is a stylish place with a nifty spiral staircase and tremendous chandeliers; the faithful flock to the DJs' ministrations like dazed survivors of the Monday to Friday grind. The DJs are pure skill and wacky theme nights keep it fresh. The venue is about to be overhauled. Multi-media gadgets, a new sound system, and drum 'n bass and 'ambient trance chill-out' areas are to be installed. Cover on Friday is HK$130 for men (plus two beers); women are free; cover on Saturday costs HK$100 for everyone. Beer is HK$55 a bottle.

CE Top (☎ 2541-5524) is a rooftop club hosting a medley of club nights including a mix of funk, jazz, disco, drum 'n bass, hip hop and raregroove. It has quite a strong gay leaning (but that's not to say it's not for straights). Follow the crowds up the hill and into the lift to the 9th floor, 37-43 Cochrane St, Central.

The area around Soho is following in the footsteps of Lan Kwai Fong and fast becoming a restaurant and entertainment centre for Hong Kong. It has a wild club scene. At the time of writing, four new clubs were poised to throw open the doors to the funky creatures of the night, including a Cuban nightclub.

Club Rosa (☎ 2801-5885) at Zona Rosa, 1 Lan Kwai Fong, Central, has DJs with a vengeance to play thumping house on one floor and cool funk on the other. It opens at 11 pm on Friday and Saturday. Also in Lan Kwai Fong, *Dillingers Steak House* (☎ 2521-2202) at 38-44 D'Aguilar St has an entry-free disco on Friday and Saturday from 11 pm.

California (☎ 2521-1345) is a bit pretentious, but really packs in the crowds, especially when the tables are cleared off the dance floor. Thursday, Friday and Saturday has no cover charge, but you'll be stung viciously on the beer (HK$60 a bottle). No shorts (trousers, not spirits).

There are a few other bars in Lan Kwai Fong with minute dance floors the size of an average telephone box.

Rock & Jazz The *Jazz Club* (☎ 2845-8477) is on the 2nd floor, California Entertainment building, Lan Kwai Fong. This venue has long been the sole salvation for true music lovers, and many jazz greats have stood on its stage. But the club also books rock, blues, folk and other kinds of acts, both local and foreign. The club is not very big, so it helps to book tickets well in advance for the bigger names. Drinks are murderously expensive (HK$52 a bottle), but there's a two-for-one happy hour from 7 to 9 pm that helps soften the blow. Tickets for local acts are around HK$100, and for overseas bands are usually anywhere from HK$200 to HK$300 (half price for members).

Except for the Jazz Club, Lan Kwai Fong doesn't have any other really serious music venues. *F-Stop* (☎ 2868-9607) is a tiny place at 14 Lan Kwai Fong that squeezes bands onto its minuscule stage on Friday and Saturday nights from 10 pm. This place is really for the teenage set; upstairs is covered with graffiti and hung together with

string and sealing wax. You can see its huge neon guitar a mile away. *Mad Dogs* (☎ 2810-1000), a rollicking British-style pub at 1 D'Aguilar St, has music three or four nights a week, usually in the form of a solo singer/guitarist. The bar has a Tsim Sha Tsui counterpart, *Mad Dogs Kowloon* (☎ 2301-2222), which also books live music occasionally.

Up on Lower Albert Rd, just on the border of the Lan Kwai Fong quadrant, is the *Dragon's Back Gallery* at the Fringe Club (☎ 2521-7251). This is the venue for a whole medley of trendy sounds from Latin jazz and mainstream jazz to rock and pop, blues, country and folk. Most nights are still free.

The *Rickshaw Jazz Room* (☎ 2525-3977) is at 22 Robinson Rd in the Mid-Levels. It features free jazz, blues, country and folk and big band jazz sounds. Give the staff a call and see what gigs are booked.

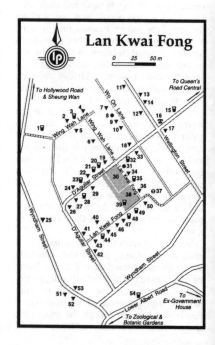

The *Fringe Club* (☎ 2521-7251), 2 Lower Albert Rd, is an excellent pub known for cheap beer and an avant-garde atmosphere. There is live music every night featuring various local folk and rock musicians.

Pubs & Bars Some of the bars are pretty pretentious (these are easy to spot). One place that bucks this trend is *Club 64* (☎ 2523-2801), 12 Wing Wah Lane. Apparently named after the Tiananmen Square massacre (64 stands for the date of the massacre on the fourth of the sixth month, or June 4th), this is still a pretty funky place to hang out. As a sign of the times, if ever there was one, the graffiti (in English and

Chinese) that used to cover the walls has been whitewashed over. Despite the new political hegemony, this is still one of the best bars in town for non-poseurs, angry young people and those who want simple, unfussy fun. From 10 am to 8 pm, Club 64 also has one of Hong Kong's better happy hours. Pints of draught beer are HK$21 and bottles cost HK$18.

More upmarket and featuring an open veranda seating area is *Le Jardin* (☎ 2526-2717) at 10 Wing Wah Lane. This is a great bar, with loads of atmosphere; a place where people seem to enjoy themselves. If you walk out of Club 64 and turn right, you will see some stairs in the corner

---

Lan Kwai Fong
蘭桂坊

PLACES TO EAT
2 Co Co Curry House;
The Curry Club
椰椰咖喱、咖喱屋
4 Bon Appetit
Vietnamese Restaurant
好開胃快餐廳
5 Good Luck Thai Restaurant
鴻運泰國美食
6 Chop Chop Café
7 Papillon
蝶軒
9 Trio's Restaurant
採美國龍蝦牛扒之家
10 Pearl Vietnamese
Restaurant
明珠越南餐廳
11 Greenlands India Club
寶軒印度餐廳
12 Yung Kee Restaurant
鏞記酒家
13 Fukuki
福喜日本料理
14 Tai Woo
太湖海鮮城
17 The Source of Health
18 Kiyotaki
清瀧日本料理

19 Beirut
22 Tutto Meglio
24 Al's Diner
25 Ashoka
雅適閣
26 Supatra's
27 Dillingers Steak House
29 McDonald's
麥當勞
30 California Tower
加州大廈
33 Haagen-Dazs
喜見達
34 Zona Rosa; Club Rosa
36 Midnight Express
38 California Entertainment
Building
加樂大廈花串日本
料理寶軒印度餐廳
40 HK Baguette
41 Vino and Olio Deli
42 Va Bene
43 Tokio Joes
45 Little Italy
46 Tutta Luna
47 Post 97
50 Yorohachi
喜八日本料理
51 Wyndham Street Thai

52 Wyndham St Deli
53 La Bodega

PUBS/CLUBS
1 Le Jardin
3 Club 64
15 Mad Dogs
20 Schnurrbart
21 Bit Point
23 Hardy's
28 Yelt's Inn
32 D'Aguilar 26
39 Café des Artistes
44 F-Stop
48 Club 1997
49 La Dolce Vita
54 Fringe Club

OTHER
8 Mountain Folkcraft
高山民藝
16 Hong Kong Telecom
Service Centre
31 Flower Stalls
花攤
37 Public Toilets
公用廁所

of Wing Wah Lane leading up to Le Jardin.

You too could get a huge, red nose and a dodgy heart in need of a triple bypass drinking at *Yelt's Inn* (☎ 2524-7796), 17-22 D'Aguilar St. This place boasts Russian vodka, a bubbly party atmosphere and extremely loud music.

Post 97 (☎ 2810-0616), 9 Lan Kwai Fong, is a very comfortable eating and drinking spot. During the daytime it's more of a coffee shop, and you can sit for hours taking advantage of the excellent rack of western magazines and newspapers. It gets very packed at night (and the lights are dimmed to discourage reading at this time), but it's a fine place to take a date.

Next door in the same building and under the same management is *Club 1997* (☎ 2810-9333), known for its really fine Mediterranean food. This place has recently become 'members only' and the policy is strictly enforced, so short-term visitors can forget it. There is a small (read 'puny') dance floor.

If you're a fan of German beer, both *Schnurrbart* (☎ 2523-7436) and *Bit Point* (☎ 2523-4700) take the time and effort to draw you a brew the right way. Most of the draught beers are Pilseners, but both have a fine selection of bottled brews as well. Schnurrbart also has a dizzying choice of German and Austrian schnapps (ask for the special menu). Bit Point has occasionally been known to serve beer in a huge glass boot.

Across the street in California Tower, *Sherman's* bar and restaurant (☎ 2801-4946) has had a refit and emerged in its new incarnation as a chromed example of aluminium chic, bathed in cold, opaque lighting. Surgeons and architects will find it fascinating.

Hardy's (☎ 2522-4448), 35 D'Aguilar St, is a rowdy watering hole where some of the patrons occasionally get up on stage to demonstrate some talent (or lack of it). *Dillingers* (☎ 2521-2202) at 38-44 D'Aguilar St is a plush steak house with a saloon bar.

Just down the street, *La Dolce Vita* (☎ 2810-8098) is as sweet as life gets. This is where the gorgeous young things go to watch each other and be watched. Go there to check out the latest in Hong Kong fashions. *Oscar's* (☎ 2804-6561) is also trendy.

The *Milk Bar* (☎ 2521-2202), Commercial building, 38-44 D'Aguilar St, with its outdoor terrace and long bar, makes for a smooth addition to the Lan Kwai Fong scene.

Up at the top of the hill, just outside Lan Kwai Fong proper is *La Bodega* (☎ 2877-5472). Though also a fully fledged, sit-down restaurant, this place has tasty tapas and a wine bar in the basement.

The *California* (☎ 2521-1345), ground floor, California Entertainment building, is perhaps the most expensive bar mentioned in this book. A friend of mine from California was once refused admission because he 'was dressed like a Californian'. Leave the beach clothes behind; it's long trousers, 'proper' footwear and collared shirts only. Skirts are acceptable, but only for women. It also has a dance floor.

Other Central Pubs & Grub Outside Lan Kwai Fong the bars all get a bit uniform and unexciting. One area that will no doubt see some action and invention will be Soho, the new restaurant ghetto around Staunton and Elgin Sts (on the other side of Victoria Prison from Lan Kwai Fong). Already home to a few bars and a queue of eateries, this part of town will (much to the horror of locals) probably continue in its parabolic pursuit of fun. Voted by readers of *HK Magazine* as the best new bar in Hong Kong in 1997, *Staunton's Bar & Café* (☎ 2973-6611), 10-12 Staunton St, is swish, cool and on the ball. The only problem is that the bar only has a conditional alcohol license: conditional on not serving any of the demon stuff after 11 pm. The situation will probably have changed by the time you read this. Also on Staunton St is *Club 1911* (☎ 2810-6681), an elegant, refined bar steeped in colonial nostalgia. Near the Mid-Levels escalator at 39 Hollywood Rd is the *Globe*

(☎ 2543-1941), hugely popular and packed out with expats.

The *Hard Rock Cafe* (☎ 2377-8168), Swire House, 11 Chater Rd, Central, does its happy hour from 3 to 7 pm. The *Mad Dogs Pub* (☎ 2810-1000), 1 D'Aguilar St, is just off trendy Lan Kwai Fong. It's a big Australian-style pub serving pub grub and drinks.

LA Cafe (☎ 2526-6863), ground floor, shop 2, Lippo Centre, 89 Queensway (near Admiralty MTR station), has a large, loyal following of late-night revellers. The mostly Mexican luncheons are not to be overlooked either, but it isn't cheap.

The *Bull and Bear* (☎ 2525-7436) on the ground floor of Hutchison House, 10 Harcourt Rd, sounds like a place for Wall St stockbrokers, but is in fact the most British-style pub in Hong Kong. English licensing laws do not apply, however, so you can go on drinking after 11 pm. All the standard pub fare (bangers and mash, mushy peas, meat pies) are available, along with a decent selection of bitters and lagers.

Hotel bars are ideal if you want a more sedate experience and a higher class of service. Try the *Captain's Bar* (☎ 2522-0111) on the ground floor of the Mandarin Oriental Hotel. After 5 pm you can't enter wearing either jeans or a collarless shirt. If you do have the right attire (and plenty of money) it's worth going in there just to drink an ice cold draught beer from one of the Mandarin's chilled silver mugs.

For the view alone, you can't beat the *Harlequin Bar* (☎ 2522-0111) on the Mandarin Oriental's 24th floor, especially at night. See Victoria Harbour in all its lighted glory while sipping your HK$65 drink. Still, the money buys not only the drink and the view but some outstanding service as well. This is a good place to go when you feel like being pampered.

Portico (☎ 2523-8893), lower ground floor, Citibank Plaza, 3 Garden Rd, opens early enough to serve breakfast. On weekdays it's basically muffins, salad and pizza. The atmosphere dramatically changes on Saturday night, however, when (from around

10 pm) live bands give rave performances. This place claims to have the longest bar in Hong Kong. It is open Monday to Saturday, from 7 am until midnight, but is closed on Sunday. *Pomeroy's* (☎ 2523-4772) is a popular hotspot on level 3 of the Pacific Place in Admiralty.

If you need to get high when you drink, take the lift up to the 56th floor of the Island Shangri-La Hotel to visit *Cyrano's* (☎ 2820-8591). The bartenders are skilled – a necessity given some of the fussy corporate types who hang out there. Good views and live jazz are a feature there and, given all this, prices are not too outrageous. It's open from 6 pm to around 2 am.

Wine Bars Had enough San Miguel and beer nuts? Hong Kong isn't the best place to head to if you want to escape the crowds, but there are some fine wine bars that will at least provide more comfort.

Brown's Wine Bar (☎ 2868-0475) in Exchange Square II, Central, has a huge wine list. *Uncle Eric's Vintage Wine Bar*, 19 On Lan St, Central, is pretty minute but a cosy spot for a quiet chat and a relaxing drink. *The Wine Room* (☎ 2525-5111) in the Furama Kempinski Hotel, 1 Connaught Rd, Central, has made a name for itself, although it only has a small selection.

Gay Bars A new bar, *Zip* (☎ 2523-3595) at 2 Glenealy Rd, takes in most of the action. Zip has gone to the length of installing an outdoor waterfall. It gets very crowded on weekends. Later in the evening, revellers usually move on to *Propaganda* (☎ 2868-1316), 1 Hollywood Rd. As Propaganda's ads are proud to proclaim, this is Hong Kong's premier gay meat market. Cover is free from Monday to Wednesday, HK$80 on Thursday, HK$110 on Friday and HK$150 on Saturday. This is a newer and larger version of a nightclub which used to operate in Wyndham St.

CE Top (☎ 2541-5524) on the 9th floor, 37-43 Cochrane St, Central, is not exclusively gay, but it's another glittering spangle on the gay map of Hong Kong.

Considerably more subdued is *Petticoat Lane* (☎ 2973-0642), 2 Tun Wo Lane, Central (where the Mid-Levels escalator cuts between Lyndhurst Terrace and Hollywood Rd). It's a small place with French decor, and is more suited to chatting than bopping. It was voted as Hong Kong's best gay bar by readers of *HK Magazine* in 1997, despite the fact that it attracts a lot of straight customers as well.

Club 97 (☎ 2586-1103 or 2810-9333), 9 Lan Kwai Fong, has a gay happy hour on Friday nights, with half price drinks and shows. Unfortunately, it is a members only club, although members are allowed to take along one person.

Wan Chai

Cinemas For movie fanatics, some cultural organisations show films occasionally. *Alliance Française* (French Institute; ☎ 2527-7825, fax 2865-3478) at 123 Hennessy Rd is one place to try. Also contact the *Goethe Institut* (German Cultural Centre; ☎ 2802-0088, fax 2802-4363) on the 14th floor of the Hong Kong Arts Centre, 2 Harbour Rd.

Wan Chai has other cinemas specialising in English-language features. These include *Cine-Art House* (☎ 2827-5015), Sun Hung Kai Centre, 30 Harbour Rd; the *New Imperial* (☎ 2893-9612), 220A Wan Chai Rd; and the *South Pacific* (☎ 2575-7363) at the South Pacific Hotel, 23 Morrison Hill Rd.

Discos & Clubs The other hub of the club galaxy revolves around Wan Chai. With a well-established reputation for marathon dances, this is where the late night crowd settles in for the wee hours. Wan Chai is one of the first destinations for naval sailors stopping in Hong Kong for a little R&R. The endless neon is mainly propped up by seedy bars (with the odd snappy watering hole), hostess clubs, hole-in-the-wall sandwich parlours and the occasional dance venue.

Neptune Disco (☎ 2528-3808), basement, Computer Centre, 54 Lockhart Rd, is a Wan Chai institution. Slightly seedy, decidedly downmarket and completely unpretentious, Neptune gets going when other clubs shut at 3 am. People mainly go to dance, and if you're not dancing this is not the place to be. Happy hour is from 4 to 8 pm and entry is free.

Over at 98 Jaffe Rd, *Neptune II* (☎ 2865-2238) lacks the character of its progenitor, but is open just as late (until around 7 am). There's a HK$140 cover charge for men that includes one drink. Women need only pay HK$50. In the same league as Neptune is *Big Apple* (☎ 2529-3461), 20 Luard Rd, thumping to club classics every weekend. It was recently elected as Hong Kong's raunchiest nightspot. Free entry.

bb's bar (☎ 2529-7702) hasn't put a foot wrong since it opened. The Blue Lizard Lounge, upstairs, has extended the bar's credibility with its Saturday dance sessions of drum'n bass and acid jazz (11 pm until late). On Sunday live jazz is performed from 8 pm. Entry free.

The Viceroy (☎ 2827-7777), 2nd floor, Sun Hung Kai Centre, is the scene of one-off live bands, the Punchline Comedy Club and Salsa nights. Discover Salsa and a whole new world from 9.45 pm onwards for HK$120. Dance parties at the Viceroy have become events to be seen.

Looking for something a bit more downmarket? You can't go lower than the *New Makati* (☎ 2866-3928), a sleazy pick-up joint at 100 Lockhart Rd, complete with dimly lit booths. Cover charge is HK$70 for men, HK$40 for women, and includes one drink.

Voted as 'Best pick-up Bar' by readers of *HK Magazine* in 1997, *Joe Bananas* (☎ 2529-1811) is a source of contention: some people rave about it, while others blast it as the trendiest, yuppiest meat market in town. There's a cover charge of HK$100 on Friday and Saturday, after 9 pm for men and after 1 am for women. The bar has two for one cocktails on Wednesday and there's a daily happy hour from 11.30 am to 10 pm. Patrons must be at least 21 years of age.

Rick's Cafe (☎ 2528-1812) at 78-82 Jaffe Rd has a new branch in Wan Chai that seems just as popular as the original in Tsim Sha Tsui. Sunday nights are energised doses of soul, rhythm and blues and hip hop laced with two-for-one alcoholic beverages. Lasses get a free shooter with every drink. Free entry.

Carnegie's (☎ 2866-6289), 55 Lockhart Rd, keeps a lot of rock memorabilia, which makes it all seem a bit Hard Rock Cafe-ish. From 9 pm on Friday and Saturday, however, the place fills up with revellers. Cover is HH$50, including one free drink. Bands are booked to play two nights a week (usually Thursday and Sunday).

Manhattan/Westworld (☎ 2824-0380) mainly draws a Cantonese crowd. Strobe lights, smoke machines and techno-pop set the scene. Manhattan/Westworld is located in the New World Harbour View Hotel in Wan Chai. Cover charge is HK$88 from Sunday to Thursday, and HK$140 on Friday and Saturday, including one free drink.

Long-awaited newcomer *Dusk till Dawn,* on the ground floor of 76 Jaffe Rd, has recently opened and is quickly making a lot of friends.

Rock & Jazz For many years the *Wanch* (☎ 2861-1621) in Wan Chai was one of the few venues for live bands. There's a lot more competition now, but the Wanch still has live music seven nights a week from 9 pm. The selection centres mainly on rock and folk, with the occasional solo singer/guitarist thrown in. Jam night is on Wednesday at 10 pm, so take your guitar along and join in with that live 'Freebird' you always wanted to do. Prices there are better than most places, and are discounted during the particularly good happy hours, which run from 3 to 9 pm daily and 1 to 4 am Friday and Saturday nights.

JJ's (☎ 2588-1234) at the Grand Hyatt, 1 Harbour Rd, Wan Chai, hosts regular appearances by Hawkeye, a funky five piece from Boston, and other bands. Cover is HK$100 from Monday to Thursday, and HK$200 on Friday and Saturday.

bb's (☎ 2529-7702), 114-120 Lockhart Rd, Wan Chai, has Sunday jazz nights (from 8 pm) and no cover charge. Call them for details.

Pubs & Bars Most of the bars are clustered along Jaffe and Lockhart Rds at the western end of Wan Chai. On the whole, these serve up decent pub grub and continental food, often with a good range of choice. Some are hybrid bars/restaurants/clubs. Like Lan Kwai Fong, on Friday and Saturday night this area is crawling with party goers and the terminally lonely looking for a place to drink or dance, or both. It's also fairly happening during the week.

Knowledgeable beer drinkers will probably like *bb's* (☎ 2529-7702), 114 Lockhart Rd. It has on tap several beers custom-brewed for it by Hong Kong's only microbrewery, the South China Brewing Company. The beer is outstanding, and in addition there is an enviable collection of bottled imports.

Delaney's Ale (☎ 2804-2880) is an authentic Irish pub incongruously located on the 2nd floor of the shiny One Capital Place building, 18 Luard Rd. This place is immensely popular, so you'll probably have to battle the pressing crowds to get to the bar. But it's worth the effort, as you can order a draught Guinness Stout poured with the care and expertise it deserves (which also makes it expensive). Delaney's Ale also has a house brew, Delaney's own real Ale, made by the South China Brewing Company. The food is good (the kitchen goes through 400 kilos of potatoes a week).

Pool players can chalk cues at the nearby *Flying Pig* (☎ 2865-3730), 2nd floor, 81-85 Lockhart Rd, an entertaining little place all decked out in aviation memorabilia and aircraft lounge seats. The pool table gets shunted aside for dancing on the weekend. Downstairs from the Flying Pig is *Ridgeways* (☎ 2866-6608), which also has a pool table.

Scattered around the area are several Tudor-style pubs with names like the *Horse & Groom, Royal Arms, Horse & Carriage,* and so on. This pub certainly doesn't feel English, but it's good enough for a (relatively) cheap beer and perhaps a plate of greasy chips.

For those who came to see the Wan Chai of Suzie Wong, there are a few girlie bars feeding off the nostalgia of tourists. Most are littered along Lockhart Rd, where the proprietors will lynch you as you walk by and march you, half-nelson applied, into a tacky world of pink neon and extortionate beer. Only for the terminally sad. The most popular of the lot is probably *Country Club 88* (☎ 2861-1009) on Luard Rd which seems to always fill every stool around its circular bar.

Finally, if you want to spend lots of money on drinks, head over to the *Champagne Bar* (☎ 2588-1234) at the Grand Hyatt Hotel, 1 Harbour Rd, in Wan Chai North. It can cost up to HK$400 for a single glass of champagne.

Hostess Clubs If your idea of a good time is paying HK$2000 to a topless waitress for a simple conversation, you should either a) have your head examined, or b) visit a hostess bar in Wan Chai. Assuming you can find a place to park the Rolls, places to check out include the *Mandarin Palace* (☎ 2575-6551), 24 Marsh Rd, and the *New Tonnochy* (☎ 2575-4276), 1 Tonnochy Rd.

Causeway Bay

Cinemas Causeway Bay is packed with cinemas, which include the following:

Jade
  (☎ 2882-1805) Paterson and Great George Sts
New York
  (☎ 2838-7380) 475 Lockhart Rd
Pearl
  (☎ 2822-2803) PJ Plaza, Paterson St, between Kingston and Great George Sts
President
  (☎ 2833-1937) 517 Jaffe Rd
UA Times Square
  (☎ 2506-2822) Times Square Complex
Windsor
  (☎ 2882-2621) Windsor House, Gloucester Rd and Great George St

Pubs & Bars Causeway Bay is relatively tame at night. But there are still some bars that do a thriving business, supported in part by those who are sick of hanging out in Lan Kwai Fong and Wan Chai.

The Jump (☎ 2832-9007) is a neat and spacious American style bar/restaurant with funky high seats. It has a mammoth menu of barbecued burgers and Cajun and Mexican cuisine. Usually hopping on the weekend, there is a HK$100 cover charge on Friday and Saturday night after 11 pm, which includes one free drink. It's located on the 7th floor, Causeway Bay Plaza II, 463 Lockhart Rd.

There are a few bars located in the Times Square shopping complex that also seem able to draw a steady crowd. *Roy's* at the new China Max (☎ 2506-2282) on the 11th floor works hard to keep its customers entertained and often has live music.

In Times Square, *La Placita* (☎ 2506-3308) has an eight piece band and more unique offerings like Brazilian dance shows (you don't see much of that in Hong Kong). There's also another version of *Oscar's* (☎ 2861-1511) packed out with suits at Podium 3, World Trade Centre, 280 Gloucester Rd.

Considerably more subdued, but also fairly unusual, is the very small *Brecht's Circle* (☎ 2577-9636), 123 Leighton Rd, an arty kind of place given more to intimate, cerebral conversation than serious raging. The decor is pseudo-German, and includes oversized portraits of Mao and Hitler.

For those with more mainstream inclinations, the *King's Arms* (☎ 2895-6557), squeezed in between two glass and steel office blocks at Sunning Plaza, Sunning Rd, is an old standby for many residents. The service can be pretty frosty, but it's still easy to stay there for several hours.

Another favourite expat hangout, for some reason, is the *Dicken's Bar* (☎ 2894-8888), located in the basement of the Excelsior Hotel, 281 Gloucestor Rd. It's a sporty establishment for those on expense accounts; on some nights it has live music. Just in case you missed the Tudor-style

Top: Despite the dominance of urban Hong Kong culture, in the rural areas of the New Territories, duck farmers are still a common sight. Eggs and duck are popular in Hong Kong restaurants and markets.
Bottom: The island of Tap Man Chau has an old-world fishing village atmosphere.

Top: Archaeological evidence indicates that Lamma has the oldest settlement in southern China.
Middle: The small town of Kam Tin contains two walled villages, Kat Hing Wai and Shui Tau. The walls were once a defence against pirates and bandits.
Bottom: Tai Mo Shan is Hong Kong's highest mountain, with an elevation of 957m.

pubs in Wan Chai, there are two more tucked away on Cannon St: *Royal's Pub* and *Shakespeare Pub*. These are mainly the domain of Hong Kong Chinese, but foreigners are made to feel welcome.

Further out in Quarry Bay is a beer-lovers' must in the form of the *East End Brewery* (☎ 2811-1907) at 23-27 Tong Chong St. Choose from a choice of almost 30 microbrewed and speciality beers from around the world, including Taikoo Brew and Aldrich Bay Pale Ale.

Stanley

There are a number of gwailo pubs that get raging in the late afternoon and continue until after midnight. A large share of this market belongs to the *Smugglers' Inn* (☎ 2813-8852), 90A Main St.

Lord Stanley's Bar & Bistro (☎ 2813-1876), 92A Main St, offers a similar atmosphere of loud music and good food. The same management owns the adjacent *Beaches* (☎ 28137313) at No 92B.

Deep Water Bay

The drinking and food scene is supplied by a single restaurant right on the beach called *Sampan East* (☎ 2812-1618). It's open from noon until 10.30 pm.

SHOPPING

Central is the main tourist shopping district on Hong Kong Island, closely followed by Wan Chai and Causeway Bay. The most glitzy of Hong Kong's tourist shopping malls is in Pacific Place, 88 Queensway, near Admiralty MTR station. Seibu Department Store is located there. The World Trade Centre and Times Square in Causeway Bay are places which aspire to provide everything under one roof. Many locals shop at Cityplaza and the adjacent Kornhill Plaza in Quarry Bay, near Tai Koo MTR station. Bear in mind that prices are slightly lower in the non-touristy neighbourhoods.

Antiques & Auctions

Hollywood Rd is a prime location if you are interested in shopping for antiques. The

shops make for fascinating browsing, with carved figures propped against antique silk screens, backed up by a medley of trinkets, boxes, busts of Mao, Zhou Enlai et al, and further hemmed in by an international assortment of ageing treasures. It's easy to get lost in some of these emporiums, but be cautious. If you don't have an eye for this line of work, step carefully through this minefield of fakes and forgeries.

If you're hunting for quality items, try Zitan (☎ 2523-7584) at 43-55 Wyndham St in Central, with its superb range of antique Chinese furniture. The Tibetan Gallery (☎ 2530-4863) at 55 Wyndham St has a rich selection of Tibetan religious art and artefacts. Also in Wyndham St is Tai Sing Company (☎ 2525-9365), well known to other dealers for quality Chinese antiques. Schoeni Fine Oriental Art (☎ 2542-3143) at 27 Hollywood Rd has a dizzying range of

HONG KONG TOURIST ASSOCIATION

Indoor and outdoor markets make for some fabulously cheap bargains.

traditional Chinese collectibles. Other well known places include Hobbs & Bishop Fine Art Ltd (☎ 2537-9838), 28 Hollywood Rd, and Luen Chai Curios Store (☎ 2540-4772) at 142 Hollywood Rd.

If you're looking for ivory substitutes, The Oriental Crafts Company (☎ 2541-8840) at 53-55 Hollywood Rd has a selection of exquisitely carved hippo teeth carvings.

For folk crafts, one of the nicest stores in town is Mountain Folkcraft (☎ 2523-2817), 12 Wo On Lane, Central, near Lan Kwai Fong. This place has batiks, clothing, wood carvings and lacquerware made by ethnic minorities in China and other Asian countries. The shop attendants are friendly and prices, while not cheap, are not outrageous either.

Don't overlook the opportunity to visit the auction houses of Sotheby's Hong Kong (☎ 2524-8121), Tower II, 18th floor, Lipo Chun Chambers, 189 Des Voeux Rd, and Christie's (☎ 2521-5396) on the 28th floor, Alexandra House, 16-20 Chater Rd. Auctions are held twice a year in April and November.

The pre-auction preview (usually held at the Furama Kempinski Hotel for Sotheby's and in the JW Marriot Hotel for Christie's) allow you to examine normally private collections and rub shoulders with the big buyers from the international art market. Both auction houses have regular sales in ceramics, jade, modern and jadeite jewellery, stamps, snuff bottles, works of art, traditional and contemporary Chinese paintings and calligraphic works.

Backpacking & Camping

The place to go is Sunmark Camping Equipment (☎ 2893-8511), 141 Wan Chai Rd, Wan Chai.

Bookshops

Times bookshops are dotted around Hong Kong and have an average range of books and stationery. Convenient branches can be found in Central, (☎ 2525-8797) on the ground floor of the Hong Kong Club building, 3 Jackson Rd; and in Causeway Bay,

shop P315-316, 3rd floor, World Trade Centre, 280 Gloucester Rd. Bookazine is somewhat similar, and (among others) has two branches in Central: on the 2nd floor of Prince's building, (☎ 2522-1785), and in the basement of Jardine House (☎ 2523-1747).

The Hong Kong Book Centre Ltd (☎ 2522-7064) at 25 Des Voeux Rd, Central, is a basement bookshop given over to a vast selection of books and magazines. This is an excellent old-fashioned browser's bookshop.

There is a *South China Morning Post* bookshop (☎ 2801-4423) at the Star Ferry terminal in Central, and another in Times Square, Matheson St, Causeway Bay. Among other branches, Jumbo Grade has a branches at shop 144, Pacific Place, Queensway (☎ 2526-3873), and in shop 134-135, Prince's building, 10 Chater Rd, Central (☎ 2521-5509).

Joint Publishing Company (☎ 2525-0105), 9 Queen Victoria St (opposite the Central Market) in Central, is an outstanding shop which has an excellent range of books about China and books and tapes for studying the Chinese language. Another good shop for China-related works is Cosmos Books Ltd (☎ 2528-3605), 30 Johnston Rd, Wan Chai. For books in French, visit Parenthèses (☎ 2526-9215) on the 4th floor of the (ironically named) Duke of Wellington House, Wellington St, Central.

A very good specialist range of business, legal and professional titles can be found in the Professional Bookshop (☎ 2526-5387) at 104A Alexandra House, Chater Rd, Central.

The Age of Aquarius (☎ 2577-4944), 1st floor, 2-6 Foo Ming St, Causeway Bay, specialises in new-age books. You can find literature on UFOs, tarot, astrology, meditation and alternative therapies.

The Government Publications Office (☎ 2537-1910), Government Office building, Queensway Government Offices, 88 Queensway, Admiralty, is open from 9 am to 4 pm daily, and 9 am to 1 pm on Saturday.

Hong Kong has very few second-hand book outlets, but occasionally a stall goes up with cheap paperbacks; there is usually one selling second-hand fiction at the Central Star Ferry terminal. Some of the junk shops at the western end of Hollywood Rd also stock old paperbacks.

Cameras & Photoprocessing
Stanley St in Central is one of the best spots in Hong Kong for buying photographic equipment; there are seven camera shops in a row and competition is keen. Everything carries price tags, though some low-level bargaining might be possible.

Photo Scientific (☎ 2522-1903), 6 Stanley St, is the favourite of Hong Kong's resident professional photographers. You might find equipment elsewhere for less, but Photo Scientific has a rock-solid reputation with labelled prices, no bargaining, no arguing and no cheating. Everything is squeezed into the shop: darkroom supplies, tripods, photographer's jackets with hundreds of pockets and every type of film.

Almost next door is Color Six (☎ 2526-0123), 18A Stanley St, which has the best photoprocessing in town. Colour slides can be professionally processed in just three hours. Many special types of film are on sale which can be bought nowhere else in Hong Kong, and all professional film is kept refrigerated (eg Kodak Ektachrome 160T and Kodak Tungsten Pro). Prices aren't perhaps the lowest in town (developing costs are HK$1.10 per exposure plus HK$12 per roll), but the quality is excellent. There are also plenty of swift developing places all over the city including the Fotomax chain which can develop in one hour for HK$75 (36 exposures).

Other reputable photographic supplies outlets include Hing Lee Camera Company (☎ 2544-7593) on the ground floor, 25 Lyndhurst Terrace, Central; and Everbest Photo Supplies Limited (☎ 2522-1985), which can be found at 28B Stanley St, Central.

Union Photo Supplies (☎ 2526-6281), 13 Queen Victoria St (next to Central Market), is excellent for colour slide processing. However, we have found camera prices higher than on Stanley St, so do a few comparisons before buying anything too expensive.

Carpets & Rugs
The bulk of Hong Kong's carpet and rug shops are clustered on Wyndham St in Central, although there are some large retailers on the Kowloon side. Noted shops include Mir Oriental Carpets (☎ 2521-5641), 52 Wyndham St, who have thousands of carpets in stock from around the world. Al Shahzadi Persian Carpet Gallery (☎ 2834-8298), 265 Queen's Rd East, has quality carpets from Afghanistan, Iran, Russia and other countries.

CDs & Music Tapes
HMV can be found in the Central building, Pedder St, Central; Swire House, Central; Windsor House, 311 Gloucester Rd, Causeway Bay; Sands building, Peking Rd, Tsim Sha Tsui; and New Town Plaza, Sha Tin. HMV also have a great range of music mags, but are expensive. The branch in the Central building is huge and open seven days a week, from 10 am to 10 pm.

Tower Records (☎ 2506-0811), 7th floor, shop 701, Times Square, Matheson St, Causeway Bay, is also a good place to look for recorded music. Prices are about the same as HMV.

KPS is another place to go for discounted CDs and music tapes. It's also a good place to buy (legal) computer software. There is a KPS branch (☎ 2868-2020) in the Prince's building, 10 Chater Rd, Central; and another branch (☎ 2890-8709), hidden above a Park N' Shop supermarket, on the 3rd floor of the Capitol Centre, 5-19 Jardine's Bazaar, Causeway Bay.

Chinese Emporiums
Chinese Arts & Crafts shops can be found in Admiralty (☎ 2523-3933), unit 230, Pacific Place, 88 Queensway; in Central (☎ 2845-0092), ground floor, Prince's building, 10 Chater Rd; in Tsim Sha Tsui (☎ 2735-4061), Star House, 3 Salisbury Rd; and in Wan Chai (☎ 2827-6667), ground floor, Lower Block, China Resources building, 26 Harbour Rd.

HONG KONG

Fakes in the Hong Kong Art Market

Fakes are a problem for potential buyers. Fake antiques from China are improving technically, often fooling inexperienced buyers and sometimes even confounding the experts. The sheer volume of fakes is also growing. During the periods of revolutionary zeal in the 1960s and 1970s, no-one would copy what were considered to be symbols of feudalism. But in the anything goes climate of the 1980s and 1990s, the copying of antique porcelain has become increasingly widespread. There's big money to be made and the most professional forgers use incredibly advanced techniques to copy valuable originals. Despite their impressive variety, many of the clay figurines and statues that you see in the shops that line Hollywood Rd are mass-produced and of little value – the decent stuff is in private collections or museums.

The authenticity of a piece is sometimes questioned, and once the word is out (even mistakenly) that a piece is fake, it can suffer heavily if sold at auction. Doubt is infectious and can rapidly erode the credibility of a piece. Generally the authenticity of, for example, a ceramic piece is discernible from the glaze, the weight, the condition of the foot rim, the mark and the painting of the design. All these factors have to be reproduced convincingly in order to fool an expert.

ℓ ℓ ℓ ℓ ℓ ℓ ℓ ℓ ℓ ℓ ℓ ℓ ℓ ℓ

The largest branch of the Yue Hwa Chinese Products Emporium chain is in Yau Ma Tei (☎ 2384-0084) at 301-309 Nathan Rd. Other branches are at Mirador Mansion, 54 Nathan Rd; and in the Park Lane Shopper's Boulevard, 143 Nathan Rd (near Kowloon Park).

There are three branches of CRC department stores on Hong Kong Island; in Central (☎ 2524-1051) at 92 Queen's Rd; Admiralty (☎ 2577-0222) 488 Hennessy Rd; and in Causeway Bay (☎ 2890-8321) at the Lok Sing Centre, 31 Yee Wo St.

Cigars

For some, cigar smoking is an almost unparalleled exotic delight. Rest assured, Hong Kong has a few cigar parlours that can furnish the needy with a Monte Cristo to round off that excellent meal. Tabaqueria Filipina (☎ 2523-8752) at 30-32 Wyndham St, Central, is a short dash from many a restaurant in the area.

Clothing

The clothing alleys in Central run between Queen's and Des Voeux Rds. One alley sells only buttons and zips. Li Yuen St sells costume jewellery, belts, scarves and shoes. Another street is devoted almost exclusively to handbags and luggage, and yet another to sweaters, tights, underwear and denims. However, high rents are starting to push out these shops and the cloth vendors have already relocated to the Western Market in Sheung Wan.

In Central, you might want to duck into Shanghai Tang (☎ 2525-7333) on the ground floor of the Pedder building, 12 Pedder St. Started up by David Tang, a flamboyant Hong Kong businessman, this one store sparked something of a fashion wave in Hong Kong with its updated versions of traditional Chinese garments. Renewed interest and appreciation of traditional Chinese lines in fashion sparked in 1997. The clothes aren't cheap, but the designs are unique and generally tasteful. Custom tailoring is available. Another company which sells traditional Chinese jackets and designs is Blanc De Chine (☎ 2524-7875) in room 201, Pedder building, 12 Pedder St, Central.

Johnston Rd in Wan Chai is perhaps the best place on Hong Kong Island to search for cheap clothes. If you like the relatively low-priced garments sold by Giordano's, you can find branches at 541 Lockhart Rd and 22 Paterson St, both in Causeway Bay.

One well known upmarket area for clothes shopping is Vogue Alley in Causeway Bay. Within a block of the intersection of Paterson and Kingston Sts there are more than 30 boutiques catering to the travellers cheque crowd. The area was once known as Food St, but the restaurants have been replaced.

The British chain Marks & Spencer has branches in Central on the 1st floor, Central Tower, Queen's Rd (☎ 2921-8303), and in shop B12, the Landmark (☎ 2921-8898); in Admiralty at units 120 and 229, Pacific Place (☎ 2921-8888); and in Causeway Bay on the ground floor, Pearl City Plaza, Paterson St (☎ 2923-7817), and in unit 313-418, 3rd floor, Times Square (☎ 2923-7970).

Hong Kong is, of course, a haven for brand names of international renown. Some of the designer fashion labels available include:

Alfred Dunhill
 (☎ 2524-4767) shop G14A, ground floor, Prince's building, 10 Chater Rd, Central; (☎ 2530-0464) shop 315-316, level 3, Pacific Place, 88 Queensway; (☎ 2893-1026) ground floor, Sogo department store, East Point Centre, 555 Hennessy Rd, Causeway Bay
Giorgio Armani
 (☎ 2530-1998) shop 18-20A, Alexandra House, 16-20 Chater Rd, Central
Hermes Boutique
 (☎ 2525-5900) G08/09, The Galleria, 9 Queen's Rd, Central; (☎ 2522-6229), level 3, Pacific Place, 88 Queensway, Central
Mothercare
 (☎ 2523-5704) shop 338-340, 3rd floor, Prince's building, 10 Chater Rd, Central; (☎ 2882-3468) shop P, 2nd floor, Windsor House, 311 Gloucester Rd, Causeway Bay
Yves Saint-Laurent
 shop M9, Mandarin Oriental shopping arcade, 5 Connaught Rd, Central; Lane Crawford, Times Square, 1 Matheson St, Causeway Bay

Computers

Most people buy computers in Kowloon where there is greater variety and prices are lower. But Hong Kong Island does have one reasonable computer arcade, Computer 88, in Windsor House, 311 Gloucester Rd, Causeway Bay. Reptron Computers (☎ 2506-3812), shops 705 and 728, Times

Square, 1 Matheson St, Causeway Bay, also has a reputation for reliability (and has three other branches).

Department Stores

Hong Kong's department stores are not cheap, so if you're looking for bargains look elsewhere. Hong Kong's original western-style department store is Lane Crawford, which has branches in Central at 70 Queen's Rd; in Admiralty at Pacific Place, 88 Queensway; and in Causeway Bay at Windsor House, 311 Gloucester Rd, and in Times Square, Matheson and Russel Sts.

Hong Kong Chinese department stores in the Central district include Wing On, which has branches at 26 and 211 Des Voeux Rd; Sincere, at 173 Des Voeux Rd; and Dragon Seed, 39 Queen's Rd.

Japanese department stores are heavily concentrated around Causeway Bay. The main branch of Daimaru is at the corner of Paterson and Great George Sts. Personally, we find the smaller Daimaru Household Square (on the corner of Kingston St and Gloucester Rd) to be more interesting. Among other retail outlets, it houses the Asahiya Japanese Bookstore. Matsuzakaya is at 6 Paterson St and Sogo is at 545 Hennessy Rd. Another good department store is Mitsukoshi at 500 Hennessy Rd.

Jewellery

King Fook and Tse Sui Luen are two chain stores which guarantee to buy back any jewellery at the current wholesale price. Of course, be sure you get a certificate and bear in mind that you need to be in Hong Kong to take advantage of the buy-back plan.

One of the most fantastic-looking King Fook branches (☎ 2822-8573) is at 30 Des Voeux Rd, Central. It is worth visiting for its sheer garishness.

Other branches can be found in Admiralty (☎ 2845-6766) at shop 216, Pacific Place; and in Causeway Bay (☎ 2576-1032) on the ground floor of Hong Kong Mansion, 1 Yee Wo St.

Tse Sui Luen shops are found in Central

(☎ 2921-8800) at Commercial House, 35 Queen's Rd; in Wan Chai (☎ 2893-2981) at 141 Johnston Rd; and in Causeway Bay (☎ 2838-6737), 467 Hennessy Rd. There is also a factory outlet in Aberdeen (☎ 2878-2618) on the ground floor, Wah Ming building, 34 Wong Chuk Hang Rd.

Pharmaceuticals

Watson's shops are all over the place, but Mannings is slightly cheaper. Branches can be found in Central , shop B, 22-23, 1st basement, the Landmark, 12-16A Des Voeux Rd (☎ 2596-0312); and in Admiralty, shop J1-J8, Queensway Plaza, Queensway (☎ 2529-1558).

Sporting Goods

The largest selection of sporting-goods shops is found in Mong Kok on the Kowloon side. Nevertheless, Hong Kong Island chips in with the following:

Bunn's Diving Equipment
 (☎ 2572-1629) ground floor, shop E and G, Kwong Sang Hong building, 188 Wan Chai Rd, Wan Chai
Mountain Services International (mountaineering equipment)
 shop 106,Vicwood Plaza, 199 Des Voeux Rd, Central
Nevada Bob's Golf
 (☎ 2868-4234) 1st floor, 33 Connaught Rd, Central
Po Kee Fishing Tackle
 (☎ 2543-7541) 6 Hillier St, Central
Quicksilver (surfwear)
 (☎ 2836-6073) 1st floor, 545 Lockhart Rd, Causeway Bay

Toys

Toys R Us (☎ 2881-1728) is the big American-owned chain on the 3rd floor of Windsor House, on the corner of Great George St and Gloucester Rd, Causeway Bay.

The New Territories

HONG KONG

For those who have the time, it's well worth taking at least a day to explore the New Territories which, together with the outlying islands, reveal a very different side of Hong Kong. Life in these more rural parts of Hong Kong is so relaxed it's hard to believe that the frantic urban sprawl is only a bus or boat ride away. Some of the views are superb, and there are good walks.

The New Territories is large – larger than Hong Kong Island, Kowloon and Lantau Island combined. Everything north of Boundary St on the Kowloon Peninsula up to the border of mainland People's Republic of China (PRC) is the New Territories. Excluding the outlying islands, the New Territories makes up 70% of Hong Kong's land area.

This is Hong Kong's bedroom – about one-third of the population lives in the New Territories, mostly in appropriately named 'new towns'. Since its inception, the New Towns Program in this area has consumed more than half of the Hong Kong government's budget, with a lot of the money spent on land reclamation, sewage, roads and other infrastructure projects.

The population of the New Territories has mushroomed from less than half a million in 1970 to the present 2.5 million, and it's expected to reach 3.5 million by the year 2000. About 60% of the new housing units have been built by the government. Chief Executive, Tung Chee Hwa, has pledged himself to building 85,000 housing units a year. Many of these will be built in the New Territories.

Alongside the construction and relentless development is a world of sacred shrines and temples, dotted along fabulous walks in mountainous and untamed countryside. Many Hong Kong residents make the New Territories their getaway for the weekend. The eastern section, most notably the Sai Kung Peninsula and the area around Clearwater Bay, has some of Hong Kong's most beautiful scenery and hiking trails

The biggest impediment to growth in the New Territories has been the lack of good transportation. This changed dramatically in 1982 with the opening of the Mass-Transit Railway (MTR) Tsuen Wan line. In the same year, the Kowloon-Canton Railway (KCR) underwent a major expansion and the system was electrified and double-tracked. The Light Rail Transit (LRT) system opened in 1988 and hoverferries now connect Tuen Mun to Central, reducing commuting time to just 30 minutes.

A whole host of infrastructure projects are envisioned for the area in the future, including a knot of expressways straddling the western New Territories, linking Kowloon with Shekou, Bao'an and Humen; expressways connecting the eastern New Territories with Shenzhen; and, incredulously, a bridge linking the westernmost tip of the New Territories with Zhuhai (using a number of islands as stepping stones). This is all part of a plan to further consolidate Hong Kong, Macau, Zhuhai and Shenzhen into an economic bulwark on the south coast of China.

The most northerly part of the New Territories, within 1km of the mainland Chinese border, is a closed area that is fenced and well marked with signs. Since the 1997 handover, it marks the boundary of the Hong Kong SAR.

MAPS
Do yourself a favour and pick up the *Countryside* series of maps. There are four maps covering the New Territories: *North-West New Territories*, *Central New Territories*, *Sai Kung & Clearwater Bay*, *North-East New Territories* and the *MacLehose Trail*. These are available from the Government Publications Centre in Hong Kong Island. The other range of maps worth keeping an eye out for are those published by Universal Publications. Waterproofed, in full colour and finely detailed, the series includes

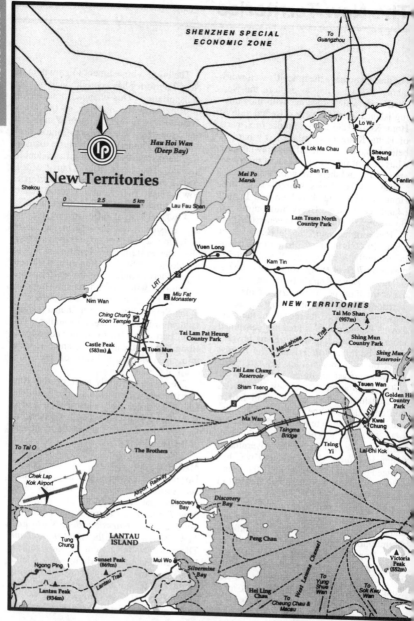

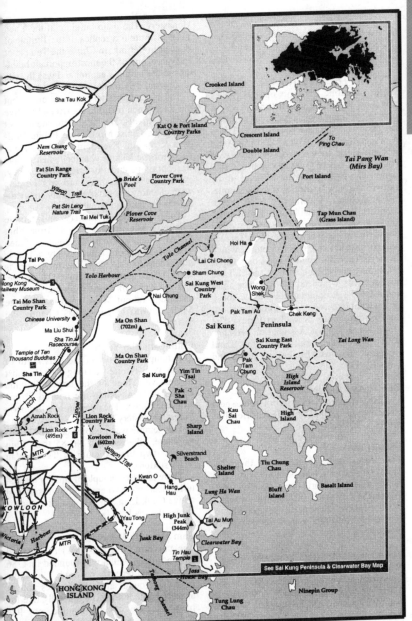

See Sai Kung Peninsula & Clearwater Bay Map

Sai Kung and Clearwater Bay, one of the most attractive regions of the New Territories. See the Maps entry in the Hong Kong Facts for the Visitor chapter for more details.

GETTING THERE & AWAY

A host of public transport options makes travelling to the New Territories easy, at least to the main towns and areas of interest. The MTR can take you as far as Tsuen Wan (on the Tsuen Wan Line) in the west or Choi Hung in the east (on the Kwun Tong Line), where you can catch buses to explore the New Territories. Travel to the north of the New territories is made simple, fast and cheap by using the KCR which connects Kowloon with Sha Tin, Tai Po Sheung Shui and Lo Wu (among other stops). In the far west of the New Territories is the light rail (LRT) option, which connects Tuen Mun with Yuen Long. Complimenting the choice of bus and rail are boat services which take in remoter areas and a few large communities on the coast. If you want to avoid using public transport, take a tour to the New Territories. The Hong Kong Tourist Association (HKTA, ☎ 2807-6177) can book you on the 'Land Between' tour, which takes six hours and costs HK$385.

GETTING AROUND

The HKTA has a handy information sheet with a map of the New Territories bus routes.

TSUEN WAN

The easiest place to reach in the New Territories, Tsuen Wan is an industrial and residential area north-west of Kowloon. While the city itself offers little in terms of atmosphere, there are a few neighbouring attractions that make the trip very worthwhile.

Yuen Yuen Institute & Western Monastery

The main attraction in Tsuen Wan is the Yuen Yuen Institute – a Taoist temple complex – and the nearby Buddhist Western Monastery. The main building at the Yuen Yuen Institute is a replica of the Temple of Heaven in Beijing. In China, the Temple of Heaven is one of the most important buildings in the nation's capitol and was the site of imperial ceremonial rites.

The large monastery is very quiet, but the Yuen Yuen Institute is extremely active during festivals. We were fortunate to visit during the Ghost Month (see Public Holidays & Special Events in the Hong Kong Facts for the Visitor chapter) when people were praying and burning ghost money, cymbals were crashing and worshippers were chanting. Vegetarian meals are available at the monastery's cafeteria.

To reach the monastery and temple complex, take minibus No 81 from Shiu Wo St, which is two blocks south of Tsuen Wan MTR station. Alternatively, a taxi is not expensive (HK$20). The monastery is about 1.5km north-east of the MTR station, and you can walk there, using the pedestrian bridge (about 400m north-east of the MTR station) to get across Cheung Pei Shan Rd.

Chuk Lam Sim Yuen

This temple complex in the hills north of Tsuen Wan is one of Hong Kong's most impressive. Three of the largest Buddha statues in Hong Kong are housed in this temple complex. The name means 'Bamboo Forest Monastery'.

This temple was established in 1927. To get there, take minibus No 85 from Shiu Wo St (two blocks south of Tsuen Wan MTR station).

There are also a couple of smaller monasteries nearby – two are on the hillside just above Chuk Lam Sim Yuen, and a third is across the road.

Sam Tung Uk Museum

The museum (☎ 2411-2001) is a walled Hakka village which was founded in 1786 and has been recently restored. Within the museum grounds are eight houses and an ancestral hall. Travellers generally like the place because it's all genuine, not like

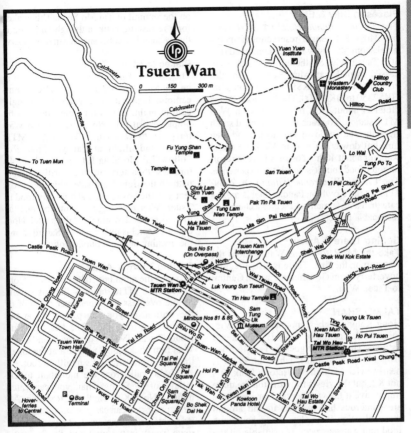

the commercial representations of what normally passes for 'Chinese culture' in Hong Kong.

The museum is a five minute walk south-east of Tsuen Wan MTR station, on Sai Lau Kok Rd. It's open from 9 am to 4 pm daily except Tuesday. Admission is free.

Airport Core Progam Exhibition Centre

If you want to look out over the world's longest combined rail and road suspension bridge and work your way through elaborate set models of the airport and peripheral

projects connected with it, the Airport Core Progam Exhibition Centre at 410 Castle Peak Rd will be right up your street. The show is actually reasonably interesting, but it's aimed at locals and visiting mainland Chinese, who find massive civil engineering projects spellbinding.

It's not that easy to reach: take bus No 234B or 53, or a No 96 green minibus from the ferry pier in Tsuen Wan. Opening times are 10 am to 5 pm Tuesday to Friday, or until 6.30 pm Saturday, Sunday and Public Holidays. Admission is free.

Places to Stay & Eat

The *Kowloon Panda Hotel* (☎ 2409-1111, fax 2409-1818, email reservations@mega-hotels.com.hk, www.hwtour.com/panda) is at 3 Tsuen Wah St, though the hotel is accessed from Kwan Mun Hau St. Doubles cost HK$1250 to HK$1950 and suites are HK$2350 to HK$6600. The Kowloon Panda Hotel is about 1km from the Tsuen Wan MTR station. To reach the hotel, head south from the station down Tai Ho Rd and then turn left down Tsuen Wan Market Rd and walk for about 400m. You may have to resort to hotel food, but it's worth the experience. The *Chianti Ristorante Italiano* (☎ 2409-1111) at the Kowloon Panda Hotel is more a cafe than a restaurant, and serves a cheap and reasonable buffet.

Getting There & Away

Take the MTR to Tsuen Wan station, the last stop on the line. There is also a regular hoverferry from Government pier in Central to Tsuen Wan.

TAI MO SHAN

Hong Kong's highest mountain is not Victoria Peak, as many tourists mistakenly assume. That honour goes to Tai Mo Shan (Big Misty Mountain), which at 957m is nearly twice as high as Victoria Peak. It's not K2, but the views from the top are quite impressive if the weather is clear, and there are numerous hiking trails in and around the peak. You'll need to bring your own food and water as none is available on the mountain. Climbing Tai Mo Shan is not too difficult, but there is no Peak Tram to the summit. The Countryside series *Central New Territories* map is the one you want for this area (see the Maps section earlier in this chapter for more details).

The area around Ng Tung Chai waterfall is scenic and worth a detour. It is near the village of Ng Tung Chai, which is a few kilometres to the north-east of Tai Mo Shan and just south of Lam Kam Rd. There is actually a series of falls and streams, reached by taking the path leading to Ng Tung Chai and the Lam Kam Rd from the radio station on the summit of Tai Mo Shan. This makes for a refreshing walk, although take care if the weather is wet because it can be slippery.

Places to Stay

The *Sze Lok Yuen* (☎ 2488-8188) hostel is on Tai Mo Shan Rd. Beds cost HK$25 and camping is permitted. It can get amazingly cold at night, at this high elevation, so be prepared. Take the No 51 bus (Tsuen Wan ferry pier to Kam Tin) at Tsuen Wan MTR station and alight at Tai Mo Shan Rd. Follow Tai Mo Shan Rd east for about 45 minutes, then turn on to a small concrete path on the right-hand side which leads directly to the hostel. You should buy food in Tsuen Wan before getting on the bus, as there is no food available at the hostel. Note that the hostel is only open on Saturday and the evening before a public holiday.

Getting There & Away

To reach the mountain, take bus No 51 from Tsuen Wan MTR station – the bus stop is on the overpass that goes over the roof of the station, or you can pick it up at the Tsuen Wan ferry pier. The bus heads up Route Twisk (Twisk is derived from 'Tsuen Wan Into Shek Kong'). Get off at the top of the pass, from where it's uphill on foot.

If you walk from the mountain to the village of Ng Tung Chai, you can catch minibus No 25K to Tai Po KCR station. Alternatively, you can carry on up to Lam Kam Rd, which runs east-west connecting with route Twisk in the west and Tai Po in the east, and clamber onto bus No 64K or 65K.

MACLEHOSE TRAIL

The 100km MacLehose Trail spans the New Territories, running from Tuen Mun in the west to Pak Tam Chung (on the Sai Kung Peninsula) in the east. The trail follows the ridge, goes over Tai Mo Shan and passes close to Ma On Shan (702m), Hong Kong's fourth highest peak. There are breathtaking views along the entire trail, which was named after Lord MacLehose, a former British governor of Hong Kong, whose hobby was walking in the hills.

If you want to hike anywhere along this trail, it is essential that you buy the map entitled *MacLehose Trail*, available from the Government Publications Centre (see Maps in the Hong Kong Facts for the Visitor chapter).

Minibus No 82 will drop you at **Pineapple Dam**, adjacent to the Shing Mun Reservoir. You can follow the **Pineapple Dam Nature Trail** (named after now subaqueous pineapple groves), past picnic sites and on around the reservoir itself. Villages bordering the reservoir were moved on when the project was under construction.

This is an area very rich in wildlife and plants, and you may see butterflies, macaque monkeys and maybe even deer. The area is also good for birdwatching. The signposted **Shing Mun Arboretum** has a wide variety of fruit trees and medicinal plants.

Not far away, stage five of the MacLehose trail takes you through some dramatic scenery. The trail leads away from Tai Po Rd (alongside Kowloon Reservoir, to the south of Shing Mun Reservoir), past Eagle's Nest (a hill), through woodland and up Beacon Hill (named after a lookout post that was stationed on the hill during the reign of Kang Xi in the Qing dynasty – this post fired up a beacon if enemy ships sailed into view), then runs along a ridge to Lion Rock (Seezee San). Near there is a junction with a path leading north to Amah Rock (for more details, see Amah Rock in the Sha Tin section in this chapter). You can take the Lion Rock path if you want, which is quite a tough haul, but worth the effort. Be careful climbing and descending, as the steps only go part of the way and it can be quite tricky. The view from the peak is stunning, with sheer cliffs and rocky crags. Alternatively, you can carry on in an easterly direction without clambering up Lion Rock, the MacLehose trail actually circumvents the summit.

Coming down from Lion Rock, the MacLehose trail leads you to Sha Tin Pass, where you may find a drinks vendor to quench the thirst you've probably acquired. From there you can either head south along

a road and pick up a bus at Tsz Wan Shan estate in Kowloon, or walk north along a path to Sha Tin (about 2km) and jump on the KCR. If you carry on along the MacLehose Trail, it will take you into the heart of Ma On Shan Country Park. The whole trail from Kowloon Reservoir to Sha Tin Pass is about 7km in length.

Those of you who really want to get the heart pounding, and plan to pick up a few blisters as well as see great scenery, can join in the annual Trailwalker event, which is a race across the MacLehose Trail. If you decide to enter, it will help if you're superfit – it's a bit like climbing up the Peak five times in a row. The Gurkhas have a team who usually win in about 13 hours. If you think you can hack it, call the Trailwalker Charitable Trust c/o Oxfam (☎ 2520-2525).

Getting There & Away

The MacLehose Trail can be accessed by bus from Tsuen Wan. Take bus No 51 (from the overpass over Tsuen Wan MTR station or from the ferry pier) to the top of Route Twisk. From there you have the choice of heading off to the east along the trail towards Tai Mo Shan or west to Tai Lam Country Park, the Tai Lam Chung Reservoir and eventually all the way to Tuen Mun (a distance of about 15km) – the western terminus of the trail. From Tuen Mun, you can catch a bus to Kowloon or a hoverferry to Central.

You can also get onto the Trail by taking bus No 72, from the Jordan Rd ferry pier in Kowloon, and getting off at the Kowloon Reservoir, on Tai Po Rd; or take a taxi from Kowloon Tong along Tai Po Rd and ask to be dropped off at Kowloon Reservoir.

WILSON TRAIL

The 78km Wilson Trail (see also the Wilson Trail entry in the Hong Kong Island chapter) begins on Hong Kong Island, disappears into the Eastern Cross-Harbour Tunnel and surfaces at Lam Tin MTR station. From there, the path zigzags south to Lei Yue Mun before turning sharply north again into the hills. The trail then takes a westward turn, heading over the summit of Tai Lo Shan (577m), and passes Lion Rock and Beacon Hill (north of Kowloon). The path makes another sharp turn northward, continues through Shing Mun Country Park, returns to civilisation near Tai Po, then disappears into the hills again at Pat Sin Leng Country Park (see the Plover Cove Reservoir section later in this chapter) before terminating at Nam Chung Reservoir, not far from the mainland Chinese border.

Parts of the trail's New Territories section overlap with the MacLehose Trail, especially in the area east of Tai Mo Shan.

TUEN MUN

This is the main new town in the north-west of the New Territories. Despite the endless rows of high-rise housing estates, there are interesting things to see.

The **Ching Chung Koon Temple** (Green Pine Temple) is just to the north of Tuen Mun. It's a huge Taoist temple dedicated to one of the eight immortals of Chinese mythology. The temple is very active during festivals. From Tuen Mun, you can easily get to the temple by taking the LRT to Ching Chung station.

Castle Peak Monastery (also known as Ching Shan Monastery or Green Mountain Monastery) is interesting, but it's very hard to reach. From Tuen Mun you need to take a taxi, but returning may be awkward unless you get the taxi to wait for you (a privilege that'll cost). The Chinese name for the monastery is Ching San Sim Yuen. It's one of the oldest monasteries in Hong Kong. The monastery takes its name from the adjacent Castle Peak which was proclaimed a sacred mountain by imperial decree in 969 AD.

Places to Stay
Getting There & Away

Bus Nos 53, 60M and 68M start from Tsuen Wan and follow the coast to Tuen Mun. Or you can take bus No 60X or 68X, both of which start from Jordan Rd ferry pier in Kowloon. Sit upstairs on the left side of the

bus for spectacular views. En route you pass another Hong Kong high-tech wonder – the world's largest seawater desalination plant at Lok An Pai. If you are coming from Yuen Long you can take the LRT.

The fastest and most fun way to get to Tuen Mun is by hoverferry. These depart from the Central Harbour Services pier in Central, Hong Kong Island. The ride takes 30 minutes and lets you off at the LRT station. There is a regular and reliable service every 15 to 20 minutes from 6.45 am to 8.30 pm.

MIU FAT MONASTERY

The Miu Fat Buddhist Monastery, in Lam Tei, houses three large golden Buddhas on the 3rd floor. This is an active monastery that preserves more of a traditional character than many smaller temples. On the 2nd floor is an excellent vegetarian restaurant, that was packed out when we were last there.

The monastery is easily reached by taking the LRT to Lam Tei from Tuen Mun, and then walking five minutes along Castle Peak Rd from the Lam Tei LRT station.

YUEN LONG

There isn't anything special at Yuen Long, but it's the last stop on the LRT line. It's not a bad place to eat lunch, but otherwise there isn't any reason to linger. Dim sum is served from 7 am to 3 pm at the *Kar Shing Restaurant* (☎ 2476-3228) in room 333, 3rd floor, Yuen Long Plaza, 249 Castle Peak Rd.

MAI PO MARSH

If you're a birdwatcher, the 300 hectare Mai Po Marsh in the north-west of the New Territories is one of the best places in Hong Kong to see your feathered friends.

The World Wide Fund for Nature (WWF, ☎ 2526-4473) can arrange for you to visit the marsh. WWF operate three hour guided tours on Saturday, Sunday and public holidays that you can join for a fee of HK$70. Alternatively, you can pay HK$100 and have unguided access to the area for the whole day from 9 am to 5 pm for HK$100. The WWF office is at 1 Tramway Path,

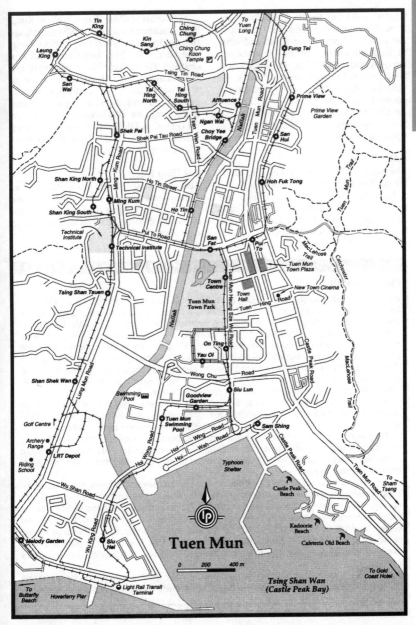

Tuen Mun

0   200   400 m

Tsing Shan Wan
(Castle Peak Bay)

HONG KONG

Central (adjacent to the Peak Tram entrance). This is also a good place to pick up the *Birds of Hong Kong* guide and other useful publications. Visitors are advised to bring binoculars, cameras, walking shoes or boots, and not to wear bright clothing. To visit Mai Po Marsh you need to have a permit from the WWF. To get there catch the KCR to Sheung Shui and then take a bus No 76K to Yuen Long, which passes the entrance of Mai Po Marsh.

KAM TIN

The small town of Kam Tin (the name means Brocade Field) contains two walled villages, Kat Hing Wai and Shui Tau. Most tourists go to Kat Hing Wai. Shui Tau is larger and less touristy, but don't expect to find remnants of ancient China.

Most other walled villages in Hong Kong have vanished under the jackhammers, although there is a good one at Ping Kong (see later in the Ping Hong section in this chapter). The walled villages are one of the last reminders that Hong Kong residents were once faced with marauding pirates, bandits and soldiers. Kam Tin is the home of the Tang clan who have lived in the town for centuries. The Tangs were high-ranking public servants in the imperial court of China in the 19th century.

Kat Hing Wai

This tiny village is 500 years old and was walled some time during the Ming dynasty (1368-1644). It's just off Kam Tin Rd and is one small street, from which a maze of dark alleys lead off.

Mai Po Marsh

Beyond the crystalline cityscape of Hong Kong, with all its bustling commerce, lies the New Territories. As well as a vast habitat for the myriad species of fauna and flora that prosper in the area, the New Territories is home to a fragile ecosystem of major importance – Mai Po Marsh.

Sitting on the edge of Deep Bay, Mai Po is a network of ponds and mudflats that every winter attract almost 70,000 waterbirds. Deep Bay and Mai Po together form an essential stopping-off place for migratory birds. Yet Mai Po's future is uncertain. The water quality in Deep Bay is among the worst around the coast of Hong Kong; the Environmental Protection Department (EPD) has found that the levels of dissolved oxygen (DO) in the water have been declining since 1988. Levels of DO fell to zero on one occasion in the 1996 summer.

As a result, the numbers of crabs and mudskippers declined sharply in 1996, and it is these that the birds use for food in winter. Although the number of birds that visited in the winter of 1996 did not decrease, anxious watchers are waiting for the knock-on effect to take place.

The pollution used to come from the vast amount of pig manure released into Deep Bay, but this has recently been curbed by a government ordinance which insists that pig slurry be treated before being flushed away. This ordinance appears to be having an effect, but a potentially larger hazard has taken its place.

Deep Bay neighbours on the city of Shenzhen in China, which is pumping out a rapidly increasing amount of sewage, 50% of which is untreated. The only real solution to this environmental threat is for the city of Shenzhen to build more sewage treatment facilities, but as the population of the city expands faster than its infrastructure, this will take time. Luckily for the beleaguered Mai Po Marsh, 1997 was one of the wettest years on record, and the large volume of rain water has flushed out and diluted many of the pollutants. The number of crabs and mudskippers has increased, but this could just reflect a temporary improvement in the region's ecology.

If the lower links of the food chain are seriously imperilled, the 270 or more species of bird that depend on Mai Po will possibly disappear, taking with them mammals such as leopard cats and otters.

The high street is packed with souvenir sellers. Just to remind you that this is indeed Hong Kong, you are expected to make a donation of HK$5 when you enter the village. Put the money in the coin slot by the entrance.

You can take photographs of the Hakka women in traditional black dress. Most of them will model for you if you pay them. Agree on a price beforehand – usually about HK$10. This is a good chance for you to practise your rusty Hakka with something like 'but I thought you said the group photo was HK$5?'.

Shui Tau

This 17th century village is famous for its carved roofs, which are ship-prow shaped and decorated with sculpted fish and dragons. Tiny traditional houses huddle inside Shui Tau's walls.

The ancestral hall in the middle of the village is used as a school in the mornings, but was originally built for the clan to worship its forebears. The ancestors' names are listed on the altar in the inner hall and on the long boards down the side. The sculpted fish, on the roof of the entrance hall, represent husband and wife and are there for good luck.

The fish is a common Chinese symbol of good luck and prosperity in most Chinese dialects. In both Mandarin and Cantonese, the word for 'fish' is pronounced the same way as the word 'plenty' or 'surplus'. To reach Shui Tau get off the bus on the outskirts of Kam Tin and walk down the road leading north.

In September 1995, Mai Po and Inner Deep Water Bay were declared a 'wetland of international importance'. The nature reserve of Mai Po marshes can be visited by contacting the World Wildlife Fund (WWF, ☎ 2526-4473), which conducts tours of the area on Sunday and public holidays. The WWF has taken more than 40,000 visitors to the area.

Greening Hong Kong If the sight of plastic bags everywhere drives you to a fit of environmental pique, don't despair. There are organisations in Hong Kong that are also concerned about the environment. Below is a list of the most prominent green groups active in Hong Kong:

Earthcare (☎ 2578-0522) focuses on animal welfare, ecology and education.
Environment Front (email envfront@rocketmail.com) is an environmental protection organisation in suburban Hong Kong.
Friends of the Earth (☎ 2528-5588) promotes all aspects relating to the protection and improvement of the living environment of Hong Kong.
Green Island Society (email ronald@falcon.cc.ukans.edu) focusses on the protection of Hong Kong wildlife and its natural habitats.
Green Lantau Association (☎ 2985-5099) is concerned with environmental issues affecting Lantau Island.
Greenpeace China (☎ 2854-8300) is technically more involved in ecological problems of a more global scale, but has an office in Hong Kong.
Green Power (email greenpow@hk.linkage.net) promotes awareness of green issues in Hong Kong.
Hong Kong Dolphinwatch (☎ 2984-1414) raises awareness of the plight of Hong Kong's pink dolphins and organises cruises for tourists to view dolphins in their natural habitat.
Produce Green (☎ 2674-1190) aims to develop green concepts.
World Wildlife Fund (WWF, ☎ 2526-1011) offers environmental protection through the use of conservation and educational measures.

Hong Kong's Vanishing Oyster Farms

The oyster farms of Lau Fau Shan, once a favoured tourist destination, are on the verge of clamming up once and for all. As a place where salt and fresh water meet and create the perfect habitat for the growth of the small bivalves, Lau Fau Shan, on the coast of Deep Water Bay, is the only part of Hong Kong suited to the cultivation of oysters. In the past tourists visited Lau Fau Shan to partake in excellent restaurant food.

However, daily production has slumped, as 80% of all oysters consumed in Hong Kong now come from over the border in Shenzhen. The reasons for this decline are several. Production costs are lower in China and oyster farming is regarded as a tough job; children from oyster growing families have left the shell-strewn shores of Lau Fau Shan behind and ventured forth to the bright lights of Hong Kong to find a new life.

In the 1970s oysters were regularly poached by thieves from across the border (some oyster farmers were even kidnapped and dragged off to China), and in 1979 the oyster farms reported a 95% loss from disease. A further blow to the industry occurred when locally grown shellfish were associated with hepatitis A and high cadmium levels. No doubt the amazing speed of growth in Shenzhen next door, with a resulting increase in levels of pollution, will also contribute to the demise of this once flourishing community of oyster farmers. Nor can the Deep Water Bay farming community, with its use of toxic chemicals, escape some of the blame.

The **Tin Hau Temple** is on the outskirts of the town and was built in 1722. The temple's absolutely enormous iron bell weighs 106kg.

Getting There & Away

To reach Kam Tin take bus No 64K, which runs from Yuen Long to Tai Po and passes Kam Tin along the way. Another option is bus No 77K between Yuen Long and Sheung Shui. Bus No 54 also goes from Yuen Long to Kam Tin. You can reach Kam Tin from Tsuen Wan by taking No 51 over the scenic Route Twisk. Whichever bus you take, sit on the top deck to enjoy the view.

PING KONG

This is another walled village, but few tourists take the time to visit. It's much more authentic than Kam Tin and you can go exploring around the farming area behind the village compound.

Getting there is a little tricky. There's a minibus, No 58K, from Sheung Shui but it's hard to find. The minibus runs from the bus stop just to the north-west of Sheung Shui KCR station (which you can get to by taking bus No 77K from Yuen Lon or Kam Tin, or the KCR from Kowloon).

The easiest way is to take a taxi from Sheung Shui to Ping Kong (about HK$30). Finding the minibus for the trip back into town is no problem.

FANLING

The main attraction in this town is the Fung Ying Sin Koon Temple, a Taoist temple for the dead. The ashes of the departed are deposited in what might be described as miniature tombs, with a photograph on each one. It's an interesting place to look around, but be respectful of worshippers. The temple is across from Fanling KCR station and is easy to find.

TAI PO

Another of the residential and industrial new towns, Tai Po is home to many of Hong Kong's high-tech industries (including the offices of the *South China Morning Post* newspaper).

Hong Kong Railway Museum

The Hong Kong Railway Museum (☎ 2653-3339) is an old train station which was built in 1913 and has recently been restored. It features trains dating back to 1911 and has

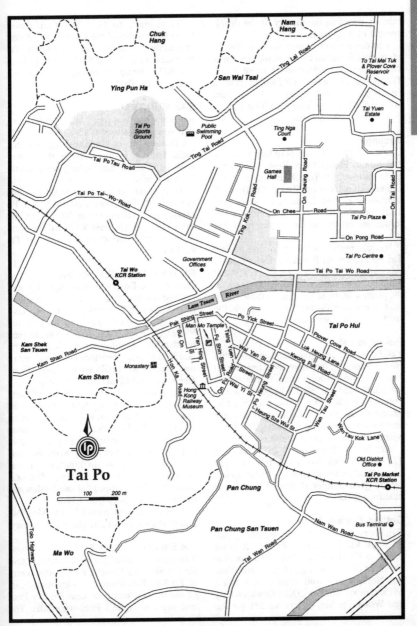

Tai Po

exhibits detailing the history of the development of local trains.

You can get to the museum from Tai Po Market KCR station by following the direction of the train tracks west for about 600m. The museum is on On Fu Rd and there are a few signs pointing the way. The museum is open daily (except Tuesday) from 9 am to 5 pm. Admission is free.

Cycling

One worthwhile activity is to hire a bicycle and ride to Plover Cove Reservoir on the north-east side of Tolo Harbour, or to the Chinese University (in Ma Liu Shui) on the south-west side of the harbour. Allow half a day for either trip. There is an inland route to the university, but the coastal route has the best views.

Bicycle rentals are easy to find around Tai Po Market KCR station. Definitely do this trip on a weekday – on weekends and holidays thousands of people descend on the place with the same idea. At these times, bikes are scarce, the rates are higher and the road is crowded with cyclists.

Places to Eat

Tai Po is not the gourmet centre of the New Territories, but there are a few decent eateries. The *Cosmopolitan Curry House* (☎ 2650-7056) at 80 Kwong Fuk Rd is regularly packed out – you may need to phone ahead to check the staff are not turning diners away at the door. The Indo-Malaysian curries are magnificent.

Nearby, the *Shalimar* (☎ 2653-7790), at 127 Kwong Fuk Rd, is an Indian curry house that's a bit hit-or-miss, but it should satisfy your hunger if you've built up a healthy appetite.

Getting There & Away

Tai Po is connected to Kowloon by the KCR at Tai Po Market station. It costs HK$8 to Kowloon for adults. You can also get there on bus No 73X from Tsuen Wan, bus No 74X to Kwun Tong (which has a MTR station), bus No 75X to Kowloon City and Wong Tai Sin, or bus No 271 (or the

N271 at night) to Tsim Sha Tsui. Buses leave from north of the Lam Tsuen River, around the area of On Chee Rd, near the Tai Po Plaza. Minibus No 501S heads to Lam Tin MTR station (coming from Sheung Shui, via Tai Po).

SAN MUN TSAI

San Mun Tsai is a small village by the sea that gets few visitors. It's a charming place – a floating mix of homes belonging to the local fishing families. Note the power cables and phone lines strung precariously between rafts.

To get there you can either get minibus No 20K to San Mun Tsai from Tai Po Market KCR station or bus No 74K to San Mun Tsai from On Chee Rd in Tai Po, north of the Lam Tsuen River and near the Tai Po Plaza.

PLOVER COVE RESERVOIR

Plover Cove Reservoir is good hiking and cycling country, and if you make the effort to go there you'll probably want to spend a full day. If you're going to hike in the Plover Cove Reservoir area be sure to pick up the HKTA information sheet on the North-East New Territories and a copy of the Universal Publications' *Sai Kung Peninsula and Clearwater Bay* map.

The reservoir was completed in 1968 and before this time Hong Kong often faced critical water shortages – water rationing was common. The reservoir was built using a very unusual technique. Rather than build a dam across a river (Hong Kong has few rivers that amount to anything), a dam was built across the mouth of a bay. The sea-water was then pumped out and fresh water pumped in – mostly from China.

Bicycles can be rented in Tai Mei Tuk and rowboats are for hire alongside the bay.

Pat Sin Leng Nature Trail

This trail is an excellent walk. It begins near the Pat Sin Leng Country Park visitor centre at Tai Mei Tuk, about half a kilometre east of the village, and ends near Bride's Pool and the two Bride's Pool waterfalls. The walk is 5km, with an elevation gain of 300m. The scenery is good, but the place gets packed on weekends – unless a typhoon comes along and clears out the tourists. Take along plenty of water, as you may not be able to buy anything on the trail. At the end of the trail, just walk along the road back to Tai Mei Tuk and catch a bus returning to Tai Po.

Alternatively, if walking has got you in the mood, continue on north to Luk Keng and clamber onto minibus No 56K to Fanling KCR station.

If you want to do more strenuous walking, detour to the nearby summit of Wong Leng, which is more than 600m high, then continue to Hok Tau Reservoir and the Country Parks centre at Hok Tau Wai. The distance from Tai Mei Tuk to Hok Tau Wai is 12km and takes about four hours. You can camp at Hok Tau Wai or walk another 1.5km to Sha Tau Kok Rd, then catch a bus to Fanling and a KCR train to Kowloon.

Places to Stay

There are camp sites at Sam A Chung and Hok Tau.

Bradbury Lodge (☎ 2662-5123) is the HKYHA's premier hostel in the New Territories. Beds cost HK$45, plus an additional HK$10 in summer if the air conditioning is turned on. Family rooms for four persons are available at HK$250 and double rooms cost HK$200. Camping is not permitted. The hostel is by the waters of Plover Cove and next to the northern tip of the Plover Cove Reservoir dam wall, a few hundred metres south of Tai Mei Tuk, on Ting Kok Rd (Ting Kok Rd is the main road that connects Tai Po with Tai Me Tuk).

To get there take the KCR to Tai Po Market station, then bus No 75K to Tai Mei Tuk and follow the access road with the sea on your right side (it's less than a five minute walk).

Bicycles can be rented in Tai Mei Tuk and rowboats are for hire alongside the bay. There are some easy hiking possibilities in the area, plus a fairly strenuous hike up into the Pat Sin Leng mountains.

Getting There & Away

To reach Plover Cove Reservoir, catch bus No 75K from Tai Po Market KCR station and take it all the way to the last stop at Tai Mei Tuk. On Sunday and public holidays bus No 75R goes on to Bride's Pool.

There is also a village bus (a blue truck with a canopy and seats on the back) that operates from Tai Po market to Tai Mei Tuk and Bride's Pool and terminates at Leng Pui/Wu Kau Tang.

TAI PO KAU

This forest reserve, between Tai Po Market KCR station and the Chinese University, is Hong Kong's most extensive woodlands and is a prime venue for birdwatching. It's a great place to get away from the crowds and a superb place to enjoy a quiet walk, except on Sunday when all the crowds will join you. To get there, take bus No 72A, which runs from Ting Kok Rd in Tai Po (north of the Lam Tsuen River) to Tai Wai, and get off at the stop before Sha Tin. You can also take bus No 72 from Shanghai St in Mong Kok (Kowloon) or a taxi (about HK$20) from Tai Po Market KCR station.

CHINESE UNIVERSITY

Ma Liu Shui is home to the Chinese University, established in 1963, which has a beautiful campus and is worth a visit.

The Institute of Chinese Studies in the Chinese University has an interesting **art museum** (☎ 2609-7416) which houses local collections as well as those from museums elsewhere in China. There's an enormous exhibition of paintings and calligraphy by Guangdong artists from the Ming period to modern times, a collection of bronze seals that are 2000 years old and a large collection of jade flower carvings.

The museum is open weekdays and Saturday from 10 am to 4.30 pm, and on Sunday and public holidays from 12.30 to 4.30 pm (closed on some public holidays). Admission is free.

If you've worked up an appetite, *Yucca De Lac Restaurant* (☎ 2961-1630) in Ma Liu Shui is a good place, with outdoor tables and a view of Tolo Harbour. There is no dim sum, but standard Chinese dishes are served (the roast pigeon is a house specialty).

You can easily reach the Chinese University by taking the KCR to University station. A free bus outside the station runs through the campus to the administration building at the top of the hill. It's easiest to take the bus uphill and then walk back down to the station.

SHA TIN

In a long, narrow valley, Sha Tin, meaning Sand Field, is a new town built mostly on reclaimed land that was a big mudflat just a few years ago. Unlike some of the other new towns, Sha Tin is both a desirable place to live and an attractive town to visit. Patches of traditional Chinese houses remain, preserving a historical look absent in many other parts of Hong Kong. Hong Kong residents flock to Sha Tin on the weekends to shop at the Sha Tin New Town Plaza, one of the biggest shopping malls in Hong Kong. In addition to the plethora of shops and restaurants, there is also a huge indoor swimming pool about 400m north of Sha Tin New Town Plaza.

Ten Thousand Buddhas Monastery

If you're big on Buddhas, head for this monastery, which sits on a hillside about 500m west of Sha Tin KCR station. Built in the 1950s, it actually has 12,800 miniature Buddha statues along the walls of the main temple, all of similar height but in slightly different poses. There is a nine level pagoda and larger-than-life statues of Buddha's followers in front of the temple.

From the main monastery area, walk up more steps to find a smaller temple housing the embalmed body of the founding monk who died in 1965. His body was encased in gold leaf and is now on display behind glass. It is considered polite to put a donation in the box next to the display case to help pay for the temple's upkeep.

The temple is open from 8 am to 6.30 pm. It's easy to reach: go through the left-hand exit at Sha Tin KCR station, and follow the signs. You'll need strong legs to climb the 400-odd steps to the complex. At the time of writing, the monastery was closed as it was undergoing repairs due to mud slides in the vicinity. Check with the HKTA (☎ 2807-6177) before heading out there.

Che Kung Temple

This is a small, but active Taoist temple between Sha Tin and Tai Wai KCR stations, which is dedicated to Che Kung, a Song dynasty general. The temple is interesting, but not as imposing as some of the larger Taoist temples (eg Wong Tai Sin in Kowloon). However, it is very popular, especially on holidays and the third day after the Chinese New Year, which is the birthday of Che Kung.

As you enter the temple grounds, old women excitedly stuff red pieces of paper with Chinese characters into your hands and then demand money. The papers appear to be a type of blessing. The old women say that 'the more money you give, the more blessing you will receive'.

From Tai Wai KCR station, you can walk to the temple. As you come out of Tai Wai KCR station, turn left and head south down Mei Tin Rd to the roundabout. Turn left again (heading east) and walk for about half a kilometre down Che Kung Miu Rd and you will come to the temple; it's on the south side of the road. Bus No 80K from Sha Tin KCR station also stops near the temple, or you can take a taxi (about HK$25).

Sha Tin Racecourse

Sha Tin is the site of Hong Kong's second racecourse. It cost HK$500 million and after seven years of building it was opened in 1980. Built almost entirely on reclaimed land, the racecourse was financed by the introduction of night racing at Hong Kong Island's Happy Valley racecourse.

On race days, entrance is HK$5. Races are held most Wednesday evenings and on weekends. Bets are easily placed at one of

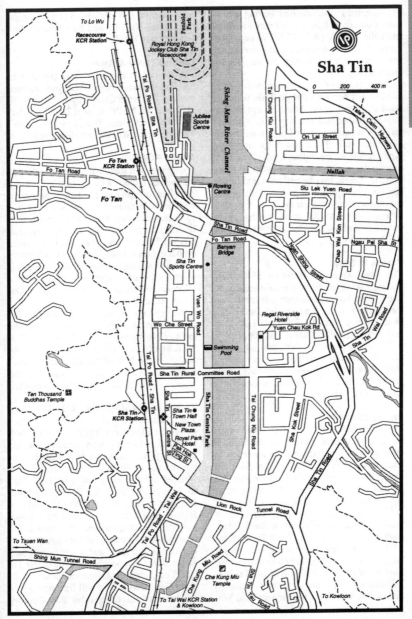

the numerous computerised betting terminals. You can pick up a list of race meetings from the HKTA (☎ 2807-6177) or if you know absolutely nothing about horseracing, you can put your money on the 'Come Horseracing Tour'.

In the centre of the racetrack is the interesting eight hectare **Penfold Park**, which is open to the public most days except on race days, Monday and the day after a public holiday. It can get packed out on weekends – an indication of just how desperate Hong Kong residents are to find a bit of greenery among the concrete housing estates. Going there to scream may be cathartic if your life savings have been trampled into the turf at the surrounding racecourse.

You can get to the racecourse by taking the KCR to either the Fo Tan or Racecourse KCR stations.

Places to Stay

The *Regal Riverside Hotel* (☎ 2649-7878, fax 2637-4748, email rrh@regal-hotels.com, www.regal-hotels.com/riverside.html), on Tai Chung Kiu Rd, is a huge three star hotel. Doubles cost from HK$2000 to HK$2400 and suites cost HK$3800 to HK$8800.

The *Royal Park Hotel* (☎ 2601-2111, fax 2601-3666, email royalprk@vol.net), 8 Pak Hok Ting St, has doubles costing from HK$1780 to HK$2480 and suites from HK$3600 to HK$5680.

Places to Eat

The multi-level Sha Tin New Town Plaza has more restaurants than you can shake a chopstick at – everything from hamburgers and pizzas to Peking duck and shark's fin soup. *Koh-I-Noor* (☎ 2601-4969), on the ground floor of New Town Plaza Phase III, is a notable place for fine Indian food.

If you're in need of a quick fix of spicy food, *Banthai Thai Cuisine* (☎ 2609-3686), shop A172, level 1, New Town Plaza Phase III, has a well deserved reputation and loyal fan base. There's also the excellent *Welcome Thai Food* (☎ 2608-0728) at 101-2 Tai Wai Rd, which is often crowded with contented diners. Tai Wai Rd is not far from Tai Wai

KCR station; exit the station and turn right onto Tsuen Nam Rd and then take the first left which is Tai Wai Rd.

Getting There & Away

Sha Tin is easy to get to – take the KCR to Sha Tin station. Alternatively you can take bus No 170 from Causeway Bay (or N170 at night), bus No 263R from Tuen Mun, bus No 48X from Tseun Wan, bus No 72 from Tai Po or bus No 299 from Sai Kung.

AMAH ROCK

It may just be a rock, but like many Chinese landmarks, there is a local legend. The story goes that for many years a fisherman's wife, with her baby on her back, stood on this spot to watch for her husband's return. The husband never came back and the gods took pity on her and transported her to heaven with a lightning bolt – a rock was left where she was standing. In Hong Kong, an amah is a servant or maid. The name of the rock in Cantonese is Mong Fu Shek or 'Gazing Out for Husband Stone'.

As you take the train south from Sha Tin towards Kowloon, Amah Rock is east of the railway line up on the hillside after Tai Wai KCR station but before the train enters the tunnel. Stage five of the MacLehose Trail passes near Amah Rock – see also the MacLehose Trail entry earlier in this chapter.

TSING SUI WAN (CLEARWATER BAY)

The southeastern point of the New Territories is the Clearwater Bay Peninsula, which is characterised by wonderfully untamed and rough contours – a wild backdrop to the modernity of urban Hong Kong. It is wedged in by Tseung Kwan O (Junk Bay) to the west and Tsing Sui Wan (Clearwater Bay) to the east – Tai Miu Wan (Joss House Bay) nestles to the south. Junk Bay is now the site of enormous land reclamation and housing development, but the eastern coastline is still unscarred and offers exceptional walks, some fine beaches and the oldest Tin Hau Temple on the Cantonese coast.

At Tai Au Mun you will find yourself in the heart of the **Clearwater Bay Country**

Park. Trails head off in various directions: you can take the small road (Lung Ha Wan Rd) north to the beach of **Lung Ha Wan** (Lobster Bay) or take the road (Tai Au Mun Lo) south to the two Clearwater Bay beaches. The sandy shores of **Clearwater Bay Beach No 1** and **Clearwater Bay Beach No 2** are lapped by clean water. In summer go during the week, as this is a popular destination and at weekends it gets very crowded.

Tai Au Mun Lo (the road leading down from Tai Au Mun) narrows just above Clearwater Bay Beach No 2, but you can carry on along the path (the bus from Choi Hung goes no further than this) away south from the two Clearwater Bay beaches past the mount of Tai Ha Shan (273m) to the venerably ancient **Tin Hau Temple**, perched on the tip of the peninsula, overlooking Joss House Bay. The place offers a view out over the waves to the island of Tung Lung Chau to the south. This temple is one of the oldest centres of spiritual power in Hong Kong and is dedicated to the protector of fisher folk, the Queen of Heaven, Tin Hau. Although the site dates back to 1266, the building itself dates from 1878. It suffered heavily during the passage of Typhoon Wanda in 1962, warranting renovation.

To the east of the temple is Clearwater Bay Golf Course and the charming village of Poi Toi O.

From the temple, hiking trails lead back to Tai Au Mun, or hikers can take the trail up Tin Ha Shan and then continue on the trail to **High Junk Peak** (Tiu Yu Yung) and then cross down to Tai Au Mun.

Getting There & Away

To get to the area, take the MTR to Choi Hung and catch bus No 91, which leaves from outside the station. The bus passes Silverstrand Beach (Ngan Sin Wan) – you can get off there and go for a dip, before heading south to Tai Au Mun. If you want to go to Lung Ha Wan, get off the bus at Tai Au Mun proper, but if you want to see the beaches in Clearwater Bay, continue on the bus, which stops above the beaches at the final station.

SAI KUNG PENINSULA

This is the garden spot of the New Territories. The Sai Kung Peninsula is the last chunk of Hong Kong, apart from the outlying islands, that remains a haven for hikers, campers, swimmers and boating enthusiasts. Pirates and tigers are no longer a problem, but hikers sometimes encounter unpleasant dogs – carry a stick, dog repellent, grenades or whatever you deem necessary.

Some of Hong Kong's best swimming beaches are on the Sai Kung Peninsula. Just keep in mind that sharks make a yearly pilgrimage to this area and attacks are not uncommon. Windsurfing equipment can be hired from the Windsurfing Centre (☎ 2792-5605), Sha Ha (just past Sai Kung). Bus Nos 94 and 99 can take you to Sha Ha from Sai Kung.

Sai Kung Town

Sai Kung town was originally a fishing village and although it's now more of a suburb, some of the feeling of the original port remains. Fishing boats still put in an occasional appearance, and down on the waterfront is a string of seafood restaurants that, despite high prices, draw patrons from all around Hong Kong. Sai Kung town is an excellent point from which to launch a walking expedition into the surrounding region and then return to for delicious food in the evening.

A short journey to one of the islands off Sai Kung town is eminently feasible. Hidden away are some excellent beaches that are worth visiting on a *kaido* (small boat). Kaidos leave from the pier on the waterfront in Sai Kung town. Most head over to **Sharp Island** (Kiu Tsui Chau) about 1.5km away. Hap Mun Bay, a sandy beach in the south of the island is served by kaidos as is Kiu Tsui Bay on the western shore. The other islands of Pak Sha Chau (White Sand Island) and Cham Tau Chau (Pillow Island) are also served by kaidos, although the service is far more irregular.

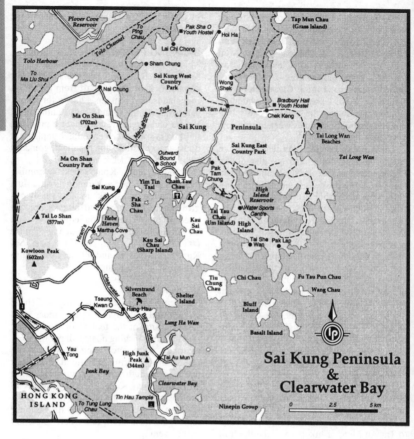

Plover Cove
Reservoir
Pak Sha O
Youth Hostel   Hoi Ha
Tap Mun Chau
(Grass Island)

To
Ping
Chau
Lai Chi Chong

Tolo Channel
Sham Chung

Tolo Harbour
Sai Kung West
Country Park

To
Ma Liu Shui
Nai Chung   Wong
Shek

Pak Tam Au   Bradbury Hall
Youth Hostel

Ma On Shan
(702m)   Sai Kung   Peninsula   Chek Keng

Tai Long Wan
Beaches

Sai Kung East
Country Park   Tai Long Wan

Ma On Shan
Country Park
Outward
Bound
School   Pak
Tam
Chung

Sai Kung
Highway   Yim Tin
Tsai   Cham Tau
Chau   High
Island
Reservoir

Pak
Sha
Chau   Tai Tau
Chau
(Um Island)   Water Sports
Centre

Tai Lo Shan
(577m)
Hebe
Haven
Martha Cove   Kau
Sai
Chau   High
Island   Tai She
Wan   Pak Lap

Kowloon Peak
(602m)   Kau Sai
Chau
(Sharp Island)

Hiram's Highway

Tiu
Chung
Chau   Chi Chau   Fu Tau Pun Chau

Wang Chau

Silverstrand
Beach   Shelter
Island

Tseung
Kwan O
Hang Hau   Bluff
Island

Clearwater Bay Road
Lung Ha Wan   Basalt Island

Yau
Tong   High Junk
Peak
(344m)   Tai Au Mun

Sai Kung Peninsula
&
Clearwater Bay

Junk Bay   Clearwater Bay

HONG KONG
ISLAND   To Tung Lung
Chau   Tin Hau Temple   Ninepin Group   0   2.5   5 km

MacLehose Trail

Also reached by kaido from Sai Kung town is the small island of **Yim Tin Tsai** (Little Salt Field), where there is a Christian Church, St Joseph's Chapel, which is the focus of the island's devout Catholic population. Yim Tin Tsai is connected to the much larger **Kau Sai Chau** by a narrow spit that becomes submerged at high tide. Kau Sai Chau is the site of the Jockey Club Kau Sai Chau Public Golf Course. A large sign at the kaido pier in Sai Kung warns of unexploded military shells still unaccounted for on some of the

islands. Areas of potential danger are clearly marked.

Places to Stay If you want to stay the night, there are a range of *camps* and *youth hostels*. A number of these hostels/camps have activities like boating, archery, swimming and walks.

Places to Eat The hungry come from miles around to see if it's true that *Pepperoni's Pizza & Cafe* (☎ 2792-2083), 1592 Po Tung Rd, dish up some of the finest pizza and pasta in Hong Kong. It's certainly excellent, and the atmosphere is both relaxing and fun – this truly is a haven for those in need of authentic Italian chow.

Just along from Pepperoni's, and under the same management, is *Al Fresco's* (☎ 2792-5296), 183D Po Tung Rd, which specialises in steaks, ribs and seafood. Both places are open from 9 am to 11 pm.

Jaspa's (☎ 2792-6388), 13 Sha Tsui Path, is opposite the playground. It serves French and Italian food. The place is often full of expats taking a break from 'noodlesville'. It's open from 9 am to 11 pm Tuesday to Sunday.

The *Tung Kee Restaurant* (☎ 2792-7453) at 96-102 Man Nin St is the place for Cantonese seafood. It's not cheap, but then the food is outstanding. Don't overlook the excellent seafood restaurants on the waterfront, some of which are hidden away in the old town section.

Sai Kung Islands Trip

There's an interesting trip over the waves from Sai Kung Town exploring the mosaic of small islands that fragment the surrounding waters.

If you have around two hours to spare, jump aboard a kaido bound for the small island of Yim Tin Tsai (Little Salt Field). The ride out from Sai Kung Town takes around 15 minutes, wending its way through a series of small islands. On your left is **Yeung Chau** (Sheep Island). You will be able to spot a burial site on the slopes of the hillside – the Chinese like to position graves with decent views of the sea. Further along on the left hand side is **Cham Tau Chau** (Pillow Island). Directly opposite on your right is **Pak Sha Chau** (White Sand Island), which has a popular beach on its northern shore. Also on the right and just ahead of Pak Sha Chau is **Dai Chaan Chau** (Big Spade Island).

Just beyond Dai Chaan Chau is the much larger island of **Kiu Tsui Chau**, which has a few popular beaches on the western shores, including **Kiu Tsui Bay**, and the small **Hap Mun Bay** to the south. A narrow sandy spit connects the island to the much smaller **Kiu Tau**.

The kaido stops at **Yim Tin Tsai**, where you can hop off onto the jetty. Yim Tin Tsai (Little Salt Field) is so named because the original inhabitants made a living from fishing and salt panning. A few minutes walk from the jetty up a small flight of steps, to the left, is the small island school of **Tsing Boor Hok Haau** (Clear Wave School). Further up the hill is the focal point of the island, the attractive **St Joseph's Chapel**. This is the only religious edifice or temple on the island, which is most unusual for Hong Kong where Tin Hau temples are usually the place of worship. Everyone on the island is Catholic and they all belong to the same clan. Apparently the villagers have maintained a devotion to the Papacy since a miraculous vision of St Peter appeared to chase away a posse of pirates who were harassing the poor fisherfolk. Further ahead is the small village of **Yim Tin Tsai**, the refuge for a handful of families.

You can return to Sai Kung Town the way you came, or via the southern route which will take you down to the south of Kiu Tsui Chau. Around the other side of the cape is the popular beach of **Hap Mun Bay**.

Finding a kaido for this trip is no problem – as soon as you walk along the promenade in Sai Kung Town you will be approached by an enthusiastic array of kaido owners trawling for fares. You will have to explain to the owner of the kaido where you want to go, how long you want to spend and which way you wish to return. The problem is that they don't speak much English. Try using the Sai Kung Peninsula & Clearwater Bay map to explain where you wish to go and how you want to return. The kaido owners should understand that you wish to remain on Yim Tin Tsai for about half an hour so that you can visit the church and take in the views before returning to the boat. The usual price for this kind of service on weekdays is around HK$150.

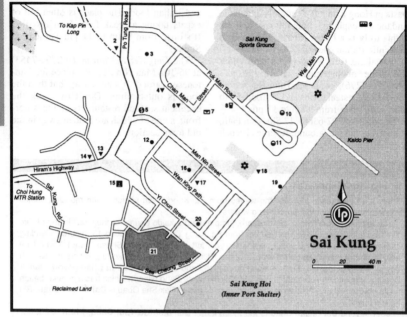

Sai Kung

0   20   40 m

The *Duke of York* (☎ 2792-8435), 42-56 Fuk Man Rd, is OK for pub grub. Specialities are the baked fish and salad, washed down with a Foster's or Carlsberg beer. This is Sai Kung's expat watering hole, and is completely packed out on Sunday.

New Castle Restaurant & Pub (☎ 2792-5225) is near McDonald's on Chan Man St. Steaks, fish and chips and snacks monopolise the menu. This place opens at noon but only gets busy in the evening. The kitchen stays open until 9 pm.

Getting There & Away To get to Sai Kung, take the MTR to Choi Hung station. Head out through exit B, which leads to Clearwater Bay Rd North. This is where you'll find the Choi Hung Estate bus station – take bus No 92 or the No 1 minibus, which is faster and more frequent, to the Sai Kung town station. The ride from Choi Hung to Sai Kung town takes about 30 minutes by bus and about 20 minutes by minibus. On weekends, the ride back tends to be slower, and the town's bus station gets extremely busy. Alternatively you can catch bus No 299 from Sha Tin (this bus also passes through Ma On Shan Village).

Hebe Haven
Bus No 92 (or preferably minibus No 1) from Choi Hung MTR station to Sai Kung town passes the small bay of Hebe Haven (or Pak Sha Wan, meaning White Sand Bay), home of the **Hebe Haven Yacht Club**. You won't have a hard time recognising the place – the yacht fleet practically chokes the harbour. Hebe Haven more than holds its own against other prestigious *gwailo* ghettos such as the Peak and Discovery Bay.

To swim at **Trio Beach** catch a sampan from Hebe Haven to the tiny peninsula (Ma Lam Wat) across the bay. The beach is

Sai Kung 西貢	7 Post Office 郵局	16 Playground 運動場
1 Catholic Cemetery 天主教墳場	8 Duke of York Pub 9 Swimming Pool 西貢公眾泳池	17 Jasper's 18 Seafood Restaurants 海鮮餐廳
2 Le Bistrol	10 Bus Terminal 巴士總站	19 Sampan Hire 租舢舨
3 Town Hall 西貢大會堂	11 Maxicab-Minibus Terminal 小巴士總站	20 7-Eleven
4 McDonald's; Wellcome Supermarket 麥當勞及惠康超級市場	12 Park N' Shop 百佳超級市場	21 Old Town 舊城
5 HongkongBank 匯豐銀行	13 Pepperoni's Pizza & Cafe	
	14 Al Fresco's Restaurant	
6 Newcastle Restaurant & Pub 新堡餐廳酒廊	15 Tin Hau Temple 天后廟	

excellent and the sampan trip should only cost a few dollars. Alternatively, walk out to the peninsula from Sai Kung town, a distance of about 2.5km one way.

Ma On Shan

At 702m, Ma On Shan is the fourth highest peak in Hong Kong after Tai Mo Shan in the New Territories and two peaks on Lantau Island (Lantau and Sunset peaks).

Ma On Shan the mountain is not to be confused with Ma On Shan the village. Ma On Shan village is another new town, with a row of high-rise housing estates and shopping malls.

Access to Ma On Shan (the mountain) is via the MacLehose Trail. The trail does not actually go over the summit, but it goes very close and the spur route to the peak is obvious. It is a steep and strenuous climb. You can walk from the mountain down to the village and get a bus to Sha Tin, then on to Kowloon by train.

You can get to the MacLehose Trail by walking from Sai Kung town or, alternatively, you can get closer to the peak by taking bus No 99 from Sai Kung town. The bus runs along Sai Sha Rd. To find the right bus stop, let the driver know you want to climb Ma On Shan. You can camp at Ngong Ping on the MacLehose trail in Ma On Shan Country Park.

Pak Tam Chung

This is the easternmost point you can reach by bus on the Sai Kung Peninsula. It's also the eastern terminus of the MacLehose Trail.

You can get to Pak Tam Chung on bus No 94 from Sai Kung town, which runs hourly. On Sunday and holidays there is also bus No 96R from Choi Hung MTR station, which runs every 20 to 30 minutes. Along the way, the bus passes Tai Mong Tsai where there is an **Outward Bound School**, an international organisation that teaches wilderness survival.

From Pak Tam Chung you can walk to High Island Reservoir, which used to be a sea channel. Both ends were blocked with dams and then the seawater was pumped out and fresh water was pumped in. The reservoir was opened in 1978.

While you're in Pak Tam Chung, visit the **Sai Kung Country Park Visitor Centre**, which has excellent maps, photographs and displays of the area's geology, fauna and flora. The centre is open every day from 9 am to 5 pm. The centre is in the south of Pak Tam Chung, just by the road from Sai Kung. It is closed on Tuesday.

From Pak Tam Chung, it's a 25 minute walk south along a trail to the **Sheung Yiu Folk Museum** (☎ 2792-6365), a restored Hakka village typical of those found in

HONG KONG

Hong Kong in the 19th century. The museum is open from 9 am to 4 pm daily, except Tuesday and some public holidays. Admission is free.

There are camp sites at Long Ke Wan (this is a bay to the south-east of High Island Reservoir), Lai Chi Chong and Yuen Ng Fan (on the western fringe of High Island Reservoir). The camp at Lai Chi Chong is popular, although more with Cantonese locals escaping the fumes and oppressive proximity of Central Hong Kong. The *Lai Chi Chong Ming Oi Siu Tong Ying* (☎ 2981-7873, fax 2981-8554) has accommodation but you have to go as a group. A room for four costs HK$208 per night, and includes a kitchen (it's about HK$80 more expensive between May and October); a range of outdoor activities are also available including canoeing (HK$480 for two), archery, orienteering, karaoke and boating (HK$10 every hour). Contact the camp for details. You can reach Lai Chi Chong by taking the ferry from Ma Liu Shui to the island of Tap Mun; this ferry stops at Lai Chi Chong (see the Tap Mun section for details). Alternatively, follow the directions for getting to Hoi Ha in this chapter and then take the trail to Lai Chi Chong.

Hoi Ha, Wong Shek, Chek Keng & Tai Long

There are several rewarding hikes in this area, but the logistics can be a bit tricky. It's highly advisable to first buy one of the *Countryside* series maps of the Sai Kung Country Park area from the Government Publications Office or the Sai Kung and Clearwater Bay map, published by Universal Publications (see the Maps section of the Hong Kong Facts for the Visitor chapter). For more information, contact the Country Parks Division of the Agriculture & Fisheries Department (☎ 2733-2132).

An attractive walk in the area starts from Hoi Ha (literally, under the sea), nestled on the coast of Hoi Ha Bay. Hoi Ha has a small beach where you can swim or have a picnic. It's is also one of the few places in Hong Kong's festering waters where coral still

grows – a large number of coral species have been recorded in the waters around the village. The WWFs is hoping to turn the area into a marine conservation area, to reverse the exodus of fish from Hoi Ha's waters and further stimulate the growth of coral. Hoi Ha has a camp site where you can pitch a tent for the night near the sea.

From Hoi Ha you can follow the path along the headland and coastline bordering Tai Tan Hoi Hap (Long Harbour) all the way to Wong Shek, from where you can catch a bus to Sai Kung or take the ferry to Ma Liu Shui. The walk covers a distance of about 6km.

Alternatively, there's an interesting walk through a few of Sai Kung's small villages, taking in a small beach. Starting at Chek Keng (Red Path) to the south-east of Wong Shek, you can follow a section of the MacLehose Trail that takes you to the small village and beach of Ham Tin (Salty Field). The path takes you through both a grassy woodland, with good views of the Sai Kung Peninsula, and the tiny village of Tai Long (Big Wave), where you can buy food and drink. The beach and village of Ham Tin are perched on the eastern coast of the Sai Kung Peninsula; from there, the MacLehose trail winds south to Sai Wan and around the High Island Reservoir. The return journey is about 8km.

Another popular clamber, starting from Chek Keng, is the ascent of the nearby Sharp Peak (468m).

Places to Stay As well as the camp site at Hoi Ha, there are a couple of hostels in the area. *Bradbury Hall* (☎ 2328-2458) in Chek Keng should not be confused with Bradbury Lodge, which is in Plover Cove Reservoir. Bradbury Hall has beds for HK$35 but you'll need to have an IYHF card. The hostel is right on the harbour facing the Chek Keng pier.

The *Pak Sha O Hostel* (☎ 2328-2327) charges HK$25 a bed and camping is permitted – don't forget to bring your IYHF membership card.

From Sai Kung town, take bus No 94 (an

hourly service from 8 am to 7 pm) towards Wong Shek pier and get off at Ko Tong village. From there, find Hoi Ha Rd and a road sign 30m ahead showing the way to Pak Sha O.

Getting There & Away Getting to Hoi Ha is not easy, unless you go on a Sunday or public holiday, when you can take minibus No 7 from Pak Tam Chung; otherwise, take a taxi from either Sai Kung or Pak Tam Chung. Bus No 94 links Sai Kung and Wong Shek pier. On Sunday and public holidays, there's a No 96R bus that runs between Wong Shek pier and Choi Hung MTR station.

To get to Chek Keng, take bus No 94 (runs hourly from 8 am to 7 pm) from Sai Kung to Yellow Stone pier, but get off at Pak Tam Au (it's the fourth bus stop after the County Park entrance, near the top of a hill). There's a footpath at the side of the road (going east) leading to Chek Keng village. Alternatively you can take the Polly Ferry from Ma Liu Shui, which departs at 8.30 am and 3.15 pm, with an extra run at 1.15 pm on Sunday and public holidays. See the following section for more details.

TOLO HARBOUR & TAP MUN CHAU

From Ma Liu Shui, ferries cruise through Tolo Harbour to Tap Mun Chau (Grass Island) and back again, calling in at various villages on the way.

Tap Mun Chau is in the north-east of the New Territories where Tolo Harbour empties into Tai Pang Wan (Mirs Bay). The island has an old-world fishing village atmosphere and is noted for its **Tin Hau Temple**, where whistling sounds can be heard at the altar during easterly winds. The temple was built during the reign of Kang Xi in the Qing dynasty. The Tin Hau Festival is very big there, although most of the celebrants come from the city.

Other attractions are **Tap Mun Cave** and the beautiful beaches on the eastern shore of the island.

Many visitors claim that Tap Mun Chau is the most interesting island of all those around Hong Kong. In many ways it's well worth the trip and you will be rewarded with the sensation of being aeons away from everything.

Unfortunately, as with many parts of Hong Kong, litter spoils many of the island's most scenic areas. It is incredible how many people dump their week's detritus on the poor little islet. There is no accommodation on the island.

Getting There & Away

The Tolo Harbour ferry is operated by the Polly Ferry Company (☎ 2771-1630). Ferries begin the journey at Ma Liu Shui, which is about a 15 minute walk from University KCR station. Ferries leave Ma Liu Shui at 8.30 am, arriving at Tap Mun Chau at 9.45 am (the ferry continues on to Wong Shek pier and Chek Keng).

On Sunday and public holidays, the first return ferry from Tap Mun Chau to Ma Liu

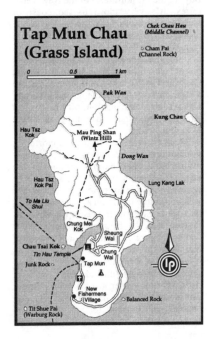

Tap Mun Chau (Grass Island)

Chek Chau Hau (Middle Channel)

Cham Pai (Channel Rock)

0   0.5   1 km

Pak Wan

Kung Chau

Hau Tsz Kok

Mau Ping Shan (Wintz Hill)

Dong Wan

Hau Tsz Kok Pai

Lung Keng Lak

To Ma Liu Shui

Chung Mei Kok

Sheung Wai

Chau Tsai Kok

Tin Hau Temple

Chung Wai

Junk Rock

Tap Mun

New Fishermens Village

Balanced Rock

Tit Shue Pai (Warburg Rock)

Shui leaves at 1.45 pm; from Monday to Saturday, the first return ferry departs at 10.40 am. The last ferry leaves Ma Liu Shui at 3.15 pm, arriving at Tap Mun Chau at 4.30 pm. The return ferry from Tap Mun Chau leaves at 5.20 pm, reaching Ma Liu Shui at 6.35 pm. You can get an up to date ferry timetable from the HKTA.

As an alternative to the Tolo Harbour ferry, an easy way to reach Tap Mun Chau is to take a kaido from Wong Shek pier, which is the last stop on bus No 94. The kaidos run once every two hours, generally between the hours of 8.30 am to 6.30 pm. This route is particularly scenic because it cruises through the narrow Tai Tan Hoi Hap (Long Harbour), which is more reminiscent of a fjord in Norway than a harbour in Hong Kong.

PING CHAU
This small island is in Tai Pang Wan (Mirs Bay) in the far north-east of the New Territories. It's very close to the coast of mainland China and used to be one of the most popular destinations for people who wanted to leave China by swimming – braving the sharks and Chairman Mao's patrol boats. The island is referred to by the Cantonese as Tung (East) Ping Chau, to differentiate it from the island of Peng Chau (same pronunciation) off Lantau. The island is very small, measuring only 2km in length.

At one time the island supported a population of 3000, but now it is virtually uninhabited. The exodus started in the mid 1960s when the islanders suddenly decided that life in a Hong Kong factory was preferable to life on a peaceful fishing isle. Perhaps another reason for the emigration was the frequent robberies conducted by pirates from the south coast of mainland China.

The island's highest point is only about 40m, but it has unusual rock layers in its cliffs that glitter after a night of rain. The island has some beautiful white sandy beaches and is good for swimming. The largest beach on the island is Cheung Sha

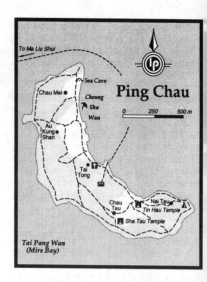

Wan, on the eastern shore. There is a small Tin Hau Temple on the south-east of the island, and some small caves dotting the cliffs.

Ping Chau is the site of Hong Kong's solitary radiation shelter, near Tai Tong (north of the pier). The island is just 12km from China's Daya Bay nuclear power station.

Places to Stay
There are several abandoned buildings crumbling on the island, but visitors are advised to bring camping equipment. There are a couple of hostels on the island, at Sha Tau (south of the pier) and in Tai Tong (to the north of the pier).

Getting There & Away
Getting to Ping Chau is quite an expedition. Unless you have your own yacht, you need to take the ferry from Ma Liu Shui (near University KCR station). The ferry is operated by the Polly Ferry Company (☎ 2771-1630). The ferry only runs on weekends. Ferries depart from Ma Liu Shui on Saturday at 9 am and 3.30 pm. The one Sunday ferry leaves Ma Liu Shui at 9 am.

There are only two return ferries from Ping Chau, at 5.30 pm on both Saturday and Sunday. Check these times since the schedule can change. Only round-trip tickets are sold (HK$50/70 for ordinary/deluxe), and the trip takes 1¾ hours. The Sunday morning ferry could well be booked out, but advance tickets are available from MTR travel service centres (eg in Tsim Sha Tsui, Causeway Bay and Admiralty). There are sporadic ferries to Wong Shek pier on the Sai Kung Peninsula, from where you can head to Choi Hung MTR station (on a Sunday) or Sai Kung town.

Outlying Islands

The outlying islands have rescued many a traveller from the mistaken belief that Hong Kong is an overpopulated ghetto of high-rises, surging crowds, rip-off tourist districts and a snarl of low-flying jets. When it's all too much and the last thing you want to see is another acre of asphalt, or yet another building site churning up dust and noise into the protesting air, it's time to dive aboard one of the ferries to the outlying islands and save your soul. Get up early, grab a ferry, sit out on the back deck and enjoy the sun and the stunning views.

Sunset on Lamma Island.

Half an hour's bounce away over the shallow waves of Hong Kong's waters is a veritable archipelago of choice. From the tranquil lanes of Cheung Chau to the monasteries and Buddhas of Lantau, Hong Kong's islands offer a world of peace and quiet, coupled with a host of sights and experiences. If it's beaches, sea air, cooler weather (in summer) and excellent seafood that make your holiday, look no further. The outlying islands are also a colourful encyclopaedia of animal and plant life and you don't have to be an entomologist to be amazed by the huge butterflies that drift on the breeze.

Some of Hong Kong's best beaches sit on the shores of the outlying islands, although these vary in quality. The remoter stretches of sand are quieter and more litter-free; camping possibilities also exist on these more secluded beaches.

Altogether there are 234 islands that make up Hong Kong, apart from Hong Kong Island itself. Together, the outlying islands make up about 20% of its total land area. Officially these islands are part of the New Territories – except for Stonecutters Island, which has become part of Kowloon thanks to land reclamation.

The outlying islands vary greatly in size and appearance. While many are little more than uninhabited rocks occasionally seen above sea level, Lantau is actually larger and higher than Hong Kong Island. Nevertheless, the number of inhabitants on the outlying islands combined is less than 100,000 people, not even 2% of Hong Kong's total.

Just a few decades ago, almost all of the habitable islands had permanent settlements supported mostly by the fishing industry. Now many of these villages are ghost towns, their inhabitants lured away by the promise of wealth in the nearby glittering metropolis. Some have travelled further than others. The actor Chow Yun Fat is a native of Lamma, and he ended up in Hollywood, via a long spell as front man in many of John Woo's ultra-violent Hong Kong movies.

While Chinese fishing families have been lured off the islands, foreigners have been moving in the opposite direction, attracted by lower housing costs and the tranquility. Expats are among the most staunch defenders of traditional island ways of life, fiercely opposing proposals to build high-rises and introduce cars to the islands. Lamma is *the* haven for expats, supported by a diverse restaurant culture and some fantastic bars.

In an ironic twist, the influx of foreigners helped developers justify more building projects. Developments such as Lantau's Discovery Bay – where matchbox high-rises now compete for a view of the sea – could be an indication of the way the islands are heading. Foreigners talk about instituting a building moratorium, but it seems unlikely. The problem is that every new resident wants to be the last.

Inconvenient transport kept the islands unspoiled, but this is changing. Discovery Bay only developed into suburbia when the introduction of high-speed ferries cut the commuting time to Central to 20 minutes. The development of the North Lantau Highway, connecting Chek Lap Kok airport on Lantau Island with Kowloon and Central erodes the sense of remoteness even more. This headlong rush to push out the high-speed ferries to the outlying islands may appear, at first glance, to threaten the seclusion that makes the islands rich. However, the islands are seeing a serious drop in beachcombers due to the recent *gwailo* exodus that has accompanied visa restrictions on those wanting to work in Hong Kong. Any sharp fall in the number of gwailos will take property prices down, and cause a rethink of the logic of a high-speed ferry option, possibly reversing the modernisation of the islands and restoring a sense of remoteness.

Cars are prohibited on all of the outlying islands except Lantau. On Lantau, a special vehicle permit is required and is not easily obtained, though this may change soon with the opening of the new airport. The only

traffic on the other islands are narrow tractors and trailers that can navigate the spindly roads. Lamma has its own ambulance, a bit wider than a fridge, that rushes around treating victims of the island's indigenous and venomous millipede.

A chronic hazard on all the islands is the dogs. Although it's illegal to have an unleashed and unmuzzled mutt in high-rise Hong Kong, the rules are largely ignored on the islands. The dogs are mostly friendly but some are fond of taking a bite out of tourists. If you are attacked, get a good look at the dog that bit you and then call the police – the owner may be tracked down and will have to pay your medical expenses and a fine.

The large number of stray dogs is in part due to thoughtless foreigners who come to Hong Kong for a brief time to work. They take on a dog and when they depart give it to a friend, who sooner or later abandons the animal.

Only those islands which are accessible by public ferry are included in this chapter. You probably won't get to visit the numerous other islands unless you can afford to charter a boat. Many of the remote islands are popular destinations for Hong Kong's fleet of yachts, where boat owners often indulge in such prohibited pastimes as nude swimming. Skinny-dipping or not, if you want to plunge into the waters in more inaccessible areas, remember that Hong Kong's waters are regularly patrolled by sharks.

The tiny islands of Tap Mun Chau and Ping Chau are covered in the New Territories chapter because they are best reached from there; the islands in this chapter are all easily accessible from Hong Kong Island.

One final word, try to avoid visiting on weekends, when it seems half of Hong Kong makes the weary pilgrimage away from skyscrapers and exhaust fumes to these oases of calm. On weekdays you will find that most of the gwailos who live on the islands are in town, along with everyone else.

ORIENTATION & INFORMATION

If you intend to do a major hike, it would be wise to equip yourself with the excellent

Countryside series of maps produced by the Crown Lands and Surveys Office. The essential map for the outlying islands is called *Countryside Series Map No 3: Lantau and Islands*. Another useful map is *Lantau Trail*. The maps are cheap and can be bought at the Government Publications Centre in the Government Offices building, 66 Queensway, Admiralty. Also look out for Universal Publications' *Lantau Island & Cheung Chau* (HK$18), which covers the two islands in great detail and is waterproof.

Worth looking out for during your sojourn in the outlying islands is the freebie magazine *The Islands' Orbital*, the outlying islands' monthly news circular. Aimed at expats living on large rocks in the waters around Hong Kong Island this mag has all sorts of useful information about festivals, shops, bars, green issues, upcoming hikes and local gossip all connected with the islands. You can generally find copies in gwailo bars on Lantau, Cheung Chau, Peng Chau and Lamma and some bars in Central. Contact the Lantau Orbital Publishing Co (☎ 2984-9780, email orbital@i-wave.net) for more details.

ACCOMMODATION
Individual hostels, guesthouses, hotels and homestays are listed in the Places to Stay sections for each island in this chapter.

For long term stays, the outlying islands give you splendid surroundings, and finding a room or an apartment on Lamma will cost far less than if you stayed in Kowloon or Hong Kong Island. You can rent a three bedroom apartment with a roof terrace on Lamma for less than HK$8000 a month. Rooms and apartments can easily be found by scanning the property pages of the daily English papers or, even better, by glancing at the advert wall just beyond the Lamma ferry terminal, which is usually plastered with offers. There you can get a share apartment or a room in a house for as little as HK$1600 a month – the cheapest Chungking Mansions' dive would be twice this amount.

Things to weigh in the balance include the cost of a one-way ferry trip to Lamma, which

costs HK$9.20 on weekdays and HK$12.50 on weekends, and takes 45 minutes. This is offset by the joy of living in an almost unspoilt Eden of banana trees and dense grasses, rolling hills, beautiful, neat fields, and total silence apart from croaking frogs (and it's cooler than Hong Kong Island or Kowloon). If you're going to live in Hong Kong for a month or so, Lamma is an excellent place to stay; it offers a jaunty nightlife scene with cheapish beer and good food. Prices will probably nose-dive further on Lamma as work visa requirements become more stringent and many expats head home.

You can book apartments in the city before your arrival at the islands. The cost of leasing a apartment can be amazingly low, especially if you're staying a week or longer. In the not-so-distant past there was an outlying islands holiday-apartment booking office next to the ferry pier in Central, but this has been wiped out (perhaps only temporarily) by a major construction project. In the meantime there are two places in Hong Kong where you can book island apartments. The Jubilee International Tour Centre (☎ 2530-0530, fax 2845-2469) is at room 302-303, Man Yee building, 60 Des Voeux Rd, Central. This office also books yachts, tour buses and even Rolls-Royces.

The other place is the Sino Centre, 582 Nathan Rd, Mong Kok, which houses numerous competing booking offices under one roof; all offer similar services.

On Cheung Chau there are booking offices for apartments right near the ferry pier (see the Cheung Chau section for details). Lantau has one such office, but it only seems to function on weekends and public holidays. The other islands do not have any booking offices for apartments, though there are some individual guesthouses and estate agents.

GETTING THERE & AWAY
The main islands are linked to Hong Kong by regular ferry services – not just for tourists but also for the locals who work in the city. The ferries are comfortable and cheap, and many have an air conditioned

top deck which costs extra. The ferries all have a basic bar that serves drinks and snacks. Smoking is prohibited on all the ferries and there is a hefty fine for offenders (maximum HK$5000), although on certain routes the rules are flouted by all and sundry, including the jovial captain, ship's mate and the rest of the crew.

There are two classes on the large ferries: ordinary and deluxe (air-con). Prices are significantly higher on weekends and holidays. For definition purposes, a weekend includes Saturday from noon onwards. There are discounts for children aged under 12 years. Seniors over 65 years can also get a discount (except in deluxe).

If you're staying on the islands and want to make a day trip into the city, definitely buy a round-trip ticket (holidays only). The ticket is only good on the day of purchase, but is 50% cheaper. The discount is not available on weekdays or on tickets sold in the city. If you decide to move to one of the islands long term, then invest in a monthly pass. The cost of a monthly pass varies from island to island.

Hoverferries also connect the islands – these cost over twice as much and go twice as fast as the normal ferries. Hoverferries are fun, but definitely not for those prone to seasickness! Eat lightly or bring a plastic bag. There is only one deck on the hoverferries, and thus only one class.

The company responsible for serving the islands is the Hongkong & Yaumati Ferry Co (☎ 2542-3081), which has a customer service centre next to the outlying islands ferry pier in Central. It operates a 24 hour schedule inquiries hotline (☎ 2525-1108). The timetables are pretty stable but are subject to slight change and certain services may be abandoned in the future. You can pick up a copy of the service timetable either at the Hongkong and Yaumati Ferry Co service centre or at the HKTA. Polly ferry (☎ 2771-1630) also runs on certain routes and is trying hard to snare more customers.

The islands are popular holiday destinations for Hong Kong residents – in fact too popular! On weekends the ferries become so crowded it's a wonder the boats don't sink.

Try to keep at least HK$20 worth of change with you and a small wad of HK$10 notes. You can buy the ticket from a booth, but you'll save time by putting the exact change into a turnstile as you enter the pier. On some of the smaller ferries the staff run out of change, so it helps to have small coins. Under no circumstances will the ticket offices change bills larger than HK$100.

If your time is limited, contact Watertours (☎ 2525-4808), which organise trips to the islands.

CHEUNG CHAU

Cheung Chau (which means Long Island in Cantonese) is 10km west of Hong Kong Island, off the south-east tip of Lantau. A one-time refuge for pirates, and later an exclusive retreat for British colonials, Cheung Chau is now the most populous of the outlying islands. Some 22,000 people, many of them commuters, are crammed onto Cheung Chau's 2.5 sq km, though very few gwailos live there.

Archaeological digs have shown that Cheung Chau, like Lamma and Lantau, was inhabited in prehistoric times. The island had a thriving fishing community 2500 years ago and a reputation for piracy from the year dot – probably started by the earliest Cantonese and Hakka settlers who supplemented their livelihood with piracy and smuggling.

When Guangzhou and Macau opened up to the west in the 16th century the island was a perfect spot from which to prey on passing ships stacked with goodies. The infamous and powerful pirate Cheung Po Tsai is said to have had his base there during the 18th century (you can visit the cave where he supposedly stashed his plunder).

Piracy and smuggling have gone, but fishing is still an important industry for a large number of the island's inhabitants, about 10% of whom live on junks and sampans anchored offshore.

There are several interesting temples on the island, the most important being the Pak

HONG KONG

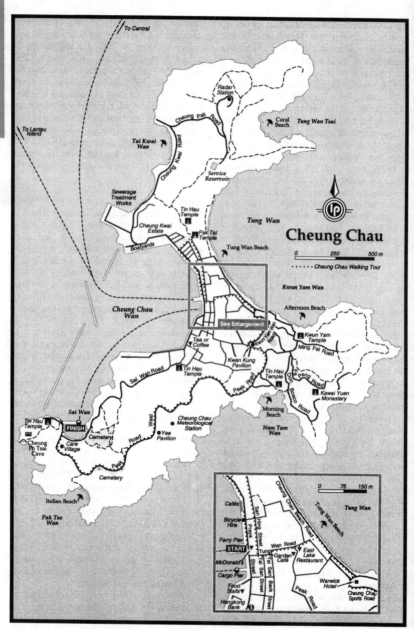

HongkongBank

HongkongBank ATMs accept a large number of international ATM systems, such as GlobalAccess, Plus and Cirrus, as well as Visa credit and debit cards. The ATM systems accepted are displayed above the ATM. Payment is in Hong Kong dollars only. Midland Bank customers can use their cash-point cards with HongkongBank machines to draw from their account in the UK, as Midland Bank is part of HongkongBank.

HongkongBank has branches dotted around Hong Kong Island and Kowloon, and are pretty easy to find (consult the maps in this book for locations). The outlying islands also have branches at the following addresses:

Cheung Chau
    (☎ 2981-1127) lot No 1116, Praya South;
    (ATM) No 19a, Pak She Praya Rd
Lamma Island
    (☎ 2982-0787)19 Main St, Yung Shue Wan
Lantau Island
    (☎ 2984-8271) DD4, Lot 667, Silvermine Bay; (☎ 2987-7348) shop G13, ground floor, Discovery Bay Plaza, Discovery Bay; (☎ 2985-7381) Minibank, 2-4 Market St, Tai O
Peng Chau
    (☎ 2983-0383) 1-3 Wing Hing St

Tai Temple, which hosts the annual Cheung Chau Bun Festival.

Cheung Chau has a few worthwhile beaches, and despite the fact that the island is getting crowded, there are still some great walks that will transport you a world away from the furious tempo of Hong Kong. None of the walks can be called strenuous – ideal if you enjoy an easy stroll among butterflies and lush vegetation. The island is packed with missionary schools, churches, retreats and cemeteries and most of the picturesque walks are easily completed in one day. The walk from Cheung Chau village to Sai Wan (see later in this section) is highly recommended.

The harbour is a colourful canvas of bobbing sampans and junks – don't forget to bring your camera for some maritime shots of Hong Kong.

As the island is crowded, it can no longer supply its own drinking water, so it's brought in by an undersea pipeline from Lantau. There's a small but mildly eclectic selection of dining possibilities and HongkongBank has an ATM in Cheung Chau village.

Cheung Chau Village

No longer really a village but a small town, the main built-up area on the island is along the narrow strip at the centre of the two headlands that make up the dumb-bell-shaped island. The waterfront is a bustling place any time of day and late into the night. If you make your way into the maze of streets and narrow alleys that make up the village you will be rewarded with a cheery collection of tumble-down shops, original historic Chinese architecture and the aromas of incense and fish hanging out to dry.

Cheung Chau Typhoon Shelter

This is the second largest typhoon shelter in Hong Kong, surpassed only by Aberdeen. As in Aberdeen, touring the typhoon shelter by boat is a must. Chartering a sampan for 20 minutes costs around HK$50 (subject to negotiation). Virtually any small boat you see in the harbour is a water taxi and can be hired for a tour. Simply wave to the boats and two or three are likely stop to offer a ride. Agree on the fare first.

Pak Tai Temple

This colourful temple is the oldest on the island and is the focus of the famous annual Bun Festival. It is dedicated to Pak Tai (see the Religion section in Facts about Hong Kong for a description of the deity). To find the temple, turn left as you get off the ferry and walk up Pak She Praya Rd along the seafront until you come to Pak She Fourth Lane (turning off to the right) and an adjacent playing ground – you will see the temple facing you and the sea.

The story goes that the first settlers from Guangdong Province in China brought Pak Tai, protector of fisherfolk (among other things), with them to Cheung Chau. Carrying the god through the village in the year 1777 is supposed to have scared away a plague. The temple was built six years later.

The temple has several historic relics. A large iron sword said to have been forged in the Song dynasty (960-1279) stands there. It was recovered from the sea by a local fisherman more than 100 years ago and presented to the god by the islanders. The sword is regarded as a symbol of good luck and its disappearance from the temple several years ago caused great consternation on the island. Fortunately, the person who took the sword was kind enough to return it. There is also a wooden sedan chair, made in 1894, which was used to carry Pak Tai around the island on festival days; and two pillars depicting dragons, hewn from hunks of granite.

Bun Festival The festival takes place in May and is famous for its bun towers – bamboo scaffolding covered with holy (bread) buns. The towers can be up to 20m high.

If you go to Cheung Chau a week or so before the festival you'll see these towers being built in the courtyard of the Pak Tai Temple.

Cheung Chau Walking Tour

If you've had it with urban Hong Kong and want a rural escape, why not catch a ferry to Cheung Chau and embark on this charming walk – it will take you past flotillas of junks, restaurants, Mahjong parlours, temples, magical trees, beaches, and some wonderful vistas of the sea and gorgeous countryside. If you see the walk through to its conclusion, it will take about 2½ hours, and the trail is not particularly strenuous. The latter part of the walk is truly lovely, and best conducted in good weather towards the end of the day for the best light conditions. Don't go on a weekend, as everyone else will be there as well. If you go on a weekday, you'll have the walk to yourself. Don't forget to take your camera!

After disembarking the ferry, turn left down Praya St, where a row of restaurants gaze out to sea. Many of these are seafood restaurants, and a few western eateries also exist – this is the place to eat at the end of the walk. Continuing along Praya St and entering Pak She Praya Rd, you will see numerous **junks** moored in the harbour. Many of these boats are the refuge of house-boat people, who make their living and their homes upon the waves. Along the side of the road you will also see a few bicycle rental shops where you can rent bikes – though it's far more fun and leisurely to stroll.

Just past Pak She Fourth Lane is a playground, and to the right of this is **Pak Tai Temple**, a temple with beautiful colours, built in the Qing dynasty and one of the most important historical monuments of Cheung Chau. This is the site of the Bun Festival, held every year in May. Leaving the temple behind you and heading back south down Pak She St, you will pass a **traditional Chinese building**, the third house on the left. The building is guarded by two stone lions, and behind them hang two posters of the door gods whose job it is to expel evil spirits. Pak She St is also the site of a number of **traditional Chinese medicine shops**, which are worth a browse, and two small **bakeries**, at 46 and 56 Pak She St, selling small Chinese cakes.

Continuing south, you will pass a small shrine to the **Earth God** on the left of the intersection of Pak She St and Kwok Man Rd. The islanders on Cheung Chau leave offerings to the Earth God who lives in objects of nature. San Hing St is a street of different flavours. **Herbalists' shops** display wares in large glass jars, the shop at No 30 sells paper money and incense *(heung)* – paper money is traditionally burned at the new year or in memory of the deceased. Shop No 68 is another incense shop – incense is burned in temples as a way of communicating with the gods. Other shops to look out for are those selling the bamboo hats worn by the fishing community in

In previous times, at an appointed hour, hundreds of people would scramble up the towers to fetch one of the buns for good luck. It was believed that the higher the bun the better the luck, so naturally it got to be something of a riot as everyone headed for the top.

This sounds like a recipe for disaster and, indeed, a serious accident occurred in 1978 when a tower collapsed. Now the buns are handed out and no-one is allowed to climb up to fetch their own.

The third day of the festival (a Sunday) is the most interesting, with a procession of floats, stilt walkers and people dressed as legendary characters.

Most fascinating are the colourfully dressed 'floating children' who are carried through the streets on long poles, cleverly strapped to metal supports hidden under their clothes. The supports include footrests and a padded seat. On Pak She St, just down from the Pak Tai Temple, there is a photo exhibition of the floating children. One of the supports for carrying them is also displayed.

During the celebrations several deities are worshipped, including Tin Hau, Pak Tai and Hung Hsing (the God of the South) – these gods are significant to people who make their living from the sea. Homage is also paid to Tou Tei, God of the Earth, and Kwun Yum, God of Mercy.

Cheung Chau. Further up is a **mahjong gambling den**, which is usually an explosion of sound as the counters are shuffled on the table. Mahjong is not encouraged by the authorities in Hong Kong, as the only legal form of gambling is horse racing – mahjong is a covert form of gambling.

As you turn the corner at the end of San Hing St and enter Tung Wan Rd, you will see a **sacred tree** on the right. This ancient banyan is believed to be inhabited by earth spirits, which explains the small shrine set up at its foot. Tung Wan Rd leads up to **Tung Wan beach**, the most popular beach on the island, where windsurfing competitions are held. If you wander along the beach towards the huge **Warwick Hotel**, walking along the road to the rear will take you up the steep Cheung Chau Sports Rd; when you see a pavilion ahead, turn right onto Kwun Yum Wan Rd (named after the God of Mercy) and pass the sports ground. A few minutes ahead is the **Kwan Kung Pavilion**, a temple dedicated to Kwan Tai, the God of War and Righteousness – the deity is also the symbol of power and loyalty. As you come out of the temple, turning left will put you on Peak Rd which will take you past a series of attractive residential properties.

The walk along Peak Rd to Sai Wan is quiet and calm, and truly beautiful. It is worth timing this walk to coincide with dusk, as the light conditions are special.

You will pass the **Cheung Chau Meteorological Station**, which offers splendid views of the island and sea. Further on is the **Yee Pavilion**, dedicated to the Chinese poet Zhang Renshi. The rocks surrounding the temple are inscribed with eulogies from fellow poets. Further ahead and through the trees is a **cemetery**, affording a quiet and solemn view out to sea. Below is a crematorium. Soon you will come to a forked road – take the fork to the right and head down to Sai Wan. You will pass through **Care Village**, a small settlement that was originally set up in 1968 with money from an American/Canadian charity. Further on is another fork in the road where you can either turn right for the **Kaido Service ferry pier**, where you can get a boat back to Cheung Chau village, or you can turn left and visit the **Cheung Po Tsai Cave** and Tin Hau Temple. The cave is supposed to have been where the Qing dynasty pirate Cheung Po Tsai stored his booty after his exploits on the South China Sea.

At one time, the pirate had unchallenged dominion over the coast of Guangdong Province. You can get into the cave, and torches are provided at the entrance. Backtracking will take you to the turning for **Tin Hau Temple**, which is dedicated to the Queen of Heaven and God of the Sea.

At the ferry pier, you can take a boat back to Cheung Chau village for HK$2 (the staff often ask for more, but HK$2 is the correct price). Boats leave every few minutes.

Offerings are made to the spirits of all fish and other animals whose lives have been sacrificed to provide food. During the four days of worship no meat is eaten and a priest reads a decree calling on the villagers to abstain from killing any animals during festival time.

The festival is unique to Cheung Chau and its origins are not really known. One popular theory is that the ceremony is to appease the ghosts of those who were killed by pirates, otherwise these ghosts would bring disasters such as typhoons to the island.

During the festival, accommodation in Cheung Chau is heavily booked and the extra ferries are always packed.

Tin Hau Temples
Cheung Chau's Tin Hau Temples, dedicated to the patron God of Fishermen, indicate the important role fishing has played on the island. One Tin Hau Temple is at the southern end of Cheung Chau village waterfront. Another is at Sai Wan on the south-west tip of the island – walk there or take a *kaido* from near the pier. A third temple is to the north of the Pak Tai Temple.

Tung Wan Beach
From the ferry pier, follow Tung Wan Rd to the east side of the island. This is where you'll find Tung Wan Beach, the biggest and most popular, but not necessarily the prettiest, beach on Cheung Chau. The best part of Tung Wan is the far southern end.

Windsurfing is a popular pastime and it is possible to rent boards. Hong Kong's only Olympic gold medal winner (in the windsurfing event at the 1996 Atlanta Olympics) grew up on Cheung Chau. The best season for this sport is autumn (see the Windsurfing section in the Hong Kong Facts for the Visitor chapter).

Other Beaches
Most of the northern headland is uninhabited, with not much more than a reservoir and a radar station. From the highlands of Cheung Chau you can get panoramic views over the island to Lamma, Lantau and Hong Kong islands. You can reach this area by climbing the path leading uphill next to the Pak Tai Temple. At the north-west corner of the island is Tai Kwai Wan, which has a sandy beach. At the north-east corner is another beach, the more isolated Tung Wan Tsai.

The southern part of Cheung Chau is perhaps the most interesting. South of Tung Wan Beach, past the Warwick Hotel, there's Kwun Yam Wan Beach. At the end of the beach a footpath takes you uphill past the small Kwun Yam Temple, dedicated to the God of Mercy. Continue up the footpath and look for the sign to the Fa Peng Knoll. The concrete footpath takes you past quiet, tree-shrouded villas.

From the knoll you can walk down to Don Bosco Rd (again look for the sign); it leads to rocky Nam Tam Wan, where swimming is possible. If you ignore Don Bosco Rd and continue straight down you will come to the intersection of Peak and Kwun Yam Wan Rds. Kwun Yam Wan Rd will take you back to Cheung Chau village.

Peak Rd is the main route to the island's cemetery. You'll pass several pavilions on the road, built for coffin bearers who have to sweat their way along the hilly climb to the cemetery. Once at the cemetery it's worth dropping down to Pak Tso Wan (Italian Beach), a sandy, isolated spot which is good for swimming. Peak Rd continues to Sai Wan (West Bay) on the south-west bulge of the island. There's a ferry pier and Tin Hau Temple there.

Cheung Po Tsai Cave
This cave in the south-west corner of the island is said to have been the hiding place of the infamous pirate, Cheung Po Tsai, who used Cheung Chau as a base.

The cave area has become a tourist attraction and there is a nearby Cheung Po Tsai Cave picnic area. The glorification of Cheung Po Tsai seems ironic, considering he had a reputation for extreme brutality, and ruthlessly robbed, murdered and tortured many people. The cave's association with Cheung Po Tsai is almost certainly apocryphal as it is very small.

You can reach the cave by walking almost 2km from Cheung Chau village, or take a kaido to the pier at Sai Wan (HK$2). From Sai Wan the walk is less than 200m.

Places to Stay

Cheung Chau is not particularly well set up for overnighters, unless you are Chinese or you want to stay at the carbuncular Warwick Hotel. Hong Kong Chinese make a beeline for the booths opposite the ferry pier that advertise rooms for the night. If you don't speak Cantonese it will be difficult to find accommodation and you will probably be ripped off. If you do manage to find someone who speaks English, be aware that prices escalate dramatically on weekends. Prices do vary greatly but you should try to negotiate cheaper rates for longer term stays.

The *Warwick Hotel* (☎ 2981-0081, fax 2981-9741) is a six storey, two star eyesore on the beach. Doubles cost HK$620 on a weekday and HK$1080 on a weekend, plus a 10% service charge and 5% tax. There are also three suites at HK$2120. The hotel has reasonable Cantonese and western-style restaurants.

Places to Eat

There are lots of little sidewalk restaurants along the waterfront where you can choose your own seafood. On Tung Wan Rd there is the *East Lake Restaurant*, which is quite popular with both locals and expats, especially in the evening when there are often outdoor tables set up.

The *Garden Café/Pub* (☎ 2981-4610) is a pleasant western style pub and restaurant where you can find such timeless classics as baked beans on toast (HK$18), eggs on toast (HK$18), fresh mushrooms on toast (HK$30), chicken and mushroom pie, chips and mushy peas (HK$58) and can even grill up a rainbow trout for you. It also has a dartboard. You can find it en route to Tung Wan Beach at 84 Tung Wan Rd.

Not far to the right of the ferry pier and near the HongkongBank at 1-2 Kin Sun Lane is *Coffee or Tea* (☎ 2986-8008), where you

naturally get coffee and tea. Another popular destination for the expat crowd in search of a decent salad is *Morocco's* (☎ 2986-9767) at 117 Praya Rd. *McDonald's* has extended it's frontier to the plot of land opposite the ferry pier; *Park N'Shop* and *Wellcome* are also on Pak She Praya Rd, so you can stock up on food and drink if you are going hiking.

Getting There & Away

Ferries to Cheung Chau leave approximately every hour between 6.25 and 12.30 am from pier 7 at the outlying islands ferry piers in Central. The last boat back to Central from Cheung Chau leaves at 11.30 pm.

The ride takes about one hour, and the adult one-way fare is HK$9.20 from Monday through to Saturday morning, and HK$12.50 on Saturday afternoon, Sunday and public holidays. The fare is halved for children who are 12 years and under and seniors. The fares for deluxe class, which lets you sit on the open-air deck on the stern, are HK$17 and HK$32 respectively. On weekdays there are also several hover-ferry trips in the morning and afternoon. The fare is HK$22 and the journey takes 35 minutes. Hoverferries leave from pier 6. Tea, coffee, soft drinks, beer and some basic snacks are available on board. Cheung Chau's fishing harbour makes for a dramatic entrance – keep your camera handy.

Getting Around

There is no motorised transport on Cheung Chau other than a few tiny cargo tractors powered by lawnmower engines.

Walking is the best way to get around Cheung Chau. Bicycles can be hired from the shop on the western waterfront, near the north end of Pak She Praya Rd – you'll have a few big hills to tackle if you're riding outside the built-up areas.

LAMMA

The third-largest island, after Lantau and Hong Kong, Lamma is home to Chinese fishers, farmers and commuters, and the hills above the main village, Yung Shue Wan, are littered with small homes and

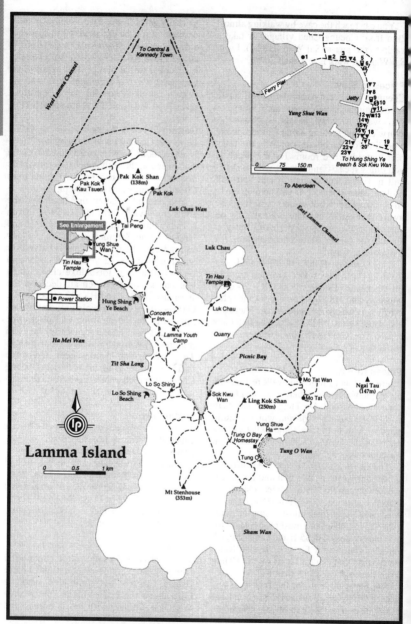

Lamma Island

apartment blocks. Known mainly for its seafood restaurants but deserving more press for its lush scenery, Lamma Island also has good beaches, beautiful hikes and some excellent pubs.

Lamma Island is also the focal point of the Hong Kong gwailo community. It is the haven of a wide spectrum of expat society: editors, poets, journalists, businessfolk, musicians, doctors and the incurably romantic. Lamma is quite beautiful and really the only place to live, if you haven't got a house on Victoria Peak. Apartment rental prices are rock bottom, and where else can you get an overgrown wilderness of banana trees in your back garden? In summer the island almost drowns in a sea of green vegetation. If you're walking around at night, watch out for the armies of frogs that jump across paths underfoot. The rustling sounds in the bushes at night are generally innocuous amphibians, but don't go anywhere near the Lamma millipede, whose bite can apparently kill a small cat.

Although low in population, archaeological evidence indicates that Lamma had the oldest settlement in all southern China. A team of 14 archaeologists doing a routine dig at Tai Wan San Tsuen unearthed evidence that there was a small village on the island 5000 to 6000 years ago. The first

expat to beach on the shores of Lamma was a Mr Jonathan Gray (in 1975) who still lives on the island. It wasn't until the early 1990s that Lamma began to take on special meaning for the armies of westerners who descended en masse to ride out the last few thrilling years of British Hong Kong. Estimates indicate that by 1996, one third of Lamma's inhabitants were foreigners. At the time of writing the population of gwailos on Lamma was dipping as a result of a change to visa restrictions.

This should push apartment prices down, but it will also eat into the profits of small businesses and restaurants that rely on expat money. Many bars could close down for good and landlords are expected to feel the pinch as apartments become vacant.

Finally, there are indications that Lamma could be attracting a more upwardly mobile expat community now that the tide of round-the-world job seekers has washed in and out. Let's just hope that South Horizons-style housing blocks don't suddenly emerge on the outskirts of Yung Shue Wan.

Lamma had no electricity until 1963. Plans to build an oil refinery on Lamma were dropped in 1973 after heated opposition from residents. Instead, Hongkong Electric constructed a huge coal-fired power station on the north-west coast of the

Archaeology on Lamma

Amazingly, there was indeed life on Lamma Island before the first gwailo poets turned up with their well-thumbed thesauri. In fact, the first community lived around the splendid little Sham Wan (Deep Bay) in the south of the island in approximately 4000 BC. These early settlers were a nomadic, maritime people known as the Yueh.

Sham Wan has turned up a whole crop of finds pointing to this early society, including Iron Age coins and pottery fragments. Whether the Central to Yung Shue Wan ferry was in operation at this time has not been fully ascertained, but judging from the ferry's archaic appearance, it's a safe bet.

By the Bronze Age, settlers on Lamma had obviously discovered that there was more to the island than Sham Wan, and settlements cropped up at Sha Po Tsuen, Yung Shue Wan and Tai Wan. Tai Wan constitutes the most significant Bronze Age site in Hong Kong, with the earth surrendering a plethora of bronze weapons to rummaging archaeologists. Discoveries indicate that the Yueh of the Bronze Age had developed into metal workers of considerable skill.

island; the two enormous smoke stacks are clearly visible from Hong Kong Island (you can get a much better view from Hung Shing Ye Beach). The road that runs across the north of the island is not a road but a concrete shell covering cables that supply the whole of Hong Kong Island with its electricity.

Meanwhile, on the south-east side of the island, the hillsides around Sok Kwu Wan are slowly being quarried away. Patrons at the bayside seafood restaurants can admire the quarry and adjacent cement plant while dining on crabs and prawns.

The most interesting way to see Lamma Island is to walk between Yung Shue Wan and Sok Kwu Wan, which takes a little over an hour. At the southern end of Yung Shue Wan there's a sign pointing to the Lamma

Youth Hostel (the hostel is mainly used as a summer camp for school kids).

Yung Shue Wan

The larger of the two main townships on Lamma, Yung Shue Wan (Banyan Tree Bay) is a small place. Plastic was the big industry there a few decades ago, but the plastics sweatshops have vanished and now restaurants and other tourist-related businesses are the main employers. There is a small Tin Hau Temple there.

Yung Shue Wan is the focus of the gwailo community. An excellent string of restaurants and bars makes a trip to Yung Shue Wan an enjoyable expedition. There's also a lot of late-night partying, plenty of stray dogs, lots of unemployment and an increasing amount of theft. The locals are appalled by this and relations between the gwailos and Chinese are generally poor. However, the community includes quite a few Chinese slackers – it's not just the gwailos who braid their hair, wear mismatched socks and get out of bed at 3 pm to tune their guitar.

Hung Shing Ye

About 25 minutes walk from the Yung Shue Wan ferry pier is Hung Shing Ye beach. This is the most popular beach on Lamma, and there's usually a fair number of people there. Arrive early in the morning and you will find it deserted. The beach is protected by a shark net. There are also a few restaurants and drink stands nearby, as well as the Concerto Inn, a hotel that also serves hot and cold drinks, as well as some mediocre western food (see Places to Stay later in this section). The nearby power station takes some getting used to; it periodically vents steam like some sort of outsize cappuccino maker.

Continuing south from Hung Shing Ye, the path climbs steeply until it reaches a Chinese-style pavilion near the top of the hill. This is a nice place to relax, despite the clear view of the power station. From this vantage point, it becomes obvious that the island is mostly hilly grassland and large boulders, with very few trees.

Heading further south from the pavilion, you soon come to a ridge where you can look down at Sok Kwu Wan. It's a beautiful sight until the quarry and adjacent cement works grind into view.

Sok Kwu Wan

Although only a small settlement, Sok Kwu Wan (Picnic Bay) supports about a dozen or more fine waterfront seafood restaurants.

There's a Tin Hau Temple as you enter the township from Lo So Shing. From Sok Kwu Wan you can head back to Hong Kong on the ferry or do some more walking. The small harbour at Sok Kwu Wan is filled with fish farms comprised of rafts from which cages are suspended. Some people live on the rafts or on boats anchored in the harbour, while others work on the rafts and commute by rowboat from their homes in the village.

Lo So Shing Beach

This is one of the nicest beaches on Lamma, and is down towards the southern part of the island on the western shore. The beach is not very big, but it's charming and has a nice cover of shade trees at the back. During the April to October swimming season there is a small snack stand and lifeguard/first aid stations in operation there. From Sok Kwu Wan, turn right from the ferry pier and follow signs initially for the youth hostel before turning left for the beach. Walking time is about 30 minutes. From Yung Shue Wan it takes around 1½ hours following the Yung Shue Wan to Sok Kwu Wan pathway and then veering right for the beach.

Mo Tat Wan

For a clean and uncrowded beach (on weekdays), it's worth making the 20 minute walk from Sok Kwu Wan to Mo Tat Wan along a path that runs along the coast. Mo Tat Wan is OK for swimming but has no lifeguards. You can also get there by ferry, but these are infrequent; the ferries start at Sok Kwu Wan, stop at Mo Tat Wan and then continue on to Aberdeen. See the Lamma Getting There & Away section in this chapter for more information.

Tung O Wan

The walk to this small and secluded beach is part of the wonder of the whole expedition to Tung O Wan (Tung O Bay). From Mo Tat Wan, take a left at the Coral Seafood Restaurant and follow the path up the hill, to Tung O Wan (signposted), through bamboo groves, lush fields and spectacular scenery. It takes about 25 minutes to reach the sleepy village of Yung Shue Ha (Under the Banyan Tree), perched on the fringes of the bay. All of the Chinese who live there are from the same clan and have the surname Chow. A member of this clan, Chow Yun Fat, is the bullet-proof star of many John Woo films. He was born and bred in Tung O Wan before making a break for stardom on the Sok Kwu Wan to Aberdeen ferry. For Hong Kong movie fans, this is clearly a place of pilgrimage.

Green Turtles

Sham Wan (Deep Bay), in the south of Lamma Island, is the only remaining beach in the whole of Hong Kong where endangered green turtles are still known to struggle onto the sand to lay their eggs. In other areas, the turtles have been repulsed in their attempts to deposit eggs by a nefarious alliance of real estate developers, construction noise and pollution.

Female turtles take 30 years to reach sexual maturity and always head back to the beach where they were born to lay their eggs. If Sham Wan catches the eye of housing estate developers, the turtles will swim away forever, taking their eggs with them. The other almost insurmountable hurdle for the long-suffering green turtle is the appetite of the locals for their eggs. In 1994 three turtles clambered ashore at Sham Wan and laid about 200 eggs, which were promptly harvested by villagers and consumed. There is hope that a sanctuary will be constructed in the future to guard against a permanent migration of the green turtle away from the shores of Hong Kong.

The bay is an unspoilt stretch of sand, punctuated by chunks of driftwood. Travellers to the bay, who fall under its spell and find it difficult to leave, will find a sympathetic welcome at the hotel-at-the-end-of-the-universe, the Tung O Bay Homestay (for more details, see Places to Stay in this section).

It's also possible to reach Sok Kwu Wan from Tung O Wan by following the beach southwards towards the small village of Tung O and taking the path to the right just before the village. The walk takes about 35 minutes, over a rugged and sublime landscape. Don't do this walk at night unless it's a full moon as there are only a few street lights at the Sok Kwu Wan end.

Sham Wan is another beautiful bay further south that can be reached by clambering over the hills and through thick undergrowth from Tung O Wan. Ask at the Tung O Bay Homestay for directions.

Mt Stenhouse

Most of the southern part of the island consists of the 353m high Mt Stenhouse. The climb to the peak and back takes no more than two hours, but the paths are rough and not well defined. The coastline is rocky and it's hard to find anywhere good to swim.

Places to Stay

Yung Shue Wan The cheapest hotel in Yung Shue Wan is the *Lamma Vacation House* (☎ 2982-0427) at 29 Main St. The smallest rooms are Chungking Mansions-style coffins for HK$150, but reasonably cushy apartments with private bath go for HK$250. Prices double on weekends. Service is not the most delightful, but an attempt at English is made.

Man Lai Wah Hotel (☎ 2982-0220) faces you as you get off the ferry. Singles and doubles cost HK$350 on weekdays, almost doubling in price on weekends. All rooms have air conditioning and an attached bath. The management speaks English.

Hung Shing Ye The classy and expensive *Concerto Inn* (☎ 2982-1668) is the nicest place to stay on Lamma. Standard rooms cost HK$523/748 on weekdays/weekends.

Tung O Wan Adventurous travellers can make it out to the *Tung O Bay Homestay* (☎ 2982-8461, fax 2982-8424) which features dorms (HK$100 per bed), double rooms (HK$350), home cooked meals, a hot tub and a sandy beach. Full breakfast is included in the price. The energetic owner throws together a cheap dinner as well if you want it. It's not the easiest place to reach, but therein lies the adventure. The hot tub can seat a party and is situated on the beach, fired up by driftwood.

The homestay is the last building in the village of Yung Shue Ha and from then on it's beach.

Places to Eat

Yung Shue Wan On the seafood front, one of the most popular places is the *Lancombe* (☎ 2982-0881), 47 Main St. It has some nice outside tables at the back, and though service is often quite slow, it gives you a chance to relax and enjoy the scenery. The deep-fried salt-and-pepper squid is excellent, as are the steamed prawns. Prices are also very reasonable.

On the way into town from the ferry pier you'll pass by the *Man Fung Seafood Restaurant* (☎ 2982-1112) and the *Sampan Seafood Restaurant* (☎ 2982-2388). The latter is popular with locals and expats, boasting an excellent view of the sea.

A favourite of the expat community is the *Lung Wah Seafood Restaurant* (☎ 2982-0791) at 20 Main St, next to the HongkongBank. This place also does a fine morning dim sum from 6 to 11 am (until noon on weekends), though it's not immediately obvious – the dim sum is kept covered in steaming baskets.

There are several western restaurants: the *Deli Lamma Café* (☎ 2982-1583), 36 Main St, serves continental fare with a Mediterranean influence, but it's pretty expensive for what you get.

Further on, *Toochka's* (☎ 2982-0159), 44 Main St, has outside seating and is popular for its Indian dishes, although it offers a continental spread.

Down near where the main street makes a sharp left is the *Waterfront* (☎ 2982-0914), Lamma's most refined eatery. There are sea views from nearly every table on its three levels, and the ambience is quite inviting. The menu includes everything from British pub grub to Thai curries and Italian pasta. It's a bit expensive, but the overall effect is very pleasant.

Health conscious eaters can curl up with a good book at the *Bookworm Café* (☎ 2982-4838) on Yung Shue Wan Main St. This is where you can tuck into a vegetarian burger or carrot cake and peruse the second-hand book selection.

Leave the dungarees behind if you want to eat all the things your doctor didn't order – like thick chips and fat pies soaked in gravy. You can get them at *Dino's* (☎ 2982-6196), 68 Main St, if you can get your order through the wall of Lamma regulars at the bar. It was about to expand upstairs at the time of writing.

Across the road is the *Aroy Thai*, with friendly service and good value Thai food; the food is nothing special but the vegetable curry is very good value. *Pizza Milano* (☎ 2982-4848), 2 Back St, is the token Italian restaurant in the locality.

Sok Kwu Wan An evening meal at Sok Kwu Wan is most enjoyable, and a good way to end a trip to the island. The restaurants are in a row along the waterfront on either side of the ferry pier.

Two good restaurants worth trying out are *The Rainbow Seafood Restaurant* (☎ 2982-8100) and the *Genuine Lamma Hilton* (☎ 2982-8220). Prices aren't much cheaper than in Hong Kong (no connection with the hotel group).

In Sok Kwu Wan, remember to carefully check the bill, as some restaurants have been known to overcharge. This doesn't always mean the staff are trying to rip you off: it may be an honest mix-up as there are usually a lot of people simultaneously clamouring for service.

Mo Tat Wan Mo Tat Wan has a wonderful waterside dining spot in the *Coral Seafood Restaurant* (☎ 2982-8328). While the food is similar to what you get at Sok Kwu Wan, the prices are lower and the surroundings better. Phone first to check if it's still open.

Entertainment
Yung Shue Wan A number of bars in Yung Shue Wan get quite busy from about 6 pm until midnight. The *Fountain Head* (☎ 2982-2118) next to HongkongBank is the most popular in Yung Shue Wan. There's good music, amiable bar staff, free salted peanuts, and decent beer at an affordable price; the rough, unpainted brick work effect inside the bar works well. You get a good mixture of expat and Chinese there; other bars are more divided.

The *Island Bar* (☎ 2982-1376) is where the real old-timers hang out. For some curious reason you have to be a member to drink there, although it seems no more than the formality of signing a members' book. The *Waterfront Bar* (☎ 2982-0914) is the yuppie pub – the beer is expensive, but it has the best western food on the island (see Places to Eat is this section).

Dino's (☎ 2982-6196) has the cheapest beer and is often pretty rowdy.

Getting There & Away
There are ferries from Central to Lamma's two main villages, Yung Shue Wan and Sok Kwu Wan. The ferries leave at regular intervals, but it's best to pick up a copy of the latest ferry schedule from the information centre of the Hong Kong & Yaumati Ferry Co near the outlying islands ferry piers in Central. The ferries leave from pier 6.

Ferries to Yung Shue Wan leave approximately every hour from 6.45 am to 12.30 am (40 minutes), but a few intervals last almost two hours. The last boat to Central from Yung Shue Wan leaves at 10.35 pm. There are seven trips a day (nine on Sunday) to Sok Kwu Wan between 8 am and 11 pm (50 minutes). The last boat from Sok Kwu Wan back to Central is at 10 pm.

The adult fare is HK$9.20 from Monday to Saturday morning, and HK$12.50 on Saturday afternoon, Sunday and public holidays. Deluxe class fares are HK$17 and HK$32 respectively, but unless it's a big boat with an open-air back deck, it's not really worth the money. Tea, coffee, soft drinks and beer can be bought on board, along with some basic snacks. An irregular service is also provided by Polly Ferries during peak hours in the morning and late afternoon.

There is also a hoverferry service between Central and Yung Shue from Monday to Friday. There are five departures from Central, at 8.10, 10 and 11.15 am and 3 and 5.50 pm. From Yung Shue Wan the hoverferry departs at 7.40, 9 and 10.30 am, noon and 3.40 pm.

There is also a smaller ferry (kaido) running between Sok Kwu Wan and Aberdeen on the south side of Hong Kong Island. The kaido makes a brief stop at Mo Tat Wan along the way. The journey between Sok Kwu Wan and Mo Tat Wan takes 10 minutes; from Mo Tat Wan to Aberdeen is 25 minutes (HK$7). There are eight departures from Aberdeen to Sok Kwu Wan from Monday to Saturday between 6.45 am and 7.25 pm, leaving roughly every hour and a half. In the other direction there are seven departures from Monday to Saturday between 6.05 am and 6.45 pm. On Sunday and public holidays the service increases to 16 trips in each direction; the earliest and latest boats from Aberdeen are 8 am and 7.55 pm, departing approximately every 45 minutes. From Sok Kwu Wan, the earliest and latest trips are 6.15 am and 7.15 pm.

There is a boat from Yung Shue Wan to Pak Kok Tsuen and then to Kennedy Town which leaves approximately every two hours. There are also occasional boats from Pak Kok Tsuen to Central, however these are not particularly useful routes for travellers.

Gwailos attending late-night parties in the city often miss the last ferry back to the island. The solution is to charter a sampan or kaido from Aberdeen. Depending on how late it is, the boat crew may want HK$200 or more for the service. Fortunately, it's often not difficult to round up 10 other inebriated late-night revellers at the pier to split the cost!

Getting Around

Like Cheung Chau, Lamma has very little motorised traffic apart from some carts used to haul seafood to the restaurants. The island's one road was built to service the power station, but you could spend a whole day there and not see a single vehicle go by. A concrete path links the two main villages, Yung Shue Wan in the north and Sok Kwu Wan in the south, but elsewhere there are mostly overgrown dirt trails. You can walk from Yung Shue Wan to Sok Kwu Wan and there is a kaido service between Sok Kwu Wan and Mo Tat Wan (see Getting There & Away).

LANTAU

Lantau means 'broken head' in Cantonese, but it also has a more appropriate name: Tai Yue Shan (Big Island Mountain). And big it is – 142 sq km, almost twice the size of Hong Kong Island. Amazingly, only about 30,000 people live on the island, compared to Hong Kong Island's 1.5 million. Most of those 30,000 are concentrated in just a couple of centres along the coast, mainly because the interior is so mountainous.

Lantau is believed to have been inhabited by primitive tribes before being settled by the Han Chinese. The last Song dynasty emperor passed through there in the 13th century during his flight from the Mongol invaders. He is believed to have held court in the Tung Chung Valley, which takes its name from a hero said to have given his life for the emperor. He's still worshipped on the island by the Hakka people, who believe he could predict the future.

Like Cheung Chau, Lantau had a reputation as a base for pirates, and is said to have been one of the favourite haunts of the 18th century pirate Cheung Po Tsai. The island was also important to the British as a trading post long before any interest was shown in Hong Kong Island.

Hong Kong's Vanishing Pink Dolphins

Although called Chinese White Dolphins (*Sousa Chinensis*), these dolphins are actually pink in colour. About 100 to 150 of these lovely mammals inhabit the coastal waters around Hong Kong, finding the brackish waters in the vicinity a perfect habitat. Unfortunately the dolphin population is being threatened by environmental pollution, and numbers are dwindling.

This threat comes in many forms, but the most prevalent and direct dangers are sewage, chemicals, over fishing and boat traffic. About 150,000 cubic metres of raw sewage is dumped into the western harbour every day (predicted to increase to 700,000 cubic metres per day by 2010), and very high concentrations of DDT and PCBs have been found in tissue samples from dolphins. Several dead dolphins have shown signs of having been entangled in fishing nets and despite the dolphins' skill at sensing and avoiding surface vessels, some show signs of having collided with boats.

The habitat of the dolphins is also being diminished by the erosion of the natural coastline of Lantau Island to make way for the new Chek Lap Kok airport. The construction of the airport has led to the reclamation of approximately nine sq km of seabed and the destruction of many kilometres of natural coastline. The north Lantau expressway has also consumed about 10km of natural coastline in its construction.

Hong Kong Dolphinwatch was founded in 1995 to raise the public's awareness of these dolphins. Promoting a policy of responsible ecotourism, Dolphinwatch offers cruises to see the pink dolphins in their natural habitat. Cruises leave on Sunday (HK$350, children under 12 years HK$175) and weekdays (HK$400/200). About 95% of Dolphinwatch cruises result in the sighting of a pink dolphin; if no dolphin is seen, passengers are offered a free trip next time. Contact Hong Kong Dolphinwatch (☎ 2984-1414, fax 2984-7799, email dolphins@hk.super.net, www.zianet.com/dolphins).

This is a particularly good place to get away from the city. There are several good mountain hikes, some interesting villages and Lantau is also the home of several important monasteries, including the Trappist Monastery and the Buddhist Po Lin Monastery. The Po Lin was rebuilt several years ago but lately it has become like a miniature Disneyland rather than a place of quiet retreat. On a hill above the monastery is the Tiantan Buddha Statue, the largest outdoor Buddha statue in the world.

Alternatively, spend the day hiking Sunset or Lantau Peak; even though urban Hong Kong can be clearly seen from the top, you'll feel like the city is in another world. Or head down to the fishing village of Tai O for street scenes that have changed little in 50 years.

More than half of the island has been designated country parkland, and there are over 70km of walking and hiking trails, as well as camping and barbecue sites. Despite its size Lantau doesn't have too many beaches, and getting to those requires some hiking.

Mui Wo

Mui Wo (Plum Nest) is on Silvermine Bay, so named for the silver mines which were once on the outskirts of the settlement. The mines were last used at the end of the 19th century and are now filled in.

About a third of Lantau's population lives in the township and surrounding hamlets. Silvermine Bay Beach is attractive, with scenic views and great opportunities for walking. The township is not a bad place for seafood restaurants. There are also a few decent gwailo bars where you can sink a pint and work out the ferry schedule back to Central (the ferries from Hong Kong Island land in Mui Wo) or plan your assault on the island.

If you have the time, a hike out to the **Silvermine Waterfall**, near the old aban-

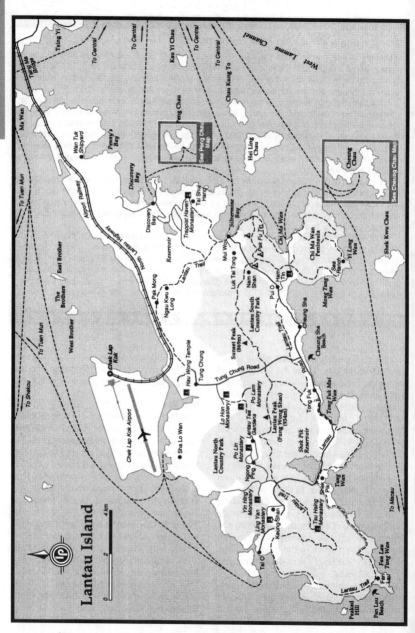

Lantau Island

doned Silvermine Cave not far to the north of Mui Wo, is an enjoyable excursion. The waterfall is quite a spectacle when it's swollen during the rainy season. En route you will pass the local **Man Mo Temple**, originally built in the reign of emperor Shen Zong of the Ming dynasty (1368-1644). Like the Man Mo Temple in Sheung Wan, it is dedicated to the civil and martial codes in society.

Silvermine Cave was mined for silver in the latter half of the 19th century; it stopped production probably due to the low quality silver ore and has now been sealed off for safety. You can reach the Man Mo Temple, the Silvermine Cave and the waterfall by walking west along Mui Wo Rural Committee Rd and then following a path north.

Pui O Beach

A little less than 5km by road from Mui Wo is the small township of Pui O, which has recently become the overflow bedroom community for gwailos wanting to get away from it all. Pui O has a decent beach and there are bicycle rental shops at hand.

Bus No 7 to Pui O leaves from Mui Wo roughly every half hour from 8.15 am till 5.30 pm and until 7 pm on Sunday and public holidays.

Trappist Haven Monastery

To the north-east of Mui Wo is the Trappist Monastery. The Trappist order was established by a clergyman in La Trappe, France, in 1644 and gained a reputation as one of the most austere orders of the Roman Catholic church. The Lantau order was established in Beijing. The Lantau monks used to run a dairy farm and sell the milk locally; the cows have been moved to Yuen Long and Trappist dairy milk now comes from over the border in China.

The monastery is not for those who like wild nightlife as the monks have all taken a vow of silence; there are signs asking visitors to keep radios and cassette players turned off and to speak in low tones.

You can get to the monastery by taking a ferry to Peng Chau (either from Mui Wo or

directly from Central) then crossing over on a kaido from the small pier just to the south of the main ferry pier. From Monday to Saturday, kaidos leave for the Trappist Monastery (the destination is Tai Shui Hang) at 11.15 and 12.15 am and 2.20 and 4.15 pm; on Sunday and public holidays the schedule is 10 am, noon and 2.30 and 4.30 pm.

There is also a ferry service from Peng Chau to Nim Shue Wan, a small bay about 500m north of the monastery. From the monastery you can easily walk to Discovery Bay (the coastal walk takes about one hour). You can also walk between the monastery and Mui Wo, but the trail is very steep in parts.

Ngong Ping

Perched 500m up in the western hills of Lantau is the Ngong Ping region, a major drawcard for Hong Kong daytrippers and foreign tourists.

Po Lin Monastery

The original temple was built in 1921, but the place has undergone considerable renovation since then. Today, Po Lin (precious lotus) is a Buddhist retreat-cum-fairground. It's a large temple complex of mostly new buildings with the simpler, older buildings tucked away behind them. From there the warm hand of friendship is offered not just to tourists but also to local film and TV companies, who frequently use it as a set.

The name 'Precious Lotus' is echoed in many lotus-like motifs decorating the monastery. The lotus is a significant emblem in Buddhist iconography as it symbolises the ability of every person to attain enlightenment. The lotus flower grows from the mud on the bottom of a pond, and from such base material evolves a thing of such beauty. This is a metaphor for transformation.

The monastery is very photogenic. The often mist-wreathed Ngong Ping plateau and Lantau Peak make for a sublime backdrop and the rows and rows of huge, pollen-yellow incense sticks arrayed in front of the temple create a meditational mood.

On a hill above the monastery is the largest outdoor bronze **Tiantau Buddha statue** in the world. The statue is 22m high – 34m if you include the pedestal. The statue was cast in 202 pieces in a factory in Nanjing, China, and then shipped to Po Lin. The current statue replaces an earlier one on the site – the one you see now was dedicated on 29 December 1993, after more than 10 years of construction. The podium that the Buddha sits upon is made up of separate chambers. In the first level are six Bodhisattva statues, each of which weighs two tonnes.

There are bigger Buddhas out there (notably the 71m high Grand Buddha in Leshan, China), but apparently these are not sitting, outdoors, or made of bronze. Even if it's not the biggest, Po Lin's Buddha is certainly impressive, and it's worth hiking up the 268 steps for a closer look, and for the surrounding views. It's open from 10 am to 6 pm. The Birthday of Buddha, around May, is a good time to be there.

Whatever you do, try to avoid visiting on a weekend. The place is flooded with day-trippers with radios and families, and consequently you're more likely to trip over a toy than a meditating monk. Visitors are requested to observe some decorum in dress and behaviour. It is also prohibited to bring meat into the grounds.

You can also spend the night there, though one traveller had a nasty early-morning encounter:

I was attacked by three dogs near Po Lin Monastery while walking around at sunrise. The stable manager was there and did nothing to call off the dogs. I just began to holler at them very loudly and backed off while they stood there, teeth bared and growling. So be careful of all the dogs!

Johanna Polsenberg

In the good old days, the approach to the Po Lin Monastery was via the Pilgrim's Path which originated from Tai O on the west coast of Lantau. This kept the numbers down and the monastery attracted a more devotional crowd. Visitors will be relieved to know they no longer need to grovel on their knees along circuitous mountain paths in permanent supplication until they arrive at the gates of the monastery.

Beside the Po Lin Monastery are the *Lantau Tea Gardens* (☎ 2985-5718), the only tea gardens in Hong Kong. The tea bushes are in desperate shape, and despite the tourist hype the whole occasion is no more than a yawnsome distraction. The world tea market doesn't rise and dip in accord with the harvest from this pitiful acreage.

Lantau Peak
Also known as Fung Wong Shan (Phoenix Mountain), this is the second-highest peak in Hong Kong at 934m. Only Tai Mo Shan in the New Territories is higher. The views from the summit are stunning and on a clear day it is possible to see Macau. Unfortunately, a number of cretins have littered the summit with plastic wrappers, Styrofoam lunch boxes and drink cans.

The easiest way to make the climb is to spend the night at the tea gardens or the SG Davis Youth Hostel. Get up at the crack of dawn and head for the summit. Many climbers get up earlier and try to reach the summit to see the sunrise – take a torch and a bundle of warm clothes as it can get pretty nippy at the top. The trail begins just to the east of the tea plantation and there is an information board there.

Also leading away from the tea plantation is another signposted trail that takes you down the northern slopes of Lantau Peak and on past wonderful views through a valley that leads to Tung Chung. This charming walk (unfortunately now disfigured by the creation of Chek Lap Kok international airport north of Tung Chung) takes you past the secluded and tranquil monastery of Po Lam and to another monastery, Lo Hon.

Lo Hon Monastery is not very old, and for those who have built up an appetite, there's a vegetarian restaurant open to travellers. Po Lin Monastery is 5km from Tung Chung, from where you can catch bus No 3 to Mui Wo or even connect with the Tung Chung line, a new railway which runs from Tung Chung New Town all the way to Kowloon and Central.

To get to Ngong Ping region, take bus No 2 from Mui Wo (via Pui O). Departures are approximately hourly from 8.20 am to 6.35 pm. The last bus back to Mui Wo leaves Po Lin at 7.30 pm. The fare is HK$9.50 from Monday to Saturday and HK$16 on Sunday and public holidays. Air conditioned buses are HK$14.50 and HK$23 respectively. The ride takes around 45 minutes. Bus No 21 connects the Po Lin Monastery with Tai O. There is also a taxi rank at the Po Lin Monastery, although it is often empty.

Lantau Trail

This 70km long footpath, runs across the island along the mountain tops and then doubles back along the coast, starting and finishing at Mui Wo. At a normal pace, the estimated walking time for the trip (not allowing for rests) is about 24 hours, but the trail is divided into 12 manageable sections.

A realistic approach is to do the middle section of the trail (the highest and most scenic part), which goes over Lantau Peak and is easily accessible from the Po Lin Monastery at Ngong Ping. From Ngong Ping to Mui Wo, via Lantau and Sunset Peaks, which is 17.5km and will take at least seven hours.

The western part of the trail – along the south-western coast of Lantau – is also very scenic. Note that the first section of the Lantau Trail is all along South Lantau Rd. There's an alternative path from Mui Wo to Nam Sham, via Luk Tei Tong.

Equip yourself with food, water, rain gear and sunscreen. Shops are few and far between along the trail. Cool drinks are available at Fan Lau in the south-west corner of the island. The next opportunity occurs three hours later at Tai O. Start out early, allowing yourself plenty of time to reach civilisation or a camp site.

The *Lantau Trail* map, published by the Country Parks Authority and available from the Government Publications Centre

in the Government Offices building, 66 Queensway, Admiralty (see Maps in the Hong Kong Facts for the Visitor chapter) is useful. Another map worth purchasing is the waterproof *Lantau Island & Cheung Chau* (HK$18) published by Universal Publications.

Tai O

For many years this village was the largest settlement on the island, but it's now in decline. A hundred years ago, along with Tung Chung village, Tai O was an important trading and fishing port, exporting salt and fish to China. Some of the salt pans are still there but many have been turned into reclaimed land and used for housing. The locals make a living from duck farming, fishing, rice growing, making shrimp paste and processing salt fish. However, young people disdain these professions and the population is declining. Processing tourists has in recent years become a major contributor to the economy.

Tai O is built partly on Lantau and partly on a tiny island about 15m from the shore – the two are connected by a bridge. For HK$10 you can take a sampan tour of the village.

A few of the old style village houses still stand, but most are being replaced by modern concrete houses. There are still many stilt houses on the waterfront as well as other shanties, including houseboats that haven't set sail for years and have been extended in such a way that these boats would never be seaworthy again. But many of these old structures have been abandoned and are slowly decaying. It's an interesting place all the same, but there are some pretty powerful odours from the fish-processing industry. The local temple is dedicated to the God of War, Kuanti.

To get to Tai O, take bus No 1 from Mui Wo. Departures are approximately half-hourly from 6 am to 1.30 am. The last bus back to Mui Wo leaves Tai O at 10.15 pm. The fare is HK$7.50 from Monday to Saturday and HK$12 on Sunday and public holidays. Air conditioned buses are HK$11 and HK$17.50 respectively. From the Po Lin Monastery, bus No 21 leaves roughly every hour from 7.30 am to 5 pm. The fare is HK$4 from Monday to Saturday and HK$8.30 on Sunday and public holidays.

There is a ferry from Central to Tai O on weekends and public holidays, departing from Central on Saturday at 9.15 am and 2.15 pm, and from Tai O on Sunday at 8.15 am. This is not the boat to take if you are in a hurry, as it takes over 2½ hours. There is also a boat to Tai O from Tsuen Wan on Sunday and public holidays that departs from Tsuen Wan at 8 am, and goes via Tuen Mun (8.45 am) and Sha Lo Wan (9.15 am).

Fan Lau

Fan Lau (Divided Flow) on the south-west tip of Lantau has a couple of very good beaches and an old fort which has been recently restored. The sea views from there are sterling. The fort was built in 1729, seeing operational service until the end of the 19th century. Fan Lau was also the site of a bitter feud over China Light and Power's plans to invade the scenery with a power station; luckily for the seagulls, the smokestacks never made it there.

Not far to the south-east of Fan Lau Fort is a stone circle, the origins and age of which are uncertain, although it is possibly a remnant from neolithic times.

To get to Fan Lau, take the coastal route of the Lantau Trail south from Tai O. If you emerge from Tai O on the path from the Tai O bus station to Leung Uk, you will intercept the Lantau Trail. You can also keep following the Lantau Trail on to Shek Pik where you can jump on a bus to Mui Wo. Alternatively, look out for boats that might take you back from Fan Lau to Tai O for around HK$300.

Cheung Sha Beach & Tong Fuk

Buses head to the Po Lin Monastery from Mui Wo along the road that hugs the southern coast. There are long stretches of good beaches (with occasional good surf) from Cheung Sha (Long Sand) to Tong Fuk on the south coast of Lantau. Both are major tourist-

beach centres. There is also a prison in Tong Fuk – but at least it's a scenic prison. Bus No 4 connects Mui Wo and Tong Fuk.

Shek Pik Reservoir

At Tong Fuk the road starts to go inland around the Shek Pik Reservoir (completed in 1963), which provides Lantau with its drinking water. Underwater pipes also supply Cheung Chau and parts of Hong Kong Island with fresh water from this reservoir. It's considered a pretty place with forest plantations and picnic spots, but the prison spoils the view. If you're feeling fit, you can walk down from Ngong Ping.

Bus No 5 connects Mui Wo with Shek Pik roughly every hour.

Chi Ma Wan

Chi Ma Wan, the peninsula in the south-east, takes its name from the large prison there. You can walk down through the Chi Ma Wan Peninsula to the beaches at Yi Long and Tai Long, but arm yourself with a map. You can also get there by kaido from Cheung Chau, though it stops at the prison and you may be asked what you're doing around there.

At the southern end of the peninsula is Sea Ranch, an upscale residential area which might be described as a 'weekend Discovery Bay'. It's not really geared towards tourism – more towards well-to-do Hong Kong residents whose villas there mostly get used on weekends.

A ferry runs from Central twice daily on weekdays (HK$25), but much more frequently on weekends (HK$30). Special bookings (☎ 2989-2128) can be made between 9.30 am and 9 pm daily.

Chi Ma Wan is also connected by ferry to Cheung Chau, Mui Wo and Peng Chau.

Tung Chung

This relatively flat farming region is centred around the village of Tung Chung, on the northern shore of Lantau. Ming dynasty annals record a village settlement in Tung Chung. There are several Buddhist establishments in the upper reaches of the valley, but the main attraction is the 19th century

Tung Chung Fort, which still has its old cannon pointing out to sea. The fort dates back to 1817, when Chinese troops were garrisoned on Lantau, and the area was also used as a base by the infamous pirate Cheung Po Tsai. The Japanese briefly occupied it during WWII, but found it of little military use and soon abandoned the neighbourhood. The fort was completely restored in 1988.

About 1km to the north is the much smaller **Tung Chung Battery**, another fort built around the same time. All that remains is a wall, but there are no plans for restoration. These ruins were only discovered in 1980, having been hidden for about a century by vegetation.

South of Tung Chung in the village of Sha Tsui Tau is the **Hau Wong Temple**, supposedly originally founded at the end of the Song dynasty, which contains a bell inscribed by the Qing dynasty Qian Long emperor. The walls of the temple are also adorned with the same emperor's musings on life in Lantau at the time.

Relatively few tourists used to go to Tung Chung because the transportation options were poor. This has changed with the opening of Chek Lap Kok airport and the transformation of Tung Chung into Tung Chung New Town. The Tung Chung railway connects the new town with Kowloon and Central, and the parallel Airport Railway emerges from Chek Lap Kok just to the north. These improvements in transport have spelt the end of Tung Chung as a peaceful historical site.

There are also a host of buses connecting Tung Chung with Kowloon and the New Territories: bus No E31 runs from Tung Chung to Tsuen Wan (where you can catch the MTR) via Tsing Yi (HK$10); bus No E32 runs to Kwai Fong MTR station, via Tsing Yi (HK$10); and bus No E33 runs from Tung Chung to Tuen Mun (HK$13). There are also a few overnight routes that serve the airport and run through Tung Chung.

Bus No 13 connects Tung Chung with Mui Wo. Departures from Mui Wo are roughly every hour between 5.45 am and 11 pm; the last bus from Tung Chung back to Mui Wo is at 11.50 pm. Departures are more frequent on Sunday and public holidays. Tung Chung and Tai O are connected by the bus No 11 route, with regular departures from Tai O between 5.20 am and 11.10 pm.

See the Lantau Peak section for details of the walk from the Lantau Tea Gardens in Ngong Ping down to Tung Chung. Otherwise hike from Mui Wo, a walk of about 4½ hours through old Hakka villages before reaching the coast and the farming settlement. Hiking from Tai O to Tung Chung takes about five hours.

Discovery Bay

Behind the romantic name of this place (appropriately shortened to Disco Bay) is the more mundane reality of an outlying sanctuary for professionals. If Chinese culture is what you're in search of, expect to be seriously shortchanged; Discovery Bay (Yue Ging Wan in Cantonese) is little more than a modern hamlet of luxury condominiums, supported by a crop of decent restaurants but devoid of history or significance. The community lives pretty much in isolation from the rest of the island and can easily be considered more a part of Central than Lantau, as many who live there commute to Hong Kong Island on the high speed ferry. If you wash up on the beach at Discovery Bay at least you'll find clean sand and reasonable food within strolling distance.

The hoverferry service from Star Ferry terminal in Central operates every 10 to 30 minutes between 6.50 am and 12.30 am, and from then there are five trips until 6.30 am. Similar services run from Discovery Bay to Central. Tickets are HK$25. There are also five high-speed air-con ferry departures on weekdays between Mui Wo and Discovery Bay at 7.45 and 11.20 am and 3.20, 4.30 and 6.30 pm. There are eight trips on Saturday, Sunday and public holidays. Tickets cost HK$11 and the trip takes about 12 minutes.

Places To Stay

Camping The cheapest accommodation options on Lantau are the government-run

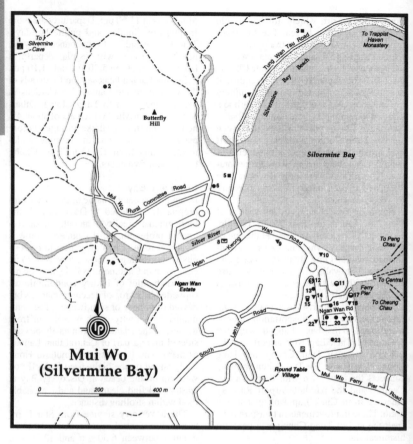

Mui Wo
(Silvermine Bay)

0   200   400 m

camp sites at Pak Fu Tin and near Pui O, Nam Shan and many places along the south coast. Other sites include Man Cheung Po (near the Tsu Hsing Monastery, north-east of Fan Lau), Kau Ling Chung and Tai Long Wan (both to the east along the coast from Fan Lau), Shek Lan Chau, Sap Long (near Ham Tin on the Chi Ma Wan Peninsula) and Tsin Yue Wan (along the coast between Fan Lau and Tai O).

The *Countryside* map or the HKTA *Hostels, Campsites and Other Accommodation in Hong Kong* leaflet will tell you where to find these campsites. There is no camping charge at most of these sites.

Mui Wo There are few good accommodation options in Mui Wo and prices skyrocket on Saturday. Hotels are clumped along the beach at Silvermine Bay.

Mui Wo Inn (☎ 2984-7225, fax 2984-8597) on Tung Wan Tau Rd is the best deal around. You can't miss the hotel as it's the one ringed by ghastly classical statues. Sunday to Friday standard doubles start at HK$280 but on Saturday the same room

Mui Wo
梅窩

1 Man Mo Temple
文武廟
2 Old Watchtower
舊更樓
3 Mui Wo Inn
4 Sea View Restaurant
海景酒家
5 Silvermine Beach Hotel
銀礦灣酒店
6 Sea Activities Centre
水上活動中心
7 Old Watchtower
舊更樓
8 Post Office; Health Clinic
郵局及診所

9 San Lee Chinese
Restaurant
生利海鮮飯店
10 Mui Wo Cooked Food
Market
梅窩熟食市場
11 Bus Terminal
巴士站
12 Hongkong Bank
匯豐銀行
13 7-Eleven
14 Lantau Fast Food; Rome
Restaurant & Bakery
大嶼山快餐、羅馬餐廳
及羅馬餐廳西餅部
15 Hippo Bar & Cafe
16 King of Bicycle
單車大王

17 Boats to Discovery Bay
去愉 瘋W之船
18 McDonald's; China Bear
麥當勞及中國熊
19 Papa Doc's Bar & Cafe
20 Wellcome Supermarket
惠康超級市場
21 Lantau Friends Bicycle
Shop
大嶼山之友單車用品
22 River Garden Restaurant
23 Middle School
中學

will cost you HK$520. Twin-bed rooms start at HK$422 (Sunday to Friday) and HK$652 (Saturday). Breakfast is included in the price.

The Savoy of Mui Wo comes in the form of the *Silvermine Beach Hotel* (☎ 2984-8295, fax 2984-1907). The most basic double is HK$880 and the smartest option is HK$1380. There are some very good discounts for long-term rentals (one month or more) during the low season. You can get a room for HK$8500 (or less if business is slack) for a month.

If you arrive at Mui Wo during the summer months, even on weekdays, you'll find a swarm of people at the pier renting holiday apartments. Not alot of English is spoken by the staff, but the holiday apartments can be readily identified by the photos on display. Not all the places being rented are in Mui Wo – many are at Cheung Sha and Pui O beaches.

Trappist Haven Monastery You can stay at the vow-of-silence monastery, but applications have to be made in writing or by phone (no, it's not a silent number). Apply to the Grand Master (☎ 2987-6286), Trap-

pist Haven, Lantau Island, PO Box 5, Peng Chau, Hong Kong. Men and women must sleep in separate dorms.

Ngong Ping People who stay at Ngong Ping normally do so to climb nearby Lantau Peak in time to catch the sunrise.

A 10 minute walk to the east of the Lantau Tea Gardens is the YHA's *SG Davis Youth Hostel* (☎ 2985-5610), which has dormitory beds and a campsite (a YHA card is required for camping too). Dorm beds cost HK$25, the campsite is HK$15. The hostel is often closed on weekdays.

If you visit in winter be sure to bring warm clothing – evenings can be amazingly chilly at this elevation. To get there from Mui Wo, catch bus No 2. From the bus stop in Ngong Ping, it's a 10 minute walk (facing the giant Buddha statue, take the paved path to your left, walk past the horse stables and turn left at the hostel sign).

Also at Ngong Ping is the *Tea Garden Hotel* (☎ 2985-5161), which has some truly grotty single rooms with shared bath for HK$170, Monday to Friday. Slightly better doubles cost around HK$200/300 on weekdays/weekends.

Cheung Sha Down by the beach you can go in search of the self-proclaimed 'smallest hotel in Hong Kong'. Contact *Babylon Villa* (☎ 2980-3145, fax 2980-3024, email Babylon@wlink.net). This cute little retreat is blessed with excellent views and a salty seawind. It only has a few rooms (different colours) with doubles at HK$480 (week-days). On weekends you have to take a package which provides one night's accom-modation, breakfast, dinner (both for two) plus a drink (wine, juice or a 'bear') for HK$1450. Other packages are available which you can check out on Babylon Villa's homepage:www.asiaonline.net.hk/~babylon.

The trouble with Babylon Villa is that you have to arrange your stay in advance. Phone first for details. Babylon Villa is at 29 Cheung Sha Lower Village; take bus No 4 from Mui Wo.

Chi Ma Wan The HKYHA and Jockey Club jointly operate the beach-side *Mong Tung Wan Hostel* (☎ 2984-1389) in the south-east corner of the island on the Chi Ma Wan Peninsula. Beds cost HK$25 and camping is permitted.

From Mui Wo, take the bus to Pui O, then walk along the road to Ham Tin. At the junction of Chi Ma Wan Rd and the temple, take the footpath to Mong Tung Wan (45 minute walk). An alternative route is to take a ferry to Cheung Chau and hire a sampan to the jetty at Mong Tung Wan – a sampan carries about 10 people including luggage, and you could find things getting a little squeezy.

Places to Eat
Mui Wo The *Mui Wo Cooked Food Market*, near the ferry terminal, harbours a large number of food stalls. Unfortunately, the food isn't great and the restaurants are not too clean.

The most expat-oriented pub/restaurant in town is *Papa Doc's Bar & Cafe* (☎ 2984-9003) at 3 Ngan Wan Rd, just beyond the *Wellcome supermarket*. Among the pub grub offerings are chilli con carne (HK$50), 8oz fillet steak (HK$85), fish and chips

(HK$65) and an all day breakfast (HK$58). A beer gut away from Papa Doc's is the *Station Café* (☎ 2984-1919), 3 Ngan Wan, serving Italian favourites. Just to the left of McDonald's is *China Bear*, a recently opened snack bar.

If you continue past the market towards the beach, you'll soon come to *San Lee Chinese Restaurant*. The food is good, the staff speak some English (and there are English menus) and prices are reasonable. Vegetarian meals are also available.

Hippo Bar & Cafe (☎ 2984-9876) is another western-style bar/restaurant combi-nation. Old faithfuls include the Hippo British breakfast (HK$55) and fish and chips (HK$60). This place is hidden in a narrow alley just behind the *Rome Restaurant & Bakery*.

Pui O Inexpensive *Nam On Thai* (☎ 2984-8491), 31 South Lantau Rd, won't dis-appoint. You probably won't be whipping your camera out to snap the decor, but the food is reliably good and the restaurant has made quite a name for itself.

Tong Fuk The *Gallery* (☎ 2980-2582) is a unique proposition in Hong Kong – a South African restaurant. At HK$25, beer is cheaper than elsewhere on Lantau. This very popular place is only open from Wednesday to Sunday and public holidays.

Ngong Ping *Po Lin Monastery* has a good reputation for its cheap vegetarian food, with a regular stream of diners passing through.

If you'd prefer to eat meat, the place to go is the *Tea Gardens Restaurant*. Facing the giant Buddha, take the paved footpath to your left and continue past the horse stables. The restaurant is on the left, near the SG Davis Youth Hostel.

Tai O This village is famous for its seafood restaurants, which are mostly unnamed. The most popular place is a decent Chinese restaurant with no English sign – to get there, cross the bridge, then go straight up to the end of the road. The restaurant is directly in front of you at the T-intersection.

Discovery Bay Most restaurants are crowded into the Discovery Bay Plaza.

Chili 'N' Spice (☎ 2987-9191), shop 102, is a popular destination for locals and vistors. The food is a pot-pourri of spicy Singaporean, Thai, and Indonesian flavours; expect to find this place wedged tight with eager eaters on weekends.

Jojo Indian Restaurant (☎ 2987-0122), shop 101, block A, is a far flung relation of the Wan Chai standby, cooking up consistently decent curries to an enthusiastic crowd.

The *Waterside Inn* (☎ 2987-0063), shop G01, is in the Discovery Bay Plaza near the ferry pier. It's a restaurant and pub with a terrace overlooking the scenic waterfront and is chock-a-block with gwailos on a Saturday night. The other trendy place in town for pub grub is *Ebeneezer's* (☎ 2987-0036), which is in the Discovery Bay Plaza at shop G06.

Getting There & Away

Boat Before travelling by boat, it's a good idea to phone the Hong Kong & Yaumati Ferry Co (☎ 2525-1108) for an update.

During the week, ferries to Mui Wo leave approximately hourly between 7 am and 12.20 am from pier 7 at the outlying islands ferry piers in Central. The journey time is around 50 minutes, but some ferries stop at the neighbouring island of Peng Chau, adding 20 minutes to the trip. The last boat from Mui Wo to Central leaves at 11.10 pm (daily). On Sunday and public holidays, ferries leave Central approximately half-hourly from 7 am to 11.30 am and then hourly until 12.20 am; ferries from Mui Wo leave hourly from 6.10 am to 2.30 pm and then half-hourly till 7.30 pm (from then on, approximately hourly till 11.10 pm).

The adult one-way fare is HK$9.70 Monday to Saturday morning, and HK$17 Saturday afternoon, Sunday and public holidays. The fare is halved for children under 12 years and seniors. Fares for deluxe class, which gives you access to the open-

air back deck, are HK$17 and HK$32 respectively.

On weekdays there are also several hoverferry trips from Central at 9.40 and 11.20 am and 2.25 and 4.25 pm. From Mui Wo departures are at 10.20 am and 12.10, 3.10 and 5.10 pm. The hoverferry takes half an hour and departs from pier 6 at the Central ferry terminal. The single fare is HK$24 (children and seniors half price). As with other HYF ferries, hot and cold drinks, beer and snacks are available.

On weekends and public holidays there are a few trips between the Star Ferry terminal in Tsim Sha Tsui and Mui Wo. On Saturday, boats leave Kowloon approximately hourly between 1 and 7 pm and on Sunday and public holidays between 9 am and 6 pm. Prices are the same as those from Central and the trip takes one hour.

The inter-island ferry connects Lantau with Peng Chau and Cheung Chau. The first ferry leaves Cheung Chau at 5.35 am, and the last ferry is at 10.10 pm; boats leave approximately every two hours and go to Peng Chau, via Chi Ma Wan and Mui Wo. There is also a small ferry between Peng Chau and Discovery Bay, as well as some late-night 'water taxis' for about HK$150.

Lantau Link With the opening of Chek Lap Kok, it's possible to get to Tung Chung New Town (just south of the new airport) by rail or road. Lantau is now connected to the New Territories and hence Kowloon and Hong Kong Island by the vast Tsing Ma Bridge, over which are carried the Airport Railway, buses, taxis and other vehicles. The Lantau Link has trains running every eight minutes to Tung Chung New Town from Central, stopping at a selection of stations. The trains take about 23 minutes to reach Tung Chung from Central.

See the Hong Kong Getting Around chapter for details of the airbuses that connect Hong Kong Island and Kowloon with Chek Lap Kok airport.

Bear in mind that travelling to Lantau by bus takes about the same amount of time as the ferry and the trip isn't as scenic

HONG KONG

(apart from the experience of crossing the Tsingma Bridge).

Getting Around

Bus Services run by the New Lantau Bus Company leave from the car park by the ferry pier in Mui Wo. On most routes the schedule is increased on weekends and public holidays to handle the flood of tourists – bus No 23 runs on weekends and public holidays only. There is a complicated pricing system for Lantau buses: weekday buses are cheaper than those on Sunday and public holidays. There are also two types of bus – the air-con version is more expensive.

Taxi If you think the bus service is lacking, just wait until you try Lantau taxis. There are only 40 taxis on the island and these don't like to pick you up on country roads. It's easiest to find taxis in Mui Wo and occasionally in Tong Fuk – elsewhere, taxis are a rare item. The taxi rank at Po Lin Monastery is usually a swirl of tumbleweeds. You could try the call service (☎ 2984-1328, 2984-1368), but don't expect any reaction.

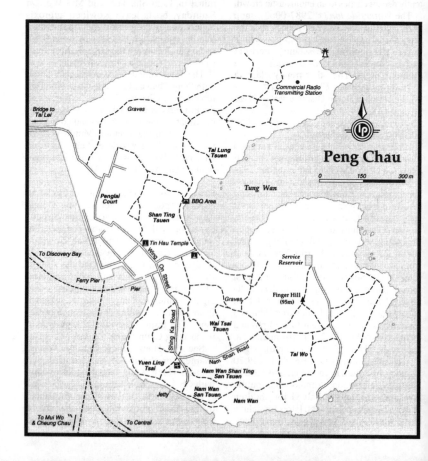

Peng Chau

Bicycle Friends Bicycle Shop (☎ 2984-8385), opposite the Park 'N' Shop in the centre of Mui Wo, rents out bikes for HK$10 per hour. The nearby King of Bicycle (bikes HK$10 per hour) hasn't yet changed its name to the People's Republic of Bicycle. During summer, bikes can also be hired on weekends from stalls in front of the Silvermine Bay Beach Hotel in Mui Wo, and from stalls in Pui O.

PENG CHAU
Shaped like a horseshoe, tiny Peng Chau is just under one sq km in area. It is inhabited by around 8000 people, making it far more densely populated than nearby Lantau.

The island is not especially beautiful, but it still has its charms. Of all the islands mentioned in this chapter, Peng Chau is perhaps the most traditionally Chinese – narrow alleys, crowded housing, a good outdoor market (near the ferry pier) and heaps of closet-sized restaurants and shops. There are a couple of small temples. Island residents claim that this is the last remaining bit of traditional Hong Kong.

Unfortunately, the government recently built the 'modern' yellow and green Penglai Court Housing Estate on Peng Chau, an abomination deplored more by the island's few gwailos than by the Chinese majority. Furthermore, on a clear day you can easily see the rapidly growing skyscraper forest across the water in Discovery Bay. Until recently the island's economy was supported by fishing and some tiny cottage industries (notably the manufacture of furniture, porcelain and metal tubes). However, these manufacturing industries are now all but dead, having moved to China where cheap labour is plentiful and no-one worries much about industrial safety or pollution.

Nowadays, weekend tourists contribute significantly to Peng Chau's coffers – Hong Kong residents head straight for the seafood restaurants and spend a small fortune on banquet-sized meals. The waiters are as likely as not to be Filipinos, as young Hong Kong women prefer working in the air conditioned office towers of Central.

There are no cars on Peng Chau and you can walk around it with ease in an hour. Climbing the island's highest point, Finger Hill (95m), will give you some light exercise and excellent views when the weather is clear. To get to Finger Hill, take a right at the Tin Hau Temple facing the ferry pier and walk along Wing On St; this gives way to Shing Ka Rd, and Nam Shan Rd leads away from this up to Finger Hill. Unfortunately, most of Peng Chau's sewage, plastic bags and Styrofoam wind up in the sea, making the otherwise pleasant beach on the east side of the island too dirty for swimming.

Places to Eat
Two popular pub/restaurant combinations are a big hit with the gwailos. The larger of the two, the *Sea Breeze Club* (☎ 2983-8785), at 38 Wing Hing St, is known for its fine T-bone steak dinners. The food is so good and reasonably priced that residents from nearby Discovery Bay take the ferry across just to dine. It packs out on Sunday, especially in the afternoon.

The *Forest Bar and Restaurant* (☎ 2983-8837) is just next door at No 38C. It's a small but cosy place with good pub grub. The owners, Tad and Iris, manage to create a welcoming atmosphere.

Getting There & Away
Most people arrive by the regular ferries from Central, but there are also hoverferries on this route. Slow ferries from Central leave roughly every hour from 7 am to 12.20 am; the last ferry from Peng Chau leaves at 11.30 pm. Ferries leave from pier 7 in Central, cost HK$9.20 (weekdays and Saturday morning) and HK$16 (Saturday afternoon, Sunday and public holidays), and take 50 minutes.

The hoverferry runs Monday to Friday, leaving Central at 9.40 and 11.20 am and 2.25 and 4.25 pm. The last hoverferry to Central takes to the sea at 5.20 pm. Hoverferries leave from pier 6 in Central, cost HK$24 and take 25 minutes.

Additionally, there is the inter-island ferry that can take you to Mui Wo and Cheung

Chau, or a smaller ferry to the Trappist Haven Monastery and Discovery Bay. You can also hire water taxis to Discovery Bay.

TUNG LUNG CHAU

Guarding the eastern entrance to Victoria Harbour is remote Tung Lung Chau (East Dragon Island). The island's position was at one time considered strategic for protection

Tung Lung Fort, at the north-east corner of the island, was eventually abandoned and is now preserved as a historical site. The fort was built in the early 18th century and

was attacked a number of times by marauding pirate bands before being disbanded in 1810. What remains is well worth a visit. Only the crumbling shell has been handed down by history, but the views are great and you can see the outline of the interior walls of the fort. There is an information hut open every day except Tuesday. Pirates, no doubt, used the island as a staging post, but there is little remaining evidence of their presence.

Humans have apparently been on Tung Lung Chau for a long time. The north-west corner of the island has some ancient rock carvings, the largest ever found in Hong Kong. Noone knows who the original artists were and the carvings are simply classified as dating back to the Bronze Age. Except for nomadic bands of weekend tourists, the island is now uninhabited.

Unless you have your own boat or charter one, the only time you can really visit Tung Lung Chau is on the weekend (although there are sporadic departures during the week, according to demand). Ferries and kaidos depart from Sai Wan Ho just east of Quarry Bay on Hong Kong Island, stop at Tung Lung Chau and then continue to Joss House Bay in the New Territories. Kaidos depart at 8.30 am and 3.30 pm, returning at 9.30 am and 5 pm. The trip from Sai Wan Ho to Tung Lung Chau takes 30 minutes (HK$20 return). The ride to Joss House Bay is significantly shorter than the trip from Sai Wan Ho, and you could go by one route and return by the other. From Joss House Bay

you can get buses to Choi Hung MTR station in Kowloon. To catch the ferry, take the MTR to Sai Wan Ho and take Exit A to Tai On St. Turn right and keep on going till you reach the quayside. Service is offered by Lam Kee Kaido (☎ 2560-9929), and if you want to charter a boat it's best to get a Cantonese speaker to make the call. A kaido will cost about HK$300. You can hire a kaido to Tung Lung Chau by asking down at the waterfront at Sai Wan Ho.

PO TOI

Po Toi is a rocky island off the south-east coast of Hong Kong Island. There is a small number of permanent residents, but who knows how much longer before they finally give up their peaceful outpost and migrate to the sin and glitter of the city just beyond their shores. This is one of the least visited islands, and that fact alone may make it worth the trip. There are no hostels where you can spend the night on Po Toi, but it is possible to pitch a

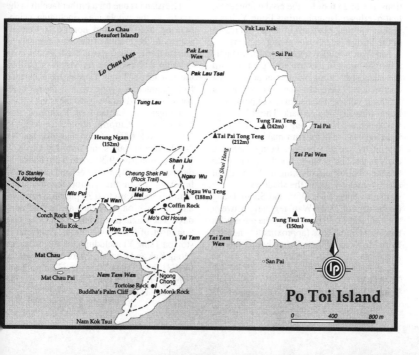

Po Toi Island

tent. At the time of writing boat services to the island had ceased. However, you could try hiring a sampan from Aberdeen though this would be very expensive.

MA WAN

Ma Wan is a flat and forested island off the north-eastern tip of the much larger Lantau Island. It was once famous as the Gate to Kowloon, where foreign ships would collect before entering Chinese waters. If you want to get away from it all, Ma Wan is hardly a beachcomber's paradise. There are two beaches but these have suffered the scourge of pollution. Swimming is allowed and a lifeguard wanders around kicking lumps of sand.

The real reason to come to Ma Wan is to take in the enormity of the Tsing Ma Bridge, the dual rail/road link spanning between Lantau, Tsing Yi and the New Territories. While catapulting the island headlong into the next century, the bridge has guaranteed an end to the island's quietude – it now functions as a huge foot for the civil engineering feat overhead. Neighbouring Tsing Yi has a special viewing platform for those interested in the bridge (see the following section).

Ma Wan's sudden transmogrification gets a further boost in the arm with plans to turn the island into a major international tourist destination. There are plans to establish a 'cultural village' theme park, and possibly a huge 'film city' theme park. The 'film park' will celebrate Hong Kong cinema and highlight local talent in the film-making industry. Optimists see the project being unveiled early in the 21st century. It will be curious to see the small island blinking in the spotlight after so many years in the shadows.

Boats connect Ma Wan and Sham Tseng (to the west of Tsuen Wan) regularly between 6.15 am and 11.30 pm – going the other way, there are regular trips (approximately hourly) from Ma Wan to Sham Tseng between 6 am and 4 pm.

TSING YI

Tsing Yi is the large island to the east of Ma Wan, disfigured by oil depots and displaying the chunky outline of a shoreline made up from reclaimed land. While not a castaway's paradise, Tsing Yi is worth a mention for being in league with Ma Wan as a huge stepping stone for the gigantic Tsing Ma Bridge. Tsing Yi makes up for its lack of beaches with the **Lantau Link Visitors Centre and Viewing Platform**, where you can savour the humungousness of the combined road and rail transport connection between the New Territories and Lantau.

The visitors centre contains models, photographs and videos of the construction process – very much for the yellow hard hat crowd. The centre is open Monday to Friday from 10 am to 5 pm (closed Wednesday), weekends (and public holidays) from 10.30 am to 6.30 pm. The viewing platform is open Sunday to Friday from 7 am to 10.30 pm; on Saturday and public holidays it's open from 7 am to 1.30 am. Admission is free; call ☎ 2495-5825 for details.

The island is due for a further facelift in the future, as the whole area (including neighbouring Ma Wan and north-east Lantau) adjusts to the reality of the vast amounts of human traffic passing overhead. Tied in with the film city complex on Ma Wan (still in the test tube), Tsing Yi may have its own film production centre with a theme hotel complex tacked on for good measure.

To reach the Lantau Link Visitors Centre and Viewing Platform, hop on the MTR to Lai Chi Kok MTR station and take bus No 243R. Regular buses run from Lai Chi Kok MTR station from 9.30 am to 5 pm on weekdays and till 6.30 pm on weekends and public holidays. From the visitors centre buses return from 10 am to 6.30 pm on weekdays, and till 8 pm on weekends and public holidays. The single fare is HK$8.80. Otherwise a number of buses en route to Tung Chung stop on Tsing Yi including: the E21 from the Mong Kok and Prince Edward MTR stations; the E31 from Tsuen Wan; the E32 from Kwai Fong MTR station (via Tsuen Wan); and the E41 from Tai Po.

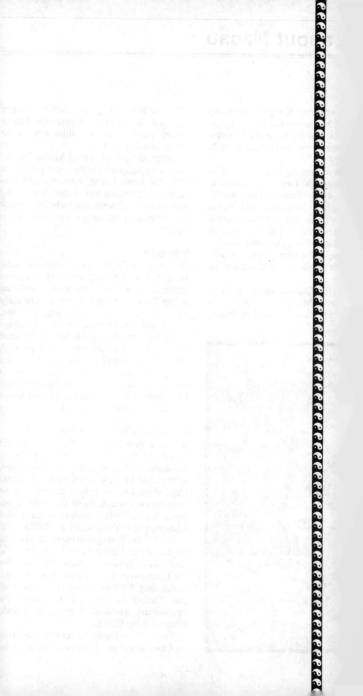

Facts about Macau

MACAU

Only 65km from Hong Kong but predating it by 300 years, Macau is the oldest European enclave in Asia. But not for much longer – Macau is due to be returned to China on 20 December 1999.

Macau is an interesting mix of cultures – a relaxed fusion of the Latin and Asian temperament. It is a city of cobbled side streets, baroque churches, fortresses and exotic street names. There are several Chinese temples and restored colonial villas, and Macau is the final resting place of many European seamen and soldiers. You will also find good-value hotels, excellent restaurants and casinos.

Apart from the Chinese gamblers, most tourists who go to Macau spend just a few hours there on a whistle-stop tour, and many who visit Hong Kong don't bother going to Macau at all – a pity, because its one of those curious places where something new can be found on every visit.

Lately, the darker side of Macau has occasionally eclipsed the fun and games. In 1997, the Triads lurched from one killing to another. No tourists were killed, but a hotel was sprayed with semi-automatic fire. Check the newspapers and the general mood before you go.

HISTORY

Macau means City of God and takes its name from A-Ma-Gau (Bay of A-Ma). At the southern tip of Macau Peninsula stands the A-Ma Temple, which dates back to the early 16th century. According to legend, A-Ma, a poor girl looking for a passage to Guangzhou, was turned away by the wealthy junk owners, so a fisherman took her on board. A storm blew up and wrecked all the junks except the boat carrying the girl. When it landed in Macau the girl disappeared, only to reappear later as a god on the spot where the fisherman built her temple.

Portuguese Trading Outpost

Macau's history is intertwined with the history of Portugal. On early voyages to India, the Portuguese had learnt of a strange, light-skinned people called the Chin, whose huge ships had once visited India. These were the enormous Chinese maritime expeditions that had been launched by the second Ming emperor, Yong Le, from 1405 to 1433.

In 1511 the Portuguese captured Malacca on the Malay Peninsula and found several junks with Chinese captains. Realising that the Chins were not a mythical people and concluding that these people had come from the 'Cathay' of Marco Polo's travels, a small party was sent northwards to open trade with the Chinese.

The first Portuguese contingent set foot on Chinese soil in 1513 at the mouth of the

CHINA

Macau Peninsula

Macau

0   1   2 km

New Macau-Taipa Bridge

Macau-Taipa Bridge

Taipa Island

Macau Airport

Taipa-Coloane Causeway

Coloane Island

CHINA

Pearl River (Zhujiang) near what is now Macau and Hong Kong.

The initial Portuguese contact with China was not successful, and for years attempts to gain a permanent trading base on the Chinese coast met with little success. However in the early 1550s an official basis for trade was established between the two countries and the Portuguese were allowed to settle on Sanchuang, a small island about 80km south-west of the mouth of the Pearl River. Sanchuang's exposed anchorage led the Portuguese to abandon the island in 1553, moving to another island closer to the Pearl River.

To the north-east was a peninsula where the Portuguese frequently anchored. It had two natural harbours – an inner harbour on the Qianshan Waterway (Qianshan Shuidao) and an outer harbour in a bay facing the Pearl River – and to its south were sheltered islands. In 1557 the Portuguese made an agreement, with some Guangzhou officials, which allowed the Portuguese to rent this peninsula – known variously as Amagao, Amacon, Aomen and Macau – apparently in return for ridding the area of marauding pirates. The Roman Catholic diocese of Macau was established in 1575 by the Holy See, however, the peninsula was never formally ceded to the Portuguese.

Macau grew rapidly as a trading centre, largely because Chinese merchants wanted to trade with foreign countries but were forbidden to go abroad. The most lucrative trade route for the Portuguese was the long circuit from the west of India to Japan and back, with Macau as the essential link between the two. Acting as agents for Chinese merchants, Portuguese traders took Chinese goods to the west coast of India and exchanged them for cotton and textiles. The cloth was then taken to Malacca to trade for spices and aromatic woods. The Portuguese then continued to Japan, where the cargo from Malacca was exchanged for Japanese silver, swords, lacquerware and fans, that would be traded in Macau for more Chinese goods.

In the 16th century the Portuguese were the carriers of all large-scale international commerce between China and Japan.

The Golden Years

By the beginning of the 17th century Macau supported several thousand permanent residents, including about a thousand Portuguese. The rest were Chinese Christian converts, Christians from Malacca and Japan, and a large number of African, Indian and Malay slaves. Large numbers of Chinese citizens worked in the town as traders, hawkers, labourers and servants.

Trade was the most important activity in the new town, but Macau also became a centre of Christianity in the Far East. Priests and missionaries accompanied Portuguese ships, although the attack was not jointly planned and the interests of traders and missionaries frequently conflicted. Among the earliest missionaries was Francis Xavier (later canonised) of the Jesuit order, who spent two years (1549–51) in Japan attempting to convert the local population before

MACAU

PATRICK HORTON

Portuguese architecture dominates the Macau skyline.

turning his attention to China. Xavier was stalled by the Portuguese, who feared the consequences of his meddling in Chinese affairs, but he made it as far as Sanchuang, where he died in December 1552. Subsequently, it was Jesuit missionaries, not traders, who were able to penetrate China beyond Macau and Guangzhou.

The Portuguese who stayed in Macau, along with their Macanese descendants, created a home away from home. Their luxurious rococo houses and splendid baroque churches were paid for with the wealth generated by their monopoly on trade with China and Japan. These structures included the Basilica de São Paulo, hailed as the greatest monument to Christianity in the East.

Apart from traders and priests, Macau attracted some colourful adventurers, eccentrics, artists and poets. Among them was Luis de Camões, Portugal's national poet, who was banished from Portugal to Goa and then to Macau in the 16th century. He is said to have written, at least part of his epic poem *Os Lusiadas*, which recounts the voyage of Vasco da Gama to India, in the enclave – though there is some dispute over whether he was ever in Macau. British artist George Chinnery spent a quarter of a century in Macau, from 1825 until his death in 1852, and is remembered for his paintings of the place and its people.

Portuguese Decline

The Portuguese decline was as rapid as its success. In 1580 Spanish armies occupied Portugal. In the early years of the 17th century the Dutch began making their presence felt in the Far East, and the Portuguese built fortresses in Macau in anticipation of Dutch attacks. Dutch attempts to take Macau included major but unsuccessful attacks in 1607 and 1627.

The Japanese soon became suspicious of Portuguese' (and Spanish) intentions and eventually, in 1637, Japan was closed to foreign trade. In 1640 the Dutch took Malacca by force. Portugal regained its independence from the Spanish in 1640, but all trade connections with China and Japan were severed as the Portuguese could no longer provide the Chinese with the Japanese silver needed for an exchange of silk and porcelain, or with spices, since the spice trade was now in the hands of the Dutch. Macau was no longer of any use to the Chinese and by 1640 the port of Guangzhou was closed to the Portuguese, leaving Macau to deteriorate rapidly into an impoverished settlement.

From the mid-18th century restrictions and regulations concerning non-Portuguese people residing in Macau were lifted. The place in effect became an outpost for European traders in China, a position it held until the British took possession of Hong Kong in 1841 and other Chinese ports were opened to foreign trade.

Until the middle of the 19th century the history of Macau was a long series of incidents involving the Portuguese, Chinese and British as the Portuguese attempted to maintain a hold on the territory. In 1850, the Portuguese made plans to attack Guangzhou, as the British had done during the Opium Wars, in order to dictate a Chinese-Portuguese treaty. A series of disasters meant this plan never came to fruition. The Portuguese were forced to settle differences with China through negotiation, although it was not until 1887 that a treaty was signed in which China effectively recognised Portuguese sovereignty over Macau.

The economic woes of Macau were more or less solved by governor Isidoro Francisco Guimarães governor from (1851-63), who introduced licensed gambling.

Macau 1900 to 1984

Macau had turned into something of a decaying backwater by the late 19th century, although it continued to serve as a refuge for Chinese fleeing war and famine in north China.

Population figures showed little signs of movement until the mid 1920s when large numbers of Chinese immigrants swelled the number of people living in Macau from 80,000 to 160,000. A steady stream of refugees from the Sino-Japanese War meant that by 1939 the population figure for

The Führer's Gold

Unbeknown to the weekend stampede of well-heeled spenders and tourists, bewitched by Macau's historical charms, are murkier quarters of business that perhaps explain why China allowed Portugal to continue to administrate the territory for so long.

Some claim that huge amounts of gold bullion from Nazi Germany, emblazoned with the stamp of the eagle and swastika, arrived in China via the small Portuguese outpost – the gold being the spoils of Nazi plunder, including that salvaged from Holocaust victims. Portugal was the recipient of vast quantities of Nazi gold in repayment for supplies to the beleaguered Third Reich during WWII and this bullion was, it is claimed, off-loaded onto China up until the 1970s. China denies the allegations, but former employees of Macau's Gold Import Commission point an accusing finger.

There is no doubt that Macau was the gateway for a steady stream of international gold after the war, but the jury is still out on the possibility that Hitler's bullion was shunted over the border into the People's Republic of China. If China was a recipient of the booty, it may explain the cosy fraternity between China and Macau.

Macau stood at 245,000. During WWII, many Europeans took refuge in Macau as the Japanese honoured Portugal's neutrality. There was another influx of Chinese refugees in 1949 when the Communists took power in China, and from 1978 until about 1980 Macau was a haven for Vietnamese boat people.

Macau's last great upset occurred in 1966, when China's Cultural Revolution spilled over into the territory. Macau was stormed by Red Guards and violent riots resulted in a few Red Guards being shot dead by Portuguese troops. The then governor reportedly proposed that Portugal should leave Macau forever but, fearing the loss of Macau's foreign trade, the Chinese backed off.

In 1974 a military coup in Portugal brought a left wing government to power, which proceeded to divest Portugal of the last remnants of its empire (including Mozambique, Angola and East Timor). Power-brokers in Lisbon tried to return Macau to China, but this was rejected by the Chinese. Some claim that the real reason China turned down the offer of reclaiming Macau was that the enclave was secretly laundering huge amounts of Nazi gold bullion, destined for China.

Until 1975 any Chinese refugee reaching Macau could obtain residency. After 1975 the policy was changed and all Chinese refugees sneaking into Macau are now regarded as illegal immigrants.

Macau Today

Once the Joint Declaration over Hong Kong was signed by Britain and China in 1984, it was inevitable that China would seek a similar agreement with Portugal on Macau's future. That agreement was finally signed in March 1987.

Under the Sino-Portuguese Pact, Macau will become a Special Administrative Region (SAR) of China for 50 years from 20 December 1999. Like Hong Kong, Macau will enjoy a 'high degree of autonomy' in all matters except defence and foreign affairs.

Unlike the uncertainty and panic that preceded the return of Hong Kong to China, Macau has approached the period of transition with little trepidation. On the whole, the enclave has avoided the prickly issues that dogged the Hong Kong handover negotiations. The Basic Law for Macau differed from its Hong Kong equivalent in that holders of foreign passports were not excluded from holding high-level posts in the post-handover administration (apart from the position of Chief Executive). There was also no stipulation that China would station troops of the PLA in Macau after the return of the territory to China.

Macau has elected a number of members of its legislature for the last 20 years, and didn't rush in proposals to widen the franchise or speed up democratisation at the last

MACAU

minute. The current legislature will continue to serve throughout the handover, unlike in Hong Kong, and Macau already has a local supreme court, side-stepping one area that became a battleground in the Anglo-Chinese Hong Kong debate.

Macau is not a colony, but a territory under the temporary administration of Portugal. This has meant that the relationship between Portugal and China has been workable. Macau has always taken its cues from China in matters regarding the administration of the territory while Hong Kong existed as a separate realm, administered according to the dictates of an independent, colonial law.

Residents were pleased that Portugal gave everyone born in Macau a Portuguese passport, allowing them the right to live anywhere in the European Union (though 70% of the population was not born in Macau and therefore don't qualify for Portuguese citizenship), while the UK hesitated on the issue. Furthermore, Macau is geographically and culturally closer to China than Hong Kong. Workers and shoppers cross the border from neighbouring Zhuhai daily, creating the sense of a united community.

But before we get too upbeat, it's important to realise that not everyone is happy about this arm-in-arm camaraderie. Despite Macau having its own Basic Law (similar to

Dicing with Death

Macau's sleepy roads and picturesque churches had a rude awakening on 8 May 1998. A string of firebombs saw 14 cars, a couple of shops and a number of motorbikes engulfed in flames; the pyrotechnics were most certainly organised by Triads. The gangland world was flexing its tattooed muscles in protest of the arrest of Macau's No 1 Big Boss, 'Broken Tooth' or Wan Kwok Koi.

The Macau Government Tourist Office (MGTO) is going to need more than a fire extinguisher to restore ailing tourist confidence. Macau is in the midst of a fully fledged Triad civil war; and the hit list has extended to leading civil servants and public officials. The number of visitors to Macau has dropped by 13%. In the midst of 1997's tit-for-tat killing spree, Macau's security chief, Manuel Monge, tried to reassure everyone that tourists were not on the Triad menu. Mr Monge's chauffeur was later shot in the head.

The Triads are known in Chinese as the 'Black Society' or the 'Black Hand Group', with extortion and violence as a motto. Inside the Triads is a vast mercenary task force of criminals, patrolling a lucrative domain of prostitution, gambling, loan-sharking and protection rackets. The Triad armoury is a hellish array of weapons ranging from meat cleavers and machetes to pistols and petrol bombs. If you default on a loan, Triad members encourage repayment by attacking you in the middle of the street with large knives. The only advice on what to do if you get on the wrong side of the Triads is, don't.

Throughout 1997 the targets of Triad violence represented the tug-of-war between gangs eager to grab what they could of shrinking profits from the world of gambling. Big money is to be made from chaperoning big spenders from mainland China who cruise into town with a cartload of money in tow. The police seem powerless to stop the knifings and shootings, but some residents are pointing the finger at police corruption and even collusion. With nothing like Hong Kong's Independent Commission Against Corruption (ICAC) in town, there's a lot of room for salary top-ups.

Three members of the Portuguese administration were killed in early 1998, signalling an upping of the stakes. Macau's Chief of Police, Antonio Marques Baptista, personally arrested Broken Tooth as he settled in for a night of gambling at the Lisboa Hotel, dressed in a Hawaiian shirt – a pet golden retriever had sniffed out a bomb on the underside of Baptista's car. Baptista himself, had previously been shot in the neck and cheek in an assasination attempt.

that inaugurated in Hong Kong), it appears to be timid when fighting for human rights and democracy. Another thorny issue is China's refusal to endow citizenship on anyone who is not of pure Chinese descent. China also does not permit dual citizenship, and has threatened to revoke the Portuguese citizenship of Macau's ethnic Chinese.

Portugal has dragged its heels on sweeping the upper echelons of the civil service of non-Chinese. The last governor of Hong Kong, Chris Patten, did a commendable job of recruiting local Chinese for most top ministerial posts in Hong Kong before the handover, whereas in Macau replacement plans have moved slowly. Complicating the

proceedings is the translation of Macau's statutes. As the government in Macau never insisted the local population learn Portuguese, translation into Chinese of these prolix documents has been an agonisingly slow affair.

Other incidents have revealed cracks beneath the optimistic façade. Lu Ping, Deputy Director of China's Hong Kong & Macau Affairs Office, launched a verbal barrage against the Macau government. Lu insisted that the statue of former Governor Joao Ferreira do Amaral be torn down because it was 'too colonial'. The statue, which was erected in 1940, was shipped off to Portugal in 1992. Sharp differences of

MACAU

Sadly, there is little chance that the culture of violence will disappear. Hong Kong cinema promotes and glorifies violence, swelling the Triad ranks with young recruits fed on a diet of popcorn and savage movies. Youngsters increasingly feel that violence is a way of life and a way to get respect. This is far more insidious than you may think. Brutality in Hong Kong cinema is expertly fused with cool images (sunglasses, slick hair, nifty suits and attitude) that are the icons of the teenage (sub) culture. Even Broken Tooth has his own homage in celluloid, imaginatively named *Casino*, which portrays him as a hero, played by Hong Kong film sensation Simon Yam. Wong Kar Wai's *As Tears Go By,* starring Andy Lau and Jacky Cheung, is an excellent film that captures the vanity of Triad members and their remorseless quest for 'face' and prestige.

There are other reasons why the Triads are restless. Macau's largest gang (of which Broken Tooth is head), the 14K, is experiencing an internal power struggle caused by tensions between the generations. The return of Hong Kong to China saw the immigration of Hong Kong Triads to Macau until a bloody war sent them packing. Hong Kong's main Triad group, the Sun Yee On, was resisted by a shaky alliance of the 14K and the Wo On Lok (Macau's other main Triad gang). The alliance apparently later collapsed. Macau's new airport has become the point of entry for Taiwan and south China gangland personalities (including the Great Circle Gang and the United Bamboo Gang).

Portugal gives the impression that it just wants out. The looming spectre of Chinese rule may promise a swift change of policy, but with Beijing keen to keep the flow of profits from gambling on tap, it's unlikely that there'll be a stop to the peninsula's main money earner.

Broken Tooth, the notorious leader of the 14K Triad gang.

opinion over the management of funds of various Macau-related foundations after the handover have ruffled some feathers. The focus was the Funação Oriente, a philanthropic foundation set up to encourage cultural links between Portugal and Asia. China was unhappy that it had no influence over this Portuguese organisation that was funded by money originating in Macau.

In the mid 1990s over-enthusiastic speculation in housing and property left a huge glut of unfilled buildings and offices. By 1995 it was estimated that there were 30,000 vacant apartments in Macau (one for every 14 residents). House prices halved in value. The economy (largely dependent on tourism and gambling) was faltering across the board, stumbling in step with the regional economic downturn. A lot of hope was pinned on the opening of the new airport in 1995, but competition from other nearby airports (eg Zhuhai), coupled with the sluggish economic figures have seen it consistently underperforming.

Let's not forget that 1997 was a grim showdown for Macau's tourist industry. There was an escalating number of gangland killings, and one hotel was raked with AK47 gunfire, the result of some bad marksmanship in the killing of a young Triad member. Gambling coughs up 40% of government revenue and is the backbone of the local economy. A lucrative market exists in chaperoning wealthy gamblers from mainland China who bring in money big-time – about two-thirds of all casino revenue. It was the struggle for this market that led to a number of Triad deaths. By the end of 1997, 29 people had been killed in Triad warfare. Any attempt to control the violence led to further savagery: 1998 saw members of the Portuguese administration dodging or stopping bullets.

Tourist arrivals were down some 36% in August 1997 compared with the same month the year before, and despite the Macau Government Tourist Office's chirpy mantra that 'eight million tourists shop with confidence in Macau' there was no avoiding the fact that coping with flying bullets and explosions needs the sort of confidence that only a Triad

upbringing can foster. Macau's struggling-tourist industry sank further under the gathering inertia of Hong Kong's equally palsied tourism figures.

This all presents a huge problem for China, set to inherit Macau, lock, stock and gun barrel on 20 December 1999. Beijing will want to have its *dangao* and eat it – it will want to hang on to the lucrative supply of gold from the enclave's gambling industry while putting down its accessory and mentor, the Triads.

On a good note, Macau is taking the preservation of its unique culture seriously. Macau has recognised that its sense of history is a fine selling point. Since 1992 about half of all buildings of historic significance have been restored. The Rua da Felicidade is one example of this energetic renovation campaign, with its brightly painted shutters and echoes of the past. Macau's heritage has been saved by a huge government investment of some HK$70 million. On top of that, the new Macau Museum will act as a tourist focus. The new museum is situated not far from the Ruinas de São Paulo.

GEOGRAPHY

Macau is divided into three main sections – the Macau Peninsula, which is attached to China at the northern tip, and the two islands of Taipa and Coloane. Taipa is directly south of the peninsula and has two bridges, each 2km in length, connecting the island to the peninsula. Coloane is south of Taipa and connected to it by a causeway.

Macau is a tiny place. It has a total land area of 23.5 sq km, including the peninsula and the two islands.

CLIMATE

Macau's climate is similar to Hong Kong's (see Climate in the Facts about Hong Kong chapter) with one minor difference – there is a delightful cool sea breeze on summer evenings. The best time to go is between October and December (autumn), as the humidity is low and the days are bright and sunny. Winter is cool but bright, with an average temperature of 14°C to 23°C, while

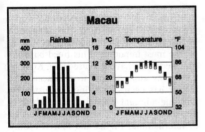

conditions become humid from about April, building up through the summer and tapering off in late September. The average temperature in summer is 27°C.

GOVERNMENT & POLITICS

Up until the handover, Macau will be regarded by the Portuguese government as Chinese territory under Portuguese administration.

In pre-handover Macau, the head of state is the president of Portugal, represented in Macau by the governor, a position that will be occupied by General Vasco Joaquim de Rocha Vieira until December 1999. The executive of Macau is composed of an eight member cabinet that includes the governor and seven secretaries (heads of government departments) appointed by the president of Portugal, upon the advice of the governor. The Chinese community in Macau is represented by a consultative committee.

There is a legislative assembly with 23 members, eight of whom are directly elected, eight elected by various 'economic interest groups', and seven appointed by the governor. Members sit for three years and elect their own president. The next elections for the legislative assembly will be held by September 2000. There are three mayors: one for the Macau Peninsula and one each for the two islands, Taipa and Coloane.

After the handover, the principle of 'one country, two systems' will operate in Macau, as in nearby Hong Kong. The Chief Executive of the SAR will be chosen by an electoral college, made up of 300 local representatives. The first legislative assembly of the new SAR will have 23 members, eight of which will be directly elected. Post-handover elections will expand the legislative assembly to 27 members, ten of which will be directly elected.

Portuguese law is currently the law of the land and Macau is part of the judicial system of Portugal.

ECONOMY

The economy is currently undergoing a period of upheaval, brought about by the regional economic downturn. The property market is sluggish and the Gross Domestic Product (GDP) growth rate has fallen significantly since its heyday rise in the early 1990s. Triad violence, apprehension over Macau's return to China and uncertainty as to the role Macau will play in the economics of the region after the handover have compounded the sense of instability.

The spin of the roulette wheel still drives Macau's economy. In the past, gambling was Macau's *raison d'être*, and although that's not as true as it once was, it's still the major cash cow. The gaming industry is monopolised by a small but wealthy Chinese business syndicate which trades under the name of STDM (Macao Travel & Amusement Co) – Sociedade de Turismo e Diversões de Macau. It was STDM that introduced the hydrofoils (later replaced with jetfoils) from Hong Kong to Macau and built the Lisboa Hotel. This group won monopoly rights on all licensed gambling in Macau in 1962. STDM's stranglehold on gambling may loosen when its licence expires in 2001.

Although Macau has long had a reputation as a gambling centre, casino gambling only got under way in 1934, when a Chinese syndicate called the Tai Hing obtained monopoly rights from the colonial government. Monopoly rights were renewed every five years and went to whichever company was willing to pay the most tax. The story goes that the original owners of the Tai Hing paid a puny tax sum, but held on to the monopoly by paying off competitors. It wasn't until after the death of the two founders of the Tai Hing that the STDM gained a monopoly on the gambling industry.

MACAU

STDM contributes 40% of government revenue through its payment of betting tax. Stitched into the fabric of the STDM empire are hotels, a television station and property. Beijing assures STDM that the dice will still be able to roll after the handover, and that casinos will be free of mainland influence. If the monopoly ends, it is possible that revenue through betting tax may fall as a result of fierce competition.

Macau closely follows the economic success formula employed in Hong Kong. It is a duty-free port and the maximum rate of salary taxation is around 15%, as in Hong Kong.

The territory has various light industries, such as fireworks, textile and toy production, but production has slowed and many companies have moved across the border to the lower labour cost haven of southern China. The main reason wages have remained low (relative to Hong Kong), despite a labour shortage, is that Macau has an agreement with China which allows a large number of Chinese workers to cross the border daily from Zhuhai. The agreement is controversial, since it weakens the position of Macau's workers to demand better wages, but it greatly benefits workers living in Zhuhai. The cheap supply of labour is attracting foreign investment.

Recent government objectives have been to encourage a diverse service sector to diminish the economic reliance on gambling. Macau entertains somewhere between six and eight million tourists a year, which is more than 12 times the local population. Over 80% of the tourists come from Hong Kong, with most of the remainder from Japan, South Korea, Taiwan, Thailand, UK and the USA.

Tourism usually generates about one-third of GDP, but with the big dip in tourist figures any reliance on this mainstay could prove ill-judged. There is a push to develop tourist facilities in the territory to shake off the strong association between holidays in Macau and gambling. The plan is to make Macau more of a family destination, based on its charm and beauty.

In recent years enormous public works projects have been initiated. The completion of Macau's US$625 million airport was by far the most important. This freed business travellers from having to use Hong Kong as a stepping stone to and from Macau. The airport has been competing for customers with the adjacent Zhuhai airport, which is also ultramodern. If Zhuhai airport opens up to international flights and tourist apathy continues unabated, then Macau airport could turn into a white elephant. Air cargo tonnage passing through Macau has also failed to achieve the expected figures.

Another big project was the construction of a deep-water port on the north-east side of Coloane Island. But keeping the port open will be a challenge – Macau's shallow harbour gets choked with mud flowing down from the Pearl River. Ships that berth there are limited in size to about 4000 tonnes.

Another scheme under way is a massive land reclamation project right on the Praia Grande, Macau's historic waterfront. It is known as the Nam Van Lakes Project because it will create two large artificial fresh-water lakes. The project has stirred considerable controversy, being opposed by conservationists and compounding the property glut in Macau. The project is due to be completed in 1999, adding a total of 20% to the land mass of the territory. The whole project will cost more than the new airport and will eventually boast a six lane waterfront highway and working and living accommodation for over 60,000 people.

The construction of Taipa City, a large high-rise housing development on Taipa Island, is a major ongoing project – the rural charm that existed there in the 1980s is well and truly gone. To handle an expected increase in motor vehicle traffic, a second bridge has been built between Taipa and the Macau Peninsula. And on the Chinese side of the border a new freeway is being built between Zhuhai and Guangzhou. This will connect with the freeway from Hong Kong to Guangzhou.

There is even talk of extending the railway from Guangzhou down to Zhuhai and maybe even into Macau. This will be a boost for the cargo trade.

The plan to link either Macau or Zhuhai with a HK$13 billion bridge to Hong Kong is another indication of the level of credence given to huge infrastructure projects in this part of the world. The idea is to enmesh the whole Hong Kong, Macau, Zhuhai and Guangzhou gold coast into an economic axis fully supported by modern communications. The ability to ship tourists in by the coach load partly underpins the logic of this monumental plan. If it makes it off the drawing board, it'll make the Tsingma Bridge in Hong Kong look like a footbridge.

Less ambitious, but an indication of Macau's imminent status change is the plan to build a US$25 million six lane bridge between Taipa Island and the neighbouring Chinese island of Hengqin. The bridge is expected to be completed by the year 2000. Work has also begun to widen the causeway between the islands of Taipa and Coloane.

In view of all this, you'd be right to conclude that Macau's image as a peaceful, colonial backwater is rapidly changing. Old-timers are appalled at the traffic and new high-rise buildings, but there is no denying that these projects will benefit the economy.

POPULATION & PEOPLE

Macau's population is approximately 420,000 but increasing rapidly at a rate of 3.8% a year. The sharp growth rate is due less to births than to a steady trickle of immigration from China.

About 98% of people live on the Macau Peninsula, thus making it one of the most crowded areas in the world. The two islands have remained essentially rural, but this will change with the completion of Taipa City, a high-rise development on Taipa Island.

The population is about 95% Chinese, and about 3% Portuguese.

EDUCATION

Under the current system, education is compulsory for children for five years, up to the age of 12 years. Despite the fact that only about 60% of 12 to 14-year-olds attend

school, the literacy rate is high. Recent immigrants from China make up a large proportion of the illiterate in the territory. As in Hong Kong, there are a large number of private schools.

Macau University (☎ 831622) on Taipa Island is the largest of Macau's 10 institutes of higher learning. It was once the small, privately owned University of East Asia, but has been renamed, taken over by the government and opened as a public university with a student body of 5000. The university is still rapidly expanding and even attracts students from Hong Kong and overseas.

Macau Polytechnic Institute (☎ 578722) at 1 Avenida da Sidonio Pais offers industrial and technical training.

ARTS

See under Arts in the Facts about Hong Kong chapter. As for the Portuguese, their art is most apparent in the old churches and cathedrals which grace Macau's skyline. It's there that you'll see some fine examples of painting, stained-glass windows and sculpture.

Music

Canto-pop from Hong Kong is of course popular in Macau (see Music in the Facts about Hong Kong chapter). If you want to browse through a selection of Portuguese music it's a good idea to try the Portuguese bookshops in town which also stock a large selection of the music of Portugal. Traditional forms of music include Portuguese folk music and the *fado*, which is a rather melancholic song form that is popular in Portugal.

SOCIETY & CONDUCT
Traditional Culture

About 95% of the population is Chinese and is culturally indistinguishable from the Hong Kong Chinese population. For more details, see the Society & Conduct section in the Facts about Hong Kong chapter.

The Portuguese minority has a vastly different culture, that has evolved under a number of different influences, including Roman, Moorish, French, Spanish, Flemish and Italian. Portuguese architectural styles

MACAU

reflect a variety of forms from Roman and Gothic through Baroque to Neoclassical, and it is to the churches of Macau that one looks for the pageantry of Portuguese building style. The colourful religious festivals are signs of a healthy and vibrant Portuguese culture in Macau and of course, Portuguese food is to be found in abundance in the territory.

Although marriages between Portuguese and Chinese are not uncommon in Macau, there has been surprisingly little assimilation between the two ethnic groups. You'll find most Portuguese cannot speak Chinese and vice versa.

Dos & Don'ts

Thongs are basically only for wearing inside your hotel room or at the beach. Sandals with a strap across the back of the ankle are generally OK, though.

See also the Gambling entry in the Macau Facts for the Visitor chapter and Society & Conduct in the Facts about Hong Kong chapter.

RELIGION

For the Chinese majority, Taoism and Buddhism are the dominant religions (see Religion in the Facts about Hong Kong chapter). However, nearly 500 years of Portuguese influence has definitely left an imprint, and the Roman Catholic church is very strong in Macau. Macau consists of a single diocese, directly responsible to the Holy See. There are approximately 23,000 adherents in the territory. The religious presence in Macau is most strongly gauged by the colourful collection of churches that grace the streets. The edifice of the Ruinas de São Paulo is testament to the power the church once wielded in Macau.

Chinese temples in Macau come alive at festival time, especially during the Chinese New Year, when huge bundles of bangers and clips of crackers are exploded.

Facts for the Visitor

HIGHLIGHTS

Although gambling is what draws most people to Macau, the fine colonial architecture and excellent walks are what make the enclave unique. Macau is a city of variegated shades, textures and moods, best appreciated on a slow wander through its narrow streets.

There are a few attractions that stand head and shoulders above the rest. The Ruinas de São Paulo are a must-see. Although only the façade remains of this edifice, it possesses such majesty that it has become an icon of Macau. At night the lit-up ruins are spectacular. The A-Ma Temple is a wonderful snapshot of Chinese religious life, especially during festivals. The Chinese New Year sees the temple resounding to music and crackers. The Kun Iam Temple in the north of the peninsula is an intriguing complex of temples dedicated to the God of Mercy. São Lourenço is a metaphor for the decaying nobility of the whole city of Macau. Other highlights include the Monte Fortress, Guia Fortress, the Leal Senado and the Penha Church. There are the tranquil islands of Taipa and Coloane which preserve a pastoral tradition despite the agenda of housing estate developers. Finally, there's no better way to round off a trip to Macau than with a fine meal at a Portuguese restaurant.

PLANNING

When to Go

Macau is a convenient escape for many Hong Kong residents, who account for over 90% of tourist arrivals in Macau. Weekends and public holidays in Hong Kong generate a flood of tourists pouring into Macau. You'd be wise to avoid these times, since hotels double their prices and rooms of any sort can be hard to find.

Chinese New Year (usually held in late January or February) is chaotic and hotel rooms are a prized commodity. This is a colourful time to visit Macau, as the city crackles with bangers and fireworks and the streets have a carnival atmosphere.

See also Public Holidays & Special Events later in this chapter for details of other special events.

For western tourists, summer (July to September) tends to be the peak travel season, although the best weather is in October and November. The Macau Grand Prix, held in the third week of November, is also a peak time for tourists.

Maps

The Macau Government Tourist Office gives out an excellent *Macau Tourist Map*. This reasonably detailed map has major streets labelled in both Portuguese and Chinese characters (useful if you are taking a taxi and the driver doesn't speak English), and includes small maps of Taipa and Coloane. Also listed are bus routes, all the major tourist sights and useful information for the traveller.

There are other maps of Macau on sale in bookshops, but these tend to be out of date and inaccurate.

What to Bring

Macau is a modern place and you'll probably be able to buy whatever you need. See also the What to Bring section in the Hong Kong Facts for the Visitor chapter.

TOURIST OFFICES

Local Tourist Offices

The Macau Government Tourist Office (MGTO, ☎ 315566, fax 510104, email promgto@macau.ctm.net, www.macau.tourism.gov.mo) is a well organised and helpful source of information. It's at Largo do Senado, Edificio Ritz No 9, next to the Leal Senado building in the square in the centre of Macau. It's open daily from 9 am to 6 pm and is staffed by multilingual personnel. It has a large selection of free leaflets on Macau.

There is a small but very helpful tourist information counter at the Jetfoil pier in Macau. The staff can answer questions and issue maps and other brochures.

Macau has a system of computerised city guides. This is a simple online service consisting of computer terminals placed at strategic locations around the city. The information available on the computers covers transport, hotels, sightseeing and daily events. You'll find the computer terminals at the Jetfoil pier, the lobby of the Leal Senado, the Lisboa Hotel, Hyatt Regency Hotel, Yaohan department store, Plaza Cultural and Livraria Portuguesa. There are also some located on the street in popular tourist areas.

The MGTO runs a tourist assistance unit to help travellers who may have run into trouble during their sojourn in Macau. The hotline for this service is ☎ 340390, and it is operated daily from 9 am to 6 pm.

Tourist Offices Abroad

On Hong Kong Island there's a useful branch of the MGTO (☎ 2549-8884, fax 2559-6513, email dnetwork@netvigator. com) next to the Macau Jetfoil pier at Destinations Network suite 1303, Shun Tak Centre, 200 Connaught Rd. If you're taking the jetfoil to Macau, you can collect all the MGTO literature and read it while you're on the boat.

Macau has overseas representative offices around the world which can assist you with planning your trip to the territory and provide you with any information and help you may need. The contact details for these offices are as follows:

Australia
  Icon Group Services Pty Ltd (☎ (02) 9264-3532, fax 9264-7046, email macau@icongs. aust.com), level 17, 456 Kent St, Sydney, NSW 2000
France
  Investment Tourism & Trade of Portugal (☎ (01) 53 83 75 95, fax 42 89 30 74), 135 Boulevard Haussman, 75008 Paris
Germany
  Representation Plus (☎ (69)-97 46 72 20, fax 97 46 71 00), Frankfurt am Main, Beethovenplatz 1-3, 60325 Frankfurt-Westend

Italy
  Investment Tourism & Trade of Portugal (☎ (2) 79 52 28, fax 79 46 22), Largo Augusto 3, 200122 Milan
Japan
  Mile Post Consultations Inc (☎ (3) 5275-2537, fax 5275-2535, email mpcsub2@ po.iijnet.or.jp), 3rd floor, Sanden building, 5-5, Kojimachi 3-chome, Chiyoda-ku, Tokyo 102
Korea (South)
  Glocom Korea (☎ (2) 778-4402, fax 778-4404, email glocom@bora.dacom.co.kr), suite 1105, Paiknam building (President Hotel) 188-3, Eulchiro 1-Ka, Chung-Ku, Seoul
Malaysia
  Pacific World Travel Sdn Bhd (☎ (3) 241-3899, fax 248-1357, email pwt@melewar. com), 2.5 and 2.6 Bangunan Angkasa Raya Jalan Ampang, 50450, Kuala Lumpur
New Zealand
  Icon Services Pty Ltd (☎ (9) 309 8094, fax 309-2832), 101 Great South Rd, Remuera, Auckland
Philippines
  Asia Pacific Project Inc (☎ (2) 817-2644, fax 813-4781), 9th floor, PDCP Bank building, Alfaro Corner Herrera St, Sacedo Village, Makati City
Portugal
  Delegacao de Macau em Lisboa (☎ (1) 793-6542, fax 796-0956), c/o Missao do Macau, Avenida 5 de Outubro, No 115, r/c, 1050 Lisboa
Singapore
  New Enterprises Pte Ltd (☎ 225-0022, fax 223-8585, email macau@drive.com.sg), 37a Smith St, Singapore 058950
Taiwan
  Compass Public Relations (☎ (2) 546-6086, fax 546-608), 3rd floor, 150 Tun Hwa North Rd, Taipei
Thailand
  Pacific Leisure (Thailand) Ltd (☎ (2) 255-05989, fax 652-0697, email manob@loxinfo. co.th), 6th floor, Maneeya Center building, 518/5 Ploenchit Rd, Bangkok 10330
UK
  Communications in Business (CiB, ☎ (0171) 771-7006, fax 771-7059, email liz@cibpr. demon.co.uk), 1 Battersea Church Rd, London SW11 3LY

USA
Asia Pacific Travel Ltd (☎ (847) 251-6421,
(800) 331-7150, fax (847) 256-5601, email
asiatour@aol.com), 2514 Laurel Lane,
Wilmette, Illinois 60091-2230

VISAS & DOCUMENTS
Visas

For most visitors, all that's needed to enter
Macau is a passport. Everyone gets a 20
day stay on arrival except Hong Kong residents (with a Hong Kong identity card,
permanent identity card or re-entry permit),
who get 90 days and Portuguese nationals
with an identity card, who can enter Macau
without a passport for an unlimited stay.
Visas are not required for visitors from
the following countries: Australia, Austria,
Belgium, Brazil, Canada, China, Denmark,
Finland, France, Germany, Greece, Hong
Kong, India, Italy, Japan, Luxembourg,
Malaysia, Mexico, the Netherlands, New
Zealand, Norway, Philippines, Republic
of Ireland, Singapore, South Africa, South
Korea, Spain, Sweden, Switzerland, Taiwan,
Thailand, the UK, Uruguay and the USA.

All other nationalities need a visa, which
can be obtained on arrival in Macau, unless
they are from countries which do not have
diplomatic relations with Portugal. Visas
cost M$100 for individuals, or M$50 for
children under 12 years. If you're part of a
tour group of 10 people or more, visas are
M$50 each. People from countries which do
not have diplomatic relations with Portugal
must obtain visas from an overseas Portuguese consulate before entering Macau.

Visa Extensions After your 20 days are up,
you can obtain a one month extension. A
second extension is not possible, although
it's easy enough to cross the border to China
and then come back again. The Immigration
Office (☎ 577338) is on the 9th floor, Macau
Chamber of Commerce building, 175 Rua
de Xangai, which is one block to the north-
east of the Hotel Beverly Plaza.

Driving Licence & Permits

Drivers must be at least 21 years of age. An
International Driver's Permit is required
and this cannot be issued in Macau unless
you already have a Macau driver's licence.
A Hong Kong driver's licence is useless
in Macau.

EMBASSIES & CONSULATES
Macau Embassies & Consulates

There is a Macau consulate in Hong Kong,
care of the British Trade Commission
(☎ 2523-0176), Bank of America Tower,
Lambeth Walk, Admiralty. Visas for China
can be picked up at the Macau Visa Office,
14th floor, 99 Avenida de Almeida Ribeiro,
just to the right of the Leal Senado. A single
entry visa is M$88, a double entry or transit
visa is M$134 and a multiple entry visa
costs M$206. The offices are open from
9.30 to 11.30 am and from 2.30 to 5.30 pm.

If you want to machete your way through
the bamboo curtain for one last time before
it gets bulldozed away on 20 December
1999, you can pick up a five day visa to
Zhuhai on the spot on the Chinese side of
the border for M$90. Only single entries
are allowed and you must stay within the
Zhuhai Special Economic Zone – you are
not allowed to wander further into China.

CUSTOMS

Customs formalities are very few and it's
unlikely you'll ever be bothered by them,
although you may be subjected to a routine
check. There is a 5% *ad valorem* duty on
the import of electrical appliances and
equipment. You're allowed to bring in a
reasonable quantity of tobacco, alcohol and
perfumes, but remember that when returning to Hong Kong the customs authorities
will only allow you to return with 1L of
spirits, 200 cigarettes, 50 cigars or 250gms
of tobacco (Hong Kong residents are only
allowed one bottle of table wine or port, 100
cigarettes or 25 cigars). There are no restrictions on the amount of foreign currency
that can be taken in or out of Macau, which
is either good or bad news for those with a
severe addiction to gambling.

Like Hong Kong, Macau customs takes
a very dim view of drugs. Note that you

MACAU

aren't supposed to take fireworks bought in Macau back to Hong Kong. See the Hong Kong Facts for the Visitor chapter for more details.

BAGGAGE STORAGE

You can store bags at the Jetfoil pier in Macau in an electronic locker that costs about M$20 to M$40 for the day, depending on the size of your bag. The lockers are on the ground floor, near the HongkongBank ATM. The way they work is that you stuff your bag in a locker, pump your money in and then a receipt feeds out, with the secret six digit combination for your locker printed on it. Read the listed instructions carefully and don't show your receipt to anyone for elucidation.

Another option is to store your luggage in a bag store at a hotel. Hotels will generally allow you to store a bag when you check out, a big convenience if you must check out by noon but don't want to return to Hong Kong until the evening.

See also the Baggage Storage section in the Hong Kong Facts for the Visitor chapter.

MONEY
Currency

Macau's currency is the pataca, normally written as M$, and one pataca is divided into 100 avos. Coins come as 10, 20 and 50 avos and one and five patacas. The notes are 5, 10, 50, 100, 500 and 1000 patacas. Commemorative gold M$1000 and silver M$100 coins have been issued, although it's hardly likely you'll see them used as currency. There are no exchange control regulations and money can be freely transferred in and out of Macau.

Exchange Rates

Because Macau's pataca is pegged to the Hong Kong dollar, exchange rates are virtually the same as for the Hong Kong dollar (for a table of exchange rates see the Money section in the Hong Kong Facts for the Visitor chapter). The pataca is pegged to the Hong Kong dollar at the rate of 103.20 patacas to HK$100 with a permissable

variation rate of up to 10%. If the Hong Kong dollar peg to the US dollar snaps, expect the pataca peg to follow suit. There are approximately eight patacas to US$1.

Exchanging Money

Cash Hong Kong dollars, including coins, are readily accepted everywhere in Macau. If you have Hong Kong dollars, it's not worth changing them into patacas, although you might make a small saving by using patacas. In Hong Kong, moneychangers often refuse to change patacas. Even worse, most Hong Kong banks won't take them either! The only place we know that will change patacas for Hong Kong dollars is the main branch of the Hang Seng Bank, at 18 Carnarvon Rd, Tsim Sha Tsui. You lose a little bit by changing them in Hong Kong rather than in Macau, and even Hang Seng Bank doesn't want the coins. You would be wise to use up all your patacas before departing Macau.

You can convert patacas into renminbi (yuan) in Macau – the best place to go is the Bank of China. Patacas are also freely converted into Portuguese escudos.

ATMs Some Jetco ATMs will work with American Express (Amex) or Visa cards. This is particularly true of the Jetco machines in the casinos – you'll find one on the 2nd floor of the Lisboa Hotel arcade.

You'll probably have better luck at the HongkongBank branch at the corner of Avenida da Praia Grande and Rua Palha. There is an Electronic Teller Card (ETC) machine there that accepts Visa and other ATM cards which use Plus, GlobalAccess and Electron. HongkongBank ATMs are also found in the arcade on the 2nd floor of the Lisboa Hotel and on the ground floor of the Jetfoil pier in Macau. Midland Bank customers can use their cash-point cards in HongkongBank ATM's and can receive payment in either Hong Kong dollars or Macau patacas. HongkongBank has an ATM hotline (☎ 5992113).

Bank of America (☎ 568821, fax 570386) has a useful ATM near the Leal Senado, which takes Visa, Jetco and Plus.

Credit Cards Major credit cards are readily accepted at Macau's hotels and casinos. Theft or loss of a credit card should be reported to the company's representative office in Hong Kong. Neither MasterCard nor Visa has a representative office in Macau. See the Hong Kong Facts for the Visitor chapter for the addresses and telephone numbers of the major credit card companies in Hong Kong.

Amex has three representative offices in Macau where you can get cash on your card, foreign exchange and other credit card services. The general office (☎ 363262) is at 23B Rua de São Paulo (not far from the Ruinas de São Paulo) and is open from 9 am to 5.30 pm. The other two branches are: (☎ 579898) shop G3, Old Wing, Lisboa hotel, open 24 hours; and (☎ 430163) block II-E Sul, Istmo Fereira do Amaral, Jardins do Mar, open from 7.30 am to 9.30 pm.

Citibank (☎ 378188, fax 578451) has a branch at 31b-c Avenida da Praia Grande. HongkongBank has a credit card centre customer service hotline (☎ 322813).

International Transfers As in Hong Kong, international telegraphic transfers are quick and efficient. The general office of the HongkongBank (☎ 553669, fax 216469) is at 639 Avenida da Praia Grande. Other banks which handle transfers are Banco Naçional Ultramarino (☎ 355111, fax 371748), 789 Avenida da Praia Grande, and Banco Comercial de Macau (☎ 569622), 572 Avenida da Praia Grande. The Amex offices (see the Credit Cards entry in this section) can arrange for cash transfers (moneyGram) but you have to have a cardholder's account.

Some Other banks that handle international transfers include: Bank of America (☎ 568821, fax 570386), 165 Avenida de Almeida Ribeiro; Banque National de Paris (☎ 562777, fax 560626), 219 Avenida da Praia Grande; and Standard Chartered Bank (☎ 378271, fax 594134), 60-64 Avenida do Infante D'Henrique.

Black Market No currency black market exists in Macau.

Costs
As long as you avoid the lurid allure of the territory's ghastly hostess clubs and don't end up on the long slippery slide to destitution promoted by the casinos of Macau, your trip should be reasonably cheap.

Bottom-of-the-barrel accommodation can be picked up for as little as M$30 for a single, and cheap eats abound. Across the board, it's far cheaper to visit Macau than to stay in Hong Kong.

Try to avoid going on weekends and public holidays, as hotels and transport to Macau are more expensive at these times.

Tipping & Bargaining
Classy hotels and restaurants will automatically hit you with a 10% service charge, which is supposedly a mandatory tip.

You can follow your own conscience, but tipping is not customary among the Chinese. Of course, porters at expensive hotels have become accustomed to handouts from well-heeled tourists.

Most shops have fixed prices, but if you buy clothing, trinkets and other tourist junk from the street markets, there is some scope for bargaining.

Macau is noticeably friendlier than Hong Kong, and therefore you should be too. Bargain politely – the rough manners of Hong Kong don't go down well in Macau, and if you're nasty you'll get nowhere in a bargaining session. Smile, tell the shop staff member that you don't have much money and would like a discount. It's a different story at the pawnshops. Bargain ruthlessly!

Pawnshops
You can literally lose your shirt gambling in Macau – the pawnbrokers sell everything. Of course, a second-hand shirt is worth peanuts. Even for a fancy gold watch or camera, you'll be lucky to get enough to pay for your jetfoil ticket back to Hong Kong. The shopping district to the east of Leal Senado on Avenida de Almeida Ribeiro has a clump of pawnshops, windows glinting with cameras, gold Rolexes and wedding rings.

MACAU

A Pawn Loser

In Macau pawnshops, it's no holds barred. These guys would sell their own mother to a glue factory. I saw a nice camera – a Ricoh KR-5 – in a pawnshop window with a M$850 price tag. That's about how much it cost new, and this camera was eight years old! I examined it and found the automatic timer was broken. After an exhaustive bargaining session, I got the price down to M$600. I bought the camera and the next day had it appraised at a camera shop. The staff told me I shouldn't have paid more than M$200. Just for fun, I took it over to another pawnshop whose staff said it was worth M$50.

James Whitham

POST & COMMUNICATIONS
Postal Rates
Domestic letters cost M$1 for up to 20g. For international mail, Macau divides the world into zones: zone 1 is east Asia, including Korea, Taiwan etc; zone 2 is everywhere else. There are special rates for China and Portugal. The rates in M$ for air mail letters, postcards and aerogrammes are as follows:

Grams	China	Portugal	Zone 1	Zone 2
10	2.00	3.00	3.50	4.50
20	3.00	4.50	4.50	6.00
30	4.00	6.00	5.50	7.50
40	5.00	7.50	6.50	9.00
50	6.00	9.00	7.50	10.50

Printed matter receives a discount of about 30% off these rates. Registration costs an extra M$12.

Sending Mail
The postal service is efficient and the clerks usually speak English. The main post office (☎ 596688) is in Leal Senado on Avenida de Almeida Ribeiro. As well as a few ordinary post offices, there are numerous mini-post offices throughout Macau. These are little red booths that sell stamps from vending machines. Large hotels like the Lisboa also sell stamps and postcards and can post letters and parcels for you.

Speedpost (EMS) is available at the main post office in Leal Senado. Other companies that arrange express forwarding are DHL (☎ 372828), Federal Express (☎ 703333) and UPS (☎ 963535).

Receiving Mail
Poste restante service is available at the main post office in Leal Senado on Avenida de Almeida Ribeiro. It's open Monday to Saturday from 9 am to 8 pm.

Telephone
Macau's telephone service provider is Companhia de Telecomunicacoes de Macau (CTM, inquiry hotline ☎ 552200). There is a useful CTM office next to Leal Senado on Avenida de Almeida Ribeiro. The clerks speak English and the office is open Monday to Saturday from 8 am until midnight and Sunday from 9 am until midnight. The main CTM office (for applying for phone service and paying bills) is on Avenida do Doutor Rodrigo Rodrigues, just up from the Lisboa Hotel. Opening hours are Monday to Saturday from 9 am to 8 pm. The phone service is good – you'll seldom have trouble with broken public phones and noisy lines. Public pay phones are mostly concentrated around the Leal Senado, and can be hard to find elsewhere. Most large hotels have a phone in the lobby and there is a courtesy phone at the MGTO.

Local calls are free from private or hotel telephones. At a public pay phone, local calls cost M$1 for five minutes. All pay phones permit International Direct Dialling (IDD).

The international access code for every country *except* Hong Kong is 00. If you want to phone Hong Kong, first dial 01 then the number you want – you don't need to dial the country code. To call Macau from abroad, the country code is 853. It is extremely expensive calling Macau from abroad, far more expensive than calling Hong Kong, so make it short. See the Telephone section in the Hong Kong Facts for the Visitor chapter for more information on making international calls.

Remember you'll need lots of change to make an IDD call unless you buy a telephone card from CTM. These are sold in denominations of M$50, M$100 and M$200. Not all phones accept these cards, so you'll have to hunt these down. Phones which accept these cards are found around Leal Senado, the Jetfoil pier and at some of the larger hotels.

The following table lists some useful telephone numbers:

Emergency	☎ 999
Police	☎ 573333
Ambulance	☎ 371333
Fire	☎ 572222
Directory Assistance (Macau)	☎ 181
Directory Assistance (Abroad)	☎ 101
Time	☎ 140
Jetfoil	☎ 7907039
Turbocats	☎ 726789

Fax & Telegraph

Most of the mid-range and above hotels have fax machines which you can use to send and receive documents. Fax machines can generally be found in the business centre of the hotel. Charges are expensive and are generally a fixed rate per page or according to the time used. If your hotel doesn't have a fax, you can send and receive faxes at the main post office (not the telephone office) on Avenida de Almeida Ribeiro.

The telephone office (not the post office) handles telegrams.

Email & Internet Access

Email services are not well developed in Macau. If you belong to a service like Compuserve or America Online, you'll have to call Hong Kong. The more expensive hotels are equipped with business centres that offer email services, and some hotels do not mind non-guests using the facilities. The charge is generally expensive and by either the half hour or the hour. Residents of Macau can apply for an Internet account through the main CTM office on Avenida do Doutor Rodrigo Rodrigues.

INTERNET RESOURCES

A good place to start a search on the World Wide Web is www.macau.net. And www.lonelyplanet.com will steer you to Lonely Planet's award-winning site. City guide information on Macau can be picked up on www.cityguide.gov.mo, which has sheets of news on sports and cultural events.

BOOKS

Books about Macau are scarce. Much of what's been published is in Portuguese, but there are a few good books in English.

Lonely Planet

Travellers heading to China should get Lonely Planet's comprehensive guide to *China* (which includes a chapter on Hong Kong and Macau). Macau is also briefly covered in Lonely Planet's *Hong Kong city guide* and *South-East Asia on a shoestring*.

Guidebooks

If you can track down a copy, it's worth getting the *Macau AOA Gambling Handbook*. This comes as part of a set which includes the *Macau Pictorial Guide* and an excellent map of Macau. The whole package costs only HK$25 and is available from most of the main bookshops in Hong Kong. If not, you could try the MGTO in Hong Kong or go directly to the publisher, AOA (☎ 2389-0352), 10th floor, 174 Wai Yip St, Kwun Tong, Hong Kong.

Behind the service counter at the MGTO on Largo do Senado there is a small collection of books and other goods for sale.

Travel

A Macao Narrative was written by Austin Coates, a well known Hong Kong magistrate, who also wrote *City of Broken Promises*. If you want the cultural lowdown on the territory, *Macau Miscellany* and *More Macau Miscellany* by Shann Davies should fill in all the gaps. Another good book is *Macau* by Cesar Guillen-Nuñez.

History & Politics

Historic Macao by CA Montalto de Jesus

MACAU

was first published in 1902 as a history of the enclave. In 1926 the author added extra chapters in which he suggested that the Portuguese government cared so little about the territory and did so little to meet its needs that it would be better if Macau was administered by the League of Nations. The Portuguese government was outraged and copies of the book were seized and destroyed.

General

There are several pictorial coffee-table books about Macau. One is simply called *Macau*, written by Jean-Yves Defay. Another, also called *Macau*, is a hardback pictorial by Leong Ka Tai & Shann Davies, that's an interesting look at Macau's history. A good coffee-table sketchbook of the colony is *Old Macau* by Tom Briggs & Colin Crisswell.

Novels set in Macau are rare but there is at least one – *Macau*, by Daniel Carney. Worth looking out for is *Macau on a Plate* by Annabel Jackson Doling if you want to experiment with local flavours in your own kitchen.

Bookshops

Finding a bookshop with a decent selection of English-language books in Macau is a headache. Some have a smattering of English-language titles, but if you want to stock up, Hong Kong is a much better bet. Most bookshops in Macau sell books either in Chinese or Portuguese. If you have to buy something, it's generally advisable to shop at the bookshops at the major hotels, where you can find a relatively decent collection of books on local themes in English.

Livraria São Paulo (☎ 323957) on Travessa do Bispo (near the cathedral) has books mainly in Portuguese and oriented towards the Catholic church, but there are some general interest English-language books and good maps of Macau. This is also one of the only bookshops in Macau that stocks Lonely Planet guides.

For Portuguese-language publications, check out Livraria Portuguesa (☎ 566442), 18-20 Rua de São Domingos. This place also has a good assortment of Portuguese music CDs.

There is a general interest bookshop inside the Plaza Cultural, basement, 32 Avenida do Conselheiro Ferreira de Almeida (near Lou Lim Ioc Gardens).

FILMS

The first ever feature film from Macau was *The Bewitching Braid* (1995), which is a bittersweet romantic comedy focusing on Macau's cultural and racial mixture, set in the 1930s.

Two films that were partly shot in Macau are the James Bond classic *The Man with the Golden Gun* (1974) and *Indiana Jones and the Temple of Doom (1984)*.

NEWSPAPERS & MAGAZINES

The *South China Morning Post* and *Hong Kong Standard* are both available from newspaper vendors on the street. If you want to get a copy of *Newsweek, Time, Asiaweek* or the *International Herald Tribune* your best bet is the bookshop at one of the top-end hotels, such as the Mandarin Oriental.

Two free monthly tourist newspapers *Macau Travel Talk* and *Welcome to Macau* are available from offices of the MGTO and from hotels. These throwaway freebies give sugar-coated coverage but come with useful maps and news about forthcoming events and shows of interest.

A selection of Macau-related Portuguese-language papers and magazines also exists, including *Futuro de Macau, O Clarim* and *Macau Hoje*. The rest of the print media market is largely dominated by the Chinese-language press.

RADIO & TV

Macau has three radio stations, two of which broadcast in Cantonese and one in Portuguese. There are no local English-language radio stations, but you should be able to pick up Hong Kong stations. Radio Macau broadcasts 24 hours a day in Portuguese.

Teledifusão de Macau (TdM) is a privately owned station that broadcasts on two channels. Shows are mainly in English and

Portuguese, although there are some Cantonese programs. It's easy to pick up Hong Kong stations in Macau (but not vice versa) and you can also receive stations from China. Hong Kong newspapers list Macau TV programs.

Hong Kong's famous satellite TV system, STAR TV, is readily available in Macau at any hotel with a cable or satellite dish hookup. Many mid-range and above hotels also have closed-circuit video channels or video disc players.

See also Radio & TV in the Hong Kong Facts for the Visitor chapter.

VIDEO SYSTEMS

Like Hong Kong, Macau uses the PAL standard for TV broadcasting and video tapes. As in Hong Kong video disc players are common. If you want to buy a video disc player in Macau, remember that although video discs are easy to buy in Macau, Hong Kong and China, getting them in the west can be difficult.

PHOTOGRAPHY & VIDEO

You can find most types of film, cameras and accessories in Macau, and photo-processing is of a high standard. A decent store for all photographic services is Foto Princesa (☎ 555959), 55-59 Avenida de Infante D'Henrique, one block east of Avenida da Praia Grande. This place sells professional film, video equipment, video tapes and binoculars, and also does quickie visa photos. Foto Nice (☎ 315678), 57 Rua da Barca, also has a large range of cameras, electronics and accessories.

Another part of town that has a concentration of camera shops is at the intersection of Rua de Ferreira do Amaral and Rua do Campo, near the Vasco da Gama Garden. Two good shops are Lua Prata (☎ 308175) at 69b Rua do Campo and Foto Maxim's (☎ 376850) at 53 Rua do Campo.

If you want somewhere handy to develop your film, there's a branch of Kodak near the MGTO in Largo do Senado. It can develop 36 exposures in one hour for M$48.

Macau offers some fantastic opportuni-

ties for photographs. The city is rich in texture and character. Be polite when photographing people and give them space – the Macau Chinese are not the most relaxed people in front of the camera; go easy on photographing locals playing mahjong as it won't be appreciated.

TIME
Like Hong Kong, Macau is eight hours ahead of GMT/UTC and does not observe daylight saving.

ELECTRICITY
Voltages & Cycles
Macau's electricity system is the same as in Hong Kong and China – 220V AC, 50Hz. There are still a few old buildings wired for 110V, but as long as you see three round holes on the outlets you can be assured it's 220V.

Plugs & Sockets
The electric outlets are three round pins, the same as Hong Kong's older design. See also Electricity in the Hong Kong Facts for the Visitor chapter.

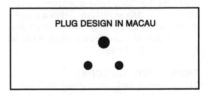

PLUG DESIGN IN MACAU

WEIGHTS & MEASURES
Macau uses the international metric system. As in Hong Kong, street markets and medicine shops sell things by the *leung* (37.5g) and the *gan* (600g).

LAUNDRY
Hidden in the alleys are many hole-in-the-wall laundry services that charge reasonable prices. The trick is to find these, as most use Chinese characters only to advertise the business. One which is relatively easy to find is Lavandaria Macau, in the same building as

San Va Hospedaria, 67 Rua de Felicidade. Another central road that has a cluster of laundries is Rua Mercadores, to the west of Largo do Senado, just off Avenida de Almeida Ribeiro. Almost all hotels offer a laundry service, but ask about the price before handing over your clothes.

TOILETS
Macau has far more public toilets per capita than Hong Kong. Good venues to find toilets include the tourist office, parks, temples, museums, casinos, fast-food restaurants, the Jetfoil pier and shopping plazas.

WOMEN TRAVELLERS
For details see the Women Travellers section in the Hong Kong Facts for the Visitor chapter.

The International Ladies Club of Macau (ILCM) invites English-speaking women of all nationalities to join. However, it's geared towards expats living in Macau, not to tourists. Activities include making friends, helping newcomers settle into Macau, organising fundraisers for charity, publishing a monthly newsletter and whatever else the membership wishes to do. There are usually several meetings a month, mostly informal get-togethers over coffee, tea or lunch. If you are interested, write to PO Box 1370, Macau.

TRAVEL WITH CHILDREN
The government is struggling to make a visit to Macau more of a family affair. However, the reality is that there is little to occupy children apart from scampering around the parks and chasing pigeons.

On the 3rd floor of the Lisboa Hotel is Children's World (☎ 569229), where kids can play video games or snooker for hours while mum and dad lose their life savings at the blackjack tables. Leave the kids there all day and they probably won't even miss you.

If you want to get rid of the kids for five days, the Hyatt Regency Hotel (☎ 831234 ext 1856) on Taipa Island has a modest proposal. For HK$4500, the hotel's summer camp will keep the kids constructively occupied with activities such as camping, scuba diving, water polo, tennis, windsurfing, ice skating, canoeing and rock climbing. Less strenuous activities include theatre, picnics, barbecues and sing-around-the-campfire social activities. The five day camps run every week from early July to late August, and children must be aged between nine and 14. The hotel can arrange to pick up the kids in Hong Kong and return them there, which gives parents a few extra days to shop in Tsim Sha Tsui. If staying at the Hyatt Regency Hotel, parents are entitled to a 25% discount by signing up the kids, though you can get the same discount by booking through Hong Kong travel agents.

USEFUL ORGANISATIONS
For those in Macau on business, some of the following organisations should be of help. The Associação Comercial de Macau (☎ 576833, fax 594513), 175 Rua de Xangai, is the chamber of commerce in Macau. The World Trade Center Macau, SARL (☎ 727666, fax 727633, email wtcmc @macau.ctm.net), 918 Avenida da Amizade, offers trade information services, and arranges conferences and exhibitions. The Instituto de Promoção do Comércio e do Investimento de Macau (Macau Trade and Investment Promotion Institute, ☎ 340090, fax 712659), 7th/8th floors, 1-3 Rua Doutor Pedro José Lobo, promotes investment and trade in Macau.

DANGERS & ANNOYANCES
More than mildly annoying is the savage internecine conflict hosted by the Triads. In 1997 this descended into a spiral of tit-for-tat killings fought mainly over diminishing returns from gambling profits. This is not a regular occurrence, but Triad activity apparently got a shot in the tattooed arm when preparations began for Hong Kong to be handed back to China. Hong Kong Triads sought to be established in Macau. The new airport also provided a gateway into the Portuguese enclave for the Triads from Taiwan.

As the Macau handover approaches, another Triad flare-up is a possibility,

MACAU

despite the MGTO's upbeat reassurances. No tourists were injured or killed in the crossfire in 1997, but a hotel had chunks taken out of it by stray bullets.

Residential burglaries and pickpocketing are also problems. Most hotels are well guarded, and if you take reasonable care with your valuables, you should avoid trouble. Cheating at gambling is a serious criminal offence, so don't even think about it.

Traffic is heavy and quite a few tourists have been hit while jaywalking. Macau police have been cracking down on jaywalkers, and although they go light on foreigners you can still get fined. Be especially careful at rush hour when the traffic (and the police) is in force. Crossing the road can be difficult as cars don't necessarily come to a halt at the pedestrian crossings (marked by black and white stripes, as used in the UK). The safest strategy is to follow the locals.

Macau has more prostitutes than almost anywhere apart from neighbouring Zhuhai and if you are a single man checking into one of the cheaper hotels (especially in the western district of Macau, near the Inner Harbour), expect to have regular sultry phone calls asking if you want a *xiaojie* (young girl). This can get very annoying as they don't take no for an answer and eventually come knocking on your door. The worst hotels normally have a welcoming committee of prostitutes loitering by the main entrance, so it is pretty obvious and these establishments can be easily avoided. The East Asia Hotel and the Capital Hotel are the two worst offenders, but are also cheap and fine in other areas. Other hotels have a more subtle policy; the manager will note single men checking in and phone at least once to see if other services are needed. Other ruses are the xiaojie on each floor to badger you. The best advice is to be firm and make sure the message gets across that you don't want company.

BUSINESS HOURS
The operating hours for most government offices in Macau are Monday to Thursday from 9 am to 1 pm and 2.30 to 5.45 pm. On Friday offices close at 5.30 pm. Private businesses keep longer hours and some casinos are open 24 hours a day, including (especially!) weekends.

Banks are normally open Monday to Saturday from 9 am to 4.30 pm.

PUBLIC HOLIDAYS & SPECIAL EVENTS
The Chinese in Macau celebrate the same religious festivals as their counterparts in Hong Kong, but there are several Catholic festivals and some Portuguese national holidays too. The tourist newspapers *Macau Travel Talk* and *Welcome to Macau*, available from the MGTO, have regular listings of events and festivals. The following are some of the more important holidays in Macau – see the Hong Kong Facts for the Visitor chapter for more details about the Chinese holidays.

New Year's Day – The first day of the year is a public holiday.

Chinese Lunar New Year – As in Hong Kong, this is a three day public holiday in late January or early February. The streets are a feast of colour and noise, with lion dances and a deafening backdrop of bangers and fireworks.

Lantern Festival – Not a public holiday, but a lot of fun, this festival occurs two weeks after the Chinese Lunar New Year.

Procession of Our Lord of Passion – Not a public holiday, but a colourful spectacle nonetheless. The procession, bearing a statue of Christ, begins in the evening from São Agostinho and goes to Macau Cathedral. The statue is kept in the cathedral overnight and the procession returns to São Agostinho the following day. The tradition is more than four centuries old.

Feast of the Earth God Tou Tei – A minor holiday for the Chinese community in March or April.

Ching Ming Festival – A major public holiday in April.

Easter – A four day public holiday in March or April (variable) from Good Friday until Easter Monday.

Anniversary of 1974 Portuguese Revolution – This public holiday on 25 April commemorates the overthrow of the Michael Caetano regime in Portugal in 1974 by a left wing military coup.

Feast of the Drunken Dragon and Feast of the Bathing of Lord Buddha – Celebrated in May, these festivals see dancing dragons in the streets of the Inner Harbour and the washing of Buddhist images in temples throughout Macau.

Procession of Our Lady of Fatima – Celebrated on 13 May, this commemorates a miracle that took place at Fatima, Portugal, in 1917. It is not a public holiday. The procession begins at Macau Cathedral and ends at Penha Church.

A-Ma Festival – This is the same as the Tin Hau Festival in Hong Kong and takes place in May. The A-Ma Temple in the south of the Macau Peninsula comes alive with festive worshippers. It's not a public holiday.

Festival of Tam Kong – A relatively minor holiday usually celebrated in May.

Camões and Portuguese Communities Day – Held on 10 June, this public holiday commemorates 16th century poet Luis de Camões.

Dragon Boat Festival – As in Hong Kong, this is a major public holiday usually held in June. Macau's races are usually held at the tip of the Macau Peninsula (Barra Fortress), but check with the MGTO to be certain.

Procession of St John the Baptist – The procession for St John the Baptist, the patron saint of Macau, is held on 10 June.

Feast of Santo António of Lisbon – This June event celebrates the birthday of the patron saint of Lisbon. A military captain, Santo António (St Anthony) receives his wages on this day from a delegation of city officials, and a small parade is held from Santo António's Church.

Battle of 13 July – Celebrated only on the islands of Taipa and Coloane, this holiday commemorates the final defeat of pirates in 1910.

Ghost Month – A Chinese festival, in August or September, a good time to visit temples in Macau.

Mid-Autumn Festival – A major public holiday in September or October.

China National Day – Already creeping in before the handover is this holiday, held on 1 October, celebrating the founding in 1949 of the People's Republic of China.

Portuguese Republic Day – A public holiday on 5 October. This holiday will be politely shown the door after the handover.

Cheung Yeung Festival – A public holiday in October.

All Saints' Day – Held on 1 November. Both All Saints' Day and the following day (All Souls' Day) are public holidays.

Portuguese Independence Day – This public holiday is celebrated on 1 December. The chances of the festivities continuing after the handover are slim.

Feast of the Immaculate Conception – Christian festival held in December; a public holiday.

Winter Solstice – Many Macau Chinese consider the winter solstice more important than Chinese Lunar New Year. There is plenty of feasting and temples are crammed with worshippers. The event is a public holiday.

Christmas – Both the 24th and 25th of December are public holidays.

The Macau Arts Festival is usually held in March and features music, drama and dance from the east and west. The Miss Macau Contest is held every August. The International Music Festival (late October to early November), is usually an intriguing mix of opera, musicals, visiting Portuguese orchestras and other musical events. Concerts are held in a number of venues around town, such as São Domingos (often given by the Oporto National Orchestra), but future events will be held in the recently constructed Macau Cultural Centre. With the opening of the new Cultural Centre, it is likely that the festival will become more large scale and significant.

Bull fights are occasionally staged during the Chinese Lunar New Year in the sports field across from the Lisboa Hotel. In September and October the International Fireworks Festival adds a splash of colour to the Macau night sky. The annual Beer Festival is a recent addition that promises to put some fizz into November.

ACTIVITIES

Future Ice Skating Rink (☎ 9892318) is on Praça de Luis Camões, on the south side of Camões Grotto & Gardens. It also features a bowling alley. If you're interested in aerobics and dance, try the Anna Escola de Danca Aerobic (☎ 518412). Those worried about going to seed can contact the Macau Powerlifting Association (☎ 562258).

Up around the Guia Lighthouse is the best track for jogging. It's also the venue for early morning *taijiquan* (t'ai chi). Another attractive route for runners is along the Avenida da Republica and around the tip of the peninsula.

There is a public swimming pool on Estrada da Vitoria near the Royal Hotel. Adjacent to the swimming pool is a gymnasium where local clubs get together to practice martial arts, taijiquan, basketball and other activities. Foreigners are a rarity there, but if you approach the locals in a friendly way you are likely to be invited to participate in their activities. The clubs have a schedule of events tacked up in the hall of the gymnasium.

Coloane Island features two decent swimming beaches: Cheoc Van Beach, which has a yacht club, and the nearby Hac Sa Beach, which also has tennis courts, ping pong tables, five-a-side football pitches, mini-golf, a swimming pool and a badminton court. Hac Sa also has a number of sea toys for rent, including windsurfers and jet skis.

Bicycles are available for hire on Taipa Island but not on the Macau Peninsula. A few hotels have exercise facilities which non-guests can use by paying a fee. The Westin Resort on Coloane features billiards, table tennis and a golf course. The health spa in the Kingsway Hotel offers hourly rates for use of the facilities: one hour M$163, 1½ hours M$208, two hours M$278 or a half-day for M$300. The Lisboa Hotel is the home of the Lisboa Snooker Club (☎ 569229).

Other useful contacts include: the Macau Sports Institute (☎ 580762), Forum de Macau, Avenida do Doutor Rodrigo Rodrigues; the Macau Athletics Association (fax 522922), PO Box 6127; and Macau Stadium (☎ 838208), Avenida Olympica, Taipa Island.

Walking

The Macau Peninsula is small enough to visit many areas on foot, and this is an excellent way to see it. Work out an itinerary first and don't expect to take in all the sights this way. Some of Macau's attractions are built on hilly ground (eg Penha Church) which can knock the stuffing out of you, but if you are reasonably fit and have more than one day to explore the city, you can take your time on Shank's pony – use your legs rather than a vehicle. In the hills of Coloane there's a hiking trail over 8km in length.

WORK

Unless you hold a Portuguese or Chinese passport, finding employment is difficult. Most Portuguese speak excellent English, so there is little need to import foreign English teachers. However, the situation is similar to that in Hong Kong before the handover, with many skilled professionals planning to leave before Macau returns to Chinese administration. This has created a number of vacancies, especially for people with specialised technical skills, but it has been offset by the regional economic downturn. The unemployment rate hovers around the 3% mark.

ACCOMMODATION

There's good and bad news. The bad news is that hotel prices in Macau continue to rise – the old dumps are being torn down and replaced with comfortable hotels, which usually charge uncomfortable prices. Nor are there dormitories like those in Hong Kong which cater to the backpacker market.

But don't close the book yet, there is good news. Macau's hotels are cheaper than those in Hong Kong. For about the same that you'd pay for a dumpy room in Hong Kong's Chungking Mansions, you can get a comfortable room in Macau with air conditioning, private bath, TV and fancy carpeting. At the very bottom end of the market, you can dig up a few places that have ultra-cheap singles and doubles – there's nothing like that in Hong Kong. In other words, you can spend a lot less on accommodation in Macau than in Hong Kong, or you can spend the same and get more for your pataca.

Hotel prices have come down in Macau, with Macau's tourist market having been sucked into the vortex of the regional downward spiral. Chances are that tourists will boycott Macau after the handover and this will bring hotel prices down more as hoteliers scramble for anything with a rucksack on it.

A few further considerations are essential before you check in. Going on the weekend or on public holidays will bring you face to face with a scarcity of rooms and hotel prices double the weekly rate. For definition purposes, 'weekend' means both Saturday and Sunday nights. Friday night is usually not a problem unless it's also a holiday. Also, during special events, like the Grand Prix or the Chinese New Year, rooms can be impossible to obtain.

Another way to save money is to avoid the high season (summer). High season prices are quoted in this book because that's when most travellers visit, but be aware that you can get substantial discounts in winter (except during Chinese New Year).

The other thing to bear in mind is that a substantial discount (up to 30% or more) is available if you book rooms through a travel agency – this only applies to three star and above hotels. If you're staying at accommodation that is two stars or lower, you'll have to bargain your own discount. If you do go through a travel agency, you can get perfectly reasonable mid-range accommodation in Macau for the same price as a dodgy firetrap in Kowloon.

If you are arriving from Hong Kong, agents offering this service can be readily found at the Shun Tak Centre (Macau Jetfoil pier). Just wander up to one at the Shun Tak Centre before you board your boat to Macau and take your time to leaf through all the hotel brochures and make your choice. You can also book your jetfoil or turbocat ticket through the same travel agent and get a discount, either separately or as a package. If you haven't booked your room before you arrive, you can do it at the Jetfoil pier in Macau. You can't get these discounts simply by showing up at the hotel and asking – only travel agents can arrange it. This is the way most Hong Kong Chinese arrange their stays in Macau and it's wise to do the same.

Camping

It seems hard to believe that in tiny, crowded Macau there could be a camping ground, but there are a couple on Coloane Island. There's a small camping ground in Seac Pai Van Park, and there's a site next to Hac Sa Beach, not far from Fernando's restaurant. Whether it's worth the trouble to go this far to save some money on a night's accommodation is something you'll have to decide. See the Coloane Island section in the Macau Islands chapter for more details.

Hostels

There is only one hostel in Macau and, like the camping grounds, it's on Coloane Island. The problem is that you can't simply show up at the hostel and ask if there's an empty bed. You must first go to the Youth Hostel Booking Office (☎ 344340, fax 960115), near the A-Ma Temple on Macau Peninsula. The office is only open during business hours, which means you can forget about it after 5.45 pm (or on weekends and public holidays). The office will sell you a voucher for M$35 which you must bring to the hostel when you check in. For more information, see the Coloane Island section in the Macau Islands chapter.

Guesthouses

By government edict, all guesthouses must have signs in both Chinese and Portuguese. Guesthouses are usually called *vila*, but sometimes are called *hospedaria* or *pensão*.

There are a few old classic guesthouses remaining in Macau – dirt cheap prices and plenty of dirt, not to mention cockroaches and other things that crawl in the night. Prices start at as little as M$30, and for that sort of money you're about one step up from the pavement in terms of comfort. These are becoming difficult to find as some of the dumps have been torn down, while others have been renovated and now offer luxurious rooms with all mod cons and prices similar to the mid-range hotels.

If you can't handle the rice-paper walls and the TB sanatorium atmosphere at the bottom of the pile, the middle ground of the guesthouse world is occupied by a galaxy of medium-priced dives where you'll pay about M$150 and up. These are generally much better than the horror stories that welcome you at Chungking Mansions and other Hong Kong backwaters. Many have brought prices down to do battle for the smaller numbers of tourists prowling the streets of Macau. Haggle hard for what it's worth. But be aware that although Macau compares favourably with Hong Kong, it's still not exactly a budget travellers' heaven.

Hotels

Macau has an incredible variety of hotels. Some are architectural museum pieces that have been fully renovated, while others are modern high-rise glass-and-concrete cylinders. The 1990s has seen an explosion in the number of hotels built.

The mid-range market is a sprawling mass of choice in Macau, and the hotels are all pretty much the same, with little to recommend one place over another. The best way to book yourself into this market is to reserve a room through a travel agent at the Shun Tak Centre in Hong Kong or at the Jetfoil pier in Macau. This way you can check into a mid-range hotel like the Sun Sun Hotel on a weekday for about M$250 – far cheaper than its equivalent in Hong Kong.

At the top of the pile there are a few places that promise the highest standards of exclusivity.

Most hotels in the middle to upper price range charge a 5% government room tax plus a 10% service charge.

FOOD

For some travellers, eating is the most rewarding part of a trip to Macau. Macau is a place to indulge the senses and feasting should take a high priority. Although Macau doesn't have the vast selection of restaurants that Hong Kong offers, the territory takes dining seriously and eateries are plentiful.

Given its cosmopolitan past, it's not surprising that the food in Macau is an exotic mixture of Portuguese and Chinese cooking, with some influence from other European countries and Africa.

The most famous local speciality is African chicken, which is chicken baked with peppers and chillies. Other specialities include *bacalhau* (cod) dishes that are served baked, grilled, stewed or boiled. The cod is imported and rather salty. Sole, a tongue-shaped flatfish, is another Macanese delicacy. There's also oxtail and ox breast, rabbit prepared in various ways, and soups like *caldo verde* and *sopa a alentejana,* made with vegetables, meat and olive oil. The Brazilian contribution is *feijoadas*, a stew made of beans, pork, potatoes, cabbage and spicy sausages. The contribution from the former Portuguese enclave of Goa on the west coast of India is spicy prawns.

Apart from cod, there's plenty of other seafood – shrimp, prawns, crab, squid and white fish. Try the baked crab or huge grilled and stuffed king prawns. There are lots of seafood restaurants where you can pick your meal from the tank at the front of the shop.

If you're going out for a meal, it's worth remembering that people eat early in Macau – in many places the dining room is clear and the chef has gone home by 9 pm.

DRINKS
Nonalcoholic Drinks

Macau doesn't produce any local specialities. The soft-drink market is dominated by imported brands from the west and Hong Kong. Chinese tea predominates in the restaurants, but Macau's supermarkets can supply you with a quick fix of Twinings and Lipton.

Alcoholic Drinks

The Portuguese influence is most visible in the many fine imported Portuguese red and white wines, port and brandy. Mateus Rosé is the most famous Portuguese wine and sells for a mere M$44. Even cheaper are bottles of red or white wine. Most are considerably more drinkable than the Chinese firewater. For lovers of fine wine, the Macau Wine Museum is a must-see. The museum takes a long look at the tradition of wine making in Portugal. See the Wine Museum entry in the Macau Peninsula chapter for further information.

Wine, spirits and beer are cheaper in Macau than in Hong Kong – even cheaper than at Hong Kong's so-called 'duty-free shops'. Part of the reason has to do with Hong Kong's 90% import tax on alcoholic beverages. In Macau, Portuguese wine carries no import duty, and other imported brews are taxed at 22%.

Wine prices vary in the restaurants but are usually not too expensive. Many people leave Macau with a bottle of Mateus tucked under their arm. You can buy wine from supermarkets and duty-free shops at the airport and the Jetfoil pier. The duty-free wine shop at the Jetfoil pier has a tremendous selection of rare and valuable wines and ports.

There is no minimum drinking age in Macau. If you're old enough to get the bottle open, you can drink whatever is inside.

ENTERTAINMENT
Gambling

Although the games in Macau are somewhat different from Las Vegas, the same basic principles apply. The most important one to remember is this – if you want to win at gambling, own a casino. In every game, the casino enjoys a built-in mathematical advantage. The casinos don't cheat the players because there's no need to. In the short-term, anyone can hit a winning streak and get ahead, but the longer you play, the more certain it is that the odds will catch up with you. There is no system that can help you win – don't believe anyone who tells you anything different!

Your best bet is to gamble for fun only. Don't bet more than you can afford to lose and don't think you can 'make up your losses' by gambling more. If you win, consider yourself lucky.

The most popular form of gambling in Macau is mahjong, played not in the casinos but in private homes. You can hear the rattle of mahjong pieces late into the night if you walk through any side street.

Macau has nine casinos and all of these operate around the clock, apart from the Victory Casino in the Macau Jockey Club. The legal gambling age in Macau is 18 years for foreigners and 21 years for residents.

Photography is absolutely prohibited inside the casinos.

If you want to play casino games that are more sophisticated than the slot machines, track down a copy of the *Macau AOA Gambling Handbook* (for more details see the Books section in this chapter).

If you defy the odds and make an absolute packet in Macau, transporting the money safely away from the casino can be arranged for you by Securicor (☎ 718600, fax 718616), 185-191 Avenida Venceslau de Morais. This company has British army trained Gurkhas at hand to look after your casino winnings.

The casinos have a dress code. Men cannot wear shorts, even relatively long ones. Men also cannot wear vests (a form of underwear), unless they have a shirt on over the vest; in Macau Chinese men love to wear cotton vests without shirts. During the summer, many male travellers run foul of these rules and are refused admission. Women are allowed to wear shorts and vests into casinos.

Neither men nor women are permitted to wear thongs (flip-flops) into casinos.

Discos & Nightclubs

Those coming to Macau in the hope of tapping into a city pulsing with the latest sounds can forget it. Macau nightlife is limited to brash and tacky floorshows and hostess clubs; strictly for visiting Hong Kong Chinese and Japanese on expense accounts. If you're a fan of feather boas, cheesy chorus lines and bad taste, this sequined world will be right up your alley.

SPECTATOR SPORTS

The Macau Stadium next to the Macau Jockey Club on Taipa Island seats 20,000 fans. At certain times of the year there are international soccer meets and track and field competitions. In November, the International Athletics Meeting is held there. The half marathon starts there and makes its way around Taipa Island before crossing to the Macau Peninsula and then returning to the stadium. The stadium has synthetic and natural grass football pitches, as well as facilities for volleyball and basketball. Contact Macau Stadium (☎ 838208), Avenida Olympica, Taipa, for details.

Top fighters, bulls and horses are flown in from Portugal for occasional bullfights; contact the MGTO (☎ 315566) for details of forthcoming fights. The MGTO can also fill you in on the Macau Open, the territory's premier golf tournament.

Another organisation that may be worth contacting for details of forthcoming events is the Macau Sports Institute (☎ 580762), Forum de Macau, Avenida do Doutor Rodrigo Rodrigues.

Grand Prix

The biggest event of the year is undoubtedly the Macau Grand Prix. As in Monaco, the streets of the town make up the race track. The 6km circuit starts near the Lisboa Hotel and follows the shoreline along Avenida da Amizade, going around the reservoir and back through the city.

The Grand Prix consists of two major races – one for cars and one for motorcycles. Both races attract many international contestants. Pedicab races are included as a novelty event.

The race is a two day event held on the third weekend in November. More than 50,000 people flock to see it and accommodation – a problem even on normal weekends – becomes rare. Be sure to book a return ticket on the jetfoil if you have to get back to Hong Kong.

Certain areas in Macau are designated as viewing areas for the races. Streets and alleyways along the track are blocked off, so it's unlikely you'll be able to get a good view without paying. Prices for seats in the reservoir stand are M$350; Lisboa stand, M$550; Mandarin Oriental stand, M$520; and Grand stand, M$600. For the practice days and qualifying events, all stands are M$100. For ticket inquires, call the MGTO on ☎ 7962287.

The Macau authorities have managed to guarantee the future of the event after the handover in 1999.

Dog Racing

Macau has a Canidrome for dog racing. It's the largest facility for greyhound racing in Asia and it's off Avenida General Castelo Branco, not far from the Barrier Gate. Greyhound races are held four times a week on Tuesday, Thursday and Saturday and Sunday, starting at 8 pm. Over 300 dogs race on each race day around the 500 yard (455m) oval track. You can call (☎ 574413) to check the schedule. On race days there are 14 races per night with six to eight dogs per race. Admission to the Canidrome costs M$2, or M$5 in the members' stand; boxes holding six persons cost M$80 for the whole group and a VIP room costs M$25.

Off-Course Betting Centres will accept bets from 5 pm onwards. The centres are in the Lisboa Hotel, Floating Casino and Jai Alai Casino.

Once a year (usually at the end of summer), the Macau Derby is held at the Canidrome. This is the year's biggest race and the winner's purse is currently M$80,000.

Horse Racing

Horse racing has a long history in Macau. In the early 1800s horse races were held outside the city walls on an impromptu course. The area around Estrada Marginal do Hipodromo in the extreme north-east corner of Macau, near the Barrier Gate, was a popular racecourse in the 1930s, but it has now been taken over by numerous apartments and factories.

Regular horse races are held at the Macau Jockey Club, on Taipa Island. For more details, see the Taipa Island section of the Macau Islands chapter.

SHOPPING

The main shopping area is along the Avenida do Infante D'Henrique and Avenida Almeida Ribeiro. Other shopping zones can be found along Rua da Palha, Rua do Campo and Rua Pedro Nolasco da Silva.

The St Dominic Market is in the alley just behind the Hotel Central and next to the MGTO. It's a good place to pick up cheap clothing.

MACAU

Fun & Games in Macau Casinos

Baccarat Also known as *chemin de fer*, baccarat has become the card game of choice for the upper crust. Its rooms are always the most classy part of any casino and the minimum wager is high – at least M$50, and up to M$1000 in some casinos. Two card hands are dealt at the same time – the player's hand and the bank's hand. The hand which scores closest to nine is the winner. Players can bet on either their own hand or the bank hand. Neither is actually the house hand. The casino deducts a percentage if the bank hand wins, which is how the house makes its profit.

If the player understands the game properly, the house only enjoys slightly better than a 1% advantage over the player.

Blackjack Also known as '21' and pontoon, this card game is easy to play, although it requires some skill. The dealer takes a card and also gives one to the player. Each card counts for a particular number of points. The goal is to get enough cards to add up as close as possible to 21 without going over. If you go over 21, then you 'bust', which means you lose. If both you and the dealer go bust at the same time, the dealer still wins and this is what gives the casino the edge over the player. If the dealer and player both get 21, it's a tie and the bet is cancelled. If the player gets 21 (blackjack) then they get even money plus a 50% bonus. Dealers must draw until they reach 16 and stand on 17 or higher. The player is free to decide when to stand or when to draw.

Dai Siu This is Cantonese for 'big-small'. The game is also known as *sik po* (dice treasure) or *cu sik* (guessing dice). It's extremely popular in Macau.

The game is played with three dice which are placed in a covered glass container. The container is then shaken and you bet that the total of the toss will be from three to nine (small) or from 10 to 18 (big). However, you lose on combinations where all three dice come up the same, like 2-2-2, 3-3-3 etc, unless you bet directly on three of a kind.

For betting big-small the house advantage is 2.78%. Betting on a specific three of a kind gives the house a 30% advantage – a sucker bet.

Fan Tan This is an ancient Chinese game practically unknown in the west. The dealer takes an inverted silver cup and plunges it into a pile of porcelain buttons, then moves the cup to one side. After all bets have been placed, the buttons are counted out in groups of four. You have to bet on how many will remain after the last set of four has been taken out. You can bet on numbers one, two, three or four, as well as odd or even.

Keno Although keno is played in Las Vegas and other western casinos, it's believed to have originated in China more than 2000 years ago. Keno was introduced to the USA by Chinese railroad workers in the 19th century.

Just by strolling around Macau's myriad lanes and narrow streets you'll stumble across bustling markets and traditional Chinese shops selling bird cages, dried herbs and medicines, and seafood, as well as bakeries and shops festooned with colourful paper offerings for the dead. If you walk east along Rua de Madeira, you'll run into a charming market street selling chickens, dried meats, sausages and fruit, bordered by small shops with carved buddhas for sale.

Another amble that will take you through a historic mercantile world is along Rua dos Mercadores which leads up to Rua da Tercena, past tailors, wok sellers, tiny jewellery shops, incense shops and other

Keno is basically a lottery. There are 80 numbers, of which 20 are drawn in each game. You are given a keno ticket and the object is to list the numbers you think will be drawn. You can bet on four numbers and if all four are among those drawn in the game, you're a winner. You can play five numbers, six, seven and so on. You have about one chance in nine million of guessing all 20 winning numbers. With only about two drawings per hour, it's a slow way to lose your money.

Pai Kao This is Chinese dominoes and is similar to mahjong. One player is designated the role of banker and the others individually compare their hands against the banker. The casino doesn't play, but deducts a 3% commission from the winnings for providing the gambling facilities.

Roulette & Boule This is a very easy game to play and we don't know why it isn't more popular in Macau. At the moment, the only roulette wheel remaining in all of Macau is at the Lisboa Hotel.

The dealer simply spins the roulette wheel in one direction and spins a ball in the opposite direction. Roulette wheels have 36 numbers plus a zero, so your chance of hitting any given number is one in 37. The payoff is 35 to one, which is what gives the casino its advantage.

Rather than betting a single number, it's much easier to win if you bet odd or even, or red versus black numbers. If the ball lands on zero, everyone loses to the house (unless you also bet the zero). If you bet red or black, or odd or even, the casino's advantage is only 2.7%.

Boule is very similar to roulette, except that it's played with a ball about the size of a billiard ball, and there are fewer numbers. Boule has 24 numbers plus a star. The payoff is 23 to one on numbers. On all bets (numbers, red or black, odd or even) the casino has a 4% advantage over the players.

Slot Machines These are the classic sucker games in any casino. Maybe the reason why slot machines are so popular is because it takes no brains to play – just put the coin in the slot and pull the handle. Some machines allow you to put in up to five coins at a time, which increases your chance of winning by five times (but costs you five times as much, so you're no better off). Contrary to popular belief, how hard or gently you pull the handle has no influence on the outcome. There are many small payoffs to encourage you to keep playing, but the goal of every slot player is to hit the grand jackpot (or megabucks as it is called in Macau).

The odds for winning on a slot machine are terrible. Machines are usually designed to give the casino a 25% advantage over the player. It's like spinning five roulette wheels at once and expecting them to all land on number seven. The more reels on the machine, the more unlikely it is they will line up for the ultimate pay off. Three reel machines give you one chance in 8000 of hitting the jackpot. You have one chance in 160,000 of lining up four reels. If you play a five reel machine, your chances of lining up all five winning numbers is one in 3.2 million.

traditional businesses. At the far end of Rua da Tercena is a flea market, where you can pick up old Macanese coins.

If you've got the habit, Macau is a bargain for booze and tobacco (including cigars and pipe tobacco). Macau has some excellent tobacconists along Avenida de Almeida Ribeiro which specialise in a wide range of cigarettes and cigars. You can't find anything like it in Hong Kong, and if you are a smoker, you'll find it irresistible.

A great road for antiques, ceramics and curios is along Rua das Estalagens and the lanes leading off it. Buy cautiously, and be aware that a large number of forgeries make their way into Macau from Zhuhai.

The largest department store in Macau is the well known Japanese retailer Yaohan. The store is near the Jetfoil pier. Central Plaza near the Leal Senado has a concentration of top-end shops such as Yves Saint Laurent.

Pawnshops are ubiquitous in Macau. It's possible to get good deals on cameras, watches and jewellery, but you must be prepared to bargain without mercy.

Macau is proud of its unusual stamps, which include portraits of everything from colonial architecture to the roulette tables and the jetfoil. Collectors' sets are on sale at the main post office. This is the place to go for your souvenir set just before the handover. Just before Hong Kong returned to China, some eager philatelists forked out tens of thousands of Hong Kong dollars for the last colonial sets.

Getting There & Away

AIR
Airports & Airlines
Macau's airport opened in December 1995, built on reclaimed land off Taipa Island and partly financed by the People's Republic of China (PRC). Construction costs ballooned from the projected M$3,500 million to M$8,900 million. It's one of the least busy airports in Asia, partly because of neighbouring Zhuhai's decision to build its own airport. The relatively small volume of passenger traffic means that immigration, customs and baggage-handling procedures are fast and efficient. Airlines serving Macau include the following:

Air France
    (☎ 712622, fax 335580) 21 Avenida do Doutor Mario Soares
Air Macau xc
    (☎ 3966888, fax 3966866, airport 8983388) Edificio Tai Wah 9-12 Andar, 693 Avenida da Praia Grande
Asiana Airlines
    (☎ 861400, fax 861404) room 22-24, mezzanine floor, Passenger terminal, Macau airport
CNAC
    (☎ 788034, fax 788036) 28th floor, D block, Bank of China building, Avenida do Doutor Mario Soares
CSA
    (☎ 787877) TTS Travel Service, Bank of China building, Avenida do Doutor Mario Soares
EVA Airways
    (☎ 861330, fax 861324) room 6, mezzanine floor, Passenger terminal, Macau airport
Korean Air
    (☎ 861480, fax 861485) room 15-18, mezzanine floor, Passenger terminal, Macau airport
Malaysia Airlines
    (☎ 787898, fax 787883, airport 8611253) 18th floor, Bank of China building, Avenida do Doutor Mario Soares
Sabena
    (☎ 750412) shares an office with Air Portugal on the ground floor, Edificio Dynasty Plaza (adjacent to Mandarin Oriental Hotel)
Singapore Airlines
    (☎ 711728, fax 711732, airport 861321) room 1001, 10th floor, Luso International building, 1-3 Rua Doutor Pedro Jose Lobo

TAP Air Portugal
    (☎ 711655, fax 711656) room 1501, 15th floor, Luso International building, Rua Doutor Pedro Jose Lobo
Trans Asia Airways
    (☎ 701777, fax 701565)11th floor, block B-C, Macau Finance Centre, 244-246 Rua de Pequim

Buying Tickets
The situation for buying tickets to or from Macau is much the same as for Hong Kong. As always, better deals on discount fares are found through travel agencies rather than from the airlines directly. Prices have recently decreased across the board due to the downturn in the regional economy.

If you're flying from a city that is directly linked by air with Macau, check as it could well be cheaper to fly straight to Macau rather than entering via Hong Kong. Macau is linked to a limited number of cities around the world, although this number is expected to grow (unless Zhuhai airport also opens up to international routes).

In the current climate of price reductions and uncertainty facing tourism in the region, check out the competition by phoning around before you buy your ticket. In general, the best deals are available through travel agents in Hong Kong, and the best way to access Macau is from there. See also the Hong Kong Getting There & Away chapter.

Travel Agencies Travel agencies in Macau that offer discounted tickets include the following:

Amigo Travel
    (☎ 337333, fax 378383) ground floor, New Wing, Lisboa Hotel
Estoril Tours
    (☎ 710361, fax 710353) ground floor, New Wing, Lisboa Hotel
Hong Kong Student Travel Macau (☎ 311100) 13 Rua do Campo
Multinational Youth Travel Agency
    (☎ 701913, fax 703056) 1023 Avenida da Amizade

MACAU

Departure Tax

Airport departure tax is M$130 for international destinations and M$80 for destinations in China, payable in either Macau patacas or Hong Kong dollars.

China

Macau is connected to a large number of cities in China. Air Macau, CSA, Xiamen Airlines and Yunnan Airlines fly to Beijing, Shanghai, Fuzhou, Xiamen, Dalian, Kunming, Haikou, Changsha, Chongqing, Shenyang, Qingdao, Xi'an, Yantai, Wenzhou and Guilin.

Europe

TAP Air Portugal operates two flights a week between Macau and Lisbon, via Bangkok. Tickets cost M$8200. At the time of writing there are twice weekly flights to Brussels, but these are due to be scrapped.

Hong Kong

For Hong Kong residents in a hurry to lose their money, East Asia Airlines (Hong Kong ☎ 2859-3359, Macau ☎ 7901040) runs a helicopter service. Flying time from Hong Kong is 20 minutes at a cost of HK$1206/1310 on weekdays/weekends – quite an expense just to save the extra 30 minutes required by boat. You'll be happy to hear that tickets are HK$4 cheaper returning to Hong Kong from Macau. There are up to 17 flights daily between 10 am and 10.30 pm. In Hong Kong, departures are from the Jetfoil pier at the Shun Tak Centre (☎ 2859-3359), 200 Connaught Rd, Sheung Wan; in Macau, departures are from the Jetfoil pier (☎ 7907240). There are no ordinary flights between Macau and Hong Kong.

Japan

No regularly scheduled direct flights exist between Macau and Japan, but Japan Air System has been running charters.

Singapore

Singapore Airlines flies between Macau and Singapore. There are two flights a week and the flight takes just over 3½ hours. Single/return tickets cost M$3700/4500.

Taiwan

You can fly from either Taipei or Kaohsiung to Macau on EVA Airways, Trans Asia Airways or Air Macau. The return fare is M$2760. EVA Airways has three flights a day to Taipei and two a day to Kaohsiung.

Thailand

Air Macau offers direct flights twice a week between Macau and Bangkok.

LAND
China

Just across the border from Macau is the town of Gongbei in the Zhuhai Special Economic Zone. The Barrier Gate (or Portas do Cerco in Portuguese) is open from 7 am until midnight.

If you want to go over to Zhuhai, you can jump on a bus (M$6) at the Kee Kwan Motors (☎ 933888) bus stop on the same side of Rua das Lorchas as the Floating Casino. Buses leave regularly, just pay the driver. Kee Kwan also has buses to Guangzhou, which leave daily at 7 am and noon and take about six hours. The single/return fares cost M$55/110. Kee Kwan also has buses to Zhongshan, but these get bogged down at customs and it's probably easier to take a bus to the border, walk across and catch a minibus to Guangzhou from the other side.

SEA
Departure Tax

Macau charges a M$22 departure tax, which is included in the ticket price. The Hong Kong government charges HK$26, included in the price of your ticket.

Hong Kong

This is by far the most popular way to enter Macau. Although Macau is separated from Hong Kong by 65km of water, the journey can be made in as little as one hour, although queues at customs can easily add another 30 minutes. There are frequent departures throughout the day. The schedule is somewhat reduced between 10 pm and 7 am, but boats run virtually 24 hours.

You have four types of vessels to choose from. There are jetfoils (single-hull jet-powered hydrofoils), turbocats (jet-powered catamarans), foil-cats (catamaran-jetfoils) and HKF catamarans (433 seats on two decks). The journey takes 55 minutes on the jetfoils and foil-cats, 60 minutes by catamaran and 65 minutes by turbocat. It's fun to take one sort of boat going to Macau, and a different one on the way back.

Most of the boats depart from the huge Macau Jetfoil pier at the Shun Tak Centre at 200 Connaught Rd, Sheung Wan, Hong Kong Island. The catamarans depart from the China ferry terminal in Kowloon.

On weekends and holidays, you'd be wise to book your return ticket in advance because the boats are often full. On weekdays the boats are rarely even half full and you'll have no problem getting a seat.

Luggage space on the jetfoils and turbocats is limited – some boats have small overhead lockers while others have storage space at the bow and stern. You are theoretically limited to 10kg of carry-on luggage (you can probably get away with more if it's not bulky), but oversized or overweight bags can be taken as checked luggage. On the HKF catamarans there is more luggage space.

You need to arrive at the pier at least 15 minutes before departure, but from our experience you'd be wise to allow 30 minutes because of occasional long queues at the immigration checkpoint, especially on the Hong Kong side (immigration works faster in Macau).

Far East Jetfoil tickets can be purchased up to 28 days in advance in Hong Kong at the pier (Shun Tak Centre) or at an MTR Travel Services Centre at any of the following MTR stations: Admiralty, Causeway Bay, Kwun Tong, Mong Kok, Tai Koo, Tsim Sha Tsui and Tsuen Wan. Telephone bookings can be made if you have a credit card by calling ☎ 2859-3333. You can pick up your ticket from the Shun Tak Centre by putting your credit card into one of the ticket machines for verification. In Macau, phone ☎ 7907039 for information. Departures are every 15 minutes from 7 am to 5 pm and then every 30 minutes to midnight. A first class ticket with Far East Jetfoils entitles you to complimentary newspapers, snacks and drinks.

Turbocat bookings can be made 28 days in advance, and you can buy your ticket with a credit card by phoning ☎ 2789-5421 in Hong Kong. Alternatively you can buy tickets at the Shun Tak Centre, at the China ferry terminal in Kowloon, or at CTS head office (☎ 2853-3533, fax 2541-9777), 4th floor, CTS House, 78-83 Connaught Rd, Central, and other travel agents. In Macau, tickets can be bought at the Jetfoil pier or at the Hotel Grandeur. For information on turbocat departures, phone ☎ 2859-7138 in Hong Kong or ☎ 726789 in Macau. Departures are every 30 minutes during the day. The VIP cabin seats up to six people, and the cost per ticket is the same whether one or six persons occupy the cabin.

HKF catamaran tickets can be booked 28 days in advance from the China ferry terminal (☎ 2736-1387, 2516-9581) in Kowloon. There are not as many departures as the options listed above, with only 12 trips between the hours of 8.30 am and 8 pm. For more information call ☎ 2516-9581 in Hong Kong.

Economy/1st class fares are listed in the following table:

Boats From Hong Kong (Prices in HK$)			
Vessel	Weekday	Weekend/Public holiday	Night (after 6 pm)
Jetfoil	137/151	148/161	168/182
Foil-cat	137/151	148/161	168/182
Turbocat	137/239	148/254	168/267
Turbocat (VIP ticket)	1434	1524	1604
HKY Catamarans	111	132	152

Shenzhen Special Economic Zone
There is a daily ferry connecting Macau to Shekou in the Shenzhen Special Economic Zone (north of Hong Kong). The boat departs Macau at 2.30 pm and arrives in Shekou at 4 pm. The fare is M$100 (child M$57) and tickets can be bought up to three days in advance from the point of departure, which is not the main Jetfoil pier in Macau, but from a pier behind the Peninsula Hotel (next to the Floating Casino).

ORGANISED TOURS
There is a growing market for tours to China from abroad, with private operators turning the heat up on CTS and CITS, the Chinese national tour operators. The pressure has caused CTS to go through an image remake, and it now has some attractive packages lined up. A typical tour commencing from abroad will take in both Hong Kong and Macau. First day: arrival in Hong Kong and spend the night in a hotel. Second day: trekking around the top sights in Hong Kong. Third day: to Macau by Turbocat – the tour takes you to the Ruinas de São Paulo, Monte Fort, Barrier Gate, Penha Hill and the Kun Iam Temple. The night is spent in a Macau Hotel and a visit to one of the territory's casinos is arranged coupled with a trip to a local restaurant. Tour operators can stitch side trips to Singapore, Malaysia, Thailand, Indonesia and other destinations into a visit to Hong Kong and Macau. Other tours worth looking out for make a start with Hong Kong and Macau before taking you on a whistle-stop tour of mainland China. Others take in fewer destinations and allow you more time to mull over sights. Tours offer a fast way to see everything with minimum hassle and can easily be booked in Hong Kong or Macau on arrival.

Tours booked in Macau are generally much better value because those booked in Hong Kong usually cost considerably more (although these tours include transportation to and from Macau and a side trip across the border to Zhuhai in China). These are usually one day whirlwind tours, departing for Macau in the morning and returning to Hong Kong the same evening. A full day whirlwind tour from Hong Kong typically costs about HK$600. Other tours allow you to spend longer in Macau but, of course, these cost more.

There is a one day tour that takes you to Shekou (in the Shenzhen Special Economic Zone north of Hong Kong), then by boat to the Zhuhai Special Economic Zone north of Macau, then to Cuiheng (former home of Dr Sun Yatsen) in Zhongshan County, then by bus to Macau, and back by jetfoil to Hong Kong by 7.30 pm. Such an escapade will cost you about HK$900, plus frayed nerves.

If you'd like a slower pace, a three to four day tour from Hong Kong to Macau, Zhuhai, Cuiheng, Shiqi, Foshan, Guangzhou and then back to Hong Kong by train, costs about HK$1700.

Finding a tour is not difficult. In Hong Kong, the ubiquitous moneychangers often have a collection of free pamphlets offering tours to Macau. The Macau Government Tourist Office (☎ 2549-8884, fax 2559-6513) and the travel agents at the Shun Tak Centre (Macau Jetfoil pier) in Hong Kong have piles of information on tours and these are probably the best places to go. One company that organises tours of Macau and Guangzhou is Grayline (☎ 2368-7111, 2721-9651). CTS is another agent worth checking out for a range of tours.

See also Organised Tours in the following Getting Around chapter.

Getting Around

TO/FROM THE AIRPORT

Airport bus AP1 leaves the airport and first zips around Taipa, passing the Jockey Club and the Hyatt and New Century hotels. It crosses the bridge and stops at the Lisboa Hotel, then takes in some other hotels in the centre (Nam Yue Hotel, Kingsway Hotel, New World Emperor Hotel, Holiday Inn, Grandeur Hotel and Fortuna Hotel), Barrier Gate (the Chinese border crossing) and terminates at the Jetfoil pier. The fare is M$6 and the bus departs every 15 minutes from 6.30 to 1.20 am.

Numerous taxis meet all incoming flights and the drivers use the meters without argument. Expect to pay roughly M$40 for a ride into the centre of town.

BUS

There are minibuses and large buses, and both offer air conditioning and frequent services. These operate from 7 am until midnight. Buses display the ultimate destination in Portuguese (eg Portas do Cerco is the Barrier Gate) and Chinese. Payment is made into a collection scoop as in Hong Kong. Note that change is not given and either Macau or Hong Kong coins are acceptable. Long-termers can buy a monthly bus pass for M$180. For questions, complaints etc, call the local bus company Transmac on ☎ 271122.

The *Macau Tourist Map* has a full list of bus routes which is useful. Another good source of information is the computerised city guides (see Tourist Offices in the Macau Facts for the Visitor chapter). These have a reasonably detailed transport chapter which shows you how to navigate by bus from one place to another.

Macau Peninsula

Buses on the Macau Peninsula cost M$2.30. The two most useful buses to travellers are probably Nos 3 and 3A which run between the Jetfoil pier and the central area near the main post office. No 3 also goes to the Chinese border, as does No 5. There are numerous other routes. The following are the most useful bus routes:

No 3
    From the Jetfoil pier past the Lisboa Hotel along Avenida Almeida Ribeiro and up to the Barrier Gate.
No 3A
    From the Jetfoil pier past the Lisboa Hotel along Avenida Almeida Ribeiro over to the cheaper hotel district in the floating casino area.
No 10
    From the Barrier Gate via the Jetfoil pier past the Macau Forum, the Lisboa Hotel, along Avenida Almeida Ribeiro and then down to the A-Ma Temple (the 10A follows a similar route).
No 12
    From the Jetfoil pier past the Macau Forum, the Lisboa Hotel and then up to the Kun Iam Temple.

The Islands

Buses to Taipa cost M$3, to Coloane Village it's M$3.50 and to Hac Sa Beach (on Coloane) it's M$4.50. The fare from Taipa to Hac Sa is M$2.50 and Coloane to Hac Sa is M$1.70. The most useful bus routes to the islands are as follows:

No 21
    From the A-Ma Temple via Avenida Almeida Ribeiro, to Taipa Village and on to Coloane.
No 22
    From the Kun Iam Temple past the Hotel Lisboa to Taipa Village.
No 25
    From the Barrier Gate via Lou Lim Ieoc Gardens past the Hotel Lisboa to Taipa, Chuk Wan and Hac Sa Beach in Coloane.
No 26A
    From Avenida Almeida Ribeiro past the Lisboa Hotel down to Taipa, Coloane Village, Chuk Wan and Hac Sa Beach.

TAXI

Taxis in Macau all have meters and drivers

are required to use them. Flagfall is M$9 for the first 1.5km, thereafter it's M$1 every 220m. There is a M$5 surcharge to go to Taipa, and M$10 to go to Coloane, but there is no surcharge on return trips. Taxis can be dispatched by radio if you ring up Vang Lek Radio Taxi Company (☎ 519519). Not many taxi drivers speak English, so it would be helpful to use the Chinese and English script on the maps in this book.

You can hire a taxi and driver for a whole day or a half day. The price as well as the itinerary should be agreed on in advance. Large hotels can usually help to arrange this.

CAR & MOTORCYCLE

Macau's streets are a teeming mass of cars plastered with go-faster stripes and stickers, giving the impression that some of the cars from the Macau Grand Prix lost their bearings and never made it back. While driving looks fun in Macau, it's strictly for the locals. If you have to join in the riot of colour and noise that is Macau's traffic, having previous rally driving experience will be a boon. Large cars are not well suited to Macau's narrow streets. Check out the number of Minis you see in Macau.

While driving on Macau Peninsula cannot be recommended, a rented car (or Moke) can be a convenient way to explore the islands. Once you're away from the transport maelstrom of the peninsula there are ample opportunities for exploring Taipa and Coloane without the stress of bumper to bumper traffic and bursts of road rage.

Motorcycles are not available for rent.

Rental

Happy Rent-A-Car (☎ 726868) is across from the Jetfoil pier in Macau. A four person Moke can be rented on weekdays for M$450 and a six person Moke for HK$500. This rate is for 24 hours and it is more expensive on weekends and public holidays. You'll need an International Driving Permit which you'll need to have held for two years. The Mokes come with a full tank of fuel and you have to return it as such (otherwise you'll be charged M$7 per

litre to fill the car up). The Moke is originally British, but the ones in Macau are custom-made Portuguese clones.

You can also rent Mokes from Avis Rent-A-Car (☎ 336789) at the Mandarin Oriental Hotel. Avis also rents cheaper Subarus that cost M$400 per day during the week and M$520 on the weekends. It's probably not necessary on weekdays, but you can book in advance at the Avis Hong Kong office (☎ 2541-2011).

Road Rules

An International Driving Permit is required theoretically – arrange it before arrival as these cannot be issued in Macau unless you already have a Macau driver's licence. Drivers must be 21 years of age or over. As in Hong Kong, you drive on the left-hand side of the road. If you do get to splutter around in a Moke, be aware that the custom in Macau is to slow down rather than to stop for pedestrians crossing the road at zebra crossings (the black and white striped road crossings). It's illegal to beep the horn (if only Hong Kong had this rule!).

If you happen to be a resident of Macau, local driver's licences are applied for at the Leal Senado. However, International Driving Permits are applied for at the Edificio do Apoio do Grande Premio (☎ 726578), near the Jetfoil pier on Avenida da Amizade.

Police in Macau are strict and there are stiff fines for traffic violators.

BICYCLE

Bikes can be rented in Taipa Village for M$12 per hour (adults) and M$8 (children). These are available in a wide variety of classes from light 10 speed racers to heavyweight clunkers.

Walking is permitted on the older Macau-Taipa Bridge, but bicycles are prohibited. The only way to take a bike across to the island is in the boot of a car. However, bikes are allowed on the Taipa-Coloane Causeway, but it's not very safe as the causeway is narrow and traffic can be heavy. One false move and you may wind up staying in Macau a lot longer than you intended.

PEDICABS

These are three wheeled bicycles, known as *triciclos* in Portuguese. In many developing countries, pedicabs (or cyclos) are used as cheap taxis. Not in Macau. The guys who ride the pedicabs are cut-throat sharks who gather like vultures around the areas where tourists congregate (eg at the Jetfoil pier and by the Lisboa Hotel). The pedicabs look cheap and should be, but being a tourist novelty can actually be more expensive than taxis. Pedicabs don't have meters (agree on a fare beforehand) and some of these move so slowly it would be quicker to strap a tortoise onto each foot. If you want to pay M$90 for 30 minutes of slow-motion Macau then go ahead. Pedicabs cannot negotiate hills, so you'll be limited to touring the waterfront and some of the narrow alleys.

ORGANISED TOURS

It's cheaper to book tours in Macau than in Hong Kong. A typical city tour (booked in Macau) of the peninsula takes three to four hours and costs about M$100 per person, often including lunch. Bus tours to the islands start at about M$40 per person. You can also book a one day bus tour across the border into Zhuhai, which usually includes a trip to the former home of Dr Sun Yatsen in Zhongshan County.

In Macau, contact the Macau Government Tourist Office (☎ 315566, fax 510104) or try one of the following tour agencies:

Asia
   (☎ 593844, fax 565060) 25B Avenida da Praia Grande
China Travel Service
   (☎ 705506, fax 706611) Xinhua building, Rua de Nagasaki
El Sol Tour
   (☎ 576522, fax 389924) ground floor, Hotel Lisboa
Guangdong
   (☎ 588807, fax 323771) 37E Avenida da Praia Grande
Hi-No-De Caravela
   (☎ 3338338, fax 566622) 6A-4C Rua de Sacadura Cabral

International
   (☎ 975183, fax 974072) Loja B, 9 Travessa do Padre Narciso
Macau Star
   (☎ 558855, fax 586702) room 511, Tai Fung Bank building, 34 Avenida Almeida Ribeiro
Macau Zhuhai
   (☎ 552739, fax 552735) room 406, Hotel Presidente, Avenida da Amizade
South China
   (☎ 706620, fax 710353) flat O, 5th floor, Nam Fong building, Avenida da Amizade

Tour Machine

The Tour Machine is a replica of a 1920s English bus, complete with leather upholstery. It's painted fire-engine red and has 'Tour Machine' painted across it in bright yellow letters. The bus seats nine people and runs on a few fixed routes past some of Macau's historic sights. You're allowed to disembark, stretch your legs and take photos along the way. There are two departures a day (11 am and 3 pm), and it sets out from the Jetfoil pier. The trip takes about two hours, so it's a good idea if you haven't much time in Macau. Tickets cost M$150 for adults and M$80 for children. The Tour Machine can also be chartered for M$200 per hour for trips in Macau, or M$300 for trips across the border into China.

If this interests you, contact Avis Rent-A-Car (☎ 336789, 314112, 567888 ext 3004) at the Mandarin Oriental Hotel.

Boat Tours

Down by the Maritime Museum (opposite the A-Ma Temple) is a small pier where you can jump onto a small boat for trips around the southern tip of the Macau Peninsula, taking in the Nam Van Lakes. For more details, see the section on the Maritime Museum in the Macau Peninsula chapter.

Blue Dolphin Sea Tours (☎ 939933, fax

930068) has day and night cruises around Macau, including the islands. The day cruise costs M$48 for a 90 minute trip, while the evening cruise takes two hours, includes a Portuguese meal on board and costs M$150. Boats depart from the pier beside the Blue Dolphin office at 12 Rua das Lorchas, just behind the Kee Kwan Motor bus stop next to the Floating Casino. You can also book tickets through travel agents and at certain hotels (eg the Lisboa Hotel and the Metropole Hotel).

Macau Peninsula

CENTRAL MACAU

Avenida de Almeida Ribeiro is the main street of Macau and is as good a place as any to start your tour. It crosses Avenida da Praia Grande just up from the waterfront and effectively divides the narrow southern peninsula from the rest of Macau. It continues down to the Lisboa Hotel where the street name becomes Avenida do Infante D'Henrique.

Jorge Alvares Statue

The monument is on Avenida da Praia Grande. Alvares was credited with being the first Portuguese to set foot on Chinese soil when he and his party landed on the island of Lingding, halfway between Macau and Hong Kong.

Leal Senado & Largo do Senado

Across the street from the GPO on Avenida de Almeida Ribeiro is the Leal Senado (Loyal Senate), which houses the municipal government offices.

The Leal Senado is the main administrative body for municipal affairs, but it once had much greater powers and dealt on equal terms with Chinese officials during the last century. It's called the Loyal Senate because it refused to recognise Spanish sovereignty when the Spanish marched into Portugal in the 17th century, and during the subsequent 60 years' occupation. When Portuguese control was re-established, the city of Macau was granted the official name of Cidade do Nome de Deus de Macau, Nao ha Outra Mais Leal or City of the Name of God, Macau, There is None More Loyal.

Above the wrought-iron gates leading to the garden, inside the main building, is an interesting bas-relief that has been the subject of some dispute. Some say the woman depicted is the Virgin Mary, sheltering all those in need of mercy. Others hold that it represents the 16th century Portuguese Queen Leonor.

Also inside the Leal Senado is the public library, open on weekdays (Monday to Friday) from 9 am to noon and 2 to 5.30 pm, and on Saturday until 12.30 pm.

Facing the Leal Senado is the magnificent Largo do Senado, the Senate Square. This square effectively constitutes the centre of Macau and is the city's focal point. A bustling thoroughfare, the Largo do Senado is bordered by magnificent colonial architecture and a number of restaurants.

São Domingos

A fine example of ecclesiastical baroque architecture is São Domingos (St Dominic's Church), built by the Spanish Order of Dominicans. The huge 17th century building has an impressive tiered altar with images of the Virgin and Child and of Our Lady of Fatima (this image is carried in procession during the Fatima Festival). There is a small museum at the back which is full of church regalia, images and paintings. The church is only open in the afternoon. To enter, ring the bell by the iron gates at the side. The church, with its distinctive cream walls and green shutters, is on Rua do São Domingos, at the northern end of Largo do Senado.

Santo António Church

A few blocks to the north of São Domingos is the modern Santo António (St Anthony's) Church. The church is memorable for having been burnt to the ground three times. Saint Anthony had military connections, and on the occasion of his feast day (13 June), an image of the saint is taken on a tour of inspection of the remnants of the city's battlements.

Camões Grotto & Gardens

In the Camões Grotto & Gardens is a memorial to Luis de Camões, the 16th century Portuguese poet who has become something of a local hero. He is said to have written his epic Os Lusiadas by the rocks in Macau, but there is no firm evidence that he was ever in

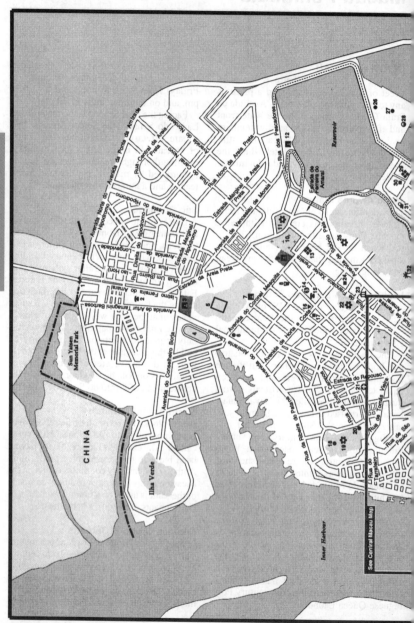

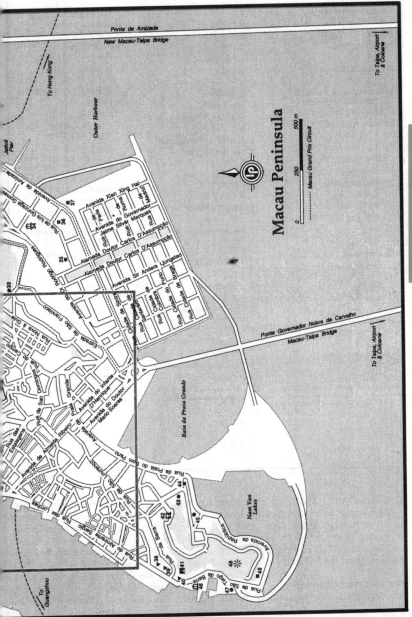

Macau Peninsula 澳門

PLACES TO STAY
17 Fu Hua Hotel
    富華酒店
24 Mondial Hotel
    環球酒店
30 Jai Alai Hotel & Casino;
    China City Nightclub
    回力球賭場
31 Nam Yue Hotel
    粵酒店
33 Guia Hotel
    東望洋酒店
35 Granduer Hotel
36 Kingsway Hotel
    金域酒店
37 Mandarin Oriental
    澳門文華東方酒店
43 Ritz
    濠璟酒店
44 Bela Vista
    峰景酒店
49 Pousada de São Tiago
    Hotel
    聖地牙哥酒店

PLACES TO EAT
16 McDonald's
    麥當勞
38 O Porto Interior
    內港
39 Restaurante Litoral
    海灣餐廳
40 A Lorcha; Barra Nova
    船屋

OTHER
1 Barrier Gate
   關閘

2 CTM Telephone Office
   澳門電訊
3 Lin Fung Miu (Lotus Temple)
   蓮峰廟
4 Canidrome
   跑狗場
5 Mong-Ha Fortress
   望廈古堡
6 Lido Theatre
7 Kuan Iam Temple
   觀音古廟
8 Talker Pub; Pyretu's Bar
9 Kun Iam Temple
   觀音堂
10 Our Lady of Piety
   Cemetery
   新西洋墳場
11 Montanha Russa Gardens
   螺絲山公園
12 Macau-Seac Tin Hau
   Temple
   天后廟
13 Pak Vai Plaza
   柏蕙廣場
14 HongkongBank
   匯豐銀行
15 CTM Telephone Office
   澳門電訊
18 Casa Garden
   Fundação Oriente
   東方基金會
19 Camões Grotto & Gardens
   白鴿巢賈梅士花園
20 Old Protestant Cemetery
   舊基督教墳場
21 Kiang Vu Hospital
   鏡湖醫院
22 Lou Lim Ioc Gardens
   廬廉若花園

23 Sun Yatsen
   Memorial Home
   孫中山紀念館
25 Flora Gardens
   龍喉花園
26 Grand Prix Control
   Tower; Stands
   賽車控制塔、賽車看臺
27 Heliport
   直升機場
28 Hong Kong-Macau Ferry
   Pier; Tourist Office
   港澳碼頭、旅遊公司
29 Yaohan Department Store;
   McDonald's; Pokka Coffee
   八佰伴及麥當勞
32 Guia Fort & Lighthouse
   松山燈塔
34 Macau Forum; Tourist
   Activity Centre; Grand Prix
   Museum; Wine Museum
   綜藝館、旅遊活動中心、
   賽車博物館、葡萄酒博
   物館
41 A-Ma Temple
   媽閣廟
42 Penha Church
   西望洋聖堂
45 Henri's Gallery
   亨利美心
46 Maritime Museum
   海事博物院
47 Youth Hostel
   Booking Office
   青年旅舍售票處
48 Barra Hill
   媽閣山

the territory. A bust of him is in the gardens – looking rather better than the man, so it is said. The gardens are a pleasant, cool and shady place, popular with the local Chinese and you may find old men playing checkers. There are good views from the top of the hill.

Old Protestant Cemetery
Beside the Camões Museum is the Old Protestant Cemetery – the resting place of numerous non-Portuguese (most Portuguese are Catholic). As ecclesiastical law forbade the burial of Protestants on Catholic soil (which effectively meant the area of Macau within the city walls), there was no burial place for the Protestants who died in the community. The territory beyond the city walls was considered Chinese soil, and the

Chinese didn't approve of foreigners desecrating their land either. The unhappy result was that the Protestants had to bury their dead either in the nearby hills (while hoping that the Chinese wouldn't notice), or else beneath the neutral territory of the Macau city walls.

Finally, the governor allowed a local merchant to sell some of his land to the British East India Company, despite a law forbidding foreign ownership of land, and the cemetery was established in 1821 – the date of 1814, above the gate, is when the cemetery committee was formed. A number of old graves were then transferred to the cemetery, which explains the earlier dates on some of the tombstones.

Among the better known people buried in the cemetery is the artist George Chinnery, noted for his portrayals of Macau and its people in the first half of the 19th century. The tombstone of Robert Morrison, the first Protestant missionary to China, records that he, 'for several years laboured alone on a Chinese version of the Holy Scriptures which he was spared to see completed'. Morrison is buried beside his wife Mary, who became one of the cemetery's first burials after dying in childbirth – 'erewhile anticipating a living mother's joy suddenly, but with a pious resignation, departed this life after a short illness of 14 hours, bearing with her to the grave her hoped-for child'. Also buried there is Lord John Spencer Churchill, an ancestor of former British Prime Minister, Sir Winston Churchill.

Other inscriptions on the tombstones indicate that ships' officers and crew are well represented. Some died from accidents such as falling off the rigging, while others died heroically, like Lieutenant Fitzgerald 'from the effects of a wound received while gallantly storming the enemy's battery at Canton'. Captain Sir Humphrey Le Fleming Stenhouse died 'from the effects of fever contracted during the zealous performance of his arduous duties at the capture of the Heights of Canton in May 1841'.

Fortune-tellers have set up shop just outside the cemetery.

Macau Cultural Centre

The recently opened Macau Cultural Centre is an imaginative and much needed addition to Macau's cultural landscape. Located at the intersection of Avenida Doutor Sun Yat Sen and Avenida Xian Xing Hai (south of the World Trade Center) just by the waters of the outer harbour, the US$100 million Macau Cultural Centre (designed by Bruno Soares) is a distinctive architectural addition to this small enclave. A walkway connects with a large tower standing in the harbour. Visitors can walk across to the tower and look out over the harbour and a 20m statue of the god Kun Iam (Kwun Yum or Kuanyin).

The interior of the museum features three museum areas and two auditoriums. Temporary displays are held on the 1st and 2nd floors, with historical and architectural exhibits on the 3rd floor, and art and ceramics in the Luis de Camões museum on the 4th floor. The larger of the two auditoriums seats 1200 people.

Ruinas de São Paulo

Some say the marvellous Ruinas de São Paulo (Ruins of St Paul's Cathedral) are the greatest monument to Christianity in the east. It is a truly magnificent piece of architecture that inspires veneration and awe, despite (or maybe because of) the fact that only the facade remains.

Built on one of Macau's seven hills, it was designed by an Italian Jesuit and built by early Japanese Christian exiles. The cathedral was finished in the first decade of the 17th century, and the crowned heads of Europe competed to present it with its most prestigious gift. All that remains is the facade, the magnificent mosaic floor and the impressive stone steps. The church caught fire during a disastrous typhoon in 1835. For a while it seemed that the whole thing might eventually fall apart, but renovation work was undertaken and finally completed in 1991.

The facade has been described as a sermon in stone, recording some of the main events of Christianity in the various carvings. At the top is the dove, representing the Holy Spirit, surrounded by stone

MACAU

carvings of the sun, moon and stars. Beneath the dove is a statue of the Infant Jesus surrounded by stone carvings of the implements of the crucifixion. In the centre of the third tier stands the Virgin Mary, with angels and two types of flowers – the peony representing China and the chrysanthemum representing Japan. To the right of the Virgin is a carving of a woman atop a seven headed hydra – the Chinese characters next to her say 'the holy mother tramples the heads of the dragon'. The fourth tier has statues of four Jesuit saints, (from the left) Francisco de Borja, St Ignatius (founder of the Jesuits), St Francis Xavier and Luis Gonzaga. On the plinth above the main door is inscribed Mater Dei (Mother of God). This inscription points to the original name of the church, the Church of Our Lady of Assumption of the Jesuit College of the Mother of God.

In 1996 **São Paulo's Museum** was opened behind the ruined church. The museum houses a number of recently unearthed artefacts, including the tomb of Father Alessandro Valignano, the Jesuit who was responsible for building Basilica de São Paulo and the Jesuit College in Macau. Father Alessandro is also given credit for establishing Christianity in Japan.

São Paulo's Museum is also home to a piece of the right arm bone of St Francis Xavier. Other bits of St Francis can be found in southern India.

Fortaleza do Monte
The Fortaleza do Monte or Monte Fort is on a hill overlooking the Ruinas de São Paulo and was built by the Jesuits around the same time. The first Portuguese settlers in Macau built their homes in the centre of the peninsula, and the fort once formed the strong central point of the old city wall. Barracks and storehouses were designed to equip the fort with the means to survive a two year siege. The cannons on the fort are the very ones that dissuaded the Dutch from further attempts to take over Macau. In 1622 a cannon ball (fired by a priest) hit a powder keg on one of the invader's ships, which exploded,

blowing the Dutch out of the water. It's the only time these cannons were ever fired in combat. Since this event occurred on St John the Baptist's Day, 24 June, he was promptly proclaimed the city's patron saint.

Now the fort is used as a public park, possessing an **observatory** and a **museum**. From it there are sweeping views across Macau. Enter the fort from a narrow cobbled street leading off Estrada do Repouso near Estrada do Cemitério. There is also a path from the fortress down to the Ruinas de São Paulo. Fortaleza do Monte is open daily from 6 am to 7 pm (May to September) and from 7 am to 6 pm (October to April).

Macau History Museum
The recently opened Macau History Museum tells the story of Macau – the history, traditions and culture of this hybrid city. The museum has been dug out from the side of the hill upon which Monte Fort sits, and can be reached by escalator from a spot near the Ruinas de São Paulo. The ground floor of the museum takes the visitor by the hand through the early history of Macau in the 16th and 17th centuries, with the floor above covering later centuries and the anthropology and ethnography of the territory. The top floor illustrates the Macau of today and of the future. The exhibits are supported by an array of CD ROMS, videos and virtual images.

St Michael's Cemetery
This beautiful Catholic cemetery is almost exactly in the centre of the Macau Peninsula, on Estrada do Cemitério. Although a few of the tombs are plain, most are stunning works of art. The whole cemetery is adorned with statues of angels. This is the largest cemetery on the peninsula, though there is an even bigger Chinese cemetery on Taipa Island.

Lou Lim Ioc Gardens
The restful Lou Lim Ioc Gardens are on Avenida do Conselheiro Ferreira de Almeida. The gardens and ornate mansion, with its columns and arches (now the Pui

GLENN BEANLAND

About 95% of Macau's population is Chinese and culturally indistingishable from the people of Hong Kong. The majority of inhabitants live on the Macau Peninsula, making it one of the most densely populated areas in the world.

JON DAVISON

JON DAVISON

GLENN BEANLAND

JON DAVISON

RUA
DE
SANTA CLARA

JON DAVISON

TONY WHEELER

JON DAVISON

TONY WHEELER

JON DAVISON

A	B	C
D	E	F
G	H	I

A: Fortaleza do Monte.
B: Ruinas de São Paulo.
C: Pastel coloured buildings abound.
D: Typical street signage.
E: Facade detail, Ruinas de São Paulo.

F: Largo do Senado.
G: Even the washing is pastel!
H: Lisboa Hotel.
I: Portuguese symbol.

Ching School), once belonged to the wealthy Chinese Lou family. The gardens are a mixture of European and Chinese plants, with huge shady trees, lotus ponds, pavilions, bamboo groves, grottoes and strangely shaped doorways. The twisting pathways and ornamental mountains are built to represent a Chinese painting and are said to be modelled on those in the famous gardens of Suzhou in eastern China. Entrance to the gardens is M$1, except Friday, when entry is free.

Sun Yatsen Memorial Home
Around the corner from the Lou Lim Ioc Gardens, at the junction of Avenida da Sidónio Pais and Rua de Silva Mendes, is a memorial home dedicated to Dr Sun Yatsen, founder of the Chinese Republic. Sun practised medicine in Macau for some years before turning to revolution and seeking to overthrow the Qing dynasty. See the Facts about Guangzhou chapter for more details.

The memorial house in Macau was built as a monument to Sun, and contains a collection of flags, photos and other relics. It replaced the original house, which blew up while being used as an explosives store. The house is open daily except Tuesday. It's open from 10 am to 1 pm and 2.30 to 5 pm.

Guia Fort & Lighthouse
The old site of the fortress, built between 1637 and 1638, occupied the highest point on the Macau Peninsula. Originally designed to defend the border with China, it came into its own as a lookout post. The 17th century chapel is the old hermitage of Our Lady of Guia – storm warnings were announced from the bell tower. The Guia Lighthouse (*guia* means 'guide' in Portuguese) is the oldest on the coast of China, first lit in 1865. The lighthouse was originally fired up by paraffin, but is now electrically powered. Also on Guia Hill is a cafe and tourist information centre.

Around the lighthouse are the only two hiking trails on the peninsula – these are also very good for jogging. One trail

circumnavigates the mountain, a total distance of 1.7km, and is called the Walk of 33 Curves. Inside this loop trail is a shorter loop, the Fitness Circuit Walk, which has 20 gymnastic-type exercise stations along the route.

You can take a cable car up to Guia Hill from the Flora Gardens on Avenida de Sidónio Pais. This cable car's claim to fame is that it's one of the world's smallest.

Flora Gardens
The Flora Gardens were once the grounds of a well-to-do Portuguese family house that burned to the ground in the 1920s after a nearby firecracker factory exploded.

This attractive garden has been recently refurbished and has a miniature zoo, along with a landscaped garden, a pond and a midget cable car that ascends nearby Guia Hill. You can enter the gardens from Avenida de Sidónio Pais.

Vasco da Gama Garden
This small garden, with its monument of Vasco da Gama, is on the corner of Rua Ferreira do Amaral and Calcada do Gaio – just to the west of the and Guia Lighthouse. Da Gama's was the first Portuguese fleet to round the southern cape of Africa and make its way to India in the 15th century.

Grand Prix Museum
This place features cars from the Macau Grand Prix. Another feature are the simulators, which let you test out your racing skills. If you'd rather not drive, you can play with the TV monitors which allow you to select any part of the circuit and see how it was covered.

The museum (☎ 7984108) is in the basement of the Macau Forum, opposite the Kingsway Hotel. It is open daily from 10 am to 6 pm. Adult tickets cost M$10, children from 11 to 18 years get in for M$5, and children under the age of 11 years can get in free.

Bus Nos 3, 3A and 32 are a sample of the buses that can get you to the museum. Otherwise it's a 10 minute journey on foot from the Jetfoil pier.

MACAU

Wine Museum

Red-nosed tourists will no doubt make a beeline to this museum, which celebrates wine production. Some of the more recent wines on display are available for tasting, but for the most part the museum is a rather inert display of wine racks and a few simple tools used by winemakers. Of course, if you have any interest in the world of wine, you will find the display fascinating. The wines are, of course, produced in Portugal.

The Wine Museum is open daily from 10 am to 6 pm; entry is M$15 for adults (including a wine tasting) and M$5 for children between the ages of 11 and 18 years. If you want, you can buy a joint-ticket for the Grand Prix Museum and the Wine Museum for M$20. The museum is housed in the Macau Forum, see the previous Grand Prix Museum entry for details on how to reach the Wine Museum.

THE SOUTH

There are a number of interesting sights on the peninsula (once known to the Chinese as the Water Lily Peninsula) to the south of Avenida de Almeida Ribeiro. A good way to start exploring this region is to walk up the steep Rua Central near the Leal Senado.

São Agostinho

Around the corner from the Leal Senado in the Largo de Santo Agostinho is São Agostinho, or St Augustine's Church. Its foundations date from 1586, though the present church was built in 1814. Among the people buried there is Maria de Moura, who in 1710 married Captain Antonio Albuquerque Coelho after he lost an arm in an attack by one of Maria's unsuccessful suitors. Unfortunately Maria died in childbirth and is buried with her baby and Antonio's arm.

São Lourenço

Heading back down to and continuing along Rua Central, you'll find yourself on Rua de São Lourenço. On the right is the mildewed São Lourenço, or St Lawrence's Church,

with its twin square towers, surrounded by palm trees. The original church was built in the 1560s from wood and eventually reconstructed in stone in the early 19th century. One of the two towers of the church formerly served as an ecclesiastical prison.

Stone steps lead to the ornamental gates, but if you want to enter use the side entrance. The church is open from 10 am to 4 pm on Sunday to Friday, until 1 pm on Saturday and closed on public holidays.

A-Ma Temple (Ma Kok Miu)

At the end of Calçada da Barra is the A-Ma Temple at the base of Penha Hill. It is dedicated to the god A-Ma (Mother). A-Ma is more commonly known as Tin Hau (Queen of Heaven).

A-Ma became A-Ma-Gao to the Portuguese, after whom Macau was named. The temple consists of several shrines dating from the Ming dynasty. The boat people of Macau go there on pilgrimage each year in April or May. The temple is actually a complex of temples, some dedicated to A-Ma and others to Kun Iam.

There are several stories about A-Ma; for more details see the Facts about Hong Kong chapter. In Macau the tale goes that she was a beautiful young woman whose presence on a Guangzhou-bound ship saved it from disaster. All the other ships in the fleet, whose rich owners had refused to give her a passage, were destroyed in a storm.

The original temple on this site was probably already standing when the Portuguese arrived, although the present building may only date back to the 17th century. The temple is built into the foot of Penha Hill and is made up of a warren of prayer halls and pavilions. Behind the temple is a climbing network of small gardens. The temple is most active with worshippers on the feast of A-Ma (in either April or May) and during the Chinese New Year, when the boulders and tiled roofs of the complex resound to the deafening explosions of bangers and crackers.

The A-Ma Temple is another venue in Macau where you will find fortune-tellers.

Maritime Museum

This museum, opposite the A-Ma Temple, is world class. It has a collection of boats and other artefacts related to Macau's seafaring past. The museum displays a flower boat, a tugboat, a Chinese fishing vessel, and a dragon boat that is used in races held during the Dragon Boat Festival.

A motorised junk moored next to the museum offers 30 minute rides around the harbour on weekends and Monday. Departures are at 10.30 and 11.30 am and 3.30 and 4.30 pm. The fare is M$15, which includes the admission fee (M$5) to the Maritime Museum.

The Maritime Museum is open from 10 am until 5.30 pm, Wednesday to Monday. It's closed on Tuesday.

Barra Hill

From the A-Ma Temple you can follow Rua de São Tiago da Barra around to Barra Hill – where the Rua de São Tiago da Barra meets the end of Avenida da Republica. At one time the hill was topped by a fortress that had great strategic importance when it was built in 1629, as ships entering the harbour had to come very close to the Macau shore.

The Pousada de São Tiago hotel has been built within the walls of the fortress and is worth seeing even if you can't afford to stay there. The hilltop is now a park, and you can circumambulate it and enjoy the views by walking along Calcada da Penha, which is closed to motorised traffic.

Governor's Residence

On the east side of the tip of the Macau Peninsula is Avenida da Praia Grande, one of the most scenic streets in the city. This is where you'll find the pink Governor's Residence, built in the 19th century as a residence for a Macanese aristocratic family. The building is not open to tourists, but you can admire the colonial architecture from outside.

Slightly further to the north on Rua Comendador Kou Ho Neng is the **Bela Vista Hotel**, Macau's equivalent to Singapore's Raffles, built at the end of the 19th century. The hotel almost slid from view into bankruptcy until it was rescued by the Mandarin Oriental Hotel Group which injected huge amounts of money into restoring the hotel to its former glory. The hotel has only eight rooms, thus adding to its exclusivity. For more details see the Places to Stay section in this chapter.

Penha Church

On a hill above the Bela Vista is the Bishop's Residence and Penha Church.

Floating Hotel or Blue Water Navy?

The purchase of an unfinished Ukrainian aircraft carrier by a company in Macau sent alarm bells ringing in defence departments around the world. We were naturally excited by the news that the company had bought the rusting hulk with plans to tow it to Macau and turn it into a floating amusement park, but more sober-minded defence analysts saw this as proof of China's determination to acquire the first semblance of a blue water navy. Taiwan is reportedly very interested in the deal, but it's not the threat to the Taipei tourist industry that has raised a few eyebrows.

An aircraft carrier would be a prize win for a China eager to extend its influence into waters previously uncharted by its military might. However, the contract prohibits the use of the carrier, which is 70% complete, for military purposes.

If the company manages to get a licence to turn it into a vast hotel cum casino, it would certainly be an imaginative transformation of the Macau skyline. It could sail to and from Hong Kong, possibly make sorties up the Pearl River, or be the thrilling venue of paint-ball weekends for would-be Triads. A huge floating nightclub would spice up Macau's nightlife (with launches ferrying clubbers to and fro) or perhaps a mammoth offshore swimming pool are other ideas that lurch to mind. Let's hope the Chinese Navy doesn't torpedo the fun and games.

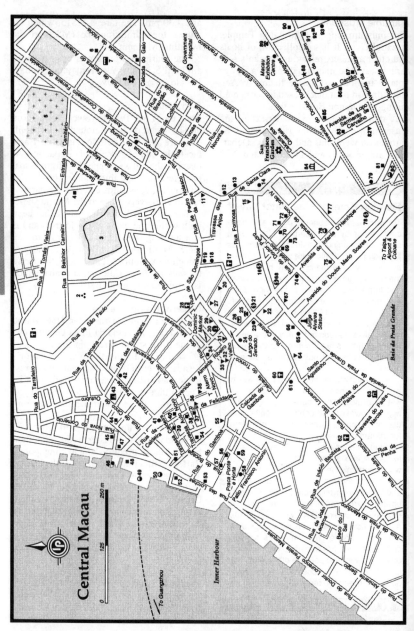

Central Macau

Central Macau
澳門中部

PLACES TO STAY
4 Holiday Hotel
假期酒店
6 Estoril Hotel
愛都酒店
9 Royal Hotel
皇都酒店
34 Central Hotel
新中央酒店
37 San Va Hospedaria
新華大旅店
38 Vila Universal;
Ko Wah Hotel
世界迎賓館、高華酒店
39 Man Va Hotel
文華酒店
40 Pensão Tai Fat
大發酒店
44 East Asia Hotel
東亞酒店
45 Vila Capital
京藝賓館
47 Grand Hotel
國際酒店
48 Peninsula Hotel
半島酒店
51 Hou Kong Hotel
濠江酒店
52 Masters Hotel
萬事發酒店
53 Vong Kong Hospedaria
皇宮旅館
54 Vila Tai Loy
大來別墅
56 London Hotel
英京酒店
57 Sun Sun Hotel
新新酒店
59 Pensão Kuan Heng
群興賓館
66 Metropole Hotel
京都酒店
69 Vila Nam Loon;
Vila Meng Meng
明明賓館
70 Pensão Nam In
藍茵酒店
71 Nam Tin Hotel
南天酒店

72 Vila Nam Pan
南濱賓館
73 Villa Tin Tin
75 Sintra Hotel
新麗華酒店
81 Lisboa Hotel
葡京酒店
83 Vila San Vu
85 Beverly Plaza Hotel
富豪酒店
86 Fortuna Hotel
財神酒店
87 Presidente
總統酒店
90 Grandeur Hotel
京澳酒店
91 Holiday Inn
假日酒店
92 New World
Emperor Hotel
新世界帝濠酒店

PLACES TO EAT
11 McDonald's
麥當勞
15 Ze do Pipo
巴比龍葡國餐廳
20 O Barril 2 Snack Bar
霸利吧
22 McDonald's; Central Plaza
麥當勞
27 McDonald's
麥當勞
29 Fairwood Fast Food;
Watson's
大快活、屈臣氏
31 Long Kei Restaurant
龍記酒家
32 Shanghai Greatwall
Restaurant
上海長城菜館
33 Restaurante Safari
金池餐廳
35 Honggei Chuenchoi
紅記川菜
36 Fat Siu Lau Restaurant
佛笑樓大餐廳
55 Black Ship Pub
& Restaurant
黑船
64 Alfonso III
亞豐素III餐廳

67 Solmar Restaurant
沙利文餐廳
77 Food Stalls
大排檔
82 Pizza Hut
必勝客

OTHER
1 Santo António Church
聖安多尼堂
2 Ruinas de São Paulo
大三巴牌坊
3 Fortaleza de Monte
中央大炮台
5 St Michael's Cemetery
聖美基西洋墳場
7 Gymnasium & Swimming
Pool
體育館及泳池
8 Vasco da Gama Garden
華士古達嘉馬花園
10 Lua da Prata
銀輝
12 Watson's Drugstore
屈臣氏
13 Cineteatro Macau
澳門戲院
14 Chinese Library
八角亭
16 HongkongBank
匯豐銀行
17 Cathedral
大教堂
18 Livraria São Paulo
19 Livraria Portuguesa
21 Bank of America
美國銀行
23 Visa Office
簽証處對外辦公室
24 Leal Senado
市政廳
25 CTM Telephone Office
澳門電訊
26 GPO
郵電局
28 São Domingo's Church
玫瑰堂
30 MGTO
澳門旅遊公司
41 Kam Pek Casino
42 Bird Cage Shop
華園雀鳥

MACAU

43	Hong Kung Temple 康公廟	
46	Floating Casino (Macau Palace) 澳門皇宮娛樂場	
49	Macau-Guangzhou Ferry Pier 往廣州客運碼頭	
50	Kee Kwan Motors (Buses to Guangzhou) 岐關車路有限公司	
58	Belissimo Supermarket	
60	São Agostinho 聖奧斯定堂	
61	Teatro Dom Pedro V	
62	São Lourenço 聖老楞佐堂	
63	Government House 澳督府	
65	Pavilions Supermarket 白利來超級市場	
68	Banco Comercial de Macau	
74	Foto Princessa 公主攝影器材行	
76	Bus Stop to Taipa & Coloane 至氹仔、路環的巴士	
78	Bank of China 中銀大廈	
79	Lisboa Casino 葡京娛樂場	
80	Airport Bus Stop 飛機場之巴士站	
84	Military Museum 軍事博物館	
88	Main Police Station 正警署	
89	CTM Telephone Office 澳門電訊	
93	Immigration Office 入境部	

From there you get an excellent view of the central area of Macau. You can also see across the Pearl River into China. In front of the church is a replica of the Grotto of Lourdes.

Government House

The Government House on Avenida da Praia Grande is pink like the Governor's Residence. Originally built for a Portuguese noble in 1849, it was acquired by the government at the end of the 19th century.

THE NORTH

The northern part of the peninsula has been more recently developed than the southern and central areas. Nevertheless, there are a few interesting historical sites in this region of Macau.

Kun Iam Temple

The Buddhist Kun Iam Temple on Avenida do Coronel Mesquita was originally founded in the 13th century, but the present buildings date from 1627. It's really a complex of temples, the most interesting in Macau, and is dedicated to the god Kun Iam (known as Kwun Yum in Hong Kong and Kuanyin in the People's Republic of China) – the God of Mercy. The image of Kun Iam is dressed in embroidered silk and flanked on either side by the 18 *arhats*. Rooms adjacent to the main hall celebrate Kuan Iam with a collection of pictures and scrolls.

This is also where the first treaty of trade and friendship between the USA and China was signed in 1844. These days it's a place for fortune-telling rather than treaties and it gets quite a lot of visitors. The terraced gardens behind the temple are very attractive; there are four ancient banyan trees with intertwined branches that symbolise marital fidelity.

Further along to the west of Avenida do Coronel Mesquita is another, smaller, Kun Iam Temple that is a hive of activity and colour, and is worth visiting.

Lin Fong Miu

Near the Canidrome is Estrada do Arco, where you'll find Lin Fong Miu (Lotus Temple). Originally a Taoist temple, the main hall is dedicated to Kun Iam. Another shrine is for A-Ma, the God of Seafarers, and another is for Guanti (Kuanti in Hong Kong), the God of War, Literature and Pawnshops. The Lin Fong Miu temple complex probably predates the arrival of the Portuguese in Macau.

Barrier Gate

The Barrier Gate (Portas do Cerco) is the gate between Macau and China. In Portuguese, Portas do Cerco literally means Gate of Siege.

Before 1980, when 'China-watching' was in vogue, Macau's Barrier Gate and Hong Kong's Lok Ma Chau attracted legions of tourists eager for that borderland *frisson* that came with being on the edge of the People's Republic of China (PRC). If you want to see it, head along Istmo Ferreira do Amaral from Lin Fong Miu (Lotus Temple).

PLACES TO STAY

Hotels in Macau are generally split geographically into price constituencies, with cheap guesthouses and mid-range hotels occupying the western reaches of the peninsula, near the Floating Casino around Rua das Lorchas and Avenida de Almeida Ribeiro, and top-end hotels in the east and centre of town. There are a few exclusive options with excellent views in the south of the peninsula.

Most people arriving from Hong Kong book their hotels in advance, often at the booking offices in the Shun Tak Centre in Sheung Wan, where the ferries from Hong Kong to Macau leave. Doing this saves a considerable amount off the walk-in rate. It is a simple matter to book your Turbo Cat ticket over to Macau and get a special deal on a hotel. Any of the countless outlets at the ferry terminal in the Shun Tak Centre can do this for you. This saves time and is a lot cheaper. If you haven't booked a place already, however, many of the mid and top-range hotels have counters at the Macau jetfoil pier – you will get a hefty discount at this booking office (up to 50% off). Some touts may also approach you offering discounts for hotels – the touts are usually reliable and are just trying to drum up business during the slow mid-week period.

If you've booked a mid or top-range hotel room, follow the crowds out to the front of the terminal where nearly all the hotels operate a shuttle bus for guests. Even if you just want to check out the hotel, jump on board. This saves a lot of time and effort.

Places to Stay – Budget

The key to finding a good, cheap room is patience. If one place charges too much, then try another. You will find that the cheap hotels are not far from each other, so don't worry if you think one place charges too much and you want to compare prices.

The tourist business has been hit in Macau and prices fluctuate quite wildly, depending on conditions. Don't necessarily think the prices quoted in this section are the lowest – bargain hard and say *'peng di la'* (make it cheaper). As long as you haven't arrived on a weekend, you should find something acceptable within half an hour or so of beginning your search. All accommodation places listed are on the Central Macau map unless otherwise noted.

Macau's true budget accommodation is not far from the centre of town. Generally these hotels form a cluster to the south-west of the Largo do Senado, around the area off Rua da Caldeira and the Rua das Lorchas, a lively area of narrow lanes, fried food stalls and shops with coloured shutters. Despite being pretty grotty, there are a few cosy retreats that won't cost too much; plus you'll be within walking distance of all the major tourist sights.

One step up from the pavement is the *Vong Kong Hospedaria* (☎ 574016) at 45 Rua das Lorchas. If you interrupt the mahjong-playing concierge he'll inform you that he has exceptionally grotty singles for M$30 and small doubles for M$40. The largest doubles are at the end of the corridor on the left and right. The walls are paper thin and the whole place is pretty grim, but what else would you expect from accommodation the same price as a couple of meals at McDonald's?

A goodie is the *San Va Hospedaria* (☎ 573701), 67 Rua de Felicidade. Situated on the road that was the hub of the old red light district (now having moved to Rua das Lorchas and around the East Asia Hotel and the Vila Capital), this place has quite a deal of charm, despite the fact that the rooms are not very clean and are separated by flimsy cardboard partitions. The atmosphere is good and the place has a homey feel about it; the rooms look unsafe and easy to break into, but the concierge and her family are always wandering around, so it's actually quite secure. Singles cost M$60 and doubles M$70, but you should be able to hammer the price down more if it's quiet.

The nearby *Vila Universal* (☎ 573247) at 73 Rua da Felicidade is more costly, with M$190 singles and M$260 doubles. The adjacent *Ko Wah Hotel* (☎ 375599) is similarly priced. The reception for the Ko Wah Hotel is on the 4th floor – be sure to check out the ancient lift. Also in the area is the *Pensão Tai Fat* (☎ 933908) at 41-45 Rua da Caldeira, which has rather damp singles/doubles for M$180/200. The staff can almost speak English, but the hotel is only passable.

Slightly further south, the *Vila Tai Loy* (☎ 939315) is on the corner of Travessa das Virtudes and Travessa Auto Novo. Singles start at M$150; the rooms are attractive and the manager is friendly. Also in the area is the *Hou Kong Hotel* (☎ 937555, fax 338884), 1 Travessa das Virtudes, which has reasonable singles for M$220 and doubles for M$280 on weekdays. The prices climb to M$309 and M$389 respectively on weekends.

Further south again on the eastern side of Praça Ponte e Horta is *Pensão Kuan Heng* (☎ 573629, 937624), 2nd floor, C block, Rua Ponte e Horta. Singles/doubles cost M$150/250, and it's clean and well managed.

Another part of Macau that has a few budget places is the area between the Lisboa Hotel and Rua da Praia Grande. This area doesn't have the character of the western district and many of the hotel owners hardly speak English, and are not really used to dealing with foreigners.

Vila Meng Meng (☎ 710064), 3rd floor, 24 Rua Doutor Pedro José Lobo, has singles at M$150. Next door is the *Vila Nam Loon*, where rooms start at M$150.

Pensão Nam In (☎ 710024), Travessa da Praia Grande, has singles with shared bath for M$110, or M$230 for a pleasant double with a private bath. On the opposite side of the alley is the *Nam Tin Hotel* (☎ 711212), a cheap looking hotel that is actually expensive – singles are M$350! *Vila Nam Pan* (☎ 572289) on the corner is also expensive for what you get, with singles for M$250.

Behind the Lisboa Hotel on Avenida de Lopo Sarmento de Carvalho is a row of pawnshops and a couple of guesthouses. The *Vila San Vu* is friendly and has good rooms for M$200. The *Jai Alai Hotel* (☎ 725599, fax 726105) is inside a sleaze circus known as China City Nightclub. It's adjacent to Yaohan department store (see the Macau Peninsula map) and close to the Jetfoil pier, but other than that there is little that can be recommended. The rooms are relatively overpriced at M$575.

Another place to check is the area north of the Lisboa Hotel on a street called Estrada de São Francisco. You have to climb a steep hill to get up to this street, but the advantage is that the hotels have a sea breeze and it's quiet. At 2A Estrada de São Francisco is *Vila Tak Lei* (☎ 577484), which has singles/doubles for M$100/200. There are a few other grottier establishments in the vicinity.

Places to Stay – Mid-Range

Most mid-range hotels in Macau are three star, and a few are four star. For some hotels, apart from the regular weekday price listed in this section, we have also included the price you could get in Hong Kong if you booked your room through a travel agent (such as Nan Hua Travel Agency (☎ 2815-0208, fax 2544-5198), room 318, Shun Tak Centre in Sheung Wan). These travel agents can be found in the same building as the departure point for Jetfoils and Turbocats for Macau. Many mid-range hotels also have telephone numbers in Hong Kong where you can book rooms.

If you can force your way through the scrum of scarlet women loitering with intent outside the *East Asia Hotel* (☎ 922433), 1A Rua da Madeira, it'll be worth it. The hotel is housed in a classic colonial-style building and, though it's been remodelled, has lost none of its charm. Spacious singles/doubles with private bath start at M$340/400; you should be able to get a double for about M$250 if you book through a travel agent in Hong Kong. There's a fine restaurant on the 2nd floor that serves dim sum for extremely reasonable prices. A few other hotels with similar prices are located in the area, but none can compare with the East Asia Hotel in terms of value for money.

The nearby *Vila Capital* (☎ 920154) at 3 Rua Constantino Brito also seems to be the Macau headquarters of the local prostitution racket. It's seedy and tacky, but has good value singles/doubles for M$230/250.

The modern looking, clean and reasonable *Sun Sun Hotel* (☎ 939393, fax 938822), 14-16 Praça Ponte e Horta, offers rooms for much less than its advertised price. The regular price is supposedly M$600, but on week days this drops to a promotional M$360 and on weekends to M$520. The rooms on the upper floors have excellent views of the Inner Harbour. The Sun Sun is very good value, especially if you book your room through a travel agent in Hong Kong; call ☎ 2517-4273 in Hong Kong for details.

Not far from the Sun Sun is the *Masters Hotel* (☎ 937572, fax 937565, HK 2598-7808) at 162 Rua das Lorchas (next to the Floating Casino). Singles/doubles on weekdays are M$280/350; if you book through a travel agent you can get a double during the week for M$250.

The *London Hotel* (☎ 937761), 4 Praça Ponte e Horta (two blocks south of the Floating Casino), has clean singles for M$230.

The *Central Hotel* (☎ 373888) is centrally located at 26-28 Avenida de Almeida Ribeiro, a short hop north-west of the GPO. Singles/doubles with a private bath cost from M$310/400.

A block to the north of the Floating Casino, at 146 Avenida de Almeida Ribeiro, is the *Grand Hotel* (☎ 921111), where singles/twins cost M$380/480. If you book through a travel agency in Hong Kong you can get a double for M$220 on weekdays or M$330 on weekends.

To the east of the Floating Casino is a street called Travessa Caldeira, where you'll find the rather scuzzy *Man Va Hotel* (☎ 388655), 32 Rua da Caldeira. Doubles cost from M$260; the more expensive rooms have a fridge.

On the north side of the Floating Casino on Rua das Lorchas is the *Peninsula Hotel* (☎ 318899). Singles/twins cost M$300/400.

This hotel is large, clean and popular. You can get a room for M$250 or less if you book in a Hong Kong travel agency.

The *Fortuna Hotel* (☎ 786333, fax 786363, HK 2517-3728), 63 Rua da Cantão, is in a useful position if you want to go and blow your inheritance in the nearby Casino Lisboa. It's a smart and clean hotel compromised by a 20,000 foot karaoke nightclub. Doubles start at M$580 but you may be able to get one for M$400 (weekdays) if you book through a travel agent in Hong Kong.

Not far across the way is the *Presidente* (☎ 553888, fax 552735, HK 2857-1533), Avenida da Amizade, which has standard doubles for M$495, deluxe doubles for M$575 and suites starting at M$1836. Booking through the hotel's Hong Kong sales office or through a travel agent may net you a double for M$360 (weekdays).

Just around the corner is the *Beverly Plaza Hotel* (☎ 782288, fax 780684, HK 2739-9928) on Avenida do Doutor Rodrigo Rodrigues. Doubles on weekdays start at M$532, with suites ranging in price from M$943 to M$1242. Booking through the hotel's Hong Kong phone number or a travel agent could net you a room for M$400.

Not far from the Guia Lighthouse is the *Guia Hotel* (☎ 513888, fax 559822) at 1-5 Estrada do Engenheiro Trigo. On weekdays doubles start from M$350, triples from M$550 and suites from M$650. You can force the price of a double down to M$300 by booking through a travel agent in Hong Kong. The hotel nightclub has 'state-of-the-art karaoke gear'; consider this a warning. Breakfast is included in the price.

Across from the Vasco da Gama Monument is the *Royal Hotel* (☎ 552222, fax 563008, HK 2543-6426), 2-4 Estrada da Vitória, a four star hotel with doubles starting at M$550. Weekday rooms can be booked through a Hong Kong travel agent for M$320.

The *Nam Yue Hotel* (☎ 726288, fax 726-726, HK 2559-0708), Avenida do Doutor Rodrigo Rodrigues, is within walking distance of the Jai Alai Casino. Doubles cost from M$585 and suites from M$1405. If you book through a Hong Kong travel agent you should be able to get a weekday double for around M$360.

Up towards the north of the Macau Peninsula is the modern, clean and bright *Fu Hua Hotel* (☎ 553838, fax 527575, HK 2559-0708), 98 Rua de Francisco Xavier Pereira. Doubles start at M$530, with triples starting at M$570. If you avoid the weekend, you can book a room through a Hong Kong travel agent for about M$310.

Once you've recovered from the affront of the external design, you'll discover that the *Kingsway Hotel* (☎ 702888, fax 702828), Rua de Luis Gonzaga Gomes, has doubles from M$500, plus its very own casino. You can pull the carpet from under the above price by booking through a travel agent and getting a weekend double for M$380.

The *Sintra* (☎ 710111, fax 510527, HK 2546-6944), Avenida Dom João IV, is centrally located near the Bank of China building. Weekday doubles cost from M$560 to M$820, but if you book through the hotel's Hong Kong number, you could get a room for M$400. A buffet breakfast is included in the price.

Also centrally located is the *Metropole Hotel* (☎ 388166, fax 330890, HK 2833-9300), 493-501 Avenida da Praia Grande, which has singles for M$396, doubles for M$443 and suites for M$759. You can hammer the weekday price down to M$280 if you book through the hotel's Hong Kong phone number or a travel agent.

The *Mondial Hotel* (☎ 566866, fax 514083, HK 2540-8180) on Rua de Antonio Basto (east side of Lou Lim Ioc Gardens). In the old wing of the building, doubles are M$360 to M$480 and suites are M$850. In the new wing of the building, doubles are M$580 to M$630 and suites are M$1050 to M$2300. If you avoid the weekend, you can check in for around M$290 by booking through a Hong Kong travel agent.

The *Grandeur Hotel* (☎ 781233, fax 785896, HK 2857-2846), Rua de Pequim, has doubles from M$650 to M$1200, and suites start at M$1500. Weekday doubles

can cost as little as M$360 if booked through a Hong Kong travel agent.

The *New World Emperor Hotel* (☎ 781888, fax 782287, HK 2724-4622), Rua de Xangai, has weekday doubles for M$570 and suites for M$1780. The staff claim 40% discounts can be arranged during the week and 20% discounts on the weekend, otherwise book through a Hong Kong travel agent and get a double for M$370.

Places to Stay – Top End

Macau doesn't have the spread of exclusive hotels that Hong Kong specialises in, but there are a few gems that will make your stay an occasion. During the summer travel season, many of the top-end places are solidly booked, even on weekdays.

The *Bela Vista* (☎ 965333, fax 965588, HK 2881-1688), Rua Comendador Kou Ho Neng, is Macau's equivalent to Hong Kong's Peninsula. It's a colonial hotel in the south of the Macau Peninsula that was going to seed until it was bought by Hong Kong's Mandarin Oriental Hotel Group. It has been painstakingly restored and has regained all of its former elegance. There are only eight rooms and suites, from M$2100 (weekdays) to M$4000 (weekdays) a night. The Bela Vista suite is the most expensive room and costs M$4000 (on weekends it goes up to M$5500). It has a glorious view from its balcony and includes a sitting room. It may be expensive, but if you want to indulge in colonial luxury, there's no better place.

Built into the remains of an old fortress, the *Pousada de São Tiago* (☎ 378111, fax 552170, HK 2803-2015) is right up there with the Bela Vista in terms of character, if not quite as luxurious. Sitting above the Avenida de Republica, the hotel commands a splendid view of the harbour, and the interior decor, with its flagstones and wooden rafters, is a delight.

Even if you don't stay, it's worth stopping for a drink on the terrace. Originally the hotel was a fortress, the Fortaleza da Barra, which was built in 1629. Doubles cost M$1380 to M$1680. The honeymoon suite is M$1850 and the most expensive suite is M$3500.

The *Mandarin Oriental* (☎ 567888, fax 594589, HK 2881-1688, email mandarin @macau.ctm.net), 956-1110 Avenida da Amizade, is not as grand as the Hong Kong Mandarin Oriental, but is still a superb five star hotel. Doubles cost M$910 from Sunday to Thursday, M$1040 on Friday and M$1300 on Saturday. Check as there may be a special package available, and try to book your room either in Hong Kong or through an agent, because you could find a weekday room for M$850. The Mandarin runs a shuttle bus from the Macau jetfoil pier – look out for the red coated assistants.

The *Lisboa Hotel* (☎ 377666, fax 567 193), Avenida da Amizade, is Macau's most famous landmark. It's difficult to find the right adjective to describe the unique architecture (orange background with white circles). Regardless of what you think of the external design, the interior is first rate. The Lisboa has the best arcade in Macau, and it is filled with shops, restaurants, banks, a billiard room and bowling alley. Doubles cost from M$1250, and suites M$1840 to M$7000. Book with a travel agent and you could get a weekday room for M$600 and blow what you save at the adjacent casino.

The *Holiday Inn* (☎ 783333, fax 782321, HK 2810-9628), Rua de Pequim, has doubles from M$688, and suites from M$1800. If you book through a Hong Kong travel agent, you could get a double on a weekday for M$450.

The *Ritz* (☎ 339955, fax 317826, HK 2739-6993), 2 Rua da Boa Vista, is in the very scenic south of the peninsula, not far from the Bela Vista. Although doubles start at M$1242, and suites at M$2392, at the time of writing some travel agents in Hong Kong were advertising rooms for M$380.

PLACES TO EAT
Main Dishes
Portuguese & Macanese *Alfonso III* (☎ 586272), 11 Rua Central, is a short stroll south from the Leal Senado. The restaurant

has won a deserved reputation among diners but tables can often be in short supply, so phone to get a status report on the size of the queue. Credit cards are not accepted.

A Lorcha (☎ 313193), 289 Rua do Almirante Sergio, is near the A-Ma Temple at the south-west tip of the peninsula. Among the fine dishes at this much-loved restaurant are African chicken, chicken with onion and tomato, and raw codfish salad.

Barra Nova (☎ 512287) is next door at 287A Rua do Almirante Sergio and is a small restaurant specialising in Portuguese dishes.

Restaurante Litoral (☎ 967878), 261 Rua do Almirante Sergio, is just a short walk north of the Maritime Museum. The decor is timbered and authentic, albeit a bit heavy, and the food is a succulent treat. The fourth restaurant in this enclave of Portuguese cuisine is *O Porto Interior* (☎ 967770), 259 Rua do Almirante Sergio.

Henri's Galley (☎ 556251) is on the waterfront at 4G-H Avenida da Republica, at the southern end of the Macau Peninsula. An old-timer on the Macau restaurant scene, Henri's is a bit tired and the prices are high.

Not far from Henri's is *Petisco Fernandes* (☎ 563865), 4F Avenida da Republica, not to be confused with Fernando's in Coloane.

Comida A Portuguesa Carlos (☎ 300315) has some of the warmest service in town, as well as outstanding food. It's the kind of place where the owner comes over and chats with you over a glass of wine. It's located at 28 Rua Bispo Medeiros, near the Lou Lim Ieoc Gardens. Credit cards are not accepted.

A Casa Macanese (☎ 974536), 32 Rua Central, may be a tiny place, but the Portuguese food is big on flavour and a hit with all who visit.

Solmar (☎ 574391) at 512 Avenida da Praia Grande is quite an institution in the restaurant world of Macau, and has recently been renovated. The strength of this place is the seafood, which is cooked with care and attention and beautifully served. The seafood soup is a thick infusion of flaky fish pieces and rich flavours.

Fat Siu Lau Restaurant (literally House of the Smiling Buddha, ☎ 573580) serves

Portuguese and Chinese food. It's at 64 Rua da Felicidade, which was once the old red-light 'Street of Happiness'. It's supposed to be the oldest Macanese restaurant in the colony, dating back to 1903 (some of the waiters appear to herald from a similar era). The speciality is roast pigeon. Credit cards are not accepted.

An excellent place to eat is *Restaurante Safari* (☎ 322239), which is tucked away at 14 Patio do Cotovelo, near the Leal Senado. It has good coffee-shop food, as well as spicy chicken, steak and fried noodles.

Ze do Pipo (☎ 374047), 95A Avenida da Praia Grande (near Rua do Campo), is a two storey splashy Portuguese restaurant. Sunday is the day to go for large and wholesome Portuguese stews.

The great *Black Ship Pub & Restaurant* (☎ 934119), in the basement at Rua do Gamboa 10AA, is a fine pub-style Portuguese restaurant. The food is rustic and filling. It's on the west side of Macau not far from the Floating Casino.

If you can't resist forking out for excellent cuisine, outstanding Portuguese food is served on the restaurant balcony of the *Bela Vista* (☎ 965333), Rua Comendador Kou Ho Neng. Opening hours are from 7 am to 3 pm and 7 to 10 pm.

If you'd like to try something different, the *Military Club* (☎ 714009), 795 Avenida da Praia Grande, serves Portuguese food in one of Macau's distinguished colonial buildings. It's open from noon to 3 pm and 7 to 11 pm.

If you enjoy revolving while you eat, you can take in a slowly circling view of China from *The Rotunda* (☎ 781233) on the 26th floor of the Grandeur Hotel on Rua de Pequim. The food's nothing special, but maybe there's some sort of pre-handover cachet in being among the last to gaze into the People's Republic with a raised wine glass of Mateus.

Chinese Rua da Felicidade is a good part of town to start hunting for hole-in-the-wall Chinese restaurants. There are loads of cheap eateries, though a number don't have English menus. If you like really, really, really hot food and want something Chinese, you can't go wrong with the *Honggei Chuenchoi* (☎ 577895), a very small Sichuan restaurant just off Rua da Felicidade at 188 Gatzai Gai. The food is fabulous and blistering, and much better than the 'Sichuan' food served in Hong Kong. A full meal won't set you back more than M$80.

The *Long Kei Restaurant* (☎ 573970) is right in the centre of the Largo do Senado, No 7B. It's a straightforward Cantonese restaurant with bright overhead lights and sparse surroundings, but it also has top notch Cantonese food and amiable waiters. There are over 350 Cantonese dishes offered. It's open from 11 am to 11 pm.

A great place for a Chinese breakfast is *Singgei* (☎ 374559), 2E Rua da Palha, just to the north of São Domingos and on the road to the Ruinas de São Paulo. If you like Chinese *juk* (rice porridge) or you're just keen to try it out, this is the place to try a sample.

There's not just porridge at this restaurant, but a whole range of tarts and cakes. A huge breakfast for four people can set you back a measly M$60 or a simple bowl of *baak juk* (white porridge) will cost you M$2.20.

Jade Restaurant (☎ 375125), 26 Avenida de Almeida Ribeiro, does morning and afternoon dim sum, and delicious Cantonese food in the evening. It's a good place for breakfast, and is open from 7 am to midnight.

Dynasty Chinese Restaurant (☎ 7933821), 2nd floor, Mandarin Oriental, is a sophisticated alternative, serving fine Cantonese cuisine from a diversity of ingredients, including chicken, goose, fish, frogs, crabs, turtles and snake.

If you want to sample abalone and don't know where to start, a small restaurant at 36 Rua da Felicidade called *Sainan Faandim* (☎ 714009), which specialises in the fish and has quite a reputation in Macau. A plate of abalone and shark's fin will set you back about M$380. There is no English sign.

Another spot famous for its abalone is the *Abalone Ah Yat Restaurant* (☎ 780807) in the Fortuna Hotel. For M$798, four people can share a set meal of abalone, a small hotpot, crispy garlic chicken and an array of seafood, plus a bottle of Portuguese wine. Another recommended speciality is the bird's nest soup.

French Excellent food, for those who want to indulge, can be found at the *Ritz Restaurant* (☎ 339955) at the Ritz. The high prices belong to Hong Kong rather than Macau, but the menu is expansive, with the stress on continental grills. The wine list is decent, though pricey.

Italian *Pizzeria Toscana* (☎ 726637), Apaia do Grande Premio de Macau, Avenida da Amizade, welcomes diners to its cosy little alcoves for some really fine pastas.

Mezzaluna (☎ 9561110), inside the Mandarin Oriental, advertises itself as a 'Cucina Italiana' and makes a fine offering in classy surroundings. The pasta is fresh and the pizzas emerge piping hot from wood fired ovens. The chef recommends either the pigeon roasted with polenta and porccini mushrooms, or the open ravioli of baby lobster with spinach and basil.

Frascati Restaurant (☎ 783333) on the 4th floor of the Holiday Inn serves Italian favourites alongside a medley of Spanish and Portuguese dishes.

Vegetarian An extremely cheap buffet meal awaits those at the *Suen Kong Restaurant* (☎ 339089), 16 Travessa de Santo Domingos. For M$19 per person (M$10 for children) you get three vegetarian choices (from a choice of 18), such as Monk's vegetables, various types of *doufu* (tofu) and noodles, and a drink. The buffet is served from 11.30 am to 2.30 pm and 6 to 10 pm.

Also in Travessa de Santo Domingos at No 12 is the *Vegetarian Pizza Restaurant* (☎ 356703), a Taiwan-style vegetarian food joint, which dishes up a range of pizzas and good value meals.

Other Asian Cuisine For those craving *bulgogi* and *kimchi*, good Korean food is served at *Restaurante Korean* (☎ 569039) in the Presidente. You can expect to pay Japanese prices for your sushi regardless of whether you buy it in Tokyo or Macau. Perhaps for this reason, Japanese restaurants tend to be inside the upmarket hotels. You'll find *Furusato* (☎ 388568) in the Lisboa Hotel.

Other Cuisine Brazilian food is available from the Ruinas de São Paulo at *Yes Brazil* (☎ 358097), 6A Travessa Fortuna.

Tunisian is what's cooking at *Sharazad Arab Cuisine* (☎ 569977), 28F Rua Bispo Medeiros. If you can't live without a daily ration of *couscous*, this restaurant could be the place for you.

Cafes *Cafe E Nata* (☎ 828534), 17B Gum Loi building, Ma Tung Ling Lane, is a popular place to stock up on breakfast essentials like cappuccino and croissants. You will find the cafe not far from the Sintra hotel. There is another branch at Rua Almirante Costa Cabral, by the Lou Lim Iok Garden.

Bolo de Arroz Pastelaria (☎ 339089), 11 Travessa de Santo Domingos, is in a small street that has a number of eateries. It has a splendid range of pastries, cheeses, cakes and aromatic coffees. A coconut tart and a coffee will cost you about M$15. Travessa de Santo Domingos is a small lane opposite the tourist office in Largo do Senado.

Those who only get going on coffee beans should pay a visit to *Pokka Coffee* (☎ 728893) on the 2nd floor of the Yaohan department store. A coffee-lovers' coffee house, this place stocks a huge range of different beans.

Street Stalls Don't overlook wandering the streets in search of stalls selling stir-fried food and *yuk gon* (dried sweet strips of pork and other meats); very popular in Macau. The best places to find these are around Rua da Caldeira, which is to the

MACAU

south of Avenida de Almeida Ribeiro in the vicinity of the cheap guesthouses.

As in other Chinese cities, the evening street markets are as cheap as cooking for yourself. Seafood is the local speciality. Eating sea snails takes a little practice. The idea is to use two toothpicks to roll the organism out of its shell, then dip it in sauce.

Food stalls are located in Rua da Escola Commercial, a tiny lane one block west of the Lisboa Hotel, next to a sports field. There are many cheap but grotty Chinese restaurants (called *casa-pasto* in Portuguese) with outdoor chairs, at night, near the Floating Casino on Rua das Lorchas.

Fast Food At the northern side of the tourist office in the plaza facing Leal Senado is the Food Plaza. You'll find a *Fairwood Fast Food* joint in the Food Plaza, which sounds far more appetising in Portuguese: Comidas Rapido Fairwood.

McDonald's is plentiful in Macau and the food is extremely cheap. See the Macau Peninsula and the Central Macau maps for a few locations.

Pizza Hut (☎ 319953) is on Avenida de Lopo Sarmento de Carvalho, in the basement of the old wing of the Lisboa Hotel. You can enter through the Lisboa Hotel shopping arcade.

Self-Catering There are lots of small grocery shops scattered around town. There are few supermarkets in the tourist zone – most supermarkets tend to be in the residential neighbourhoods. *Belissimo Supermarket* is the main supermarket near the budget hotels in the western area of town. *Pavilions Supermarket* on Avenida da Praia Grande has a wide selection of imported food and drinks. The largest supermarket in Macau is on the 2nd floor of *Yaohan department store* close to the Jetfoil pier.

ENTERTAINMENT
Cinemas
Macau is not strong on foreign films and cinemas lack the sophistication and variety offered in Hong Kong. The *Cineteatro*

Macau (☎ 572050) is on Rua de Santa Clara, down the street from Watson's Drugstore. The main theatre often has good quality films in English, as well as Hong Kong movies. On rare occasions, there might be a French film showing at the *Alliance Française* (☎ 965342), Veng Fu San Chun.

Theatre
Teatro Dom Pedro V (☎ 939646) on Largo St Augustine is a beautiful old theatre used for occasional special events (music festivals, drama performances etc).

The shows are irregular and there is no schedule. The Macau Government Tourist Office (MGTO) might have information, but it's most likely that you'll have to check with the theatre. This theatre is geared towards the local and expat community rather than foreign tourists.

Billiards & Pinball
The shopping arcade at the *Lisboa Hotel* includes a video games centre, to keep the kids busy, and a billiards room for the grown-up kids.

Discos & Nightclubs
Macau makes unimaginative and limp efforts to scrub off its indelible reputation for ghastly hostess clubs and cheesy floorshows. If you want to dance, do it in Hong Kong and get it out of your system before you visit Macau. Nightlife in Macau is generally put on for those who have come to gamble or spend money on prostitutes; as a result, there's nowhere for anyone with style or good taste.

The *Skylight Disco* (☎ 780923) in the Presidente hotel has no cover charge, but you have to buy a drink for M$70; it's more of a hostess club and quite a sad affair. Other hotels have discos, and cover charges vary from M$60 to M$150, with one or two free drinks. The *Fortuna Nightclub* in the Fortuna Hotel is a huge warehouse of a nightclub patrolled by hostesses and reverberating to the elegant strains of discordant karaoke. Most places are pay to get in, pray to get out.

Large scale venues tend to appeal to Hong Kong and mainland Chinese. The *Savoy Nightclub* in the Lisboa Hotel is a huge, brightly lit place with a M$200 cover charge. The club features a Filipino band and floor show.

The 'Crazy Paris Show' is performed nightly in the Mona Lisa Hall of the Lisboa Hotel and is similar to the revue-style shows in Las Vegas. Shows scheduled from Sunday to Friday are at 8.30 and 10 pm. On Saturday, shows are at 8.30, 10 and 11 pm. Admission is M$90 on weekdays or M$100 on weekends. There is no admittance for anyone under 18 years.

The *China City Nightclub* is near the Jetfoil terminal. This is basically a male-oriented girlie club, with hostesses that circulate and keep the clientele smiling. There is even a scantily clad hostess in the men's washroom who hands paper towels to customers. Admission is M$200 and there may be additional charges for the time spent simply talking with the hostesses. The whole building gives the impression of being an absolute sleaze pit. The edifice is home to the Jai Alai Casino, Jai Alai Hotel, several pawnshops, a movie theatre, the Darling Thai Massage & Sauna, the Taipan Health Spa and the Show Palace, which features Russian strippers that dance on the tables. Single male travellers who go anywhere near the place will almost certainly be accosted by pushy touts explaining the virtues of a particular establishment's services.

Karaoke

These are everywhere and the music is mostly Canto-pop. Every hotel of any size has a karaoke bar. To find one, just look for the sign saying 'OK'. If you know any Cantonese or Mandarin songs, you'll be on cloud nine – if you don't, you won't.

Pubs

Near the Kun Iam Temple at 104 Rua de Pedro Coutinho is *Talker Pub* (☎ 550153, 528975). Just next door at No 106 is *Pyretu's Bar* (☎ 581063). Both places open

around 8 pm but don't get moving until after 9 pm and often don't close until sunrise. These two pubs draw young expats from as far as Hong Kong.

The *Jazz Club*, 9 Rua da Alabardas, lives up to its name in large part because it hosts an annual jazz festival. On Friday and Saturday night live bands usually perform, and on other evenings excellent recorded music is played. The Jazz Club is just behind São Lourenço (St Lawrence's Church).

Tribo (☎ 455234), 306 Rua Nova da Areia Preta, is a new and popular hotspot for those after something a bit different. The accent is on African music and there's a small dancefloor.

Oskar's Pub, in the Holiday Inn, draws a large number of local expats. Happy hour is from 5 to 9 pm and a pint of Carlsberg will set you back a reasonable M$19.

Bar da Guia in the Mandarin Oriental is decorated with a Grand Prix motif. There is a live band at 9 pm nightly, a midget dancefloor and a big-screen TV broadcasting sporting matches.

Bar da Montanha Russa (☎ 302731), Estrada Ferreira de Amaral, is popular with the locals as both a bar and a Portuguese restaurant. It's easy to find, being right inside Montanha Russa Gardens (see the Macau Peninsula map). Beer is M$12 a bottle during happy hour.

Worth looking out for is the microbrewed Macau Golden Ale and Praia Grande Amber Ale. Brewed by the Macau Brewing Co, the beers make a change from the usual generic lagers that are shipped into the territory. The beer is served in many of the hotel bars, including the Holiday Inn, the Lisboa Hotel and the Mandarin Oriental.

Casinos

None of the casinos in Macau offer the atmosphere or level of service considered minimal in Las Vegas. There are no seats for slot machine players and no cocktail waitresses offering free drinks to gamblers. Incredibly, the casinos don't even have 'change girls' walking the casino floor giving change to slot players so they can keep playing.

An obnoxious custom is that the dealers will tip themselves 10% of your winnings without asking! Any dealer doing this in Las Vegas would be immediately fired, and possibly subject to criminal prosecution. In Macau's casinos the dealers don't talk to the customers and no one smiles. Perhaps smiling is against the rules?

Nevertheless, the casinos have no trouble attracting customers and are usually jam-packed. One thing the casinos have in common with Las Vegas is that there are no clocks or windows – no sense letting people know how late it is, lest they be tempted to stop playing and go to bed. With the exception of the tiny Casino Victoria on Taipa Island, all casinos in Macau stay open daily, 24 hours, unless there is a major typhoon. A rundown of the casino battlefield follows.

Lisboa Casino Though it's by no means the newest casino in town, the Lisboa is still the largest and liveliest. When typhoon signal eight is hoisted and all the other casinos shut down, only this one stays open.

The Lisboa feels more comfortable than the other casinos – maybe this is because it has four storeys of spacious gambling halls. The adjacent hotel offers the comforts of a good but overpriced shopping arcade, fine restaurants and a video arcade to keep the kids busy while mum and dad lose their life savings at the blackjack tables.

There is a big meter in the casino which shows how much will be paid if you hit the grand jackpot on the five reel slot machines. The total shown on the meter increases until someone hits 'megabucks', then the meter is reset to zero and starts again. Of all the gambling halls in Macau, this one comes closest to matching the grandeur of a Las Vegas casino.

Floating Casino Officially, the name is Macau Palace, but everyone calls it the Floating Casino. Built in an old, converted ferry anchored on the west side of Macau, the concept conjures up romantic images of riverboat gambling, but the reality is somewhat different. Apart from being earthquake-proof, there's little else to recommend.

Inside, it's a very crowded, windowless, smoke-filled box where players climb over each other to get at the tables. It's one of Macau's oldest casinos, and the players are serious and oblivious to all else but the next roll of the dice.

Kam Pek Casino The original Kam Pek Casino used to look like a Salvation Army soup kitchen, but the new one near the Floating Casino has been considerably improved. The Kam Pek is known as a 'neighbourhood casino' and it appeals mainly to the locals – foreign tourists are made to feel unwelcome. The slot machines are the only ones in Macau to work with Macau patacas (the other casinos require Hong Kong dollars).

Mandarin Oriental Hotel Casino This place appeals to the upper crust and has a stuffed-shirt atmosphere. Men often wear neckties and the women dress in formal gowns. Even the hotel lobby looks like a museum. The Mandarin Oriental is to the south of the Jetfoil pier.

Jai Alai Casino Known as the Palacio de Pelota Basca in Portuguese, this casino once distinguished itself as the venue for *jai*

HONG KONG TOURIST ASSOCIATION
Mahjong is not played in the casinos, but in the homes and cafes around Macau.

alai (pronounced hi-a-lie) games. Jai alai is reputed to be the world's fastest ball game and is popular in many Latin American countries, particularly Cuba and Mexico. The game is similar to handball, racquetball or squash. The ball is three quarters the size of a baseball and harder than a golf ball. Each player alternatively catches it and throws it with his plethora – an elongated wicker basket with an attached leather glove that is strapped to his wrist. As with horse racing and dog racing, jai alai is something else for gamblers to wager on.

Sadly, the jai alai games are no more. The game just never caught on with visitors from Hong Kong, and the present-day Jai Alai Casino only has standard table games and slots. Nevertheless, this casino remains popular, partially because it's close to the Jetfoil pier, thus giving arriving visitors their first chance to gamble (or departing visitors their last chance).

Kingsway Hotel Casino Close to the Jai Alai Casino is the Kingsway. This is Macau's newest casino and aspires to be the best, with fancy decor and expensive fittings. Games are the same as elsewhere, but the minimum bets at some tables are too high for many players.

Macau Islands

The two islands of Taipa and Coloane perfectly round off a trip to Macau. While the Macau Peninsula is where the vast majority of the territory's population live and do business, Taipa and Coloane are pockets of calm and tranquillity languishing in a seemingly permanent siesta. Gorgeous colonial architecture presides over a land of sleepy lanes and an equally somnolent population. The motionless haze that blankets the two islands makes a day on Taipa and Coloane a long one; after wandering around the plentiful beaches and visiting the island churches, what better way to relax than to rest your feet and submit to the local rhythm of siestas and long meals.

A few large-scale projects have recently threatened to shake the islands from their torpor. The once backward Taipa now has two major hotels, a university, horse racing track, high-rise apartments and an airport. A golf course and deepwater port on Coloane herald the new era of change at any cost. There are plans to connect Taipa and the neighbouring Chinese isle of Hengqin with a huge bridge. Work is also proceeding apace to widen the causeway between Taipa and Coloane. But all of this has failed to arouse the islands from their forgetful reverie. A visit to Taipa and Coloane is still a charming experience.

TAIPA ISLAND

When the Portuguese first sighted Taipa (Tamzai in Chinese) it was actually two islands, but over the past few centuries the east and west halves have joined – one of the more dramatic demonstrations of the power of the siltation process occurring within the huge Pearl River Delta. Siltation continues and, if the mud flats to the south of Taipa Village are any indication, Taipa and Coloane are destined to become one island.

Traditionally a province of duck farmers and junk builders, with a small fireworks industry to satisfy the insatiable demand for bangers and crackers, Taipa is rapidly becoming urbanised. Resisting the onslaught of progress is a sleepy rebellion of Portuguese colonial churches and buildings, Buddhist temples, overgrown esplanades and lethargic villages. In fact it's still easy to experience the traditional charms of the island by going straight to Taipa Village.

Taipa Village

This village on the southern shore of Taipa island has picture-book charm, unruffled by the overblown development just to the north. It is a leisurely sprawl of Chinese shops and restaurants, punctuated here and there by grand colonial remains. Take your time to wander slowly around the village, which, although not crammed with sights, should leave something of its tranquil mood with you.

Down by the seafront, the **Avenida da Praia** is a tree-lined esplanade that has sadly been robbed of its seafront perch. Siltation has overwhelmed the beach and it has become a mud flat extending almost all the way to Coloane at low tide. Nevertheless, the place musters considerable charm with its wrought-iron benches and old-world character, and provides a beautiful opportunity for a stroll.

The few Macanese who lived on Taipa sought refuge in this colonial ghetto of smart apartments by the sea. One of the houses has been preserved as the **Taipa House Museum** and is open to the public. Artificially aged to recreate the atmosphere of the time, the museum is a snapshot of life at the turn of the century. The family who lived there would probably have been involved in the local administration, staunch Catholics and of quite modest means. It's open every day, except Monday, from 9.30 am to 1 pm and from 3 to 5.30 pm.

From the Taipa House Museum, walk west and up a few steps to find **Our Lady of Carmel Church**, built in 1885. When we

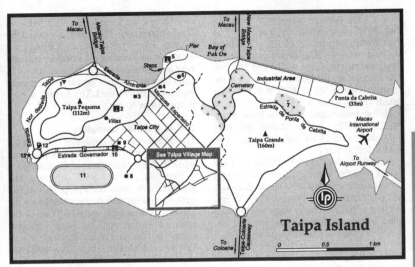

Taipa Island 仔

1 Rasa Sayang Restaurant
   莎洋
2 Pou Tai Un Temple
   菩提園
3 Hotel Hyatt Regency
   凱悦酒店
4 New Century Hotel
   新世紀酒店

5 Kun Iam Temple
   觀音廟
6 Macau University
   澳門大學
7 United Chinese Cemetery
   孝思墳場
8 Kartodrome
   小車場
9 Grandview Hotel
   君怡酒店

10 Four-Faced Buddha
   四面佛
11 Horse Racetrack & Macau
   Jockey Club
   澳門賽馬會
12 Petrol Station
   加油站
13 Police Station
   警察局

last visited, a Chinese wedding was in progress, later spilling out in a shower of confetti onto the Avenida da Praia.

The rest of the village is much more Chinese in appearance. There is a small Tin Hau Temple on the Largo Governador Tamagnini Barbosa, at the south-west corner of the village, very close to the main bus stop and bicycle rental shops. There are also a couple of small temples/shrines along Rua de Fernão Mendes Pinto, itself a beautiful, narrow, walled road along which cars squeeze their way. Just around the corner on

Rua do Regedor is a **Pak Tai Temple**. **Rua do Cunha** is a street with many tiny shops.

Macau Jockey Club

The Macau Jockey Club opened on Taipa Island in 1991. Also known as the Hippodrome, it's Macau's venue for horse racing. If you know your quinellas from your trifectas and six-ups, this is the place to go. The five storey grandstands can accommodate 18,000 spectators and are air conditioned. Unlike the race tracks at Hong Kong's Happy Valley and Sha Tin, the Macau

Jockey Club operates throughout the summer. Now Hong Kong residents can lose their money any season of the year. Races are held twice weekly (although not on set days) and race times are at 1.15 and 7.15 pm. The entrance fee is M$20 for visitors and the minimum bet is M$10. Call ☎ 820868 for details (Hong Kong ☎ 800-967-822). There is also an information office in Hong Kong (☎ 2517-0872). A free shuttle bus runs between Lisboa Hotel and the racecourse, via the Jetfoil pier.

Outside the Macau Jockey Club is a Four Faced Buddha shrine. There are several similar statues worldwide – one in Bangkok and another in (brace yourself) Las Vegas. Praying to the Buddha is supposed to bring good fortune, which is what you will undoubtedly need in Macau's casinos.

Kartodrome

You may have heard of the canidrome; well now there's the kartodrome. This venue is for go-cart racing. Officially, it's called the Karting School (or Escola de Karting), but locals prefer to call it the Kartodromo. Just why anyone would need to go to school to learn how to operate a go-cart is something we haven't determined. The Karting School is open from 10 am to 6 pm.

United Chinese Cemetery

The cemetery on the north-east corner of the island is worth a look. Resting in peace are those from the triumvirate of Chinese faiths – Buddhist, Taoist and Confucian. The graves face the open sea, a propitious and attractive vista for their occupants. Among the graves is a 30m-high statue of Tou Tei, the earth god. Some say Tou Tei is a bit perturbed by the newly constructed Macau international airport nearby. No doubt the sacred laws of *fung shui* (geomancy) have been jostled a bit in the wake of the huge jets.

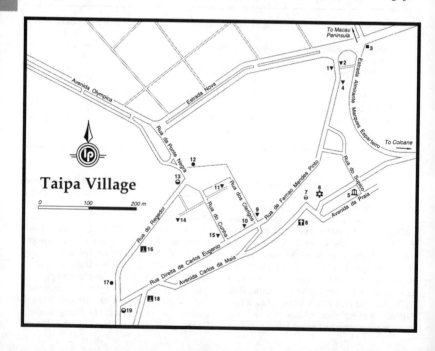

Kun Iam Temple
Walking downhill from Macau University along Estrada Almirante (back towards the Hyatt Regency), you should find some stone steps off to your right going down towards the sea. Follow these a short distance and you'll reach the very small Kun Iam Temple. It was built by the sea to worship Kun Iam, a god who protects sailors.

Pou Tai Un Temple
Less than 200m to the south-west of the Hyatt Regency is Pou Tai Un Temple, the largest temple on the island. It overlooks the tennis courts of the Hyatt. If you're around during lunch time, the temple operates a vegetarian restaurant – the vegetables are said to be grown in the temple's own garden. See the Places to Eat section in this chapter for details.

From the temple you can walk back to the Hyatt Regency and catch a bus to Taipa Village at the south end of the island, or you could walk the 1.5km distance.

Places to Stay
Unfortunately, there's nothing on Taipa for budget travellers. If you want to live in style, however, you should have no problem. The *Hyatt Regency* (☎ 831234, fax 830195, HK 2559-0168) has everything you'd expect in a five star hotel. Facilities include tennis courts, squash courts, a nearby golf course,

a fully equipped weights and exercise room, play areas for the kiddies, swimming pool and a pool-side bar. Facilities for the business traveller include a business centre and a conference room. Restaurants in the hotel dish up Cantonese, Macanese and Portuguese food, and there's also a deli if you want to surround yourself with the aromas of olive oil, cheese and other fine foods. Doubles range from M$990 to M$1380, and suites from M$2800 to M$10,000. If you book through a travel agency, you should be able to get a room for M$630 during the week. The hotel operates its own shuttle bus to the Macau Peninsula.

The *New Century Hotel* (☎ 831111, fax 832222, HK 2581-9863) is just across the street from the Hyatt Regency and also has a five star rating. Doubles are M$1100 to M$1650 and suites cost M$3000 to M$20,000. Booking through a travel agency should get you a room during the week for as little as M$480. The hotel also offers 'bargain' apartments available for rent by the month. These cost M$20,500 to M$22,500 per month for two bedrooms or M$27,000 to M$29,000 per month for three bedrooms.

The *Grandview Hotel* (☎ 837788, HK 800-933-966, fax 837777), 142 Estrada Governador, Albano de Oliveira, is not far from the Macau Jockey Club. If you don't want to watch the horses, you can take advantage of the hotel's swimming pool or badminton

MACAU

Taipa Village
仔村

1 Hon Seng Korean Restaurant
韓國烤燒火鍋
2 Restaurante Mediterraneo
地中海葡國餐廳
3 Taipa Hotel
格蘭酒店
4 O'Manel
阿曼諾葡國餐廳
5 Taipa House Museum
住宅式博物館

6 Carmel Garden
十字公園
7 Public Toilet
公用廁所
8 Our Lady of Carmel Church
9 Restaurant Estrela do Mar
海星餐室
10 Restaurante Panda
熊貓葡國餐廳
11 Pinocchio
木偶葡國餐廳
12 Fire Station
消防站

13 Bus Stop
巴士站
14 A Petisqueira
國美食天地
15 Galo Restaurant
公雞葡國餐廳
16 Pak Tai Temple
北地廟
17 Bicycle Hire
租單車處
18 Tin Hau Temple
天后廟
19 Main Bus Stop
巴士站

courts. If you book through a travel agent, you should be able to get a room during the week for around M$390. There is a scheduled shuttle bus service which travels between the Jetfoil pier, Lisboa Casino and the hotel.

At the time of writing, the *Taipa Hotel* was being constructed in Taipa village on the corner of Estrada Nova and Estrada Almirante Marques Esparteiro. It doesn't look like it'll be cheap, but its in a picturesque location.

Places to Eat

Taipa Village has several good medium-priced restaurants. Best known for its excellent Portuguese food, *Restaurante Panda* (☎ 827338) is at No 4-8 Rua Direita de Carlos Eugenio.

Rua do Cunha is chock-a-block with small restaurants. *Galo* (☎ 827317), 47 Rua do Cunha (easily recognised by the picture of a rooster above the door), is a quaint addition to the row of eateries. Also on Rua do Cunha are a couple of tiny Chinese restaurants worth popping into for a quick meal. *Seng Cheong* (☎ 827-589), 30 Rua do Cunha, is famous for its fried fish balls (M$28) and its steamed eel (M$100). *Tai Tung*, 16 Rua do Cunha, has a popular dish of soya sauce chicken (M$120) and roast meat dishes. *Restaurante Italian* (☎ 827387), 46 Rua do Cunha, offers a fair range of Italian favourites.

Not far away is *Pinocchio* (☎ 827128) at 4 Rua do Sol, an obscure alley near the fire station. Recommended dishes include grilled squid, deep-fried sardines and roast lamb, which is a treat.

Also in an obscure alley is the excellent *A Petisqueira* (☎ 825354), 15 Rua de São Joao; staff can present you with a decent wine list and a fine selection of dishes. *Restaurante Mediterraneo* (☎ 825069) on Rua de Fernão Mendes Pinto is an exquisite, reasonably priced little place. Just next door at No 88 is *O'Manel* (☎ 827571), and across the street is the Hon Seng Korean Restaurant (☎ 827205), where you can consume vast amounts of barbecued meat.

Elsewhere on the island, a good veggie option is the restaurant at *Pou Tai Un Temple* (☎ 811007), not far from the Hyatt Regency. The food's not that cheap, but it's the perfect retreat for lovers of Chinese vegetarian cooking. The restaurant's open from 9 am to 8 pm.

If you're looking for pricier international cuisine, the *Flamingo* (☎ 831234) at the Hyatt Regency, specialises in Portuguese and Macanese cuisine (African chicken is M$75), with a strong accent on seafood.

The Hyatt has another classy restaurant, the *Canton Tea House* (☎ 831234), which does excellent dim sum and other Cantonese fare. The menu also has a variety of vegetarian dishes, although it's all quite pricey.

For those on a budget, the best deal is the *student cafeteria* at Macau University.

Entertainment

The Hyatt Regency is the centre of Taipa's upscale nightlife. *The Bar* has an American theme and is decked out with photos of Hollywood stars. Drinks are expensive, but there is a happy hour from 5 to 7 pm.

The Namsan area of Taipa village has a number of pubs that have cropped up over the years. Take your pick from the *Cheers Pub* (☎ 821846), Estrada Governador Albano de Oliveira, Jardim Namsam; *Patio das Cantigas,* Avenida de Kwong Tung; the *Irish Pub*; *Bar dos Namorados*; or *Café Marseilles*.

As you might imagine, the *Hyatt Regency* has an upmarket casino. It's also fairly small and doesn't radiate the atmosphere of chaos that many gamblers enjoy. On the other hand, if you're attracted by high-stakes gambling, this is the place.

The *Casino Victoria* is the other casino on the island. It's hard to take this casino seriously, as it's basically just a gaming room at the Macau Jockey Club. It's only open on race days from 11 am to 3 pm.

COLOANE ISLAND

Once a popular destination for pirates, Coloane islanders (Lowaan in Chinese) fought off the last assault by South China Sea buccaneers in 1910. The island still celebrates the anniversary of the victory every 13 July. The beaches of the island no longer resound to the whistle of cannon balls or the clash of broadswords – Coloane instead attracts large numbers of camera-wielding tourists to its slumbering main village and sandy coastline. While Coloane is free of high-rise developments, a number of hotels, villas and even a golf course have sprouted near the previously pristine beaches. Still, for the moment the island is largely unspoilt and will probably remain that way for a few years yet.

Seac Pai Van Park

About a kilometre south of the causeway is the 20 hectare Seac Pai Van Park. There is a fountain and well-tended gardens, but the most notable feature is the **aviary** behind Balichao Restaurant. It contains a number of rare species of bird, and a display room which catalogues a wide range of the local fauna and flora. There is also a recently built **Museum of Nature and Agriculture**, which is open from Tuesday to Sunday, from 10.30 am to 4.30 pm. The park is open from 8 am to 6 pm, from Tuesday to Sunday. Admission is M$5, if you plan to visit the aviary. It costs M$20 if you want to rent a table in the picnic area. The park also has a camping area.

Hiking Trails

Behind Seac Pai Van Park are two hiking trails. The longest is simply called the Coloane Trail (Trilho de Coloane), and the entire loop walk is 8.6km. The shorter North-East Coloane Trail (Trilho Nordeste de Coloane) is near Kau-O, and the total length is 6.2km.

Coloane Village

The only town on the island, this is still largely a fishing village in character, although in recent years tourism has given the local economy a big boost. The village is an attractive relic of old Macau which hopefully will survive the transformation gripping the islands. Strolling around Coloane village's narrow and cluttered lanes, bordered on each side by pastel-shaded shops and restaurants, is a joy.

At the northern end of town are numerous **junk-building sheds**. Just how long this business can last is debatable; siltation threatens to make the harbour a mud flat within a decade. You can walk to the sheds and see how the junks are built, but take along a big stick as several of the sheds are guarded by vicious, xenophobic dogs!

If you arrive by bus, you'll be dropped off near the village roundabout. If you walk one short block to the west, you'll see the waterfront. From there you'll get a good view of China. It's so close one could easily swim across the channel. In fact, many people used to do just that to escape from China.

A sign near the waterfront points towards a **Sam Seng Temple** to the north. This temple is very small – not much more than a family altar. Just past the temple is the village pier. Walking south along Avenida de Cinco de Outubro, you'll soon come to the main attraction in this village, the **Chapel of St Francis Xavier**. This fascinating chapel was built in 1928 to honour St Francis Xavier, who died on nearby Sanchuang Island in 1552. He had been a missionary in Japan, and to this day Japanese come to Coloane to pay their respects.

A fragment of arm bone which once belonged to St Francis Xavier used to be kept in the chapel. In 1978 several boxes of martyrs' bones were also left in the chapel. These were the bones of the Portuguese and Japanese Christians who were martyred in Nagasaki in 1597, the Vietnamese Christians killed in the early 17th century and the Japanese Christians killed in a rebellion in Japan during the 17th century. In 1995 the bones were returned to St Joseph's Seminary and, in 1996, the bones of St Francis were relocated to the new São Paulo Museum (see the Macau Peninsula chapter).

Near the chapel is a **monument** surrounded by cannon balls to commemorate the successful final battle against pirates in these islands in 1910.

South of the chapel is a library and a sign pointing towards a Kun Iam Temple. This temple is tiny – not much more than an altar inside a little walled compound. Although there are no signs to indicate the path, if you walk just a little further past the stone wall you'll find a considerably larger and more interesting **Tin Hau Temple**.

At the very southern end of Avenida de Cinco de Outubro is a **Tam Kong Temple**. Tam Kong is the Taoist God of Seafarers. Inside is a whale bone, more than a metre long, which has been carved into a model of a ship – complete with a dragon's head and a crew of men in pointed hats. The temple custodian enthusiastically welcomes foreigners and then holds up a little placard in English soliciting donations for the maintenance of the temple. Such donations are voluntary, so let your conscience be your guide.

Cheoc Van Beach
About 1.5km down the Estrada de Cheoc Van from Coloane Village is Cheoc Van Beach. The name means Bamboo Bay. You can swim in the ocean (there are public changing rooms) or at the pool in Cheoc Van Park for a fee. The pool is M$15 for adults and M$5 for kids, and is open from 8 am to 9 pm. Cheoc Van Beach also has a yacht club, where you can inquire about boat rentals. To get there, take bus No 21A to Hac Sa Beach and ask the driver to drop you at 'juk wan hoi tan'; he'll drop you off at the top of a road leading down to the beach, or there's also a flight of steps.

Hac Sa Beach
Hac Sa, which means 'Black Sand', is the largest and most popular beach in Macau. The sand does indeed have a grey to black colour and this makes the water look somewhat polluted, but actually it's perfectly clean and fine for swimming. The area is beautiful, and on a clear day you can see the mountains on Hong Kong's Lantau Island.

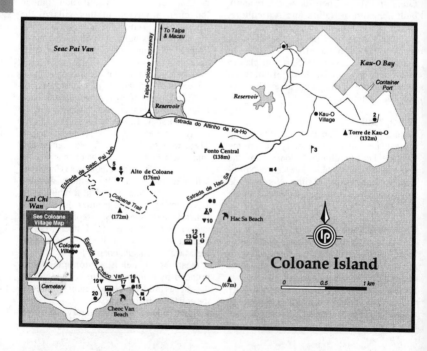

Just near the bus stop is **Hac Sa Sports & Recreation Park**. There seems to be just about everything there: a swimming pool (M$15 adults, M$5 kids), tennis courts (M$30 per hour, M$60 after 7 pm; you can also hire racquets and balls), a five-a-side football ground (M$70 per hour), a mini-golf course (M$10 per hour), ping pong tables (M$5 per hour) and badminton courts (M$10 per hour). The facility is open from 10 am to 9 pm. At the far end of Hac Sa Beach is a place to rent windsurfers and – if you can stand the noise – jet skis.

The **golf course** at the Westin Resort is open to non-guests as well, but you have to pay. Green fees for 18 holes are M$600 from Monday to Friday and M$800 on weekends, not including a 5% tax.

Bus No 21A provides frequent service to Hac Sa. On weekends the buses are even more frequent.

Kau-O Village

At the eastern end of Coloane is Kau-O Village, but it's not likely that you'll want to go there. It's not very attractive because of the neighbouring cement and power plants. There is also a leprosarium. In the past, there was a Vietnamese refugee camp, but this has long since been closed and demolished.

Following the tradition of putting things there that Macau's government would rather the tourists didn't see, a deep-water container port is being built.

Perhaps the most interesting sight in town is the church called Our Lady of Sorrows, which has a large bronze crucifix above the north door.

Places to Stay

Camping If you have a tent, there's an area for camping at Hac Sa beach, just to the right and behind Fernando's, not far from the bus stop and next to the beach. The place looked pretty on last inspection; the area seems clean and there are toilets and showers.

Youth Hostels The very clean *Pousada de Juventude* youth hostel (☎ 882050), also known as *Vila Dom Bosco*, is at Cheoc Van Beach. Off season (basically winter) it's pretty easy to get in there, but during peak season (summer and holidays) competition for beds is keen. Big youth groups tend to book this place out during school holidays (there are only 35 beds).

Another complication is that you can't simply show up at the hostel and ask to check in. You must first visit the Youth

---

Coloane Island 路環

1 Power Plant
發電所
2 Catholic School Centre
天主教學校
3 Golf Course
高爾夫球場
4 Westin Resort
威斯登酒店
5 Seac Pai Van Park
石排灣公園
6 Balichao Restaurant
金龍餐廳
7 Aviary
鳥舍

8 Waterscooter & Windsurfer Rentals
摩托艇及風帆租用處
9 Camping Site
野營場
10 Fernando's
法蘭度餐廳
11 Public Toilets; Showers
公用廁所及淋浴
12 Bus Stop
巴士站
13 Swimming Pool; Tennis Courts
泳池及網球場

14 Pousada de Juventude Youth Hostel
路環竹灣青年旅舍
15 Yacht Club
帆船俱樂部
16 Pousada de Coloane
竹灣酒店
17 Snack Bar; Changing Rooms
咖啡館
18 Swimming Pool
游泳池
19 La Torre
斜塔餐廳
20 Villas
別墅

Hostel Booking Office (☎ 344340), which is near the A-Ma Temple on the Macau Peninsula. This office is only open Monday to Friday from 9 am to 1 pm and 2.30 to 5.45 pm. The booking office will book your bed and sell you a voucher which you then take to the hostel when you want to check in. An International Youth Hostel Federation (IYHF) card is needed.

The hostel is closed from 10 am to 3 pm, and lights are out from 11 pm until 7 am. The weekday rate for a dormitory bed is M$40 for foreigners and M$25 for Macau residents, rising to M$80 and M$50 respectively on weekends. The hostel has a small kitchen, a small garden and a couple of double rooms.

Hotels Very close to Cheoc Van Beach is a luxury hotel, the *Pousada de Coloane* (☎ 882143, fax 882251, HK 2540-8180). This relaxed and appealing hotel has doubles ranging from M$680 to M$750. The hotel has its own sauna and swimming pool, and is well known for its excellent Sunday lunch buffet. It also has a deal where, if you spend M$700 or more (for two) at the hotel's restaurant, you get a night's free accommodation.

The *Westin Resort* (☎ 871111, fax 871 122, HK 2803-2015, www.westin.com), 1918 Estrada de Hac Sa, is a five star resort complex on the east side of Hac Sa Beach. The emphasis is on villas and a country club atmosphere, as indicated by the 18 hole golf course and eight tennis courts, squash courts, swimming pools, outdoor Jacuzzi, sauna and gymnasium. During the week, the cheapest double rooms start at M$900, and suites at M$4500.

Places to Eat
Not far from the roundabout at Coloane Village is *Cacarola* (☎ 882226), 8 Rua dos Gaivotas, probably the most loved of all the restaurants in town. Here you can find simple and honest Portuguese cuisine served to an appreciative audience. *O'Pescador* (☎ 880197), near the post office at 87-91 Rua da Cordoaria, also does wholesome

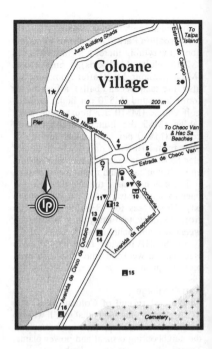

Portuguese food. The *Restaurant Alem Mar*, close to Cacarola, serves excellent Cantonese food.

Right next to the Chapel of St Francis Xavier at 8 Rua Caetano is the small and cheap *Nga Tim Café* (☎ 882086) The food is Sino-Portuguese, and while the restaurant's not an oil painting, the view outside is. If it's a sunny day, take a seat in the outside section and savour both the scenery and the food.

Next to the swimming pool at Cheoc Van Park is a fine Italian restaurant, *La Torre* (☎ 880156), which has some very flavoursome pastas and pizzas. A cheaper alternative is the *Snack Bar* (☎ 328528), just above the changing rooms by the beach.

At Hac Sa Beach, *Fernando's* (☎ 882531) deserves honourable mention for some of the best food in Macau. The atmosphere is also pleasant, but it can get crowded in the

Coloane Village
路環市區

1 Police Station
　警察局
2 Police Training Centre
　警察學院
3 Sam Seng Temple
4 Restaurant Alem Mar
　碧瑤海鮮家鄉菜館
5 Public Toilets
　公用廁所

6 Bus Stop
　巴士站
7 Health Clinic
　衛生部
8 Bus Stop
　巴士站
9 O'Pescador
　海夫海鮮屋
10 Post Office; Telecom
　郵局
11 Nga Tim Café

12 Chapel of St Francis Xavier
　聖方濟各聖堂
13 Library
　圖書館
14 Kun Iam Temple
　觀音廟
15 Tin Hau Temple
　天后廟
16 Tam Kong Temple
　譚公廟

MACAU

evening. The restaurant is at the far end of the car park, close to the bus stop. Famed for its seafood, Fernando's has a devout clientele and an almost legendary profile in good-dining circles. No credit cards.

Balichao (☎ 870098) is delightfully situated in Seac Pai Van Park, and serves fine Portuguese food from noon until 11 pm.

From the selection of hotel restaurants on Coloane Island, the *Kwun Hoi* (☎ 871111) at the Westin Resort is worth noting for its sumptuous views and superb Cantonese cuisine. The set lunch served from Monday to Friday is excellent value at M$88.

The restaurant at the *Pousada de Coloane* (☎ 882143), by Cheoc Van beach, has verandah dining and Portuguese food. The M$100 Sunday lunch buffet is great value. Check before you go, as the hotel sometimes offers a free night's accommodation to diners consuming enough food and wine on the premises to satisfy the hotel's accountants.

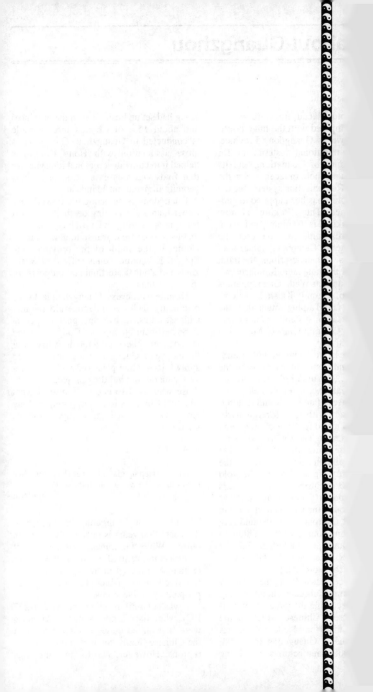

Facts about Guangzhou

Hong Kong and Macau are mere specks on the map compared with the huge political entity known as Guangdong Province. 'Canton' is the traditional western name for both the province of Guangdong and its capital city, Guangzhou. In recent years, the official pinyin Romanisation system (see the Language chapter) has been applied to geographical names. Thus 'Peking' is now 'Beijing', 'Nanking' is 'Nanjing', and so on. However, in this guide we have used the more familiar term 'Cantonese' rather than 'Guangdongnese' when describing the food, the people and the language. Similarly, we have used the familiar Wade-Giles spellings of Sun Yatsen, Chiang Kaishek, Kuomintang (KMT) and Taiping rather than the pinyin Romanisation system – Sun Yixian, Jiang Jieshi, Guomindang (GMD) and Daibing respectively.

The Cantonese are regarded with a mixture of envy and suspicion by many in the rest of China. Guangdong's topography and unique dialect, its remoteness from traditional centres of authority and its longstanding contact with the 'foreign barbarians' created a strong sense of autonomy and self-sufficiency. The Cantonese spearheaded Chinese emigration to the USA, Canada, Australia and South Africa in the mid-19th century, spurred on by the gold rushes in those countries and by the wars and growing poverty in China. Bustling Chinatowns around the world are steeped in the flavours of Cantonese cuisine and ring with the singsong sounds of the Cantonese dialect and Canto-pop melodies. See the boxed text entry 'The Ones That Got Away' in this chapter for more details.

The province basked in the healthy regional economic climate encompassing Hong Kong, becoming the target for investment by Overseas Chinese. Much of the manufacturing that Hong Kong was famous for is now done in Guangdong (by 1993, more than 30,000 manufacturers from Hong Kong had set up businesses in the province) and about 15% of China's foreign trade is conducted in Guangzhou. Guangdong's close association with Hong Kong has helped it to cultivate a regional idiosyncrasy that finds vigorous expression in its burgeoning film and music industries.

Guangdong is an economic powerhouse rather than a sightseeing destination. Most foreigners visiting the province are there on business or are in transit to other parts of China. In the south of the province, the Special Economic Zones (SEZs) of Shenzhen and Zhuhai are financial outposts for the new China.

Despite its success, Guangzhou lacks the originality, facilities and modernity of other Chinese cities, such as Shanghai. It appears to be hell-bent on copying Hong Kong and is in danger of becoming too derivative. For the most part, Guangzhou is a traffic-locked sprawl, its skyline plastered with huge advertisements and building projects. But, for those who want to get a glimpse of what 'the real China' is like as opposed to Hong Kong, Guangzhou is an easily accessible starting point.

HISTORY

China is a sleeping giant. Let her sleep, for when she awakes, she will astonish the world.

Napoleon

The history of Guangdong Province over the past 2000 years is only known to us in outline. While the Chinese were carving out a civilisation centred on the Yellow River (Huang He) region in the north, the south remained a semi-independent tributary peopled by native tribes.

It was not until the Qin dynasty (221-207 BC), when the Chinese states of the north were first united under a single ruler, that the Chinese finally conquered the southern regions. However, revolts and uprisings

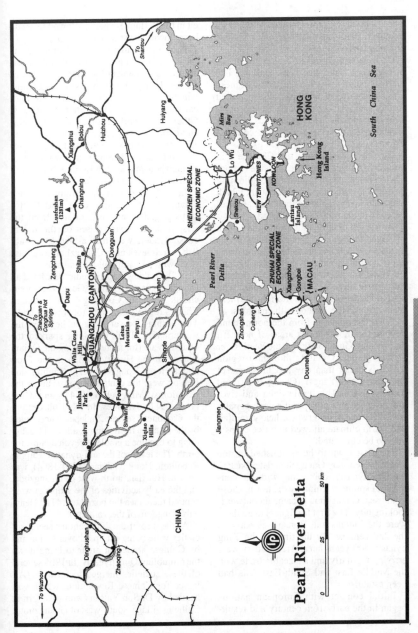

Pearl River Delta

were frequent and the Chinese settlements remained small and dispersed among a predominantly aboriginal population.

Chinese emigration to the region began in earnest around the 12th century. The original native tribes were killed by Chinese armies, isolated in small pockets or pushed further south – like the Li and Miao peoples who now inhabit the mountainous areas of Hainan Island off the southern coast of China.

By the 17th century the Chinese had outgrown Guangdong. The pressure of population forced them to move into adjoining Guangxi Province and into Sichuan, which had been ravaged and depopulated after rebellions in the mid-17th century.

As a result of these migrations, the people of Guangdong are not a homogeneous group. The term Cantonese is sometimes applied to all people living in Guangdong Province, but there are significant minorities, including the Hakka people, who started moving southward from the northern plains around the 13th or 14th centuries.

What the migrants from the north found beyond the mountainous areas of northern and western Guangdong was the Pearl River Delta (Zhujiang), cutting through a region which is richer than any in China, except for around the Yangzi (Chang Jiang) and Yellow rivers. The fertile delta and river valleys were able to support a huge population. The many waterways, heavy rainfall and warm climate allowed two rice crops a year to be cultivated.

The first town to be established on the site of present-day Guangzhou dates back to the Qin dynasty, coinciding with the conquest of southern China by the north. Close to the sea, Guangzhou became an outward-looking city. The first foreigners to go there were the Indians and Romans as early as the 2nd century. By the time of the Tang dynasty 500 years later, Arab traders were arriving regularly and a sizeable trade with the Middle East and South-East Asia had been established.

Initial contact with European nations began in the early 16th century and result-

ed in the Portuguese being allowed to set up base downriver at Macau in 1557.

Next the Jesuits came and aroused the interest of the imperial court with their scientific and technical knowledge. This was mainly through their expertise in astronomy, which permitted the all-important astrological charts to be produced more accurately. Other Jesuits worked as makers of fountains and curios, or as painters and architects. In 1582 the Jesuits were allowed to establish themselves at Zhaoqing, a town west of Guangzhou, and later in Beijing, but overall their influence on China was negligible.

In 1685 the imperial government opened Guangzhou to foreign trade, and British ships began to arrive regularly from the East India Company bases on the Indian coast. Traders were then allowed to establish warehouses near Guangzhou as a base from which to ship out tea and silk.

In 1757 a new imperial edict restricted all foreign trade to a single Guangzhou merchants' guild, the Co Hong – a reflection of China's relative contempt for western trade. The ensuing power struggle between the westerners and the Co Hong sparked the Opium Wars (for more details on the Opium Wars, see the History section in the Facts about Hong Kong chapter). Nanjing and Beijing were the centres of power under the isolationist Ming (1368-1644) and Qing (1644-1911) dynasties. In the 19th century the Cantonese sense of independence, aided by the distance from Beijing, allowed Guangdong to become a cradle of revolt against the north. The leader of the anti-dynastic Taiping Rebellion, Hong Xiuquan (1814-1864), was born in Huaxian, north-west of Guangzhou, and the early activities of the Taipings were centred there (see the boxed text 'The Heavenly Kingdom of the Taiping').

At the turn of the 20th century secret societies were being set up all over China and by Chinese abroad in order to bring down the crumbling Qing dynasty. In 1905 several of these societies merged to form the Alliance for Chinese Revolution, which was headed by Dr Sun Yatsen (who was born in Cuiheng village, south-west of Guangzhou).

GLENN BEANLAND

Setting sail on the Pearl River.

A	B	C
D	E	F
G	H	I

A: Sun Yatsen monument.
B: Children playing on the steps of the Sacred Heart Church.
C: Zhen Hai Tower, Yuexiu Park.
D: Colonial architecture, Shamian Island.
E: Sculpture of the Five Rams.
F: Street scene, Shamian Island.
G: Sacred Heart Church.
H: Locals enjoying Yuexiu Park.
I: Temple of Six Banyan Trees.

The Heavenly Kingdom of the Taiping

The Taiping rebellion in the middle of the 19th century ranks among the most frenzied and calamitous uprisings in Chinese history. What makes it remarkable was its claim: that Hong Xiuquan, the leader of the Taipings, was the brother of Jesus and the son of God and had been sent down to exterminate 'demons', who were personified by the Qing dynasty and its supporters.

Born into a Hakka family in Guangdong, not far from Guangzhou, and having failed the official examinations that would have taken him onto the career ladder among the Qing elite, Hong Xiuquan first came into contact with Christianity through Protestant missionaries in Guangzhou in the mid-1830s. After failing the official examinations for the third time, Hong had a dream of a bearded man and a younger man who he later interpreted, in a flash of realisation after reading some Christian tracts, as being God the Father and Jesus, his son. It is believed that he repeatedly read the character for his surname, 'Hong' (the character means 'flood'), in the Chinese translation of the bible he possessed; and he made strong associations between the biblical flood and his mission on earth to wipe out evil.

Collecting around him a flock of believers attracted by his zeal, self-belief and drive, Hong soon had a formidable army of the faithful who sought to establish the Heavenly Kingdom of Great Peace on earth, and to overthrow the Qing dynasty in the process. God was the one true god and traditional Chinese beliefs (such as Confucianism) were heretical and wayward.

By 1850, Hong Xiuquan's followers were estimated as numbering more than 20,000 and were a capable military force, regimented by a strict morality that forbade opium smoking, took serious measures against corruption, and established separate camps to divide men and women. A communal treasury was set up to take charge of the finances of the Taiping community. Led by daring officers, the Taiping army dispatched itself on a remarkable series of conquests that took it through Hunan, Hubei and Anhui, eventually setting up the Taiping capital in Nanjing, which fell to the rebels in March 1853. The Manchu population of Nanjing was slaughtered in affirmation of Hong's plan to rid China, and the world, of demons.

For 11 years the Taiping held sway over their conquered domain, with Hong ruling over all as the Heavenly King. Hong further regimented the rules governing the Taiping faithful, creating a society ordered by spartan and inflexible decrees all intent on eliminating inequality. However, it is believed that a power struggle emerged among the leadership of the Taiping, and it resulted in the murder of those in positions of great influence. Hong managed to reassert his authority, but in the process he had eliminated his most useful advisers.

The Taiping failed in its northern expedition to take Beijing and Shanghai. Taiping economic strategies similarly failed, and the strict codes of conduct left many bitter and complaining; Hong also failed to align himself and his cause with other simultaneous anti-Qing rebellions – all of this led to an erosion of the power and influence of the Taiping. Qing soldiers, led by Zeng Guofan, eventually retook Nanjing in 1864, soon after Hong Xiuquan's death. Zeng Guofan reported to the emperor that none of the 100,000 rebels in Nanjing surrendered – they all committed suicide.

The fanaticism of the Taiping was incredible, and despite its strongly anti-Manchu character, the event clearly questions the notion that Christianity has no place in China. Even though Hong arrogated upon himself the heretical (to Protestants and Catholics) title of son of God, the Taiping were responsible for, among other things, a vast translation and publishing program of Christian scriptures and writings, and it was their aim to spread these ultimately to the four corners of the earth.

Further Reading: *God's Chinese Son – The Taiping Heavenly Kingdom of Hong Xiuquan* by Jonathan Spence.

GUANGZHOU

In 1911 the Imperial court announced the nationalisation of the railways. The move was viewed by provincial governors and wealthy merchants as an attempt to restrict their autonomy. In Wuhan in central China the army staged a coup, seizing control of the city, and the heads of many other provinces declared their loyalty to the rebels. By the year's end, most of southern China had repudiated Qing rule and given its support to Sun Yatsen's alliance. On 1 January 1912 he was proclaimed president of the Chinese Republic, but it was a republic in name only, since most of the north was controlled by local warlords left over from the Qing era.

In the wake of these events, China underwent an intellectual revolution. Study groups and other political organisations sprang up everywhere and members included Zhou Enlai and Mao Zedong. In 1921 several Chinese Marxist groups banded together to form the Chinese Communist Party (CCP).

By this stage Sun Yatsen had managed to secure a political base in Guangzhou and set up a government made up of surviving members of the Kuomintang (KMT), the party which had emerged as the dominant revolutionary political force after the fall of the Qing dynasty. In shaky alliance with the Communists, the KMT began training a National Revolutionary Army (NRA) under the command of Chiang Kaishek, who had met Sun in Japan some years before. Sun died in

Cultural Revolution

Mao Zedong's extreme political views, his opposition to the bureaucratisation of the Chinese Communist Party (CCP), his role in the economic disaster known as the Great Leap Forward and the disintegration of Sino-Soviet relations placed the leader in an uncomfortable position with the Party. Many Party members thought that he should be put out to pasture, and Mao himself felt that his vision of the continuing Chinese revolution was becoming increasingly unheeded. One man who sought to change all this was Lin Biao, the minister of defence and head of the People's Liberation Army (PLA).

In the early 1960s, Lin had a collection of Mao's sayings compiled into a book that was to become known simply as the *Little Red Book*, though its real title was *Quotations from Chairman Mao*. Using his position, Lin saw to it that the book became the subject of study sessions for all PLA troops. At the same time PLA propaganda writers produced another significant literary effort, *The Diary of Lei Feng*. Lei was a PLA soldier who had devoted his life to Mao, and who died when run over by a truck while trying to save a friend. While it's possible that comrade Lei never existed, the book was introduced into the school system to provide lessons in selfless heroism. Mao, who endorsed the book with his own calligraphy, exhorted the people to learn from the PLA, which was under his and Lin's control, bypassing the authority of the Party.

The Cultural Revolution was sparked by a play, *The Dismissal of Hai Jui*, written by Yao Wenyuan, which was a thinly disguised criticism of Mao. When Beijing papers would not publish Mao's criticism of the play, he turned to the Shanghai newspapers. Jiang Qing, Mao's wife and an erstwhile Shanghai B-grade stage and film actress, held a forum in Shanghai in 1966 to expound her views on the need for a socialist purification of the arts. The stage was set for what is properly known as the Great Proletarian Cultural Revolution.

From this point, events moved swiftly and unpredictably. A multitude of complicated factors turned what started as a purge of the arts into a movement that swept the entire nation into four years of chaos. Divisions within the Party, political intrigues and broad discontent in the general Chinese populace came together in an explosion of pent-up frustration. For his part, Mao was fed up with the bureaucratisation of the Party and the slow pace of change; Lin had ambitions to put his PLA at the vanguard of Chinese cultural policy-making; and throughout China millions of

1925 and by 1927 the KMT was ready to launch its Northern Expedition – a military venture under the command of Chiang designed to subdue the northern warlords.

However, Chiang was also engaged in a power struggle within the KMT. So as the NRA moved on Shanghai (then under the control of a local warlord whose strength had been undermined by a powerful industrial movement organised in the city by the Communists), Chiang took the opportunity to massacre both the Communists and his enemies in the KMT.

By mid-1928 the Northern Expedition had reached Beijing and a national government was established, with Chiang holding the highest political and military positions. The

Communists who survived the massacres made their famous Long March to the Jinggang Mountains, on the Hunan-Jiangxi border, and other mountainous areas of China. From there they began a war against the KMT, which lasted just over 20 years and ended in victory for the Communists in 1949. Mao Zedong became chairman of the CCP and essentially the country's leader until his death in 1976. During his reign, Mao presided over numerous crises, including the Korean War in 1950-53, the economically disastrous Great Leap Forward, a traumatic split with the Soviet Union and the chaotic Cultural Revolution.

The early 70s saw the Chinese dispirited and psychologically scarred by the events

ordinary people had been stifled by the control of the CCP and angered by official corruption and petty power-mongering.

In Beijing, wall posters went up at Beijing University attacking the university administration. Mao officially sanctioned the wall posters and criticisms of party members by university staff and students and, before long, students were being issued red armbands and taking to the streets. The Red Guards *(hongweibing)* had been born. By August 1966 Mao was reviewing mass parades of the Red Guards, chanting and waving copies of his little red book.

Nothing was sacred enough to be spared the brutal onslaught of the Red Guards as they went on a rampage through the country. Universities and secondary schools were shut down; intellectuals, writers and artists were dismissed, killed, persecuted or sent to labour in the countryside; publication of scientific, artistic, literary and cultural periodicals ceased; temples were ransacked and monasteries disbanded; and many physical reminders of China's 'feudal', 'exploitative' or 'capitalist' past, including temples, monuments, and works of art, were destroyed.

Many innocent people were denounced as 'capitalist roaders'. Deng Xiaoping's son, Deng Pufang, was crippled for life when Red Guards threw him out of a 4th floor window. Red Guard factions even

Mao Zedong

battled each other, and the country seemed to be moving towards civil war and financial collapse.

By the end of January 1967 the PLA was ordered to break up all 'counter-revolutionary organisations', an edict that the PLA interpreted as all groups with interests contrary to their own. Thousands of Chinese were killed in the ensuing struggles, notably in Sichuan and in Wuhan, where the PLA took on a coalition of 400,000 Red Guards and workers' groups, killing over a thousand people. The struggles continued into September of 1967. 'Ultra-left tendencies' were condemned and the PLA was championed as the sole agent of 'proletarian dictatorship'.

The PLA gained the upper hand over the Red Guards, but the army launched its own brand of terror that resulted in untold thousands being killed or imprisoned. Events took a new turn when Mao died in 1976. Soon after, members of the Gang of Four, led by Mao's wife, Jiang Qing, were arrested. Jiang remained imprisoned until 1991, when she committed suicide.

GUANGZHOU

of the Cultural Revolution, most of them employed in state enterprises that doled out pay cheques whether workers did anything or not. The Chinese system was one in which politics were in command, the philosophy of which is well summed up in the Cultural Revolution saying: 'a socialist train running late is better than a revisionist train running on time'.

In the middle of 1977 Deng Xiaoping, an accused 'capitalist roader' who had twice been purged for his views, returned to power and was appointed to the positions of vice-premier, vice-chairman of the party and chief of staff of the People's Liberation Army (PLA). Final power now passed to the collective leadership of the six member Standing Committee of the CCP, which included Deng. The China the CCP took over was racked with problems – a backward country in desperate need of modernisation. Deng adopted what became known as 'pragmatic economic policies' – China remains officially socialist while 'temporarily' adopting capitalist economic incentives in order to modernise the country.

In 1978 China embarked on its Four Modernisations (agriculture, industry, national defence, and science and technology) in earnest. The Deng Xiaoping years saw a slow but sure freeing up of the Chinese economy, and by the early 90s it had become the fastest growing economy in the world. But many agree that the Four Modernisations should be expanded to include a fifth, namely democracy. Throughout it's 5000 year history, China has been plagued by the lack of a system for orderly succession. Deng was well aware that the orderly succession of power was essential for the CCP if it was to avoid the fate of communism in the former USSR.

By 1994 Deng had gradually dwindled into a state of physical and political catatonia, crippled by old age and bad health, and rumours claimed that he was being kept alive by the nation's most skilled *qigong* experts (the ancient Chinese therapy for restoring health in the body by regulating *qi*, or energy). Deng died on 19 February 1997, aged 92. For some time he had paved the way for a succession that would preserve his reformist zeal and the integrity of the Party. Jiang Zemin was head of the seven member Standing Committee of the Politburo (which had in effect been running China's affairs), and he was groomed to replace Deng as China's leader. At the 14th Congress of the CCP in October 1992, Jiang Zemin (then General Secretary of the Party) was appointed State President.

After Deng's death Jiang Zemin quickly consolidated his position amid considerable consternation from the west as to his plans for the country. However, China appears to be too far down the road of economic reform to have the time for reactionary opinion. Jiang Zemin's authority has since been strengthened and his position has apparently been confirmed. Jiang Zemin attempted this on one front by seeking to align the CCP with patriotic themes.

Since the mid-1990's there has been a more pronounced nationalist aspect to Party propaganda and China's internal and foreign

Deng Xiaoping

affairs. And the highly unpopular former Prime Minister Li Peng (who is universally blamed by the people of China for deciding to send the troops into Tiananmen Square for an 'incident' with the students in 1989) was elbowed out of the picture in 1998 to make way for the much admired former economics minister Zhu Rongji. Zhu Rongji has the unenviable task of decommissioning state-controlled firms, which has the potential to put tens of thousands of people out of work. It is this issue, more than any other in contemporary China, that threatens to pull the delicate fabric of society apart.

And there are other tensions in Chinese society. In 1996 the Party instigated its infamous Strike Hard campaign to take a tough line on the accelerating spiral of crime afflicting China (the country is so vast and so badly policed that the most appalling crimes go unpunished): the execution of numerous high profile criminals was a strategy designed to strike terror into the hearts and minds of China's criminal establishment. Many are concerned that the justice system in China fails to provide adequate representation for the accused; judgements are rapidly reached, and death sentences dished out like parking tickets.

Further social unrest (and terrorism) came to China in 1997 with riots by native Uighurs in the north-eastern Xinjiang Province, and subsequent bombings on buses in Beijing and Wuhan by Muslim terrorists left many dead. China-ccupied Tibet is another powder keg.

GEOGRAPHY

Guangdong Province lies on the south-east coast of China and occupies just 1.8% of China's total land area. The dominant feature is the Pearl River Delta, a fertile plain which supports a huge population and provides a natural harbour. The river forms a natural transport system and is the chief reason for Guangzhou's existence as an economic hub. Guangzhou, the capital of Guangdong Province, is the sixth largest city in China. Not surprisingly, the Cantonese have a much closer affection for Hong Kong than Beijing – Guangzhou is a mere 120km north-west of Hong Kong but 2300km from the national capital.

Guangzhou was originally three cities. The inner city was enclosed by sturdy walls and was divided into the new and old cities. The outer city was everything outside these walls. The building of the walls began during the 11th century and was completed in the 16th century. The walls were 15km in circumference, 8m high and between 5m and 8m thick. Not surprisingly, the walls have since come down to make way for roads, apartment blocks and fast-food barns.

Foreigners tend to gravitate towards two main parts of town: Shamian Island in the west, which attracts tourists and business travellers; and the Greenery in the east, a complex of expensive expat apartments which has, among other things, the American School and a computer shopping arcade.

CLIMATE

Most of Guangdong Province has a subtropical climate, but temperatures tend to be more variable further inland. Winter tends to be dreary – chilly, damp and overcast, but temperatures are not extreme.

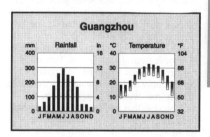

ECOLOGY & ENVIRONMENT

If you think Hong Kong could do with a little more green space, wait until you see Guangzhou and its environs. Massive economic development (18% growth rate between 1981 and 1994) has come at a price. There has been little planning or prediction as to the possible consequence for the environment.

Most of what's left of Guangdong's flora and fauna is found to the north of Guangzhou. From Guangzhou southwards to Hong Kong and Macau, what was farmland 20 years ago is now a hellscape of roads, dockyards, factories, chimneys and workers' apartments. The environment is particularly blighted along waterways, which means most of the Pearl River Delta.

By 1995, acid rain accounted for 50% to 90% of the delta's precipitation, which finally prompted the authorities to put a ban on new thermal power plants. The amount of chemical and human sewage that floods out of Shenzhen is threatening to turn Deep Bay in the north-east of Hong Kong into an environmental tragedy.

At least the wake-up call has come and someone is paying attention. The Guangdong authorities are planning to spend US$7 billion between 1996 and 2001 on environmental protection. But many say it is too little, too late. Hong Kong, which is tiny by comparison and hardly a shining example of ecological saintliness, spent US$1 billion on environmental protection in 1996.

There is also a move to reinstate the position of agriculture within the province. The Pearl River Delta's output of rice has fallen by 24% since 1981, and the plan is to remove Guangdong's current reliance on imports to satisfy its needs. There has been an exodus of people from the traditional farmlands to the city factories, where pay is a pittance but considerably more than what they were able to earn from working in agriculture.

A process that will have to be reversed is the conversion of arable land to make way for mass construction.

GOVERNMENT & POLITICS

Every revolution evaporates, leaving behind only the government slime of a new bureaucracy.
Franz Kafka

Precious little is known about the inner workings of the Chinese government, but westerners can make some educated guesses as to what goes on.

The highest authority rests with the Standing Committee of the Communist Party Politburo. Below it is the 210 member Central Committee, made up of younger Party members and provincial Party leaders. At the grass-roots level, considerable authority is exercised by Party representatives at every level in the PLA, universities, local government and industries. They, in turn, are responsible to the Party officials in the hierarchy above them, thus ensuring strict central control. Although elections are held for the lowest level positions in the party, democracy in the western sense does not exist.

Throughout the system, there are various antagonistic factions. Governing the country seems to involve a delicate balance between these rivals; as a result, government is often unable to make any significant policy decisions at any level.

Things are somewhat different in Guangdong Province. While paying lip service to the official line taken by the socialist leadership in Beijing, Guangdong officials from the governor down have continued to push their own programmes of economic liberalisation. Although political liberalisation is not possible at present, officials have a relaxed attitude and are much more interested in making money than in controlling people's lives. Guangdong's quest for autonomy was given a setback in March 1998 by the appointment of Li Changchun as Party secretary for Guangdong. It is the first time in more than a decade that a non-Cantonese has been given the top job. The indication is that Beijing wants to keep a closer eye on Guangdong, which has so far enjoyed a significant degree of freedom.

The basic unit of government organisation is the work unit, or *danwei*. Every Chinese is a member of one. Nothing can proceed without the work unit's say-so. The danwei decides if a couple can marry or divorce, and when they can have a child. The danwei also assigns housing, sets salaries, handles mail, recruits Party members, keeps files on each unit member, arranges transfers to other jobs or other parts of the country, and gives permission to travel abroad. Work unit members are also compelled to attend propaganda meetings that the government calls 'political education'.

ECONOMY

China's economic policies have undergone a radical change since the death of Mao Zedong. Under Mao, China had largely isolated itself from other nations, apprehensive that economic links would create a dependency on other states.

This has all changed. Foreign investment, most of it funnelled into China via Hong Kong, has transformed the country. Not surprisingly, Guangdong has benefited more than any other province, and Guangzhou has become one of China's biggest boom towns.

While capitalist-style reforms have undeniably boosted growth to record levels in China, the country still claims to be a socialist state. This is at least partly true – the economy is littered with state-run enterprises that do nothing but lose money and soak up subsidies. When China's leaders recently endorsed a wide-ranging plan to sell off huge chunks of the state enterprise apparatus, Guangdong didn't need much encouragement to get on with it. The province is a past master at the game – since 1993, about a thousand state enterprises have been sold in the province. The big sell-off, although an essential feature of economic reform in China, is likely to have far-reaching effects on the Chinese population. Victims of the auction-house environment will add to the already huge armies of the unemployed. Riots over pay and appalling work conditions are becoming an increasingly popular way of expressing worker grievances.

The economy of Guangdong continues to expand, although at a slower rate than following Deng Xiaoping's southern tour to the province in 1992, when he called on Guangdong to match the great industrialised economies of East Asia and to set an example to the rest of China. Foreign investment in Guangdong is down as firms look to cities such as Shanghai, which offer better facilities, industrial estates, communications and transport options. Other areas of China are beginning to make better business sense to foreign investors, and this is at least partly due to the fact that the rest of the country is making inroads into the successes that were previously the monopoly of Guangdong. In 1991 Guangdong Province was the recipient of 42% of all foreign investment in China, but this was down to 27% by 1995.

Even so, Guangdong's figures are still at the top. Responsible for 39% of total exports from China and 26% of foreign investment in 1996, the province is still in good shape. Guangdong is still at the top of the provincial league tables, but its overall rate of growth has slowed. Economic forecasts predict that more investment will move away from Guangdong to other regions of China.

Local government planners are trying to reverse this trend by pouring vast amounts of money into colossal infrastructure projects that will tighten the link between Guangdong and Hong Kong and the rest of China. A 40km bridge across the Pearl River Delta is in the offing; it will connect the area to major roads in south-western China. A bridge joining Shenzhen and Hong Kong is under construction and more expressways for the province are planned.

The return of Hong Kong to China cannot be overemphasised, and the presence of the ex-colony on the coast of Guangdong will have an enormous economic and political effect on the province. The transferral of sovereignty to China has increased the country's population by 0.5% and its GDP has increased by almost 25%. Although politically Guangdong and Hong Kong are separate entities, they are now closer than any other time in the last 150 years. Hong Kong comes back to China equipped with a first rate economy, huge foreign investment, a sophisticated financial sector and all the know-how of a successful capitalist entity.

POPULATION & PEOPLE

China's population is more than 1.2 billion,

The Ones That Got Away

One product that China has always exported in abundance is the refugee. This should come as no surprise, since the nation's history includes long episodes of poverty, dictatorship, war, famine and revolution.

Of the millions who have fled the turbulence in China most have gone to neighbouring countries in South-East Asia. Ethnic Chinese communities have long been established in places like Thailand, the Philippines, Vietnam, Indonesia and Malaysia. In Singapore, ethnic Chinese make up 80% of the population.

Hong Kong and nearby Macau have also largely been populated by refugees fleeing first the chaos of China's 1945 revolution, and later the Cultural Revolution. Large numbers of ethnic Chinese have migrated to the west, establishing various 'Chinatowns' in such places as New York, San Francisco, London and Melbourne.

This outflow of people has not always been welcomed by the Chinese government. In 1718 the Manchu emperor attempted to halt Chinese emigration with an imperial edict recalling all subjects who were in foreign lands. Finding this ineffectual, in 1728 the court issued another proclamation declaring that anyone who did not return to China would be banished forever and those captured would be executed. Chinese emigration was only made legal by the Convention of Peking that ended the fourth Opium War in 1860.

Members of China's Diaspora usually refer to themselves collectively as 'Overseas Chinese'. In his book *Lords of the Rim*, author Sterling Seagrave estimates the number of Overseas Chinese at 55 million. This figure included the 6.5 million Chinese in Hong Kong. The figure also includes the 21 million residents of Taiwan over whom China claims sovereignty (the Taiwanese view their status rather differently).

Overseas Chinese represent less than 5% of the Chinese on the planet, yet they claim more wealth than the remaining 95% who live in China. Ethnic Chinese minorities have provided much of the capital, know-how and hard work that have turned many South-East Asian countries into

and with a national growth rate of 1.2% annually, it is expected to hit 1.3 billion by the year 2000.

According to the last official census, Guangdong Province's population is about 63 million. More than 98% of the inhabitants are Han Chinese; the rest belong to small minority groups, such as the Miao and Li.

The assimilation of southern China was a slow process, reflected in the fact that the southerners referred to themselves as men of Tang (of the Tang dynasty, 618-907), while the northerners referred to themselves as men of Han (of the Han dynasty, 206 BC to 220 AD).

The northerners regarded their southern compatriots with disdain, or as one 19th century northern account put it:

The Cantonese ... are a coarse set of people ... Before the times of Han and Tang, this country was quite wild and waste, and these people have sprung forth from unconnected, unsettled vagabonds that wandered here from the north.

Despite the nasty rhetoric, the Cantonese are widely admired for their entrepreneurial skills. Of all the Chinese ethnic groups, the Cantonese have probably been the most influenced by foreign cultures and products.

Almost everyone in southern Guangdong has relatives in Hong Kong who for years have been storming across the border loaded down with the latest fashions, and gifts of electronic appliances, music tapes (legal), smuggled video tapes (illegal) and even motorcycles.

economic tigers. Without a doubt, these people have proven to be an economic asset almost wherever they go.

Unfortunately, being economically successful does not necessarily make them popular. Various leaders in South-East Asia and elsewhere have railed against the Overseas Chinese as 'parasites, exploiters, oppressors' and countless other unprintable terms. One king of Thailand referred to the Chinese as 'the Jews of the Orient' – and just like the Jews, the Chinese have occasionally been murdered en masse. In Indonesia in 1965, thousands of Overseas Chinese were slaughtered in what started out as a purge of Communists, but soon developed into a bloody free-for-all. In 1978, Vietnam seized the property of most of the country's Overseas Chinese – hundreds of thousands fled on rickety boats providing the world with a new term, 'boat people'. While mass slaughter and seizure of property is not currently fashionable, discrimination certainly still exists. In modern-day Brunei, Overseas Chinese are not permitted to obtain citizenship – essentially, they're stateless persons.

The vast majority of Overseas Chinese are from distinct Chinese linguistic groups, most of which are near the Chinese coast. This includes the Cantonese (the majority of Hong Kong residents), the Fujianese (sometimes called the Hokkien) and the Chaozhou (formerly spelt Teochew). There are also many Hakka, who originate from Henan Province in northern China. The Hakka first moved to the Guangdong and Fujian provinces in the south to escape severe persecution in their homelands. The Hakka are proud to point out that their group has managed to produce three national leaders all at once: China's Deng Xiaoping, Taiwan's Lee Tenghui and Singapore's Lee Kuan Yew.

One of the great ironies is that – having been driven from China by the country's tumultuous politics – Overseas Chinese have been supplying most of the capital and technical expertise that is driving China's economic boom. A startling 80% of the foreign investment in China comes from Overseas Chinese (that is, if you include Hong Kong and Taiwan). China has long recognised the value of Overseas Chinese investment, and has assiduously courted its exiles to be patriotic and invest in the motherland.

EDUCATION
According to official figures 81.5% of China's population is literate.

ARTS
Politics invades every aspect of life in China, and much of what Hong Kong residents see in the movies or even in museums is considered inappropriate for China's masses.

The art scene in China is slowly being liberalised, but it is still choked by conformity and haunted by the spectre of central control.

The new Guangzhou Art Museum is a step in the right direction – housed in an impressive building, it is currently the largest museum of art in the People's Republic of China.

Music & Dance
Taiwanese and Hong Kong bands are the most popular music played in Guangzhou. The Cantonese of Guangdong Province generally like the same music as their compatriots across the border in Hong Kong, which means that the early hours of the morning reverberate with the endless strains of karaoke. Songs are either about unrequited love, requited love or fierce loyalty to the motherland. Irony generally does not exist in Chinese song writing.

Attempts to tailor Chinese classical music, song and dance to more western tastes have resulted in a Frankenstein's monster of Broadway-style spectaculars and epic film scores. One Chinese rock star, Cui Jian, released a big hit called 'Rock for the New Long March'. And in an attempt to show that China's ageing leaders are also hip, government officials authorised a disco version of 'The East is Red'.

Occasionally groups of China's disaffected youth coalesce into bands that take inspiration from the tragic acts such as Nirvana and Manic Street Preachers. This sort of music acts as a template upon which the band members can hammer out all the angst of their generation; a youth subculture is developing in China that is fighting its own war against conformity and the demands of very conservative Chinese traditions.

On another note, Chinese opera and traditional music still has an enthusiastic fan base, although generally the audience belongs to the older generation. In Guangzhou Chinese opera is performed at the Friendship Theatre (☎ 8666-2743), 696 Renmin Beilu. The Friendship Theatre is also the venue for classical music performances. Another spot that hosts musical performances is the Huang Hua Gang Theatre (☎ 8776-5491), 96 Xianlie Zhonglu.

SOCIETY & CONDUCT
Traditional Culture
Traditional culture has taken a beating in China since the Communists came to power in 1949. Much of what was traditional Chinese culture was supplanted by politics in a series of campaigns and sometimes bloody purges. Indeed, the whole point of the Cultural Revolution of the 1960s was to erase traditional Chinese culture and start out with a clean slate (for more details, see the boxed text 'Cultural Revolution' in the History section earlier in this chapter).

Nonetheless, traditional Chinese culture is staging a comeback, thanks mainly to the influence of Hong Kong, Taiwan and overseas Chinese communities. This revival comes in many forms – religion, architecture, classic books (which were once banned), music, re-establishing festivals and resurrecting nearly forgotten practices such as qigong. Full-form Chinese characters are making a reappearance in mainland China, despite being banned in part and replaced by a simplified

form (only a few thousand characters were ever simplified, while the majority are still full-form). As traditional characters are more complicated and attractive, they are used a lot in advertising and by those who wish to project the impression of being learned and refined.

The government has even dusted off Confucianism, long disdained by the Communists as a feudalistic practice. This may have much to do with politics, however, as Confucius emphasised the importance of obedience to the established powers.

Dos & Don'ts
After Hong Kong, which resembles one big fashion show, you may actually find Guangzhou to be a relief. Most people in China dress casually, partly because of poverty and partly because Communist ideology glorifies peasants and workers. Foreigners can get away with wearing almost anything as long as it isn't overly revealing.

In summer, shorts are OK for men and women and many Chinese men walk around outdoors bare-chested. However, shy western men with a lot of body hair should not try this, as displaying a hairy chest in public will attract a large crowd of enthusiastic onlookers. Men with hairy chests should wear a T-shirt when swimming. Children may actually pull your body hair to test if it's real!

The novelty of seeing foreigners has pretty much worn off in today's China, especially in the large cities. But you still bump into the odd posse of bumpkins from the countryside who go slack-jaw at the sight of a foreigner. If this happens, just take it in your stride and try not to overreact. The staring only intensifies if you make wild movements or if you stare back – if you don't do anything, the person staring at you will reach the dull conclusion that you are human after all and will look away.

RELIGION
The situation is similar to that in Hong Kong and Macau (for more details see the Religion section of the Facts about Hong Kong

The Dying Rooms

It has long been the case in China that parents prefer boys over girls. Boys are cherished largely because young men have a moral duty in Chinese society to support their elderly parents. By contrast, a woman joins her husband's family when she gets married, and her moral duty is to support her in-laws when they get old. For many Chinese parents, a baby girl represents a financial liability. All this is nothing new – for centuries, the only way for Chinese parents to recoup their investment in raising a girl was to sell her (either to a brothel or as a wife to an older man). Very poor Chinese parents have sometimes solved the 'problem' by murdering their newborn female babies.

Since China adopted a one child family policy in 1979, the situation has worsened. All estimates are crude guesses, but a number of sources have suggested that about 15 million female babies have 'disappeared' since 1979. The figure is based on the (skewed) official birth statistics which show many more male births than female. While many girls are aborted before birth, there is some disturbing evidence to indicate that older girls are 'aborted', at several months or years of age.

Even China's supporters were shocked by a documentary called *The Dying Rooms*, which was released in early 1996. Using a hidden video camera, a documentary team funded by the UK's Channel Four posed as members of an American charity group and managed to film the inside of four Chinese orphanages. Unlike the showcase orphanages shown to foreigners wishing to adopt Chinese children, the four orphanages in the documentary looked more like concentration camps.

The children in the video were tied up with ropes and were clearly starving to death. The video also revealed that all the children, with the exception of a few handicapped boys, were girls. Informal interviews with the caretakers at the orphanage, secretly filmed, indicated that most of the children were abandoned by their parents. The staff implied that they fully expected all these children to die, not from disease but from sheer neglect and starvation.

Kate Blewett, who led the documentary team, took care not to attack the one child family policy, which for all its flaws may be the only way for China to tackle its severe overpopulation problem. 'We don't want to criticise the one child policy, but we do want to focus on the problems it is causing which can be solved', said Blewett.

The documentary also featured a tour of a privately funded orphanage where the children were well treated. 'We were very keen to show what could be done with the right attitude', Blewett added.

Before the documentary was shown, the Chinese government was asked to give a response to the allegations of neglect and death in the orphanages. The government's shrill response became the final sequence to the documentary when it was publicly shown: 'The so-called dying rooms do not exist in China at all. Our investigations confirm that those reports are vicious fabrications made out of ulterior motives. The contemptible lie about China's welfare work in orphanages cannot but arouse the indignation of the Chinese people, especially the great numbers of social workers who are working hard for children's welfare'.

The Chinese government later rolled out stage-managed happy smiling couples showing off their well-cared-for 'adopted' children.

Whether or not the Chinese government knowingly starves unwanted children to death can be debated, but the government did little to help its image when the Philip Hayden Charitable Foundation came to China's aid a few weeks later. Perhaps naively, the foundation thought the problem might simply be a lack of cash, and decided to launch a fundraising dinner for the orphans at a luxury hotel in Beijing. Lots of important people were invited to the fundraiser, including the US ambassador to China, Jim Sasser, American-Chinese author Amy Tan, prominent American business people and about half the American Chamber of Commerce in Beijing. All up, about 450 people bought tickets at US$720 apiece, raising more than US$30,000. But before Tan could deliver the opening speech, the Beijing police showed up and declared the fundraiser an illegal gathering. The guests were ordered to leave.

chapter), the basic difference being that all forms of religion were harshly suppressed during the Cultural Revolution. Priests, nuns and monks were imprisoned, executed or sent to labour in the countryside while temples and churches were ransacked and converted into factories and warehouses. Since the early 1980s, temples have been restored, at least for the sake of tourism. There has been a religious revival, but a main feature of temples in China is that they are usually devoid of worshippers. Chinese Communist Party members are not permitted to belong to any religious organisation.

Catholics have a particularly hard time – loyalty to the Pope is regarded as treason and priests are still rotting in prison for refusing to denounce the Holy See. The government has set up a Catholic church which does not recognise the Vatican.

Facts for the Visitor

HIGHLIGHTS

Guangzhou is an interesting city and a worthwhile place to visit, but it would be dishonest to describe it as beautiful. The main attraction is the feeling of being in China – the street markets, temples, food, chaos, surprising prosperity amid crushing poverty etc. The same could be said for most of the area around Guangzhou, known as the Pearl River Delta.

On the other hand, there are some major attractions in and around Guangzhou. Within the city itself are a few charming diversions like Shamian Island, Yuexiu Park and the Pearl River Cruise. The new Guangdong Art Museum is a stunning addition to the cultural landscape and the Qingping Market is morbidly fascinating, but not recommended for animal lovers. The Southern Yue Tomb Museum and Chen Clan Academy get good reviews from travellers.

Scenic beauty can also be found outside the city. Highlights include: Zhaoqing and Dinghushan to the west, Xiqiao Hills to the south-west, Lotus Mountain to the southeast and the White Cloud Hills just north of the city.

Previously the exclusive province of missionaries fired with Christian zeal, Guangzhou is attracting more and more expats. This has created a community that is serviced by an increasing number of bars, restaurants and nightspots.

PLANNING

When to Go

Since the weather is tolerable almost any time of year, your main consideration will be avoiding the crowds. One rule to remember is to avoid travelling on weekends and (even more so) at public holiday times, such as Easter and Chinese Lunar New Year. At these times everything is booked out as herds of Hong Kong residents stampede across the border, leaving trampled foreign tourists in their wake. Accommodation in

Guangzhou is also difficult to find during the Guangzhou Fair, held twice a year in April and October. For more detail about public holidays, see the Public Holidays & Special Events section in this chapter.

What Kind of Trip?

Apart from the language barrier, there's nothing to stop you from tackling Guangzhou single-handed. The places covered in this section are not far apart and are easily accessible by public transport. If you would prefer to go on a tour, a good place to start would be to contact either China International Travel Service (CITS) or China Travel Service (CTS) for information on trips organised to Guangdong. See the Tourist Office section in this chapter for contact details.

Maps

Finding maps of Guangzhou and other Chinese cities is easy enough – if you can read Chinese characters. To find one in English, look in the gift shops of the major hotels. Recommended are the maps of *Guangzhou* and *Shenzhen* by Universal Publications of Hong Kong, which show both Chinese and English place names. You can't buy these maps in mainland China, but they are available at most Hong Kong bookshops for around HK$18.

What to Bring

While you can now buy almost everything you need in China, certain things are difficult to find. This is doubly true if you can't speak Chinese. To preserve your sanity, bring some reading material. Due to censorship, good books in English are scarce in China. And don't expect to find a convenience store on every Guangzhou corner as you do in Hong Kong.

Your biggest problem will be finding pharmaceutical items. Expats living in Guangzhou were much relieved when the first

Watson's chemist (the Hong Kong chain stores) opened in the city. Unfortunately, there are many everyday pharmaceuticals which you may suddenly need when no Watson's is in sight.

With this in mind, bring enough of your everyday pharmaceutical needs to last your entire trip in Guangzhou and beyond. For more information, see the What to Bring section in the Hong Kong Facts for the Visitor chapter.

TOURIST OFFICES
Local Tourist Offices
Tragically, mainland China doesn't have any equivalent to the Hong Kong Tourist Association or the Macau Government Tourist Office. What the mainland does have are mammoth government-owned travel agencies with branch offices all over the country and abroad. In recent years there has been a proliferation of government-owned travel agencies, but the biggies have always been CITS and CTS. The levels of service are for the most part prehistoric, and dealing with these agencies can be a frustrating experience.

There is a hulking CITS office (☎ 8666-6271, fax 8667-8048) at 179 Huanshi Lu, next to Guangzhou train station. It has little information for travellers, generally serving as a ticketing office for train, plane and boat travel, but even this function is being made increasingly redundant by all the hotel booking services and private operations in town. The staff have even been known to ask for a tip before handing over information.

CTS (☎ 8333-6888, fax 8333-2247) is at 10 Qiaoguang Lu, Haizhu Square (next to the Hotel Landmark Canton).

Probably more helpful are the host of small expat travel agents that have set up to occupy the massive market niche left by the user-hostile Chinese agents. At the time of writing there were a few that could enlighten you about Guangzhou or book you into a travel program to surrounding areas. China Merchants International Travel Co (☎ 8354-2827, fax 8354-4099) advertises that its staff speak English, French,

German, Japanese and Korean, and seem pretty upbeat. Another company on the 'put CITS out of business' bandwagon is Xpat Travel Planners (☎ 8350-7967). Flick through the pages of the freebie expat magazine *Clueless in Guangzhou* (available at branches of DHL, expat pubs, clubs, restaurants and dives scattered about town) for ads from this entrepreneurial group.

Tourist Offices Abroad
CITS and CTS in Hong Kong and abroad are under separate management, and are therefore more efficient than the Guangzhou-based tourist offices. It's worth getting in touch before you set out to China, as these offices can mail you brochures and answer any queries you may have (in English).

CITS Outside China, CITS is usually known as China National Tourist Office (CNTO). CITS in Hong Kong and CNTO offices overseas are located as follows:

Australia
   (☎ (02) 9290 4057, fax 9290 1958) 19th floor, 44 Market St, Sydney NSW 2000
France
   (☎ (01) 42 96 95 48, fax 42 61 54 68) 116 Avenue des Champs-Elysées, 75008, Paris
Germany
   (☎ (069) 528-465, fax 528-490) 6 Ilkenhans Strasse, 6000, Frankfurt M 50
Hong Kong
   Main Office (☎ 2725-5888), 12th floor, Tower A, New Mandarin Plaza, 14 Science Museum Rd, Tsim Sha Tsui East; Central Branch (☎ 2810-4282, fax 2868-1657), 18th floor, Wing On House, 71 Des Voeux Rd, Central
Israel
   (☎ (03) 522-6272, fax 522-6281) 19 Frishman St, PO Box 3281, Tel-Aviv 61030
Japan
   (☎ (03) 3433-1461, fax 3433-8653) 6th floor, Hamamatsu Cho building, 1-27-13 Hamamatsu-Cho, Minato-Ku, Tokyo
Singapore
   (☎ 221-8681, fax 221-9267) No 17-05 Robina House, 1 Shenton Way, Singapore 0106
UK
   (☎ (0171) 935-9427, fax 487-5842) 4 Glenworth St, London NW1

USA
  Los Angeles Branch (☎ (818) 545-7504, fax 545-7506), suite 201, 333 West Broadway, Glendale, CA 91204; New York Branch (☎ (212) 760-9700, fax 760-8809), suite 6413, 350 Fifth Ave, New York, NY 10118

CTS Overseas representatives include the following:

Australia
  (☎ (02) 9211 2633, fax 9281 3595) ground floor, 757-759 George St, Sydney, NSW 2000
Canada
  (☎ (1604) 872-8787, fax 045-4219) 556 West Broadway, Vancouver, BC V5Z 1E9; (☎ (1416) 979-8993, fax 979-8220) suite 306, 438 University Ave, Toronto, Ontario M5G 2K8
France
  (☎ (01) 44 51 55 66, fax 44 51 55 60) 32 Rue Vignon, 75009, Paris
Germany
  (☎ (30) 393-4068, 391-8085) 5 Beusselstrabe, D-10553, Berlin; (☎ (69) 2385-2228, fax 232-324) 14 Düsseldorfer Strasse, 6000, Frankfurt M1
Hong Kong
  Head Office (☎ 2853-3533, fax 2541-9777), 4th floor, CTS House, 78-83 Connaught Rd, Central; Central Branch (☎ 2525-2284, fax 2868-4970), 2nd floor, China Travel building, 77 Queen's Rd, Central; Kowloon Branch (☎ 2315-7188, fax 2721-7757), 1st floor, Alpha House, 27-33 Nathan Rd, Tsim Sha Tsui
Indonesia
  (☎ (21) 629-4452, fax 629-4836) PT Cempaka Travelindo, 97 Jalan Hayam Wuruk, Jakarta-Barat
Japan
  (☎ (03) 3273-5512, fax 3273-2667) 103 Buyoo building, 3-8-16, Nihombashi, Chuo-Ku, Tokyo
Korea (South)
  (☎ (822) 566-9361, fax 557-0021) 8th floor, Jung Oh building, 163-4 Samsung-Dong, Kangnam-Ku, Seoul
Macau
  (☎ 705506, fax 706611) Xinhua building, Rua de Nagasaki
Malaysia
  (☎ (03) 201-8888, fax 201-3268) ground floor, 112-114 Jalan Pudu, 55100, Kuala Lumpur

Philippines
  (☎ (02) 733-1396, fax 733-1431) 801-803 Gandara St (corner Espeleta St), Santa Cruz, Manila
Singapore
  (☎ 532-9988, fax 535-4912) 1 Park Rd, No 03-49 to 52, People's Park Complex, Singapore, 059108
Thailand
  (☎ (02) 226-0041, fax 226-4712) 559 Yaowaraj Rd, Sampuntawong, Bangkok 10100
UK
  (☎ (0171) 836-9911, fax 836-3121) CTS House, 7 Upper St Martins Lane, London WC2H 9DL
USA
  (☎ (1415) 398-6627, fax 398-6669) 575 Sutter St, San Francisco, California 94102

VISAS & DOCUMENTS
Visas
The visa requirements for visiting mainland China are totally different from Hong Kong and Macau (even if they are officially part of China): virtually all foreigners need a visa to visit China.

Visa charges depend on the country you hail from. American passport holders will generally be charged the most. You'll normally be issued a one month single-entry visa for HK$90 (the prices are listed in Hong Kong dollars as many travellers apply for their visas in Hong Kong). The visa is only good for one month from the date of entry you specify on your application. It is possible to get three month visas, but only if you apply through a travel agent.

You can also obtain a dual-entry visa for HK$180, a three month multiple-entry visa for HK$500 or a six month multiple-entry visa for HK$700. The multiple-entry visa is in fact a business visa which permits you to stay for 30 days at a time but cannot be extended inside China. You can get a multiple-entry visa even if you don't have a work permit. You can obtain a six month multiple-entry visa if you can provide a business card with your name and a business address in China on it.

It normally takes two days to process a visa application, but if you're in a hurry, you

GUANGZHOU

can obtain an express visa in one day for an extra charge.

Heaps of travel agencies and even some guesthouses can get visas for you. This saves you the hassle of queuing, but you'll pay an extra service charge. CTS charges a massive whack for running around with your passport, while other agents are much cheaper. Time Travel Service Limited (☎ 2366-6222, fax 2739-5413), 16th floor, A block, Chungking Mansions, Tsim Sha Tsui, is far cheaper and can get you set up with a visa by 6 pm if you deliver your passport to its office by 11 am.

If you don't mind queuing, the cheapest visas can be obtained from the Visa Office of the Ministry of Foreign Affairs of the People's Republic of China (☎ 2893-9812), 5th floor, low block, China Resources building, 26 Harbour Rd, Wan Chai, Hong Kong Island. It's open Monday to Friday from 9 am to 12.30 pm and 2 to 5 pm; Saturday until 12.30 pm.

Visas can also be obtained at the China border crossing at Lo Wu; however, this costs a whopping HK$360 for a single-entry visa, and you might not even get the usual 30 day stay.

Visa applications require one photo. You're advised to have one entire blank page in your passport. You'll have to part with your passport while your visa application is processed, so be sure you have enough money, especially if you need the passport to cash travellers cheques.

Visa Extensions Visa extensions are handled by the Foreign Affairs Section of the local PSB (the police force); extensions cost US$3 for most nationalities, but some pay US$6 and others get it free. The general rule is that you can get one extension of one month's duration. At an agreeable PSB you may be able to wangle more time, especially with cogent reasons like illness (except HIV/AIDS), transport delays or a pack of Marlboros, but second extensions are usually only granted for one week with the understanding that you are on your way out of China.

Re-Entry Visas Most foreign residents of China have multiple-entry visas and don't need a re-entry visa. However, there might be other requirements (tax clearance, vaccinations etc) – if in doubt, check with the PSB before departing.

Driving Licence & Permits
Visitors to China are not allowed to drive, so there is no need to bring an International Driving Permit. However, foreign residents can obtain a Chinese driving permit. To obtain this, you need your original driver's licence from your home country. This can be exchanged for a Chinese driver's licence. When you leave China, you get your original driver's licence back.

Other Documents
Given the Chinese preoccupation with official bits of paper, it's worth carrying around a few business cards, student cards, and anything else that's printed and laminated in plastic.

If you are in China on business, it's a good idea to get some business cards printed with your name and your job title in Chinese. The Chinese love to hand these around to everyone, so you might as well join in (bring large quantities). Hong Kong is a good place to get business cards made.

Chinese bicycle-renters often expect a deposit or other security for the bikes. Sometimes you may be asked to leave your passport, but you should insist on leaving some other piece of ID or a deposit instead. It's most useful if you have an old expired passport for this purpose. Some hotels also require you to hand over your passport as security, even if you've paid in advance – again, an old passport is handy.

Foreigners who live, work or study in China will be issued with a number of documents. The most important of these documents is the so-called 'green card', or residence permit. Foreigners living in China say that if you lose your green card, you might want to leave the country rather than face the music. Resembling a small passport, the card is issued for one year and must be renewed annually. When you leave China at the end of your stay, your card is taken from you.

If you are a student studying in China, you will be issued with a foreign student's card, which lends you a certain amount of kudos with the local Chinese. Sometimes you can use it to get into the ultra-cheap hotels that are usually out of bounds to foreigners. It used to be possible to get Chinese-price rail tickets with the card, but now that there is no discrepancy between the foreigners' and the Chinese price, this advantage has disappeared.

Photocopies

Married couples should have a copy of their marriage certificate with them. This is especially true if the wife is ethnic Chinese or looks like she could be – the authorities are hyper-sensitive about foreign males 'insulting' Chinese women.

A photocopy of the pages of your passport (eg the page with your photo and passport number, and the page with your China visa) could be useful in the event that you lose your passport or it is stolen. It makes it so much easier when you tell your consulate the bad news.

EMBASSIES & CONSULATES
Chinese Embassies & Consulates

Australia
   (☎ (02) 6273 4780, 6273 4781) 15 Coronation Drive, Yarralumla, ACT, 2600
Canada
   (☎ (613) 234-2706, 234-2682) 515 St Patrick St, Ottawa, Ontario, KIN 5H3
Denmark
   (☎ 31 61 10 13) 12 Oregaards alle, DK 2900 Hellerup, Copenhagen 2900
France
   (☎ (01) 47 23 36 77) 11 George V, 75008 Paris
Germany
   (☎ (0228) 361-095) 125-300 Kurfislrstenalle, Bonn 2
Italy
   (☎ (06) 3630-8534, 3630-3856) 00135 Roma Via Della Camilluccia 613, Rome
Japan
   (☎ (03) 3403-3380, 3403-3065) 3-4-33 Moto-Azabu, Minato-ku, Tokyo 106

Netherlands
   (☎ (070) 355 15 15, 355 92 09) 7 Adriaan Goekooplaan, 2517 JX The Hague
New Zealand
   (☎ (04) 587-0407) 104 Korokoro Rd, Petone, Wellington
Sweden
   (☎ (08) 767 87 40, 767 40 83) 56 Ringvagen, 18134 Lidings
UK
   (☎ (0171) 636-5197) 49 Portland Place, London W1N 3AH
USA
   (☎ (202) 338-6688) 2300 Connecticut Ave NW, Washington, DC 20008

Consulates in Guangzhou

It's a good idea to register with your consulate as soon as you reach Guangzhou.

The US consulate might better be called the 'Emigration Information Centre'. If you go there with some other intention besides emigrating to the USA, the staff will be so happy to see you they might throw a party.

Australia
   (☎ 8335-0909, fax 8335-0718) room 1509, GITIC Plaza Hotel, 339 Huangshi Donglu
Canada
   (☎ 8666-0569, fax 8667-2401) room 801, China Hotel Office Tower, Liuhua Lu
France
   (☎ 8667-7522, fax 8332-1960) unit 1160, China Hotel, Liuhua Lu
Germany
   (☎ 8192-2566, fax 8192-2599) 103 Shamian Beijie, Shamian Island
Japan
   (☎ 8334-3019, fax 8333-8972) 1st floor, Garden Hotel Tower, 368 Huanshi Dong Lu
Malaysia
   (☎ 8739-5661, fax 8739-5669) 3rd floor, Ramada Pearl Hotel, 9 Mingyue 1-Lu, Dongshan district
Poland
   (☎ 8186-1854, fax 8186-2872) 63 Shamian Dajie, Shamian Island
Thailand
   (☎ 8188-6968 ext 3312, fax 8187-9451) 1st floor, White Swan Hotel, 1 Shamian Nanjie, Shamian Island
UK
   (☎ 8335-1354, fax 8333-6485) 2nd floor, GITIC Plaza Hotel, 339 Huanshi Dong Lu

GUANGZHOU

USA
(☎ 8188-8911, fax 8186-2341) 1 Shamian Nanjie, Shamian Island
Vietnam
(☎ 8652-7908, fax 8358-1000) 13 Taojin Bei Lu

CUSTOMS

Chinese border crossings have gone from being severely traumatic to exceedingly easy. While there seems to be lots of uniformed police around, the third degree at customs seems to be reserved for Hong Kong residents smuggling pornography rather than the stray foreigner.

You'll note that there are clearly marked 'green channels' and 'red channels', the latter reserved for those with such everyday travel items as refrigerators, motorcycles and TV sets.

You're allowed to import 600 cigarettes or the equivalent in tobacco products, 2L of alcohol and one pint (0.5L) of perfume. You're also allowed to import 900m of movie film, and a maximum of 72 rolls of still film. The importation of fresh fruit is strictly prohibited.

It's illegal to import any printed material, film, tapes etc 'detrimental to China's politics, economy, culture and ethics'. But don't be too concerned about what you take to read. As you leave China, any tapes, manuscripts, books etc 'which contain state secrets or are otherwise prohibited for export' can be seized. If you're hoping to export antiques from China, check with the authorities first. There are restrictions on what you can legally export, and infringement of these laws are severe. Cultural relics, handicrafts, gold and silver ornaments, and jewellery purchased in China have to be shown to customs on leaving.

BAGGAGE STORAGE

Most hotels in Guangzhou and elsewhere in China have luggage storage rooms (jìcúnchù or xínglì) where you can safely leave your bags for a small fee. This service is always available to guests at the hotel (sometimes for free), even after you've checked out (save your check-in receipt). This service is sometimes offered to non-guests, but don't count on it.

There are also luggage storage rooms at all train stations. At Guangzhou station there's a den of thieves, so you'd be wise to use the safer facilities at Guangzhou East station.

MONEY
Currency

The basic unit of currency is the yuan – designated in this book by a 'Y'. In spoken Chinese, the word *kuai* is often substituted for yuan. Ten *jiao* make up one yuan. In spoken Chinese, it's pronounced *mao*. Ten *fen* make up one jiao, but these days fen are becoming rare because these are worth so little.

China has another name for its currency, the Renminbi (RMB), which means 'people's money'. It's issued by the Bank of China. Paper notes are issued in denominations of one, two, five, 10, 50 and 100 yuan; one, two and five jiao; and one, two and five fen. Coins are in denominations of one yuan; five jiao; and one, two and five fen. The one fen note is small and yellow, the two fen note is blue, and the five fen note is small and green – all are next to worthless.

Be careful, there are plenty of fake bills about, especially of larger denominations (Y50 and Y100 notes). If you get the money from a bank, it will presumably be OK.

Exchange Rates

Australia	A$1	=	Y4.70
Canada	C$1	=	Y5.30
France	Ffr1	=	Y1.40
Germany	DM1	=	Y4.72
Hong Kong	HK$1	=	Y1.07
Japan	¥100	=	Y5.85
Korea (South)	W100	=	Y0.62
Netherlands	G1	=	Y4.18
New Zealand	NZ$1	=	Y4.10
Philippines	P1	=	Y0.19
Singapore	S$1	=	Y4.66
Switzerland	Sfr1	=	Y5.76
Taiwan	NT$1	=	Y0.24
Thailand	1B	=	Y0.20
UK	UK£1	=	Y13.92
USA	US$1	=	Y8.28

Exchanging Money

Foreign currency and travellers cheques can be changed at the main centres of the Bank of China, tourist hotels, some big department stores, the airport, border crossings and international ferry wharves. If you want to change money at the airport on departure from Guangzhou, it's important to remember that you have to do it before entering the immigration queue. Of course, if your next stop is Hong Kong, you can easily unload your excess Chinese currency there.

Unlike in Hong Kong, the exchange rates are pretty much the same all over and no hidden commissions are charged. One annoyance is that a few five star hotels only change money for guests – you can always make up a room number.

Always be sure to keep enough money on you to last for at least a few days. Public holidays can pose a big problem: even hotels don't want to do business because a bank can't be called for the latest official rates.

Whenever you change foreign currency into Chinese currency you'll be given a money-exchange voucher recording the transaction. If you've got any leftover RMB when you leave the country and want to re-convert it to hard currency, you must have some of those vouchers – 50% of what you originally exchanged can be re-exchanged on departure. The government is saying that you must spend the rest while in China.

You can ignore the preceding if your next stop is Hong Kong, since Hong Kong moneychangers are willing to exchange RMB. However, if you're flying directly from Guangzhou to another country, you'd better get rid of all your RMB at the airport.

Cash The easiest foreign currencies to exchange are US dollars and Hong Kong dollars. Forget about Macau patacas.

Shop vendors used to be keen to get at your Hong Kong dollars and give you change in RMB, but now it seems difficult to off-load Hong Kong dollars.

The last time we were in Guangzhou, McDonald's gave us a free meal rather than accept a HK$100 note. The best thing is to change all your Hong Kong dollars either at the Bank of China or in one of the many top-end hotels.

Travellers Cheques You actually get a much better exchange rate on travellers cheques than you do for cash. Travellers cheques in US dollars are the easiest cheques to exchange.

ATMs For a long time, ATMs in Guangzhou refused to accept any plastic that wasn't from mainland China. The situation is still pretty backward, but you can now withdraw cash on your Visa or MasterCard from several Bank of China ATMs, including the Friendship Store, the Bank of China in the Garden Hotel and at GITIC Plaza.

Credit Cards Credit cards are not nearly as readily accepted in Guangzhou as in Hong Kong or Macau. Major hotels will accept them, but elsewhere don't expect to get much use out of your card.

American Express (Amex, ☎ 8331-1888 ext 70111, fax 8331-3535) is in room C1, ground floor, central lobby, Guangdong International Hotel, 339 Huanshi Dong Lu.

International Transfers China's decrepit banking system is notoriously slow when it comes to doing international transfers. In some cases you may wait weeks for your money. If you really need money transferred to you, it would be much better to do it through Hong Kong or Macau.

If you must do an international transfer in Guangzhou, talk to some of the representative offices of foreign banks. These are not authorised to do international transfers, but can advise you on the best method. Some foreign bank representatives include: HongkongBank (☎ 8667-7061 ext 1363), Sumitomo Bank (☎ 8778-4988), Standard Chartered Bank (☎ 8778-8813), Societe Generale (☎ 8778-2688), Citibank (☎ 8332-1711) and ANZ Bank (☎ 8331-1490).

Black Market In every edition of this book we warn people not to use the black market.

GUANGZHOU

Nevertheless, we get a constant stream of letters from people telling us how they got ripped off changing money on the street. Certainly, if you look like a foreigner and hang around Guangzhou for long, you will be approached by the 'change money' people.

If you deal with them you will get robbed. It's that simple.

One trick is for the moneychanger to first hand over his wad of moolah for you to count, then he takes your money and puts it in his pocket. He then says he thinks he's made a mistake and says he wants to recount the money he has just handed you. If you hand it back you will get a fine view of his heels as he legs it down the street.

Costs

China is experiencing rapid inflation, and for that reason most of the prices quoted hereafter are in US dollars. China devalues its currency periodically, but prices in US dollars terms have remained relatively stable. It's possible that China will opt for large devaluation before the year 2000, as the over-appreciation of the yuan is hitting Chinese exports hard.

Although Guangzhou is cheaper than Hong Kong or Macau, it's not as cheap as you would expect given the low wages. The main reason is the deliberate government policy of squeezing as much money as possible out of foreign tourists. Things are slowly improving: foreigners used to pay triple for train fares and about 30% more than locals for airfares. This has now balanced out.

Accommodation is usually the biggest expense. If foreigners were allowed to stay in the ubiquitous Chinese *zhaodaisuo* (guesthouses), they could save a packet. As it is, foreign barbarians are herded together into PSB approved hotels that are all above a certain price.

If you get into a dormitory, Guangzhou is cheap; otherwise, your daily living expenses could be higher than in Hong Kong.

Hotel restaurants in Guangzhou have grown accustomed to charging high prices for food, but you can get around this by eating at hole-in-the-wall restaurants. You should be able to live comfortably on US$30 per day in Guangzhou.

Tipping & Bargaining

In Communist China, tipping is not normally a custom. Even in today's Guangzhou, you'll find that many a restaurateur will refuse to accept tips from you.

Bribery is another matter. Don't be blatant about it, but if you need some special service, it's customary to offer someone a cigarette and just tell them 'Go ahead and keep the pack – I'm trying to quit'. In China, a 'tip' is given before you receive the service, not after.

Since foreigners are so frequently overcharged in China, bargaining becomes essential. You can bargain in shops, hotels, with taxi drivers, but not everywhere. In large stores where prices are clearly marked, there is usually no latitude for bargaining. In small shops and street stalls, bargaining is expected, but there is one important rule to follow – be polite. There is nothing wrong with asking for a discount, if you do so with a smile.

In 'face-conscious' China, any nastiness or intimidation on your part is likely to make the vendor more recalcitrant and you'll be overcharged.

You should keep in mind that entrepreneurs are in business to make money. Your goal should be to pay the Chinese price, as opposed to the foreigners' price. If you can do that, you've done well.

Guangzhou was different bargaining-wise. Even official-looking shops on the tourist trail with marked prices were prepared to offer huge discounts. Most people in our tour party didn't ask. I looked at a tea set in the souvenir shop attached to the Sun Yatsen Memorial Middle School for which they were asking Y1200. The sales assistant was pressing me to buy it – I said no, too expensive, much cheaper in Hong Kong. She asked how much in Hong Kong – I had forgotten the exact figure, but told her I thought it was about Y400. She said OK!

Cilla Taylor

Consumer Taxes

Although big hotels and fancy restaurants may add a tax or 'service charge' of 10% or more, all other consumer taxes are included in the price tag.

POST & COMMUNICATIONS
Postal Rates

With China's rapid inflation, postal rates can escalate suddenly, so use the following only as a general guide. Rates per kilogram are of course cheaper for printed matter, small packets and parcels:

Letters (up to 20g)
  Local city Y0.10; elsewhere in mainland China Y0.20; Hong Kong, Macau and Taiwan surface mail Y0.60; Hong Kong, Macau and Taiwan airmail Y0.80; international surface mail Y2.20; international airmail Y2.90
Postcards
  Local city Y0.10; elsewhere in mainland China Y0.15; Hong Kong, Macau and Taiwan surface mail Y0.40; Hong Kong, Macau and Taiwan airmail Y0.60; international surface mail Y1.60; international airmail Y2.30
Aerogrammes
  Hong Kong, Macau and Taiwan Y0.60; other countries Y2.80
EMS (Speedpost)
  Domestic EMS parcels up to 200g, Y23; each additional 200g, Y5. For international EMS, rates vary according to country. For nearby Asian countries (Japan, Korea etc) for up to 500g costs Y148.

Sending Mail

The international postal service seems efficient, and air-mailed letters and postcards will probably take around five to 10 days to reach the destination. If possible, write the country of destination in Chinese, as this should speed up delivery. Domestic post is amazingly fast, perhaps one or two days from Guangzhou to Beijing. Within a city, mail may be delivered the same day it's sent.

As well as the local post offices, there are branch post offices in most major tourist hotels where you can mail letters, packets and parcels (the contents of packets and parcels are checked by post office staff). Even at cheap hotels you can usually post letters from the front desk – reliability varies, but in general it's OK. In some places, you may only be able to post printed matter from these branch offices. Other parcels may require a customs form to be attached at the town's main post office, where contents will be checked.

Large envelopes are a bit hard to come by – try the department stores. Most post offices supply tape, string, glue and sometimes cloth bags. The huge Liuhua Post Office adjacent to Guangzhou train station has a massive selection of cardboard boxes.

For tourists staying on Shamian Island, the nearest major post office is at 43 Yanjiang West Lu, near the river. This is one of the post offices authorised for sending parcels overseas. Otherwise, there is a post office conveniently located in the White Swan Hotel, opposite the youth hostel.

Postcards are hard to find in Guangzhou. If you don't want to bring some from Hong Kong or Macau, try the shopping arcades in the large hotels (the book shop in the White Swan Hotel has stocks).

Courier Service Private couriers offering express document and parcel service include the following:

Asian Express
  (☎ 8659-0616)
DHL
  (☎ 8664-4668, fax 8335-1647) 37 Xiaobei, Xiatangxi Lu. DHL has centres at the China Hotel, Garden Hotel, Guangdong Trade Centre, GITIC Plaza, Huangpu Trade Centre, International Financial building Centre and the White Swan Hotel.
Federal Express
  (☎ 8386-2026, fax 8386-2012) room 1356-1357, Garden Tower, Garden Hotel, 368 Huanshi Donglu
Trans China
  (☎ 8666-3388 ext 2803)
United Parcel Service
  (☎ 8775-5778) room 2103, South Tower, Guangzhou World Trade Centre, 371-375 Huanshi Donglu

Receiving Mail

Adjacent to Guangzhou train station is the

GUANGZHOU

main post office, locally known as the Liuhua Post Office (☎ 8666-2735, *liúhuā yóu jú*). You can collect poste restante letters here, although there is no poste restante window. Names are written on a notice board, and you are supposed to see if your name is there and then find someone (but who?) to get the letter for you. Most of the names are in Chinese, so yours should stand out. The best plan is to arrange a hotel booking in advance and have all mail forwarded to the hotel.

It's worth noting that some foreigners living in China have had their mail opened or parcels pilfered before receipt – and some have had their outgoing mail opened and read. This seems to affect tourists less, although letters with enclosures will almost certainly be opened. Your mail is less likely to be opened if it is sent to cities that handle high volumes of mail, like Guangzhou.

Officially, China forbids several items from being mailed to it – the regulations specifically prohibit 'reactionary books, magazines and propaganda materials, obscene or immoral articles'. You also cannot mail Chinese currency abroad, or receive it by post. Like elsewhere, mail-order hashish and other recreational chemicals will not amuse the authorities.

Telephone

China's creaky phone system is being overhauled, at least in major cities. Whereas just a few years ago calling from Guangzhou to Shanghai could be an all-day project, you can now just pick up a phone and dial direct. International calls have also become much easier.

Most hotel rooms are equipped with phones from which local calls are free. Local calls can also be made from public pay phones (there are some around but not many). China's budding entrepreneurs try to fill the gap – people with private phones run a long cord out the window and stand on street corners, allowing you to use the phone to place local calls for around Y1 each. Long-distance domestic and international calls are not always possible on these

phones, but ask. In the lobbies of many hotels, the reception desks have a similar system – free calls for guests, Y1 for non-guests, and long-distance calls are charged by the minute. If you call from the business centre of one of the smarter hotels, you'll pay through the nose for it.

You can also place both domestic and international long-distance phone calls from telecommunications offices. Be aware that dealing with these offices can be a nuisance. Communication with the clerk can be a problem, and the procedure is usually a cumbersome haul through forms and long waits for a free booth. The Guangzhou telephone office is across from the Guangzhou train station on the east side of Renmin North Lu, though there is little need to go there, as you can most likely make your call from your hotel. Domestic long-distance rates in China vary according to distance, but are incredibly cheap. International calls are relatively expensive. Calls to Hong Kong and Macau are considered international calls; calls to Hong Kong are cheap, but don't call Macau unless you're being held at gunpoint – it's unbelievably expensive.

If you are expecting a call, either international or domestic, try to advise the caller beforehand of your hotel room number. The operators frequently have difficulty understanding foreign names, and the hotel receptionist may not be able to locate you.

Direct Dialling   Domestic Direct Dialling (DDD) and International Direct Dialling (IDD) calls are cheapest if you can find a phone that accepts magnetic cards. These phones are usually available in the lobbies of major hotels, at least in big cities, and the hotel's front desk should also sell the phone cards. These cards come in two denominations, Y20 and Y100. For an international call, you'll need the latter.

If card phones aren't available, you can usually dial direct from the phones in the business centres found in most luxury hotels. You do not have to be a guest at these hotels to use these facilities, but they are excruciatingly expensive.

You should be able to dial direct from your hotel room. You'll have to ask the staff at your hotel what the dial-out code for a direct line is (it's often either No 9 or 7 on most switchboards). Once you have the outside line, dial 00 (the international access code – always the same throughout China) followed by the country code, area code and the number you want to reach. If the area code begins with zero (like 03 for Melbourne, Australia) omit the first zero.

Check with the hotel management first about call charges. Also check that you won't be charged if you leave the phone to ring at the other end or if you just get an engaged tone. Some of the hotel switchboards charge you even if you fail to get through, if you hang on the line for more than 30 seconds.

For DDD, it's useful to know the area codes of China's cities, which all begin with zero. If you're dialling China from abroad, omit the first zero from each code. China's country code is 86. Some important area codes in Guangdong Province include: Foshan 0757, Guangzhou 020, Shenzhen 0755, Zhaoqing 0758, Zhongshan 07654 and Zhuhai 0756.

Some useful telephone numbers are the same in every Chinese city (excluding Hong Kong and Macau). Some examples include the following:

Police	☎ 110
Ambulance	☎ 120
Fire	☎ 119
Local and International Directory Assistance	☎ 114
Domestic Long-Distance Directory Assistance	☎ 116
Operator Assistance – Domestic Long-Distance	☎ 113
Operator Assistance – International	☎ 103
AT&T Service (English)	☎ 10811
Time	☎ 117
Tourist Hotline	☎ 8667-7422
Weather Forecast	☎ 121

If you are planning to move to Guangzhou for business or to study, you can get a telephone installed in your apartment, but there is a long waiting list as the rest of the Chinese population are also queuing up. For a mobile telephone (analogue system) the cost is Y13,000. Digital phones are available and cost more – Y15,000. Mobile phones are available immediately; there's no queue for them.

Those living on a budget, such as foreign students, may well find pagers a more realistic option. Pagers are more common than telephones in China, making it the world's second largest pager market after the USA. Those with a residence permit can obtain a pager in just a couple of weeks.

Pagers for use in Guangzhou only cost Y15 a month. For a pager useable throughout China, the price rises to Y80 per month. The paging market was opened to free competition in 1993. There are now more than 1700 paging operators in China, so it's difficult to say which company is best.

The market for cellular phones and pagers is dominated by the US company Motorola and Sweden's Ericsson. The Chinese don't yet manufacture cellular phones but they do make pagers, which even the locals will tell you are junk.

If you are going to make regular calls abroad and plan to stay in Guangzhou a while, try Global One (☎ 8331-2822), a combined venture by Deutsche Telecom, France Telecom and Sprint, which offers large discounts on international calls (on a fibre optic network).

Fax, Telegraph & Telex

Major hotels usually operate a business centre complete with telephone, fax and telex service, not to mention photocopying, and sometimes the use of typewriters and word processors. As a rule, you do not have to be a guest at the hotel to use these services, but you certainly must pay. Prices seem to be pretty uniform regardless of the hotel, but it's still not a bad idea to ask the rates first.

International fax and telexes cost either about Y20 per minute (with a three minute minimum charge) or you get charged at the international rate for the connection.

GUANGZHOU

Email & Internet Access

Guangzhou is not well organised for email. If you don't have a resident's visa, then you'll have to do your email by calling long-distance to Hong Kong at about Y8 per minute. Also try phoning GITICNet (see later in this entry), who may be able to offer you temporary usage of its service. Otherwise, you can use the business centres at the smarter hotels, which generally have an email facility. At many of these hotels, you don't have to be a guest, but it's not cheap. The business centre at the White Swan hotel charges Y80 for half an hour. A few Internet cafes have come and gone, with no permanent settlement at the time of writing. Ask at your hotel for any news on recent arrivals.

China is a big disappointment when it comes to the Internet. At present, there are only two authorised Internet Service Providers (ISPs) in mainland China (compared to 33 in Hong Kong). Internet users have to register with the government, and content is carefully monitored. Obviously, the authorities fear they can't control all that dangerous information being tossed around on the Internet.

If you have residency in Guangzhou, the best option for getting access to the Internet is GITICNet (☎ 8331-1888 ext 72312/72347), which has a registration fee of Y150, an installation fee of Y120 and a monthly charge of Y230 (unlimited line use). Otherwise you can log on temporarily for eight hours for Y100.

The other ISP in town is Chinanet, a more cumbersome arrangement which involves you going in person and applying at the Guangzhou Post and Telecommunications department in Tianhe in the east of the city.

Registration for Chinanet is Y100, with a monthly service charge of Y20 plus Y0.20 per minute. This is probably the cheaper option, depending on how much you plan to use the facility, but the staff at GITICNet speak English and are generally more helpful.

INTERNET RESOURCES

The best Web site for what's going on in Guangzhou is the homepage of the expats survival magazine, *Clueless in Guangzhou.* look it up on at www.nease.net/~clueless and get the latest info on pubs, clubs and events in the city.

BOOKS
Lonely Planet

In addition to the book you're holding, other Lonely Planet guides to the region include the *Hong Kong* city guide, *China* and *South-West China*.

History & Politics

An excellent book that sets part of its action in Guangzhou is *God's Chinese Son*, by Jonathan Spence, charting the parabolic rise to power of the leader of the Taipings, Hong Xiuquan. The Taipings believed that Hong Xiuquan was the son of the Christian God and the brother of Jesus. Their rebellion almost signalled the end of the Qing dynasty. Read this book and get a unique glimpse of Chinese passions, beliefs and the insolubly tragic nature of Chinese history.

The Search for Modern China, also by Jonathan Spence, is the definitive work, often used as a textbook in college courses. If you want to understand the PRC, this is the book to read. Sumptuously illustrated, it's a bit big to carry all the way to China and better taken in before hitting the road. A much lighter read is *The Walled Kingdom*, the classic history of China from 2000 BC to the present day by the recently deceased Witold Rodzinski.

A dimmer view of China under Deng Xiaoping is taken by Italian journalist Tiziano Terzani in *Behind the Forbidden Door*. Terzani, once an avid socialist, became disillusioned after living in China from 1980 to 1984, when he was finally booted out for his critical reporting.

An intriguing and popular book is *The New Emperors* by Harrison Salisbury. The 'emperors' he refers to are Mao Zedong and Deng Xiaoping.

Seeds of Fire – Chinese Voices of Conscience is an anthology of blistering eloquence from authors such as Wei Jingsheng, Liu Qing, Wang Xizhe and Xu Wenli (imprisoned for their roles in the Democracy Movement) and the poet Sun Jingxuan. Wei Jingsheng's description of Q1, China's top prison for political detainees, is utterly horrific.

The issue of human rights is covered in Amnesty International's *China – Violations of Human Rights*, a grim aspect of the country that should not be ignored.

Cultural Revolution The best seller seems to be *Life and Death in Shanghai* by Nien Cheng. The author was imprisoned for six years, and this is her gripping story of survival.

Other stories from this period include *Born Red* by Gao Yuan and *Son of the Revolution* by Liang Heng & Judith Shapiro.

The Chinese People Stand Up by Elizabeth Wright examines China's turbulent history from 1949 up to the brutal suppression of pro-democracy demonstrators in 1989.

The Soong Dynasty by Sterling Seagrave is one of the most popular books on the corrupt Kuomintang (KMT) period. Unfortunately, the author severely damaged his credibility when he later published *The Marcos Dynasty*, which some argue contains more rumour than fact.

The Private Life of Chairman Mao is banned in China. The author, Dr Li Zhisui, was the personal physician to Mao Zedong. Despite the Communist Party's attempts to depict Mao as a paragon of virtue, Dr Li asserts that the old chairman in his later years spent nearly all his free time in bed with teenage girls.

General

There are numerous books about China but rather few dealing specifically with Guangzhou or Guangdong Province. One of the few is *Kwangtung or Five Years in South China* by the English Wesleyan minister Reverend John Arthur Turner, who worked as a missionary in China from 1886 to 1891. His book was originally published in 1894.

Another early account of western contact with China comes from the Jesuit priest and missionary Matteo Ricci, who was permitted to take up residence at Zhaoqing near Guangzhou in the late 16th century, and in Beijing in 1601. An English translation of his diaries has been published under the title *China in the 16th Century – the Journals of Matteo Ricci 1583-1610*. This book is not easy to find.

Other rare books about Guangzhou include *Canton in Revolution – The Collected papers of Earl Swisher, 1925-1928*. Also, Ezra Vogel's *Canton Under Communism* covers the history of the city from 1949 to 1968.

The best known English fiction about China is *The Good Earth* by Pearl Buck.

If you want to read a weighty Chinese classic, you could try *Journey to the West*, available in English in a four volume set in Guangzhou and some Hong Kong bookshops. Condensed versions are available in paperback editions.

The Dream of the Red Chamber (also known as *The Story of the Stone*) by Cao Xueqin, is a Chinese classic written in the late 18th century. It's not an easy read. Again, look for the condensed version.

The third great Chinese classic is *Outlaws of the Marsh*. This is also available in abridged form.

A moving and popular book is *Wild Swans* by Jung Chang. The author traces the lives of three Chinese women: the author's grandmother (an escaped concubine with bound feet), her mother and herself.

If you want to make inroads into understanding the Chinese creative instinct, *The Path of Beauty – a study of Chinese aesthetics* by Li Zehou is an excellent introduction to the field.

NEWSPAPERS & MAGAZINES
Chinese-Language Publications

There are nearly 2000 national and provincial newspapers in China. The main one is *Renmin Ribao* (the People's Daily), with nationwide circulation. It was founded in 1946 as the official publication of the Central Committee of the Communist Party. It is diabolically boring, but is actu-

GUANGZHOU

ally slowly improving, despite the front page monopoly of Communist Party news and photos of gleeful peasants.

At the other end of the scale there is China's version of the gutter press, several hundred 'unhealthy papers' and magazines hawked on street corners and bus stations in major cities with nude or violent photos, and stories about sex, crime, witchcraft, miracle cures and UFOs. These have been severely criticised by the government for the obscene and racy content. It is also extremely popular. There are also about 40 newspapers for minority nationalities.

Foreign-Language Publications

China publishes various newspapers, books and magazines in a number of European and Asian languages. The only English-language newspaper is the *China Daily*, first published in June 1981. The paper is a crashing bore, but for many a traveller on the road in China, it cultivates a sort of twisted affection due to the lack of alternatives.

In Guangzhou, however, you should be able to find copies of popular imported English-language magazines like *Time*, *Newsweek*, *Far Eastern Economic Review*, the *International Herald Tribune* and the *Economist*. A censored edition of Hong Kong's *South China Morning Post* is also available. You can find these publications at major hotels.

Well worth hunting down is *Clueless in Guangzhou*, put out monthly by the pioneering owner of Kathleen's (a popular bar/restaurant in the north-east of the city). This is a lifeline thrown out to those bewildered by the strangeness of Guangzhou. If you want to tap into a well-fed pool of news of the latest bars, clubs, restaurants and events in Guangzhou, you'll find this magazine at a number of locations, including most of the foreign consulates, some larger hotels, many expat bars and hangout dives plus DHL centres around town (eg at the China Hotel, Garden Hotel, GITIC Plaza and White Swan Hotel).

Guangdong Citylife is a bi-monthly colour tourist information journal recently given a kick in the pants by the appearance of *Clueless in Guangzhou*. It looks snazzy and has some useful information, but is just as vapid as its predecessor, *Welcome to China – Guangdong*. You can find copies of this free magazine at counters of most of the larger hotels.

News Agencies

China has two news agencies, the New China (Xinhua) News Agency and the China News Service. The New China News Agency is a national organisation with its headquarters in Beijing and branches in each province, as well as in the army, Hong Kong and many foreign countries. It provides news for the national, provincial and local papers, and radio stations, transmits radio broadcasts abroad in foreign languages, and is responsible for making contact with and exchanging news with foreign news agencies. In Hong Kong, this agency acts as the unofficial embassy.

The main function of the China News Service is to supply news to overseas Chinese newspapers and journals, including those in Hong Kong and Macau. It also distributes Chinese documentary films abroad.

RADIO & TV

Chinese TV is broadcast in either Cantonese or Mandarin. The only English-language programs are the news on CCTV4 from 10 to 10.30 pm and the occasional subtitled foreign movie or educational show (for those attempting to learn English).

The situation is not hopeless. After years of attempts to tear down the TV antennas and jam foreign broadcasting, many Guangzhou residents now have access to satellite dishes and receive Hong Kong's transmission of the latest bourgeois and subversive episodes of western programs, which the authorities believe have ruinous influences on the moral and ideological uprightness of the Chinese.

Nevertheless, what you get to see on satellite is also sanitised. The Chinese government forced Hong Kong's STAR TV to delete the BBC World News. In China, you are only supposed to watch good, wholesome movies like *The Terminator* and *Natural Born Killers*.

In the border areas of Shenzhen and Zhuhai it is easy to pick up uncensored English-language broadcasts from Hong Kong stations.

Fascinating local dramas on TV include a regular spot for the Guangzhou PSB, who reel off an endless list of cars that have run red lights (the presenters have perfected that sort of malicious half-smile enjoyed by the Chinese authorities). It would be far more economical just to list the few cars that didn't shoot the lights.

VIDEO SYSTEMS
Like Hong Kong, China uses the PAL video system. See also the Video Systems entry in the Hong Kong Facts for the Visitor chapter for more detailed information.

PHOTOGRAPHY & VIDEO
In China you'll get a fantastic run for your money; for starters there are 1.2 billion portraits to work your way through. Religious reasons for avoiding photographs are absent among the Han Chinese – some guy isn't going to stick a spear through you for taking a picture of his wife and stealing part of her soul – though you probably won't be allowed to take photos of statues in many Buddhist temples.

A lot of Chinese still cannot afford a camera, and resort to photographers at tourist places. The photographers supply dress-up clothing for that extra touch. The subjects change from street clothing into spiffy gear, and sometimes even bizarre costumes and make-up for the shot. Others use cardboard props such as opera stars or boats.

The standard shot is one or more Chinese standing in front of something significant. Temples, waterfalls, heroic statues or important vintages of calligraphy are considered suitable backgrounds. At amusement parks, Mickey Mouse and Donald Duck get into nearly every photo; Ronald McDonald and the Colonel of KFC fame are favourite photo companions at these prestigious restaurants. If you hang around these places you can sometimes click off a few portrait photos for yourself, but don't be surprised if your photo subjects suddenly drag you into the picture as an exotic prop.

Film & Equipment
Imported film is relatively expensive, but Japanese companies like Fuji and Konica now have factories in China. This has

---

Ad Nauseam

Advertising for the foreign market is one area the Chinese are still stumbling around. A TV advertisement in Paris for Chinese furs treated viewers to the bloody business of skinning and cadavers in the refrigerator rooms before the usual parade of fur-clad models down the catwalk.

It would be fun to handle the advertising campaigns for their more charming brands. There's Pansy underwear (for men) or you can pamper your stud with Horse Head facial tissues. Wake up in the morning with a Golden Cock alarm clock (since renamed Golden Rooster). You can start your breakfast with a glass of Billion Strong Pulpy C Orange Drink, or finish your meal with a cup of Imperial Concubine Tea. For your trusty portable radio it may be best to stay away from White Elephant batteries, but you might try the space-age Moon Rabbit variety. Long March car tyres should prove durable, but what about the ginseng product with the fatal name of Gensenocide?

Rambo toilet paper must be the toughest stuff around, but its rival Flying Baby seems to have vanished. Smokers can pick up a pack of Puke cigarettes.

The characters for Coca-Cola translate as 'tastes good, tastes happy' but the Chinese must have thought they were really on to something when the 'Coke adds life' slogan was mistranslated and claimed the stuff could resurrect the dead. And as a sign of the times, one enterprising food vendor has started a chain store named Capitalist Road.

GUANGZHOU

brought the price of colour print film down to what you'd pay in the west, sometimes less. While colour print film is available almost everywhere, it's almost always 100 ASA (21 DIN). Video cassettes are becoming increasingly easy to find.

Black and white film can be found in Guangzhou's larger department stores, but in general it's hard to buy in China, colour photos are all the rage.

In general, colour slide film is also hard to find. Check out major hotels, department stores and Friendship Stores if you get caught short. When you do find slide film, it's usually expensive and sometimes out of date, though last year's slide film is still better than none. Ektachrome and Fujichrome can be found in Guangzhou. Kodachrome and Agfachrome are virtually non-existent in China or Hong Kong.

Polaroid film is rumoured to exist, but if you need the stuff in mainland China, you'd better bring your own supply from Hong Kong or elsewhere.

Finding special lithium batteries used by many cameras is pretty easy in large cities like Guangzhou. Some cameras have a manual mode that allows you to continue shooting with a dead battery, though the light meter won't work. Fully automatic cameras just drop dead when the battery goes.

Video cameras were once subject to shaky regulations, but there seems to be no problem now. In fact, nearly every member of the holidaying Chinese business set has a video camera, so finding film is easy. The biggest problem is recharging your batteries off the strange mutations of plugs in China, so bring all the adapters you can, and remember that they use 220V.

Motion picture film is hard enough to find in the west these days, and next to impossible in China, where it is tightly controlled by authorities.

Restrictions

Photography from planes and photographs of airports, military installations, harbour facilities and train stations are prohibited; bridges may also be a touchy subject.

Taking photos is not permitted in most museums, at archaeological sites and in many temples, mainly to protect the postcard and colour slide industry. These rules are enforced if the enforcers happen to be around. If you plan to photograph something that is prohibited, at least take the precaution of starting with a new roll of film. That way, if the film gets ripped out of your camera, you haven't lost too much.

You're allowed to bring in 8mm movie cameras, but 16mm or professional equipment may raise eyebrows with customs.

Photographing People

Some Chinese shy away from having their photo taken, and even duck for cover. Others are proud to pose and will ham it up for the camera, and they're especially proud if you're taking a shot of their kid. Nobody expects any payment for photos, so don't give any or you'll set a precedent.

There are three basic approaches to photographing people. One is the polite 'ask for permission and pose it' shot, which is sometimes rejected. Another is the 'no-holds barred and upset everyone' approach. The third is surreptitious, standing half a kilometre away with a 1m long telephoto lens. Many Chinese will disagree with you on what constitutes good subject matter; they don't really see why anyone would want to take a street scene, a picture of a beggar or a shot of butchered dogs on display in the market. The notion of photographing negative scenes or shots flooded with urban angst does not compute in some Chinese minds.

Another objection often brought up is that the subject is not 'dignified' – be it a labourer straining down the street with a massive load on his hand-cart, or a barrel of excrement on wheels. The official line is that peasants and workers are the glorious heroes of China, but you'll have a tough time convincing your photo subject of this.

Photoprocessing

Major cities like Guangzhou and Shenzhen are equipped with the latest Japanese photoprocessing machines. Quality colour prints can be turned out in one or two hours at reasonable cost.

It's a different situation with colour slides. Ektachrome and Fujichrome can be processed in Guangzhou, but this can be expensive and quality is not assured. If you don't want your slides scratched, covered with fingerprints or over developed, save the processing until you get home or to Hong Kong. Kodachrome film cannot be processed on the mainland. Undeveloped film can be sent out of China and, going by personal experience only, the dreaded X-ray machines do not appear to be a problem.

TIME

Time throughout mainland China is set the same as Hong Kong, eight hours ahead of GMT/UTC. China experimented with daylight-saving time but has now dropped it.

ELECTRICITY

Voltages & Cycles

As in Hong Kong, China uses AC 220V, 50 Hz. The only difference is in the design of the electrical outlets. There are at least four permutations of electric outlet designs.

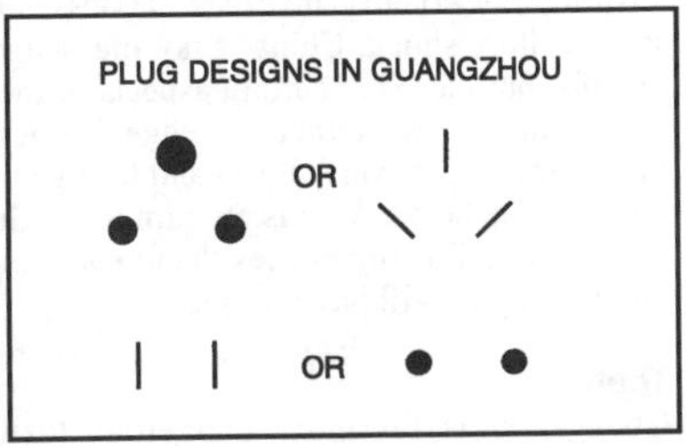

Plugs & Sockets

Conversion plugs are easily purchased in Hong Kong, but are damn near impossible to find in Guangzhou. Battery chargers are widely available, but these are generally the bulky style which are not suitable for travelling – buy a small one in Hong Kong.

Power failures occasionally happen, especially during summer when everyone turns on their air conditioner. Given this situation, a torch (flashlight) is essential survival gear. Chinese torches are indeed torturous – half the time these don't work and the bulbs seldom last as long as the batteries. Bring a small but good quality torch from Hong Kong or elsewhere.

WEIGHTS & MEASURES

The international metric system is in use. Local Chinese units of weight are still used in markets: the *leung* (37.5g) and the *catty* or the *gan* (600g).

LAUNDRY

Most hotels have a laundry service, but check the prices first. Some places charge so much you could buy new clothes cheaper. Many travellers wind up washing their clothes by hand. If you plan on doing this, dark clothes are better since the dirt doesn't show up so clearly. China's ubiquitous washing powder product is called white cat, or *baimao*.

TOILETS

Toilet paper is never provided in the toilets at bus and train stations or other public buildings (mainly because people steal it), so you'd be wise to keep a stash of your own with you at all times. Only in big modern hotels can you hope to find a supply of toilet paper.

In hotels, the toilets are clearly labelled in English, but in most public buildings only Chinese is used. To avoid embarrassment, try to remember:

男	女
MEN	WOMEN

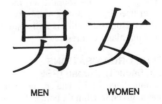

In Guangzhou you may encounter squat toilets – basically, a hole in the floor that usually flushes. Try not to lose your footing. A variation on the theme is a ditch with water running through it. Both the hole and the ditch take some getting used to. The Chinese, though, appear to have difficulty adapting to western toilets. In big hotels or fast-food restaurants where western-style toilets are available, you'll often find big black footprints and urine on the seats.

In many places, the plumbing system cannot adequately handle toilet paper. In that case, you should toss the paper into a waste basket provided for just that purpose.

WOMEN TRAVELLERS

Western women report relatively little sexual harassment in China. The biggest complaints come from women with Asian features; indeed, some have been raped.

All women visitors should take the precaution of dressing conservatively. Beach wear especially should be conservative. Bikinis will attract spectators and public nudity will get you arrested.

GAY & LESBIAN TRAVELLERS

In 1992 the Chinese government caught up with most of the world and declared that homosexuality was not illegal. The authorities instructed police to cease detaining men who confined their sexual activities to their home and ruled that there was no legal reason to separate cohabiting lesbian couples.

The gay scene is still underground in mainland China, and lacks the confidence of its counterpart in Hong Kong. Even in Hong Kong, it is only in the last few years that the gay scene has found itself increasingly serviced by a growing number of bars and clubs. Homosexuality is still anathema to most mainland Chinese.

USEFUL ORGANISATIONS
Public Security Bureau (PSB)

The Public Security Bureau (*gōng'ān jú*) is the name given to China's police, both uniformed and plain-clothes. Its responsibilities include suppression of political dissidence,

crime detection, preventing foreigners and Chinese from having sex with each other (no joke), mediating family quarrels and directing traffic. The Foreign Affairs Branch (*wài shì kē*) of the PSB deals with foreigners. This branch is responsible for issuing visa extensions.

In Guangzhou, the PSB (☎ 8333-1060) is at 863 Jiefang Bei Lu, opposite the road that leads to Zhenhai Tower in Yuexiu Park, only a 15 minute walk from the Dongfang Hotel.

The United States Information Service, usually just called USIS (☎ 8335-4269), is on the restaurant floor of the Garden Hotel.

Business Organisations

The American Chamber of Commerce (☎ 8335-1476) is in the Guangdong International Hotel next to the GITIC Plaza.

Other associations that could be of use are the Australian Business Association (☎ 8384-9883), the Association of British Commerce China (☎ 8552-5117), the Canadian Business Forum (☎ 8552-5117) and the Italian Institute of Foreign Trade (☎ 8667-0013).

DANGERS & ANNOYANCES

Visiting any country involves hassles and some culture shock. China is not the worst for this, but there are certain aspects of the culture that set westerners on edge. It does little good to get overly upset and lose your temper. The best advice is to learn to laugh it off. The following entries detail some of the things you will have to live with.

Theft

Guangzhou is far more dangerous than either Hong Kong or Macau. As one of China's boom towns, the city has attracted a large number of migrants from the countryside in search of the proverbial pot of gold. Needless to say, most become disillusioned when they find themselves camped out on the pavement with no prospects for employment. Many turn to begging and theft. The situation is set to get worse with the surging unemployment figures that characterise China at present. Guangzhou taxis have plastic shields or wire screens separating the driver from the passengers. Before these became mandatory, many drivers were attacked and some were killed.

For foreigners, there is little physical danger in walking the streets, but pickpockets are a problem, especially on crowded buses. You should also be cautious of bag snatchers, especially around the train stations. Some thieves use bicycles as their getaway vehicles. Another tactic is to slit your bag or pocket open with a razor blade and remove the contents. The PSB are worthless in such cases.

Violent crime is also increasing. Knife wielding gangs attack passengers on trains and jump off as the train approaches a station. So far, the criminals have shown a preference for robbing Chinese and leaving foreigners alone, but this is starting to change. If you are going to travel long distances by bus, stash your rucksack where you can see it. This is difficult if you are

Killing the Rooster to Frighten the Monkey

It's hard to say how China's crime rate compares with those in other countries, though the country has its share of rapists and murderers. White-collar crime is also a big problem, and the Chinese newspapers regularly report arrests, and even the occasional execution of people who committed fraud or embezzlement.

The crackdown on corruption has been given extensive coverage in the official press. In Shanghai, the sons of three senior cadres were executed for attacks on women. A Shanghai Party official was also jailed for life for accepting over Y30,000 in bribes. Although such sentences were intended to show that all are equal before the law, the centuries-old system of privilege for high officials and their relatives is unlikely to receive more than a dent.

When the minister and vice-minister of astronautics embezzled US$46 million in foreign exchange they were rebuked with 'serious disciplinary warnings within the Party'. Meanwhile, local pickpockets get the death penalty.

Juvenile crime is a growing problem in China's cities. The types of crime committed include murder, rape and theft of large sums of money. The official view is that they are victims of 'spiritual pollution' – influenced by images of foreign criminal cliques portrayed in mass media. Other factors such as unemployment and disillusionment are rarely blamed.

Justice in China seems to be dispensed entirely by the police, who also decide the penalty. The ultimate penalty is execution, which serves the purpose of 'killing the rooster to frighten the monkey' or, to phrase this in official terms, 'It is good to have some people executed so as to educate others'. With no independent judiciary, people charged with a crime have little chance of beating a conviction unless they're well connected.

China has become famous for its periodic crackdown campaigns. When official word comes down that it's time to get tough on crime, the newspapers routinely report impressive-sounding figures – thousands of people arrested, many executions. To judge from official figures, these anti-crime campaigns are a resounding success. The police seem to have little difficulty filling their quota. How many of these people really committed the crimes in question is another matter.

The standard manner of dispatching convicted criminals is with a bullet in the back of the head. Afterwards, a mug shot and maybe even a photo of the extinguished body appears in the newspapers or even gets pinned up on a public noticeboard. Such executions are generally performed at mass gatherings, often at a stadium but sometimes in front of bus or train stations. The train station routine has become less popular in recent years, mainly because some foreign tour groups would occasionally disembark from their train just in time to see someone get their head blown off. Should you by chance happen upon such a spectacle, taking photos may be a bad idea.

GUANGZHOU

taking an overnight bus, unless you take your gear to bed with you – gangs are known to wander around stealing everyone's belongings while they sleep.

PSB officers often show a stunning lack of interest in getting involved when someone reports a crime. Rather than respond to individual complaints, the situation is handled collectively with periodic high-profile crackdown campaigns.

Terrorism

Well, there's not much you can do about this, but China has joined the list of nations who suffer from terrorism. Guangdong has not been hit yet, but Beijing and Wuhan have both been the victims of bombs planted on public buses by Uighur separatists.

The Uighurs are a Muslim minority that live in the vast north-western expanse of Xinjiang Province. Separatist demonstrations were ruthlessly put down by Beijing's iron fist in early 1997, which led to a bomb exploding on a packed bus in the Xidan district of the nation's capital. It is thought that a couple of people died in the explosion.

About a year later a larger bomb took out a bus in Wuhan, killing a larger number of people, although exact figures were not forthcoming. These two events were the only ones released to the world's press, and other terrorist attacks could well have occurred within the huge interior of China that have not been reported to the outside world.

Spitting

Clearing your throat and discharging the phlegm onto the floor or out the window (to the peril of those below) is perfectly acceptable in China. Everyone does it – any time, any place. This is the main medium for the spread of TB. It's not so bad in summer, but in winter, when many people are afflicted by the notorious 'China Syndrome', you'll have a hard time trying to keep out of the crossfire!

Littering

The environmental movement has not reached China. Rather than carry the garbage down the stairs once a day, many Chinese find it more convenient to dump it out the window. (You get a hint of this in Hong Kong at Chungking Mansions – just look in the light wells in the centre of the building.) Sewer grates are also convenient garbage dumps. Restaurants and street vendors usually dump all uneaten food down the sewer, much to the joy of the rats who inhabit the underworld.

If you take a boat cruise on the Pearl River, sit on the lower deck. You can watch in astonishment as it rains garbage from the upper deck. Of course, every boat has a rubbish bin and some people use it, which is why a shipmate comes along about once an hour and dumps the contents overboard.

Nevertheless, the streets in China are reasonably clean, but not because civic-minded citizens are careful with their rubbish. The government employs a small army of people who do nothing all day but sweep up the continual mess, otherwise the country would be quickly buried in it.

Noise

In recent years the Chinese government has launched an anti-noise pollution campaign. Look out for billboards emblazoned with a huge crossed-through ear presiding over busy intersections swarming with honking traffic. The government is on a loser with this one. The Chinese are generally much more tolerant of noise than most westerners. People watch TV at ear-shattering volumes, drivers habitually lean on the horn, telephone conversations are conducted in high-decibel rapid-fire screams, and most of China seems to wake uncomplainingly to the sound of jackhammers and earth-moving vehicles. If it's peace and quiet you want, Guangzhou is not the place for you, head for a remote part of China – try the desert in Xinjiang, or a mountain-top in Tibet.

Pushing & Shoving

When Mao was alive, leftists in western countries pointed to China as a model of harmony and happiness, where smiling peasants joined hands and worked together in a cooperative effort to build a better Chinese society.

Undoubtedly, many of them were dismayed when they finally did get to visit the PRC and saw what the Chinese go through to get on a bus. No cooperative effort here, just panicked mobs frantically pushing, shoving and clawing. Those who want to get off are shoved right back inside by those who want to get on. In a few notorious incidents (mostly involving overcrowded ferries) people have actually been trampled to death.

Queuing does not exist in China, and there's no point pretending that it does by trying to form a line. You will quickly notice that there is no line at the bank, just a melee of people digging their elbows into each others ribs. The only advice we can offer is to join in the melee, as any polite gesture or attempt at an organised queue will be trampled into the ground.

All of this helps explain the decline of the controlled economy in China and its replacement with the logic of market forces – the people of this huge country work hard, and push and shove to get what they want before anyone else does.

Price Gouging

Overall, Nathan Rd in Hong Kong is worse when it comes to price gouging, but Guangzhou is hardly a hotbed of honesty. It probably wouldn't matter if foreigners were only charged double, but you might be charged five times the going rate for some simple service such as doing laundry or a shoe repair. Needless to say, it's always wise to negotiate the price beforehand.

While we're on the subject, try not to buy any of the tourist souvenir items on sale in the top-end hotel shopping arcades. Prices in these emporiums of extortion are often 500% higher than what you would find if you hunt around for yourself. Refer to the Shopping section in this chapter for advice on where to shop.

LEGAL MATTERS

The PSB is responsible for introducing and enforcing regulations concerning foreign-

ers. So, for example, it bears responsibility for exclusion of foreigners from certain hotels. If this means you get stuck for a place to stay, the PSB can direct you to an expensive hotel.

There are a few ways you can inadvertently have an unpleasant run-in with the PSB. The most common way is to overstay your visa. Foreign males who are suspected of being 'too friendly' with Chinese women could have trouble with the PSB. Foreign missionaries who enter China on a tourist visa and proceed to proselytise are routinely arrested.

If you do have a run-in with the bureau, you may have to write a confession of your guilt and pay a fine. In more serious cases, you can be expelled from China (at your own expense). If you proclaim political views of an alien nature (eg wearing a T-shirt that says 'Remember Tiananmen'), sooner or later you will be escorted to the border. But in general, if you aren't doing anything particularly nasty like smuggling suitcases of dope or weapons through customs, the PSB will probably not throw you in prison.

If you do get arrested, you should insist on the right to contact staff at your country's embassy.

BUSINESS HOURS

In 1995, the working week in mainland China was reduced to five days (it had previously been six) – so the residents of Guangzhou actually work fewer days than their more affluent counterparts in Hong Kong and Macau.

Banks, offices and government departments are open Monday to Friday. As a rough guide only, banks open around 8 to 9 am, close for two hours in the middle of the day, and reopen until 5 or 6 pm.

Many parks, zoos and monuments have similar opening hours, and are also open on weekends and often at night. Shows at cinemas and theatres conclude at about 9.30 or 10 pm.

Restaurants are open for early-morning breakfast, sometimes as early as 5.30 am, until about 7.30 am, then open for lunch and again for dinner around 5 to 9 pm. Chinese eat early and go home early – by 9 pm you'll probably find the chairs stacked and the cooks heading home. Privately run restaurants are usually open all day, and often late into the night, especially around train stations.

Long-distance bus and train stations open the ticket offices around 5 or 5.30 am before the first trains and buses pull out. Apart from a one or two hour break in the middle of the day, these often stay open until about 11 or 11.30 pm.

PUBLIC HOLIDAYS & SPECIAL EVENTS

The Chinese have nine national holidays during the year, as follows:

New Year's Day
    1 January
Chinese Lunar New Year
    The first day of the first moon (usually at the end of January or the beginning of February).
International Working Women's Day
    8 March
International Labour Day
    1 May
Youth Day
    4 May
Children's Day
    1 June
Anniversary of the founding of the Chinese Communist Party (CCP)
    1 July
Anniversary of the founding of the Chinese People's Liberation Army (PLA)
    1 August
National Day
    1 October

International Labour Day celebrations in China have been slightly muted in recent years with the winding down of state controlled enterprises and subsequent massive layoffs; Youth Day commemorates the Beijing student demonstrations of 4 May 1919 when the Versailles Conference gave Germany's 'rights' in the city of Tianjin to Japan; and National Day celebrates the founding of the PRC in 1949.

ACTIVITIES

Check out the magazine *Clueless in Guangzhou* for up to the minute details on organisations that arrange a whole spectrum of sports fixtures including football, rugby, floorball and aerobic classes.

Fitness Clubs

While swimming pools and gymnasiums exist for the Chinese public, these are generally overcrowded and in poor condition. You'll find better facilities at the tourist hotels. Most hotels in big cities like Guangzhou permit non-guests to use the gyms, pools, saunas, tennis courts etc on a fee basis. This is not a bad idea if you're staying for a month or more. Monthly fees typically start at around US$50.

Golf

The Guangzhou Luhu Golf and Country Club (☎ 8350-7777, fax 8358-7777) boasts an 18 hole golf course and fitness complex. It's within the grounds of Luhu Park on the southern slope of the White Cloud Hills. Non-member fees are as follows: nine holes cost Y374 (weekdays) and Y641 (weekends); 18 holes cost Y705 (weekdays) and Y1069 (weekends).

Elsewhere in Guangdong Province, both Shenzhen and Zhuhai boast a number of golf courses. See the relevant chapters in this book for details.

Running

While jogging through the black clouds of petrol fumes on Renmin Lu may not be the best way to clear out the lungs, there are a few alternatives. Hash House Harriers meet regularly to jog in the countryside surrounding Guangzhou. The group meets every Saturday afternoon at Kathleen's (☎ 8359-8045). You need to take Y40 for the bus and soft drinks for the trip.

Taijiquan

If you don't mind getting up at the crack of dawn, you can join the Chinese in any park for an early morning *taiji (t'ai chi)* exercise session. This is an excellent way to keep fit and an opportunity to see the Chinese in one of their favourite pastimes.

Tennis

The Garden Hotel has two courts, and there are also very good courts at Tianhe Stadium. If you're staying on Shamian Island, check its map in the Guangzhou City chapter for the location of the courts on the south of the island.

COURSES

As China continues to experiment with capitalism, universities have found it increasingly necessary to raise funds and not depend so much on state largesse. For this reason, most universities welcome fee-paying foreign students.

Most of the courses offered are in Chinese language studies, but other possibilities include Chinese medicine, acupuncture, painting, music etc. If you have the money, almost anything is possible.

There is a considerable variation in the quality of instruction and the prices charged. Tuition alone typically runs from US$1000 to US$3000 per year, sometimes double, and it may depend on your nationality. The university is supposed to arrange your accommodation (no, it's not free). You'll find that living conditions vary from reasonably comfortable to horrific.

If possible, try not to pay anything in advance. Show up at the school to assess the situation, and talk to other foreign students to see if they're satisfied. Once you've handed over the cash, don't expect a refund.

Language

There is a growing number of places where you can learn either Mandarin or Cantonese. This used to be the sole province of the universities, but with the growth in the number of expats working in Guangzhou, a number of schools are offering Chinese language classes.

ALTEC (☎ 8777-5167) offers a 12 week course (48 hours) in Mandarin for Y2000. Class groups are limited to eight people, so you don't end up in the back row of a warehouse sized classroom. ProFe (☎ (13) 8277-8600) also tutors in Mandarin.

The Chinese Language Centre of Zhongshan University in Guangzhou, 135 Xingang Xilu, is an excellent place to study either Mandarin or Cantonese. Courses are typically four hours per day, five days a week and cost Y6650 per semester. Dormitory accommodation for students is approximately Y25 to Y35 per day.

Consult the expat magazine *Clueless in Guangzhou* for schools advertising for students; otherwise, you can advertise in the magazine yourself for a teacher, especially if you find the going rates at most schools too expensive.

Traditional Medicine

Acupuncture and herbal medicine classes attract many foreign students. By far the most popular venue for this is the Traditional Chinese Medicine Hospital (☎ 8188-6504, *zhōngyī yīyuàn*) at 16 Zhuji Lu (near Shamian Island).

WORK

This is far easier than it used to be and as a result there is a flourishing expat society in Guangzhou. With the growing number of foreign firms setting up, there is an increasing need to hire knowledge and expertise, so a growing band of foreigners is heading to Guangzhou for work. For an idea of available jobs, consult *Clueless in Guangzhou*, which has a ever-growing section devoted to employment ads.

As the expat community grows, so does the number of bars and restaurants where it is possible to angle for work. For other types of work keep your eyes open as employment can surface in unexpected quarters, as the following illustrates:

A friend of mine called Tom, an American law student studying Mandarin in China, had been introduced to this guy who was scouting for western faces for a Cherokee Jeep ad that was to go on national TV. I managed to get in on the deal as well, and it was a scream. There was this other guy called Sergei, a rather intense Russian ex-officer from the Afghanistan campaign. Tom and

The Point of it All

Can you cure people by sticking needles into them? The Chinese think so, and they've been doing it for thousands of years. Now the technique of acupuncture is gaining popularity in the west. In recent years, many westerners have made the pilgrimage to China either to seek treatment or to study acupuncture. Guangzhou is a particularly popular place both for patients and for students who want to learn more about this ancient medical technique (see Traditional Medicine in the previous Courses section for more details).

Having needles stuck into you might not sound pleasant, but if done properly it doesn't hurt. Knowing just where to insert the needle is crucial. Acupuncturists have identified more than 2000 insertion points, but only about 150 are commonly used.

The exact mechanism by which acupuncture works is not fully understood. The Chinese talk of energy channels or meridians which connect the needle insertion point to the particular organ, gland or joint being treated. The acupuncture point is sometimes quite far from the area of the body being treated.

There are several schools of thought among acupuncturists. The most common school in China is called the Eight Principles School. Another is the Five Elements School.

As with herbal medicine, acupuncture works depending on the acupuncturist and the condition being treated. Like herbal medicine, acupuncture tends to be more helpful for treating long-term conditions (such as chronic headaches) than sudden emergencies (eg acute appendicitis).

However, there are times when acupuncture can be used for an acute condition. For example, surgical operations have been performed using acupuncture as the only anaesthetic. In this case,

I had to stand in front of these two jeeps and declare (in Chinese) that the jeeps were ours (I didn't have a clue how to drive at the time). Sergei meanwhile would drive by in his jeep and we'd turn and wave woodenly after him like the stilted actors we were. It was all a joke, but we were paid decent money and a big meal was thrown in plus the ignominy of watching ourselves on TV every night. I stopped going to the local market when the stallholders started to gather around me, asking if it was really me on TV. The pressures of fame!

English Tutoring

There are also opportunities to teach English and other foreign languages. Teaching in China is not a way to get rich – pay is roughly US$180 a month, payable in RMB rather than foreign currency. While this is about four times as much as the average urban Chinese worker earns, it won't get you far after you've left China. There are usually some fringe benefits, like free or low-cost housing and special ID cards that get you discounts on trains and flights. As a worker in China, you will be assigned to a 'work unit', but unlike the locals, you'll be excused from political meetings and the God-like controls over your life that the typical Chinese has to endure.

Two topics that cannot be discussed in the classroom are politics and religion. Foreigners teaching in China have reported spies being placed in their classrooms.

Doing Business

At one time, China was the world's most advanced nation. The Chinese invented gunpowder, rockets, the printing press and paper currency. How did such an advanced nation fall so far behind? Probably because the Chinese also invented bureaucracy.

In bureaucratic China, even simple things can be made difficult – renting property, getting a telephone installed, hiring staff, paying taxes etc can generate mind-boggling quantities of red tape. Many foreign business people who have worked in China say that success is usually the a small electric current (from batteries) is passed through the needles, which are usually inserted in the head.

While some satisfied patients give glowing testimonials about the prowess of acupuncturists, others are less impressed. The only way to find out is to try it for yourself.

While acupuncture itself is relatively harmless, one should not forget that AIDS and hepatitis B can be spread easily by contaminated needles. In Hong Kong disposable acupuncture needles are routinely used, but this is not necessarily the case elsewhere in China. Back-alley acupuncturists who reuse needles are still common in many parts of Asia. If you're going to experiment with acupuncture outside Hong Kong, first find out if the doctor has disposable needles. If not, you can buy your own needles, which you can take to the doctor (check first if the doctor is willing). You need to consult with the doctor to find out what size and gauge of needles you should buy.

Massage is another traditional healing technique loosely related to acupuncture. The Chinese variety is somewhat different from the popular techniques practised by people in the west. One traditional Chinese method employs cups placed on the patient's skin. A burning piece of alcohol-soaked cotton is briefly put inside the cup to drive out the air before it is applied. As the cup cools, a partial vacuum is produced, leaving a nasty looking but harmless mark on the skin. The mark goes away after a few days. Other methods include blood-letting and scraping the skin with coins or porcelain soup spoons.

Moxibustion is a variation on the theme. Various types of herbs, rolled into what looks like a ball of fluffy cotton, are held near the skin and ignited. This method can be spiced up by igniting the herbs on a slice of ginger. The idea is to apply the maximum amount of heat possible without burning the patient. This heat treatment is supposed to be good for diseases such as arthritis.

result of dogged persistence. Many give up completely.

If you have a business interest in China and you need help, consult one of the associations listed under Business Organisations in this chapter. Otherwise, make sure that you have researched your area thoroughly and sounded out advice from business experts or consultants before you make a visit to China.

Buying is simple, selling is more difficult, but setting up a business in China is a whole different can of worms.

If yours is a high-technology company, you can go into certain economic zones and register as a wholly foreign-owned enterprise. In that case you can hire people yourself without going through the government, enjoy a three year tax holiday, obtain long-term income tax advantages, and import duty-free personal items for corporate and expat use. The alternative is listing your company as a representative office, which does not allow you to sign any contracts in China – these must be signed by the mother company. The Foreign

Service Company (FESCO) is where you hire employees. FESCO currently demands around US$325 per month per employee, 75% of which goes to the government.

It's easier to register as a representative office. First find out where you want to set up (a city or special economic zone), then go through local authorities (there are no national authorities for this). Go to the local Commerce Office, Economic Ministry, Foreign Ministry or any ministry that deals with foreign economic trade promotion. Setting up in a 'high-technology zone' is recommended if you can qualify, but where you register depends on what type of business you're doing. Your embassy can advise you.

The most important thing to remember when you go to register a company is not to turn away when you run into a bureaucratic barrier. Bureaucrats will tell you that everything is 'impossible'. In fact, anything is possible – it all depends on your *guanxi* ('connections'; see later in this section). Whatever you have in mind is negotiable – the rules are not necessarily rules at all.

Tax rates vary from zone to zone, authority to authority – it seems to be negotiable, but 15% is fairly standard in economic zones. Every

GUANGZHOU

economic zone has a fairly complete investment guide in English and Chinese – your embassy's economic council might have one, and these investment guides are becoming very clear (but even all these printed 'rules' are negotiable).

Red tape is not the only obstacle foreign investors have to face. It's very common that once a foreign-owned business gets up and running successfully, the military or the police suddenly move in Mafia style and demand to become your 'joint-venture partner'. That is to say, they demand 50% of your earnings. If you don't agree to this, you'll simply be harassed out of business. Many (if not most) expat-owned pubs and restaurants have fallen into this trap. Indeed, it's one of the things that most worries Hong Kong business people. Already several large Hong Kong businesses have been forced to take on Chinese state-run companies as 'business partners'.

The other worry that has forced a number of large foreign companies to pull the plug on venturing into China is that the companies technology may be stolen by a potential joint-venture partner. This has led to a hugely declining investment in China on the part of foreign firms who were once so eager to get into the market.

The vital ingredient to success in the Byzantine business world of China is *guanxi*, which loosely means connections. With the right guanxi, previously insoluble problems evaporate before your eyes and all's hunky dory. Without guanxi, even the simplest venture rapidly bogs down. Once you know who pulls the strings, take him (or her) out for dinner and spoil them with presents until you see the glint in their eye that signals guanxi has been established.

ACCOMMODATION
The PSB prohibits foreigners from staying in the dirt cheap Chinese hotels. Private guesthouses, such as Hong Kong's Chung-king Mansions, are also forbidden. At present, there is only one real budget hotel remaining in Guangzhou, the Guangzhou Youth Hostel on Shamian Island, and it often fills up.

Fortunately, there are a few tricks to keeping the hotel bill down. The simplest way is to share a room. Usually a second person can stay in the room for no extra cost. Also be aware that there is some confusion in terms: what most Chinese hotels call a 'single room' is a room with one bed. If two people sleep in a single room in the same bed, it's still a single room (and priced accordingly). A 'double room' is in fact a room with twin beds – up to four people could stay in a 'double room' for the same price as a single traveller. The vast majority of China's hotel rooms are actually doubles, and you pay for that second bed whether you use it or not. Rooms with three and four beds can also be found.

Discounts
If you're a foreign student in the PRC, you can get a discount on room prices. Students usually have to show their government-issued 'green card', though sometimes a fake 'white card' will do the trick. Foreign experts working in China usually qualify for the same discounts as students.

If you are really stuck for a place to stay, it sometimes helps to phone or visit the local PSB and explain your problem. Just as the PSB makes the rules, the PSB can break the rules. A hotel not approved for foreigners can be granted a temporary reprieve by the PSB; all it takes is a phone call from the right official. Unfortunately, getting such an exemption is not easy.

Hotel Etiquette
Most hotels have an attendant on every floor. The attendant keeps an eye on the hotel guests. This is partly to prevent theft and partly to stop you from bringing locals back for the night.

To conserve energy, in many cheaper hotels hot water for bathing is only available in the evening, sometimes only for a few hours a night, or once every three days. It's worth asking when/if the hot water will be turned on. Hot water for drinking is delivered in thermos flasks which can be refilled upon request.

The policy at every hotel in China requires that you check out by noon to avoid being charged extra. If you check out between noon and 6 pm, there is a charge of 50% of the room price – after 6 pm you have to pay for another full night.

The trend in China over the last few years has been to equip every room, even in the cheap hotels – with TV sets permanently turned to maximum volume. The Hong Kong-style ultra-violent movies are noisy enough, but the introduction of Nintendo-style video games and karaoke microphones (which can be attached to TV sets) has added a new dimension to the cacophony. The combination of screams, screeches, shootings, songs, rings, gongs, beeps and buzzers that reverberate through the vast concrete corridors could force a statue to run away. Many hotels also have a karaoke parlour on a particular floor; try not to book the room just above it, as the singing usually gets going late in the evening, building to a crescendo at around 2 am.

Something to be prepared for is lack of privacy – what happens is that you're sitting starkers in your hotel room, the key suddenly turns in the door and the room attendant casually wanders in. Don't expect anyone to knock before entering. Some of the better hotels have a bolt that will lock the door from the inside, but most budget hotels are not so well equipped. Your best protection against becoming an unwilling star in a live nude show is to prop a chair against the door.

The method of designating floors in mainland China is the same as used in the USA, but different from that used in Hong Kong, Australia or the UK. What would be the 'ground floor' in Hong Kong is the '1st floor' on the mainland, the 1st is the 2nd, and so on. However, there is some inconsistency, and a few Hong Kong-owned hotels in southern China use the British system.

Rental Accommodation

Most Chinese people live in government subsidised housing which is almost always dirt cheap. For foreigners, the situation is totally different.

If you're going to be working for the Chinese government as a teacher or other type of foreign expert, you'll almost certainly be provided with cheap or low-cost housing. Conditions probably won't be luxurious, but the cost should be minimal.

The news is not good for those coming to China to do business or work for a foreign company. The cheap apartments available to the Chinese are off-limits to foreigners, which leaves you with two choices, a hotel or a luxury apartment in a compound specifically designated for foreigners.

If you live in a hotel, you might be able to negotiate a discount for a long-term stay, but it's not guaranteed. Due to the increasing number of foreigners working in Guangzhou, there is a wider range of accommodation available. Monthly rental prices for apartments and villas start at US$500 and reach US$15,000 or more.

One estate agent that has expat experience is Guangzhou Zhongli Properties Agency Ltd (☎ 8778-5418, fax 8775-2957), unit 3002, North Tower, World Trade Centre, 371-375 Huanshi Dong Lu. This agent can also arrange domestic help for you, fill your apartment with furniture and advise on other aspects you may need to know about living in Guangzhou.

Another agency that can help you to locate suitable accommodation is Uni-Wide Consultants Ltd (☎ 8755-2456, fax 8755-0015), room 1408, Metro Plaza, 183 Tianhe Bei Lu, Tianhe.

Increasingly, Hong Kong-style expat and high-living Chinese residential estates are cropping up. These are self-contained blocks of apartments that incorporate underground parking, imported appliances and fixtures, health clubs, cafes, bars and sports facilities. One example is Gold Arch Riverdale (☎ 8736-3279), on Ersha Island.

Considering the sky-high rents, buying a apartment or villa might seem like a good idea for companies with cash. It's actually possible, but the rules vary from city to city. In some cities, only Overseas Chinese are

GUANGZHOU

permitted to buy luxury villas. Real estate speculators from Taiwan do a roaring trade. Shenzhen has long been in the business of selling apartments to Hong Kong residents, who in turn rent the apartments out to others. Foreigners can buy apartments in some cities (at astronomical prices), and doing this can actually gain you a residence permit.

As for simply moving in with a Chinese family and paying them rent, forget it. The PSB will swoop down on you (and the hapless Chinese family) faster than ants at a picnic.

FOOD

While lacking the range and finesse of the Hong Kong restaurant universe, Guangzhou is developing quickly and new eateries are constantly flinging open the doors.

Food in Guangzhou is similar to what you'll find in Hong Kong, except that there's a good deal of wildlife on the menu. Snake, monkey, pangolin (an armadillo-like creature), bear, giant salamander, turtle and racoon are among the exotic tastes that can be catered for, not to mention the more mundane dog, cat and rat dishes. For a comprehensive list of dishes (with script) see the Language chapter.

One look at the people fishing in the sewage canals around Guangzhou might dull your appetite for Pearl River trout.

Western food is increasing in range and availability, as more and more expats zero in on Guangzhou for work. Expat restaurants are either set up by expats (who have moved in to occupy the market niche) or by entrepreneurial Chinese who smell rich pickings in the air.

Most of the smart restaurants are still at top-end hotels, but there is a thriving market for the pub grub scene. Fast food is well represented by McDonald's, KFC and Pizza Hut.

DRINKS
Nonalcoholic Drinks

Aside from the ubiquitous tea, China has come up with a few surprisingly good local soft drinks. A local speciality is the orange and honey flavoured Jianlibao; brush your teeth after drinking this – it's a real filling-loosener. Oddities include lychee-flavoured carbonated drinks and orange drinks with strange pieces of something floating in them. Suannai is an excellent sweet liquid yoghurt that you slurp out of bottles with a straw.

Alcoholic Drinks

Most Chinese firewater has little appeal to western tastes. Famous brews like Shaoxing and Maotai taste like they could take the paint off a car. If you smoke, try to hold the ember of your cigarette away from any of the vapours, as they have a low flash point. If you end up quaffing this stuff in a drinking match with one of the locals, make sure you eat about eight pizzas beforehand. Rice wine *(mi)* is meant for cooking, but it's also a cheap drink, though the next morning you'll feel like your brain is made of cottage cheese.

Most Chinese beers are OK and extremely cheap. Rumour has it that formaldehyde is used as a preservative in the cheaper local varieties, which is why your hands start shaking after a few bottles, but the national beers, like Tsingtao, are great. It's actually a German beer – the town where it is made, Tsingtao (now spelled Qingdao) was once a German concession. The Chinese inherited the brewery when the Germans were kicked out. Guangzhou is also known for it's local Zhujiang (Pearl River) brand. San Miguel has a brewery in Guangzhou.

The Chinese also do a few sweet grape wines. The stuff is drinkable, but otherwise unremarkable. The two most popular labels are Great Wall and Dynasty.

ENTERTAINMENT

The expat invasion and the growing liberalisation of China has led to a micro-boom in Guangzhou nightlife. Nightclubs, bars and clubs open and close with abandon as the youth of China experiment with new-found sights and sounds.

Although Guangzhou doesn't have the spread that Hong Kong offers, the city appears keen to catch up. There's definitely a feeling of excitement in today's Guangzhou that was absent just a few years ago and the face of the city is quickly changing.

A host of western-style bars and restaurants provide welcome refuge for people on the run from rice and karaoke. Apart from those listed in the Guangzhou City chapter, for a full list of newly opened bars and clubs consult the entertainment section of the freebie magazine *Clueless in Guangzhou*.

Warning
Besides any mental damage you may suffer from visiting karaoke bars, these places can be ruinous to your budget. There have been disturbing reports that the 'Tokyo Nightclub Syndrome' has hit Guangzhou. Basically, foreigners (chiefly male) sitting in a karaoke bar are suddenly joined by an attractive young woman (or maybe several women) who 'just want to talk'. A few drinks are ordered, maybe just Coke or orange juice, and at the end of an hour's conversation a bill of perhaps US$500 or so is presented to the hapless foreigner. The drinks might only cost US$10, but the other US$490 is a 'service charge' for talking to the women, who are in fact bar hostesses.

Even more sinister is that these women approach foreigners on the street, ostensibly just to 'practise their English'. Somewhere in the conversation they suggest going to a 'nice place', which happens to be a karaoke bar. What they fail to mention is that they work for the bar and get a percentage of the profits for every sucker they bring in.

It needs to be mentioned that the victims of these schemes are not only western foreigners. Overseas Chinese, Hong Kong residents, Macanese, Taiwanese and even mainland Chinese who appear to have money are also targeted. This rip-off system seems to be spreading.

SPECTATOR SPORT
Horse Racing
That most bourgeois of capitalist activities, gambling, has staged a comeback in Guangzhou with the opening of the Guangzhou

Horse Racing Track *(pǎo mǎ chǎng)*. Chairman Mao is no doubt doing somersaults in his tomb. Gambling is actually still illegal throughout mainland China, but the Guangdong government manages to get around this inconvenience by calling it an 'intelligence competition'. Races are held twice weekly in the evenings. The racing season is in winter (December to February), but the exact times are subject to change.

Football & Rugby
Regular matches are held at Tianhe Stadium in the north-east of the city.

SHOPPING
The Chinese produce some interesting items for export – tea, clothing, Silkworm missiles – the latter not generally for sale to the public. Another huge speciality lies in pirate CDs, which gets right up the noses of foreign film and music companies. The quality of pirate video CD films is generally diabolical, and even though you can pick up films that have only just come out in the west, these are often filmed in cinemas, so occasionally a head in silhouette pops into view, or you see the usherette's torch beam cutting through the blackness. The quality of music CDs is, of course, much better, but you won't find much of a selection.

The Chinese economy has been fuelled since the early 1980s by manic consumer spending, reflected in the growing number of department stores in the major cities. Unfortunately, quality has often not kept pace with quantity. There is an awful lot of junk on sale: zippers that break the first time you use them, music cassette players (some with whirling, flashing lights) that last a week, electric appliances that go up in smoke the first time it's plugged in etc.

Given this state of affairs, you might wonder how China manages to successfully export so much. The simple fact is that export items are made to a much higher standard, while junk is dumped on the local markets. Always test zippers, examine stitching and, in the case of electrical appliances, plug it in and make sure it won't electrocute you before handing over the cash. Chinese sales clerks expect you to do this; you'll be considered a fool if you don't.

The intersection of Beijing Lu and Zhongshan Lu is the top shopping area in Guangzhou. Here many excellent shops spread out along both streets. The central section of Jiefang Lu is also good. Otherwise, shopping in Guangzhou is becoming more and more focused in the large department stores.

Department Stores

Guangzhou's department stores have certainly changed over the past decade. Visitors from the 1980s recall finding everyday consumer goods for sale, such as jackhammers, lathes, anti-aircraft spotlights and 10,000V transformers. These days, you're more likely to find video tape players, electric guitars and Nintendo games.

Large stores include Nanfang (nánfáng dàshà) at 49 Yanjiang 1-Lu, just to the east and opposite the main entrance to the Cultural Park. You can also enter the store from the Yanjiang Lu side by the Pearl River.

On the corner of Beijing Lu and Xihu Lu is the Guangzhou Department Store (guǎngzhōu bǎihuò dàlóu). The other main department store in town is the Dongshan Department Store (dōngshān bǎihuò dàlóu), just south of Zhongshan 1 Lu and north of Dongshanhu Park.

Friendship Stores

There are two Friendship Stores in Guangzhou. The main one is next to the Baiyun Hotel on Huanshi Lu. It's adjacent to the Friendship Cafe. This store has a particularly good supermarket, so if you have a craving for Cadbury chocolate bars or Swiss cheese, this is the place.

The other Friendship Store is near the China Hotel on the corner of Liuhua Lu and Jiefang North Lu. Both Friendship Stores accept all main credit cards and can arrange shipment of goods back to your country.

Shopping Malls

In Teem Plaza on Tian He Rd is the Teem shopping mall. Teem Plaza is in Tianhe, set to become a major hub of the new Guangzhou. Tianhe contains China's tallest building (for the present), the Sky Plaza (80 storeys), and is likely to develop into the shopping axis for the city.

Nam Fong International Plaza (nánfāng guójì guǎngchǎng) is immediately to the east of the Friendship Store on Huanshi Lu. It has a decent Hong Kong-style supermarket, and its mall is heavily geared towards luxury items like jewellery, perfume, cosmetics and the latest fashions.

Antiques

Guangzhou has its antique market in the alleys off Daihe Lu (see the West Guangzhou map in the Guangzhou City chapter). It's very informal and consists mostly of people peddling wares from their windows or the back of a truck. It can be very interesting, but be aware that few of these 'antiques' are very old and many may be fake. Still, it's good fun to explore.

The Friendship Stores have antique sections, but don't expect to find a bargain. Only antiques that have been cleared for sale to foreigners may be taken out of the country. When you buy an item that is more than 100 years old it will come with an official red wax seal attached. This seal does not necessarily indicate that the item is an antique. You'll also get a receipt of sale which you must show to customs when you leave the country; otherwise, the antique will be confiscated. Imitation antiques are sold everywhere. Some museum shops sell replicas of pieces on exhibit.

On the left of the Cultural Park and tucked away down a small street is a fascinating antiques market full of ceramics, jade and other collectibles. The owners of the stalls all trip over each other to show you the cream of the crop. Haggle hard. On the west of Shamian Island, on Shamian Sijie, is a string of souvenir shops selling paintings, clothes and calligraphy. The road leading up to the Temple of the Six Banyan Trees is also chock-a-block with souvenir shops bursting with ceramics and jade. The

Guangzhou Antique Shop at 172 Wende Bei Lu has a reasonable range of (not cheap) souvenir items.

Arts & Crafts

Brushes, paints and other art materials may be worth checking: a lot of this stuff is being imported by western countries, so you should be able to pick it up cheaper at the source. Scroll paintings are sold everywhere and are invariably expensive, partly because the material on which the paintings are done is expensive. There are many street artists in China who sit on the sidewalk making drawings and paintings on the spot and selling them to passers-by.

Beautiful kites are sold in China and are worth getting just to hang on your wall. Paper rubbings of stone inscriptions are cheap and make nice wall hangings when framed. Papercuts are sold everywhere and some are exquisite.

Jade and ivory jewellery is commonly sold in China, but watch out for fakes. Remember that every ivory item bought brings the African elephant closer to extinction, and that countries such as Australia and the USA prohibit the importation of ivory. We strongly urge you not to buy ivory goods.

The Jiangnan Native Product Store at 399 Zhongshan 4-Lu has a good selection of bamboo and baskets, and the Guangzhou Arts and Crafts Market is convenient at 284 Changdi Dama Lu, near the Aiqun Hotel.

No prizes for guessing the speciality at the Guangzhou Pottery Store, 151 Zhongshan 5-Lu.

Bicycles

If you think you can handle the anarchy of Guangzhou's streets on two wheels, head over to Fucheng Bicycle Industry at 350 Dezheng Zhong Lu, which has a decent selection of bicycles.

Books, Posters & Magazines

The gift shops at major hotels might seem like a strange place to shop for books, but these often have a decent collection of English-language maps, books and foreign magazines, such as *Time, Newsweek, Far Eastern Economic Review* and the *Economist*. You can find lower prices in Guangzhou's Chinese bookshops, but the foreign magazines are priced the same everywhere. The Holiday Inn seems to have one of the better bookshops in town.

The largest bookshop is the Guangzhou Book Centre, opposite Teem Plaza in Tianhe. The Foreign Language Bookshop at 326 Beijing Lu has mostly textbooks and some notable English classics, but the pickings are slim if you want contemporary blockbusters.

The Xinhua Bookshop at 336 Beijing Lu is the other main Chinese bookshop in the city. It has a good collection of maps, which are often better than those you can buy on the street. Most are in Chinese characters, though some maps have both Chinese characters and pinyin. It also has lots of wall posters and reproductions of Chinese paintings.

Music

Unfortunately, Guangzhou still suffers from the appalling range of music that typifies the rest of mainland China. If you like Richard Clayderman, you'll have a field day. There is a music shop next to the Guangzhou Antique Shop, 172 Wen De Lu, that has a large selection of classical CDs.

Sporting Goods

Datong Lu, on the western side of Ersha Dao (Ersha Island), has a decent selection of sports shops.

Stamps

Some travellers seem to think they can buy stamps cheaply in China and sell them for a profit at home, but it rarely works out that way. Nevertheless, China produces some beautiful stamps, and if you're a collector, they're worth checking out. The Guangzhou Stamp Company is at 151 Huanshi Xi Lu, west of the train station.

Getting There & Away

AIR

While Hong Kong is a great place to find cheap airfares, Guangzhou is not. Tickets purchased within mainland China are invariably more expensive (usually much more) than those purchased elsewhere. For example, buying a Melbourne to Guangzhou ticket will be cheaper if you purchase the ticket in Melbourne rather than Guangzhou. On the mainland, there is almost no such thing as discounting. This is in sharp contrast to Hong Kong, where cut-throat competition and discounting are the norm.

For this reason, prices quoted in this chapter are what you'd pay in China. If you're after the cheapest flights you can get from outside mainland China, see the Hong Kong Getting There & Away chapter.

Aside from being more expensive, flights into Guangzhou are not numerous. Only a handful of airlines fly into the city, mostly from neighbouring Asian countries. The situation will probably improve in the future, but for now the easiest way to reach Guangzhou by air is to fly into Hong Kong and then change flights.

On the other hand, Guangzhou is a major hub for domestic flights to other parts of mainland China.

Airports & Airlines

To give pilots a challenge, Guangzhou's Baiyun airport is right next to the White Cloud Hills, Guangzhou's only mountains. It's 12km north of the city centre. A new airport is planned at Huadu outside Guangzhou, but it most likely won't be open before 2003.

On domestic and international flights, the free baggage allowance for an adult passenger is 20kg in economy class and 30kg in 1st class. You are also allowed 5kg of hand luggage, though this is rarely weighed.

For years, Civil Aviation Administration of China (CAAC) was China's only domestic and international carrier. It has now

been broken up and private carriers have been allowed to operate. CAAC is now the umbrella organisation for the numerous subsidiaries, such as Air China, China Eastern, China Southern, China Northern, China Southwest, China Northwest, Great Wall, Shanghai, Shenzhen, Sichuan, Xiamen, Xinjiang and Yunnan airlines.

CAAC still publishes a combined international and domestic timetable in both English and Chinese, in April and November each year. These can be obtained for free in Hong Kong, but can be hard to find in Guangzhou (or indeed, anywhere in mainland China). It's important to realise that many of CAAC's flights are technically charters, even if it does run according to a regular schedule. If you purchase one of these 'charter' tickets, there will be no refund for cancellations and no changes are permitted. Don't count on the CAAC staff to tell you this.

It is possible to buy all of your domestic CAAC tickets from some non-Chinese airlines that have reciprocal arrangements with CAAC; however, this is generally not a good idea. First of all, it saves you no money whatsoever. Secondly, the tickets issued by travel agencies need to be exchanged for a proper stamped ticket at the appropriate CAAC offices in China. These offices have at times refused to honour 'foreign' tickets. Furthermore, CAAC flights are sometimes cancelled. If this happens, you'll have to return the ticket to the seller to get a refund. Your best bet is to buy your tickets directly from a CAAC office.

While CAAC's service has improved, some of its affiliated airlines fly pretty dodgy looking old Russian jets which will make you sorry you didn't purchase extra life insurance. Fortunately, on major routes such as Hong Kong to Guangzhou you're likely to fly on a new Boeing or Airbus. All the CAAC-affiliated airlines are listed in the CAAC timetable and sell tickets through

CAAC offices; some even have the CAAC logo on the tickets. The telephone number for Baiyun airport is ☎ 8657-8901; for airport flight information, call ☎ 8666-6123.

In Guangzhou, you'll find the following airline offices:

Air China
  (☎ 8668-1319, fax 8668-1286) 917 Renmin Lu
China Eastern
  (☎ 8668-1688 ext 3362, fax 8667-1104) 1st floor, Leizhou Hotel, 88 Zhanqian Lu
China Northern Airlines
  (☎ 8668-2488)
China Northwest Airlines
  (☎ 8330-8058/9212, fax 8330-9212) 197-199 Dongfeng Xilu
China Southern Airlines
  (☎ 8657-8901, fax 8664-4623) Baiyun airport
China Southwest Airlines
  (☎ 8666-5581)
Hainan
  (☎ 8669-9999) 99 Zhanqian Lu
Japan Air Systems
  (☎ 8669-6688, fax 8666-5603) room A-201, China Hotel, Liuhua Lu
Malaysia Airlines
  (☎ 8335-8828, 8335-8868) shop M04-05, Garden Hotel, 368 Huanshi Lu
Singapore Airlines
  (☎ 8335-8999, 8335-8886) mezzanine floor, Garden Hotel, 368 Huanshi Lu
Thai Airways
  (☎ 8382-4333)
Vietnam Airlines
  (☎ 8382-7187)

Australia
There are flights directly between Guangzhou and either Melbourne or Sydney. The standard return fare is US$1199.

China
There are four daily flights between Hong Kong and Guangzhou on China Southern Airlines. A one-way airfare is US$85; a return ticket costs double. The flight takes 35 minutes; the first flight leaves Guangzhou at 8.25 am and the last at 6.20 pm.

Japan
JAS flies from Guangzhou to Osaka. An economy return ticket costs US$800.

Malaysia
Kuala Lumpur is connected directly with Guangzhou on Malaysia Airlines. The economy return airfare is US$846.

Singapore
Both Singapore Airlines and CAAC fly the Guangzhou to Singapore route. Economy return tickets cost US$624.

Thailand
CAAC offers Guangzhou to Bangkok flights for US$300 (economy return).

USA
There are three flights per week from Los Angeles to Guangzhou on Southern Airlines; a return flight costs US$1380.

Vietnam
The only direct flight between Ho Chi Minh City (Saigon) and China is to Guangzhou. All other Vietnam to China flights are via Hanoi. The Guangzhou to Hanoi flight (US$299 return) takes 1½ hours; Guangzhou to Ho Chi Minh City (US$430 return) takes 2½ hours.

Departure Tax
If leaving China by air, the departure tax is Y90. The domestic airport departure tax is Y15.

LAND
Bus
There are several long-distance bus stations in Guangzhou. Different stations serve different routes, though there is quite a lot of overlap.

The Provincial bus station (adjacent to Guangzhou train station) serves many long-distance destinations, such as Guilin, Macau, Zhanjiang and Zhongshan.

The Liuhua bus station (opposite the Guangzhou train station and not to be confused with the Guangzhou City bus station) has a number of buses to destinations within Guangdong, Guangxi and Hainan including: Shantou (Y140 sleeper), Guilin (Y182 sleeper), Conghua (Y15), Haikou (Y149

GUANGZHOU

sleeper), Chaozhou (Y140 sleeper), Zhao-qing (Y21), Foshan (Y16), Shenzhen (Y40) and Zhuhai (Y40). Next door is the Baiyun bus station, which has minibuses to Foshan and Shenzhen. Both the Baiyun and the Liuhua bus stations are east of the Guang-zhou City bus station and do not have signs in English or pinyin.

Guangfo bus station serves Foshan, Taiping, Zhongshan and Zhuhai. It can be found on the south side of Zhongshan 8 Lu (further along to the west of Zhongshan 7 Lu), just north of Liwanhu Park. Nearby is the Xijiao bus station (to the west of Guangfo bus station on the intersection of Huangsha Lu and Zhongshan 8 Lu), which is also useful for getting to towns in the Pearl River Delta. Places served from there include Shenzhen, Zhongshan and Zhuhai.

The small Dashatou bus station is near the Dashatou Wharf and serves Taiping, Zhanjiang, Zhongshan and Wuzhou. It's not used much and foreigners may find it diffi-cult to make themselves understood unless they can speak Chinese.

The Panyu bus station is also called the Shayuan bus station, and serves Lianhua-shan and Panyu.

The Baiyun Lu bus station is one place where you can get buses to Conghua Hot Springs, but most people use the Guangzhou City bus station. It's in East Guangzhou, north-west of Ersha Island on Baiyun Lu.

The Yuexiunan bus station is a remote one that you aren't likely to use – all of its routes are better served by the larger sta-tions. Ditto for the Sanyuanli bus station.

Distant destinations are serviced by sleeper buses, which are more expensive but worth taking because you can sleep away most of the journey.

Train

Guangzhou is blessed with extensive inter-national and domestic train services. But in socialist China, trains do not have classes – instead you have hard seat, hard sleeper, soft seat and soft sleeper.

Except on the trains which serve some of the branch or more obscure lines, hard seat is not in fact hard but padded. But it is hard on your sanity, and if you're travelling a long distance you'll get little sleep on the upright seats.

Hard-seat carriages get packed to the gills, the lights stay on all night, passengers spit on the floor, you can asphyxiate from cigarette smoke, and the carriage speakers endlessly drone news, weather, information and music. Hard seat is OK for a day trip; some foreigners can't take more than five hours of it, while others have a threshold of 12 hours or even longer. A few brave, pen-niless souls have even been known to travel long distance this way – some roll out a mat on the floor under the seats and go to sleep on top of the gob, chicken bones, peanut shells and other litter.

Hard sleepers are comfortable and only a fixed number of people are allowed in the sleeper carriage. The carriage is made up of doorless compartments with six bunks in three tiers. The sheets, pillows and blankets are all provided. It does very nicely as a budget hotel.

The best bunk to get is a middle one, since the lower one is invaded by all and sundry who use it as a seat during the day, and the top one has little headroom. The top bunks are also where the cigarette smoke floats about and it's usually stinking hot up there in summer, even when the fans are on full blast.

The worst possible bunks are the top ones at either end of the carriage or right in the middle – they're right up against the speak-ers and you'll get a rude shock at about 6 am. Lights and speakers in hard sleeper go out at around 9.30 to 10 pm. Competition for hard sleepers has become keen in recent years, and you'll be lucky to get one on short notice.

On short journeys (such as Shenzhen to Guangzhou) some trains have soft-seat carriages. The seats are comfortable and overcrowding is not permitted. Smoking is prohibited, a significant advantage unless you enjoy asphyxiation. If you want to smoke in the soft-seat section, you can do so only by going out into the corridor between cars. Soft seats cost about the same as hard sleepers, but they're well worth it. Unfortunately, carriages with soft seats are a rarity.

Soft sleeper is the luxury class. Softies get the works, with four comfortable bunks in a closed compartment – complete with straps to stop the top fatso from falling off in the middle of the night, wood panelling, potted plants, lace curtains, tea set, clean washrooms, carpets (so no spitting) and often air conditioning. As for those speakers, not only do you have a volume control, you can turn the bloody things off.

Soft sleeper costs twice as much as hard sleeper, and almost the same price as flying (on some routes even more than flying). It's relatively easy to get soft sleeper because few Chinese can afford it; however, the growing class of *nouveaux riches* plus high-ranking cadres (who charge it to their expense accounts) have upped the demand for soft sleepers, so you might wind up in a hard seat no matter how much cash you've got. Travelling in soft sleeper should be experienced once – it gives you a good chance to meet the ruling class.

Trains head north from Guangzhou to just about everywhere in China including Beijing, Shanghai, Qingdao, Kunming, Chengdu, Hangzhou, Fuzhou, Shaoxing, Foshan, Zhongqing, Xian and Tianjin. Sleepers can be booked several days in advance at CITS in Guangzhou (east of the Guangzhou train station). Otherwise, you can book your ticket at the ticketing office (in the eastern part of the Guangzhou train station) to the right of Guangzhou train station. The ticket office is open from 5.30 am to 10.30 pm.

Guangzhou train station is a nightmare – mobs of people do battle for a limited number of seats and only the fit survive. Add to that an army of thieves and pickpockets, and it's not hard to see why many foreigners opt for the bus. If you want to go by train, however, there is a way to be spared all this. Many trains depart from Guangzhou East train station *(guǎngzhōu dōng zhàn)*. This station is newer, considerably cleaner and definitely safer. There is also a special foreigners' ticket window.

In Future A high-speed railway line is being constructed between Hong Kong and Guangzhou which should reduce the trip to perhaps an hour or so. A new line is also under construction from Guangzhou to the Zhuhai Special Economic Zone near Macau. Yet another line is being built along the east coast with the goal of connecting Guangzhou to Fujian Province. Don't expect to be making use of all these marvellous additions to the Chinese railway system for a long while.

Hong Kong

Bus The six lane super highway from Hong Kong to Guangzhou has reduced the bus journey to around three hours. The expressway will eventually be extended to make a 240km loop from Hong Kong to Guangzhou to Macau.

Citybus operates express buses on the Hong Kong to Guangzhou route. The bus journey takes about three hours and costs HK$160. Departures in Kowloon are from the Guangdong bus station on Canton Rd (between Austin and Jordan Rds). There are also departures from Admiralty Mass Transit Railway (MTR) station on Hong Kong Island and City One in Sha Tin (New Territories). In Hong Kong you can ring Citybus (☎ 2736-3888) for the latest information.

In Guangzhou, you catch these buses from major hotels, popular spots being the White Swan and Victory Hotels (both on Shamian Island); the GITIC Plaza International, Landmark, China and Liuhua Hotels. Phone the relevant hotel to get a schedule. There are also regular coaches that depart from outside the China International Travel Service (CITS) building near the Guangzhou train station that cost Y180.

Train The express through train between Hong Kong and Guangzhou is comfortable and convenient. It covers the 182km route in just under two hours.

Departures are from the Kowloon station of the Kowloon-Canton Railway (KCR). You must complete immigration exit formalities at the station before boarding. Therefore, you'd best arrive about 45 minutes before train departure time, as the gate closes 20 minutes before the train departs.

Departures from Hong Kong are at 8.35, 9.25 and 11.35 am, and 12.55 pm. One-way, 2nd class tickets for the high-speed express trains are HK$220 (child HK$110); 1st class costs HK$250. Prices can increase across the board by HK$40 during 'high season' (meaning during public holidays or whenever Guangzhou hosts a major trade fair).

When returning to Hong Kong, the toilets on the train close once you cross the border, so if you need to use them think about it early. There's a long wait to get through immigration in Hong Kong, and then there are crowds lining up for the toilet.

To reach the Kowloon KCR station from Tsim Sha Tsui, take green minibus No 6 from Hankow Rd (south side of Peking Rd opposite the HMV CD store).

In Hong Kong, tickets can be booked up to seven days before departure at China Travel Service (CTS) or the Kowloon KCR station. Return tickets are also sold, but only seven to 30 days before departure.

Departures from Guangzhou are from the Guangzhou East train station. Trains leave at 8.40 and 10 am, and 3.15 and 5.45 pm. A 2nd class one-way ticket costs Y242, and 1st class is Y275. In Guangzhou, CITS or CTS both sell train tickets but not for same-day departure. Hotels can also get you tickets if you give them enough notice. Same-day tickets must be bought on the ground floor of the Guangzhou East train station.

You're allowed to take bicycles on the express train, and these are stowed in the freight car.

Macau

Bus If you want to go directly from Macau, Kee Kwan Motors, across the street from the Floating Casino, sells bus tickets. One bus takes you to the border at Zhuhai and a second takes you to Guangzhou four hours later. The trip takes about five hours in all. Single tickets cost HK$55 and return tickets are HK$110. From Monday to Friday, buy your ticket in the evening before departure.

This international bus route is not necessarily the best way to make this journey. Having to get off the Macau bus, go through immigration and customs, wait for all your fellow passengers (and their enormous luggage), and then reboard another bus is a time-wasting and confusing exercise.

It's usually faster to cross the Macau and Zhuhai border by foot and catch a minibus from Zhuhai to Guangzhou. In Macau, bus No 3 runs between the Jetfoil pier and the China border via the Lisboa Hotel, Avenida Almeida Ribeiro and the Floating Casino.

Shenzhen

Bus In Shenzhen, coaches line up near the Hong Kong border at the Luohu bus station (opposite Shenzhen train station). The fares are posted on a sign beside the coaches, and at the time of writing were Y55. The drivers in Shenzhen often ask for Hong Kong dollars, but will accept Renmimbi (RMB). Most minibuses take the expressway, which reduces travel time to approximately two hours.

Minibuses from Guangzhou to Shenzhen, operate from several locations. These are most numerous at the Guangzhou city bus station in front of the Liuhua Hotel. Buses leave from there every thirty minutes (Y45), but there are numerous other departure points, such as other hotels (eg the China Hotel, Y55), Liuhua bus station and at the airport.

Minibuses speed to Shenzhen from the Baiyun bus station next to the Liuhua bus station, and large buses also head to Shenzhen (Y55) from the large CITS opposite the Guangzhou train station.

Train The local hard-seat train from Shenzhen to Guangzhou is cheap, but it makes a lot of stops en route, taking about 2½ hours. Hard seats are Y48. Slow trains leave from Guangzhou train station.

The double-decker express train is much more convenient and only takes just over an hour. Trains leave regularly from the Guangzhou East train station between 7 am and 9 pm. Soft seats cost Y80.

In Guangzhou, you can buy train tickets from CITS or hotel service desks several days in advance. Otherwise, you can join the queues at the train station.

Zhuhai

Bus From the Zhuhai bus station (next to the Yongtong Hotel), you can catch minibuses to Guangzhou. Some of the buses discharge passengers at Guangzhou's Xijiao bus station (near to the Guangfo bus station), which is just a short taxi ride from Shamian Island.

Buses leave from the long-distance bus station in Guangzhou every half an hour from 7.30 am to 6.30 pm for Zhuhai (Y34). These buses take you to the Gongbei district just on the border with Macau. Unscheduled minibuses to Zhuhai also cruise in front of the Guangzhou train station and leave when full (Y30). There are also direct buses from Guangzhou's Baiyun airport to Zhuhai. The journey takes about three hours and costs Y50.

Guilin & Yangshuo

Bus Buses for Guilin leave from the Liuhua bus station opposite the Guangzhou train station. Tickets (sleepers) are Y182 and the trip takes about 15 hours, but you can get off at Yangshuo if you don't want to go all the way to Guilin.

SEA

Travel to China by boat is usually less stressful than the trains or buses. The problem is that the number of services is being eroded and, at the time of writing, there were only a few possibilities for those wanting to travel by sea. This is a shame, but the reality is that the majority of Chinese now travel by train, plane and automobile, and the ferries are being slowly squeezed out of the picture.

The most popular boat is the overnight ferry to Guangzhou (it survives with a severely reduced schedule). Other services are the overnight ferry or the fast ferry to Zhaoqing. Some travellers make use of the fast catamarans plying the route from

Hong Kong to Shenzhen, Huangtian airport (also in Shenzhen), Zhuhai and Zhongshan. For details, see the Getting There & Away sections for these cities in the Around Guangzhou chapter.

CTS is the main booking agent for boats, but it charges for the service. You can get cheaper tickets at the China ferry terminal on Canton Rd in Kowloon, but the level of English spoken there is low. The company that operates these ferries also has a booking office (☎ 2885-3876) at 24 Connaught Rd West, but the language of business there is Cantonese.

Departure Tax

There is no departure tax from China if you leave by boat.

Hong Kong

There are two types of ships plying the route between Hong Kong and Guangzhou: Turbocats and a slow, overnight ferry.

In Hong Kong, ferry tickets to Guangzhou can be bought at the pier or from CTS. In Guangzhou, you can buy tickets at the pier, but you must pay in Hong Kong dollars.

Turbocats depart from the China ferry terminal in Tsim Sha Tsui. Turbo Cat (☎ 2851-1700) has two trips daily to East River Guangzhou (the Guangzhou Economic Zone), departing at 7.15 am and 1.30 pm; tickets are HK$250 from Kowloon and HK$225 from Guangzhou, and the journey takes two hours.

From the East River Guangzhou ferry terminal in Guangzhou, departures to Hong Kong are at 10.30 am and 4.30 pm. An economy ticket costs HK$189, 1st class is HK$284 and the VIP cabin costs HK$1704. Ring ☎ 8222-2555 in Guangzhou for details and ticket bookings.

The Pearl River Shipping Company also runs an overnight ferry, but the schedule is capricious and business is under threat from the faster Turbocats and the increased rail traffic. Ask at your hotel for any information on the service. At the time of writing, there were only five departures per month. The boat departs from Hong Kong at the China ferry terminal in Tsim Sha Tsui at 9 pm and arrives in Guangzhou the following morning at 6 am (though you cannot disembark until 7 am). In Guangzhou, the boat departs at 9 pm and arrives in Hong Kong at 6 am.

There are dormitory beds in 2nd class, which are quite comfortable – the biggest problem might be noisy neighbours. A 1st class ticket gets you a bed in a four person cabin with private bath. Special class is a two person cabin with bath. VIP class is like your own little hotel room.

Tickets in Guangzhou can be bought at the Zhoutouzui Wharf (☎ 8444-8218) and cost from HK$138 to HK$406. If you can't get a cabin or a bunk, buy a seat ticket and go to the purser's office to upgrade *(bǔpiào)* as soon as you are on board. The purser distributes leftover bunks and cabins, but get in quick if you want one.

Bus No 31 (not trolleybus No 31) will drop you off near Houde Lu in Guangzhou, which leads to Zhoutouzui Wharf (see the West Guangzhou map). To get from the wharf to Guangzhou train station, walk up to the main road, cross to the other side and take bus No 31 all the way to the station.

Zhaoqing to Wuzhou to Yangshuo

The quickest way to get to Wuzhou is the rapid ferry service, which takes between 4½ and five hours. It costs Y160, and departures are at 7.30 and 9 am, and 12.30 and 2 pm. Boats go via Zhaoqing (Y80), which is an excellent way to visit the city. Tickets are sold at the Dashatou Wharf (☎ 8383-3691) and departures are from the Rapid Ferry terminal, which is 100m east of Dashatou. Bus No 7 travels from the Guangzhou train station to the wharf.

The old 24 hour service is still running, but most of the ferries have been upgraded, so you can do the trip in a bit more comfort than was the case in the past: Y77 will get you a two bed cabin, Y50 a four bed cabin and penny pinchers can sleep with the masses for Y35. Boats depart from Dashatou Wharf at 12.30, 2.30 and 9 pm.

It is possible to buy a combined bus/boat ticket from Guangzhou to Yangshuo via

Wuzhou, but there are plenty of buses available in Wuzhou for Yangshuo and Guilin, many of them timed with the arrival of boats from Guangzhou. From Wuzhou you can return to Hong Kong directly by boat. These boats depart from Wuzhou at 7.30 am on odd-numbered dates and take 10 hours.

Other Destinations

At the time of writing, the service to Shanghai from Dashatou Wharf had been suspended; it might have started again by the time you read this. The same applies to the ferry services to Haikou, Dalian, Qingdao and Liuzhou.

ORGANISED TOURS

If time and convenience are more important than money, the brief tours to Guangzhou from Hong Kong are worth considering. Although expensive, you will never be able to complain about not being shown enough. Itineraries are invariably jam-packed with as much as can possibly be fitted into a day. The Chinese expect stamina from their foreign guests.

There are innumerable variations on the theme. A tour could just take in Guangzhou, but it could be expanded to include Shenzhen, Zhuhai and Macau. The best information on tours is available from Hong Kong travel agents, CITS or CTS. Both agencies keep a good stock of leaflets and information on a range of tours to the mainland. You usually have to book tours one or two days in advance. Essentially, the same tours can be booked from CTS in Macau.

Judging by the mail we receive at Lonely Planet, many people who have booked extended tours through CTS and CITS have been less than fully satisfied. Although the one day tours seem to be OK, tours further afield frequently go awry. Most complaints have been about overcharging, substandard accommodation and tours being cut short. No refunds are given – if you cancel you forfeit the full amount.

Thankfully, expat travel agencies have come onto the scene. China Merchants International Travel Co (☎ 8354-2827) has a whole host of possible tours that take in both Guangdong and more far-flung destinations. It arranges five day trips to Yunnan, desert tours to Ningxia and Inner Mongolia (taking in camel riding through the Tengger desert and Mongolian wrestling) and even trips to

Tibet. Closer to home are two day, two night trips to Guilin and Yangshuo. Why not give the office a bell and see what is on offer? See the Tourist Offices section in the Guangzhou Facts for the Visitor chapter for further addresses of tour agencies that may be able to help.

Getting Around

Guangzhou proper extends for 60 sq km, with most of the interesting sights scattered throughout, so seeing the place on foot is impractical. None of the transport options are pleasant however, and the only alternative to riding wedged against someone's armpit on one of the public buses is to take a grid-locked taxi and watch the meter climb.

Guangzhou's traffic conditions are in a state of mob rule. Be careful when crossing the road and use 360° vision, as vehicles come from all directions.

TO/FROM THE AIRPORT

Guangzhou's Baiyun airport is 12km out of town near the Baiyun Hills. There is a regular airbus that runs from the Civil Aviation Administration of China (CAAC) office near the train station to the airport for Y3.

Just outside the entrance to the airport is a taxi ramp. Taxis leaving from there are metered. Don't go with the taxi touts unless you want to be ripped off. When you get into a taxi, tell the driver *dǎ biǎo* (turn on the meter). The cost should be between Y30 and Y40 depending on the size of the taxi and where you are headed in town.

BUS

Guangzhou has an extensive network of motor and electric trolley-buses which will get you just about anywhere you want to go. Unfortunately the network hasn't figured on the sheer mass of humanity living in Guangzhou, all of whom travel by bus. As soon as a bus pulls into view, the genteel granny you were just chatting to at the bus stop is transformed into a bag swinging human tank.

Bumper to bumper traffic also serves to slow public transport down during peak hours and can make getting around Guangzhou a frustrating experience. You just have to be patient. Never expect anything to move rapidly and allow lots of time to get to the station to catch your train. Some-times you may find it's best to give up and walk.

Announcements on the buses of impending stops are delivered in Mandarin and Cantonese, but not in English, so try and place yourself near the driver so that he can motion for you to get off at your stop. Buses in Guangzhou generally run from 6 am to 10 pm.

It's worth getting a detailed map of the city (for the bus routes) from one of the hawkers outside either of the train stations or at one of the hotels. There are too many bus routes to list all here, but a few of the important routes are:

No 31
　Runs along Gongye Dadao Bei, east of Zhoutouzui Wharf, crosses Renmin Bridge and goes straight up Renmin Lu to Guangzhou train station at the north of the city.
No 30
　Runs from Guangzhou train station eastwards along Huanshi Lu before turning down Nonglin Xia Lu to terminate in the far east of the city. This is a convenient bus to take if you want to go from the train station to the Baiyun or Garden hotels.
No 5
　Starting from Guangzhou train station, this bus takes a similar route to No 31, but instead of crossing Renmin Bridge it carries on along Liu'ersan Lu, which runs by the northern side of the canal separating the city from Shamian Island. Get off there and walk across the small bridge to the island.

Minibus

Minibuses seating 15 to 20 people ply the streets on set routes. If you can find out where it is going, minibuses are a good way to avoid the crowded buses. The front window usually displays a sign with the destination written in Chinese characters.

TRAIN

Guangzhou is constructing a subway and a small section of Line 1 officially opened for just a few days on 1 July 1997 to coincide with China's takeover of Hong Kong. In many ways a metaphor for the stop-start nature of modern China, the subway rapidly closed again, being open as a showcase for visiting civil engineers and dignitaries and not for the public. When it does open, it will be a cause for unmitigated joy for travellers, freeing them as it will from the dictatorship of Guangzhou's leviathan buses.

The official opening date for the subway line is now September 1999. When completed, it will be 18.5km long and will have 16 stations. Line 1 will certainly be very useful to visitors; it starts out from Guangzhou East train station, then passes major shopping areas along Zhongshan Lu and stops near the popular Shamian Island before terminating on the south side of the Pearl River. If you want to pop in and check out developments, the Huangsha station near Shamian Island is open for you to peruse, although you won't get onto a train until the official grand opening.

Work has started on Line 2, which will roughly run north-south. It will also have 16 stations, but there are already proposals to extend this line. It will probably not be opened before the year 2000.

Still on the drawing board is a surface train (light rail transit system) which will run towards east Guangzhou.

CAR & MOTORCYCLE

In spite of numerous optimistic rumours and predictions, self-drive rental cars of the Avis and Hertz genre have still not made a debut in Guangzhou. On the other hand, renting a car with a driver is rapidly developing into a cottage industry. Prices are highly negotiable and depend on type of vehicle and distance travelled. In reality, this isn't much different to booking a taxi for a whole day (or several days). Large hotels charge high prices for arranging vehicle rentals. Small hotels charge less, or just try asking a porter or waiter – everyone in Guangzhou seems to have a friend or relative who is doing business.

Resident expats with a Chinese driver's licence can purchase a car and drive it themselves, but there are restrictions on travel outside the city. In general, foreigners are permitted to drive their own vehicles almost anywhere in the Pearl River Delta, but not beyond. This basically means you can drive from Guangzhou to Hong Kong, Macau and all points in between. As for going elsewhere, the rules are ill-defined, though trips to Zhaoqing by car seem to be permissible. Foreigners who have been in trouble for this particular offence have mostly been caught when checking into hotels far from Guangzhou.

Under certain circumstances, expats can get permission to import a foreign-made vehicle into China duty free.

Driving is on the right side of the road in mainland China, the opposite to Hong Kong and Macau.

Resident foreigners can also purchase a motorbike, either with or without a sidecar. In China, both driver and passenger are required to wear a safety helmet. Theoretically, you need an International Driving Permit, but you can also drive on your national licence. Motorbikes are, however, prohibitively expensive – a 400cc Honda will cost you over Y70,000. It appears that the price is high to dissuade citizens of the city from buying motorbikes. Driving a motorbike in Guangzhou is also an extremely hazardous pastime; traffic rules are Machiavellian, the centre of Guangzhou is a protesting knot of vehicles and the road surface is almost lunar with potholes and bumps.

TAXI

Taxis are available from the main hotels 24 hours a day. You can also catch a taxi outside the train stations or hail one on the street. Demand for taxis is great, particularly during the peak hours from 8 to 9 am and during lunch and dinner hours.

Taxi drivers in Guangzhou take long shifts so watch out for sleepy cabbies. The last time we took a taxi in Guangzhou, the driver almost dozed off at the wheel. As soon as he was paid, he draped himself over

GUANGZHOU

the steering wheel and started snoring. Considering the nightmarish traffic conditions on the roads in Guangzhou, this is extremely dangerous.

Taxis are equipped with meters and drivers use them unless you've negotiated a set fee in advance. The cost depends on what type of vehicle it is. Flagfall for each type of taxi is the same (Y7) but the charge per 1km after flagfall differs depending on the size of the taxi. The cost per kilometre (after flagfall) is displayed on a little sticker on the right rear window. For the cheapest taxis, the sticker displays the number 2.2; you are taken 1km for Y7 and after that you are charged the rate of Y2.20 for every additional kilometre (the meter clicks Y1.10 for every 500m). The taxis marked Y2.60 cost Y2.60 per km after flagfall. Taxis marked Y2.80 cost Y2.80 per km after flagfall. A taxi from Shamian Island to Guangzhou East train station will cost you about Y35.

Taxis can be hired for a single trip or chartered on an hourly or daily basis. The latter is worth considering if you've got the money or if you're in a group which can

split the cost. If you hire for a set period of time, negotiate the fee in advance and make it clear which currency you will pay with.

Motorcycle Taxi

A fine example of China's budding free-enterprise reforms, people who own motorcycles hang around train stations and bus stops to solicit passengers. It is required that passengers wear a safety helmet, and the drivers will supply one. There are no meters on motorcycles, so get the fare established in advance. In general, a ride on a motorcycle will be at least 30% cheaper than a regular taxi.

BICYCLE

Shamian Island usually has somewhere you can rent a bike. The bike rental outlets move around, so ask at your hotel for details. Usually rental is Y2 per hour or Y20 per day, plus a large deposit (Y400). Before hiring a bike, take a look at the traffic on the streets of Guangzhou and check whether the brakes are working to make sure it's not a death-trap.

Guangzhou City

SHAMIAN ISLAND

Shamian *(shāmiàn)* is a blessed retreat from the bustle of Guangzhou's streets. All activities are conducted in low gear on Shamian – pedestrians saunter rather than walk, cars idle rather than drive, birds sing and lazy tennis matches stretch out into the late afternoon. The island has shades of Paris' *rive gauche* in its serenity and crumbling history, and is an ideal place to wander around and inhabit the past. Unfortunately, instead of the Seine flowing by the northern banks of Shamian, you are greeted by a slow moving effluence that emerges as if from the pages of a Dickensian horror story. The river is a grotesque clot of blackness.

Shamian means 'sand surface', which is all this island was until foreign traders were permitted to set up warehouses there in the middle of the 18th century. Land reclamation has increased its area to its present size: 900m east to west by 300m north to south. The island became a British and French concession after they defeated the Chinese in the Opium Wars, and is covered with decaying colonial buildings which once housed trading offices and residences.

The French Catholic church has been restored and stands on the main boulevard. The boulevard itself is a gentle stretch of gardens, trees and bird song. Just to the west of the White Swan Hotel is the 'Church of Christ', which is an active church again, after doing time as a workshop. It is managed by the Guangdong Christian Council.

Today most of the buildings are used as offices or apartment blocks, some with the front doors flung open, reveal old wooden staircases climbing into cavernous interiors. The German consulate on the far west of the island is a recent Teutonic addition to this European enclave.

Slowly but surely the island is being gentrified. Sidewalk cafes, bars and boutiques have sprung up, while the police patrol to keep beggars off the island.

QINGPING MARKET

Three bridges connect the north side of Shamian Island to the rest of the city. Directly opposite the middle bridge, on the city side, is the entrance to Qingping Market *(qīngpíng shìchǎng)* – Guangzhou's largest and most interesting market – on Qingping Lu.

The market came into existence in 1979. Although such private markets are a feature of all Chinese cities today, it was one of Deng Xiaoping's more radical economic experiments at that time. Deng probably did not realise that he was also creating one of Guangzhou's more radical tourist attractions – if you want to buy, kill or cook it yourself, this is the place to come, since the market is more like a take-away zoo.

Near the entrance you'll find the usual selection of medicinal herbs and spices, dried starfish, snakes, lizards, deer antlers, dried scorpions, leopard and tiger skins, bear paws, semi-toxic mushrooms and bark. Further up you'll find death row, where sad-eyed monkeys rattle at the bars of their wooden cages, tortoises crawl over each other in shallow tin trays, owls sit perched on boxes full of pigeons and fish paddle around in small tubs. Here you can get bundles of frogs, live scorpions (some people like them fresh), giant salamanders, pangolins, dogs, cats and racoons, alive or contorted by recent violent death – which may just swear you off meat for the next few weeks.

The market spills out into Tiyun Lu, which cuts east-west across Qingping Lu. Further north is another area supplying vegetables, flowers, potted plants and goldfish. There are small and cheap food stalls in the streets around the perimeter of the market.

Qingping's days are numbered. The market is to be moved in the near future to make way for high-rises. Apparently the scheme has the full support of the animals.

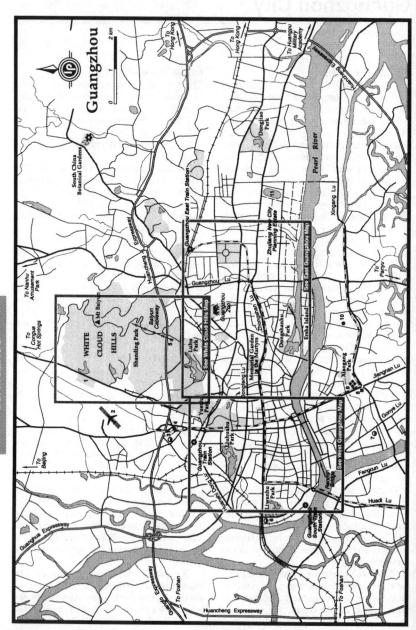

GUANGDONG MUSEUM OF ART

The recently opened Guangdong Museum of Art (guǎngdōng měishùguǎn) cost Y140 million to build and is China's largest art museum to date. This fabulous museum contains 12 exhibition halls, with a huge space outside devoted to sculpture. On show are modern Chinese works, and there are plans to host international exhibitions. Anyone interested in contemporary Chinese art will find this museum fascinating; even the building is an architectural event. Also on display within the museum are works of sculpture and ceramics.

The museum (☎ 8737-4468) can be found on the south of Ersha Island. It is open from Tuesday to Sunday, from 9 am to 5 pm; admission is Y10.

TEMPLE OF THE SIX BANYAN TREES

The Temple of Six Banyan Trees' (liù róng sì huā tǎ) history is vague, but it seems that the first structure on this site, called the Pre-

cious Solemnity Temple, was built during the 6th century and was ruined by fire in the 10th century. The temple was rebuilt at the end of the 10th century and renamed the Purificatory Wisdom Temple because the monks worshipped Hui Neng, the sixth patriarch of the Chan (Zen) Buddhist sect. Today it serves as the headquarters of the Guangzhou Buddhist Association.

The temple was given its present name by Su Dongpo, a celebrated poet and calligrapher of the Northern Song dynasty who visited the temple in the 11th or 12th century. He was so enchanted by the six banyan trees growing in the courtyard (no longer there) that he contributed two large characters for 'Six Banyans'.

Within the temple compound is the octagonal Flower Pagoda, the oldest and tallest in the city at 55m. Although it appears to have only nine storeys from the outside, inside it has 17 storeys. It is said that Bodhidharma, the Indian monk considered to be the founder of the Chan sect, once spent a night here, and owing to the virtue of his presence the pagoda was rid of mosquitoes forever.

It's worth climbing the pagoda, although if you are tall, you might end up with a collection of bruises, as the doorways on the way up are very low. As you come down, go anti-clockwise for the quickest descent; otherwise, its easy to get lost.

The temple stands in central Guangzhou, on Liurong Lu just to the west of Jiefang Bei Lu. The main hall was rebuilt in 1984. One shrine houses a statue of Hui Neng.

The temple complex is now a major tourist attraction, but it is an active temple – be sensitive about taking photographs of monks and worshippers. Inside the Kuanyin Temple is a huge golden effigy of Kuanyin (the God of Mercy), to whom women burn incense and pray.

I would like to suggest that you make a point of reminding readers that many of the temples listed are 'working', they're not there for tourists. At Liu Rong Si ... some American and French tourists were happily snapping shots of the kneeling worshippers; some even snuck up in front of the

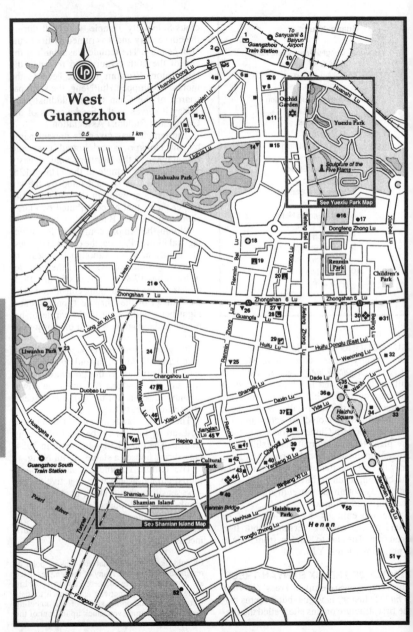

West Guangzhou
广州西部

PLACES TO STAY
4　Zhanqian Hotel
　　站前酒店
6　Liuhua Hotel
　　流花宾馆
7　Hotel Equatorial
　　贵都酒店
12　Overseas Chinese Hotel
　　华侨酒店
13　Leizhou Hotel
　　雷州酒店
15　Dongfang Hotel
　　东方宾馆
32　Lido Hotel
　　丽都大酒店
34　Hotel Landmark
　　Canton; CTS
　　华厦大酒店、
　　中国旅行社
35　Guangzhou Hotel
　　广州宾馆
38　Furama Hotel; GD Hotel
　　富丽华大酒店、
　　广东大酒店
40　Aiqun Hotel
　　爱群大厦
41　New Asia Hotel
　　新亚酒店
42　Bai Gong Hotel
　　白宫酒店
43　Xinhua Hotel;
　　Datong Restaurant
　　新华酒店、
　　大同饭店

PLACES TO EAT
8　Friendship Theatre;
　　Furusato Japanese
　　Restaurant
　　友谊剧院、日本餐馆
14　Koreanna Barbecue
　　Restaurant
　　金大庄菜根香素菜馆
23　Banxi Restaurant
　　泮溪酒家
25　McDonald's; Pizza Hut;
　　Watson's; Park N' Shop
　　麦当劳、必胜客
　　屈臣氏、百佳超级市

26　Five Rams Muslim
　　Restaurant
　　五羊回民饭店
27　Caigenxiang (Veg)
　　Restaurant
39　KFC
　　肯德基
45　Snake Restaurant
　　蛇餐馆
46　Guangzhou Restaurant
　　广州酒家
48　Taotaoju Restaurant
　　陶陶居酒家
50　Buddhist World
　　Vegetarian Restaurant
　　佛世界素食社
51　Pizza Hut; KFC
　　必胜客、肯德基

OTHER
1　GPO
　　邮政总局（流花邮局）
2　Provincial Bus Station
　　广东省汽车客运站
3　Guangzhou City Bus
　　Station
　　广州市汽车客运站
5　Liuhua Bus Station
　　流花车站
9　Telephone Office
　　国际电话大楼
10　CAAC; CITS
　　中国民航、
　　中国国际旅行社
11　Guangzhou Fair
　　广州出口商品交易会
16　Sun Yatsen Memorial
　　Hall
　　孙中山纪念堂
17　Provincial Government
　　省政府
18　Guangzhou People's
　　Hospital No 1
　　第一人民医院
19　Bright Filial Piety
　　Temple
　　光孝寺
20　Temple of the Six
　　Banyan Trees
　　六榕寺花塔
21　Chen Clan Academy
　　陈氏书院、陈家祠

22　Guangfo Bus Station
　　广佛车站
24　Antique Market
　　古玩市场
28　Huaisheng Mosque
　　怀圣寺光塔
29　Five Genies Temple
　　五仙观
30　Guangzhou
　　Department Store
　　广州百货大厦
31　Xinhua Bookstore
　　新华书店
33　Tianzi Pier
　　天字码头
36　Guangdong Trade
　　Centre
　　广东贸易中心
37　Sacred Heart Church
　　石室教堂
44　Nanfang Department
　　Store
　　南方大厦
47　Jade Market; Hualin
　　Temple
　　玉市场、华林寺
49　Xidi Pier
　　西堤码头
52　Zhoutouzui Wharf
　　洲头嘴码头

GUANGZHOU

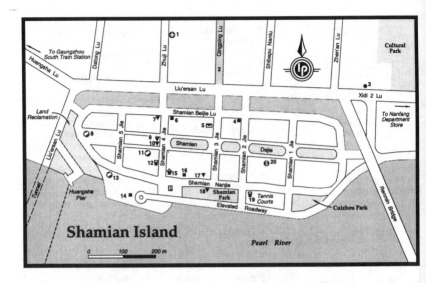

Shamian Island

Pearl River

0   100   200 m

altar to do so. My Chinese friend said her blood was close to boiling ... she did indeed seem awfully close to losing her temper.

On Liurong Lu, outside the temple, is a colourful array of souvenir shops selling ceramics, jade and religious ornaments. There is also a bustling fruit and meat market on Ruinan Lu, on the right just before you reach the temple itself. Entrance to the temple is Y1. Tickets for climbing the pagoda are Y5.

BRIGHT FILIAL PIETY TEMPLE

The Bright Filial Piety Temple (guāngxiào sì) is one of the oldest in Guangzhou. The earliest Buddhist temple on this site possibly dates as far back as the 4th century. The place has particular significance because Hui Neng was a novice monk here in the 7th century. The temple buildings are of much more recent construction, as the original buildings were destroyed by fire in the mid-17th century. The main temple is a deep and impressive construction equipped with golden figures. The temple is on Hongshu Lu, just west of the Temple of Six Banyan Trees.

FIVE GENIES TEMPLE

The Five Genies Temple (wǔ xiān guān) is held to be the site of the appearance of the five rams and celestial beings in the myth of Guangzhou's foundation (see the Yuexiu Park entry later in this chapter). The stone tablets flanking the forecourt commemorate the various restorations that the temple has undergone. The present buildings are comparatively recent, as the earlier Ming dynasty buildings were destroyed by fire in 1864.

The large hollow in the rock in the temple courtyard is said to be the impression of a celestial being's foot; the Chinese refer to it as the 'Rice-Ear Rock of Unique Beauty'. The great bell, which weighs five tonnes, was cast during the Ming dynasty and is 3m high, 2m in diameter and about 10cm thick. It's known as the 'calamity bell', since the sound of the bell, which has no clapper, is a portent of calamity for Guangzhou city.

At the rear of the main tower stand life-size smiling stone figures, which appear to represent four genies. In the temple forecourt are four statues of rams, and inside the temple are inscribed steles.

Shamian Island 沙面	9 Kiu Mei Restaurant 侨美食家	5 Post Office 邮局
PLACES TO STAY	10 Li Qin Restaurant 利群饮食店	8 German Consulate 德国领事馆
4 Guangdong Victory Hotel (New Annexe) 胜利宾馆（新楼）	17 New Litchi Bay Restaurant 新荔枝湾酒楼	11 Polish Consulate 波兰领事馆
6 Guangdong Victory Hotel 胜利宾馆	18 Lucy's Bar & Restaurant 露丝酒吧餐厅	12 Shamian Bar 沙面吧
14 White Swan Hotel 白天鹅宾馆	**OTHER**	13 US Consulate 美国领事馆
15 Guangzhou Youth Hostel 省外办招待所	1 Hospital of Traditional Chinese Medicine 中医医院	19 Lankwaifong Bar 兰桂坊酒吧
16 Shamian Hotel 沙面宾馆	2 Qingping Market 清平市场	20 Bank of China 中国银行
PLACES TO EAT	3 Antiques Market; McDonald's 古玩市场、麦当劳	
7 Victory Bakery 胜利饼屋		

The temple is south of the Temple of Six Banyan Trees, at the end of an alleyway off Huifu Xi Lu. It runs west off Jiefang Zhong Lu. The temple is open daily from 9 am to noon and from 1.30 to 5 pm; the entry fee is Y1.

SACRED HEART CHURCH
This impressive edifice is known to the Chinese as the House of Stone *(shí shì jiàotáng)*, as it is built entirely of granite. Designed by the French architect Guillemin, the church is an imitation of a European Gothic cathedral. Four bronze bells in a building to the east of the church were cast in France; the original coloured glass was also made in France, but almost all of the coloured glass has gone. The site was originally the location of the office of the governor of Guangdong and Guangxi provinces during the Qing dynasty, but that building was destroyed by British and French troops at the end of the Second Opium War in the 19th century. The area was leased to the French following the signing of the Sino-French Tianjin Treaty. Construction of the church began in 1863 and was completed in 1888, during the reign of Guangxu.

It's on Yide Lu, not far from the river, and is closed, except on Sunday when masses are held. All are welcome.

Another church you may find interesting is the Zion Christian Church at 392 Renmin Lu. The building is a hybrid, with traditional European Gothic outlines and Chinese eaves. It's an active place of worship.

HUAISHENG MOSQUE
The original mosque on this site is said to have been established in 627 AD by the first Muslim missionary to China, possibly an uncle of Mohammed. By all accounts the original mosque was the first Islamic building in China and proof of the early communication between the two cultures. The present Huaisheng Mosque *(huáishèng sì guāngtǎ)* was built in the Qing dynasty (1644-1911) as the original mosque was destroyed in a fire in 1343. The name of the mosque means 'Remember the Sage', in memory of the prophet.

Inside the grounds of the mosque is a minaret, which because of its flat, even appearance is known as the Guangta, or Smooth Tower. It stands on Guangta Lu, which runs eastwards off Renmin Zhong Lu.

GUANGZHOU

478 Guangzhou City – Orchid Garden

ORCHID GARDEN

The Orchid Garden (*lánpǔ*) was originally laid out in 1957 and has over a hundred varieties of orchids. It's a fabulous place in summer, but a dead loss in winter when all you will see are rows of flowerpots.

The admission fee includes tea by the small pond. The park is open daily from 7.30 to 11.30 am and 1.30 to 5 pm; closed on Wednesday. It's at the northern end of Jiefang Bei (North) Lu, not very far from Guangzhou train station. The admission fee is Y8.

MOHAMMEDAN TOMB & BURIAL GROUND

The Mohammedan Tomb and Burial Ground (*mùhǎn mò dé mù*) is situated in the Orchid Garden at the top of Jiefang Bei Lu, and is thought to be the tomb of the Muslim missionary who built the original Huaisheng Mosque. There are two other Muslim tombs outside the town of Quan-zhou on the south-east coast of China, thought to be the tombs of other missionaries sent by Mohammed.

The Guangzhou tomb is in a secluded bamboo grove behind the Orchid Garden; continue north along Jiefang Bei Lu past the entrance to the Orchid garden, walk through the narrow gateway ahead and take the narrow stone path on the right.

Behind the tomb compound are Muslim graves and a monumental stone arch. The tomb came to be known as the Tomb of the Echo or the Resounding Tomb due to the noises that reverberate through the inner chamber of the building.

CULTURAL PARK

The Cultural Park (*wénhuà gōngyuán*), just north-east of Shamian Island, was opened in 1956. Not your average Chinese park, this one provides you with a whole medley of alternatives, including dodgem cars (*pèngpèngchē*), a miniature fun fair, big wheel, weights room, theatre, dolphin acts at Ocean World and even a flight simulator which will set you back Y20 unless you're a kiddie (Y15).

HAIZHUANG PARK

Haizhuang Park (*hǎizhuàng gōngyuán*), across the Pearl River, would be a nondescript park but for the remains of what was once Guangzhou's largest monastery, the Ocean Banner Monastery. It was founded by a Buddhist monk in 1662, and in its heyday the grounds covered 2.5 hectares. After 1911 the monastery was used as a school and soldiers' barracks. It was opened to the public as a park in the 1930s.

Religious services stopped at the temple during the Cultural Revolution, but continue today. The temple is home to three huge golden buddhas, and in the rear courtyard lay visitors burn incense and pray. An adjacent building houses thousands of miniature shrines, each with a photograph of the deceased.

The temple, the gate to the park and other fixtures are slowly being restored, and the area gradually beautified. During the day the grounds are full of old men chatting, playing cards and checkers, and airing their pet birds.

Bus Nos 10, 16 and 25 all go to the park; bus No 10 can be picked up on Liu'ersan Lu which faces Shamian Island.

YUEXIU PARK

Yuexiu Park (*yuèxiù gōngyuán*) is the biggest park in Guangzhou, covering 93 hectares, and includes Zhenhai Tower, the Sun Yatsen Monument and the Sculpture of the Five Rams.

The Sculpture of the Five Rams, erected in 1959, is the symbol of Guangzhou. It is said that long ago five celestial beings wearing robes of five colours came to Guangzhou riding through the air on rams. Each carried a stem of rice, which they presented to the people as an auspicious sign from heaven that the area would be free from famine forever. Guangzhou means 'Broad Region', but from this myth it takes its other name, City of Rams – or just Goat City.

Zhenhai Tower, also known as the Five Storey Pagoda, is the only part of the old city wall that remains. From the upper storeys it commands a view of the city to the south and

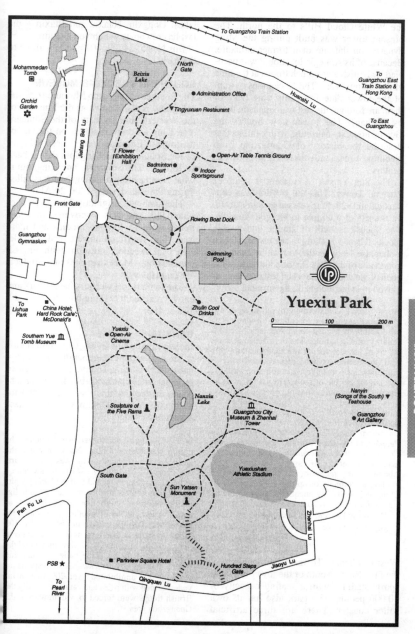

the White Cloud Hills to the north. The present tower was built during the Ming dynasty, on the site of a former structure. Because of its strategic location it was occupied by British and French troops at the time of the Opium Wars. The 12 cannons in front of the tower date from this time (five of them are foreign, the rest were made in nearby Foshan). The tower now houses the Guangzhou City Museum, with exhibits that describe the history of Guangzhou from Neolithic times until the early part of this century.

The Sun Yatsen Monument is south of Zhenhai Tower. This tall obelisk was constructed in 1929, four years after Sun's death, on the site of a temple to the god Kuanyin. The obelisk is built of granite and marble blocks. There's nothing to see inside, though a staircase leads to the top where there's a good view of the city. On the south side of the obelisk the text of Sun's last testament is engraved in stone tablets on the ground:

For 40 years I have devoted myself to the cause of national revolution, the object of which is to raise China to a position of independence and equality among nations. The experience of these 40 years has convinced me that to attain this goal, the people must be aroused, and that we must associate ourselves in a common struggle with all the people of the world who treat us as equals. The revolution has not yet been successfully completed. Let all our comrades follow the principles set forth in my writings *Plans for National Renovation*, *Fundamentals of National Reconstruction*, *The Three Principles of the People* and the *Manifesto of the First National Convention of the Kuomintang*, and continue to make every effort to carry them into effect. Above all, my recent declaration in favour of holding a national convention of the people of China and abolishing unequal treaties should be carried into effect as soon as possible.

This is my last will and testament.

(Signed) Sun Wen

11 March 1925

West of Zhenhai Tower is the Sculpture of the Five Rams. South of the tower is a large sports stadium with a seating capacity of 40,000 people. The park also has its own roller coaster. There are three artificial lakes: Dongxiu, Nanxiu and Beixiu – the last has rowboats which you can hire.

Bus Nos 5, 24, 29, 101 and 103 all go to the park.

SOUTHERN YUE TOMB MUSEUM

The Southern Yue Tomb Museum *(nán yuè wáng mù)* is also known as the Museum of the Western Han Dynasty of the Southern Yue King's Tomb. It stands on the site of the tomb of Emperor Wen, the second ruler of the Southern Yue Kingdom dating back to 100 BC. The Southern Yue Kingdom is what the area around Guangzhou was called during the Han dynasty (206-20 AD).

The tomb was originally 20m under Elephant Hill and was discovered in 1983; inside were 15 funerary bodies and more than 1000 sacrificial objects made of jade.

It's an excellent museum with English explanations. More than 500 rare artefacts are on display.

The tomb is just west of Yuexiu Park and can be reached by taking bus No 5, 24, 29, 101 or 103.

SANYUANLI

In the area north of Guangzhou train station is the nondescript neighbourhood of Sanyuanli *(sānyuánli)*. Today, it's an area of factories and apartment blocks, which obscures the fact that this place was notable for its role in the first Opium War. A Chinese leaflet relates that:

In 1840, the British imperialists launched the opium war against China. No sooner had the British invaders landed on the western outskirts of Guangzhou on 24 May 1841 than they started to burn, slaughter, rape and loot the local people. All this aroused Guangzhou people's great indignation. Holding high the great banner of anti-invasion, the heroic people of Sanyuanli together with the people from the nearby 103 villages took an oath to fight against the enemy at Sanyuan Old Temple. On 30 May, they lured the British troops to the place called Niulangang where they used hoes, swords and spears as weapons and annihilated over 200 British invaders armed with rifles and cannons. Finally the British troops were forced to withdraw from the Guangzhou area.

A little-visited monument *(kàngyīng jìniàn bēi)* commemorates the struggle that took place at Sanyuanli. You will pass Sanyuanli on the journey from Guangzhou city to Baiyun airport.

OTHER SIGHTS

The **Peasant Movement Institute** *(nóngmín yùndòng jiǎngxí suǒ)* can be found at 42 Zhongshan 4 Lu. It was a former training ground for Communist aspirants to copy the good examples set by peasants; the institute is now a revolutionary museum.

Continuing along Zhongshan 3 Lu, you will come to the **Memorial Garden to the Martyrs** *(lièshì língyuán)* which commemorates the failed Guangzhou Communist uprising of 11 December 1927; the memorial garden is laid out on Red Flower Hill *(honghuagang)*, which was one of the execution grounds.

The **Chen Clan Academy** *(chén shì shū yuàn; chén jiā cí)* on Zhongshan 7-Lu is a family shrine housed in a large compound built between 1890 and 1894. The compound encloses 19 traditional-style buildings along with numerous courtyards, stone carvings and sculptures. Bus Nos 19, 107 and 104 all pass by.

The **Sun Yatsen Memorial Hall** *(sūn zhōngshān jìniàn táng)* on Dongfeng Zhonglu, opposite Renmin Park was built in honour of Sun Yatsen, with donations from Overseas Chinese and Guangzhou citizens. Construction began in January 1929 and finished in November 1931. The memorial hall is an octagonal Chinese monolith some 47m high and 71m wide; its seating capacity is about 4000.

Liuhua Park *(liúhuāhú gōngyuán)* is an enormous park on Renmin Bei Lu containing the largest artificial lake in the city. It was built in 1958, a product of the ill-fated Great Leap Forward. Ornithologists may be interested in the bird island, which is home to thousands of our feathered friends. The entrance to the park is on Renmin Bei Lu. Bus Nos 19, 107 and 104 stop nearby.

Guangzhou Zoo *(guǎngzhōu dòngwùyuán)* was built in 1958 and is one of the three largest zoos in China and one of the better ones, however in China this doesn't mean much. The cages have been designed with no consideration for the animal's natural habitat – consisting of concrete walls and floor and iron bars. A number of the animals show obvious distress. On the positive side the cages are kept clean and the park is beautiful. At the gate of the zoo is a recently constructed aquarium, **Ocean World**, which contains a number of aquatic diversions such as sealion and dolphin shows, a shark tank and an underwater tunnel. Ocean World is open every day from 9 am to 5.30 pm, and tickets are Y90 for adults and Y45 for children. It's on Xianlie Zhong Lu in the north-east of the city; bus No 6 goes there.

Guangdong Provincial Museum *(guǎngdōng shěng bówùguǎn)* houses exhibitions of archaeological finds from around Guangdong Province, but overall isn't too good. You'll find it on the corner of Yuexiu Bei (North) Lu and Wenming Lu, one big block south of the Peasant Movement Institute.

PEARL RIVER CRUISES

The northern bank of the Pearl River is one of the most interesting areas of Guangzhou, filled with people, markets and dilapidated buildings, while the southern side takes its inspiration from Victoria Harbour in Hong Kong: it is a growing forest of enormous neon advertisements.

A tourist boat ride down the Pearl River *(zhūjiāng yóulǎnchuán)* runs daily from 3.30 to 5 pm and costs Y10. Boats leave from the Xidi pier just east of Renmin Bridge. The ride takes you down the river as far as Ersha Island, and then returns to Renmin Bridge.

From April to October there are night cruises for tourists. These are becoming increasingly colourful as more and more neon goes up on the southern shore of the river. Departures are from Xidi pier (☎ 8333-0397), just south of the Nanfang Department Store. Bookings can be made at many hotels around town, including the Shamian Hotel on Shamian Island. Tickets

GUANGZHOU

GUANGZHOU

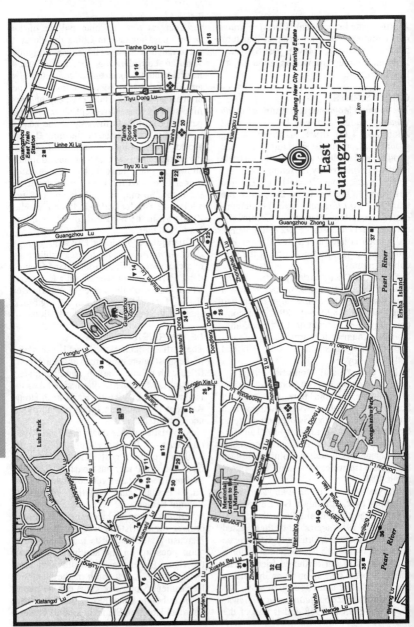

East Guangzhou 广州东部

PLACES TO STAY

2 Star Hotel
景星酒店

3 Zhejiang Building
(Fuchun Hotel)
浙江大厦（富春宾馆）

7 GITIC Plaza Hotel;
McDonald's
广东国际大酒店、
麦当劳

10 Baiyun Hotel
白云宾馆

12 Holiday Inn
文化假日酒店

19 Overseas Chinese
Friendship Hotel
华侨友谊大厦

22 Tianhe Guesthouse
天河宾馆

27 Hakkas Hotel
嘉应宾馆

28 Ocean Hotel
远洋宾馆

29 Cathay Hotel
国泰宾馆

30 Garden Hotel
花园酒店

35 GITIC Riverside Hotel
广信江湾大酒店

37 Ramada Pearl Hotel
凯旋华美达酒店

PLACES TO EAT

4 My Home Hunan
Restaurant
我家

5 Banana Leaf Curry House
蕉叶风味屋

6 KFC
肯德基

8 Hill Bar
小山酒吧

11 Kathleen's Cafe & Bar
嘉芙莲

14 Cafe Elles

21 Tianhe Palace
(Thai Restaurant)
天河皇宫潮泰酒楼

26 L'Africain
非洲吧

OTHER

1 Luhu Golf & Country Club
麓湖高尔夫乡村俱乐部

9 Friendship Store
友谊商店

13 Mausoleum of the 72
Martyrs
黄花岗七十二烈士墓

15 Guangzhou Book Centre
广州购书中心

16 The Greenery
名雅苑

17 Computer Shopping
Arcade
广州电脑城

18 Electronics Market
电子品市场

20 Tianhe Shopping Mall
天河城

23 One Love Disco
艳阳天酒吧

24 Meilihua Plaza
美丽华广场

25 Hollwood East Disco
荷李活东

31 Peasant Movement
Institute
农民运动讲习所

32 Guangdong Provincial
Museum
广东省博物馆

33 Dongshan Department
Store
东山百货

34 Baiyun Lu Bus Station
白云路汽车站

36 Dashatou Wharf
大沙头码头

GUANGZHOU

sold at the pier are Y38, and the boat runs from 7.30 to 9 pm.

The White Swan Hotel on Shamian Island also offers an evening cruise from 7.30 to 9 pm between Monday and Thursday. Tickets are Y50. On Saturday and Sunday dinner is included, and tickets are Y250.

PLACES TO STAY
Places to Stay – Budget
Guangzhou City This is not such a safe option (and we don't recommend it to women), but if you're getting off the train, it might be worth checking out what's on offer with the usual galaxy of touts who operate there. They will come rushing at you as you exit the station, waving photo books or simple placards advertising cheap rooms. Some of these places are Chinese only; some touts don't seem to care who they take.

Shamian Island This remains a popular place to look for cheapish hotels in reasonably pleasant and quiet surroundings. It is quieter and more attractive than the rest of the city, you are much more likely to meet other travellers there and the bars are better. To get to Shamian Island, take bus No 5 from Huanshi Lu; the bus stop is on the opposite side of the road and just to the west of Guangzhou train station. The bus runs along Liu'ersan Lu on the northern boundary of the canal which separates Shamian Island from the rest of Guangzhou. Four footbridges connect Shamian Island to the city. When the Guangzhou subway eventually opens, the Huangsha station will be the one closest to Shamian Island.

Near the massive White Swan Hotel is the *Guangzhou Youth Hostel* (☎ 8188-4298, *guǎngzhōu qingnian zhāodàisuǒ*) at 2 Shamian 4 Jie. By default, this place wins the title of 'backpacker headquarters' in Guangzhou, since there is almost nothing else in this price range open to foreigners. The hostel was gutted by a fire in 1992, but has now been reopened with fancy decor. The staff are not particularly friendly, but it's cheap (despite the foreigners' mark-up). The dormitories have just three beds per room and cost Y60 per person. Double rooms cost Y160.

Places to Stay – Mid-Range
Baiyun Airport The *Baiyun International Hotel* (☎ 8663-8838, fax 8665-9020) is practically located for those who don't want to stray far from the airport. Doubles start at Y440 in this three star hotel.

South-West Guangzhou The *Shamian Hotel* (☎ 8191-2288, fax 8191-1628, *shāmiàn bīnguǎn*), 50 Shamian Nanjie, is only a few steps to the east of the Guangzhou Youth Hostel on Shamian Island. Doubles with twin beds start at Y280. This is an attractive, charming and popular hotel.

Also on Shamian Island are two branches of the *Guangdong Victory Hotel* (☎ 8186-2622, fax 8186-2413, *shènglì bīnguǎn*). Both of these are fairly upmarket, though the branch at 54 Shamian Daijie is the cheaper of the two, with double rooms from Y280 upwards. The branch at 53 Shamian Beijie (despite the consecutive number these are on the same side of the road and about a five minutes walk from each other) has standard doubles at Y530, with triples at Y600.

The *Aiqun Hotel* (☎ 8186-6668, fax 8188-3519, *aìqún dà jiǔdiàn*) is at 113 Yanjiang Xi Lu (on the corner of Changdi Lu). Opened in 1937 but fully refurbished, this grand old place overlooks the Pearl River. Given the high standards, prices are reasonable at

Y248/298 for singles/doubles. Pricier rooms have river views. The hotel seems to have restaurants tucked away in every corner, including an interesting one on the rooftop that revolves.

The *Bai Gong Hotel* (☎ 8188-2313, fax 8188-9161, *bái gōng jiǔdiàn*) is a pleasant and friendly place to stay, though it's in a very noisy part of town, near the river at 17 Renmin Nan Lu. Singles are Y198 for standard or Y238 for deluxe with doubles at Y238 or Y318. From Guangzhou station, take bus No 31 and get off at the river.

Across the street is the *New Asia Hotel* (☎ 8188-4722, *xīnyà jiǔdiàn*), 10 Renmin Lu, where singles/doubles are Y238/Y248. The hotel is an old but elegant looking place, popular with Hong Kong residents. Two stars.

Just to the south of the New Asia is the *Xinhua Hotel* (☎ 8188-2688, fax 8186-8809, *xīnhuá dà jiǔdiàn*) at 4 Renmin Lu. This is another large, Chinese-speaking place geared towards the Hong Kong crowd; singles/doubles start at Y198/248.

The *GD Hotel* (☎ 8188-3601, fax 8188-3667, *guǎngdōng dà jiǔdiàn*) is at 294 Changdi Lu, one block north of the Aiqun Hotel and next to the fancier Furama Hotel. It's a large and attractive hotel, with singles/doubles for Y180/210. Two stars.

The *Furama Hotel* (☎ 8186-3288, fax 8186-3388, *fùlìhuá dà jiǔdiàn*), 316 Changdi Lu, is a splashy place near the river. Rooms start at Y418 and suites start from Y907. Three stars.

The *Guangzhou Hotel* (☎ 8333-8168, fax 8333-0791, *guǎngzhōu bīnguǎn*) is on the north side of Haizhu Square. Doubles cost from Y483 (although discounts are often available, pushing the price down to Y387). Three stars.

The *Lido Hotel* (☎ 8332-1988, fax 8332-3413, *lìdū dà jiǔdiàn*), 182 Beijing Lu, is on Guangzhou's main shopping street. Doubles start at Y352 and suites start from Y968. Three stars.

North-West Guangzhou Zhanqian Lu has a number of hotels in the middle price range. At 90 Zhanqian Lu is the *Overseas Chinese*

Hotel (☎ 8666-3488, fax 8666-3230, *huáqiáo jiǔdiàn*). Singles/doubles start at Y298/368, and you get a good discount by booking through CTS. Three stars.

A popular option is the *Leizhou Hotel* (☎ 8668-1688, fax 8667-0075, *léizhōu jiǔdiàn*) at 88 Zhanqian Lu. Rooms are priced between Y250 and Y300.

The *Zhanqian Hotel* (☎ 8667-0348, *zhànqián jiǔdiàn*), 81 Zhanqian Lu, has twin rooms for Y200 and triples for Y260.

The *Liuhua Hotel* (☎ 8666-8800, fax 8666-7828, *liúhuā bīnguǎn*) is the large building directly opposite Guangzhou train station at 194 Huanshi Lu. Doubles start at Y380.

The *Hotel Equatorial* (☎ 8667-2888, fax 8667-2582, *guìdū jiǔdiàn*), 931 Renmin Bei (North) Lu, is a short walk from Guangzhou train station and offers decent doubles for around Y280.

North-East Guangzhou This is Guangzhou's exclusive neighbourhood. High-rise hotels and office blocks are being built like mad. If there's any part of Guangzhou determined to mimic Hong Kong's skyscraper canyons, this is it.

The *Hakkas Hotel* (☎ 8777-1688, fax 8777-0788, *jiāyìng bīnguǎn*), 418 Huanshi Lu, is aimed at the business traveller. Doubles are Y480, although it often offers discounts. Four stars.

Zhejiang Building (☎ 8777-2998; fax 8775-3564, *zhèjiāng dàshà*), 85 Xianlie Lu, is also known as the *Fuchun Hotel (fù'chūn bīnguǎn)*. Prices start at Y250.

The *Overseas Chinese Friendship Hotel* (☎ 8551-3298, fax 8551-8992, *huáqiáo yǒuyí dàshà*), 44 Tianhe Dong Lu, has good doubles for Y333. *Tianhe Guesthouse* (☎ 8551-5888, fax 8551-4996, *tiānhé bīnguǎn*), 188 Tianhe Lu, has doubles from Y280.

The *Star Hotel* (☎ 8755-2888, *jǐngxīng jiǔdiàn*), Linhe Xi Lu, is just south of Guangzhou East train station. This place has decent doubles for Y580. Four stars.

Places to Stay – Top End
South-West Guangzhou One of the best

hotels in this area is the *White Swan Hotel* (☎ 8188-6968, fax 8186-2288, *báitiāné bīnguǎn*) at 1 Shamian Nanjie on Shamian Island. It has an excellent range of facilities, including 11 restaurants and bars, a complete shopping arcade and Rolls-Royce rental. There is a whole range of rooms with standard/deluxe doubles at US$120/160 and executive suites at US$250 (plus 10% service charge). Five stars.

On Haizhu Square is the *Hotel Landmark Canton* (☎ 8335-5988, fax 8333-6197, *huáshà dà jiǔdiàn*), where rates for standard doubles are Y630 and suites start at Y980. Four stars.

South-East Guangzhou The *GITIC Riverside Hotel* (☎ 8383-9888, fax 8381-4508, *guǎngxìn jiāngwān dà jiǔdiàn*), 298 Yanjiang Zhong Lu, is a towering modern hotel overlooking the river. Doubles are Y530 to Y730. Four stars.

The *Ramada Pearl Hotel* (☎ 8737-2988, fax 8737-7481, *kǎixuán huáměidá jiǔdiàn*), 9 Mingyue 1 Lu (near the waterfront), is a favourite in this development area of the city. Doubles cost Y630. Four stars.

North-West Guangzhou *Parkview Square* (☎ 8666-5666, fax 8667-1741, *yuèxiù tiān'ān dàshà*), 960 Jiefang Bei (North) Lu, has singles/doubles at Y480/480. Four stars.

The *Guangdong Guesthouse* (☎ 8333-2950, fax 8333-2911, *guǎngdōng yíng bīnguǎn*), 603 Jiefang Bei (North) Lu, has standard doubles at Y536. It's an exclusive looking place, with its own grounds and a wall around it. A sign by the lobby reminds you that 'proper attire' is required at all times. This place is about half way between Guangzhou train station and the Pearl River. Four stars.

The *Dongfang Hotel* (☎ 8666-9900, fax 8666-2775, *dōng fāng bīnguǎn*) is at 120 Liuhua Lu near Jiefang North Lu and next to the China Hotel. One of the hotel's greatest attractions is the beautiful garden in the central courtyard, where there are a number of restaurants. Doubles begin at Y690, but you can often get discounts. It's

GUANGZHOU

about a 15 minute walk from Guangzhou train station and bus No 31 runs right by. Five stars.

Home to the Hard Rock Cafe is the *China Hotel* (☎ 8666-6888, fax 8667-7014, *zhōngguó dàjiŭdiàn*), Liuhua Lu, a traditional Chinese piece of architecture built in 1948 and one of the best hotels in Guangzhou, with excellent facilities. Double rooms start at US$140 (plus a 10% service charge). Five stars.

The *Central Hotel* (☎ 8657-8331, fax 8659-2316, *zhōngyāng jiŭdiàn*), 33 Jichang Lu, is north of Guangzhou train station, on the way to the airport. Doubles begin at Y570. Four stars.

North-East Guangzhou The *Baiyun Hotel* (☎ 8333-3998, fax 8333-6498, *báiyún bīnguăn*), 367 Huanshi Dong Lu, is one of the oldest (but still excellent) hotels in this part of town. Doubles begin at Y380. Three stars.

Opposite the Baiyun Hotel is the *Garden Hotel* (☎ 8333-8989, fax 8332-4534, *huāyuán jiŭdiàn*) at 368 Huanshi Dong Lu. This place positively drips with elegance; it's one of the most spectacular hotels in China. The hotel is topped by a revolving restaurant, and there's a snooker hall and a lobby large enough to park a jumbo jet. Doubles start at Y700. The hotel has special packages on weekends. Five stars.

Also in the same neighbourhood is the *Ocean Hotel* (☎ 8776-5988, fax 8776-5475, *yuănyáng bīnguăn*) at 412 Huanshi Dong Lu. Doubles begin at Y500, with deluxe doubles at Y750. Four stars.

Immediately to the north-west of the Ocean Hotel is the *Holiday Inn* (☎ 8776-6999, fax 8775-3126, *wénhuà jiàrì jiŭdiàn*), 28 Guangming Lu (a tiny side street off Huanshi Lu). Doubles cost from Y570. Four stars.

Yuehai Hotel (☎ 8777-9688, fax 8778-8364, *yuèhăi dàsha*) is far to the north-east, at 472 Huanshi Dong Lu. Standard doubles start at Y437.

The *Cathay Hotel* (☎ 8386-2888, fax 8384-2606, *guótài bīnguăn*), 376 Dong Lu, is slightly cheaper than its neighbours at Y400 for a double. Three stars.

At 63 storeys, the *GITIC Plaza Hotel* (☎ 8331-1888, fax 8331-1666, email sales @gitic.com.cn, *guăngdōng guójì dà jiŭdiàn*), 339 Huanshi Lu, was once the tallest building in China. Double rooms start at US$140, and suites start at US$170 and rise to US$2600. Five stars.

South of the River The south side of the Pearl River is a rapidly developing area. The best place in this district is the *Plaza Canton Hotel* (☎ 8441-8888, fax 8442-9645, *jiāngnán dà jiŭdiàn*), 348 Jiangnan Lu. Doubles begin from Y500. Four stars.

PLACES TO EAT
The Chinese have a saying: to enjoy the best in life, one has to be 'born in Suzhou, live in Hangzhou, eat in Guangzhou and die in Liuzhou'. Suzhou is renowned for beautiful women, Hangzhou for scenery and Liuzhou for the finest wood for coffin-making. It's too late for us to be born in Suzhou, we don't like the weather in Hangzhou and we have no enthusiasm for dying in Liuzhou, but when it comes to eating, Guangzhou is a pretty good place to stuff your face.

Chinese
On Shamian Island most budget travellers still head for the old favourite, the *Li Qin Restaurant* (*lì qún yishídiàn*) on Shamian 4-Jie. It's built around a tree that emerges through the roof. It's cheap and the food is excellent.

Try the spicy fried dried bean curd (*làchaŏ dòugān*) and the sweet and sour chicken (*tángcù jīkuai*). If you like hot and spicy dishes, tuck into the spicy chicken (*làjiāo jīdīng*). The restaurant is also very popular with local Chinese, which is a good sign.

Right next door is the *Kiu Mei Restaurant* (☎ 8188-4168, *qiáoměi shíjiā*). Prices are at least 50% higher than at the Lin Qin, but the environment is more cheery and the chairs infinitely more comfortable. The food is superb.

The *New Litchi Bay Restaurant (xīn lìzhī wān jiŭlóu)* is just to your right as you face the Shamian Hotel on Shamian Nanjie. All kinds of seafood squiggles and squirms in fish tanks near the entrance, but the most exotic dish is snake. Before choosing your eel or cobra, ask the price – some of these creatures cost more than the tanks they're kept in.

Also on Shamian Island is the *Victory Restaurant*, attached to the Victory Hotel. Prices are amazingly reasonable for such a high standard of service. An English menu is available.

Back on the mainland, the China Hotel, near Yuexie Park, is where you'll find *Food St*, an arcade offering what could be considered gourmet food at very reasonable prices.

One of the city's most famous restaurants is the *Guangzhou* (☎ 8188-8388, *guăngzhōu jiŭjiā*), 2 Wenchang Lu near the intersection with Dishipu Lu. It boasts a 70 year history and in the 1930s came to be known as the 'first house in Guangzhou'. Its kitchens were staffed by the city's best chefs and the restaurant was frequented by the most important people of the day. The four storeys of dining halls and private rooms are built around a central garden courtyard, where potted shrubs, flowers and landscape paintings are intended to give the feeling (at least to the people in the dingy ground-floor rooms) of 'eating in a landscape'. Specialities of the house include shark fin soup with shredded chicken, chopped crab meatballs and braised dove. It's even got camel's hump on the menu. It does tend to be expensive and reservations are sometimes necessary.

For excellent Muslim-Chinese cuisine, and if you want to escape pork for a while, check out the *Five Rams Muslim Restaurant (wŭyáng huímín fàndiàn)*, a huge place at 325 Zhongshan Liu Lu, right on the corner of Renmin Lu and Zhongshan Lu. Try the boiled mutton slices *(shuàn yángroù)* and the crispy goose *(cuìpí huŏé)*.

In the west of Guangzhou, the *Banxi* (☎ 8181-5718, *bànxī jiŭjiā*), 151 Longjin Xi Lu, is the biggest restaurant in the city, and opened in 1947. It's noted for its dumplings,

stewed turtle, roast pork, chicken in tea leaves and a crab-meat-shark fin consommé. Its famed dim sum is served from about 5 to 9.30 am, at noon and again at night. Dim sum includes fried dumplings with shrimp, chicken gizzards, pork and mushrooms – even shark fin dumplings. You can try crispy fried egg rolls stuffed with chicken, shrimp, pork, bamboo shoots and mushrooms. Monkey brains are steamed with ginger, scallions and rice wine, and then steamed a second time with crab roe, eggs and lotus blossoms.

If you like spicy hot Hunan food, you might want to try *My Home Hunan Restaurant* (☎ 8359-8045) at the north end of Taojin Lu up in north-east Guangzhou. This is traditional Hunan food, which is searingly hot. It differs from Sichuan food in that the Hunan Chinese *chīlà bùchīmá*, which, roughly translated, means they love hot food, but don't go in for the mouth numbing herbs that Sichuan chefs use.

While on the subject of Sichuan food, there are a couple of restaurants that make a fair stab at *shuĭzhŭ rŏupiàn* and other fiery delights that will have you pouring beer down your neck. Try either the *Puli Chuancai Restaurant* (☎ 8775-1685, *pŭli chuāncàiguăn*), 744 Dongfeng Dong Lu, or the *Laoshuren Hotpot Restaurant* (☎ 8380-6853, *lăoshŭrén huŏguōchéng*), 2nd floor, Chenyu building, Jianshe Hengma Lu, is not far from the Old Shanghai Restaurant. The latter specialises in Sichuan hotpots which fire up the winter months in Guangzhou.

Shanghai cooking can be sampled at the *Old Shanghai Restaurant* (☎ 8384-1417, *lăoshàghăi*), 2nd floor, 48 Jianshe Liu Malu, and the *Peace Restaurant* (☎ 8667-1731), 2nd floor, Parkview Square, 960 Jiefang Bei Lu.

A very popular restaurant is *Taotaoju* (☎ 8181-5769, *táotáojū*) at 20 Dishipu Lu. Originally built as a private academy in the 17th century, it was turned into a restaurant in the late 19th century. Dim sum is the speciality there; you choose sweet and savoury snacks from the selection on trolleys that are wheeled around the restaurant. Other

GUANGZHOU

specialities include the trademark Taotao ginger and onion chicken *(táotáo jiāngcōng jī)*. Taotaoju mooncakes are very popular during the Moon Festival in mid-Autumn.

One of Guangzhou's 'famous' restaurants is located in Beijing Lu. The *Wild Animals Restaurant (yěwèixiāng fàndiàn)* at No 247 is where you can feast on dog, cat, deer, snake and bear. Spare a thought for the tiger, which was once served up at this restaurant like there was no tomorrow; indeed, you might spare a thought for all the wild animals on the menu.

Just to the west of Renmin Lu at 43 Jianglan Lu is the *Snake Restaurant* (☎ 8188-3811, *shé cānguǎn*), announced by a large neon sign and the knot of snakes in the window. The restaurant was originally known as the 'Snake King Moon' and has an 80 year history. To get to the restaurant, you have to walk down Heping Lu, which runs west from Renmin Lu. After a short distance turn right onto Jianglan Lu and follow it around to the restaurant on the left-hand side. If you want to sink your fangs into snake breast meat stuffed with shelled shrimp, stir-fried colourful shredded snakes, three snake thick soup or just plain, simple fried snake, this is the place for you. Wash it all down with a glass of snake's blood mixed with Chinese wine. It has an English menu.

If eating reptilian dishes really takes your fancy, then you could check out the *Turtle Restaurant* (☎ 8188-5943, *dòujīnshān fànzhuāng*), 75 Guangta Lu, not far from the Huaisheng Mosque. Eating turtle flesh is considered by the Cantonese to do wonders for your skin.

Japanese
Furusato (☎ 8667-9898, *rìběn cānguǎn*), next to the Friendship Theatre on Renmin Lu, is one of the few Japanese restaurants in Guangzhou city.

Korean
Koreanna Barbecue Restaurant (☎ 8186-2828, *jīndàzhuāng*), 360 Renmin Bei Lu, is a popular spot. If you haven't experienced a Korean barbecue before, now's your big chance. Vegetarians, give this place a wide berth.

Thai
Banana Leaf Curry House (☎ 8334-1288, *jiāoyèfēngwèi wū*), 8 Luhu Lu (in the Broadcasting and Television Hotel just north of Huanshi Dong Lu), *Tianhe Palace* (☎ 8757-8268 ext 5, *tiānhé huánggōng cháotài jiǔlóu*), 3rd floor, Baifu Centre, Tiyi Xi Lu and *Golden Elephant Thai Restaurant* (☎ 8188-5137), 2nd floor, 317 Renmin Zhong Lu, are three places in the city that serve spicy Thai cuisine.

Vegetarian
The *Caigenxiang Vegetarian Restaurant* (☎ 8334-4363, *càigēnxiāng sùshíguǎn*), 167 Zhongshan 6-Lu, is Guangzhou's most famous venue for vegie meals. It's also one of the few places in the city where you don't have to worry about accidentally ordering dog, cat or monkey brains.

Less famous, but certainly worth tracking down, is the *Buddhist World Vegetarian Restaurant (fó shìjiè sùshí shè)*. It's situated on Tongfu Lu on the south side of the Pearl River.

Fo You Yuan (☎ 8188-7157, *fó yǒu yuán sùshíguǎn*), another Buddhist vegetarian restaurant, fries up meat-free delicacies at 74 Shangjiu Lu, not far from the corner with Renmin Nan Lu. The food is prepared to look like and have the same texture as meat, as is the tradition with Chinese Buddhist cooking.

Western
If you'd like western food that is more avant-garde than an Egg McMuffin, try *Kathleen's Cafe and Bar* (☎ 8359-8045, *jiāfúlián*). It's near the Friendship Store and the Baiyun Hotel at 60 Taojin Lu. This bar and restaurant is very popular among the expats in Guangzhou. Recommended dishes include the marinated burger and chicken breast. The resourceful Kathleen is the publisher of *Clueless in Guangzhou*, so her fancy eatery is worth a visit to get the low-down on the latest places to see in town.

The *Hard Rock Cafe* (☎ 8666-6888, *yìngshí cāntīng*), in the basement of the China Hotel, dishes up the usual Buffalo wings, steak and chips etc, albeit with a hefty price tag.

The *Cafe de Paris* (☎ 8441-8888) in the Plaza Canton Hotel at 348 Jiangnan Dadao Zhong Lu is French right down to the white table cloths.

A popular restaurant for Italian cuisine is *Milano's Cafe* (☎ 8753-0594, *mǐlán xīcāntīng*), 3 Xincheng Beijie near Tianhe Dong Lu.

There are a couple of delis in town where you can stock up on those vital necessities the rest of China denies you. *AFT Gourmet Downunder* (☎ 8750-1473), 11/104 Xincheng Nanjie (not far from the Greenery), has all the usuals: meats, salami, a variety of cheeses and yoghurts, tortillas, spices and fine wines. There's also the *China Hotel Deli* (☎ 8666-6888) in the China Hotel, which has a similar selection.

Cheap Eats

Small government-owned dumpling (*jiǎozi*) restaurants are cheap and the food is usually good, but the service leaves a lot to be desired. Before you get your food you must pay the cashier and obtain tickets which you take to the cook. Especially when the staff are busy, customers tend to be ignored, so if you want something to eat you have to be aggressive. Just watch how the Chinese do it. Join the push and shove match, or come back in the off-peak hours.

Innumerable *street stalls* are open at night in the vicinity of the Aiqun Hotel. If you walk around the streets, and particularly along Changdi Dama Lu on the north side of the hotel, you'll find sidewalk stalls dishing up frogs, toads and tortoises. At your merest whim these will be summarily executed, thrown in the wok and fried. It's a bit like eating in an abattoir, but at least there's no doubt about the freshness. These stalls are open till about 5 am.

Other places you should check out for late night eats are the stalls on Wende Lu. At the junction of Wende Lu and Wenming Lu,

north-east of the Lido Hotel, are a bunch of eateries that open from midnight to about 6 am. This is cheap food territory.

Huifu Dong Lu is another goodie for late night feasts. West of Wende Lu, this gets going earlier, starting at about 6 pm, with the chefs clearing up at around 3 am.

Closer to Shamian Island is Zhen'an Lu, which runs north-south off Liu'ersan Lu. Cheap food is cooked from about 6 pm until way past the witching hour at 3 am.

Anyone for hot dog? The Chinese believe that dog meat has tonic properties that fight off colds and flu, so it's only served during the winter months. If it's January and you need your flu shot, all sorts of doggie dishes are available from little *back-alley restaurants* along Liu'ersan Lu north of Shamian Island (and elsewhere).

Another road pop-ular for dog dishes is Huifu Lu – ask for *xiang rou* (*heung yuk* in Cantonese) or 'fragrant meat', which is how cooked dog meat is described.

By the way, only black dogs are thought to be good medicine, a big break for the St Bernards.

Cafes

A growing number of coffee-starved expats has forced the opening of the first cafes in Guangzhou. At the time of writing, *Cafe Elles* (☎ 8764-2939) at 119 Shuiyin Erheng Lu and *Cafeto Coffee Break* (☎ 8350-1132) at 6-8 Taojin Lu could both guarantee you a decent, steaming cup of coffee.

Fast Food

McDonald's made its debut in Guangzhou in 1993, and has become all the rage with face-conscious Chinese. While cheeseburgers on sesame buns rarely turn heads in the west, McDonald's is considered one of Guangzhou's most prestigious restaurants, the venue for cadre birthday parties and other important gatherings.

On Sunday, the restaurants pack out as the city's chic social climbers get dressed up in their best and order a banquet of Chicken McNuggets which they enjoy in air conditioned comfort.

There are umpteen McDonald's and *KFCs* in the city – see the Guangzhou maps for a few locations.

Fairwood Fast Food (dà kuàihuó) is a branch of the Hong Kong instant food chain of the same name (which means 'big happy'). You'll know this place by the red plastic clown face by the door. As fast food goes, you could certainly do worse. There is a Fairwood in the basement of the Nam Fong International Plaza next to the Friendship Store on Huanshi Lu, and another on Jiefang Lu just to the north and east of Guangzhou train station.

The China Hotel's *Hasty Tasty Fast Food* shop (which opens on to Jiefang Lu) is China's home-grown answer to instant capitalist cuisine. Despite the egg and chips being soaked in more grease than a major oil tanker spillage, the food is great for refugees from rice and noodles. There is a picture on the wall of fish and chips in newspaper (English style). Observant diners will notice that the newspaper article reports social instability in Hong Kong and the need there for a labour movement.

ENTERTAINMENT

Back in the days of Mao, 'nightlife' often meant revolutionary operas featuring evil foreign devils who eventually were defeated by heroic workers and peasants frantically waving copies of Mao's 'Little Red Book'. Even as late as 1990, the only thing in Guangzhou for foreign visitors to do at night was go to bed. Then came cocktail lounges

Up in Smoke

China has the world's largest number of smokers, a fact you'll be pointedly reminded of if you travel in the hard-seat section on trains. A typical Chinese smoker puffs away three packs or more daily.

Some westerners speculate that cigarette smoking is a more effective means of reducing China's population than the one child family policy. Although the government launched an anti-smoking campaign in 1996, there is little indication that this is being taken seriously. Nor is it likely to be, since tax revenue from tobacco sales is a major source of income for the government. It also seems that few are heeding the warnings to be careful with lit cigarettes – in hotel rooms, note the burns on the carpets, bed sheets and furniture. Perhaps it's a good thing that Chinese hotels are made from bricks and concrete rather than wood.

As with drinking hard liquor, smoking in public is largely a male activity. Young women who smoke in public may be regarded as morally corrupt. This is not to say that no Chinese women smoke, but most who have the habit prefer to light up in private. Conversely, men tend to smoke like chimneys in public and frequently ignore 'no smoking' signs in public places.

If you're the sort of person who gets upset by people smoking in public places like buses and restaurants, either change your attitude, leave the country or buy a gas mask – the Chinese typically laugh off any attempts to tell them not to smoke.

The Chinese place considerable prestige value on smoking foreign cigarettes. Brands such as Marlboro, Dunhill and 555 are expensive, widely available and the ultimate status symbol for aspiring Chinese yuppies. Not surprisingly, the counterfeiting of foreign cigarettes has become a profitable cottage industry.

As for rolling your own cigarettes, you occasionally see the older Chinese doing this, but young people sneer at such a proletarian activity. They prefer to spend a full day's pay on a pack of imported cigarettes.

Many foreigners consider Chinese tobacco to have the gentle aroma of old socks, but some good quality stuff is grown, mostly in Yunnan Province. Chinese-made Red Pagoda Mountain *(hóng tǎ shān)* cigarettes cost more than Marlboros. Many foreigners are familiar with Double Happiness *(shuāngxǐ)* cigarettes, the only brand so far that has been developed for export.

at joint-venture hotels, bowling alleys, STAR TV, and now a proliferation of bars and discos catering to a mixed expat and local crowd. You'll still have to choose your discos carefully (unless you're deaf or happen to enjoy Canto-pop), but no longer is the music selection limited to renditions of the national anthem, 'The East is Red'.

Pubs & Bars

Shamian Island is a good place to begin. The island has a population of will-o'-the-wisp bars and cafes, and you can be assured that many of those mentioned here have either packed up and left, changed name, gone up or downmarket or just vanished.

One worthy survivor on Shamian Park, is *Lucy's* (☎ 8187-4106, *lùsī jiŭbā cāntīng*), a very American bar that serves an extremely value-for-money pint of beer. The food is also excellent, of the grilled chicken and steak variety, and the decor (perfect for homesick Americans) is almost as retro as the price tag on the drink. If you're planning to go to Shanghai, get drunk at Lucy's first, it's miles cheaper.

Other bars on Shamian Island try to hit the right note, but mostly don't quite make it. These include the *Lankwaifong Bar* (☎ 8191-9722), which tries to recreate the bustle and excitement of the Hong Kong night spot with little success, and the *Shamian Bar*, a pricey and tacky alternative.

The *Hill Bar* (☎ 8359-0206, *xiăoshānbā*), 367 Huanshi Lu, next to the Baiyun Hotel, is good for both pub grub and a mellow drinking session. The excellent food is remarkably inexpensive. On Saturday the place keeps going until the sun comes up – it has an excellent juke box which pumps out a fine selection of tunes. There's no dance floor, but nobody will mind if you throw back a few Tequila slammers and start jumping on the table.

Discos & Clubs

If it's dancing you want, try the *One Love Bar* (☎ 8737-1720, *yànyángtiān*), which has a large beer garden, dance floor and live music upstairs. Dancing starts at 10 pm and

goes on till 2 am. Entry is Y10 and a large beer is Y30. It's on the north-west corner of Dongfeng Dong Lu and Guangzhou Dadao.

In the same area, another place to be seen in is *L'Africain* (☎ 8778-2433, *fēizhoūba*), on the corner of Dongfeng Dong Lu and Nonglin Xia Lu. It is a bar that has dancing till 2 am on weekdays and till 4 am on weekends. This is where the crowds settle in for the early hours.

A massive disco complex comes in the form of *Hollywood East* (☎ 8766-0303, *hélihuódōng*), Dongjun Plaza, 838 Dongfeng Dong Lu. Inside, you'll find the *Jurassic Disco* (open till 3 am) and the *Oscar Lounge*, which is a venue for live bands.

The *Rock and Roll Club* (☎ 8890-8088, *gŭnshí jùlèbù*), down near the river at 101 Yanjiang Xi Lu, is another popular dance venue at the time of writing, with live bands, floor shows, karaoke, catwalk and disco all rolled into one. Entrance is Y60 during the week and Y80 at weekends. Opposite is the *Top Show Disco* (☎ 8188-7968, *yănwùtái*), a similar sort of place parked by the Pearl River. Techno is on the menu at *Star East* (☎ 8384-3559) in the Garden Hotel. Deafeningly noisy, this is the place to come if you want to shout at the barman all night while he shrugs his shoulders. Entry is Y50 on weekends.

The *Face Club* on Taojin Lu (opposite My Home Hunan Restaurant) and further up from Kathleen's, is in the building with the face on it. A quieter sort of spot, this is the place to come when you've no energy left but can't face hitting the sack.

Hard Rock Cafe (☎ 8666-6888), in the basement of the China Hotel, has a disco from 10 pm to 2 am from Sunday to Thursday and from 10.30 pm to 3 am on weekends. The cover charge is Y50, but the beer is pricey. Live music is also on the menu.

Other bars and clubs include *42nd Street* (☎ 8776-5603), 399 Huanshi Dong Lu (not far from Kathleen's), and *Catwalk* (☎ 8666-6888 ext 2068) in the China Hotel.

What remains is very much falling prey to the inexorable march of bad taste, as exemplified by karaoke parlours. If you want to include karaoke as one of your really genuine experiences of modern China, try the aptly named *Sing High Karaoke Club*, at the White Swan Hotel. Knock back a few stiff ones, grab the golden microphone, swallow hard and try to remember the melody for 'Desperado' as everyone cheers you on.

Cinemas

Cinemas that show decent western films are a rarity; however, international films are screened (in the original tongue) at the *Film Library of the Haizhu Culture Centre* (☎ 8448-9893). It screens five films a day, seven days a week.

Opera & Theatre

Chinese drama and opera is periodically performed at the *Friendship Theatre* (☎ 8666-2743), 696 Renmin Bei Lu. Tickets are Y80, Y120 and Y180.

Classical Music

Musical performances are sometimes held at the *Huanghuagang Theatre* (☎ 8776-5491), 96 Xianlie Zhong Lu. Tickets range from Y80 to Y200. The Guangzhou Symphony Orchestra also performs at the *Friendship Theatre* (see the Opera/Theatre entry for details).

Rock & Jazz

Live bands perform at the *Hard Rock Cafe*, *Oscar Lounge*, *One Love Bar*, *Rock and Roll Club* and *Kathleen's Cafe and Bar*. For details, see the earlier entries for these venues.

Around Guangzhou

WHITE CLOUD HILLS

The White Cloud Hills *(báiyún shān)*, in the north-eastern suburbs of Guangzhou, are an offshoot of Dayu Ling, the chief mountain range of Guangdong Province. The hills were once dotted with temples and monasteries, though no buildings of any historical significance remain. Famous as a resort since the Tang and Song dynasties, the area is being thematically restored to attract Hong Kong tourists, and now sports water-slides, a decent golf course, botanical gardens and a sculptural park, among other popular sights.

A tourist brochure describes the hills as 'the first spectacular scene of Guangzhou' (the lawless traffic conditions are a close second), and they're really not bad when the weather obliges. Despite being very much for the Chinese, the hills can provide relaxing walks in sometimes lovely scenery.

The highest peak in the White Cloud Hills is **Star Touching Hill** (382m, *mōxīng líng*). On a clear day, you can see a panorama of the city – the Xiqiao Hills to one side, the North River and the Fayuan Hills on the other side, and the sweep of the Pearl River. Unfortunately, clear days are becoming a rarity in Guangzhou.

The Chinese rate the evening view from **Cheng Precipice** as one of the eight sights of Guangzhou. The precipice takes its name from a Qin dynasty tale:

It is said that the first Qin Emperor, Qin Shi Huang, heard of a herb which would confer immortality on whoever ate it. Cheng On Kee, a minister of the emperor, was dispatched to find it. Five years of wandering brought Cheng to the White Cloud Hills, where the herb grew in profusion. On eating the herb, he found that the rest of it disappeared. In dismay and fearful of returning empty-handed, Cheng threw himself off the precipice, but having been assured immortality from eating the herb, he was caught by a stork and taken to heaven.

The precipice, formerly the site of the oldest monastery in the area, was named in his memory. However, these days it is usually just called the White Cloud Evening View *(báiyún wǎnwàng)*.

Getting There & Away

The White Cloud Hills are about 15km north of Guangzhou and make a good half-day excursion. Express buses leave from Guangwei Lu, a little street running off Zhongshan 5-Lu to the west of the Children's Park, about every 15 minutes. The trip takes between 30 and 60 minutes, depending on traffic. Also, bus No 24 can take you from Dongfeng Zhong Lu, just north of Renmin Park, to the cable car at the bottom of the hill near Lu Lake. The cable car covers a short stretch for Y30 (return).

LOTUS MOUNTAIN

Lotus Mountain *(liánhuā shān)* is an old Ming dynasty quarry site 46km to the southeast of Guangzhou. It is a possible day trip from Guangzhou, though it is of more interest to Guangzhou residents than to travellers with a busy itinerary.

The stonecutting at Lotus Mountain ceased several hundred years ago and the cliffs have eroded to a state where they look almost natural. On the mountain is an assortment of temples and pagodas, including the **Old Lotus Tower**, which was built in 1664. During the Opium War, Lotus Mountain served as a major line of defence against the British forces.

Getting There & Away

Both bus and boat connections are available, but the boat is more interesting. Boats depart from Xidi pier (☎ 8333-0397) just south of the Nanfang Department Store on Yanjiang Xi Lu. There is an individual service that leaves from Xidi pier at 8.30 am for Y25, but probably the best option is to get the earlier, luxury one day tour, which leaves the same pier at 8 am and returns from Lotus Mountain at 3.15 pm. Tickets are Y38 and available at Xidi pier. The boat takes about one hour to reach Lotus Mountain.

Buses depart from the Lihua bus station opposite the Guangzhou train station. In theory the bus should be faster than the boat, but with Guangzhou's traffic jams the time works out to be about the same.

The major hotels in Guangzhou also run tours to Lotus Mountain, as does CTS in Hong Kong. Naturally, it is cheaper to organise your own tour.

CONGHUA HOT SPRINGS

Conghua Hot Springs *(cōnghuà wēnquán)* are 85km north-east of Guangzhou in a pleasant forested valley with a river flowing through it. The springs are unlikely to be of much interest to foreign visitors, but they have been big business with the Chinese since the 1930s. Nowadays the hot spring water, which can reach 73°C, is piped into the bathrooms of fairly expensive tourist hotels, and the area has generally been developed into an ugly resort.

There is no shortage of hotels in the area, and visitors are greeted by touts representing the smaller, cheaper establishments (expect over Y150 for a double). Prices of Y300 and upwards prevail at the better hotels.

Getting There & Away

Buses to Conghua depart throughout the day from the Liuhua bus station (opposite the Guangzhou train station, *liúhuā chēzhàn)*, the Guangzhou City bus station and from the Baiyun Lu bus station *(báiyún chēzhàn)*. Buses are very frequent and cheap (Y10), but some buses go directly to the hot springs (about three hours, depending on traffic), while others go to the town of Conghua, from where you will have to get another bus (20 minutes) to the hot springs. Make sure you are on the right bus and ask for *wēnquán* (hot springs).

FOSHAN

Foshan (Buddha Hill, *fóshān)*, just 28km south-west of Guangzhou, is for the most

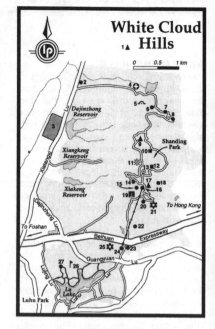

White Cloud Hills

part a drab diversion that wouldn't warrant a mention, were it not for its Ancestor Temple, which has emerged as a popular destination for local and Overseas Chinese tourists.

Like all tourist attractions worth their salt in China, there is a legend connected with Foshan. In this case, the story involves three Buddha statues which mysteriously disappeared, only to be rediscovered hundreds of years later in the Tang dynasty (618-907). Foshan also has a reputation as a handicrafts centre.

Information

CITS (☎ 335-3338, fax 335-2347) is in the Foshan Hotel at 75 Fenjiang Nan Lu. CTS (☎ 222-3828) is in the Overseas Chinese Hotel at 14 Zumiao Lu.

Ancestor Temple

Foshan's No1 tourist attraction, the Ancestor Temple *(zǔ miào)* is one of those temples

GUANGZHOU

White Cloud Hills 白云山

1 Wulei Peak (247m)
五雷岭
2 Guangzhou Foreign
Language Institute
广州外语学院
3 Dongfang Amusement Park
东方乐园
4 Liaoyang Clinic
疗养院
5 Hero Cave
英雄洞
6 Mingzhu Building
明珠楼
7 Billowing Pines Villa
松涛别墅
8 White Cloud Billowing
Pines
白云松涛

9 Star Touching Peak (382m)
摩星岭
10 Shanzhuang Inn
山庄旅舍
11 South Sky Viewpoint
锦绣南天
12 Twin River Villa
双溪别墅
13 Nine Dragon Spring
九龙泉
14 Embrace Clouds Pavilion
抱云亭
15 Cheng Precipice
白云晚望
16 Upper Cable Car Station
白云索道上部站
17 Southern Sky First Peak
天南第一峰
18 Cloud Crag
云岩（郑仙岩）

19 Nengren Temple
能仁寺
20 Keqi Teahouse
可憩茶座
21 White Flower Garden
白花园
22 Shengjian Village School
省建村学校
23 Rongchang Flower Market
荣昌花场
24 Lower Cable Car Station
白云索道下部站
25 Baitai Garden
白台花园
26 Luhu Golf & Country Club
麓湖高尔夫球乡村俱乐部
27 Honghu Building
鸿鹄楼

that has been through so much re-building that its name and function have drifted apart from each other. The original 11th century temple may have been a place of ancestor worship, but from the mid-14th century it has enshrined a 2.5 tonne bronze statue of Beidi, the Taoist god of the water, and all its denizens, especially fish, turtles and snakes.

Because much of south China was prone to floods, people often tried to appease Beidi by honouring him with temples and carvings of turtles and snakes. Outside the Ancestor Temple is a statue of 'the casted iron beast of flood easing' – a one horned buffalo. Statues like this were placed near the river at times of flood to hold back the waters.

Among other historical fragments are some caricatures of British imperialists on the stone plinths outside the temple and a huge ridge-tile covered with a whole galaxy of ceramic figures. The Ancestor Temple is open daily from 8.30 am to 4.30 pm. Bus Nos 1, 9 and 11 go to the temple from the Foshan train station.

Getting There & Away
Foshan is an easy day trip from Guangzhou.

There are frequent minibuses from the Guangfo bus station (*guǎngfó qìchē zhàn*), which is on Zongshan 8 Lu. Alternatively, there are less frequent services from the Liuhua bus station near the Liuhua Hotel, and opposite the Guangzhou train station. The Baiyun bus station next to the Liuhua bus station also has minibuses to Foshan. If you are in the Shamian Island area of Guangzhou, just wait on Liu'ersan Lu and you will see minibuses heading west, many of which are going to Foshan (Y8). Put your hand out and one will stop. Minibuses take about an hour, but can take longer in Guangzhou's horrific traffic. Foshan is also connected to a number of cities by air.

Train services between Guangzhou and Foshan are faster than the buses (30 minutes), but are only really worth it if you are staying in the Guangzhou train station area. If you add on the time getting to the station and queuing for a ticket, it could take longer.

There are five buses a day from the Revolving Palace Hotel (☎ 228-5622, *xuángōng jiǔdiàn*) in the city centre, at 1 Zumiao Lu to Zhuhai (Y37), and one bus every day to Kowloon (Y267).

For the busy business traveller, there are now direct express trains to/from Hong Kong. There is one service from Foshan to Kowloon which leaves at 10.39 am, and takes three hours (Y256). Going the other way, the train departs from Kowloon at 2.45 pm. Buses from Foshan to Guangzhou leave regularly from the Foshan long-distance bus station near the Foshan train station. Foshan is connected to a number of cities in China by air.

Getting Around

You won't have to look too hard for the two wheeled taxis – these will be looking for you. Motorcycle drivers wearing red safety helmets greet minibuses arriving from Guangzhou and practically kidnap disembarking passengers. The drivers assume that every foreigner wants to head for the Ancestor Temple. If that's not where you want to go, make it clear straight away. There aren't too many pedicabs, but you will see them about town. Foshan's pedicabs are really designed for hauling freight – there are no seats, just a cargo area behind the driver. The fares are negotiable.

SHIWAN

Two km south-west of Foshan, Shiwan township *(shìwān)* is known mostly for its porcelain factories. Although there is nothing of outstanding scenic interest there, you might want to take a look if you have an interest in pottery. Bus Nos 9 and 10 go to Shiwan from the Foshan train station, via the Ancestor Temple. From the Ancestor Temple, you could easily walk to Shiwan in 30 minutes.

XIQIAO HILLS

Xiqiao Hills *(xīqiáo shān)* are another scenic spot, made up of caves, crags, peaks, lakes and waterfalls, these hills are 68km south-west of Guangzhou and 28km south-west of Foshan. Seventy-two peaks (basically hills) make up the area. At the foot of the hills is the small market town of Xiqiao, and around the upper levels of the hills are scattered several centuries-old villages. Popular sights

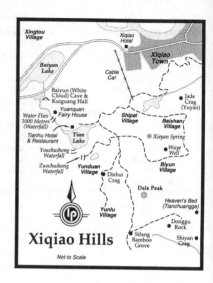

Xiqiao Hills

(at least for the Chinese) include a waterfall called **Water Flies 1000 Metres** *(fēi liútiān chi)* and **White Cloud Cave** *(báiyún dòng)*. Most of the area is made accessible by stone paths. It's popular with Chinese tourists, but foreigners of any kind are rare.

Getting There & Away

Buses to the hills depart from the Foshan bus station on Daxin Lu, which runs west off Jiefang Nan Lu. Ask at your hotel in Guangzhou about one day tours that visit Guangzhou, Foshan, Shiwan and the Xiqiao Hills. These tours are usually good value, but the commentary will undoubtedly be delivered in Chinese.

ZHAOQING

Zhaoqing *(zhàoqìng)*, home to craggy limestone rock formations similar to those around Guilin, is rated highly among the attractions of Guangdong. Despite not having the appeal of Yangshuo, Zhaoqing is an attractive city with far more character than Guangzhou or Foshan.

As the city is a major tourist destination for the Chinese, most of whom head directly for the Seven Star Crags, you can always escape to the nearby mountainous Dinghushan, which makes for a charming walk among temples, pools, brooks, ponds and lush scenery.

Orientation
Zhaoqing, 110km west of Guangzhou on the Xi River, is bounded to the south by the river and to the north by the lakes and crags that make up Seven Star Crags Park. The main attractions can be easily seen on foot.

Information
There is a branch of CTS (☎ 227-6660) next to the Texas Cowboy Fastfood situated on Duanzhou Wu Lu. CITS (☎ 282-2091) has a branch at 46 Renmin Nan Lu.

Things to See
Zhaoqing's premier attraction, the **Seven Star Crags** *(qī xīng yán)*, is a group of limestone towers – a peculiar geological formation abundant in the paddy fields of Guilin and Yangshuo. Legend has it that the crags were actually seven stars that fell from the sky to form a pattern resembling the Big Dipper.

All of the crags have exotic names and some have legends:

From Ming dynasty times onwards it was said that if you stood under Stone House Crag on clear moonlit nights, you could hear the celestial strains of music played by the Jade Emperor, the supreme god of Taoism, as he gave a banquet for the rest of the gods. Furthermore, a tablet known as Horse Hoof Tablet, one of many inscribed tablets at the site of the crags, was dented by the hoof of an inquisitive celestial horse as he alighted on the shores of Star Lake.

The crags are home to myriad inscriptions and limestone caves that you can explore. A boat can take you from the southern tip of Zhongxin Lake (Paifang Square) and speed you across to a bridge that crosses over to the crags. At this point you have to pay an entrance fee, or you can just turn right and keep walking in a big circle. This way, you avoid the fee and can go all the way around

Xing Lake among the willow and kapok trees, and take in the views.

On Tajiao Lu in the south-east of the city, the nine storey **Chongxi Pagoda** *(chóngxī tǎ)* was in a sad state after the Cultural Revolution, but was restored in the 1980s. On the opposite bank of the river are two similar pagodas.

The **Yuejiang Temple** *(yuèjiāng lóu)* is a restored temple about 30 minutes walk from the Chongxi Pagoda, which is just back from the waterfront at the eastern end of Zheng Dong Lu.

Places to Stay
Zhaoqing is not the place to stay for budget accommodation, but there are a few relatively cheap establishments in town.

The least expensive hotel around is the *Flower Tower Hotel* (☎ 223-2412, *huātǎ jiǔdiàn*), 5 Gongnong Bei Lu. Doubles range from Y100 to Y200.

For sheer character and scenery, try the predictably named *Star Crag Hotel* (222-6688, fax 222-4112, *xīngyán bīnguǎn*) slap bang in the middle of the crags. Take a boat over and walk around Xing Lake to the northern side, where you will see signs leading to the hotel, which is hidden behind a wall of bamboo. Cut through the bamboo and you will see a crumbling flight of steps leading up to the hotel, past almost vertical grass slopes. It's a haul with a backpack, but it's well worth it. Doubles/triples start at Y150/Y198. You can also get there by taxi.

The *Jinbi Hotel* (☎ 222-3888, fax 222-3328, *jīnbì dàjiǔdiàn*) is in a good location on Tianning Lu. Singles are Y168, with deluxe doubles for Y288. A 30% discount is available. Opposite, at 77 Tianning Bei Lu, is the *Duanzhou Hotel* (☎ 223-2281, *duānzhōu dàjiǔdiàn*), a reasonable option with doubles from Y180.

The *Huaqiao Hotel* (☎ 223-2952, fax 223-1197, *huáqiáo dàshà*), 90 Tianning Bei Lu, has an excellent location with doubles starting at Y288.

The *Star Lake Hotel* (☎ 222-1188, fax 223-6688, *xīnghú dàjiǔdiàn*), 37 Duanzhou Lu, is the best of Zhaoqing's hotels and

GUANGZHOU

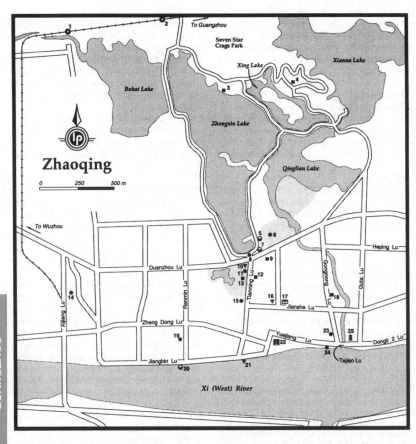

has a full range of near international-class services with rooms from Y565.

Places to Eat

Just take a stroll along Duanzhou Lu for affordable eats. Look for the restaurants selling *zōngzi* – rice, pork and other oddments steamed in a lotus leaf; these triangular snacks can be seen hanging outside the restaurants. Tianning Lu is another good area for restaurants.

Texas Cowboy Fastfood (*dézhoūniúzai*) next to the Huaqiao Hotel, cooks up fried chicken, pizza, hamburgers, French toast and Chinese food. *KFC* has flown into town and is currently roosting on Jianshe Lu near the post office.

Shopping

There is a lively night market that sets up on Tianning Lu outside the Jinbi Hotel. Stalls are flung up and on show are antiques, curios, ceramics, Qing dynasty water pipes, old watches, wood carvings, jade ornaments and just about anything else you can think of. Bargains like an engraved solid silver

Zhaoqing 肇庆

PLACES TO STAY
3 Songtao Hotel
松涛宾馆
4 Star Crag Hotel
星岩宾馆
9 Star Lake Hotel
星湖大厦
11 Huaqiao Hotel
华侨大厦
12 Jinbi Hotel
金碧大酒店
13 Duanzhou Hotel
端州大酒店
18 Flower Tower Hotel
花塔酒店

PLACES TO EAT
10 CTS;
Texas Cowboy Fastfood
中国旅行社,
德州牛仔快餐

16 KFC
肯德基
21 Floating Restaurant
海鲜舫

OTHER
1 Zhaoqing Train Station
肇庆火车站
2 Seven Star Crags Train
Station
七星岩火车站
5 Long Distance Buses
长途公共汽车
6 Star Lake Amusement Park
星湖游乐园
7 Local Bus Station
公共汽车站
8 Paifang Square
牌坊广场
14 Plum Monastery
梅庵
15 Xinhua Bookstore
新华书店

17 Post Office
邮局
19 CITS
中国国际旅行社
20 Passenger Ferry Terminal
肇庆港客运站
22 Yuejiang Temple
阅江楼
23 Boat Tickets for Hong Kong
售票处
24 Zhaogang Pier
(Boats for Hong Kong)
肇港码头
25 Chongxi Pagoda
崇禧塔

late-Qing dynasty pipe (weighing about 350g) for Y100 have been picked up there. Be on your guard though, as much of the stuff is fake, especially the ceramics.

Getting There & Away

Bus Buses to Zhaoqing leave from Guangzhou's west bus station and from the long-distance bus station, near Guangzhou train station. There are five departures daily, the fare is Y17 and the trip takes about three hours. Try to avoid returning to Guangzhou on a weekend afternoon.

Privately run minibuses operate between Zhaoqing and Guangzhou. In Zhaoqing the minibus ticket office is inside the main gate of the Seven Star Crags Park; tickets are Y33 and there are 14 departures daily. The buses leave from near the local bus station to the right of Paifang Square; minibuses also leave from there for Shenzhen (Y30).

Train Be careful – there are two train stations in Zhaoqing. All trains stop at the main

(Zhaoqing) train station (*zhàoqìng huǒchē zhàn*) but only train Nos 351 and 356 stop at the Seven Star Crags station (*qīxīngyán huǒchē zhàn*). If you get into a taxi and say you want to go to the train station, drivers will automatically assume you mean the main one.

There are four trains daily to Guangzhou (Y28). Trains from Guangzhou take two to three hours. All trains also stop at Foshan. Train Nos 16 and 78 connect Zhaoqing and Shenzhen – you do not need to get off at Guangzhou if you wish to go straight through. Direct trains to Kowloon cost Y319.

Boat This is the best way to get to Zhaoqing. There are direct high-speed ferries from Guangzhou to Zhaoqing (the ferries continue to Wuzhou) from the Dashatou ferry terminal. Ferries take two hours (Y80), and there are four departures daily (the last one is at 2 pm). Slow boats from Guangzhou leave from Dashatou and take 10 hours. Boats from Zhaoqing to Guangzhou leave

GUANGZHOU

from the passenger ferry terminal at the southern end of Renmin Lu.

Jetcats (jet-powered catamarans) speed from Zhaoqing to Hong Kong at 2 pm, take four hours and cost Y218. Boats leave from Zhaogang pier, and tickets can be bought just up the road on Gongnong Nan Lu. Boats from Ducheng to Zhuhai go via Zhaoqing; you can get on board at 1.30 pm.

Getting Around

The local bus station is on Duanzhou Lu, a few minutes walk east of the intersection with Tianning Lu and next to Paifang Square. Bus No 1 runs to the ferry terminal on the Xi River. Zhaoqing train station is a long haul, but can be reached on bus No 2, from the local bus station. A taxi to Zhaoqing train station will set you back Y12.

DINGHUSHAN

One of the most attractive spots in Guangdong, Dinghushan (*dǐnghú shān*) is 20km east of Zhaoqing, This accessible mountainous area offers a myriad of walks among pools, springs, ponds, temples, nunneries, woods and charming scenery. You probably need half a day there, as there is a lot to cover. If you get stranded on the mountain, you can crash the night in the Qingyun Resort (*qìngyún dùjiàcūn*) near the famed Qingyun Temple.

Minicab and taxi drivers wait at the bus stop at Dinghushan to ferry you around, but if you have time, journey on foot and take it all in slowly. Bus No 15 goes to Dinghushan from the bus station to the right of Paifang Square on the southern tip of Zhongxin Lake. You can also reach Dinghushan by train from Guangzhou; there are two trains daily.

SHENZHEN

'You think you're brave till you go to Manchuria, you think you're well-read till you reach Beijing and you think you're rich till you set foot in Shenzhen' goes an

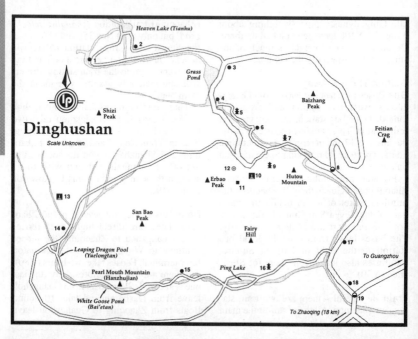

oft-coined maxim of today's China. The locals of China's north-east have always been a rough-and-ready lot and Beijing's residents have a long history of learning, but you can give the knives and broken bottles a miss, forgo the books and the erudition, and head straight for Shenzhen if you want to be rolling in it.

Shenzhen (shēnzhèn) is officially labelled a Special Economic Zone (SEZ), whereas its border-town neighbour Hong Kong is a Special Administration Region (SAR). The Shenzhen SEZ came into existence in 1980. Three other SEZs were established at the same time: Zhuhai (near Macau), Shantou in the eastern part of Guangdong Province and Xiamen in Fujian Province.

Shenzhen is not particularly interesting to visit, and the majority of foreigners who go there are on business. If you are visiting Shenzhen with a briefcase, the city will mesmerise with its sense of opportunity. Shenzhen pulls in entrepreneurs, rebels and the downright desperate from all over China like a vast whirlpool. But if you are travelling in quest of Chinese culture and history, it doesn't have quite the same allure. Coming from the north, Shenzhen City seems like a tacky introduction to Hong Kong; coming from the south, it seems like a ghastly prologue to China. Most travellers give the place a wide berth.

The northern part of the SEZ is walled off from the rest of China by an electrified fence to prevent smuggling and to keep back the hordes of people trying to emigrate illegally into Shenzhen and Hong Kong. Hong Kong has gone back to China, but the fence remains – in fact it's probable that the voltage has gone up. There is a checkpoint when you leave the SEZ. You don't need your passport to leave, but you will need it to get back in, so don't leave it in your hotel if you decide to make a day trip outside Shenzhen.

History

Shenzhen was no more than a fishing village until it won the equivalent of the National Lottery and became a SEZ in 1980. Developers added a stock market, glittering hotels, office blocks and a population of two million to the existing fish market; the only fishnets you see now are on the legs of Shenzhen's prostitutes. Like many fortune winners, the city attracted a lot of unwanted friends (two thirds of its residents have no permit to live there and beggars throng the streets) and its morals have gone soft (prostitution and sleaze are endemic). A surging crime rate is another of its less appealing statistics: it jumped 66% in 1994.

Shenzhen has no doubt been a fabulous commercial success, but it's a place without culture or spirit, a kit city driven on by the worst excesses of vice and avarice. In other words, if it's high rises and the high life you want, stay in Hong Kong, and if

GUANGZHOU

Dinghushan 鼎湖山

1 Cliff-Face Plank Path 连天栈道
2 No 1 Hydroelectric Station 水电一站
3 No 2 Hydroelectric Station 水电二站
4 Twin Rainbow Bridge 双虹飞堑
5 Tingpu Pavilion 听瀑亭
6 Sun Yatsen Swimming Area 孙中山游泳处
7 Half Mountain Pavilion 半山亭
8 Bus Station 鼎湖山汽车站
9 Tea Flower Pavilion 花茶阁
10 Qingyun Temple 庆云寺
11 Qingyun Resort 庆云度假村
12 Gulong Spring 古龙泉
13 White Cloud Temple 白云寺
14 Leaping Dragon Nunnery 跃龙庵
15 Lion's Roar Rock 狮吼石
16 Crane Viewing Pavilion 望鹤亭
17 Archway 牌楼
18 Kengkou Store 坑口商店
19 Kengkou Bus Station 坑口汽车站

and if you want history, anywhere else is an improvement.

Orientation

The name 'Shenzhen' refers to three places: Shenzhen City (opposite the Hong Kong border crossing at Lo Wu); Shenzhen Special Economic Zone (SEZ); and Shenzhen County, which extends several kilometres north of the SEZ. Most of the hotels, restaurants and shopping centres are in Shenzhen City, along Renmin Lu, Jianshe Lu and Shennan Lu.

In the western area of the SEZ is the port of Shekou, where you can get a hover-ferry to Hong Kong. Shenzhen University is also in the west, as are the holiday resorts of Shenzhen Bay and Honey Lake. The main attraction in the eastern part of the zone is the beach at Xiaomeisha.

Information

Tourist Offices There are two branches of CITS. The one most convenient for arriving travellers is the office in the Shenzhen train station. Otherwise there is a branch (☎ 217-6615) in the lobby of the Guangxin Hotel on Renmin Nan Lu that sells train and plane tickets, while tourist enquiries are dealt with in room 1102 (☎ 218-2660) of the same building. CTS has a branch at the Wah Chung International Hotel (☎ 223-8060) on Shennan Lu. CTS must be doing well, as it has its own jewellery store next to the Dawah Hotel called the 'China Travel Service Jewellery Co'.

Visas A visa-free stay of up to 72 hours is permitted in Shenzhen. However, without a visa you cannot continue on to Guangzhou. Alternatively, you can get a visa at the Shenzhen border crossing, though it is expensive.

Public Security The Foreign Affairs Branch of the PSB (☎ 557-2114) is at 174 Jiefang Lu.

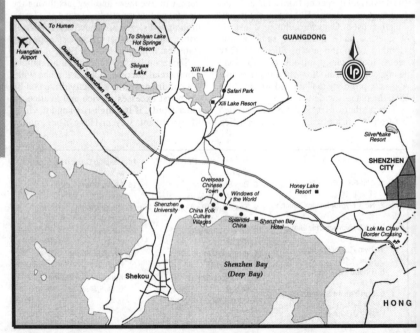

Money Shenzhen effectively operates with a dual currency system – Chinese yuan and Hong Kong dollars. If you pay for things in HK dollars, you will get RMB as change and will effectively lose out on every transaction, so change some of your dollars into yuan. Hotels will change money, or you can do it right at the Hong Kong border crossing. There is also a large Bank of China at 23 Jianshe Lu.

Black market moneychangers will often approach you on the street and yell '*gǎngbì*' (Hong Kong dollars). Like elsewhere in China, moneychangers are skilled rip-off artists.

HongkongBank, on Chunfeng Lu, has an ATM which accepts Hong Kong-issued ETC cards, plus foreign cards which use the Cirrus system.

You can also get money out on your Visa or MasterCard. Midland Bank cashpoint card holders can withdraw money from their accounts directly.

Post & Communications The post office is at the north end of Jianshe Lu and is often packed out – a great place to practise sumo wrestling techniques.

For express delivery of packages, phone DHL (☎ 339-5592) for details. EMS (☎ 223-5345, speedpost) has an office at 13 Jianshe Lu, just north of the junction with Shennan Lu.

The telecommunications office is in a separate building on Shennan Lu, but most hotels now offer IDD service right from your room.

Rates to Hong Kong are very low, but not as low the other way around. Many of the large hotels sell phone cards in the following denominations: Y20, Y50, Y100 and Y200; the office also has public telephones, usually in the hotel foyer, where you can make international calls. The huge Shunhing Square building has a number of public phones where you can make international calls.

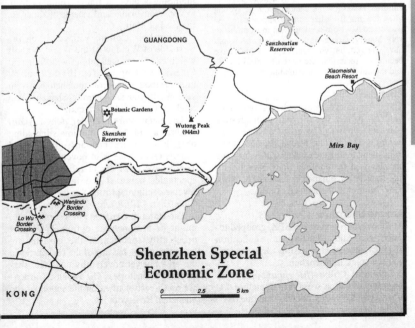

For direct dialling to Shenzhen, the area code is 0755.

Maps Chinese-character maps of Shenzhen are widely available from stalls near the Shenzhen train station and elsewhere. There is at least one edition that is partially in English, though you may have to hunt around to find it. The Universal Publications map of Shenzhen (HK$18) can be picked up in Hong Kong, although the edition available at the time of writing was quite out of date.

Dangers & Annoyances Shenzhen acts as a mecca for beggars from all over the country. They mainly congregate on Jianshe Lu and Renmin Nan Lu, tenaciously following foreigners in search of alms. If you do give them money, this is generally the green light for the rest to pursue you. A traveller writes:

> I was walking down Renmin Nan Lu at night when a young girl, followed by a small posse of children, asked me if I wanted a *xiǎojie* (young girl). Judging from her scruffy appearance, she was obviously from a village and most probably very hungry. Goodness knows what she would have charged, but you can bet it wouldn't have been much more than the price of a meal for her and the kiddies standing behind her.

Shenzhen City

There isn't much in Shenzhen City (*shēnzhèn shì*) to see, but it's still an interesting place to explore. The urban area near the border is a good place for walking. Most visitors spend their time exploring the shopping arcades and restaurants along Renmin Lu and Jianshe Lu, pursued by tribes of beggars, their families and extended families.

Around Shenzhen

At the western end of the SEZ, grouped together near Shenzhen Bay, are a collection of tacky attractions possibly of interest if you are stuck in Shenzhen.

Splendid China (*jiù zhōnghuá*) is an assembly of China's sights in miniature that allows you to 'visit all of China in one day'.

You get to see Beijing's Forbidden City, the Great Wall, Tibet's Potala Palace, the Shaolin Temple, the gardens of Suzhou, the rock formations of Guilin, the Tianshan Mountains of Xinjiang, the Stone Forest in Yunnan, Huangguoshu Falls and even some sights in Taiwan. The catch is that everything is reduced to one fifteenth of its real size. Foreigners give this place mixed reviews. Some find it intriguing while others call it a 'bad Disneyland without the rides'.

Windows of the World (*shìjiè zhīchuāng*) takes the concept of Splendid China one step further by providing models of sights in foreign countries. Thus you can admire miniaturised versions of the Eiffel Tower and the Golden Gate Bridge. (See the following paragraph for transport details.)

China Folk Culture Villages (*zhōngguó mínzú wénhuà cūn*) gives you the chance to see real-life ethnic minorities (including *gwailo* wandering around). On show are over 20 re-creations of minority villages, including a cave, a Lama Temple, drum tower, rattan bridge and a statue of Kuanyin, the God of Mercy.

China Folk Culture Villages is on the west side of Window of the World, both of which can be reached (along with Splendid China) by taking bus No 101 (Y4) or by minibus (both leave from the Shenzhen train station). If you are entering Shenzhen via Shekou, you could take a taxi.

The **Safari Park** (*yěshēng dòngwùyuán*) features a wide range of animals including deer, lions, tigers, baboons, giraffes and zebras. Our advice is to boycott the place. There have been recent reports of brutal spectacles being staged in an effort to reverse declining profits. See the boxed text 'Shenzhen – It's a Jungle' for more details.

The **Botanic Gardens** (*zhíwù gōngyuán*) might be a more sane option. While not necessarily spectacular, the gardens are spacious, green and one of the few places in the area not yet covered by concrete, skyscrapers or factories. The Botanic Gardens are north-east of town on the shores of the Shenzhen Reservoir.

Activities

Hong Kong residents with a passion for golf often head to Shenzhen because the green fees are lower and the golf courses more spacious. For information, contact the Shenzhen Golf Club (☎ 330-888). The club has a contact office in Hong Kong (☎ 2890-6321) in Hang Lung Centre at Paterson and Yee Wo Sts in Causeway Bay.

There is also the Shenzhen Famous Businessmen's Outdoor Sport Club (☎ 336-3698 ext 11906) in room 1906 of the Grand Skylight Hotel (*gélán yúntiān dà jiǔdiàn*) at 68 Shennan Lu.

Places to Stay – Budget

The bad news is that there are no dormitories in Shenzhen. But the good news is that

---

Shenzhen – It's a Jungle

The Shenzhen Tourism Corporation has tried to boost declining tourist figures to its Safari Park by playing the desperate card of sadistic animal shows. In 'anything goes' Shenzhen, the Safari Park is another smear on the happy image of China that the national tourist board is desperate to project.

Peppering up the bland show are savage horse fights between two stallions, goaded into a frenzy in front of a mare. The horses gouge chunks out of each other and leave the ring bloodied and crippled. For those who find entertainment in such pastimes as soaking cats in petrol and applying a naked flame, it's a crowd puller. If this all gets a bit yawnsome, there's the sideline attraction of Malayan bears being made to walk upright in bright costumes, encouraged by tugging on the rings ventilating their nostrils.

Maybe this is all unsurprising, considering Shenzhen is China's frontier town, governed by a dubious morality spawned from backlash *laissez-faire* economics. Bogged down in appalling crime figures, its sense of decency reeling from the effects of an economic tempest, Shenzhen is an unfortunate gateway into China.

---

in Shenzhen you can get a much larger and more luxurious room than you could in Hong Kong for the same amount of money. There is nothing really budget priced where foreigners can stay, and cheap rooms mean anything under Y300. Hotels in Shenzhen typically give discounts from Monday to Friday, as much as 40% off the regular price. This is also partially offset by a 10% tax, plus (in some hotels) an additional 5% surcharge. One cheapy that was grudgingly taking foreigners at the time of writing was the *Kouan Guesthouse (kǒoàn zhaōdaisuǒ)*, a grotty establishment near the Bank of China on Shennan Lu. The doubles (no toilet) go from Y110, while doubles (with toilet) start at Y160.

Nearby is the *Yat Wah Hotel* (☎ 558-8530, *rìhuá bīnguǎn*), next to a colourful miniature Disneyland Kindergarten on the north-west corner of Shennan Lu and Heping Lu, just to the west of the railway tracks. The outside looks slightly tattered, but the rooms are large and bright. Room prices are Y168 for singles and doubles, and there is a 20% discount from weekdays.

The *Shentie Hotel* (☎ 558-4248, *shēntiĕ dàshà*) has more upmarket rooms, coupled with a good location on Heping Lu (apart from the adjacent railway line) and offers a 20% discount on its listed price of Y268 for double rooms.

The *Kingwu Hotel* (☎ 232-6666, fax 232-6983, *jīnghú dà jiǔdiàn*), 66 Renmin Lu, is centrally located and easy to find. Singles/doubles are Y130/250. The *Hong Yan Hotel* (☎ 225-4168, fax 225-4268, *hóngyàn jiǔdiàn*) on Renmin Lu is quite a smart place. Double rooms are Y239 to Y269.

The *Jingpeng Hotel* (☎ 222-7190, fax 222-7191, *jīngpéng bīnguǎn*) on Shennan Lu is an attractive place that offers good value for the money. However, it's a rather long walk from the border station. Doubles with twin beds are Y248.

The *Guangxin Hotel* (☎ 217-6615, *guāng xìn jiǔdiàn*) at 22 Renmin Lu is not a bad option. Doubles are reasonably cheap at Y250 (although it can be more expensive on the weekends).

GUANGZHOU

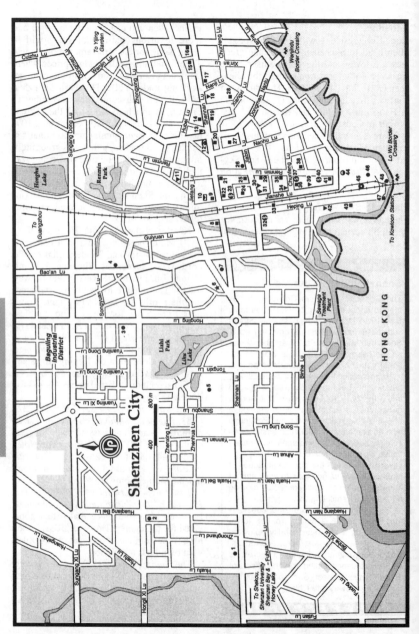

The *Petrel Hotel* (☎ 223-2828, fax 222-1398, *hǎiyàn dàjiǔdiàn*) on Jiabin Lu is a 29 storey tower with standard single/double rooms costing from Y288/391. If you are perplexed by the name, the hotel's brochure explains – 'Petrel hover at sea of the red sun shine upon'.

Shenzhen Hotel (☎ 223-8000, fax 222-9422, *shēnzhèn jiǔdiàn*) at 156 Shennan Dong Lu has doubles from Y258 and deluxe doubles from Y278.

Places to Stay – Mid-Range
In Shenzhen, 'mid-range' would have to be defined as a hotel costing between Y300 and Y600.

Shenzhen City 深圳市

PLACES TO STAY
8 Yat Wah Hotel
   日华宾馆
9 Kouan Guesthouse
   口岸招待所
14 Gold Hotel
   富丽华大酒店
15 Jingpeng Hotel
   京鹏宾馆
16 Nam Fong International Hotel
   南方国际大酒店
17 Tung Nam International Hotel
   东南国际大酒店
19 Far East Grand Hotel; Cafe de Coral
   远东大酒店
20 Guangdong Hotel
   粤海酒店
21 Wah Chung International Hotel; CTS
   华中国际酒店、中国旅行社
22 Shenzhen Hotel
   深圳酒店
24 Nanyang Hotel
   南洋酒店
25 Petrel Hotel
   海燕大酒店
27 Landmark Hotel; Piazza Cafe
   富苑酒店
28 Sunshine Hotel; JJ Disco
   阳光酒店
29 Guangxin Hotel; McDonald's; CITS
   广信酒店、麦当劳、中国国际旅行社

33 Shen Tieh Building; Tiecheng Restaurant
   深铁大厦、铁城食街
35 Hong Yan Hotel
   鸿雁大酒店
36 Century Plaza Hotel
   新都酒店
38 Kingwu Hotel
   京洳大酒店
41 Shangri-La Hotel; Pan Hsi Restaurant; Henry J Bean's Bar & Grill; The Shang Palace
   香格里拉大酒店、泮溪酒家、亨利酒吧
43 Forum Hotel
   富临大酒店
47 Overseas Chinese Hotel
   华侨酒店

PLACES TO EAT
11 McDonald's
   麦当劳
13 KFC
   肯德基
18 McDonald's
   麦当劳
30 Pizza Hut
   必胜客
31 Banxi Restaurant
   泮溪酒家
34 Luohu Restaurant
   罗湖餐厅
39 McDonald's
   麦当劳
42 Fairwood Fast Food
   大快活

OTHER
1 CAAC
   航空大厦

2 China Eastern Airlines
   中国东方航空公司
3 Xinhua Bookstore
   新华书店
4 Wall Street Disco
   华尔街
5 Shenzhen City Hall
   深圳市政府
6 PSB
   公安局外事科
7 Shunhing Square Building (Diwang Commercial Centre); Hard Rock Cafe
   信兴广场（地王商业中心）硬石餐厅
10 Post Office
   邮局
12 Telecommunications Building
   电信大楼
23 Bank of China (Large)
   中国银行
26 International Trade Centre
   国贸大厦
32 Bank of China
   中国银行
37 Hongkong Bank
   汇丰银行
40 Bank of China (Small)
   中国银行
44 Luohu Bus Station
   罗湖汽车站
45 Shenzen Train Station; Dragon Inn; CITS
   火车站、港龙大酒店、中国国际旅行社
46 Luohu Commercial Plaza
   罗湖商业城
48 Customs & Immigration
   联检大楼

GUANGZHOU

The *Wah Chung International Hotel* (☎ 223- 8060, *huázhōng guójì jiǔdiàn*) at 140 Shennan Lu has a very central location. Spacious singles/doubles cost Y300/380; suites are priced at Y440. You can get 20% off the above prices from Monday to Friday.

For a convenient location, you can hardly beat the *Dragon Inn* (☎ 232-9228, fax 233-4585, *gǎnglóng dà jiǔdiàn*), which is on the ground floor of the Shenzhen train station. Compared to most of the train station hotels in China, this one is relatively luxurious (with prices to match). Standard doubles are Y580 and suites range from Y1100 to Y1800. Large discounts were available at the time of writing.

The *Guangdong Hotel* (☎ 222-8339, fax 223-4560, *yuèhǎi jiǔdiàn*) is a sparkling glass and concrete edifice on Shennan Lu. Doubles cost Y567 to Y727; suites are Y941 to Y2782.

In the same neighbourhood as the preceding is the *Far East Grand Hotel* (☎ 220-5369, fax 220-0239, *yuǎndōng dà jiǔdiàn*), 104 Shennan Lu. Singles are Y478 and doubles are Y498 to Y588.

Nam Fong International Hotel (☎ 225-6728, fax 225-6936, *nánfāng guójì dà jiǔdiàn*) is an attractive place at 55 Shennan Lu. Doubles cost Y580 to Y1070.

The *Gold Hotel* (☎ 218-0288, fax 217-7436, *fùlìhuá dà jiǔdiàn*) at 97 Shennan Lu is quite a bargain for what appears to be a luxury hotel. It even offers 40% discounts during off-peak times. Regular rates for doubles are Y680 on weekends; the same room during the week will cost Y408.

Places to Stay – Top End

As in Guangzhou, you can get a good discount at top-end places by booking through CTS in Hong Kong. Monday to Friday off-season rates are also discounted. The following are regular rates.

If you really want to go 1st class, the *Shangri-La Hotel* (☎ 233-0888, fax 233-9878, www.Shangri-La.com, *xiānggé lǐlā dà jiǔdiàn*) has it all. It's on Jianshe Lu facing the train station and is topped by a revolving restaurant – The Tiara. Service is excellent and overall standards are right at the top. Doubles cost from Y1680, while suites start at Y2993. Five stars.

The *Century Plaza Hotel* (☎ 232-0888, fax 233-4060, HK 2598-0363, *xīndū jiǔdiàn*) is an excellent hotel on Chunfeng Lu, between Jianshe Lu and Renmin Lu. Standard/deluxe doubles are Y960/1070. As with other hotels, room prices are discounted during the week. Four stars.

The *Forum Hotel* (☎ 558-6333, fax 556-1700, *fùlín dà jiǔdiàn*) is at 67 Heping Lu, just to the west of the train station. This place discounts up to 37% from Monday to Friday during the low season. Regular prices for doubles are Y1100. Four stars.

The excellent *Sunshine Hotel* (☎ 223-3888, fax 222-6719, *yáng guāng jiǔdiàn*) is at 1 Jiabin Lu. Doubles start at Y970, but can be discounted by up to 40%. You can book rooms through the hotel's Hong Kong agent (☎ 2575-5989). Five stars.

The *Landmark Hotel* (☎ 217-2288, fax 229-0473, email Landmark@szwd.net.cn, www.szwd.net. cn/~Landmark, *fùyuàn jiǔdiàn*) is at 2 Nanhu Lu. Singles/doubles start at Y1550/1550. You can also book through its Hong Kong agent on ☎ 2375-6580. Five stars.

Places to Stay – Resorts

These Chinese-oriented paradise escapes are unlikely to be of much interest to the average foreign visitor (when they can fly to Thailand or Malaysia instead). These offer discos, saunas, swimming pools, golf courses, horseback riding, roller coasters, supermarkets, palaces, castles, Chinese pavilions, statues and monorails. The huge dim sum restaurants become nightclubs in the evening, with Las Vegas-style floor shows. Expect to pay upwards of Y400 for a double. As with hotels, resorts in Shenzhen offer discounts averaging 20% Weekdays.

Honey Lake Resort (☎ 370-5061, fax 370-5045, *xiāngmì hú dùjià cūn*) is nearest to town, situated next to Honey Lake in the futian district of Shenzhen. This is pretty much the largest resort in town.

Shenzhen Bay Hotel (☎ 660-0111, fax 660-0139, *shēnzhèn wān dàjiǔdiàn*) is situated on Shennan Lu, wedged between the Window of the World and the China Folk Cultural Village, looking out over Shenzhen Bay.

Shiyan Lake Hot Springs Resort (☎ 996-0143, *shíyán hú wēnquán dùjià cūn*) can be found on the shores of Shiyan Lake, 40km to the north-west of Shenzhen. The resort is famous for its Yulu hot spring and is popular with the Chinese business set.

Xiaomeisha Beach Resort (☎ 555-0000, *xiǎoméishā dàjiǔdiàn*) is about 30km to the east of Shenzhen on the coast, and despite being just down the road from China's Dayawan Nuclear Power Station *(dàyàwān hédiànzhàn)*, is a popular resort packed with aquatic amusements and beach activities.

Xili Lake Resort (☎ 666-0022, fax 666-0521, *xīlì hú*) can be found near the Safari Park on the shores of Xili Lake. Camping facilities can be found at the resort.

The easiest way to get to the resorts is to take a minibus from the train station area in Shenzhen. These are operated by the hotels and only accept payment in Hong Kong dollars. The privately run minibuses that run up and down Shennan Lu are cheaper and accept payment in RMB. Buses to the resorts leave just east of the Shenzhen train station.

Places to Eat

Shenzhen train station has a collection of reasonably priced take-away food stalls, fast-food eateries and cafes.

Dim sum breakfast and lunch is available in all but the scruffiest hotels. Usually the dim sum restaurants are on the 2nd or 3rd floor, rather than by the lobby. Prices are slightly lower than in Hong Kong.

One of the best places, if you are sticking to a budget yet want to sample some fantastic food, is *Tiecheng Restaurant (tiěchéng shíjiē)*, on the same side of the road and just up from the Shentie Hotel (the restaurant doesn't have an English sign, but it's on a corner). The food is excellent, the staff helpful (although not many of them speak English) and prices are very low. Try

the *suāncàiyú*, a fantastic Sichuan soup with sour cabbage and huge chunks of fish floating in it. For Y20 you get a massive bowl which is a meal in itself. There is an English menu, but the Chinese menu is far more tasty – ask one of the staff for a recommendation.

One of Shenzhen's best restaurants is the *Pan Hsi Restaurant* (☎ 223-8081, *bànxī jiǔjiā*) next to the Shangri-La Hotel.

Opposite the Century Plaza Hotel is the *Luohu Restaurant (luóhú dàjiǔjiā)*, which is one of the most popular restaurants in the city centre. At night it's noticeable a long way off for its decorations and bright lights.

Shenzhen is the site of China's first *McDonald's* (that is, outside of Hong Kong). Whether or not you want to eat, you might wish to visit for historical reasons. The restaurant is to the north of Jiefang Lu.

Pizza Hut is on Jiabin Lu, near the intersection with Jianshe Lu.

Fairwood Fast Food (dà kuàihuó) offers Hong Kong-style fast food – not bad actually. The easiest branch to find is on the west side of Heping Lu, just north of the flashy Forum Hotel.

Hard Rock Cafe (☎ 246-1671) is at hand for those on the run from noodles, rice and Canto-pop. It is in the huge Shunhing Square building (otherwise known as the Diwang Commercial Centre) on Shennan Dong Lu. *Henry J Bean's Bar and Grill* in the Shangri-La Hotel does a fine spread of American favourites.

The top-end hotels are where you'll find high quality international and Chinese cuisine. The *Shang Palace* (☎ 233-0888) in the Shangri-La Hotel cooks up the very best in Cantonese cuisine. The *Piazza Cafe* in the Landmark Hotel has a fine buffet that is good value at Y86.

Entertainment

The *Wall Street Disco* (☎ 589-0388), 16 Bao'an Nan Lu is a cavernous place that has free entry Monday to Friday and Y40 entry on weekends. It's open till 3 am.

Hard Rock Cafe (☎ 246-1671) in the Shunhing Square building on Shennan

GUANGZHOU

Dong Lu flings open its doors at 11.30 am, but the dancing doesn't start until 10.30 pm. Last dancers are thrown out at 3 am. Entry is Y50, Monday to Thursday; Y70 on weekends. Soft drinks will set you back Y20 and a cool Y40 for beer. Ladies night is on Thursday. The Hard Rock Cafe occasionally hosts live bands.

JJ Disco (☎ 223-3888 ext 3008) is a popular club in the very smart Sunshine Hotel. It is on the 1st floor in B block.

Henry J Bean's Bar and Grill (☎ 233-0888 ext 8270) in the Shangri-La Hotel is a quieter sort of place, although it also periodically has live music.

Shekou (Snake Mouth), on the far side of Shenzhen Bay, harbours a large number of expats and consequently a variety of popular watering holes that might make the trip out to the port town worthwhile. Hotspots include the *Red Rooster Bar and Restaurant* (☎ 667-1511), Shunfa building, 1st Industry Rd; *Casablanca Bar and Restaurant* (☎ 667-6576), Bitao Yuan, 1st Industry Rd and *China Beach Bar and Restaurant* (☎ 669-8080), Ming Hua Rd. To get to Shekou, jump on either minibus No 49 or 439, which leave from the Shenzhen train station.

Shopping
On the flyovers to the east of Shenzhen train station, and around the Luohu Commercial City *(luóhú shāngyè chéng)* are whole avenues of stalls selling ceramics and curios for souvenir and antique hunters. Don't expect to find trophies from Beijing's Summer Palace, but it's a colourful and varied selection.

There is also a flock of art and antique shops at the western end of Chunfeng Lu, near the Century Plaza Hotel, that have a varied, although pricey selection. If you see anything that sparks your interest, either haggle hard or look around for cheaper versions.

Opposite the Shen Tieh building on Heping Lu is a branch of Wellcome, the Hong Kong supermarket chain, where you can stock up on cheese, biscuits, milk and other goodies.

The towering Shunhing Square building is a great piece of architecture and also the focus of top-notch shopping, hosting a medley of famous brand outlets such as Hugo Boss and Bally.

Getting There & Away
Air Shenzhen's Huangtian airport (airport hotline ☎ 777-6789) is rapidly becoming one of China's busiest. There are flights to most major destinations around China, but it is often significantly cheaper to fly from Guangzhou.

Air tickets can be purchased from most hotels, such as the Shen Tieh building (☎ 558-4248) or the Guangxin Hotel. CITS also provides air tickets, and there is a small airline ticketing office on the 2nd floor of the Shenzhen train station. If you don't mind trekking out there, the two airline offices can be found as follows: CAAC (☎ 324-1440), Shennan Lu just west of Huaqiang Nan (South) Lu; and China Eastern Airlines (☎ 322-2931), on the corner of Hongli Xi Lu and Huaqiang Bei (North) Lu.

Bus From Hong Kong, bus services to Shenzhen are run by Citybus (☎ 2736-3888) and the Motor Transport Company of Guangdong & Hong Kong, from China Hong Kong City in Kowloon. Buses leave at 7.30, 8.30, 9 and 9.30 am, and 2 pm. From Shenzhen, you can jump on a Citybus double-decker bus at the stop next to the Shangri-La Hotel. For further information and tickets, contact CTS at the Wah Chung International Hotel, or Citybus.

Long-distance buses leave from the Luohu bus station *(luóhú qìchēzhàn)* next to the train station; destinations include Shantou (Y120) and Chaozhou (Y140). There is also an air-con service to Guangzhou (Y55), which takes two hours.

Buses travel frequently between Shenzhen and Guangzhou. In Shenzhen, departures are from just east of the train station next to the Hong Kong border crossing. The fare is Y55 and the ride takes two hours. In Guangzhou, buses depart from the Guangzhou City bus station near Guangzhou train station.

Minibuses also run directly from Guangzhou's Baiyun airport to Shenzhen.

Train The Kowloon-Canton Railway (KCR) offers the fastest and most convenient transport to Shenzhen from Hong Kong. Trains to the border crossing at Lo Wu begin from Kowloon station in Tsim Sha Tsui East. See the Getting Around chapter in the earlier Hong Kong section for more details, including information on the new double-decker express train that covers the distance for HK$66.

There are frequent local trains between Guangzhou and Shenzhen, and the journey takes 2½ hours. Ticket prices are Y41 (hard seat) and Y65 (soft seat). There is also a fast service that takes 1½ hours and costs Y70. The queues can be appalling at the train station, so if you are staying overnight, see if your hotel can get you a ticket.

Car It is possible to drive across the Hong Kong-Shenzhen border, but it makes little sense to do so given the convenience of public transport. There is also a pretty long queue of vehicles at the border checkpoints.

The original border crossing is at Man Kam To on the Hong Kong side; called Wenjindu on the Chinese side. Another border crossing was opened at Lok Ma Chau in 1991.

Boat There are 11 jetcat departures daily between Shekou (a port on the west side of Shenzhen) and Hong Kong. Four of these go to the China ferry terminal in Kowloon, while the rest go to the Macau ferry terminal on Hong Kong Island. Ticket prices are Y120 and Y155, depending on class, and the trip takes one hour. To get to Shekou Port pier, take either minibus No 49 or 439 from the Shenzhen train station.

There are six departures daily to the China ferry terminal in Hong Kong from the Shenzhen Fuyong ferry terminal (*shēnzhèn fúyǒng kèyùnzhàn*) at the airport. The trip takes one hour and 10 minutes; ticket prices are Y161 (economy) and Y261 (1st class).

There is one jetcat departure daily from Shekou to Macau. It departs from Shekou at 11 am and arrives at noon. Tickets are Y93. Ferries leave every half an hour for Zhuhai from Shekou. The trip takes one hour and costs Y65.

Even-numbered days of the month have a service from Shekou to Guangzhou which leaves at 9 pm and arrives at 5 am (the boat returns from Guangzhou on odd-numbered days). There is also a daily boat to Haikou (not on Sunday) from Shekou which leaves at 3.30 pm, costs Y323 and takes 18 hours.

Getting Around
To/From The Airport There are shuttle buses between the Huangtian airport and the CAAC office at Shennan Lu. Minibuses and taxis are also available, but remember that getting to the airport can take a long time in Shenzhen's traffic. Bus No 501 goes from the train station to the airport; bus Nos 502 and 504 stop at the Guangxi Hotel en route to the airport.

Getting to Huangtian airport by direct bus from Hong Kong is also possible. Citybus No 505 costs HK$150 and tickets can be bought from CTS in Hong Kong. Another place in Hong Kong selling these tickets is MTR Travel, which has offices in the following MTR stations: Admiralty, Causeway Bay, Central, Kwun Tong, Mong Kok, Tai Koo, Tsim Sha Tsui and Tsuen Wan. The schedule is limited and subject to change, so ring Citybus (☎ 2736-3888) to inquire about changes. Currently, departures from Hong Kong are in the morning only at 7.45, 8, 9.15, 9.30 and 9.45 am.

Bus & Minibus The government-run city buses are not nearly as crowded as elsewhere in China. However, destinations are written exclusively in Chinese.

The minibuses are faster, privately run and cheap, but if you can't read the destination in Chinese characters, you will need help.

Taxi Taxis are abundant but not so cheap, because the drivers have been spoilt by free-spending tourists. There are no meters, so negotiate the fare before you get in. Make sure you understand which currency is being negotiated – drivers will usually ask for payment in Hong Kong dollars.

HUMEN

The small city of Humen *(hǔmén)* on the Pearl River is of interest only to history buffs who are curious about the Opium Wars that led directly to Hong Kong's creation as a British colony. At the end of the first Opium War, after the Treaty of Nanjing, there was a British Supplementary Treaty of the Bogue, signed on 8 October 1843. The Bogue Forts *(shājiǎo pàotái)* at Humen is now the site of an impressive museum. There are many exhibits, including large artillery pieces and other relics, and the actual ponds in which Commissioner Lin Zexu had the opium destroyed.

Getting there is a hassle. Few buses go directly to Humen, but buses and minibuses travelling from Shenzhen to Guangzhou go right by. You could ask to be let off at the Humen access road, and then get a taxi, hitch or walk the 5km into town. Minibuses do travel from Guangzhou to Humen and leave half-hourly (Y20) from outside the Xiangjiang Hotel (to the right of the Guangzhou train station as you face it).

ZHUHAI

Like Shenzhen to the east, Zhuhai *(zhūhǎi)* is a boom town, doing very well out of the South China Gold Coast. In true rags to riches style, Zhuhai was built from the soles up on what was farmland not long ago. Travellers from the 1980s (even late 1980s) remember Zhuhai as a small agricultural town with a few rural industries and a peaceful beach.

That's all history now – the Zhuhai of today not only has the usual SEZ skyline of glimmering five star hotels and big-name factories, it has its own aerotropolis to boot (servicing a spotless and ultra-modern airport).

Zhuhai is mainly a business destination offering little in the way of interest to the in-

dependent traveller; that said, Zhuhai is a lot prettier and cleaner than Shenzhen. Zhuhai is more laid-back than Shenzhen and definitely cleaner than Guangzhou (for now, at least). Also, there's more of a sense of community in Zhuhai. There are no school children on the streets of Shenzhen – the city belongs purely to the yuppy generation and the beggars that pursue them along the street.

If you're looking for an easily accessible getaway from Hong Kong and Macau, but with all the modern conveniences, Zhuhai is worth a visit. The city is so close to the border with Macau that a visit can be arranged as a day trip; alternatively, you can use Zhuhai as an entry or exit point for the rest of China.

If you're in two minds, perhaps the words of Jiang Zemin can help you decide: 'I have been in a lot of places in the country, Zhuhai is the best one, it is suitable for tourism and holidays, Zhuhai tourism has boundless prospects'. Obviously, either Jiang doesn't do a lot of travelling or he got a nice backhander from CITS for that one.

Orientation

Zhuhai City is a sprawling municipality and Special Economic Zone (SEZ) larger in land area than all of Hong Kong. The central area is opposite Macau and is divided into three main areas. The area nearest the Macau border is called Gongbei, and is the main tourist area, with lots of hotels, restaurants and shops. To the north-east is Jida, the eastern part of which has Zhuhai's harbour *(jiǔzhōu gǎng)*. Xiangzhou is the northern-most part of Zhuhai's urban sprawl.

West of the central area it's flat and fertile delta country. Until recently, the west was entirely farmland, but land reclamation and factory building should be taken as a sign of the urban horrors to come.

Information

Tourist Office There is a helpful CTS office (☎ 888-6748) next to the Huaqiao Hotel on Yingbing Dadao. The staff are unusually keen to speak English and assist you with any inquiries.

Visas Like Shenzhen, Zhuhai permits a visa-free stay for up to 72 hours, but at the moment it's not available to British nationals.

No matter what your nationality, this type of visa limits your stay to the Zhuhai SEZ, and you cannot continue northwards to Guangzhou unless you have a regular Chinese visa.

Public Security The PSB (☎ 822-2459) is in the Xiangzhou district, on the corner of Anping Lu and Kangning Lu.

Money The Bank of China is a gleaming building next to the towering Yindo Hotel on the corner of Yuehai Lu and Yingbin Dadao. You can also change money in most hotels, but another good place in the Gongbei district is the Nan Tung Bank on the corner of Yuehai Lu and Shuiwan Lu. There is an official moneychanger at the Macau border crossing. The black marketeers hanging out by the border crossing are basically thieves.

Post & Communications The most useful post office is on Yuehai Dong Lu. You can

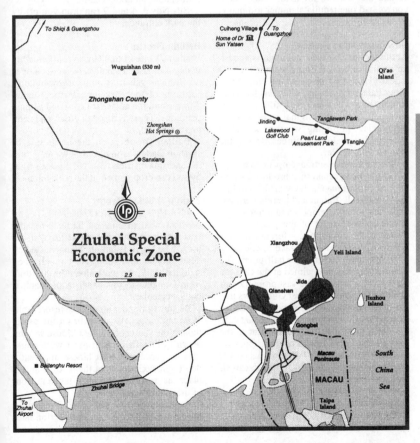

make IDD calls from your room in most hotels. The area code for Zhuhai is 0756.

Maps Hawkers sell maps around the area in front of the Yongtong Hotel by the border with Macau. The map in the *Zhuhai Tourist Guide* is bilingual, quite flash as Chinese maps go, and easy to use.

Dangers & Annoyances Zhuhai's pavements are full of gaping holes that could potentially disable you if you fell into one. Out of familiarity, the locals can steer around the holes at night like bats, but if you've had one tequila slammer too many, tread carefully.

New Yuan Ming Palace
At the foot of Dashilin mountain is a monumental symbol of China's future tourist industry. The first phase of the New Yuan Ming Palace *(yuánmíng xīnyuán)* has been completed at a cost of Y600 million. This is a reproduction of the original imperial Yuan Ming Palace in Beijing, which was torched by British and French forces during the second Opium War.

The impressive entrance opens to a huge adventure playground of reproduced sights from around China and the world, including the Great Wall, Italian and German castles, halls, restaurants, temples and a huge lake.

The colossal scale of the project is reflected in the ticket price – foreigners have to pay Y140 (locals only have to cough up Y80), although children are half-price. The whole affair is clearly aimed at the Chinese market, who make up the vast proportion of visitors. The *Zhuhai Tourist Guide* says that 'Its existence provides an important base for Chinese patriotism education' – in that case it's unlikely to include a monument to the folly of the Great Leap Forward. Opening hours are from 9 am to 7.30 pm. Bus Nos 1, 13, 25, 30, 40, 60, 201, 202 and 205 can all take you there.

Haibin Park
Haibin Park *(hǎibīn gōngyuán)* in the Jida district just keeps on developing. At one time it was only trees, but now there's a swimming pool, shooting range, roller-skating rink, windmill, barbecue pits and the Zhuhai Mermaid.

The mermaid, symbol of Zhuhai, is a statue just off the coast. She looked great until the new highway obscured the view. The park is attractive and a great respite from the streets.

Not far from Haibin Park is **Jiuzhou Cheng**. From the outside, you will probably think it's some kind of restored Ming dynasty village. Inside, you'll find that it's a fashionable shopping centre.

Bus Nos 2, 4 and 9 can drop you off by the park entrance.

Bailian Grotto
Bailian (White Lotus) Grotto *(báilián dòng gōngyuán)* is in a small park on the slopes of Banzhangshan (Camphor Mountain). Features of the park include the Huatuo Temple and the adjacent Dashi and Liujiao pavilions. There is also the **Jidan Gardens** and a few villas.

Bailian Grotto is on the north side of Jiuzhou Dadao, which runs between Gong-bei and Jida districts. Bus No 2 passes right by and can drop you off at the park entrance.

Zhuhai Holiday Resort
Zhuhai Holiday Resort (ZHR, *zhūhǎi dùjià cūn*)just west of Jiuzhou harbour has the best beach in Zhuhai – or at least, it did have. The beach is largely being wasted by development and there isn't much open sand left. Still, the walk along the coastline from Gongbei to this beach is pleasant, if not spectacular.

Be sure to wander around the resort itself. You can't say it's not a beautiful place, though the statue of Mickey Mouse waving doesn't quite fit in with most westerners' idea of paradise. The Chinese apparently don't agree. Carloads of them come to this place just to get their picture taken in front of the giant Disney rodent.

For more details, see the ZHR entry in the Places to Stay – Top End section later in this chapter.

Pearl Land Amusement Park

At the northern end of Zhuhai SEZ is the Pearl Land Amusement Park (☎ 331-1170, *zhēnzhū lèyuán*), a land of Ferris wheels, roller coasters and various other rides capable of allowing you to see your lunch for the second time.

The park is open from 9 am to 5.30 pm. Minibuses running from Zhuhai north to Cuiheng can drop you off at Pearl Land.

Lakewood Golf Club

Adjacent to Pearl Land is the Lakewood Golf Club (☎ 338-0656, *zhūhǎi cuihú gāo'ěrfū qiú huì*). Facilities include a 36 hole championship golf course, club house, putting green and driving range. If belting a little white ball isn't your style, the other major feature is the **Zhuhai International Racing Circuit**. This is the first formula-one race track in China; contact CTS for a schedule of forthcoming events. See the previous Pearl Land Amusement Park entry for details about getting there.

Places to Stay

The good news is that hotels in Zhuhai are slightly cheaper than in Shenzhen. The bad news is that there really isn't much in the budget range. There are no dormitories open to foreigners. As might be expected, hotel prices rise by at least 10% on weekends and public holidays.

The accommodation situation has been made more complicated by the Zhuhai PSB, which has placed many perfectly acceptable hotels off-limits to foreigners. This includes many hotels which accepted foreigners just a few years ago. The excuse given for this is to 'improve the standards for our foreign guests', but the reality has to do with covering up Zhuhai's growing reputation as a haven for prostitution. It's not that prostitution has been cracked down on, it's just that foreigners can no longer stay in the hotels which have made a speciality out of this business. While a nightly parade of young women ply their trade along the eastern end of Yuehai Lu, the message from the Zhuhai PSB is that this service is strictly for the domestic market (which now includes Hong Kong residents).

Places to Stay – Mid-Range

The *Zhuhai Quzhao Hotel* (☎ 888-6256, *gǒngběi dàshà*) is the cheapest around, with singles from Y178 and doubles from Y198.

Facing you as you stumble across the border and in the same building as the Gongbei bus station is the *Yongtong Hotel* (☎ 888-8887, fax 888-4187, *yǒngtōng jiǔdiàn*). Because of its good location and affordable price, it's now the favoured place for backpackers. Doubles start at Y278.

Another hotel traditionally cheaper than the rest, the *Lianhua Hotel* (☎ 888-5637, *liánhuā dàshà*), 13 Lianhua Lu, has re-opened after redecorating and has standard doubles from Y300. At the time of writing, a 60% discount off room prices were available as a promotion.

A little further from the border is the *Overseas Chinese Hotel* (☎ 888-5183, *huáqiáo dà jiǔdiàn*), on the north side of Yuehua Lu between Yingbin Dadao and Lianhua Lu, right next to the Gongbei Market. Singles/doubles are Y196/196. The *Fortune Hotel* (☎ 888-0888, fax 887-3787, *fúhǎi dà jiǔdiàn*) is on Changsheng Lu. Doubles start at Y230; suites start at Y434.

The *Overseas Chinese Guesthouse* (☎ 888-6288, *huáqiáo bīnguǎn*) on Yingbin Dadao, one block north of Yuehai Lu, has doubles from Y315 and suites from Y476.

The *Bu Bu Gao Hotel* (also known as the *Popoko Hotel*, ☎ 888-6628, fax 888-9992, *bùbùgāo dà jiǔdiàn*) is at 2 Yuehai Lu, on the corner of Shuiwan Lu, near the waterfront. Doubles cost from Y303.

Adjacent to the Gongbei Palace Hotel is the *Jiuzhou Hotel* (☎ 888-6851, fax 888-5254, *jiǔzhōu jiǔdiàn*). Singles/doubles cost from Y255/Y273 and breakfast is thrown in for free. It's located at 19 Shuiwan Lu, near Qiaoguang Lu.

The *Good World Hotel* (☎ 888-0222, fax 889-2061, *hǎo shìjiè jiǔdiàn*), 82 Lianhua Lu, is a fine place for the price. Doubles are from Y330, suites from Y650. There is a 10% surcharge, with another 10% on

GUANGZHOU

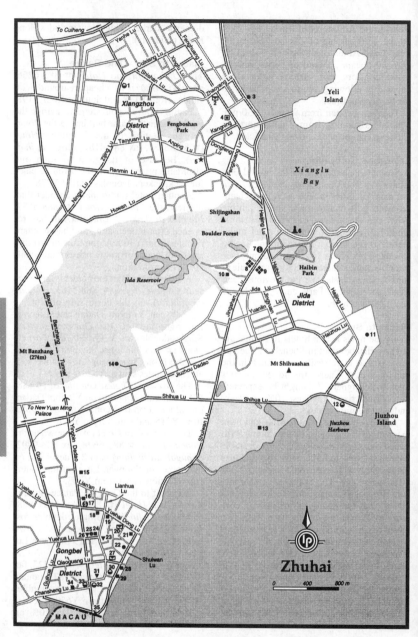

To Cuiheng

Yanhe Lu

Cuiliang Lu

Shishan Lu

Xingfu Lu

Fengzhuang Lu

Zhaoyang Lu

● 3

● 1

Xiangzhou

District

Fengboshan
Park

4 ■

Kangning

Taoyuan Lu

Anping Lu

Dongfeng Lu

Fenghuang Lu

Kangning Lu

Zijing Lu

Renmin Lu

Ningxi Lu

5 ★

*Xianglu
Bay*

Huwan Lu

Shijingshan
▲

Boulder Forest

▲ 6

7 ■

Haijing Lu

8 ■ ● 9

10 ■

Haibin Lu

Haibin
Park

Jida Reservoir

Jida Lu

Jingshan Lu

Jingshan Lu

Yuanlin Lu

*Jida
District*

Haizhou Lu

Mt Banzhang
(274m) ▲

Mount Banzhang Tunnel

14 ●

Jiuzhou Dadao

Mt Shihuashan
▲

Haijing Lu

● 11

To New Yuan Ming
Palace

Shihua Lu

Shihua Lu

Shouwan Lu

12 ○

*Jiuzhou
Island*

● 13

Jiuzhou
Harbour

Guihua Lu

Yinbin Dadao

■ 15

Lianan Lu

Lianhua
Lu

Yuehai Lu

■ 17

18 ■

Yuehai Dong Lu

19 ■

25 24

26 ● 23

22 ●

21 ■

Yuehua Lu

Gongbei

Qiaoguang Lu

District

27 ●

Shuiwan
Lu

30 ● ■ 28

31 ● ● 29

34 ■

● 32

Guihua Lu

Chansheng Lu

35 ●

■ MACAU

Zhuhai

0   400   800 m

weekends or 20% on public holidays, offset
by periodic 30% discounts.

Places to Stay – Top End
The best place within striking distance of the
border is the *Yindo Hotel* (☎ 888-3388, fax
888-3311, *yíndū jiǔdiàn*), on Yingbin Dadao
in Gongbei district. Its services range from
a coffee shop, bar and shopping arcade to
massage centre, sauna and bowling alley.
Rates for doubles and singles both start at
Y820. This is Zhuhai's only five star hotel,
and easily the best in town.

The *Gongbei Palace Hotel* (☎ 888-6833,
fax 888-5686, *gōngběi bīnguǎn*) is the most
luxurious place close to the border. It's by
the waterfront at 21 Shuiwan Lu near
Qiaoguang Lu, about a one minute walk
from the border crossing. Among the facilities are a disco, video game arcade, sauna
and swimming pool (including water slide).

Unfortunately, the 'beach' is just for looking
– it's too rocky for swimming. The hotel
also runs bus tours of the surrounding area.
Doubles are Y520 to Y650, and you can
check into a villa suite for Y1350, or Y1760
if you want the sea view. There is a 15%
service charge.

The *Guangdong Hotel* (☎ 888-8128) at
30 Yuehai Lu is a flashy place with double
rooms costing from Y730 and suites from
Y1500 to Y5000. The price is subject to a
15% surcharge.

The *Zhuhai Hotel* (☎ 333-3718, fax 333-
2339, *zhūhǎi bīnguǎn*) close to the Jida
reservoir is meant to be a playground for the
upper classes. It doesn't have the benefit of
a beach or a casino, and nearby Macau is
more interesting, so it's hard to see the attraction. Nevertheless, Hong Kong residents
keep coming, and the hotel caters to them
with a sauna, tennis courts, billiard room,

Zhuhai 珠海

PLACES TO STAY
10 Zhuhai Hotel
珠海宾馆
13 Zuhai Holiday Resort
珠海度假村
15 Huaqiao Hotel; CTS
华侨宾馆、中国旅行社
16 Yindo Hotel
银都酒店
18 Good World Hotel
好世界酒店
19 Guangdong Hotel
粤海酒店
21 Bu Bu Gao (Popoko) Hotel
步步高大酒店
24 Overseas Chinese Hotel
华侨大酒店
28 Gongbei Palace Hotel
拱北宾馆
29 Jiuzhou Hotel
九洲酒店
30 Yongtong Hotel;
Gongbei Bus Station
永通酒店、长途汽车站
34 Fortune Hotel
福海大酒店

PLACES TO EAT
23 Fairwood Fast Food
大快活
26 McDonald's
麦当劳
31 Restaurant Row
餐厅

OTHER
1 Xiangzhou Bus Station
香洲汽车站
2 Post Office
邮局
3 Xiangzhou Harbour
香洲码头
4 Martyrs' Mausoleum
烈士陵园
5 PSB
公安局
6 Zhuhai Mermaid Statue
珠海渔女
7 Shijingshan Tourist Centre
石景山旅游中心
8 Jiuzhou Cheng
(Shopping Mall)
九洲城

9 Duty Free Shopping
Centre
珠海免税商城
11 Helicopter Pad
直升机场
12 Jiuzhou Harbour
Passenger Terminal
九洲港客运站
14 Bailian Grotto
白莲洞公园
17 Bank of China
中国银行
20 Post Office
邮店局
22 Beauty Salons
美容院
25 Gongbei Market
拱北市场
27 Post Office
邮局
32 Local Bus Station
拱北公共汽车总站
33 Zhuhai-Gongbei Bus
Company
珠海拱北客运站
35 Customs & Immigration
海关

swimming pool, nightclub and even ma-hjong rooms. For all that, it's still quite reasonable – double rooms cost Y450 to Y700 and villas start at Y900. There is a 15% surcharge.

The *Zhuhai Holiday Resort* (☎ 333-2038, fax 333-2036, *zhūhǎi dùjià cūn*), or ZHR for short, is a four star complex with spacious grounds. At one time it had the best beach in Zhuhai, but the sand has nearly disappeared after recent construction work. Still, its amenities include a bowling alley, roller-skating rink, tennis courts, club house, go-kart racing, horse riding, camel riding, disco, karaoke, video parlour and sauna. On the downside, service seems to have fallen off. The resort is on the shoreline north-east of Gongbei near Jiuzhou Harbour. Single rooms in the main hotel are Y795 on weekends (Y722 Monday to Friday), and you can try the villas for Y3110 (weekends) or Y2700 (Monday to Friday). There is a 15% surcharge.

Places to Eat

The area near the Macau border crossing has the most of everything – restaurants, bakeries, night markets and street vendors. Right near the border crossing is *Maxim's* (☎ 888-5209) at 4 Lianhua Lu, the Hong Kong fast-food chain famous for its cakes. It's a good place to catch a quick breakfast.

The ubiquitous Hong Kong chain *Fairwood Fast Food (dà kuàihuó)* has made its debut in Zhuhai. You'll find it close to the corner of Lianhua Lu and Yuehua Lu.

The north-east corner of Youyi Lu and Yingbin Dadao is Zhuhai's unofficial food alley. There is a good collection of *streetside restaurants* plus a few *street vendors*.

McDonald's has opened at last in Gongbei, on the corner of Yuehua Lu and Yingbin

You Are What You Eat

The Chinese notion of 'health food' (*yàoshàn*) differs somewhat from that of the west. While western health food emphasises low-fat, high-fibre and a lack of chemical additives, the Chinese version puts its main emphasis on the use of traditional ingredients and herbs.

It is a widely held belief in China that overwork and sex wears down the body and that such 'exercise' will result in a short life. To counter the wear and tear, some Chinese practice *jinbu* (the consumption of tonic food and herbs). This can include, for example, drinking raw snake's blood or bear's bile, or eating deer antlers, all of which are claimed to improve vision, strength and sexual potency.

In a literal interpretation of 'you are what you eat', it's widely believed that consuming tiger meat will produce a miraculous increase in one's vigour and virility. Rhinoceros horn has long been touted as a tonic for whatever ails you. Eating monkey's brain is said to increase intelligence, and may also explain the behaviour of Beijing's taxi drivers.

Environmentalists are not too happy about the consumption of tiger meat and rhinoceros horn, given that both tigers and rhinos are endangered species. To be fair, the Chinese government has cracked down on the practice, and much of what gets passed off nowadays as ultra-expensive tiger meat and rhino horn is in fact fake.

Animal rights activists have sharply criticised the method used to obtain bear's bile – by strapping a living bear into a metal vest and running a tube into the creature's liver. However, China has reacted to such criticism the same way the country reacts to reports of human rights violations – by telling everyone that this is one of China's 'internal affairs'.

If the animal rights activists happen to be British, the Chinese remind them of Britain's rude behaviour in the Opium War of 1841; if the critics are Americans, they get reminded of 19th century slavery in the southern USA; the Aussies get reminded about mistreatment of the aborigines. No word yet on just what the bears get told.

Dadao; apparently you had to queue for two hours on its opening day, which kind of defeats the purpose of 'fast food'.

Getting There & Away

Air Zhuhai has a glittering new airport, and has flights to most cities in China, although it has no international routes as yet. Domestic destinations include Beijing (Y1240), Shanghai (Y1120) and Hangzhou (Y970). There are also regular flights to Guangzhou. The airport could well serve international flights in the future; it probably doesn't yet out of deference to Macau international airport just down the road.

Macau Simply walk across the border. In Macau, bus Nos 3 and 5 lead to the Barrier Gate, from where you make the crossing on foot. Taxis from the Hong Kong ferry area cost around HK$22. The Macau-Zhuhai border is open from 7 am to midnight.

Guangzhou Buses to Zhuhai depart from the Guangzhou City bus station near Guangzhou train station. Minibuses from this station are air-con and leave according to a posted schedule. Buses for Zhuhai also leave from the Liuhua bus station, which is opposite the Guangzhou train station (Y40). From Zhuhai, buses leave from the main bus station, to the west of the customs building (the border checkpoint). Buses from Zhuhai to Guangzhou depart every 25 minutes from 6.50 am to 4 pm, and air conditioned services cost Y47. The journey takes three hours. There are also buses for Guangzhou (Y50) that leave from just to the west of the Yongtong Hotel.

Hong Kong Jetcats between Zhuhai and Hong Kong do the trip in about 70 minutes. From the China ferry terminal on Canton Rd in Tsim Sha Tsui, boats depart at 7.45, 9.30 and 11 am, and 2.30 and 5 pm. Boats from the Macau ferry terminal in Central depart at 8.40 am, noon and 4 pm. It is, however, only marginally slower (and less expensive) to take a ferry to Macau and then a taxi to Zhuhai.

Going the other way, departures are from Jiuzhou Harbour in Zhuhai at 8 and 9.30 am, and 1, 3 and 5 pm to Tsim Sha Tsui, and at 10.30 am, and 2 and 5.30 pm to Central. Tickets cost Y140.

Shenzhen Ferries operate between the port of Shekou in Shenzhen and Jiuzhou Harbour in Zhuhai. There is a variety of craft plying this route – the fastest take only 50 minutes, while the old clunkers take about twice as long. There are departures every fifteen minutes from 7.30 am to 6 pm. The cost is Y65 and the journey takes one hour.

Other Destinations From the bus station to the west of the customs building (the border checkpoint) there are buses to Foshan (Y50), Zhaoqing (Y70), Haikou (Y165 sleeper), Guilin (Y140 sleeper) and Shantou (Y130 sleeper). From there, minibuses also speed to Zhongshan (Y15).

Getting Around

To/From the Airport Zhuhai's airport is about 40km south-west from the city centre, which makes travel to and from it a hassle. A taxi will be expensive (over Y100); alternatively, take bus No 201 to Sanzao *(sānzào)* from the bus station in Xiangzhou, and then change to bus No 105, which will take you direct to the airport. Alternatively, a CAAC shuttle bus runs reasonably regularly to the airport from the CAAC office near McDonald's (Y15).

Bus & Minibus Zhuhai has a clean and efficient bus system. The buses are new and not like the hulking monsters that grind around Guangzhou. Minibuses ply the same routes as the larger buses and cost Y2 for any place in the city.

Taxi You are most likely to use taxis to shuttle between your hotel and the boats at Jiuzhou Harbour. Zhuhai taxis have no meters and fares are strictly by negotiation. Drivers typically try to charge foreigners double. A fair price from the Macau border to Jiuzhou Harbour is around Y20.

GUANGZHOU

AROUND ZHUHAI

In the village of Cuiheng *(cuíhēng cūn)*, north of the city limits of Zhuhai, is **Dr Sun Yatsen's Residence** *(sūn zhōngshān gùjū)*. A republican, enemy of the Qing dynasty and China's most famous revolutionary, Dr Sun Yatsen was born in a house on this site on 12 November 1866. That house was torn down after a new home was built in 1892. This second house is still standing and is open to the public.

There are frequent minibuses to Cuiheng from the bus station just to the west of the customs building in Gongbei.

ZHONGSHAN

The administrative centre of the county by the same name, Zhongshan City *(zhōngshān shì)* is also known as Shiqi. An industrial city, there is little to see or do there, though you may pass through the place if you are doing the circuit from Cuiheng to Zhongshan Hot Springs.

If you get stranded for an hour or so, the one and only scenic spot in town is **Zhongshan Park**, which is pleasantly forested and dominated by a large hill *(yāndūn shān)* topped with a pagoda. It's visible from most parts of the city, so it's easy to find.

Zhongshan Hot Springs

The Zhongshan Hot Springs *(zhōngshān wēnquán)* resort has indoor hot springs and a golf course. If you're a real enthusiast of either activity, you might want to spend a night there. Otherwise, you'll probably just want to look around briefly and then head back to Gongbei. Accommodation is available at the *Zhongshan Hot Springs Hotel* (☎ 668-3888, fax 668-3333) from Y300 for doubles plus 10% service charge.

Minibuses to Zhongshan from Zhuhai leave regularly from the bus station to the west of the customs building in Gongbei (Y15). The minibuses will drop you by the entrance to the resort, then it's a 500m walk to the hotel. For a couple of yuan you can hire someone to carry you on the back of a bicycle. You won't have to look for these people, as they'll be looking for you. To get back to Gongbei, flag down any minibus you see passing the resort entrance.

Health

In general, health conditions in Hong Kong, Macau and southern China are good, but a little awareness of potential hazards could prevent illness from ruining your trip.

PREDEPARTURE PLANNING
Immunisations

There are no specific vaccination requirements for Hong Kong or Macau. For Guangzhou and southern China, the only vaccination requirement is yellow fever if you are coming from a yellow fever infected area.

However, this doesn't mean that you shouldn't get any vaccinations. Remember that the further off the beaten track you go the more necessary it is to take precautions. Be aware that there is often a greater risk of disease with children and in pregnancy.

Plan your vaccinations in advance as some of them require more than one injection, while other vaccinations should not be given together. It is recommended you seek medical advice at least six weeks before travel.

Record all vaccinations on an International Certificate of Vaccination, available from your doctor or government health department.

Discuss your requirements with your doctor, but vaccinations you should consider for this trip include:

Hepatitis A This is the most common travel-acquired illness after diarrhoea, and can put you out of action for weeks. Havrix 1440 and VAQTA are vaccinations which provide long term immunity (possibly more than 10 years) after an initial injection and a booster at six to 12 months. Gamma globulin is ready-made antibody collected from blood donations. It should be given close to departure because, depending on the dose, it only protects for two to six months. A combined hepatitis A and hepatitis B vaccination, Twinrix, is also available. This combined vaccination is recommended for people wanting protection against both types of viral hepatitis. Three injections over a six month period are required.

Typhoid This is an important vaccination to have where hygiene is a problem. Available either as an injection or oral capsules.

Diphtheria & Tetanus Diphtheria is a throat infection and tetanus is a wound infection; both can be fatal. Everyone should have these vaccinations. After an initial course of three injections, boosters are necessary every 10 years.

Hepatitis B China is one of the world's great reservoirs of hepatitis B infection. This disease is spread by blood or by sexual activity. Vaccination involves three injections, the quickest course being over three weeks with a booster at 12 months.

Polio This serious, easily transmitted disease is still prevalent in China. Everyone should keep up to date with this vaccination. A booster every 10 years maintains immunity.

Rabies Vaccination should be considered by those planning to spend a month or longer in China, especially if they are cycling, handling animals, caving or travelling to remote areas, or for children (who may not report a bite). Pretravel rabies vaccination involves having three injections over 21 to 28 days. If someone who has been vaccinated is bitten or scratched by an animal they will require two booster injections of vaccine, those not vaccinated require more.

Japanese B Encephalitis This mosquito-borne disease is not common in travellers, but occurs in Asia. Consider the vaccination if spending a month or longer in a high risk area, making repeated trips to a risk area or visiting during an epidemic. It involves three injections over 30 days. The vaccine is expensive and has been associated with serious allergic reactions so the decision to have it should be balanced against the risk of contracting the illness.

Tuberculosis TB risk to travellers is usually very low. For those who will be living with or closely associated with local people in high risk areas, such as Asia, Africa and some parts of the Americas and the Pacific, there may be some risk. As most healthy adults do not develop symptoms, a skin test before and after travel to determine whether exposure has occurred may be considered. A vaccination is recommended for children living in these areas for three months or more.

521

HEALTH

Medical Kit Check List

Consider taking a basic medical kit including:

- [ ] **Aspirin** or paracetamol (acetaminophen in the USA) – for pain or fever.
- [ ] **Antihistamine** (such as Benadryl) – useful as a decongestant for colds and allergies, to ease the itch from insect bites or stings, and to help prevent motion sickness. Antihistamines may cause sedation and interact with alcohol so care should be taken when using them; take one you know and have used before, if possible.
- [ ] **Antibiotics** – useful if you're travelling well off the beaten track, but they must be prescribed; carry the prescription with you.
- [ ] **Loperamide** (eg Imodium or Lomotil) for diarrhoea; prochlorperazine (eg Stemetil) or metaclopramide (eg Maxalon) for nausea and vomiting.
- [ ] **Rehydration mixture** – for treatment of severe diarrhoea; particularly important for travelling with children.
- [ ] **Antiseptic** such as povidone-iodine (eg Betadine) – for cuts and grazes.
- [ ] **Multivitamins** – especially for long trips when dietary vitamin intake may be inadequate.
- [ ] **Calamine lotion** or **aluminium sulphate spray** (eg Stingose) – to ease irritation from bites or stings.
- [ ] **Bandages** and **Band-Aids**
- [ ] **Scissors, tweezers** and a **thermometer** (note that mercury thermometers are prohibited by airlines).
- [ ] **Cold and flu tablets** and throat lozenges. Pseudoephedrine hydrochloride (Sudafed) may be useful if flying with a cold to avoid ear damage.
- [ ] **Insect repellent, sunscreen, lip salve** and **water purification tablets.**
- [ ] **Syringes,** in case you need injections in a country with medical hygiene problems. Ask your doctor for a note explaining why they have been prescribed.

Malaria Medication

Antimalarial drugs do not prevent you from being infected but kill the malaria parasites during a stage in their development and significantly reduce the risk of becoming very ill or dying.

Expert advice on medication should be sought, as there are many factors to consider, including the area to be visited, the risk of exposure to malaria-carrying mosquitoes, the side effects of medication, your medical history, and whether you are a child or adult or pregnant. Travellers to isolated areas in high risk countries may like to carry a treatment dose of medication for use if symptoms occur.

Health Insurance

Although you may have medical insurance in your own country, it is probably not valid in Hong Kong, or Guangzhou. But ask your insurance company anyway – you *might* already be covered. You also *might* be automatically covered if you hold a valid International Student Identity Card (ISIC), GO 25 International Youth Travel Card or International Teachers' Identity Card (ISTC) – ask at the place where you purchased the card.

A travel insurance policy is a very good idea – the best ones protect you against cancellation penalties on advance-purchase flights, against medical costs through illness or injury, against theft or loss of possessions and against the cost of additional air tickets if you get really sick and have to fly home. Cover depends on the insurance and your type of ticket, so ask both your insurer and the ticket-issuing agency to explain where you stand. Ticket loss is also covered by travel insurance.

Some policies offer lower and higher medical expense options; the higher ones are chiefly for countries such as the USA which have extremely high medical costs. There is a wide variety of policies available so check the small print.

Some policies specifically exclude 'dangerous activities', which can include scuba diving, motorcycling, and even trekking. A locally acquired motorcycle licence is not valid under some policies. Check that the policy covers ambulances or an emergency flight home.

You may prefer a policy which pays doctors or hospitals directly rather than having to pay on the spot and claim later. If you have to claim later make sure you keep all documentation. Some policies ask you to call back (reverse charges) to a centre in your home country where an immediate assessment of your problem is made.

Buy travel insurance as early as possible. If you buy it the week before you fly, you may find, for instance, that you're not covered for delays to your flight caused by strikes or other industrial action that may have started or been threatened before you took out the insurance.

Paying for your airline ticket with a credit card often provides limited travel accident insurance and you may be able to reclaim the payment if the operator doesn't deliver. Ask your credit-card company what it's prepared to cover.

Student travel offices are one place to inquire about relatively inexpensive insurance policies. Better travel agencies also sell travel insurance policies – do a little checking around before you buy. Again, read the fine print – the coverage may be cheap, but very limited.

Travel Health Guides

If you are planning to be away or travelling in remote areas for a long period of time, you may like to consider taking a more detailed health guide.

Staying Healthy in Asia, Africa & Latin America, Dirk Schroeder, Moon Publications, 1994. Probably the best all-round guide to carry; it's compact, detailed and well organised.

Travellers' Health, Dr Richard Dawood, Oxford University Press, 1995. Comprehensive, easy to read, authoritative and highly recommended, although it's rather large to lug around.

Where There is No Doctor, David Werner, Macmillan, 1994. A very detailed guide intended for such travellers as Peace Corp workers, going to work in underdeveloped countries.

Travel with Children, Maureen Wheeler, Lonely Planet Publications, 1995. Includes advice on travel health for younger children.

There are also a number of excellent travel health sites on the Internet. From the Lonely Planet home page there are links at www.lonelyplanet.com/weblinks/wlprep.htm to the World Health Organisation and the US Center for Disease Control & Prevention.

Other Preparations

Make sure you're healthy before you start travelling. If you are going on a long trip make sure your teeth are OK. If you wear glasses take a spare pair and your prescription.

If you require a particular medication, take an adequate supply as it may not be available locally. Take part of the packaging showing the generic name, rather than the brand, which will make getting replacements easier. It's a good idea to have a legible prescription or letter from your doctor to show that you legally use the medication to avoid any problems.

BASIC RULES
Food

The Chinese are pretty conscientious about handling food and there is little to worry about. If you want to be particularly cautious, then avoid shellfish and seafood, which are at risk of spoilage (due to lack of refrigeration) and water pollution. Some of the rivers and bays in China are positively toxic, yet you often see people fishing in them. Better restaurants only buy fish that are raised in commercial ponds, and the fish are kept alive in aquariums until just before cooking – unfortunately, not all restaurants are so scrupulous. Steaming does not make shellfish safe for eating.

If a place looks clean and well run and the vendor also looks clean and healthy, the food is probably safe. In general, places that are packed with travellers or locals will be fine, while empty restaurants are questionable. The food in busy restaurants is cooked and eaten quite quickly with little standing around and is probably not reheated.

If you are buying your own vegetables from the market in Hong Kong or Macau, be aware that a lot of the food is imported from Guangdong Province where human

HEALTH

manure is commonly used as fertiliser. Washing and soaking all produce well is essential (especially leafy vegetables) unless you want to pick up a dose of hepatitis A. The same, of course, applies to all vegetables bought in Guangzhou.

Water

The government insists that Hong Kong's tap water is perfectly safe to drink and does not need to be boiled. However, most local Chinese boil it anyway, more out of habit than necessity. In urban areas there should be no problem with tap water, although in some agricultural backwaters in the New Territories and outlying islands, surface water may be contaminated by fertiliser. If you're going to be hiking in the countryside, be sure to bring an adequate supply of water and avoid drinking unboiled surface water. Bottled water is widely available from shops.

In Macau, the water supply is purified and chlorinated and considered safe to drink. Nevertheless, many locals boil it anyway. Distilled or mineral water is widely available from shops.

In Guangzhou and surrounds, tap water is chlorinated and safe for brushing teeth, but it's still advisable to boil it before drinking. Virtually all hotels provide flasks with boiled water. Bottled water is widely available from kiosks and stores.

Water Purification

The simplest way of purifying water is to boil it thoroughly. Vigorously boiling should be satisfactory; however, at high altitude water boils at a lower temperature, so germs are less likely to be killed. Boil it for longer in these environments.

Consider purchasing a water filter for a long trip. There are two main kinds of filter. Total filters take out all parasites, bacteria and viruses, and make water safe to drink. They are often expensive, but they can be more cost effective than buying bottled water. Simple filters (which can even be a nylon mesh bag) take out dirt and larger foreign bodies from the water so that chemical solutions work much more effectively;

if water is dirty, chemical solutions may not work at all. It's very important to read the specifications when buying a filter, so that you know exactly what it removes from the water and what it doesn't. Simple filtering will not remove all dangerous organisms, so if you cannot boil water it should be treated chemically.

Chlorine tablets (Puritabs, Steritabs or other brand names) will kill many pathogens, but not some parasites like giardia and amoebic cysts. Iodine is more effective in purifying water and is available in tablet form (such as Potable Aqua). Follow the directions carefully and remember that too much iodine can be harmful.

Swimming Water

Most beaches in Hong Kong fall below the World Health Organisations levels for safe swimming, due to unacceptable pollution. Water is tested at each beach every two weeks and judgements made based upon the level of E Coli bacteria present in the sample. At the start of the swimming season, the health authorities list the beaches that are deemed safe enough for swimming. Swimming in polluted water can give rise to such conditions as diarrhoea, ear, nose and throat infections, skin infections or hepatitis A. It is much safer to go to the beach for a tan and to admire the view.

MEDICAL PROBLEMS & TREATMENT

Self-diagnosis and treatment can be risky, so you should always seek medical help. Although we do give drug dosages in this chapter, they are for emergency use only. Correct diagnosis is vital.

An embassy, consulate or five star hotel can usually recommend a local doctor. Antibiotics should ideally be administered only under medical supervision. Take only the recommended dose at the prescribed intervals and use the whole course, even if the illness seems to be cured earlier. Stop immediately if there are any serious reactions and don't use the antibiotic at all if you are unsure that you have the correct one. Some people are allergic to commonly pre-

Nutrition

If your food is poor or limited in availability, if you're travelling hard and fast and therefore missing meals, or if you simply lose your appetite, you can soon start to lose weight and place your health at risk.

Make sure your diet is well balanced. Cooked eggs, tofu, beans, lentils and nuts are all safe ways to get protein. Fruit you can peel (bananas, oranges or mandarins for example) is usually safe (melons can harbour bacteria in their flesh and are best avoided) and a good source of vitamins. Try to eat plenty of grains (including rice) and bread. Remember that although food is generally safer if it is cooked well, overcooked food loses much of its nutritional value. If your diet isn't well balanced or if your food intake is insufficient, it's a good idea to take vitamin and iron pills.

In hot climates make sure you drink enough – don't rely on feeling thirsty to indicate when you should drink. Not needing to urinate or small amounts of very dark yellow urine is a danger sign. Always carry a water bottle with you on long trips. Excessive sweating can lead to loss of salt and therefore muscle cramping. Salt tablets are not a good idea as a preventative, but in places where salt is not used much adding salt to food can help.

scribed antibiotics such as penicillin or sulpha drugs; carry this information when travelling, eg on a indentifying bracelet.

You can buy almost any medication across the counter in Hong Kong, or get it by prescription.

If you need any vaccinations while in Hong Kong, the Port Health office (☎ 2961-8852) can give you a low cost jab for cholera and typhoid. It occasionally stocks other vaccines, depending on which epidemics are ravaging this part of Asia. Port Health has two branch offices: Kowloon (☎ 2368-3361), room 905, Government Offices, Canton Rd, Yau Ma Tei; and Hong Kong

Island (☎ 2961-8840), 18th floor, Wu Chung House, 213 Queen's Rd East, Wan Chai.

Hospitals

Although Hong Kong's medical care is of a high standard, there is a real shortage of qualified medical staff. This is because China's takeover has driven many of the best medical staff to emigrate in droves to western countries. This has led some cynics to suggest that perhaps the best place to get sick in Hong Kong is at the airport.

Hong Kong and Macau's public hospitals charge much less than private clinics, but you may have to wait a long time to see a doctor. Residents pay less than foreign visitors. Most four and five star hotels have resident doctors.

Public hospitals in Hong Kong include:

Princess Margaret Hospital
(☎ 2310-3111) Lai Chi Kok, Kowloon
Prince of Wales Hospital
(☎ 2636-2211) 30-32 Ngan Shing St, Sha Tin, New Territories
Queen Elizabeth Hospital
(☎ 2710-2111) Wylie Rd, Yau Ma Tei, Kowloon
Queen Mary Hospital
(☎ 2819-2111) Pok Fu Lam Rd, Pok Fu Lam

There are some excellent private hospitals in Hong Kong, but the prices reflect the fact that these operate at a profit. Some of the better private hospitals include:

Adventist
(☎ 2574-6211) 40 Stubbs Rd, Wan Chai, Hong Kong Island
Baptist
(☎ 2339-8888) 222 Waterloo Rd, Kowloon Tong
Canossa
(☎ 2522-2181) 1 Old Peak Rd, Mid-Levels, Hong Kong Island
Grantham
(☎ 2518-2111) 125 Wong Chuk Hang Rd, Deep Water Bay, Hong Kong Island
Hong Kong Central
(☎ 2522-3141) 1B Lower Albert Rd, Central, Hong Kong Island
Matilda & War Memorial
(☎ 2849-0111, 2849-0777) 41 Mt Kellett Rd, The Peak, Hong Kong Island

HEALTH

St Paul's
(☎ 2890-6008) 2 Eastern Hospital Rd, Causeway Bay, Hong Kong Island

There are two government-run hospitals in Macau:

Government Hospital
(☎ 51449, 313731) Estrada de a São Francisco
Kiang Vu
(☎ 371333) Estrada do Repouso and Rua Coelho do Amaral

Hospitals in Guangzhou include:

Guangzhou No 1 People's Hospital
(☎ 8333-3090, *dìyī rénmín yīyuàn*) 602 Renmin Lu
Sun Yatsen Memorial Hospital
(☎ 888-2012) 107 Yanjiang Lu
The Red Cross Hospital
(☎ 8444-6411)

Resident foreigners in Guangzhou may be interested in the health services offered by SOS International (☎ 8759-5357) at The Greenery, 55-79 Huayang Jie, Tiyu Dong Lu. It can arrange house calls in the Guangzhou area and has a 24 hour emergency doctor. Other expat medical services can be found at the New Pioneer International Medical Centre (☎ 8384-8228) at the Peace World Plaza, next to the Garden Hotel. It has an emergency medical hotline: ☎ 8384-8911.

If you break a tooth on a stone chip in your rice, head over to the Guangdong Dental Hospital (☎ 8440-3983), south of the river at 366 Jiangnan Boulevard, which has English-speaking dentists at hand.

Guangzhou is the place to go if you want to be treated with acupuncture and herbs. Just next to Shamian Island and the Qingping Market is the Traditional Chinese Medicine Hospital (☎ 8188-6504, *zhōngyī yīyuàn*) at 16 Zhuji Lu. Another option is the Liwanqu Traditional Chinese Medicine Hospital (☎ 8181-8679), 32 Zhoumen Xijie, Zhongshan 8 Lu (at the east end of town).

Qigong

Kungfu meditation, known as *qigong*, is used both as a form of self-defence training and as a healing technique in Chinese medicine. *Qi* represents life's vital energy. Qigong can be thought of as energy management – practitioners try to project their qi to perform nearly magical acts.

Qigong practitioners occasionally give impressive demonstrations, driving nails through boards with their fingers or putting their fists through a brick wall. Less spectacular but potentially more useful is the ability to heal others. Typically, practitioners place their hands above or next to the patient's body without actually making physical contact. To many foreigners this looks like a circus act, and even many Chinese suspect that it's nothing than quackery. However, there are many who claim that they have been cured of serious illness through qigong, even after more conventional doctors told them that their condition was hopeless.

In China during the Cultural Revolution, qigong practitioners were denounced as a superstitious link to the bourgeois past. Many practitioners were arrested and all were forced to stop. It is only recently that qigong has made a comeback, but many of the highly skilled practitioners are no longer alive.

Does qigong work? It isn't easy to say, but there is a theory in medicine that all doctors can cure one-third of their patients regardless of what method is used.

ENVIRONMENTAL HAZARDS
Fungal Infections
Fungal infections occur more commonly in hot weather and are found on the scalp, between the toes or fingers, in the groin and on the body (ringworm). You get ringworm (which is a fungal infection, not a worm) from infected animals or other people. Moisture encourages these infections.

To prevent fungal infections wear loose, comfortable clothes, avoid artificial fibres, wash frequently and dry yourself carefully. If you do get an infection, wash the infected area at least daily with a disinfectant or medicated soap and water, and rinse and dry well. Apply an anti-fungal cream or powder like tolnaftate (Tinaderm). Try to expose the infected area to air or sunlight as much as possible, and wash all towels and underwear in hot water, change them often and let them dry in the sun.

Heat Exhaustion
Dehydration and salt deficiency can cause heat exhaustion. Take time to acclimatise to high temperatures, drink sufficient liquids and do not do anything that is too physically demanding.

Salt deficiency is characterised by fatigue, lethargy, headaches, giddiness and muscle cramps; salt tablets may help, but adding extra salt to your food is better.

Anhydrotic heat exhaustion, caused by an inability to sweat, is quite rare. It is likely to strike people who have been in a hot climate for some time, rather than newcomers.

Heatstroke
This serious, occasionally fatal, condition can occur if the body's heat-regulating mechanism breaks down and the body temperature rises to dangerous levels. Long, continuous periods of exposure to high temperatures and insufficient fluids can leave you vulnerable to heatstroke.

The symptoms are feeling unwell, not sweating very much (or at all) and a high body temperature (39°C to 41°C or 102°F to 106°F). Where sweating has ceased the skin becomes flushed and red. Severe, throbbing headaches and lack of coordination will also occur, and the sufferer may be confused or aggressive. Eventually the victim will become delirious or convulse. Hospitalisation is essential, but in the interim get victims out of the sun, remove their clothing, cover them with a wet sheet or towel and then fan continually. Give fluids if they are conscious.

Jet Lag
Jet lag is experienced when a person travels by air across more than three time zones (each time zone usually represents a one hour time difference). It occurs because many of the functions of the human body (such as temperature, pulse rate and emptying of the bladder and bowels) are regulated by internal 24 hour cycles.

When we travel long distances rapidly, our bodies take time to adjust to the 'new time' of our destination, and we may experience fatigue, disorientation, insomnia, anxiety, impaired concentration and loss of appetite. These effects will usually be gone within three days of arrival, but to minimise the impact of jet lag:

- Rest for a couple of days prior to departure.
- Try to select flight schedules that minimise sleep deprivation; arriving late in the day means you can go to sleep soon after you arrive. For very long flights, try to organise a stopover.
- Avoid excessive eating (which bloats the stomach) and alcohol (which causes dehydration) during the flight. Instead, drink plenty of non-carbonated, non-alcoholic drinks such as fruit juice or water.
- Avoid smoking.
- Make yourself comfortable by wearing loose-fitting clothes and perhaps bringing an eye mask and ear plugs to help you sleep.
- Try to sleep at the appropriate time for the time zone you are travelling to.

Motion Sickness
Eating lightly before and during a trip will reduce the chances of motion sickness. If you are prone to motion sickness try to find a place that minimises movement near the wing on aircraft, close to amidships on boats, near the centre on buses. Fresh air usually helps; reading and cigarette smoke don't.

Commercial motion-sickness preparations, which can cause drowsiness, have to be taken before the trip commences. Ginger (available in capsule form) and peppermint (including mint-flavoured sweets) are natural preventatives.

HEALTH

Prickly Heat

Prickly heat is an itchy rash caused by excessive perspiration trapped under the skin. It usually strikes people who have just arrived in a hot climate. Keeping cool, bathing often, drying the skin and using a mild talcum or prickly heat powder or resorting to air conditioning may help.

Sunburn

You can get sunburnt surprisingly quickly, even through cloud. Use a sunscreen, hat, and barrier cream for your nose and lips. Calamine lotion or Stingose are good for mild sunburn. Protect your eyes with good quality sunglasses, particularly if you will be near water, sand or snow.

INFECTIOUS DISEASES
Influenza

Upper respiratory tract infections (URTIs), or the common cold, are the most common ailment to afflict visitors to China. The Chinese call it *ganmao*. Transmission rates are high because of the crowding and the cold. China also has a special relationship with the influenza virus. You may not remember the notorious 'Hong Kong flu' of 1968, but you may have heard of the more recent 'Bird flu' epidemic in 1997. There have been various other influenza strains named after Chinese cities. This is because China is the production house for new strains of influenza virus. The reason for this is thought to be the proximity in which people live to ducks and pigs, which are the reservoirs for the two other main populations of the virus. This provides the opportunity for the viruses to chop and change, reappearing in different forms or strains.

During winter, practically the entire population of 1.2 billion is stricken with ganmao. URTIs are aggravated by cold weather, poor nutrition and China's notorious air pollution. Smoking makes it worse, and half the population of China smokes. Overcrowded conditions increase the opportunities for infection. Another reason is that Chinese people spit a lot, which helps spread the disease. It's a vicious circle: they're sick

> ### Everyday Health
>
> Normal body temperature is up to 37°C or 98.6°F; more than 2°C (4°F) higher indicates a high fever. The normal adult pulse rate is 60 to 100 beats per minute (children 80 to 100, babies 100 to 140). As a general rule the pulse increases about 20 beats per minute for each °C (2°F) rise in fever.
>
> Respiration (breathing) rate is also an indicator of illness. Count the number of breaths per minute: between 12 and 20 breaths is normal for adults and older children (up to 30 for younger children, 40 for babies). People with a high fever or serious respiratory illness breathe more quickly than normal. More than 40 shallow breaths a minute may indicate pneumonia.

because they spit and they spit because they're sick.

Winter visitors to China should bring a few favourite cold remedies. These can easily be purchased from any good pharmacy in Hong Kong or Macau. Such items can be found elsewhere in China, but with considerably more difficulty.

Symptoms of influenza include fever, weakness, sore throat and a feeling of malaise. Any URTI, including influenza, can lead to complications such as bronchitis and pneumonia, which may need to be treated with antibiotics. Seek medical help in this situation.

Finally, if you can't get well in China, leave the country and take a nice holiday on a warm beach in Thailand.

Diarrhoea

Simple things like a change of water, food or climate can all cause a mild bout of diarrhoea, but a few rushed toilet trips with no other symptoms is not indicative of a major problem.

Dehydration is the main danger with any diarrhoea, particularly in children or the elderly, as dehydration can occur quite quickly. Under all circumstances *fluid replacement* (at least equal to the volume being lost) is the most important thing to remember. Weak black tea with a little sugar, soda water, or soft drinks allowed to go flat and diluted 50% with clean water are all good. For severe diarrhoea a rehydrating solution is preferable to replace minerals and salts lost. Commercially available oral rehydration salts (ORS) are very useful; add them to boiled or bottled water. In an emergency you can make up a solution of six teaspoons of sugar and a half teaspoon of salt to a litre of boiled or bottled water. You need to drink at least the same volume of fluid that you are losing in bowel movements and vomiting. Urine is the best guide to the adequacy of replacement – if you have small amounts of concentrated urine, you need to drink more. Keep drinking small amounts often. Stick to a bland diet as you recover.

Lomotil or Imodium can be used to bring relief from the symptoms, although they do not actually cure the problem. Only use these drugs if you do not have access to toilets, eg if you *must* travel. For children under 12 years, Lomotil and Imodium are not recommended. Do not use these drugs if the person has a high fever or is severely dehydrated.

In certain situations antibiotics may be required: diarrhoea with blood or mucus (dysentery), any fever, watery diarrhoea with fever and lethargy, persistent diarrhoea not improving after 48 hours and severe diarrhoea. In these situations gut-paralysing drugs like Imodium or Lomotil should be avoided.

A stool test is necessary to diagnose which kind of dysentery you have, so you should seek medical help urgently. Where this is not possible the recommended drugs for dysentery are norfloxacin 400mg twice daily for three days or ciprofloxacin 500mg twice daily for five days. These are not recommended for children or pregnant women. The drug of choice for children would be co-trimoxazole (Bactrim, Septrin, Resprim) with dosage dependent on weight. A five day

course is given. Ampicillin or amoxycillin may be given in pregnancy, but medical care is necessary.

Amoebic dysentery has a gradual onset of symptoms, with cramping abdominal pain and vomiting less likely than with other types of dysentery; fever may not be present. It will persist until treated and can recur and cause other health problems.

Giardiasis is another type of diarrhoea. The parasite causing this intestinal disorder is present in contaminated water. The symptoms are stomach cramps, nausea, a bloated stomach, watery, foul-smelling diarrhoea and frequent gas. Giardiasis can appear several weeks after you have been exposed to the parasite. The symptoms may disappear for a few days and then return; this can go on for several weeks. Tinidazole, known as Fasigyn, or metronidazole (Flagyl) are the recommended drugs. Treatment is a 2g single dose of Fasigyn or 250mg of Flagyl three times daily for five to 10 days.

Hepatitis

Hepatitis is a general term for inflammation of the liver. It is a common disease worldwide. The symptoms are fever, chills, headache, fatigue, feelings of weakness and aches and pains, followed by loss of appetite, nausea, vomiting, abdominal pain, dark urine, light-coloured faeces, jaundiced (yellow) skin and the whites of the eyes may turn yellow. **Hepatitis A** is transmitted by contaminated food and drinking water. The disease poses a real threat to the traveller. In China, the disease may be spread because of the Chinese custom of everybody eating from a single dish rather than using separate plates and a serving spoon. It is a good idea to use the disposable chopsticks now freely available in most restaurants in China, or else buy your own chopsticks and spoon.

If you think you have hepatitis, you should seek medical advice, but there is not much you can do apart from resting, drinking lots of fluids, eating lightly and avoiding fatty foods. People who have had hepatitis should avoid alcohol for some time after the illness, as the liver needs time to recover.

Hepatitis E is transmitted in the same way, and can be very serious in pregnant women.

There are almost 300 million chronic carriers of **Hepatitis B** in the world. It is spread through contact with infected blood, blood products or body fluids, for example, through sexual contact, unsterilised needles and blood transfusions, or contact with blood via small breaks in the skin. Other risk situations include having a shave, tattoo or having your body pierced with contaminated equipment. The symptoms of type B may be more severe and may lead to long term problems. **Hepatitis D** is spread in the same way, but the risk is mainly in shared needles.

Hepatitis C can lead to chronic liver disease. The virus is spread by contact with blood, usually via contaminated transfusions or shared needles. Avoiding these is the only means of prevention.

HIV & AIDS

The Human Immunodeficiency Virus (HIV) develops into the Acquired Immune Deficiency Syndrome (AIDS), which is a fatal disease. HIV is a major problem in many countries. Any exposure to blood, blood products or body fluids may put the individual at risk. The disease is often transmitted through sexual contact or dirty needles – vaccinations, acupuncture, tattooing and body piercing are potentially as dangerous as intravenous drug use. HIV/AIDS can also be spread through infected blood transfusions; some developing countries cannot afford to screen blood used for transfusions.

China does not issue visas to foreigners known to be HIV positive, and foreigners who wish to work in China must submit to an AIDS test. Those who test HIV positive at Chinese hospitals are routinely deported. Beijing isn't known for respecting an individual's right to confidentiality.

Under British rule, Hong Kong has been fairly tolerant towards people living with HIV/AIDS. For example, AIDS testing is free at all public hospitals in Hong Kong and medical records are kept strictly confidential. For this reason alone, Hong Kong is a good place to get an AIDS test. Not only are the testing facilities reliable, but the government does not deport people who test positive for the disease.

If you do need an injection, ask to see the syringe unwrapped in front of you, or take a needle and syringe pack with you. Fear of HIV infection should never preclude treatment for serious medical conditions.

Intestinal Worms

These parasites are most common in rural, tropical areas. The different worms have different ways of infecting people. Some may be ingested on food, including undercooked meat, and some enter through your skin. Infestations may not show up for some time and, although they are generally not serious, if left untreated some can cause severe health problems later. Consider having a stool test when you return home to check for these and determine the appropriate treatment.

Sexually Transmitted Diseases

For decades, the authorities pretended that prostitution, premarital and extra-marital sex simply didn't exist in the People's Republic of China, and that Sexually Transmitted Diseases (STDs) were a foreign problem. The Cultural Revolution may be over, but the sexual revolution is booming in China and STDs are spreading rapidly. The sexual revolution reached Hong Kong long ago, as did the STDs that go with it.

Gonorrhoea, herpes and syphilis are among these diseases; sores, blisters or rashes around the genitals, discharge or pain when urinating are common symptoms. In some STDs, such as the wart virus or chlamydia, symptoms may be less marked or not observed at all, especially in women. Syphilis symptoms eventually disappear completely but the disease continues and can cause severe problems in later years. While abstinence from sexual contact is the only 100% effective prevention, using condoms is also effective. The treatment of gonorrhoea and syphilis is with antibiotics. The different STDs each require specific antibiotics. There is no cure for herpes or AIDS.

Typhoid

Typhoid fever is a dangerous gut infection caused by contaminated water and food. Medical help must be sought.

In its early stages sufferers may feel they have a bad cold or flu on the way, as early symptoms are a headache, body aches and a fever which rises a little each day until it is around 40°C (104°F) or more. The victim's pulse is often slow, relative to the degree of fever present – unlike a normal fever where the pulse increases. There may also be vomiting, abdominal pain, diarrhoea or constipation.

In the second week the high fever and slow pulse continue and a few pink spots may appear on the body; trembling, delirium, weakness, weight loss and dehydration may occur. Complications such as pneumonia, perforated bowel or meningitis may occur.

The fever should be treated by keeping the victim cool and giving them fluids, as dehydration is a danger. Ciprofloxacin 750mg twice a day for 10 days is the recommended dosage for adults.

Chloramphenicol is recommended in many countries. The adult dosage is two 250mg capsules, four times a day. Children aged between eight and 12 years should have half the adult dose; and younger children one-third the adult dose.

INSECT-BORNE DISEASES

Filariasis, leishmaniasis, lyme disease and typhus are all insect-borne diseases, but they do not pose a great risk to travellers. For more information see Less Common Diseases later in this chapter.

Malaria

This serious and potentially fatal disease is spread by mosquito bites. There is no risk of malaria in Hong Kong or Macau, but there is a risk in Guangdong, mainly in rural areas, especially in summer.

If you are travelling in endemic areas it is extremely important to avoid mosquito bites and to take tablets to prevent this disease. Symptoms range from fever, chills and sweating, headache, diarrhoea and abdominal pains to a vague feeling of ill-health. Seek medical help immediately if malaria is suspected. Without treatment malaria can rapidly become more serious and can be fatal.

If medical care is not available, malaria tablets can be used for treatment. You need to use a malaria tablet which is different to the one you were taking when you contracted malaria. The standard treatment dosages are: mefloquine, three 250mg tablets and a further two tablets six hours later, or fansidar, single dose of three tablets. If you were previously taking mefloquine and cannot obtain fansidar, alternatives are halofantrine (three doses of two 250mg tablets every six hours) or quinine sulphate (600mg every six hours). There is a greater risk of side effects with these dosages than in normal use if used with mefloquine, so medical advice is preferable.

Travellers are advised to prevent mosquito bites at all times. The main messages are:

- Wear light coloured clothing.
- Wear long trousers and long sleeved shirts.
- Use mosquito repellents containing the compound DEET on exposed areas (prolonged overuse of DEET may be harmful, especially to children, but its use is considered preferable to being bitten by disease-transmitting mosquitoes).
- Avoid wearing perfume or aftershave.
- Use a mosquito net impregnated with mosquito repellent (permethrin) – it may be worth taking your own.
- Impregnating clothes with permethrin effectively deters mosquitoes and other insects.

Dengue Fever

There is no preventative drug available for this mosquito-spread disease which can be fatal in children. A sudden onset of fever, headaches and severe joint and muscle pains are the first signs before a rash develops. Recovery may be prolonged.

HEALTH

Japanese B Encephalitis

This viral infection of the brain is transmitted by mosquitoes. Most cases occur in rural areas as the virus exists in pigs and wading birds. Symptoms include fever, headache and alteration in consciousness. Hospitalisation is needed for correct diagnosis and treatment. There is a high mortality rate among those who have symptoms; of those that survive many are intellectually disabled.

CUTS, BITES & STINGS

Rabies is passed through animal bites. See Less Common Diseases following this section for details of this disease.

Bedbugs & Lice

Bedbugs live in various places, but particularly in dirty mattresses and bedding, evidenced by spots of blood on bedclothes or on the wall. Bedbugs leave itchy bites in neat rows. Calamine lotion or Stingose spray may help.

All lice cause itching and discomfort. They make themselves at home in your hair (head lice), your clothing (body lice) or in your pubic hair (crabs). You catch lice through direct contact with infected people or by sharing combs, clothing and the like. Powder or shampoo treatment will kill the lice, and infected clothing should then be washed in very hot, soapy water and left in the sun to dry.

Bites & Stings

Bee and wasp stings are usually painful rather than dangerous. However, in people who are allergic to them severe breathing difficulties may occur and urgent medical care is necessary. Calamine lotion or Stingose spray will give relief and ice packs will reduce the pain and swelling. There are some spiders with dangerous bites but antivenenes are usually available. Scorpion stings are notoriously painful and in some parts of Asia, the Middle East and Central America can actually be fatal. Scorpions often shelter in shoes or clothing.

Except during the dead of winter, mosquitoes are a year-round annoyance in Hong Kong, even in the urban jungles of Kowloon and Central. They are especially annoying at night when you're trying to sleep. Electric mosquito zappers are useful, but are too heavy for travelling. A portable innovation is 'electric mosquito incense', also known as 'vape mats' or 'mosquito mats'. Mosquito mats and the mosquito mat electric heater are sold in grocery stores and supermarkets all over Hong Kong, Macau and southern China. The mats emit a poison – breathing it over the long-term may have unknown health effects, though all the manufacturers of this stuff insist that it is safe. Avoid buying electric mosquito repellers that emit a high-frequency note imitating the sound of the male mosquito (only pregnant female mosquitoes bite and theoretically fly away when confronted by a male); recent test indicate that these do not work and may in fact attract more mosquitoes.

Mosquito incense coils accomplish the same thing as the vape mats and require no electricity, but the smoke is nasty. Mosquito repellent is somewhat less effective than incense, but is probably less toxic and gives protection outdoors where incense is impractical. Look for brands that contain DEET (diethyl toluamide). Sleeping under a blowing electric fan all night (not recommended during winter) may help keep mosquitoes away.

There are various fish and other sea creatures which can sting or bite dangerously or are dangerous to eat. Local advice is the best suggestion.

Cuts & Scratches

Wash well and treat any cut with an antiseptic such as povidone-iodine. Where possible avoid bandages and Band-Aids, which can keep wounds wet. Coral cuts are notoriously slow to heal and if they are not adequately cleaned, small pieces of coral can become embedded in the wound.

Leeches & Ticks

Leeches may be present in damp rainforest conditions; they attach themselves to your skin to suck your blood. Trekkers often get them on their legs or in their boots. Salt or a lighted cigarette end will make them fall off. Do not pull them off, as the bite is then more likely to become infected. Clean and apply pressure if the point of attachment is bleeding. An insect repellent may keep them away.

You should always check all over your body if you have been walking through a potentially tick-infested area, as ticks can cause skin infections and other more serious diseases. If a tick is found attached, press down around the tick's head with tweezers, grab the head and gently pull upwards. Avoid pulling the rear of the body as this may squeeze the tick's gut contents through the attached mouth parts into the skin, increasing the risk of infection and disease. Smearing chemicals on the tick will not make it let go and is not recommended.

Snakes

The term 'snake' is used by the Cantonese to describe someone who smuggles illegal aliens into Hong Kong. However, we speak here of the non-human kind.

The countryside of Hong Kong in particular is home to some poisonous snakes which you'd be wise to avoid. Most dangerous are the cobras, and some species show very little shyness about living near areas inhabited by people. The king cobra is most dangerous by far, but fortunately it's not common and avoids contact with humans. Two common poisonous snakes include the green bamboo pit viper and coral snake. There are a number of poisonous freshwater snakes and sea snakes. Non-poisonous snakes include rat snakes (which find plenty to eat in Hong Kong), copperhead racers, pythons and boas.

To minimise your chances of being bitten always wear boots, socks and long trousers when walking through undergrowth where snakes may be present. Don't put your hands into holes and crevices, and be careful when collecting firewood.

Snake bites do not cause instantaneous death and antivenenes are usually available. Immediately wrap the bitten limb tightly, as

Snakes & Bladders

The Chinese believe that eating snake gall bladder dispels wind, promotes blood circulation, dissolves phlegm and soothes one's breathing. Snake meat is said to remedy all sorts of ailments, including anaemia, rheumatism, arthritis and asthenia (abnormal loss of strength). Way back in the 1320s the Franciscan friar Odoric visited China and commented on the snake-eating habits of the southern Chinese: 'There be monstrous great serpents likewise which are taken by the inhabitants and eaten. A solemn feast among them with serpents is thought nothing of'.

you would for a sprained ankle, and then attach a splint to immobilise it. Keep the victim still and seek medical help, if possible with the dead snake for identification. Don't attempt to catch the snake if there is a possibility of being bitten again. Tourniquets and sucking out the poison are now comprehensively discredited.

Sharks

In addition to the shopkeepers along Nathan Rd, there are several other species of sharks in Hong Kong. The tiger shark seems to be particularly nasty – there is typically about one fatal attack on humans every year. Most of these attacks have occurred at beaches in the Sai Kung area of the New Territories. If you want to swim, stick to the beaches that are guarded by shark nets.

LESS COMMON DISEASES

The following diseases pose a small risk to travellers, and so are only mentioned in passing. Seek medical advice if you think you may have any of these diseases.

Cholera

This is the worst of the watery diarrhoeas and medical help should be sought. Outbreaks of cholera are generally widely

HEALTH

reported, so you should avoid such problem areas. *Fluid replacement is the most vital treatment* – the risk of dehydration is severe as you may lose up to 20L a day. If there is a delay in getting to hospital then begin taking tetracycline. The adult dose is 250mg four times daily. It is not recommended for children under nine years nor for pregnant women. Tetracycline may help shorten the illness, but adequate fluids are required to save lives.

Filariasis

This is a mosquito-transmitted parasitic infection found in many parts of Africa, Asia, Central and South America and the Pacific. Possible symptoms include fever, pain and swelling of the lymph glands; inflammation of lymph drainage areas; swelling of a limb or the scrotum; skin rashes and blindness. Treatment is available to eliminate the parasites from the body, but some of the damage already caused may not be reversible. Medical advice should be obtained promptly if the infection is suspected.

Leishmaniasis

A group of parasitic diseases transmitted by sandfly bites, found in many parts of the Middle East, Africa, India, Central and South America, and the Mediterranean. Cutaneous leishmaniasis affects the skin tissue causing ulceration and disfigurement, and visceral leishmaniasis affects the internal organs. Seek medical advice as laboratory testing is required for diagnosis and correct treatment. Avoiding sandfly bites is the best precaution. Bites are usually painless, itchy and are yet another reason to cover up and apply repellent.

Lyme Disease

Lyme disease is a tick-transmitted infection which may be acquired throughout North America, Europe and Asia. The illness usually begins with a spreading rash at the site of the tick bite, and is accompanied by fever, headache, extreme fatigue, aching joints and muscles, and mild neck stiffness. If untreated, these symptoms usually resolve over several weeks but over subsequent weeks or months disorders of the nervous system, heart and joints may develop. Treatment works best early in the illness. Medical help should be sought.

Rabies

Rabies is a fatal viral infection found in many countries. Many animals can be infected (such as dogs, cats, bats and monkeys) and it is their saliva which is infectious. Any bite, scratch or even lick from a warm-blooded, furry animal should be cleaned immediately and thoroughly. Scrub with soap and running water, and then apply alcohol or iodine solution. Medical help should be sought promptly to receive a course of injections to prevent the onset of symptoms and death.

Tetanus

Tetanus occurs when a wound becomes infected by a germ which lives in soil and in the faeces of horses and other animals. It enters the body via breaks in the skin. All wounds should be cleaned promptly and adequately and an antiseptic cream or solution applied. Use antibiotics if the wound becomes hot, throbs or pus is seen. The first symptom may be discomfort in swallowing, or stiffening of the jaw and neck; this is followed by painful convulsions of the jaw and whole body. The disease can be fatal.

Tuberculosis (TB)

TB is a bacterial infection usually transmitted from person to person by coughing but may be transmitted through consumption of unpasteurised milk. Milk that has been boiled is safe to drink, and the souring of milk to make yoghurt or cheese also kills the bacilli. Travellers are usually not at great risk as close household contact with the infected person is usually required before the disease is passed on.

TB resulted in 310 deaths in Hong Kong in 1996 and in the first nine months of 1997 there were more than 5000 new cases. There are approximately 100 new cases per

100,000 people in Hong Kong annually compared to 10 new cases annually per 100,000 people in other industrialised countries.

The vaccine for TB is called BCG and is most often given to school children. The disadvantage of the vaccine is that, once given, the recipient will always test positive to the TB skin test.

Typhus

Typhus is spread by ticks, mites or lice. It begins with fever, chills, headache and muscle pains followed a few days later by a body rash. There is often a large painful sore at the site of the bite and nearby lymph nodes are swollen and painful. Typhus can be treated under medical supervision. Seek local advice on areas where ticks pose a danger and always check your skin (including hair) carefully for ticks after walking in a danger area such as a tropical forest. A strong insect repellent can help, and serious walkers in tick areas should consider having their boots and trousers impregnated with benzyl benzoate and dibutylphthalate. See also the Leeches & Ticks entry in the previous Cuts Bites & Stings section.

WOMEN'S HEALTH
Gynaecological Problems

STDs are a major cause of vaginal problems. Symptoms include a smelly discharge, painful intercourse and sometimes a burning sensation when urinating. Male sexual partners must also be treated. Medical attention should be sought, and remember in addition to these diseases HIV or hepatitis B may also be acquired during exposure. Besides

abstinence, the best preventative is to practise safe sex using condoms.

Antibiotic use, synthetic underwear, sweating and contraceptive pills can lead to fungal vaginal infections when travelling in hot climates. Maintaining good personal hygiene, and wearing loose-fitting clothes and cotton underwear will help to prevent these infections. Fungal infections, characterised by a rash, itch and discharge, can be treated with a vinegar or lemon-juice douche, or with yoghurt. Nystatin, miconazole or clotrimazole pessaries or vaginal cream are the usual treatment.

Pregnancy

It is not recommended to travel to some places while pregnant as some vaccinations normally used to prevent serious diseases are not advisable in pregnancy, eg yellow fever. In addition, some diseases, such as malaria, are much more serious for the mother (and may increase the risk of a stillborn child) in pregnancy.

Most miscarriages occur during the first three months of pregnancy. Miscarriage is not uncommon, and can occasionally lead to severe bleeding. The last three months should also be spent within reasonable distance of good medical care. A baby born as early as 24 weeks stands a chance of survival, but only in a good modern hospital.

Pregnant women should avoid all unnecessary medication, though vaccinations and malarial prophylactics should still be taken where needed. Additional care should be taken to prevent illness, and particular attention should be paid to diet and nutrition. Alcohol and nicotine, for example, should be avoided.

Language

HONG KONG

While the Chinese have about eight main dialects, around 70% of the population of China speaks the Beijing dialect (commonly known as Mandarin) which is the official language of the People's Republic of China (PRC). Hong Kong's two official languages are English and Cantonese. Cantonese is a southern Chinese dialect, spoken in Guangzhou, Guangdong Province, parts of Guangxi Province, Hong Kong and Macau.

While Cantonese is used in Hong Kong in everyday life and is the official language of the territory, English is still the primary language of commerce, banking and international trade, and is also used in the law courts. However, many have noticed a sharp decline in the level of English-speaking proficiency. Those Hong Kong Chinese who speak excellent English are usually also the wealthiest, and many of them have emigrated. Many secondary schools in Hong Kong, who previously taught all lessons in English, had to make the transition to Cantonese in autumn 1998, which has exacerbated the decline. Generally, the Hong Kong Chinese cannot compare with their cousins in Singapore, who often speak English at near first language levels.

On the other hand, the ability to speak Mandarin is on the increase. There has been a large percentage of Mandarin speakers in Hong Kong since the 1950s because so many refugees fled from China. Until recently, the younger generation has generally not bothered studying Mandarin, preferring English as a second language. The new political realities are changing attitudes. For a Cantonese native speaker, Mandarin is far easier to learn than English but it's the last thing that many school children want to learn. Hong Kong Chinese are, on the whole, very lazy about learning Mandarin and it's not rare to hear Cantonese and Mandarin being spoken in a sort of fusion.

Short-term English-speaking visitors can get along fine in Hong Kong without a word of Cantonese, especially in the tourist zones. Street signs and public transport information are presented in both English and Cantonese, so there's no problem getting around.

The Word on the Street

While Hong Kong's expatriate community tries to speak the Queen's English, some Chinese words have been incorporated into the local English vernacular. Taipan means a big boss, usually in a large company, which is referred to as a hong. A godown is a warehouse. An amah is a servant, usually a woman who babysits and takes care of the house.

A *cheongsam* (*qipao* in Mandarin) is a tight-fitting Chinese dress with a slit up the side. You may well see receptionists at upmarket restaurants wearing these, and it's also the gown favoured by honeymoon brides. The dress originated in Shanghai and was banned in China during the Cultural Revolution.

A foreigner is often referred to as a *gwailo* – a Cantonese word which literally means ghost person, but is more accurately translated as 'foreign devil'. It used to have a negative connotation, but these days many foreigners call themselves gwailo without giving it a second thought. More polite terms would be *sai yan* (westerner) or *ngoi gwok yan* (foreigner).

The word *shroff*, frequently used in Hong Kong, is not derived from Chinese – it's an Anglo-Indian word meaning cashier.

Finally there is the word *junk*. It might be rubbish in English, but to the Chinese it's a mid-sized fishing boat. The traditional models had sails, but these days diesel engines do the job.

Most expatriates in Hong Kong never learn the local language. This is mainly because they spend their time in the company of other expats. Of course, the foreigners willing to expend the considerable effort required to learn Cantonese are rewarded with a level of understanding and camaraderie not achievable otherwise.

GUANGZHOU

What a difference a border makes. Cantonese is still the most popular dialect in Guangzhou and the surrounding area, but the official language of the PRC is the Beijing dialect or *putonghua,* usually referred to in the west as Mandarin. In Guangdong you can use either Mandarin or Cantonese.

MACAU

While Portuguese is the official language of Macau, Cantonese is the language of choice for about 95% of the population. Most Chinese in Macau are unable to speak Portuguese. English is regarded as a third language, even though it's more commonly spoken than Portuguese. Mandarin (*putonghua*) is understood by more than half the Chinese population. With so many immigrants turning up in Zhuhai from north China and working in Macau, and with Macau poised to return to China, Mandarin is becoming an essential tool for business.

Within the Macau educational system, English is now the main language of instruction and children begin learning it in elementary school – if you're having trouble communicating, your best bet is to ask a young person.

SPOKEN CHINESE

Cantonese differs from Mandarin as much

Cantonese Pluck

The Cantonese of Hong Kong are a plucky lot, and display an ethnic chauvinism rarely encountered in the rest of China. Despite being latecomers to the Chinese empire (1997), the Cantonese of Hong Kong (who call themselves Heunggongyan) consider themselves to be perfect exemplars of what it means to be Chinese. This is all despite being colonised and exposed to western ways for 150 years. The northern Chinese call the southern Chinese 'southern barbarians', while southern Chinese call those who hail from the north of China, 'northern barbarians'.

The Cantonese dialect is also considered by those in Hong Kong as being true 'Chinese', a notion that flabbergasts northern Chinese, who speak Mandarin and look upon Cantonese as an uncivilised aberration. In fact, the Cantonese have a point, as it is argued that the language is closer to that spoken in earlier ages in China.

Tang dynasty poetry tends to rhyme better when read aloud in Cantonese rather than in Mandarin (Putonghua). It also keeps a fair number of classical Chinese expressions in its daily vocabulary, while Mandarin has shorn itself of many of these. It is not rare to meet Cantonese who claim that Mandarin is not Chinese, but an invention.

Chinese from northern China are recognised as being Chinese as opposed to *gwailo* (unless they have spent time in the USA or the west, which means the Chinese/gwailo dividing line blurs considerably) but are not considered to have reached the zenith of Chinese culture as occupied by the Heunggongyan. By the same token, Chinese from other parts of China are almost universally suspicious of the Cantonese.

Gwailos are treated with ambivalence, because they represent modernity, style and prosperity, while at the same time being barbaric. Indians *(a cha)* living in Hong Kong are almost universally looked down upon by Hong Kong Chinese, even though Indians are respected for their diligence and competence with languages (including Cantonese).

as French differs from Spanish. Speakers of both dialects can read Chinese characters, but a Cantonese speaker will pronounce many of the characters differently from a Mandarin speaker. For example, when Mr Ng from Hong Kong goes to Beijing the Mandarin-speakers will call him Mr Wu. If Mr Wong goes from Hong Kong to Fujian Province the character for his name will be read as Mr Wee, and in Beijing he is Mr Huang.

WRITTEN CHINESE

Officially, written Chinese has about 50,000 characters or pictographs. Most of these have become archaic but about 6000 remain in common use, and there are at least 2000 essential characters you'd need to know to read a newspaper.

While many of the basic Chinese characters are in fact highly stylised 'pictures' of what they represent, most of those in common use (around 90%) are actually compounds of a 'meaning' element and a 'sound' element.

The written language allows Chinese people from around the country to overcome the barrier posed by more than 200 different dialects. Both Cantonese and Mandarin speakers can understand the same newspaper but if they read it aloud it would sound like two different tongues. Hong Kong also has 150 of its own Chinese characters which are used solely to represent colloquial Cantonese words. These are not understood by speakers of other dialects, or even some Cantonese speakers from the mainland.

Hong Kong, like Taiwan, uses the original 'complex' character set, as opposed to the system of simplified characters adopted by China in the 1950s in a bid to increase literacy. The result is that many of the characters you'll see in Hong Kong look quite different from their counterparts in China. In Hong Kong, Chinese characters can be read from left to right, right to left, or top to bottom. In China the government has been trying to get everyone to read and write from left to right.

BODY LANGUAGE

Hand signs are used a lot in China. The thumbs-up sign has a long tradition as an indication of excellence, or *guā guā jiào*.

The Chinese have a system for counting on their hands. If you can't speak the language, it would be worth your while to at least learn Chinese finger counting. The symbol for number 10 is to form a cross with the index fingers, but many Chinese just use a fist.

CANTONESE
Romanisation

The PRC uses a Romanisation system known as *pinyin* which, while very accurate, only works for the Mandarin dialect. You cannot use it to Romanise Cantonese.

For Cantonese the situation is far messier. Unfortunately, several competing systems of Romanisation exist and no single one has emerged as an official standard. Hong Kongers are not forced to learn Romanisation in school, so asking a Cantonese native speaker to Romanise a Chinese character produces mixed results. The lack of an established standard creates a good deal of confusion for foreigners trying to master the vagaries of Cantonese pronunciation.

A number of Romanisation schemes have come and gone, but at least three have survived and are currently used in Hong Kong: Meyer-Wempe, Sidney Lau and Yale. You are likely to encounter all three of them if you make any serious study of the language.

The Meyer-Wempe system is the oldest in current use. Until Sidney Lau came along, it was the one most likely to appear on maps, street signs and in books about Hong Kong. The reason for its popularity is simply its age – the first past the post usually has the best chance of becoming the standard because people resist change. Unfortunately, Meyer-Wempe is also highly confusing. One of its oddities is the use of apostrophes in words to distinguish aspirated sounds (pronounced with a puff of air) from unaspirated sounds. Map and book publishers tend to drop the apostrophes, thus leaving readers unable to distinguish 'p' from 'b' and 't' from 'd'.

The Sidney Lau system fixed this defect and several others. Lau was the principal of the Government Language School for civil servants, and he also broadcast the popular *Cantonese by Radio* teaching series which started in 1961. The Sidney Lau system has been widely adopted by publishers. Sidney Lau is the author of the excellent, but chunky, *A Practical Cantonese-English Dictionary* and an exhaustive six volume Cantonese course.

In this language guide we use the Yale system. It's the most phonetically accurate and the one generally preferred by foreign students. It's the system adopted by the Chinese University of Hong Kong for the New Asia Yale in China Language Institute. There are a number of textbooks and dictionaries based on this system.

The following table illustrates the notable differences between the three major Romanisation systems:

Meyer-Wempe	Sydney Lau	Yale
p'	p	p
p	b	b
t'	t	t
t	d	d
k'	k	k
k	g	g
ch'	ch	ch
ts	j	j
k'w	kw	kw
kw	gw	gw
s,sh	s	s
i,y	y	y
oo,w	w	w
oeh	euh	eu
ui	ui	eui
un	un	eun
ut	ut	eut
o	o	ou
oo	oo	u
ue	ue	yu

Some have wondered about the placement of spaces and hyphens in Chinese words. 'Hong Kong' is sometimes written 'Hongkong', though you will probably not see 'Shanghai' written as 'Shang Hai' or 'Beijing' as 'Bei Jing'. Chinese often hyphenate their given names, so you may find Sun Yatsen written as Sun Yat-sen. The confusion comes from the fact that every syllable in Chinese is written with a separate character, but when transcribed into Romanised form a name is usually written as a multisyllabic word.

In Mandarin there is a standard rule – names are kept as one word (thus 'Shanghai' and 'Beijing'). However, Cantonese has not adopted any such standard, so in this book we use what is most commonly accepted (thus 'Hong Kong'). The hyphenation of names is falling into disuse and is therefore best avoided.

Pronunciation

The following Romanisation system is a simplified version designed to help you pronounce the Cantonese words and phrases in this book as quickly and easily as possible. As such it glosses over some aspects of pronunciation that you would need to know if you planned to study the language in depth. Note that the examples given reflect British pronunciation.

a	as in 'father'
ai	as the 'i' in 'find', but shorter
au	as the 'ou' in 'bout'
e	as in 'let'
ei	as the 'a' in 'say'
eu	as 'e' + the 'ur' in 'urn' (with pursed lips)
i	as the 'ee' in 'see'
iu	similar to the word 'you'
o	as in 'got'; as in 'go' when word-final
oi	as the 'oy' in 'boy'
oo	as in 'soon'
ou	as the word 'owe'
u	as in 'put'
ue	as in 'Sue'
ui	as 'oo' + 'ee'

Consonants are generally pronounced as in English. Some that may give you trouble are:

j	as the 'ds' in 'suds'
ch	as the 'ts' in 'tsar'
ng	as in 'sing'; practise using this sound at the beginning of a word

Tones

Chinese languages have many homonyms (sound-alike words). Thus, the Cantonese word for 'silk' sounds the same as the words for 'lion', 'private', 'poem', 'corpse' and 'teacher'. What distinguishes the meaning of each word are changes in a speaker's pitch (tones) and the context of the word within the sentence. Mandarin has four tones but Cantonese has seven (although you can easily get by with six).

The best way to learn tones is by ear, ideally from a teacher who takes the time to distinguish each one clearly. The system we use to show tones in this language guide is based on the Yale Romanisation system. It's designed to make pronunciation of Cantonese tones as simple as possible and may not necessarily reflect what you come across where official transliteration systems are used.

In the Yale system six basic tones are represented: three 'level' tones which do not noticeably rise or fall in pitch (high, middle and low) and three 'moving' tones which either rise or fall in pitch (high rising, low rising and low falling). Remember that it doesn't matter whether you have a high or low voice when speaking Cantonese as long as your intonation reflects relative changes in pitch. The following examples show the six basic tones – note how important they can be to your intended meaning:

high tone: represented by a macron above a vowel, eg *fōo* (husband)
middle tone: represented by an unaccented vowel, eg *foo* (wealthy)
low tone: represented by the letter 'h' after a vowel, eg *fooh* (owe); note that when 'h' appears at the beginning of a word it is still pronounced, elsewhere it signifies a low tone

middle tone rising: represented by an acute accent, eg *fóo* (tiger)
low falling tone: represented by a grave accent followed by the low tone letter 'h', eg *fòoh* (to lean)
low rising tone: represented by an acute accent and the low tone letter 'h', eg *fóoh* (woman)

Useful Phrases

Even if you never gain fluency, knowing a few simple Cantonese phrases can be useful. Hong Kong is not known as a very friendly place, yet even a small attempt to speak the local vernacular will bring smiles to the faces of Chinese people you meet. The following phrase list should help get you started. For a more in depth guide to Cantonese, with loads of information on grammar and pronunciation plus a comprehensive phrase list, get hold of Lonely Planet's *Cantonese phrasebook*.

Pronouns

I
 ngóh 我
you
 néhìh 你
he/she/it
 kúhìh 佢
we/us
 ngóh dēih 我哋
you (pl)
 néhìh dēih 你哋
they/them
 kúhìh dēih 佢哋

Greetings & Civilities

Hello, how are you?
 néhìh hó ma? 你好嗎?
Fine.
 géih hó 幾好
Fine, and you?
 géih hó, néhìh nē? 幾好，你呢?
So so.
 màh má déih 麻麻地
Good morning.
 jó sàhn 早晨
Goodbye.
 bāàhìh baàhìh, joìh gin 拜拜/再見

See you tomorrow.
 tìng yahìh joìh gin 聽日再見
Thank you very much.
 *dōh jē saàhìh, m
  gōìh saàhìh* 多謝哂／唔該哂
Thanks. (for a gift or
special favour)
 dōh jē 多謝
Thanks. (making a
request or purchase)
 m gōìh 唔該
You're welcome.
 m sáìh haàhk hēìh 唔駛客氣
Excuse me. (after
bumping into someone)
 duìh m juhèh 對唔住
I'm sorry.
 m hó yi si 唔好意思
Don't worry about it.
 m gán yiùh 唔緊要
Please wait a moment.
 *chéng dáng yāt
  jahn* 請等一陣
Excuse me. (calling
someone's attention)
 m gōìh 唔該

Small Talk

What is your surname? (polite)
 chéng mahn gwaìh sing?
 請問貴姓？
My surname is ...
 síùh sing ...
 小姓 ...
My name is ...
 ngóh giùh ...
 我叫 ...
This is Mr/Mrs/Ms (Lee).
 *nì wáìh hahìh (léhìh) sìn sāàhng/
  taàhìh táahìh/síùh jé*
 呢位係(李)先生／太太／小姐
Glad to meet you.
 hó gō hing yihng sìk néhìh
 好高興認識你
Please hurry up.
 m gōìh faàhìh dì
 唔該快啲
Please slow down.
 m gōìh mahàhn dì
 唔該慢啲

Can you please help me take a photo?
 *hóh m hóh yíh bōng ngóh yíng
  jēùhng séùhng a?*
 可唔可以幫我影張相呀？
Is it OK to take a photo?
 hóh m hóh yíh yíng séùhng a?
 可唔可以影相呀？

Language Difficulties

Do you speak English?
 néhìh sìk m sìk góng yìng mán a?
 你識唔識講英文呀？
Do you understand?
 néhìh mìhng m mìhng a?
 你明唔明？
I understand.
 ngóh mìhng 我明
I don't understand.
 ngóh m mìhng
 我唔明
Can you repeat that please?
 chéng joìh góng yat chi?
 請再講一次？
What is this called?
 nì goh giùh māt yéh a?
 呢個叫乜嘢呀？

Accommodation

Do you have any rooms available?
 yáhùh mó fóng a?
 有冇房呀？
I'd like a (single/double) room.
 *ngóh séùhng yiùh yāt gāàhn
  (dāàhn yàhn/séùhng yàhn) fóng*
 我想要一間(單人／雙人)房
I'd like a quiet room.
 *ngóh séùhng yiùh yāt gāàhn
  jihng dì gē fóng*
 我想要一間啲嘅房
How much per night?
 géìh dōh chín yāt máhàhn a?
 幾多錢一晚呀？
Can I get a discount if I stay longer?
 juhèh nohìh dì yáhùh mó jit kaùh a?
 住耐啲有冇折扣呀？

Shopping

How much is this?
 nī goh géìh dōh chín a?
 呢個幾多錢呀？

Glossary of Hong Kong Place Names

Aberdeen	香港仔	Hong Kong Arts Centre	藝術中心
Admiralty	金鐘	Hong Kong Convention	
Admiralty Centre	金鐘廊	& Exhibition Centre	香港會議展覽中心
Alexandra House	亞歷山大大廈	Hong Kong Cultural	
		Centre	香港文化中心
Bank of China	中國銀行	Hong Kong Island	香港島
		Hong Kong Park	香港公園
Causeway Bay	銅鑼灣	Hung Hom	紅磡
Central	中環		
Central Building	中建大廈	Ice House St	雪廠街
Chai Wan	柴灣		
Chater Rd	遮打道	Jade Market	玉器市場
Chek Lap Kok Airport	赤鱲角機場	Jardine House	怡和大廈
Cheung Chau	長洲	Jardine's Bazaar	渣甸街
Chungking Mansions	重慶大廈		
Connaught Rd	干諾道中	Kai Tak Airport	香港啓德國際機場
		KCR (Kowloon	
D'Aguilar St	德忌笠街	Canton Railway)	九廣鐵路
Des Voeux Rd	德輔道	Kowloon	九龍
Discovery Bay	愉景灣		
		Ladder St	樓梯街
Exchange Square	交易廣場	Lai Chi Kok	荔枝角
		Lamma Island	南丫島
Fanling	粉嶺	Lan Kwai Fong	蘭桂坊
		Lantau Island	大嶼山
Happy Valley	跑馬地	Lippo Centre	力寶中心
Hollywood Rd	荷利活道		
Hongkong and		Macau Ferry Terminal	港澳碼頭
Shanghai Bank	匯豐銀行	Mid-Levels	半山區

That's very expensive.
hó gwaìh
好貴
Can you reduce the price?
pèhng dī dāk m dāk a?
平啲得唔得呀?
I'm just looking.
ngóh sīn táih yāt táih
我先睇一睇

Getting Around

airport	*gēih chèhùhng*	機場
bus stop	*bā sí jahàhm*	巴士站
pier	*máh tàhùh*	碼頭
subway station	*dèih tit jahàhm*	地鐵站
north	*bāk*	北
south	*nàhàhm*	南
east	*dūng*	東
west	*sāih*	西

I'd like to go to ...
ngóh séuhng huìh ...
我想去 ...
Where is the ...?
... háih bìn doh a?
喺邊度呀?
Does this (bus, train etc) go to ...?
huìh m huìh ... a?
去唔去 ... 呀?
How much is the fare?
gèih dōh chín a?
幾多錢呀?

Mong Kok	旺角	Stanley	赤柱
MTR		Star Ferry	天星
(Mass Transit Railway)	地下鐵路	St George's Building	聖佐治大廈
Nathan Rd	彌敦道	Swire House	太古大廈
New Territories	新界		
Noon Day Gun	午炮	Tai O	大澳
		Tai Po	大埔
Ocean Park	海洋公園	Temple St Night Market	廟街夜市
Pacific Place	太古廣場	Tiger Balm Gardens	胡文虎花園
Peak Tram	山頂纜車	The Landmark	置地廣場
Pedder St	畢打街	Tsim Sha Tsui	尖沙咀
Prince's Building	太子行	Tsuen Wan	荃灣
Quarry Bay	鰂魚涌	Victoria Park	維多利亞公園
Queen's Rd, Central	皇后大道中	Victoria Peak	山頂
Repulse Bay	淺水灣	Wan Chai	灣仔
		Wellington St	威靈頓街
Sai Kung	西貢	Worldwide Plaza	環球大廈
Sai Kung Peninsula	西貢半島	Wyndham St	雲咸街
Sha Tin	沙田		
Shek O	石澳	Yau Ma Tei	油麻地
Sheung Shui	上水	Yuen Long	元朗
Sheung Wan	上環	Yuen Po St Bird Garden	園圃街雀鳥公園
Shun Tak Centre	信德中心		
Silvermine Bay	梅窩		
Standard Chartered Bank	渣打銀行	Zoological & Botanical Gardens	香港動植物公園

I want to get off at ...
ngóh séuhng háih ... lohk chē
我想喺 ... 落車
Stop here please. (taxi, minibus)
m gōih, nì doh yáhùh lohk
唔該，呢度有落
How far is it to walk?
hàahng loh yiùh géih nohih a?
行路要幾耐呀？
Where is this address please?
m gōih, nì goh dēih jí háih bìn doh a?
唔該，呢個地址喺邊度呀？
Please write down the address for me.
m gōih sé goh dēih jí bêih ngóh
唔該寫個地址俾我

Numbers

0	*lìhng*	零
1	*yāt*	一
2	*yih (léhùhng)*	二(兩)
3	*sāahm*	三
4	*sēih*	四
5	*ng*	五
6	*luhk*	六
7	*chāt*	七
8	*baàht*	八
9	*gáùh*	九
10	*sahp*	十
11	*sahp yāt*	十一
12	*sahp yih*	十二
20	*yih sahp*	二十
21	*yih sahp yāt*	二十一

30	*sāàhm sahp*	三十
100	*yāt baàhk*	一百
101	*yāt baàhk lìhng yāt*	一百零一
110	*yāt baàhk yāt sahp*	一百一十
112	*yāt baàhk yāt sahp yih*	一百一十二
120	*yāt baàhk yih sahp*	一百二十
200	*yih baàhk*	二百
1000	*yāt chīn*	一千
10,000	*yāt mahàhn*	一萬
100,000	*sahp mahàhn*	十萬

one million *yāt baàhk mahàhn* 一百萬

Health

I'm sick.
  ngóh yáhùh bēng
  我有病
My friend is sick.
  ngóh pàhng yáhùh yáhùh bēng
  我朋友有病
I need a doctor.
  ngóh yiùh tāih yī sāng
  我要睇醫生
It hurts here.
  nī doh m sùèh fuhk
  呢度唔舒服
I have asthma.
  ngóh hāàhùh chúèhn
  我哮喘
I have diarrhoea.
  ngóh tó ngōh
  我肚痾
I'd like to see a female doctor.
  ngóh yiùh wán yāt wàih núhìh
    yī sāng
  我要搵一位女醫生
I'm allergic to (antibiotics/penicillin).
  ngóh duìh (kong sāng so/
    pòòhn nèhìh sāih làhm) gwoh mán
  我對(抗生素/盤尼西林)過敏

Emergencies

Help!
  gaùh mēng a! 救命呀！
Watch out!
  síùh sām! 小心！
Thief!
  chéùhng yéh a! 搶嘢呀！
Call the police!
  giùh gíng chaàht! 叫警察！

Call an ambulance!
  giùh gaùh sēùhng chē! 叫救傷車！

Food

Do you have an English menu?
  yáhùh mó yīng mán chāàhn páàhìh a?
  有冇英文餐牌呀？
Can you recommend any dishes?
  yáhùh māt yéh hó gaàhìh siùh a?
  有乜嘢好介紹呀？
I'm a vegetarian.
  ngóh sihk jāàhìh 我食齋
I'd like the set menu please.
  ngóh yiùh goh to chāàhn
  我要個套餐
Please bring me a knife & fork.
  m gōìh béîh ngóh yāt foòh dō chā
  唔該俾我一副刀叉
Please bring the bill.
  m gōìh, mààhìh dāàhn
  唔該，埋單

Cantonese

barbecued pork		
chā sīùh		叉燒
stir-fried pea sprouts		
cháùh dahùhmìhùh		炒豆苗
stir-fried kale (cabbage)		
chīngcháùh gaìhlán		清炒芥蘭
roast pigeon		
sāng sīùh gap		生燒鴿
steamed garoupa (fish)		
with soy sauce dressing		
chīngjīng sehkbān		
yùhèh		清蒸石斑魚
deep-fried salt &		
pepper spareribs		
jiùhyìhm ngaùhpaìh		椒鹽牛排
fried rice noodles with		
beef & green peppers		
sihjiùh ngaùhhó		豉椒牛河
stir-fried broccoli with		
scallops		
sāìhlanfā daìhjí		西蘭花帶子
pan-fried lemon chicken		
sīnnìhng jīnyúèhngaìh	鮮檸煎軟雞
'drunken' prawns		
(steamed in rice wine)		
taìhbahk juìhyūng		
hā		大白醉翁蝦

barbecued pork buns
   chā sīùh bāùh   叉燒包
steamed rice flour rolls
with shrimp, beef or pork
   chéùhng fén   腸粉
fried green vegetable
of the day
   chīng cháùh
   sìhchohìh   清炒時菜
fried spring rolls
   chūn gúèhn   春卷
fried chicken's feet
   fuhng jáùh   鳳爪
steamed dumplings
with pork, shrimp &
bamboo shoots
   fún gwó   粉果
fried crispy noodles
with shredded chicken
   gāihsī cháùhmihn   雞絲炒麵
dry-fried noodles
   gōn sīùh yīmihn   干燒伊麵
shrimp dumplings
   hā gáùh   蝦餃
fried rice flour triangles
(with pork inside)
   ham súìh gohk   鹹水角
rice in lotus leaf
   hòh yihp fahn   荷葉飯
steamed spare ribs
   paìh gwāt   排骨
steamed beef balls
   sān jūk ngaùh yohk   山竹牛肉
pork & shrimp
dumplings
   sīùh maìh   燒賣
deep-fried taro puffs
   wohòh gohk   芋角

Chiu Chow

stewed broccoli with
black mushrooms
   bākgū sāìhlanfā   北菇西蘭花
cold sweet bird's nest
soup (dessert)
   bīngfā gōngyin   冰花宮燕
baked lobster in light
pepper sauce
   chùhèhnjīùh
   gohklùhnghā   川椒焗龍蝦

fried shredded beef
with green pepper
   chīngjīùh
   ngaùhyohksī   清椒牛肉絲
shark's fin soup
   dahìh yùhèhchi tōng   大魚翅湯
fried kale with dried fish
   fōngyùhèh gailán   方魚芥蘭
stewed Tianjin cabbage
with minced chicken
   gāìhyùhng
   sihùhchohìh   雞茸紹菜
steamed crab
   jīng háìh   蒸蟹
deep-fried spiced duck
   ja nghēùhng ngap   炸五香鴨
cold appetiser platter
of four meats/seafood
   seìhsēk pingpún   四色拼盤

Peking (Beijing) & Northern Chinese

Peking duck
   bākgīng tìhnngap   北京填鴨
noodles with shredded
pork & bean sprouts
   bākgīng fūngcháùh
   lāìhmihn   北京風炒拉麵
tianjin cabbage &
black mushrooms
   bākgūpa
   jūnbahkchohìh   北菇扒津白菜
pan-fried spring onion
cakes
   chōngyaùh béng   蔥油餅
beggar's chicken
   fohòhgwaìh gāìh   富貴雞
fried shredded beef
with chilli sauce
   gōncháùh
   ngaùhyohksī   干炒牛肉絲
sauteed prawns in
chilli sauce
   gōngbaùh dahìhhā   宮爆大蝦
clear soup with chicken,
prawn & abalone
   sāmsīn tōng   三鮮湯
steamed minced pork
dumplings
   sīnyohk síùhlòhng
   bāùh   鮮肉小龍包

Shanghai

sauteed pea sprouts
*chīngcháuh
dahùhmìhùh* 清炒豆苗

sauteed scallops
with vegetables
fehìhchuìh yùhèhdaìh 翡翠玉帶

Shanghai cabbage
with ham
fótúih síùhchohìh 火腿小菜

braised minced pork
balls with vegetables
hòhngsīùh sījítaùh 紅燒獅子頭

deep-fried chicken
ja jígāìh 炸子雞

'drunken' chicken in
cold rice wine marinade
juìh gāìh 醉雞

cold spiced beef
nghēùhng ngaùhyohk 五香牛肉

fried Shanghai noodles
with pork
*sehùhnghóìh
chōcháùh* 上海粗炒

hot-&-sour soup
sūèhnlaht tōng 酸辣湯

sweet-&-sour yellow
croaker fish
*sùhngsúèh
wòhngyùhèh* 松鼠黃魚

Sichuan (Szechuan) & Hunan

suteed shredded beef
& green pepper
*chīngjíùh
ngaùhyohksī* 清椒牛肉絲

noodles in spicy
peanut soup
dan dan mihn 擔擔麵

fried fish in sweet &
sour sauce
*chuìhpèhìh
wòhngyùhèhpin* 脆皮黃魚片

pan-fried spicy
string beans
*gōnbīn seìhgwaìh
dahùh* 干煸四季豆

sauteed diced chicken
& peanuts in chilli sauce
gōngbaùh gāìhdīng 宮爆雞丁

sauteed shrimp in
chilli sauce
gōngbaùh mìhnghā 宮爆明蝦

duck smoked in
camphor wood
jēùhngcha háùh ngap 樟茶烤鴨

'grandma's beancurd'
in spicy sauce
mapòh dahùhfohòh 麻婆豆腐

peppery hot-&-sour
soup with shredded meat
sūèhnlaht tōng 酸辣湯

sauteed eggplant in
spicy fish sauce
yùhèhhēùhng kéìhjí 魚香茄子

Vegetarian

fried rice with diced
pineapple
bōlòh cháùhfahn 菠蘿炒飯

black mushroom soup
chīngdūn bākgū tōng 清燉北菰湯

spring rolls
chūn gúèhn 春卷

spicy bean-curd rolls
fohòhpèhìh gúèhn 腐皮卷

braised bamboo shoots
& black mushrooms
gūmgū súnjīm 金菇筍尖

mock chicken, barbecued
pork or roast duck
jaìhlóùhmehìh 齊鹵味

stewed mixed vegetables
lòhhohn chohìh 羅漢菜

fried noodles with
vegetables
lòhhohnjāìh yīmihn 羅漢齊伊麵

cabbage rolls
yèhhchohìh gúèhn 椰菜卷

Noodles

fishball noodles
yùhèhdán mihn 魚蛋麵

beef balls with rice
noodles
ngaùhyúèhn hó 牛河丸

shrimp dumpling noodles
sīnhā wùhntūn mihn 鮮蝦雲吞麵

vegetable noodles
chohìhyúèhn mihn 菜遠麵

fish & beef balls with
rice noodles
   sēùhngyúèhn hó   雙丸河
steamed vegetables
with oyster sauce
   hòhyaùh yechohìh   蠔油野菜
congee with fish slices
   yùhpin jūk   魚片粥
Singapore fried
noodles (spicy)
   sīngjāùh cháùhmáìh 星洲炒米
fried rice with egg,
shrimp & spring onion
   yèhùhngjāùh
    cháùhfahn   楊州炒飯
curried beef on
white rice
   gāléìh ngaùhyohk
    fahn   咖喱牛肉飯

MANDARIN

Most foreigners are more successful at learning Mandarin than Cantonese. The Chinese government set about popularising it in the 1950s. A large percentage of foreigners living and working in China manage to gain a reasonable level of fluency in the spoken language, but the written form is another story.

Pinyin

In 1958 the Chinese officially adopted a system known as pinyin as a method of writing Mandarin using the Roman alphabet. The original idea was to eventually do away with characters altogether and use only pinyin. Tradition dies a slow death, however, and the idea has gradually been abandoned.

Pinyin is often used on shop fronts, street signs and advertising billboards but don't expect Chinese people to be able to use it, as it never really took off as the main form of written Chinese.

In the countryside and the smaller towns you may not see any signs in pinyin, so unless you speak Chinese you'll need a phrasebook with Chinese characters. Although pinyin is helpful, it's not an instant

key to communication, as westerners usually don't get the pronunciation and intonation of the Romanised word correct. Pinyin as it appears on signs captures the sound approximately, but does not include the tones, which are essential to vebal communication.

Since 1979 all translated texts of Chinese diplomatic documents and Chinese magazines published in foreign languages have used the pinyin system of spelling names and places. The system replaces the old Wade-Giles and Lessing systems of Romanising Chinese script. Thus, in pinyin 'Mao Tse-tung' becomes *mao zedong*; 'Chou En-lai' becomes *zhou enlai* and 'Peking' becomes *beijing*. The name of the country remains as it has been generally written: 'China' in English and *zhongguo* in pinyin.

Pronunciation

The following is a rough description of the sounds produced in spoken Mandarin Chinese. You'll find that most pinyin letters are pronounced as they would be in English but we list a few which may cause considerable difficulty.

In pinyin, apostrophes are occasionally used to separate syllables. So, you can write *ping'an* to prevent the word being pronounced as *pin'gan*.

a	as in 'father'
ai	as the 'i' in 'high'
ao	as the 'ow' in 'cow'
e	as the 'u' in 'fur'
ei	as the 'ei' in 'weigh'
i	as the 'ee' in 'meet'; as the 'oo' in 'book' after **c**, **ch**, **r**, **s**, **sh**, **z** or **zh**
ian	as the word 'yen'
ie	as the word 'yeah'
o	as in 'or'
ou	as the 'oa' in 'boat'
u	as in 'flute'
ui	as the word 'way'
uo	as 'w' followed by the 'o' in 'or'
yu	as the German 'ü' – pucker your lips and try saying 'ee'
ü	as the German 'ü'

The English 'v' sound doesn't occur in Chinese. For beginners, the trickiest consonants are **c**, **q** and **x** because their pronunciation isn't remotely similar in English. Other than **n**, **ng** and **r**, consonants never occur at the end of a syllable.

c	as the 'ts' in 'bits'
ch	as in English, but with the tongue curled back
h	as in English, but articulated from the throat
q	as the 'ch' in 'chicken'
r	as the 's' in 'pleasure'
sh	as in English, but with the tongue curled back
x	as the 'sh' in 'shine'
z	as the 'ds' in 'suds'
zh	as the 'j' in 'judge' but with the tongue curled back

Tones

Mastering tones is tricky for the untrained western ear, but with practice it can be done.

Four basic tones are used in Mandarin, which makes it easier to learn than Cantonese. As in Cantonese, changing the tone changes the meaning. For example, in Mandarin the word *ma* can have four distinct meanings depending on which tone is used:

high tone:	*mā*	'mother'
rising tone:	*má*	'hemp' or 'numb'
falling-rising tone:	*mǎ*	'horse'
falling tone:	*mà*	'scold' or 'swear'

Useful Phrases

The following list of survival phrases in Mandarin will help get you started.

If you want to arm yourself more fully for your travels, Lonely Planet's *Mandarin Chinese phrasebook* contains a comprehensive guide to grammar and pronunciation plus an array of useful words and phrases for most occasions. It uses both simplified Chinese characters and pinyin. Lonely Planet's *Cantonese phrasebook* can also be used throughout Guangdong.

Pronouns

I
   wǒ   我
you
   nǐ   你
he, she, it
   tā   他/她/它
we, us
   wǒmen   我们
you (plural)
   nǐmen   你们
they, them
   tāmen   他们

Greetings & Civilities

Hello.
   nǐ hǎo   你好
Goodbye.
   zàijiàn   再见
Thank you.
   xièxie   谢谢
You're welcome.
   búkèqi   不客气
I'm sorry.
   duìbùqǐ   对不起

Small Talk

May I ask your name?
   nín guìxìng?   您贵姓?
My (sur)name is ...
   wǒ xìng ...   我姓 ...
Where are you from?
   nǐ shì cōng
   nǎr láide?   你是从 哪儿来的?
I'm from ...
   wǒ shì cōng ... láide   我是从 ... 来的
No. (don't have)
   méi yǒu   没有
No. (not so)
   búshì   不是
I'm a foreign student.
   wǒ shì liúxuéshēng   我是留学生
What's to be done now?
   zěnme bàn?   怎么办?
It doesn't matter.
   méishì   没事
I want ...
   wǒ yào ...   我要 ...
No, I don't want it.
   búyào   不要

Countries

Australia
  àodàlìyà   澳大利亚
Canada
  jiānádà   加拿大
France
  fǎguó   法国
Germany
  déguó   德国
New Zealand
  xīnxīlán   新西兰
Spain
  xībānyá   西班牙
Sweden
  ruìdiǎn   瑞典
Switzerland
  ruìshì   瑞士
UK
  yīngguó   英国
USA
  měiguó   美国

Language Difficulties

I understand.
  wǒ tīngdedǒng   我听得懂
I don't understand.
  wǒ tīngbudǒng   我听不懂
Do you understand?
  dǒng ma?   懂吗?
Could you speak
more slowly please?
  qīng nǐ shuō màn   请你说慢一点,
  yīdiǎn, hǎo ma?   好吗?

Visas & Documents

passport
  hùzhào   护照
visa
  qiānzhèng   签证
visa extension
  yáncháng qiānzhèng   延长签证
Public Security Bureau
  gōng'ān jú   公安局
Foreign Affairs Branch
  wài shì kē   外事科

Money

How much is it?
  duōshǎo qián?   多少钱?

Is there anything
cheaper?
  yǒu piányi yìdiǎn   有便宜一点
  de ma?   的吗?
That's too expensive.
  tài guìle   太贵了
Bank of China
  zhōngguó yínháng   中国银行
change money
  huàn qián   换钱

Post

post office
  yóujú   邮局
letter
  xìn   信
envelope
  xìnfēng   信封
package
  bāoguǒ   包裹
air mail
  hángkōng xìn   航空信
surface mail
  píngyóu   平邮
stamps
  yóupiào   邮票
postcard
  míngxìnpiàn   明信片
aerogramme
  hángkōng xìnjiàn   航空信件
poste restante
  cúnjú hòulǐnglán   存局候领栏
express mail (EMS)
  yóuzhèng tèkuài
  zhuāndì   邮政特快专递
registered mail
  guà hào   挂号

Communications

telephone
  diànhuà   电话
telephone office
  diànxùn dàlóu   电讯大楼
telephone card
  diànhuà kǎ   电话卡
international call
  guójì diànhuà   国际电话
collect call
  duìfāng fùqián
  diànhuà   对方付钱电话

direct-dial call
zhíbō diànhuà 直拨电话
fax
chuánzhēn 传真

Time

What's the time?
jǐ diǎn? 几点？
... hour ... minute
... diǎn ... fēn ... 点 ... 分
3.05
sān diǎn wǔ fēn 3点5分
now
xiànzài 现在
today
jīntiān 今天
tomorrow
míngtiān 明天
day after tomorrow
hòutiān 后天
yesterday
zuótiān 昨天
Wait a moment.
děng yī xià 等一下

Toilets

Men/Women 男/女
toilet (restroom)
cèsuǒ 厕所
toilet paper
wèishēng zhǐ 卫生纸
bathroom (washroom)
xǐshǒu jiān 洗手间

Accommodation

Is there a room vacant?
yǒu méiyǒu kōng fángjiān?
有没有空房间？
Yes, there is/No, there isn't.
yǒu/méiyǒu
有/没有
Can I see the room?
wǒ néng kànkan fángjiān ma?
我能看看房间吗？
I don't like this room.
wǒ bù xǐhuan zhèijiān fángjiān
我不喜欢这间房
Are there any messages for me?
yǒu méiyǒu liú huà?
有没有留话？

May I have a hotel namecard?
yǒu méiyǒu lǚguǎn de míngpiàn?
有没有旅馆的名片？
Could I have these clothes washed, please?
qíng bǎ zhè xiē yīfú xǐ gānjìng, hǎo ma?
请把这些衣服洗干净，好吗？

hotel
lǚguǎn 旅馆
tourist hotel
bīnguǎn/fàndiàn/ 宾馆/饭店/
jiǔdiàn 酒店
reception desk
zǒng fúwù tái 总服务台
dormitory
duōrénfáng 多人房
single room
dānrénfáng 单人房
twin room
shuāngrénfáng 双人房
bed
chuángwèi 床位
economy room
(no bath)
pǔtōngfáng 普通房
standard room
biāozhǔn fángjiān 标准房间
deluxe suite
háohuá tàofáng 豪华套房

Directions

Where is the ...?
... zài nǎlǐ? ... 在哪里？
I'm lost.
wǒ mílùle 我迷路了
Turn right.
yòu zhuǎn 右转
Turn left.
zuǒ zhuǎn 左转
Go straight ahead.
yìzhí zǒu 一直走
Turn around.
wàng huí zǒu 往回走
alley
nòng 弄
boulevard
dàdào 大道
lane
xiàng, hútóng 巷\胡同

map	
dìtú	地图
road	
lù	路
section	
duàn	段
street	
jiē, dàjiē	街，大街
No 21	
21 hào	21号

Getting Around

I want to go to ...	
wǒ yào qù ...	我要去 …
I want to get off.	
wǒ yào xiàchē	我要下车
What time does it depart/arrive?	
jǐdiǎn kāi/dào?	几点开/到？
How long does the trip take?	
zhècì lǚxíng yào huā	这次旅行要花
duōcháng shíjiān?	多长时间？
Please use the meter.	
dǎ biǎo	打表
luggage	
xíngli	行李
left-luggage room	
jìcún chù	寄存处
one ticket	
yìzhāng piào	一张票
two tickets	
liǎngzhāng piào	两张票
buy a ticket	
mǎi piào	买票
refund a ticket	
tuì piào	退票
taxi	
chūzū chē	出租车
microbus taxi	
miànbāo chē,	
miǎndī	面包车，面的

Air

airport	
fēijīchǎng	飞机场
charter flight	
bāojī	包机

CAAC ticket office	
zhōngguó mínháng	中国民航
shòupiào chù	售票处
one way ticket	
dānchéng piào	单程票
return ticket	
láihuí piào	来回票
boarding pass	
dēngjì kǎ	登机卡
reconfirm	
quèrèn	确认
cancel	
qǔxiāo	取消
bonded baggage	
cúnzhàn xínglǐ	存栈行李

Bus

bus	
gōnggòng qìchē	公共汽车
minibus	
xiǎo gōnggòng qìchē	小公共汽车
long-distance bus station	
chángtú qìchē zhàn	长途汽车站
When is the first bus?	
tóubān qìchē jǐdiǎn kāi?	头班汽车几点开？
When is the last bus?	
mòbān qìchē jǐdiǎn kāi?	末班汽车几点开？
When is the next bus?	
xià yìbān qìchē jǐdiǎn kāi?	下一班汽车几点开？

Train

train	
huǒchē	火车
ticket office	
shòupiào chù	售票处
railway station	
huǒchē zhàn	火车站
hard-seat	
yìngxí, yìngzuò	硬席，硬座
soft-seat	
ruǎnxí, ruǎnzuò	软席，软座
hard-sleeper	
yìngwò	硬卧
soft-sleeper	
ruǎnwò	软卧

platform ticket
  zhàntái piào   站台票
Which platform?
  dìjǐhào zhàntái?   第几号站台？
upgrade ticket
(after boarding)
  bǔpiào   补票
subway (underground)
  dìxiàtiě   地下铁
subway station
  dìtiě zhàn   地铁站

Bicycle
bicycle
  zìxíngchē
  自行车
I want to hire a bicycle.
  wǒ yào zū yíliàng zìxíngchē.
  我要租一辆自行车
How much is it per day?
  yìtiān duōshǎo qián?
  一天多少钱？
How much is it per hour?
  yíge xiǎoshí duōshǎo qián?
  一个小时多少钱？
How much is the deposit?
  yājīn dūoshǎo qián?
  押金多少钱？

Food
For more information see the Food section in the Facts for the Visitor chapter.

At the Restaurant
I don't eat dog.
  wǒ bú chī gǒuròu   我不吃狗肉
I don't want MSG.
  wǒ bù yào wèijīng   我不要味精
I'm vegetarian.
  wǒ chī sù   我吃素
not too spicy
  bú yào tài là   不要太辣
(cooked) together
  yíkuàir   一块儿
restaurant
  cāntīng   餐厅
menu
  cài dān   菜单
bill (cheque)
  mǎi dān/jiézhàng   买单/结帐

set meal (no menu)
  tàocān   套餐
to eat/let's eat
  chī fàn   吃饭
chopsticks
  kuàizi   筷子
knife
  dāozi   刀子
fork
  chāzi   叉子
spoon
  tiáogēng/tāngchí   调羹/汤匙

Condiments
black pepper
  hújiāo   胡椒
garlic
  dàsuàn   大蒜
ginger
  jiāng   姜
hot pepper
  làjiāo   辣椒
hot sauce
  làjiāo jiàng   辣椒酱
honey
  fēngmì   蜂蜜
jam
  guǒ jiàng   果酱
ketchup
  fānqié jiàng   蕃茄酱
salt
  yán   盐
sesame seed oil
  zhīmá yóu   芝麻油
soy sauce
  jiàng yóu   酱油
sugar
  táng   糖
vinegar
  cù   醋

Sauces & Styles
'fish-resembling'
  yúxiāng   鱼香
fried
  chǎo   炒
oyster sauce
  háoyóu   蚝油
red cooked
  hóngshāo   红烧

sweet & sour
  tángcù 糖醋
yellow bean
  huángdòu 黄豆

Soup
bean curd &
vegetable soup
  dòufǔ cài tāng 豆腐菜汤
egg drop soup
  jīdàn tāng 鸡蛋汤
hot & sour soup
  suānlà tāng 酸辣汤
mushroom & egg soup
  mógū dànhuā tāng 蘑菇蛋花汤
three kinds of
seafood soup
  sān xiān tāng 三鲜汤
vegetable soup
  shūcài tāng 蔬菜汤
wanton soup
  húndùn tāng 馄饨汤

Rice
steamed white rice
  mǐfàn 米饭
fried rice with beef
  niúròusī chǎofàn 牛肉丝炒饭
fried rice with pork
  ròusī chǎofàn 肉丝炒饭
fried rice & vegetables
  shūcài chǎofàn 蔬菜炒饭
fried rice with egg
  jīdàn chǎofàn 鸡蛋炒饭

Vegetables
bean curd casserole
  shāguō dòufǔ 沙锅豆腐
bean curd &
mushrooms
  mógū dòufǔ 蘑菇豆腐
fried beansprouts
  sù chǎo dòuyá 素炒豆芽
fried cauliflower &
tomato
  chǎo fānqié càihuā 炒蕃茄菜花
aubergine
  qiézi 茄子

beans
  hélándòu 荷兰豆
bok choy
  báicài 白菜
brocolli
  gānlán 甘蓝
cauliflower
  càihuā 菜花
four season beans
  sìjìdòu 四季豆
french beans
  biǎndòu 扁豆
snow peas
  wāndòu biǎndòu 豌豆扁豆
mushroom
  mógū 蘑菇
mushroom
  pínggū 平菇
mushroom
  xiānggū 香菇
potato
  tǔdòu 土豆
pumpkin
  nánguā 南瓜
sweet potato
  yùtou 芋头
tofu
  dòufu 豆腐
tomato
  xīhóngshì 西红柿
wooden ear mushroom
  mùěr 木耳

Top Twenty Dishes
spicy chicken with
peanuts
  gōngbào jīdīng 宫爆鸡丁
shredded pork &
green beans
  biǎndòu ròusī 扁豆肉丝
pork & sizzling
rice crust
  guōbā ròupiàn 锅巴肉片
double cooked
fatty pork
  huíguō ròu 回锅肉
sweet & sour
pork fillets
  tángcù lǐjǐ/ 糖醋里脊/
  gǔlǎo ròu 古老肉

pork cooked with
soy sauce
   jīngjiàng ròusī　　精酱肉丝
'wooden ear'
mushrooms & pork
   mùěr ròu　　木耳肉
pork & green peppers
   qīngjiāo ròu piàn　　青椒肉片
'strange tasting' pork
   guàiwèi ròusī　　怪味肉丝
dry cooked beef
   gānbiàn niúròu sī　　干煸牛肉丝
beef & tomato
   fānqié niúròupiàn　　番茄牛肉片
sizzling beef platter
   tiěbǎn niúròu　　铁板牛肉
'fish-resembling' meat
   yúxiāng ròusī　　鱼香肉丝
egg & tomato
   fānqié chǎodàn　　番茄炒蛋
red cooked aubergine
   hóngshāo qiézi　　红烧茄子
'fish-resembling'
aubergine
   yúxiāng qiézi　　鱼香茄子
fried vegetables
   sùchǎo sùcài　　素炒素菜
garlic beans
   sùchǎo biǎndòu　　素炒扁豆
spicy tofu
   málà dòufu　　麻辣豆腐
'home-style'tofu
   jiācháng dòufu　　家常豆腐

Seafood Dishes

shrimp with peanuts
   gōngbào xiārén　　宫爆虾仁
fish in soy sauce
   hóngshāo yú　　红烧鱼
fish in sour soup
   suān yú tāng　　酸鱼汤

Other Dishes

beef with green peppers
   *qīngjiāo niúròu
piàn*　　青椒牛肉片
beef with oyster sauce
   háoyóu niúròu　　蚝油牛肉

beef braised in
soy sauce
   hóngshāo niúròu　　红烧牛肉
pork & fried onions
   *yángcōng chǎo
ròupiàn*　　洋葱炒肉片
pork with eggs &
vegetables
   mùxū ròu　　木须肉
pork with oyster sauce
   háoyóu ròusī　　蚝油肉丝
sauteed shredded pork
   qīngchǎo ròusī　　清炒肉丝
spicy pork cubelets
   làzi ròudīng　　辣子肉丁
pork cubes & cucumber
   huángguā ròudīng　　黄瓜肉丁
pork & soy sauce
   jiàngbào ròudīng　　酱爆肉丁
shredded pork fillet
   chǎo lǐjī sī　　炒里脊丝
fried pork slices
   liūròupiàn　　熘肉片
fried pork
   guòyóu ròu　　过油肉
ribs
   páigǔ　　排骨
scallops & kidney
   xiānbèi yāohuā　　鲜贝腰花
crispy chicken
   xiāngsū jī　　香酥鸡
chicken & cashews
   yāoguǒ jīdīng　　腰果鸡丁
chicken in soy sauce
   hóngshāo jīkuài　　红烧鸡块
lemon chicken
   níngméng jī　　柠檬鸡
spicy chicken pieces
   làzi jīdīng　　辣子鸡丁
tangerine chicken
   júzi jī　　桔子鸡
Beijing Duck
   běijīng kǎoyā　　北京烤鸭

Unusual Food

dogmeat
   gǒu ròu　　狗肉
goat, mutton
   yáng ròu　　羊肉

kebab
ròu chuàn 肉串
pangolin
chuānshānjiǎ 穿山甲
ratmeat
lǎoshǔ ròu 老鼠肉
snake
shé ròu 蛇肉

Snacks

beef noodles in soup
niúròu miàn 牛肉面
beef rib noodles
dàpái miàn 大排面
chinese ravioli
shuǐjiǎo 水饺
dough stick
yóutiáo 油条
dry 'burning' noodles
rán miàn 燃面
egg & flour omelette
jiān bǐng 煎饼
fried noodles
('chaomein')
chǎomiàn 炒面
fried noodles & beef
niúròu chǎomiàn 牛肉炒面
fried noodles & pork
ròusī chǎomiàn 肉丝炒面
fried shuijiao
guōtiē 锅贴
hotpot
huǒguō 火锅
noodles with beef
(soupy)
niúròu tāng miàn 牛肉汤面
noodles & egg
jīdàn miàn 鸡蛋面
rice noodles
fěn miàn 粉面
soupy casserole
qìguō 汽锅
spicy hotpot
málàtàng 麻辣烫
steamed bun
mántou 馒头
steamed dumpling
bāozi 包子
steamed shuijiao
zhēngjiǎo 蒸饺

stewed casserole
shāguō 砂锅

Desserts

caramelised banana
básī xiāngjiāo 拔丝香蕉
eight treasure rice
bābǎofàn 八宝饭
sweet glutinous ball
tāngyuán 汤圆

Fruit

apple
píngguǒ 苹果
banana
xiāngjiāo 香蕉
coconut
yēzi 椰子
longan
lóngyǎn 龙眼
loquat
pípa 枇杷
lychees
lìzhī 荔枝
mandarins
gānzi 柑子
mango
mángguǒ 芒果
pear
lízi 梨子
persimmon
shìzi 柿子
pineapple
bōluó 菠萝
pomelo
yòuzi 柚子
rambutan
hóngmáodān 红毛丹
sugar cane
gānzhé 甘蔗

Drinks

For more information about Chinese beverages, see the Drinks section in the Facts for the Visitor chapter.

Cheers!
gānbēi 干杯
beer
píjiǔ 啤酒

LANGUAGE

Chinese spirits		
báijiǔ	白酒	
red grape wine		
hóng pútáo jiǔ	红葡萄酒	
rice wine		
mǐ jiǔ	米酒	
whisky		
wēishìjì jiǔ	威士忌酒	
white grape wine		
bái pútáo jiǔ	白葡萄酒	
vodka		
fútèjiā jiǔ	伏特加酒	
Coca-Cola		
kěkǒu kělè	可口可乐	
coconut juice		
yézi zhī	椰子汁	
coffee		
kāfēi	咖啡	
coffee creamer		
nǎijīng	奶精	
fizzy drink (soda)		
qìshuǐ	汽水	
fruit juice		
guǒzhī	果汁	
mango juice		
mángguǒ zhī	芒果汁	
milk		
niúnǎi	牛奶	
mineral water		
kuàng quán shuǐ	矿泉水	
orange juice		
liǔchéng zhī	柳橙汁	
pineapple juice		
bōluó zhī	波萝汁	
soybean milk		
dòujiāng	豆浆	
tea		
chá	茶	
water (boiled)		
kāi shuǐ	开水	
yoghurt		
suānnǎi	酸奶	
hot		
rède	热的	
ice cold		
bīngde	冰的	

Numbers

0	*líng*	零
1	*yī, yāo*	一，么

2	*èr, liǎng*	二，两
3	*sān*	三
4	*sì*	四
5	*wǔ*	五
6	*liù*	六
7	*qī*	七
8	*bā*	八
9	*jiǔ*	九
10	*shí*	十
11	*shíyī*	十一
12	*shí'èr*	十二
20	*èrshí*	二十
21	*èrshíyī*	二十一
100	*yìbǎi*	一百
200	*liǎngbǎi*	两百
1000	*yìqiān*	一千
2000	*liǎngqiān*	两千
10,000	*yíwàn*	一万
20,000	*liǎngwàn*	两万
100,000	*shíwàn*	十万
200,000	*èrshíwàn*	二十万

Health

hospital		
yīyuàn	医院	
laxative		
xièyào	泻药	
anti-diarrhoea		
medicine		
zhǐxièyào	止泻药	
rehydration salts		
shūwéizhí dīnà	舒维质低钠	
fā pàodìng	发泡锭	
aspirin		
āsīpǐlín	阿斯匹林	
antibiotics		
kàngjùnsù	抗菌素	
condom		
bìyùn tào	避孕套	
tampon		
wèishēng mián tiáo	卫生棉条	
sanitary napkin		
(Kotex)		
wèishēng mián	卫生棉	
sunscreen (UV) lotion		
fáng shài yóu	防晒油	
mosquito coils		
wénxiāng	蚊香	
mosquito pads		
diàn wénxiāng	电蚊香	

Emergencies

I'm sick.
wǒ shēng bìng 我生病

I'm injured.
wǒ shòushāng 我受傷

Fire!
huǒ zāi! 火災

Help!
jiùmìng a! 救命啊

Thief!
xiǎo tōu! 小偷

emergency
jǐnjí qíngkuàng 緊急情況

hospital
yīyuàn 醫院

emergency room
jízhěn shì 急诊室

police
jǐngchá 警察

foreign affairs police
wàishì jǐngchá 外事警察

pickpocket
páshǒu 勒忒

rapist
qiángjiānzhě 強姦者

PORTUGUESE

Although there's no compelling reason for you to learn Portuguese while in Macau, there are a few words that are useful to know for reading street signs and maps.

admiral	*almirante*
alley	*beco*
avenue	*avenida*
bay	*baía*
beach	*praia*
big	*grande*
bridge	*ponte*
building	*edifício*
bus stop	*paragem*
cathedral	*sé*
church	*igreja*
courtyard	*pátio*
district	*bairro*
fortress	*fortaleza*
friendship	*amizade*
garden	*jardim*
guesthouse	*hospedaria* or *vila*
guide	*guia*
hill	*alto* or *monte*
hotel	*pousada*
island	*ilha*
lane	*travessa*
library	*biblioteca*
lighthouse	*farol*
lookout point	*miradouro*
market	*mercado*
moneychanger	*casa de cambio*
museum	*museu*
of	*da, do*
path	*caminho*
pawn shop	*casa de penhores*
pier	*ponte-cais*
police	*polícia*
post office	*correios*
restaurant (small)	*casa de pasto*
road	*estrada*
rock, crag	*penha*
school	*escola*
small hill	*colina*
square	*praça*
square (small)	*largo*
steep street	*calçada*
street	*rua*
teahouse	*casa de chá*

Glossary

amah – a servant, usually a woman, who cleans houses and looks after the children. Older Chinese women from the countryside used to find work as amahs, but in Hong Kong the job is mostly done by Filipinos and other South-East Asian migrant workers.

chau – a Cantonese word meaning 'land mass'; you'll see it everywhere, like in the outlying islands (Cheung Chau, Peng Chau etc)

cheongsam – originating in Shanghai, a fashionable tight-fitting Chinese dress with a slit up the side. Often worn on special occasions, it's also the favoured gown for a bride departing on her honeymoon.

chim – sticks that are used to divine the future. They're shaken out of a box onto the ground and then 'read'.

congee – watery rice porridge

dai pai dong – open-air street stalls; great places to enjoy tasty dishes from a sidewalk folding table, especially at night

dragon boat – a long and narrow boat used in races on Dragon Boat Day

fleecy – a sweet cold drink usually containing red or green mung beans, and sometimes pineapple and other fruit

fungshui – literally 'wind-water', the Chinese art of geomancy that aims to balance the elements of nature

gam bei – 'cheers' or 'bottoms up', literally 'dry glass'

godown – a warehouse, usually located on or near the waterfront

gongfu – or 'kungfu' as it is known in the west; the basis of many Asian martial arts

gwailo – a foreigner, particularly a westerner. In Cantonese the term means 'ghost person' and is interpreted as 'foreign devil', and stems from the 19th century when westerners began to come to China in force.

Hong Kong residents claim the term no longer has any negative connotation, though some foreigners are less than fond of the name.

Hakka – a Chinese ethnic group who speak a different dialect from Cantonese; some Hakka people still lead traditional lives as farmers in the New Territories

HKTA – Hong Kong Tourist Association

hong – a company, usually engaged in trade. Often used to refer to Hong Kong's original trading houses, such as Jardine Matheson or Swire, which have grown to become major conglomerates.

II – illegal immigrant

joss – luck, fortune

joss sticks – incense

junk – originally referred to Chinese fishing and war vessels with square sails. Now applies to the diesel-powered, wooden pleasure yachts which can be seen on Victoria Harbour.

kaido – a small to medium-sized ferry which makes short runs on the open sea, usually used for non-scheduled service between small islands and fishing villages

karaoke – a system that allows you to sing along to the recorded melody of songs. A popular social activity among the Chinese, it takes place in bars, specialised 'karaoke lounges' and private homes. The word 'karaoke' (meaning 'empty music') was borrowed from Japan, which bears responsibility for its invention.

KCR – Kowloon-Canton Railway

KMB – Kowloon Motor Bus

LRT – Light Rail Transit

mahjong – popular Chinese card game played among four persons with tiles engraved with Chinese characters

mai dan – the bill or check in a restaurant
MTR – Mass Transit Railway

oolong – high grade Chinese tea, partially fermented

PLA – People's Liberation Army
PRC – People's Republic of China

sampan – a motorised launch that can only accommodate a few people and is too small to go on the open sea. It's mainly used for inter-harbour transport.
SAR – Special Administrative Region. Hong Kong is now known as Hong Kong SAR, a region of China that is under special administration.
shroff – an Anglo-Indian word meaning 'cashier'
snake – a smuggler of illegal immigrants

taijiquan – slow-motion shadow boxing, a form of exercise; commonly shortened to *taiji* (*t'ai chi* in the west)
taipan – big boss of a large company

Tanka – a Chinese ethnic group who traditionally live on boats. Somewhat looked down upon by other Chinese groups, they are among Hong Kong's original inhabitants.
Triad – Chinese secret society. Originally founded to protect Chinese culture from the influence of usurping Manchurians, their modern-day members are little more than gangsters. Hong Kong's Triads are mainly involved in drug-running, prostitution and protection rackets.

URBTIX – Urban Ticketing System

walla walla – a motorised launch used as a water taxi and capable of short runs on the open sea

yum cha – dim sum meal, literally 'drink tea'

wan – the Cantonese word for 'bay' which pops up on all sorts of maps

Index

TEXT

Map references are in **bold** type.

A
Aberdeen (HK) 247, **248-9**
Aberdeen Country Park (HK)
    230
accommodation
    Cheung Chau (HK) 315
    Cheung Sha (HK) 332
    Chi Ma Wan (HK) 332
    Chungking Mansions (HK)
        183-8
    Coloane Island (M) 409
    Guangzhou 454-6, 483-6
    Hong Kong 107-12
    Hong Kong Island 247-52
    Hung Shing Ye (HK) 320
    Kowloon (HK) 183-93
    Macau 363-5

Macau Peninsula (M) 391-5
Mirador Arcade (HK) 188-9
Mui Wo (HK) 330-1
Ngong Ping (HK) 331
outlying islands (HK) 308
Plover Cove Reservoir (HK)
    293
Sai Kung Town (HK) 298
Sha Tin (HK) 296
Shenzhen (G) 505-9
Tai Mo Shan (HK) 284
Taipa Island (M) 405-6
Tsuen Wan (HK) 284
Tuen Mun (HK) 286
Tung O Wan (HK) 320
Yung Shue Wan (HK) 320
Zhaoqing (G) 497-8
Zhuhai (G) 515-8
Admiralty (HK) **218**

AIDS *see* HIV/AIDS
air travel
    air tickets 143-51, 371
    air travel glossary 142-3
    airline offices 139-43, 460-1
    airport 155-6, 375, 468
    to/from Guangzhou 460-7
    to/from Hong Kong 139-51
    to/from Macau 371-2
    to/from Shenzhen 510
    to/from Zhuhai 519
    travel agencies 371
Airport Core Progam Exhibition
    Centre (HK) 283
Airport Railway (HK) 140, 155
Amah Rock (HK) 285, 296
A-Ma Temple (M) 386
Ancestor Temple (G) 494-5
apartments 110-12

560

BOXED TEXT

Ad Nauseam 443
Air Travel Glossary 42
Archaeology on Lamma 318
Art in Hong Kong 30
Cantonese Pluck 537
Card Tricks 187
Chek Lap Kok Airport 144
Cheung Chau Walking Tour 312
Chinese Gods 40
Chinese Zodiac 32
Cultural Revolution 418
Dicing with Death 344
Dying Rooms, The 427
Elvis Lives! .... in Lan Kwai Fong, and he's Cantonese 216
Everyday Health 528
Fakes in the Hong Kong Art Market 276
Floating Hotel or Blue Water Navy? 387
Führer's Gold, The 343

Fun & Games in Macau Casinos 368
Gate of Heavenly Peace, The 19
Giving Some Stick 499
Glossary of Hong Kong Place Names 542
Greening Hong Kong 289
Green Turtles 319
Heavenly Kingdom of the Taiping, The 416
Herbal Medicine 208
HongkongBank 311
Hong Kong's Vanishing Oyster Farms 290
Hong Kong's Vanishing Pink Dolphins 323
International Dialling Codes 58
Jardine Matheson 231
Killing the Rooster to Frighten the Monkey 447
Lais, Damned Lais 205

Last Governor, The 60
Leung Kwok Hung 26
Mad Dogs & Chinamen 80
Mai Po Marsh 288
Nutrition 525
Ones that Got Away, The 424
Pawn Loser, A 356
Point of it All, The 452
Qigong 526
Sai Kung Islands Trip 299
Shenzhen – It's a Jungle 505
Snakes & Bladders 533
Taiwan and Hong Kong 21
Tour Machine 377
Triads, The 116
Typhoons 23
Unmansionables 184
Up in Smoke 490
Where have all the Rickshaws Gone? 164
Word on the Street, The 536
You Are What You Eat 518

LONELY PLANET TRAVEL ATLASES

Lonely Planet has long been famous for the number and quality of its guidebook maps. Now we've gone one step further and produced a handy companion series: Lonely Planet travel atlases – maps of a country produced in book form.

Unlike other maps, which look good but lead travellers astray, our travel atlases have been researched on the road by Lonely Planet's experienced team of writers. All details are carefully checked to ensure the atlas corresponds with the equivalent Lonely Planet guidebook.

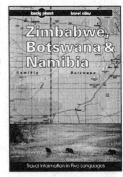

The handy atlas format means no holes, wrinkles, torn sections or constant folding and unfolding. These atlases can survive long periods on the road, unlike cumbersome fold-out maps. The comprehensive index ensures easy reference.

- full-colour throughout
- maps researched and checked by Lonely Planet authors
- place names correspond with Lonely Planet guidebooks
  – no confusing spelling differences
- legend and travelling information in English, French, German, Japanese and Spanish
- size: 230 x 160 mm

Available now:
Chile & Easter Island • Egypt • India & Bangladesh • Israel & the Palestinian Territories •Jordan, Syria & Lebanon • Kenya • Laos • Portugal • South Africa, Lesotho & Swaziland • Thailand • Turkey • Vietnam • Zimbabwe, Botswana & Namibia

---

LONELY PLANET TV SERIES & VIDEOS

Lonely Planet travel guides have been brought to life on television screens around the world. Like our guides, the programmes are based on the joy of independent travel, and look honestly at some of the most exciting, picturesque and frustrating places in the world. Each show is presented by one of three travellers from Australia, England or the USA and combines an innovative mixture of video, Super-8 film, atmospheric soundscapes and original music.

Videos of each episode – containing additional footage not shown on television – are available from good book and video shops, but the availability of individual videos varies with regional screening schedules.

Video destinations include: Alaska • American Rockies • Australia – The South-East • Baja California & the Copper Canyon • Brazil • Central Asia • Chile & Easter Island • Corsica, Sicily & Sardinia – The Mediterranean Islands • East Africa (Tanzania & Zanzibar) • Ecuador & the Galapagos Islands • Greenland & Iceland • Indonesia • Israel & the Sinai Desert • Jamaica • Japan • La Ruta Maya • Morocco • New York • North India • Pacific Islands (Fiji, Solomon Islands & Vanuatu) • South India • South West China • Turkey • Vietnam • West Africa • Zimbabwe, Botswana & Namibia

The Lonely Planet TV series is produced by:
Pilot Productions
The Old Studio
18 Middle Row
London W10 5AT UK

For video availability and ordering information contact your nearest Lonely Planet office.

Music from the TV series is available on CD & cassette.

PLANET TALK

Lonely Planet's FREE quarterly newsletter

We love hearing from you and think you'd like to hear from us.

*When...*is the right time to see reindeer in Finland?
*Where...*can you hear the best palm-wine music in Ghana?
*How...*do you get from Asunción to Areguá by steam train?
*What...*is the best way to see India?

For the answer to these and many other questions read PLANET TALK.

Every issue is packed with up-to-date travel news and advice including:

- a letter from Lonely Planet co-founders Tony and Maureen Wheeler
- go behind the scenes on the road with a Lonely Planet author
- feature article on an important and topical travel issue
- a selection of recent letters from travellers
- details on forthcoming Lonely Planet promotions
- complete list of Lonely Planet products

To join our mailing list contact any Lonely Planet office.

Also available: Lonely Planet T-shirts. 100% heavyweight cotton.

LONELY PLANET ONLINE

Get the latest travel information before you leave or while you're on the road

Whether you've just begun planning your next trip, or you're chasing down specific info on currency regulations or visa requirements, check out Lonely Planet Online for up-to-the-minute travel information.

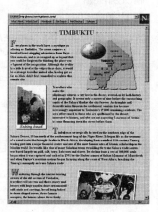

As well as travel profiles of your favourite destinations (including maps and photos), you'll find current reports from our researchers and other travellers, updates on health and visas, travel advisories, and discussion of the ecological and political issues you need to be aware of as you travel.

There's also an online travellers' forum where you can share your experience of life on the road, meet travel companions and ask other travellers for their recommendations and advice. We also have plenty of links to other online sites useful to independent travellers.

And of course we have a complete and up-to-date list of all Lonely Planet travel products including guides, phrasebooks, atlases, Journeys and videos and a simple online ordering facility if you can't find the book you want elsewhere.

www.lonelyplanet.com
or
AOL keyword: lp

LONELY PLANET PRODUCTS

Lonely Planet is known worldwide for publishing practical, reliable and no-nonsense travel information in our guides and on our web site. The Lonely Planet list covers just about every accessible part of the world. Currently there are nine series: *travel guides, shoestring guides, walking guides, city guides, phrasebooks, audio packs, travel atlases, Journeys – a unique collection of travel writing and Pisces Books - diving and snorkeling guides.*

EUROPE

Amsterdam • Andalucia • Austria • Baltic States phrasebook • Berlin • Britain • Canary Islands• Central Europe on a shoestring • Central Europe phrasebook • Czech & Slovak Republics • Denmark • Dublin • Eastern Europe on a shoestring • Eastern Europe phrasebook • Estonia, Latvia & Lithuania • Finland • France • French phrasebook • Germany • German phrasebook • Greece • Greek phrasebook • Hungary • Iceland, Greenland & the Faroe Islands • Ireland • Italian phrasebook • Italy • Lisbon • London • Mediterranean Europe on a shoestring • Mediterranean Europe phrasebook • Paris • Poland • Portugal • Portugal travel atlas • Prague • Romania & Moldova • Russia, Ukraine & Belarus • Russian phrasebook • Scandinavian & Baltic Europe on a shoestring • Scandinavian Europe phrasebook • Slovenia • Spain • Spanish phrasebook • St Petersburg • Switzerland •Trekking in Spain • Ukrainian phrasebook • Vienna • Walking in Britain • Walking in Italy • Walking in Switzerland • Western Europe on a shoestring • Western Europe phrasebook

Travel Literature: The Olive Grove: Travels in Greece

NORTH AMERICA

Alaska • Backpacking in Alaska • Baja California • California & Nevada • Canada • Chicago • Deep South• Florida • Hawaii • Honolulu • Los Angeles • Mexico • Mexico City • Miami • New England • New Orleans • New York City • New York, New Jersey & Pennsylvania • Pacific Northwest USA • Rocky Mountain States • San Francisco • Seattle • Southwest USA • USA phrasebook • Washington, DC & the Capital Region

Travel Literature: Drive thru America

CENTRAL AMERICA & THE CARIBBEAN

• Bahamas and Turks & Caicos • Bermuda • Central America on a shoestring • Costa Rica • Cuba • Eastern Caribbean • Guatemala, Belize & Yucatán: La Ruta Maya • Jamaica

Travel Literature Green Dreams: Travels in Central America

SOUTH AMERICA

Argentina, Uruguay & Paraguay • Bolivia • Brazil • Brazilian phrasebook • Buenos Aires • Chile & Easter Island • Chile & Easter Island travel atlas • Colombia Ecuador & the Galápagos Islands • Latin American Spanish phrasebook • Peru • Quechua phrasebook • Rio de Janeiro • South America on a shoestring • Trekking in the Patagonian Andes • Venezuela

Travel Literature: Full Circle: A South American Journey

ISLANDS OF THE INDIAN OCEAN

Madagascar & Comoros • Maldives • Mauritius, Réunion & Seychelles

AFRICA

Africa - the South • Africa on a shoestring • Arabic (Moroccan) phrasebook • Cairo • Cape Town • Central Africa • East Africa • Egypt • Egypt travel atlas• Ethiopian (Amharic) phrasebook • The Gambia & Senegal • Kenya • Kenya travel atlas • Malawi, Mozambique & Zambia • Morocco • North Africa • South Africa, Lesotho & Swaziland • South Africa, Lesotho & Swaziland travel atlas • Swahili phrasebook • Tunisia • Trekking in East Africa • West Africa • Zimbabwe, Botswana & Namibia • Zimbabwe, Botswana & Namibia travel atlas

Travel Literature: Mali Blues • The Rainbird: A Central African Journey • Songs to an African Sunset: A Zimbabwean Story

MAIL ORDER

Lonely Planet products are distributed worldwide. They are also available by mail order from Lonely Planet, so if you have difficulty finding a title please write to us. North American and South American residents should write to 150 Linden St, Oakland CA 94607, USA; European and African residents should write to 10a Spring Place, London NW5 3BH; and residents of other countries to PO Box 617, Hawthorn, Victoria 3122, Australia.

NORTH-EAST ASIA

Beijing • Cantonese phrasebook • China • Hong Kong • Hong Kong, Macau & Guangzhou • Japan • Japanese phrasebook • Japanese audio pack • Korea • Korean phrasebook • Kyoto • Mandarin phrasebook • Mongolia • Mongolian phrasebook • North-East Asia on a shoestring • Seoul • Taiwan • Tibet • Tibet phrasebook • Tokyo
Travel Literature: Lost Japan

MIDDLE EAST & CENTRAL ASIA

Arab Gulf States • Arabic (Egyptian) phrasebook • Central Asia • Central Asia phrasebook • Iran • Israel & the Palestinian Territories • Israel & the Palestinian Territories travel atlas • Istanbul • Jerusalem • Jordan & Syria • Jordan, Syria & Lebanon travel atlas • Lebanon • Middle East • Turkey • Turkish phrasebook • Turkey travel atlas • Yemen
Travel Literature: The Gates of Damascus • Kingdom of the Film Stars: Journey into Jordan

ALSO AVAILABLE:

Brief Encounters • Travel with Children • Traveller's Tales • Not the Only Planet

INDIAN SUBCONTINENT

Bangladesh • Bengali phrasebook • Bhutan • Delhi • Goa • Hindi/Urdu phrasebook • India • India & Bangladesh travel atlas • Indian Himalaya • Karakoram Highway • Nepal • Nepali phrasebook • Pakistan • Rajasthan • South India • Sri Lanka • Sri Lanka phrasebook • Trekking in the Indian Himalaya • Trekking in the Karakoram & Hindukush • Trekking in the Nepal Himalaya
Travel Literature: In Rajasthan • Shopping for Buddhas

SOUTH-EAST ASIA

Bali & Lombok • Bangkok • Burmese phrasebook • Cambodia • Ho Chi Minh City • Indonesia • Indonesian phrasebook • Indonesian audio pack • Indonesia's Eastern Islands • Jakarta • Java • Laos • Lao phrasebook • Laos travel atlas • Malay phrasebook • Malaysia, Singapore & Brunei • Myanmar (Burma) • Philippines • Pilipino phrasebook • Singapore • South-East Asia on a shoestring • South-East Asia phrasebook • South-West China • Thailand • Thailand's Islands & Beaches • Thailand travel atlas • Thai phrasebook • Thai audio pack • Thai Hill Tribes phrasebook • Vietnam • Vietnamese phrasebook • Vietnam travel atlas

AUSTRALIA & THE PACIFIC

Australia • Australian phrasebook • Bushwalking in Australia • Bushwalking in Papua New Guinea • Fiji • Fijian phrasebook • Islands of Australia's Great Barrier Reef • Melbourne • Micronesia • New Caledonia • New South Wales • New Zealand • Northern Territory • Outback Australia • Papua New Guinea • Papua New Guinea phrasebook • Queensland • Rarotonga & the Cook Islands • Samoa • Solomon Islands • South Australia • Sydney • Tahiti & French Polynesia • Tasmania • Tonga • Tramping in New Zealand • Vanuatu • Victoria • Western Australia
Travel Literature: Islands in the Clouds • Sean & David's Long Drive

ANTARCTICA

Antarctica

THE LONELY PLANET STORY

Lonely Planet published its first book in 1973 in response to the numerous 'How did you do it?' questions Maureen and Tony Wheeler were asked after driving, busing, hitching, sailing and railing their way from England to Australia.

Written at a kitchen table and hand collated, trimmed and stapled, *Across Asia on the Cheap* became an instant local bestseller, inspiring thoughts of another book.

Eighteen months in South-East Asia resulted in their second guide, *South-East Asia on a shoestring*, which they put together in a backstreet Chinese hotel in Singapore in 1975. The 'yellow bible', as it quickly became known to backpackers around the world, soon became *the* guide to the region. It has sold well over half a million copies and is now in its 9th edition, still retaining its familiar yellow cover.

Today there are over 350 titles, including travel guides, walking guides, language kits & phrasebooks, travel atlases and travel literature. The company is the largest independent travel publisher in the world. Although Lonely Planet initially specialised in guides to Asia, today there are few corners of the globe that have not been covered.

The emphasis continues to be on travel for independent travellers. Tony and Maureen still travel for several months of each year and play an active part in the writing, updating and quality control of Lonely Planet's guides.

They have been joined by over 80 authors and 200 staff at our offices in Melbourne (Australia), Oakland (USA), London (UK) and Paris (France). Travellers themselves also make a valuable contribution to the guides through the feedback we receive in thousands of letters each year and on our web site.

The people at Lonely Planet strongly believe that travellers can make a positive contribution to the countries they visit, both through their appreciation of the countries' culture, wildlife and natural features, and through the money they spend. In addition, the company makes a direct contribution to the countries and regions it covers. Since 1986 a percentage of the income from each book has been donated to ventures such as famine relief in Africa; aid projects in India; agricultural projects in Central America; Greenpeace's efforts to halt French nuclear testing in the Pacific; and Amnesty International.

'I hope we send people out with the right attitude about travel. You realise when you travel that there are so many different perspectives about the world, so we hope these books will make people more interested in what they see. Guidebooks can't really guide people. All you can do is point them in the right direction.'

– Tony Wheeler

LONELY PLANET PUBLICATIONS

Australia
PO Box 617, Hawthorn 3122, Victoria
tel: (03) 9819 1877 fax: (03) 9819 6459
e-mail: talk2us@lonelyplanet.com.au

USA
150 Linden St
Oakland, CA 94607
tel: (510) 893 8555 TOLL FREE: 800 275-8555
fax: (510) 893 8572
e-mail: info@lonelyplanet.com

UK
10a Spring Place,
London NW5 3BH
tel: (0171) 428 4800 fax: (0171) 428 4828
e-mail: go@lonelyplanet.co.uk

France:
1 rue du Dahomey, 75011 Paris
tel: 01 55 25 33 00 fax: 01 55 25 33 01
e-mail: bip@lonelyplanet.fr

World Wide Web: http://www.lonelyplanet.com
or *AOL keyword: lp*